W9-DHU-755

HARRAP'S
FRENCH AND ENGLISH
Business
DICTIONARY

HARRAP'S
FRENCH AND ENGLISH

Business

DICTIONARY

Edited by

FRANÇOISE LAURENDEAU
JANE PRATT
PETER COLLIN

HARRAP
LONDON · PARIS · STUTTGART

First published in Great Britain 1981
by Harrap Limited
19–23 Ludgate Hill, London EC4M 7PD

Third Impression 1982

© *Harrap Limited* 1981

ISBN 0 245-53455-5

Text set in 9/10 pt VIP Times, printed and bound
in Great Britain at The Pitman Press, Bath

PREFACE

This new *French and English Business* Dictionary includes terms and expressions used in a wide range of commercial contexts: Banking, Stock Exchange, Accountancy, Insurance, Commerce, Law. Also included are specific terms relating to EEC commercial practices. The work has been based on terms commonly found in commercial correspondence, business newspapers and magazines put out by commercial companies, banks, etc.

The aim of the dictionary is to provide a basic translating tool for everyday business language. As in all Harrap dictionaries, the emphasis has been laid on providing practical examples to show terms and phrases used in context— rendering the dictionary of great value to the translator, the businessman, the secretary, the sales manager, the business-school student.

In addition to the main text, the dictionary provides useful supplementary material concerning international currencies, international organizations and their abbreviations, comparison between balance sheets in English and French to mention but a few.

It should be noted that in contrast to other business dictionaries, the *Harrap's French and English Business Dictionary* gives only the strictly commercial meanings of words, leaving non-commercial meanings for a general dictionary. Superfluous non-business matter has been kept to the absolute minimum.

We want to thank all those who worked on this dictionary, in particular Marie-Noëlle Gérard of Bristol Polytechnic, the late C. B. Johnson and Janet Kernachan.

F.L.
J.P.
P.H.C.

PRÉFACE

Ce nouveau dictionnaire, le *Harrap's French and English Business Dictionary*, contient des termes et expressions employés dans la langue des affaires, c'est-à-dire des termes de banque, d'assurance, de comptabilité, de Bourse, de commerce, de publicité et de nombreux termes juridiques et autres expressions propres aux affaires de la CEE.

Comme tous les autres dictionnaires Harrap, le *Business Dictionary* a pour politique de donner autant d'exemples que possible. Ces exemples proviennent de lettres d'affaires, de journaux et revues économiques aussi bien que de matériel publicitaire émis par des entreprises commerciales, des banques et autres organisations. Notre dictionnaire devient ainsi un outil précieux pour le traducteur, l'homme d'affaires, la secrétaire, le directeur commercial ou l'étudiant de l'école de commerce.

Le *Harrap's French and English Business Dictionary* contient un supplément dans lequel on trouve une foule de renseignements utiles tels que les listes des devises internationales, d'organisations nationales et internationales et leur sigle sans oublier plusieurs pages, en français et en anglais, tirées du rapport annuel bilingue d'une société.

Le *Harrap's French and English Business Dictionary* étant un dictionnaire pour spécialistes, les éditeurs ont pris soin de ne donner que la traduction du sens commercial des mots à moins qu'une traduction plus générale n'ait été considérée utile même dans le domaine des affaires.

Nous tenons à remercier les personnes qui ont travaillé à ce dictionnaire, dont en particulier Marie-Noëlle Gérard de Bristol Polytechnic, C. B. Johnson† et Janet Kernachan.

F.L.
J.P.
P.H.C.

ABBREVIATIONS USED IN THE DICTIONARY— ABRÉVIATIONS UTILISÉES DANS LE DICTIONNAIRE

a.	adjective	adjectif
abbr.	abbreviation	abréviation
Adm:	administration	administration
adv.	adverb	adverbe
adv.phr.	adverbial phrase	locution adverbiale
Aut:	motoring; motor industry	automobilisme; industrie automobile
Av:	aviation; aircraft	aviation; avions
Bank:	banking	opérations de banque
Book-k:	book-keeping	comptabilité
Cmptr:	computers; data processing	ordinateurs; informatique
coll.	collective	collectif
Const:	construction industry	industrie du bâtiment
Corr:	correspondence	correspondance
Cust:	customs	douane
EEC:	Common Market term	terme du Marché commun
esp.	especially	surtout
etc.	et cetera	et caetera
f.	feminine	féminin
F:	colloquialism	familier; style de la conversation
Fin:	finance	terme de finance
FrC:	French Canadian	mot utilisé au Canada français
Hist:	history	histoire
Ind:	industry	industrie
Ins:	insurance	assurance
inv.	invariable	invariable
Journ:	journalism	journalisme
Jur:	legal term	terme de droit
Lt.phr.	latin phrase	locution latine
m.	masculine	masculin
Meas:	weights and measures	poids et mesures
MIns:	marine insurance	assurance maritime
Mkt:	advertising and marketing	publicité et marketing
n.	noun	nom
NAm:	United States and Canada	États-Unis et Canada
Nau:	nautical term	terme de marine
num.	numeral	numéral
occ.	occasionally	parfois
Pej:	pejorative	péjoratif
pers.	person	personne
Pharm:	pharmacy	pharmacie
pl.	plural	pluriel
PN:	public notice	avis au public
PolEc:	political economy; economics	économie politique
Post:	postal services	postes
pref.	prefix	préfixe
prep.phr.	prepositional phrase	locution prépositive
Publ:	publishing	édition
qch.	something	quelque chose
qn	someone	quelqu'un
Rail:	railways/railroads	chemins de fer
Rtm:	registered trademark	marque déposée

ABBREVIATIONS USED IN THE DICTIONARY
ABRÉVIATIONS UTILISÉES DANS LE DICTIONNAIRE

Scot:	Scotland; Scottish	mot utilisé en Écosse
sg.const.	singular construction	avec verbe au singulier
s.o.	someone	quelqu'un
Stat:	statistics	statistiques
StExch:	Stock Exchange	terme de Bourse
sth.	something	quelque chose
SwFr:	Swiss French	mot utilisé en Suisse
Tchn:	technical	terme technique
Th:	theatre	théâtre
Tp:	telephone	téléphone
Trans:	transport	transports
TV:	television	télévision
Typ:	typography	typographie
US:	United States	États-Unis
usu.	usually	d'ordinaire
v.	verb	verbe
Veh:	vehicles	véhicules
v.i.	intransitive verb	verbe intransitif
v.pr.	pronominal verb	verbe pronominal
v.tr.	transitive verb	verbe transitif
WTel:	telephone, telegraph	téléphone, télégraphe

/	synonym or alternative	synonyme ou alternative
=	nearest equivalent (of an institution an office, etc., when systems vary in the different countries)	équivalent le plus proche (d'un terme désignant une institution, une charge, etc., dans les cas où les systèmes varient dans les différents pays)

ENGLISH-FRENCH

A

abandonment, *n. MIns:* délaissement *m* (d'un navire).

abatement, *n.* rabais *m*/réductión *f*/remise *f* (sur le prix); **abatement of taxes,** dégrèvement *m* d'impôt.

abeyance, *n.* **work in abeyance,** travail *m* en souffrance; **the matter is still in abeyance,** la question est toujours pendante/en suspens.

above-the-line, *a. Book-k: (of expenses, etc.),* (dépenses, etc.) au-dessus de la ligne.

absenteeism, *n.* absentéisme *m.*

absorb, *v.tr. (a)* **to absorb a surplus,** résorber un excédent/un surplus *(b)* **the business has been absorbed by a competitor,** l'entreprise a été absorbée par un concurrent.

absorption, *n.* absorption *f* (d'une entreprise par une autre, etc.).

abstract, *n.* résumé *m*/abrégé *m*/sommaire *m*/précis *m*/extrait *m*/analyse *f*; **to make an abstract of an account,** faire le relevé d'un compte/faire un relevé de compte; **abstract of an article,** sommaire/précis d'un article.

accept, *v.tr.* **to accept a bill,** accepter un effet; **to accept (delivery of/shipment of) goods,** prendre livraison de marchandises.

acceptance, *n. (a)* acceptation *f*/effet accepté/effet à payer; **to present a bill for acceptance,** présenter une traite à l'acceptation; **acceptance bank/acceptance house,** banque *f* d'escompte d'effets étrangers/banque d'acceptation *(b)* réception *f* (d'un article commandé); **qualified acceptance,** acceptation sous réserve; **unconditional acceptance,** acceptation sans réserve.

accepting, *a.* **accepting house,** banque *f* d'acceptation.

acceptor, *n.* tiré *m*; accepteur *m* (d'une lettre de change).

access, *n.* **to have access to the books of a company,** prendre communication des livres d'une société.

accident, *n.* **industrial accident,** accident *m* du travail; **accident insurance,** assurance *f* contre les accidents; **accident policy,** police *f* d'assurance accidents.

accommodation, *n.* **accommodation bill,** billet *m* de complaisance/effet *m* de complaisance.

accord, *n.* **accord and satisfaction,** libération *f* (d'une obligation) à titre onéreux.

accordance, *n.* **in accordance with your instructions,** en conformité avec/conformément à vos ordres; suivant vos ordres.

according, *prep. phr.* **according to instructions,** selon/suivant/d'après les ordres; conformément aux ordres.

account, *n. (a)* compte *m*/note *f*; **let me have your account,** envoyez-moi votre note/votre compte; **detailed/itemized account,** compte détaillé; **accounts payable,** compte de passif; dettes *fpl* à court terme; dette passive; **accounts receivable,** compte d'actif; valeurs *fpl* réalisables à court terme; dette active; **to**

have an account/a credit account/NAm: **a charge account with s.o.**, avoir un compte/un compte d'achats/un compte permanent chez qn; être en compte (avec qn); **charge it to my account,** inscrivez-le/mettez-le à mon compte; **account card,** carte f de crédit (d'un magasin); **cash or account?** avez-vous un compte chez nous?/vous réglez comptant? **to pay a sum on account,** donner une somme en acompte/à compte/à valoir; verser un acompte/un à-valoir/une provision; **to pay £10 on account,** donner un acompte de £10; **to account rendered/as per account rendered,** suivant compte remis/suivant relevé remis; **to settle an account,** régler une note/un compte (b) **the accounts (of a firm, etc.),** la comptabilité (d'une entreprise, etc.); **accounts department,** (service m de) la comptabilité; **profit and loss account,** compte des pertes et profits; **income and expenditure account,** compte des dépenses et recettes; **cash account,** compte de caisse; NAm: **operating account,** compte d'exploitation; **purchase account,** compte d'achats; **trading account,** compte d'exploitation; **capital account,** compte de capital; **sales account,** compte des ventes; **advertising account,** budget m de publicité; **contra account,** compte contre-partie; **account book,** livre m de comptes; registre m de comptabilité; **to keep the accounts,** tenir les livres/les écritures f/les comptes/la comptabilité; **to keep separate accounts,** faire bourse à part; **to keep (a) strict account of expenses,** tenir un compte rigoureux des dépenses (c) Bank: **bank account,** compte en banque; **current account,** compte courant; **deposit account** = compte d'épargne; **(National) Girobank account** = compte chèque postal (CCP); **loan account,** compte de prêt; crédit m; compte d'avances; **cheque**/NAm: **checking account,** compte (de) chèques (CC); **joint account,** compte joint/conjoint; **office account,** compte professionnel/commercial; **savings account,** compte d'épargne/de caisse d'épargne; compte sur livret; **credit ac-**

count, compte créditeur; **debit account,** compte débiteur; **to open an account,** (se faire) ouvrir un compte; **account number,** numéro m de compte; **to pay money into one's account,** verser de l'argent à son compte/faire créditer son compte d'une somme/alimenter son compte; **to pay s.o.'s salary directly into his account,** verser le salaire de qn par virement direct sur son compte; **to apply for an account,** faire une demande d'ouverture de compte; **to overdraw an account,** mettre un compte à découvert; **statement of account,** relevé m de compte; **exchange equalization account,** fonds m de stabilisation des changes (d) StExch: **account day,** la liquidation (boursière) (e) exposé m/état m/mémoire m/note f; **account of expenses,** état/note de dépenses; **account of one's transactions,** état/exposé de ses opérations (f) **to set up in business on one's own account,** s'installer à son compte/prendre à son compte/se mettre à son compte.

accountable, a. **accountable receipt,** reçu certifié/pièce f comptable.

accountancy, n. 1. comptabilité f; expertise f comptable 2. tenue f de(s) livres.

accountant, n. (a) agent m comptable; comptable mf; **chief accountant,** chef m de la comptabilité/chef comptable (b) **chartered accountant (CA)**/NAm: **certified public accountant (CPA),** (i) expert m comptable/FrC: comptable agrégé (CA) (ii) conseiller fiscal.

account for, v.tr. Book-k: **to account for (sth.),** comptabiliser (une dépense, etc.).

accounting, n. comptabilité f; expertise f comptable; **cost accounting,** comptabilité de prix de revient; **standard cost accounting,** méthode des coûts standards; **accounting of variable costs,** comptabilité analytique des coûts variables; **accounting period,** exercice m; **accounting machine,** machine f comptable; tabulatrice f; **accounting policies,** méthodes f comptables; **accounting sys-**

tem, plan *m* comptable; **automatic accounting,** mécanographie *f.*

accredited, *a.* accrédité/autorisé/attitré.

accrual, *n.* accumulation *f.*

accrue, *v.i.* (*of interest*) courir/s'accumuler; **interest accrues (as) from . . .,** les intérêts *mpl* courent à partir de . . . .

accrued, *a.* (intérêt) couru/(intérêt) accumulé à recevoir; **accrued charges/ expenses,** effets *mpl* à payer/frais (ac)cumulés; **accrued income,** effets à recevoir.

accumulate, *v.i.* **to allow one's dividends to accumulate,** laisser accumuler ses dividendes; **accumulated dividends,** dividendes accumulés.

accumulation, *n.* **accumulation of capital/ capital accumulation,** accumulation *f* du capital.

acknowledge, *v.tr.* **to acknowledge (receipt of) a letter,** accuser réception d'une lettre; **I acknowledge receipt of your letter,** j'accuse réception de votre lettre/j'ai bien reçu votre lettre.

acknowledg(e)ment, *n.* (*a*) reçu *m*/ quittance *f* (d'un paiement) (*b*) **acknowledg(e)ment (of receipt),** accusé *m* de réception (d'une lettre, etc.).

acquittance, *n.* acquittement *m* (d'une dette).

across-the-board, *a.* **an across-the-board increase,** une augmentation générale.

act[1], *n.* **1. Companies Act,** loi *f* sur les sociétés; **Factory Act/Health and Safety at Work Act,** loi sur les accidents du travail; **Finance Act,** loi de finances **2. act of God,** (cas *m* de) force majeure/cas fortuit; fléau *m*/désastre naturel.

act[2], *v.i.* (*a*) **to act as (secretary, etc.),** exercer les fonctions de (secrétaire, etc.) (*b*) **to act on a letter,** donner suite à une lettre (*c*) **to act for/on behalf of s.o.,** agir au nom de qn/représenter qn.

acting, *a.* suppléant; intérimaire; **acting manager,** directeur intérimaire.

action, *n.* **1. (to take) industrial action,** (*i*) (voter/organiser un) mouvement revendicatif (*ii*) se mettre en grève **2.** *Jur:* **action at law,** action *f* en justice/procès (civil ou criminel); **legal action,** action juridique/procès; **action for libel,** procès/ plainte *f* en diffamation; **action for damages,** action en dommages et intérêts; **action for payment,** action en paiement; **action for an account,** action en reddition de compte; **to bring an action against s.o.,** intenter une action contre qn/intenter un procès à qn/exercer des poursuites *f* contre qn/déposer une plainte contre qn/(faire) appeler qn en justice.

active, *a.* **active balance,** balance *f* excédentaire; **active money,** monnaie circulante; **active partner,** commandité *m*; **active population,** population active; *StExch:* **these shares are very active,** ces valeurs sont très allantes; **there is an active demand for oils,** les valeurs pétrolières sont très recherchées.

actual, 1. *a.* (*a*) **to give the actual figures,** donner les chiffres réels; **actual employment,** emploi effectif; **the figures represent the actual value,** les chiffres représentent la valeur réelle (*b*) **actual cost,** prix *m* (*i*) d'achat (*ii*) de revient **2.** *n.pl.* **the actuals,** les chiffres réels.

actuary, *n.* actuaire *m.*

ad, *n.* *F:* annonce *f*; **to put an ad in the paper,** insérer une annonce dans le journal; **classified/small ads,** annonces classées/ petites annonces.

add, *v.tr. & i.* (*a*) **to add the interest to the capital,** ajouter l'intérêt au capital (*b*) **to add up a column of figures,** additionner une colonne de chiffres (*c*) **the assets add up to two million(s),** l'actif *m* s'élève à deux millions; **the figures don't add up,** les chiffres sont faux; **the accounts won't add up,** je n'arrive pas à faire accorder/balancer les comptes (*d*) **this adds to our expenses,** cela augmente (le montant de) nos dépenses.

adder, *n. Cmptr:* additionneur *m.*

adding, *n.* addition *f;* **adding machine,** machine *f* à calculer/à additionner.

addition, *n.* (*a*) addition *f;* **additions to the staff,** adjonction *f* de personnel (*b*) **addition to the stock,** augmentation *f* de capital (par incorporation de réserves).

additional, *a.* **additional charges,** supplément(s) *m;* **additional investment,** investissement *m* supplémentaire; **additional payment,** supplément; **additional clause,** avenant *m.*

address[1], *n.* adresse *f;* **business address,** (*i*) (*of company*) (adresse du) siège social (*ii*) (*of person*) adresse du bureau; **home address,** adresse du domicile.

address[2], *v.tr.* (*a*) **to address a letter,** mettre/écrire l'adresse sur une enveloppe; **please address all enquiries to . . .,** faire parvenir toute demande de renseignements à . . . (*b*) **he is to address the meeting,** il doit prendre la parole à la réunion.

addressed, *a.* (enveloppe, etc.) qui porte l'adresse (du destinataire); **this parcel is addressed to me,** ce colis m'est adressé; **please send a stamped addressed envelope (sae),** pour la réponse joindre une enveloppe timbrée portant votre a-dresse.

addressee, *n.* destinataire *mf.*

addressing, *n.* **addressing machine,** machine *f* à adresser.

Addressograph, *n.* (*Rtm: of machines manufactured by Addressograph Multigraph Corporation*) Adressographe *m;* machine *f* à imprimer les adresses.

adjourn, 1. *v.tr.* **to adjourn a meeting,** ajourner une réunion 2. **v.i. the meeting adjourned at 3 o'clock,** on a levé la séance à 3 heures.

adjournment, *n.* ajournement *m*/renvoi *m* (d'une séance).

adjudicate, *v.tr.* juger; adjuger; **to adjudicate a claim,** adjuger une récla-

mation; **to adjudicate s.o. (to be) bankrupt,** déclarer qn en état de faillite.

adjudication, *n.* jugement *m*/décision *f*/ arrêt *m;* **adjudication order/adjudication of bankruptcy,** jugement déclaratif de faillite; **adjudication of a bankrupt's debts,** répartition *f* des dettes d'un failli.

adjudicative, *a. Jur:* (acte) déclaratif/ déclaratoire.

adjudicator, *n.* arbitre *m;* juge *m.*

adjust, *v.tr.* r(é)ajuster (les salaires); **income adjusted for inflation,** revenu réel compte tenu de l'inflation.

adjuster, *n.* **average adjuster,** dispa(t)cheur *m*/ajusteur *m.*

adjustment, *n.* **tax adjustment,** redressement fiscal; **wage adjustment,** r(é)ajustement *m* des salaires.

adjustor, *n.* = **adjuster.**

adman, *n. F:* publicitaire *m.*

admin, *n. F:* = **administration.**

administered, *a.* **administered price,** prix imposé.

administration, *n.* administration *f*/ gestion *f* (des affaires).

administrative, *a.* administratif; **administrative details,** détails *m* d'ordre administratif; **administrative expenses,** frais *mpl* d'administration/de gestion.

admission, *n.* **admission (fee),** (prix *m* d')entrée *f;* **admission free,** entrée libre; **admission 50p** = entrée 1 Fr.

admittance, *n.* **no admittance,** entrée interdite.

adopt, *v.tr.* approuver (les minutes d'un conseil d'administration); **to adopt a resolution (at a meeting),** adopter une motion (à une réunion).

ad valorem, *Lt. phr.* **ad valorem duty/tax,** droit *m*/taxe *f* sur la valeur; droit/taxe ad valorem; droit proportionnel; **to pay a**

duty ad valorem, payer un droit sur/ d'après la valeur des marchandises; **ad valorem revenue stamp,** timbre fiscal selon la valeur.

advance[1], *n.* **1.** (*a*) **to pay in advance,** payer d'avance; **to pay a sum in advance,** verser une provision/des provisions; avancer des paiements; **duty payable in advance,** droit *m* exigible d'avance; **fixed in advance,** fixé à l'avance; (prix) forfaitaire; *Corr:* **thanking you in advance,** en vous remerciant d'avance; avec mes remerciements anticipés (*b*) **advance payment,** provision; arrhes *fpl*; **advance booking,** location *f*/réservation *f* de places (à l'avance) **2.** (*a*) avance *f* (de fonds); à-bon-compte *m inv*; à-valoir *m inv*; **bank advance,** avance bancaire; **cash advance,** avance en numéraire; **advance on current account,** avance en compte courant; **to make an advance of £10 to s.o.,** faire à qn une avance de £10/avancer £10 à qn; **advance account,** compte *m* d'avances; **advance on a contract,** acompte *m* sur contrat; arrhes; **advance against security,** avance/prêt *m* sur nantissement; **advances on securities,** prêts sur titres; **standing advance,** avance permanente; **secured advances,** avances sur garanties; **unsecured advances,** avances à découvert/sur notoriété (*b*) augmentation *f*/hausse *f* (de prix); renchérissement *m*; **the general advance in prices,** la hausse/l'augmentation générale des prix; **there is an advance on wheat,** les blés ont subi une hausse.

advance[2], **1.** *v.tr.* (*a*) **to advance s.o. money,** avancer/prêter de l'argent à qn; **I will advance him £1000 on your note of hand,** je lui avancerai/je lui ferai une avance de £1000 sur un billet de vous; **sum advanced,** avance *f*/provision *f*; arrhes *fpl*; mises *f* hors (*b*) augmenter/ hausser (les prix) **2.** *v.i.* (*of shares, etc.*) augmenter de prix/monter; **prices are advancing,** les prix *m* augmentent/montent.

advancement, *n.* **1. economic advance-**

ment, essor *m* économique **2.** avancement *m*/promotion *f*.

adverse, *a.* **adverse budget,** budget *m* déficitaire; **adverse balance of trade,** balance *f* commerciale déficitaire.

advert, *n. F:* réclame *f*/annonce *f*.

advertise, *v.tr. & i.* (*a*) **to advertise in a paper,** (faire) insérer/mettre une annonce dans un journal; **to advertise for a translator,** faire paraître une annonce pour recruter les services d'un traducteur (*b*) faire de la réclame/de la publicité (pour un produit); **to advertise widely to launch sth. on the market,** faire appel à la grande publicité pour lancer un article; **(goods) as advertised (on television),** (marchandises *f*) conformes à la spécification publicitaire (télévisée).

advertisement, *n.* (*a*) publicité *f*/réclame *f*/annonce *f* publicitaire (*b*) (*in newspaper*) annonce; **classified advertisements,** annonces classées/petites annonces; **advertisement manager,** annoncier *m*.

advertiser, *n.* annonceur *m*.

advertising, *n.* publicité *f*/réclame *f*; annonces *fpl*; **advertising account,** budget *m* de publicité; **advertising agency,** agence *f* publicitaire/de publicité; **advertising agent,** agent *m* de publicité; annoncier *m*; **advertising campaign,** campagne *f* de publicité; **advertising expenses,** dépenses *f* de la publicité; **advertising manager,** chef *m* de la publicité; **advertising medium,** organe *m* de publicité; **advertising media,** supports *m* publicitaires; **advertising schedule,** programme *m* des annonces; **advertising sheet,** feuille *f* d'annonces; **advertising space,** espace *m*/emplacement *m* réservé à la publicité; **cheapness can be a bad advertising point,** le bon marché peut être une contre-publicité; **competitive advertising,** publicité concurrentielle.

advice, *n.* (*a*) **advice note/letter of advice,**

lettre *f*/note *f* d'avis; **as per advice,** suivant avis (*b*) **until further advice,** jusqu'à nouvel avis; **to take legal advice,** consulter un avocat; **we have received advices from Hong Kong,** nous avons reçu des avis/des informations *f* de Hong Kong.

advise, *v.tr.* **to advise a draft,** aviser d'une traite/donner avis d'une traite.

affidavit, *n.* déclaration écrite sous serment/affidavit *m.*

affiliated, *a.* **affiliated company,** filiale *f*/ société affiliée.

affreightment, *n.* affrètement *m.*

afloat, *a.* **to keep (s.o., a business) afloat,** renflouer (qn, une entreprise); **to keep bills afloat,** faire circuler des effets.

aforesaid, *a. & adv. Jur:* susmentionné/ susdit / mentionné ci-dessus / mentionné plus haut.

after, *prep.* (*of a bill of exchange*) **after date,** délai *m* de date; **after sight,** délai de vue.

agency, *n.* (*a*) agence *f*/bureau *m*; **sole agency for a firm,** représentation exclusive d'une maison; **news/press agency,** agence de presse; **employment agency,** bureau/agence de placement; **estate agency,** agence immobilière; **land agency,** agence foncière; **customs agency,** agence en douane; **shipping agency/forwarding agency,** agence maritime; **travel agency,** agence de voyage(s)/de tourisme; **literary agency,** agence littéraire; **agency account,** compte *m* agence; **agency agreement,** contrat *m* de mandat/traité *m* d'agence/accord *m* du mandataire; **agency contract,** contrat d'agence; **agency fee,** prestation *f* (*b*) *Bank:* (*i*) succursale *f*/agence (de banque) (*ii*) direction *f* (d'une succursale)/agence (de banque) (*c*) comptoir *m* (à l'étranger).

agenda, *n.* ordre *m* du jour/programme *m* (d'une réunion); **to draw up an agenda,**

dresser l'ordre du jour; **to place a question on the agenda,** inscrire une question à l'ordre du jour.

agent, *n.* agent *m*/représentant *m*; **agent for the firm of . . .,** représentant de la maison . . .; **appointed/authorized agent,** mandataire *mf*; (agent) agréé (*m*); fondé *m* de pouvoir; **to be sole agent for . . .,** avoir la représentation exclusive de . . .; **sole agent for a brand,** seul dépositaire/concessionnaire d'une marque; agent (commercial) exclusif; **commission agent,** commissionnaire *m* en marchandises; **fiscal agent,** représentant fiscal; **forwarding agent/transit agent,** transitaire *m*; **insurance agent,** agent d'assurances; **local agent,** agent sur le terrain; (**real-)estate agent,** agent immobilier; **general business agent,** agent d'affaires; **literary agent,** agent littéraire; **universal agent,** mandataire général.

aggregate, *a.* total/global; **aggregate economic activity,** ensemble *m* des activités économiques; **aggregate output,** production globale; **aggregate demand/supply,** demande/offre globale; **aggregate net increment,** accroissement global net.

agio, *n.* **1.** agio *m*; prix *m* du change; **agio account,** compte *m* d'agio **2.** commerce *m* du change.

agiotage, *n.* agiotage *m.*

agree, *v.tr.* **to agree the accounts/the books,** faire accorder les livres; **the figures were agreed between the accountants,** les chiffres ont été acceptés (d'un commun accord) par les experts-comptables.

agreed, *a.* convenu; forfaitaire; **agreed price,** prix convenu; **contract at an agreed price,** contrat *m* à forfait/contrat forfaitaire; **agreed consideration,** (*i*) prix convenu (*ii*) contrepartie convenue.

agreement, *n.* **1.** convention *f*/acte *m*/ contrat *m*/traité *m*/arrangement *m*; **written agreement,** convention écrite; **agreement for sale,** contrat/acte de vente;

collective agreement, contrat collectif; **collective wage agreement,** convention collective des salaires; **to work by agreement,** entreprendre un travail à prix convenu/à forfait; **to break an agreement,** rompre un marché; **to enter into an agreement with s.o.** passer un traité/un contrat avec qn; **an agreement has been concluded between the two parties,** un accord est intervenu entre les deux parties; **to sign an agreement,** signer un contrat/une convention; **to sign a legal agreement,** s'engager (par) devant notaire (**to do sth.,** à faire qch.); **to abide by the agreement,** s'en tenir à la convention/ s'en tenir à ce qui a été convenu **2.** accord *m*/entente *f*; **as per agreement,** comme (il a été) convenu; **by mutual agreement,** de gré à gré/à l'amiable/d'un commun accord; **marketing agreement,** accord de commercialisation; **General Agreement on Tariffs and Trade (GATT),** Accord général sur les tarifs douaniers et le commerce.

agricultural, *a.* (produit, etc.) agricole; **agricultural show,** exposition *f* agricole/ comice *m* agricole; **common agricultural policy (CAP),** politique agricole commune.

agriculture, *n.* agriculture *f*.

air, *n.* **by air,** par avion/par voie aérienne; **air cargo,** transport *m* par avion; **air transport,** transports aériens; **air company,** compagnie *f* de navigation aérienne; **air carrier,** (*i*) transporteur aérien (*ii*) compagnie aérienne; **air travel,** voyages *mpl* par avion; **air letter,** aérogramme *m*.

aircraft, *n. inv.* avion *m*/appareil *m*; **charter aircraft,** (*i*) avion affrété/avion nolisé/(avion) charter *m* (*ii*) avion-taxi *m*; **aircraft charter agreement,** contrat *m* d'affrètement aérien; **commercial aircraft,** avion commercial; **the aircraft industry,** l'industrie *f* aéronautique; **aircraft manufacturer/aircraft constructor,** constructeur *m* d'avions/avionneur *m*.

airfreight[1]**,** *v.tr.* acheminer/transporter par avion.

airfreight[2]**,** *n.* (*i*) transport *m* par avion (*ii*) fret *m*/frais *mpl* (de transport par avion).

airline, *n.* ligne aérienne/compagnie aérienne/service *m* de transports aériens.

airmail[1]**,** *n.* (*a*) poste aérienne; service postal aérien; **by airmail,** par avion (*b*) courrier *m* par avion; **airmail letter,** lettre (envoyée) par avion; **airmail paper,** papier *m* avion/papier pelure; **airmail sticker,** collant *m* 'par avion'.

airmail[2]**,** *v.tr.* envoyer/expédier (une lettre, etc.) par avion.

airport, *n.* aéroport *m*.

album, *n.* album *m*/(disque) 33 tours *m*/ (disque) 30 cm.

all-in, *a.* **all-in price,** prix *m* tout compris/prix forfaitaire; *Ins:* **all-in policy,** police *f* tous risques.

allocate, *v.tr.* allouer/assigner (qch., à qn, à qch.); **to allocate a sum to sth.,** affecter/assigner une somme à qch.

allocation, *n.* **1.** (*a*) allocation *f*/affectation *f* (d'une somme); **allocation of capital,** affectation des investissements; **allocation to reserve funds,** dotation *f* au fonds de réserve/au compte de provisions (*b*) répartition *f* (de dépenses, etc.); attribution *f* (de fonctions) (*c*) **allocation of contract,** adjudication *f*; **allocation to the lowest tender,** adjudication au mieux-disant; **allocation to the highest bidder,** adjudication à la surenchère **2.** part assignée/somme assignée.

allonge, *n.* allonge *f* (d'une lettre de change).

allot, *v.tr.* répartir/distribuer (des actions); **all the shares have been allotted,** toutes les actions ont été réparties.

allotment, *n.* (*a*) affectation *f* (d'une
somme à un but) (*b*) **allotment of shares,**
attribution *f* d'actions; **letter of allotment,** (lettre *f* d')avis *m* de répar-
tition/lettre d'allocation; bulletin *m* de
souscription; **payment in full on allotment,** libération *f* à la répartition; **to pay
so much on allotment,** payer tant lors de la
répartition.

allow, *v.tr.* (*a*) **to allow s.o. a discount,**
consentir/accorder/faire une remise à
qn; **to allow 5%,** déduire 5%/faire une
remise de 5%; **to allow 5% interest on
deposits,** allouer/attribuer 5% d'intérêt
sur les dépôts (*b*) **to allow a claim,**
admettre un recours (*c*) **to allow for sums
paid in advance,** faire déduction des
sommes payées d'avance; **packing is not
allowed for,** (le prix de) l'emballage n'est
pas compris/inclus; **after allowing for
. . .,** déduction faite de . . .; **to allow for
the tare,** défalquer la tare; **to allow so
much for carriage,** (*i*) ajouter (*ii*) déduire tant pour le port (*d*) **to allow s.o.
£500 a year,** allouer à qn la somme
annuelle de £500.

allowable, *a.* admissible/admis/permis/
légitime; **allowable claim,** réclamation *f*
recevable; **allowable expense,** dépense *f*
déductible/dépense remboursable.

allowance, *n.* **1. cost-of-living allowance,**
indemnité *f* de vie chère/de cherté de
vie; **accommodation allowance,** indemnité de logement; **income tax allowance,**
déduction *f* avant impôt/déduction
fiscale; **personal allowance,** abattement *m* à la base; **earned income allowance,** déduction au titre de revenus
salariaux ou professionnels; **office/enter-
tainment allowance,** frais *mpl* de bureau/
de représentation; **travel(ling) allowance,** indemnité de déplacement; **foreign currency allowance,** allocation en
devises **2.** (*a*) remise *f*/rabais *m*/déduc-
tion/concession *f*; **to make an allowance
on an article,** faire/accorder un rabais
sur un article; **allowance (for bad quality, etc.),** réfaction *f* (*b*) provisions *fpl*;

allowance to cashier for errors, tare *f* de
caisse; passe *f* de caisse; **allowance for
exchange fluctuations,** provisions pour
fluctuations du change; **allowance for
loss,** provisions pour pertes; **depreciation
allowance/wear-and-tear allowance,** provisions pour amortissement.

amalgamate, 1. *v.tr.* amalgamer/fusion-
ner (des sociétés, etc.); unifier (des
industries); **to amalgamate shares,** fusionner des actions **2.** *v.i.* (*of companies*)
fusionner/opérer une fusion.

amalgamation, *n.* fusion *f*/fusionnement
m (de deux sociétés, *Fin:* d'actions);
amalgamation of industries, fusion industrielle.

amazing, *a.* **amazing offer!** offre exceptionnelle!

amend, *v.tr.* (*a*) **to amend a resolution,**
amender une proposition (*b*) rectifier
(un compte).

amendment, *n.* (*a*) amendement *m* (d'une
proposition) (*b*) rectification *f* (d'un
compte).

amortizable, *a.* amortissable.

amortization, *n.* amortissement *m* (d'une
dette, etc.); **amortization quota,** cote *f*/
taux *m* d'amortissement; **authorized quota amortization,** contingent *m* d'amortissement autorisé.

amortize, *v.tr.* amortir (une dette).

amount[1], *n.* somme *f*/montant *m*/total *m*
(d'une facture, etc.); valeur *f*; **amount of
expenses,** chiffre *m* de la dépense;
amount paid, somme versée; **amount
paid on account,** acompte versé; **what is
the amount of their turnover?** quel est
leur chiffre d'affaires? **amount invested
(in a company),** mise *f* de fonds; **amounts
of stock negotiable,** quotités *f* de titres
négociables; **amounts to be made good,**
masse créancière; **amount insured/
amount of the risk,** montant assuré;
amount written off, amortissement *m*;

Book-k: **amount brought in,** report *m* des exercices antérieurs; **amount carried forward,** report à nouveau/somme à reporter; **amount entered twice,** double emploi *m*.

amount[2], *v.i.* (*of money, etc.*) s'élever/se monter (to, à); **the stocks amount to 2 500,** les stocks *m* s'élèvent à 2 500/atteignent 2 500.

analyse, *v.tr.* **to analyse an account,** dépouiller/décomposer un compte.

analysis, *n.* analyse *f*; **analysis of an account,** dépouillement *m*/décomposition *f*/ analyse d'un compte; **economic analysis,** analyse économique; **statistical analysis,** analyse statistique; **cost-benefit analysis,** analyse des coûts et rendements/analyse coût-profit; **cost-effectiveness analysis,** étude *f* de coût et d'efficacité; **job analysis,** analyse des tâches; **operating costs analysis,** comptabilité *f* analytique d'exploitation; **project analysis,** étude de projet; **sales/market analysis,** analyse des ventes/du marché; **supply and demand analysis,** analyse de l'offre et de la demande; **systems analysis,** analyse des systèmes.

analyst, *n.* analyste *mf*.

analytical, *a.* **analytical training,** formation *f* par étapes.

annual, *a.* annuel; **annual leave,** congé annuel; **annual abstract of statistics,** annuaire *m* de statistiques; **he has an annual salary of £5000,** il gagne cinq mille livres par an.

annualized, *a.* **the annualized figures,** le montant total pour un an.

annually, *adv.* annuellement; tous les ans.

annuitant, *n.* rentier, -ière (en viager).

annuity, *n.* **1. annuity in redemption of debt,** annuité *f* **2.** rente *f* (annuelle); **government annuity,** rente sur l'État; **perpetual annuity,** rente perpétuelle; **terminable annuity,** rente à terme; annuité résiliable; **life annuity,** rente viagère; **annuity in reversion/reversion-** ary **annuity,** rente réversible; **survivorship annuity,** rente viagère avec réversion; **deferred annuity,** annuité différée; **contingent annuity,** annuité contingente; **to invest money in an annuity/to buy an annuity,** placer son argent en viager/à fonds perdu.

annul, *v.tr.* annuler/résilier/résoudre (un contrat).

annullable, *a.* (contrat) annulable/résiliable/résoluble.

annulling[1], *a.* qui annule; **annulling clause,** clause *f* abrogatoire.

annulling[2], **annulment,** *n.* annulation *f*/ résiliation *f*/abrogation *f*/résolution *f* (d'un contrat, etc.).

answer[1], *n.* réponse *f*; **in answer to your letter,** en réponse à votre lettre.

answer[2], *v.tr.* **I answered this letter,** j'ai répondu à cette lettre; **to answer the telephone,** répondre au téléphone; prendre une communication.

answering, *a.* **answering service,** repondeur *m* (téléphonique); répondeur-enregistreur.

antedate, *v.tr.* antidater (un document, etc.).

anti-inflationary, *a.* **anti-inflationary measures,** mesures anti-inflationnistes.

anti-trust, *a.* anti-trust *inv*; **anti-trust laws,** législation *f* anti-trust.

appeal, *n.* **sales appeal,** attraction commerciale.

appear, *v.i.* apparaître/figurer/être inscrit; **item which appears in the books,** article *m* qui figure dans les livres.

applicant, *n.* **applicant for a job,** candidat(e) à un emploi/postulant(e); **applicant for a patent,** demandeur *m* d'un brevet; **applicant for shares,** souscripteur *m* à des actions; **applicant for a trademark,** déposant *m* d'une marque.

application, *n.* (*a*) **application (for a job, for a patent),** demande *f* (d'emploi, de brevet); **application form,** formule *f* de demande (d'emploi, etc.); bulletin *m* d'abonnement (à un journal); **to send in/to submit an application,** faire une demande (par écrit); **samples are sent on application,** on envoie des échantillons sur demande (*b*) *Fin:* **application for shares,** souscription *f* d'actions; demande de titres en souscription; **payable on application,** payable à la souscription; **application form,** bulletin de souscription (à des actions); **application money,** versement *m* de souscription; **application receipt,** reçu *m* de souscription.

apply, 1. *v.tr.* **to apply a payment to a particular debt,** imputer/affecter un paiement à une dette spécifiée 2. *v.i.* (*a*) **to apply for a job,** poser sa candidature à un poste; solliciter/postuler un emploi; **apply within,** s'adresser ici; **to apply in writing,** écrire; **to apply in person,** se présenter (*b*) **to apply for shares,** souscrire (à) des actions.

appoint, *v.tr.* **to appoint s.o. to a post,** nommer qn à un emploi/désigner qn à un poste.

appointee, *n.* candidat(e) retenu(e)/choisi(e); nouveau/nouvelle titulaire d'un poste.

appointed, *a.* (*i*) **appointed agent,** agent attitré (*ii*) **our newly appointed sales manager,** notre nouveau chef de vente/le chef de vente que nous venons de nommer.

appointment, *n.* 1. (*for business*) entrevue *f*; **to make/fix an appointment with s.o.,** fixer un rendez-vous/donner rendez-vous (à qn); **to make an appointment with s.o. for three o'clock,** prendre un rendez-vous pour trois heures; **to break an appointment,** manquer au rendez-vous; **to cancel an appointment,** annuler un rendez-vous; **to meet s.o. by appointment,** avoir (un) rendez-vous avec qn; **have you an appointment?** avez-vous un rendez-vous? **by appointment only,** sur rendez-vous 2. (*a*) nomination *f*/dési-

gnation *f* (de qn à un emploi) (*b*) (*of shop, etc.*) **by appointment to Her Majesty,** fournisseur breveté/attitré de sa Majesté (*c*) poste *m*/emploi *m*; **to hold an appointment,** être préposé à un emploi; (*in newspaper*) **appointments vacant,** offres *f* d'emploi; **appointments wanted,** demandes *f* d'emploi.

apportion, *v.tr.* répartir/ventiler (les frais).

apportionment, *n.* partage *m*/répartition *f*/imputation *f*/affectation *f* (d'impôts, de dépenses, etc.); ventilation *f* (de frais, etc.).

appraisal, *n.* estimation *f*/évaluation *f*; expertise *f*; **market appraisal,** évaluation *f* du marché; **investment appraisal,** appréciation *f* des investissements.

appreciate, *v.i.* (*of goods, etc.*) augmenter de valeur/augmenter de prix/monter de prix/accuser une plus-value; **appreciated surplus,** plus-value; **the franc has appreciated in terms of other currencies,** le franc s'est apprécié vis-à-vis des autres monnaies.

appreciation, *n.* 1. appréciation *f* (du prix/de la valeur de qch.); estimation *f* (de la valeur de qch.); évaluation *f* 2. augmentation *f*/hausse *f* de valeur; amélioration *f*/valorisation *f*/plus-value *f*; **these shares show an appreciation,** ces actions *f* ont enregistré une plus-value; **appreciation of assets,** plus-value d'actif; **appreciation of the exchange,** plus-value du change; **appreciation in prices,** amélioration des cours/des prix.

apprentice[1], *n.* apprenti(e).

apprentice[2], *v.tr.* **to apprentice s.o. to s.o.,** placer/mettre qn en apprentissage chez qn.

apprenticeship, *n.* apprentissage *m*; **serve one's apprenticeship with s.o.,** faire son apprentissage chez qn.

appro, *n. F:* **on appro,** à l'essai/à condition;

to buy (sth.) on appro, acheter (qch.) à condition/à l'essai.

appropriate, *v.tr.* destiner/affecter/consacrer **(a sum to/for a purpose,** une somme à un projet); **funds appropriated for the new library,** fonds affectés à la nouvelle bibliothèque; **appropriated profits,** bénéfices distribués.

appropriation, *n.* affectation *f* de fonds; attribution *f*/distraction *f* (d'une somme); **appropriation account,** compte *m* d'affectation; **appropriation of payment to a debt,** imputation *f* d'un paiement à une dette; **appropriation to the reserve,** dotation *f* au compte de provisions; **prior appropriation,** prélèvement *m* prioritaire.

approval, *n.* **1.** approbation *f*/agrément *m*; **subject to approval/for approval,** soumis à l'approbation; **to submit for approval (by s.o.),** soumettre à l'approbation (de qn) **2.** ratification *f*/homologation *f* (d'un document) **3.** (*a*) **on approval,** à condition/à l'essai; **to buy sth. on approval,** acheter qch. à l'essai/à condition; **tools sent on approval,** outils envoyés à titre d'essai; **book sent on approval,** livre envoyé à l'examen/en communication (*b*) *NAm:* **approvals,** marchandises envoyées à l'essai.

approve, *v.tr.* approuver/sanctionner (une action); ratifier/homologuer (un document); agréer (un contrat); approuver (les comptes); **read and approved,** lu et approuvé; **the proposal was approved (of),** la proposition a été approuvée/agrée.

approximation, *n.* approximation *f*/évaluation approximative.

arbitrage, *n.* (*a*) *Fin:* arbitrage *m;* **stock arbitrage,** arbitrage sur des valeurs (*b*) *PolEc:* **arbitrage syndicate,** syndicat *m* arbitragiste.

arbitrate, 1. *v.tr.* arbitrer/juger/trancher (un différend) **2.** *v.i.* décider en qualité d'arbitre; arbitrer.

arbitration, *n.* **1.** arbitrage *m*; **arbitration board,** commission *f* paritaire d'arbitrage; **procedure by arbitration,** procédure arbitrale; **settlement by arbitration,** règlement *m* par arbitrage; solution arbitrale; **to refer a question to arbitration,** soumettre une question à l'arbitrage; **to submit an affair for arbitration,** soumettre un différend à l'arbitrage; **difference submissible to arbitration,** litige *m* arbitral; **to go to arbitration,** soumettre un différend à l'arbitrage/recourir à l'arbitrage; **arbitration tribunal,** tribunal arbitral; **arbitration court/court of arbitration,** tribunal arbitral; **arbitration clause,** clause *f* d'arbitrage; clause compromissoire; **arbitration analysis,** analyse arbitrale **2. arbitration of exchange,** arbitrage du change.

arbitrator, *n.* arbitre *m*; arbitre-juge *m*; amiable compositeur *m*; compromissaire *m*.

area, *n.* (*a*) **shopping area,** quartier commerçant (*b*) **free trade area,** zone *f* de libre-échange; **currency area,** zone monétaire; **the sterling/dollar/franc area,** la zone sterling/dollar/franc (*c*) **growth area,** secteur *m* de croissance; **problem area,** zone critique.

arrangement, *n.* **to make an arrangement/to come to an arrangement with s.o.,** faire un arrangement avec qn; **price by arrangement,** prix *m* à débattre/à discuter/à négocier; (*after bankruptcy*) concordat *m*.

arrears, *n.pl.* arriéré *m*/arrérages *mpl*; **arrears of wages,** arrérages de salaires/rappel *m* de salaires; **arrears of interest,** intérêts moratoires/arriérés/échus et non payés; arrérages; **to let one's rent fall into arrears,** être en retard pour payer son loyer; **salary with arrears effective as from March 1st,** augmentation *f* avec effet rétroactif au 1er mars.

arrival, *n.* arrivage *m* (de marchandises); **arrival (of a plane, etc.),** arrivée *f* (d'un avion, etc.), (*on letters*) **to await arrival,** prière d'attendre l'arrivée.

arrive, *v.i.* **to arrive at a price,** calculer/ fixer un prix; parvenir à un prix/convenir d'un prix.

article[1], *n.* **1.** article *m*/clause *f* (d'une convention, d'un traité); **articles of apprenticeship,** contrat *m* d'apprentissage; **he is under articles,** il fait son apprentissage/il est en apprentissage; **articles of a partnership,** contrat de société/acte *m* d'association; **the articles of a contract,** les stipulations *f* d'un contrat; **articles of association,** statuts *m* (d'une société à responsabilité limitée); **appointed/provided by the articles,** statutaire; **under the articles/in accordance with the articles,** statutairement; (*of sale, contract*) **articles and conditions,** cahier *m* des charges **2.** article *m*; produit *m*; marchandise *f*; **to put an article on the market,** lancer un produit sur le marché.

article[2], *v.tr.* **to article s.o. to an architect,** placer qn (comme élève) chez un architecte; **articled clerk,** clerc d'avoué/de notaire (lié par un contrat d'apprentissage).

assess, *v.tr.* **to assess the damage,** évaluer les dommages/les dégâts; **to assess the damages at £100,** fixer les dommages et intérêts à £100; **to assess a property (for taxation),** évaluer une propriété.

assessment, *n.* évaluation *f*; **assessment of damages,** évaluation des dommages et intérêts; **tax assessment,** détermination *f* de l'assiette de l'impôt/de l'assiette fiscale; **additional tax assessment,** redressement fiscal.

asset, *n.* (*a*) *pl.* **assets,** actif *m*/avoir(s) *m(pl)*; masse active (d'une liquidation après faillite); **available assets,** actif disponible/liquide; **capital assets,** actif immobilisé/valeurs immobilisées; **circulating assets,** capitaux circulants; **current assets,** actif circulant/valeurs *f* disponibles/valeurs réalisables; **fixed assets,** immobilisations (corporelles)/actif immobilisé/valeurs immobilisées/actif sta-

ble; **frozen assets,** fonds bloqués/non liquides; **intangible assets,** actif incorporel/immobilisations (incorporelles); **liquid assets,** actif liquide; **net tangible asset value,** valeur comptable nette; *NAm:* **quick assets,** actif disponible/ négociable; **realizable assets,** actif réalisable; **personal assets,** biens *m* meubles; **real assets,** biens immobiliers; **excess of assets over liabilities,** excédent *m* de l'actif sur le passif; **assets brought in,** apport *m* (*b*) **asset turnover,** rotation *f* des capitaux; **asset value,** valeurs *fpl* des actifs; **asset valuation,** réserve *f*/provision *f* pour évaluation d'actif.

assign, *v.tr.* assigner (**to,** à); **to assign a right to s.o.,** attribuer un droit à qn/faire cession d'un droit à qn; **to assign shares to s.o.,** transmettre/céder des actions à qn.

assignation, *n.* cession *f*/transfert *m* (de dettes, etc.); **assignation of shares/of patent,** transmission *f* d'actions/de brevet; **deed of assignation,** acte *m* de transfert; acte attributif.

assignee, *n.* cessionnaire *mf* (d'une créance, etc.); ayant cause *m*.

assignment, *n.* (*a*) cession *f*/transfert *m* (de biens, de dettes, etc.); **deed of assignment,** acte attributif/acte de transfert (*b*) **job assignment,** affectation *f* des tâches.

assignor, *n.* cédant(e).

assistance, *n.* **financial assistance,** appui financier.

assistant[1], *a.* auxiliaire; adjoint; **assistant manager,** sous-directeur *m*.

assistant[2], *n.* aide *mf*; adjoint(e)/auxiliaire *mf*; collaborateur, -trice; **shop assistant,** vendeur, -euse; **personal assistant (PA),** assistant(e)/secrétaire particulier, -ière.

associate[1], *a.* **associate company,** société affiliée; **associate director,** directeur adjoint.

associate[2], *n.* associé(e); adjoint(e); **business associate,** associé(e).

association, *n.* association *f;* société *f;* **trade association,** association professionnelle; **employers' association,** syndicat patronal; **producers' association,** syndicat de producteurs.

assume, *v.tr.* **to assume all risks,** assumer tous les risques.

assurance, *n.* assurance *f;* **life assurance,** assurance sur la vie/assurance-vie *f;* **assurance company,** compagnie *f* d'assurances; **assurance policy,** police *f* d'assurance.

assure, *v.tr.* **to assure s.o.'s life,** assurer la vie de qn; **to assure one's life,** s'assurer (sur la vie); **to have one's life assured,** se faire assurer sur la vie.

assured, *n.* assuré(e).

assurer, assuror, *n.* assureur *m.*

attachment, *n.* effet *m* d'une assurance; papillon *m* (attaché à une police d'assurance).

attention, *n.* **your orders shall have our best attention,** vos commandes seront exécutées avec le plus grand soin; **(for the) attention (of) Mr X,** à l'attention de M. X.

attorney, *n.* (*a*) agréé(e) (au tribunal de commerce) (*b*) procureur *m*/fondé *m* de pouvoir; **attorney in fact,** mandataire *m;* **power of attorney,** procuration *f*/mandat *m*/pouvoirs *mpl* (*c*) *NAm:* avocat *m* (inscrit au Barreau); *NAm:* **district attorney** = procureur de la République.

attractive, *a.* **attractive prices,** prix intéressants.

attributable, *a.* **attributable profits,** bénéfices *m* distribuables.

auction[1], *n.* **(sale by) auction/auction sale,** vente *f* à l'enchère/aux enchères/à l'encan; (vente à la) criée *f;* adjudication publique/vente publique; **by auction,** par voie d'adjudication; **to sell goods by auction/***NAm:* **at auction,** vendre des marchandises aux enchères; **to put sth. up to/for auction,** mettre qch. à l'enchère; **auction room,** salle *f* des ventes; **Dutch auction,** vente à la baisse/au rabais.

auction[2], *v.tr.* vendre (qch.) à l'enchère/aux enchères/à l'encan; mettre (qch.) aux enchères; vendre à la criée; **to auction sth. off,** vendre qch. aux enchères (pour s'en débarrasser).

auctioneer, *n.* **1. auctioneer and valuer,** commissaire-priseur *m* **2.** (*at a sale*) directeur *m* de la vente.

audio(-)typing, *n.* dactylographie *f* audio-magnéto.

audio(-)typist, *n.* dactylo *f* audio-magnéto; audio-copiste *mf.*

audit[1], *n.* vérification *f*/apurement *m* des comptes; vérification(s) comptable(s); audit *m*/contrôle *m;* **audit manager,** directeur *m*/chef *m* du service d'audit; **external audit,** audit/contrôle externe; **internal audit,** audit/contrôle interne.

audit[2], *v.tr.* vérifier/apurer/examiner (des comptes); **to audit the accounts of a company,** vérifier et certifier la comptabilité d'une société.

auditing, *n.* vérification *f* et certification *f* des écritures; apurement *m;* **balance-sheet auditing,** contrôle *m* du bilan.

auditor, *n.* vérificateur *m* comptable/audit(eur) *m*/réviseur *m*/commissaire *m* aux comptes (d'une société); censeur *m* (d'une compagnie d'assurances); **auditor's final discharge,** quitus *m;* **external auditor,** audit(eur) externe; **internal auditor,** audit(eur)/vérificateur interne.

auditorship, *n.* commissariat *m* des comptes.

authenticate, *v.tr.* authentifier.

authorize, *v.tr.* autoriser; **to authorize the payment (of a sum),** mandater une somme.

authorized, *a.* **authorized agent,** mandataire *mf;* **authorized capital,** capital social/nominal; **authorized dealer,** concessionnaire *mf*/distributeur agréé.

automated, *a.* automatisé.

automatic, *a.* automatique; **automatic data processing (ADP),** traitement *m* automatique des données.

automation, *n.* automatisation *f.*

availability, *n.* disponibilité *f* (de matériaux, etc.); (durée et rayon de) validité *f* (d'un billet); **subject to availability,** selon disponibilité.

available, *a.* (*a*) disponible; (*of pers.*) libre; **available at all branches,** en vente dans toutes nos succursales; **no longer available,** qu'on ne peut plus se procurer; introuvable; **items available in stock,** disponibilités *f* du stock; **available assets,** actif *m* disponible/liquide; **available funds,** fonds *m* liquides/fonds disponibles/disponibilités; **capital that can be made available,** capitaux *m* mobilisables; **sum available for dividend,** affectation *f* aux actions (*b*) valable; **(ticket) available on day of issue only,** (billet) valable le jour d'émission seulement.

average¹, *n.* (*a*) moyenne *f*; **sales average,** moyenne des ventes; **weighted average,** moyenne pondérée (*b*) *MIns:* avarie(s) *f(pl)*; **particular average,** avarie particulière; **general average,** avaries communes; **free from average,** franc d'avaries; **average adjustment/average statement,** dispache *f*; **average adjuster,** ajusteur *m* dispacheur *m*; **average bond,** compromis *m* d'avarie.

average², *a.* moyen; **average cost per unit,** coût unitaire moyen; **average price,** prix moyen; **average specimen,** échantillon normal; **average due date,** échéance moyenne; **taking as a basis the average figures for the last five years,** en adoptant comme base la moyenne des cinq dernières années.

average out, *v.i.* faire la moyenne de; **it**

averages out at ..., cela donne en moyenne ....

averager, *n. MIns:* répartiteur *m* d'avaries/dispacheur *m.*

averaging, *n. St Exch:* moyennes *fpl*; communes *fpl.*

avoidance, *n.* **avoidance of an agreement (owing to breach, etc.),** résolution *f*/annulation *f*/résiliation *f* d'un contrat; (*in a contract*) **condition of avoidance,** condition *f* résolutoire; **action for avoidance of contract,** action *f* en nullité; **avoidance of contract owing to mistake or misrepresentation,** rescision *f*; **tax avoidance,** évasion fiscale.

avoirdupois, *n.* poids *m* du commerce; **ounce avoirdupois,** once *f* avoirdupois/once du commerce.

award¹, *n.* arbitrage *m*; sentence arbitrale/décision *f* (arbitrale)/adjudication *f*; **to make an award,** rendre un jugement (arbitral); prononcer/rendre un arrêt; **to enforce an award,** rendre obligatoire une sentence; **to set aside an award,** annuler une sentence.

award², *v.tr.* adjuger/décerner (**sth. to s.o.,** qch. à qn); adjuger (un marché); **to award a wage increase,** accorder une augmentation de salaire; **to award damages,** accorder des dommages-intérêts.

awarding, *n.* adjudication *f* (d'un marché).

axe¹, *n. F:* **the axe,** coupe *f* (dans les prévisions budgétaires); réductions *fpl* (sur les traitements); diminutions *fpl* (de personnel); **to give s.o. the axe,** se débarrasser de qn/sa(c)quer qn.

axe², *v.tr. F:* **to axe public expenditure,** porter la hache dans les dépenses publiques; **to axe officials,** renvoyer des fonctionnaires (pour des raisons d'économie).

B

back¹, *n.* dos *m*/verso *m* (d'un chèque); **bills as per back,** effets *m* comme au verso; **back to back loan/operation,** opération *f* de face à face; contrat *m* de prêt direct.

back², *a.* **back orders,** commandes *f* en attente/en retard; **back interest,** arrérages *mpl*; **back pay/payment,** rappel *m* de traitement; **back rent,** arriéré *m* de loyer.

back³, *v.tr.* **to back s.o.,** financer/soutenir qn; **to back a bill,** avaliser/endosser un effet/donner son aval *m* à un effet.

backdate, *v.tr.* antidater; **the contract is backdated,** le contrat est antidaté; **increase backdated to May 1st,** augmentation *f* avec effet rétroactif au 1ᵉʳ mai.

backer, *n.* (*a*) **backer of a bill,** avaliseur *m*/ donneur *m* d'aval/avaliste *m* (*b*) commanditaire *m* (*c*) **financial backer,** bailleur, -euse de fonds; **the enterprise has an American backer,** le bailleur de fonds est américain.

backing, *n.* (*a*) **backing of the currency,** garantie *f* de la circulation (*b*) **financial backing,** fonds *mpl*; aide financière.

backlog, *n.* arriéré *m*; **backlog of orders,** commandes non exécutées.

back-up, *a.* **back-up service,** service *m* après-vente.

backwardation, *n.* déport *m*.

bad, 1. *a.* **bad debt,** mauvaise créance/ créance irrécouvrable/créance douteuse **2.** *n.* **he is 50 francs to the bad,** il est en perte de 50 francs.

bail, *n.* **to go bail for s.o.,** se porter garant de qn/caution pour qn.

bailee, *n.* dépositaire *mf* (de biens sous contrat).

bailer, *n.* = **bailor.**

bailment, *n.* (acte *m* de) dépôt *m*; contrat *m* de gage/de dépôt.

bailor, *n.* déposant(e) (de biens sous contrat).

balance¹, *n.* (*a*) solde *m*/reliquat *m* (d'un compte); **credit balance/balance in hand,** solde créditeur; **debit balance,** solde débiteur; **balance carried forward/balance to next account,** report /solde à reporter; **balance brought forward,** report/solde reporté; **balance due,** reste dû/solde (de compte); **payment of balance,** paiement *m* pour solde de compte; **to pay the balance,** régler le solde; **balance book,** livre *m* d'inventaire; **trial balance,** balance générale (*b*) **balance of trade,** balance commerciale; **balance of payments,** balance des paiements.

balance², 1. *v.tr.* balancer (un compte); compenser (une dette); **to balance the books,** clôturer les comptes; dresser/ établir le bilan; **to balance the budget,** équilibrer le budget; **to balance an adverse budget,** rétablir un budget déficitaire **2.** *v.i.* (*of accounts*) balancer/ s'équilibrer.

balance sheet, *n.* inventaire *m* comptable; bilan *m* (d'entreprise); tableau *m* de comptabilité; **off the balance sheet,** hors de bilan.

balancing, *n.* **balancing of accounts,** règlement *m*/arrêté *m* de comptes.

bale¹, *n.* balle *f*/ballot *m* (de marchandises, etc.); **bale of cotton,** balle de coton (pesant de 160 à 500 livres); **bale of paper,** ballot (de dix rames) de papier.

bale[2], *v.tr.* emballer/emballotter/empaqueter (des marchandises).

baling, *n.* mise *f* en balles.

ballasting, *n.* lestage *m.*

bang, *v.tr. StExch:* **to bang the market,** faire baisser les prix/écraser le marché/casser les cours.

bank[1], *n.* (*a*) banque *f*; **central bank,** banque centrale/banque d'émission; **commercial bank,** banque de dépôt; **the High Street banks,** les grandes banques centrales; **land bank,** banque territoriale/banque hypothécaire; crédit foncier; **merchant bank,** banque d'affaires; **private bank,** banque privée; **savings bank,** caisse *f*/banque d'épargne; **National Savings Bank,** Caisse nationale d'épargne; **the Bank of England,** la Banque d'Angleterre; **the World Bank,** la Banque Mondiale; **bank account,** compte *m* en banque/compte bancaire; **bank acceptance,** acceptation *f*; **bank annuities,** rente perpétuelle/fonds consolidés; **bank bill,** effet (tiré par une banque sur une autre); **bank book,** livret *m*/carnet *m* de banque; **bank credit,** crédit bancaire; **bank clerk,** employé(e) de banque; **bank manager,** directeur *m* de banque; **bank messenger,** garçon *m* de recettes; **bank holiday,** (jour de) fête *f* légale (où les banques n'ouvrent pas); **bank rate,** taux (officiel) de l'escompte; **bank roll,** ressources *f* monétaires (*b*) (bureau de) banque.

bank[2], *v.tr. & i.* mettre/déposer (de l'argent) à la banque; **he banked his salary,** il a déposé son salaire à la banque; **to bank with . . .,** avoir un compte (bancaire) chez . . .; **where do you bank?** qui est votre banquier?/à quelle banque avez-vous votre compte?/avec quelle banque faites-vous affaire?

bankable, *a.* (effet *m*) bancable/banquable/négociable (en banque).

banker, *n.* banquier *m*; **banker's card,**

carte *f* de crédit/de garantie (d'une banque); **banker's draft,** traite *f*; **banker's order,** ordre de virement *m* bancaire.

banking, *n.* **1.** opérations *fpl* de banque; **banking house,** maison *f* de banque/établissement *m* bancaire; **big banking houses,** maisons de haute banque; *NAm:* **banking account,** compte *m* en banque/compte bancaire; **banking hours,** heures *f* d'ouverture de la banque; **banking business,** trafic *m* bancaire **2.** profession *f* de banquier; la banque.

banknote, *n.* billet *m* de banque.

bankrupt[1], *a. & n.* (commerçant) failli (*m*); **fraudulent/negligent bankrupt,** banqueroutier, -ière; **to go bankrupt,** (*i*) faire faillite (*ii*) (*fraudulently*) faire banqueroute; **to be bankrupt,** être en faillite; **to adjudge/to adjudicate s.o. bankrupt,** déclarer/mettre qn en faillite; **bankrupt's certificate,** concordat *m*; **undischarged bankrupt,** failli non réhabilité.

bankrupt[2], *v.tr.* mettre (qn) en faillite.

bankruptcy, *n.* (*a*) faillite *f*; *Jur:* **act of bankruptcy,** acte *m* manifeste d'insolvabilité (entraînant la faillite); **petition in bankruptcy,** dépôt *m* de bilan; **to present/to file one's petition in bankruptcy,** déposer son bilan; **the Bankruptcy Act,** le code de procédure régissant les faillites (*b*) **fraudulent bankruptcy,** banqueroute *f*/faillite frauduleuse.

bar, *n. Mkt:* **bar code,** code-barre *m.*

bargain[1], *n.* (*a*) marché *m*/affaire *f*; **a good bargain,** une bonne affaire/un bon marché/un marché avantageux; **a bad bargain,** une mauvaise affaire; **to strike a bargain with s.o.,** conclure/faire un marché avec qn; *StExch:* **bargains done,** cours faits; **time bargain,** marché à terme/à livrer; vente *f* à livrer; *Jur:* **bargain and sale,** contrat *m* de vente impliquant le transfert de la propriété à titre onéreux (*b*) **bargain counter,** rayon *m* des soldes; **bargain basement,** sous-sol *m* d'économie; **bargain hunter,** chercheur, -euse d'occasions/acheteur, -euse à la recherche de soldes; **bargain offer,** offre exceptionnelle; **bargain sale,** marchandises *fpl* en solde *m*; vente-réclame *f*; **bargain price(s),** prix *m* de solde/prix exceptionnel(s); (*of article*) **a real bargain,** une véritable occasion/une occasion unique/une aubaine.

bargain[2], *v.i.* (*a*) entrer en négociations; négocier/traiter (**with s.o.,** avec qn); faire un marché (avec qn) (*b*) (*haggle*) **to bargain with s.o.,** marchander avec qn; **to bargain over a second-hand book,** marchander un livre d'occasion.

bargaining, *n.* marchandage *m*; **bargaining unit,** groupement négociateur; **bargaining position,** situation *f* permettant de négocier; **bargaining power,** pouvoir *m* de négociation; pouvoir de contestation; **free collective bargaining,** négociations collectives; **collective bargaining agreement,** convention collective.

barrel, *n.* fût *m*/tonneau *m* (de vin, de bière); caque *f* (de harengs); baril *m* (de pétrole).

barrier, *n.* barrière *f*/obstacle *m*/entrave *f*; **customs barrier,** barrière douanière; **trade barrier,** barrière commerciale.

barrister, *n.* **barrister (at law),** avocat *m*.

barter[1], *n.* échange *m*/troc *m*.

barter[2], *v.* (*a*) *v.tr.* **to barter sth. for sth.,** échanger qch. contre qch./troquer une chose contre une autre (*b*) *v.i.* faire le commerce d'échanges/faire le troc.

base, *n. Bank:* **base rate,** taux *m* de base (bancaire).

basic, *a.* **basic pay,** salaire *m* de base/de départ; **basic commodity,** denrée *f* témoin.

basket, *n. PolEc:* **the shopping basket,** le panier de la ménagère; **basket of currencies,** panier de monnaies.

batch, *n.* lot *m* (de marchandises, etc.).

batched, *a.* **batched consignment/dispatch,** envoi groupé.

bay, *n.* **loading bay,** quai *m* de chargement.

bear[1], *n. StExch:* baissier *m*/spéculateur *m* à la baisse; **bear speculation,** spéculation *f* à la baisse; **to sell a bear,** vendre à découvert.

bear[2], *StExch:* (*a*) *v.tr.* **to bear the market,** chercher à faire baisser les cours (*b*) *v.i.* spéculer à la baisse; prendre position à la baisse.

bear[3], *v.tr.* **to bear interest,** porter intérêt.

bearer, *n.* **bearer (of a letter/of a cheque)** porteur, -euse (d'une lettre/d'un chèque); **bearer bond,** obligation *f* au porteur; **cheque made payable to the bearer,** chèque (payable) au porteur.

bearing, *a.* **interest-bearing capital,** capital productif d'intérêts/capital qui rapporte.

bearish, *a. StExch:* **bearish tendency,** tendance *f* à la baisse.

bed, *n.* **bed and breakfast,** chambre *f* avec petit déjeuner; *StExch:* **bed and breakfast deal,** aller et retour *m*.

behalf, *n.* **payment on behalf of s.o.,** (*i*) versement *m* au compte/à l'acquit *m* de qn (*ii*) de la part qn/au nom de qn.

beneficial, *a.* **beneficial owner/beneficial occupant,** usufruitier, -ière.

benefit[1], *n.* **1. fringe benefits,** avantages sociaux **2.** prestation *f*/indemnité *f*/allocation *f*; **industrial injuries benefit,** indemnité pour accidents du travail; **social security benefits,** prestations sociales; **unemployment benefit,** indemnité de chômage; **sickness benefit/medical benefit,** indemnité de maladie/prestation de l'assurance-maladie; **to pay out benefits,** verser des prestations.

benefit[2], **1.** *v.tr.* faire du bien/être avantageux/profiter à (qn/qch.); **a steady ex-**

change rate benefits trade, un taux d'échange stable est avantageux au commerce/favorise le commerce **2.** *v.i.* **to benefit by/from, sth.,** profiter de qch./ gagner à qch./se trouver bien de qch./ tirer avantage de qch.; **to benefit from a rise in prices,** profiter/tirer profit d'une hausse de prix.

bestseller, *n.* best-seller *m*; (*of book*) succès *m* de librairie/best-seller.

best-selling, *a.* à grand succès/de grosse vente.

bid¹, *n.* (*a*) enchère *f*/offre *f*/mise *f*; **to make a bid of £15 000 for a property,** (*i*) faire une offre de £15 000 pour un immeuble (*ii*) mettre une enchère de £15 000 sur un immeuble; **to make the first bid,** faire la première mise; **to make a higher/further bid,** surenchérir/faire une offre plus élevée; **cash bid,** offre au comptant; **higher/further bid,** offre supérieure/ surenchère *f*; **closing/last bid,** dernière mise/dernière enchère; **takeover bid,** offre publique d'achat (OPA) (*b*) StExch: NAm: **bid and asked,** l'offre et la demande.

bid², *v.tr. & i.* **1.** (*at auction sale*) **to bid for sth.,** faire une offre pour qch./mettre une enchère sur qch.; **to bid a high price,** offrir une grosse somme; **to bid £10,** faire une offre de dix livres/miser dix livres; **to bid another pound,** faire une surenchère d'une livre; **to bid over s.o./more than s.o.,** enchérir sur qn/surenchérir; **to bid in (a lot),** racheter un lot (pour le compte du vendeur); **the buyers were bidding (up) well,** les enchères montaient vite **2. to bid for the new hospital,** faire une soumission pour le nouvel hôpital.

bidder, *n.* (*at sale*) enchérisseur, -euse; **there were no bidders,** il n'y a pas eu de prenants; **the lowest bidder,** le moins disant; **the highest bidder,** le plus offrant/ le dernier enchérisseur/l'adjudicataire *m*; **allocation to the highest bidder,** adjudication *f* à la surenchère/au plus offrant.

bidding, *n.* enchères *fpl*/mises *fpl*; **the bidding was very brisk,** les enchères

étaient vives; la vente a été bonne/a bien marché; **to start the bidding for a picture at £5 000,** mettre un tableau à prix £5 000.

big, *a.* **to earn big money,** gagner gros; **there's big money in it,** cela rapporte/ rapportera gros; **big drop in prices,** forte baisse de prix; **to do a big trade,** faire de grosses affaires.

bill¹, *n.* **1.** note *f*/facture *f*/mémoire *m*; **to make out a bill,** dresser/faire/établir/ rédiger une facture; **the bill was made out to me/in my name,** la facture a été émise/faite à mon nom; **to pay a bill,** payer/régler une facture; **you have not paid your bill,** vous n'avez pas réglé (la facture/la note/l'addition); vous n'avez pas payé votre facture; **shall I charge it on the bill?** faut-il le facturer/le porter sur la note? **to foot the bill,** payer la note/les dépenses; **wages bill,** masse globale des salaires; *Jur:* **bill of costs,** état *m* de frais **2.** (*a*) effet *m*/papier *m* (de commerce); **accommodation bill,** billet *m* de complaisance; **bill of exchange,** lettre *f* de change/ traite *f*; **bill of debt,** reconnaissance *f* de dette; **long bill,** effet à long terme; **short bill,** effet à court terme; **sight bill/bill payable at sight,** effet payable à vue/à présentation; **term bill,** effet à terme; **usance bill,** effet à usance; **bills payable,** effets à payer; **bills receivable,** effets à recevoir; **bills in hand,** effets en portefeuille/portefeuille *m* effets; **bills in a set,** effet en plusieurs exemplaires; **bill broker/discounter,** courtier *m* de change/agent *m* de change (*b*) NAm: billet de banque; **five-dollar bill,** billet de cinq dollars (*c*) **exchequer bill,** bon *m* du Trésor (britannique) **3.** affiche *f*/écriteau *m*; **stick no bills!** défense d'afficher! **4. bill of lading,** (*i*) Nau: connaissement *m* (*ii*) Rail: NAm: feuille *f* d'expédition; *Cust:* **bill of entry,** déclaration *f* (d'entrée) en douane; **bill of sight,** déclaration (en douane) provisoire; **transit bill,** passavant *m*; **victualling bill,** autorisation *f* d'embarquer des provisions soumises aux droits **5. bill of sale,** acte *m* de vente/contrat *m* de vente/facture.

bill², *v.tr.* facturer (des marchandises); **they billed me twice for the spare parts,** les pièces de rechange m'ont été facturées deux fois.

biller, *n. NAm:* **1.** (*pers.*) facturier, -ière **2.** (machine) facturière/machine *f* à facturer.

billing, *n.* facturation *f* (de marchandises); **billing machine,** machine *f* à facturer/facturière *f*.

bimonthly, *a.* (*i*) deux fois par mois (*ii*) tous les deux mois.

bind, *v.tr.* obliger (par contrat).

binder, *n.* **1.** convention *f* liant le vendeur **2. loose-leaf binder,** reliure *f*/classeur *m* à anneaux.

binding, *a.* obligatoire; **legally binding,** qui oblige en droit; **binding agreement,** obligation *f* irrévocable; **decision binding on all parties,** décision *f* obligatoire pour tous; **obligation binding on all parties,** obligation solidaire.

biodegradable, *a.* biodégradable.

birthplace, *n.* lieu *m* de naissance.

biweekly, *a.* (*a*) deux fois par semaine (*adj. only*) bihebdomadaire (*b*) tous les quinze jours.

black, 1. *a.* **black market,** marché parallèle/marché noir; **black economy,** économie *f* parallèle **2.** *n. F:* **in the black,** solvable/sans dettes.

blackleg, *n.* briseur *m* de grève.

black list¹, *n.* liste noire.

blacklist², *v.tr.* inscrire/mettre (qn, une entreprise, etc.) sur la liste noire.

blank¹, *a.* **blank credit,** crédit *m* en blanc/dont le montant n'est pas spécifié; **blank cheque,** (*i*) chèque *m* en blanc (*ii*) *NAm:* **blank check,** (formule de) chèque.

blank², *n.* (*in document, etc.*) blanc *m*/case *f*; **to fill in the blanks (of a form),** remplir (une formule); **cheque signed in blank,** chèque signé en blanc; **endorsement in**

blank/blank endorsement, endossement *m* en blanc/titre au porteur.

blanket, *a.* général/applicable à tous les cas; **blanket order,** commande globale/d'une portée générale; **blanket mortgage,** hypothèque générale; **blanket policy,** police globale (tous risques); *Rail: etc:* **blanket rate,** tarif *m* de groupe/tarif global.

blister, *n.* **blister pack,** emballage-bulle *m*/emballage transparent.

block, *n.* (*a*) **block of shares,** tranche *f* d'actions; **block booking,** location *f* (de places de théâtre, de films, etc.) en bloc; **block purchase,** achat *m* en bloc (*b*) **to write in block letters,** écrire en caractères d'imprimerie/en majuscules/en lettres moulées/en capitales.

blue, *a.* **blue chip,** valeur sûre/valeur de père de famille/titre *m* de premier ordre/blue chip.

blurb, *n.* (*a*) baratin *m* publicitaire (*b*) texte *m* publicitaire sur la jaquette d'un livre/sur la bande de nouveauté.

board, *n.* (*a*) conseil *m*/comité *m*; **price control board,** commission *f* de contrôle des prix; **advisory board,** comité consultatif; **marketing board,** office *m* de régularisation de vente; fonds *m* de stabilisation du marché; **board of directors,** direction générale (d'une société); **executive board,** conseil d'administration; **the bank is represented on the board,** la banque fait partie du conseil; **board meeting,** réunion *f* du conseil d'administration; **Board of Trade,** Ministère du Commerce et de l'Industrie (*b*) *Nau:* **free on board (fob),** franco bord (*c*) **board and lodging/room and board,** chambre et pension; **half board,** demi-pension *f*; **full board,** pension complète.

boardroom, *n.* salle *f* (de réunion) du conseil (d'administration).

body, *n.* **professional bodies,** organisations professionnelles.

bogus, *a.* **bogus company**, (*i*) société *f* qui n'existe pas/société fantôme (*ii*) société véreuse.

bona fide, *a. & adv.* de bonne foi; sérieux; **bona fide offer**, offre sérieuse.

bonanza, 1. *n.* **the new store proved (to be) a bonanza**, le nouveau magasin est devenu une vraie mine d'or 2. *a.* prospère/favorable; **bonanza year**, année *f* de prospérité/d'abondance.

bond¹, *n.* **1.** (*a*) engagement *m*/contrat *m* (*b*) *Jur:* obligation *f*/engagement; **to enter into a bond (with s.o.)**, contracter une obligation/un engagement (envers qn); **mortgage bond**, titre *m*/obligation hypothécaire; **contract bond/performance bond**, garantie *f* d'exécution (d'un contrat) (*c*) *Fin:* bon *m*; *NAm:* obligation; **Treasury bonds**, bons du Trésor; **registered bond**, bon nominatif; **government bonds**, (*i*) rentes *f* sur l'État (*ii*) titres de rente 2. *Cust:* dépôt *m*/entrepôt *m*; (*of goods*) **to be in bond**, être à l'entrepôt de la douane; **tobacco in bond**, tabac *m* en garenne; **goods out of bond**, marchandises sorties de l'entrepôt; **to take goods out of bond**, dédouaner des marchandises/faire sortir des marchandises de l'entrepôt de la douane; **taking out of bond**, dédouanage *m*; **bond note**, acquit-à-caution *m*.

bond², *v.tr. Cust:* entreposer/mettre en dépôt/mettre à l'entrepôt (des marchandises).

bonded, *a.* **1.** *Cust:* (*of goods*) entreposé/en dépôt/en entrepôt/en douane; **bonded warehouse**, entrepôt *m* de douane 2. *Fin:* (dette) garantie par obligations.

bonder, *n.* (*pers.*) entrepositaire *m*.

bondholder, *n. Fin:* obligataire *m*/détenteur *m* d'obligation.

bonding, *n. Cust:* entreposage *m* (de marchandises).

bonus, *n.* gratification *f*/sursalaire *m*/surpaie *f*/boni *m*/bonification *f*/prime *f*; part *f* de bénéfice/intéressement *m*; **work on a bonus system**, travail *m* à la prime; **cost-of-living bonus**, indemnité *f* de vie chère/de cherté de vie; **bonus share**, action gratuite/action d'attribution/action donnée en prime; **bonus on shares**, dividende *m* supplémentaire/bonification sur les actions; *Ins:* **bonus to policy holder**, bénéfice additionnel alloué aux assurés; **no-claims bonus**, bonification pour nonsinistre/bonus *m*; **Christmas bonus** = gratification du jour de l'an/de fin d'année; 13ᵉ mois, **group bonus**, prime collective/d'équipe; **output bonus/** *NAm:* **merit bonus**, prime de rendement.

book¹, *n.* **1.** livre *m*; **the book trade**, l'industrie *f* du livre; **book publishing**, l'édition *f*; **book club**, club *m* du livre; **book token**, chèque-livre *m* **2.** registre *m*; **account book**, livre de comptes/registre de comptabilité/livre *m* journal; **to keep the books (of a firm)**, tenir les livres/les écritures/la comptabilité (d'une maison); **bill book**, échéancier *m* d'effets; **purchase book/bought book**, journal *m* des achats; **sales book**, journal des ventes; **waste book**, main courante; **book of original entry**, journal; **book credit**, crédit *m* compte; **book debts**, comptes fournisseurs; **book entry**, écriture *f* (comptable); **book value**, valeur *f* comptable; **bank book**, livret *m*/carnet *m* de banque; **cash book**, livre de caisse; **cheque book**, carnet de chèques/chéquier *m*; **order book**, carnet de commandes.

book², *v.tr.* (*a*) inscrire/enregistrer (une commande)/prendre note d'(une commande); **we are heavily booked**, nous avons beaucoup de commandes à exécuter/notre carnet de commandes est bien rempli (*b*) retenir (une chambre à l'hôtel); retenir/réserver/louer (une place au théâtre); réserver (une place dans un avion, etc.); **to book s.o. into a hotel**, retenir une chambre d'hôtel pour qn; **to book a ticket through to Paris**, prendre un billet direct pour Paris; **we are booked up/fully booked**, c'est complet/il n'y a plus de places/il n'y a plus de chambres disponibles.

booking, *n.* location *f*/réservation *f*; **booking office,** guichet *m*/bureau de réservation/de location; **booking clerk,** préposé(e) à la location/au guichet/à la vente des billets; **double booking,** survente *f.*

book(-)keeper, *n.* teneur, -euse de livres/commis *m* aux écritures.

book(-)keeping, *n.* tenue *f* de(s) livres/comptabilité *f*; **single-entry book-keeping,** comptabilité/tenue de livres en partie simple; unigraphie *f*; **double-entry book-keeping,** comptabilité/tenue de livres en partie double; digraphie *f.*

booklet, *n.* livret *m*/brochure *f*; **descriptive booklet,** notice descriptive (d'une machine, etc.).

bookseller, *n.* libraire *m*; **secondhand bookseller,** bouquiniste *m*; **new and secondhand bookseller,** librairie *f* de neuf et d'occasion; **bookseller and publisher,** libraire-éditeur *m.*

bookselling, *n.* (commerce de) librairie *f*; commerce/vente *f* des livres.

bookwork, *n.* tenue *f* de(s) livres/des écritures.

boom[1], *n.* boom *m*/essor *m* économique/vague *f* de prospérité/(période de) haute conjoncture.

boom[2], *v.i.* être en hausse; **trade/business is booming,** les affaires *f* marchent bien/sont en plein essor.

booming, *a.* we have a **booming economy,** nous traversons une période d'essor économique.

boost[1], *n.* to give a **boost to an industry,** relancer une industrie.

boost[2], *v.tr.* augmenter; **to boost production,** relancer/augmenter la production.

boosting, *n.* réclame *f*/battage *m.*

booth, *n. NAm:* stand *m* (d'exposition).

borrow, *v.tr. & i.* emprunter (**from,** à); **to borrow (money) from s.o.,** faire un emprunt à qn/emprunter (de l'argent) à qn; **to borrow on mortgage,** emprunter sur hypothèque; **to borrow on/at interest,** emprunter à intérêt; **to borrow long,** emprunter à long terme/à longue échéance; **to borrow short,** emprunter à court terme; *StExch:* **to borrow stock,** (faire) reporter des titres.

borrowed, *a.* emprunté/d'emprunt; **borrowed capital,** capitaux empruntés/d'emprunt.

borrower, *n.* emprunteur, -euse; **borrower's credit,** crédit *m* de l'emprunteur.

borrowing, *n.* emprunts *mpl*; **financed by borrowing,** financé par des emprunts; **borrowing power,** capacité *f* de crédit.

boss, *n.* patron *m*; contremaître *m.*

bottom, 1. *n.* the **bottom has fallen out of the market,** le marché s'est effondré 2. *a.* **bottom price,** le prix le plus bas.

bottomry, *n. Nau:* hypothèque consentie sur un navire (pour fournir les fonds nécessaires à son voyage); (emprunt *m* à la) grosse aventure; contrat *m* en gros; **bottomry interest,** profit *m* maritime.

bought, *see* **buy**[1].

bounce, *v.i. F:* **I hope this cheque won't bounce,** j'espère que ce n'est pas un chèque sans provision.

bouncer, *n. F:* chèque *m* sans provision.

bouncing, *a. F:* **bouncing cheque,** chèque *m* sans provision.

bounty, *n.* prime *f* d'encouragement; prime (à l'exportation, etc.); subvention *f*; **system of bounties,** système *m* de primes.

boutique, *n.* (*a*) (petit) magasin de modes (*b*) (*in department store*) boutique *f*; **teenage boutique,** le coin/la boutique des jeunes.

box[1], *n.* (*a*) boîte *f*; **(cardboard) box,** (caisse box   22   bring out

en) carton *m* (*b*) **cash box,** caisse *f* (*c*) **PO Box 301,** boîte *f* postale 301/BP 301; (*in advertisments*) **Box number 301,** Référence 301/Ref. 301 (*d*) case *f* (d'un formulaire) (*e*) **letter box/post box/** *NAm:* **mail box,** boîte aux lettres (*f*) *Trans:* **black box,** contrôlographe *m*/ disque *m* de Sheila.

box², *v.tr.* emboîter/encaisser/encartonner (qch.)/mettre (qch.) dans une boîte; coffrer; **to box an article for sale,** conditionner un article pour la vente.

boxed, *a.* dans une boîte/dans un étui/sous étui.

bracket, *n.* tranche *f* (de revenus); fourchette *f* (de salaires); **the middle income bracket,** la tranche des revenus moyens; **tax bracket,** tranche *f* d'imposition.

brain-drain, *n.* fuite *f*/exode *m*/drainage *m* des cerveaux/des spécialistes.

branch¹, *n.* (*a*) **the different branches of industry,** les différentes branches de l'industrie (*b*) succursale *f*/filiale *f* (d'une société, d'une maison de commerce); succursale agence *f*/comptoir *m* (d'une banque); **branch manager,** directeur de (la) succursale (d'une banque); (*of a business*) **main branch,** établissement principal/maison mère; **branch office,** (*i*) agence *f* (*ii*) bureau *m* de quartier; **this shop has a branch in Lyon,** ce magasin a une succursale à Lyon.

branch², *v.i.* (*of an organization, etc.*) **to branch out into . . .,** étendre ses activités *f*/son commerce à . . .

brand, *n.* (*a*) marque *f* (de fabrique); **brand image,** image *f* de marque; **a good brand of cigars,** une bonne marque de cigares (*b*) sorte *f*/qualité *f* (d'une marchandise).

branded, *a.* **branded goods,** produits *m* de marque; **branded petrol** = supercarburant *m*/F: super *m*.

breach, *n.* **breach of contract,** rupture *f* de

contrat; **breach of warranty,** violation *f* de garantie.

break, *v.tr.* **to break a contract,** résilier/rompre un contrat.

breakage, *n.* (*i*) casse *f*/avarie *f* (*ii*) colis endommagé/avarié; **to pay for breakages,** payer la casse.

break down, *v.tr.* ventiler (les dépenses); **to break down an account,** faire un décompte/faire le détail d'un compte.

breakdown, *n.* analyse *f*/décomposition *f*/ détail *m*; **statistical breakdown,** analyse statistique; **breakdown of expenses,** ventilation des dépenses/décompte *m*.

break even, *v.i.* équilibrer son budget; ne faire ni pertes ni profits/rentrer dans ses frais/dans son argent.

break-even, *a.* **break-even deal,** affaire blanche; **break-even point,** seuil *m* de rentabilité; point mort.

break up, *v.i.* (*of meeting*) se séparer; **when the meeting broke up,** à l'issue de la réunion.

breakup, *n.* **breakup price,** prix *m* de liquidation.

bridging, *a.* **bridging facility/loan,** crédit *m* provisoire/crédit de relais; **bridging value,** valeur *f* de récupération.

bring down, *v.tr.* (*a*) *Book-k:* **balance brought down,** solde *m* à nouveau (*b*) abaisser/faire baisser (les prix); avilir (la monnaie, les prix); **to bring down the price of an article to £5,** baisser le prix d'un article jusqu'à £5.

bring forward, *v.tr.* **to bring forward an amount,** reporter une somme; **brought forward,** à reporter; report *m*.

bring in, *v.tr.* (*of capital investment*) **to bring in interest,** rapporter/porter intérêt; **investment that brings in 6%,** placement *m* qui porte intérêt à 6%/qui rapporte un intétêt de 6%.

bring out, *v.tr.* introduire (des valeurs sur le marché); **to bring out a new book,**

publier/lancer un nouveau livre; **to bring out a new washing machine,** lancer/ mettre sur le marché une nouvelle lessiveuse.

brisk, *a.* actif/animé; **brisk trade,** commerce actif; **brisk market,** marché actif/ animé; **business is brisk,** les affaires *f* marchent.

British, *a.* (*i*) britannique/de la Grande-Bretagne (*ii*) anglais/d'Angleterre; **British goods,** produits anglais/marchandises anglaises.

broadside, *n. NAm:* dépliant *m.*

brochure, *n.* brochure *f*/dépliant *m*; prospectus *m* publicitaire.

broker, *n.* (*a*) courtier *m* (de commerce); **bill broker,** courtier de change; **cotton broker,** courtier en coton; **insurance broker,** courtier/agent *m* d'assurances/ assureur *m*; **ship broker,** courtier maritime; **broker's contract,** courtage *m* (*b*) *StExch:* (**stock**)**broker,** agent de change/ courtier en valeurs mobilières; **intermediate broker,** intermédiaire *m* (en Bourse); **outside broker,** courtier marron/courtier non autorisé; **running broker,** remisier *m.*

brokerage, *n.* **1.** (*profession of broker*) courtage *m*; **outside brokerage,** affaires *fpl* de banque **2.** (frais de) courtage *m.*

broking, *n.* courtage *m.*

bubble, *n.* **bubble pack,** emballage-bulle *m*/emballage *m* transparent.

buck, *n. F:* dollar *m* (américain).

bucket-shop, (*a*) *F:* bureau *m* d'un courtier marron (*b*) agence *f* de voyages à prix réduits.

budget[1], *n.* (*a*) budget *m*; prévisions *f* budgétaires; **balanced budget,** budget équilibré; **budget constraint,** contrainte *f* budgétaire; **budget deficit,** déficit *m* budgétaire; **cash budget,** budget de trésorerie; **flexible budget,** budget flexible/adaptable; **to fix the budget,** établir le budget; **to balance the budget,** équilibrer le budget; **family/household**

budget, budget familial; **master budget,** budget global; **publicity budget,** budget de publicité/publicitaire; **sales and marketing budget,** budget commercial/des ventes; **operating budget,** budget d'exploitation; *Parl:* **budget statement for the year,** situation *f* budgétaire de l'année; **to open/to introduce the budget,** présenter le budget (*b*) **budget account,** compte *m* crédit (avec mensualités payées d'avance) / compte d'abonnement / compte permanent; **budget department,** rayon *m* des prix modiques/sous-sol *m* d'économie; **budget prices,** prix avantageux/ raisonnables/modiques (*c*) *Bank:* **budget account** = compte crédit.

budget[2], *v.i. Fin: Parl:* **to budget for (a certain expenditure),** budgetiser (certaines dépenses); **I have to budget for the whole year,** il me faut établir mon budget pour toute l'année.

budgetary, *a.* budgétaire; **budgetary policy,** politique *f* budgétaire; **budgetary control,** contrôle *m* budgétaire/gestion prévisionnelle.

budgeting, *n.* (*i*) budgétisation *f* (*ii*) établissement *m* du budget.

build, *v.tr. esp. NAm:* **to build (sth.) into a product,** incorporer (qch.) dans un produit.

building, *n.* (*a*) bâtiment *m*/édifice *m*; **office building,** édifice de bureaux; **public buildings,** édifices publics (*b*) construction *f*; **building contractor,** entrepreneur *m* de bâtiments; **building land,** terrain(s) *m* à bâtir; **building plot,** lotissement *m*; **building estate,** lotissement; **building materials,** matériaux *m* de construction; **building society** = (*i*) coopérative/société immobilière (*ii*) = crédit foncier; **the building trades,** les industries *f* du bâtiment; le bâtiment/la construction.

build up, *v.tr.* (*a*) **to build up one's business,** développer son affaire *f*/son commerce (*b*) faire de la publicité pour (un produit).

build-up, *n.* publicité *f*; campagne *f* publicitaire.

bulk, *n.* (*a*) **in bulk,** en grande quantité; en bloc; **to buy in bulk,** acheter en gros/en grosse quantité; **bulk buying is cheaper,** c'est moins cher d'acheter en grande/ grosse quantité (*b*) en vrac; **to ship (sth.) in bulk,** transporter (qch.) en vrac.

bulky, *a.* volumineux/encombrant; **bulky cargo,** chargement volumineux.

bull[1], *n. StExch:* haussier *m*/spéculateur *m* à la hausse; **bull transaction,** opération *f* à la hausse; **to buy a bull,** acheter à découvert.

bull[2], *StExch:* (*a*) *v.tr.* **to bull the market,** chercher à faire hausser les cours (*b*) *v.i.* spéculer à la hausse (*c*) *v.i.* (*of stocks, etc.*) être en hausse.

bullion, *n.* or *m* en barres; or/argent *m* en lingot(s); matières *fpl* d'or ou d'argent; valeurs *fpl* en espèces; *Fin:* métal *m*; **bullion reserve,** réserve *f* métallique.

bullish, *a. StExch:* **bullish tendency,** tendance *f* à la hausse.

bumper, *a.* **bumper crop,** récolte magnifique/exceptionnelle.

burden, *n. NAm:* frais généraux.

bureau, *n.* bureau *m*/agence *f*; **employment bureau,** bureau/agence de placement; **visitors' bureau,** centre *m* d'accueil.

bushel, *n.* boisseau *m* (8 gallons, approx. 36 litres).

business, *n.* (*a*) les affaires *f*; **business is business,** les affaires sont les affaires; **what's his line of business?** qu'est-ce qu'il fait (comme métier)? **to do business with s.o.,** faire affaire avec qn; **to lose business,** perdre de la clientèle; **shop that does a thriving business,** commerce *m* qui fait de bonnes affaires; **to be in business,** être dans les affaires; **to give up business,** se retirer des affaires; **to go out of business,** (*i*) faire faillite (*ii*) fermer boutique; **I'm going to London on business,** je vais à Londres pour affaires; **to be away on business,** être en déplacement (pour affaires); **how's business?** comment vont les affaires? **business is slow,** les affaires ne marchent pas; **volume of business,** volume *m* de la production; **to talk business,** parler affaires; **big business,** les grosses affaires; les consortiums *m*; les trusts *m*; **the tourist trade is big business today,** le tourisme est une affaire de grande importance aujourd'hui (*b*) entreprise *f*/maison *f*/firme *f*/établissement *m*; fonds *m* de commerce; **a profitable business,** une entreprise lucrative/rentable; **to run a business,** diriger un commerce; **to set up in business,** ouvrir un magasin/un commerce; **he is the owner of a small business,** il est propriétaire (*i*) d'une petite entreprise (*ii*) d'un petit commerce/d'un petit magasin; **the small business sector,** la petite entreprise; **his business is near the station,** son établissement/son atelier *m*/son usine *f* est près de la gare (*c*) **business agent,** agent *m* d'affaires; **business bank,** banque *f* d'affaires; **business card,** carte *f* (de visite) d'affaires; **business call,** visite *f* d'affaires; **business career,** carrière *f* dans les affaires; **business centre,** centre *m* des affaires; **business college/school,** école (supérieure) de commerce; **business concern,** entreprise commerciale; **business correspondence,** correspondance commerciale; **business hours,** heures *f* d'ouverture/de bureau/d'affaires; **business letter,** lettre commerciale; **business lunch,** déjeuner *m* d'affaires; **business management,** gestion *f* d'entreprise; **business manager,** directeur commercial; **business name,** raison commerciale/nom commercial; **business quarter,** quartier commerçant; **business trip,** voyage *m* d'affaires; **business world,** le monde des affaires; **business year,** exercice *m* (financier).

businessman, *n.m.,* (*i*) homme d'affaires (*ii*) commerçant; **to be a good businessman,** s'entendre aux affaires.

businesswoman, *n.f.* (*i*) femme d'affaires (*ii*) commerçante.

bust, *a. F:* **to go bust,** faire faillite.

buy[1], *v.tr. & i.* acheter (**sth. from s.o.,** qch. à qn); **to buy for cash,** acheter au comptant;

to buy in bulk/wholesale, acheter en gros/en grande quantité; **to buy on credit,** acheter à crédit/à terme; **bought of,** doit à.

buy², *n.* achat *m*; affaire *f*; **it's a good buy,** c'est un bon placement/c'est une occasion/une affaire; **to make a bad buy,** faire un mauvais achat/une mauvaise affaire/ un mauvais placement.

buy back, *v.tr.* racheter.

buyer, *n.* **1.** acheteur, -euse; acquéreur *m*; preneur, -euse; **potential/prospective buyer,** acheteur potentiel/éventuel; **buyer's market,** marché *m* à la baisse; **buyer's option,** prime *f* acheteur **2.** (*for firm*) acheteur; commissionnaire *m* d'achat; **head buyer/chief buyer,** acheteur, -euse principal(e).

buy in, *v.tr.* (*a*) (*at auction sale*) racheter (pour le compte du vendeur) (*b*) s'approvisionner de (denrées, etc.) (*c*) *StExch:* **to buy in against a client,** exécuter un client (*d*) (*at auction sale*) **the diamonds were bought in at £65 000,** les diamants ont été retirés de la vente à £65 000.

buying, *n.* achat(s) *m(pl)*; **speculative buying,** achats spéculatifs; (*in shop*) **impulse buying,** achat d'impulsion/achat stimulé; **shop buying,** achats professionnels (à la Bourse); **buying back,** rachat *m*; **buying in,** rachat; approvisionnement *m*; *StExch:* exécution *f* (d'un client); **buying order,** ordre *m* d'achat; **buying out,** désintéressement *m* (d'un associé); *Fin:* exclusion *f* (d'un actionnaire) par voie d'achat; **buying up,** accaparement *m* (des denrées).

buy into, *v.i.* **to buy into a company,** acheter des actions d'une société.

buying out, *v.tr.* désintéresser (un associé, etc.); **we bought him out for £90 000,** nous lui avons acheté sa part/son intérêt *m* dans l'affaire pour £90 000; nous avons payé son commerce £90 000.

buy up, *v.tr.* acheter (qch.) en masse; rafler/accaparer (des denrées, etc.).

by-product, *n.* sous-produit *m*/(produit) dérivé *m*.

C

cabinet, *n.* filing cabinet, fichier *m*/classeur *m*.

cable¹, *n.* câble *m*/câblogramme *m*; cable address, adresse *f* télégraphique.

cable², (*a*) *v.tr.* câbler (un message) (*b*) *v.tr. & i.* to cable (to) s.o., câbler à qn/aviser qn par câble/envoyer un câble à qn.

cablegram, *n.* câblogramme *m*/câble *m*.

calculate, *v.tr. & i.* (*a*) calculer/évaluer; supputer; estimer (*b*) faire un calcul/compter.

calculating, *adj.* calculating machine, machine *f* à calculer; calculatrice *f*.

calculation, *n.* calcul *m*; estimation *f*; to make a calculation, faire un calcul/calculer; to be out in one's calculations, être loin de son compte; rough calculation, calcul approximatif.

calculator, *n.* machine *f* à calculer; calculatrice *f*; electronic calculator, calculatrice électronique; calculator with a listing, calculatrice imprimante.

calendar, *n.* calendrier *m*; calendar month, mois civil/commun; calendar year, année civile.

call¹, *n.* 1. (*claim*) demande *f* (d'argent); *Fin:* appel *m* de fonds/de versement; call letter, avis *m* d'appel de fonds; payable at call, payable sur demande/à présentation/à vue; money at call/money on call/call loan/call money, prêt *m*/argent *m* à court terme/prêt remboursable à demande; withdrawal at call, retrait *m* à vue 2. *StExch:* call option, option *f*

d'achat; call premium, prime *f* de remboursement; call on a hundred shares, option de cent actions; call of more, faculté *f* du double/achat *m* d'encore autant à prime; call of twice more, achat du double à prime 3. appel *m*/communication *f* (téléphonique); call box, cabine *f* (téléphonique); local call, communication urbaine; person-to-person call, appel avec préavis; transferred charge call/*NAm:* collect call, appel en PCV; trunk call/long distance call, communication interurbaine; to take/to receive a (phone) call, prendre/recevoir un appel 4. visite *f*; to do a round of calls, faire une tournée.

call², *v.tr. & i.* 1. to call s.o. on the telephone, téléphoner à qn/appeler qn au téléphone 2. to call on s.o., rendre visite à qn/aller voir qn (chez lui, au bureau) 3. to call a strike, ordonner une grève/lancer un ordre de grève.

callable, *a.* callable bonds, obligations *f* remboursables avant échéance/obligations avec amortissement anticipé.

called-up, *a.* called-up capital, capital appelé.

call for, *v.i.* to call for a wage increase, demander/réclamer une augmentation de salaire.

call in, *v.tr.* (*a*) retirer (une monnaie) de la circulation (*b*) to call in one's money, faire rentrer ses fonds.

calling in, *n.* retrait *m* (de monnaies).

call off, *v.tr.* to call off a deal, rompre/

annuler un marché; **the strike was called off,** on a annulé la grève/mis fin à la grève.

campaign, *n.* **sales campaign,** campagne *f* de vente; **advertising campaign,** campagne publicitaire/de publicité; **press campaign,** campagne de presse.

can¹, *n.* **1.** bidon *m* (de lait, d'huile) **2.** cannette *f* (en métal); boîte *f* (de conserve, de bière).

can², *v.tr.* mettre en conserve (de la viande, etc.).

cancel, *v.tr.* **1.** annuler (un chèque/une dette/une commande/une réunion); faire remise d'(une dette); *Jur:* annuler/résilier/résoudre/révoquer/rescinder (un marché, un contrat); décommander (une réunion, des marchandises, qn); infirmer (un contrat); **to consider an agreement as cancelled,** considérer un contrat comme nul et non avenu; **to cancel a stamp,** oblitérer un timbre **2.** *Book-k:* contrepasser; (*of two entries*) **to cancel each other,** s'annuler.

cancellation, *n.* annulation*f*/révocation*f*/résiliation *f* (d'un contrat, d'une vente, d'une commande); résolution *f* (d'une vente).

cancelled, *a.* annulé/décommandé/révoqué/supprimé; (contrat) nul et non avenu/rescindé.

canned, *a.* (*of food*) en boîte/en conserve.

cannery, *n.* conserverie *f.*

canning, *n.* mise *f* en conserve; **canning industry,** conserverie *f*/industrie *f* des conserves alimentaires; **canning factory,** conserverie.

canvass¹, *n.* sollicitation *f* (de commandes); prospection *f* (de la clientèle).

canvass², *v.tr. & i.* solliciter (des commandes); **to canvass s.o.,** solliciter la clientèle de qn/démarcher qn; **to canvass for customers,** prospecter la clientèle; **to**

canvass from door to door, faire du porte(-)à(-)porte.

canvasser, *n.* démarcheur, -euse; placier *m* (de marchandises).

canvassing, *n.* sollicitation *f*/démarchage *m.*

capacity, *n.* **1.** (*a*) rendement *m*; débit *m*; **manufacturing capacity/production capacity,** capacité *f* de production; **yield capacity,** productivité *f*; **to work at full capacity,** travailler à plein rendement; **capacity output,** production *f* maximum; **idle capacity,** potentiel non utilisé; **capacity utilization rate,** taux *mpl* d'utilisation de la capacité; **excess capacity,** surcapacité *f*; **plant capacity,** capacité de l'usine; **profit-earning capacity,** rentabilité *f*; (*b*) **capacity (content),** capacité (d'un tonneau, etc.); **storage capacity,** capacité de stockage **2.** (*talent, ability*) capacité (**for,** pour, de); aptitude *f* (à faire qch.); **business capacity,** capacité pour les affaires **3. to have the capacity to do sth.,** être qualifié pour faire qch.; savoir/pouvoir faire qch.; **in the capacity of . . .,** en qualité de . . .; **to act in one's official capacity,** agir dans l'exercice de ses fonctions.

capital, *n.* capital *m*/capitaux *mpl*/fonds *mpl*; **authorized/registered/nominal/capital,** capital autorisé/capital déclaré/capital social; **capital account,** compte *m* de capital; **capital accumulation,** accumulation *f* de capital; **capital allowances,** déductions (fiscales) sur frais d'établissement; **capital assets,** actif *m* immobilisé/valeurs immobilisées; **capital bonus,** actions gratuites; **capital budget,** budget *m* d'investissement; **capital expenditure/outlay,** dépenses *fpl* en capital/mise *f* de fonds/frais *mpl* d'établissement; **capital gains/profits,** plus-value *f*; **capital gains tax,** impôt *m* sur les plus-values; **capital goods,** biens *mpl* d'équipement; **capital loss,** moins-value *f*; **capital market,** marché *m* des capitaux/marché financier; **capital movements,** mouvements *mpl* des capitaux; *NAm:* **capital stock,** capital social/capital-actions; **capital structure,** plan financier; **circulating capital,** capital circulant/roulant; **fixed capital,** capital fixe; **human capital,** capital humain; **issued capital,** capital émis; **paid-up capital,** capital versé; **share capital,** capital social/capital-actions; **subscribed capital,** capital souscrit; **uncalled capital,** capital non appelé/actions non libérées; **venture capital,** capital risque; **working capital,** capital d'exploitation/capital de roulement/fonds de roulement/actifs circulants; **company with a capital of . . .,** société au capital social de . . ..

capitalism, *n.* capitalisme *m.*

capitalist, 1. *a.* capitaliste **2.** *n.* (*a*) capitaliste *mf*; **the great capitalists,** les grands financiers; la haute finance (*b*) bailleur *m* de fonds.

capitalization, *n.* capitalisation *f* (des intérêts, etc.); **market capitalization,** capitalisation par le marché; **capitalization issue,** attributions *fpl* d'actions gratuites; **capitalization of reserves,** incorporation *f* de réserves au capital.

capitalize, *v.tr.* capitaliser (une rente, etc.); **your income, if capitalized, would run to . . .,** votre revenu, en termes de capital, se monterait à . . .; **company capitalized at £100 000,** société *f* au capital de £100 000; **capitalized value,** valeur capitalisée.

capture, *v.tr.* **to capture the market,** accaparer la vente/conquérir le marché.

car, *n.* **(motor) car,** automobile *f*/voiture *f*; **the car industry,** l'industrie *f* de l'automobile; **car manufacturer,** constructeur *m* (d')automobile(s); **car insurance,** assurance *f* automobile; **company car,** voiture de fonction.

card, *n.* (*a*) **business card,** carte *f* de visite professionnelle; **(bank) cheque card/cheque guarantee card,** carte chèque/carte de crédit/carte de garantie (d'une banque); **credit card,** carte accréditive/

carte de crédit (*b*) **show card,** (*i*) étiquette *f* (de vitrine, etc.) (*ii*) carte d'échantillons (*c*) (*for card index*) fiche *f*; **card index,** fichier *m*; **tab(ulating) card/punch card,** carte mécanographique; **punched card,** carte perforée; **card punch,** perforateur *m*/perforatrice *f* de cartes (*d*) **letter card,** carte-lettre *f*; **reply card,** carte-réponse *f* (*e*) carte (de sécurité sociale); *F:* **to get one's cards,** être renvoyé; **to give s.o. his cards,** renvoyer qn; (*f*) **clock card,** carte de pointage.

cardboard, *n.* carton *m*/cartonnage *m*; **fine cardboard,** bristol *m*; **corrugated cardboard,** carton d'emballage/carton ondulé; **cardboard box,** boîte *f* en carton/carton *m*.

card-index, *v.tr.* mettre (des informations) sur fiches.

card-indexing, *n.* mise *f* sur fiches.

care, *n.* **care of** (^c/_o) **Mr X.,** aux (bons) soins de M. X/chez M. X.

cargo, *n.* (*a*) cargaison *f*/chargement *m*/marchandises *fpl*; **to take on/to take in/to embark cargo,** charger des marchandises/prendre du fret/prendre un chargement; **full cargo,** plein chargement; **air cargo,** fret aérien; **deck cargo,** pontée *f*; **general/mixed cargo,** cargaison mixte/marchandises diverses; **cargo outward,** chargement/fret *m* d'aller; **cargo homeward,** chargement/fret de retour (*b*) **cargo boat/cargo ship,** cargo *m*; **cargo plane,** avion-cargo *m*; avion *m* de fret.

carriage, *n.* fret *m*/port *m*/transport *m*; **carriage free,** franc de port/franco; **carriage paid,** (en) port payé; **carriage forward,** (en) port dû; **carriage (expenses),** frais *mpl* de port/de transport; **to pay the carriage,** payer le factage/le camionnage/le transport.

carrier, *n.* (*a*) entrepreneur *m* de transports; transporteur *m*; camionneur *m* (*b*) **carrier bag,** sac *m* (à provisions).

carry, *v.tr.* **1.** transporter (des marchandises, etc.); camionner (des marchandises)

2. (*i*) adopter (une proposition) (*ii*) faire adopter/faire passer (une proposition); (*of a bill, etc.*) **to be carried,** passer/être adopté/être voté **3.** (*a*) **to carry interest,** porter intérêt; **to carry an interest of 4%,** rapporter un intérêt de 4% (*b*) (*of shop*) avoir (des marchandises) en magasin/en stock; **we don't carry this brand of cigar,** nous ne vendons pas cette marque de cigares **4.** *StExch:* (*of broker*) accorder un crédit à (un client).

carry forward, *v.tr. Book-k:* **balance carried forward,** report à nouveau; **to carry an item forward,** reporter un article/faire un report; **to be carried forward,** à reporter.

carrying, *n. NAm:* **1. carrying charges,** frais *mpl* de possession/de jouissance; **carrying cost,** frais financiers **2. carrying cost/value,** valeur *f* comptable.

carry on, *v.tr.* **to carry on a trade/a business,** exercer/diriger un commerce; diriger une entreprise.

carry-over, *n.* report *m*; **carry-over rate,** taux *m* de report.

carry over, *v.tr.* **1.** *Book-k:* faire un report/reporter (une somme d'une page à une autre); **to carry over a balance,** reporter un solde **2.** *StExch:* **to carry over stock,** reporter des titres; prendre des titres en report; **stock carried over,** titres *mpl* en report.

cartage, *n.* (*a*) transport *m* par voiture/par camion; camionnage *m* (*b*) frais *mpl* de transport.

cartel, *n.* cartel *m*.

carter, *n.* camionneur *m*.

carton, *n.* (*a*) carton *m* (*b*) boîte *f*/étui *m* en carton; **a carton of 200 cigarettes,** une cartouche de 200 cigarettes.

cartridge, *n.* **film cartridge,** chargeur *m*; **ink cartridge,** cartouche *f* d'encre.

case¹, *n.* **(packing) case,** caisse *f*/boîte *f* (d'emballage); **case of goods,** caisse de marchandises; **glass case/show case,** vitrine *f*.

case², *n.* **law case,** affaire contentieuse.

case³, *v.tr.* **to case goods,** emballer des marchandises/mettre des marchandises en caisse(s).

cash¹, *n.* (*no pl*) espèces *fpl*; numéraire *m*; argent comptant; valeurs *fpl* en espèces; **hard cash,** argent liquide; **cash balance,** solde/actif/solde de caisse; **cash budget,** budget *m* de trésorerie; **cash discount,** escompte *m* (de caisse)/remise *f*/escompte sur paiement (au) comptant; **cash float,** caisse *f*; **cash management,** gestion *f* de trésorerie; **cash price,** prix *m* au comptant; **to buy for cash,** acheter (au) comptant; **cash purchase,** achat *m* (au) comptant; **to pay cash,** payer comptant; **to pay in cash,** payer en espèces; **cash butcher,** boucher qui ne fait pas de crédit; **cash payment/settlement in cash/cash down,** paiement *m* (au) comptant/versement *m*/règlement *m* en espèces; **cash reserve,** encaisse *f* liquide; **to sell for cash,** vendre (au) comptant; **cash transaction/cash sale,** transaction *f*/vente *f* au comptant; **cash with order,** payable à la commande; **terms cash/cash terms,** payable au comptant; **cash less discount,** comptant avec escompte; **cash on delivery (COD),** paiement à la livraison; (livraison) contre remboursement; **cash account,** compte *m* de caisse; **cash book,** livre *m* de caisse; **cash and carry,** libre-service *m* de demi-gros; marchandises *fpl* à emporter contre paiement (au) comptant; payer prendre; **cash store,** magasin *m* qui ne vend pas à crédit; *Jur:* **cash offer,** offre réelle; *Fin:* **cash shares,** actions *f* de numéraire/en numéraire; **shares issued for cash,** actions émises contre espèces; **securities dealt for in cash,** valeurs au comptant; **cash at maturity,** valeur aux échéances; *Book-k:* **cash in hand,** fonds *mpl* espèces en caisse/caisse *f*/encaisse disponible; **petty cash,** petite caisse; **ready cash,** argent *m* en main/liquide; **to have cash in hand,** avoir de l'argent en caisse; **to keep the cash,** tenir la caisse; **to balance the cash,** faire la caisse; **cash box,** caisse/cassette *f*; **cash desk,** caisse; **would you please go to the cash desk,** veuillez passer à la caisse; **cash dispenser,** guichet *m* automatique de banque; **cash register,** caisse enregistreuse; caisse comptable.

cash², *v.tr.* **1.** toucher/encaisser (un chèque/un mandat-poste); encaisser (un effet, un coupon); escompter (un effet) **2. to cash a cheque for s.o.,** verser à qn le montant d'un chèque.

cashable, *a.* encaissable/payable (à vue).

cash-book, *n.* livre *m* de caisse; **counter cash-book,** chiffrier *m*; main courante de caisse; **paid cash-book,** main courante de sorties de caisse.

cash flow, *n.* cash flow *m*; marge *f* brute d'autofinancement (MBA); **discounted cash flow (DCF),** cash flow actualisé; **they have cash flow problems,** ils ont des problèmes de trésorerie.

cashier, *n.* caissier, -ière/préposé(e) à la caisse; **cashier's desk/office,** caisse *f*/comptoir-caisse *m*; **she's the cashier,** elle tient la caisse.

cash in, 1. *v.i.* (*a*) (*of salesman, etc.*) verser sa recette à la caisse; régler ses comptes (*b*) (*after attendance at board meeting, etc.*) toucher ses jetons **2.** *v.tr.* **to cash in a cheque,** toucher un chèque.

cash up, *v.i.* faire la caisse.

cask, *n.* (*a*) barrique *f*/baril *m*/fût *m*/futaille *f*/tonneau *m*; **to put wine into casks,** mettre le vin en fût(s)/en tonneau(x)/en barrique; **wine in the cask,** vin en fût/en cercles; vin en pièce; vin logé (*b*) (*for dry goods*) boucaut *m*.

casting, *a.* **casting vote,** voix prépondérante (accordée au président d'un conseil, etc., quand les avis sont également partagés); **the chairman has the casting vote,** la voix du président est

prépondérante; **to give the casting vote,** départager les voix/les votes.

casual, *a.* **casual labour,** main-d'œuvre occasionnelle/temporaire; **casual worker,** travailleur, -euse/employé(e) occasionnel(le).

catalogue¹, *NAm:* **catalog,** *n.* catalogue *m*/liste *f*/répertoire *m*/nomenclature *f*; **mail order catalogue,** catalogue (d'achat par correspondance); **trade catalogue,** catalogue général (complet)/tarif *m*; **to buy by catalogue,** acheter par catalogue.

catalogue², *NAm:* **catalog,** *v.tr.* cataloguer/inscrire (qch.) dans un catalogue.

cater, *v.i.* **to cater for (schools, etc.).** préparer les repas pour (les écoles, etc.)

caterer, *n.* restaurateur *m*; traiteur *m*.

catering, *n.* (*a*) **catering department,** rayon *m* d'alimentation (d'un grand magasin) (*b*) **the catering industry,** restauration *f*; **the catering was done by Messrs X,** la maison X a fourni/préparé le repas.

cattle, *n. coll. inv.* bétail *m*; bestiaux *mpl*; **cattle market,** marché *m* aux bestiaux.

caveat, *n. Jur:* (*a*) opposition *f* (**to,** à); **to enter/put in a caveat,** former/mettre opposition (**against,** à); **caveat against unfair practices,** avertissement *m* contre la concurrence déloyale (*b*) avis *m* d'opposition (au renouvellement d'un brevet d'invention, etc.); **caveat emptor,** aux risques de l'acheteur.

ceiling, *n.* plafond *m*; **price ceiling,** plafond des prix; **output has reached its ceiling,** la production plafonne; **prices have reached the ceiling of . . .,** les prix plafonnent à . . .; **ceiling price,** prix plafond; **monetary ceilings,** plafonds monétaires; **to fix a ceiling to a budget,** fixer un plafond à un budget.

central, *a.* **central purchasing office,** centrale *f* d'achats.

centre, *NAm:* **center,** *n.* **business centre,**

centre *m* des affaires; **commercial centre,** centre commercial; **industrial centre,** centre industriel; **shopping centre,** centre commercial; *FrC:* centre d'achat(s); **tourist centre,** centre de tourisme.

cereal, *a. & n.* céréale *f*; **cereal crops,** céréales.

certificate, *n.* (*a*) certificat *m*; **bearer certificate,** titre au porteur; **loan certificate,** titre *m* de prêt; **negotiable exchange certificate,** certificat d'échange négociable; **savings certificate,** bon *m* d'emprunt/bon d'épargne; **scrip certificate,** certificat provisoire; **share/stock certificate,** certificat d'action(s); **registered share certificate,** certificat nominatif d'action(s); *Bank:* **certificate of deposit,** bon de caisse; **certificate of insurance,** attestation *f* d'assurance; **certificate of compliance,** certificat de conformité; **certificate of approval,** certificat d'homologation; **certificate of origin,** certificat d'origine; *Nau:* **certificate of damage,** certificat d'avarie; **certificate of receipt,** certificat de chargement; **certificate of registration,** certificat d'inscription maritime; **tonnage certificate,** certificat de jauge; *Av:* **certificate of airworthiness,** certificat de navigabilité; *Aut:* **test certificate** = certificat d'aptitude à rouler; **international certificate for motor vehicles,** certificat international pour automobiles (*b*) *Jur:* **(bankrupt's) certificate** = (acte *m* de) concordat *m* (entre un failli et ses créanciers).

certificated, *a.* **1.** diplômé/titré **2.** *Jur:* **certificated bankrupt,** failli *m*/concordataire *mf*.

certify, *v.tr.* (*a*) certifier/déclarer/attester; **to certify (this) a true copy,** certifier copie conforme; **certified as a true copy,** copie certifiée conforme; *Fin:* **certified transfers,** transferts déclarés (*b*) authentiquer/homologuer/légaliser (un document); **certified cheque,** chèque certifié/*FrC:* chèque visé (pour provision); *NAm:* **certified letter** = lettre recommandée.

cession, *n.* **1.** cession *f*; abandon *m* (de marchandises/de droits) **2.** *Jur:* cession de biens (aux créanciers).

cessionary, **1.** *a.* cessionnaire **2.** *n. Jur:* ayant cause *m*.

chain-store, *n.* (*a*) magasin *m* à succursales (multiples) (*b*) succursale *f* (de grand magasin).

chair[1], *n.* fauteuil *m* (de président); **to be in the chair,** occuper le fauteuil présidentiel/présider/diriger les débats; **to be voted into the chair,** être élu président; **Mr X was in the chair,** M. X présidait la réunion/la réunion était sous la présidence de M. X; **to speak from the chair,** parler en tant que président; **to leave/vacate the chair,** lever la séance; **to support the chair,** se ranger à l'avis du président; **to address/appeal to the chair,** s'adresser/en appeler au président; **chair! (chair!),** à l'ordre!

chair[2], *v.tr.* **to chair a meeting,** présider une réunion.

chairman, *n.* (*a*) président(e); **to act as chairman,** présider (une séance); **a committee with Mr X as chairman,** un comité sous la présidence de M. X; **Mr Chairman/Madam Chairman,** Monsieur le Président/Madame la Présidente; **chairman's report,** rapport (annuel) du président (*b*) **he was chairman of the firm for ten years,** il a été président/président-directeur général de la maison pendant dix ans.

chairmanship, *n.* présidence *f*; **under the chairmanship of Mr X,** sous la présidence de M. X.

chairperson, *n.* président(e) *m(f)*.

chairwoman, *n.f.* présidente (d'une séance, etc.).

chamber, *n.* **Chamber of Commerce,** Chambre *f* de commerce; **Chamber of Trade,** Chambre de métiers.

chandler, *n.* **ship chandler,** fournisseur *m* maritime.

change¹, *n.* (small) change, monnaie *f*; to give change for £2, donner/rendre la monnaie de £2; keep the change, gardez la monnaie; change machine, changeur *m* de monnaie.

change², *v.tr.* to change a £5 note into francs, changer un billet de £5 en francs; could you change me a note? pouvez-vous me faire de la monnaie.

changer, *n.* money changer, courtier *m* de change.

channel, *n.* to go through the official channels, suivre la filière/la voie hiérarchique/les degrés *m* hiérarchiques; to open up new channels for trade, créer de nouveaux débouchés pour le commerce; channels of distribution, canaux *m* de distribution.

charge¹, *n.* frais *mpl*/prix *m*; admittance/entry charge, (prix d')entrée *f*; there is no charge (for admittance), l'entrée est gratuite; advertising charges, frais de publicité; list of charges, tarif *m*; scale of charges, barème *m* des prix; handling charges, frais de manutention; inclusive charge, tarif tout compris; extra charge, supplément *m*; customs charges, frais de douane; bank charges, frais bancaires; capital charge, intérêt *m*/service *m* des capitaux (investis); interest charges, intérêt *m* (à payer); NAm: charge account, compte *m* (d'achats); NAm: charge plate, carte *f* de crédit; to make a charge for sth., compter qch.; no charge is made for packing, on ne compte pas l'emballage/l'emballage n'est pas facturé/l'emballage est gratuit; free of charge, (*i*) exempt de frais/sans frais (*ii*) gratis/franco (*iii*) à titre gratuit/à titre gracieux; at a charge of . . ., moyennant . . .; at a small charge, moyennant une faible rétribution; charge forward, frais à percevoir à la livraison; (en) port dû; service charge, prestation *f* (de service).

charge², *v.tr.* (*a*) charger/imputer/passer en perte; to charge an account with all the expenses, charger un compte de tous les frais; to charge the postage to the customer, débiter les frais de poste au client; commission charged by the bank, commission prélevée par la banque; to charge an expense on/to an account, imputer/passer/mettre une dépense à un compte; to charge a sum to the debit of an account, inscrire/passer une somme au débit d'un compte; débiter un compte d'une somme; charge it on the bill, portez-le sur la note/facturez-le (*b*) property charged as security for a debt, immeuble affecté à la garantie d'une créance (*c*) to charge s.o. £5 for sth., prendre/compter/demander £5 à qn pour qch.; we are charging you the old prices, nous vous faisons encore les anciens prix; to charge ten francs a metre, demander dix francs du mètre; how much will you charge for the lot? pour combien me faites-vous le tout?/combien demandez-vous pour le tout?/quel est votre prix pour le tout?

chargeable, *a.* (*a*) à la charge (to, de); repairs chargeable to/against the owner, réparations *f* à la charge du propriétaire (*b*) *Fin:* sum chargeable to a reserve, somme *f* imputable sur une réserve.

chargee, *n. Jur:* créancier privilégié.

chargehand, *n. Ind:* chef *m* d'équipe.

chart, *n.* activity chart, graphique *m* des activités; organization chart, organigramme *m*; flow chart, graphique *m* d'évolution.

charter¹, *n.* 1. charte *f*/statuts *mpl* (d'une société); privilège *m*; bank charter, privilège de la banque 2. *Nau: Av:* affrètement *m*; charter plane, (avion) charter *m*; charter flight, vol *m* charter; on charter, (*i*) affrété (*ii*) loué (*iii*) sous contrat 3. *Nau:* charter (party), chartepartie *f*/contrat *m* d'affrètement.

charter², *v.tr.* 1. instituer (une compagnie) par charte/accorder une charte à (une compagnie, etc.) 2. affréter/noliser (un navire, un avion); prendre (un navire) à fret; to charter a coach, affréter un car.

chartered, *a.* **1. chartered company,** compagnie privilégiée/à charte; **chartered bank,** banque privilégiée; **chartered accountant (CA)** = expert *m* comptable **2. chartered ship,** navire affrété; **chartered aircraft/plane,** avion affrété/nolisé/charter.

charterer, *n. Nau:* affréteur *m.*

chartering, *n.* affrètement *m* (d'un navire, etc.); **chartering agent,** agent *m* d'affrètement.

cheap, *a. & adv.* (*a*) (à) bon marché/(à) bon compte/pas cher; **exceptionally cheap article,** article *m* très bon marché; **cheap rate,** tarif réduit; **to buy sth. cheap,** acheter qch. (à) bon marché/à bon compte/pour pas cher; **cheaper,** (à) meilleur marché/à meilleur compte; moins coûteux/moins cher; **it comes (out)/works out cheaper to buy 10 kilos,** on a avantage à acheter 10 kilos à la fois/cela revient moins cher d'acheter 10 kilos à la fois; **to obtain cheaper credit,** obtenir du crédit à meilleur compte; **cheaper and cheaper,** de moins en moins cher; **cheapest,** le meilleur marché/le moins cher; **dead/dirt cheap,** à vil prix/pour rien/à un prix défiant toute concurrence; **it's dirt cheap,** c'est donné/c'est d'un bon marché ridicule; *F:* (*of shopkeeper*) **he's very cheap,** il n'est pas cher/il ne prend pas cher; **to buy sth. on the cheap,** acheter qch. au rabais/à bas prix (*b*) *Fin:* **cheap money,** facilités d'escompte/argent *m* à bon marché.

cheaply, *adv.* (à) bon marché/à bas prix/à peu de frais; **they can manufacture more cheaply than we do,** ils sont à même de fabriquer à meilleur marché que nous.

cheapness, *n.* bon marché/bas prix (de qch.).

check¹, *n.* **1.** (*restraint*) frein *m*; **to put a check on production,** freiner la production **2.** contrôle *m*/vérification *f* (d'un compte, etc.); **check sample,** échantillon *m* témoin **3. luggage/baggage check,** bulletin *m* de bagages **4.** addition *f*/facture *f* **5.** *NAm:* = **cheque.**

check², *v.tr.* **1.** enrayer (la hausse des prix); freiner (la production) **2.** vérifier/apurer (un compte); examiner (des documents); **all the sales are checked,** toutes les ventes sont contrôlées; **to check (off/over) goods,** vérifier des marchandises; **to check and sign for goods on delivery,** réceptionner des marchandises **3.** *NAm:* enregistrer (des bagages).

check in, (*a*) *v.i.* (*at hotel*) s'inscrire à l'arrivée/se faire enregistrer; (*at airport*) se présenter à l'enregistrement (*b*) *v.tr.* (*at airport*) **to check one's luggage in,** (*i*) (faire) enregistrer ses bagages (*ii*) mettre ses bagages à la consigne.

check-in, *n.* (*at airport*) **check-in time is 30 minutes prior to departure,** (à l'aéroport) les voyageurs sont priés de se présenter à l'enregistrement 30 minutes avant l'heure du départ; **check-in counter,** guichet *m* d'enregistrement (de départ).

checking, *n.* **1.** contrôle *m*/vérification *f*; apurement *m*; pointage *m* **2.** *NAm:* **checking account,** compte *m* en banque/compte de chèques.

check out, *v.i.* (*at hotel*) régler (sa note) au départ; quitter l'hôtel.

checkout, *n.* (*a*) (*in supermarket*) **checkout (point),** caisse *f* (de sortie) (*b*) **checkout time is at 12 noon,** les clients doivent quitter la chambre avant midi (le jour du départ.).

checkroom, *n. NAm:* consigne *f.*

cheque, *n.* chèque *m:* **bank cheque,** chèque bancaire; **cheque for ten pounds,** chèque de dix livres (sterling); **cheque to order,** chèque à ordre; **cheque to bearer,** chèque au porteur; **crossed cheque,** chèque barré; **open/uncrossed cheque,** chèque ouvert/non barré; **blank cheque,** chèque en blanc; **certified cheque,** chèque certifié/*FrC:* visé; **pay cheque,** (chèque de) traitement *m*/salaire *m*; **stale cheque,** chèque périmé; **traveller's cheque,** chèque de voyage; **cheque without cover/worthless cheque/***F:* **dud**

cheque/bouncing cheque, chèque sans provision; **cheque book,** carnet *m* de chèques/chéquier *m*; **cheque paper,** papier *m* de sûreté; **cheque counterfoil/ stub,** talon *m* de chèque/souche *f*; **to cash a cheque,** toucher un chèque; **to make out a cheque to . . . .,** établir/faire un chèque à l'ordre de . . .; **to pay by cheque,** régler par chèque; **to pay a cheque into the bank/into one's account,** déposer un chèque à la banque/verser de l'argent à son compte; **to refer a cheque to drawer,** refuser d'honorer un chèque; **to stop a cheque,** suspendre le paiement d'un chèque; **to write (out)/to draw a cheque,** faire/émettre un chèque.

chief, *a.* **chief accountant,** chef comptable; **chief executive,** directeur général.

chip, *n.* **1. blue chip (investment),** investissement sûr/de père de famille/titre *m* de premier ordre/blue chip **2.** *Cmptr:* **(silicon) chip,** puce *f*.

chit, *n.* note *f*/facture *f* (de consommation) (dans un club).

choice, *a.* **choice article,** article *m* de choix/article surfin; **choice quality,** qualité *f* de choix; **choice raisins,** raisins *m* surchoix; **choice wine,** vin *m* de première qualité; vin de marque.

circular, 1. *a.* **circular letter,** (lettre) circulaire *f*/lettre collective; **circular letter of credit,** lettre de crédit circulaire **2.** *n.* (*a*) (lettre) circulaire/lettre collective (*b*) prospectus *m*.

circularize, *v.tr.* envoyer/expédier (des circulaires/des prospectus).

circulate, 1. *v.i.* (*of money*) **to circulate freely,** circuler librement; rouler **2.** *v.tr.* (*a*) mettre en circulation/émettre (des billets de banque) (*b*) = **circularize.**

circulating[1], *a.* circulant; *Fin:* **circulating capital,** capitaux circulants/roulants.

circulating[2], *n.* circulation *f*; *Fin:* **circulating medium,** agent *m* monétaire/monnaie *f* d'échange/moyen *m* d'échange.

circulation, *n.* (*a*) **circulation of capital,** roulement *m*/circulation *f* des capitaux; **to withdraw capital from its natural channels of circulation,** enlever des capitaux à leur circuit naturel (*b*) (*of money*) **to be in circulation,** circuler; **notes in circulation,** billets *m* en circulation; **credit circulation,** circulation *f* fiduciaire (*c*) **circulation (of a newspaper),** tirage *m* (d'un journal); **newspaper with a wide circulation,** journal à grand/gros tirage.

City (the), *n.* la Cité de Londres (centre des affaires); **City man,** homme d'affaires (de la Cité de Londres); financier *m*; **he's in the City,** il est dans la finance (dans la Cité de Londres); *Journ:* **City article,** bulletin financier/compte rendu de la Bourse et du commerce; **The City,** Bourse/finance/ commerce; **City editor,** rédacteur *m* de la rubrique financière.

claim[1], *n.* **1.** revendication *f*/réclamation *f*; **wage claims,** revendications de salaire/salariales **2.** droit *m*/titre *m*/ prétention *f* (**to sth.,** à qch.); **legal claim to sth.,** titre juridique à qch.; **to put in a claim,** faire valoir ses droits **3.** *Jur:* (*debt*) créance *f*; **claims and liabilities,** créances et engagements *m*; **contractual claim,** créance contractuelle; **preferential claim,** créance privilégiée; privilège *m* du créancier **4.** *Ins: Jur:* réclamation *f*; **claim form,** formulaire *m* de réclamation; **claims manager,** chef *m* du service des réclamations; **to lay claim to sth.,** déposer une réclamation; **to set up a claim,** faire une réclamation; **to make/put in a claim for damages,** demander une indemnité/ réclamer des dommages et intérêts; **disputed claims office,** le contentieux; **small claims court,** cour *f* des petites créances.

claim[2], *v.tr.* réclamer/revendiquer (un droit, etc.); *Ins:* **to claim damages,** réclamer des dommages et intérêts.

claimant, *n.* prétendant(e); revendicateur, -trice; *Jur:* réclamant(e); demandeur, -eresse; partie requérante; **rightful claimant,** ayant droit *m*; **claimant for a patent,** demandeur d'un brevet.

claim back, *v.tr.* to claim back VAT, récupérer la TVA.

claimer, *n.* = claimant.

claiming, *n.* réclamation *f*/revendication *f*; *Jur:* claiming back, action *f* en restitution.

clamp-down, *n.* clamp-down on credit, resserrement *m* du crédit.

class, *n.* *Av:* economy class, classe *f* économique; first class, première classe; *Rail:* second class coach, wagon *m* de seconde/de 2e classe; to travel first/second class, voyager en première/en seconde.

classification, *n.* job classification, classification *f* des fonctions.

clause, *n.* clause *f*/article *m* (d'un traité); clauses of a law, dispositions *f* d'une loi; additional clause, clause additionnelle; *Ins:* avenant *m* (d'une police); clauses governing a sale, conditions *f* d'une vente; customary clause, clause d'usage; formal clause, clause de style; penalty clause, clause pénale; arbitration clause, clause compromissoire; saving clause, clause de sauvegarde/clause restrictive; réservation *f*; restrictive clauses, modalités *f*.

clean, *a.* *Fin:* clean bill, effet *m* libre; clean receipt, reçu *m* sans réserve.

clear¹, *a.* 1. (*a*) clear profit, bénéfice clair et net; clear loss, perte sèche (*b*) *Jur:* three clear days, trois jours francs 2. clear accounts, comptes *m* en règle.

clear², *v.tr.* 1. to clear goods, solder/liquider des marchandises; to clear, (en) solde; must be cleared, vente *f* à tout prix 2. to clear a ship, expédier un navire; faire la déclaration à la sortie; to clear goods through customs, passer des marchandises en douane/dédouaner des marchandises/retirer des marchandises de la douane 3. to clear 10%, réaliser 10% tous frais payés/faire un bénéfice net de 10%; not to clear one's expenses, ne pas faire

ses frais; I cleared a hundred pounds, cela m'a rapporté cent livres net 4. *Fin:* compenser (un chèque); to clear a bill, régler un effet.

clearance, *n.* 1. clearance (sale), vente *f* de soldes; liquidation *f* 2. *Cust: Nau:* acquit *m*/acquittement *m* (de marchandises); déclaration *f* en douane à la sortie/dédouanement *m*; congé *m*; clearance inward(s), (*i*) déclaration d'entrée (*ii*) permis *m* d'entrée; acquit; clearance outward(s), (*i*) déclaration de sortie (*ii*) permis de sortie; congé des douanes; clearance certificate, lettre *f* de mer; to effect customs clearance, procéder aux formalités de la douane 3. *Bank:* compensation *f* (d'un chèque).

clearing, *n.* 1. clearing (off) of goods/merchandise, liquidation *f*/solde *m* 2. (*a*) acquittement *m* des droits (sur des marchandises)/dédouanement *m* (*b*) clearing (off) of a debt, acquittement (d'une dette) (*c*) liquidation (d'un compte) (*d*) *Fin:* compensation *f*/clearing *m* (de chèques); under the clearing procedure, par voie de compensation; clearing agreement, accord *m* de compensation/de clearing; clearing bank, banque *f* de clearing; *Fin:* clearing house, chambre *f* de compensation; to pass a cheque through the clearing house, compenser un chèque.

clear off, *v.tr.* to clear off a debt, rembourser une dette.

clerical, *a.* (*a*) clerical error, faute *f* de copiste; *Book-k:* erreur *f* d'écritures (*b*) clerical work, travail de bureau; clerical worker, employé(e) de bureau; clerical staff, personnel *m* de bureau; employés de bureau.

clerk¹, *n.* 1. employé(e) de bureau; commis *m*; bank clerk, employé(e)/commis de banque; chief clerk/senior clerk/head clerk, chef *m* de bureau; commis principal/premier commis; junior clerk, petit employé; shipping clerk, (commis) expéditionnaire *m*/employé(*e*) à l'expédition; **filing clerk**/*NAm:* **file clerk,** préposé(e)/employé(e) aux dossiers; **records clerk,** employé(e) aux archives; **booking clerk,** préposé(e) au guichet/à la location/à la vente des billets **2.** *NAm:* (*a*) **sales clerk,** vendeur, -euse/commis (de magasin) (*b*) préposé(e) à la réception (d'un hôtel).

clerk[2], *v.i. NAm:* travailler comme employé(e) de bureau/de banque/comme vendeur, -euse dans un magasin.

clerkess, *n.f. Scot:* employée de bureau.

client, *n.* client(e); **our clients,** nos clients/ notre clientèle *f.*

clientele, clientèle, *n.* clientèle *f* (d'un magasin/d'un restaurant, etc.).

clock, *v.i.* **to clock in,** pointer à l'arrivée; **to clock out,** pointer au départ/à la sortie.

clocking, *n.* **clocking in,** pointage *m* à l'arrivée; **clocking out,** pointage à la sortie/au départ.

close, 1. *v.tr.* (*a*) *Book-k:* **to close the books,** balancer les comptes (*b*) clôturer/arrêter (un compte); **to close the yearly accounts,** arrêter les comptes de l'exercice; conclure/clore (un marché/une négociation); *StExch:* liquider (une opération); *Jur:* clôturer (une faillite) **2.** *v.i.* (*a*) *StExch:* **the shares closed at £10,** les actions *f* ont clôturé/terminé à £10 (*b*) (*of shop*) **closed,** (magasin) fermé; **closed on Saturdays,** fermé le samedi **3. closed shop,** monopole syndical de l'embauche; entreprise *f*/atelier *m* qui n'embauche que du personnel syndiqué **4. closed end (investment) trust,** société *f* d'investissement à capital fixe.

close down, 1. *v.tr.* fermer (une usine, etc.) **2.** *v.i.* (*of factory*) fermer; arrêter/ cesser la production; chômer; (*of shop*) fermer boutique.

close out, *NAm:* **1.** *v.tr.* (*a*) solder (des marchandises)/écouler (des marchandises) à bas prix (*b*) fermer/arrêter/

clôturer (un compte) **2.** *v.i.* fermer boutique.

closing[1], *a.* dernier/final; **the closing bid,** la dernière enchère; **closing date (for application),** date *f* limite; **closing prices,** derniers cours/prix *m* de clôture; **the closing quotations,** les cotes *f* en clôture; **closing stock,** stock *m* à l'inventaire.

closing[2], *n.* **1.** fermeture *f* (d'un magasin); fermeture/chômage *m* (d'une usine); **Sunday closing,** chômage du dimanche; repos *m* hebdomadaire; **closing time,** heure *f* de (la) fermeture (d'un pub); **early closing day,** jour *m* où les magasins sont fermés l'après-midi **2.** (*i*) clôture *f* (d'un compte) (*ii*) règlement *m* (d'un compte); clôture/conclusion *f* (d'un marché/d'une affaire); levée *f*/clôture (d'une séance).

closing down, *n.* **1.** cessation *f* de commerce **2.** fermeture *f*/chômage *m* (d'une usine); fermeture/liquidation *f* (d'un magasin); **closing down sale,** solde *m* de fermeture.

closing out, *n. NAm:* fermeture *f*/ liquidation *f* (d'un magasin); **closing out sale,** solde *m* de fermeture.

closure, *n. NAm:* **closure at 6 pm,** fermeture *f* à 18 heures.

clothing, *n. coll.* habillement *m*/vêtements *mpl*; **article of clothing,** vêtement *m*; **the clothing trade,** l'industrie *f* du vêtement/de l'habillement; *NAm:* **clothing store,** magasin *m* de drapier/de confections.

co-creditor, *n. Jur:* cocréancier, -ière.

code, *n.* **post(al) code,** code *m* postal; *WTel:* **area code,** indicatif départemental/*FrC:* régional; **country code,** indicatif du pays; **international code,** préfixe *m* d'accès à l'automatique international.

co-director, *n.* codirecteur, -trice; co-administrateur *m*.

coin, *n.* **1.** pièce *f* de monnaie; **gold coins,** pièces d'or **2.** *coll.* (*no pl*) monnaie(s) *f* (*pl*)/pièces/numéraire *m*/espèces *fpl*;

coin and bullion, métal monnayé et métal en barres; **in coin,** en espèces/en numéraire **3. coin machine/coin-operated machine/coin-in-the-slot machine,** distributeur *m* automatique.

coinage, *n.* (*a*) système *m* monétaire (d'un pays) (*b*) monnaie(s) *f*(*pl*); numéraire *m.*

co-insurance, *n.* coassurance *f.*

collapse[1], *n.* (*a*) débâcle *f* (d'un établissement) (*b*) *Fin:* **the collapse of the market,** l'effondrement *m* du marché/des cours de la Bourse; **the collapse of the franc,** la dégringolade du franc.

collapse[2], *v.i.* (*of prices*) s'effondrer.

collar, *n.* **blue collar worker,** employé manuel; **white collar worker,** employé *m* de bureau.

collateral, *a. & n.* **collateral (security)/collateral evidence,** garantie additionnelle/accessoire/complémentaire; nantissement *m* subsidiaire; **to lodge as collateral,** fournir en nantissement.

collect[1], *v.tr.* percevoir/lever/recouvrer (des impôts); toucher (une traite); **to collect a debt,** recouvrer/récupérer/ faire rentrer une créance; **to collect moneys due,** faire la recette (des traites).

collect[2], (*a*) *a. NAm:* **collect call,** appel *m* (téléphonique) en PCV; **to make a collect call,** *FrC:* (faire) renverser les frais (d'appel) (*b*) *adv. NAm:* **to call collect,** faire un appel en PCV; **to send a parcel collect,** envoyer un colis en port dû/payable à destination.

collectable, *a.* (*of money*) recouvrable/récupérable; (*of tax*) percevable; (*of coupon*) encaissable.

collecting, *a.* **collecting clerk,** garçon *m* de recettes; **collecting banker,** banquier encaisseur; **collecting agency,** banque *f* de recouvrement; **collecting department,** service *m* de recouvrement.

collection, *n.* (*a*) perception *f*/recouvrement *m*/levée *f*/rentrée *f* (des impôts) (*b*) encaissement *m*; **bill for collection,** effet *m* à l'encaissement; **list of bills for collection,** bordereau *m* d'encaissement; **collection bank,** banque *f* d'encaissement; **collection charges,** frais *m* d'encaissement/de recouvrement; **statement of collections,** décompte *m* des encaissements; **collection rates,** tarifs *m* d'encaissement; **to hand in for collection,** donner à l'encaissement; **to send for collection,** envoyer à l'encaissement.

collective, *a.* collectif; **collective bargaining,** négociation *f* de convention collective; **collective contract,** contrat collectif.

collector, *n.* (*a*) encaisseur *m* (d'un chèque, etc.) (*b*) *Adm:* percepteur *m* (des contributions directes); receveur *m* (des contributions indirectes).

column, *n.* colonne *f.*

combine, *n.* combinaison financière; entente industrielle; cartel *m*; trust *m*; **horizontal combine,** cartel horizontal/consortium *m.*

commerce, *n.* commerce *m*; **Chamber of Commerce,** Chambre *f* de commerce.

commercial[1], *a.* commercial; **commercial artist,** dessinateur, -trice de publicité; **commercial attaché,** attaché commercial; **commercial bank,** banque commerciale/de commerce; banque de dépôt; **commercial college,** école supérieure de commerce; **commercial court,** tribunal *m* de commerce; **commercial designer,** dessinateur, -trice de publicité; **commercial efficiency (of a machine),** rendement *m* économique/effet *m* utile (d'une machine); **commercial law,** droit commercial/le Code de commerce; **commercial paper,** effet commercial; **commercial port,** port *m* de commerce; **commercial district,** quartier commerçant; **commercial traveller,** représentant *m*/voyageur *m* de commerce; courtier *m*; **commercial television,** télévision commerciale; **commercial value,** valeur marchande; **sample**

of no commercial value, échantillon *m* sans valeur marchande; commercial vehicle, véhicule *m* utilitaire.

commercial², *n. WTel: TV:* émission *f* publicitaire.

commercialism, *n.* esprit commercial; *Pej:* mercantilisme *m.*

commercialization, *n.* commercialisation *f.*

commercialize, *v.tr.* commercialiser.

commercially, *adv.* commercialement.

commission, *n.* 1. commission *f*/pourcentage *m*; commission on sale, commission sur vente; sale on commission, vente *f* à (la) commission; three per cent commission, trois pour cent de commission; to charge/to receive 5% commission, prendre/toucher une commission de 5%; to appoint s.o. as buyer on commission, commissionner qn; illicit commission, remise *f* illicite/*F:* pot *m* de vin; commission agent, représentant *m* à la commission; commissionnaire *m* en marchandises 2. control commission, commission de contrôle.

committee, *n.* comité *m*/commission *f* conseil *m*; to be on/to sit on a committee, être membre/faire partie d'un comité; management committee, conseil d'administration; joint production committee, comité d'entreprise; the Stock Exchange Committee = la Chambre syndicale des agents de change.

commodity, *n.* marchandise *f*/denrée *f*/produit *m*; commodities such as tea, coffee and sugar, denrées telles que le thé, le café et le sucre; primary commodity/basic commodity, produit de base; standard commodity, bien *m* étalon; article *m* de référence; rice is the staple commodity of China, le riz est la ressource principale de la Chine; commodity market, marché *m* de matières premières, métaux et denrées; commodity exchange, bourse *f* des matières premières et denrées; commodity credits, crédits commerciaux; commodity money/com-modity currency, monnaie *f* marchandise; international commodity agreements, accords internationaux sur les produits de base.

common, *a.* ordinaire; *NAm:* common stock/common equity, actions *f* ordinaires.

community, *n.* (*a*) the (European) Community, la communauté européenne (*b*) business community, milieu *m* d'affaires.

commutation, *n.* commutation ticket, carte *f* (d'abonnement).

commute, *v.i.* voyager chaque jour entre sa résidence et son travail.

commuter, *n.* personne *f* qui voyage chaque jour entre sa résidence et son travail; *F:* banlieusard; commuter belt, banlieue *f*; zone des villes dortoirs; commuter train, train de banlieue.

company, *n.* (*a*) société *f*/compagnie *f*/entreprise *f*; joint stock company, société anonyme par actions; limited (liability) company/company limited by shares, (*i*) société à responsabilité limitée (SARL) (*ii*) société anonyme (SA); private company = société à responsabilité limitée; public company = société anonyme (SA); affiliated/subsidiary company, filiale *f*/compagnie affiliée; dependant/daughter company, compagnie/société captive; assurance company/insurance company, compagnie d'assurances; bogus company, société fantôme; family company, société de famille; joint venture company, société d'exploitation en commun; management company, société de gérance; compagnie d'exploitation; parent company, compagnie mère; real estate company, société immobilière; shipping company, compagnie de navigation; Companies Act, loi *f* sur les sociétés; name of a company, raison sociale; and Co., et Cie; to form/to incorporate a company, constituer une société; to liquidate/to wind up a company, liquider une société; a (good) company man, un homme qui se dévoue aux intérêts de l'entreprise; one company

town, agglomération construite pour les employés d'une entreprise (*b*) corporation *f* de marchands; **the City Companies,** les corporations de la Cité de Londres.

comparability, *n.* **pay comparability,** alignement *m* des salaires (sur ceux d'autres industries).

compensate, *v.tr.* (*a*) **to compensate s.o. for sth.,** dédommager/indemniser qn de qch.; **to compensate a workman for injuries,** dédommager un ouvrier pour blessures (*b*) rémunérer (qn).

compensation, *n.* (*a*) compensation *f*; (*for loss/injury*) dédommagement *m*; (*for damage*) indemnité *f*/indemnisation *f*; *Jur:* réparation civile/composition *f*; *EEC:* **monetary compensation amount,** montant *m* compensatoire monétaire; **to pay s.o. compensation in cash,** indemniser qn en argent (*b*) **executive compensation,** rémunération *f* des cadres.

compete, *v.i.* **to compete with s.o.,** faire concurrence à qn/concurrencer qn; **we cannot compete successfully with . . .,** nous ne pouvons pas soutenir la concurrence de . . ./nous ne pouvons pas lutter contre . . .; **to compete with one another,** se faire concurrence.

competence, competency, *n.* attributions *fpl* (d'un fonctionnaire); *Jur:* compétence *f*; **this lies within his competence,** cela rentre dans ses attributions; **to be within the competence of a court,** être de la compétence/du ressort d'un tribunal; **to fall beyond the competence of . . .,** ne pas relever/ne pas être de la compétence de . . .

competent, *a.* **1.** capable; **I am looking for a competent manager,** je cherche un gérant qualifié/compétent **2.** compétent (**in a matter,** en une matière); **competent to do sth.,** capable de faire qch.; compétent/qualifié pour faire qch. **3.** *Jur:* (tribunal) compétent.

competing, *a.* **competing firms,** entre-prises concurrentielles; **competing products,** produits concurrents.

competition, *n.* concurrence *f*; **free competition,** libre concurrence; **monopolistic competition,** concurrence monopolistique; **unfair competition,** concurrence déloyale.

competitive, *a.* concurrentiel/concurrent/compétitif; **in competitive conditions,** en conditions de concurrence; **competitive price,** prix concurrentiel/compétitif; prix défiant toute concurrence; **competitive products,** produits concurrents/compétitifs; **full competitive costs,** coûts concurrentiels intégraux; **competitive supply and demand,** l'offre et la demande concurrentielles; **competitive bidding,** appel *m* d'offres.

competitiveness, *n.* compétitivité *f* (des prix, des produits).

competitor, *n.* concurrent(e); rival(e); **my competitors in trade,** mes concurrents.

complaint, *n.* (*a*) plainte *f*; **the complaints by the employers of the scarcity of skilled labour,** les plaintes formulées par les patrons sur la rareté de la main-d'œuvre spécialisée (*b*) plainte/réclamation *f*; **to lodge/make a complaint against s.o.,** porter plainte contre qn/déposer une plainte contre qn; **to lodge a complaint with s.o.,** réclamer auprès de qn; **complaints office,** service *m* des réclamations.

completion, *n.* **completion of a contract,** signature *f* d'un contrat.

complex, *n.* centre *m*/complexe *m* (industriel).

complimentary, *a.* **complimentary copy (of a book),** exemplaire (d'un livre) envoyé à titre gracieux; **complimentary ticket,** billet *m* de faveur.

composition, *n.* (*a*) atermoiement *m* (avec ses créanciers) (*b*) arrangement *m*/accommodement *m* (avec ses créanciers); concordat préventif (à la faillite); **to make a composition,** composer; **composition of fifty pence in the pound,** décharge *f* de cinquante pour cent.

compound[1], *a. Book-k:* **compound entry,** article composé/collectif/récapitulatif; *Fin:* **compound interest,** intérêts composés.

compound[2], *v.i.* composer/transiger/concorder/arriver à un concordat/faire un compromis/s'accommoder/s'arranger (avec ses créanciers).

Comptometer, *n. Rtm:* machine *f* à calculer.

computable, *a.* calculable.

computation, *n.* (*a*) compte *m*/calcul *m*/estimation *f*; **to make a computation of sth.,** faire le calcul de qch./calculer/estimer qch; **at the lowest computation it will cost . . .,** en mettant les choses au plus bas, cela va coûter . . . (*b*) **electronic computation,** calcul électronique.

computational, *a.* de calcul; **computational error,** erreur *f* de calcul.

compute, *v.tr.* compter/calculer.

computer, *n.* ordinateur *m*; calculateur *m*; **all-purpose computer,** calculateur universel; **analog computer,** ordinateur analogique; **digital computer,** calculateur numérique; **electronic computer,** ordinateur électronique; **computer control,** gestion *f* par ordinateur; **computer department/computer service,** service *m* informatique; **computer accounting,** comptabilité *f* par ordinateur; **computer analyst,** analyste *mf*; **computer expert,** informaticien, -ienne; **computer engineer,** ingénieur informaticien; **computer programmer,** programmeur,-euse; **the computer industry,** l'industrie *f* (de l')informatique.

computerize, *v.tr.* (*a*) informatiser/équiper (une organisation) d'ordi-

nateurs (*b*) **to computerize wages,** informatiser des salaires.

computerized, *a.* **computerized data,** données enregistrées (sur ordinateur); données mises/placées en mémoire.

computing, *n.* évaluation *f*/estimation *f*; calcul *m*; **computing machine,** machine *f* à calcul; **computing equipment,** unités *fpl* d'ordinateur; **computing speed/computing time,** vitesse *f*/durée *f* de calcul.

concealment, *n. Jur:* dissimulation *f* de certains faits/de défauts (de la marchandise); *Fin:* **concealment of assets,** dissimulation d'actif.

concern, *n.* entreprise *f*/affaire *f*/exploitation *f*/maison *f* (de commerce, etc.); fonds *m* de commerce; **business concern,** entreprise commerciale; **the whole concern is for sale,** toute l'entreprise est mise en vente/est à vendre; **going concern,** affaire qui marche; (*of shop, etc.*) **to be sold as a going concern,** à vendre avec fonds.

concession, *n.* (*a*) concession *f*; **mining concession,** concession minière (*b*) **(price) concession,** réduction *f*; **tax concession,** avoir fiscal.

concessionary, **1.** *a.* (*a*) (compagnie *f*, etc.) concessionnaire (*b*) (subvention, etc.) concédé (*c*) **concessionary fare,** tarif *m* de faveur **2.** *n.* concessionnaire *mf*.

condition, *n.* **1.** condition *f*; **conditions of sale,** conditions de vente; **conditions laid down in an agreement,** stipulations *f* d'un contrat; **conditions of the contract,** cahier *m* des charges; **conditions of employment,** conditions d'emploi; *Fin:* **terms and conditions of an issue,** modalités *f* d'une émission; **express condition,** condition expresse; **implied condition,** condition tacite; **on condition,** sous réserve **2.** état *m*/situation *f*; état d'entretien (du matériel, etc.); **working conditions (in a factory),** conditions de travail (dans une usine); **in good (working) condition,** en bonne condition/en bon état (de marche); **in bad condition,** en mauvais état; (*of goods*) **in fair condition,** acceptable(s); **economic conditions,** conditions économiques; conjoncture *f*; **the condition of the market,** l'état du marché; **minimum cost condition,** hypothèse *f* du coût minimum.

conference, *n.* **1.** conférence *f*/entretien *m*/consultation *f*; **to be in conference with one's colleagues,** être en conférence/en consultation avec ses collègues; **the secretary is in conference,** le secrétaire est occupé **2.** congrès *m*; conférence; colloque *m*; **publishers' conference,** congrès d'éditeurs.

consideration, *n.* **1. for a consideration,** moyennant paiement; **contract without consideration,** contrat *m* sans contrepartie; **agreed consideration,** prix convenu; contrepartie convenue; **for good consideration,** (*i*) à titre amical (*ii*) à titre onéreux **2.** cause *f*/provision *f* (**for,** de); **to give consideration for a bill,** provisionner une lettre de change; **consideration given for a bill of exchange,** cause *f* d'un billet.

consign, *v.tr.* consigner/envoyer/expédier (des marchandises) (**to s.o.,** à qn/à l'adresse de qn); envoyer (des marchandises) en consignation (à qn).

consignation, *n.* consignation *f*; **to ship goods to the consignation of s.o.,** consigner des marchandises à qn; envoyer des marchandises en consignation à qn.

consignee, *n.* consignataire *mf*; destinataire *mf*; **bareboat consignee,** consignataire de la coque.

consignment, *n.* **1.** (*a*) envoi *m*/expédition *f* (de marchandises); **goods for consignment to the provinces and abroad,** articles *m* à destination de la province et de l'étranger; **consignment note,** (*i*) lettre *f* de voiture; bon *m*/bordereau *m* d'expédition (*ii*) *Rail:* récépissé *m* (*b*) **on consignment,** en consignation/en dépôt (permanent) **2.** (*goods sent*) envoi/arrivage *m* (de marchandises); **your consignment of books has arrived,** votre envoi de livres nous est

bien parvenu; **I am expecting a large consignment of . . .,** j'attends un fort arrivage de . . ..

consignor, *n.* consignateur,-trice/expéditeur, -trice.

consolidate, *v.tr.* (*a*) consolider/unir/réunir (deux entreprises, etc.) (*b*) *Fin:* consolider/unifier (une dette).

consolidated, *a.* (*a*) consolidé/intégré; *Fin:* **consolidated accounts,** comptes consolidés/intégrés; **consolidated annuities,** fonds consolidés; **consolidated balance-sheet,** bilan consolidé; **consolidated cash transactions,** récapitulation *f*/regroupement *m* des opérations de caisse (*b*) réuni; **consolidated shipping,** compagnie des armateurs réunis.

consolidation, *n.* **1.** *Fin:* regroupement *m* (d'actions) **2.** consolidation *f*/unification *f* (d'une dette).

consols, *n.pl. Fin:* fonds consolidés/les consolidés *m*; **consols certificate,** titre consolidé.

consortium, *n.* consortium *m*.

consultancy, *n.* **consultancy firm,** cabinet *m* d'ingénieur(s)-conseil(s)/etc.

consultant, *n.* conseil *m*/consultant(e); **engineering consultant,** ingénieur-conseil *m*; **management consultant,** conseiller *m* de gestion/de direction; **tax consultant,** conseil fiscal; **consultant service,** assistance *f* technique.

consulting, *a.* **consulting engineer,** ingénieur-conseil *m*.

consumable, *a.* (*a*) (aliment *m*) consommable; *PolEc:* consomptible; **consumable goods,** produits *m* de consommation (*b*) *n.pl.* **consumables,** aliments/comestibles *m*/denrées *f*.

consumer, *n.* consommateur, -trice; **gas consumers,** les abonnés *m* du gaz; *PolEc:* **producers and consumers,** producteurs *m* et consommateurs; **consumer council,** comité (consultatif) des consommateurs;

consumer goods, biens *m* de consommation; **consumer durables,** biens de consommation durables; **consumer credit,** crédit *m* à la consommation; **consumer research,** recherche *f* des besoins des consommateurs; **consumer society,** société *f* de consommation; **consumer spending/consumer expenditure,** dépenses *fpl* de consommation; **consumer price index,** indice *m* des prix à la consommation.

consumption, *n.* consommation *f*; **home consumption,** consommation intérieure; (*of car*) **petrol consumption,** consommation d'essence; **for current consumption,** destiné à la consommation courante; **unfit for human consumption,** non comestible.

contact, *n.* **contact man,** agent *m* de liaison.

container, *n.* (*a*) récipient *m*; réservoir *m*; bac *m* (pour aliments); boîte *f*/caisse *f* (*b*) *Trans:* conteneur *m*/container *m*; **container ship,** (navire) porte-conteneurs *m*; **container shipping,** transports *m* maritimes par conteneurs; **container berth,** poste *m* à quai pour navires porte-conteneurs; **to put into containers,** conteneuriser.

containerization, *n. Trans:* conteneurisation *f*; transport *m* par conteneurs; **the dock strike was against containerization,** la grève des dockers avait pour origine l'opposition à l'adoption des conteneurs.

containerize, *v.tr.* conteneuriser.

contango¹, *n. StExch:* (*i*) report *m* (*ii*) taux *m* de report; **contango day,** jour *m* des reports; **money on contango,** capitaux *mpl* en report; **contangoes are low,** les reports sont bon marché; **payer of contango,** reporté *m*.

contango², *v.tr. & i. StExch:* reporter (une position).

contangoable, *a. StExch:* reportable.

content, *n.* contenu *m* (d'une bou-

teille/d'une boîte/d'un colis); **work contents,** contenu du travail.

contingency, *n.* **contingency fund,** fonds *m* de prévoyance; **contingency reserve,** réserve *f* de prévoyance; *pl.* **contingencies,** faux frais/frais divers; **to provide for/to allow for contingencies,** parer à l'imprévu/tenir compte de l'imprévu.

contingent, *a.* (*a*) éventuel/fortuit/accidentel/aléatoire; **contingent expenses,** dépenses imprévues; **contingent profit,** profit *m* aléatoire (*b*) *NAm:* conditionnel.

continuation, *n. StExch:* **continuation operation,** opération *f* de report.

contra¹, *n. Book-k:* **per contra,** par contre; **as per contra,** en contrepartie/porté ci-contre; **settlement per contra,** compensation *f*; **to settle a debt per contra,** compenser une dette avec une autre; **contra entry,** article *m* inverse/écriture *f* inverse; **contra account,** compte *m* d'autre part; compte contrepartie; jumelage *m*.

contra², *v.tr. Book-k:* contrepasser (des écritures, etc.).

contraband, *n.* contrebande *f*; **contraband goods,** marchandises *f* de contrebande.

contract¹, *n.* **1.** (*a*) contrat *m*/convention *f*; **contract of employment,** contrat de travail; **group contract,** contrat collectif; **simple contract,** contrat ordinaire; **social contract,** convention sociale; **to bind oneself by contract,** s'engager par contrat/contractuellement; **to acquire sth. under a contract,** acquérir/obtenir qch. par contrat; **to draw up a contract,** dresser/rédiger un contrat; **to sign a contract,** signer un contrat; **to void a contract,** annuler un contrat; **under contract,** lié par contrat (*b*) acte *m* de vente; contrat translatif de propriété; **law of contract,** droit *m* des obligations; **contract note,** note *f*/bordereau *m* de contrat; *StExch:* avis *m* d'exécution; **private contract,** contrat sous seing privé; **by private**

contract, à l'amiable/de gré à gré **2.** entreprise *f*; soumission *f*; adjudication *f*; convention forfaitaire; marché *m*; **building contract,** contrat d'entreprise; **to make a contract for supplying wood,** faire/passer un marché pour une fourniture de bois; **contract for a bridge,** entreprise d'un pont; **contract work/work by contract/on contract,** travail *m* à l'entreprise/à forfait; **contract price,** prix *m* forfaitaire; *Adm:* prix de série; **to enter into a contract,** (*i*) (*of pers.*) passer un contrat (**with,** avec) (*ii*) (*of thg*) faire partie d'un contrat; **contract labour,** main-d'œuvre contractuelle; **worker on contract,** contractuel, -elle; **to put work up for contract,** mettre un travail en adjudication; **to put work out to contract,** mettre un travail à l'entreprise; **to place/to give/to award a contract,** concéder/adjuger l'exécution (d'un travail); passer un contrat (à qn) pour l'exécution (d'un travail); **to tender for a contract,** soumissionner à une adjudication; **to get/to secure a contract for sth.,** être déclaré adjudicataire d'un contrat; **conditions of contract,** cahier *m* des charges; **conditions as per contract,** conditions contractuelles; **contract date,** date contractuelle; **breach of contract,** rupture *f* de contrat; *Jur:* **action for breach of contract,** action *f* en rescision/pour inexécution d'un contrat; action contractuelle; **action for specific performance of contract,** action en exécution de contrat; **penalty for non-fulfilment of contract,** peine contractuelle; **to claim under a contract,** intenter une action en exécution de contrat.

contract², *v.* **1.** *v.tr.* (*a*) **to contract to do sth.,** entreprendre de faire qch./s'engager par traité à faire qch. (*b*) **to contract a loan,** faire/contracter un emprunt **2.** *v.i.* **to contract for a supply of sth.,** entreprendre une fourniture de qch.; **to contract for work,** prendre qch. à l'entreprise; **to contract with s.o.,** traiter avec qn; faire/passer un marché avec qn; **the work was contracted out to s.o.,** on a donné le travail à un sous-traitant; **to contract out (of an agreement),** rompre un contrat; **to contract in,** s'engager par contrat préalable.

contracting, *a.* **contracting party,** contractant *m*/parties contractantes; *esp.* adjudicataire *mf*.

contractor, *n.* entrepreneur *m*; **haulage contractor,** entrepreneur de transports.

contractual, *a.* contractuel/forfaitaire; **contractual claims,** créances contractuelles.

contribution, *n.* contribution *f*/apport *m*/cotisation *f*; **contribution pro rata,** quote-part *f*; **employer's and employee's contributions,** cotisations patronales et ouvrières; **health insurance contributions,** colisations maladies; **National Insurance contribution** = cotisation de la Sécurité sociale; **to pay one's (National Insurance) contributions,** cotiser à la Sécurité sociale; *Fin:* **contribution of capital,** apport de capitaux; **contribution to the capital of a company,** contribution au capital d'une compagnie/apport d'actif.

contributor, *n. Fin:* **contributor of capital,** apporteur *m*/société apporteuse/personne apporteuse de capitaux.

contributory, **1.** *n.* actionnaire *mf* responsable proportionnellement à son apport **2.** *a.* **contributory pension plan,** régime de retraite financé par les cotisations patronales et ouvrières.

control¹, *n.* **1.** autorité *f*; **to have control of a business,** être à la tête d'une entreprise **2.** contrôle *m*; **budgetary control,** contrôle *m* budgétaire; **credit control,** encadrement *m* des crédits; **(foreign) exchange control,** contrôle des changes; **price control,** réglementation *f*/contrôle (des prix); **quality control,** contrôle de (la) qualité; **stock control,** contrôle/gestion *f* des stocks.

control², *v.tr.* **1.** diriger/réglementer (des affaires); **to control a business,** diriger une entreprise/être à la tête d'une entreprise **2.** **to control inflation,** contenir l'inflation; **to control the rise in the cost of living,** enrayer la hausse du coût de la vie.

controlled currency, monnaie dirigée; **controlled economy,** économie dirigée; **controlled market,** marché réglementé; **controlled prices,** prix réglementés/ taxés.

controller, *n.* (*i*) vérificateur *m* des comptes (*ii*) directeur des services comptables.

controlling, *a.* **controlling interest (in a firm),** majorité *f*/participation *f* majoritaire/participation qui donne le contrôle (dans une société).

convene, 1. *v.tr.* convoquer/réunir (une assemblée); réunir/assembler (une conférence, etc.); **to convene a meeting of shareholders,** convoquer une assemblée d'actionnaires **2.** *v.i.* s'assembler/se réunir/se rencontrer.

conversion, *n.* (*a*) détournement *m* de fonds (*b*) *StExch:* conversion *f* (d'un titre); **conversion issue,** émission *f* de conversion; **conversion loan,** emprunt *m* de conversion; **conversion price,** prix *m* de conversion.

convert, *v.tr.* **to convert funds to another purpose,** affecter des fonds à un autre usage/à d'autres fins; *Jur:* **to convert funds to one's own use,** détourner des fonds.

convertibility, *n.* convertibilité *f* (d'une monnaie, d'une obligation).

convertible, *a.* *Fin:* **convertible bond,** obligation *f* convertible (en actions); **convertible currencies,** monnaies *f* convertibles.

cook, *v.tr.* *F:* **to cook the books,** falsifier/ truquer/tripoter les comptes.

cooking, *n.* *F:* **cooking of accounts,** falsification *f*/trucage *m* des comptes; irrégularités *fpl* d'écriture; tripotage *m* de caisse.

cooling off, *a.* **cooling off period,** délai *m* de réflexion.

co-op = **cooperative,** *n.* la coopé.

cooperative, 1. *a.* **co-operative society,** société coopérative/coopérative *f* **2.** *n.* coopérative *f*; **agricultural co-operative,** coopérative agricole.

co-owner, *n.* copropriétaire *mf.*

co-ownership, *n.* copropriété *f.*

copartner, *n.* coassocié(e)/coparticipant(e).

copartnership, *n.* coassociation *f*/coparticipation *f*; société *f* en nom collectif; **industrial copartnership,** actionnariat ouvrier.

coproperty, *n.* copropriété *f.*

coproprietor, *n.* copropriétaire *mf.*

copy, *n.* (*a*) copie *f*/transcription *f* (d'une lettre, etc.); *Typ:* **carbon copy,** double *m*/ copie (au papier carbone)/duplicata *m*; **top copy,** original *m*; **rough copy,** brouillon *m*; **fair copy,** copie (au net) (*b*) *Jur:* expédition *f* (d'un acte/d'un titre); **certified copy,** copie authentique; **certified true copy,** pour copie conforme/ copie certifiée (conforme); copie authentique; **true copy,** copie conforme; **file copy,** exemplaire *m* des archives (*c*) (*of a book*) exemplaire *m*; **presentation copy,** spécimen gratuit; (*of magazine, etc.*) numéro *m.*

copying, *n.* **copying machine,** duplicateur *m.*

copyright[1], *n.* propriété *f* littéraire; copyright *m*; droit *m* d'auteur; **copyright act,** loi *f* sur les droits d'auteurs; **out of copyright,** (tombé) dans le domaine public; **infringement of copyright,** violation *f* des droits d'auteur; **copyright reserved,** tous droits réservés/droit de publication réservé; **copyright notice,** mention *f* de réserve; *Journ:* mention d'interdiction.

copyright[2], *v.tr.* déposer (un livre à la Bibliothèque Nationale).

copyright[3], *a.* (livre) qui est protégé par des droits d'auteur; (article) dont le droit de reproduction est réservé; (livre) qui n'est pas dans le domaine public; **copyright (in all countries),** tous droits de reproduction et de traduction réservés (pour tous les pays).

copyrighted, *a.* (*of book*) déposé.

copyrighting, *n.* dépôt légal (d'une publication).

copywriter, *n.* concepteur-rédacteur *m.*

corn, *n. coll.* grains *mpl*/blé(s) *m*(*pl*)/ céréales *fpl:* **Corn Exchange,** bourse *f* des céréales; halle *f* aux blés; **corn chandler/ dealer/merchant,** marchand *m* de blé/de grains; grainetier *m;* **corn trade,** commerce *m* des grains/des céréales.

corner[1], *n.* monopole *m;* trust *m* d'accapareurs; corner *m;* **to make a corner in wheat,** accaparer le blé.

corner[2], *v.tr.* accaparer (une denrée, le marché).

cornering, *n.* accaparement *m* (d'une denrée).

corporate, *a.* corporatif/de société; **corporate body,** corporation *f;* **corporate name,** raison sociale; **corporate image,** image *f* de marque; **corporate profit,** profit *m* des sociétés.

corporation, *n.* **1.** société enregistrée; compagnie *f* **2.** *Fin:* (*a*) **corporation stocks,** emprunts *mpl* de ville (*b*) **corporation tax,** impôt *m* sur les sociétés.

correspond, *v.i.* **1. to correspond to sample,** être conforme à l'échantillon **2. to correspond with s.o.,** correspondre avec qn/écrire à qn/échanger des lettres avec qn.

correspondence, *n.* (*a*) correspondance *f*/ échange *m* de lettres; **to be in correspondence with s.o.,** être en correspondance avec qn (*b*) correspondance/courrier *m;* **correspondence clerk,** correspondancier *m.*

correspondent, *n.* correspondant(e).

corresponding, *a. Book-k:* **correspond-**

ing entry, écriture *f* conforme/de conformité.

cost[1], *n.* **1.** coût *m*/frais *mpl;* **cost of living,** coût de la vie; **increased cost of living,** augmentation *f* du coût de la vie; **cost-of-living allowance/bonus,** indemnité *f* de cherté de vie/de vie chère; **the cost of an undertaking,** les frais d'une entreprise; **costs to be borne by . . .,** frais à la charge de . . .; **first cost/prime cost,** coût premier; prix initial; **actual cost/net cost/cost price,** prix de revient/prix d'achat/prix coûtant; **gross cost,** prix de revient brut; **total cost,** coût total; **to sell at cost (price),** vendre au prix coûtant; **to sell under cost price,** vendre à perte; **cost analysis,** analyse *f* des charges/du prix de revient; **fixed cost,** coût constant/fixe; **incidental cost,** faux frais; **operating costs,** frais d'exploitation; **cost, insurance and freight,** coût, assurance, fret (CAF); **cost keeping,** comptabilité de prix coûtants; **cost account,** compte *m* des charges; **cost accountant,** comptable *mf* de prix de revient; **cost accounting,** comptabilité *f* de prix de revient/comptabilité analytique; **full cost accounting,** méthode de capitalisation du coût entier; **cost book,** livre *m* de(s) charges; *StExch:* **cost of a share,** valeur *f* d'achat d'une action; **cost of acquisition and disposal (of securities),** frais d'acquisition et de cession (de titres) **2.** *pl. Jur:* frais d'instance; dépens *mpl;* **to pay costs,** payer les condamnations/les frais et dépens; **order to pay costs,** exécutoire *m* de dépens.

cost[2], **1.** *v.i. & tr.* coûter; **how much does it cost?** combien cela coûte-t-il? **it costs five pounds,** cela coûte cinq livres **2.** *v.tr.* **to cost an article,** établir le prix de revient d'un article; **to cost a job,** évaluer le coût d'une entreprise/d'un travail.

cost-benefit, *n.* **cost-benefit analysis,** analyse *f* coût-profit/analyse des coûts et rendements.

cost-effective, *a.* rentable.

cost-effectiveness, *n.* **cost-effectiveness analysis,** étude *f* de coût et efficacité.

costing, *n.* établissement *m* du prix de revient/évaluation *f* du coût; **direct costing,** méthode *f* des coûts variables; **full costing,** méthode de capitalisation du coût entier; **production costing,** comptabilité analytique/industrielle.

cotton, *n.* coton *m*; **cotton industry,** industrie cotonnière/du coton; **cotton trade,** commerce *m* des cotons; **cotton broker,** courtier *m* en coton; **cotton goods/stuffs,** tissus *m* de coton; cotonnades *f*.

counsel, *n.* avocat-conseil *m*.

counter, *n.* (*a*) (*in bank, etc.*) guichets *mpl*/caisse *f*; **payable over the counter,** payable au guichet (*b*) (*in shop*) comptoir *m*; **sold over the counter,** vendu (au) comptant; **drugs sold over the counter,** médicaments vendus sans ordonnance; **to sell under the counter,** vendre en cachette; **goods from under the counter,** des marchandises *f* de l'arrière-boutique; **counter hand,** vendeur, -euse.

counterfoil, *n.* souche *f*/talon *m* (de chèque, de quittance); **counterfoil book,** cahier *m*/carnet *m*/registre *m*/livre *m* à souche.

countermand, *v.tr.* **to countermand the order for sth.,** décommander qch.; **unless countermanded,** sauf contrordre/sauf contravis.

counterpart, *n.* duplicata *m*/double *m* (d'un document); contrepartie *f*; **tally counterpart,** souche *f* (d'un reçu).

counting-house, *n.* bureau *m*/service *m* de la comptabilité; la comptabilité.

coupon, *n.* coupon *m*; **(free) gift coupon,** bon-prime *m*; **coupon redeemable for cash,** timbre *m*/chèque *m* ristourne; **reply coupon,** coupon-réponse *m*; *Fin:* **interest coupon,** coupon (d'intérêts); **cum coupon,** coupon attaché; **ex coupon,** coupon détaché; **due date of coupon,** échéance *f* de coupon; **outstanding coupons,** coupons en souffrance.

court, *n.* *Jur:* cour *f*/tribunal *m*.

covenant, *n.* **1.** convention *f*; **deed of covenant,** pacte *m*/engagement *m* **2.** *NAm:* **the lessee is a good covenant,** le locataire a une bonne capacité de remboursement/une solvabilité assurée.

cover¹, *n.* (*a*) couverture *f*/provision *f*/ garantie *f*; *Fin:* marge *f* de sécurité; **to operate with/without cover,** opérer avec couverture/à découvert; **call for additional cover,** appel *m* de marge; *Ins:* **full cover,** garantie totale; **cover note,** lettre *f* de couverture; *Jur:* **to lodge stock as cover,** déposer des titres en nantissement (*b*) (*in restaurant*) **cover charge,** couvert *m* (*c*) **to send sth. under separate cover,** faire parvenir qch. sous pli séparé.

cover², *v.tr.* (*a*) couvrir (un risque/son banquier); (*of creditor*) **to be covered,** être à couvert; **to cover a bill,** faire la provision d'une lettre de change; *StExch:* **to cover short sales/shorts,** se racheter; **to cover a short account,** couvrir un découvert; **to cover by buying back,** se couvrir en rachetant; **the application is covered,** la souscription est couverte; *Ins:* **he is covered against fire,** son assurance *f* couvre le risque d'incendie/il est assuré contre les incendies (*b*) **to cover one's expenses,** faire ses frais/couvrir ses dépenses/rentrer dans ses frais; **to cover a deficit,** combler un déficit.

coverage, *n.* *Ins:* couverture *f*/provision *f*/ garantie *f*.

covering, *a.* **1. covering letter,** lettre explicative; lettre d'introduction/lettre annexe; lettre de confirmation; **covering note,** garantie *f* **2.** *StExch:* **covering purchases,** rachats *m*.

crab, *n.* *Publ:* **crabs,** invendus *mpl* (retournés à l'éditeur).

crash¹, *n.* **financial crash/business crash,** débâcle financière/krach *m*.

crash[2], *v.i.* (*of business*) faire faillite; (*of prices*) s'effondrer.

crate, *n.* cageot *m* (à légumes)/caisse *f* à claire-voie.

creation, *n.* **the job creation programme** = le pacte pour l'emploi.

credit[1], *n.* (*a*) crédit *m*; **to give s.o. credit,** faire crédit à qn; **to sell on credit,** vendre à crédit/à terme; **long credit,** crédit à long terme; **blank credit/open credit,** crédit en blanc/à découvert; **revolving credit,** crédit renouvelable; **credit bank/credit establishment,** banque *f*/établissement *m* de crédit; **credit facilities,** facilités *f* de paiement; **credit union,** société *f* de crédit; *Bank:* **letter of credit,** accréditif *m*/lettre de créance/de crédit/lettre accréditive; **documentary letter of credit,** crédit documentaire; **permanent credit,** accréditif permanent; **credit account,** (*i*) compte créditeur (*ii*) compte crédit d'achats; **to open a credit account with s.o.,** ouvrir un crédit chez qn; **to open a credit,** loger un accréditif; **to give s.o. credit facilities,** accréditer qn (auprès d'une banque); **to open credit facilities with a bank,** loger un accréditif sur une banque; **to give s.o. a bank credit,** ouvrir un crédit en banque à qn/accréditer qn; **credit card,** carte *f* de crédit/carte accréditive; **credit circulation,** circulation *f* fiduciaire; **credit insurance,** assurance *f* contre les mauvaises créances; **credit rating,** degré *m* de solvabilité; **credit worthy,** qui a une réputation de solvabilité/digne de confiance; **credit worthiness,** degré/réputation de solvabilité; **to live on credit,** vivre à crédit; **no credit (allowed),** on ne fait pas (de) crédit (*b*) *Book-k:* **debit and credit,** doit *m* et avoir *m*; **credit side,** avoir; **credit balance,** solde créditeur; **account showing a credit balance,** compte bénéficiaire; *Bank:* **credit note,** note *f* d'avoir/note de crédit/bordereau *m* de crédit; *Bank:* **credit slip,** bulletin *m* de versement; **to enter/put a sum to s.o.'s credit,** porter une somme au crédit/à l'actif de qn;

alimenter le compte de qn; **to pay in a sum to s.o.'s credit,** payer une somme à la décharge de qn; **bank credit,** crédit bancaire; **investment credits,** crédit d'impôt/avoir fiscal; **tax credits,** (*i*) déductions fiscales (*ii*) *StExch:* avoir *m* fiscal; **frozen credits,** créances gelées.

credit[2], *v.tr.* **to credit an account with a sum/to credit a sum to an account,** créditer un compte d'une somme/créditer une somme à un compte/porter une somme au crédit d'un compte/passer (un montant) en profit.

creditor, *n.* **1.** créancier, -ière; **to be s.o.'s creditor for 1000 francs,** devoir 1000 francs à qn; **simple-contract creditor,** créancier chirographaire/créancier en vertu d'un contrat sous seing privé; **joint creditor,** cocréancier, -ière; (*in bankruptcy*) **creditor of a creditor,** créancier en sous-ordre **2.** créditeur, -trice; *Book-k:* (*of balance*) **creditor side,** crédit *m*/avoir *m* **3.** *pl.* **creditors,** dette passive.

cross, *v.tr.* barrer (un chèque); **crossed cheque,** chèque barré.

currency, *n.* unité *f* monétaire (d'un pays)/monnaie *f*; devise *f*; **payable in currency,** payable en espèces; **foreign currency,** (*i*) monnaie étrangère (*ii*) devise étrangère; **bill in foreign currency,** effet *m* en devises étrangères; **decimal currency,** système monétaire décimal; **foreign currency allowance,** allocation *f* en devises; **hard currency,** devise forte; **soft currency,** devise faible; **legal (tender) currency,** monnaie légale/courante/libératoire; **paper currency,** papier-monnaie *m*/monnaie fiduciaire; **silver currency,** monnaie/numéraire *m* d'argent; **currency note,** coupure *f*/billet *m* (de banque); **currency-note** *f*; **questions of currency,** questions *f* monétaires.

current, *a.* **current account,** (*a*) compte courant (*b*) *StExch:* liquidation courante; **money on current account,** dépôt *m* à vue; **current liabilities,** passif *m* exigible/exigibilités *fpl*; dette *f* à court terme; **current assets,** actif *m* réalisable et disponible/actifs de roulement; **current price,** prix courant/prix du marché; **the current rate of exchange in Paris,** le taux de change en cours à Paris; **current quotations,** cours *mpl* actuels; **money that is no longer current,** monnaie qui n'est plus courante/qui n'a plus cours; **current loan,** prêt en cours/non remboursé/consenti.

custom, *n.* **1.** (*a*) (*of business*) clientèle *f* (*b*) patronage *m*/pratique *f* (du client); **to lose s.o.'s custom,** perdre un client/perdre la clientèle de qn; **custom(-)built/custom(-)made,** (fait) sur mesure; adapté aux goûts/aux besoins du client **2.** *pl* **customs,** douane *f*; **customs broker,** agent *m* en douane; **customs declaration,** déclaration *f* de/en douane; **customs duties,** droits *m* de douane; **customs house,** (bureau *m* de) douane; **customs officer,** douanier *m*; **customs regime/tariff,** régime/tarif douanier; **customs union,** union douanière; **to get/to go through customs,** passer la douane/en douane/par la douane; **to get/to take sth. through the customs,** faire passer qch. à la douane;

customs examination/formalities, formalités *f* de douane; **customs clearance,** dédouanement *m*; **to effect customs clearance,** procéder aux formalités de la douane/dédouaner.

customer, *n.* (*of shop, etc.*) client(e); (*of bank, etc.*) déposant(e); **current account customer,** titulaire *mf* d'un compte courant; (*of public house, etc.*) consommateur *m*; (*of restaurant, etc.*) **regular customer,** habitué(e).

cut[1], *n.* réduction *f* (de prix, de dépenses); **salary cuts/cuts in salary,** réductions de salaires/sur les traitements.

cut[2], (*a*) *v.tr.* **to cut (back) prices,** baisser les prix; **to cut (back) production,** diminuer la production (*b*) *p.p.* **cut price,** prix *m* de rabais; **to sell at cut price,** vendre au rabais/au dessous des cours.

cutback, *n.* réduction *f*/diminution *f* (de la production/d'un budget).

cut-throat, *a.* **cut-throat competition,** concurrence acharnée.

cutting, *n.* **cutting (down) of prices,** réduction *f* des prix/rabais *m*.

cycle, *n.* cycle *m*; **economic cycle/trade cycle,** cycle économique.

D

dabble, *v.i.* **to dabble on the Stock Exchange,** boursicoter.

dabbler, *n.* **dabbler on the Stock Exchange,** boursicoteur *m*/boursicotier *m*.

dabbling, *n. StExch:* boursicotage *m*.

daily, *a.* journalier/quotidien/de tous les jours; **daily consumption,** consommation journalière; **daily paper,** (journal) quotidien *m;* **daily returns,** recettes journalières/relevés journaliers; *Fin:* **daily loans,** prêts *m* au jour le jour; *StExch:* **daily closing prices,** cours de clôture quotidiens.

dairy, *n.* **1.** laiterie *f*; **co-operative dairy,** coopérative laitière; **dairy farming,** industrie laitière; **dairy produce,** produits laitiers **2.** (*shop*) laiterie/crémerie *f*.

dairying, *n.* l'industrie laitière.

damage[1]**,** *n.* **1.** dommage(s) *m(pl)*/dégât(s) *m(pl)*; (*to ship, cargo*) avarie(s) *f(pl)*; **damage in transit,** avaries de route; **to suffer damage,** subir un dommage; **the insurance will pay for the damage,** les assurances *f* vont payer les dommages; *Ins:* **damage survey,** expertise *f* des dégâts/des avaries **2.** *pl. Jur:* dommages-intérêts *mpl*/dommages et intérêts/indemnité *f*; **to bring an action for damages against s.o./to sue s.o. for damages,** poursuivre qn en dommages-intérêts; **to be liable for damages,** être tenu des dommages-intérêts; (*in respect of act committed by third party*) être civilement responsable; **to claim £1 000 damages,** réclamer des dommages-intérêts/une indemnité de £1 000; **to pay the damages,** payer/acquitter les condamnations.

damage[2]**,** *v.tr.* endommager/abîmer; avarier (une marchandise).

damaged, *a.* avarié/endommagé/abîmé/qui a subi un dommage; **damaged goods,** marchandises avariées.

damp down, *v.tr.* **to damp down the market,** freiner le marché; **to damp down consumption,** réduire la consommation.

data, *n.pl.* (*occ. with sg. const.*) données *f*/information(s) *f*/renseignements *m*; **data acquisition,** collecte *f* de données; **data processing,** (*i*) l'informatique *f* (*ii*) traitement *m* de l'information/des données; **data processing department,** service *m* informatique/mécanographique; **data handling,** interprétation *f*/manipulation *f*/traitement de données; **data bank,** banque *f* de(s) données; fichier central; **data processing card,** carte perforée/mécanographique.

date[1]**,** *n.* (*a*) date *f*; **date stamp,** timbre *m* dateur; **date of delivery,** date/jour *m* de livraison (*b*) **up to date,** à jour; **I am up to date with my work,** mon travail est à jour; **to bring/to keep sth. up to date,** mettre/tenir qch. à jour (*c*) **to date,** à ce jour/jusqu'ici; **interest to date,** intérêts *m* à ce jour (*d*) **out of date,** (passeport/chèque, etc.) périmé; (vêtement) démodé (*e*) *Fin:* **date of a bill,** terme *m*/échéance *f* d'un billet; **three months after date/at three months' date,** à trois mois de date/d'échéance; **date of maturity/due date,** (date d')échéance; **final/latest date,** terme de rigueur; **to buy at long date,** acheter à long terme; **to pay at fixed dates,** payer à échéances fixes.

49

date², *v.tr.* (*a*) dater (une lettre, etc.); **the cheque is dated March 24th,** le chèque a été émis le 24 mars/est daté du 24 mars; **to date back,** antidater; **to date forward,** postdater (*b*) composter (un billet); **dating and numbering machine,** composteur *m*.

dated, *a.* daté; **thank you for your letter dated June 15th,** je vous remercie de votre lettre datée/en date du 15 juin; (*in compounds*) *Fin:* **long-dated,** à longue échéance; **short-dated,** à courte échéance.

day, *n.* **1.** (*a*) jour *m*; journée *f*; **day off,** jour de congé; **eight-hour day,** journée de huit heures; **pay day,** jour de paie; **working day,** jour ouvrable; *StExch:* **pay day/settlement day/settling day,** jour de liquidation/de règlement (*b*) **day labour,** travail *m* à la journée; **day labourer,** journalier *m*/ouvrier *m* à la journée; *Ind:* **day shift,** équipe *f* de jour; (*of workman*) **to be on day shift,** être de jour; *Rail: etc:* **day return,** (billet *m* d')aller et retour *m* (valable pour un jour); *Fin:* **day bill,** effet *m* à date fixe; **day-to-day loan,** prêt *m* au jour le jour; **one-day option,** prime *f* au lendemain; **last-day money,** emprunt *m* remboursable fin courant **2.** (= *24 hours*) **clear day,** jour franc/plein; **ten clear days' notice,** préavis *m* de dix jours francs.

daybook, *n.* livre journal *m*/livre *m* de commerce/main courante/brouillard *m*.

dead, *a.* **1.** (*inactive*) **dead season,** morte-saison *f;* **dead period,** période *f* d'inactivité; *Fin:* **dead money,** argent mort/qui dort; **dead loan,** emprunt *m* irrécouvrable; **dead market,** marché mort; **dead freight,** faux fret; dédit *m* pour défaut de chargement **2. dead loss,** perte sèche.

deadline, *n.* date *f* limite; **to meet a deadline,** faire qch. dans un délai prescrit.

deadweight, *n. Nau:* portée *f* en poids/chargement *m* en lourd/port *m* en lourd; **deadweight cargo,** marchandises lourdes; **deadweight cargo capacity,** port en

marchandises; **ton deadweight,** tonneau *m* de portée en lourd/d'affrètement.

deal¹, *n.* affaire *f*/marché *m*; **it's a deal,** c'est (une affaire) entendu(e); marché conclu! **to call off a deal,** annuler un marché; **fair deal,** prix juste; **financial deal,** opération financière/transaction *f;* **firm deal,** marché ferme; **cash deal,** transaction *f* au comptant; **deal on joint account,** opération *f* en participation; **option deal,** opération à prime; **package deal,** contrat global/panier *m*; **even deal,** opération blanche; **swap credit deal,** facilités *f* de crédit réciproques; **a big deal,** une grosse affaire; **deal on the Stock Exchange,** coup *m* de Bourse.

deal², *v.i.* **1. to deal with a piece of business,** se charger d'une affaire; **to deal with an order,** donner suite à une commande **2. to deal with s.o.,** traiter/négocier avec qn; **to deal in leather/in wool,** faire le commerce des cuirs/des laines; **I don't deal in that line,** je ne fais pas cet article; *Fin:* **to deal in options,** faire le commerce des primes.

dealer, *n.* (*a*) négociant *m* (**in,** en); distributeur *m* (**in,** de); stockiste *m* (*b*) marchand(e)/fournisseur *m* (**in,** de); **retail dealer,** détaillant(e); **wholesale dealer,** grossiste *mf*; **secondhand dealer,** revendeur, -euse; brocanteur, -euse; **exchange dealer,** courtier *m* de change/cambiste *m*; **authorized dealer,** concessionnaire *mf;* distributeur agréé; **art dealer,** marchand(e) de tableaux; **you can obtain this article from your usual dealer,** vous trouverez cet article chez votre fournisseur habituel (*c*) *StExch:* marchand de titres.

dealing, *n.* **1. dealing in wool/in wines,** commerce *m* des laines/des vins; *StExch:* **dealings for the account/for the settlement,** négociations *f* à terme; **forward dealings,** négociations/opérations *f* de change à terme; **option dealing(s),** opérations à prime/à option **2. to have dealings with s.o.,** être en relations d'affaires/faire affaire/traiter avec qn **3. fair/square dealing,** loyauté *f*/honnêteté *f* (en affaires).

dear, *a.* **1.** cher/coûteux; (*of food, etc.*) **to get dear/dearer,** augmenter/renchérir; **apples are much dearer this year,** le prix des pommes a beaucoup augmenté cette année; **this shop is very dear,** ce magasin vend très cher; **dear money,** argent cher **2. Dear Madam,** Madame/Mademoiselle; **Dear Mr Collin,** Cher Monsieur (Collin); **Dear Sir,** Monsieur; **Dear Sirs,** Messieurs.

debenture, *n. Fin:* obligation *f* (nongarantie); **first/second/third debenture,** obligation de premier/de deuxième/de troisième rang; **bearer debenture,** obligation au porteur; **convertible debenture,** obligation convertible (en action); **mortgage debenture,** obligation hypothécaire; **issue of debentures/debenture issue,** émission *f* d'obligations; **unissued debentures,** obligations à la souche; **debenture bond,** titre *m*/certificat d'obligation; **debenture capital,** capital-obligations *m*; **debenture holder,** détenteur, -trice, d'obligations/obligataire *mf*; **debenture loan,** emprunt *m* obligataire; **debenture register,** registre *m* des obligataires; **debenture stock,** obligations.

debit¹, *n. Book-k:* débit *m*/doit *m*; **debit and credit,** doit et avoir *m*/débit et crédit *m*; **debit (entry),** article *m* au débit; **to enter sth. on the debit (side) of an account,** porter/inscrire qch. au débit d'un compte; **debit note,** note *f*/bordereau *m* de débit; **debit account,** compte débiteur; **debit balance,** solde débiteur; **account showing a debit balance,** compte déficitaire/qui présente un déficit; **debit column,** colonne *f* des débits; **by direct debit,** par prélèvement *m* bancaire (automatique).

debit², *v.tr. Book-k:* **1.** débiter (un article/un compte); **to whom shall I debit the amount?** au débit de qui dois-je porter le montant? **2. to debit s.o. with a sum,** porter une somme au débit de qn/débiter (le compte de) qn d'une somme.

debitable, *a.* **charge debitable to the profit and loss account,** charge *f* à porter au débit du compte des profits et pertes.

debt, *n.* dette *f*; créance *f*; **bad debt,** mauvaise créance/créance irrécouvrable; **doubtful debt,** créance douteuse; dette véreuse; **good debt,** bonne créance/dette; **debt due,** créance exigible; **privileged debt,** dette privilégiée; **secured debt,** créance garantie; **debt owed by us/by the firm,** dette passive; **debt owed to us,** dette active/créance; **to be in debt,** être endetté/avoir des dettes; **to run into debt,** s'endetter; **floating debt,** dette publique flottante/dette non consolidée/dette courante; **funded debt/consolidated debt,** fonds consolidés; dette consolidée; dette publique en rentes sur l'État; **debt collector,** agent *m* de recouvrements; **debt security,** titre *m* de créance.

debtor, *n.* **1.** débiteur *m*; **joint debtor,** co-débiteur **2.** *Book-k:* **debtor side,** débit *m*/doit *m*; **debtor account,** compte débiteur; **debtor and creditor account,** compte par doit et avoir; *pl.* **debtors,** dette active.

decile, *n. Stat:* décile *m*.

decimal, 1. *a.* **decimal point,** virgule *f* (3.5 = 3,5)/*FrC:* point *m* (décimal); **decimal system,** système décimal **2.** *n.* décimale *f*.

decimalization, *n.* décimalisation *f*.

decimalize, *v.tr.* appliquer le système décimal.

decimate, *v.tr.* **we have to decimate our workforce,** il nous faut réduire notre main-d'œuvre.

decision, *n.* **to make a decision,** prendre une décision; **decision making,** prise *f* de décision(s).

declaration, *n.* (*a*) **statutory declaration,** attestation *f*; **declaration of bankruptcy,** jugement déclaratif de faillite; **declaration of income,** déclaration *f* de revenu; **VAT declaration,** déclaration de TVA;

customs declaration, déclaration de/en douane (b) StExch: declaration of options, réponse f des primes.

declare, v.tr. Cust: have you anything to declare? avez-vous quelque chose à déclarer? nothing to declare, rien à déclarer (b) StExch: to declare an option, répondre/donner la réponse à une prime (c) to declare s.o. bankrupt, constater l'état de faillite de qn; Fin: to declare a dividend of 10%, déclarer un dividende de 10%.

declared, a. declared dividend, dividende déclaré; declared value, valeur déclarée.

decontrol, v.tr. libérer (le commerce, etc.) des contraintes du gouvernement; to decontrol the price of meat, détaxer la viande; to decontrol prices/to decontrol wages, débloquer les prix/débloquer les salaires.

decrease¹, n. diminution f/baisse f/décroissance f/amoindrissement m; decrease in price, baisse de prix; decrease in value, diminution de valeur/moins-value f; the decrease in wheat, la raréfaction du blé; our imports are on the decrease, nos importations f sont en baisse.

decrease², v.i. diminuer/décroître/s'amoindrir/aller en diminuant/aller en décroissant; our imports are decreasing, nos importations f diminuent/baissent.

deduct, v.tr. déduire/défalquer/retrancher (from, de); to deduct sth. from the price, décompter/déduire qch. du prix/rabattre qch. sur le prix; to deduct a sum (of money), décompter une somme; to deduct 5% from the salaries, faire une retenue de/précompter 5% sur les salaires; after deducting . . ., après déduction de . . ./déduction faite de . . .; to be deducted, à déduire.

deductible, a. déductible.

deduction, n. décompte m/déduction f/défalcation f/imputation f (from a quantity, sur une quantité); (of pay) retenue f; after deduction of taxes, après déduction des impôts; deduction from salary/

deduction at source, retenue sur le salaire/précompte m.

deed, n. Jur: acte notarié sur papier timbré et signé par les parties contractantes; deed privately executed by the parties/private deed, acte sous seing privé; deed of assignment, acte attributif; acte de transfert; to draw up a deed, rédiger un acte; title deed, titre (constitutif) de propriété; acte; deed of covenant, pacte m/engagement m; deed of partnership, acte constitutif/acte de société; deed of transfer, feuille f de transfert.

defalcation, n. NAm: détournement m de fonds.

default¹, n. (a) Jur: défaut m de comparaître (b) default in paying, défaut de paiement/non-paiement; default interest, intérêts mpl pour défaut de paiement/intérêts moratoires; in default of payment, à défaut de paiement.

default², v.i. ne pas faire face à ses engagements/manquer à ses engagements.

defaulter, n. partie défaillante/débiteur défaillant.

defect, n. défaut m/imperfection f/défectuosité f/vice m (de construction)/tare f; latent defects, défauts/vices cachés; manufacturing defect, défaut de fabrication; patent defects, défauts/vices apparents.

defendant, n. Jur: défendeur, -eresse.

deferment, n. deferment of payment, délai m de paiement.

deferred, a. (of share, etc.) différé; deferred stock, actions différées; deferred calls on shares, appels différés sur actions; deferred charges, frais reportés/différés; deferred liabilities, passif reporté; deferred payment, (i) paiement différé (ii) paiement par versements échelonnés; deferred results, résultats m à longue échéance.

deficiency, n. (a) découvert m; to make up a deficiency, combler un déficit (b) déficit budgétaire/découvert; **deficiency bills/deficiency advances,** avances *f* provisoires/crédits *m* budgétaires/crédits intérimaires; collectifs *m* budgétaires (*c*) **deficiency payment,** subvention compensatrice (aux agriculteurs, etc.).

deficit, *n.* déficit *m*/excédent *m* de dépenses/découvert *m*; **budget that shows a deficit,** budget *m* déficitaire; **to make good/make up the deficit,** combler le déficit.

deflate, *v.tr.* **to deflate (the currency),** amener la déflation de la monnaie; diminuer la circulation fiduciaire.

deflation, *n. Fin:* déflation *f.*

deflationary, *a.* (politique) de déflation; (mesures) déflationnistes.

defray, *v.tr. NAm:* défrayer (qn)/couvrir les frais (de qn).

degearing, *n.* diminution *f*/réduction *f* du ratio d'endettement; désendettement *m.*

del credere, *a. & n.* **del credere (commission),** (commission) ducroire *m*; **del credere agent,** agent *m* ducroire.

delete, *v.tr.* **delete where inapplicable,** rayer la (les) mention(s) inutile(s).

deliver, *v.tr.* livrer/délivrer (des marchandises); **delivered free,** livraison gratuite/expédié franc de port/livraison franco; **deliver free as far as the French border,** livraison franco frontière française; **delivered on board,** rendu à bord; **goods delivered at/to any address,** livraison *f* à domicile.

delivery, *n.* (*a*) **delivery of goods,** livraison *f*/transport *m*/envoi *m*/factage *m* de marchandises; **parcels awaiting delivery,** colis *m* en souffrance; **delivery area,** réception *f* des marchandises; **delivery office,** bureau *m* de distribution; **delivery order form,** bulletin *m* de livraison; **delivery note,** bon *m* de réception; **delivery price,** prix rendu; **delivery van,** voiture *f*/camion *m* de livraison; **express/special delivery,** par exprès *m*; **recorded delivery,** envoi recommandé; **for immediate**

delivery, à livrer de suite; **free delivery,** envoi livraison franco; **delivery within a month,** délai de livraison, moins d'un mois; **delivery man/boy/girl,** livreur, -euse; **to pay on delivery,** payer à la livraison/livrer contre remboursement; **cash on delivery (COD),** livraison contre remboursement/payable à la livraison; **delivery date,** date *f* de livraison; **purchase for future delivery,** achat *m* à terme; **to accept/to take delivery of sth.,** prendre livraison de qch. (*b*) *Fin:* **delivery of stocks,** cession *f*/remise *f* de titres; **to take delivery of stocks,** prendre livraison de titres; (*of stocks*) **for delivery,** au comptant; **to sell for delivery,** vendre à couvert; **sale for delivery,** vente *f* à livrer (*c*) *Jur:* tradition *f* (d'un bien, d'une marchandise).

demand, *n.* **1.** (*a*) demande *f*/réclamation *f*/revendication *f*/requête *f*; *Jur:* sommation *f*; **the Trade Union demands,** les revendications syndicales; **payable on demand,** payable sur demande/à vue/à bureau ouvert/à présentation; **promissory note payable on demand,** billet *m* payable à volonté/sur demande; **demand bill,** traite *f* à vue; *Fin:* **demand deposit,** dépôt *m* à vue (*b*) (*for taxes, rates*) avertissement *m*; (*for bills*) **final demand,** dernier rappel **2.** demande; **supply and demand,** l'offre *f* et la demande; **to be in (great) demand,** être (très) demandé/recherché; **to be in little demand,** être peu demandé/peu recherché.

demonetization, *n.* démonétisation *f.*

demonstration, *n.* (*of apparatus*) démonstration *f* (d'un appareil); **demonstration model,** appareil *m* ayant servi aux démonstrations/appareil de démonstrations.

demonstrator, *n.* démonstrateur, -trice.

demurrage, *n.* **1.** *Nau:* (*a*) surestarie(s) *f*(*pl*) (*b*) indemnité *f* de/pour surestaries **2.** *Rail:* (*a*) magasinage *m* (*b*) droits *mpl* de magasinage **3.** *Fin:* retenue pour frais de fabrication (perçue sur l'or en barres versé à la Banque d'Angleterre).

denomination, *n.* **coins of all denominations,** pièces *f* de toutes valeurs; **(notes of) small denominations,** petites coupures.

department, *n.* (*a*) département *m*/ service *m*/branche *f*; **accounts department,** (service de) la comptabilité/ services comptables; **after-sales department/customer service department,** service après-vente; **(capital-)issue department,** service des émissions; **complaints department,** service des réclamations; **design department,** service technique; **dispatch department,** service des expéditions; **equipment/supply department,** service du matériel/service fournisseur; **export department,** service des exportations; **head of department,** chef *m* de service; **legal department,** service du contentieux; **personnel department,** service du personnel; **to solve a problem between the departments concerned,** résoudre un problème interdépartemental (*b*) (*in shop*) rayon *m*; comptoir *m*; **dress department,** rayon des robes; **department store,** grand magasin/magasin à rayons.

departmental, *a.* (*a*) départemental/qui se rapporte à un service; **departmental manager,** chef *m* de service/de rayon (*b*) **departmental store,** grand magasin/ magasin à rayons.

deposit[1], *n.* **1.** *Bank:* dépôt *m*; **bank deposit,** dépôt bancaire/en banque; **deposit bank,** banque *f* de dépôt; **deposit money,** monnaie scripturale; **minimum deposit,** acompte *m* minimum; **on deposit,** en dépôt; **deposit account** = compte *m* d'épargne; **fixed deposit/deposit for a fixed period,** dépôt à échéance fixe; argent *m* en dépôt à terme; **deposit at seven days' notice,** dépôt à sept jours de préavis; **deposit slip,** bordereau *m*/ bulletin *m* de versement; **safe deposit,** dépôt en coffre-fort **2.** (*a*) *Bank:* consignation *f* (d'une somme) (*b*) caution *f*/ cautionnement *m*; (*for contract*) arrhes *fpl*; (*for apartment*) caution; (*for bottle*)

consigne *f*; (*on bottles*) **no deposit** = (bouteilles) non consignées; **to leave/to make/to pay a deposit on sth.,** verser une somme/un acompte en garantie de qch.; donner des arrhes/verser une provision; **to leave £10 as (a) deposit,** verser un acompte de £10 **3.** *Publ:* **legal deposit,** dépôt légal.

deposit[2], *v.tr.* (*a*) déposer (de l'argent à la banque); **to deposit documents with a bank,** mettre des documents en dépôt dans une banque; *Publ:* **to deposit duty copies of a publication (for copyright),** déposer des exemplaires d'un livre (= dépôt légal) (*b*) **to deposit £100,** verser £100 d'arrhes/verser £100 à titre de provision; *Cust:* **to deposit the duty (repayable),** cautionner les droits.

depositary, *n.* dépositaire *mf*/consignataire *mf*.

depositor, *n. Bank:* déposant(*e*); **depositor's book,** livret nominatif.

depository, *n.* **1.** dépôt *m*/magasin *m*/ entrepôt *m*; **furniture depository,** garde-meubles *m inv* **2.** = **depositary.**

depot, *n.* dépôt *m*/entrepôt *m*; **goods depot,** dépôt de marchandises/hangar *m* à marchandises; **petrol storage depot,** dépôt d'essence.

depreciate, **1.** *v.tr.* (*a*) déprécier/rabaisser (la valeur de qch.); avilir (les marchandises); **to depreciate the franc,** déprécier/dévaloriser le franc (*b*) amortir (le mobilier, l'outillage, etc.) **2.** *v.i.* se déprécier/diminuer de valeur; (*of prices, shares, etc.*) baisser.

depreciation, *n.* (*a*) dépréciation *f*/dévalorisation *f* (de la monnaie); dépréciation (du matériel); moins-value *f* (des actions); avilissement *m* (des marchandises); **shares that show a depreciation,** actions *f* qui ont enregistré une moins-value/une baisse (de prix) (*b*) *Ind: Book-k:* **annual depreciation,** dépréciation annuelle/amortissement annuel; **depreciation rate,** taux *m* d'amortissement; **accelerated deprecia-tion,** amortissement accéléré; **straight line method of depreciation,** méthode *f* de l'amortissement constant/méthode linéaire.

depress, *v.tr.* faire languir/faire végéter (le commerce); faire baisser (le prix de qch.).

depressed, *a.* (marché) languissant/dé-primé/dans le marasme.

depression, *n.* crise *f*/affaissement *m*/marasme *m*/stagnation *f* (des affaires); **economic depression,** dépression *f* éco-nomique/récession *f*.

deputy, *n.* fondé *m* de pouvoir; repré-sentant *m* (de qn); délégué *m* (d'un fonctionnaire); **to act as deputy for s.o.,** suppléer qn; **deputy chairman,** vice-président *m*; **deputy manager/manager-ess,** directeur adjoint/directrice adjointe; **deputy managing director,** directeur général adjoint.

description, *n.* désignation *f* (de mar-chandises); **Trade Descriptions Act,** loi *f* qui empêche la publicité mensongère (*b*) **job description,** description *f* d'un poste/définition *f* d'une fonction.

design, *n.* dessin *m*/type *m*/modèle *m*/conception *f* (d'une machine/d'un pro-duit); **industrial design,** dessin industriel; **product design,** conception d'un produit; **our latest design,** notre dernier modèle; **car of the latest design,** voiture *f* dernier modèle; **The Design Centre,** Centre *m* d'exposition de modèles.

designation, *n.* désignation *f* (d'une mar-chandise).

designer, *n.* (*i*) **project designer,** concep-teur (-projeteur) *m* (*ii*) dessinateur, -trice.

desk, *n.* **1.** (office) desk, bureau *m*; **desk pad,** (*i*) sous-main *m inv* (*ii*) bloc-notes *m*; **desk work,** travail *m* de bureau **2.** caisse *f*; **pay at the desk,** payez à la caisse; (*in hotel*) **reception desk,** la réception.

despatch, *n.* & *v.* = **dispatch**[1, 2].

determination, *n.* **1.** détermination *f*/fixation *f* (d'une date/des prix) **2.** *Jur:* expiration *f* (d'un contrat, etc.); ré-siliation *f* (d'un contrat).

determine, *v.tr.* **1.** déterminer/fixer (une date/des prix); **conditions to be deter-mined,** conditions *f* à définir **2.** *Jur:* **to determine a contract/a lease,** résilier un contrat/un bail.

devaluation, *n.* dévaluation *f*.

devalue, *v.tr.* dévaluer; **the franc has been devalued,** le franc a été dévalué; **the franc has devalued by 3%,** le franc s'est dévalué de 3%.

development, *n.* (*a*) exploitation *f*/mise *f* en valeur (d'une région); **development area,** zone *f* de développement/zone d'aménagement (*b*) **research and deve-lopment,** recherche *f* et développement.

deviation, *n.* (*a*) *MIns:* déroutement *m* (d'un navire, entraînant l'annulation des polices d'assurance et de la charte-partie) (*b*) *Stat:* **standard deviation,** déviation normale.

device, *n.* dispositif *m*/système *m*/mécanisme *m*.

dial, *v.tr.* & *i.* composer (un numéro de téléphone); **to dial direct,** obtenir une communication par voie automatique.

dialling, *n.* **dialling code,** indicatif *m*/préfixe *m*; **dialling tone,** tonalité *f*; **international direct dialling,** automati-que *m* international.

diary, *n.* agenda *m*/calendrier *m*/semainier *m*; **bill diary,** carnet *m* d'échéances/échéancier *m*; **desk diary,** bloc *m* calendrier; agenda de bureau.

Dictaphone, *n.* *R.t.m.* Dictaphone *m*/appareil *m* à dicter.

dictate, *v.tr.* dicter (une lettre).

dictating, *n.* dictée *f* (d'une lettre); **dictat-ing machine,** appareil *m* à dicter.

dictation, *n.* dictée *f*.

difference, *n.* différence *f*/écart *m* (**be-**

tween, entre); **differences in price**, écarts de prix; *StExch:* **difference between cash and settlement prices**, report *m*; **speculation in difference and contangoes**, spéculation *f* sur les différences et les reports.

differential, 1. *a.* **differential duties**, droits différentiels; **differential tariff**, tarif différentiel **2.** *n.* écart *m* (de prix, de salaires); **wage differentials**, hiérarchie salariale.

dilution, *n.* **dilution of equity**, dilution *f* du bénéfice par action.

dip, *v.i.* (*of shares, etc.*) baisser.

direct[1], *v.tr.* diriger/mener/gérer/régir/administrer (une entreprise).

direct[2], *a.* **direct costing**, méthode *f* des coûts *m* variables; *Bank:* **direct debit**, prélèvement *m* bancaire automatique; **direct expenses**, charges directes; **direct labour**, main-d'œuvre directe; **direct tax**, impôt direct; **direct taxation**, contribution directe.

direction, *n.* (*a*) direction *f*/administration *f* (d'une société); conduite *f* (des affaires) (*b*) **directions for use**, mode *m* d'emploi.

director, *n.* directeur *m*/administrateur *m* (d'une société); **managing director**, directeur général; **chairman and managing director**, président-directeur général (P-DG); **board of directors**, conseil *m* d'administration/direction générale.

directorate, *n.* (conseil d')administration *f*.

directorship, *n.* direction *f*; poste *m*/fonctions *fpl* de directeur; **during his directorship**, pendant sa direction.

directory, *n.* **commercial directory**, annuaire *m* du commerce; **street directory**, guide *m* des rues; **telephone directory**, annuaire (des téléphones).

directress, *n.f. NAm:* directrice.

disburse, *v.tr.* débourser (de l'argent).

disbursement, *n.* **1.** déboursement *m*/versement *m*/paiement *m* **2.** *pl.* **disbursements**, déboursé *m*/frais *mpl*/débours *mpl*.

discharge[1], *n.* **1.** (*i*) déchargement *m* (d'un navire) (*ii*) déchargement/débarquement *m*/débardage *m* (d'une cargaison) **2.** *Jur:* **discharge in bankruptcy/order of discharge**, réhabilitation *f* (d'un failli) **3.** (*a*) paiement *m* (d'une dette) (*b*) quittance *f*/décharge *f*/libération *f*/acquit *m*; **in full discharge**, pour acquit; **final discharge**, quitus *m*.

discharge[2], *v.tr.* **1.** (*i*) décharger (un navire) (*ii*) décharger/débarquer (une cargaison) **2.** *Jur:* réhabiliter/décharger (un failli); **discharged bankrupt**, failli réhabilité **3.** acquitter/liquider/solder (une dette); payer (une dette/un compte); apurer (un compte); faire l'apurement *m* (d'un compte); **to discharge one's liabilities**, payer/régler ses dettes **4. to discharge an employee**, renvoyer/congédier un employé.

dischargeable, *a.* **1.** (failli *m*) réhabilitable **2.** (dette) acquittable/payable.

discount[1], *n.* **1.** remise *f*/rabais *m*/escompte *m*/ristourne *f*; **to give a discount**, faire une remise; **to sell sth. at a discount**, vendre qch. au rabais; **discount for quantities**, réduction *f* sur la quantité; **discount for cash**, escompte (sur paiement) au comptant/escompte de caisse; **trade discount**, remise/escompte d'usage; **additional discount**, surremise *f*; **to allow a discount of 10%/a 10% discount**, consentir un rabais de dix pour cent; **discount price**, prix *m* faible **2.** *Fin:* escompte; **bank discount**, escompte en dehors; **true discount**, escompte en dedans; **discount house**, (*i*) banque spécialisée dans l'escompte des effets de commerce/banque d'escompte (*ii*) *NAm:* magasin *m* de demi-gros/magasin minimarge; **discount rate**, taux *m* d'escompte; **discount store**, magasin de demi-gros; (*of shares*) **to be/to stand at a**

discount, être en perte/accuser une perte.

discount[2], *v.tr. Fin:* escompter (un effet)/ prendre (un effet) à l'escompte/faire l'escompte d'(un effet); **to discount a rise in shares,** escompter sur une hausse des valeurs; **discounted value,** valeur actualisée.

discountable, *a. Fin:* escomptable.

discounter, *n.* **1.** (*pers.*) escompteur *m* **2.** *NAm:* (= **discount store**) magasin *m* de demi-gros/magasin minimarge.

discounting, *n.* escompte *m*; actualisation *f*; **discounting banker,** banquier *m* escompteur.

discrepancy, *n.* écart *m*/différence *f*; **statistical discrepancy,** écart statistique; **there is a discrepancy in the accounts,** les comptes *m* ne sont pas justes.

discretionary, *a. StExch:* **discretionary order,** ordre *m* à appréciation.

dishonour, *v.tr.* **to dishonour a bill,** ne pas honorer/ne pas accepter un effet/refuser de payer un effet; **dishonoured cheque,** chèque impayé/non honoré.

disinvestment, *n.* désinvestissement *m.*

dismiss, *v.tr.* **to dismiss an employee,** congédier/licencier un employé; **to be dismissed,** recevoir son congé/être congédié/se faire mettre à la porte.

dismissal, *n.* renvoi *m*/congédiement *m*/ licenciement *m/F:* mise *f* à pied.

dispatch[1], *n.* expédition *f*/envoi *m*; **dispatch service/dispatch department,** service *m* des expéditions; **dispatch manager,** chef *m* du service des expéditions; **dispatch note,** bulletin *m*/bordereau *m* d'expédition.

dispatch[2], *v.tr.* **1.** expédier/envoyer/acheminer (une lettre/des marchandises); **to dispatch goods to Paris,** acheminer des marchandises sur/vers Paris **2.** expédier (une affaire).

dispatcher, *n.* expéditeur, -trice.

dispatching, *n.* expédition *f*/envoi *m*/ acheminement *m* (des marchandises/des lettres).

dispenser, *n.* appareil *m*/étui *m*/ distributeur *m*; **automatic dispenser,** distributeur automatique; **cash dispenser,** distributeur automatique de billets.

displaced, *a. StExch:* **displaced shares,** actions déclassées.

displacement, *n. St Exch:* déclassement *m* (d'actions).

display[1], *n.* étalage *m*/exposition *f* (de marchandises); **display pack,** emballage *m* de présentation/emballage présentoir; **display window/display cabinet/display case,** vitrine *f*; **display unit/stand,** présentoir *m*; *Cmptr:* **visual display unit/terminal (VDU/VDT),** visuel *m*/console *f* de visualisation.

display[2], *v.tr.* étaler/exposer (des marchandises).

disposable, *a.* (*a*) disponible; **disposable income,** surplus *m*/revenu *m* disponible; **disposable funds,** disponibilités *f*/valeurs *f* disponibles (*b*) à jeter après usage/ jetable.

disposal, *n.* **1.** disposition *f*/cession *f* (onéreuse)/vente *f* (de biens); **for disposal,** à vendre/à céder; **disposal of securities,** cession de titres **2.** **to have a car at one's disposal,** disposer d'une voiture.

dispose, *v.i.* **to dispose of goods/of an article,** écouler (des marchandises)/vendre/ placer (un produit); **to dispose of one's business,** céder son fonds.

dispute, *n.* **labour dispute,** conflit *m* du travail.

distribute, *v.tr.* être concessionnaire d'un produit/vendre/distribuer (un produit).

distribution, *n.* (mise *f* en) distribution *f*; répartition *f*; **distribution channel/network,** circuit *m*/réseau *m* de distribution; **distribution costs,** frais *mpl* de distribution/coût *m* de la distribution; **distribution manager,** chef *m* de la distribution; **distribution slip,** bordereau *m* de circulation/liste *f* de(s) destinataires; *Fin: (in bankruptcy)* **distribution of debts,** répartition des dettes.

distributor, *n.* distributeur, -trice (d'automobiles, etc.).

district, *n.* **district bank,** banque régionale; **district manager,** directeur régional.

disturbed, *a. StExch:* **disturbed market,** marché agité.

diversification, *n.* **product diversification,** diversification *f* des produits.

diversify, *v.tr.* **to diversify production,** diversifier la production.

dividend, *n.* dividende *m*; *(from cooperative society)* ristourne *f*; **dividend on shares,** dividende d'actions; **final dividend,** solde *m* de dividende; **interim dividend,** dividende intérimaire; **cum dividend/*NAm:* dividend on,** avec le dividende/coupon attaché; **ex dividend/*NAm:* dividend off,** ex-dividende/sans intérêt; **dividend warrant,** chèque-dividende *m*/coupon d'arrérages.

dock, *n.* bassin *m* (d'un port); *(wharf)* **loading dock,** embarcadère *m*; **unloading dock,** débarcadère *m*; **the docks,** les docks *m*.

docker, *n.* docker *m*/débardeur *m*.

docket, *n.* (*a*) étiquette *f*/fiche *f* (*b*) bordereau *m* (de livraison, etc.) (*c*) récépissé *m* (de douane).

document, *n.* document *m*/pièce *f*/titre *m*/ papier *m*; **legal document,** acte *m* authentique; **commercial documents,** papiers d'affaires; **working document,** document de travail.

documentary, *a.* documentaire; **documentary bill,** traite *f* documentaire;

traite accompagnée de documents; **documentary credit,** crédit *m* documentaire.

dole, *n.* allocation *f*/indemnité *f* de chômage.

dollar, *n.* (*i*) dollar (canadien/australien/ malais/etc.) (*ii*) dollar (américain); **a five dollar bill,** un billet de cinq dollars; **dollar area,** zone *f* dollar; **dollar balances,** balances *f* dollar; **dollar crisis,** crise *f* du dollar; **dollar premium,** prime *f* sur le dollar.

domestic, *a.* (commerce) intérieur; **domestic production,** production nationale; **domestic products,** denrées *f* du pays.

domicile¹, *n.* domicile *m*.

domicile², *v.tr.* domicilier (un effet); **bills domiciled in France,** traites *f* payables en France.

domiciliation, *n.* domiciliation *f* (d'un effet).

door-to-door, *a.* **door-to-door transport/ canvassing/selling,** porte à porte *m*; **to be a door-to-door salesman,** être placier *m*/ faire du porte à porte.

down, *a.* **down payment,** (*i*) acompte *m* (*ii*) versement *m* à la commande/versement initial.

downward, *a.* **downward trend (of prices),** tendance *f* à la baisse.

dozen, *n.* douzaine *f*; **two dozen eggs,** deux douzaines d'œufs; **half a dozen,** une demi-douzaine; **to sell articles in (sets of) dozens/by the dozen,** vendre des articles à la douzaine.

draft¹, *n.* (*a*) tirage *m* (d'un effet) (*b*) traite *f*/lettre *f* de change/mandat *m*/ disposition *f*/effet *m*; bon *m* (sur une banque); **banker's draft,** chèque *m* bancaire; **time draft,** traite/effet à terme; **to make a draft on s.o.,** faire traite/tirer sur qn (*c*) **draft contract,** projet *m* de contrat.

draft², *v.tr.* rédiger (un acte/un projet); **to draft a letter,** faire le brouillon d'une lettre; **to draft a contract,** préparer/faire le projet d'un contrat.

drafter, *n.* rédacteur, -trice (d'un acte, etc.).

drafting, *n.* rédaction *f* (d'un acte, etc.).

drain, *n.* **drain of money,** drainage *m* de capitaux; **drain on the resources,** cause *f* d'épuisement des ressources; **the brain drain,** la fuite/l'exode *m*/le drainage des cerveaux (vers l'étranger).

draughtsman, -woman, *n.* dessinateur, -trice industriel, -elle.

draw, *v.tr.* (*a*) **to draw a commission,** prélever/demander une commission (*b*) **to draw money from the bank/from an account,** retirer de l'argent de la banque/d'un compte; **to draw one's salary,** toucher son salaire (*c*) **to draw (a cheque) on a bank,** tirer un chèque sur une banque/fournir sur une banque; **to draw three months' bill on London,** fournir à 3 mois sur Londres (*d*) **money drawing interest,** argent *m* qui produit des intérêts.

drawback, *n. Cust:* draw-back *m*/remise *f*.

drawee, *n.* tiré *m* (d'une lettre de change).

drawer, *n.* tireur *m* (d'une lettre de change).

drawing, *n.* traite *f* (de chèques, d'effets); **drawing on s.o.,** disposition *f* sur qn; **drawing account,** compte courant pour frais de représentation.

draw up, *v.tr.* établir/dresser/rédiger (un bilan).

dress up, *v.tr. NAm:* **the accounts were dressed up,** les comptes avaient été falsifiés.

drive, *n.* campagne *f*; **sales drive,** campagne de vente.

drop[1]**,** *n.* **1.** chute *f*/baisse *f*/abaissement *m*; **drop in prices,** chute/ baisse de prix; **heavy drop in cottons,** débâcle *f* des cotons; **sales show a drop of 10%,** les ventes *f* accusent une régression/enregistrent une baisse de 10%; *Fin:* **drop in value/in takings,** moins-value *f*. **2.** *F:*

livraison *f*; **I have four drops to make,** j'ai quatre livraisons à faire.

drop[2]**,** *v.i.* (*of prices*) baisser; *Fin:* **receipts have dropped,** les recettes *f* ont baissé/ accusent une moins-value; *StExch:* **shares dropped a point,** les actions *f* ont reculé d'un point; **the pound dropped 10% against the dollar,** la livre a baissé de 10% contre le dollar.

dry, *a.* (*a*) **dry money,** argent sec (*b*) **dry goods,** (*i*) marchandises sèches (*ii*) *NAm:* articles *m* de nouveauté; étoffes *f*/tissus *m*; mercerie *f*; **dry goods store,** magasin *m* de nouveautés; *Nau:* **dry cargo,** cargaison sèche.

dud, *F:* **1.** *a.* (*a*) **dud stock,** marchandises *f* invendables; rossignols *mpl* (*b*) **dud cheque,** chèque *m* sans provision; **dud note,** faux billet de banque **2.** *n.* **the note was a dud,** le billet était faux.

due, *a.* **1.** (*of debt*) exigible; **not due,** inexigible; **bill due on 1st May,** effet *m* payable le premier mai; **contributions still due,** cotisations *f* à percevoir; **balance due (to us),** solde créditeur; **balance due (by us),** solde débiteur; **debts due to us/to the firm,** dettes actives/créances *f*; **debts due by us/by the firm,** dettes passives; **amounts due within one year,** échéances à moins d'un an; **sums due from banks,** créances sur les banques; **bond due for repayment,** obligation amortie; *NAm:* **due bill,** reconnaissance *f* de dette; **to fall/become due,** échoir/ arriver à échéance/venir à échéance; **past due,** en souffrance; **when due,** à l'échéance; **due date,** (date d') échéance/(date d') exigibilité *f*; **redemption before due date,** remboursement/amortissement anticipé **2. in due form,** dans les formes voulues/ en bonne forme/en règle/dans les règles; **contract drawn up in due form,** contrat rédigé en bonne et due forme; **receipt in due form,** quittance régulière **3.** *n.* commande notée.

due-date, *v.tr.* coter (un effet).

dues, *n.pl.* droits *m*/frais *mpl*; **taxes and**

dues, impôts *m* et taxes *f*; **market dues,** hallage *m*; **port dues,** droits de port.

dull, *a.* (marché) calme/inactif/lourd/plat/ inanimé/languissant; **the dull season,** la morte-saison; **business is dull,** les affaires *f* languissent/le marché est calme.

dul(l)ness, *n.* stagnation *f*/calme *m* (des affaires); inactivité *f*/inaction *f*/peu d'activité (du marché).

duly, *adv.* **1.** dûment; **duly authorized representative,** représentant dûment accrédité; **I duly received your letter of . . .,** j'ai bien reçu votre lettre du . . . **2.** en temps voulu/en temps utile; **I duly sent it back,** je l'ai renvoyé en temps voulu.

dummy, *a. & n.* (*of pers.*) mannequin *m*; (*of book, etc.*) maquette *f*; **dummy (pack),** emballage *m* factice; **dummy box,** boîte *f* factice.

dump, *v.tr.* **to dump goods on a foreign market,** écouler à perte des marchandises à l'étranger/faire du dumping.

dump bin, *n.* *Mkt:* panier *m* (présentoir).

dumper, *n.* **1.** commerçant *m* (*esp.* exportateur *m*) qui fait du dumping **2. dumper truck,** camion *m* à benne.

dumping, *n.* dumping *m*/délestage *m*; **panic dumping,** délestage de panique.

duplicate[1], *a.* double/en double; **duplicate receipt,** duplicata *m* d'un reçu.

duplicate[2], *n.* duplicata *m*/double *m*/ contrepartie *f* (d'un écrit); **in duplicate,** (en) double/en duplicata/en double exemplaire; **to draw a bill of exchange in duplicate,** tirer une lettre de change en duplicata.

duplicate[3], **1.** *v.i. Book-k:* (*of entry*) to

duplicate with another, faire double emploi avec un autre **2.** *v.tr.* **to duplicate a circular letter,** reproduire/tirer une lettre circulaire à plusieurs exemplaires (au duplicateur)/polycopier une lettre circulaire.

duplicating, *n.* **1.** répétition *f*; **duplicating book,** manifold *m* **2.** reproduction *f*/tirage *m* à plusieurs exemplaires (au duplicateur); **duplicating machine,** duplicateur *m*/machine *f* à polycopier; **duplicating paper,** papier *m* pour duplicateurs.

duplication, *n.* répétition *f*/reproduction *f*; *Book-k:* double emploi *m* (d'une écriture).

duplicator, *n.* duplicateur *m*/machine *f* à polycopier.

durable, 1. *a.* durable; **durable goods,** (*i*) biens permanents/biens d'équipement/ biens durables (*ii*) biens/produits *m* d'usage **2.** *n.* (**consumer**) **durables,** biens durables.

dutiable, *a.* soumis à des droits; passible de droits/imposable/taxable; *Cust:* soumis aux droits de douane/*F:* déclarable.

duty, *n.* droit *m*; **customs duty,** droit(s) de douane/droit(s) d'entrée; **liable to duty,** passible de droits; soumis aux droits; **duty on silk,** droits d'entrée sur les soieries; **duty-paid goods,** marchandises acquittées/dédouanées; **to take the duty off goods,** exonérer des marchandises; **stamp duty,** droit de timbre.

duty-free, *a.* exempt de droit/franc de tout droit; (importé) en franchise de douane; **duty-free shop,** magasin *m*/ boutique *f* hors taxe; **duty-free goods,** marchandises *f* hors taxe.

E

early, *a.* **1. early closing day,** jour *m* où les magasins sont fermés l'après-midi **2. at an early date,** prochainement/sous peu/bientôt; **at your earliest convenience,** le plus tôt (qu'il vous sera) possible/dès que possible.

earmark, *v.tr.* **to earmark funds for a purpose,** assigner/affecter une somme à un projet.

earn, *v.tr.* gagner (de l'argent); **to earn interest,** recevoir de l'intérêt; **to earn one's living by writing,** gagner sa vie en écrivant.

earnest, *n.* **earnest (money),** arrhes *fpl*; dépôt *m* de garantie.

earning, *a.* profitable/qui rapporte/lucratif; **earning capacity/power,** (*i*) capacité *f* bénéficiaire (*ii*) profitabilité *f*/rentabilité *f*.

earnings, *n.pl.* **1.** salaire *m*; appointements *mpl*; **loss of earnings,** perte *f* de salaire **2.** profits *m*/bénéfices *m*/gains *m*/revenus *mpl* (d'une entreprise); **earnings per share,** bénéfice/gain par action; **earnings performance,** rentabilité *f*; **earnings power,** capacité *f* bénéficiaire; **gross earnings,** bénéfices bruts/recettes brutes; **invisible earnings,** revenus *m* invisibles; **price earnings ratio (PER),** taux *m* de capitalisation des bénéfices/ratio *m* cours-bénéfices/price earnings ratio.

easement, *n. Jur:* servitude *f*.

easy, *a.* **1. by easy payments/on easy terms,** avec facilités *f* de paiement **2. easy market,** marché *m* tranquille/calme; **share prices are easier today,** le prix des actions fléchit.

echelon, *n.* **the higher echelons of industry,** les niveaux/les échelons supérieurs de l'industrie.

economic, *a.* **1.** qui se rapporte à l'économie politique; (problème situation) économique; **economic crisis,** crise *f* économique; **economic growth,** croissance *f* économique; **economic policy,** politique *f*/système *m* économique; **economic sanctions,** sanctions *f* économiques; **economic situation,** conjoncture *f* économique; **economic trend,** évolution *f*/conjoncture économique; **European Economic Community (EEC),** Communauté économique européenne (CEE) **2. economic rent,** loyer bon marché.

economical, *a.* économique; **economical car,** voiture *f* économique.

economics, *n.pl.* (*usu. with sg. const.*). **1.** l'économique *f*/science *f* économique/économie *f* politique; **welfare economics,** l'économie du bien-être **2.** rentabilité *f* (d'un projet); **the economics of town planning,** les aspects financiers de l'urbanisme.

economist, *n.* **(political) economist,** économiste *m*; **agricultural economist,** agronome *m*.

economize, **1.** *v.i.* **to economize on food,** économiser/faire des économies sur la nourriture **2.** *v.tr.* **to economize £500 on rent,** économiser £500 sur le prix du loyer.

economy, *n.* **1.** économie *f* (d'argent, de

temps, etc.); **to practise economy/ economies,** économiser; *Aut:* **economy run,** concours *m* de consommation; *Av:* **to travel (in) economy class,** voyager en classe économique **2.** (*a*) **controlled economy,** économie dirigée; **economy of scale,** économie d'échelle; **mixed economy,** économie mixte; **open economy,** économie ouverte; **planned economy,** économie planifiée; **political economy,** économie politique (*b*) **to disturb the economy of the country,** déranger l'économie/le régime économique du pays.

edge, *n.* **competitive edge,** avance concurrentielle/sur les concurrents.

effect[1], *n.* **1.** (*a*) effet *m*/action *f*/influence *f*; résultat *m*/conséquence *f* (d'un fait) (*b*) (*of regulation, etc.*) **to take effect/to come into effect,** entrer en vigueur; **to take effect on/with effect from January 1st,** applicable à compter du/qui entre en vigueur le 1er janvier; **to remain in effect,** demeurer en vigueur/être toujours en vigueur (*c*) sens *m*/teneur *f* (d'un document); **with a proviso to the effect that . . .,** avec une clause conditionnelle portant que . . ./dont la teneur est que . . .; **we have made provisions to this effect,** nous avons pris des dispositions dans ce sens **2.** *pl.* **personal effects,** effets/biens personnels; *Jur:* **movable effects,** biens meubles/effets mobiliers; *Bank:* **no effects,** pas de provision/défaut *m* de provision.

effect[2], *v.tr.* effectuer/accomplir/opérer/ réaliser/exécuter (qch.); **to effect a payment,** effectuer un paiement; **to effect customs clearance,** procéder aux formalités douanières; **to effect a settlement between two parties,** arriver à un accord entre deux parties/réussir à mettre les deux parties d'accord; *Book-k:* **to effect a corresponding entry,** passer une écriture conforme.

effective, *a.* (*a*) effectif; *PolEc:* **effective demand,** demande effective; **effective management,** direction *f*/gestion *f* efficace; **effective yield,** rendement effectif;

Fin: **effective money,** monnaie effective/réelle (*b*) *Adm:* **effective date,** date *f* d'entrée en vigueur; **effective on/as from October 10th,** applicable à partir du 10 octobre/qui entre en vigueur le 10 octobre.

effectiveness, *n.* efficacité *f*; **cost effectiveness,** coût-efficacité *m*.

effectual, *a.* (contrat) valide; (règlement) en vigueur.

efficiency, *n.* **1.** (*a*) efficacité *f* (du travail, etc.); performance; **with a high degree of efficiency,** exceptionnellement performant; **economic efficiency,** efficience *f*/ efficacité économique; **technical efficiency,** efficacité technique (*b*) productivité *f*/rendement *m* (d'une machine); (*in chain production*) **motion efficiency,** rendement du geste; **efficiency expert,** expert *m* en organisation/en rendement (*c*) bon fonctionnement (d'une administration, etc.) **2.** (*of pers.*) capacité *f*/rendement; valeur professionnelle (de la main-d'œuvre); *Ind:* **efficiency wages,** salaire proportionné à la production/basé sur le rendement.

efficient, *a.* (*a*) (*of method, work*) efficace; **efficient working (of apparatus),** bon fonctionnement (d'un appareil) (*b*) **efficient machine,** (*i*) machine *f* à bon rendement (*ii*) machine d'un fonctionnement sûr (*c*) (*of pers.*) capable/compétent/habile.

efficiently, *adv.* **1.** efficacement **2.** avec compétence.

efflux, *n. PolEc:* **efflux of capital,** exode *m* de capitaux; **efflux of gold,** sortie *f* d'or.

elastic, *a. PolEc:* (offre, demande) élastique.

elasticity, *n. PolEc:* **the elasticity of supply and demand,** l'élasticité *f* de l'offre et de la demande.

electronic, *a.* électronique; **electronic**

computer, calculateur *m* électronique; **electronic data processing (EDP),** traitement *m* électronique de l'information (TEI); **the EDP industry,** l'industrie *f* de l'informatique; **electronic engineer/electronic specialist,** électronicien, -ienne/ingénieur électronicien.

electronics, *n.pl.* (*usu. with sg. const.*) électronique *f*; **electronics industry,** industrie *f* électronique; **electronic specialist/engineer/technician,** electronicien, -ienne/ingénieur électronicien.

embargo[1], *n.* embargo *m*; séquestre *m*; *Nau:* saisie *f*; **to lay an embargo on a ship,** mettre l'embargo sur un navire/frapper un navire d'embargo/saisir un navire; (*of ship, goods*) **to be under an embargo,** être séquestré; **to put/to impose an embargo on the import of horses,** mettre l'embargo sur/défendre l'importation des chevaux; **to lift/to remove an embargo,** lever un embargo.

embargo[2], *v.tr.* mettre l'embargo sur/ frapper d'embargo/séquestrer (un navire, des marchandises).

embark, *v.tr.* (*of ship*) prendre à bord (des marchandises, etc.).

embarkation, *n.* embarquement *m*; **port of embarkation,** port *m* d'embarquement.

embezzle, 1. *v.tr.* détourner/distraire/ s'approprier (des fonds) **2.** *v.i.* commettre des détournements (de fonds).

embezzlement, *n.* détournement *m* de fonds/appropriation *f* de fonds.

emergency, *n.* circonstance *f* critique/ nécessité urgente/cas urgent/cas pressant; imprévu *m*.

emolument, *n.* appointements *mpl*/ traitement *m*/rémunération *f*/émoluments *mpl*.

employ, *v.tr.* (*a*) employer (qn) à son service; **to employ twenty workmen,** employer vingt ouvriers (*b*) (*only of new staff*) embaucher.

employed, 1. *a.* employé; **to be fully employed,** travailler à plein temps; **gainfully employed,** rémunéré; **the gainfully employed population,** la population active; **capital employed,** capital investi **2.** *n.* **employers and employed,** le patronat et le salariat/les patrons et les ouvriers.

employee, *n.* employé(e); **the employees of a firm,** le personnel d'une maison; **relations between management and employees,** relations *f* entre la direction et le personnel; **to take on employees,** engager/recruter du personnel; embaucher de la main-d'œuvre.

employer, *n. Ind: etc:* patron, -onne/chef *m* d'entreprise; **the big employers of labour,** les grands employeurs de main-d'œuvre; **body of employers,** patronat *m*; **organization of employers/ employers' association,** organisation patronale/syndicat patronal; **chamber of employers,** chambre patronale; **employers' liability insurance,** assurance *f* des patrons contre les accidents du travail; assurance réparation; **employer's contribution,** cotisation patronale.

employment, *n.* **1.** (*use*) emploi *m* (de l'argent, etc.) **2.** (*occupation*) emploi/ travail *m*/place *f*/situation *f*/occupation *f*; *PolEc:* **full employment,** plein-emploi; **full-time employment,** travail à plein temps; **part-time employment,** travail à mi-temps/travail à temps partiel; **temporary employment,** travail temporaire; **to be without employment,** être sans emploi/sans travail/en chômage; **to find alternative employment for an employee,** transférer un(e) employé(e)/placer un(e) employé(e) ailleurs; **to give s.o. employment,** donner un emploi à qn; **employment bureau/employment agency/ employment office,** bureau *m*/agence *f* de placement; (*for workmen*), **employment agency,** service *m* d'embauche/de la main-d'œuvre; **employment exchange/**

NAm: **employment bureau** = agence nationale pour l'emploi (ANPE); **employment tax,** taxe *f* sur l'emploi; **conditions of employment,** conditions *f* d'embauche; **security of employment/guaranteed employment,** sécurité *f* de l'emploi.

emporium, *n.* **1.** entrepôt *m*; centre *m* de commerce; marché *m* **2.** grand magasin.

empties, *n.pl.* caisses *f* vides; bouteilles *f* vides; **returned empties,** emballages retournés vides; **empties are not returnable,** on ne reprend pas les bouteilles vides.

emption, *n. Jur:* achat *m*; **right of emption,** droit *m* d'emption/droit d'achat.

encash, *v.tr.* encaisser/toucher (un chèque); **when encashed,** après encaissement.

encashable, *a.* encaissable.

encashment, *n.* **1.** encaissement *m* **2.** recette *f*/rentrée *f*.

enclose, *v.tr.* **to enclose sth. in a letter,** joindre qch. à une lettre; **letter enclosing a cheque,** lettre *f* contenant un chèque; **enclosed herewith,** sous ce pli; **enclosed please find . . . ,** veuillez trouver ci-inclus/ci-joint/sous ce pli . . . .

enclosure, *n.* pièce annexée/incluse; annexe *f*; le document ci-joint; **enclosures,** pièces jointes (PJ).

end¹, *n.* bout *m*/fin *f* (du mois, etc.); issue *f* (d'une réunion); terme *m* (d'un procès, etc.); **to come to an end,** prendre fin; arriver à son terme; **at the end of the month/of the year,** à la fin du mois/de l'année; **at the end of the six months allowed,** au bout des six mois; **end product,** produit manufacturé/article fini.

end², **1.** *v.tr.* finir/terminer/achever; conclure (un discours); clore/clôturer (une séance) **2.** *v.i.* finir/se terminer (**at/in,** dans/en); **your subscription ends on May 31st,** votre abonnement *m* expire le 31 mai.

endorse, *v.tr.* endosser (un chèque); **to endorse a bill,** avaliser/endosser/donner son aval *m* à un effet; **to endorse a bill of exchange,** endosser une lettre de change; **to endorse over a bill to s.o.,** transmettre par voie d'endossement une lettre de change à qn; **to endorse back a bill to drawer,** contre-passer un effet au tireur; **an endorsed driving licence,** un permis de conduire portant la mention d'une infraction.

endorsee, *n. Fin:* endossataire *mf*/ bénéficiaire *mf* (d'un billet par endos); tiers porteur d'un chèque.

endorsement, *n.* (*a*) *Fin: etc:* endossement *m*/endos *m* (d'un chèque, d'une lettre de change); aval *m* (d'un effet) (*b*) *Ins:* avenant *m*.

endorser, *n. Fin:* endosseur, -euse/ cessionnaire *m* (d'un chèque, etc.); avaliste *m*/avaliseur *m* (d'un effet); **second endorser (of bill),** tiers porteur *m*.

endowment, *n. Ins:* (**pure**) **endowment assurance/endowment policy,** assurance *f* en cas de vie; assurance à capital différé/à terme fixe/à dotation; **combined endowment and whole-life insurance,** assurance en cas de vie et de décès; (**ordinary**) **endowment assurance,** assurance mixte; **endowment mortgage,** hypothèque liée à une assurance en cas de vie.

engineer, *n.* (*a*) ingénieur *m*; **civil engineer,** (*i*) ingénieur des travaux publics; ingénieur civil (*ii*) = ingénieur des ponts et chaussées (*b*) **consulting engineer,** ingénieur conseil; **management/industrial engineer,** ingénieur en organisation/ d'exploitation/des méthodes; **project/ design engineer,** ingénieur d'études; **planning/work-study engineer,** ingénieur de planification/en organisation; **programming engineer,** ingénieur programmeur/de programmation; **production engineer,** ingénieur (chargé) de la production; **sales engineer,** ingénieur commercial/chef *m* du service des ventes;

technical sales engineer, ingénieur technico-commercial.

engineering, *n.* (*a*) ingénierie *f*; **civil engineering,** génie civil; les travaux publics (*b*) **human engineering,** ergonomie *f*; **industrial engineering,** organisation industrielle; **management engineering,** organisation de la gestion des entreprises; **production engineering,** technique *f* de la production; **methods engineering/process engineering,** étude *f* des méthodes industrielles; **engineering department,** service *m* technique; **engineering and design department,** bureau *m* d'études; **engineering consultant,** ingénieur *m* conseil.

enquiry, *n. see* **inquiry.**

enter, 1. *v.tr.* (*a*) *Cust:* **to enter goods,** déclarer des marchandises en douane; **to enter a ship (inwards, outwards),** faire la déclaration (d'entrée, de sortie) (*b*) comptabiliser (une dépense, etc.); **to enter (up) an item in the ledger,** inscrire/porter un article au grand(-)livre; passer une écriture; **to enter (up) an amount in the profits,** employer une somme en recette **2.** *v.i.* (*a*) **to enter into relations with s.o.,** entrer en relations avec qn/entamer des relations avec qn; **to enter into business,** entrer dans les affaires; **to enter into negotiations with s.o.,** engager des négociations avec qn; **to enter into partnership with s.o.,** s'associer à/avec qn; **to enter into a bargain/an agreement/a contract,** conclure un marché/un engagement; passer un contrat (**with,** avec) (*b*) *Jur:* **to enter into the rights of a creditor,** demeurer subrogé aux droits d'un créancier.

entering, *n.* **entering (up),** inscription *f*/enregistrement *m*/comptabilisation *f*; **entering clerk,** commis *m* aux écritures.

enterprise, *n.* **free enterprise,** la libre entreprise; **private enterprise,** l'entreprise privée/le secteur privé; **state enterprise,** le secteur public; **small-scale enterprise,** entreprise artisanale.

entertainment, *n.* **entertainment expenses,** frais *mpl* de représentation.

entitlement, *n.* (*on forms*) montant auquel on a droit; ce qui revient de droit; **holiday entitlement,** congé annuel payé auquel les salariés ont droit.

entrepôt, *n.* entrepôt *m*; **entrepôt port,** port franc.

entry, *n.* **1.** *Book-k:* (*a*) passation *f* d'écriture/inscription *f* (dans un livre de commerce); **single-entry bookkeeping,** comptabilité *f* en partie simple; **double-entry bookkeeping,** comptabilité en partie double (*b*) article *m*/écriture *f*; **to contra an entry,** contre-passer une écriture; **to make an entry,** passer une écriture; **to make an entry of a transaction,** passer une transaction en écriture; **to make an entry against s.o.,** débiter qn; **compound entry,** article composé/collectif/récapitulatif; **contra entry,** contre-passation *f*/contre-passement *m*; **post entry,** écriture postérieure/subséquente; **wrong entry,** faux emploi **2.** *Cust:* **custom-house entry/customs entry,** passage *m* en douane; **to pass a customs entry of manufactured goods,** faire une déclaration en douane de produits manufacturés; **to make an entry of goods,** déclarer des marchandises à la douane; **(bill of) entry/entry inwards,** déclaration *f* d'entrée (en douane); **entry under bond,** acquit-à-caution *m*; **post entry,** déclaration additionnelle.

envelope, *n.* enveloppe *f*; **aperture envelope,** enveloppe à panneau découpé/à fenêtre découpée; **adhesive envelope,** enveloppe gommée; **airmail envelope,** envelope avion; **envelope with metal fastener,** pochette *f*; **window envelope/panel envelope,** enveloppe à fenêtre; **to put a letter in an envelope,** mettre une lettre sous enveloppe; **in a sealed envelope,** sous pli cacheté; **envelope file,** chemise *f* (de carton); **stamped addressed envelope (s.a.e),** enveloppe timbrée/affranchie portant (votre) adresse (pour la réponse).

equalization, *n.* **1.** *Fin:* régularisation *f*
(de dividendes); *Adm:* péréquation *f* (de
contributions, de traitements) **2.** *EEC:*
exchange equalization account, fonds *m*
de stabilisation des changes.

equalize, *v.tr.* **to equalize wages,** faire la
péréquation des salaires; **to equalize dividends,** régulariser les dividendes.

equalizing, *n.* péréquation *f* (des prix, des
salaires).

equation, *n.* **equation of payments,**
échéance commune (de billets de
change).

equip, *v.tr.* outiller/monter (une usine); **to
equip a workman with tools,** outiller un
ouvrier; **to equip a works with new plant,**
équiper une usine d'un matériel neuf.

equipment, *n.* matériel *m*/équipement
m; machines *fpl*; outillage *m*; **heavy
equipment,** matériel lourd; **equipment
leasing,** crédit–bail mobilier; **capital
equipment,** biens *m* d'équipement/biens
durables; capitaux *m* fixes; **technical
equipment,** capital *m* technique.

equity, *n.* **1.** *Jur:* droit *m* (équitable);
equity of redemption, droit de rachat,
après forclusion, d'un bien hypothéqué
2. **shareholders'/stockholders' equity,**
capitaux *mpl*/fonds *m* propres; avoir des
actionnaires; **equity capital,** capital actions; *pl.* **equities/**NAm:** common equities,** actions *f* ordinaires.

equivalence, *n.* *Fin:* **equivalences of exchange,** parités *f* de change.

equivalent, 1. *a.* équivalent; **to be equivalent to sth.,** être équivalent à qch./
équivaloir à qch. **2.** *n.* *PolEc:* **man equivalent,** unité-travailleur *f.*

ergonomics, *n.pl.* (*usu. with sg. const.*)
ergonomie *f.*

ergonomist, *n.* ergonomiste *mf.*

error, *n.* erreur *f*/faute *f*/méprise *f*; **error
of calculation,** erreur de calcul/faux calcul; **error in printing,** coquille *f*; **typing**

error, faute de frappe; **errors and omissions excepted,** sauf erreur ou omission;
sent by error, envoyé par erreur.

escalate, *v.i.* (*of prices*) monter /augmen-
ter rapidement,

escalation, *n.* hausse *f*/augmentation *f*
(rapide) (des prix).

escape, *n.* **escape clause,** clause *f*
échappatoire.

escrow, *n.* **held in escrow,** déposé en main
tierce/*FrC:* entiercé; *NAm:* **escrow account,** compte bloqué; compte à
échéance/à terme.

establish, *v.tr.* fonder (une maison de
commerce); édifier (un système); créer/
fonder (une agence); **to establish a tax
on tobacco,** taxer le tabac; **to establish
oneself in business,** s'établir dans les
affaires; **to establish oneself in a job,** se
faire une (bonne) réputation.

establishment, *n.* **1.** établissement *m*
(d'une industrie, etc.); création *f* (d'un
système, d'un bureau); fondation *f*
(d'une maison de commerce) **2.**
établissement/maison *f*; **business establishment,** maison de commerce; **establishment charges,** frais généraux/dé-
penses *f* de la maison **3.** **to be on the
establishment/to form part of the establishment,** faire partie du personnel **4.**
the Establishment, les classes dirigean-
tes.

estate, *n.* **1.** (*a*) bien *m*; domaine *m*;
immeuble *m*; **real estate,** biens immobiliers (*b*) succession *f* (d'un défunt); **estate
duty,** droits *mpl* de succession (*c*) actif *m*
(d'un failli) **2.** (*a*) terre *f*/propriété *f*;
country estate for sale, domaine à vendre
(*b*) **housing estate,** (*i*) lotissement *m* (*ii*)
cité ouvrière; groupe *m* de H.L.M.; **indus-
trial/trading estate,** zone industrielle (*c*)
(real) estate agent, agent immobilier;
(real) estate agency, agence immobilière;
agence de location.

estimate[1], *n.* **1.** aperçu *m*/évaluation *f*/
calcul *m*; **rough estimate,** estimation approximative; **these figures are only a**

rough estimate, ces chiffres sont très approximatifs; **conservative estimate,** évaluation prudente **2.** devis (estimatif)/état estimatif/état appréciatif; **building estimate,** devis de construction; **estimate of expenditure,** chiffre prévu pour les dépenses; **printing estimate,** devis d'imprimerie; **preliminary estimate/rough estimate,** devis de prévision/devis approximatif/avant-projet *m*; **estimate on demand,** devis sur demande; **to put in an estimate,** établir un devis; soumissionner; **to ask for an estimate,** faire évaluer/faire estimer qch..

estimate², *v.tr.* estimer/évaluer/apprécier (les frais); évaluer (la production d'un puits de pétrole, etc.).

estimated, *a.* **estimated cost,** coût estimatif/estimation *f*; **estimated value,** valeur estimée; **it is only an estimated figure,** ce n'est qu'une estimation.

estimation, *n.* estimation *f*/appréciation *f*/évaluation *f*/calcul *m* (des frais, etc.).

Eurocheque, *n.* eurochèque *m*.

Eurocurrency, *n.* **the Eurocurrency market,** le marché des eurodevises *f*.

Eurodollar, *n.* eurodollar *m*.

Euromarket, *n.* euromarché *m*.

Eurobond, *n* euro-obligation *f*.

evaluation, *n.* étude *f*/analyse *f*; **job evaluation,** évaluation *f* d'un emploi.

evasion, *n.* **tax evasion,** fraude fiscale/fraude à l'impôt.

ex, *prep.* **1. ex warehouse** = en magasin; **ex wharf/ex quay** = à quai; **price ex works/ex factory,** prix *m* départ usine/prix sortie (d')usine **2.** (*without*) *Fin:* **ex allotment,** ex-répartition; **stock ex rights,** titre *m* ex-droit; **shares quoted ex dividend,** actions citées ex-dividende/sans intérêts; coupon détaché/ex-coupon; **this stock goes ex coupon on August 1st,** le coupon de cette action se détache le premier août.

excess, *n.* excédent *m* (de poids, de dépenses, etc.); **excess of expenditure over revenue,** excédent des dépenses sur les recettes; **excess charges/excess fare,** supplément *m*/surcharge *f*; **excess luggage,** excédent de bagages; **excess supply,** surproduction *f*; **excess weight,** excédent de poids/surpoids *m*; **in excess,** en surplus; *Ins:* **excess clause,** franchise *f*; **excess profits,** (*i*) surplus *m* des bénéfices (*ii*) bénéfices exceptionnels/extraordinaires; *Fin:* **excess profits tax,** impôt *m* sur les bénéfices exceptionnels.

exchange¹, *n.* **1.** échange *m* (de marchandises); **exchange and barter,** troc *m*; (**car, etc. taken in) part exchange,** reprise *f* **2.** *Fin:* (*a*) change *m*; devises *fpl*; **dollar exchange,** change du dollar/en dollar(s); **(foreign) exchange broker/dealer,** agent *m* de change/cambiste *m*; **exchange control,** contrôle *m* des changes; **exchange list,** la cote des changes; **exchange market,** marché *m* des changes; **exchange premium/premium on exchange,** agio *m*/prix *m* du change; **exchange value,** valeur *f* d'échange; **fixed/direct exchange,** le certain; **foreign exchange,** devises (étrangères)/change étranger; **foreign exchange transaction,** opération *f* de change; **rate of exchange/exchange rate,** cours *m*/taux *m* du change; **at the current rate of exchange,** au cours du jour; au taux de change courant/en vigueur; (*at the top of foreign bill*) **exchange for £ . . .,** bon pour . . . (*b*) **bill of exchange,** effet *m*/traite *f*/lettre *f* de change; **short exchange,** papier court; **first of exchange,** première *f* de change; primata *m* de change; **second of exchange,** seconde *f* de change; copie *f* de change **3.** bourse *f* (des valeurs); **Commodities Exchange/**(*in London*) **the Royal Exchange,** Bourse de commerce; **the Stock Exchange,** la Bourse; **Corn Exchange,** Bourse des céréales; halle *f* aux blés; **employment exchange,** l'agence nationale pour l'emploi (ANPE) **4. telephone exchange,** central *m* téléphonique.

exchange², *v.tr.* (*a*) échanger (des marchandises); **to exchange a dress for one of a bigger size,** échanger une robe contre une de la taille au-dessus (*b*) **to exchange contracts,** signer les contrats de vente et d'achat d'une propriété (*c*) **to exchange francs for pounds,** changer des francs en livres.

exchangeable, *a.* **1.** échangeable (**for,** contre); **exchangeable value,** valeur *f* d'échange.

exchanger, *n.* échangeur, -euse; *Jur:* échangiste *m*.

exchanging, *n.* échange *m* (de marchandises); troc *m* (de denrées).

exchequer, *n.* (*in the UK*) **the Exchequer,** (*i*) la trésorerie; le fisc (*ii*) le Trésor public (*iii*) = le Ministère des Finances; **the Chancellor of the Exchequer** = le Ministre des Finances; **exchequer bill,** bon *m* du Trésor.

excisable, *a.* imposable; (*of goods*) soumis aux droits de régie.

excise[1], *n.* **1.** droit *m*; contributions indirectes **2.** service *m* des contributions indirectes; la régie; **Customs and Excise,** la Régie; **Excise officer,** (*i*) receveur *m* des contributions indirectes (*ii*) employé *m* de la régie; **excise duties,** droits de régie; **excise tax,** impôt indirect; *Cust:* **excise bond,** acquit-à-caution *m*.

excise[2], *v.tr.* imposer (une denrée etc.)/frapper (qch.) d'un droit de régie; soumettre (qn) à un droit de régie.

exciseman, *n.m.* employé de la régie.

exclusive, 1. *a.* exclusif; **exclusive rights,** droits exclusifs (de vendre)/exclusivité *f* **2.** *prep.* **exclusive of wrappings,** emballage non compris; **exclusive of taxes,** hors taxe (HT).

exclusivity, *n.* exclusivité *f*.

executive, *n.* directeur, -trice; cadre *m*; chef *m* de service; **chief executive,** directeur général; **executive officer,** cadre supérieur; *NAm:* **Chief executive officer (CEO)** = président-directeur général (P-DG); **account executive,** chargé *m*/

responsable *m* de budget; **sales executive,** directeur/cadre commercial; **junior executive,** jeune cadre; **senior executive,** cadre supérieur.

exempt[1], *a.* exempt/dispensé/exempté (**from,** de); **exempt from taxation,** exempt d'impôts.

exempt[2], *v.tr.* **to exempt s.o. (from sth.),** exempter/exonérer/dégrever qn (d'un impôt, etc.).

exemption, *n.* exemption *f*/exonération *f*/ dégrèvement *m* (d'impôt); **exemption clause,** clause *f* d'exonération.

exercise[1], *n.* (*a*) exercice *m* (de ses fonctions, etc.) (*b*) *StExch:* **exercise of an option,** levée *f* d'une prime.

exercise[2], *v.tr.* (*a*) exercer (ses fonctions, etc.) (*b*) *Fin:* **to exercise an option,** lever une prime/une option/l'option.

ex gratia, *a.* **ex gratia payment,** paiement *m* à titre de faveur.

exhibit[1], *n.* objet *m*/marchandise *f* exposé(e).

exhibit[2], *v.tr.* **1. to exhibit large profits,** faire ressortir de gros bénéfices **2. to exhibit goods in shop windows,** mettre/ exposer des marchandises à l'étalage/en vitrine.

exhibition, *n.* **1.** exposition *f*/étalage *m* (de marchandises, etc.) **2.** (*a*) exposition; **Ideal Home Exhibition** = Salon *m* des Arts ménagers (*b*) **exhibition room/hall,** salon d'exposition; **exhibition stand,** stand *m* (d'exposition).

exhibitor, *n.* (*at exhibition*) exposant(e).

expansion, *n.* **1. currency expansion,** expansion *f* monétaire **2.** (*a*) expansion (d'un commerce, etc.) (*b*) *PolEc:* relance *f* (économique).

expenditure, *n.* **1.** (*spending*) dépense *f* (d'argent, etc.) **2.** (*amount spent*) dépense(s)/frais *mpl*; **it entails heavy expenditure,** cela entraîne une forte dépense/de fortes dépenses; **capital ex-**

penditure, immobilisations *fpl*; **current expenditure,** frais d'exploitation.

expense, *n.* **1.** dépense *f*/frais *mpl*; **book published at author's expense,** livre publié à compte d'auteur; **at great expense,** à grands frais; **regardless of expense,** sans regarder à la dépense; **it is not worth the expense,** c'est trop cher pour ce que c'est **2.** (*a*) **expense account,** note de frais professionnels (*b*) frais *mpl*; **business expenses,** frais généraux; **incidental expenses,** faux frais; **legal expenses,** frais d'avocat/de notaire; **preliminary expenses (of a company),** frais d'établissement (d'une société); **petty expenses,** menues dépenses; **running expenses,** (*i*) (*of car*) frais d'entretien (d'une voiture) (*ii*) (*of business*) frais d'exploitation; **travelling expenses,** frais de représentation/de déplacement; **to cut down on expenses,** réduire les frais/les dépenses; **all expenses paid,** tous frais payés/remboursés; **no expenses,** exempt de frais; (*on bill*) (retour) sans frais/sans protêt.

expensive, *a.* coûteux/cher; **to be expensive,** coûter cher.

expert, *n.* expert *m*/spécialiste *mf*; **the experts,** les gens *m* du métier/les spécialistes; **he is an expert in this field,** il est expert en la matière/il s'y connaît; **expert's report,** expertise *f*.

expertise, *n.* évaluation *f*/expertise *f*.

expiration, *n.* échéance *f* (d'un marché à prime); fin *f* (d'un terme); **expiration of a lease,** expiration *f* d'un bail; *Ins:* **expiration of a policy,** expiration déchéance *f* d'une police; **to repay before the expiration of a period,** rembourser par anticipation.

expire, *v.i.* (*of term, etc.*) expirer/échoir/prendre fin/venir à échéance/à expiration; **expired bill,** effet périmé; *Ins:* **expired policy,** police échue; **his passport has expired,** son passeport est expiré/périmé.

expiry, *n.* expiration *f*/fin *f*/échéance *f*/

terminaison *f* (d'un terme); terme *m* (d'une période); **expiry date,** date à laquelle qch. vient à expiration/date d'échéance.

export[1], *n.* **1.** marchandise exportée; *pl.* **exports,** (*i*) articles *m* d'exportation (*ii*) exportations *f* (d'un pays); **invisible exports,** exportations invisibles; **visible exports,** exportations visibles; **to increase exports to Britain,** augmenter les exportations vers la Grande-Bretagne **2.** exportation/sortie *f*; **export agent,** commissionnaire exportateur; **export trade,** commerce *m* d'exportation; **export duty,** droit(s) *m*(*pl*) de sortie; *EEC:* **export restitution/refund,** restitution *f* à l'exportation; **prohibition of exports,** prohibitions *fpl* de sortie.

export[2], *v.tr.* exporter (des marchandises) (**from,** de).

exportation, *n.* exportation *f*/sortie *f* (de marchandises).

exporter, *n.* exportateur, -trice.

exporting, *a.* (marchand, pays, etc.) exportateur.

express, *a.* **express,** exprès (*inv*); **express letter,** lettre *f* exprès; **express delivery,** livraison *f* par exprès.

extend, *v.tr.* **1. to extend credit to s.o.,** accorder des facilités de crédit à qn **2.** prolonger (un délai); proroger (l'échéance d'un billet); *Bank:* **to extend the validity of a credit until March,** proroger jusqu'en mars l'échéance d'un accréditif.

extension, *n.* **1.** *Book-k:* transport *m*/report *m* (d'une balance) **2.** (*growing*) extension *f*/accroissement *m* (des affaires, etc.) **3.** prolongation *f* (d'échéance, etc.); **to get an extension of time,** obtenir un délai/une prorogation de délai; **arrangement for an extension of time,** atermoiement *m*; *Bank:* **extension of credit,** prolongation d'un accréditif **4.** *Tp:* **extension 136,** poste *m* 136.

external, *a.* (*of trade, etc.*) étranger/

extérieur; **external account** = compte *m* d'étranger/*FrC:* compte de non-résident.

extra, 1. *a.* en sus/en plus; supplémentaire; **extra charge,** prix *m* en sus; supplément *m*; **to charge extra,** percevoir un supplément; facturer en sus; *Ins:* **extra premium,** surprime *f* **2.** *adv.* **service extra,** service non compris

3. *n.pl.* **extras,** frais *m*/dépenses *f* supplémentaires.

extraordinary, *a.* **to call an extraordinary (general) meeting (EGM) of the shareholders,** convoquer d'urgence les sociétaires/convoquer une assemblée générale extraordinaire; *Book-k:* **extraordinary items,** profits exceptionnels, pertes exceptionnelles.

F

face, *n.* **1. face value,** valeur nominale; valeur faciale (d'un timbre) **2.** recto *m* (d'un document, etc.).

facility, *n.* **1.** facilité *f*; **facilities for payment,** facilités de paiement; **overdraft facilities,** facilités de caisse **2.** *usu. pl.* installations *fpl*; **storage facilities,** entrepôt *m*/magasin *m*; **transport facilities,** moyens *m* de transport; *Nau:* **harbour facilities,** installations portuaires; *Trans:* **loading and unloading facilities,** installations/quais *m* de chargement et de déchargement; **we have no facilities for it,** nous ne sommes pas équipés/outillés pour cela.

facsimile, *n.* fac-similé *m*; **copy in facsimile,** copie *f* fac-similaire.

factor, *n.* **1.** (*pers.*) (*a*) agent *m* (dépositaire); courtier *m* de marchandises (*b*) factor *m*/société *f* d'affacturage **2.** facteur *m*/indice *m*/coefficient *m*; **cost factor,** facteur coût.

factorage, *n.* (*a*) courtage *m*/commission *f* (*b*) commission d'affacturage.

factoring, *n.* affacturage *m*; **factoring charges,** commission *f* d'affacturage.

factory, *n.* usine *f*/fabrique *f*; **biscuit factory,** biscuiterie *f*; **car factory,** usine d'automobiles; **shoe factory,** fabrique de chaussures; **factory unit,** unité *f* de fabrication; **factory-installed component,** pièce *f* d'origine; **factory hand/factory worker,** ouvrier, -ière d'usine; **factory inspector,** inspecteur *m* du travail; **factory inspection,** inspection *f* du travail; **factory overheads,** frais généraux de fabrication; **factory price,** prix *m* (sortie) usine.

failed, *a.* **failed firm,** maison *f* en faillite.

failing[1], *n.* faillite *f*.

failing[2], *prep.* à défaut de; **failing payment within thirty days,** à défaut de paiement dans les trente jours; **failing your advice to the contrary,** sauf avis contraire de votre part.

failure, *n.* **1. failure to pay a bill,** défaut *m* de paiement d'un effet **2.** (*a*) insuccès *m*/non-réussite *f*; avortement *m* (d'un projet, etc.); échec *m* (dans une entreprise) (*b*) faillite *f*.

fair[1], *n.* foire *f*/exposition *f*/salon *m*; **book fair,** salon/foire du livre; **world fair,** exposition universelle.

fair[2], *a.* **to have a reputation for fair (and square) dealing,** avoir une réputation de loyauté en affaires; **fair deal,** prix *m* juste; **to charge a fair price,** vendre à un prix modéré/raisonnable; **to make fair profits,** réaliser des bénéfices raisonnables; **fair trade,** libre échange basé sur des conditions de réciprocité; **fair wages,** salaire *m* équitable; **fair wear and tear,** usure normale.

faith, *n.* **good faith,** bonne foi; loyauté *f*; **purchaser in good faith,** acquéreur *m* de bonne foi.

faithfully, *adv. Corr:* (**we remain) yours faithfully,** veuillez agréer nos meilleures salutations/nos salutations distinguées/nos respectueuses salutations; recevez l'expression de nos sentiments distingués/de nos sentiments les meilleurs.

fake[1], *n.* faux *m*; contrefaçon *f*; falsification *f*/imitation *f*.

fake², *v.tr.* contrefaire/truquer/falsifier (des calculs); **faked balance-sheet,** bilan truqué.

fall¹, *n.* baisse *f* (des prix, des actions); **heavy fall,** forte baisse/débâcle *f*; **fall of the currency,** dépréciation *f* de la monnaie; chute *f* des cours; **fall in the minimum lending rate,** baisse/fléchissement *m* du taux officiel de l'escompte; *StExch:* **dealing for a fall,** opération *f* à la baisse; **to buy on a fall,** acheter à la baisse.

fall², *v.i.* (*a*) (*of price*) baisser/subir une baisse; (*of money*) se déprécier; (*of value*) baisser/diminuer/fléchir (*b*) **to fall due,** venir à échéance.

fall back, *v.i.* (*a*) *StExch: Fin:* se replier; **shares fell back a point,** les actions se sont repliées d'un point (*b*) **to fall back on one's capital,** avoir recours à/recourir à son capital.

falling¹, *a.* **falling market,** marché orienté à la baisse/avec tendance à la baisse/en baisse; **to sell on a rising market and buy on a falling market,** vendre en hausse et acheter en baisse; **the falling pound,** la livre qui se dévalorise/qui se déprécie.

falling², *n.* (*a*) abaissement *m*/baisse *f* (de prix); fléchissement *m*/baisse (de la valeur de qch.) (*b*) *StExch: Fin:* **falling back,** repli *m* (*c*) **falling off,** diminution *f*/décroissement *m* (de chiffres, de taux, etc.); dépérissement *m* (d'une industrie); ralentissement *m* (de commandes, des affaires).

fall off, *v.i.* (*of profits*) diminuer; **the takings are falling off,** les recettes *f* diminuent.

false, *a.* 1. (*incorrect*) faux; **false weight,** faux poids 2. **false balance-sheet,** faux bilan 3. (*sham*) (*of document, etc.*) forgé; (*of coin, etc.*) faux/contrefait.

falsification, *n.* falsification *f* (des comptes, etc.).

falsify, *v.tr.* falsifier (un document); fausser (un bilan).

fancy, *a.* (*a*) **fancy goods,** nouveautés *f*/

objets *m* de fantaisie; *NAm:* **fancy chocolates,** chocolats *m* de choix/surchoix (*b*) **fancy price,** prix trop élevé/fantaisiste.

fare, *n.* prix *m* du billet/du voyage/de la place; (*in taxi*) prix de la course; **full fare/adult fare,** (billet) plein tarif/place entière; *Av:* **full fare,** (classe) plein service; **half fare (ticket),** (billet/place) demi-tarif *m*/demi-place *f*; **single fare,** prix du billet simple/d'un aller (simple); **return fare**/*NAm:* **round-trip fare,** prix d'un (billet) aller (et) retour.

farm, *n.* ferme *f*/exploitation *f* agricole; **dairy farm,** ferme laitière; **fish farm,** établissement *m* piscicole; **poultry farm,** exploitation avicole/élevage de volailles; **sheep farm,** élevage *m* de moutons; **farm labourer,** ouvrier *m* agricole.

farmer, *n.* agriculteur *m*/cultivateur, -trice/exploitant(e) agricole.

farming, *n.* exploitation *f* agricole; culture *f*/agriculture *f*; **mixed farming,** polyculture *f*; **single-crop farming,** monoculture *f*; **fish farming,** pisciculture *f*/élevage *m* de poissons; **poultry farming,** aviculture *f*/élevage *m* de volailles; **sheep farming,** élevage de moutons; **stock farming,** élevage de bestiaux; **farming lease,** bail *m* à ferme.

farm out, *v.tr.* **to farm out work,** donner un travail à un sous-traitant/donner un travail en sous-traitance.

favourable, *a.* (*of terms, etc.*) bon/avantageux; **on favourable terms,** à bon compte.

feasibility, *n.* **feasibility report,** rapport *m* de faisabilité; **feasibility study,** étude *f* préalable/étude de faisabilité.

federation, *n.* fédération *f*; **employers' federation,** syndicat patronal.

fee, *n.* (*a*) honoraires *mpl* (d'un médecin consultant, d'un avocat, etc.); jeton *m* de présence (d'un administrateur); prestation *f* (de services); redevance *f*; **finders'**

fee, commission *f*; prestation; **to draw one's fees,** toucher ses honoraires, etc. (*b*) droit *m*; **admission fee,** (droit d')entrée *f*; **patent fee,** taxe *f* de droits de brevet; **registration fee,** droit d'inscription; **subscription fee,** prix *m* de l'abonnement (à un journal, etc.); cotisation *f* (à une organisation); **for a small fee,** moyennant une légère redevance; **to charge a fee,** demander (une prestation de service, des honoraires, etc.)

fetch, *v.tr.* (*i*) rapporter (*ii*) atteindre (un certain prix); **it fetched a high price,** cela s'est vendu cher; **it won't fetch much,** cela ne rapportera pas beaucoup; **the table will fetch about £200,** la table rapportera dans les £200.

fiat, *n.* *Fin: NAm:* **fiat money,** monnaie fiduciaire/fictive; papier-monnaie *m* inconvertible.

fictitious, *a.* fictif; **fictitious assets,** actif fictif; *Fin:* **fictitious bill,** traite *f* en l'air.

fiduciary, *a.* *Jur: Fin:* (prêt, monnaie, etc.) fiduciaire.

field, *n.* (*a*) marché *m* (pour un produit) (*b*) **field work,** démarchage *m* auprès de la clientèle (*c*) **field of activity,** sphère *f*/secteur *m* d'activité.

fifty-fifty, *a.* **a fifty-fifty venture,** un accord d'entreprise en coparticipation à 50%.

figure, *n.* (*a*) chiffre *m*; **in round figures,** en chiffres ronds; **to work out the figures,** faire les calculs; **to find a mistake in the figures,** trouver une erreur de calcul; **sales figures,** chiffre d'affaires/chiffres de vente; **his income runs into five figures,** il a un revenu de plus de dix mille livres (par an); **we cannot allow you credit beyond this figure,** nous ne pouvons pas vous accorder un crédit plus important/un crédit au-delà de ce montant (*b*) *pl.* **figures,** données *f* numériques/détails chiffrés (d'un projet, etc.); statistiques *f*; **the figures for next year look good,** les

statistiques pour l'année prochaine semblent favorables.

figuring, *n.* chiffrage *m* (des dépenses, etc.).

file[1], *n.* **1.** classeur *m*; **card-index file,** fichier *m* **2.** *pl.* **files,** archives *f*; dossier *m*; **we have placed your report in/on the file,** nous avons ajouté votre rapport au dossier; **file copy,** exemplaire *m*/pièce *f* d'archives.

file[2], *v.tr.* **1.** classer (des fiches, des documents, etc.) **2. to file one's petition (in bankruptcy),** présenter une requête de mise en faillite/déposer son bilan; **to file an application for a patent,** déposer une demande de brevet.

filing, *n.* classement *m* (de documents, de fiches, etc.); rangement *m*; **filing cabinet,** fichier *m*/(meuble-) classeur *m*; **filing tray/filing basket,** corbeille *f* pour correspondance/pour documents à classer; **filing drawer,** tiroir *m* classeur; **filing clerk,** employé(e) au classement; **filing system,** (méthode *f* de) classement.

fill, *v.tr.* **1. to fill a post/a vacancy,** suppléer/pourvoir à une vacance; nommer qn à un poste **2. to fill an order,** exécuter une commande.

fill in, *v.tr.* remplir (un formulaire, une formule, un bordereau); **to fill in the date,** insérer la date.

fill out, *v.tr.* *NAm:* remplir (un formulaire, une formule, un bordereau).

fill up, *v.tr.* remplir (un formulaire, une formule, un bordereau).

final, *a.* final/dernier; **final date (for payment),** délai *m* de rigueur; **final demand (for payment),** dernier rappel; **final instalment,** dernier versement/versement libératoire; **final product,** produit fini.

finance[1], *n.* finance *f*; **public finance,** finances publiques; **high finance,** la haute finance; **the world of finance,** le monde de la finance; **questions of finance,** la finance/les questions financières; **finance company/finance house,** société *f* de crédit/de prêt; **finance development corporation,** fonds *m* de développement économique.

finance², *v.tr.* financer/commanditer (qn, une entreprise, etc.); supporter tous les frais d'(une entreprise); **we have someone to finance the business,** nous avons un bailleur de fonds; **to finance the cost of the undertaking,** fournir les fonds nécessaires à l'entreprise.

financial, *a.* financier; **financial assistance,** appui financier; **financial adviser/consultant** = conseil fiscal; **financial news,** informations financières; **financial position,** situation financière; **financial resources,** ressources *f*/finances *f*; **financial statement,** situation *f* de trésorerie/état financier; bilan *m*; **the financial world,** le monde de la finance; **financial year,** exercice *m* (comptable); année *f* budgétaire.

financially, *adv.* financièrement; **financially sound,** solvable/solide au point de vue financier.

financier, *n.* **1.** financier *m*/homme *m* de finance **2.** bailleur *m* de fonds.

financing, *n.* financement *m* (d'une entreprise, etc.); **compensatory official financing,** financement compensatoire officiel.

find, *v.tr.* (*a*) **to find the money for an undertaking,** procurer les capitaux/fournir l'argent pour une entreprise (*b*) **I pay her £20 all found,** je lui donne £20 tout compris.

findings, *n.* **clear report of findings,** certificat *m* de conformité.

fine¹, *n.* amende *f*; **to have to pay a fine of £300,** avoir une amende de £300 à payer.

fine², *v.tr.* **to fine s.o.,** condamner qn à une amende.

fine³, *a.* **fine bills,** beau papier; **fine trade paper,** papier de haut commerce/de premier ordre.

fine⁴, *adv.* **prices are cut very fine,** les prix *m* sont au plus bas; **profits cut very fine,** profits réduits à presque rien.

fire, *v.tr.* **to fire s.o.,** mettre qn à la porte/licencier qn/renvoyer qn.

firm¹, *n.* maison *f* de commerce/société (commerciale); société en nom collectif; entreprise *f*/firme *f*; **name/style of a firm,** raison sociale; **a large firm,** une grosse entreprise.

firm², *a.* (*of market, offer, sale*) ferme; (*of contango rates*) tendu; **firm stock,** valeur ferme/soutenue; **these shares remain firm at . . .,** ces actions se maintiennent à . . .; **article in firm demand,** article constamment demandé.

firmness, *n.* **the firmness of the pound,** la bonne tenue de la livre.

first, *n.* (*a*) *Fin:* **first of exchange,** première *f*/primata *m* de change (*b*) *pl.* **firsts,** articles *m* de première qualité/produits *m* surchoix (*c*) **first-line manager,** agent *m* de maîtrise (*d*) **first in first out/ FIFO** = premier entré premier sorti/ FIFO.

fiscal, *a.* fiscal; **fiscal period/fiscal year,** exercice *m* (financier); année *f* budgétaire.

fitting, *n.* (*a*) **made in three fittings,** fabriqué en trois tailles; (*of shoes*) en trois largeurs (*b*) **fitting out,** aménagement *m* (d'un magasin, etc.).

fix, *v.tr.* fixer/établir (une indemnité, un prix, le taux de l'intérêt, etc.); **to fix the budget,** déterminer le budget; **to fix a meeting for three o'clock,** fixer une séance pour trois heures; **the date is not yet fixed,** la date n'est pas encore fixée/déterminée/arrêtée; **on the date fixed,** à la date prescrite.

fixed, *a.* **1. fixed charges,** frais *m* fixes; **fixed cost,** coût *m* fixe/constant; **fixed price,** prix *m* fixe/forfaitaire; prix fait/coté; **fixed in advance,** forfaitaire/à forfait; **fixed deposit,** dépôt *m* à terme (fixe)/à échéance fixe; **fixed income,** revenu *m* fixe; **fixed salary,** appointements *m* fixes/salaire *m* fixe/un fixe; **fixed-interest security,** valeur *f* à intérêt fixe **2. fixed capital/assets,** capital fixe/capital immobilisé/immobilisations *fpl*/valeurs immobilisées.

fixing, *n.* (*a*) fixation *f*/établissement *m*/détermination *f* (des prix, des droits, etc.) (*b*) **price fixing,** contrôle illégal des prix (par un cartel, etc.).

fixture, *n.* **fixtures and fittings (f&f),** reprise *f.*

flat, *a.* (*a*) **flat market,** marché calme/languissant (*b*) **flat rate,** taux *m* fixe/tarif *m* fixe/forfait *m*/tarif forfaitaire; **flat rate of pay,** taux uniforme de salaires; **flat-rate subscription,** abonnement *m* à forfait; *NAm:* **flat quotation,** cotation *f* sans intérêts.

fleet, *n.* **fleet of cars,** parc *m* automobile; flotte *f* de véhicules.

flexibility, *n.* **price flexibility,** flexibilité *f* des prix.

flexible, *a.* **flexible budget,** budget *m* adaptable/flexible; **flexible prices,** prix *m* flexibles; **flexible (working) hours,** horaire *m* flexible/souple/variable.

flexi(-)time, *n.,* **flex-time,** *n.* horaire *m* souple/flexible/variable.

flight, *n.* (*a*) (*of aircraft*) vol *m* (*b*) **the flight of capital,** l'exode *m*/la fuite des capitaux (vers l'étranger).

float[1], *n.* caisse *f*/monnaie *f.*

float[2], *v.tr.* **1.** créer/fonder/lancer (une compagnie, etc.); **to float a loan,** émettre/lancer un emprunt **2. to float the pound,** laisser flotter la livre (sterling).

floatation, *n.* lancement *m* (d'un emprunt, etc.); émission *f* d'actions.

floater, *n.* **1.** (*pers.*) lanceur *m* (d'une compagnie, etc.) **2.** (*a*) *StExch: F:* titre *m* de premier rang (*b*) *Ins:* police flottante (*c*) (*i*) prêt *m* (*ii*) argent emprunté.

floating[1], *n.* **the floating of the pound,** le flottement de la livre (sterling).

floating[2], *a.* **1. floating cargo,** cargaison *f* sur mer **2. floating capital/assets,** capital circulant / flottant / mobile / disponible; fonds *mpl* de roulement/capitaux roulants; **floating debt,** dette flottante; **floating exchange rate,** taux de change flottant; **floating pound,** la livre (sterling) qui flotte/flottante; *Ins:* **floating policy,** police flottante.

floor, *n.* **1. the factory floor,** l'atelier *m* **2.** *NAm:* (*in shop*) **floor manager,** chef *m* de rayon.

floorwalker, *n.* (*in a store*) inspecteur, -trice; surveillant(e); chef *m* de rayon; (*in a bank*) surveillant(e).

flotation, *n.* = **floatation.**

flotsam, *n.* épave(s) flottante(s); **flotsam and jetsam,** choses *fpl* de flot et de mer.

flourish, *v.i.* (*of business, etc.*) être florissant/prospérer; **trade will flourish,** le commerce prendra de l'extension/deviendra florissant.

flourishing, *a.* **flourishing trade,** commerce *m* prospère.

flow[1], *n.* (*a*) **flow of capital,** mouvement *m* de capital (*b*) **cash flow,** cashflow *m*; produit *m* disponible; **discounted cash flow (DCF),** cashflow actualisé (méthode DCF); **they have cash flow problems,** ils ont des problèmes de trésorerie (*c*) **flow chart,** graphique *m* d'évolution.

flow[2], *v.i.* (*of money*) circuler.

flow in, *v.i.* (*of money*) affluer.

flow-through, *a. NAm:* (*of tax*) **flow-through method of accounting,** méthode *f* de l'impôt exigible.

fluctuate, *v.i.* (*of markets, values*) fluctuer/osciller; **prices fluctuate between £2000 and £2500,** les prix flottent/varient entre £2000 et £2500.

fluctuating, *a.* (*of prices, etc.*) oscillant/ fluctuant/variable.

fluctuation, *n.* **fluctuation of the franc,** fluctuation *f*/variation *f* du (cours du) franc.

fold (up), *v.i.* F: (*of business, etc.*) cesser les affaires/fermer boutique.

folder, *n.* **1.** dépliant *m*/prospectus *m* **2.** (*for papers, etc.*) chemise *f*/carton *m*/ dossier *m*.

folio[1], *n. Book-k:* **posting folio,** rencontre *f*.

folio[2], *v.tr. Book-k:* paginer (un registre, etc.) à livre ouvert.

following, *a. StExch:* **following settlement/following account,** liquidation suivante.

follow up, *v.tr.* faire suivre (une lettre) d'une seconde lettre.

follow-up, *n.* relance *f* (du client, de la publicité, etc.); **follow-up work,** travail *m* complémentaire; **follow-up letter,** (lettre de) rappel *m*.

food, *n.* (*a*) aliments *mpl*; **food counter/**(*in large store*) **food hall/food store/food department,** rayon *m* d'alimentation; **food packaging,** emballage *m* des produits alimentaires; **food products,** produits *m* alimentaires/comestibles *m*/denrées *f*; **food and drink trade,** la restauration; **the food industry,** l'industrie *f* alimentaire; **food manufacturer,** fabricant *m* de produits comestibles; **food value,** valeur nutritive (*b*) aliment; **canned/tinned foods,** conserves *f* (alimentaires)/aliments en conserve/aliments en boîtes; **health foods,** produits (d'alimentation) naturels.

foodstuffs, *n.pl.* produits *m* alimentaires/ produits d'alimentation/denrées *f* (alimentaires)/comestibles *m*; **essential foodstuffs,** denrées de première nécessité.

foolscap, *n.* papier *m* ministre; (papier) tellière (*m*).

foot[1], *n. Meas:* pied (anglais) *m* (= 0.3048 m).

foot[2], *v.tr.* **1. to foot the bill,** payer la note/les dépenses **2.** *NAm:* **to foot (up) an account,** additionner un compte.

force, *n.* (*a*) **to be in force,** être en vigueur; **to come into force,** entrer en vigueur; **rates in force,** tarifs *m* en vigueur (*b*) **sales force,** équipe *f* de vente.

forced, *a.* **forced sale,** vente forcée; *Fin:* **forced currency,** cours forcé.

force down, *v.tr.* **to force down prices,** faire baisser les prix.

force up, *v.tr.* **to force up prices,** faire hausser/faire monter les prix.

forecast[1], *n.* **sales forecast,** prévision *f* des ventes; **forecast operating budget,** budget *m* d'exploitation prévisionnel; **forecast plan,** plan prévisionnel.

forecast[2], *v.tr.* prévoir/faire des prévisions; **he forecasts sales of £1m,** il prévoit un chiffre de vente de £1 m.

foreclose, *v.tr. Jur:* **to foreclose the mortgagor (from the equity of redemption)/to foreclose the mortgage,** saisir/poursuivre la vente de l'immeuble hypothéqué.

foreclosure, *n. Jur:* forclusion *f*; saisie *f* (d'une hypothèque).

foreign, *a.* étranger; **foreign currency,** devises *f* étrangères; **foreign exchange,** devises (étrangères)/change (étranger); **foreign exchange transfer,** transfert *m* de devises; **foreign exchange broker,** courtier *m* en devises; **foreign goods,** marchandises qui viennent de l'étranger; **foreign money order,** mandat international; **Foreign Office,** Ministère *m* des Affaires étrangères/*FrC:* Ministère des Affaires extérieures; **foreign trade,** commerce extérieur.

foreman, *n.m.* contremaître.

forfeit[1], *n.* (*a*) (*for non-performance of contract*) dédit *m*; (*for a contract*), clause *f* de dédit (*b*) *StExch:* **to relinquish the forfeit,** abandonner la prime.

forfeit[2], *v.tr.* perdre (qch.) par confiscation; *Jur:* **to forfeit a patent,** déchoir d'un brevet.

forfeiting, *n.* affacturage *m* à forfait.

forfeiture, *n.* **1.** *Jur: Fin:* déchéance *f*/ forfaiture *f* (d'un droit, etc.); **action for forfeiture of patent,** action *f* en déchéance de brevet **2.** bien(s) confisqué(s).

forge, *v.tr.* contrefaire (une signature, des billets de banque).

forged, *a.* (document, billet de banque, etc.) faux/contrefait/falsifié; **forged document,** faux *m.*

forgery, *n.* **1.** contrefaçon *f* (d'une signature, de billets de banque); falsification *f* (de documents) **2.** faux *m*; **the signature was a forgery,** la signature était contrefaite.

form¹, *n.* **1. receipt in due form,** quittance régulière/en bonne forme **2. (printed) form,** formule *f*/formulaire *m*/bulletin *m*; **printed form of receipt,** formule de quittance; **form for bill of exchange,** formule d'effet de commerce; **form 20,** formulaire numéro 20; **form of tender,** modèle *m* de soumission; **inquiry form,** bulletin de demande de renseignements; **application form,** (*i*) formulaire de demande (*ii*) (*for shares*) bulletin de souscription; **blank form,** formulaire en blanc; **order form,** bulletin de commande; *Bank:* **cheque form,** (*i*) formule (*ii*) volant *m* (de chèque) (*iii*) chèque *m*; **listing forms,** bordereaux *m* en blanc; **form of return,** feuille *f* de déclaration (de revenu, etc.).

form², *v.tr.* former/organiser/constituer (une société, etc.).

formation, forming, *n.* constitution *f* (d'une société, etc.); **capital formation,** formation *f* de capital.

forward¹, *a.* *StExch:* **forward deals/sales,** opérations *f*/ventes *f* à terme; **forward exchange contract,** opération *f* de change à terme; **forward market,** marché *m*

à terme; *Bank:* **forward rates,** taux *m* pour les opérations à terme.

forward², *adv.* **1.** (*a*) **to date forward a cheque,** postdater un chèque; **a forward dated cheque,** un chèque postdaté; **carriage forward,** (en) port dû; **charges forward,** frais *m* à percevoir à la livraison (*b*) **to buy forward,** acheter à terme; **to sell forward,** vendre à terme **2.** *Book-k:* **to carry the balance forward,** reporter le solde à nouveau; **(carried) forward,** à reporter; report *m.*

forward³, *v.tr.* (*a*) expédier/envoyer/ transiter (des marchandises, etc.); **to forward sth. to s.o.,** faire parvenir qch à qn; **to forward goods to Paris,** diriger des marchandises sur Paris; acheminer des marchandises sur/vers Paris (*b*) transmettre/faire suivre/réexpédier (une lettre); **to be forwarded/please forward,** (prière de) faire suivre/faire suivre s.v.p.

forwarder, *n.* (*a*) expéditeur, -trice (d'un colis, etc.)/envoyeur, -euse (d'un paquet, etc.) (*b*) = **forwarding agent.**

forwarding, *n.* (*a*) expédition *f*/envoi *m*; acheminement *m* (d'un colis); **forwarding agent,** entrepreneur *m* de transports/(agent) expéditeur (*m*)/transporteur *m*; transitaire *m*; **forwarding agency,** entreprise *f* de transports; société *f*/compagnie *f*/maison *f* d'expédition; maison de transit, **forwarding time,** durée *f* d'acheminement; **international forwarding,** transport international; **forwarding instructions,** indications *f* concernant l'expédition (*b*) réexpédition *f* (d'une lettre); **forwarding address,** adresse *f* de réexpédition/nouvelle adresse.

foul, *a.* **foul bill of lading,** connaissement *m* avec réserves.

founder, *n.* fondateur *m* (d'une maison de commerce/d'une société); **founder's shares,** parts *f* bénéficiaires/de fondateur.

fraction, *n.* (*a*) fraction *f*/nombre *m* fractionnaire; **fractions of a franc are charged as a franc,** l'addition est arrondie au franc supérieur (*b*) *Fin:* fraction/rompu *m* (d'action, d'obligation).

fractional, *a.* fractionnaire; **fractional part,** fraction *f*; **fractional coins,** monnaie *f* divisionnaire/d'appoint; *NAm:* **fractional note,** (billet *m* de banque de) petite coupure.

franc, *n.* franc *m* (français, suisse, belge, etc.); **franc account,** compte (tenu) en francs.

franchise, *n.* **1.** contrat *m* de franchisage **2.** *MIns:* minimum d'avaries au-dessous duquel l'assureur est libéré de toute responsabilité/franchise *f*.

franchisee, *n.* franchisé(e).

franchiser, *n.* **1.** franchisé(e) **2.** franchiseur *m*.

franchising, *n.* franchising *m*/franchisage *m*; **franchising operation,** franchisage.

franchisor, *n.* franchiseur *m*.

frank, *v.tr.* **to frank a letter,** affranchir une lettre.

franking, *a.* **franking machine,** machine *f* à affranchir les lettres.

fraud, *n.* fraude *f*; **to obtain sth. by fraud,** obtenir qch. par fraude/frauduleusement; **frauds relating to goods,** tromperie *f* sur la marchandise.

fraudulent, *a.* frauduleux; **fraudulent balance-sheet,** faux bilan; **fraudulent transaction,** transaction frauduleuse/ entachée de fraude; **fraudulent clause (in a contract),** clause dolosive; **fraudulent bankrupt,** banqueroutier frauduleux.

fraudulently, *adv.* frauduleusement/par fraude; **goods imported fraudulently,** marchandises passées en fraude.

free¹, *a.* **1.** *Fin:* **to set money free,** mobiliser de l'argent/débloquer des fonds; **setting**

free, mobilisation *f* (de l'argent) **2.** franc (**of,** de); **interest free of tax,** intérêts nets d'impôts/exempts d'impôt/en franchise d'impôt; **interest-free,** en franchise d'intérêt; **(interest) free credit,** crédit gratuit; **post free,** en franchise postale; *Cust:* **free of duty/duty free,** exempt de droits d'entrée; en franchise douanière; **to import sth. free of duty/ duty free,** faire entrer qch. en franchise; **free list,** liste *f* d'exemptions **3.** **free sample,** échantillon gratuit; **free of charge,** gratuit(e); **free ticket,** billet gratuit/de faveur; **free trial,** essai gratuit; **we are sending you the machine for free trial,** nous vous envoyons l'appareil gratuitement à l'essai/à titre d'essai; **free demonstration in the home,** démonstration *f* à domicile à titre gracieux; **delivery free,** franc de port; sans frais de transport; **delivered free as far as the French frontier,** livraison franco frontière française; **free on rail,** franco wagon; **free alongside ship (FAS)/free at quay/on wharf,** franco long du bord; franco (à) quai; vente FAS; **free over side,** franco allège; **free on board (FOB),** franco à bord; vente FOB **4.** **free port,** port franc; **free trade,** libre-échange *m*; **free trade area,** zone *f* de libre-échange; **free trade policy,** politique *f* antiprotectionniste/ politique libre-échangiste/ politique de libre-échange; **free trader,** (*i*) libre-échangiste *mf*/antiprotection(n)iste *mf* (*ii*) *NAm:* commerçant indépendant des consortiums.

free², *adv.* franc de port/en port payé/ franco; **free of charge,** gratuitement; **catalogue sent free on request** = demandez notre catalogue gratuit.

free³, *v.tr.* (*a*) mettre (des denrées réglementées) en vente libre (*b*) détaxer (des denrées taxées).

freehold, *n.* **freehold property,** propriété *f* sans réserve; pleine propriété.

freephone, *n.* libre-appel *m*.

freepost, *n*, libre-réponse *f*.

freeze¹, *n*. **1. prices and wages freeze**, blocage *m* des prix et des salaires **2. deep freeze**, congélateur *m*/surgélateur *m*.

freeze², *v.tr*. **1. to freeze credits**, bloquer les crédits; **to freeze wages**, bloquer les salaires **2.** congeler/surgeler (des aliments).

freeze out, *v.tr*. étrangler (une maison de commerce qui vous fait concurrence).

freezer, *n*. freezer *m*/congélateur *m*/surgélateur *m*; **chest freezer**, congélateur bahut; **upright freezer**, congélateur vertical/droit.

freezing, *n*. blocage *m* (des salaires, des crédits, d'une dette, etc.).

freight¹, *n*. **1.** fret *m*; transport maritime et aérien; *NAm:* transport par camion/par trains; **air freight**, transport aérien; **sent by air freight**, envoyé par avion **2.** (*a*) fret/cargaison *f*/chargement *m* (d'un navire); **to take in freight**, prendre du fret; **dead freight**, (*i*) faux fret (*ii*) dédit *m* pour défaut de chargement; **home freight/onward freight**, fret de retour (*b*) marchandises (transportées); *NAm:* **freight train**, train *m* de marchandises; *NAm:* **freight car**, wagon *m* à/de marchandises; *Av:* **freight plane**, avion *m* de fret; **freight depot**, gare *f* de marchandises; **freight elevator**, monte-charge *m inv*; **freight shipping**, messageries *f* maritimes **3.** fret; (frais de) port *m*/transport; **freight by weight**, fret au poids; **to pay the freight**, payer le fret; **freight charges paid**, port payé.

freight², *v.tr*. **1.** affréter (un navire) **2. to freight (out) a ship**, donner un navire à fret **3.** charger (un navire) **4.** (*i*) transporter des marchandises (*ii*) faire transporter/envoyer des marchandises (par bateau, par avion, *also NAm:* par camion, par train).

freightage, *n*. **1.** affrètement *m* **2.** fret *m*/cargaison *f* **3.** *NAm:* frais *mpl* de transport/fret.

freighter, *n*. **1.** affréteur *m* (d'un navire) **2.** consignataire *m* (de marchandises à

transporter) **3.** entrepreneur *m* de transports; exportateur *m* **4.** (*a*) cargo *m*; navire *m* de charge (*b*) *Av:* avion *m* de fret.

freightliner, *n*. train *m* de marchandises en conteneurs.

fringe, *n*. **fringe benefits**, avantages *m* accessoires; suppléments *m* de salaire (en nature); avantages sociaux; **fringe market**, marché marginal.

front, *n*. **1. front man**, (*i*) prête-nom *m* (*ii*) représentant(e) (d'une société); porte-parole *m* (d'une organisation) **2. he demanded the money up front**, il a demandé d'être payé en avance.

frozen, *a*. (*a*) *Fin:* **frozen assets**, fonds *m* non liquides/fonds gelés/fonds bloqués; **frozen credits**, créances gelées/crédits bloqués (*b*) **frozen food(s)**, produits surgelés/congelés.

frustrated, *a*. **frustrated exports**, produits destinés à l'exportation en souffrance.

full¹, *a*. **full fare**, (*i*) (billet) plein tarif/place entière (*ii*) *Av:* (classe) plein service; **full measure**, mesure *f* juste/mesure comble; **full price**, prix fort; **full payment**, remboursement intégral; **full weight**, poids *m* juste; *Ins:* **full cover**, garantie totale; *Fin:* **full discharge**, quitus *m*.

full², *n*. **money refunded in full**, remboursement complet; vous serez intégralement remboursé de la somme versée; **capital paid in full**, capital entièrement versé; **in full of all demands**, pour fin de compte/pour solde de tout compte; **acceptance in full of the conditions**, acceptation intégrale des conditions.

full-time, **1.** *adv*. **to work full-time**, travailler plein temps **2.** *a*. **full-time employment**, emploi *m* à temps complet/à plein temps; **full-time employee**, employé(e) qui travaille à plein temps.

fully, *adv*. pleinement/entièrement/complètement; **fully paid**, payé inté-

gralement; **until fully paid,** jusqu'à règlement complet/parfait paiement;
capital fully paid (up), capital entièrement versé; **fully paid shares,** actions
entièrement libérées.

functional, *a.* fonctionnel; **functional approach,** démarche *f* pragmatique.

fund[1], *n.* (*a*) fonds *m*; caisse *f*; **International
Monetary Fund (IMF),** Fonds Monétaire
International (FMI); **pension fund/
retirement fund,** caisse de retraites (*b*) *pl.*
funds, fonds; masse *f*; ressources *f*
pécuniaires; **funds of a company,** fonds
social/masse sociale; (*of company*) **to
make a call for funds,** faire un appel de
capital; **funds on which an annuity is
secured,** assiette *f* d'une rente; *Bank:* **no
funds,** défaut *m* de provision/manque *m*
de fonds; pas d'encaisse; **not sufficient
funds,** (chèque) sans provision; **sinking
fund,** fonds d'amortissement (*c*) *pl.*
funds, la Dette publique; les fonds publics; la rente sur l'État; les bons du
Trésor; **fund holder,** rentier, -ière.

fund[2], *v.tr.* *Fin:* **1.** consolider (une dette
publique) **2. to fund money,** placer de
l'argent dans les fonds publics; acheter
des bons du Trésor **3.** pourvoir (une
société, etc.) de fonds/verser des fonds
(dans une société).

funded, *a.* **funded capital,** capitaux investis; **long-term funded capital,** capitaux
consolidés à long terme; **funded debt,**

dette consolidée; **funded property,** biens
mpl en rentes.

funding, *n.* consolidation *f* (d'une dette);
assiette *f* (d'une rente); **funding loan,**
emprunt *m* de consolidation.

further, *a.* **further orders,** commandes
ultérieures/nouvelles commandes; **further to your letter of the 15th,** (comme)
suite à/en réponse à votre lettre du 15
courant; **further to your telephone call,**
(comme) suite à notre conversation
téléphonique; **further to our letter,** nous
référant à notre lettre; **a further £50 on
account,** un nouvel acompte de cinquante
livres; **to ask for a further credit,** demander un crédit supplémentaire; **for further
particulars,** pour (obtenir de) plus amples renseignements.

future, *a.* **your future orders,** vos
nouvelles commandes; **future delivery,**
livraison *f* à terme; **goods for future
delivery,** marchandises *f* livrables
ultérieurement/à terme; *Fin:* **exchange
for future delivery,** opérations *f* de
change à terme; **to sell for future delivery,**
vendre livrable à terme.

futures, *n.pl.* *Fin:* opérations *f*/
transactions *f* à terme; **(quotations for)
futures,** cotations *f*/livraisons *f* à terme;
futures market, marché *m* à terme; **selling of futures/sale for futures,** vente *f* à
forfait/à découvert.

G

gain[1], *n.* **1.** (*profit*) gain *m*/profit *m*/bénéfice *m*; **capital gains tax,** impôt *m* sur les plus-values **2.** (*increase*) accroissement *m*/augmentation *f*.

gain[2], *v.tr. & i.* gagner; bénéficier (de); faire un profit.

gallon, *n. Meas:* gallon *m* (**Imperial gallon** = 4,546 litres; **US gallon** = 3,785 litres); (*of car*) **28 miles to the gallon** = 10 litres au 100 (kilomètres).

gamble[1], *n.* affaire *f* où l'on risque fort de perdre; **pure gamble,** pure spéculation/affaire de chance.

gamble[2], *v.i.* **to gamble on the Stock Exchange,** boursicoter/jouer à la Bourse/spéculer.

gambler, *n.* **gambler on the Stock Exchange,** joueur, -euse/spéculateur, -trice/boursicoteur, -euse.

gambling, *n.* **gambling on the Stock Exchange,** spéculation *f*.

gap, *n.* écart *m*; **gap study,** étude *f* des écarts; **market gap,** créneau *m*; **trade gap,** déficit commercial; découvert *m* de la balance commerciale; **the dollar gap,** la pénurie de dollars.

gas, *n. NAm:* = **petrol.**

gazette, *n.* **London Gazette** = Le Journal officiel/l'Officiel.

gazump, *v.tr.* (*i*) revenir sur une promesse de vente pour accepter une suroffre (*ii*) faire une suroffre (dans l'immobilier); **I have been gazumped,** quelqu'un a fait une suroffre qui a été acceptée et l'affaire est tombée à l'eau.

gazumping, *n.* suroffre *f*; surenchère *f* des prix (dans l'immobilier).

gear, *v.tr.* (*a*) **wages geared to the cost of living,** salaires indexés au coût de la vie; **a company geared up for expansion,** une société tournée/orientée vers l'expansion (*b*) **highly geared company,** société avec ratio d'endettement élevé.

gearing, *n. Fin:* (*i*) effet *m* de levier (*ii*) ratio *m* d'endettement.

general, *a.* (*a*) **general meeting,** assemblée générale; (*on agenda of meeting*) **general business,** questions diverses; **general expenses,** frais généraux; *MIns:* **general average,** avaries communes; **general balance-sheet,** bilan *m* d'ensemble; **general bill of lading,** connaissement collectif; **General Agreement on Tariffs and Trade (GATT),** Accord général sur les tarifs douaniers et le commerce; **general ledger,** grand(-)livre *m*; **general partnership,** société (commerciale) en nom collectif (*b*) **general store(s),** alimentation générale.

generic, *n. NAm: Pharm:* (produit) générique *m*; **branded generic,** générique de fantaisie; **commodity generic,** générique vrai.

genuine, *a.* (*a*) authentique/véritable; **genuine article,** article garantie d'origine (*b*) **genuine purchaser,** acheteur sérieux.

genuineness, *n.* authenticité *f* (d'une marque de fabrique, etc.).

get, *v.tr.* **1.** (*a*) (*i*) se procurer/obtenir (*ii*) acheter; **I got this car cheap,** j'ai eu/j'ai acheté cette voiture (à) bon marché (*b*) recevoir/gagner; **to get £5000 a year,** gagner £5000 par an; **to get 10% interest,** recevoir un intérêt de 10%; **I get only a small profit,** il ne me revient/je n'en retire qu'un léger bénéfice **2.** recevoir (une lettre, etc.); **I got his answer this morning,** j'ai eu/j'ai reçu sa réponse ce matin **3. he got himself appointed chairman,** il s'est fait nommer président **4. he got (himself) into debt,** il s'est endetté **5. I can't get hold of him,** je n'arrive pas à le joindre **6. he gets on well with his colleagues,** il s'entend bien avec ses collègues **7. we must get down to work,** il nous faut nous mettre au travail.

get through, *v.tr.* **to get sth. through the customs,** (faire) passer qch. à la douane.

get up, *v.tr.* apprêter/présenter (un article pour la vente); habiller (des bouteilles).

getup, get-up, *n.* façon *f*/présentation *f* (de marchandises); habillage *m* (de bouteilles); présentation (d'un livre).

giant, *a.* **giant packet,** carton géant.

gift, *n.* (*a*) don *m*; donation *f*; *Jur:* **as a gift,** à titre d'avantage; **deed of gift,** (acte *m* de) donation entre vifs (*b*) cadeau *m*; **gift shop,** magasin *m* de nouveautés; **gift cheque/token,** chèque-cadeau *m*; **gift coupon/gift voucher,** bon-cadeau *m* (*c*) (*on presentation of coupons*) prime *f*.

gilt, *n.* = gilt-edged stock.

gilt-edge(d), *a.* *StExch:* **gilt-edged stock(s)/securities,** fonds *m* d'État; valeurs *f* de haute qualité/de premier choix/*F:* valeurs de père de famille.

giro, *n.* *Bank:* **Giro (bank) system,** giro bancaire; **Giro cheque,** chèque *m* de virement; **bank giro transfer,** virement *m* bancaire.

Girobank, *n.* *Post:* = service *m* de chèques postaux; **Girobank account** = compte courant postal/compte chèque postal (CCP).

give, *v.tr.* **1.** (*a*) donner; **to give a good price**

for sth., donner/payer un bon prix pour qch.; **what did you give for it?** combien l'avez-vous payé? **I'll give you £10 for it,** je vous en donnerai £10; **what will you give me for it?** combien m'en offrez-vous? **to give a week's notice,** donner ses huit jours (de préavis) (*b*) *StExch:* **to give for the call,** acheter la prime à livrer; **to give for the put,** acheter la prime à recevoir **2.** (*at shop*) **I gave him an order for ten new cars,** je lui ai passé une commande de dix voitures neuves **3. investment that gives 10%,** placement *m* qui rapporte 10%.

giveaway, *n.* *F:* **giveaway (price),** prix *m* dérisoire; **it's a giveaway!** c'est donné!

give on, *v.tr.* *StExch:* faire reporter (des titres).

glass, *n.* **1.** (*a*) **the glass industry,** l'industrie *f* du verre/la verrerie (*b*) (*on parcel*) **glass** = (*sur un colis*) fragile.

glut[1], *n.* surabondance *f*/pléthore *f* (d'une denrée, etc.); *Fin:* **glut of money,** pléthore de capitaux.

glut[2], *v.tr.* encombrer/inonder/écraser/surcharger (le marché); créer une pléthore sur (le marché).

glutting, *n.* **glutting of the markets,** encombrement *m*/engorgement *m* des marchés.

godown, *n.* comptoir *m* (colonial) (dans les pays orientaux).

go down, *v.i.* (*of prices, value*) baisser.

going, *a.* **1.** qui marche; **going concern,** affaire *f* qui marche/prospère **2. the going price,** le prix courant/actuel.

gold, *n.* (*a*) or *m*; **gold content,** teneur *f* en or (*b*) *Fin:* **gold currency/gold money,** monnaie *f* d'or; **pièces** *fpl* d'or/en or; **gold specie,** or monnayé; **gold bullion,** or en lingots; **gold coin and bullion,** encaisse *f* or; **gold franc,** franc *m* or; **France's gold reserves,** le stock/la réserve d'or de la France; **the gold standard,** l'étalon-or *m*; **gold ratio,** rapport *m* de l'encaisse en or à la monnaie en circulation; **export/**

outgoing gold point, point *m* de sortie de l'or/gold-point *m* de sortie; **import/incoming gold point,** point d'entrée de l'or/gold-point d'entrée; *StExch:* **gold bond,** obligation *f* or; **gold shares**/*F: s.pl.* **golds,** valeurs *f* aurifères.

goods, *n.pl.* (*a*) *Jur:* biens *m*/effets *m*/biens meubles (*b*) marchandises *f*/denrées *f*/objets *m*/articles *m*; **capital goods,** biens d'équipement; **consumer goods,** biens de consommation; **luxury goods,** articles de luxe; **manufactured goods,** produits fabriqués/manufacturés; **perishable goods,** denrées périssables; *esp. NAm:* **soft goods,** articles de nouveauté; **hard goods,** biens d'équipement; **wet goods,** liquides *m* (*c*) *Rail:* **goods train,** train *m* de marchandises; **goods station/goods depot,** gare *f*/dépôt *m* de marchandises.

goodwill, *n.* goodwill *m*/survaleur *f*/actif incorporel; fonds *m* de commerce.

go-slow, *a. & n.* **go-slow (strike),** grève perlée; **go-slow policy,** politique *f* d'attente.

go up, *v.i.* (*of prices, etc.*) monter/augmenter; **the cost of living is going up,** le coût de la vie augmente; **the bidding went up to £200,** les enchères *f* ont monté jusqu'à £200.

grace, *n.* **days of grace,** (*i*) délai (accordé pour le paiement d'un effet) (*ii*) *Ins:* délai (accordé pour le paiement des primes d'assurance sur la vie); **to give a creditor seven days' grace,** accorder à un créancier sept jours de grâce/de faveur.

grade[1], *n.* (*of employee*) échelon *m*; (*of products*) **high-grade/top-grade/choice-grade,** de qualité supérieure/de (tout) premier choix; surchoix; *F:* (de qualité) extra; **low-grade/below-grade,** de qualité inférieure; *Aut:* **high-grade/premium-grade petrol** = supercarburant *m*/super *m*; **low-grade petrol** = ordinaire *m*.

grade[2], *v.tr.* **1.** classer/trier (des marchandises, etc.) selon leur qualité/calibrer **2.**

graded tax, (*i*) impôt progressif (*ii*) impôt dégressif; **graded advertising rates,** tarif d'annonces dégressif **3. graded hotels,** hôtels classés.

grading, *n.* (*of employee*) échelon *m*.

graduate[1], *n.* diplômé(e); licencié(e); **graduate entry,** échelon *m* d'entrée pour les diplômés; **graduate training scheme,** programme *m* de formation professionnelle pour les diplômés.

graduate[2], *v.tr.* **to graduate a tax according to the taxpayer's income,** établir un impôt proportionnellement au revenu du contribuable; **graduated pension scheme** = régime *m* de retraites complémentaires (obligatoires); **graduated income tax,** impôt progressif; impôt proportionnel au revenu du contribuable; **graduated taxation,** taxes imposées par paliers.

gram, *n. Meas:* gramme *m* (*abbr:* g) (= 0.0353 oz); **250 gram(s)/250g,** 250 grammes/250g.

grand, *a.* **grand total,** total global/général.

grant[1], *n.* aide *f* pécuniaire; subvention *f*/allocation *f*/prime *f*; **grant-aided,** subventionné par l'État.

grant[2], *v.tr.* accorder/allouer (une subvention à qn); **to grant a loan,** consentir un prêt; **to grant an overdraft,** consentir un découvert (**to,** à); *Jur:* **to grant bail,** accorder une liberté (provisoire) à qn sous caution.

gratuity, *n.* pourboire *m*/gratification *f*.

green, *a.* **green franc,** franc vert; **green pound,** livre verte; **green rate,** taux vert.

grid, *n.* **grid structure,** structure *f* en grille; **managerial grid,** grille *f* de gestion.

gross[1], *n.* douze douzaines *f*/grosse *f*; **six gross of pencils,** six grosses de crayons; **great gross,** douze grosses.

gross[2], *a.* (*a*) brut; **gross amount,** montant brut (d'une facture, etc.); **gross cost,** prix de revient brut; **gross margin,** marge brute/profit brut; **gross proceeds,** produit brut (d'une opération commerciale ou financière); **gross profit,** bénéfice brut; **gross loss,** perte brute; **gross national income,** revenu national brut; **gross national product (GNP),** produit national brut (*b*) **gross weight,** poids brut; **gross (register) ton,** tonneau *m* de jauge brute; **gross (register) tonnage,** (tonnage *m* de) jauge brute/tonnage brut (*c*) *MIns:* **gross average,** grosse(s) avarie(s) commune(s).

gross³, *v.tr.* produire un montant brut/donner des recettes brutes; **they grossed £10 million,** cela leur a rapporté brut £10 millions.

group, *n. Ind: etc:* groupe *m*/groupement *m*/société *f*/groupe d'entreprises/groupe industriel; **the Shell Group,** le Groupe Shell.

growth, *n.* accroissement *m*/augmentation *f* (en quantité)/développement *m* (des affaires); expansion *f* (des affaires, d'une maison de commerce); **economic growth,** développement/croissance *f* économique; **growth index,** indice *m* de croissance; **growth industry,** industrie *f* en croissance rapide; **growth share/stock,** valeur *f* de croissance; **growth of productivity,** accroissement *m* de la productivité; **sales growth,** accroissement/augmentation des ventes; **rate of growth,** taux *m* d'expansion/de croissance/d'accroissement.

guarantee¹, *n.* **1.** (*pers.*) garant(e); caution *f*; **to go guarantee for s.o.,** se porter garant de qn/se porter caution pour qn/cautionner qn **2.** garantie *f*; **certificate of guarantee,** bulletin *m* de garantie; **under guarantee,** sous garantie; **I bought it secondhand, without guarantee,** je l'ai acheté d'occasion et sans garantie; **guarantee of a bill of exchange,** aval *m* d'une lettre de change; **guarantee fund,** fonds *m* de garantie; **guarantee company/guarantee society,** société *f* de sécurité; **guarantee commission,** ducroire *m* **3.** (*security*) garantie/cautionnement *m*; **to leave £5 as a guarantee,** verser un cautionnement de £5; **to secure all guarantees,** s'assurer toutes les garanties nécessaires.

guarantee², *v.tr.* **1.** (*a*) garantir/cautionner (qn, qch.)/se porter garantie/se porter caution pour (qn, qch.); **to guarantee a debt,** garantir une dette (*b*) **to guarantee an endorsement,** avaliser la signature (sur une traite); **to guarantee a bill of exchange,** avaliser une lettre de change **2.** garantir (une montre, un appareil)/vendre sous garantie; **watch guaranteed for two years,** montre garantie pour deux ans.

guaranteed, *a.* (*a*) garanti; **guaranteed bonds/stocks,** obligations/valeurs garanties (*b*) (*of bill*) signé pour aval/avalisé.

guarantor, *n.* garant(e)/caution *f*/répondant(e); avaliste *m*/donneur *m* d'aval (d'une lettre de change); **to stand as guarantor for s.o.,** appuyer qn de sa garantie/cautionner qn/se porter garant de qn.

guaranty, *n.* = guarantee¹ **2.** and **3.**

guesstimate, *n. F:* estimation approximative.

guild, *n. Hist:* corporation *f*; **merchant guild,** g(u)ilde *f* de commerçants; **trade guild,** corps *m* de métier.

H

habilitate, *v.tr. NAm:* avancer les fonds pour l'exploitation (d'une usine).

habilitator, *n. NAm:* bailleur *m* de fonds.

haggle, *v.i.* marchander.

half, 1. *n.* moitié *f*; **the first half of the year,** la première moitié de l'année; **reduced by half,** réduit de moitié **2.** *a.* demi; **half day,** demi-journée *f*; **to work half days,** faire des demi-journées; *NAm:* **half a dollar,** (valeur de) cinquante cents; **a half dozen/half a dozen,** une demi-douzaine; **a rebate of half percent,** une ristourne d'un demi pour cent; **at half price,** à moitié prix; **on half profits,** de compte à demi; *StExch:* **half commission,** remise *f*; **half commission, man,** remisier *m*.

half-dollar, *n. NAm:* (pièce de) cinquante cents.

halfpenny, *n.* pièce de ½ penny; **he gave me the change in halfpennies,** il m'a rendu la monnaie en pièces de ½ penny.

half(-)year, *n.* semestre *m*; **first half(-)year,** semestre de janvier/d'hiver; **second half(-)year,** semestre de juillet/d'été.

half-yearly, 1. *a.* semestriel; **half-yearly meeting,** assemblée semestrielle; **to draw up the half-yearly accounts,** dresser le bilan semestriel; **half-yearly dividend/payment,** semestre *m* **2.** *adv.* par semestre/tous les six mois.

hallmark[1], *n.* poinçon *m* (de contrôle, de maître) (sur les objets d'orfèvrerie).

hallmark[2], *v.tr.* poinçonner (l'orfèvrerie).

hammer[1], *n.* marteau *m* (de commis-saire-priseur); **to come under the hammer,** être mis/vendu aux enchères.

hammer[2], *v.tr.* (*a*) *StExch:* (*of stockbroker*) **hammered,** déclaré insolvable/exécuté (*b*) *F:* **to hammer prices,** faire baisser les prix (*c*) **to hammer out a contract,** signer un contrat (après de longues négociations).

hammering, *n.* déclaration d'insolvabilité (d'un courtier, etc.).

hand, *n.* **1.** (*a*) (*of business, etc.*) **to change hands,** changer de propriétaire (*b*) **to have so much money in hand,** avoir tant d'argent disponible; **cash in hand,** encaisse *f*; montant *m* en caisse; **stock in hand,** marchandises *fpl* en magasin; **work in hand,** travail *m* en cours/en chantier (*c*) **work on hand,** travail en cours; travail à faire; **goods left on hand,** marchandises non vendues/laissées pour compte (*d*) **your order is not to hand at present,** l'article que vous avez commandé n'est pas disponible en ce moment **2.** (*pers.*) ouvrier, -ière; manœuvre *m*; **to take on hands,** embaucher de la main-d'œuvre **3.** signature *f*; *Jur:* **to set one's hand to a deed,** apposer sa signature à un acte; **note of hand,** billet *m* à ordre.

handbook, *n.* manuel *m* (de références).

handicraft, *n.* artisanat *m*/travail artisanal.

hand in, *v.tr.* remettre/déposer qch.; **to hand in one's resignation,** démissioner/donner sa démission.

handle, *v.tr.* (*a*) **to handle a lot of money,** manier de grosses sommes d'argent; **we don't handle these goods,** nous ne tenons pas ces articles; **we can handle orders for overseas,** nous prenons des commandes pour l'étranger; **we are in a position to handle any sort of business,** nous sommes à même d'exécuter n'importe quelle opération (*b*) (*on parcels*) **handle with care** = fragile.

handler, *n.* manutentionnaire *mf.*

handling, *n.* (*a*) manutention *f* (de marchandises, etc.); **handling charges,** frais *mpl* de manutention; **industrial handling,** manutention industrielle; **handling capacity,** capacité *f* de traitement (*b*) distribution *f.*

hand(-)made, *a.* fait (à la) main/fabriqué à la main.

hand over, *v.tr.* remettre (qch. à qn); **the letter was handed over to him personally,** on lui a remis la lettre en main(s) propre(s).

handout, *n.* (*a*) prospectus *m*/circulaire *f* publicitaire (*b*) cadeau *m* publicitaire.

handshake, *n.* *F:* **golden handshake,** indemnité *f* de départ/cadeau *m* d'adieu; **to give s.o. a golden handshake,** remercier qn de ses services en le dédommageant grassement.

handwork, *n.* travail *m* à la main; travail manuel.

handwriting, *n.* **send your application in your own handwriting,** envoyez une demande manuscrite.

harbour, *n.* port *m*; **commercial harbour,** port commercial; **fishing harbour,** port de pêche; **harbour dues,** droits *m* de port/de mouillage; **harbour installations/harbour facilities/harbour works,** installations *f* portuaires.

hard, *a.* **1.** *Fin:* (*of stock, rates, etc.*) soutenu/ferme **2. article that is hard to sell,** article difficile à vendre/qui ne se vend pas bien/d'écoulement difficile **3. hard currency,** devise *f* forte.

harden, *v.i. Fin:* (*of shares, etc.*) **to harden (up),** se raffermir; **prices are hardening,** les prix *m* sont en hausse/se raffermissent.

hardening, *n.* (*of prices*) raffermissement *m.*

hardness, *n.* *Fin:* tension *f* (du marché, des actions).

hard sell, *n.* publicité poussée à fond/publicité agressive/battage *m* (publicitaire); **to give s.o. the hard sell,** imposer une vente à qn.

hardware, *n.* *Cmptr:* matériel *m*/hardware *m.*

haul^1**,** *n.* transport *m*; **length of haul,** distance *f* de transport; **short haul,** transport à/sur courte distance; **medium haul,** transport à/sur moyenne distance; **long haul,** transport sur longue distance/à grande distance.

haul^2**,** *v.tr.* transporter (des marchandises) par camion/camionner.

haulage, *n.* **1.** roulage *m*/camionnage *m*; **haulage contractor,** entrepreneur *m* de transports/de roulage; **road haulage,** transports routiers; **road haulage depot,** gare routière (de marchandises) **2.** (*costs*) frais *mpl* de roulage/de transport.

haulier, *n.* (*a*) entrepreneur *m* de transports (*b*) entreprise *f* de roulage.

hawk, *v.tr.* colporter (des marchandises); crier des marchandises.

hawker, *n.* (*a*) colporteur *m*/marchand ambulant/camelot *m* (*b*) (*of fruit, vegetables*) marchand des quatre saisons.

hawking, *n.* colportage *m*; **share hawking,** colportage de titres.

head, *n.* **1.** (*headings*) **he signed heads of agreement,** il a signé le protocole d'accord **2.** (*pers.*) (*a*) chef *m* (d'une entreprise); directeur, -trice; **head of department,** chef de service; (*in store*) chef de rayon (*b*) **head agent,** agent principal; **head clerk,** premier commis/commis principal; chef de bureau; **head foreman,** chef d'atelier; **head office,** siège social/bureau principal **3. to pay so much per**

head/so much a head, payer tant par tête/par personne.

headed, *a.* **headed notepaper,** papier *m* à en-tête.

head-hunter, *n.* chasseur *m* de tête.

heading, *n.* (*a*) en-tête *m* (d'une page, d'une lettre, d'une facture) (*b*) rubrique *f*; **see under the heading 'sales',** voir sous la rubrique "vente".

headquarters, *n.pl.* siège social/bureau principal; **to have its headquarters at . . .,** avoir son siège à . . ..

health, *n.* santé *f*; **health insurance,** assurance *f* maladie.

hear, *v.tr. Corr:* **hoping to hear from you soon,** dans l'espoir de vous lire bientôt.

heavy, *a.* **1. the market is heavy,** le marché est lourd **2. heavy expenditure,** dépenses *f* considérables/grosses dépenses; **heavy industry,** industrie lourde; **heavy losses,** lourdes/fortes pertes; **heavy percentage,** pourcentage élevé; **heavy sales,** ventes massives; **contangoes are heavy,** les reports sont chers **3.** (*oppressive*) **heavy tax,** impôt lourd; **heavy charge on the budget,** charge onéreuse pour le budget.

hedge[1], *n. StExch:* **hedge (operation),** (*i*) arbitrage *m* (*ii*) (opération de) couverture *f*; **hedge against inflation,** sauvegarde *f*/couverture *f* contre l'inflation; **hedge clause,** clause de sauvegarde (insérée dans un contrat).

hedge[2], *v.i. & tr. StExch:* (*i*) faire une opération d'arbitrage/arbitrer (des valeurs) (*ii*) se couvrir; **to hedge by a sale for the account,** se couvrir par une vente à terme.

hedger, *n. StExch:* arbitragiste m.

hedging, *n.* (*a*) *StExch:* arbitrage *m*/opération *f* de couverture/hedging *m* (*b*) *NAm:* contrepartie *f*.

hereafter, *adv.* ci-après/ci-dessous.

hereby, *adv.* **we hereby declare that . . .,** nous déclarons, par la présente, que . . ..

herewith, *adv.* **I am sending you herewith,** je vous envoie ci-joint/ci-inclus/sous ce pli.

hidden, *a. Fin:* **hidden reserves,** réserves secrètes/occultes.

high[1], **higher, highest,** *a.* (*a*) **high/higher executives,** cadres supérieurs; **to be in a high position,** être haut placé (*b*) **high prices,** prix élevés; **to fetch a high price,** se vendre cher; **highest price,** chiffre *m* maximum; **the highest and lowest prices,** cours *m* extrêmes; **to make a higher bid,** faire une offre supérieure; **high rate of interest,** taux d'intérêt élevé (*c*) **the highest efficiency,** (*i*) la plus grande compétence (*ii*) le rendement maximum.

high[2], *adv.* (*of price*) **to run high,** être élevé; **expenditure is running high,** les dépenses *f* sont élevées.

high[3], *n.* **prices have reached a new high,** les prix *m* ont atteint un nouveau maximum; **to reach an all-time high,** atteindre un nouveau record/plafond; *StExch:* **highs and lows,** les (cours) extrêmes/les cours les plus hauts et les cours les plus bas.

high-grade, *a.* (marchandise, etc.) de première qualité/de (premier) choix; **high-grade petrol,** supercarburant *m*/super *m*.

high-level, *a.* **high-level staff,** les cadres supérieurs; **high-level decision,** décision prise à un niveau supérieur.

highly, *adv.* **1. highly placed official,** haut fonctionnaire **2. his services are highly paid,** ses services sont largement rétribués/on paie très cher ses services.

high-pressure, *a.* **high-pressure salesman,** vendeur importun/agressif/qui force la main; **high-pressure salesmanship,** l'art *m* de vendre coûte que coûte (en forçant la main).

high-quality, *a.* de première qualité/de premier ordre/de (premier) choix.

hire¹, *n.* **1.** (*a*) *NAm:* embauchage *m* (de main-d'œuvre) (*b*) location *f* (d'une voiture, etc.); **cars for hire,** voitures à louer; **car hire service,** location *f* de voitures; **hire car,** voiture de location (*c*) **hire purchase,** (*i*) achat *m* à crédit/à tempérament (*ii*) location-vente *f*; **hire purchase agreement,** contrat *m* de location-vente; **to buy sth. on hire purchase,** acheter qch. à crédit/à tempérament **2.** (*i*) salaire *m* (*ii*) prix de la location.

hire², **1.** *v.tr.* (*a*) *esp. NAm:* engager (un ouvrier, un employé); **the personnel manager has the power to hire and fire,** le chef du personnel a tous droits d'embauche et de renvoi (*b*) louer (une voiture, etc.)/prendre (qch.) en location **2.** *v.i. NAm:* **he hired (himself) out as a waiter,** il a accepté un emploi comme garçon de restaurant.

hired, *a.* **hired car,** voiture *f* de location.

hire out, *v.tr.* donner en location.

hiring, *n.* (*a*) embauchage *m* (d'un ouvrier) (*b*) location *f* (d'une voiture, etc.).

historical, *a.* **historical cost,** valeur *f* à l'origine.

hive off, *v.tr.* (*a*) *F:* mettre de côté/mettre à l'écart (*b*) **the subsidiary company will be hired off,** la filiale deviendra indépendante.

hoarding, *n.* **1.** thésaurisation *f* (de capitaux) **2.** panneau *m* d'affichage.

hold, *v.tr.* **1. to hold stocks as security,** détenir des titres en garantie; **to hold stocks for a rise,** conserver des valeurs en vue d'une hausse **2. this product is still holding its own after all these years,** ce produit, lancé depuis des années, se vend toujours bien **3.** tenir (une séance); **the Motor Show is held in October,** le Salon de l'Automobile a lieu/se tient au mois d'octobre; **to hold an auction,** faire/

procéder à une vente aux enchères; **the meeting will be held at 8 p.m.,** la réunion aura lieu à huit heures du soir **4.** *Tp:* **hold the line please,** ne quittez pas, s'il vous plaît; **the line's engaged, will you hold?,** voulez-vous attendre que le poste soit libre?

hold back, *v.i.* **buyers are holding back,** les acheteurs *m* s'abstiennent.

holder, *n.* (*a*) (*pers.*) détenteur, -trice (de titres, d'une lettre de change); porteur, -euse (de titres, d'un effet); titulaire *mf* (d'un droit, d'un poste, d'un permis, d'un compte en banque, d'une carte de crédit); concessionnaire *mf* (d'un brevet, d'une marque, d'un produit); propriétaire *mf* (d'une terre); **holder of insurance policy,** assuré(e); *Jur:* **holder (on trust) of s.o.'s securities,** dépositaire *mf* des valeurs de qn; **holders of debt claims,** créanciers *m*; **holder in due course,** porteur régulier/de bonne foi (*b*) **message holder,** classe-notes *m*/spirale *f* de classement.

holding, *n. Fin:* avoir *m* (en actions); effets *mpl* en portefeuille; dossier *m*; holding *m*; **he has holdings in several companies,** il est actionnaire de plusieurs sociétés; **cross holdings,** participations croisées; **holding company,** (société) holding *m*/société de portefeuille/société de contrôle.

hold over, *v.tr.* arriérer/différer (un paiement); **bills held over,** effets *m* en souffrance/en suspens.

hold up, **1.** *v.tr.* **goods held up at the customs,** marchandises *f* en consigne/en souffrance/immobilisées à la douane; **payment is held up,** (*i*) on refuse de régler tout de suite (*ii*) les paiements sont suspendus **2.** *v.i.* **the shares held up well,** les actions se sont bien défendues; **the market is holding up well,** le marché tient toujours.

holiday, *n.* (*a*) (jour de) fête *f*/jour férié; **statutory/legal/official/national/ public/bank holiday,** fête légale (*b*) (jour de) congé *m* (*c*) **a month's holiday,** un mois de vacances; **paid holidays,** congé payé; **the summer holidays,** les grandes vacances; **to stagger holidays,** étaler les vacances.

home, *n.* **1. the Ideal Home Exhibition** = le Salon des Arts Ménagers **2.** (*a*) *NAm: Ind:* **home office,** siège social (d'une compagnie) (*b*) (*referring to the nation*) **the Home Office,** le Ministère de l'Intérieur; **home trade,** (*i*) commerce intérieur (*ii*) cabotage national; **home market,** marché intérieur; **home products/home produce,** produits nationaux/du pays.

home-made, *a* (fait) maison; **home-made bread,** pain *m* maison.

homeward, *a.* **homeward freight,** fret *m* de retour; **homeward journey,** voyage *m* de retour.

homewards, *adv. Nau:* **loading homewards,** chargement *m* pour le retour; chargement de retour; **cargo homewards,** cargaison *f* de retour.

honorary, *a.* (*a*) (emploi, service) honoraire/non rétribué/bénévole; **honorary duties,** fonctions *f* sans rétribution/travail à titre gratuit/travail bénévole (*b*) **honorary president,** président *m* d'honneur/honoraire.

honour[1], *n.* **acceptance (of protested bill) for honour,** acceptation *f* par intervention; **the acceptor for honour,** l'avaliste *m*; le donneur d'aval; **act of honour,** acte *m* d'intervention; **for the honour of . . .,** pour l'honneur de . . ..

honour[2], *v.tr.* **to honour a bill,** faire honneur à/honorer/payer une lettre de change; **honoured bill,** traite payée/acquittée; **to honour one's signature,** honorer/faire honneur à sa signature.

horizontal, *a.* (*a*) *NAm:* **horizontal increase in salaries of 10%,** augmentation *f* uniforme de 10% sur toutes les rétributions (*b*) **horizontal integration,** intégration *f* horizontale.

horsepower, *n.* (*abbr.* **h.p.**), cheval-vapeur (*abbr.* **c.v.**) *m*.

hosiery, *n.* **hosiery (trade),** bonneterie *f*; **hosiery counter,** département *m*/rayon *m* des bas et chaussettes.

hostess, *n.f. Av:* **air hostess,** hôtesse de l'air; **ground hostess,** hôtesse au sol.

hotel, *n.* hôtel *m*; **hotel accommodation,** chambre *f* d'hôtel; **hotel bill/expenses,** frais de séjour à l'hôtel; **hotel manager,** le directeur de l'hôtel; **private/residential hotel** = pension *f* de famille; **the hotel trade,** l'industrie hôtelière/l'hôtellerie *f*.

hour, *n.* heure *f*; **to pay s.o. by the hour,** payer qn à l'heure; **to be paid £5 an hour,** être payé £5 (de) l'heure; **output per hour,** puissance *f* horaire/rendement *m* à l'heure; **eight-hour day,** journée *f* (de travail) de huit heures; **37-hour week,** semaine de 37 heures; **business hours,** heures d'affaires/de bureau; heures d'ouverture et de clôture; **office hours,** heures de bureau; **I do this work out of hours,** je fais ce travail en dehors de mes heures (de bureau, d'atelier, etc.); **rush/peak hours,** heures de pointe/d'affluence.

hourly, **1.** *a* (débit, rendement, salaire) par heure/à l'heure/horaire; **hourly paid workers,** ouvriers payés à l'heure; **hourly rate,** tarif *m* horaire **2.** *adv* toutes les heures; d'heure en heure.

house, *n.* **1.** maison *f*; **house property,** immeubles *mpl*; **to invest in house property,** placer son argent en immeubles; **house duty/tax,** taxe *f* d'habitation; **house agent,** agent immobilier; **house agency,** agence immobilière **2.** (*a*) **finance house,** maison de finance; **publishing house,** maison d'édition (*b*) **house magazine,** journal *m* de la maison; **house telephone,** téléphone intérieur; *Fin:* **house bill,** lettre de change creuse (*c*) *StExch:* **the House,** la Bourse; **members of the House,** agents *m* de change.

household, *n. PolEc:* ménage *m*/famille *f*.

householder, *n.* propriétaire *mf*/occupant(e) (d'une maison).

house-to-house, *a.* (vente, etc.) à domicile; **house-to-house canvassing,** le porte(-)à(-)porte/démarchage *m.*

hovercraft, *n.* aéroglisseur *m*; *F:* hovercraft *m.*

hoverport, *n.* hoverport *m.*

hull, *n. MIns:* corps *m*; **hull insurance,** assurance *f* sur corps; **hull underwriter,** assureur *m* sur corps.

hundredweight, *n.* (*abbr.* **c.w.t.**), (*a*) poids *m* de 112 livres/quintal *m* (= 50 kg) (*b*) poids de 100 kilogrammes.

hush-money, *n.* pot *m* de vin.

hydrofoil, *n.* hydroglisseur *m.*

hypermarket, *n.* hypermarché *m.*

hypothecate, *v.tr. Jur:* hypothéquer (une terre); déposer (des titres) en nantissement.

hypothecation, *n.* fait *m* d'hypothéquer; inscription *f* hypothécaire/nantissement; **letter of hypothecation,** lettre *f* hypothécaire.

I

idle, *a.* (*a*) (*of employees*) qui chôme/en chômage; (*of machine*) au repos/arrêté (*b*) (*of money*) **to lie idle,** dormir; **capital lying idle,** capital oisif; fonds dormants/ inemployés/improductifs/morts; **to let one's money lie idle,** laisser dormir son argent.

illegal, *a.* illégal.

illegality, *n.* illégalité *f.*

illegally, *adv.* illégalement.

illicit, *a.* illicite; **illicit profits,** profits *m* illicites.

image, *n.* **brand image,** image de marque; **corporate image,** image de marque (de l'entreprise).

immovable, *Jur:* **1.** *a.* **immovable property,** biens immobiliers/biens immeubles; **seizure of immovable property,** saisie immobilière **2.** *n. pl.* **immovables,** biens immobiliers/biens immeubles.

immunity, *n.* exemption *f* (**from,** de); **to claim immunity from certain taxes,** demander à être exempté/exonéré/dispensé de certains impôts.

impact, *n.* répercussion(s) *f*(*pl*)/impact *m*; **the impact of high wages on production costs,** l'incidence *f* des hauts salaires sur les prix de revient; **the impact of a publicity campaign,** l'impact d'une campagne publicitaire.

impersonal, *a.* **impersonal account,** compte fictif.

implement, *v.tr.* exécuter (un projet); appliquer (une loi).

implementation, *n.* application *f*/exécution *f*/mise à effet (d'un règlement, d'un programme).

import¹, *n.* (*a*) *usu. pl.* **imports,** (*i*) (*coll.*) importations *f* (*ii*) articles *m* d'importation; **the imports and exports of a country,** les importations et les exportations *f* d'un pays; **visible and invisible imports,** importations visibles et invisibles (*b*) **import agent,** commissionnaire importateur; **import ban,** prohibition *f*/interdiction *f* d'importation; prohibition d'entrée; **import duty,** droit *m* d'entrée/de douane; **import firm,** maison *f* d'importation; **import licence/permit,** licence *f*/permis *m* d'importation; **import list,** (*i*) liste *f* des importations (*ii*) tarif *m* d'entrée; **import quotas,** contingentement *m* des importations; **import trade,** commerce *m* d'importation; commerce passif; **import (and) export company,** entreprise *f* d'import-export.

import², *v.tr.* importer (des marchandises); **imported goods,** articles *m* d'importation/importations *f*; **goods imported from France,** produits de provenance française/importations françaises.

importable, *a.* importable.

importation, *n. NAm:* **1.** importation *f* (de marchandises); **for temporary importation,** en franchise *f* temporaire **2.** (article d')importation.

importer, *n.* (*a*) importateur, -trice (*b*) maison d'importation.

importing¹, *a.* importateur; **the importing countries,** les pays importateurs; **importing house,** maison *f* d'importation.

91

importing[2], *n.* importation *f* (de marchandises).

impose, *v.tr.* **to impose a tax on sugar,** imposer le sucre/taxer le sucre/frapper le sucre d'une taxe; **to impose a tax on small business,** imposer les petits commerces.

imposition, *n.* imposition *f*/impôt *m*/taxe *f*; *pl.* contributions *f*.

impound, *v.tr.* *Jur:* (*a*) confisquer/saisir (des marchandises) (*b*) faire déposer (des documents) au greffe.

impounding, *n.* *Jur:* (*a*) arrêt *m*/saisie *f* (de marchandises) (*b*) prise *f* de possession (de documents).

imprest, *n.* *Adm:* avance *f* de fonds (à un fournisseur de l'État); **imprest account,** compte *m* d'avances (à montant fixe); **imprest system,** comptabilité *f* de prévision.

imprint, *n.* **publisher's imprint,** nom *m* de l'éditeur; **published under the Harrap imprint,** publié par la maison Harrap.

imprinter, *n.* **(credit card) imprinter,** presse imprimante (de cartes de crédit).

improve, **1.** *v.ind.tr.* **to improve on s.o.'s offer,** enchérir sur l'offre de qn **2.** *v.i.* (*a*) s'améliorer; **his business is improving,** son commerce est en voie de relèvement; **business is improving/things are improving,** il y a une amélioration dans les affaires/les affaires reprennent (*b*) (*of prices, markets*) monter; être en hausse.

improved, *a.* (*a*) (*of invention, method*) perfectionné (*b*) **improved offer,** offre supérieure.

improvement, *n.* amélioration *f*; **job improvement,** amélioration des tâches; **house improvement,** travaux *mpl* de modernisation (d'une maison).

impulse, *n.* **impulse buying,** achat spontané/achat d'impulsion.

imputed, *a.* **imputed payments,** paiements imputés; **imputed value,** valeur imputée/implicite.

in, *a.* **in tray,** entrées *fpl*; *Fin:* **in book,** livre *m* du dedans/registre *m* des chèques à rembourser.

incentive, *n.* **incentive pay,** primes *fpl* de rendement; **incentive scheme,** programme *m* de stimulants salariaux/de salaires au rendement; **group incentive,** prime (de rendement) d'équipe/prime collective; **production incentives,** primes de rendement.

inch, *n.* *Meas:* pouce *m* (= 2.54 cm).

incidence, *n.* incidence *f*.

incidental, **1.** *a.* **incidental expenses**/*n.pl.* **incidentals,** faux frais/frais accessoires; dépenses imprévues.

in-clearing, *a.* *Fin:* **in-clearing book,** livre *m* du dedans/registre *m* des chèques à rembourser.

include, *v.tr.* comprendre/renfermer/ embrasser; **including carriage,** y compris le port/port compris; **up to and including December 31st,** jusqu'au 31 décembre inclusivement.

inclusive, *a.* **inclusive sum,** somme globale/totale; **all inclusive/inclusive price/ inclusive terms,** (prix) tout compris; **inclusive of all taxes,** toutes taxes comprises (TTC); **from 4th to 12th February inclusive,** du 4 au 12 février inclusivement.

income, *n.* **1.** revenu *m*/revenus *mpl*; **annual income,** revenu annuel; **source of income,** source(s) *f(pl)* de revenu; **earned income,** (*i*) revenu(s) du travail (*ii*) revenus salariaux (*iii*) revenus professionnels; **unearned income/private income,** rente(s) *f(pl)*; revenus non professionnels; **to have a private/an unearned income of £3000 a year,** avoir trois mille livres de rente; **land that brings in a good income,** terre *f* de bon rapport; **income group/income bracket,** tranche *f* de salaire/de revenu; **higher-income/ lower-income/middle-income groups,** groupes *m* (de contribuables) à revenus élevés/faibles/moyens; **incomes policy,** politique *f* des revenus; *PolEc:* **gross**

national income, revenu national brut; **income tax,** impôt *m* (cédulaire) sur le revenu; **income-tax return,** déclaration fiscale/déclaration *f* de revenu/déclaration d'impôt sur le revenu **2.** recettes *fpl*/revenus/rentrées *fpl*/bénéfice *m*; **income statement/statement of income,** compte de pertes et profits; résultat *m* (de l'exercice)/résultat d'exploitation/compte de résultat; **net income,** bénéfice net; **income debenture,** obligation *f* à revenu variables.

incomings, *n.pl.* recettes *f*/revenus *m*/rentrées *f*; **his incomings and outgoings,** ses recettes et ses dépenses *f*.

incontestability, *n. Ins:* **incontestability clause,** clause *f* d'incontestabilité.

inconvertible, *a.* (*of paper money, etc.*) inconvertible (**into,** en).

incorporate, 1. *v.tr.* constituer (une association) en société commerciale **2.** *v.i.* se constituer en société commerciale.

incorporated, *a. NAm:* **incorporated company (Inc.),** association constituée en société commerciale/société enregistrée/société autorisée.

incorporation, *n.* constitution *f* (d'une association) en société commerciale.

increase¹, *n.* (*a*) augmentation *f*/accroissement *m*/progression *f*; **increase of capital,** augmentation de capital; **increase in price,** augmentation de prix/hausse *f* de prix; **increase in the cost of living/cost-of-living increase;** hausse du coût de la vie; **increase in value (of property, etc.),** plus-value *f* (d'une propriété, etc.); **increase in wages/pay increase(s),** augmentation/relèvement *m*/hausse *f* de salaire(s); **I've had an increase in salary,** j'ai reçu une augmentation (de salaire)/*F:* j'ai été augmenté; **an increase of 30% on last week('s),** une augmentation/une plus-value de 30% sur la semaine dernière (*b*) **to be on the**

increase, augmenter/aller en augmentant.

increase², 1. *v.i.* augmenter/progresser; grandir; croître; **to increase in size,** augmenter de volume; **to increase in value,** augmenter de valeur; **to increase in price,** devenir plus cher; augmenter de prix; **to go on increasing,** aller en augmentant **2.** *v.tr.* augmenter (la production); relever/augmenter (les salaires); augmenter/majorer (les prix, les impôts); **to increase the expenditure,** augmenter la dépense.

increment, *n.* **1.** augmentation *f*; **a salary of £6000 plus annual increments of . . .,** un salaire de £6000 avec augmentation annuelle de . . . **2.** profit *m*; (*of land, shares*) **unearned increment,** plus-value *f*.

incremental, *a.* **incremental cost,** coût marginal.

incur, *v.tr.* courir (un risque); éprouver/subir (une perte); contracter (des dettes); faire (les frais).

indebted, *a.* endetté; **to be heavily indebted to s.o.,** devoir une forte somme à qn.

indebtedness, *n.* endettement *m.*

indemnification, *n.* **1.** indemnisation *f*/dédommagement *m* (**of s.o.** de qn) **2.** indemnité *f*/dédommagement/compensation *f*; **to pay a sum of money by way of indemnification,** payer une somme à titre d'indemnité.

indemnify, *v.tr.* indemniser/dédommager (qn) (**for a loss,** d'une perte).

indemnity, *n.* **1.** garantie *f*/assurance *f* (contre une perte, etc.); **indemnity bond/(letter of) indemnity,** cautionnement *m*/(lettre de) garantie **2.** indemnité *f*/dédommagement *m*/compensation *f*; **to pay full indemnity to s.o.,** indemniser qn totalement/de tous ses frais; **receiver of an indemnity,** indemnitaire *mf.*

indent¹, *n.* commande *f* de marchandises/ordre *m* d'achat; *esp.* commande reçue de l'étranger.

indent[2], *v.i.* **to indent on s.o. for sth.**, passer une commande (de qch) à qn.

indenter, *n.* client *m* qui passe une commande de marchandises venant de l'étranger.

indenture[1], *n. Jur:* (*a*) acte *m*; contrat *m* synallagmatique; contrat bilatéral/réciproque (*b*) *usu.pl.* **indentures**, contrat d'apprentissage.

indenture[2], *v.tr.* (*a*) lier (qn) par contrat; **indentured labour**, main-d'œuvre engagée à long terme (*b*) mettre (qn) en apprentissage (**to s.o.**, chez qn) (sous contrat).

index, *n.* **1.** (*pl.* **indexes**) (*a*) index *m*/table *f* alphabétique (*b*) répertoire *m*/catalogue *m*; **card index**, fichier *m* **2.** (*pl.* **indices**) **index number** (nombre) indice *m*; **growth index**, indice de croissance; **consumer price index**, indice des prix à la consommation; **cost of living index**, indice du coût de la vie; **retail price index**, indice des prix de détail; **wholesale price index**, indice des prix de gros; **overall index**, indice général.

indexation, *n.* indexation *f.*

index-linked, *a.* indexé sur l'indice du coût de la vie.

indicator, *n.* **retail-price indicator**, indice *m* des prix de détail; **all-items indicator**, indice général des cours; *PolEc:* **economic indicators**, indicateurs d'alerte/*F:* clignotants *m.*

indirect, *a.* indirect; **indirect charges/indirect expenses**, frais généraux/charges indirectes; **indirect labour**, main-d'œuvre indirecte; **indirect selling**, vente indirecte; **indirect taxes**, impôts indirects.

indorse, *v.tr.* = **endorse**.

induction, *n.* **induction course**, stage *m* de mise au courant/d'accueil.

indulge, *v.tr.* accorder un délai à (une

lettre de change, au payeur d'une lettre de change).

indulgence, *n.* délai *m* de paiement (accordé au payeur d'une lettre de change).

industrial, *a.* (*a*) industriel; **industrial centre**, centre industriel; **industrial complex/industrial estate**, complexe industriel/zone industrielle; **industrial exhibition**, salon *m* de l'industrie; **industrial training**, formation *f* à l'usine/dans l'entreprise (*b*) **industrial dispute**, conflit ouvrier/du travail; **industrial unrest**, agitation ouvrière; conflits sociaux; **industrial relations**, relations industrielles/professionnelles; **industrial disease**, maladie professionnelle; **industrial injuries**, accidents *m* du travail; **industrial insurance**, assurance contre les accidents du travail (*c*) *PolEc:* **industrial unit**, atelier *m* (*d*) *Fin:* **industrial bank**, banque industrielle; **industrial shares**/*n.pl.* **industrials**, valeurs industrielles.

industrialism, *n.* industrialisme *m.*

industrialist, *n.* industriel *m.*

industrialization, *n.* industrialisation *f.*

industrialize, **1.** *v.tr.* industrialiser **2.** *v.i.* s'industrialiser.

industry, *n.* (*a*) industrie *f*; **basic industry**, industrie de base; **processing industry**, industrie de transformation (*b*) **growing/growth industry**, industrie en plein essor; **consumer goods industry**, industrie de consommation (*c*) **cottage industry**, industrie artisanale/artisanat *m*; **heavy industry**, l'industrie lourde; **light industry**, l'industrie légère; **primary industry**, industrie primaire/secteur *m* primaire; **sector of industry**, secteur industriel; branche *f* d'industrie (*d*) **agricultural industries**, industries agricoles; **aircraft industry**, industrie aéronautique; **building industry**, industrie du bâtiment/le bâtiment; **chemical industry**, industrie chimique; **engineering industry**, industrie mécanique; **hotel industry**, industrie hôtelière; **mining industry,** industrie minière/industrie extractive; **metal industry,** industrie métallurgique; **motor industry/car industry,** industrie automobile; **oil industry/petroleum industry,** industrie pétrolière/industrie du pétrole; **plastics industry,** industrie pétrochimique; **precision industry,** industrie de précision; **service industry,** (*i*) secteur tertiaire (*ii*) société de services; **shipping industry,** (*i*) industrie des transports maritimes (*ii*) industrie de constructions navales.

inefficiency, *n.* (*a*) inefficacité *f* (des mesures prises, etc.) (*b*) incapacité (professionnelle); incompétence *f*/manque *m* de compétence.

inefficient, *a.* (*a*) (*of measure, etc.*) inefficace/ineffectif (*b*) (*of pers.*) incapable/incompétent.

inelastic, *a.* (demande, etc.) fixe/qui ne change pas.

inertia, *n.* **inertia selling,** vente *f* par obtention abusive/frauduleuse de commande.

inexecution, *n.* inexécution *f* (d'un contrat, etc.)

inexpensive, *a.* peu coûteux/bon marché/(qui ne coûte) pas cher.

inexpensively, *adv.* (à) bon marché/à bas prix/à peu de frais/à bon compte; **to live inexpensively,** vivre économiquement/à peu de frais.

inferior, *a.* inférieur; **inferior goods,** marchandises inférieures; **inferior quality,** qualité inférieure/mauvaise qualité.

inflate, *v.tr.* (*a*) grossir/charger (un compte); gonfler (une facture) (*b*) hausser/faire monter (les prix) (*c*) *PolEc:* **to inflate the currency,** accroître artificiellement la circulation fiduciaire; recourir à l'inflation.

inflated, *a.* (*a*) (prix) exagéré/gonflé (*b*) *PolEc:* **inflated currency,** circulation fiduciaire artificiellement accrue.

inflation, *n.* *PolEc:* **rate of inflation,** taux *m* d'inflation; **the danger of inflation,** le danger inflationniste; **creeping inflation,** inflation rampante; **galloping inflation,** inflation galopante; **measures to combat inflation,** mesures déflationnistes; **monetary inflation,** inflation monétaire; **inflation of the currency,** inflation fiduciaire; **cost-push inflation,** inflation par les coûts; **demand-pull inflation,** inflation par la demande.

inflationary, *a.* (politique, etc.) inflationniste/d'inflation; **inflationary spiral,** spirale *f* inflationniste; **inflationary tendency,** tendance *f* inflationniste/à l'inflation.

inflationism, *n.* *PolEc:* inflationnisme *m.*

inflow, *n.* afflux *m* (de marchandises, etc.).

influx, *n.* entrée *f*/afflux *m*; **influx of gold,** afflux d'or.

inform, *v.tr.* *Corr:* **we are writing to inform you of the dispatch of . . . ,** nous vous avisons de l'envoi de . . . ; **I am pleased to inform you that . . . ,** j'ai le plaisir/l'honneur de vous annoncer/de vous informer que . . . ; **I regret to have to inform you that . . . ,** j'ai le regret de vous annoncer/de vous faire savoir que . . . ; **we are informed that . . . ,** on nous apprend/on nous fait savoir/on nous informe que . . . .

information, *n.* renseignement(s) *m(pl)*/information(s) *f(pl)*; **all the necessary information,** tous (les) renseignements utiles; **I am sending you for your information/by way of information . . . ,** je vous envoie à titre d'information/de renseignement . . . ; *Adm:* **information copy,** copie *f* pour information; **(strictly) confidential information,** renseignement (strictement) confidentiel; **information retrieval,** recherche *f* documentaire (de données); **information technology,** informatique *f*; **piece of information,** renseignement; indication *f*; **request for information,** demande *f* de renseignement(s); **for further information apply to . . . ,** pour de plus amples renseignements s'adresser à/écrire à . . . ; **processing of infor-**

mation, traitement *m* de l'information; *Adm:* **information bureau,** bureau *m* de renseignements/centre *m* d'information; **tourist information bureau** = Syndicat *m* d'Initiative.

infrastructure, *n. PolEc: Adm:* infrastructure *f*.

infringe, *v.tr.* **to infringe a patent,** (*i*) contrefaire un objet breveté (*ii*) empiéter sur un brevet; **to infringe a copyright,** violer les droits d'auteur.

infringement, *n.* **infringement of a patent,** contrefaçon *f* (d'un brevet); **infringement of (literary) copyright,** contrefaçon (littéraire); violation *f* des droits d'auteur.

ingot, *n.* lingot *m* (d'or, d'argent); **ingot gold,** or *m* en lingot.

initial[1], *a.* **initial capital,** capital initial/ d'apport; **initial (capital) expenditure/ expenses/investment/outlay,** frais *mpl* de premier établissement; **initial cost,** coût initial; (*of manufactured product*) prix *m* de revient; **initial value,** valeur *f* de départ.

initial[2], *v.tr.* parafer/parapher/viser (une lettre, un document).

inject, *v.tr.* **to inject capital into a business,** injecter du capital dans une entreprise.

injection, *n.* **injection of capital into a business,** injection *f*/apport *m* de capital dans une entreprise.

injured, *a.* **injured party,** partie lésée.

inland, *a.* **inland trade,** commerce intérieur; **inland postage rates,** (tarif *m* d')affranchissement *m* en régime intérieur; **inland bill,** traite *f* sur le pays; effet *m*/lettre *f* de change sur l'intérieur; **inland revenue,** contributions (directes et indirectes); **the (Commissioners of) Inland Revenue/the Inland Revenue (Department),** le fisc; **inland revenue stamp,** timbre fiscal.

inquiry, *n.* **inquiry office,** bureau de ren-

seignements; *Corr:* **with reference to your inquiry of May 5th . . .,** en réponse à votre demande du 5 mai . . ..

inscribed, *a. Fin:* **inscribed stock,** actions inscrites (au grand-livre).

insider, *n. StExch:* **the insiders,** les initiés.

insolvency, *n.* insolvabilité *f*; **to be in a state of insolvency,** être insolvable/en état de cessation de paiements.

insolvent, 1. *a.* (débiteur, société) insolvable; **to become insolvent,** être en état de cessation de paiements; **to declare oneself insolvent,** déposer son bilan **2.** *n.* failli *m*.

inspect, *v.tr.* inspecter/visiter (une fabrique, etc.); contrôler/vérifier (les livres d'un négociant); vérifier/inspecter (une machine, etc.).

inspecting[1], *a.* **inspecting officer,** inspecteur *m*.

inspecting[2], *n.* inspection *f*; **inspecting order,** ordre *m* d'inspection.

inspection, *n.* (*a*) examen *m*/vérification *f* (de documents, etc.); **to buy goods on inspection,** acheter des marchandises sur examen; *Publ:* **inspection copy,** spécimen *m* (*b*) inspection *f*/visite *f* (d'un établissement, etc.); contrôle *m* (du personnel, du matériel, etc.); **periodical inspection of factories,** visite périodique des fabriques; **tour of inspection,** inspection; **sanitary inspection,** visite/contrôle sanitaire; **to make an inspection,** faire une inspection; *Cust:* **inspection order,** bon *m* de visite; *Adm:* **inspection stamp,** (*i*) cachet *m* de vérification (*ii*) (*punch*) poinçon *m* de contrôle.

inspector, *n.* inspecteur, -trice; **inspector of taxes,** inspecteur/contrôleur *m* des contributions directes; **inspector of weights and measures,** vérificateur *m* des poids et mesures.

instability, *n.* instabilité *f* (financière).

instal(l)ment, *n.* fraction *f* (de paiement); acompte *m*; paiement *m* à compte; versement *m*; mensualité *f*; **annual instalment,** annuité *f*; **debt payable by annual instalments,** dette *f* annuitaire; **final instalment,** paiement pour solde/versement libératoire; **to pay an instalment,** verser un acompte; faire un versement; **to pay in/by instalments,** payer par versements; échelonner/fractionner les paiements; **payable in two instalments,** payable en deux versements; **payable in monthly instalments,** payable par mensualités *f*; **repayable by instalments,** remboursable par paiements à terme/par versements échelonnés/en plusieurs versements; *NAm:* **to buy on the instalment plan,** acheter à tempérament/à crédit; *NAm:* **instalment credit,** crédit à tempérament; **to vote credits in instalments,** voter des crédits par tranches.

instant, *a.* (*abbr.* **inst.**) *Corr:* courant; **my letter of the 5th inst.,** ma lettre du 5 courant/du 5 ct.

institute, *v.tr.* **to institute proceedings against s.o.,** intenter un procès contre qn.

institution, *n. Fin:* **credit institution,** établissement *m* de crédit; **investment institution,** société *f* de placement.

institutional, *a.* (*a*) **institutional advertising,** publicité *f* de prestige (*b*) **institutional investors,** investisseurs *mpl* institutionnels/grand investisseurs.

instruction, *n. Corr:* **we await your instructions,** nous attendons vos instructions/vos ordres; **instructions for use,** mode *m* d'emploi.

instrument, *n. Jur:* instrument *m*/acte *m*/document *m*; **negotiable instrument,** effet *m* de commerce; titre *m* au porteur.

insurable, *a.* assurable; **insurable interest,** intérêt *m* pécuniaire.

insurance, *n.* **1.** (*a*) assurance *f*; **to take out an insurance on sth./against a risk,** contracter une assurance/prendre une assurance/s'assurer/se faire assurer contre un risque; **his furniture was covered by an**

insurance, il avait assuré son mobilier; **to pay the insurance on a car,** payer l'assurance/les primes d'assurance d'une voiture; **accident insurance,** assurance contre les accidents/assurance-accidents *f*; **burglary insurance/theft insurance,** assurance contre le vol; **credit insurance,** assurance crédit; **endowment insurance,** (*i*) assurance en cas de vie (*ii*) assurance à terme fixe; **fire insurance,** assurance contre l'incendie/assurance-incendie *f*; **health insurance/private medical insurance,** assurance maladie; **life insurance,** assurance sur la vie/assurance-vie *f*; **marine insurance,** assurance maritime; **motor/car insurance,** assurance-automobile *f*; *NAm:* **no fault insurance,** assurance non-responsabilité/sans égard à la responsabilité; **personal liability insurance,** assurance responsabilité civile; **third-party liability insurance,** assurance au tiers; **workmen's compensation insurance/employers' liability insurance,** assurance (des employeurs) contre les accidents du travail; **whole life insurance,** assurance-décès; **all risks insurance/all-in insurance/comprehensive insurance,** assurance tous risques; assurance multirisque; *SwFr:* assurance casco; **collective insurance/group insurance,** assurance collective; **double insurance,** assurance cumulative; **index(-linked) insurance,** assurance indexée (*b*) **insurance agent,** agent *m* d'assurance(s); **insurance broker,** courtier *m* d'assurance(s); assureur *m*; **insurance charges,** frais *m* d'assurance; **insurance company,** compagnie/société d'assurance; **insurance money,** indemnité *f* d'assurance; **insurance policy/contract,** police *f*/contrat *m* d'assurance; **insurance premium,** prime *f* d'assurance; **he's in insurance,** il est/il travaille dans les assurances (*c*) *Adm:* **national insurance,** assurance sociale; **unemployment insurance,** assurance chômage.

insure, 1. *v.tr.* (*i*) assurer (*ii*) faire assurer (des marchandises, un mobilier, etc.); **to insure one's life,** s'assurer sur la vie/se faire assurer sur la vie/contracter une assurance-vie 2. *v.i.* **to insure against theft,** s'assurer/se faire assurer contre le vol.

insured, *a. & n.* assuré(e); **the house was insured,** la maison était assurée; **insured value,** valeur assurée; *Post:* **parcel insured for £5,** colis chargé avec valeur déclarée £5.

insurer, *n.* assureur *m.*

intangible, *a.* **intangible assets/**n.pl.* **intangibles,** valeurs immatérielles; actif incorporel/immobilisations incorporelles.

intascale, *n.* (= **inter-tanker nominal freight scale**) barème mondial des taux de fret nominaux.

inter, *pref.* **inter(-)company items,** opérations intersociétés.

interbank, *a.* (opération, etc.) entre banques; **interbank loans,** prêts *m* de banque à banque.

interbranch, *a.* (opérations) entre succursales (d'une même entreprise).

interdepartmental, *a.* interdépartemental; *Adm: etc:* **interdepartmental problems,** problèmes communs à plusieurs services.

interest, *n.* (*a*) *Fin:* intérêt *m*; **compound interest,** intérêt composé; **simple interest,** intérêt simple; **accrued interest,** intérêt couru/produits financiers à recevoir; **fixed interest,** intérêt fixe; **high interest,** intérêt élevé/gros rendement; **interest charges,** frais financiers; **interest coupon/warrant,** coupon *m* (d'intérêt); **interests due/payable,** intérêts échus/à recevoir; **interest income,** revenu *m* d'intérêt/produits financiers; **interest on capital,** intérêt du capital; **interest on a loan,** intérêt sur prêt; **interest on £100,** intérêt sur £100; **interest rate/rate of interest,** taux *m* d'intérêt/de l'intérêt; **long-term interest rate,** taux d'intérêt à long terme; **the interest rate is 4%,** le taux

d'intérêt est de 4%; **to bear/to yield/to carry interest,** porter intérêt/rapporter; **shares that yield a 5% interest,** actions *f* portant intérêt au taux de 5%; **interest-bearing loan,** prêt *m* à intérêt; **interest-bearing securities,** titres *m* qui produisent des intérêts; **interest-free,** sans intérêt; **interest-free credit,** crédit gratuit; **to pay interest,** payer des intérêts; **money earning no interest,** argent improductif/dormant; **to allow interest to accumulate,** laisser courir des intérêts (*b*) intérêt/participation *f*; **majority interest,** participation majoritaire; **minority interest,** participation minoritaire; **to have an interest in the profits,** participer aux bénéfices; **I have no vested interests in the business,** je n'ai pas de capitaux/je n'ai pas d'intérêts/je ne suis pas intéressé dans cette entreprise; **his interest in the company is £10 000,** il a une commandite de £10 000.

interested, *a.* **the interested parties,** les parties intéressées; *Jur:* **interested party,** ayant droit *m.*

interim, *a.* **interim dividend,** dividende *m* intérimaire; **interim report,** rapport *m* intérimaire.

intermediate, *a.* *Fin:* **intermediate credit,** crédit *m* à moyen terme; **intermediate goods/products,** biens intermédiaires.

internal, *a.* **internal revenue,** recettes fiscales; **internal trade,** commerce intérieur.

international, *a.* international; **international law,** droit international.

intertrade, *n.* commerce *m* réciproque.

intervention, *n.* *EEC:* **intervention price,** prix *m* d'intervention.

intrinsic, *a.* **intrinsic value,** valeur *f* intrinsèque.

introduce, *v.tr.* lancer (une marchandise); *StExch:* introduire (des actions).

introductory, *a.* **introductory price/offer,** (*i*) prix *m* de lancement/de vente publicitaire/prix-réclame *m* (*ii*) vente-réclame *f*.

invalid, *a.* périmé/qui n'est pas valable/qui n'est plus valable.

invalidate, *v.tr.* invalider/rendre invalide (un contrat).

invalidation, *n.* invalidation *f* (d'un document, d'un contrat).

invalidity, *n.* invalidité *f* (d'un contract, etc.).

inventory[1], *n.* **1.** inventaire *m*; **to take/to draw up an inventory**, faire/dresser un inventaire; **inventory of fixtures**, état *m* des lieux; **inventory book**, livre *m* d'inventaires; *Book-k:* **book inventory**, inventaire comptable; **ingoing inventory**, inventaire d'entrée (dans un immeuble); **outgoing inventory**, inventaire de sortie (d'un immeuble); **inventory with valuation**, inventaire avec prisée **2.** *NAm:* (*a*) stock(s) *m(pl)*; **inventory management/control**, gestion *f* des stocks/du stock; **inventory turnover**, rotation *f* des stocks (*b*) (établissement, levée d')inventaire.

inventory[2], *v.tr.* inventorier (les biens de qn); dresser l'inventaire (des biens de qn); **furniture that inventories at £1 000**, meubles *mpl* dont l'inventaire se monte à £1 000.

invest, *v.tr. Fin:* placer/investir (son argent, des fonds); **to invest money**, faire des placements; **to invest money in a business**, mettre de l'argent/placer des fonds dans un commerce; **to invest one's money to good account**, faire valoir son argent; **money invested in an annuity**, argent constitué en viager; **capital invested**, mise *f* de fonds; capital engagé/investi; *Ind:* capital d'établissement; **to invest in real estate**, faire des placements immobiliers.

investment, *n. Fin:* placement *m*/investissement *m* (de capitaux); mise *f* de fonds; (titre de) participation *f*; **fixed investment**, (montant des) immobilisations *f*; **good investment**, placement avantageux; **safe investment**, placement sûr/valeur *f* de tout repos; **long-term investment**, placement à long terme; **short-term investment**, placement à court terme; **investment in real estate**, placements/investissements immobiliers; **investments in securities**, placements en valeurs; **employee investment in the capital of a business**, actionnariat ouvrier; **to make investments**, investir des capitaux/faire des investissements/faire des placements; **(list of) investments**, portefeuille *m* titres; valeurs en portefeuille; dossier *m*; **investment company**, société *f* de portefeuille/d'investissement(s)/de placement(s); **investment credit**, crédit *m* d'investissement; **investment market**, marché *m* des capitaux; **investment securities/investment stock**, valeurs en portefeuille/valeurs de placement; valeurs classées; **investment trusts**, sociétés de placement(s); fonds *m* de placement(s).

investor, *n.* actionnaire *mf*; investisseur *m*; **small/private investors**, petits actionnaires/petits épargnants; l'épargne privée/la petite épargne.

invisible, *PolEc:* **1.** *a.* **invisible exports**, exportations *f* invisibles; **invisible imports**, importations *f* invisibles **2.** *n.pl.* **invisibles**, invisibles *m*.

invitation, *n. Fin:* **invitation to the public (to subscribe to a loan)**, appel *m* au public (pour la souscription d'un emprunt); **invitation for tenders**, appel d'offres.

invite, *v.tr. Fin:* **to invite shareholders to subscribe (a new issue)**, faire un appel de fonds.

invoice[1], *n.* facture *f* (de débit); note *f* (de frais); **shipping invoice**, facture d'expédition; **invoice of origin/original invoice**, facture originale; **the amount was included in my invoice**, le montant m'a été facturé; **to make out an invoice**, établir/faire une facture; **to settle an invoice**, régler une facture; **as per invoice**, suivant la facture; **invoice book**, facturier *m*; copie *f* des factures; livre *m* des achats; **invoice clerk,** facturier, -ière; **invoice price,** prix *m* de facture; **invoice work,** travaux *mpl* de facturation.

invoice[2], *v.tr.* facturer (des marchandises)/porter (une marchandise) sur une facture.

invoicing, *n.* facturation *f* (de marchandises, de frais d'emballage, etc.); **invoicing machine,** machine *f* à facturer; facturière *f*; **VAT invoicing,** facturation de la TVA.

inward, *a.* **inward charges,** frais *m* à l'entrée (d'un navire dans un port); **inward bill of lading,** connaissement *m* d'entrée; **inward manifest,** manifeste *m* d'entrée; **inward mission,** visite *f* d'un groupe d'hommes d'affaires venant de l'étranger; *Book-k:* **inward payment,** paiement reçu; encaissement *m*.

inwards, *adv.* pour l'importation; **clearance inwards,** (*i*) déclaration *f* d'entrée (*ii*) permis *m* d'entrée.

IOU, *n.* (= I owe you) reconnaissance *f* (de dette)/billet *m* à ordre.

irrecoverable, *a.* (créance *f*) irrécouvrable.

irredeemable, *a. Fin:* (fonds *m*) irrachetable/irréalisable/irremboursable; (papier *m*) non convertible; **irredeemable bonds** *n.pl.* **irredeemables,** obligations *f* non amortissables.

irregulars, *n.pl. NAm:* articles *m* de deuxième qualité/de qualité moyenne.

issuance, *n. NAm:* émission *f*.

issue[1], *n.* (*a*) *Adm: Fin:* émission *f* (d'un emprunt, de billets de banque, d'actions, de timbres, etc.); **capitalisation issue/ scrip issue/bonus issue,** action gratuite;

home currency issues, billets émis à l'intérieur du pays; **issue premium,** prime *f* d'émission; **issue price,** taux *m* d'émission; *Bank:* **issue department,** service *m* des émissions; **rights issue,** droits préférentiels de souscription (*b*) *Adm:* **issue card,** carte *f* (de) sortie de stock (*c*) **the latest issue of a magazine,** le dernier numéro d'une revue.

issue[2], *v.tr.* émettre (des billets de banque, des timbres, etc.); **to issue a letter of credit,** fournir une lettre de crédit; **to issue a draft on s.o.,** fournir une traite sur qn.

issued, *a,* **issued capital,** capital émis/souscrit; **number of shares issued,** nombre d'actions émises.

issuing[1], *a. Fin:* **issuing company,** société émettrice; **issuing house,** banque *f* de placement.

issuing[2], *n.* émission *f*.

item, 1. *adv. Book-k.* item 2. *n.* (*a*) article *m*; **please send us the following items,** prière de nous envoyer les articles suivants (*b*) *Book-k:* écriture *f*/article; poste *m*/détail *m*; **cash item,** article de caisse; **item of expenditure/expense item,** article/chef *m* de dépense; **credit item,** poste créditeur; **balance-sheet items,** détails du bilan; **to give the items on an invoice,** donner les détails d'une facture/détailler une facture; **this item does not appear in our books,** cette écriture ne figure pas dans nos livres (*c*) **the second item of the contract,** l'article deux du contrat; **the items on the agenda,** les questions *f* à l'ordre du jour.

itemize, *v.tr.* détailler (une facture, etc.); **itemized account,** compte spécifié/détaillé.

J

jacket, *n.* book jacket, jaquette *f.*

jet, *n.* jet (aeroplane)/jet-propelled aircraft, avion *m* à réaction/jet *m*; jumbo jet, (avion) gros porteur/jumbo-jet *m.*

jetliner, *n.* avion commercial à réaction/avion de ligne à réaction.

jetsam, *n.* marchandise jetée à la mer (pour alléger le navire).

jingle, *n.* (advertising) jingle, ritournelle *f* publicitaire.

job, *n.* 1. tâche *f*/ouvrage *m*/travail (particulier); to do a job, exécuter/faire un travail; job ticket, bon *m* de travail; job wage, salaire *m* à forfait; precision job, travail *m* de précision 2. emploi *m*/place *f*/poste *m*/ fonctions *fpl*/situation *f/F:* job *m*/ boulot *m*; off-the-job training, formation extérieure/institutionnelle; on-the-job training, apprentissage *m*/formation sur le tas; to look for a job, chercher un emploi/du travail; to lose one's job, perdre son emploi/sa place; to resign/throw up one's job, donner sa démission; to be out of a job, être en chômage/sans travail; *Adm:* job analysis, analyse *f* de la tâche/de la fonction; job assignment, assignation *f* des tâches; Job Centre = Agence nationale pour l'emploi (ANPE); job classification, classification *f* des emplois; job creation, création *f* d'entreprise/d'emplois; job description, description *f* d'un poste/d'une fonction; 600 job reductions/600 jobs lost, 600 suppressions *f* d'emploi; job satisfaction, satisfaction *f* dans le travail; job security, sécurité *f* d'emploi; job specification, spécification de la fonction 3. job lot, soldes *mpl*; articles *mpl*/marchandises *fpl* d'occasion;

articles dépareillés; lot *m* de marchandises; to buy a job lot of books, acheter des livres en vrac; to buy sth. as a job lot, acheter qch. à forfait; job-lot quantities, petites séries (de fabrication).

jobber, *n.* 1. ouvrier, -ière à la tâche 2. revendeur *m*; (*in contract work*) sous-entrepreneur *m* 3. *StExch:* (stock) jobber, contrepartiste *m.*

jobbing[1], *a.* 1. qui travaille à la tâche/à la pièce; jobbing workman, (ouvrier) façonnier (*m*); ouvrier à la tâche; ouvrier à façon; jobbing gardener, jardinier *m* à la journée 2. *Typ:* jobbing hand, homme *m* en conscience; jobbing work, ouvrage *m* de ville.

jobbing[2], *n.* 1. (*i*) ouvrage *m* à la tâche; (*ii*) travail *m* à façon 2. commerce *m* d'intermédiaire; vente *f* en demi-gros 3. *StExch:* (*a*) courtage *m* (de titres en gros et en détail); *Pej:* stock jobbing, agiotage *m* (*b*) jobbing in contangoes, arbitrage *m* de reports 4. *Typ:* travaux *mpl* de ville.

jobless, 1. *a* sans travail/en chômage 2. *n.* the jobless, less sans-travail *inv*/les chômeurs.

join, *v.tr.* 1. the documents joined to the report, les documents annexés au procès-verbal 2. (*a*) to join a company, (commencer à) travailler chez . . . (*b*) to join an association, adhérer à une organisation/ devenir membre d'une société.

joint, *a.* 1. (*of work, etc.*) commun/en commun/conjoint; joint commission, commission *f* mixte; joint committee, comité *m* mixte/paritaire; joint orders/ ordering, groupage *m* de commandes; joint report, rapport collectif; joint undertaking/venture, entreprise *f* en participation; coparticipation *f*; *Bank:* **joint account,** compte joint/compte (en) commun; **deal on joint account,** opération *f* en participation; *Fin:* **joint shares,** actions indivises; **joint stock,** capital social; **joint stock bank,** société *f* de dépôt; **joint stock company,** société anonyme par actions; *Publ:* **edition published at the joint expense of publisher and author,** édition (faite) en participation **2.** co-/associé; **joint author,** coauteur *m*; **joint beneficiaries,** bénéficiaires conjoints/indivis; **joint creditor,** cocréancier, -ière; **joint debt,** dette *f* conjointe; **joint debtor,** codébiteur *m*; **joint director/directress,** codirecteur, -trice; **joint holder,** codétenteur *m*; **joint management,** cogérance *f*/cogestion *f*/codirection *f*; **joint manager/manageress,** cogérant(e)/codirecteur, -trice; **joint obligation,** coobligation *f*; **joint owner,** copropriétaire *mf*; **joint ownership,** copropriété *f*; **joint partner,** coassocié(e); **joint partnership,** coassociation *f*; **joint production,** coproduction *f*; **joint purchase,** coacquisition *f*; **joint purchaser,** coacquéreur *m*; **joint seller,** covendeur, -euse; **joint surety (contract),** cautionnement *m* solidaire; **joint tenant,** colocataire *mf*.

jointly, *adv.* ensemble/conjointement; **we manage the firm jointly,** nous sommes cogérants de la maison; **to start a company jointly with . . . ,** créer une société en commun avec . . . ; **to possess sth. jointly,** posséder qch. conjointement/indivisément/par indivis; *Jur:* **jointly liable/jointly responsible,** solidaire; **to act jointly,** agir solidairement; **jointly and severally liable,** responsables conjointement et solidairement.

journal, *n.* (*a*) *Book-k:* (livre) journal (*m*); **journal entry,** écriture *f* comptable (*b*) revue *f*; **do you subscribe to our (professional) journal?** êtes-vous abonné à notre revue professionnelle?

journalism, *n.* journalisme *m.*

journalist, *n.* journaliste *mf.*

journalize, *v.tr. Book-k:* porter (une écriture comptable) au journal/journaliser.

judge, *n.* juge *m.*

judgement, *n.* **to give judgement,** prononcer un jugement/un arrêt.

jump^1, *n.* **jump in prices,** brusque hausse *f* des prix; **rents have gone up with a jump,** les loyers ont fait un bond.

jump^2, *v.i.* **prices have jumped 10%,** les prix *m* ont monté/progressé de 10%.

jumpy, *a.* **the market is jumpy,** le marché est instable.

junior, *a. & n.* (*a*) (*in rank*) junior; subalterne (*m*); **junior clerk,** petit commis; **junior executive,** jeune cadre; **office junior,** employé(e) subalterne; **junior partner,** associé(e) en second; adjoint *m* (*b*) *Fin:* **junior stocks,** actions *f* de dividende.

jurisdiction, *n.* juridiction *f*; compétence *f*; **general jurisdiction of a court,** compétence générale d'une cour; **this matter does not come within our jurisdiction,** cette matière n'est pas de notre compétence.

K

kaffirs, *n.* valeurs or sud-africaines.

keen, *a.* **keen competition,** concurrence acharnée/âpre; **there is a keen demand for these stocks,** ces fonds sont activement recherchés; **keen prices,** prix compétitifs.

keep, *v.tr.* **1. keep dry,** craint l'humidité; **keep upright,** ne pas renverser **2. to keep an appointment,** aller à un rendez-vous **3. to keep the books,** tenir les livres/les écritures/la comptabilité **4.** tenir/avoir en magasin (des marchandises) **5. to keep prices down,** empêcher les prix de monter/d'augmenter; **to keep prices up,** maintenir les prix fermes **6. to keep £10 back from s.o.'s salary,** retenir (une somme de) £10 sur le salaire de qn.

key, *n.* (*a*) **key money,** pas *m* de porte (*b*) d'une importance capitale/vitale; **key factor,** facteur *m* clé; **key post,** poste *m* clé; **key industry,** industrie *f* clé; **key man,** cheville *f* (ouvrière)/pilier *m*/pivot *m* (d'un établissement, d'une organisation); **key personnel/workers/staff,** personnel *m* de base.

kickback, *n.* ristourne *f*; dessous-de-table *m*.

kilo/kilogram(me), *n. Meas:* kilogramme *m*/kilo *m* (*abbr.* kg) (= 2.2046 lb).

kilometre, *n. Meas:* kilomètre *m* (*abbr.* km) (= 0.6214 mile); **distance in kilometres,** distance *f* kilométrique.

kind, *n.* **to pay in kind,** payer en nature.

king-size(d), *n.* (format) géant; **king-sized cigarettes,** cigarettes extra longues.

kite, *n. Fin: F:* cerf-volant *m*; traite *f* en l'air; billet *m* de complaisance; **kite flyer,** tireur *m* en l'air/à découvert; **kite flying,** tirage *m* en l'air/en blanc; **to fly/to send up a kite,** tirer en l'air/tirer en blanc.

kitty, *n.* cagnotte *f*/caisse commune (d'un groupe).

knock, *n. Aut: Ins:* **knock-for-knock agreement,** convention entre compagnies d'assurance par laquelle chacune s'engage à dédommager son client, en cas d'accident, sans chercher à départager les responsabilités.

knockdown, *a.* **knockdown prices,** prix *m* minimums/les prix le plus bas; prix (de) réclame/prix-choc.

knock down[2], *v.tr.* **to knock down prices,** abaisser/réduire les prix considérablement.

knock-on, *n.* **they said that the knock-on effect of increases would be large,** ils ont dit que la répercussion des augmentations de salaires serait considérable.

know-how, *n.* savoir-faire *m*; expertise *f*; connaissances *f* techniques.

L

label[1], _n._ (_a_) étiquette _f_; **address label,** étiquette-adresse; **gummed label,** étiquette gommée; **(self-)adhesive/stick-on label,** étiquette adhésive/autocollante; auto-collant _m_; **tie-on label,** étiquette à œillet; **price label,** étiquette (portant le prix) (_b_) label _m_/étiquette; **own label goods,** marque _f_ d'un magasin particulier; **quality label,** label/étiquette de qualité; **guarantee label,** label/étiquette de garantie.

label[2], _v.tr._(_a_) étiqueter; apposer/attacher une étiquette à/coller une étiquette sur (un paquet, etc.) (_b_) attribuer un label (de garantie, de qualité, etc.) à (un produit).

labelling, _n._ (_a_) étiquetage _m_ (_b_) attribution _f_ d'un label (de garantie, de qualité).

labour, _n._ **1.** travail _m_; **manual labour,** travail manuel; travail de manœuvre; **material and labour,** main d'œuvre _f_ et matériel _m_; _Tail:_ tissu _m_ et façon _f_; **division of labour,** division _f_ du travail **2.** (_a_) main d'œuvre travailleurs _mpl_; **cheap labour,** main d'œuvre à bon marché; **labour force,** (_i_) effectif _m_; main d'œuvre (_ii_) _PolEc:_ population active; **local labour,** main d'œuvre locale; **skilled labour,** main d'œuvre qualifiée/spécialisée; **cost of labour,** prix _m_ de la main d'œuvre; **shortage of labour,** pénurie _f_/crise _f_/rareté _f_ de la main d'œuvre; **labour intensive industry,** industrie qui dépend d'une main d'œuvre considérable (_b_) **capital and labour,** le capital et la main d'œuvre; **labour disputes/conflicts/troubles,** conflits _m_ du travail; **labour unrest,** agitation ouvrière/malaise ouvrier; **labour market,** marché du travail; **labour relations,** relations syndicales/relations du travail; **Minister of Labour,** Ministre _m_ du travail; **International Labour Organization,** Organisation Internationale du Travail.

labourer, _n._ ouvrier _m_; travailleur manuel; **agricultural labourer,** ouvrier agricole.

labour-saving, _a._ qui rend le travail plus facile; **labour-saving device** = appareil électroménager.

lack[1], _n._ manque _m_/absence _f_/pénurie _f_ (de capitaux, de main d'œuvre, etc.); **lack of funds,** pénurie de fonds; **for lack of sufficient data,** à défaut de données suffisantes.

lack[2], _v.tr._ manquer de (disponibilités, etc.); faire défaut; **he lacks experience,** manque d'expérience; **they lack capital,** les capitaux _m_ leur font défaut.

laden, _a._ _Nau:_ chargé; **fully laden ship,** navire _m_ en pleine charge; **laden in bulk,** chargé en vrac; **laden draught,** tirant _m_ d'eau en charge.

lading, _n._ (_a_) chargement _m_ (d'un navire) (_b_) embarquement _m_/mise _f_ à bord (de marchandises); **bill of lading,** connaissement _m_.

land[1], _n._ _Jur:_ terre(s) _f(pl)_; fonds _m_ de terre/biens-fonds _m_/propriété foncière; **land and buildings,** terrains _m_ et bâtiments _m_; **land tax,** contributions foncières (sur les propriétés non bâties); **land agent,** (_i_) intendant _m_/régisseur _m_ d'un domaine; administrateur foncier (_ii_) agent immobilier; **land agency,** (_i_) agence immobilière (_ii_) gérance _f_ d'immeubles/de propriétés; **land registration,** inscription *f* (d'un bien-fonds) au cadastre; **land register,** registre *m* du cadastre; **land registry (office),** bureau *m*/service *m* du cadastre.

land², *v.tr.* **1.** débarquer (des marchandises **2.** *v.i. Av:* atterrir.

landed, *a.* **landed cost,** prix *m* à quai.

landing, *n.* (*i*) *Nau: etc.* débarquement *m*/ mise *f* à quai (*ii*) *Av:* atterrissage *m*; **landing certificate,** certificat *m* de déchargement; **landing charges,** frais *mpl* (*i*) de déchargement (*ii*) *Av:* d'atterrissage; **landing permit/order,** permis *m* (*i*) de débarquement (*ii*) *Av:* d'atterrissage.

landlady, *n.* la propriétaire.

landlord, *n.* le propriétaire.

landowner, *n.* propriétaire *m* foncier.

language, *n.* **business language,** langue *f* des affaires/langage de gestion; **computer language/machine language,** langage machine.

lapse¹, *n.* **1.** déchéance *f* (d'un droit) **2.** laps *m* de temps; **after a lapse of three months,** après un délai de trois mois/au bout de trois mois.

lapse², *v.i. Jur:* (*of right, patent, etc.*) se périmer/tomber en désuétude; *Ins:* (*of policy, etc.*) cesser d'être en vigueur; **to have lapsed,** être périmé.

lapsed, *a.* (billet, etc.) périmé; *Jur:* (droit) périmé; (contrat) caduc.

large, *a.* **a large sum,** une grosse/forte somme; une somme considérable; **to incur large losses,** éprouver/subir des pertes sensibles; **to trade on a large scale,** traiter des affaires sur une grande échelle.

last, *a.* **last in first out (Lifo),** dernier entré, premier sorti.

late¹, *a.* **1. late delivery,** livraison retardée **2. latest date,** terme *m* de rigueur/délai *m* de rigueur **3. latest models,** derniers modèles; **the very latest improvements,** les tout derniers perfectionnements.

late², *adv.* en retard.

launch, *v.tr.* **to launch a product,** lancer un produit/mettre un produit sur le marché.

launching, *n.* lancement *m* (de nouveaux produits).

launder, *v.tr.* lessiver; **the money is laundered,** on lessive l'argent/on fait le lessivage de l'argent.

law, *n.* **1.** (*a*) **labour laws,** législation *f* du travail (*b*) loi *f*; *PolEc:* **law of supply and demand,** loi de l'offre et de la demande; **law of diminishing returns,** loi des rendements décroissants **2.** droit *m*; **commercial law/mercantile law/law merchant,** droit commercial; code *m* de commerce; **Company law,** droit des sociétés; **international law,** droit international; **maritime law,** droit maritime; **law of contract** = droit des obligations **3.** (*justice*) **case law,** jurisprudence *f*; **court of law,** cour *f* de justice; tribunal *m*; **to go to law,** avoir recours à la justice/recourir à la justice/aller en justice; **action at law,** action *f* en justice; **law costs,** frais *mpl* de procédure; **law department,** bureau *m*/ service *m* du contentieux; le contentieux.

lawful, *a.* **1.** légal **2.** permis/licite; **lawful trade,** trafic *m* licite **3.** (droit etc.) légitime; (contrat) valide; **lawful currency,** cours légal.

lawfully, *adv.* légalement; légitimement.

lawfulness, *n.* légalité *f*; légitimité *f*.

lawsuit, *n.* procès *m*; poursuites *f* judiciaires; litige *m*; *F:* affaire *f*; **to bring a lawsuit against s.o.,** intenter un procès à qn.

lawyer, *n.* (*i*) avocat *m* (*ii*) avoué *m*.

lay-away, *n.* **lay-away plan,** vente réservée/vente à terme.

laying off, *n.* licenciement *m* (de la main d'œuvre).

lay-off, *n. Ind:* (période de) licenciement *m* (temporaire); chômage *m* technique; **the lay-offs,** les employés en chômage technique.

lay off, *v.tr.* (*a*) licencier/renvoyer temporairement (des ouvriers); mettre des employés en chômage technique (*b*) *Ins:* **to lay off a risk,** effectuer une réassurance.

leading, *a.* (*a*) **leading shares,** valeurs dirigeantes/marquantes; **a leading shareholder,** un des principaux actionnaires/un gros actionnaire (*b*) **available from all leading jewellers,** en vente chez tous les grands bijoutiers; **one of the leading firms in the country,** une des plus importantes entreprises du pays (*c*) **leading article,** article *m* (de) réclame.

leaf, *n.* volant *m* (d'un chèque).

lease[1], *n.* (*a*) *Jur:* bail *m*; **long lease,** bail à long terme/à longue échéance; bail emphytéotique; **operating lease,** contrat *m* de location-exploitation; **to take (sth.) on lease,** louer/prendre (qch.) à bail; affermer (une terre); **to take out a lease on a house,** louer une maison/prendre une maison à bail; **to renew a lease,** renouveler un bail; **to sign a lease,** signer un bail; **expiration of a lease,** expiration *f* d'un bail; **my lease runs out in May,** mon bail expire en mai (*b*) **oil and gas leases,** concessions pétrolières et gazéifères.

lease[2], *v.tr.* **1. to lease (out),** louer/céder (une maison) à bail; affermer (une terre) **2.** prendre (une maison) à bail/louer (une maison); affermer (une terre).

lease-back, *n.* cession *f* de bail/cession-bail *f*.

leasehold, 1. *n.* (*a*) tenure *f* à bail, *esp.* tenure en vertu d'un bail emphytéotique (*b*) immeuble *m* loué à bail **2.** *a.* tenu à bail.

leaseholder, *n.* locataire *mf*.

leasing, *n.* (*i*) crédit-bail *m*/leasing *m* (*ii*) location-vente *f*; **equipment leasing,** crédit-bail mobilier.

leather, *n.* cuir *m*; **the leather industry,** l'industrie *f* du cuir; **fancy leather goods,** maroquinerie *f*.

leave, *n.* **leave (of absence),** congé *m*; autorisation *f*/permission *f* de s'absenter; **sick leave,** congé de maladie; **annual leave,** congé annuel; **leave pay,** salaire *m* de congé; **on leave,** en congé.

ledger, *n. Book-k:* grand(-)livre *m*/livre *m* de comptabilité générale; **bought ledger,** grand(-)livre des achats; **sales ledger,** grand(-)livre des ventes; **ledger clerk,** employé(e) aux écritures; **loose-leaf ledger,** grand(-)livre biblorhapte; **payroll ledger,** grand(-)livre de paie.

legal, *a.* **1.** légal; licite; **legal commerce,** commerce *m* licite **2.** (*a*) légal; judiciaire; juridique; selon les lois; **legal charges,** (*i*) (*in an action*) frais *m* judiciaires (*ii*) (*in a transaction*) frais juridiques; **legal document,** acte *m* authentique/document *m* juridique; **legal entity,** personne civile/morale (*b*) (*of bank, etc.*) **legal department,** service *m*/bureau *m* du contentieux; le contentieux; **legal expert,** jurisconsulte *m*; avocat *m* conseil; **legal adviser,** conseiller *m* juridique; **to take legal advice,** consulter un avocat/un notaire; **to take legal action,** engager des poursuites judiciaires.

legality, *n.* légalité *f*.

legalization, *n.* légalisation *f*.

legalize, *v.tr.* légaliser/certifier/authentiquer (un document).

legally, *adv.* légalement; (*i*) licitement (*ii*) judiciairement (*iii*) juridiquement; **legally responsible,** responsable en droit.

lend, *v.tr.* **to lend sth. to s.o./to lend s.o. sth.,** prêter qch. à qn; **to lend money at interest,** prêter de l'argent à intérêt; **lend against security,** prêter sur nantissement; **to lend stock on contango,** placer des titres en report.

lender, *n.* prêteur, -euse.

lending, *n.* prêt *m* (d'un objet, d'argent); *Fin:* prestation *f* (de capitaux); *StExch:* placement *m* (de titres en report); **lending bank,** banque *f* de crédit; **lending limit,** plafond *m* de crédit; **lending officer,** agent prêteur (d'un établissement de crédit); *Bank:* **minimum lending rate,** taux (officiel) de l'escompte.

less, 1. *a.* **of less value,** d'une valeur moindre/de moindre valeur; **quantities/ sums less than . . .,** quantités *f*/sommes *f* au-dessous de . . . **2.** *prep.* **purchase price less 10%,** prix *m* d'achat moins 10%; **interest less tax amounts to £50,** les intérêts nets s'élèvent à £50 **3.** *n.* **to sell sth. at less than cost price,** vendre qch. à moins du prix de revient/à un prix inférieur au prix de revient.

lessee, *n.* **1.** locataire *mf* (à bail) (d'un immeuble, etc.); preneur, -euse **2.** concessionnaire *mf.*

lessor, *n.* bailleur, -eresse; propriétaire *mf.*

let, *v.tr.* louer (une maison); **house to (be) let,** maison *f* à louer.

let-out, *n.* *F:* **let-out (clause),** clause *f* échappatoire.

letter, *n.* (*a*) lettre *f*; **business letter,** lettre d'affaires/lettre commerciale; **covering letter,** note/lettre explicative; lettre d'introduction/lettre d'envoi; **follow-up letter,** lettre de relance (à un client); **letter file,** classeur *m* de lettres/classe-lettres *m inv*; **letter of acknowledgement,** accusé *m* de réception; **letter of application,** lettre de demande (d'emploi, etc.); **letter of appointment,** lettre de nomination/d'affectation; **letter of complaint,** (lettre de) réclamation *f*; **letter of reference,** lettre de recommandation; **set-form letter,** lettre type/lettre passe-partout/lettre modèle; **side letter,** papillon *m* (*b*) *Post:* **air(mail) letter,** (*i*) lettre par avion (*ii*) aérogramme *m*; **express letter,** lettre exprès; **letter rate,** tarif (d'affranchissement des) lettres; **registered letter,** lettre recommandée; **to send a letter first class** = envoyer une lettre à tarif normal; **to send a letter second class** = envoyer une lettre à tarif réduit (*c*) **letters patent,** brevet *m* d'invention (*d*) **letter of advice,** lettre d'avis; **letter of credit,** lettre de crédit; **letter of exchange,** lettre de change; **letter of guaranty,** lettre d'aval; *StExch:* **letter of allotment,** avis *m* d'attribution/de répartition.

letter-card, *n.* carte-lettre *f.*

letting, *a.* **letting agency,** agence *f* de location.

level[1], *n.* niveau *m* (des prix, des salaires, etc.); **to maintain prices at a high level,** maintenir les prix à un niveau élevé.

level[2], *v.tr.* niveler (des cours, des taux, etc.).

levelling, *n.* nivellement *m* (des revenus, etc.).

level off, *v.i.* (des prix, etc.) se stabiliser.

level out, *v.i.* (*of prices*) s'équilibrer.

leverage, *n.* (*i*) ratio *m* d'endettement (*ii*) effet *m* de levier.

leveraged, *a.* **the company is highly leveraged,** la société est fortement endettée.

levy[1], *n.* **1.** perception (d'une taxe, d'un impôt) **2.** impôt *m*/contribution *f*; **capital levy,** prélèvement *m* sur le capital; *EEC:* **(variable import) levy,** prélèvement *m* (à l'importation).

levy[2], *v.tr.* (*a*) percevoir (une taxe, un impôt); **to levy a duty on goods,** imposer des marchandises; frapper des marchandises d'un droit (*b*) **£50 a year is levied on members salaries for the pension fund,** les traitements des membres sont sujets à un prélèvement annuel de £50 comme contribution à la caisse de retraite.

levying, *n.* perception *f* (d'impôts).

liability, *n.* **1.** (*a*) *Jur:* responsabilité *f*; **joint liability,** responsabilité conjointe/

collective; **several liability,** responsabilité séparée; **joint and several liability,**
responsabilité (conjointe et) solidaire/
solidarité *f* (*b*) **third party liability,**
responsabilité au tiers (*c*) **limited liability,** responsabilité limitée; **limited
liability company,** (*i*) société *f* à
responsabilité limitée (*ii*) société
anonyme (*d*) **employer's liability,**
responsabilité patronale/de l'employeur
(pour les accidents du travail) (*e*) **absolute
liability,** responsabilité totale/obligation
inconditionnelle; **contractual liability,**
responsabilité contractuelle; obligation
contractée souscrite **2.** *Fin:* (*a*) **contingent liability,** (*i*) engagements éven-
tuels; passif éventuel/exigible (*ii*) tierce
caution; *Bank:* **contingent liability in respect of acceptances,** débiteurs *mpl* par
aval (*b*) *pl.* **liabilities,** ensemble *m* des
dettes; obligations/valeurs passives/det-
tes passives; le passif; (*in bankruptcy*)
masse passive (d'une liquidation après
faillite); **assets and liabilities,** actif *m* et
passif; **current liabilities,**dettes à court
terme/passif exigible/exigibilités *f*; **deferred liabilities,** passif reporté; **long-
term liabilities,** dettes/passif à long terme; **to meet one's liabilities,** faire face à
ses engagements/à ses échéances (*c*)
(*on bills of exchange*) encours *m*; **liability as drawer,** encours tiré; **liability as
maker/as transferor,** encours cédant.

liable, *a.* **1.** *Jur:* responsable/passible (**for,**
de); **liable at law,** responsable civilement
2. sujet/assujetti/tenu/astreint (**to,** à);
redevable/passible (**to,** de); **liable to
stamp duty,** assujetti au timbre; **liable to a
tax,** assujetti à un impôt; redevable/
passible d'un impôt; **dividends liable to
income tax,** dividendes soumis à l'impôt
sur le revenu; **to make sth. liable to a tax,**
assujettir qch. à un impôt **3.** sujet/exposé
(**to,** à); **goods liable to go bad,** marchandises *f* susceptibles de s'avarier.

libel, *n.* diffamation *f*; **to sue for libel,**
intenter un procès en diffamation.

liberate, *v.tr. Fin:* **to liberate capital,**
mobiliser des capitaux.

liberation, *n. Fin:* **liberation of capital,**
mobilisation *f* de capitaux.

licence[1]**,** *n.* permis *m*/autorisation *f*/
licence *f*/privilège *m*; **licence to sell beer,
wines and spirits,** permis/licence de débit
de boissons; **trading licence,** carte *f* de
commerce; **manufacturing licence,** brevet *m*/licence de fabrication; **exclusive
licence,** licence exclusive; **made/manu-
factured under licence,** construit/
fabriqué sous licence; **import licence,**
licence d'importation; **export licence,**
licence d'exportation; **licence holder,**
titulaire *mf* d'un permis; **driving licence,**
permis de conduire; **heavy goods (vehicle)
licence,** permis poids lourds.

licence[2]**,** *v.tr. NAm:* =**license**[1].

license[1]**,** *v.tr.* accorder un permis/une
autorisation/une licence/un privilège à
(qn); **licensed to sell beer, wines and
spirits,** autorisé à vendre des boissons
alcoolisées/*FrCan:* licencié; **to be licensed to sell sth.,** avoir un permis de vente/
avoir l'autorisation de vendre qch.

license[2]**,** *n. NAm:* =**licence**[1].

licensed, *a.* autorisé(e); **licensed premises** = débit *m* de boissons (avec licence
de plein exercice).

licensee, *n.* titulaire *mf*/détenteur, -trice
d'un permis (pour vendre de l'alcool).

licensing, *n.* autorisation *f* (à faire qch.);
octroi *m* d'un permis/d'une autorisation
(à qn); **cross licensing,** concession *f*
réciproque de licences; **licensing requirements,** conditions *f* d'autorisation;
licensing acts/laws, lois relatives aux
débits de boissons (alcooliques).

lien, *n. Jur:* privilège *m* (sur un bien
meuble, etc.); droit *m* de rétention;
general lien, privilège général; **vendor's
lien,** privilège du vendeur; **(possessory)
lien on goods,** droit de rétention de
marchandises.

life, *n.* (*a*) **working life,** période *f*/années
fpl d'activité (*b*) **life annuity/life pen-**

sion, pension/rente viagère; pension à vie; **life interest,** usufruit *m* (d'un bien); viager *m*; rente viagère; **life tenant,** usufruitier (*c*) *Ins:* **life assurance/life insurance,** assurance *f* sur la vie/assurance-vie *f* (*d*) *Fin:* **life of a loan,** durée *f* d'un emprunt; **(product) life expectancy,** durée *f* (utile) (d'un produit)/courbe *f* de vie (d'un produit).

limit, *n.* (*a*) **age limit,** limite *f* d'âge; **time limit,** délai *m* (de paiement, etc.); **size limit/weight limit,** limite de dimension/ de poids; **limit of free delivery area,** rayon *m*/périmètre *m* de livraison gratuite; *Fin: etc:* **credit limit/limit of credit,** limite/ plafond *m* d'un crédit; **they set voluntary limits to their exports,** ils autolimitent leurs exportations/ils appliquent une limitation volontaire de leurs exportations.

limitation, *n.* **1.** limitation *f*/restriction *f*; **limitation of liability,** limitation de responsabilité **2.** *Jur:* prescription (extinctive); **term of limitation,** délai *m* de prescription; (*in a suit*) **time limitation,** péremption *f*.

limited, *a.* limité/borné/restreint; **limited market,** marché étroit/restreint; **the expenditure, however limited . . .,** les dépenses, si réduites soient-elles . . .; **limited (liability) company (Ltd),** (*i*) société *f* à responsabilité limitée (SARL) (*ii*) société anonyme (SA); **limited partnership,** société en commandite; *StExch:* **limited prices,** cours limités.

limiting, *a.* limitatif; *Jur:* **limiting clause,** clause/condition restrictive (d'un contrat, etc.).

line, *n.* **1. air line,** compagnie *f* aérienne; **shipping line,** compagnie de navigation; messageries *f* maritimes **2.** série *f* (d'articles); gamme *f* (de produits); **leading lines,** articles *m*/spécialités *f* de réclame **3. assembly line,** chaîne *f* de montage **4.** *Bank:* **credit line,** ligne *f* de crédit/ autorisation *f* de crédit **5. line organ-**

ization, organisation hiérarchique/verticale; **line and staff organization,** structure mixte.

liner, *n.* (*i*) paquebot *m* de grande ligne/ liner *m* (*ii*) (avion) gros porteur *m*; **cargo liner,** navire de charge régulier; **liner freighting,** affrètement *m* à la cueillette; **liner rate,** fret *m* à (la) cueillette.

liquid, *a. Fin:* (argent) liquide/disponible; **liquid assets,** valeurs *f* disponibles/actif *m* liquide/disponibilités *fpl*; **liquid debt,** dette *f* liquide/claire.

liquidate, *v.tr.* liquider (une société, une dette); amortir (une dette); mobiliser (des capitaux).

liquidation, *n.* liquidation *f* (d'une société, d'une dette); amortissement *m* (d'une dette); mobilisation *f* (de capitaux); (*of company*) **to go into liquidation,** déposer son bilan; **compulsory liquidation,** liquidation forcée; **voluntary liquidation,** liquidation volontaire; **liquidation subject to supervision of court,** liquidation judiciaire.

liquidator, *n.* liquidateur, -trice (d'une société en liquidation).

liquidity, *n. Fin:* liquidité *f* (d'une dette); **cash liquidity,** liquidités; **liquidity ratio,** coefficient *m*/taux *m* de liquidité.

list¹, *n.* (*a*) liste *f*; bordereau *m*; inventaire *m* (d'actif, de passif, de portefeuille); *Fin:* **list of applicants/of applications,** liste des souscripteurs (à un emprunt, etc.); *StExch:* **list of quotations,** bulletin *m* des cours; **official list,** cote officielle; *Cust:* **free list,** liste des marchandises importées en franchise; *Bank: etc:* **list of investments,** (bordereau de) portefeuille *m*; **list of bills for collection/for discount,** bordereau d'effets à l'encaissement/à l'escompte; bordereau d'encaissement/ d'escompte; **mailing list,** liste d'envoi; liste des abonnés (*b*) **list price,** prix *m* (de) catalogue; prix public; **(current) price list,** tarif *m*; **market price list,** mercuriale *f*.

list², *v.tr.* inscrire/mettre/porter (des

listing	110	loan

noms, etc.) sur une liste; enregistrer (qch.); inventorier (des marchandises, etc.); *Cmptr:* lister; *Fin:* **listed securities/stock,** valeurs cotées/inscrites à la cote (officielle); **these articles are listed in the catalogue,** ces articles figurent dans le catalogue.

listing, *n. Cmptr:* liste *f*/listage *m*; sortie *f* d'imprimante.

liter, *n. NAm:* = **litre.**

literature, *n.* prospectus *m*/brochures *fpl.*

litre, *n. Meas:* litre *m* (*abbr.* l) (= 0.2200 gallon).

live, *a. Fin:* **live claims,** créances *f* valables/ qui subsistent (à l'égard d'un établissement de crédit).

lively, *a. Fin:* (*of market*) animé.

living, *n.* **1. cost of living,** coût *m* de la vie; **standard of living,** niveau *m* de vie **2. living allowance,** indemnité *f* de séjour; **living wage,** minimum vital.

load[1], *n.* (*a*) charge *f*/chargement *m* (d'un camion, d'un navire, d'un avion, etc.); **average load,** charge moyenne; **axle load,** charge par essieu; **commercial load/pay load,** charge utile; **constant/dead load,** charge constante/poids à vide/poids mort; **load carrying capacity,** charge utile; charge maximale/charge limite; **load limit,** charge limite; **maximum load,** charge maximale; **permitted pay load/ regulation carrying capacity,** charge utile réglementaire; **test load,** charge d'essai **lorry load**/*NAm:* **truck load,** charge complète (*b*) (*contents of vehicle*) camion *m* (de gravier, etc.); chargement *m*; cargaison *f* (d'un navire).

load[2], **1.** *v.tr.* (*a*) charger (un camion, un navire, etc.) (*b*) *Ins:* majorer (une prime); imposer une surprime **2.** *v.i.* (*of ship, etc.*) **to be loaded,** prendre charge; faire la cargaison; **loading for Bombay,** en charge pour Bombay; **ship loading,** navire *m* en chargement/en charge.

loaded, *a.* **1.** (camion, navire, etc.) chargé **2.** *Ins:* **loaded premium,** prime majorée.

loading, *n.* **1.** chargement *m* (d'un camion, d'un wagon, d'un navire, d'un avion); **bulk loading,** chargement en vrac; **loading point,** point *m* de chargement; **loading ramp/rack,** rampe *f* de chargement; **loading chute,** couloir *m* de chargement; **loading board,** pont volant; **loading bay,** quai *m* de chargement **2.** *Ins:* surprime *f*/ majoration *f* (d'une prime).

loan[1], *n.* **1.** (*i*) (*money lent*) prêt *m*/avance *f* (*ii*) (*money borrowed*) emprunt *m*/ avance *f*; **loan capital/loan stock,** capital-obligations *m*; **loan at interest,** prêt à intérêt; **loan at call/loan repayable on demand,** prêt/emprunt remboursable sur demande; **loan at notice,** prêt/emprunt à terme; **dead loan,** emprunt irrécouvrable; **long-term loan,** prêt/emprunt à long terme; **short(-term) loan,** prêt/emprunt à court terme; **time loan,** prêt/emprunt à terme fixe; **loan by the week,** prêt/emprunt à la petite semaine; **loan on collateral,** prêt sur gage/ sur nantissement; **loan on mortgage/ mortgage loan,** emprunt hypothécaire/ sur hypothèque; **loan on securities/on stock,** emprunt sur titres; **loan on trust,** prêt d'honneur; **secured loan,** prêt/ emprunt garanti; **unsecured loan/loan without security/loan on overdraft,** prêt/emprunt à découvert; **tied loan,** prêt conditionnel/emprunt à emploi spécifié; *MIns:* **loan on respondentia,** prêt/emprunt à la grosse sur facultés; **loan office,** (*i*) caisse *f* d'emprunts (*ii*) maison *f* de prêts; **loan bank,** caisse de prêt; **loan society/company,** société *f* de crédit; **loan charges,** frais financiers; **loan department,** service *m* des crédits; **loan certificate,** titre *m* de prêt; **to apply for a loan,** demander/solliciter un prêt; **application for a loan,** demande *f* de prêt; **to allow/to grant a loan,** accorder/consentir un prêt; **to contract/to raise/to take up a loan,** contracter/faire un emprunt; **to collect a loan,** toucher un emprunt; **to repay a loan,** amortir/rembourser un emprunt **2.** *Fin:* emprunt; **bank loan,** emprunt bancaire/de la banque; **government loan,** emprunt d'État; **public loan,** emprunt public; **per-petual loan,** emprunt perpétuel; **person-al loan,** emprunt personnel; **consolida-tion loan/funding loan,** emprunt de con-solidation; **consolidated loan,** emprunt consolidé; **conversion loan,** emprunt de conversion; **debenture loan,** emprunt obligataire; **indexed loan,** emprunt in-dexé; **to issue a loan,** émettre/lancer un emprunt; **issue of a loan,** émission *f* d'un emprunt; **to float a loan,** lancer un emprunt; **to subscribe to a loan,** souscrire à un emprunt.

loan[2], *v.tr.* prêter (**sth. to s.o.,** qch. à qn).

locking up, *n.* **locking up of capital,** immo-bilisation *f* de capitaux.

lock out, *v.tr. Ind:* lock(-)outer (le person-nel); fermer (les ateliers).

lockout, *n. Ind:* lock-out *m inv.*

lock up, *v.tr. Fin:* **to lock up capital,** immobiliser/bloquer/engager/des capi-taux.

loco, *adv.* loco; **loco price,** prix *m* loco.

lodge, *v.tr.* déposer/remettre; **to lodge money with s.o.,** consigner/déposer de l'argent chez qn; confier/remettre de l'argent à qn; **to lodge securities with a bank,** déposer des titres dans une ban-que; **securities lodged as collateral,** titres déposés/remis en nantissement.

lodging, lodg(e)ment, *n.* dépôt *m*/ consignation *f*/remise *f* (d'argent, de valeurs) (**with,** chez).

logo, *n.* logotype *m*.

long-dated, *a. Fin:* à longue échéance; **long-dated bills,** billets *m*/papiers *m* à longue échéance.

long-distance, *a.* **long-distance (tele-phone) call,** communication interur-baine; **long-distance lorry driver,** routier *m*.

longstanding, *a.* ancien; de longue date; de vieille date; **longstanding accounts,** notes dues depuis longtemps/vieux comptes.

long-term, *a.* à long terme; **long-term credit,** crédit *m*/emprunt *m* à long terme; **long-term debt,** dette *f* à long terme; **long-term policy,** politique *f* à long terme/à longue échéance.

loophole, *n.* échappatoire *f*/porte *f* de sortie.

loose, *a.* **loose cash/change,** menue mon-naie; **loose goods,** marchandises *f* en vrac.

lorry, *n.* camion *m*; **five-ton lorry,** camion de cinq tonnes; **heavy lorry,** camion lourd/de fort tonnage; poids lourd; **arti-culated lorry,** semi-remorque *fm*; **lorry driver,** conducteur *m*/chauffeur *m* (*i*) de camion (*ii*) de poids lourd; *F:* routier *m*.

lose, *v.tr. (a)* perdre (qch.) *(b)* **to lose in value,** perdre de sa valeur *(c)* **to lose a customer,** perdre un client.

loss, *n.* **1.** perte *f*; **loss of custom,** perte de clientèle; **loss of market,** perte de marché **2.** *(a)* déficit *m*; **to sustain/suffer heavy losses,** subir de grosses/fortes pertes; **to make up one's losses,** compenser ses pertes; **dead loss,** perte sèche; **to sell at a loss,** vendre à perte/mévendre; **sale of goods at a loss,** mévente *f* de marchandi-ses; **to cut one's losses,** faire la part du feu *(b) Ins:* sinistre *m*; **to estimate the loss,** évaluer le sinistre; **loss assessment,** fixation des dommages; **(actual) total loss,** perte totale **3.** *Ind: Trans:* freinte *f*/ frainte *f*/diminution *f* (de poids d'un produit en cours de fabrication ou de transport); **loss in transit,** freinte/déchet *m* de route.

loss(-)leader, *n.* article-réclame *m*/ article *m* en réclame (vendu à perte); article/produit *m* d'appel.

lot, *n.* **1.** *Fin:* **the debentures are redeemed by lot,** les obligations sont rachetées par voie de tirage **2.** *(a) (at auction)* lot *m (b)* lot; paquet *m*; **lot of goods,** lot de mar-chandises; **to buy in one lot,** acheter en bloc; *Fin:* **lot of shares,** paquet de titres/ d'actions; **to sell shares in small lots,** vendre des actions par petits paquets.

lottery, *n.* loterie *f*; **lottery ticket,** billet *m* de loterie; *Fin:* **lottery loan,** emprunt *m* à lots.

low[1], *a.* bas; **low price,** bas prix; prix faible; **low wages,** salaires peu élevés; **at a low figure/at a low price,** à bas prix/à bon compte/à bon marché; **to keep prices low,** maintenir les prix bas; **the lowest price,** le dernier prix; **prices are at their lowest,** les prix sont au plus bas; **the rate of exchange is low,** le taux du change est bas.

low[2], *n.* **the share index has reached an all-time low,** l'indice des actions est descendu à son plus bas niveau; **to reach a new low,** descendre à un niveau encore jamais atteint.

lower, *v.tr.* rabaisser (un prix); **to lower rents,** diminuer/baisser les loyers; **to lower the minimum lending rate,** abaisser le taux de l'escompte.

lowering, *n.* **lowering of prices,** rabais *m*/réduction *f* (de prix).

luggage, *n.* bagages *mpl;* **hand luggage/cabin luggage,** bagages à main; **free luggage allowance,** franchise de bagages; **luggage registration office,** (bureau d') enregistrement *m* (des bagages); **registered luggage,** bagages enregistrés; **(un)checked luggage,** bagages (non) enregistrés.

lump, *n.* **1. to sell sth. in the lump,** vendre qch. en bloc/en gros/globalement; **lump sum,** (*i*) montant global/somme globale; prix global (*ii*) prix forfaitaire; paiement *m* forfaitaire; **lump sum contract,** forfait *m* **2.** *F:* **the Lump,** ouvriers indépendants (qui évitent le fisc).

luxury, *n.* **luxury goods,** articles *m*/produits *m*/objets *m* de luxe; **luxury tax,** taxe *f* de luxe.

M

machine, *n.* (*a*) (*for office use, etc.*) **adding machine,** machine à additionner/à calculer; **copying machine,** machine à (poly)copier; duplicateur *m*; **dictating machine,** machine à dicter (*b*) **machine production,** production *f* en série/production à la machine/production mécanisée; **machine work,** travail *m* à la machine; usinage *m*; **machine made,** fait à la machine/en série; **vending machine,** distributeur *m* automatique (*c*) **the industrial machine,** les rouages *m*/l'organisation *f* de l'industrie.

machinery, *n.* **administrative machinery,** l'appareil administratif/la machine administrative; *Fin:* **compensation machinery,** mécanisme de compensation.

macro-economic, *a.* macro-économique.

macro-economics, *n.pl.* macro-économie *f*.

made, *a.* fait/fabriqué/confectionné; **made in France,** fabriqué en France; **French made cars,** voitures de fabrication française; *see also* **make**[2].

made-up, *a.* **made-up box,** caisse assemblée.

mag, *n.* = **magazine.**

magazine, *n.* revue *f*/publication *f*; périodique *m*; **fashion magazine,** journal *m*/revue de mode; **illustrated magazine,** revue illustrée/magazine *m*; *Publ:* **magazine rights,** droits *m* de reproduction dans les périodiques.

magistrate, *n.* magistrat *m*; **magistrates' court,** tribunal *m* d'instance.

mail[1], *n.* **1.** courrier *m*; lettres *fpl*; **incoming mail,** courrier (à l')arrivée; **outgoing mail,** courrier (au) départ; **inward mail,** courrier en provenance (*i*) de l'étranger (*ii*) de la province; **outward mail,** courrier (en partance) (*i*) pour l'étranger (*ii*) pour la province; **to open one's mail/to deal with one's mail,** dépouiller/lire son courrier; **we put it in the mail yesterday,** nous l'avons mis à la poste hier **2. mail order,** commande *f* par correspondance; **mail order business,** (achat et) vente *f* par correspondance (VPC)/sur catalogue; **mail order firm/house,** maison *f* de vente par correspondance; **mail order catalogue,** catalogue *m* de vente par correspondance **3. direct mail advertising,** publicité directe (par correspondance).

mail[2], *v.tr.* envoyer par la poste/expédier (une lettre, un paquet) par la poste/mettre (une lettre) à la poste.

mailable, *a.* qu'on peut envoyer par la poste.

mailing, *n.* envoi *m* (publicitaire) par la poste/publipostage *m*; **direct mailing,** publicité directe (par correspondance); **mailing list,** liste *f* de diffusion; liste d'adresses; **mailing piece/mailing shot,** prospectus *m*/dépliant *m*/envoi *m* (de publicité directe); **please add our name to your mailing list,** veuillez nous faire parvenir régulièrement votre documentation/vos catalogues/vos tarifs.

main, *a.* principal; premier; essentiel; **main office,** direction (générale); siège social; **factory contained in three main buildings,** usine *f* en trois corps de bâtiment.

maintain, *v.tr.* (*a*) entretenir (des relations, une correspondance) (*b*) **to maintain the exchange above the gold-point,** maintenir le change au-dessus du gold-point; **the dividend maintains at 5%,** le dividende se maintient à 5%.

maintenance, *n.* **1. resale price maintenance,** prix imposés **2.** (*a*) entretien *m*/conservation *f* (du matériel, des bâtiments, etc.); maintenance *f*; **planned maintenance,** maintenance programmée/entretien systématique; **preventive maintenance,** entretien préventif; **routine maintenance/scheduled maintenance,** entretien courant/périodique/de routine; **maintenance allowance,** allocation *f* d'entretien; **maintenance charges/maintenance expenses,** frais *mpl* d'entretien; **maintenance equipment,** matériel *m* d'entretien; **maintenance personnel/maintenance staff,** personnel *m* d'entretien/équipe(s) *f(pl)* d'entretien; **maintenance engineer,** ingénieur *m*/technicien *m* d'entretien (*b*) **maintenance programme/maintenance project,** programme *m* de maintenance; **maintenance requirements,** moyens *m* de maintenance exigés/indispensables; **maintenance resources,** moyens de maintenance (dont on dispose); **maintenance service,** location *f* entretien **3.** *Jur:* aide pécuniaire (apportée à une des parties).

majority, *n.* majorité *f* (des voix, etc.); **absolute majority,** majorité absolue; **majority decision,** décision prise à la majorité (des voix); **majority holding/interest/stake,** participation *f* majoritaire.

make[1], *n.* (*a*) façon *f*/forme *f*/fabrication *f*/construction *f* (*b*) marque *f* (d'un produit); **of French make,** de fabrication française; **our own make,** notre propre marque; **cars of all makes,** voitures de toutes marques; **a good make (of car, etc.),** (voiture, etc.) de marque connue/d'excellente fabrication; **standard make,** marque courante.

make[2], *v.tr.* **1.** (*a*) fabriquer/faire/ construire (une machine, une boîte, etc.) (*b*) *Fin:* **to make a promissory note,** souscrire un billet à ordre; **to make a bill of exchange,** libeller une lettre de change (*c*) **to make a deal**/to make a payment, effectuer/faire un versement (*d*) **to make a speech,** faire un discours (*e*) **to make an appointment,** prendre rendez-vous **2.** (*acquire*) faire (de l'argent); **to make £100 a week,** gagner/se faire £100 par semaine; **to make profits,** réaliser des bénéfices; **to make a deal,** conclure un marché/faire une affaire (avec qn); **to make a good deal by . . .,** tirer beaucoup de profit de . . .; (*of goods*) **to make a price,** rapporter un prix; **the prices made yesterday,** les cours pratiqués hier **3.** faire la fortune de . . .; **the cotton trade made Manchester,** l'industrie cotonnière a fait la prospérité de Manchester.

make out, *v.tr.* faire/établir/dresser (une liste, etc.); dresser/rédiger (un mémoire); établir/dresser/relever (un compte); **to make out a cheque to . . .,** faire/libeller/établir un chèque à l'ordre de . . .; **to make out a document in duplicate,** établir un document en double (exemplaire).

make over, *v.tr.* céder/transférer/transmettre (sth. to s.o., qch. à qn).

maker, *n.* (*a*) fabricant *m* (de drap, etc.); constructeur *m* (de machines); **biscuit maker,** fabricant de biscuits; **maker's price,** prix *m* de fabrique/prix départ usine (*b*) **maker (of a promissory note),** signataire *mf* (d'une lettre de change).

make up, 1. *v.tr.* (*a*) compléter/parfaire (une somme); exécuter (une commande); combler/suppléer à (un déficit); **to make up the difference,** combler la différence; **to make up the even money,** faire l'appoint (*b*) **to make up back payments,** régler/solder l'arriéré; **the lost day will be made up,** la journée chômée sera récupérée (*c*) faire (un paquet); **to make up goods into a parcel,** faire un paquet des marchandises (*d*) (*i*) faire/ confectionner/façonner (des vêtements) (*ii*) dresser (une liste) (*iii*) établir/arrêter (un compte) (*iv*) clôturer (les comptes); dresser (un bilan); **customer's own material made up** = on travaille à façon/tailleur *m* à façon; **to make up one's accounts,** arrêter ses comptes (*e*) rassembler/réunir (une compagnie); rassembler (une somme d'argent) (*f*) **the payments make up a considerable total,** ces versements atteignent une somme considérable **2.** *v.i.* (*a*) **to make up for one's losses,** compenser ses pertes; **that will make up for your losses,** cela vous dédommagera de vos pertes (*b*) **to make up on a competitor,** gagner sur un concurrent.

making, *n.* **1.** fabrication *f* (de la toile, du papier); confection *f*/façon *f* (de vêtements); construction *f* (d'une machine); création *f* (d'un poste); **decision making,** prise *f* de décision; **the making of a profit,** la réalisation d'un bénéfice **2. making up,** (*i*) compensation *f* (**for losses,** de pertes) (*ii*) arrêté *m* (de comptes); clôture *f* (d'un bilan); *StExch:* **making up price,** cours *m* de compensation.

maladjustment, *n. PolEc:* **maladjustment in the balance of trade,** déséquilibre *m* dans la balance commerciale.

maladministration, *n.* mauvaise administration/mauvaise gestion.

mala fide, *a. & adv. Jur:* de mauvaise foi.

mammoth, *a.* géant/énorme/gigantesque/colossal; **mammoth reduction,** énorme réduction; **on a mammoth scale,** sur une échelle colossale; **mammoth size,** paquet *m* géant.

man[1], *n.m.* **1.** homme; **a married man,** un homme marié; **a single man,** un homme non marié/célibataire/un célibataire; **a salaried man,** un salarié **2.** (*a*) **men's department,** rayon *m* (de vêtements pour) hommes (*b*) **the men on a site,** les ouvriers d'un chantier.

man[2], *v.tr.* fournir du personnel à (une organisation, etc.); assurer le service d'(une machine)/la manœuvre d'(un appareil); **to man a night-shift,** composer une équipe de nuit; **to man a stand,** (*i*) affecter du personnel à un stand/assurer la surveillance d'un stand (*ii*) garder un stand/surveiller un stand.

manage, *v.tr.* conduire (une entreprise, etc.); administrer/diriger/gérer (une affaire, une société, une banque, etc.); régir/gérer (une propriété, une exploitation agricole, etc.); mener (une affaire); **to manage s.o.'s affairs,** gérer les affaires de qn.

manageable, *a.* (*of undertaking*) praticable/faisable; **business grown too big to be manageable,** entreprise devenue si grosse qu'on ne peut plus la diriger.

management, *n.* **1.** gestion *f*/administration *f*/direction *f*/management *m* (d'une entreprise, d'une société etc.); **business management,** administration; gestion des affaires; **divisional management,** gestion cellulaire/par département; **office management,** organisation *f* des bureaux; **personnel/staff management,** direction *f*/administration *f* du personnel; **production management,** gestion/organisation de la production; **sales management,** direction commerciale/administration des ventes; **management accounting,** comptabilité *f* de gestion; **management chart,** organigramme *m*; **management committee,** comité *m* de direction; **management consultant,** ingénieur-conseil *m*; conseil *m* en gestion; conseiller *m* de direction; **management by objectives (MBO),** direction par objectifs (DPO); **management operating system,** système intégré de gestion; **management science,** science *f* de la gestion; **management team,** équipe *f* de direction; **management techniques,** techniques *f* de gestion; **management theory,** théorie *f* de la gestion de l'entreprise; **bad management,** mauvaise organisation; **owing to bad management,** faute d'organisation; **under new management,** (*i*) changement *m* de propriétaire (*ii*) nouvelle direction **2.** *coll.* les administrateurs *m*/les directeurs *m*/les dirigeants *m* (d'une société); l'administration/la direction; **general management,** direction générale; **joint management,** co-direction *f*; **management training,** formation des cadres; **middle management,** cadres moyens; **supervisory management,** maîtrise *f*; **top management,** cadres supérieurs/dirigeants; haute direction; **the management regrets any inconvenience caused by the rebuilding,** la direction s'excuse auprès des ses clients de tout inconvénient causé par les travaux (de construction).

manager, *n*. **1.** (*i*) directeur *m*/gérant *m* (d'une société, etc.); administrateur *m* (*ii*) régisseur *m* (d'une propriété); **account manager,** chargé *m*/responsable *m* de budget; **advertising/publicity manager,** chef *m* de publicité/directeur de la publicité/responsable du service (de) publicité; **art manager,** directeur artistique; **assistant manager,** sous-directeur *m*/sous-chef *m*; **branch manager,** directeur de succursale; **business manager,** (*i*) gérant d'affaires (*ii*) directeur commercial (*iii*) *Journ:* administrateur (*iv*) *Th:* impresario *m* (d'une chanteuse, etc.); (*in store*) **department manager,** chef de rayon (dans un grand magasin); **departmental manager,** (*i*) chef *m* de service (*ii*) (*in shop*) chef de rayon; **deputy manager,** directeur adjoint; **distribution manager,** chef de distribution; **district manager,** directeur régional; **engineering manager,** directeur technique; **general manager,** directeur général; **hotel manager,** directeur d'hôtel; **joint manager,** directeur adjoint/cogérant; **marketing manager,** directeur commercial/du marketing; **middle manager,** cadre moyen; **office manager,** chef de bureau; **personnel/staff manager,** chef/directeur du personnel; **plant manager,** directeur d'usine; **production manager,** directeur de la production; *Publ:* chef *m* de fabrication; **purchasing manager,** chef des achats; **sales manager,** directeur commercial; **senior manager,** cadre supérieur; **works manager,** chef du service (des) ateliers **2.**

Jur: **receiver and manager,** administrateur (d'une faillite, etc.); syndic *m* de faillite.

manageress, *n.f.* directrice/gérante; **joint manageress,** directrice adjointe/cogérante.

managerial, *a.* directorial; **the managerial staff,** les cadres *m*; **managerial control,** contrôle *m* de direction; **managerial position,** poste *m* de commande; poste de cadre; **managerial structure,** hiérarchie *f*.

managership, *n.* direction *f*/gérance *f*; intendance *f*; gouvernement *m* (d'une entreprise, etc.).

managing, *a.* **managing board,** comité *m* de direction; **managing director,** directeur général; **chairman and managing director,** président-directeur général (P-DG).

mandate, *n. Bank:* **mandate form,** lettre de signatures autorisées.

mandatory, *a.* obligatoire.

man-hour, *n.* heure *f* de travail (d'un homme)/heure d'ouvrier.

manifest[1], *n.* (*a*) *Nau:* (**inward, outward**) **manifest,** manifeste *m* (d'entrée, de sortie) (*b*) *Av:* état *m* de chargement.

manifest[2], *v.tr. Nau:* (*a*) déclarer (une cargaison) en douane (*b*) faire figurer (une marchandise) sur un manifeste.

manipulate, *v.tr. Pej:* **to manipulate accounts,** tripoter/cuisiner/arranger des comptes; *StExch:* **to manipulate the market,** agir sur le marché/travailler le marché; provoquer des mouvements de Bourse.

manipulation, *n. Pej:* tripotage *m*; **manipulation of the market,** tripotages en Bourse; agiotage *m*.

manipulator, *n. Pej:* tripoteur *m*; *StExch:* agioteur *m*.

man-made, *a.* artificiel/synthétique; **man-made fibres**, fibres *f* synthétiques.

manned, *a.* (*a*) (*of administrative, technical agency*) = service assuré; **the service is manned 24 hours a day**, il y a une permanence (*b*) (*of machine, apparatus, stand*) = surveillance assurée.

manning, *n.* affectation *f* de personnel (à une organisation, au fonctionnement d'une machine, etc.).

manpower, *n. coll. Ind:* main-d'œuvre *f*; effectifs *mpl*; **manpower forecasting**, prévision *f* de l'emploi; **manpower management**, gestion *f* d'effectifs/gestion de l'emploi; **manpower planning**, planification *f* de l'emploi; **shortage of manpower**, crise *f* de main-d'œuvre/d'effectifs.

manual[1], *n.* manuel *m* (d'utilisation).

manual[2], *a.* manuel; **manual labour**, la main-d'œuvre; **manual work**, travail manuel; travail de manœuvre; **manual worker**, un(e) manuel(le)/travailleur manuel/travailleuse manuelle; **manual operation**, fonctionnement *m* à la main.

manually, *adv.* manuellement/à la main.

manufacture[1], *n.* **1.** fabrication *f* (d'un produit industriel); confection *f* (de vêtements, etc.); **articles of foreign manufacture**, articles fabriqués à l'étranger/de fabrication étrangère **2.** *usu. pl.* produits fabriqués/manufacturés.

manufacture[2], *v.tr.* fabriquer/manufacturer (un produit industriel); confectionner (des vêtements, etc.); **manufactured goods**, produits manufacturés.

manufacturer, *n.* (*i*) fabricant *m* (*ii*) industriel *m*; **cloth manufacturer**, fabricant de draps; **boiler manufacturer**, constructeur *m* de chaudières; **manufacturer's price**, prix *m* (de) fabrique.

manufacturing[1], *a.* industriel; **manufacturing town**, ville industrielle.

manufacturing[2], *n.* fabrication *f*; confection *f* (de vêtements); **economic manufacturing quantity**, quantité *f* économique de production; **manufacturing capacity**, capacité *f* de production; **manufacturing control**, contrôle *m* de fabrication; **manufacturing costs/manufacturing overheads**, frais *mpl* de fabrication; **manufacturing industry**, industrie de fabrication; **manufacturing process**, procédé *m* de fabrication.

margin[1], *n.* **1.** (*a*) marge *f*/écart *m*; **the margin between the rates of interest**, l'écart entre les taux d'intérêt; **profit margin**, marge bénéficiaire; **gross margin**, marge brute; **net margin**, marge nette; **margin of error**, marge d'erreur; **to allow a margin for error**, prévoir une marge d'erreur; **margin of £100 for unforeseen expenses**, disponibilité *f* d'imprévus de £100; **the margin of permitted fluctuation**, la marge de fluctuation; **safety margin**, marge de sécurité (*b*) *Fin:* marge de garantie/couverture *f*/provision *f* (versée à un courtier); **margin call**, appel de marge **2.** marge (d'une page, etc.); **to write sth. in the margin**, écrire qch. en marge; faire une note marginale.

margin[2], *v.i.* (*esp. NAm:*) *StExch:* **to margin (up)**, verser les couvertures requises.

marginal, *a.* **1.** marginal; **marginal cost**, coût marginal; **marginal costing/cost pricing**, comptabilité marginale/méthode des coûts marginaux; **marginal return on capital**, rendement marginal du capital; **marginal profit**, bénéfice marginal; **firm with only a marginal profit**, entreprise marginale; **marginal productivity**, productivité marginale; **marginal revenue**, revenu marginal; **marginal utility**, utilité marginale **2.** marginal/en marge; **marginal note**, annotation marginale.

marine, **1.** *a.* **marine insurance**, assurance *f* maritime **2.** *n.* **merchant/mercantile marine**, marine marchande/de commerce.

maritime, *a.* maritime; **maritime law,** droit *m*/législation *f* maritime; **maritime loan,** (*i*) prêt *m* (*ii*) emprunt *m* à la grosse; *Ins:* **maritime peril,** péril *m*/fortune *f* de mer; **maritime risk,** risque *m* maritime/ risque de mer; **maritime trade,** commerce *m* maritime.

mark¹, *n.* **certification mark,** marque *f* de garantie; (*on gold and silver*) (**assay**) **mark,** poinçon *m* de garantie.

mark², *v.tr.* **1.** marquer/chiffrer/estampiller (des marchandises); **marked 'breakable',** revêtu de la mention 'fragile' **2. to mark (the price of) an article,** fixer le prix d'un article; *StExch:* **to mark stock,** coter des valeurs.

mark³, mark *m*/Deutschmark *m*.

mark down, *v.tr.* **to mark down (the price of) goods,** baisser le prix de marchandises/démarquer des marchandises; *StExch:* **prices have been marked down,** les cours se sont inscrits en baisse.

mark-down, *n.* rabais *m*/remise *f*.

market¹, *n.* **1.** marché *m*; **covered market,** halle(s) *f(pl)*/marché couvert; **open-air market,** marché en plein air; **cattle market,** marché aux bestiaux; **fish market,** marché aux poissons; **market day,** jour *m* de marché; **market place,** la place du marché; **to go to the market,** aller au marché **2.** (*a*) **the Common Market,** le Marché commun; **foreign market/overseas market,** marché extérieur/marché d'outre-mer; **free/ open market,** marché libre; *StExch:* **to buy shares on the open market,** acheter des actions en bourse; **home market,** marché intérieur; **the teenage market,** le marché des adolescents/des jeunes (*b*) **capital market,** marché financier; **commodity market,** marché de matières premières; **cotton market,** marché du coton; **foreign exchange market,** marché des changes; **forward exchange market,** marché des changes à terme; **international money market,** marché monétaire international; **world market,** marché mondial; **settlement market,**

marché à terme (des valeurs); **the property market,** le marché immobilier; **stock market/the market,** marché des valeurs/la Bourse (des valeurs) (*c*) **black market,** marché noir; **to buy on the black market,** acheter au noir; **buyer's market,** marché à la baisse; **fringe market,** marché marginal; **grey/ semi-black market,** marché gris; **jumpy market,** marché instable; **limited market,** marché étroit; **official market,** marché officiel; **seller's market,** marché à la hausse; **steady market,** marché ferme/soutenu; **unofficial market/***NAm:* **over-the-counter market,** marché hors cote (*d*) **market analysis,** analyse de marchés; **market appraisal,** évaluation du marché; **market forces,** tendances du marché; **market forecast,** prévisions du marché; **market intelligence,** information commerciale; **market opportunity/gap/opening,** créneau *m*; **market price,** prix du marché/cours (de la bourse); **market rate of discount,** taux *m* d'escompte hors banque; **market research/market study,** étude de marché; **market trend,** tendance *f* du marché (à long terme); **market value,** valeur marchande/prix *m* du marché; **down market,** bas de gamme; **up market,** haut de gamme; **up market store,** magasin (de) haut de gamme/magasin chic/magasin de luxe; **to be in the market for sth.,** être acheteur/chercher à acheter quelque chose; **to be on the market/to come into the market/onto the market,** être en vente; **to buy at the top of the market,** acheter au prix/au cours le plus élevé; **to corner a market,** monopoliser un marché; **his house is on the market,** sa maison est à vendre; **he put his house on the market,** il a mis sa maison en vente; **to find a market for sth.,** trouver un débouché pour qch.; **to find a ready market,** trouver à vendre facilement; **to make a market/to rig a market,** se porter contrepartiste (occulte); **market rigger,** contrepartiste occulte; **market rigging,** contrepartie *f* occulte; **to price oneself out of the market,** perdre sa clientèle en demandant trop cher; **the bottom has fallen out of the market,** le marché s'est effondré.

market[2], *v.tr.* vendre; trouver des débouchés *m* pour (ses marchandises); lancer (un produit).

marketability, *n.* valeur marchande/commerciale (d'un produit).

marketable, *a.* (*a*) (*of goods*) vendable; d'un débit facile (*b*) **marketable securities,** titres de placement; **marketable value,** valeur marchande/vénale.

marketing, *n.* commercialisation *f*/marketing *m*/marchéage *m*/mercatique *f* (d'un produit); **creative marketing,** créativité commerciale; **marketing agreement,** accord *m* de commercialisation; **marketing costs,** frais *mpl* de commercialisation; **marketing department,** service *m* du marketing; **marketing manager,** directeur *m* commercial/chef *m* du marketing/directeur du marketing; **marketing mix,** marketing *m* mix; stratégie commerciale; **marketing policy,** politique *f* de commercialisation; **marketing specialist,** mercaticien, -ienne.

marking, *n. StExch:* cotation *f* (des valeurs).

mark up, *v.tr.* augmenter le prix de (qch.); majorer un prix/une facture; *StExch:* **prices have been marked up,** les cours sont en hausse.

mark-up, *n.* marge *f* (bénéficiaire); augmentation *f*/majoration *f* (d'un prix); **mark-up pricing,** fixation *f* du prix au coût moyen majoré; **we operate a 2.5 times mark-up,** nous appliquons une marge de 2,5/notre marge est de 2,5.

mart, *n.* **1.** centre *m* de commerce; marché *m*; **money mart,** marché monétaire **2.** (auction) mart, salle *f* de vente; **car mart,** marché (des) autos.

mass, *n.* (*large quantity*) **mass production,** fabrication *f*/production *f* en série; **mass-production car,** voiture *f* de série; **mass unemployment,** chômage massif.

mass-produce, *v.tr.* fabriquer en série; **mass-produced cars,** voitures de série.

matched, *a. StExch: NAm:* **matched orders,** ordres couplés d'achat et de vente (pour stimuler le marché).

matching, *n. StExch: NAm:* application *f.*

material, *n.* **1.** matière *f*; matériau *m*; **raw material(s),** matière(s) première(s); **unprocessed/unrefined material,** matière brute/non traitée (industriellement); **synthetic material,** matière/produit synthétique; **building materials,** matériaux de construction **2.** *Tex:* tissu *m*; étoffe *f*; **dress materials,** tissus (de confection) **3.** matériel *m*; **artists' materials,** matériel d'artiste; **camping material,** matériel de camping.

materiality, *n.* (*in accounts*) importance *f* (relative) (d'une erreur, d'un élément); pertinence *f* (d'un procédé, etc.).

matter, *n.* **1.** (*a*) **matter of dispute,** sujet *m* de controverse (*b*) **postal matter,** lettres *fpl* et paquets postaux; **printed matter,** imprimé *m* **2.** affaire *f*/chose *f*/cas *m*; **we'll deal with this matter tomorrow,** nous nous occuperons de ce problème demain; **business matters,** affaires; **money matters,** affaires d'argent; *Jur:* **in the matter of the Companies Act,** vu la loi sur les Sociétés; **a matter of business,** une question d'affaires; **that will cost you a matter of £50,** cela vous coûtera dans les £50/une cinquantaine de livres.

mature[1], *a.* (*a*) **mature economy,** économie *f* en pleine maturité (*b*) *Fin:* (papier) échu.

mature[2], *v.i. Fin:* (*of bill*) échoir; arriver à échéance; **bills to mature,** papier *m* à échéance.

matured, *a. Fin:* échu; **matured capital,** capitaux *mpl* dont la date de paiement est échue; **matured bonds,** obligations échues.

maturity, *n.* (*a*) *Fin:* **(date of) maturity,** échéance *f* (d'une traite, d'un billet);

payable at maturity, payable à l'échéance (*b*) *NAm:* **current maturities,** versements *mpl* (sur une dette à long terme) exigibles à moins d'un an/ exigibles à court terme.

maximization, *n.* maximation *f*/maximisation *f*; **profit maximization,** maximisation du profit/des profits; **the maximization of total utility,** la maximisation de l'utilité totale.

maximize, *v.tr.* maximaliser/maximiser; porter (qch.) au maximum.

maximizing = **maximization.**

maximum, 1. *n.* maximum *m;* **to the maximum,** au maximum; **up to a maximum of. . .,** jusqu'à concurrence de . . .; **to raise production to a maximum,** porter la production au maximum **2.** *a.* maximum; *occ.* maximal(e); **maximum efficiency,** maximum de rendement; **maximum load,** charge *f* maximale/limite; **maximum price,** prix *m* maximum; **maximum output,** rendement *m* maximum.

mean, *a.* moyen; **mean price,** prix moyen; **mean due date,** échéance moyenne/ commune; **mean tare,** tare commune.

means, *n.pl.* moyens *mpl* (de vivre); ressources *fpl*; **private means,** ressources personnelles/fortune personnelle; **this car is beyond my means,** cette voiture est hors de ma portée/n'est pas dans mes prix; *Adm:* **means test** = enquête *f* sur la situation (de fortune).

measure[1]**,** *n.* **1.** (*a*) mesure *f*; **linear measure,** mesure linéaire; **square measure,** mesure de superficie/de surface; **cubic measure,** mesure de volume; **liquid measure,** mesure de capacité (pour les liquides); **dry measure,** mesure de capacité (pour les matières sèches); **weights and measures,** poids *m* et mesures (*b*) *Tail:* **made to measure,** fait sur mesure(s); **to have a suit made to measure,** se faire faire un costume sur mesure(s) (*c*) *Nau:* cubage *m*; jaugeage *m*; **measure goods,** marchandises *f* de

cubage/d'encombrement **2.** (*instrument for measuring*) (*a*) mesure (à grains, à lait, etc.) (*b*) **tape measure,** centimètre *m* (de couturière)/mètre *m* à ruban **3.** mesure/démarche *f*/manœuvre *f*; **security/ safety measures,** mesures de sécurité; **measures of conciliation,** voies *f* d'accommodement; **as a measure of economy/as an economy measure,** par mesure d'économie; **deflationary measures,** mesures déflationnistes.

measure[2]**,** *v.tr.* (*a*) mesurer (une distance, etc.) (*b*) **to measure the tonnage of a ship,** jauger un navire (*c*) *Tail:* mesurer (qn)/prendre les mesures/prendre les mensurations (de qn).

measurement, *n.* **1.** mesure *f*; mesurage *m*; **performance measurement,** mesure de la performance; **productivity measurement,** mesure de la productivité **2.** *Nau:* (*a*) jaugeage *m* (d'un navire) (*b*) cubage *m*/encombrement *m* (du fret); **measurement converted into weight,** cubage converti en poids; **to pay for cargo by measurement,** payer le fret au cubage/au volume; **measurement freight,** fret selon encombrement/selon volume; **measurement goods,** marchandises *f* de cubage/ d'encombrement; **measurement ton,** tonneau *m* d'encombrement/de mer **3.** *Tail:* **to take a customer's measurements,** mesurer un client/prendre les mesures/ prendre les mensurations d'un client.

mechanism, *n.* mécanisme *m*; **banking mechanism,** mécanisme bancaire; **discount mechanism,** mécanisme de l'escompte; **price mechanism,** mécanisme des prix.

mechanization, *n.* mécanisation *f*.

mechanize, *v.tr.* mécaniser (une industrie).

media, *n.* média *m*; **TV is a media,** la télévision est un média; **advertising media,** média publicitaire; **the new mass media,** les nouveaux mass(-)média.

mediate, *v.i.* (*of pers.*) agir en médiateur/servir de médiateur/servir d'intermédiaire (**between . . . and . . .,** entre . . . et . . .).

mediation, *n.* médiation *f*/intervention (amicale); **offer of mediation,** offre *f* d'intervention; **through the mediation of . . .,** par l'entremise *f* de . . ..

mediator, *n.* médiateur, -trice/intermédiaire *mf*/arbitre *m*.

medical, *a.* **medical certificate,** certificat médical; *Ind:* **medical officer,** médecin *m* du travail.

medium, *n.* (*a*) intermédiaire *m*/entremise *f*; **through the medium of the press,** par l'intermédiaire de la presse/par voie de presse (*b*) moyen *m* (de communication, etc.); agent *m*/organe *m*; **advertising medium,** organe de publicité/support *m* publicitaire.

medium-size(d), *a.* de grandeur moyenne; **small and medium-size firms,** petites et moyennes entreprises (PME).

medium-term, *a.* **medium-term finance,** financement *m* à moyen terme.

meet, 1. *v.tr.* (*a*) rejoindre/revoir (qn); **to arrange to meet s.o.,** donner (un) rendez-vous à qn; fixer un rendez-vous avec qn; **I arranged to meet him at three o'clock,** j'ai pris rendez-vous avec lui pour trois heures (*b*) faire la connaissance de (qn); **it was a great pleasure to meet you/meeting you,** je suis enchanté d'avoir fait votre connaissance; **I hope to meet you soon,** j'espère avoir sous peu le plaisir de faire votre connaissance (*c*) faire des concessions *f* à (qn); **I'll do my best to meet your price,** on peut s'arranger quant au prix (*d*) satisfaire à (un besoin, une demande); **to meet the demand,** satisfaire à la demande; **to meet s.o.'s requirements,** donner satisfaction à qn; **he met my request by saying that . . .,** en réponse à ma demande il a dit que . . . (*e*) faire honneur à/faire bon accueil à/accueillir (un effet, une lettre de change); honorer (un chèque); **to meet one's commitments,** faire honneur à ses engagements; remplir ses engagements (*f*) **to meet expenses,** faire face aux dépenses/à ses dépenses; subvenir aux frais; **he met all expenses,** il a subvenu à tout **2.** *v.i.* (*a*) (*of pers.*) se rencontrer/se voir (*b*) (*of society, assembly*) se réunir (en session); s'assembler (*c*) **to meet with a loss,** éprouver/subir une perte; **to meet with a refusal,** essuyer un refus.

meeting, *n.* assemblée *f*/réunion *f*/séance *f*; **annual general meeting (AGM),** assemblée générale annuelle; **board meeting,** réunion du conseil d'administration; **meeting place/meeting point,** lieu *m* de réunion; rendez-vous *m*; **to hold a meeting,** tenir une réunion; **the association holds its meetings at . . .,** l'association *f* se réunit à . . .; **the meeting will be held tomorrow at 3 o'clock,** la réunion est prévue pour demain/aura lieu demain à 3 heures; **notice of meeting,** convocation *f*; **to call a meeting of shareholders,** convoquer les actionnaires; *Jur:* **meeting of creditors,** assemblée de créanciers; **at the meeting in London,** à la séance tenue à Londres; **to open the meeting,** déclarer la séance ouverte; **to dissolve the meeting,** lever la séance; **to address the meeting,** prendre la parole; **to put a resolution to the meeting,** mettre une résolution aux voix.

member, *n.* membre *m* (d'une société, etc.); **ordinary members/paying members of an association,** cotisants *m*; **member countries of the EEC,** les pays membres de la CEE.

membership, *n.* **1.** qualité *f* de membre; adhésion *f*; **qualifications for membership,** conditions *f*/titres *m* d'éligibilité; **conditions of membership,** conditions *f* d'adhésion/d'admission; **membership card,** carte *f* de membre/de sociétaire; **to apply for membership,** faire une demande d'adhésion; **to pay one's membership (fee),** payer sa cotisation/son abonnement *m*; **to renew one's membership,**

renouveler sa carte (de membre) **2.** (*a*) nombre *m* de membres/effectif *m* (d'une société, etc.); **club with a membership of a thousand,** club *m* de mille membres (*b*) **the opinion of the majority of our membership,** l'avis *m* de la majorité de nos membres.

memo, *n. F:* mémo *m*; **memo pad,** bloc-notes *m*.

memorandum, *n.* **1.** mémorandum *m*; note *f*; **to make a memorandum of sth.,** prendre note de qch.; noter qch. **2.** (*a*) mémoire *m* (d'un contrat, d'une vente, etc.); sommaire *m* des articles (d'un contrat) (*b*) *Jur:* **memorandum of association,** charte constitutive d'une société à responsabilité limitée; acte *m* de société; **memorandum and articles of association,** statuts *mpl* **3.** note *f*; circulaire *f* **4.** bordereau *m*; **memorandum book,** carnet *m*/calepin *m*/agenda *m*.

menswear, *n.* vêtements *mpl* pour hommes.

mercantile, *a.* marchand/commercial/commerçant/de commerce; **mercantile operations,** opérations *f* mercantiles; **mercantile nation,** nation commerçante; **mercantile broker,** agent *m* de change; **mercantile agency,** agence commerciale; **mercantile agent,** agent commercial; **mercantile marine,** marine marchande; **mercantile law,** droit commercial/code *m* de commerce.

merchandise[1]**,** *n.* marchandise(s) *f*(*pl*).

merchandise[2]**,** *v.i.* marchandiser.

merchandising, *n.* marchandisage *m*/merchandising *m*.

merchant[1]**,** *n.* (*a*) négociant, -ante; commerçant, -ante; marchand, -ande en gros; **wine merchant,** négociant en vins (*b*) *Scot: & NAm:* marchand, -ande/boutiquier, -ière **2.** *a.* (*a*) marchand; du commerce; **merchant bank,** banque *f* d'affaires; **merchant marine/merchant navy/merchant service/merchant shipping,** marine marchande; **mer-**

chant ship/merchant vessel, navire marchand/navire de commerce.

merchantable, *a.* **1.** en état d'être livré au commerce; vendable **2.** de débit facile/de bonne vente.

merchantman, *n.* navire marchand/navire de commerce.

merge, 1. *v.tr.* fusionner (deux systèmes, etc.); amalgamer (**sth. in/into sth.,** qch. avec qch.) **2.** *v.i.* (*of banks, etc.*) s'amalgammer/fusionner.

merger, *n. Fin:* fusion *f* (de plusieurs sociétés en une seule); absorption (d'une société par une autre); **industrial merger,** fusion/concentration *f* industrielle; **merger company,** sociétés réunies.

merging, *n.* fusionnement *m*.

merit, *n.* **1.** mérite *m*; **to discuss the merits of sth.,** discuter le pour et le contre de qch. **2.** valeur *f*/mérite; *Ind: etc:* **merit bonus,** prime *f* de rendement; **merit rating,** (*i*) appréciation *f* du mérite (*ii*) notation *f* du personnel.

message, *n.* message *m*; communication *f* (téléphonique, etc.); **advertising message,** message publicitaire; **to leave a message for s.o.,** laisser un message/un mot pour qn; **I'll give him the message,** je lui transmettrai le message.

messenger, *n.* (*a*) messager, -ère; courrier *m* (*b*) commissionnaire *m*; **by messenger,** par porteur; **auctioneer's messenger,** garçon de salle; **office messenger,** garçon *m* de bureau; coursier, -ière.

Messrs, *n.m.pl.* Messieurs, *abbr.* MM. **Messrs J. Martin & Co.,** Messieurs J. Martin & Cie.

meter, *n.* **1.** *NAm:* = **metre 2.** compteur *m* (à gaz, à eau, d'électricité).

method, *n.* (*a*) (*research, science*) méthode *f* (*b*) méthode/manière *f* (**of doing sth.,** de faire qch.); procédé *m* (pour faire qch.); modalités *fpl*; **method of payment,** modalités de paiement; *Ind:*

production method, procédé(s) de fabrication; **method of operation,** méthode d'exploitation; **method of working,** méthode de travail; **sampling method,** échantillonnage *m*/sondage *m* (*c*) *Ind:* **methods engineer,** ingénieur *m* des méthodes; **methods engineering/methods study,** étude *f* des méthodes; **methods office,** bureau *m* des méthodes; **time and methods study,** étude des temps et des méthodes.

methodical, *a.* méthodique.

metre, *n. Meas:* mètre *m* (*abbr.* **m**) (= 1.0936 yards); **square metre,** mètre carré; **cubic metre,** mètre cube; **stacked cubic metre,** stère *m* (de bois).

metric, *a. Meas:* métrique; **metric unit,** unité *f* métrique; **the metric system,** le système métrique; **metric ton,** tonne *f* (métrique); (*of country*) **to go metric,** adopter le système métrique.

metricate, *v.tr. & i.* introduire/adopter le système métrique.

metrication, *n.* adoption *f*/introduction *f*/ utilisation *f*/du système métrique.

microcomputer, *n.* micro-ordinateur *m.*

micro-economic, *a.* micro-économique.

micro-economics, *n.pl.* micro-économie *f.*

microfiche, *n.* microfiche *f.*

microfilm, *n.* microfilm *m.*

microprocessor, *n.* microprocesseur *m.*

mid, *a.* mi-/du milieu; **from mid June to mid August,** de la mi-juin à la mi-août; *StExch:* **mid month account/settlement,** le 15 du mois/la liquidation de quinzaine.

middle, *n.* **middle management,** cadres moyens.

middleman, *n.m.* intermédiaire *m & f.*

mile, *n. Meas:* mille *m*; **five miles,** cinq milles (= huit kilomètres); **speed limit of 50 miles an hour,** vitesse limitée à 50 milles à l'heure/= à 80 kilomètres à l'heure; **my car does 25 miles to the gallon/25 miles per gallon (m.p.g.)** = ma voiture consomme (environ) onze litres aux 100 kilomètres (11L/100 km).

mileage, *n.* distance *f* en milles/ = kilométrage *m*; **daily mileage** = parcours kilométrique journalier; (*for taxi, etc.*) **mileage rate** = tarif *m* au kilomètre; **mileage allowance,** indemnité *f* de déplacement.

mill, *n.* usine *f*; **cotton mill,** filature *f* de coton.

milligram, *Meas:* milligramme *m* (*abbr.* **mg**) (0.0154 grain).

millilitre, *n. Meas:* millilitre *m* (*abbr.* **ml**).

millimetre, *n. Meas:* millimètre *m* (*abbr.* **mm**) (= 0.0394 in); **millimetre scale,** échelle *f* millimétrique.

million, *n.* million *m*; **one thousand million(s),** un milliard; **two million men,** deux millions d'hommes; (*of pers.*) **worth millions/worth ten million(s),** riche à millions/ dix fois millionnaire; **a two-million pound machine,** une machine coûtant deux millions de livres.

minicomputer, *n.* mini-ordinateur *m.*

minimal, *a.* minimal/minimum; **minimal amount,** (*i*) quantité *f* minimum (*ii*) montant *m* minimum; **minimal value,** valeur minimale/minimum; **minimal weight,** poids *m* minimum.

minimization, *n.* minimisation *f*/réduction *f* au minimum.

minimize, *v.tr.* minimiser/réduire au minimum; **to minimize a loss,** atténuer une perte.

minimizing, *n.* = **minimization.**

minimum, *pl.* 1. *n.* minimum *m*; **to reduce expenses to a minimum,** réduire les frais au minimum 2. *a.* **minimum quantity,** quantité *f* minimum; **minimum prices,** prix *m* minimums/minima; **the minimum number of shares,** le nombre minimum d'actions; **(index-linked) minimum wage,** = salaire minimum interprofessionnel de croissance (SMIC).

minor, *a.* petit/menu/peu important/ mineur(e); **minor expenses,** menus frais.

minority, *n.* minorité *f*; **minority holding/interest/stake,** participation *f*/intérêt *m* minoritaire.

mint[1], *n.* **the Mint** = l'Hôtel *m* de la Monnaie/l'Hôtel des Monnaies/la Monnaie; **in mint condition,** à l'état (de) neuf; *Fin:* **mint par,** pair *m* intrinsèque/pair théorique.

mint[2], *v.tr.* **to mint money,** frapper de la monnaie/battre monnaie.

mintage, *n.* **1.** monnayage *m*; frappe *f* de la monnaie **2.** espèces monnayées (de telle date, de telle Monnaie) **3.** droit *m* de monnayage; droit de frappe.

minute, *n.* (*a*) **minutes of a meeting,** procès-verbal *m*/compte-rendu *m* d'une réunion; **to confirm the minutes of the last meeting,** approuver le procès-verbal de la dernière réunion; **to read the minutes (of a meeting),** lire le procès-verbal (d'une réunion); **to take the minutes of a meeting,** rédiger le procès-verbal d'une réunion; **minute book,** (*i*) registre *m* des procès-verbaux/des délibérations (*ii*) *Adm:* journal *m* de correspondance et d'actes (*b*) **Treasury minute,** approbation *f* de la Trésorerie; communiqué *m* de la Trésorerie.

misapplication, *n.* emploi injustifié (d'une somme d'argent); détournement *m* (de fonds).

misapply, *v.tr.* faire un emploi injustifié (d'une somme d'argent); détourner (des fonds).

misappropriate, *v.tr.* détourner (des fonds).

misappropriation, *n.* détournement *m* (de fonds); malversation *f*.

miscalculate, *v.tr.* mal calculer (une somme, etc.).

miscalculation, *n.* faux calcul/calcul erroné; mécompte *m*; erreur *f* de calcul/erreur de compte.

miscellaneous, *a.* varié; divers; **miscellaneous shares,** valeurs diverses; **miscellaneous expenses,** (frais) divers *mpl*.

miscount[1], *n.* (*a*) erreur *f* de calcul; faux calcul (*b*) erreur d'addition.

miscount[2], (*a*) *v.tr.* mal compter (*b*) *v.i.* faire une erreur de calcul.

misdate, *v.tr.* mal dater (une lettre, un chèque, etc.).

misdirect, *v.tr.* mal adresser/mal acheminer (une lettre).

misenter, *v.tr.* *Book-k:* contre-poser.

misentry, *n.* *Book-k:* contre-position *f*.

mismanage, *v.tr.* mal conduire/mal diriger/mal administrer/mal gérer (une affaire, une entreprise).

mismanagement, *n.* mauvaise administration/mauvaise gestion.

misprint, *n.* coquille *f*.

misrepresent, *v.tr.* dénaturer des faits; présenter (des faits) sous un faux jour; faire un faux rapport/une fausse déclaration.

misrepresentation, *n.* faux rapport/ faux exposé/fausse déclaration.

misroute, *v.tr.* mal acheminer (un paquet, etc.).

misrouting, *n.* erreur *f* d'acheminement d'un paquet, etc.); fausse direction.

Miss, *n.* mademoiselle *f*; **Miss Thomas,** Mademoiselle (Mlle) Thomas.

mission, *n.* **trade mission,** mission *f* commerciale.

mistake, *n.* erreur *f*/faute *f*; méprise *f*; **mistake in labelling,** erreur d'étiquetage; **mistake in the date,** erreur de date; **to make a mistake,** faire une faute; commettre une faute/une erreur; se méprendre/ se tromper.

misuse, *n.* abus *m*/mauvais usage/emploi abusif/mauvais emploi (de qch.); **misuse of authority,** abus d'autorité; *Jur:* **fraudulent misuse of funds,** détournement *m* de fonds; abus de confiance.

mixed, *a.* mixte; **mixed economy,** économie *f* mixte; *Ins:* **mixed policy,** police *f* au temps et au voyage; **mixed sea and land risks,** risques *m* mixtes maritimes et terrestres; *Nau:* **mixed cargo,** cargaison *f* mixte.

mobility, *n.* mobilité *f* (des capitaux, de la main d'œuvre, du personnel).

mobilizable, *a.* mobilisable.

mobilization, *n.* mobilisation *f* (de capitaux, etc.).

mobilize, *v.tr.* mobiliser (des capitaux, etc.).

mock-up, *n.* maquette *f*.

model, *n.* (*a*) modèle *m*/maquette *f*/ modèle réduit (*b*) **new model (of a car),** nouveau modèle (d'une voiture) (*c*) (*pers.*) mannequin *m* (*d*) **econometric models,** modèles prévisionnels.

moderate, *a.* modéré/moyen/raisonnable; **moderate price,** prix modéré/modique/moyen; **moderate income,** revenu *m* modique.

modernization, *n.* modernisation *f*.

modernize, *v.tr.* moderniser; rénover.

modular, *a. Const: etc:* modulaire; fait d'éléments normalisés (préfabriqués); **modular construction/modular design,** construction au moyen d'éléments normalisés.

monetary, *a.* monétaire; **monetary area,** zone *f* monétaire; **monetary convention,** convention *f* monétaire; **monetary policy/monetary management,** politique *f* monétaire; **monetary reform,** réforme *f*/ assainissement *m* monétaire; **monetary**

standard, étalon *m* monétaire; **monetary unit,** unité *f* monétaire; **European Monetary System (EMS),** système *m* monétaire européen (SME); **International Monetary Fund (IMF),** Fonds *m* monétaire international (FMI).

money, *n.* **1.** monnaie *f*; argent *m*; espèces *fpl*; numéraire *m*; (*coins*) **gold/silver money,** monnaie d'or/d'argent; **to coin/to mint money,** frapper de la monnaie; *Bank:* **bank money/deposit money,** monnaie de banque/monnaie scripturale; **commodity money,** monnaie marchandise; **current money,** monnaie qui a cours; **divisional/fractional money,** monnaie divisionnaire/monnaie d'appoint; **fiduciary money,** billets *mpl* sans couverture; **money of account,** monnaie de compte; **paper money,** monnaie de papier; billets *mpl* (de banque); papier-monnaie *m*; **token money,** monnaie fiduciaire; *Fin:* **cheap/easy money,** argent à bon marché; **call money/money at call,** argent remboursable sur demande; argent/dépôt *m* à vue; **danger money,** prime *f* de risque(s); **hot money,** capitaux *mpl* fébriles; **money rate,** taux *m* de l'argent; **money market,** marché monétaire/marché des changes; marché financier; **money supply,** masse *f* monétaire; **price of money,** loyer *m* de l'argent; **ready money,** argent comptant/argent liquide; **to pay in ready money,** payer (au) comptant; *Post:* **money order,** mandat (postal)/mandat-poste *m*; **international/foreign money order,** mandat international; **to be worth a lot of money,** (*i*) (*of thg*) valoir cher/ avoir de la valeur (*ii*) (*of pers.*) être riche/avoir de la fortune; **to be short of money,** être à court d'argent; **to get one's money back,** (*i*) se faire rembourser (*ii*) rentrer dans ses fonds **2.** *Jur: pl:* **moneys/monies** argent/fonds *mpl*; **monies paid out,** versements (opérés); **monies paid in,** recettes (effectuées); **public monies,** deniers publics; le trésor public; **sundry monies owing to him,** diverses sommes à lui dues; **monies owing to us,** nos créances *f*.

moneylender, *n.* prêteur *m* (d'argent); maison *f* de prêt.

moneymaker, *n.* (commerce, etc.) qui rapporte.

money-spinner, *n.* (produit, etc.) qui rapporte; mine *f* (d'argent).

monopolist, *n.* monopoliste *m* & *f.*

monopolistic, *a.* monopolistique; monopolisant; monopolisateur.

monopolization, *n.* monopolisation *f.*

monopolize, *v.tr.* monopoliser/accaparer (une denrée, etc.).

monopoly, *n.* monopole *m*; **to have a monopoly of sth.**/*NAm:* **on sth.,** avoir le monopole de qch.; avoir l'exclusivité *f* de qch.; **State monopoly,** monopole d'État; **monopoly control,** contrôle *m* monopolistique.

monopsony, *n.* monopsone *m.*

month, *n.* mois *m*; **calendar month,** mois du calendrier/mois civil; **in the month of August,** au mois d'août; **at the end of the (current) month,** fin courant; **once a month,** une fois par mois; mensuellement; **a month's credit,** un mois de crédit; *Fin:* **bill at three months,** papier *m* à trois mois (d'échéance); **to pay an employee by the month,** mensualiser un employé.

monthly[1], *a.* (*a*) mensuel; **monthly payment/monthly instalment,** mensualité *f*; **monthly statement (of account),** relevé *m*/situation *f* de fin de mois (*b*) *Rail: etc:* **monthly season ticket,** carte *f* (d'abonnement) valable pour un mois; (*on underground*) = carte orange.

monthly[2], *adv.* mensuellement/une fois par mois/chaque mois/tous les mois.

moonlight, *v.i. F:* faire du travail noir/travailler au noir.

moonlighter, *n. F:* personne qui fait du travail (au) noir.

moonlighting, *n. F:* travail (au) noir.

mop up, *v.tr.* **losses that mop up all the profits,** pertes *f* qui engloutissent tous les bénéfices.

moratorium, *n. Fin:* moratorium *m*/moratoire *m*; **to announce a moratorium,** décréter un moratoire; **debt for which a moratorium has been granted,** dette *f* moratoire.

moratory, *a.* moratoire.

mortgage[1], *n.* hypothèque *f*; **blanket mortgage/general mortgage,** hypothèque générale; **chattel mortgage,** hypothèque mobilière/hypothèque sur biens meubles; **discharge of a mortgage,** mainlevée *f* d'une hypothèque; **first/prior mortgage,** hypothèque de premier rang/première hypothèque; **second mortgage,** seconde hypothèque; **burdened/encumbered with mortgage,** grevé d'hypothèque; **by/on mortgage,** hypothécairement; **to borrow on mortgage,** emprunter sur hypothèque; **to create a mortgage,** constituer une hypothèque; **to foreclose a mortgage,** saisir un bien hypothéqué; **to raise a mortgage,** contracter une hypothèque; **to buy a house on mortgage,** prendre une hypothèque pour acheter une maison; **to secure a debt by mortgage,** hypothéquer une créance; **to register a mortgage on a property,** inscrire une hypothèque sur un bien; **to pay off/redeem a mortgage,** purger une hypothèque; **mortgage bond/mortgage debenture,** obligation *f* hypothécaire; **first mortgage bonds,** obligations de première hypothèque; **mortgage charge,** affectation *f* hypothécaire; **mortgage creditor,** créancier *m* hypothécaire; **mortgage debtor,** débiteur *m* hypothécaire; **mortgage deed,** contrat *m* hypothécaire; **mortgage registrar,** conservateur *m* des hypothèques; **mortgage registration,** inscription *f* hypothécaire; **mortgage registry,** conservation *f* des hypothèques.

mortgage[2], *v.tr.* hypothéquer (une terre, un immeuble, des titres); engager/mettre en gage (des marchandises, des titres); déposer (des titres) en nantissement; **mortgaged estate,** domaine hypothéqué.

mortgageable, *a.* hypothécable.

mortgagee, *n.* créancier *m* hypothécaire.

mortgager, mortgagor, *n.* débiteur *m* hypothécaire.

motion, *n.* **1.** mouvement *m*; *Ind: etc:* **motion analysis,** analyse *f* des mouvements; **motion efficiency,** rendement *m* du geste; **time and motion consultant,** organisateur-conseil *m*; **time and motion study,** étude *f* des temps et des mouvements **2.** (*a*) motion *f*/proposition *f*; **to carry a motion,** faire adopter une motion; **to put forward the motion,** mettre la proposition aux voix; **to speak for the motion/to support the motion,** soutenir la motion; **to speak against the motion,** soutenir la contrepartie (*b*) *Jur:* demande *f*/requête *f*.

motivated, *a.* **the staff must be motivated,** le personnel doit être motivé.

motivation, *n.* motifs *mpl*/motivation *f*.

motivational, *a.* **motivational studies/ research,** études *f*/recherche *f* de motivation.

motivator, *n.* mobile *m*/motivation *f*.

motive, *n.* **profit motive,** motivation *f* par le profit.

mount up, *v.i.* croître/monter/augmenter.

moveable, 1. *a. Jur:* mobilier/meuble; **moveable effects,** effets mobiliers; **moveable property,** biens *m* meubles **2.** *n.pl.* **moveables,** (*a*) mobilier *m* (*b*) *Jur:* biens mobiliers/biens meubles; meubles *mpl* (meublants).

movement, *n. PolEc: etc:* circulation *f* (des capitaux, etc.); mouvement *m* (de baisse, de hausse) (des prix, des valeurs, en bourse); activité (du marché); **free movement of labour/of workers,** libre circulation des travailleurs/de la main d'œuvre; **cyclical movements,** mouvements cycliques/conjoncturels.

move up, *v.i. StExch:* (*of shares*) se relever/reprendre (de la valeur).

Mr, (*form of address*) **Mr Thomas,** Monsieur/M. Thomas.

Mrs, (*form of address*) **Mrs Thomas,** Madame/Mme Thomas.

Ms, M/s, (*form of address*) **Ms, M/s Thomas,** (*i*) Mademoiselle/Mlle Thomas (*ii*) Madame/Mme Thomas.

multimillionaire, *a. & n.* multimillionnaire (*mf*)/milliardaire (*mf*).

multinational, *a. & n.* **multinational company,** (société) multinationale *f*.

multiple, *a.* multiple; **multiple management,** direction *f* multiple; **multiple stores,** magasin *m* à succursales (multiples); **multiple ownership,** multipropriété *f* (d'un immeuble, etc.); *PolEc:* **multiple-use principle,** principe *m* de polyvalence.

multiplication, *n.* multiplication *f*.

multiplier, *n.* multiplicateur *m*.

multiply, 1. *v.tr.* multiplier; **to multiply two numbers together,** multiplier deux nombres l'un par l'autre **2.** *v.i.* multiplier/ faire une multiplication.

mutual, *a.* mutuel/réciproque; **to arrange a transaction on mutual principles/on mutual terms,** conclure un marché stipulant un échange de services/avec stipulation de réciprocité; **mutual benefit society,** société *f* de secours mutuels; **member of a mutual benefit society,** mutualiste *mf*; **mutual assurance,** coassurance *f*; **mutual assurance company,** société *f* d'assurances mutuelles; mutuelle *f*; *NAm:* **mutual funds/***n.pl.* **mutuals** = société *f* d'investissement à capital variable (SICAV).

N

naked, *a.* sans garantie; **naked debenture,** obligation *f* chirographaire/sans garantie.

name, *n.* **1.** nom *m*; **full name,** nom et prénoms *mpl*; *StExch:* **name day,** deuxième jour *m* de liquidation; **name of a firm/of a company/corporate name,** raison sociale (d'une maison de commerce, d'une société); **the company trades under the name of . . .,** la société a pour dénomination . . . **name of an account,** intitulé *m* d'un compte; **name of the payee,** nom du bénéficiaire; **brand name,** marque *f* de fabrique; **registered (trade) name,** nom déposé; **to set/put one's name to a document,** signer un document/apposer sa signature à un document; **list of names,** liste nominative; **the shares are in my name,** les actions *f* sont à mon nom **2.** réputation *f*/ renommée *f*; **trademark with a good name,** marque réputée; **a big name in the business world,** un nom bien connu dans le monde des affaires.

named, *a.* nommé; **on the named day/ on the day named,** à jour nommé; *Ins:* **party named/person named,** accrédité(e); **named policy/policy to a named person,** police nominative.

national, *a.* national; de l'État; **National debt,** la dette publique; **(gross, net) national income,** revenu national (brut, net); **(gross, net) national product,** produit national (brut, net); **national expenditure,** dépenses *fpl* de l'État.

nationality, *n.* nationalité *f.*

nationalization, *n.* nationalisation *f*/ étatisation *f* (d'une industrie, etc.).

nationalize, *v.tr.* nationaliser/étatiser (une industrie, etc.); **nationalized industry,** industrie nationalisée.

natural, *a.* naturel; **natural gas,** gaz naturel; **natural resources,** ressources *f* naturelles; **natural resources company,** exploitation *f* de diverses ressources naturelles.

nature, *n.* **nature of contents,** nature *f*/ désignation *f* du contenu.

navigation, *n.* navigation *f*; **navigation company,** compagnie *f* de navigation/de transports maritimes; **navigation dues,** droits *m* de navigation.

neglected, *a. StExch:* **neglected stocks,** fonds négligés/délaissés.

negligence, *n.* négligence; **through negligence,** par négligence; *Jur:* **criminal negligence,** négligence coupable/criminelle; **gross negligence,** négligence grave; *Ins:* **negligence clause,** clause *f* (de) négligence.

negotiability, *n.* négociabilité *f* (d'un effet de commerce).

negotiable, *a. Fin: etc:* (effet, titre, etc.) négociable; **stocks negotiable on the Stock Exchange,** titres négociables en Bourse; **not negotiable,** (*i*) non négociable (*ii*) (*on cheque*) non à ordre.

negotiate, **1.** *v.tr.* (*a*) négocier/traiter (une affaire) (*b*) **to negotiate a bill,** négocier une lettre de change **2.** *v.i.* (*a*) **to be negotiating with s.o. for . . .,** être en pourparlers avec qn au sujet de . . .; négocier une affaire avec qn (*b*) **they refuse to negotiate,** ils refusent de négocier.

negotiation, *n.* négociation *f* (d'un emprunt, d'une lettre de change); **under negotiation,** en (cours de) négociation; **by negotiation,** par (voie de) négociations; de gré à gré; **the price is a matter for negotiation,** le prix est à débattre; **to be in negotiation with s.o.,** être en pourparler(s) avec qn; **to enter into negotiations with s.o./to start negotiations with s.o.,** engager/entamer des négociations avec qn; entrer en pourparlers/entamer des pourparlers avec qn; **to break off negotiations,** rompre les négociations; **to resume negotiations,** reprendre les négociations; **joint negotiations,** négociations paritaires.

negotiator, *n.* négociateur, -trice.

nervous, *a.* (*of market*) agité/instable.

net[1], **1.** *a.* (*of weight, price, etc.*) net; **net amount,** montant net; **net asset,** valeur nette; **net income,** revenu net; **net margin,** marge nette; **net present value,** valeur actuelle nette; **net proceeds of a sale,** produit net d'une vente; **net profit,** bénéfice net; **net receipts,** recettes nettes; **net weight,** poids net; **net worth,** situation nette; **terms strictly net,** sans déduction; payable au comptant **2.** *n.* le (poids, prix, montant) net.

net[2], *v.tr.* **1.** (*of pers.*) toucher net/gagner net (tant de bénéfices, etc.); **I netted (a full profit of) £2000,** (*i*) cela m'a rapporté un bénéfice net de £2000 (*ii*) il me reste £2000 net **2.** (*of enterprise, etc.*) rapporter net/produire net (une certaine somme).

nett, *a.* = **net**[1].

network, *n.* réseau *m*; **broadcasting networks,** réseaux de transmission; **distribution network,** réseau de distribution.

never-never, *n.* F: **to buy sth. on the never-never,** acheter qch. à crédit/à tempérament.

new, *a.* **1.** (*a*) nouveau; **new issue (of shares),** nouvelle émission (d'actions); **under new management,** changement *m* de direction; **new shares,** actions nouvelles; **two new shares for each five shares held,** deux actions nouvelles pour cinq anciennes; **to open up new channels for trade,** créer de nouveaux débouchés au commerce **2.** neuf; **as new,** à l'état (de) neuf.

news, *n.pl.* (*usu. with sg. const.*) **1.** nouvelle(s) *f(pl)*/actualités *fpl*; **news agency,** agence *f* de presse **2.** **financial news,** chronique financière/informations financières.

newsagent, *n.* marchand(e)/dépositaire *mf* de journaux.

newsletter, *n.* bulletin *m* (d'informations); circulaire *f*.

newspaper, *n.* journal *m*.

nickel, *n.* (*a*) nickel *m* (*b*) (pièce de) 5 cents (au Canada et aux USA).

night, *n.* nuit *f*; **night work,** travail *m* de nuit; **to do night work/to be on night duty/***F:* **to work nights/to be on nights,** travailler la nuit/*F:* être de nuit; **night shift,** équipe *f* de nuit; **he's on (the) night shift,** il est de nuit; *Bank:* **night safe,** coffre(-fort) *m* de nuit.

nil, *n.* (*on report sheet, etc.*) néant *m*; **the balance is nil,** le solde est nul.

nomenclature, *n.* nomenclature *f*.

nominal, *a.* **1.** (*a*) nominal/de peu d'importance; **nominal rent,** loyer insignifiant (*b*) *Book-k:* **nominal accounts,** comptes d'exploitation générale; **nominal ledger,** grand(-)livre général; *Fin:* **nominal capital,** capital nominal/social; **nominal price,** prix théorique/nominal/fictif; **nominal value,** valeur nominale; **nominal wages,** salaire nominal **2.** nominatif; **nominal list (of shareholders),** liste nominative (des actionnaires).

nominate, *v.tr.* (*a*) nommer/choisir/désigner (qn); **to nominate s.o. to a post,** nommer qn à un emploi (*b*) proposer/présenter (un candidat).

nomination, *n.* nomination *f.*

nominee, *n.* **1.** (*for an annuity, etc.*) personne dénommée/désignée **2.** (*for a post*) personne nommée/choisie; candidat(e) désigné(e)/choisi(e) **3.** prête-nom *m; Jur:* personne interposée.

non-acceptance, *n.* non-acceptation *f;* refus *m* d'acceptation (d'un effet, d'une traite).

non-assessable, *a. Adm:* (revenu, etc.) non imposable.

non-assessment, *n. Adm:* non-imposition *f* (d'un revenu, etc.).

non-cancellable, *a.* non résiliable.

non-capitalized, *a.* non capitalisé.

non-contributory, *a.* **non-contributory pension scheme,** caisse *f* de retraite sans versements de la part des bénéficiaires.

non-cumulative, *a. Fin:* **non-cumulative shares,** actions non cumulatives.

non-current, *a.* **non-current liabilities,** passif *m* non exigible/passif à long terme.

non-delivery, *n.* non-livraison *f;* défaut *m* de livraison; non-réception *f* (de marchandises, etc.); non-remise *f* (d'une lettre).

none, *pron. Adm:* (*in schedules, forms, etc.*) néant.

non-execution, *n.* non-exécution *f* (d'un contrat, etc.).

non-executive, *a.* **non-executive director,** administrateur *m.*

non-forfeiture, *n. Jur:* non-déchéance *f/* non-résiliation *f/*prolongation *f/*reconduction *f; Ins:* **non-forfeiture clause,** clause *f* de reconduction automatique.

non-fulfilment, *n.* non-exécution *f* (d'un contrat, etc.).

non-liability, *n. Jur:* non-responsabilité *f;* **non-liability clause,** clause *f* de non-responsabilité.

non-member, *n.* **open to non-members,** ouvert au public.

non-negotiable, *a.* (billet, etc.) non-négociable.

non-participating, *a. Ins:* (police) sans participation aux bénéfices.

non-payment, *n.* non-paiement *m;* défaut *m* de paiement; **in case of non-payment,** en cas de non-paiement; à défaut de paiement; faute *f* de paiement.

non-profit, *a.* **non-profit organization,** société *f* sans but lucratif.

non-profit-making, *a.* (*a*) déficitaire (*b*) **non-profit-making organization,** société *f* sans but lucratif.

non-recurring, *a.* **non-recurring expenditure,** frais *m*/dépenses *f* extraordinaires.

non-resident, *n.* non-résident(e); **bar open to non-residents,** bar ouvert au public.

non-returnable, *a.* perdu; **non-returnable packing,** emballage perdu/non repris; bouteille non consignée.

non-smoker, *n. Trans:* **non-smoker compartment,** compartiment non-fumeurs.

non-taxable, *a. Adm:* (revenu) non imposable.

non-union, *a.* (ouvrier) non syndiqué.

non-unionist, *n.* non-syndiqué(e).

non-warranty, *n.* non-garantie *f;* **non-warranty clause,** clause *f* de non-garantie.

notarial, *a. Jur:* (*a*) (*of functions, etc.*) notarial (*b*) (*of deed, etc.*) notarié.

notary, *n. Jur:* notaire *m;* **contract drawn up before a notary,** contrat fait devant notaire.

note[1]**,** *n.* **1.** note *f*/mémorandum *m* **2.** (*a*) billet *m*/bordereau *m;* **commission note,** bon *m* de commission; **discount note,** bordereau d'escompte; **credit note,** note/facture *f* d'avoir; bordereau de crédit;

debit note, note/bordereau de débit; **note of hand,** reconnaissance *f* (de dette); billet (simple); **promissory note,** billet à ordre (simple) (*b*) **advice note,** bon de livraison; **delivery note,** bon de réception; **dispatch note,** bulletin *m*/bordereau/feuille *f* d'expédition (*c*) *StExch:* **contract note,** bordereau d'achat/de vente; **customhouse note,** bordereau de douane/facture douanière **3.** billet (de banque); **hundred franc note,** coupure *f*/billet de cent francs.

note[2], *v.tr.* **we duly note that . . .,** nous prenons bonne note (de ce) que . . .; **you will note that there is an error in the account,** nous vous faisons remarquer qu'il s'est glissé une erreur dans le compte; **we have noted your order,** nous avons pris bonne note de votre commande.

notice, *n.* **1.** (*a*) avis *m*/notification *f*; **notice of delivery,** avis/bon *m* de réception (*b*) préavis *m*; avertissement *m*; **until further notice,** jusqu'à nouvel ordre/jusqu'à nouvel avis/jusqu'à avis contraire (*c*) (*at work*) préavis *m* (de congé); **to give one's notice,** donner sa démission; **period/term of notice,** délai-congé *m*/délai *m* de congé/délai de préavis; **to give six months' notice,** donner un préavis de six mois; **to require three months' notice,** exiger un préavis de trois mois (*d*) délai *m*; **at short notice,** à bref délai; **can be delivered at three days' notice,** livrable dans un délai de trois jours; *Fin:* **realizable at short notice,** réalisable à court terme; *Bank:* **deposit at seven days' notice,** dépôt *m* à sept jours de préavis; **notice of withdrawal,** mandat *m* (*e*) **notice (to quit),** (avis de) congé *m*; *Jur:* intimation de vider les lieux; **to give notice (to a tenant),** donner congé/signifier son congé à un locataire; **to be under notice to quit,** avoir reçu son congé; **what notice do you require?** quel est le terme du congé? **to give notice,** (*i*) (*of landlord*) donner congé à un locataire

(*ii*) (*of tenant*) donner congé au propriétaire; **you have to give a month's notice,** il faut donner congé un mois d'avance.

notification, *n.* avis *m*/notification *f*/annonce *f* (d'un fait, etc.); **letter of notification,** lettre notificative.

notify, *v.tr.* **to notify s.o. of sth.,** avertir/aviser qn de qch.; notifier qch. à qn; **to be notified of sth.,** recevoir notification de qch.; être avisé/averti de qch.

notions, *n.pl. NAm:* (*in store*) **notions department,** rayon *m* de la mercerie.

novation, *n. Jur:* novation *f* (de contrat, etc.).

novelty, *n.* (article de) nouveauté *f*.

null, *a. Jur: etc:* (*of decree, etc.*) nul; **null and void,** nul et de nul effet/nul et sans effet/nul et non avenu; **to declare a contract null and void,** déclarer un contrat nul et non avenu; **to render null,** annuler/infirmer (un décret, etc.).

nullification, *n.* annulation *f*/infirmation *f*.

nullify, *v.tr.* annuler/infirmer (un acte).

number[1], *n.* **1.** nombre *m*; **total number of shares,** nombre total d'actions; **number of hours worked,** nombre d'heures de travail; *PolEc:* **index number,** nombre index **2.** (*a*) numéro *m*; **reference number,** numéro de référence/d'abonnement, etc.; **order number,** numéro de commande; **lot number,** numéro de lot; (*in hotel*) **room number,** numéro de chambre; *Ind:* **serial number,** numéro de série/de fabrication; **telephone number,** numéro de téléphone; *Bank:* **cheque number,** numéro de chèque (*b*) **the latest number (of a magazine),** le dernier numéro (d'une revue).

number[2], *v.tr.* (*consecutively*) numéroter.

numerical, *a.* (valeur, etc.) numérique; **numerical analysis,** analyse *f* numérique; **numerical data,** données *f* numériques.

O

objective, *n.* but *m*/objectif *m*; **long-term objective**, objectif lointain; **short-term objective**, objectif à court terme; **management by objectives (MBO)**, direction *f* par objectifs (DPO).

obligate, *v.tr.* **1.** *Jur:* **to obligate s.o. to do sth.**, imposer à qn l'obligation de faire qch.; **to be obligated to do sth.**, avoir l'obligation de faire qch. **2.** *NAm: Fin:* (*a*) obliger (un bien) (*b*) affecter (des fonds, des crédits).

obligation, *n.* (*a*) obligation *f*; **to be under an obligation (to do sth)**, être dans l'obligation de/être forcé de/être tenu de (faire qch.); **you are under no obligation**, sans engagement *m* de votre part; **without obligation**, sans engagement; (*in shop*) **no obligation to buy** = entrée libre (*b*) *Jur:* **joint and several obligation**, obligation solidaire.

obsolescence, *n.* (*a*) obsolescence *f*/vieillissement *m*/désuétude *f*; *Ind:* obsolescence (d'un outillage); **built-in obsolescence**, obsolescence prévue systématiquement; **planned obsolescence**, obsolescence prévue/désuétude calculée (*b*) *Ins:* **obsolescence clause**, clause *f* de vétusté.

obsolescent, *a.* obsolescent; qui tombe en désuétude.

obsolete, *a.* obsolescent; vieilli.

obtainable, *a.* procurable; **where is that book obtainable?** où peut-on se procurer ce livre?

occupancy, *n.* **1.** *Jur:* possession *f* à titre de premier occupant **2.** (*a*) occupation *f*/habitation *f* (d'un immeuble); *NAm:*

industrial occupancy, location *f* par une entreprise industrielle; (*of house, etc.*) **immediate occupancy**, possession immédiate (*b*) *NAm:* immeuble occupé; appartement occupé.

occupant, *n.* (*a*) (*i*) occupant(e) (d'un lieu) (*ii*) locataire *mf* (d'une maison) (*b*) *Jur:* premier occupant.

occupation, *n.* **1.** *Jur:* prise *f* de possession (d'un bien à titre de premier occupant) **2.** métier *m*/emploi *m*/profession *f*; **what is his occupation?** quel est son métier? quel est son emploi?

occupational, *a.* **occupational disease**, maladie professionnelle; **occupational hazards**, risques professionnels/risques du métier.

occupier, *n.* occupant(e).

occupy, *v.tr.* **1.** occuper/habiter (une maison, etc.) **2.** occuper/remplir (une fonction, un emploi); **to occupy an important post**, occuper un poste important.

ocean-going, *a.* **ocean-going ship**, navire *m* au long cours/long-courrier *m*.

odd, *a.* **1.** (*a*) (nombre) impair (*b*) **a hundred-odd packing cases**, cent et quelques caisses; une centaine de caisses; **a few odd grammes over**, quelques grammes de plus; **keep the odd change/the odd money**, gardez la monnaie; **to make up the odd money**, faire l'appoint **2.** (*a*) disparate; (*of one of a set, of a pair*) dépareillé; **odd one (of pair)**, demi-paire *f* (*b*) **odd lot**, (*i*) solde *m* (*ii*) lot *m* d'appoint **3.** non usuel; **odd size**, dimension spéciale/non courante; **odd sizes**, tailles non suivies.

oddment, *n.* article dépareillé; article en

solde; coupon *m* d'étoffe; *pl.* **oddments,** fins *f* de série.

off, 1. *adv.* (*a*) **the deal is off,** le marché est rompu; **the strike is off,** la grève n'aura pas lieu (*b*) **to allow 5% off for cash payment,** faire une réduction/une remise de 5% pour paiement (au) comptant; **5p off,** remise/réduction de 5p **2.** *prep.* (*a*) **to take sth. off the price,** faire une remise; **a third off everything,** rabais général d'un tiers; **to borrow money off s.o.,** emprunter de l'argent à qn (*b*) **to have/to take time off (work),** avoir du temps (de) libre; **an afternoon off,** un après-midi de congé; **day off,** jour *m* de congé; **to give the staff a day off,** donner congé à son personnel pour la journée; **to arrange to take two days off,** se libérer pour deux jours.

off-licence, *n.* (*i*) licence *f* permettant exclusivement la vente des boissons alcoolisées à emporter (*ii*) bar *m*/magasin *m* qui vend des boissons alcoolisées à emporter.

offer[1], *n.* (*a*) offre *f*/proposition *f*; **firm offer,** offre ferme; **(this house is) under offer,** on a fait une offre d'achat (pour cette maison); **verbal offer,** offre verbale; **written offer,** offre écrite; **to make an offer (for sth.),** faire une offre (pour qch.); **that's the best offer I can make,** c'est le plus que je puis offrir; c'est mon dernier mot; **we made a better offer,** nous avons fait une suroffre (*b*) **on offer,** en réclame/en vente; **special offer,** article *m* (en) réclame; offre spéciale (*c*) *NAm:* **job offers,** offres d'emploi (*d*) **offer for sale,** mise *f* sur le marché.

offer[2], *v.tr.* (*a*) offrir; **he was offered the post,** on lui a offert le poste (*b*) **to offer goods (for sale),** mettre des marchandises en vente; **house offered for sale,** maison mise en vente (*c*) *StExch:* **prices offered,** cours offerts/cours vendeurs.

offering, *n.* offre *f*; mise *f* sur le marché (de nouvelles actions).

office, *n.* **1.** (*a*) fonctions *fpl*; **to perform the office of secretary,** faire office de secrétaire; **to be in office,** être au pou-

voir; exercer une fonction (*b*) charge *f*/emploi *m*/place *f*/fonctions; **high office/important office,** poste élevé **2.** (*a*) bureau *m*; étude *f* (d'un avocat, d'un notaire); cabinet *m*; **branch office,** succursale; **business office,** bureau commercial; **head office/registered offices (of a company),** bureau principal/bureau central/siège social; administration centrale; **office boy,** garçon de bureau; **office building/office block,** immeuble *m* de bureaux/bâtiment administratif; **office copy,** double *m*; **office equipment,** matériel *m* de bureau; **office expenses,** frais *mpl* de bureau; **office hours,** heures *f* de bureau; **office management,** organisation *f* des bureaux; **office manager,** chef *m* de bureau; **office premises/office space,** locaux *mpl* pour bureaux; **office requisites/office supplies,** articles *m*/fournitures *f* de bureau; **office staff,** personnel *m* de bureau; **for office use only,** (cadre) réservé à l'administration; **office work,** travail *m* de bureau; **office worker,** employé(e) de bureau (*b*) **private office,** cabinet particulier; **the manager's office,** le bureau du directeur; **the secretary's office,** le sécrétariat (*c*) **booking office/(***in theatre***) box office,** bureau de location; guichet *m*; **cash office,** la caisse; **inquiry office,** bureau des renseignements; **tourist office,** bureau de tourisme; Syndicat d'Initiative (*c*) **the Audit Office,** la Cour des comptes.

officer, *n.* **customs officer,** douanier *m*; *NAm:* **executive officer,** cadre supérieur; administrateur *m*; directeur *m*; **training officer,** directeur *m* de formation/cadre chargé de la formation professionnelle.

official, 1. *a.* (*a*) officiel; **official document,** document officiel; **to act in one's official capacity (as),** agir en sa qualité de . . . (*b*) (*of statement, source, journal, etc.*) officiel; *Fin:* **official list,** cote officielle; **official market,** marché officiel; parquet *m*; **official quotations,** cours *m* officiel; *Bank:* **official rate,** taux *m* d'escompte officiel; **official receiver,** syndic *m* au règlement judiciaire/syndic de faillite; **official strike,** grève officielle/réglementaire (c) *Post:* (*on Government envelopes*) **official paid** = franchise postale **2.** *n.* fonctionnaire *m*; *Pej:* bureaucrate *m*; **higher officials,** hauts fonctionnaires; **minor officials,** petits fonctionnaires.

officialese, *n.* jargon administratif.

officially, *adv.* officiellement; **stock quoted officially,** valeurs admises à la cote officielle.

offload, *v.tr.* débarquer (un excédent de marchandises, etc.).

off-peak, *a.* **off-peak day,** jour creux; **off-peak season,** période creuse.

off-season, 1. *n.* morte-saison *f* **2.** *adv.* pendant la morte-saison **3.** *a.* hors saison; **off-season tariff,** tarif *m* hors saison.

offset[1], *n.* (*a*) compensation *f*/dédommagement *m*; **as an offset to my losses,** en compensation de mes pertes (*b*) *Book-k:* compensation (d'une écriture).

offset[2], *v.tr.* compenser (des pertes, etc.).

offtake, *n.* écoulement *m* (de marchandises, etc.).

off-the-job, *a.* **off-the-job training,** formation extérieure/institutionelle.

oil, *n.* (*a*) huile *f*; **crude oil,** pétrole brut/le brut; **diesel oil,** gas-oil *m*; **fuel oil,** (*i*) pétrole (*ii*) mazout *m*; **oil field,** gisement *m* pétrolifère/gisement de pétrole; **oil producing countries,** pays producteurs de pétrole; **oil refinery,** raffinerie *f* de pétrole; **oil rig,** appareil *m* de sondage; installation *f* de forage; (*offshore*) plate-forme (pétrolière); **oil tanker,** pétrolier *m* (*b*) *StExch:* **oil market,** marché pétrolier; **oil prices** prix pétroliers; **oil products,** produits pétroliers; **oil shares/oils,** valeurs pétrolières/les pétroles.

oligopoly, *n. PolEc:* oligopole *m*.

ombudsman, *n.m.* ombudsman; médiateur; protecteur du citoyen.

omnium, *n. StExch:* omnium *m*.

on, *prep.* **1.** (*a*) sur; **tax on tobacco,** taxe sur le tabac (*b*) **to be on the committee,** être membre du comité; **to be on the staff,** faire partie du personnel **2. on a commercial basis,** sur une base commerciale; **on an average,** en moyenne; **interest on capital,** intérêt *m* d'un capital; **to borrow money on security,** emprunter de l'argent sur nantissement; **to retire on a pension of £5000 a year,** prendre sa retraite avec une pension de £5000 par an; **to buy sth. on good terms,** acheter qch. à d'excellentes conditions **3.** (*a*) **on Monday,** lundi (prochain ou dernier); **on Mondays,** le(s) lundi(s); **on April 3rd,** le trois avril; **on and after the 15th,** à partir du quinze; à dater du quinze; **on or about the 12th,** vers le douze (*b*) **on account,** à valoir; **on application/on request,** sur demande; **on condition,** sous réserve; **on examination,** après examen; **on hand,** disponible; **on trial,** à l'essai; **payable on demand,** payable sur demande/à vue; **payable on sight,** payable à vue **4. on the cheap,** à bon marché **5. on sale,** en vente; **on display,** exposé; en vitrine **6. I am here on business,** je suis ici pour affaires; **on holiday,** en congé/en vacances; **to be (working) on sth.,** travailler à qch. **7.** (*a*) **decision binding on s.o.,** décision *f* obligatoire pour qn/qui lie qn (*b*) **cheque on a bank/on Paris,** chèque *m* sur une banque/sur Paris.

oncost, *n.* frais généraux.

one, 1. *num.a.* un **2.** *n.* (*a*) **number one,** numéro un (*b*) **goods that are sold in ones,** marchandises *f* qui se vendent à la pièce/à l'unité; **two for the price of one,** deux pour le prix d'un (*c*) *StExch:* unité *f*; unité de mille livres (au prix nominal des actions); **to issue shares in ones,** émettre des actions en unités.

one-legged, *a. F:* (contrat, etc.) inégal.

one-off, *a.* (article) spécial/hors série; *Publ:* (livre) qui ne fait pas partie d'une série.

one-price, *a.* **one-price counter,** rayon *m* à

prix unique; **one-price store,** magasin *m* à prix unique/prix *m* unique.

onerous, *a.* **1.** (devoir, impôt, etc.) onéreux **2.** *Jur: esp. Scot:* **onerous contract,** contrat *m* à titre onéreux.

one-sided, *a.* (*of contract*) unilatéral; inégal.

one-way, *a.* **one-way packing,** emballage perdu; **one-way ticket,** aller *m* (simple).

on-the-job, *a.* **on-the-job training,** formation *f* pratique; apprentissage *m*/ formation sur le tas/sur le terrain.

open¹, *a.* **1.** (*a*) ouvert; *PolEc:* **the policy of the open door/the open-door policy,** la politique de la porte ouverte (*b*) (*of box, etc.*) ouvert; (*of parcel*) défait; (*of envelope*) (*i*) non cacheté (*ii*) décacheté (*c*) **open all (the) year round,** ouvert toute l'année; **the offices are open from ten to five,** les bureaux sont ouverts de dix heures à cinq heures (*d*) *StExch:* **to buy on the open market,** acheter en Bourse **2. open to any reasonable offer,** disposé à considérer toute offre raisonnable **3. to keep a job open,** ne pas pourvoir à un emploi **4.** (*a*) **open contract,** contrat *m* dont toutes les stipulations ne sont pas encore arrêtées (*b*) *MIns:* **open policy,** police flottante/d'abonnement; police d'assurance ouverte **5.** *Fin:* **open account,** compte ouvert; compte courant; **open cheque,** chèque ouvert/non barré; **open credit,** facilité *f* de caisse; découvert *m* par caisse; **open ticket,** billet ouvert.

open², **1.** *v.tr.* (*a*) décacheter (une lettre); défaire (un paquet); (*on box*) **open here,** côté à ouvrir; **to open the mail,** dépouiller le courrier (*b*) **to open a new shop,** ouvrir un nouveau magasin; **the company is opening its own bank,** la société va ouvrir sa propre banque (*c*) commencer; **to open negotiations,** entamer/engager des négociations (*d*) **to open a bank account,** (se faire) ouvrir un compte bancaire; **to open a line of credit,** ouvrir un crédit (*e*) **to open a loan,** ouvrir un emprunt **2.** *v.i.* (*a*) (*of shop, etc.*) ouvrir; **the bank opens at ten,** la banque ouvre (ses portes) à dix

heures; **as soon as the season opens,** dès l'ouverture *f* de la saison (*b*) *StExch:* **coppers opened firm,** les valeurs *f* cuprifères ont ouvert fermes.

open-end, *a.* **open-end mortgage,** hypothèque qui peut être changée/ modifiée; *NAm: Fin:* **open-end trust/ fund** = société *f* d'investissement à capital variable (SICAV).

open-ended, *a.* (*of agreement, etc.*) sans limites fixes; non déterminé; extensible; **open-ended trust** = société *f* d'investissement à capital variable (SICAV).

opening¹, *n.* **1.** (*a*) ouverture *f* (d'un magasin, d'un bureau; d'un compte, d'un crédit); décachetage *m* (d'une lettre); dépouillement *m* (du courrier) (*b*) **opening of an additional workshop,** mise *f* en service d'un nouvel atelier (*c*) ouverture (de négociations) (*d*) **the opening (up) of new markets/of new channels of trade,** l'ouverture de nouveaux débouchés (pour une marchandise); **have you any openings for school-leavers?** avez-vous des débouchés pour les jeunes qui quittent l'école? (*e*) **opening hours,** heures *f* d'ouverture; **late opening Friday** = nocturne *m* le vendredi; **opening time,** heure d'ouverture (d'un *pub*).

opening², *a.* *Book-k:* **opening entry,** écriture *f* d'ouverture; *StExch:* **opening price,** (*i*) cours *m* d'ouverture/premier cours (d'une séance boursière) (*ii*) cours d'introduction (d'une nouvelle valeur en bourse).

open up, *v.tr.* (*a*) **to open up a country to trade,** ouvrir un pays au commerce (*b*) ouvrir (une boutique, une maison de commerce, une succursale).

operate, **1.** *v.i.* (*a*) opérer; agir; **to operate without cover,** opérer à découvert (*b*) **the rise in wages will operate from January 1st,** l'augmentation *f* des salaires entrera en vigueur le premier janvier (*c*) *StExch:* **to operate for a rise,** spéculer à la hausse; **to operate for a fall,** spéculer à la baisse; **to operate against one's client,** faire de la contrepartie **2.** *v.tr.* (*a*) (*i*) (*of* *pers.*) **to operate a machine,** faire fonctionner un appareil (*ii*) (*of machine*) **how to operate** = fonctionnement *m* (*b*) gérer/diriger (une maison de commerce, etc.).

operating, *n. NAm:* **chief operating officer** = président-directeur général; **operating budget,** budget *m* d'exploitation; **operating costs,** frais *m* d'exploitation; **operating losses,** pertes *f* d'exploitation; **operating profits,** bénéfices *m* d'exploitation.

operation, *n.* **a firm's operations,** les activités *f* d'une entreprise; **operations breakdown,** décomposition *f* des tâches; **operations management,** gestion *f* des opérations; *StExch: Bank:* **bank operation,** opération *f* bancaire; **credit operation,** opération à terme; **stock exchange operation,** opération de Bourse.

operational, *a.* (*a*) opérationnel; **operational costs,** coûts opérationnels; **operational efficiency,** efficacité opérationnelle; **operational planning,** planification *f* des opérations; **operational research (OR),** recherche opérationnelle (RO) (*b*) **to become operational,** être (mis) en service/en marche.

operative, **1.** *a.* (*a*) **to become operative,** entrer en vigueur/prendre effet; **the rise in wages has been operative since May 1st,** l'augmentation des salaires est entrée en vigueur le premier mai (*b*) **the operative side of an industry,** les ateliers *m* **2.** *n.* (*pers.*) ouvrier, -ière; artisan(e).

operator, *n.* (*a*) opérateur, -trice; **(telephone) operator,** opérateur, -trice/téléphoniste *mf*; **switchboard operator,** standardiste *mf*; **to call the operator,** appeler la standardiste/la téléphoniste (*b*) opérateur (d'une machine); **operator's handbook,** manuel *m* de l'utilisateur (*c*) exploitant *m* (d'une entreprise) (*d*) *StExch:* boursier; *m* **operator for a fall,** spéculateur *m* à la baisse; **operator for a rise,** spéculateur *m* à la hausse.

opinion, *n.* (*a*) **opinion poll/survey,** sondage *m* (d'opinion) (*b*) *Jur:* **to take counsel's opinion,** consulter un avocat/un conseiller juridique.

opportunity, *n.* **1.** occasion *f* (favorable); **Equal Opportunity Commission** = commission *f* d'égalité des chances; **investment opportunities,** occasion d'investissement; **job opportunities,** débouchés *m*; **market opportunity,** créneau *m*; **unique sales opportunities,** occasions exceptionnelles **2. opportunity cost,** coût *m* de substitution/coût d'opportunité; **productive opportunity,** possibilité *f* de production; **the industry is rising to the height of its opportunity,** l'industrie *f* atteint peu à peu son développement maximum.

optimal, *a.* optimal; optimum; **optimal resource allocation,** répartition optimale des ressources.

optim(al)ization, *n.* optimisation *f*.

optim(al)ize, *v.tr.* optimiser.

optimum, 1. *n.* optimum *m* **2.** *a.* **optimum conditions,** les conditions les meilleures; les conditions optima/optimales; **optimum employment of resources,** emploi *m* optimum des ressources.

option, *n.* **1.** option *f* (d'achat); **to rent a building with option of purchase,** prendre un immeuble (*i*) en crédit-bail (*ii*) en location-vente **2.** *StExch:* option; **call option,** option d'achat; **double option,** double option/stellage *m*; **option day,** (jour de) la réponse des primes; **option dealings/trading,** opérations à prime/à option; **options market,** marché *m* à options; marché à primes; **option rate,** dont; **put option,** option de vente; **put and call option,** double option/stellage; **to declare an option,** donner la réponse/répondre (à une prime, à une option); **to take up an option,** lever une option/une prime.

optional, *a.* facultatif; **optional extras,** accessoires *m* au choix (de l'acheteur); **optional retirement at sixty,** retraite *f* à soixante ans sur demande.

optionee, *n.* bénéficiaire *mf* d'options.

order[1], *n.* **1.** (*a*) **in order,** en règle; **is your passport in order?** est-ce que votre passeport est en règle? (*b*) en bon état; **machine in good (working) order,** machine *f* en bon état (de fonctionnement, de marche); **out of order,** hors service; (téléphone) en dérangement **2. pay to the order of J. Martin,** payez à l'ordre de J. Martin; **pay J. Martin or order,** payez à J. Martin ou à son ordre; **bill to order/order bill,** billet *m* à ordre; **cheque to order/ order cheque,** chèque *m* à ordre **3.** commande *f*/ordre *m*; **order book,** carnet *m* de commandes; **phone order,** commande par téléphone; **standing order,** commande permanente; (*in restaurant*) **have you given your order?** avez-vous commandé? **to fill an order,** exécuter une commande; **to place an order with (s.o.)/to give (s.o.) an order,** faire/passer une commande à (qn); commander qch. chez qn; **he gave us an order for five tons of fertilizer,** il a commandé/il nous a passé une commande de cinq tonnes d'engrais; **cash with order,** payable à la commande; **order form,** bon *m*/bulletin *m* de commande; **to put goods on order,** commander des marchandises; **economic order quantity,** quantité *f* économique à commander; **it's on order,** c'est commandé; **by order and for account of J. Martin,** d'ordre et pour compte de J. Martin; (*of furniture, etc.*) **made to order,** fabriqué sur commande/à la demande **4.** (*goods ordered*) **to deliver an order,** livrer une commande **5.** (*a*) **order to pay/order for payment,** ordonnance *f* de paiement; **order to view,** permis *m* de visiter (une maison à vendre, etc.) (*b*) bon *m*; **delivery order,** bon de livraison; **issue order,** bon de sortie (de magasin, etc.); **purchase order,** bon d'achat/de commande (*c*) mandat *m*; **order on a bank,** mandat sur une banque; **to pay by banker's order,** payer par virement bancaire; **postal order/money order,** mandat-poste *m*; *Bank:* **standing order,** ordre de transfert permanent.

order[2], *v.tr.* commander/demander/commissioner (qch.); faire/passer une com-

mande; **to order goods from Paris,** commander des articles de Paris; **to order a taxi,** demander un taxi/faire venir un taxi.

ordinary, *a.* (*a*) ordinaire; normal; courant; **ordinary scale of remuneration,** barème courant de rémunération (*b*) *Fin:* **ordinary share,** action *f* ordinaire.

organization, *n.* **1.** organisation *f*; *Ind:* **organization and methods (O and M),** méthodes *f* et organisation; **functional organization/staff organization,** organisation fonctionnelle/horizontale; **line organization,** structure hiérarchique/verticale; **organization chart,** organigramme *m* **2.** organisation/organisme *m* (politique, international, etc.); **travel organization,** organisation de tourisme/de voyage.

organize, *v.tr.* organiser; **organized labour** = les organisations ouvrières.

organizer, *n.* organisateur, -trice.

organizing, *n.* organisation ; **organizing committee,** comité *m* d'organisation.

orientation, *n.* orientation *f*; **customer orientation,** orientation du client.

oriented, *a.* orienté; **profit-oriented organization,** entreprise *f* à but lucratif; **export-oriented economy,** économie orientée vers les exportations.

origin, *n.* origine *f*; **country of origin,** pays *m* de provenance; **goods of foreign origin,** marchandises *f* de provenance étrangère; *Cust:* **certificate of origin,** certificat *m* d'origine.

original, 1. *a.* (*a*) original; initial/premier/ primitif; **original cost,** coût *m* d'acquisition/coût initial; **original value,** valeur initiale/à l'origine; **original packing,** emballage *m* d'origine; *Fin:* **original capital,** capital d'origine/primitif (*b*) **original bill/ cheque/receipt,** primata *m* de traite/de chèque/de quittance; **original document,** (*i*) *Book-k:* pièce *f* comptable (*ii*) *Jur:* primordial *m*; **original invoice,** facture originale 2. *n.* original *m* (d'une facture, etc.); *Fin:* primata (d'une traite); **to copy sth. from the original,** copier qch. sur l'original.

ounce, *n. Meas:* once *f*; (*measure of weight*) **avoirdupois ounce** = 28,35 g; **Troy ounce** = 31,1035 g; (*measure of capacity*) **fluid ounce** = 28 cl.

out, 1. *adv.* (*a*) **the workmen are out (on strike),** les ouvriers sont en grève; **money out (on loan),** argent prêté; prêts *mpl* (*b*) dans l'erreur; **to be out in one's calculations,** être loin du compte; s'être trompé dans ses calculs; **he is five pounds out (in his accounts),** il a une erreur de cinq livres (dans ses comptes) (*c*) **the lease is out,** le bail est expiré **2.** *prep. phr.* **out of season,** hors (de) saison; **my passport is out of date,** mon passeport est périmé; **out of stock,** épuisé; **to be out of work,** être en chômage **3.** *a.* **out (tray),** (corbeille à courrier) sorties *fpl*; *Book-k:* **out book,** livre *m* du dehors.

outbid, *v.tr.* (*at auction*) enchérir (sur qn)/surenchérir/faire une surenchère.

outbidding, *n.* surenchère *f*.

outbound, *a.* (*a*) (navire) en partance; (avion, train) en partance (*b*) (navire, avion) effectuant un voyage d'aller (*c*) **outbound freight,** fret *m* de sortie.

out-clearing, *n. Fin: Bank:* **out-clearing book,** livre *m* du dehors.

outflow, *n. Fin:* **outflow of gold currencies,** sortie *f* d'or; **inflow and outflow of currencies,** opérations *fpl* sur devises.

outgo, *n. NAm:* dépenses *fpl*/sorties *fpl* de fonds.

outgoing, *a.* (*a*) *Ind:* **outgoing shift,** équipe sortante/relevée (*b*) **outgoing mail,** courrier *m* (*i*) à expédier (*ii*) au départ (*c*) *Fin:* **outgoing gold-point,** gold-point *m* de sortie.

outgoings, *n.pl.* dépenses *fpl*/frais *mpl*/ débours *mpl*; sorties *fpl* (de fonds); **the outgoings exceed the incomings,** les

dépenses excèdent les recettes; il y a plus de sorties que de rentrées.

outlay, *n.* frais *mpl*/dépenses *fpl*/débours *mpl*; investissement *m*; **first/initial/ capital outlay,** première mise de fonds/ frais d'établissement; **to get back/recover one's outlay,** rentrer dans ses fonds; **without any great outlay/considerable outlay,** (*i*) sans mise de fonds importante (*ii*) à peu de frais.

outlet, *n.* débouché *m* (pour marchandises); **retail outlet,** magasin *m*.

out-of-court, *a.* **out-of-court settlement,** règlement *m* à l'amiable.

out-of-date, *a.* **out-of-date cheque,** chèque périmé.

out-of-pocket, *a.* **out-of-pocket expenses,** menues dépenses; débours *mpl*; **to be left out-of-pocket,** payer les frais/en être pour ses frais.

output, *n.* production *f*/rendement *m* (d'un travailleur, etc.); **this represents 25% of the total output,** cela représente 25% de la production totale; **daily output of a worker,** production journalière/ rendement journalier d'un ouvrier; **unit price of output,** prix *m* unitaire du produit; **output per hour,** production horaire/production à l'heure; **capacity/ maximum/peak output,** production maximale/maximum; rendement maximal/ maximum; **output bonus,** prime *f* de rendement; **output ceiling,** plafond *m* de la production; **input-output tables,** tableaux *m* d'échanges industriels.

outright, *adv.* **to buy sth. outright,** acheter qch. (au) comptant; **to buy rights outright,** acquérir des droits en bloc.

outsell, *v.tr.* **1.** (*of goods*) (*i*) se vendre en plus grande quantité que/être plus demandé que (qch.) (*ii*) se vendre plus cher que (qch.) **2.** vendre plus (qu'un autre).

outside, *a.* (*a*) **outside worker,** ouvrier, -ière à domicile (*b*) *StExch:* **outside**

broker, courtier *m* marron/coulissier *m*; **outside market,** marché *m* hors cote; coulisse *f*.

outsider, *n. StExch:* courtier *m* marron; courtier libre.

outsize, *n.* grande taille/taille exceptionnelle; (*in men's clothes*) très grand patron; **outsize dress,** robe *f* en taille exceptionnelle; **outsize shoes,** pointure *f* hors série.

outstanding, *a.* (compte) impayé/dû; à percevoir; (paiement) arriéré/en retard; (intérêt) échu; **outstanding debts (due to us),** créances *f* (à recouvrer); **total of bills/credits outstanding at any (given) time,** en-cours *m*; **outstanding coupons,** coupons *m* en souffrance; **outstanding shares,** actions en cours/en circulation; **outstanding notes,** billets *m* effectivement en circulation; **there is nothing outstanding,** tout est réglé.

out-turn, *n.* production nette/rendement net.

outvote, *v.tr.* obtenir une majorité sur/l'emporter sur (qn); **we were outvoted,** la majorité des voix a été contre nous.

outward, *a.* **outward voyage,** voyage *m* d'aller; **outward cargo,** cargaison *f*/ chargement *m* d'aller; **the outward and the homeward voyages,** l'aller *m* et le retour; **outward bill of lading,** connaissement *m* de sortie; **outward freight,** fret *m* de sortie; **outward mission,** visite *f* (d'un groupe d'hommes d'affaires) à l'étranger/ mission *f* à l'étranger.

outwork, *n.* travail *m* (fait) à domicile.

outworker, *n.* employé(e) qui travaille à domicile.

over, 1. *prep.* (*a*) **over fifty pounds,** plus de cinquante livres; **not over 250 grams,** jusqu'à 250 g; **he receives tips over and above his wages,** il reçoit des pourboires en plus/en sus de son salaire (*b*) **an increase of 10% over last year,** une augmentation de 10% par rapport à l'année dernière (*c*) **over the last three years,** au cours des trois dernières années **2.** *adv.* (*a*) **difference over or under,** différence *f* en plus ou en moins (*b*) **bills held over,** effets *m* en souffrance/en suspens **3.** *n.* **over in the cash,** excédent *m* dans l'encaisse; **shorts and overs,** déficits *m* et excédents; **we agree to supply 5% overs,** nous acceptons de vous fournir un excédent de 5% (du nombre commandé).

overage, *n. NAm:* excédent *m*/surplus *m*.

overall, *a.* (*a*) hors tout; total; **overall length,** longueur totale/hors tout; **overall consumption,** consommation totale (*b*) général; global; total; **overall demand,** demande globale; **overall efficiency,** (*i*) efficacité totale (*ii*) rendement global; **overall plan,** plan *m* d'ensemble; **overall company objectives,** objectifs globaux de l'entreprise; **overall financial budget deficit,** impasse *f* budgétaire; **overall indexation,** indexation généralisée.

overassessment, *n.* surtaux *m*.

overbid[1], *n.* (*a*) surenchère *f*; suroffre *f* (*b*) enchère exagérée/offre exagérée.

overbid[2], **1.** *v.tr.* surenchérir; enchérir sur (qn) **2.** *v.i.* (*at sale*) faire une offre exagérée.

overbook, *v.i.* **to be overbooked,** avoir accepté des réservations *f* en surnombre.

overbooking, *n.* réservations *f* en surnombre; surbooking *m*.

overbought, *a. StExch:* (marché) surévalué.

overbuy, *v.i.* acheter au delà de (*i*) ses moyens (*ii*) ce qu'on pourra écouler.

overcapacity, *n. PolEc:* surcapacité *f*.

overcapitalization, *n. Fin:* surcapitalisation *f*.

overcapitalize, *v.tr. Fin:* surcapitaliser (une société).

overcharge[1], *n.* excédent *m*; surmarquage *m*; survente *f*; **to pay a £5 overcharge,** payer £5 d'excédent/payer £5 en trop; **overcharge on an account,** majoration *f* d'un compte.

overcharge[2], *v.tr.* faire payer trop cher un article à (qn); surmarquer (un article); survendre (un article); **you have overcharged me £2,** vous m'avez compté £2 en trop; **to overcharge (on) an account,** majorer une facture/compter qch. en trop sur une facture.

overconsumption, *n.* surconsommation *f.*

overdevelop, *v.tr. PolEc:* surdévelopper.

overdevelopment, *n. PolEc:* surdéveloppement *m.*

overdraft, *n.* **(bank) overdraft,** découvert *m* (d'un compte); solde débiteur; **unsecured overdraft,** découvert en blanc; **to allow s.o. an overdraft of £1000,** accorder à qn un découvert de £1000; **to grant a firm overdraft facilities,** consentir des facilités de caisse à une maison.

overdraw, *v.tr. Bank:* **to overdraw (one's account),** mettre son compte à découvert; tirer à découvert; **account overdrawn,** compte (à) découvert/désapprovisionné; **to be overdrawn at the bank,** avoir un découvert à la banque.

overdue, *a.* (*of account*) arriéré/échu/en retard/en souffrance; **interest on overdue payments,** intérêts *m* moratoires; **the interest is overdue,** l'intérêt n'a pas été payé à l'échéance.

overemployment, *n.* suremploi *m.*

overestimate, *v.tr.* surévaluer (qch.)/ surestimer (la valeur de qch.).

overextend, *v.pr.* **to overextend oneself,** prendre des engagements *m* en excès de ses moyens (financiers).

overfreight, *n.* poids *m* en excès; surcharge *f.*

overfull, *a.* **overfull production,** production *f* excédentaire.

overhead, 1. *a.* (*a*) **overhead expenses/ costs,** frais généraux (*b*) **overhead projection,** rétroprojection *f*; **overhead projector (OHP),** rétroprojecteur *m* **2.** *n.pl* **overheads,** frais généraux (d'administration, de fabrication, etc.).

overindustrialization, *n.* surindustrialisation *f.*

overinsurance, *n.* surassurance *f.*

overinsure, *v.tr.* surassurer.

overissue[1], *n. Fin:* surémission *f*/émission excessive (de papier-monnaie, etc.).

overissue[2], *v.tr. Fin:* faire une surémission de (papier-monnaie, etc.).

overlapping, *n.* **overlapping of two jobs,** chevauchement *m* de deux emplois; empiétement *m* d'un emploi sur l'autre.

overload, *v.tr.* surcharger (un navire, le marché, etc.); **overloaded market,** marché alourdi/surchargé.

overman, *v.tr.* **to be overmanned,** avoir un personnel trop nombreux; avoir un surplus de main-d'œuvre.

overmanning, *n.* **the industry suffers from overmanning,** l'industrie souffre d'un excédent de personnel/de main-d'œuvre.

overnight, *n. Fin:* **overnight loans,** prêts *m* du jour au lendemain.

overpay, *v.tr.* surpayer; trop payer (qn); **overpaid workmen,** ouvriers surpayés/ trop payés; **it appears that I am overpaid,** il paraît que je suis payé au-dessus du taux normal; il paraît que mon salaire est trop élevé.

overpayment, *n.* (*a*) surpaye *f*/surpaie *f*/ paiement *m* en trop; (*of taxes*) trop-perçu *m* (*b*) rémunération/rétribution excessive (d'un employé, etc.).

overproduce, *v.tr. & i.* surproduire.

overproduction, *n.* surproduction *f.*

overrate, *v.tr.* **1.** surévaluer/surestimer/ surfaire (la valeur d'une action, etc.) **2.** *Adm:* surtaxer (un contribuable à l'impôt foncier).

overriding, *a.* principal; essentiel; (redevance, etc.) prioritaire/de priorité/de premier rang; **overriding importance,** importance primordiale; *Jur:* **overriding clause,** clause *f* dérogatoire.

overrun, *n.* *NAm:* (*a*) **overrun (costs),** excédent *m* du coût estimé (*b*) excédent/surplus *m* (de production, etc.).

overseas, 1. *a.* (commerce, etc.) d'outre-mer; **overseas debt,** dette extérieure; **overseas market,** marché étranger/d'outre-mer **2.** *adv.* **from overseas,** d'outre-mer.

overseer, *n.* surveillant(e); inspecteur, -trice; *Ind:* contremaître, -tresse; chef *m* d'atelier.

oversell, *v.tr.* vendre plus (de qch.) qu'on ne peut livrer.

oversold, *a.* *StExch:* (marché) sous-évalué.

overspend[1], *v.tr.* dépenser au-delà de (ses moyens, etc.); **to overspend one's income by £1000,** dépenser £1000 de plus que le montant de son revenu; *Fin:* **amount overspent,** découvert *m.*

overspend[2], *n.* découvert *m.*

overstaffed, *a.* qui a un personnel trop nombreux/un excédent de personnel.

overstock[1], *n.* (*a*) surplus *m*/excédent *m* (d'un stock)/surstock *m* (*b*) *n.pl.* *NAm:* **overstocks,** surplus *m*/excédent *m* (d'un stock)/surstock.

overstock[2], *v.tr.* encombrer (le marché, etc.) (**with,** de); **to overstock a shop with (sth.),** encombrer un magasin de stocks (de qch.).

oversubscribe, *v.tr.* *Fin:* sursouscrire (une émission).

oversubscription, *n.* *Fin:* **oversubscription of a loan,** sursouscription *f* d'un emprunt.

overt, *a.* **market overt,** marché public.

overtax, *v.tr.* surtaxer/surimposer (qn).

over-the-counter, *a.* **over-the-counter sales,** ventes *f* au comptant; **over-the-counter market,** marché *m* des valeurs hors cote.

overtime, 1. *n.* *Ind:* (*a*) heures *f* supplémentaires (de travail); surtemps *m*; **an hour of overtime/an hour's overtime,** une heure supplémentaire; **overtime ban,** grève des heures supplémentaires (*b*) **the salary does not include overtime,** les heures supplémentaires ne sont pas comprises/comptées dans le salaire **2.** *adv.* **to work overtime/to be on overtime,** faire des heures supplémentaires.

overvaluation, *n.* surestimation *f* (de la valeur de qch.) surévaluation *f* (de qch.).

overvalue[1], *n.* survaleur *f* (des monnaies).

overvalue[2], *v.tr.* surévaluer; estimer/ évaluer (un objet) au-dessus de sa valeur.

overweight, 1. *n.* (*a*) surpoids *m*; poids *m* en excès (*b*) excédent *m* (de bagages) **2.** *a.* au-dessus du poids réglementaire; **parcel 50 grams overweight,** colis *m* qui excède de 50 grammes le poids réglementaire/qui a un excédent de 50 grammes.

owe, *v.tr.* devoir; **to owe s.o. sth./to owe sth. to s.o.,** devoir qch. à qn; **the sum owed (to) her,** le montant qui lui est dû; **I still owe you for the petrol,** je vous dois encore l'essence/j'ai encore à vous payer l'essence.

owing, *a.* dû; **all the money owing to me,** tout l'argent qui m'est dû; **the moneys/**

monies owing to us, nos créances *f*; **the rent owing,** l'arriéré *m* du loyer.

own, *v.tr.* posséder; **majority-owned subsidiaries,** filiales dans lesquelles × détient une participation majoritaire; **50% owned company,** société détenue à 50%; **State-owned company,** compagnie étatisée/qui appartient à l'État.

owner, *n.* propriétaire *mf*; exploitant(e); possesseur *m*; patron, -onne (d'une maison de commerce); **rightful owner,** possesseur légitime; *Jur:* ayant droit *m*; **sole owner,** propriétaire unique; **bare owner,** nu propriétaire; **owner-occupied,** occupé par le propriétaire; **owner-occupier,** propriétaire occupant *m*; **ship owner,** armateur *m*.

ownership, *n.* (droit de) propriété *f*; possession *f*; participation *f* (dans une société); *Jur:* **bare ownership,** nue propriété; **common ownership,** collectivité *f*; **joint ownership,** copropriété *f*; **private ownership,** (régime de) propriété privée; **change of ownership,** (*i*) *Jur:* mutation *f* (*ii*) *P.N:* changement *m* de propriétaire; *Jur:* **claim of ownership,** action *f* pétitoire.

P

p, *abbr.* = penny, *pl.* pence; one p, un penny; a book costing 50p, un livre qui coûte cinquante pence; a 10p (postage) stamp, un timbre de dix pence; a half p, un demi-penny; 10p off, remise *f* de 10p/10 pence.

pack[1], *n.* paquet *m*; ballot *m* (de marchandises, etc.); balle *f* (de coton, etc.); *NAm:* pack of cigarettes, paquet de cigarettes; pack goods, marchandises *f* en balle(s) (*b*) blister pack/bubble pack, emballage-bulle *m*.

pack[2], *v.tr.* emballer/empaqueter (des marchandises).

package[1], *n.* 1. (*i*) empaquetage *m*/emballage *m* (*ii*) conditionnement *m* 2. (*a*) paquet *m*/colis *m*; ballot *m* (*b*) *NAm:* package store, débit *m* où on vend des boissons à emporter 3. package deal, contrat global; panier *m*; package tour, voyage *m* à prix forfaitaire; *Ins:* package policies, garanties *f* multirisques; *Cmptr:* progiciel *m*; accounting package, progiciel de comptabilité.

package[2], *v.tr.* (*i*) empaqueter/emballer (*ii*) conditionner.

packaging, *n.* (*i*) empaquetage *m*/emballage *m* (*ii*) conditionnement *m*; packaging industries, industries *f* de conditionnement.

packet, *n.* (*a*) paquet *m* (de thé, de biscuits, de cigarettes, etc.); packet soup, potage *m* en sachet (*b*) (postal) packet, colis (postal).

packing, *n.* 1. emballage *m*/empaquetage *m*; packing charges, frais *mpl* d'emballage; packing extra, emballage non compris/en sus; packing included, emballage compris; packing case, caisse *f*/boîte *f* d'emballage; packing crate, caisse (d'emballage); packing cloth/canvas, toile *f* d'emballage; packing slip, bon *m* de livraison 2. matériel *m* d'emballage; non-returnable packing, emballage perdu.

pad[1], *n.* bloc *m* (de papier à écrire, etc.); desk pad, sous-main *m inv*; memo pad/scribbling pad, bloc-notes *m*; inking pad, tampon encreur.

pad[2], *v.tr.* gonfler (un budget, un relevé de dépenses, etc.).

paid, *a.* 1. appointé/payé/rétribué/rémunéré/salarié; paid assistant, aide rétribué(e); paid holidays, congés payés; paid work, travail rémunéré/rétribué; paid worker, (travailleur, -euse) salarié(e) 2. (*a*) (*of goods, etc.*) payé; (*on bills*) pour acquit/payé/acquitté; paid bills, rentrées *fpl*; paid cash book, main courante de dépenses/de sorties (*b*) *Fin:* paid up capital, capital appelé/versé; paid up shares, actions libérées; tax paid, (*i*) impôt payé (*ii*) net versé.

pallet, *n.* palette *f*; plate-forme *f* de manutention.

palletization, *n.* palettisation *f* (des marchandises).

palletize, *v.tr.* palettiser (des marchandises); mettre (des marchandises) sur palette(s); palletized goods, marchandises palettisées/sur palette(s).

panel, *n.* 1. advertisement panel, panneau *m* d'affichage/de publicité; panneau-réclame *m* 2. consumer panel, groupe-témoin *m*/panel *m* de consommateurs.

panic, *n.* **panic buying,** (faire des) achats *mpl* de précaution.

paper, *n.* **1.** (*a*) papier *m*; **blotting paper,** (papier) buvard *m*; **carbon paper,** papier carbone; **brown paper/wrapping paper,** papier kraft/papier d'emballage; **grease-proof paper,** papier beurre/papier jambon/papier parcheminé; **typing paper,** papier pour machine à écrire/*F:* papier machine; **ruled/lined paper,** papier réglé (*b*) **a sheet/a piece of paper,** une feuille/un morceau de papier; **paper bag,** pochette *f*/sac *m* de papier (*c*) **the paper industry,** l'industrie du papier; **paper manufacture,** (usine de) papeterie *f*; **paper manufacturer,** fabricant *m* de papier (*d*) **paper profits,** profits fictifs/théoriques **2.** (*a*) écrit *m*/document *m*/pièce *f*; **the papers of a firm,** les écritures *f* d'une entreprise; **relevant papers,** pièces justificatives; **ship's papers,** papiers/documents de bord; **clearance papers,** papiers d'expédition (*b*) **paper clip/paper fastener,** attache *f* métallique; trombone *m* (*c*) *Fin:* papier valeur; **accommodation paper,** papier de complaisance; **bankable/unbankable paper,** papier bancable/non bancable; **commercial/mercantile/trade paper,** papier commercial/de commerce; **guaranteed paper,** papier fait; **long paper,** papier à long terme; **short paper,** papier à court terme; **negotiable paper,** papier négociable; **paper securities,** papiers valeurs/titres *m* fiduciaires (*d*) billets *mpl* (de banque); **paper money/paper currency,** papier-monnaie *m* **3.** journal *m*; **daily paper,** quotidien *m*; **weekly paper,** hebdomadaire *m*; **Sunday paper,** journal du dimanche; **trade paper,** revue *f* (de commerce) spécialisée.

paperwork, *n.* travail *m* de bureau; VAT makes a lot of paperwork for shopkeepers, la TVA complique les écritures des commerçants.

par, *n. Fin:* pair *m*; **above par,** au-dessus du pair; **below par,** au-dessous du pair; **par of exchange,** pair du change; **par value,** valeur *f* au pair/valeur nominale; **repayable at par,** remboursable au pair; **to issue shares at par,** émettre des actions au pair.

parcel[1], *n.* paquet *m*/colis *m*; **to make/do up a parcel,** faire un paquet; **to do up goods into parcels,** empaqueter des marchandises; **parcel(s) delivery,** livraison *f*/remise *f* de colis à domicile; factage *m*/service *m* de messageries; **parcels-delivery company,** entreprise *f* de factage; **parcel(s) office,** (bureau des) messageries *f*; **parcel post,** service *m* (*i*) des colis postaux (*ii*) de messageries; **to send sth. by parcel post,** envoyer qch. comme colis postal/par colis postal; **parcel rates,** tarif *m* colis postal.

parcel[2], *v.tr.* empaqueter; **to parcel up a consignment of books,** mettre en paquets/emballer un envoi de livres.

parent, *n.* **parent company,** société mère/maison mère.

pari passu, *Lt. phr.* pari passu (**with,** avec).

parity, *n.* **1.** *Fin:* exchange at parity, change *m* à (la) parité/au pair; **fixed parity,** parité fixe; **parity of exchange,** parité de change; **parity ratio,** rapport *m* de parité; **parity table,** table *f* des parités; **parity value,** valeur *f* au pair **2.** *n.pl.* **parities,** taux *mpl* des changes.

part, *n.* (*a*) **as part of this expansion programme,** dans le cadre de ce programme d'expansion; **it is part of his job to . . . ,** il lui appartient de . . . (*b*) **to pay in part,** payer partiellement; **to contribute in part to the expenses,** contribuer en partie/partiellement aux frais (*c*) *Ind:* pièce *f*/élément *m*; **spare parts,** pièces détachées/de rechange (*d*) **part owner,** copropriétaire *mf*; **part ownership,** copropriété *f*; indivision *f* (*e*) **to work part time,** travailler à temps partiel/à mi-temps; **part time worker/part timer,** employé(e) qui travaille à temps partiel/à mi-temps (*f*) **part exchange,** reprise *f*; **part load,** charge incomplète; **part payment,** acompte *m*; *Nau:* part

shipment, expédition partielle/chargement partiel.

partial, *a.* partiel; en partie; **partial damage to goods,** avarie *f* d'une partie de la marchandise; **partial loss,** perte partielle/sinistre partiel; **partial acceptance of a bill,** acceptation partielle d'une traite.

participation, *n.* participation *f* (**in sth.,** à qch.); **worker participation,** participation des salariés/participation ouvrière/intéressement *m* du personnel; *Bank: Ins:* **participation loan,** crédit syndical.

participative, *a.* participatif; **participative management,** direction participative.

particular, 1. *a.* particulier; spécial 2. *n.* détail *m*/particularité *f*; **to give particulars of sth.,** donner des détails de qch.; **particulars of an account,** détail d'un compte; **to give full particulars,** donner les menus détails/tous les détails; **to ask for fuller particulars about sth.,** demander des précisions *f*/des indications *f* supplémentaires sur qch.; **for further particulars apply to . . .,** pour tous renseignements/pour obtenir des renseignements supplémentaires, écrire à/s'adresser à . . .; **particulars of sale,** description *f* de la propriété à vendre; cahier *m* des charges; *Book-k:* **the particulars of an entry,** le libellé d'un article/d'une écriture (comptable).

partition, *n. Ins:* **partition of average,** répartition *f* d'avaries.

partly, *adv.* partiellement; en partie; **partly paid (up) (share, capital),** (action) non (complètement) libérée; (capital) non entièrement versé; **partly secured creditor,** créancier partiellement nanti.

partner, *n.* associé(e); **active partner,** (associé) commandité *m*; **contracting partner,** contractant(e); **full partner,** associé à part entière; **general partner,** associé en nom collectif; **joint partner,** coassocié(e); **junior partner,** associé en second; **sleeping/dormant partner,** (associé) commanditaire *m*; bailleur *m* de fonds; **senior partner,** associé principal.

partnership, *n.* 1. association *f*/société *f*; **deed of partnership,** contrat *m* de société/d'association; **to enter/go into partnership with s.o.,** s'associer à/avec qn; **to take up a partnership in a business,** s'associer à/avec qn; s'intéresser dans une affaire; **to take s.o. into partnership,** s'adjoindre un associé/prendre qn comme associé; **to dissolve a partnership,** dissoudre une association; **deed/articles of partnership,** contrat de société/d'association 2. société; **general partnership,** société commerciale en nom collectif; **limited partnership,** (société en) commandite (simple); **limited partnership/partnership limited with shares,** (société en) commandite par actions; **industrial partnership,** participation *f* des salariés aux bénéfices/participation ouvrière/intéressement *m* du personnel.

party, *n.* 1. *Adm: etc:* **working party,** comité *m* d'étude/groupe *m* de travail 2. (*a*) *Jur:* **party (to a suit, to a dispute),** partie *f*; **the contracting parties,** les parties contractantes (*b*) **to become a party to an agreement,** devenir partie à un contrat; **parties to a bill of exchange,** intéressé(e)s à une lettre de change; **a third party,** un tiers/une tierce personne; **to deposit a sum in the hands of a third party,** déposer une somme en main tierce; **for the account of a third party,** pour compte d'autrui; **payment on behalf of a third party,** paiement *m* par intervention; **third party insurance,** assurance *f* au tiers; **third party risks,** risques *m* de préjudice au tiers.

pass[1], *n.* laissez-passer *m inv*; **pass book,** carnet *m*/livret *m* de banque.

pass[2], *v.tr.* 1. **to pass a dividend,** conclure un exercice sans payer de dividende; **passed dividend,** dividende non déclaré 2. (*a*) **pass an invoice,** approuver une facture; (*of company*) **to pass a dividend of 5%,** approuver un dividende de 5% (*b*) **to pass a resolution,** passer/voter/adopter une résolution 3. *Book-k:* **to pass an item to**

current account, passer/porter un article en compte courant.

passenger, *n.* (*on train*) voyageur, -euse; (*on ship, aircraft*) passager, -ère; **passenger train,** train *m* de voyageurs.

passport, *n.* passeport *m.*

patent[1], **1.** *a.* (*a*) *Jur:* **letters patent,** brevet *m* d'invention/d'inventeur (*b*) **patent goods,** articles brevetés; **patent medicine,** spécialité *f* pharmaceutique **2.** *n.* (*a*) brevet d'invention; **patent relating to improvements,** brevet de perfectionnement; **to take out a patent for an invention,** prendre un brevet pour une invention/faire breveter une invention; **patent applied for/patent pending,** demande (de brevet) déposée; **infringement of a patent,** contrefaçon *f*; (*of invention*) **patent expired,** invention tombée dans le domaine public; **commissioner of patents,** directeur *m* de brevets; **patent agent,** agent *m* en brevets (d'invention); **patent engineer,** ingénieur *m* conseil (en matière de propriété industrielle); **patent office,** bureau *m* des brevets; **patent rights,** propriété industrielle; **patent rolls,** registres *m* portant nomenclature des brevets d'invention; **patent trading,** échange *m* de brevets (*b*) invention/fabrication brevetée.

patent[2], *v.tr.* protéger par un brevet/faire breveter (une invention); prendre un brevet pour (une invention).

patentable, *a.* brevetable.

patented, *a.* breveté.

patentee, *n.* titulaire *mf* d'un brevet.

pattern, *n.* **1.** échantillon *m*; **pattern book/card,** livre *m*/carte *f* d'échantillons **2.** patron *m* (de robe, etc.) **3.** **price pattern,** structure *f* de(s) prix; **the normal pattern of trade,** la tendance normale du marché.

pawn[1], *n.* **in pawn,** en gage; **to put sth. in pawn,** mettre qch. en gage/engager qch.; déposer qch. au crédit municipal; **to take**

sth. out of pawn, dégager/désengager qch.; **pawn ticket,** reconnaissance *f* (de dépôt de gage).

pawn[2], *v.tr.* (*a*) mettre (qch.) en gage; engager (qch.) (*b*) *StExch:* **pawned stock,** titres *mpl* en pension.

pawnbroker, *n.* prêteur sur gage(s); commissionnaire *m* au crédit municipal.

pawnee, *n.* prêteur, -euse sur gage(s).

pawner, *n.* *Jur:* emprunteur, -euse sur gage(s).

pawnshop, *n.* bureau *m* de prêt sur gage(s)/mont-de-piété *m*; crédit municipal.

pay[1], *n.* **1.** salaire *m*; appointements *mpl*; traitement *m* (d'un cadre); **back pay,** rappel *m* de traitement/arrérage *m* de salaire; **basic pay,** salaire de base; **equal pay,** égalité *f* des salaires (entre hommes et femmes); **holidays with pay,** congés payés; **rate of pay,** taux *m* de salaire; **severance pay,** indemnité *f* de cessation d'emploi; **take-home pay,** salaire net/ traitement net (moins impôt, etc. retenu à la source); **unemployment pay,** allocation *f*/indemnité/secours *m* de chômage; **to draw one's pay,** toucher son salaire/son traitement/son mois; **pay day,** jour *m* de paie; **pay slip,** bulletin *m*/feuille *f* de paie; **pay cheque,** chèque *m* de règlement/de traitement/de salaire; **pay packet/pay envelope** = salaire (payé en espèces); **pay policy,** politique salariale; **pay talks,** négociations *fpl* salariales **2.** **pay desk,** caisse *f*; **pay office,** caisse; guichet *m* **3.** **pay phone,** téléphone payant; **pay TV,** télévision *f* à péage.

pay[2], *v.tr. & i.* (*a*) **to pay s.o. £100,** payer £100 à qn; **he paid him £100 for it,** il le/la lui a payé(e) £100; **how much do you pay for tea?** combien payez-vous le thé? **you have paid too much for it,** vous l'avez payé trop cher; **to pay cash (down)/spot cash,** payer (argent) comptant/payer (au) comptant; **to pay in advance,** payer d'avance; **to pay in full,** payer intégralement/en totalité; *NAm:* **to pay as you go,** (*i*) payer ses factures promptement (*ii*) ne jamais dépenser plus que l'on ne gagne; **£1000 to be paid in four instalments,** £1000 payable en quatre versements; **advance to be paid back within a year,** avance *f* remboursable dans un an au plus tard; **to pay sth. (down) on account,** verser une (somme à titre de) provision; verser des arrhes *f* (*b*) **pay as you earn (PAYE)**/*NAm:* **pay as you go** = retenue *f* (de l'impôt sur le revenu) à la source; **to pay at maturity/at due date,** payer à échéance; **to pay on demand/ on presentation,** payer à vue/à présentation; **dividend paid out of capital,** dividende prélevé sur le capital; **pay to the order of . . .,** payez à l'ordre de . . .; (*on cheque*) **pay self/pay cash,** payez à (l'ordre de) moi-même; **to pay a cheque into the bank/to pay in a cheque,** remettre/déposer un chèque à la banque; faire porter un chèque au crédit de son compte/sur son compte; **to pay money into s.o.'s account,** verser de l'argent au compte de qn (*c*) payer (ses employés, etc.); **to be paid by the hour/by the week,** être payé à l'heure/à la semaine; **badly paid job,** situation mal payée/mal rémunérée; **to pay (off) a debt,** payer/solder/liquider/régler/acquitter (une dette); **to pay (off) a creditor,** rembourser/désintéresser un créancier; **to pay off a mortgage,** purger une hypothèque; **to pay a bill/an account,** payer/régler un compte; acquitter une facture; (*on receipted bill*) **paid,** pour acquit/payé; **carriage paid,** (en) port payé (par l'envoyeur); *Cust:* **to pay duty on sth.,** payer des droits sur qch. (*e*) **business that doesn't pay,** affaire *f* qui ne rapporte pas/qui n'est pas rentable.

payable, *a.* payable/acquittable; (emprunt) remboursable; **payable at sight/to order/to bearer,** payable à vue/à ordre/ au porteur; **payable on presentation,** payable à vue/à présentation; **payable on delivery,** payable à la livraison; **bill payable in one month,** lettre *f* de change à une usance/à trente jours; **payable on the 15th**

prox., valeur au 15 prochain; **to make (a bill, a cheque) payable to s.o.,** faire/ libeller (un billet, un chèque) à l'ordre de qn; **cheque payable to bearer,** chèque *m* au porteur; **bonds made payable in francs,** bons libellés en francs; **accounts payable/** *NAm: n.* **payables,** comptes fournisseurs; **rates payable by the tenant,** impôts locatifs/charges locatives; *Book-k:* **bills payable book,** échéancier *m*.

payback, *n.* récupération *f* (du capital investi); **payback period,** délai *m* de récupération.

paycheck, *n. NAm:* chèque *m* de traitement/de salaire.

PAYE, *abbr:* = **pay as you earn,** retenue *f* (de l'impôt sur le revenu) à la source.

payee, *n.* (*a*) bénéficiaire *mf*; **payable at address of payee,** payable à domicile (*b*) porteur *m* (d'un effet).

payer, *n.* **tax payer,** contribuable *mf*; *StExch:* **payer of contango,** reporté *m*.

paying[1], *a.* **1. paying guest,** pensionnaire *mf* **2.** (*of business, etc.*) rentable/lucratif/profitable/qui rapporte **3.** payant; **paying third system,** système *m* du tiers payant.

paying[2], *n.* **1.** paiement *m*/versement *m* (d'argent) **2.** (*a*) **paying back,** remboursement *m*/restitution *f* (d'un emprunt) (*b*) versement (d'argent à la banque, etc.); **paying-in slip,** bulletin *m* de versement/de paiement; **paying-in book,** carnet *m* de versements (*c*) **paying off,** (*i*) liquidation *f*/règlement *m*/amortissement *m* (d'une dette); purge *f* (d'une hypothèque) (*ii*) congédiement *m* (des ouvriers, etc.) (*d*) **paying out/up,** déboursement *m*; débours *m*.

payload, *n.* charge payante/charge commerciale/charge utile (d'un véhicule); *Av:* poids *m* utile.

payment, *n.* (*a*) paiement *m*/versement *m* (d'argent); **cash payment,** paiement (au) comptant/en argent comptant; **down payment,** acompte *m*/arrhes *fpl*/provision *f*; **on payment of £100,** contre paiement de £100/moyennant (le paiement de) £100; **payment by cheque,** paiement par chèque; **payment in cash,** paiement en espèces/en numéraire; **payment in full,** paiement intégral; *StExch:* **payment in full on allotment,** libération *f* (d'actions) à la répartition; **payment on account,** paiement partiel / versement / acompte / provision/arrhes; **subject to payment,** à titre onéreux/moyennant paiement; **without payment,** à titre gracieux/à titre bénévole (*b*) paiement/règlement *m* (d'une dette); remboursement *m* (d'un créancier); **deferment of payment,** délai *m* de paiement; **deferred payment,** paiement différé/retardé; **non payment,** défaut *m* de paiement; **payment by instalments,** paiement par versements/paiement échelonné; **payment of balance,** paiement pour solde; **payment of interest,** paiement des intérêts; **to authorize payment,** autoriser le paiement d'un compte (*c*) **to present a cheque for payment,** présenter un chèque à l'encaissement; **to stop payment of a cheque,** faire opposition à un chèque (*d*) salaire *m*; **back payment,** rappel *m*/arrérage *m* de salaire; **payment by results,** salaire *m* au rendement.

pay off, *v.tr. & i.* congédier (des ouvriers, etc.).

pay-off, *n. NAm:* (*a*) paiement *m*/ règlement *m* (*b*) **£40 000 pay-off for company head,** indemnité *f* de £40 000 offerte au président de la société.

pay out¹, *n. NAm:* récupération *f* (d'un investissement).

pay out², *v.tr. & i.* payer/débourser/ verser.

payroll, *n.* livre *m* de paie/registre *m* des salaires; **to be on the payroll,** faire partie du personnel.

pay up, *v.tr. & i.* payer; se libérer (de ses dettes, etc.).

peak, *n.* **peak hours,** heures de pointe; **peak output,** (niveau) record (*m*) de production; **peak year,** année *f* record; **production was at its peak,** la production était à son maximum.

pecuniary, *a.* pécuniaire; **pecuniary difficulties,** embarras financiers; ennuis *m* d'argent; *Jur:* **for pecuniary gain,** dans un but lucratif; **pecuniary offence,** délit puni d'une amende.

pedlar, *n.* colporteur *m.*

peg¹, *n.* **1. off the peg clothes,** vêtements *m* de confection; le prêt-à-porter; **to buy a dress off the peg,** acheter une robe de confection **2.** *Fin:* **crawling peg,** parité *f* à crémaillère/parité rampante/taux *m* de change rampant/flottant.

peg², *v.tr.* **1. to peg (back) prices,** bloquer les prix; **pegged prices,** prix *m* de soutien **2.** *StExch: Fin:* **to peg the market,** stabiliser le marché (en achetant et en vendant); maintenir le marché ferme; *esp.* maintenir le cours du change.

pegging, *n. StExch: Fin:* stabilisation *f* (du marché, etc.); blocage *m* (de la livre sterling, des prix, etc.); soutien *m* des prix.

pen, *n.* stylo *m; Cmptr:* **light pen,** photostyle *m.*

penalty, *n.* (*a*) amende *f* (pour retard de livraison, etc.) (*b*) *Adm:* sanction (pénale); (*in contract*) **penalty clause,** clause pénale (de dommages-intérêts); **penalty for non-performance of contract,** dédit *m.*

pence, *n.pl. see* **penny.**

pending, *a.* (*a*) (négociations) en cours; *Jur:* (affaire) en instance; **patent pending,** demande de brevet déposée (*b*) **pending tray,** travail en attente/en souffrance.

penetrate, *v.tr.* pénétrer (des marchés étrangers, etc.).

penny, *n.* **1.** *pl.* **pence** (*abbr.* **p**)

(*coin* = *1/100th of £1*) penny *m*; **a ten pence piece/a ten p piece,** une pièce de dix pence; **one half penny,** un demi penny; **a five pence stamp,** un timbre de 5 pence; (*value*) **I paid 60 pence for it,** je l'ai payé 60 pence **2.** *NAm:* (*coin*) *pl.* **pennies,** cent *m*.

pension, *n.* (*a*) pension *f*; **Government pension,** pension de/sur l'État; **old age pension** = assurance-vieillesse *f*; **widow's pension,** pension de veuve/pension réversible/de réversion (*b*) **pension plan/ scheme,** régime *m* de retraite; **contributory pension plan,** régime de retraite financé par les cotisations patronales et ouvrières; **earnings related pension plan,** régime de retraite proportionnelle; **graduated pension scheme** = régime de retraites complémentaires (obligatoires)/ retraite des cadres; *NAm:* **voluntary pension plan,** plan bénévole de retraite; **pension funds,** caisses *f* de retraite; **to retire on a pension,** prendre sa retraite; **to commute a pension,** liquider une pension.

pensionable, *a.* **1.** (*of pers.*) qui a droit à une pension/à sa retraite **2.** (*of injury, etc.*) qui donne droit à une pension; **pensionable age,** âge *m* de la mise à la retraite **3.** (emploi) donnant droit à pension.

pensioner, *n.* bénéficiaire *mf* d'une pension; **old age pensioner (OAP),** retraité(e).

pensioning, *n.* **pensioning (off),** mise *f* à la retraite.

pension off, *v.tr.* **to pension s.o. off,** mettre qn à la retraite.

peppercorn, *n.* **peppercorn rent,** loyer nominal.

per, *prep.* (*a*) par; *Jur:* **per pro,** par procuration (*b*) **as per invoice,** suivant facture; selon/d'après facture; **as per sample,** conformément à l'échantillon; **credited as per contra,** crédité ci-contre (*c*) **ten francs per kilo,** dix francs le kilo; **100 km per hour,** 100 kilomètres à l'heure/100 kilomètres-heure/100 Km/h; **per cent,** pour cent; **seven per cent interest,** intérêt de sept pour cent (*d*) **per annum/per year,** par an; **how much do you earn per annum?** quel est votre salaire annuel? **to receive so much per year,** recevoir tant par an; **per week,** par semaine; **per day/per diem,** par jour; *NAm:* **the per diem,** le salaire journalier; **per capita income/income per capita,** salaire individuel (*e*) **per-share earnings,** bénéfices *m* par action.

percentage, *n.* pourcentage *m*; **percentage of profit,** pourcentage de bénéfices; **directors' percentage of profits,** tantième *m*.

percentile, *n. Stat:* centile *m*.

performance, *n.* **1.** exécution *f* (d'un contrat); **performance bond,** garantie *f* d'exécution/de bonne exécution **2.** (*i*) fonctionnement *m*/marche *f* (d'une machine) (*ii*) rendement *m*/performance *f* (d'un appareil, etc.); **performance rating,** rendement effectif **3.** rendement/résultat *m*; **performance against objectives,** réalisations comparées aux projets; **performance appraisal/evaluation,** évaluation *f* du rendement; **job performance,** rendement au travail; **earnings performance,** rentabilité *f*.

peril, *n. MIns:* **peril(s) of the sea,** fortune *f* de mer; risque(s) *m*(*pl*) de mer.

period, *n.* **1.** période *f*; durée *f*; délai *m*; **for a period of three months/for a three months' period/for a three-month period,** pendant (une période de) trois mois; **to discharge a liability within the agreed period,** liquider une créance dans les délais convenus; *Bank:* **deposit for a fixed period,** dépôt *m* à terme fixe **2.** **accounting period,** exercice *m*; **period under review,** exercice écoulé.

periodical, **1.** *a.* périodique **2.** *n.* périodique *m*/publication *f* périodique; journal *m*.

perishable, 1. *a.* périssable; sujet à s'altérer/à se détériorer; *Nau:* **perishable cargo,** denrées *f* périssables; chargement *m* périssable **2.** *n.pl.* **perishables,** denrées périssables.

perks, *n.pl.* avantages sociaux; privilèges *mpl.*

permanency, *n.* emploi permanent.

permanent, *a.* (*a*) permanent; **permanent job,** situation permanente; **to be on the permanent staff (of a firm),** avoir un emploi permanent/être titulaire d'un poste (*b*) *Fin:* **permanent assets,** actif immobilisé; capital immobilisé.

permission, *n.* permission *f*; autorisation *f*; **written permission,** autorisation écrite.

permit, *n.* **1.** permis *m*; permission *f*/ autorisation *f*; **building permit,** permission/autorisation/permis de construire; **work permit,** permis de travail **2.** *Cust:* acquit-à-caution *m*; passavant *m*.

perpetual, *a.* perpétuel/à vie; **perpetual loans,** emprunts perpétuels; **perpetual inventory,** inventaire permanent.

perquisites, *n.pl.* = **perks.**

person, *n.* personne *f*; individu *m*; **private person,** (simple) particulier *m*; **to act through a third person,** passer par une tierce personne/par personne interposée; **the persons concerned,** les intéressés; **person named,** accrédité(e); **policy to a named person,** police nominative; **to be delivered to the addressee in person,** à remettre en main(s) propre(s); *Tp: NAm:* **person-to-person call,** appel avec préavis.

personal, *a. Cust:* **articles for personal use/personal effects,** effets usagers/ effets personnels; *Bank:* **personal account,** compte (en banque) personnel/ particulier; *Fin:* **personal income,** revenu personnel; **personal share,** action nominative; *Com:* **personal selling,** vente directe au consommateur; *Ins:* **personal accident insurance,** assurance *f* contre les accidents corporels/contre les accidents à personnes; *Adm:* (*on letter*) **personal,** personnel; **personal assistant (PA),** secrétaire particulier, -ière; assistant(e); *Tp:* **personal call,** appel *m* avec préavis.

personalize, *v.tr.* personnaliser; **personalized sales techniques,** publicité personnalisée; **personalized cheque,** chèque personnalisé.

personalty, *n. Jur:* biens *m* meubles/ effets mobiliers; **to convert realty into personalty,** ameublir un bien; **conversion of realty into personalty,** ameublissement *m* d'un bien.

personnel, *n. Ind: etc:* personnel *m*; **personnel department,** service *m* du personnel; **personnel manager/officer,** directeur *m*/chef *m* du personnel; **personnel management,** direction *f*/administration *f*/gestion *f* du personnel; **personnel rating,** appréciation *f* du personnel.

pertinent, *a.* **pertinent cost,** coût approprié.

petition, *n.* **petition in bankruptcy,** (*i*) requête *f* des créanciers (*ii*) requête du négociant insolvable; **to file a petition in bankruptcy,** déposer son bilan.

petrodollar, *n.* pétrodollar *m.*

petrol, *n.* essence *f*; **petrol consumption,** consommation *f* d'essence; **petrol station,** station-service *f*; **premium grade petrol/four star petrol,** supercarburant *m*/ *F:* super *m.*

petroleum, *n.* pétrole *m*; **crude petroleum,** pétrole brut/le brut; **refined petroleum,** pétrole raffiné; **the petroleum industry,** l'industrie pétrolière/ du pétrole; **petroleum products,** produits pétroliers.

petty, *a.* **petty cash,** petite caisse; menue monnaie; **petty cash book,** livre *m* de petite caisse; **petty expenses,** menues dépenses.

phase in, *v.tr.* adopter/introduire progressivement (de nouvelles méthodes, etc.); mettre en place progressivement (de nouvelles installations, etc.).

phase out, *v.tr.* éliminer progressivement (de vieilles méthodes, etc.); éliminer/ remplacer progressivement (de vieux équipements, etc.).

phone[1], *n.* F: téléphone *m*; **to be on the phone,** (*i*) être/parler au téléphone (*ii*) être abonné au téléphone; **to answer the phone,** répondre au téléphone; **to speak to s.o. on the phone,** parler à qn au téléphone; **phone book,** annuaire *m* téléphonique/du téléphone; **phone box,** cabine *f* téléphonique; **phone call,** appel *m* (téléphonique)/coup *m* de téléphone/ coup de fil.

phone[2], *v.tr. & i.* **to phone s.o.**, téléphoner à qn/appeler qn au téléphone/donner un coup de fil à qn; **I'll phone you,** je vous téléphonerai; **to phone for sth.,** demander qch./faire venir qch. par téléphone; **to phone for a taxi,** appeler un taxi/ téléphoner pour faire venir un taxi; **to phone a piece of news,** téléphoner une nouvelle.

photocopier, *n.* photocopieur *m*/photo-copieuse *f*/copieur *m*.

photocopy[1], *n.* photocopie *f*.

photocopy[2], *v.tr.* photocopier.

photostat[1], *n.* **photostat (copy),** photostat *m*.

photostat[2], *v.tr. & i.* faire un photostat.

physical, *a.* physique; *NAm:* **physical inventory,** inventaire *m* (du matériel, des marchandises, etc.).

picket[1], *n. Ind: etc:* **flying pickets,** piquets de grève volants; **strike pickets/picket line,** piquets de grève/de grévistes.

picket[2], *v.tr.* **to picket a factory,** faire le piquet de grève; se tenir en faction devant une usine (pour en interdire l'accès); **the workers are picketing the factory,** les ouvriers font le piquet de grève devant l'usine.

picketing, *n. Ind: etc:* **there is no picket-**

ing, il n'y a pas de piquets de grève (en faction); **secondary picketing,** piquet *m* de grève devant une entreprise étrangère au conflit.

pick up, *v.i.* **business is picking up,** les affaires *f* reprennent; **prices are picking up,** les cours *m* reprennent.

piece, *n.* pièce *f* (de drap, etc.); **to sell sth. by the piece,** vendre qch. à la pièce; *Tex:* **piece goods,** marchandises *f*/tissus *m* à la pièce; *Ind:* **piece work,** travail *m* à la pièce/aux pièces; travail à la tâche; **piece rate,** salaire *m* à la pièce/aux pièces; **to be paid piece rates**/*esp. NAm:* **by the piece,** être payé à la pièce.

piecework, *n.* travail *m* (rémunéré) aux pièces/travail à la tâche.

pie-chart, *n.* graphique *m* circulaire (à secteurs).

pigeonhole, *n.* case *f*/casier *m* (pour le courrier).

pilot, *n.* **pilot factory/pilot plant,** usine *f* pilote; installation *f* d'essai; **pilot project,** projet *m* pilote; **pilot series,** présérie *f*.

pint, *n. Meas:* (*i*) pinte *f* = 0,568 litre; *Fr.C:* chopine *f* (*ii*) *NAm:* = 0,473 litre; **imperial pint,** pinte légale.

pioneer[1], *n.* pionnier *m*; **pioneer products,** innovations *f*.

pioneer[2], *v.i.* innover.

placard, *n.* écriteau *m*; affiche *f*/placard *m*.

place[1], *n. Fin: Bank:* **place of payment,** lieu *m* de paiement.

place[2], *v.tr.* **1.** placer/mettre; **to place an amount (of money) to s.o.'s credit,** verser une somme au crédit de qn; **to place goods,** placer/vendre des marchandises; **difficult to place,** de vente/d'écoulement difficile; **to place an order (for goods),** placer/passer une commande; **to place a loan,** placer/négocier un emprunt; **to place £10 000 in bonds,** investir £10 000/faire un placement de £10 000 en obligations; **to place a contract,** adjuger/concéder un contrat **2.** trouver un emploi à (qn); **I could place her as a typist,** je pourrais lui trouver un travail de dactylo/la caser comme dactylo.

placement, *n. esp. NAm:* placement *m* (des capitaux, etc.).

placing, *n.* placement *m*/écoulement *m*/vente *f* (de marchandises, d'actions); placement (d'un emprunt).

plan[1], *n.* plan *m*/projet *m*/programme *m*; **general plan,** plan d'ensemble; **action plan,** plan d'action; *Fin:* **investment plan,** plan d'investissement; **savings plan,** plan (d')épargne; *PolEc:* **economic plan,** plan économique; **five year plan,** plan quinquennal; *StExch:* **stock option plan/stock purchase plan,** plan d'options sur titres.

plan[2], *v.tr. PolEc:* planifier (la production, etc.).

planned, *a. PolEc:* planifié; **planned economy,** économie dirigée/planifiée; dirigisme *m* économique; **planned maintenance,** entretien *m* systématique.

planner, *n. PolEc:* planificateur, -trice; **town planner,** urbaniste *mf*.

planning, *n.* **1. town planning,** urbanisme *m*; aménagement *m* des villes; **planning permission** = permis *m* de construire **2.** *PolEc: etc:* dirigisme *m*/planification *f*/planning *m*; **economic planning,** planification économique **3.** *Ind:* **company/corporate planning,** planification dans l'entreprise; **long-term planning,** planification à long terme; **short-term planning,** planification à court terme; **planning and allocation of resources,** estimation *f* des besoins et répartition *f* des moyens; **planning, programming and budgeting system (PPBS),** rationalisation *f* des choix budgétaires (RCB); **planning department,** service *m* planning/bureau *m* de planning; **product planning,** plan de développement des produits; **sales planning,** planification/planning des ventes.

plant, *n. Ind:* (*a*) appareil(s) *m*(*pl*)/outillage *m*; équipement (industriel)/matériel (industriel); **plant hire,** location

f d'équipement; **to equip with plant,** outiller (*b*) usine *f*; **plant capacity,** capacité *f* de l'usine; **plant layout,** schéma *m* d'installation; **plant manager,** directeur *m* d'usine.

pledge[1], *n.* gage *m*/nantissement *m*; **pledge holder,** détenteur, -trice, de gage(s); **unredeemed pledge,** gage non retiré; **to borrow on pledge,** emprunter sur gage; **to give/put sth. in pledge,** donner/mettre qch. en gage; **to hold in pledge,** (dé)tenir en gage/en nantissement; **to realize a pledge,** réaliser un gage; **to redeem a pledge,** retirer un gage; **to set aside as a pledge,** affecter en gage.

pledge[2], *v.tr.* donner/mettre (qch.) en gage; déposer (qch.) en gage/en nantissement/en garantie; engager/gager (qch.); **to pledge one's property,** engager/gager son bien; **to pledge securities,** déposer des titres en garantie/en nantissement.

pledgee, *n. Jur:* (créancier) gagiste *m*; prêteur, -euse sur gage(s).

pledger, *n.* emprunteur, -euse sur gage(s).

ploughback, *n.* bénéfices *mpl* réinvestis.

plough back, *v.tr.* **to plough back the profits into the company,** réinvestir/réinjecter les bénéfices dans la société.

ploughing back, *n.* **ploughing back of profits,** autofinancement *m*; affectation *f* de profits aux investissements.

plow back, *NAm:* = **plough back.**

plug[1], *n. F:* (*a*) *Publ: NAm:* ouvrage *m* qui se vend mal (*b*) réclame (tapageuse)/battage *m*.

plug[2], *v.tr. F:* faire l'article/faire de la réclame/faire du battage pour (un produit, etc.).

plunge, *v.i. StExch:* risquer de grosses sommes.

plunger, *n. StExch:* (spéculateur, -trice) risque-tout (*m inv*).

plus, 1. *prep.* plus; **purchase price plus brokerage,** le prix *m* d'achat plus le courtage **2.** *a.* (*a*) (*of quantity, number, etc.*) positif (*b*) **on the plus side of the account,** à l'actif du compte; **plus or minus difference,** différence *f* en plus ou en moins **3.** *n.* avantage *m*/atout *m* **4.** *adv.* she earns **£6 000 plus,** elle reçoit un salaire de plus de £6 000.

pocket, *n.* **to be in pocket,** faire un bénéfice/un gain; **to be £10 in pocket,** prendre un bénéfice de £10; gagner £10; **to be out of pocket (over a transaction),** être en perte; ne pas retrouver son argent; ne pas rentrer dans ses fonds; **to be £10 out of pocket,** essuyer une perte de £10/en être de sa poche pour £10.

point, *n.* **1.** (*a*) **point of arrival/of departure,** point *m* d'arrivée/point de départ; **loading/unloading point,** point de chargement/point de déchargement (*b*) **point of sale,** point/lieu *m* de vente; **point-of-sale material,** matériel *m* de publicité sur le lieu de vente/matériel PLV (*c*) **break-even point,** point mort/seuil *m* de rentabilité **2.** *StExch:* (*of price*) **to decline/to lose one point,** baisser d'un point; **to gain/to rise one point,** gagner un point/hausser d'un point; **silver-point,** silver-point *m*; **silver import point,** silver-point d'entrée; **silver export point,** silver-point de sortie.

policy[1]**,** *n.* (*a*) politique *f*; ligne *f* de conduite; tactique *f*; **economic policy,** politique économique; **exchange policy,** politique en matière de change; **free trade policy,** politique de libre échange; **policy of deflation,** politique de déflation/politique déflationniste; **prices and incomes policy,** politique des prix et des salaires; **to adopt a policy,** adopter une ligne de conduite (*b*) **company policy,** politique de l'entreprise; **policy statement,** rapport annuel; **product policy,** politique de lancement d'un produit (sur le marché); **sales policy,** politique de vente; **our policy is to satisfy our customers,** nous avons pour politique de satisfaire nos clients.

policy[2]**,** *n.* **(insurance) policy,** police *f* (d'assurance); **(fully) comprehensive/all-risks policy,** (police) omnium (*m*)/police tous risques; **life insurance policy,** police d'assurance (sur la) vie; **joint policy,** police conjointe; **master/general policy,** police générale; **standard policy,** police type; **policy for a specific amount,** police à forfait; **policy holder,** titulaire *mf*/détenteur, -trice d'une police d'assurance; assuré(e); **to draw up/make out a policy,** établir une police; **to take out a policy,** prendre une police/souscrire à une police (d'assurance) (*b*) *MIns:* **marine insurance policy,** police d'assurance maritime; **cargo policy,** police sur facultés; **floating policy/open policy,** police d'abonnement/police ouverte/police flottante; **hull/ship policy,** police sur corps; **time policy,** police à temps.

poll, *n.* **(public) opinion poll,** sondage *m* d'opinion (publique); **Gallup poll,** sondage Gallup; **to carry out a poll,** faire un sondage.

pool[1]**,** *n.* (*a*) groupe *m* (de travail); pool *m*; **typing pool,** service général de dactylographie; central *m* dactylographique; pool de dactylos (*b*) groupement *m* (pour opérations en commun); syndicat *m* de placement/de répartition (de marchandises, de commandes, etc.) (*c*) *PolEc: etc:* fonds commun/*F:* pool.

pool[2]**,** *v.tr.* (*a*) mettre en commun (ses capitaux, ses bénéfices, etc.); grouper (ses moyens) (*b*) grouper (les commandes).

pooling, *n.* mise *f* en commun (de fonds, etc.); groupement *m* (des intérêts, des commandes, etc.); **pooling arrangements,** dispositions *fpl* de mise en commun (des ressources); **pooling of interests (method),** (méthode) de groupement/de fusion/de mise en commun des intérêts (de deux sociétés).

poor, *a.* pauvre; **poor quality,** qualité inférieure; mauvaise qualité; **poor qual-**

ity goods, *F:* camelote *f*; **it's of poor quality,** c'est de la camelote.

popular, *a.* populaire/à la mode/goûté du public; **popular prices,** prix *m* à la portée de tous.

popularity, *n.* popularité *f*; succès *m* (d'un produit, etc.) auprès du (grand) public.

population, *n.* population *f*; **population statistics,** statistique(s) *f(pl)* démographique(s); **floating population,** population flottante; **the working/the active population,** la population active.

port, *n.* port *m*; **the port of London,** le port de Londres; **inland port,** port intérieur; **river port,** port fluvial; **in port,** au port; **to call at a port,** faire escale à un port; relâcher dans un port; **port of call,** port d'escale; **port authority,** autorité *f* portuaire; **port capacity,** capacité *f* portuaire; **port charge/dues,** droits *mpl* de port; **fishing port,** port de pêche; **commercial port,** port de commerce/port marchand; **free port,** port franc; **oil port,** port pétrolier; **open port,** port ouvert.

portable, *a.* portatif; transportable; mobile; roulant; **portable typewriter,** machine à écrire portative.

porter, *n.* porteur *m* (de bagages, etc.); chasseur *m*/garçon *m* (d'hôtel); **bank porter,** garçon de recette.

porterage, *n.* **1.** transport *m*/manutention *f*/factage *m* (de marchandises, de colis); **porterage facilities,** service *m* de porteurs **2.** prix *m*/frais *mpl* de transport; factage.

portfolio, *n.* (*a*) cartable *m* (pour documents, etc.) (*b*) portefeuille *m* (d'assurances, etc.) (*c*) *Fin:* **securities in portfolio,** valeurs *f* en portefeuille; **portfolio management,** gestion *f* de portefeuille.

position, *n.* **1.** *Post: Bank:* guichet *m*; **position closed,** guichet fermé **2.** état *m*/situation *f*; **financial position,** situation financière; **the cash position is not good,** la situation de la caisse laisse à désirer; **what is the position of the firm?** quelle est la situation (financière) de cette maison? **3.** **key position,** position *f* clé; **position of trust,** poste *m* de confiance.

possession, *n.* possession *f*/jouissance *f* (**of,** de); **to take possession of an estate,** entrer en possession/avoir la jouissance d'un bien; *Jur:* **actual possession,** possession de fait; **vacant possession,** libre possession (d'un immeuble); **house to let with vacant possession,** maison *f* à louer avec jouissance immédiate/avec possession immédiate.

possessor, *n.* propriétaire *mf*; *Jur:* possesseur *m*.

post[1]**,** *v.tr.* **1. to post (up),** placarder; coller (des affiches, etc.); afficher (un avis, etc.); **the market rates are posted (up),** les cours sont affichés **2.** *MIns:* porter (un navire) disparu **3.** *NAm:* **to post an entry,** passer une écriture.

post[2]**,** *n.* (*a*) courrier *m*; **by return of post,** par retour du courrier; **the first post,** la première distribution (*b*) la poste; **the Post Office** = les Postes et Télécommunications *f*; **to send sth. by post,** envoyer qch. par la poste (*c*) **post office,** (bureau de) poste; **Post Office (PO)** = Postes et Télécommunications (P et T); **sub post office,** bureau auxiliaire (des postes); bureau de quartier; **post office clerk,** employé(e) des postes; **post office directory,** annuaire *m* des postes; **post office box, (PO Box),** boîte postale (BP)/*FrC:* case postale.

post[3]**,** *n.* poste *m*/emploi *m*; **the post is still vacant,** vous n'avons pas encore pourvu à cet emploi.

post[4]**,** *v.tr.* (*a*) **to post a letter,** mettre une lettre à la poste/poster une lettre; **I'll post it to you,** je vous l'enverrai par la poste (*b*) *Book-k:* **to post (up) the books,** passer les écritures *f*; **to post an entry,** passer écriture d'un article; **to post an item in the ledger/to post up an item,** porter/inscrire/passer/reporter/rapporter/transcrire un article au grand(-)livre; **to post up the ledger,** arrêter le grand(-)livre; mettre le grand(-)livre à jour.

postage, *n.* affranchissement *m*/port *m*; tarif postal (d'une lettre, etc.); **postage stamp,** timbre-poste *m*; (*on insufficiently stamped letter*) **additional postage,** surtaxe (postale); **postage included,** port compris; **postage paid,** affranchi; port payé/port perçu; **postage free,** franc de port/franco *inv*.

postal, *a.* postal; **postal authorities,** l'Administration *f* des Postes; **postal charges,** frais *mpl* d'envoi/frais de port (d'une lettre, etc.); **postal money,** monnaie postale; **postal order,** mandat-poste *m*; **postal rates,** tarifs *mpl* postaux; **postal receipt,** récépissé postal; **postal services,** les services postaux/les Postes *f* et Télécommunications *f*; les postes; **postal transfer,** virement postal; **postal tranfer form,** mandat *m* de virement.

postcard, *n.* carte postale.

postcode, *n.* code postal.

postdate, *v.tr.* postdater (un chèque, un document).

poster, *n.* affiche murale; placard *m* (de publicité).

poste restante, *n.* poste restante.

post free, *adv.* franc de port/sans frais de poste.

posting, *n.* (*a*) envoi *m* (d'une lettre) par la poste; mise *f* à la poste (d'une lettre); **certificate of posting,** récépissé postal (*b*) *Book-k:* passation *f* (d'écritures); report *m*/entrée *f* (au grand(-)livre); transcription *f* (du journal).

postpaid, *a.* affranchi; port payé.

postpone, *v.tr.* remettre/ajourner/renvoyer à plus tard/reporter à plus tard/différer/reculer (un départ, un projet, etc.); **to postpone a payment,** différer un paiement.

postponement, *n.* remise *f* à plus tard; ajournement *m* (d'une réunion, d'une cause); renvoi *m* (d'une cause); sursis *m*.

potential, 1. *a.* **potential buyer/customer,** acheteur/client éventuel; **potential man-**ager = futur cadre **2.** *n.* potentiel *m*; **industrial potential,** potentiel industriel; **growth potential,** potentiel de croissance; **market potential,** potentiel du marché; **sales potential,** potentiel de vente.

pound, *n.* **1.** (*poids*) livre *f* (= 453,6 grammes); **to sell sth. by the pound,** vendre qch. à la livre; **40 pence a pound,** quarante pence la livre **2.** (*monnaie*) **pound (sterling),** livre *f* (sterling); **pound note,** billet *m*/coupure *f* d'une livre; **five pound note (£5),** billet de cinq livres (£5).

poundage, *n.* **1.** (droit *m* de) commission *f*; remise *f* de tant par livre (sterling) **2.** taux *m* de tant par livre (de poids).

poverty, *n.* **poverty line,** seuil *m* de pauvreté.

power, *n.* **1.** pouvoir *m*; **earning power,** capacité *f* bénéficiaire; **purchasing power,** pouvoir d'achat **2.** (*a*) pouvoir/influence *f*/autorité *f*; **executive power,** pouvoir exécutif (*b*) **to act with full powers,** agir de pleine autorité.

practice, *n.* **1.** (*a*) habitude *f*/coutume *f*/usage *m*; **trade practices,** usages commerciaux (*b*) *Ind:* technique *f*/méthodes *fpl*; **shop practice,** technique d'atelier; **management practices,** procédures *f* de gestion **2.** clientèle *f* **3.** (*a*) (*of doctor, lawyer, etc.*) **to be in practice,** exercer (*b*) étude *f* (d'un avocat); cabinet *m* (d'un médecin); **private practice,** cabinet (médical) privé.

precinct, *n.* **shopping precinct,** (*i*) centre commercial (*ii*) galerie marchande; **pedestrian precinct,** (*i*) rue piétonnière (*ii*) aire piétonnière.

pre-empt, *v.tr.* acheter/acquérir (une propriété, un monopole, etc.) par priorité.

pre-emption, *n.* *Jur:* (droit de) préemption *f*.

pre-emptive, *a.* **pre-emptive right,** droit *m* de préemption.

pre-emptor, *n.* acquéreur (en vertu d'un droit de préemption).

preference, *n.* (*a*) préférence *f* (*b*) *PolEc:* tarif *m*/régime *m* de faveur; traitement préférentiel; préférence; **imports entitled to preference,** importations *f* ayant droit à un régime de faveur (*c*) droit *m* de priorité; *Fin:* **preference stock/ shares,** actions privilégiées/de priorité; **liquidity preference,** préférence pour la liquidité; *Jur:* **preference clause,** pacte *m* de préférence.

preferential, *a.* **1.** (*a*) (traitement, etc.) préférentiel; **preferential price,** prix *m* de faveur (*b*) *Cust:* **preferential duty,** préférences *fpl* douanières; **preferential tariff,** tarif préférentiel/de faveur **2.** *Jur:* **preferential claim/preferential right,** droit *m* de préférence; privilège *m*; **creditor's preferential claim,** droit de préférence/privilège du créancier; **preferential creditor,** créancier privilégié; **preferential debt,** créance privilégiée; **preferential dividend,** dividende privilégié/dividende de priorité.

preferred, *a. Fin:* **preferred creditors,** créanciers privilégiés; **preferred stock,** actions privilégiées/de priorité.

prefinancing, *n.* préfinancement *m*; **prefinancing of export transactions,** (crédits de) préfinancement d'exportations.

prejudice[1], *n.* préjudice *m*/tort *m*/ dommage *m*; **without prejudice to any claim they may otherwise have,** sans préjudice pour tous les droits et recours qu'ils pourraient avoir; **without prejudice,** sous toutes réserves; **to the prejudice of . . .,** au préjudice de . . ..

premises, *n.pl.* local *m*/immeuble *m*; **business premises,** locaux commerciaux; **shop premises,** (locaux à l'usage de) magasin(s) *m(pl)*; **drinks to be consumed on the premises,** boissons à consommer sur place; **off the premises,** hors de l'établissement.

premium, *n.* **1.** prime *f*/prix *m*/récom-
pense *f*; *Ind:* **premium bonus,** prime de rendement **2.** (*a*) **(insurance) premium,** prime (d'assurance); **additional/extra premium,** surprime *f*; **annual premium,** prime annuelle; **low-premium insurance,** assurance *f* à prime réduite (*b*) reprise locative/redevance *f* (à payer au début d'un bail); **flat to let, no premium,** appartement *m* à louer sans reprise **3.** *Fin:* (*a*) **(exchange) premium,** agio *m*; prix du change; **dollar premium,** prime sur le dollar; **premium on gold,** agio sur l'or; **the (quoted) premium,** le report (*b*) *StExch:* **issue premium,** prime d'émission; **share premium,** prime d'émission; **to issue shares at a premium,** émettre des actions au-dessus du pair/de leur valeur nominale; **premium on redemption,** prime de remboursement; **premium (savings) bonds,** obligations *f* à primes (*c*) **antiques are at a premium,** les antiquités (*i*) sont très recherchées (*ii*) se vendent à prix d'or **4. premium grade petrol** = supercarburant *m*/*F:* super *m*.

prepack, prepackage, *v.tr.* conditionner; emballer.

prepaid, *a.* payé d'avance/prépayé; (*of letter, etc.*) affranchi; **carriage prepaid,** port payé; payé au départ; franc de port/franco *inv*; *WTel:* **prepaid answer/ reply prepaid,** réponse payée/prépayée.

prepay, *v.tr.* payer/régler (qch.) d'avance; prépayer; affranchir (une lettre, etc.).

prepayment, *n.* paiement *m* d'avance; paiement par anticipation; affranchissement *m* (d'une lettre, etc.).

present[1], *a.* actuel; d'aujourd'hui; **the present year,** l'année courante; **present value,** valeur actuelle; **present capital,** capital appelé.

present[2], *v.tr.* présenter; **to present a bill for payment,** présenter un billet à l'encaissement; **to present a bill for acceptance,** présenter une traite à l'acceptation.

presentation, *n.* présentation *f*; **cheque**

payable on presentation, chèque *m* payable à présentation/à vue; **payable on presentation of the coupon,** payable contre remise du coupon.

presentment, *n.* presentment of a bill (for acceptance), présentation *f* d'une traite à l'acceptation.

preservative, *n.* agent conservateur/de conservation; **without artificial colour or preservatives,** sans colorant ni agent de conservation.

preside, *v.i.* (*a*) to preside at/over a meeting, présider une réunion (*b*) exercer les fonctions de président.

president, *n. esp. NAm:* président-directeur général (d'une société anonyme).

press, *n.* to pass (a book) for press, donner le bon à tirer.

press-button, *n.* press-button industry, industrie entièrement automatisée.

pressure, *n.* pression *f*; **financial pressure,** embarras financiers; **pressure group,** groupe *m* de pression.

prestige, *n.* prestige *m*; **prestige advertising,** publicité *f* de prestige.

prestocking, *n.* préstockage *m*.

pre-tax, *a.* pre-tax profit, bénéfice brut/avant impôt.

preventive, *a.* preventif; **preventive maintenance,** entretien préventif; **preventive measures,** mesures préventives/de précaution.

price[1], *n.* (*a*) prix *m*; **actual price,** prix réel; **administered price,** prix imposé; **agreed price,** prix convenu; **the asking price of this house is too high,** le prix qu'on demande pour cette maison est trop élevé; **basic price,** prix initial; **cash price,** prix du comptant; **catalogue price,** prix public/prix (de) catalogue/prix fort (de vente); **ceiling price,** prix plafond; **competitive price,** prix compétitif; **cost price,** prix coûtant/prix de revient; **current**

price, prix actuel/courant/pratiqué; **cut price,** prix de rabais; **direct price,** prix de gros; **discount price,** prix de rabais; **firm price/steady price,** prix ferme; **fixed price,** prix fixe/prix forfaitaire; forfait *m*; **floor price,** prix plancher; **full price,** prix fort; *Rail: Th: etc:* **half price,** demi-place *f*; demi-tarif *m*; **children travel at half price,** les enfants paient demi-tarif; **to sell sth. at half price,** vendre qch. à moitié prix; **high price,** prix élevé; **inclusive price,** prix tout compris/tous frais compris; **list price,** prix (de) catalogue/prix public; **low price,** bas prix; **at a low price,** à bas prix/à un prix avantageux; **lowest price/rock bottom price,** le prix le plus bas/le dernier prix; **manufacturer's price,** prix de fabrique; **manufacturer's recommended price (MRP),** prix conseillé/recommandé; **marked price,** prix marqué; **moderate price,** prix modique/modéré; **net(t) price,** prix net; **purchase price,** prix d'achat; prix coûtant; **recommended price,** prix conseillé; **at a reduced price,** à prix réduit/au rabais; **retail price,** prix de détail; **retail price maintenance (RPM),** prix imposé; **standard price,** prix officiel/prix taxé; **trade price,** prix de demi-gros; **wholesale price,** prix de gros; **price control,** contrôle des prix; **price cutting/slashing,** forte réduction des prix; **price index,** indice des prix; **price level,** niveau des prix; **(current) price list,** tarif *m*; **price mechanism/system,** régime *m* des prix; **price range,** échelle *f*/éventail *m* des prix; **price regulation,** réglementation *f* des prix; **price war,** guerre *f* des prix; **what price is that book?** combien coûte ce livre? quel est le prix de ce livre? **what price did you pay for it?** combien cela vous a-t-il coûté? combien l'avez-vous payé? **to increase in price,** augmenter de prix; **to push up prices,** faire monter les prix; **to mark up/mark down prices,** augmenter/baisser les prix; **to quote/to name a price,** faire un prix (*b*) *Bank: Fin:* price of money, loyer *m* de l'argent; **price ring,** monopole *m* des prix (*c*) *StExch:* closing price, cours *m* de fermeture; **market price,** cours du marché/de la

Bourse; **market price list,** mercuriale *f; at* **current market price,** suivant le cours du marché; **opening price,** (*i*) cours d'introduction (*ii*) cours d'ouverture; **put and call price,** cours de l'option; **price bid,** cours demandé; **price differential,** différence *f* des prix; **price earnings ratio (PER),** taux de capitalisation des bénéfices/ratio cours-bénéfices/price earnings ratio; **price for the account,** cours à terme; **price of option/option price,** cours de la prime; **spot price,** cours du comptant; **slump in prices,** effondrement *m* des prix/des cours.

price², *v.tr.* **1.** déterminer le prix (de qch.); fixer un prix pour (qch.); **the book is priced at £4 net,** le livre se vend (au prix de) £4 net **2.** s'informer du prix de (qch.) **3. to price competitors out of the market,** fixer des prix si bas que les concurrents ne peuvent continuer à vendre; **we shall be priced out of the market/we shall price ourselves out of the market,** nos prix (trop élevés) nous feront perdre le marché **4.** *PolEc:* valoriser (une quantité).

pricey, *a. F:* cher/coûteux; **too pricey,** trop cher.

pricing, *n.* détermination *f*/établissement *m*/fixation *f* du prix (**of sth.,** de qch.); évaluation *f*; **competitive pricing,** fixation concurrentielle des prix; **pricing policy,** politique *f* des prix.

primage, *n. Nau:* primage *m.*

primary, *a.* **primary product,** matière première/produit brut; produit de base; **primary industries,** secteur *m* primaire; *NAm:* **primary earnings per share,** bénéfices premiers par action.

prime, *a.* **1.** premier; principal; de premier ordre; **prime cost,** prix *m* coûtant; prix de revient (de production) **2.** (*a*) excellent/de qualité supérieure/de première qualité; **prime quality meat,** viande *f* de première qualité/de premier choix; viande surchoix; **prime (grade) beef,** bœuf de premier choix (*b*) *Fin:* **prime bills,** papier commercial de premier ordre; **prime bond,** obligation *f* de

premier ordre; *NAm:* **prime (lending) rate** = taux *m* de base/taux d'escompte (pour les *prime bills*).

principal, *n.* (*a*) *Jur:* (*in transaction*) mandant *m*/commettant *m*; **principal and agent,** mandant et mandataire *m* (*b*) *StExch:* donneur *m* d'ordre (*c*) capital *m* (d'une dette); **principal and interest,** capital et intérêts *mpl.*

print-out, *n. Cmptr:* sortie *f* d'imprimante; listage *m*/listing *m*; **print-out calculator,** calculatrice à imprimante.

prior, *a.* préalable/précédent; antérieur; (**to sth.,** à qch.).

priority, *n.* priorité *f*; antériorité *f*; **to have priority,** avoir la priorité/être prioritaire; *Jur:* **priority of a creditor,** privilège *m*/priorité d'un créancier; *StExch:* **priority shares,** actions *f* de priorité.

private, *a.* **1.** privé; **private and confidential,** secret et confidentiel; **private conversation,** entretien privé; **private interview,** (*i*) entretien *m* à huis clos (*ii*) entretien privé; **to mark a letter "private",** marquer sur une lettre "confidentiel"/"personnel"; *Jur:* **private agreement/contract/treaty,** acte *m* sous seing privé; sous-seing *m* **2. private bank,** banque privée; **private company,** société à responsabilité limitée; **private enterprise/industry/the private sector,** le secteur privé **3. private income/money/means,** rentes *fpl*; fortune personelle; **private property,** (*i*) propriété privée (*ii*) = entrée interdite.

pro = **procuration.**

probate, *v.tr. Jur:* homologuer/entériner (un document).

probation, *n.* **period of probation,** période *f*/stage *m* probatoire; **to take s.o. on probation,** prendre qn à l'essai.

problem, *n.* problème *m*; **problem analysis,** analyse *f* de problème(s); **problem area,** source *f* de difficultés/d'incidents (techniques); zone *f* critique.

procedure, *n.* procédure *f*/marche *f* à

suivre/méthode *f*; **administrative procedure,** méthodes administratives; **order of procedure,** règles *fpl* de procédure.

proceed, *v.i.* (*a*) **negotiations are now proceeding,** des négociations *f* sont en cours (*b*) *Jur:* **to proceed against s.o.,** procéder contre qn; poursuivre qn (en justice); intenter un procès à/contre qn.

proceedings, *n.pl.* (*a*) débats *mpl* (d'une assemblée) (*b*) *Jur:* (**legal**) **proceedings,** procès *m;* poursuites *f* judiciaires/en justice; **to take/institute proceedings (against s.o.),** intenter une action/un procès (à, contre qn); engager/entamer des poursuites (judiciaires) (contre qn); introduire une instance.

proceeds, *n.pl.* produit *m*/montant *m* (d'une vente, etc.); **the net proceeds,** les recettes nettes.

process, *v.tr.* (*a*) *Adm: esp. NAm:* faire l'analyse préalable (*i*) de documents (*ii*) de candidats à un poste (*b*) *Ind:* traiter (des aliments, des produits industriellement); **processed cheese,** fromage industriel.

processable, *a.* (information) traitable.

processing, *n.* (*a*) traitement *m*; **data processing/information processing,** traitement des données (de l'information); informatique *f*; **word processing,** traitement *m* de textes (*b*) *Adm: esp. NAm:* examen *m*/analyse *f* préalable (*i*) de documents, etc. (*ii*) de candidats à un poste.

processor, *n.* **data processor,** ordinateur *m*; **word processor,** machine *f* de traitement de textes; éditeur *m* de textes.

procuration, *n.* (*a*) négociation *f* (d'un emprunt); (*abbr:* **pro**); **per pro (pp),** par procuration (*b*) **procuration (fee),** commission payée (à un agent) pour l'obtention d'un prêt.

procurator, *n. Jur:* fondé *m* de pouvoir.

produce[1], *n. coll.* produits *mpl*/denrées *fpl*; **home/inland produce,** produits du pays/produits indigènes; **foreign pro-** duce, produits étrangers/exotiques; **agricultural produce,** produits agricoles; **farm produce,** produits de ferme/produits fermiers; **market garden produce,** produits maraîchers; **raw produce,** matières premières.

produce[2], *v.tr.* **1.** présenter/produire (des documents); **I can produce the documents,** je peux fournir les documents **2.** *Ind:* fabriquer (des marchandises) **3.** rapporter; **shares that produce five per cent,** actions *f* qui rapportent un intérêt de cinq pour cent.

producer, *n.* producteur, -trice; fabricant *m* (**of,** de); **producers' co-operative,** coopérative *f* de production; **producer goods,** biens *m* de production/d'équipement.

producing[1], *a.* producteur; productif; **producing capacity,** capacité *f* de production; productivité *f*; **producing centre,** centre *m* de production; **producing country,** pays producteur; **producing industry,** industrie productrice.

producing[2], *n.* = **production 1.**

product, *n.* produit *m*; *Ind:* **basic product,** produit de base; **by-product,** dérivé *m*; **end product/finished product,** produit fini; **secondary product,** produit secondaire; sous-produit *m*; **semi-manufactured product,** produit semi-fini/semi-produit; **waste products,** déchet *m*/produits de rejet; **product advertising,** publicité *f* de produit; **product analysis,** analyse *f* de produit; **product design,** conception *f* du produit; **product image,** image *f* de produit; **product line/range,** gamme *f* de produits; *PolEc:* **gross national product (GNP),** produit national brut (PNB).

production, *n.* **1.** production *f*/communication *f* (de documents); **on production of (your ticket, etc),** sur présentation de (votre billet, etc.) **2.** (*a*) production/fabrication *f* (de marchandises); **batch production,** fabrication par lots; **mass production,** production/fabrication en série; **planned production,** production planifiée/dirigée; **production to order,**

production sur commande; **rate of production**, taux *m* de (la) production (*b*) **production chart/sheet**, graphique *m* d'évolution (de la production); **production cost**, coût *m*/frais *mpl* de production; **production department**, service *m* de la production; **production engineering**, organisation *f* de la production; **production line**, chaîne *f* de montage; **production line system**, production/travail *m* à la chaîne; **to work on a production line**, travailler à la chaîne; **production management**, gestion *f* de la production; **production manager**, chef *m*/directeur, -trice de la production; *Publ:* chef de fabrication; **production plant**, usine *f*; **production unit**, (*i*) unité *f* (*ii*) équipe *f* de production.

productive, *a.* (*a*) productif; (capital) productif d'intérêts; (travail) productif; **the productive life (of a machine),** la vie physique (d'une machine) (*b*) profitable/utile.

productivity, *n.* productivité *f*/rendement *m*; **productivity bonus**, prime *f* de rendement; **productivity deal**, contrat *m* de productivité; **productivity drive/campaign**, campagne *f* de productivité.

profession, *n.* profession *f*; métier *m*.

proficiency, *n.* compétence *f* (**in a subject**, en une matière); **proficiency in English**, connaissance *f* pratique de l'anglais.

proficient, *a.* capable/compétent.

profile, *n.* profil *m*; **company profile**, profil d'entreprise; **customer profile**, profil de la clientèle; **job profile**, description *f* de fonction; **market profile**, profil du marché.

profit, *n.* profit *m*/bénéfice *m*; **capital profit**, plus-value *f*; **clear profit**, profit net; **gross profit**, profit brut; **net (operating) profit**, bénéfice net (d'exploitation); **profit balance**, solde *m* bénéficiaire; **profit graph**, courbe *f* de rentabilité; **profit and loss**, pertes et profits; **profit and loss account**, compte *m* de résultats; **profit margin**, marge *f* bénéficiaire; **profit optimization**, optimisation *f* des profits; **profit target**, objectif *m* de profits; **profit tax**, impôts sur les bénéfices; **profit after tax(ation)**, bénéfice net/bénéfice après impôt; **profit before tax(ation)**, bénéfice brut/bénéfice avant impôt; **to bring/to yield/to show a profit**, donner un bénéfice; **to derive a profit from sth.**, retirer un profit de qch.; **to make a large profit**, réaliser de gros bénéfices; (*of business*) **to move into profit**, devenir rentable; **to sell sth. at a profit**, prendre/faire un bénéfice sur une vente; **profit-earning**, rentable; **profit-earning (capacity)**, rentabilité *f*; **profit-making**, réalisation *f* de bénéfices; **profit-making association**, association *f* à but lucratif; **non profit-making association**, association à but non lucratif/sans but lucratif; *Ind:* **profit-sharing (scheme)**, participation *f* aux bénéfices; intéressement *m*; participation ouvrière; participation des salariés; intéressement du personnel aux fruits de l'expansion; **profit-sharing employee**, employé(e) intéressé(e); **profit-sharing bond**, obligation participante; *PolEc:* **profit system**, économie basée sur le profit; économie de libre entreprise; **profit-taking**, prise *f* de bénéfices.

profitability, *n.* rentabilité *f*; profitabilité *f*.

profitable, *a.* profitable/avantageux; (*of speculation, etc.*) lucratif; (emploi) rémunérateur; (*of business*) rentable.

profiteer[1], *n.* profiteur *m*/affairiste *mf*.

profiteer[2], *v.i.* faire des bénéfices excessifs.

profiteering, *n.* mercantilisme *m*; affairisme *m*.

profitless, *a.* sans profit; **profitless deal**, affaire blanche.

pro forma, *n. & adj. phr.* pro forma (**invoice**), facture pro forma.

programme[1], *NAm:* **program** *n.* programme *m*; **development programme,** programme de développement; **investment programme,** programme d'investissements; **research programme,** programme de recherche(s); **training programme,** programme d'instruction/de formation/d'entraînement; **to draw up/arrange a programme,** arrêter un programme/dresser un emploi du temps.

programme[2], *NAm:* **program,** *v.tr. Cmptr:* programmer; **programmed management,** gestion programmée.

programmer, *n. Cmptr:* programmeur, -euse.

programming, *n. Cmptr:* programmation *f*; **programming department,** service *m* (de la) programmation; **programming manager,** chef *m* du service (de) programmation; **programming staff,** personnel chargé de la programmation.

progress, *n.* avancement *m* (d'un travail, etc.); *Ind:* **progress of the work through the different departments,** cheminement *m* des pièces à travers les différents services; **progress report,** compte rendu (de l'avancement) des travaux/rapport périodique; **the work is now in progress,** le travail est en voie d'exécution/en cours; **the negotiations in progress,** les négociations *f* en cours.

progression, *n.* progression *f*; **salary progression curve,** courbe *f* d'augmentation de salaire.

progressive, *a.* progressif; **progressive tax,** impôt progressif; **progressive increase in taxation,** progressivité *f* de l'impôt; *Fin:* (*of interest*) **at a progressive rate,** à taux progressif.

prohibitive, *a.* (prix) prohibitif/inabordable; *Cust:* (droits) prohibitifs; **the price of caviare is prohibitive,** le caviar est hors de prix.

project, *n.* projet *m*; plan *m*; **capital project evaluation,** étude *f* de projet d'investissement; **project analysis,** étude de projet.

projected, *a.* **projected sales,** ventes prévues.

projection, *n.* projection *f*; prévision *f*; **profit projection,** projection des profits.

promise, *n.* promesse *f*; **promise to pay,** promesse de payer.

promissory, *a.* **promissory note,** billet *m* à ordre.

promote, *v.tr.* **1.** promouvoir (qn); donner de l'avancement à (qn); **to promote s.o. to a post,** promouvoir qn à un poste plus élevé; **to be promoted,** être promu; avancer; recevoir de l'avancement **2.** (*a*) encourager (un projet, etc.) (*b*) **to promote a company,** lancer/fonder une société (*c*) (*i*) lancer (un produit) (*ii*) stimuler la vente (d'un produit).

promoter, *n.* (*a*) **company promoter,** promoteur *m*/fondateur *m* d'une société anonyme; *Fin:* **promoters' shares,** parts *f* de fondateurs (*b*) **sales promoter,** promoteur des ventes.

promotion, *n.* **1.** promotion *f*/avancement *m*; **to gain promotion,** avoir/recevoir/obtenir de l'avancement; **promotion by seniority,** avancement à l'ancienneté; **prospect/chance of promotion,** possibilité d'avancement; (*in ads*) poste d'avenir/poste évolutif **2.** fondation *f* lancement *m* (d'une société anonyme); promotion (immobilière); **promotion money,** frais *mpl* de fondation (d'une société anonyme); frais d'établissement; coût *m* de premier établissement **3.** lancement (d'un produit); stimulation *f* (de la vente d'un produit); **promotion budget,** budget promotionnel; **promotion team,** équipe promotionnelle; **sales promotion,** promotion des ventes.

promotional, *a.* promotionnel; **promotional campaign/sale,** campagne/vente promotionnelle; **promotional material,** matériel *m* de promotion/promotionnel/publicitaire.

prompt, 1. *a.* (*a*) prompt; vif/rapide; diligent; **prompt service,** service *m* rapide (*b*) immédiat; instantané; **prompt**

reply, réponse *f* par retour du courrier (*c*) **prompt cotton,** coton *m* livrable sur-le-champ et comptant **2.** *n.* terme *m* (de paiement); délai *m* limite; **prompt note,** mémoire *m* de vente (avec indication du délai de paiement); **prompt day,** jour *m*/ date *f* de paiement.

promptly, *adv.* promptement.

property, *n.* **1.** (droit de) propriété *f*; **literary property,** propriété littéraire **2.** (*a*) propriété/biens *mpl*/avoir(s) *m*(*pl*); **private/public property,** propriété privée/publique; *Jur:* **funded property,** biens en rentes; **personal property,** biens personnels/mobiliers; effets personnels; **damage to property,** dommages matériels (*b*) immeuble(s) *m*(*pl*); propriété (foncière)/terre *f*; **property developer,** promoteur immobilier/constructeur-promoteur; **property loan,** prêt immobilier; **property market,** le marché immobilier/ l'immobilier *m*; **property tax,** impôt foncier; **property for sale,** immeuble/maison *f* à vendre; propriété à vendre.

proportion, *v.tr.* **to proportion one's expenditures to one's profits,** mesurer ses dépenses sur ses profits.

proportional, *a.* proportionnel; en proportion (**to,** de); proportionné (**to,** à); **compensation proportional to the damage,** compensation proportionnelle au dommage subi; *Adm:* **proportional assessment,** coéquation *f*; **proportional scale,** échelle proportionnelle.

proportionment, *n.* distribution proportionnelle/au prorata.

proposal, *n.* proposition *f*/offre *f*; **to make a proposal,** faire/formuler une proposition; **proposals for . . .,** propositions relatives à . . .; **proposal of insurance,** proposition d'assurance.

propose, *v.tr.* proposer; **to propose a candidate,** proposer un candidat; **to propose a motion,** faire une motion.

proposition, *n.* (*a*) proposition *f*/offre *f* (*b*) *F:* affaire *f*; **it's a big proposition,** c'est

une grosse affaire; **paying proposition,** affaire rentable/qui rapporte.

proprietary, *a.* **proprietary insurance company,** compagnie *f* d'assurance à primes; **proprietary article,** spécialité *f*/ article breveté; **proprietary medicine,** spécialité *f* pharmaceutique.

proprietor, *n.* propriétaire *mf*; **hotel proprietor,** propriétaire/patron *m* d'un hôtel.

proprietorship, *n.* (*a*) droit *m* de propriété (*b*) propriété *f*/possession *f*.

proprietress, *n.f.* propriétaire *f*; patronne (d'une hôtel, etc.).

pro rata, *adv. & a. phr.* au prorata/proportionnel.

prorate, *v.tr. Fin: etc:* partager proportionnellement.

prospect, *n.* (*a*) perspective *f*/expectative *f*; **market prospects,** perspectives commerciales; **no prospect of agreement,** aucune perspective d'accord (*b*) **future prospects of an undertaking,** perspectives d'avenir d'une entreprise (*c*) *NAm:* client éventuel/possible.

prospective, *a.* **prospective buyer,** acheteur éventuel.

prospectus, *n.* **1.** prospectus *m inv* **2.** *Fin:* appel *m* de souscription publique.

protect, *v.tr.* protéger; sauvegarder (les intérêts de qn, etc.); *StExch:* **to protect a book,** défendre une position; **to protect a bill of exchange,** garantir le bon accueil d'une lettre de change; faire provision pour une lettre de change.

protective, *a.* protecteur; *PolEc:* **protective tariff,** tarif protecteur.

protest[1]**,** *n.* **1.** protêt *m*; **certified protest,** protêt authentique; **protest for non-acceptance,** protêt faute d'acceptation; **protest for non-payment,** protêt faute de paiement; **to make a protest,** lever/faire protêt **2. ship's protest,** rapport *m* de mer; déclaration *f* d'avaries; procès-verbal *m* des avaries; **to note a protest,** faire un rapport de mer.

protest[2], *v.tr.* **to protest a bill,** (faire) protester un effet/une lettre de change; lever protêt d'une lettre de change.

prototype, *n.* prototype *m*; **exhibit prototype,** prototype de démonstration; **prototype car,** voiture *f* prototype; *Ind:* **prototype series,** présérie *f*.

prove up, *v.i. NAm:* (*a*) donner satisfaction (*b*) **to prove up on a claim,** faire valoir ses droits à une revendication; **to prove up on a concession,** accomplir toutes les formalités requises pour obtenir une concession.

provide, 1. *v.i.* pourvoir à; prévoir; **expenses provided for in the budget,** dépenses prévues au budget; **this has been provided for,** on y a pourvu; *Ins:* **this risk is not provided for in the policy,** ce risque n'est pas prévu dans la police; **to provide for a bill,** faire provision pour une lettre de change **2.** (*a*) *v.tr.* stipuler (**that,** que + *ind.*); **the contract provides that . . .,** dans le contrat il est stipulé que . . . (*b*) fournir; **to provide s.o. with sth.,** fournir qch. à qn; pourvoir/munir/fournir/approvisionner qn de qch.; **to provide a bill with acceptance,** revêtir un effet de l'acceptation.

provision, *n.* (*a*) **we have made provisions to this effect,** nous avons pris des dispositions dans ce sens (*b*) *Book-k:* provisions *fpl*/réserve *f* (*c*) *pl.* **provisions,** provisions (de bouche)/comestibles *m*; *NAm:* **provision store,** alimentation *f* (*d*) clause *f* stipulation *f* (d'un contrat); **there is no provision to the contrary,** il n'y a pas de clause contraire.

provisional, *a.* provisoire; **provisional duties,** fonctions *f* intérimaires/temporaires.

provisionally, *adv.* provisoirement/par provision/par intérim; **to sign an agreement provisionally,** signer un engagement sous condition.

proviso, *n.* clause conditionnelle; condi-

tion *f* (d'un contrat); stipulation *f*; **with the proviso that . . .,** à condition que . . ..

provisory, *a.* (*of clause, etc.*) qui énonce une stipulation; conditionnel.

proxy, *n.* (*a*) *Jur:* procuration *f*; **by proxy,** par procuration (*b*) (*of pers.*) mandataire *mf*.

psychology, *n.* psychologie *f*; **economic psychology,** psychologie économique; **industrial psychology,** psychologie industrielle/psychotechnique *f*.

public, 1. *a.* **public expenditure,** dépense *f* publique; **public finance,** finances publiques; **public holiday,** fête légale; **public image,** image *f* de marque; **public relations (PR),** relations publiques; **public sector,** secteur *m* publique; **public transport,** transports *mpl* en commun; (*of firm*) **to go public,** émettre/placer des actions dans le public **2.** *n.* **the (general) public,** le (grand) public.

publicity, *n.* publicité *f*/réclame *f*; **advance publicity,** publicité d'amorçage; **publicity bureau/agency,** bureau *m*/agence *f* de publicité; **publicity campaign,** campagne *f* de publicité; **publicity department,** la publicité; **publicity expenses,** dépenses *f* publicitaires; **publicity man,** publicitaire *m*; **publicity manager,** chef *m* de (la) publicité.

publicize, *v.tr.* faire de la publicité/de la réclame pour (un produit).

puff[1], *n.* réclame (tapageuse).

puff[2], *v.tr.* prôner/pousser/vanter (ses marchandises).

pull down, *v.tr.* **to pull down prices,** faire baisser les prix.

purchase[1], *n.* (*a*) achat *m*; **cash purchase,** achat au comptant; **credit purchase,** achat à crédit; *Book-k:* **purchase book/purchase journal,** livre *m* des achats; *StExch:* **purchase contract,** bordereau *m* d'achat; **purchase money,** prix *m* d'achat; **purchase method,** méthode *f* d'achat au prix coûtant; **purchase price,** prix d'achat/prix coûtant; **purchase tax,** taxe *f* à l'achat; **to make a purchase,** faire un achat (*b*) loyer *m*; **sold at twenty years purchase,** vendu moyennant vingt ans de loyer.

purchase[2],*v.tr.* acheter/acquérir/faire l'acquisition de qch.; **to purchase for cash,** acheter (au) comptant; **to purchase sth. on credit,** acheter qch. à crédit.

purchaser, *n.* (*a*) acheteur, -euse; acquéreur *m*; (*at auction*) adjudicataire *mf*; **purchasers' association,** coopérative *f* d'achats (*b*) preneur, -euse; **to have found a purchaser for sth.,** avoir (trouvé) preneur pour qch.

purchasing[1], *a.* **purchasing party,** acquéreur; (*at auction*) partie *f* adjudicataire.

purchasing[2], *n.* achat *m*/acquisition *f*; *NAm:* **purchasing agent,** acheteur; **purchasing costs,** frais *mpl* de passation de commande; **purchasing department,** service *m* de l'approvisionnement; service des achats; **purchasing manager,** chef *m* des achats; *PolEc:* **purchasing power,** pouvoir *m* d'achat.

pure, *a. Ins:* **pure premium,** prime nette.

purpose, *n.* but *m*/raison *f*; **for tax purposes,** pour le calcul de l'impôt.

put[1], *n. StExch:* **put option,** option *f* de vente; **put of more,** la demande de plus;

l'encore autant *m*; **put and call,** double option/stellage *m*.

put[2], *v.tr.* **1.** mettre; **to put an article on sale,** mettre un article en vente; **to put a new article on the market,** lancer une marchandise; **to put an advertisement in the paper,** (faire) insérer une annonce dans le journal; **to put one's signature to sth.,** signer qch.; *Book-k:* **to put an amount in the receipts/in the expenditure,** employer une somme en recette/en dépense; *StExch:* **to put stock at a certain price,** délivrer/fournir des actions à un certain prix; **to put money into an undertaking,** verser des fonds/placer de l'argent dans une affaire **2. to put a resolution to the meeting,** présenter une résolution à l'assemblée; **I shall put your proposal to the Board,** je porterai votre proposition à la connaissance du conseil d'administration; **to put a resolution to the vote,** mettre une résolution aux voix.

put out, *v.tr.* (*a*) **to put out work,** donner du travail en sous-traitance; donner du travail à faire à domicile (*b*) **to put out money at interest,** placer de l'argent.

put up, *v.tr.* (*a*) fournir (une somme d'argent); **to put up the money for an undertaking,** fournir les fonds d'une entreprise (*b*) **to put up prices,** monter/augmenter les prix.

Q

qualification, *n.* **1.** aptitude *f*/compétence *f*/talent *m*/capacité *f*; **to have the necessary qualifications for a job,** avoir la compétence nécessaire pour remplir une fonction; posséder les qualités requises/les titres *m*/les qualifications *f* nécessaires pour un poste; **professional qualifications,** qualification professionnelle **2. qualification shares,** actions *f* statutaires.

qualified, *a.* **1.** qui a les qualités requises (pour un poste, etc.); **to be qualified to do sth.,** être qualifié pour faire qch.; **qualified accountant,** comptable diplômé; **qualified persons,** personnes compétentes/personnes qualifiées **2.** restreint/mitigé/modéré; **qualified acceptance,** acceptation conditionnelle/sous condition (d'une traite, etc.); **qualified approval,** approbation avec réserve.

qualify, *v.i.* acquérir les qualifications professionnelles/les connaissances requises/l'expérience *f* nécessaire (**for sth.,** pour qch.); **he is not qualified,** il ne possède pas les qualifications requises/les diplômes nécessaires.

qualifying, *a.* **1. qualifying period,** période *f* d'essai **2.** *Fin:* **qualifying shares,** actions *f* statutaires.

quality, *n.* **1.** (*a*) qualité *f*; **of good/high quality,** de bonne qualité/de qualité supérieure; **poor quality goods,** marchandises *f* de qualité inférieure; **of first rate quality/of the best quality,** de première qualité; de premier choix (*b*) **quality control (QC),** contrôle *m* de la qualité; **quality goods,** marchandises *f* de qualité; **quality newspaper,** journal sérieux.

Quango, *n.* (**Quasi autonomous non-governmental organization**) = société nationale de service public.

quantify, *v.tr.* déterminer la quantité de (qch); mesurer/évaluer avec précision.

quantity, *n.* **1.** (*a*) quantité *f*; **a small quantity of . . .,** une petite quantité de . . .; **a (large) quantity of . . .,** une (grande) quantité de . . .; **to buy sth. in large quantities,** acheter qch. en grande quantité/en quantité considérable; **quantity rebate/discount,** remise *f* sur la quantité; *Cust:* **the quantity permitted,** la tolérance/la quantité permise (de tabac, etc.); **economic manufacturing quantity,** quantité économique de production (*b*) *Const:* **to survey a building for quantities,** faire le toisé d'un immeuble; **bill of quantities,** devis *m*; **quantity surveyor,** métreur *m* vérificateur; **quantity surveying,** (faire un) métré/toisé **2. marketable quantity of shares,** quotité *f* négociable de valeurs.

quart, *n. Meas:* le quart d'un gallon/*Fr.C:* pinte *f*; **a quart of milk,** *FrC:* une pinte de lait; (**British quart** = 1 litre 136; **American liquid quart** = 0 litre 946; **American dry quart** = 1 litre 101).

quarter, *n.* **1.** quart *m*; **three quarters,** trois quarts; **three and a quarter,** trois et un quart; **a quarter (of a pound) of coffee,** un quart (de livre) de café; **a quarter cheaper,** d'un quart meilleur marché; **I can buy it for a quarter of the price,** je peux l'avoir au quart du prix/quatre fois moins cher **2.** trimestre *m*; terme *m* (de loyer); **every quarter I receive a statement of account,** on m'envoie un relevé de compte tous les trimestres/tous les 3 mois; **a quarter's rent,** un terme/un trimestre (de loyer); **quarter day,** (jour de) terme.

quarterly, 1. *a.* trimestriel; **quarterly statement,** relevé (de compte) trimestriel **2.** *n.* publication trimestrielle **3.** *adv.* trimestriellement; par trimestre; tous les 3 mois.

quasi, *pref. & a.* quasi; **quasi contract,** quasi-contrat *m*; **quasi-money,** quasi-monnaie *f.*

quay, *n.* quai *m*; (*of goods*) **ex quay,** à prendre/livrable à quai.

quayage, *n.* droit(s) *m(pl)* de quai.

quick, *a.* rapide; **quick recovery,** reprise *f* rapide; **quick returns,** profits *m* rapides; **quick sale,** prompt débit; vente *f* facile; **quick assets,** actif *m* disponible/actif négociable/disponibilités *f.*

quiet, *a.* calme; **quiet market,** marché *m* calme; **business is very quiet,** les affaires *f* sont très calmes.

quorum, *n.* quorum *m*; nombre suffisant; nombre voulu; **to have/to form a quorum,** atteindre le quorum.

quota, *n.* (*a*) quote-part *f*/quotité *f*; cotisation *f*; **to contribute one's quota,** payer/apporter sa quote-part; *Adm:* **taxable quota,** quotité *f* imposable (*b*) contingent *m*/quota *m*; **sales quota,** quota de ventes (*c*) **quota sampling,** sondage *m* par quota (*d*) taux *m* de contingen-

tement; **import/export quotas,** quotas d'importation/d'exportation; **quota system (of distribution),** contingentement; **to fix quotas for an import,** contingenter une importation/déterminer les quotas d'une importation.

quotable, *a. StExch:* (valeur, etc.) cotable.

quotation, *n.* (*a*) *StExch:* cotation *f*/cote *f*/ cours *m*/prix *m*; **actual quotations,** cours effectifs; prix effectifs cotés; **closing quotation,** cours *m* de clôture; *NAm:* **flat quotation,** cotation sans intérêt; **the latest quotations,** les derniers cours; **stock admitted to quotation,** valeurs admises à la cote officielle; **to seek a share quotation,** faire une demande d'admission à la cote (*b*) *Ind:* devis *m*; **quotation for paint,** prix pour la peinture.

quote[1], *n. F:* = **quotation.**

quote[2], *v.tr.* **1.** *Adm:* (*in reply*) **please quote this number,** prière de rappeler ce numéro **2.** (*a*) établir/indiquer/fixer (un prix); **to quote s.o. a price for sth.,** fixer à qn un prix pour qch. (*b*) *StExch:* coter (une valeur); **quoted company,** société *f* dont les actions sont inscrites à la cote officielle; **quoted price,** cours *m* inscrit à la cote officielle; **quoted shares/stock,** actions inscrites à la cote officielle/ valeurs cotées en Bourse; **shares quoted at 90p,** valeurs qui cotent à 90p.

R

rack rent, *n.* (*i*) loyer à la valeur du marché; prix courant d'un loyer (*ii*) loyer *m* exorbitant.

rail, *n.* chemin *m* de fer/voie ferrée; **free on rail,** franco wagon; **price on rail,** prix *m* sur le wagon.

railroad, *n. NAm:* = **railway.**

railway, *n.* chemin *m* de fer/voie ferrée; **railway transport,** transport *m* ferroviaire/par chemin de fer; **works with railway facilities,** usine *f* avec facilités d'accès/avec raccordement au réseau ferroviaire.

raise¹, *n. NAm:* augmentation *f* (de salaire); **I've had a raise,** j'ai reçu une augmentation de salaire/j'ai été augmenté.

raise², *v.tr.* **1. to raise a question,** soulever une question **2.** *NAm:* **to raise a cheque,** (*i*) augmenter (frauduleusement) le montant d'un chèque (*ii*) faire un chèque **3.** (*a*) **to raise capital,** mobiliser des fonds/procurer des capitaux; **to raise funds by subscription,** réunir des fonds par souscription; **to raise money,** trouver/se procurer de l'argent (*b*) **to raise taxes,** lever des impôts; **to raise a loan,** (*i*) lancer (*ii*) émettre un emprunt (*c*) **the dividend is raised by 25%,** le dividende marque une progression/a augmenté de 25%.

raising, *n.* **1.** relèvement *m*/hausse *f*/augmentation *f*; **the raising of the minimum lending rate,** le relèvement du taux officiel de l'escompte **2.** (*a*) levée *f* (d'un impôt); (*i*) lancement *m* (*ii*) émission *f* (d'un emprunt) (*b*) mobilisation *f* (de fonds).

rake in, *v.tr. F:* amasser (de l'argent).

rake-off, *n. F:* pourcentage *m* (illicite ou non); commission *f*/ristourne *f*; **to get a rake-off on each sale,** toucher une commission/un pourcentage/une guelte sur chaque vente.

rally¹, *n.* reprise *f* (des prix); reprise/redressement *m* des affaires.

rally², *v.i. StExch:* **shares rallied,** les actions se sont redressées/ont repris.

rallying, *n.* reprise *f*/redressement *m* (des prix, etc.).

random, 1. *n.* **at random,** au hasard **2.** *a.* aléatoire; (fait) au hasard; **random sampling,** échantillonnage *m* aléatoire; **random check,** contrôle *m* par sondage(s); *Stat:* **random error,** erreur *f* aléatoire.

range¹, *n.* (*a*) **price range,** échelle *f*/éventail *m* des prix; **range of products,** gamme *f* de produits; **range of sizes,** éventail/choix *m* de dimensions; **salary range,** éventail de salaires (*b*) **range of activities,** rayon *m* d'action.

range², *v.i.* **incomes ranging from £5 000 to £6 000,** revenus *m* de l'ordre de £5 000 à £6 000.

rank¹, *n.* **1. the rank and file of union members,** la masse des syndiqués **2.** *Fin:* rang *m* (d'une créance, d'une hypothèque, etc.); **to assign a rank to a debt,** assigner un rang à une créance; *Stat:* **rank order statistics,** méthodes *f* statistiques de rang.

rank², 1. *v.tr. Jur:* **to rank creditors (in bankruptcy),** colloquer des créanciers **2.** *v.i.* (*a*) (*of creditor, claimant, etc.*) **to rank**

after s.o., prendre rang/passer après qn; **to rank before s.o.,** prendre rang/passer avant qn/avoir la priorité; **to rank equally with s.o.,** prendre/avoir le même rang que qn (*b*) *Jur:* (*of claim in bankruptcy*) être accepté à la vérification des créances; **to rank after sth.,** (*i*) (*of mortgage*) prendre rang après qch. (*ii*) (*of share*) être primé par qch.; **to rank before sth.,** (*i*) (*of mortgage*) prendre rang avant qch. (*ii*) (*of share*) avoir la priorité (sur qch.); **to rank equally with sth.,** prendre le même rang que qch.; **preference shares of all issues shall rank equally,** les actions de toutes les émissions prendront (le) même rang.

ranking, *n.* **1.** rang *m*; *Jur:* **ranking of a creditor,** collocation *f* de créanciers **2.** hiérarchie *f*.

ratable, *a.* = **rateable.**

rate[1], *n.* **1.** taux *m*; **birth rate,** (taux de) natalité *f*; **to be paid at the rate of £5 an hour,** être payé au taux de/à raison de £5 l'heure **2.** (*a*) taux/prix *m*/tarif *m*; **average rate,** taux/tarif moyen; **fixed rate,** taux/tarif/prix forfaitaire; **flat rate,** taux/tarif/prix uniforme; **full rate,** plein tarif; **letter rate,** tarif lettre; **night rates,** tarifs de nuit; **postal rates,** tarifs postaux; *Cust:* **preferential rates,** tarifs de faveur/préférentiels; **rates of insurance,** taux/tarifs d'assurance; **rates of pay,** barème *m* des salaires; **reduced rate,** tarif réduit; **standard rate,** tarif normal/uniforme; **rate fixing,** tarification *f*; **to fix a rate,** tarifer (*b*) taux/pourcentage *m*; **rate of interest/interest rate,** taux d'intérêt; **rate of return,** rentabilité/taux de rendement (*c*) *Bank:* **bank rate,** taux de l'escompte; **base rate,** taux de base; **minimum lending rate,** taux (officiel) de l'escompte; *NAm:* **prime rate,** taux de l'escompte (pour les *prime bills*) (*d*) cours *m*/taux; **rate of exchange/exchange rate,** cours/taux du change; **the rate of the dollar,** le cours du dollar; **to-day's rate,** le cours du jour (*e*) *StExch:* **backwardation rate,** cours/taux de

déport; **carry-over/contango rate,** cours/taux de report; **forward rate,** cours/taux (pour les opérations) à terme; **market rate,** taux du marché (*f*) ratio *m*; **rate of turnover,** ratio de rotation des stocks **3.** (*a*) taux d'un impôt local (= centime le franc) (*b*) impôts locaux, (*i*) contribution foncière (*ii*) impôt mobilier; cotisation *f*; **rates and taxes,** impôts et contributions.

rate[2], *v.tr.* **1.** estimer/évaluer (qch.)/fixer la valeur de (qch.) **2.** (*a*) imposer/taxer (qn, qch.); tarifer (qch.); **to rate s.o./a property at a certain sum,** taxer qn/un immeuble à tant; **heavily rated building,** immeuble fortement grevé (*b*) *Ins:* **to rate s.o. up,** faire payer à qn une prime plus élevée.

rateable, *a.* **1.** évaluable **2.** imposable; **rateable value,** (*i*) loyer matriciel/valeur locative imposable (d'un immeuble) (*ii*) évaluation cadastrale (d'un terrain à bâtir).

ratepayer, *n.* contribuable *mf*.

ratification, *n. Jur:* ratification *f*/homologation *f*/validation *f*.

ratify, *v.tr. Jur:* ratifier/sanctionner/valider/homologuer; **to ratify a contract,** approuver un contrat.

rating, *n.* **1.** (*a*) estimation *f*/évaluation *f* (d'une pièce de monnaie/etc.) (*b*) tarification *f* (des transports, etc.); taxation (d'une marchandise); répartition *f* des impôts locaux (*c*) classement *m*/classification *f* (d'une auto, etc.) **2.** évaluation (assignée à qch.); **credit rating,** réputation *f* de solvabilité; **market rating,** cours *m* en Bourse; **merit rating,** appréciation *f* du mérite; (*of machine*) **performance rating,** rendement effectif; **personnel rating,** appréciation du personnel; **work-force rating,** notation *f* de la main-d'œuvre.

ratio, *n.* **1.** raison *f*/rapport *m*/coefficient *m*/ proportion *f*/ratio *m*; **in the ratio of one to three,** dans le rapport/dans la proportion de un à trois; sous-triple; **ten-to-one**

ratio, proportion décuple; **accounting ratio,** ratio comptable; **capital-output ratio,** ratio d'intensité de capital; *Fin: Book-k:* **cash ratio,** coefficient de trésorerie; **current ratio/liquid(ity) ratio/ ratio of quick current assets to current liabilities,** coefficient de liquidité; **debt ratio,** ratio d'endettement; **price-earnings ratio,** rapport cours-bénéfices; **profit-volume ratio,** rapport profit sur ventes; **ratio of working expenses;** *NAm:* **operating ratio,** coefficient d'exploitation 2. taux *m*; **cover ratio,** taux de couverture; **mark-up ratio,** taux de marge.

rationale, *n.* analyse raisonnée/exposé raisonné (d'un procédé).

rationalization, *n.* rationalisation *f* (d'une industrie, etc.); organisation rationnelle (de l'industrie).

rationalize, *v.tr.* rationaliser (une industrie, etc.).

rationing, *n.* rationnement *m*; **capital rationing,** rationnement de capitaux.

rat-race, *n.* *F:* **the rat-race,** le panier de crabes/la foire d'empoigne/la course au bifteck.

raw, *a.* **raw material,** matière(s) première(s); matériaux bruts; *Cmptr:* **raw data,** données brutes/à traiter/non traitées.

re, *prep.* **re your letter of March 8th,** relativement à/me référant à/au sujet de votre lettre du 8 mars.

react, *v.i.* (*of prices*) réagir.

reaction, *n.* réaction *f*; **sharp reaction of sterling on the foreign market exchange,** vive réaction du sterling sur le marché des changes.

read, *v.tr.* lire (un livre, une lettre, etc.); *Adm:* **read and approved,** lu et approuvé **to read a report (to the meeting),** donner lecture d'un rapport (à l'assemblée).

readjust, *v.tr.* **to readjust the wage structure,** r(é)ajuster les salaires.

readjustment, *n.* **the unions are demanding a readjustment of the wage structure,** les syndicats *m* réclament un r(é)ajustement des salaires.

readvertise, *v.tr.* annoncer de nouveau/ faire passer une annonce de nouveau.

readvertisement, *n.* deuxième annonce (pour le même poste).

ready, *a.* 1. **ready money,** argent comptant/liquide; **to pay in ready money,** payer (au) comptant 2. **goods that meet with a ready sale,** marchandises *f* de vente courante/marchandises qui s'écoulent rapidement.

ready-to-wear, *a.* **ready-to-wear clothes,** (le) prêt-à-porter.

real, *a.* 1. véritable/réel; **real cost,** coût réel; **real income,** revenu réel; **real terms,** termes *m* réels/effectifs; *Cmptr:* **real time,** temps *m* réel; *Fin:* **real value,** valeur effective; **real wages,** salaires réels 2. *Jur:* **real estate,** propriété immobilière/biens immobiliers/immeubles *mpl*; (*landed property only*) propriété foncière/biens fonciers; bien-fonds *mpl*; *NAm:* **real estate agent,** agent immobilier; **real estate agency,** agence *f* immobilière; **real estate leasing,** crédit-bail *m* immobilier.

realizable, *a.* (*a*) (projet) réalisable (*b*) **realizable assets,** capital *m* réalisable; **assets that are hardly realizable,** capital *m* difficile à convertir (en espèces)/difficilement réalisable.

realization, *n.* (*a*) réalisation *f* (d'un projet, etc.) (*b*) *Fin:* conversion *f* en espèces; réalisation (d'un placement, d'une propriété); mobilisation *f* (d'une indemnité); **realization account,** compte de liquidation (*c*) *Jur:* conversion (de biens meubles) en biens immeubles.

realize, *v.tr.* (*a*) réaliser (un projet, etc.)

(b) *Fin:* convertir (des biens) en espèces; vendre/réaliser (une propriété, un placement); mobiliser (une indemnité); **these shares cannot be realized,** il n'y a pas de marché pour ces titres (c) réaliser (des bénéfices) (d) *Jur:* convertir (des biens meubles en biens immeubles) (e) (*of goods*) **to realize a high price,** atteindre/rapporter un bon prix.

realtor, *n. NAm:* agent immobilier.

realty, *n. Jur:* (a) bien immobilier (b) *coll.* biens immobiliers; (biens) immeubles *mpl.*

reapply, *v.i.* faire une nouvelle demande; écrire de nouveau.

reappoint, *v.tr.* réintégrer (qn) dans ses fonctions.

reappraisal, *n.* réévaluation *f.*

reasonable, *a.* raisonnable; **reasonable prices,** prix modérés/raisonnables/abordables; **reasonable offer,** offre *f* acceptable/raisonnable.

reassess, *v.tr.* (a) réévaluer/reviser le taux d'imposition (d'un contribuable) (b) réévaluer (des dommages, un immeuble, etc.).

reassessment, *n.* (a) révision *f* du taux d'imposition (b) réévaluation *f.*

reassign, *v.tr.* **to reassign funds to their original use,** réaffecter des fonds à leur destination première.

reassignment, *n.* réaffectation *f* (de fonds).

reassurance, *n. Ins:* réassurance *f.*

reassure, *v.tr. Ins:* réassurer.

rebate, *n.* **1.** rabais *m*/remise *f*/escompte *m*; bonification *f*/ristourne *f*; remboursement *m*; (*on goods not up to sample*) réfaction *f*; **to allow a rebate on an account,** faire une remise sur un compte; *Adm:* **tax rebate,** dégrèvement *m*/crédit *m* d'impôt.

rebound, *n.* **sharp rebound of the market,** reprise vigoureuse du marché.

recapitalization, *n. Fin:* changement *m* de la structure financière (d'une société).

recapitalize, *v.tr. Fin:* **to recapitalize a company,** changer la structure financière d'une société.

recede, *v.i.* décliner (en valeur); *StExch:* **oil shares receded three points,** les pétroles *m* ont reculé/baissé de trois points.

receipt[1], *n.* **1.** (a) recette *f*; *pl.* **receipts,** recettes/rentrées *f*/encaissements *m*; **receipts and expenditure,** recettes et dépenses *f*; **receipts and payments,** rentrées et sorties *f* (b) réception *f*; **to acknowledge receipt of a letter,** accuser réception d'une lettre; **I am in receipt of your letter of June 9th,** j'ai bien reçu votre lettre du 9 juin; **on receipt of (this letter, your parcel),** au reçu de/dès réception de (cette lettre, votre envoi); **to pay on receipt,** payer à (la) réception; **within ten days of receipt,** dans les dix jours suivant réception **2.** reçu *m*/récépissé *m*/acquit *m*/quittance *f* (**for goods, money,** de marchandises, d'argent); **customs receipt,** récépissé de douane; **formal receipt,** quittance comptable; **receipt book,** carnet *m* de quittances; **receipt for a loan,** reconnaissance *f* de dette; **receipt form,** formule *f* d'acquit; **receipt for payment,** acquit/quittance/reçu; **receipt in full (discharge),** reçu pour solde de tout compte; **receipt on account,** reçu à valoir; **receipt for a registered parcel,** récépissé postal (d'un envoi recommandé); **receipt stamp,** timbre *m* de quittance/timbre-quittance *m*; **rent receipt,** quittance de loyer; **warehouse receipt,** récépissé d'entrepôt: *Fin:* **application receipt for shares,** récépissé de souscription à des actions; **to give a receipt,** donner un reçu; **send it with the receipt,** envoyez-le avec la facture acquittée.

receipt[2], *v.tr.* acquitter/quittancer/décharger (une facture); (*with rubber stamp*) apposer le tampon "acquitté"/"pour acquit" sur (une facture); **to receipt a bill in the margin,** émarger une facture.

receivable, *a.* **accounts receivable**/*NAm:* **receivables,** *n.* créances *f*; dettes actives; actif *m*; **bills receivable,** (*i*) effets *m* à recevoir (*ii*) comptes clients *m*.

receive, *v.tr.* recevoir (une nouvelle, une lettre, etc.); **on receiving your letter,** dès réception de votre lettre; **I have received your letter,** votre lettre m'est parvenue; j'ai bien reçu votre lettre; **to receive money,** recevoir/toucher de l'argent; **to receive one's salary,** toucher son salaire; **received the sum of £100,** reçu la somme de £100; (*on bill*) **received with thanks,** acquitté/payé/pour acquit.

receiver, *n.* **1.** (*a*) personne *f* qui reçoit (qch.); destinataire *mf* (d'une lettre, etc.); *Jur:* réceptionnaire *mf* (d'un envoi) (*b*) *NAm:* receveur *m* (des deniers publics); **receiver's office,** recette *f* (*c*) *Jur:* **receiver in bankruptcy/official receiver,** syndic *m* au règlement judiciaire; syndic de faillite; **to be in the hands of the receiver,** être en règlement judiciaire (*d*) *StExch:* **receiver of contango,** reporteur *m* **2.** (telephone) **receiver,** récepteur *m*/écouteur *m*.

receivership, *n.* **to go into receivership,** se mettre en règlement judiciaire.

receiving[1], *a.* **receiving clerk,** réceptionnaire *mf*; **receiving department,** service *m* de la réception.

receiving[2], *n.* (*a*) réception *f*; **receiving of goods,** réception de marchandises; **receiving certificate,** certificat *m* de réception; **receiving office,** (*i*) *Post:* bureau *m* de réception (*ii*) *Rail:* bureau de(s) messageries (*b*) *Jur:* **receiving order,** mandat *m* d'action; ordonnance *f* de mise sous séquestre.

reception, *n.* **1.** (*at hotel*) **the reception desk/office,** la réception/le bureau de réception; *NAm:* **reception clerk,** réceptionniste *mf*/préposé(e) à la réception; **chief reception clerk,** chef *m* de (la) réception **2.** (bureau d')accueil *m* **3.** réception (officielle, etc.).

receptionist, *n.* préposé(e) à la réception/réceptionniste *mf* (d'un hôtel, etc.); (*in tourist centre, etc.*) hôtesse d'accueil; **head receptionist,** chef *m* de (la) réception.

recession, *n.* *PolEc:* récession *f*; dépression *f*; crise *f* économique; (*of business*) ralentissement *m* des affaires.

recipient, *n.* destinataire *mf* (d'une lettre, etc.); bénéficiaire *mf* (d'un chèque, d'un effet); *Jur:* donataire *mf*; **recipient of an allowance,** allocataire *mf*.

reciprocal, *a.* réciproque/mutuel; **reciprocal concessions,** concessions *f* réciproques; *Jur:* **reciprocal contract,** contrat réciproque/bilatéral; *StExch:* **reciprocal holdings,** participations croisées.

reciprocate, *v.tr.* *Book-k:* **to reciprocate an entry,** passer écriture conforme; passer une écriture en conformité.

reckon, **1.** *v.tr* compter/calculer/faire le compte de; supputer (une somme, etc.); **to reckon the cost of sth.,** calculer les frais de (qch.) **2.** *v.i.* compter/calculer.

recognition, *n.* **brand recognition,** identification *f* d'une marque.

recognized, *a.* **recognized agent,** agent accrédité; **recognized merchant,** commerçant attitré.

recommend, *v.tr.* recommander; **to recommend s.o. to an employer,** recommander qn à un employeur; **to recommend a candidate for a post,** recommander un candidat pour un emploi; **to recommend a (good) hotel,** recommander un (bon) hôtel; **recommended price,** prix *m* recommandé/conseillé.

recommendation, *n.* **1.** recommandation *f*; **I have come on the recommendation of one of your customers,** je viens sur la recommandation d'un de vos clients; *Fin:* **recommendation of a dividend,** proposition *f* de dividende **2.** **stockbroker's list of recommendations,** liste *f* de placements conseillés par un courtier.

reconcile, *v.tr.* *Book-k:* **to reconcile one**

account with another, faire accorder un compte avec un autre.

reconciliation, *n. Book-k:* ajustement *m* (des écritures); **reconciliation account,** compte collectif.

reconstruction, *n.* reconstitution *f* (d'une société, etc.); **economic and financial reconstruction,** restauration économique et financière.

record[1], *n.* **1.** (*a*) note *f*/mention *f*; **to be shown only as a record,** ne figurer que pour mémoire (*b*) registre *m* **2.** *pl.* **records,** archives *f*; registres *m* **3.** carrière *f*/dossier *m*/antécédents *mpl* (de qn); **service record,** état *m* de service **4.** record *m*; **record figure,** chiffre *m* record; **record production/output,** production *f* record/sans précédent; **record year,** année *f* record.

record[2], *v.tr.* enregistrer; *Adm:* recenser (des faits, etc.); **(to send a letter by) recorded delivery,** (envoyer une lettre) en recommandé.

record-breaking, *a.* **record-breaking production,** production *f* record.

recording, *n.* (prise de) note *f* (d'une commande).

recoup, *v.tr.* **1.** dédommager (qn); **to recoup (one's losses),** se rattraper (de ses pertes); récupérer son argent **2.** *Jur:* défalquer/faire le décompte de (qch.).

recoupment, *n. NAm:* dédommagement *m.*

recourse, *n. Fin: Jur:* **to have recourse to the endorser of a bill,** avoir recours contre l'endosseur d'un effet; **endorsement without recourse,** endossement *m* à forfait; **to reserve right of recourse,** se réserver le recours/un droit de recours; **recourse against third parties,** recours contre des tiers.

recover, *v.tr. & i.* (*a*) regagner (de l'argent perdu, etc.); recouvrer/regagner/rentrer en possession de (ses biens); rentrer dans (ses dépenses); recouvrer/récupérer/faire rentrer (une créance); **to recover**

one's money, récupérer son argent/rentrer en possession de son argent/se rembourser; **to recover money advanced,** récupérer ses avances; **to recover damages from s.o.,** obtenir des dommages-intérêts de qn; se faire dédommager par qn (*b*) **the market is recovering,** le marché reprend/se ranime; **oils recovered five pence,** les valeurs pétrolières ont remonté de cinq pence; **prices are recovering,** les prix *m* se relèvent/les cours *m* reprennent.

recoverable, *a.* (*of loss, etc.*) recouvrable/récupérable.

recovery, *n.* **1.** recouvrement *m*/récupération *f*; **losses beyond/past recovery,** pertes *f* irrécupérables; **recovery of debts,** recouvrement de créances; **recovery of expenses,** recouvrement des dépenses/récupération des frais **2.** *Jur:* **recovery of payment made by mistake,** répétition *f* d'indu; **action for recovery of property,** (action en) revendication *f*; **recovery of damages,** obtention *f* de dommages-intérêts **3.** redressement *m*/relèvement *m* (économique, etc.); reprise *f* (des affaires); **trade recovery/industrial recovery,** reprise/relance *f* économique; **recovery of prices,** reprise des cours.

recredit, *v.tr. Book-k:* faire une extourne.

recruit, *v.tr.* recruter (du personnel).

recruiting, recruitment, *n.* recrutement *m* (de personnel).

rectification, *n.* rectification *f*/correction *f* (d'une erreur, etc.).

rectify, *v.tr.* rectifier/corriger (un calcul, une erreur); *Book-k:* **to rectify an entry,** modifier/rectifier une écriture.

recurrent, *a.* **recurrent expenses,** dépenses *f* qui reviennent périodiquement.

recycle, *v.tr.* recycler (des journaux, etc.).

red, *n. F:* **to be in the red/to go into the red,** avoir un découvert/un compte *m* à découvert; **to be out of the red,** avoir un compte créditeur.

redeem, *v.tr.* (*a*) racheter/dégager (une propriété, un nantissement, etc.) (*b*) rembourser (une obligation, une annuité, etc.); **to redeem a bill,** honorer une traite; **to redeem a debt,** amortir une dette/se libérer d'une dette; **to redeem a mortgage,** (*i*) (*of mortgagor*) éteindre une hypothèque (*ii*) (*of purchaser of mortgaged property*) purger une hypothèque (*c*) obtenir le remboursement (d'obligations remboursables, etc.); encaisser (un bon de caisse, etc.).

redeemable, *a.* *Fin:* (*of stock, etc.*) rachetable/remboursable/amortissable.

redeeming, *n.* (*a*) rachat *m*/dégagement *m* (d'un objet mis en gage, d'une propriété hypothéquée) (*b*) remboursement *m*/amortissement *m* (d'une obligation); **redeeming of a mortgage,** (*i*) (*by mortgagor*) extinction *f* d'une hypothèque (*ii*) (*by purchaser of mortgaged property*) purge *f* d'une hypothèque.

redemption, *n.* (*a*) *Fin:* remboursement *m*/amortissement *m* (d'une obligation); rachat *m*/*Jur:* rédemption *f* (d'un emprunt, d'une concession); **debt redemption,** amortissement de la dette publique; **interim redemption/redemption before due date,** amortissement/remboursement anticipé; **optional redemption date,** remboursement à période d'option; **redemption date,** amortissement obligatoire; **redemption fund,** caisse *f* d'amortissement; **redemption loan,** emprunt d'amortissement; **redemption premium,** prime *f* de remboursement; **redemption table,** plan *m* d'amortissement (d'une dette, etc.); **redemption value/price,** valeur *f* de rachat/de remboursement; **redemption yield,** rendement sur remboursement; **terms of redemption,** (*i*) condition *f* de rachat/de remboursement (*ii*) plan d'amortissement (*b*) **redemption (of a pledge, of a security),** dégagement *m*/retrait *m* (d'un gage, d'un nantissement); **re-demption of a mortgage,** (*i*) (*by mortgagor*) extinction *f* (*ii*) (*by purchaser of mortgaged property*) purge *f* d'une hypothèque (*c*) *Jur:* **sale with power/option of redemption,** vente *f* avec faculté de rachat; vente à réméré; **covenant of redemption,** pacte *m* de rachat.

redeploy, *v.tr.* *Adm: Ind:* réorganiser (un service); redistribuer/reclasser/procéder à une nouvelle répartition de (la main-d'œuvre, etc.).

redeployment, *n.* *Adm: Ind:* réorganisation *f* (d'un service); réorganisation/reclassement *m* (de la main-d'œuvre).

rediscount[1], *n.* **1.** réescompte *m* **2.** *F:* papier réescompté.

rediscount[2], *v.tr.* réescompter.

rediscountable, *a.* réescomptable.

redistribute, *v.tr.* redistribuer.

redistribution, *n.* redistribution *f*; nouvelle distribution.

reduce, *v.tr.* réduire/baisser/rabaisser/diminuer (le prix, etc.); **reduced to £5 from £10,** prix réduit de £10 à £5; **to reduce taxes,** alléger les impôts; **to reduce the rates on a house,** dégrever un immeuble; **to reduce expenses,** diminuer/réduire les dépenses; *Ind:* **to reduce the output,** ralentir la production; **to reduce the working week from 42 to 40 hours,** ramener la semaine de 42 heures à 40 heures; **to reduce the cost of living,** faire baisser le coût de la vie.

reduced, *a.* réduit; **reduced goods,** soldes *mpl*; **reduced price,** prix réduit; **bought at reduced prices,** acheté à prix réduit/à rabais/en solde; **reduced assessment on property,** dégrèvement *m*.

reduction, *n.* (*a*) réduction *f*/diminution *f*/baisse *f* (des prix, des salaires); **cost reduction,** réduction des frais; **reduction of taxes/of taxation,** allègement *m*/dégrèvement *m* d'impôts; **reduction of expenses,** réduction *f* des dépenses; **reduction of share capital,** réduction du capital social; **staff reduction,** réduction du personnel; **600 job reductions,** 600 suppressions d'emploi (*b*) rabais *m*/remise *f*; **to make a reduction on an article,** faire un rabais/une remise sur un article.

redundancy, *n.* licenciement *m*; chômage partiel; **redundancy pay(ment),** indemnité *f*/prime *f* de licenciement; **voluntary redundancy,** départ *m* volontaire.

redundant, *a.* **redundant capital,** surplus *m* (de capital)/capital en trop; *Ind:* **to be made redundant,** être (déclaré en surnombre et) licencié; (*as a result of automation*) être en chômage techn(olog)ique.

re-employ, *v.tr.* reprendre/réembaucher (qn); remployer/réemployer (qch.).

re-employment, *n.* réemploi *m* (de qn, qch.); *Fin:* remploi *m* (de fonds).

re-engage, *v.tr.* rengager/réembaucher (des employés).

re-establish, *v.tr.* rétablir; **to re-establish a company's credit,** raffermir le crédit d'une maison.

re-establishment, *n.* rétablissement *m*.

re-export[1], *n.* réexportation *f*; **re-export trade,** commerce *m* intermédiaire/réexportation *f*.

re-export[2], *v.tr.* réexporter.

re-exportation, *n.* réexportation *f*.

refer, 1. *v.tr.* (*of bank*) **to refer a cheque to drawer,** refuser d'honorer un chèque (faute de provision); **referred to drawer,** retour au tireur **2.** *v.i.* **I shall have to refer (back) to the board,** il faudra que je consulte le conseil de direction; **to refer to a document,** se reporter à un document; **referring to your letter,** (comme) suite à votre lettre/(nous, me) référant à votre lettre.

referee, *n.* **1.** *Jur:* arbitre *m*/médiateur *m*; **board of referees,** commission arbitrale **2.** répondant(e)/personne *f* à qui on peut s'en rapporter pour obtenir des références sur qn.

reference, *n.* **1.** (*a*) renvoi *m* (d'une affaire) devant arbitre; renvoi/référence *f* (d'une question à une autorité, etc.) (*b*) compétence *f*/pouvoirs *mpl* (d'un tribunal); **terms of reference of a commission/order of reference,** délimitation *f* des pouvoirs d'une commission; mandat *m*/attributions *fpl* d'une commission; **under these terms of reference,** aux termes des instructions données **2. with reference to your letter of June 9th,** nous référant à votre lettre/comme suite à votre lettre du 9 juin **3.** (*at head of letter*) **our reference,** N/Réf(érence); **your reference,** V/Réf(érence); **please quote this reference number,** numéro à rappeler; **when replying quote reference no. RL3U,** adresser sous référence RL3U **4.** (*a*) renseignements *mpl*; références *fpl* (d'employé, etc.); **to give a reference (about s.o.),** fournir des références sur qn; **to take up s.o.'s references,** prendre des renseignements sur qn; **to have good references,** avoir de bonnes références/de bonnes recommandations; **to ask for references,** solliciter une recommandation; **letter of reference,** lettre de recommandation (*b*) répondant(e); personne *f* à qui on peut s'en rapporter pour obtenir des références sur qn; **who are your references?** quelles sont les personnes que vous pouvez donner en référence? **to give s.o. as a reference,** se recommander/se réclamer de qn; **you may use my name as (a) reference,** vous pouvez donner mon nom comme référence.

refinancing, *n.* refinancement *m*.

reflate, *v.tr. PolEc:* ranimer/relancer (l'économie, etc.).

reflation, *n. PolEc:* relance (économique).

refloat, *v.tr. Fin:* (*a*) émettre de nouveau

(un emprunt) (*b*) renflouer (une entreprise, une société).

refresher, *n*. **to attend a refresher course,** se recycler/suivre un cours de recyclage.

refrigerate, *v.tr. Ind:* réfrigérer/garder au réfrigérateur; **refrigerated lorry,** camion frigorifique/réfrigéré; **refrigerated ship,** navire *m* frigorifique.

refrigeration, *n*. réfrigération *f*; **to keep under refrigeration,** garder au réfrigérateur; **refrigeration plant,** installation *f* frigorifique.

refund[1], *n*. (*a*) remboursement *m*; **to obtain a refund,** être remboursé/se faire rembourser/obtenir un remboursement (*b*) *Jur:* restitution *f* d'indu.

refund[2], **1.** *v.tr.* (*a*) rembourser (de l'argent, un paiement) (**to s.o.,** à qn); **to refund s.o.,** rembourser qn; **to refund the cost of postage,** rembourser les frais de port; **to have one's money refunded,** obtenir un remboursement; **money refunded if not satisfied,** satisfaction garantie ou argent remis (*b*) ristourner (un paiement en trop); restituer (de l'argent) **2.** *v.i. Jur:* faire restitution d'indu.

refundable, *a*. remboursable (**over 25 years,** sur une période de 25 ans); (*when hiring*) **deposit refundable,** caution *f*/ acompte *m* remboursable; **bottle with refundable deposit,** bouteille consignée.

refunding, *n*. remboursement *m*; **refunding loan,** emprunt *m* de remboursement; **refunding clause,** clause *f* de remboursement.

refusal, *n*. **1.** (*a*) refus *m*; **refusal to pay,** refus de paiement (*b*) **refusal of goods,** refus de marchandises **2.** droit *m* de refuser; droit de préemption; **to have (the) first refusal,** avoir la première offre de qch..

refuse, *v.tr.* **1.** refuser (une offre, etc.) **2.** (*a*) rejeter/repousser (une requête) (*b*) **to refuse to pay,** refuser de payer.

region, *n*. **it will cost in the region of £50,** cela coûtera dans les £50/environ £50.

register[1], *n*. (*a*) registre *m*; journal *m*; *Adm: etc:* sommier *m*; *Cust:* **register of goods in bond,** sommier d'entrepôt; *Nau:* **ship's register,** livre *m* de bord; **to enter an item in a register,** rapporter/ inscrire/noter/mettre un article sur/ dans un registre; **register of debenture holders,** registre/livre des obligataires; **register of shareholders,** registre/livre des actionnaires: **share register,** registre des actions (*b*) **commercial register,** registre de commerce (tenu par un commerçant); *Adm:* **companies register/ register of companies/trade register** = registre du commerce; **cadastral/land register,** registre du cadastre.

register[2], *v.tr.* enregistrer/inscrire/immatriculer/enrôler; **to register a company,** immatriculer (une société) au registre du commerce; **to register a security,** immatriculer une valeur; **to register a trademark,** déposer une marque de fabrique.

registered, *a*. (*a*) enregistré/inscrit/immatriculé; **registered design,** modèle déposé (*b*) *Fin:* **registered bond/ debenture,** obligation nominative; **registered stock/securities,** effets/titres nominatifs; **registered value,** valeur enregistrée/constatée (*c*) *Post:* **registered letter/parcel,** (*i*) lettre recommandée/ colis recommandé; (envoi en) recommandé *m* (*ii*) lettre/colis avec valeur déclarée; **by registered post,** en recommandé (*d*) **registered office(s),** siège social.

registering, *n*. (*a*) enregistrement *m*/ inscription *f*/immatriculation *f* (*b*) *Post:* recommandation *f* (d'une lettre, d'un colis).

registrar, *n*. employé(e)/préposé(e) aux registres; *Adm:* **registrar of mortgages,** conservateur *m* des hypothèques; **companies registrar/registrar of companies,** directeur *m* du registre des sociétés.

registration, *n*. enregistrement *m*/ inscription *f*; immatriculation *f* (d'une valeur, etc.); **land registration,** inscription au cadastre; *Fin:* **registration and transfer fees,** droits *m* d'inscription et de transfert; **registration certificate,** matricule *f*; **registration fees,** (*i*) *Post:* taxe *f* de recommandation (*ii*) *Adm:* droit d'inscription (*iii*) frais *mpl* d'enregistrement; **registration number,** (*i*) *Aut:* numéro *m* d'immatriculation/numéro minéralogique (*ii*) *Adm:* numéro matricule; **registration of luggage,** enregistrement des bagages; **registration of mortgages,** inscriptions hypothécaires/des hypothèques; **registration of (a) trademark,** dépôt *m* d'une marque de fabrique.

registry, *n.* (*i*) bureau *m* de l'enregistrement (*ii*) greffe *m*; **land registry,** bureau du cadastre; **registry books,** livres *m* d'ordre/registres *m*; *Nau:* **certificate of registry,** lettre *f* de mer; **port of registry,** port *m* d'attache.

regression, *n.* **regression analysis,** analyse *f* de régression.

regular, *a.* **1.** régulier; **regular customer,** (bon) client *m*; habitué(e); **regular income,** revenu régulier; **regular staff,** employés permanents **2.** *Ind:* **regular model,** modèle courant; type courant; **regular price,** prix *m* ordinaire/prix de règle.

regulate, *v.tr.* régler; réglementer; **the price is regulated by supply and demand,** le prix est déterminé par l'offre et la demande; **regulated price,** prix réglementé.

regulation, *n.* **1.** règlement *m*/réglementation *f* (des affaires, etc.) **2.** règlement/arrêté *m*/ordonnance *f*/prescription *f*; **regulations,** règlement(s)/réglementation/prescriptions/dispositions *f*; **customs regulations,** règlements de la douane; **safety regulations,** règles *fpl* de sécurité.

reimbursable, *a.* remboursable (**over 25 years,** sur une période de 25 ans).

reimburse, *v.tr.* **1.** rembourser (de l'argent) **2. to reimburse s.o. (for) sth.,** rembourser qn de qch.; désintéresser qn; **to be reimbursed,** (*i*) rentrer dans ses frais/se rembourser (*ii*) obtenir un remboursement.

reimport[1], *n.* réimportation *f*.

reimport[2], *v.tr.* réimporter.

reimportation, *n.* réimportation *f*.

reinflate, *v.tr.* relancer/ranimer (l'économie).

reinstate, *v.tr.* réintégrer (qn) (dans ses fonctions); **to reinstate s.o. in his former job,** réaffecter qn à son premier emploi.

reinstatement, *n.* réintégration *f* (de qn dans ses fonctions).

reinsurance, *n.* *Ins:* réassurance *f*; contre-assurance *f*; **reinsurance policy,** police *f* de réassurance.

reinsure, *v.tr.* *Ins:* réassurer.

reinsurer, *n.* *Ins:* réassureur *m*.

reinvest, *v.tr.* *Fin:* (*a*) replacer (des fonds); trouver un nouveau placement pour (des fonds) (*b*) réinvestir/reverser des bénéfices (dans une entreprise).

reinvestment, *n.* *Fin:* (*a*) nouveau placement (*b*) bénéfices réinvestis.

reissue[1], *n.* (*a*) *Fin:* nouvelle émission (de billets de banque, etc.) (*b*) nouvelle édition/réédition *f* (d'un livre).

reissue[2], *v.tr.* *Fin:* émettre de nouveau (des actions, etc.).

reject[1], *n.* (pièce de) rebut *m*; **export reject,** article (de rebut) non destiné à l'exportation; **reject shop,** magasin *m* de marchandises défectueuses.

reject[2], *v.tr.* (*a*) rejeter/repousser (une offre, une proposition) (*b*) refuser (des marchandises, un candidat, etc.).

relate, *v.i.* se rapporter/avoir rapport/avoir trait (**to,** à); **agreement relating to . . .,** convention *f* ayant trait à . . . .

---

related, *a.* (*a*) **related company**, société affiliée; **related markets**, marchés liés (*b*) **earnings(-)related pension**, pension proportionelle au salaire.

relation, *n.* (*a*) **in/with relation to . . .**, en/pour ce qui concerne . . . (*b*) *pl.* relations *f*; **to have business relations with s.o.**, être en relations d'affaires avec qn; **industrial relations**, relations industrielles; **labour relations**, relations syndicales; relations ouvrières; relations du travail; **labour-management relations**, rapports patrons-ouvriers; **public relations (PR) officer**, chef *m* du service des relations avec le public/des relations publiques.

release[1], *n.* **1.** (*a*) décharge *f*/libération *f* (**from an obligation**, d'une obligation) (*b*) **day release**, congé de formation rémunéré; jour de permission accordé aux employés d'une maison pour se perfectionner (*c*) (*of records, etc.*) **new release**, (dernière) nouveauté/vient de paraître (*d*) *Cust:* **release of wine from bond**, congé pour le transport des vins; **release of goods against payment**, libération de marchandises **2.** acquit *m*/quittance *f*/reçu *m*.

release[2], *v.tr.* **1.** (*a*) décharger/acquitter/libérer (qn d'une obligation); libérer (un débiteur) (*b*) sortir/mettre en vente (un nouveau disque, etc.) (*c*) **to release funds**, débloquer des fonds **2.** *Jur:* (*a*) **to release a debt/a tax**, remettre une dette/un impôt; faire (à qn) la remise d'une dette/d'un impôt (*b*) abandonner/renoncer à (un droit, une créance).

reliability, *n.* (*of machine*) fiabilité *f*.

reliable, *a.* (*of person*) sérieux/digne de confiance/sur qui on peut compter/à qui on peut se fier; (renseignement) sûr; (*of machine*) fiable/sûr; **reliable firm**, maison *f* de confiance; **reliable guarantee**, garantie *f* solide; **to have sth. from a reliable source**, tenir qch. de bonne source/de source sûre.

relief, *n.* **tax relief**, réduction *f*/dégrèvement *m* d'impôt; allègement *m* (fiscal).

reminder, *n.* (*a*) (lettre de) rappel *m*; avertissement *m*; **reminder of account due/of due date**, rappel d'échéance (*b*) *Publ:* (lettre de) relance *f*.

remission, *n.* remise *f* (d'une dette, etc.); **remission of a tax**, remise d'un impôt; détaxe *f*; **remission of taxes**, exonération *f*.

remit, *v.tr.* remettre (une dette) (*b*) **to remit a sum of money to s.o.**, envoyer/remettre une somme à qn; faire remise d'une somme à qn; **kindly remit by cheque**, prière de régler par chèque.

remittance, *n.* règlement *m*; **send your remittance (to)**, faites parvenir votre règlement (à).

remnant, *n.* coupon *m* (de tissu); **remnants**, soldes *m*; fins *f* de série.

remunerate, *v.tr.* (*a*) rémunérer (**s.o. for his services**, qn de ses services) (*b*) rémunérer/rétribuer (un service).

remuneration, *n.* rémunération *f* (**for**, de)/rétribution *f*/paiement *m*; **in remuneration for . . .**, en rémunération de . . . .

remunerative, *a.* (travail, prix) rémunérateur.

render, *v.tr.* **to render an account to s.o.**, remettre un compte à qn; **as per account rendered/to account rendered**, suivant compte remis.

renew, *v.tr.* renouveler; **to renew a lease**, renouveler un bail; **to renew one's subscription to a newspaper**, se réabonner à un journal; **to renew a bill**, prolonger une lettre de change; *Fin:* **to renew the coupons of a share certificate**, recouponner un certificat d'action.

renewal, *n.* **renewal (of subscription)**, réabonnement *m* (**to**, à); **renewal of a bill**, atermoiement *m*/prolongation *f* d'une lettre de change; **renewal of a lease**, renouvellement *m* d'un bail; *Fin:* **renewal of coupons,** recouponnement *m*.

rent[1], *n.* (*a*) loyer *m*; (prix de) location *f* (d'une maison, etc.); **high rent,** gros loyer/loyer élevé; **low rent,** petit loyer/loyer peu élevé; **nominal/peppercorn rent,** loyer symbolique; **rent free,** gratuit; **to owe three months' rent,** devoir trois mois de loyer; **quarter's rent,** terme *m* (*b*) **ground rent,** redevance *f* emphytéotique/rente foncière.

rent[2], *v.tr.* (*a*) (*let*) louer (une maison) (*b*) (*hire*) louer/prendre en location (une maison, etc.); **rented car,** voiture *f* de location/de louage; **to rent a house from the tenant,** sous-louer une maison (*c*) **this house rents at £200 a month,** cette maison se loue £200 par mois.

rental, *n.* (*a*) loyer *m*/location *f*; prix *m* de la location; **car rental,** location de voitures; **rental value,** valeur locative (d'un immeuble); **yearly rental,** redevance annuelle/loyer annuel (*b*) revenu locatif/revenu provenant des loyers.

renting, *n.* location *f*/louage *m* (d'une maison, d'une voiture, etc.).

reopen, 1. *v.tr.* rouvrir (un compte, etc.) **2.** *v.i.* **the shops will reopen on Monday,** la réouverture des magasin aura lieu lundi.

reopening, *n.* réouverture *f* (d'un magasin, etc.); **reopening day,** jour *m* de réouverture.

reorder[1], *n.* (*i*) commande renouvelée (*ii*) réapprovisionnement *m*; **reorder level/point,** seuil *m* de réapprovisionnement.

reorder[2], *v.tr.* renouveler une commande/faire une nouvelle commande (d'une marchandise, etc.)/commander à nouveau; faire une commande de réapprovisionnement.

reorganization, *n.* réorganisation *f*.

reorganize, 1. *v.tr.* réorganiser (les finances) **2.** *v.i.* (*of company, etc.*) se réorganiser.

rep, *n.* *F:* (= **representative**) représentant(e)/délégué(e) commercial(e).

repack, *v.tr.* rempaqueter/remballer/rencaisser (des marchandises).

repacking, *n.* rempaquetage *m*/remballage *m*/rencaissage *m* (de marchandises).

repair[1], *n.* réparation *f* (d'un bâtiment, d'une machine, etc.); **to be under repair/to be undergoing repairs,** être en réparation.

repair[2], *v.tr.* réparer/*F:* retaper (un bâtiment, une machine, etc.).

repay, *v.tr.* rembourser (qn) (**for,** de); **to repay a debt,** rembourser/payer une dette; **to repay a debt in full,** amortir une dette; **to repay s.o.,** rembourser qn.

repayable, *a.* remboursable (**over 25 years,** sur une période de 25 ans).

repayment, *n.* remboursement *m* (d'une somme); **bond due for repayment,** obligation amortie.

repeat[1], *n.* **repeat (order),** commande renouvelée.

repeat[2], *v.tr.* renouveler (une commande); (*of special offer*) **cannot be repeated,** sans suite.

replace, *v.tr.* remplacer (qn, qch.).

replaceable, *a.* remplaçable.

replacement, *n.* (*a*) remplacement *m*/substitution *f*; **replacement cost,** coût *m* de remplacement; *Ins:* **replacement markets,** débouchés *m*/marchés *m* de (produits de) remplacement(s); **replacement value,** valeur *f* de remplacement (*b*) *Ind:* pièce *f* de rechange/pièce détachée (*c*) (*pers.*) remplaçant(e).

reply[1], *n.* réponse *f*; **in reply to your letter,** en réponse à votre lettre/(comme) suite à votre lettre; *Post:* **reply card,** carte-réponse *f*; (**international**) **reply coupon,** coupon-réponse (international);

(*of telegram, envelope*) **reply paid,** réponse payée.

reply[2], *v.i.* répondre (**to,** à).

report[1], *n.* (*a*) rapport *m* (**on,** sur); compte rendu; (*of meeting*) procès-verbal *m*; exposé *m*; récit *m* (d'une affaire); **to make/draw up a report on sth.,** faire/rédiger un rapport sur qch.; **to present a report to s.o. on sth.,** présenter/soumettre un rapport à qn sur qch.; **annual report (of a company),** rapport de gestion (d'une société); **audit(ors) report,** rapport des commissaires (aux comptes); **chairman's/ manager's/president's report,** rapport du président; **progress report,** rapport périodique; rapport d'avancement (des travaux); **treasurer's report,** rapport financier; *StExch:* **stock market report,** bulletin *m* des cours de la Bourse; *Nau:* **damage report,** rapport d'avarie(s) (*b*) nouvelle *f;* **newspaper report,** reportage *m*; **to confirm a report,** confirmer une nouvelle.

report[2], *v.tr.* (*a*) rapporter (un fait); rendre compte de (qch.); **to report progress to s.o.,** tenir qn au courant de la marche d'une affaire; **to report to s.o./to report on sth.,** envoyer/présenter un rapport à qn; faire un rapport sur qch./rendre compte de qch. (*b*) **please report to our branch in Paris,** veuillez vous rendre/vous présenter à notre succursale de Paris; *Cust:* **to report a vessel,** déclarer un navire; faire la déclaration d'entrée.

represent, *v.tr.* représenter (une maison de commerce, etc.)

representation, *n.* (*a*) représentation *f;* **worker representation,** représentation du personnel (*b*) **joint representation,** démarche collective.

representative, 1. *a.* typique; **representative sample,** échantillon *m* type 2. *n.* représentant(e); **educational representative,** délégué(e) pédagogique; **foreign representative,** représentant(e) à l'étranger; **sales representative,** représentant(e) (de commerce)/délégué(e) commercial(e);

sole representatives of a firm, seuls représentants d'une société; **trade representative,** délégué(e) commercial(e).

reprocess, *v.tr.* recycler.

reprocessing, *n.* recyclage *m.*

repudiate, *v.tr.* nier (une dette); refuser d'honorer (un contrat).

repurchasable, *a.* rachetable.

repurchase[1], *n.* rachat *m/Jur:* réméré *m*; **sale with option of repurchase,** vente *f* à réméré.

repurchase[2], *v.tr.* racheter; **sale with right to repurchase,** vente *f* à réméré.

request[1], *n.* demande *f*/prière *f*/requête *f*; **request for money/funds,** demande d'argent/de crédits; **samples sent on request,** échantillons *m* sur demande.

request[2], *v.tr.* **to request s.o. to do sth.,** demander à qn de faire qch./prier qn de faire qch.; **as requested,** conformément à vos instructions/(comme) suite à votre demande.

requisition, *n.* demande *f*; **requisition for materials/for supplies,** demande de matériaux; commande *f* de fournitures; **requisition number,** numéro *m* de référence (d'une demande).

resale, *n.* revente *f* (d'un fonds de commerce, etc.); **resale price maintenance (RPM),** prix imposé(s) (par le fabricant); **resale value,** valeur *f* à la revente.

resaleable, *a.* revendable.

rescind, *v.tr.* annuler/résoudre/résilier/ rescinder (un contrat).

rescindable, *a.* annulable/résiliable/rescindable.

rescinding[1], *a.* (clause, etc.) abrogatoire.

rescinding[2], **rescission,** *n.* recision *f*/ annulation *f*/résolution *f*/résiliation *f* (d'un contrat).

research[1], *n.* recherche *f;* **advertising research,** études *f* publicitaires; **con-**

sumer research, recherche des besoins des consommateurs; economic research, études économiques; field research, prospection f sur le terrain; industrial research, recherche appliquée; market research, étude de(s) marchés; marketing research, recherche commerciale; product research, recherche de produits; research and development, recherche et mise au point; research and development department, atelier m/service m d'études; research centre/department, centre m/service de recherche; bureau m d'études; research work, recherches/travaux de recherche; research worker/assistant, (i) chercheur m (scientifique) (ii) documentaliste mf; to do research/to be engaged in research, faire des recherches/de la recherche.

research², v.i. & tr. faire des recherches (scientifiques, etc.) (sur qch.).

researcher, n. (a) chercheur m (scientifique) (b) documentaliste mf.

reservation, n. réserve f/restriction f; to enter a reservation in respect of a contract, apporter une réserve à un contrat (b) réservation f; to make a reservation, retenir (une place, une chambre, etc.).

reserve¹, n. 1. réserve f (d'argent, etc.); Fin: bank reserves, réserves bancaires; cash reserves, réserve de caisse; contingency reserve, réserve de prévoyance; legal reserve, réserve légale; reserve account, compte m de réserve/de provisions; reserve for bad debts, réserves/provisions f pour créances douteuses; reserve capital, capital m de réserve/provision; reserve currency, monnaie f de réserve; reserve deposit, dépôt m de couverture; reserve fund, fonds m de réserve/de prévoyance; statutory reserve, réserve statutaire; to draw on the reserves, puiser dans les réserves; in reserve, en réserve 2. (a) Bank: under reserve, sauf bonne fin (b) (at auction) reserve price, mise f à prix/prix m initial minimal.

reserve², v.tr. réserver; to reserve a room at a hotel, retenir une chambre d'hôtel; to reserve a table (at a restaurant), retenir/réserver une table (au restaurant); to reserve a seat, retenir, réserver/louer une place; Publ: all rights reserved, tous droits (de reproduction, etc.) réservés.

reshipment, n. réexpédition f (de marchandises).

resign, (a) v.tr. résigner (une fonction)/se démettre (de ses fonctions)/donner sa démission (b) v.i. démissionner/donner sa démission/résigner ses fonctions/sa charge.

resignation, n. démission f; to give (in)/to hand in/to send in/to tender one's resignation, donner sa démission/démissionner.

resistance, n. résistance f; consumer resistance, résistance des consommateurs.

resolution, n. résolution f/proposition f; to put a resolution to the meeting, soumettre/proposer une résolution; to pass/carry/adopt a resolution, adopter une résolution/une proposition; to reject a resolution, rejeter une proposition/une résolution.

resource, n. (a) ressource f; resource allocation, allocation f/affectation f des ressources; financial resources, ressources financières; limited resources, moyens limités (b) pl. NAm: Fin: actif disponible/liquide.

respect¹, n. with respect to . . ./in respect of . . ., en ce qui concerne . . ./concernant . . ./quant à . . . .

respect², v.tr. to respect a clause in a contract, respecter une clause dans un contrat.

respite, n. to grant a respite for payment, différer un paiement.

responsibility, n. responsabilité f; allocation of responsibilities, répartition f des responsabilités; linear responsibility, responsabilité hiérarchique; without responsibility on our part, sans engagement *m* ni responsabilité de notre part.

responsible, *a.* **1. responsible to s.o.,** responsable devant qn; **the commission is responsible to the government,** la commission relève du gouvernement; **to be responsible for s.o.,** répondre de qn; **to be responsible for sth.**, être responsable de qch. **2.** (*a*) capable/compétent/digne de confiance/sur qui on peut compter; **a responsible man,** un homme sérieux (*b*) **responsible job,** poste *m* qui entraîne des responsabilités; responsabilité *f.*

restitution, *n. EEC:* **export restitution,** restitution *f* (à l'exportation).

restock, *v.tr.* réapprovisionner (un magasin); **to restock with wine,** se réapprovisionner en vin.

restocking, *n.* réapprovisionnement *m* (d'un magasin).

restraint, *n.* **restraint of trade/trade restraint,** atteinte *f* à la liberté du commerce; restriction *f* de concurrence (entre sociétés); **wage restraint,** restriction salariale; limitation *f* des salaires.

restrict, *v.tr.* restreindre (les dépenses, la production, etc.); **to restrict credits,** encadrer le crédit; **restricted credit,** crédit restreint; **restricted market,** débouchés réduits.

restriction, *n.* restriction *f*/limitation *f*; **credit restrictions,** encadrement *m*/ restriction du crédit; **import restrictions,** restrictions sur les importations; **restriction of expenditure,** réduction *f* des dépenses.

restrictive, *a.* restrictif; **restrictive clause,** clause restrictive; **restrictive indorsement,** endossement restrictif; **restrictive practices,** (*i*) *Ind:* pratiques restrictives (*ii*) *Jur:* ententes *f.*

restructure, *v.tr.* restructurer.

restructuring, *n.* restructuration *f.*

result, *n.* résultat *m* (**of,** de); **payment by**

results, salaire *m* au rendement; **trading results,** résultats de l'exercice/de l'exploitation; **to yield results,** donner des résultats.

retail[1], *n.* détail *m*; vente *f* au détail; **to sell goods by**/*NAm:* **at retail,** vendre des marchandises au détail/détailler des marchandises; **retail dealer,** marchand(e) au détail/détaillant(e)/marchand détaillant/ marchand qui fait le détail; **retail price,** prix *m* de détail; **retail price index,** indice *m* des prix de détail; **the retail trade,** le détail; **wholesale and retail business,** commerce *m* de gros et de détail.

retail[2], **1.** *v.tr.* détailer/vendre au détail (des marchandises) **2.** *v.i.* (*of goods*) se vendre au détail/se détailler; **these pencils retail at 8p,** ces crayons se détaillent à 8p/le prix de détail de ces crayons est de 8p.

retailer, *n.* marchand(e) au détail/détaillant(e)/marchand détaillant/marchand qui fait le détail.

retain, *v.tr.* (*a*) **to retain s.o.'s services,** retenir les services de qn (*b*) **retaining fee,** honoraires versés à qn pour s'assurer son concours éventuel; provision *f*/ avance *f*/acompte *m.*

retained, *a.* **retained earnings,** bénéfices non distribués.

retainer, *n.* provision *f*/avance *f*/acompte *m*; **to pay a retainer,** verser une avance/ une provision.

retention, *n.* **retention money,** retenue *f* de garantie.

retest, *n. Ind: etc:* contre-essai *m.*

retire, 1. (*a*) *v.tr.* mettre (qn) à la retraite (*b*) *Fin:* retirer/rembourser (un effet) **2.** *v.i.* se démettre (de ses fonctions); démissionner; **to retire (from business),** se retirer des affaires; **to retire (on a pension),** prendre sa retraite.

retired, *a.* (négociant, etc.) retiré des affaires; (fonctionnaire) retraité/à la retraite; **retired pay,** pension *f* de retraite.

retirement, *n.* **1.** retraite *f*; **early retirement,** retraite anticipée/pré(-)retraite; **optional retirement,** retraite sur demande; **compulsory/mandatory retirement,** retraite d'office; **retirement on account of age,** retraite par limite d'âge; **retirement pension,** (pension de) retraite; retraite de vieillesse **2.** *Fin:* retrait *m*/ remboursement *m* (d'un effet); retrait (de monnaies).

retiring, *n.* **retiring age,** âge *m* de la retraite.

retrain, 1. *v.tr.* recycler (qn) **2.** *v.i.* se recycler.

retraining, *n.* recyclage *m* (de qn); **job retraining,** recyclage.

retrenchment, *n.* réduction *f* (des dépenses); **policy of retrenchment,** politique *f* d'économies/de redressement.

retrieval, *n.* **information retrieval (system),** (système de) recherche *f* documentaire.

retroactive, *a.* (avec effet) rétroactif.

retrospective, *a.* (avec effet) rétroactif.

return[1], *n.* **1.** retour *m*; (*a*) *Post:* **by return (of post),** par retour (du courrier) (*b*) *Rail: etc:* **day return,** billet d'aller et retour (bon pour la journée seulement); **cheap day return,** billet d'aller et retour à tarif réduit (bon pour la journée seulement); **return fare,** prix *m*/tarif *m* de l'aller et retour; **return journey,** (*i*) (voyage de) retour (*ii*) voyage (d')aller et retour; **to buy a return (ticket),** prendre un (billet d')aller et retour (*c*) **empty return,** retour à vide; **loaded return,** retour en charge; **return cargo/freight,** cargaison *f*/chargement *m*/fret *m* de retour **2.** (*a*) *pl.* **returns,** recettes *f*/rentrées (provenant des ventes); **quick returns,** un prompt débit/une vente rapide (*b*) revenu *m*/gain *m*/profit *m*/rendement *m*; **to bring (in) a fair return,** rapporter un

bénéfice raisonnable; **gross return,** rendement brut; **rate of return,** rentabilité *f*/ taux *m* de rendement; **return on capital invested,** rentabilité/taux de rendement des capitaux investis; *PolEc:* **law of diminishing returns,** loi *f* du rendement non proportionnel **3.** (*a*) renvoi *m*/retour; réexpédition *f* (de marchandises avariées, etc.); **return (of bill to drawer),** contre-passation *f*/contre-passement *m* (d'un effet de commerce); **on sale or return,** (marchandises) vendues avec faculté de retour/en dépôt (avec reprise des invendus)/à condition; **to deliver goods on sale or return,** livrer des marchandises en dépôt temporaire; *Post:* **return address,** adresse *f* de l'expéditeur (*b*) *pl.* **returns,** (*of books, newspapers*) invendus *m*/rendus *m*/retours *m*/bouillons *m* (*c*) ristourne *f* (d'une somme payée en trop); *Fin:* **return of a capital sum,** remboursement *m* d'un capital; **return commission,** commission allouée en retour **4.** (*a*) rapport officiel; état *m*/ exposé *m*; compte rendu/relevé *m*; statistique *f*; *Adm:* recensement *m* (de la population, etc.); **nil return,** état néant; **the official returns,** les relevés officiels; **return of expenses,** état de frais/de dépenses; **sales returns,** statistique des ventes; **bank return,** situation *f* de la banque; **the weekly bank return,** le bilan hebdomadaire; **quarterly return,** rapport trimestriel; **sales return,** statistique des ventes; **trade returns,** statistique de commerce (*b*) **income tax return,** (*i*) déclaration *f* de revenu/déclaration d'impôts/déclaration fiscale (*ii*) formule *f*/ formulaire *m* de déclaration d'impôts.

return[2], *v.tr.* **1.** rendre (un dépôt, etc.); rembourser (un emprunt); **to return an amount paid in excess,** ristourner/ rembourser une somme payée en trop; **to return an article,** retourner une marchandise; **returned books,** invendus *mpl*; **returned empties,** bouteilles consignées/ reprises *f*; **returned goods,** rendus *m*/retours *m*; *Fin:* **to return a bill to drawer,** contre-passer un effet; *Post:* **return to sender,** retour à l'envoyeur **2.** *Fin:*

rapporter/donner (un bénéfice); **invest-ment that returns good interest,** placement *m* qui produit un intérêt élevé/placement avantageux **3. to return one's income at £4 000,** faire une déclaration de £4 000 de revenu; **the liabilities are returned at £10 000,** le passif est estimé/évalué à £10 000.

returnable, *a.* qui peut être rendu/renvoyé/retourné; restituable; **return-able bottle,** bouteille consignée; (*on goods*) **not returnable,** sans consigne/non consigné; ne peut être échangé ni rendu.

returning, *n.* renvoi *m* (de marchandises, etc.).

revalorization, *n. Fin:* revalorisation *f* (du franc, etc.).

revalorize, *v.tr. Fin:* revaloriser (le franc, etc.).

revaluation, *n.* réévaluation *f* (des actifs, etc.); réestimation *f; Fin:* revalorisation *f* (du franc, etc.).

revalue, *v.tr.* réestimer; réévaluer (une propriété, etc.); *Fin:* revaloriser (le franc, etc.).

revenue, *n.* **1.** revenu *m*/rentes *fpl*; rapport *m* (**from an estate,** d'une terre); **advertising revenue,** recettes *fpl* de publicité **2.** *Adm:* **Inland Revenue**/*NAm:* **Internal Revenue,** le fisc; **the revenue authorities,** les agents *m* du fisc; **revenue office,** (bureau de) perception *f;* **revenue officer,** inspecteur *m* des contributions.

reversal, *n. Book-k:* contre-passement *m;* annulation *f* (d'une écriture).

reverse[1], *a. Book-k:* **reverse entry,** écriture *f* inverse.

reverse[2], *v.tr. Book-k:* **to reverse an entry,** contre-passer/annuler une écriture.

reversing, *n. Book-k:* **reversing of entry,** contre-passation *f*/contrepassement *m* d'une écriture.

reversion, *n. Jur:* réversion *f;* **annuity in reversion on the death of the holder,** rente *f* réversible après la mort du titulaire.

reversionary, *a.* (droit) de réversion; **reversionary annuity,** annuité *f* réversible; rente viagère avec réversion.

review[1], *n.* **1. financial review,** examen financier **2.** *Publ:* revue *f;* périodique *m.*

review[2], *v.tr.* **to review salaries,** réviser les salaires.

revive, 1. *v.i.* (*of business, commerce*) reprendre/se relever; **industry is reviv-ing,** l'industrie *f* commence à revivre/l'in-dustrie se relève; **credit is reviving,** le crédit se rétablit **2.** *v.tr.* relancer (l'économie); **to revive trade,** ranimer/revivifier le commerce.

revolving, *a.* **revolving credit,** crédit *m* sur acceptation renouvelée; **credit-revolv-ing,** (avec) crédit renouvelable.

rider, *n.* ajouté *m*/annexe *f*/papillon *m* (d'un document); allonge *f* (d'un effet de commerce).

rig[1], *n. StExch:* (*i*) hausse *f* factice (*ii*) baisse *f* factice; coup *m* de bourse.

rig[2], *v.tr. Fin: StExch:* **to rig the market,** spéculer/agioter; provoquer (*i*) une hausse factice (*ii*) une baisse factice.

rigger, *n. StExch:* spéculateur *m*/agioteur *m.*

rigging, *n. StExch:* spéculation *f;* agiotage *m.*

right, *n.* (*a*) droit *m*/titre *m;* privilège *m; Jur:* **rights granted by contract,** droits contractuels (*b*) *Fin:* **application rights,** droit(s)/privilège de souscription; **rights issue,** droit préférentiel de souscription; **with right of transfer,** avec faculté de transfert (*c*) *Publ:* **foreign rights,** droits étrangers; **publishing rights,** droits d'édition; **all rights reserved,** tous droits réservés.

rightful, *a.* (*a*) légitime/véritable; en droit; **rightful owner,** propriétaire *mf* légitime (*b*) (*of claim*) légitime/juste/justifié.

ring, *n.* (*a*) syndicat *m;* cartel *m* (*b*) *StExch:* **the Ring,** le Parquet.

ring back, *v.tr. Tp:* rappeler (qn).

ring off, *v.i. Tp:* raccrocher.

ring up, *v.tr. Tp:* **to ring s.o. up,** téléphoner à qn/donner un coup de téléphone à qn/appeler qn au téléphone (*b*) enregistrer (une somme) (sur une caisse enregistreuse).

rise[1], *n.* augmentation *f*/élévation *f*/hausse *f* (de prix); augmentation (de salaire); renchérissement *m* (des denrées); **the rise in the price of petrol,** la hausse du prix de l'essence; **rise in value,** augmentation de valeur; plus-value *f*; **rise in the minimum lending rate,** relèvement *m* du taux de l'escompte; **the rise in the cost of living,** la hausse du coût de la vie; la montée des prix; *StExch:* **to speculate on/operate for a rise,** jouer à la hausse; **to ask (one's employer) for a rise,** demander une augmentation (de salaire).

rise[2], *v.i.* (*of prices*) monter; **prices are rising,** les prix *m* montent; **prices have risen considerably,** les prix ont subi une forte hausse; **bread has risen by 5p,** le (prix du) pain a augmenté de 5p; **everything has risen (in price),** tout a augmenté de prix/tout a renchéri.

risk, *n.* (*a*) risque *m*/péril *m*/aléa *m*/hasard *m*; **the risks of an undertaking,** les aléas d'une entreprise; **to run/to incur a risk,** courir un risque; **calculated risk,** risque calculé (*b*) **risk capital,** capital *m* risque; **risk management,** gestion *f* des risques dans l'entreprise (*c*) *Ins:* risque; **risk subscribed,** risque assuré; **theft/fire/war risk,** risque de vol/d'incendie/de guerre; **at owner's risks,** au(x) risque(s) du propriétaire; **risks and perils at sea,** risques et périls de la mer; péril de mer; fortune *f* de mer; **comprehensive all risks policy,** police *f* tous risques; **third-party risk,** risque de recours de tiers; **tenant's third-party risk,** risque locatif; (*pers., thg*) **a good/bad risk,** un bon/mauvais risque; **to underwrite a risk,** souscrire un risque.

rival, *a. & n.* rival(e); concurrent(e).

road, *n.* route *f*; chemin *m*; voie *f*; **road transport,** transports routiers; **to be on the road,** (*i*) être représentant (*ii*) (*of representative*) être en tournée/en déplacement.

rock, *n.* **rock(-)bottom price,** le prix le plus bas; **prices have reached rock bottom,** les prix sont au plus bas.

rocket, *v.i.* (*of prices*) monter en flèche.

roll back, *v.tr. NAm:* baisser (un prix) à son niveau précédent.

roll-over, *a.* **roll-over credit,** crédit *m* roll-over/prêt *m* bancaire en euro-devises à moyen terme et à taux variable.

roster, *n.* liste *f*/rôle *m*/feuille *f*; *Adm:* **promotion roster/advancement roster,** tableau *m* d'avancement; **duty roster,** tableau de service.

rotation, *n.* rotation *f*; **job rotation,** rotation des postes.

rough, *a.* approximatif; **rough average,** moyenne approximative; **rough calculation,** calcul approximatif; **rough estimate,** évaluation *f* en gros; estimation approximative/devis approximatif; **rough sketch,** ébauche *f* (de projet).

round, *a.* (*a*) **round dozen,** bonne douzaine; **round figure,** chiffre rond; **in round figures,** en chiffres ronds; **round sum,** compte rond (*b*) *NAm:* **round trip,** voyage *m* d'aller et retour/aller et retour.

roundsman, *n.m.* livreur.

roundtrip, *a. NAm:* **roundtrip fare,** tarif *m* aller-retour.

round up, *v.tr.* arrondir une somme (au chiffre supérieur).

route[1], *n.* itinéraire *m*; route *f*/voie *f*/chemin *m*; **commercial/trade route,** route commerciale; **shipping route,** route de navigation.

route[2], *v.tr.* router/acheminer (un envoi).

routeman, *n.m. NAm:* livreur.

routine, *n.* routine *f*; **office routine,** travail courant de bureau; **routine work,** (*i*) (travail de) routine/affaires courantes (*ii*) travail routinier.

routing, *n.* routage *m*/acheminement *m* (d'un colis, etc.).

royalty, *n.* **royalties,** droits *mpl* d'auteur/ royalties *fpl*/redevances *fpl* (du(e)s à un inventeur, au détenteur de la propriété littéraire ou artistique d'une œuvre); **oil royalties,** redevances pétrolières; **royalty of 10% on the published price,** droit de 10% sur le prix fort.

rule[1], *n.* règle *f*; règlement *m*; **company rules,** règlements internes/de la maison; **operating rules,** règles d'exploitation.

rule[2], *v.i.* **prices are ruling high,** les prix restent élevés; les prix se maintiennent; **the prices ruling at the moment,** les prix qui se pratiquent en ce moment.

rule off, *v.tr.* **to rule off an account,** clore/arrêter/régler un compte.

ruling, 1. *a.* **ruling price,** cours actuel; cours/prix *m* du jour **2.** *n.* décision *f*/ jugement *m*.

run[1], *n.* **trial run,** essai *m*; **the run of the market,** les tendances *f* du marché; **run on the market,** ruée *f* (sur les valeurs en bourse); **a run on oils,** une ruée sur les valeurs pétrolières; **a run on the banks,** un retrait massif de dépôts bancaires; **there was a great run on that line,** ces marchandises *f* ont été écoulées rapidement.

run[2], **1.** *v.i.* (*a*) **the bill has fifteen days to run,** l'effet a quinze jours à courir; **the lease has only a year to run,** le bail n'a plus qu'un an à courir (*b*) (*of amount, number*) **to run to . . .,** monter/s'élever à . . .; **the increase in business may run to tens of thousands (of pounds),** l'augmentation *f* du chiffre d'affaires pourra bien être de l'ordre de dizaines de milliers de livres (*c*) **prices are running high,** les prix sont élevés/en général les prix sont plutôt élevés **2.** *v.tr.* (*a*) **to run a cheap line,** vendre un article (à) bon marché/en

réclame (*b*) **to run (a business, a shop, a hotel),** diriger (une affaire); tenir (un magasin, un hôtel).

runback, *v.i.* (*of shares*) diminuer de valeur/baisser.

run down, *v.tr.* **the company is being run down,** la société réduit/diminue son niveau d'activité.

run(-)down, 1. *n.* réduction *f* (du personnel) **2.** *a.* **a rundown investment,** une mauvaise affaire/un mauvais investissement.

run into, 1. *v.i.* **to run into debt,** faire des dettes/s'endetter; **the debts run into hundreds of pounds,** la dette s'élève à des centaines de livre **2.** *v.tr.* **that will run me into considerable expenses,** cela me coûtera cher/m'entraînera des frais considérables.

runner, *n.* (*a*) messager *m*/courrier *m* (*b*) *Fin:* démarcheur *m*.

running[1], *a.* **1. running account,** compte courant **2. running cost,** frais *mpl* d'exploitation **3. for 5 days running,** pendant 5 jours consécutifs/cinq jours de suite.

running[2], *n.* (*a*) marche *f*/fonctionnement *m* (d'une machine, etc.); (*of car, etc.*) **running costs,** frais *mpl* d'entretien (*b*) direction *f* (d'un hôtel, etc.); exploitation *f* (d'une compagnie); **running expenses,** frais d'exploitation.

run up, *v.tr.* (*a*) laisser grossir (un compte); laisser accumuler (des dettes); **I ran up a bill for £100,** à la fin je devais £100 (*b*) (*at auction*) **to run up the bidding,** pousser les enchères.

rush, *n.* **1. the rush hour,** les heures *f* d'affluence/de pointe; **a rush period,** (*i*) une poussée (d'affaires, etc.) (*ii*) (*at shop*) heure(s) *f* d'affluence (de la clientèle) **2.** hâte *f*/empressement *m*; **rush order,** commande urgente; **rush work/rush job,** travail de première urgence.

rushed, *a.* **1.** débordé de travail **2.** (travail) fait à la va-vite/bâclé.

S

sack¹, *n. F:* **to get the sack,** être renvoyé/mis à la porte/sa(c)qué; **to give s.o. the sack,** renvoyer qn/mettre qn à la porte/sa(c)quer qn.

sack², *v.tr. F:* renvoyer (qn)/mettre (qn) à la porte/sa(c)quer (qn)/congédier (qn).

sacrifice¹, *n.* vente *f* à perte; **to sell sth. at a sacrifice,** sacrifier (des marchandises); vendre qch. à perte/à toute offre acceptable.

sacrifice², *v.tr.* sacrifier un article/vendre à perte/vendre à très bas prix.

s.a.e., (= stamped addressed envelope), enveloppe *f* affranchie.

safe, 1. *n.* coffre-fort *m*; *Bank:* **night (deposit) safe,** coffret *m* de nuit 2. *a.* (*a*) **to place deposit/securities in safe custody,** mettre des valeurs en dépôt (*b*) **safe investment,** placement sûr/de tout repos/de père de famille.

safe-deposit, *n.* (*i*) coffre-fort *m*; coffre *m* (*ii*) dépôt *m* en coffre-fort.

safeguard, *v.tr.* sauvegarder/protéger; **to safeguard the interests of shareholders,** sauvegarder les intérêts des actionnaires.

safe-keeping, *n.* sécurité *f*/sûreté *f*; **to place securities in the bank for safe-keeping,** mettre des valeurs en dépôt à la banque.

safety, *n.* sûreté *f*/sécurité *f*; **safety regulations,** règles *fpl* de sécurité; **safety stock,** stock *m* de sécurité/stock tampon; *Ind:* **safety factor,** facteur *m*/coefficient *m* de sécurité; **safety vault,** chambre forte/blindée (d'une banque, etc.).

sag¹, *n.* baisse *f*/diminution *f*/fléchissement *m* (des valeurs, etc.).

sag², *v.i.* (*of prices*) baisser/fléchir; **prices are sagging,** les prix *m* fléchissent/baissent.

sagging, 1. *n.* baisse *f*/fléchissement *m*/affaissement *m*/diminution *f* (des prix, du marché, des valeurs, etc.) 2. *a.* (*of prices, etc.*) en baisse.

salaried, *a.* 1. **salaried worker,** employé salarié; **salaried staff,** personnel qui touche un traitement/des appointments; **lower salaried staff,** cadres *m* moyens; **higher salaried staff,** cadres supérieurs 2. (travail) rétribué/rémunéré/salarié.

salary, *n.* salaire *m*; traitement *m*/appointements *mpl*; rémunération *f*; **to draw one's salary,** toucher son salaire/ses appointements; **fixed salary,** salaire fixe/*F:* fixe *m*; **starting salary,** rémunération *f* de départ; **salary increase,** augmentation *f* de salaire; **salary structure,** structure *f* des salaires/des traitements.

sale, *n.* 1. vente *f*; **bill of sale,** acte *m* de vente; **cash sale,** vente au comptant; **credit sale,** vente à crédit; **ready sale,** vente facile; écoulement *m* rapide; **sale contract,** (*i*) contrat *m* de vente (*ii*) *StExch:* bordereau *m* de vente; **sale value,** valeur marchande; valeur vénale; **goods for which there is a sure sale,** marchandises *f* de vente/d'un bon débit; **goods for which there is no sale,** articles *m* hors de vente/articles qui n'ont pas de marché; **for sale,** à vendre; **business for sale,** fonds *m* à céder; **house for sale,** maison à vendre; **to put sth. up for sale,** mettre qch. en vente; **not for sale,** (cet article n'est) pas à vendre; **not for general sale/not for sale to the general public,** hors commerce; **for quick sale,** pour vente/

liquidation rapide; **on sale,** en vente; **on sale in all leading stores,** en vente/ vendu dans tous les grands magasins; **sale by private treaty/contract/agreement,** vente à l'amiable/de gré à gré; **sale by sealed tender,** vente par soumission cachetée; **sale with option of repurchase,** vente à réméré/avec faculté de rachat; *StExch:* **sale for the account,** vente à terme *(b)* **sales analysis,** analyse *f* des ventes; *Ind:* **sales area,** secteur *m*/ territoire *m* (de vente); **sales book,** journal *m* des ventes; facturier *m*; **sales campaign/drive,** campagne *f* de ventes; **sales department,** services *mpl* commerciaux/service des ventes; **sales force,** équipe *f* de vente; **sales forecast,** prévision *f* des ventes; **sales manager,** directeur *m*/chef *m* du service des ventes; directeur *m* commercial; **sales policy,** politique *f* de vente; **sales promotion,** promotion *f* de(s) vente(s); **sales room,** salle *f* des ventes (aux enchères); *NAm:* **sales slip,** ticket *m* de caisse; **sales talk,** arguments *mpl* de vente/boniment *m*; **sales tax,** taxe à l'achat; **sales turnover/ sales figures/sales,** chiffre *m* d'affaires *(c)* **sale by auction/auction sale/sale to the highest bidder,** vente à l'enchère/aux enchères; criée *f*/vente à la criée; vente publique; (*at auction*) **day's sale,** vacation *f*; **sale ring,** cercle *m* d'acheteurs; *Jur:* **compulsory sale,** adjudication forcée **2.** solde *m*; **(clearance) sale,** solde (de marchandises); **(bargain) sale,** vente au rabais; **closing-down sale,** solde de fermeture; liquidation *f*; *NAm:* **on sale,** en solde; **the sales are on,** c'est l'époque des soldes; **to put stock in the sale,** mettre du stock en solde/solder du stock; **sale goods,** soldes *mpl*; **sale price,** prix *m* de solde.

saleability, *n.* qualité marchande (d'un article); facilité *f* d'écoulement.

saleable, *a.* (*of goods, etc.*) vendable/de vente facile; de vente courante; **readily saleable,** qui se vend bien; **saleable value,** valeur marchande.

saleroom, *n.* salle *f* de(s) vente(s).

salesclerk, *n. NAm:* vendeur, -euse.

salesgirl, *n.f.* vendeuse.

saleslady, *n.f.* vendeuse.

salesman, *n.m.* vendeur.

salesmanship, *n.* l'art *m* de vendre.

salesperson, *n.* vendeur, -euse.

saleswoman, *n.f.* vendeuse.

sample¹, *n.* (*a*) échantillon *m* (de tissu, de vin, etc.); **free sample,** échantillon gratuit; **reference sample,** contre-échantillon *m*; **representative sample,** échantillon type; **to send sth. as a sample,** envoyer qch. à titre d'échantillon; **to buy sth. from sample,** acheter qch. d'après échantillon/sur montre; **sample book,** collection *f* d'échantillons; **sample card,** carte *f* d'échantillons; **sample packet (of sth.),** paquet *m* échantillon (de qch.); **up to sample,** conforme à l'échantillon *(b)* **random sample,** échantillon aléatoire.

sample², *v.tr.* prendre/prélever un échantillon/échantillonner; déguster (des vins).

sampling, *n.* (*a*) dégustation *f* (de vins); échantillonnage *m* de marchandises *(b)* **random sampling,** échantillonnage aléatoire *(c)* **cluster sampling,** sondage *m* en grappes; **sampling error,** erreur *f* d'échantillonnage/de sondage; **sampling method,** méthode *f* de sondage.

satisfaction, *n.* (*a*) acquittement *m*/ paiement *m*/liquidation *f* (d'une dette); désintéressement *m* (d'un créancier) *(b)* satisfaction *f*; **consumer satisfaction,** satisfaction du consommateur; **job satisfaction,** satisfaction dans le travail.

satisfy, *v.tr.* payer/liquider (une dette); s'acquitter (d'une dette, d'une obligation); remplir (une condition); satisfaire à (une demande).

saturate, *v.tr.* saturer (le marché); **the market is saturated,** le marché est saturé.

saturation, *n.* **market saturation,** saturation *f* du marché; **saturation point,** point *m* de saturation; **the market has reached saturation point,** le marché est saturé.

save, 1. *v.tr.* **to save money,** économiser/épargner/mettre de côté (de l'argent); **to save time,** faire une économie de temps **2.** *v.i.* **to save on sth.,** économiser sur qch.; **to save (up),** économiser pour l'avenir/faire des économies/épargner (son argent); **save as you earn (SAYE)** = économie à la source.

saver, *n.* épargnant(e).

saving, 1. *n.* (*a*) économie *f*/épargne *f*; **labour saving,** (*i*) économie de travail (*ii*) *Ind:* économie de main-d'œuvre (*b*) *pl.* **savings,** économies; **savings account,** compte *m* (de caisse) d'épargne; compte sur livret; **Savings plan,** plan d'épargne à long terme; **(National) Savings Bank** = Caisse (Nationale) d'Épargne; **(National) savings certificate** = bon *m* d'épargne **2.** *a.* **saving clause,** clause *f* de sauvegarde/clause restrictive/restriction *f*.

scab, *n.* briseur *m* de grève.

scale[1], *n.* (*a*) échelle *f*; **scale of prices/of charges,** échelle/gamme *f* des prix; **scale of salaries/salary scale,** échelle/barème *m* des salaires; **sliding scale,** échelle mobile (des salaires, des prix); **standard scale (of machine part sizes, etc.),** échelle des calibres (*b*) échelle (d'une carte etc.); **scale model,** maquette *f*/modèle réduit; **small-scale firm,** petite entreprise; **to do sth. on a small/large scale,** faire qch. sur une petite/une grande échelle.

scale[2], *v.tr.* **to scale up prices by 5%,** augmenter les prix de 5%; **to scale down production,** ralentir/diminuer la production.

scaling, *n.* graduation *f* (des prix, des salaires, etc.); **scaling down,** réduction *f* à l'échelle; **scaling up,** augmentation *f* à l'échelle.

scarce, *a.* (*of commodities*) rare.

scarceness, scarcity, *n.* rareté *f*; manque *m*/pénurie *f* (de qch.); **scarcity of labour,** manque/pénurie de main-d'œuvre.

schedule[1], *n.* **1.** (*a*) *Jur:* annexe *f* (aux statuts d'une société, etc.) (*b*) bordereau *m*/note explicative **2.** (*a*) nomenclature *f* (de pièces, etc.); inventaire *m* (de machines, etc.); barème *m* (de prix); **schedule of charges,** liste officielle des taux; tarif *m* (*b*) *Adm:* cédule *f* (d'impôts) (*c*) *Jur:* (*in bankruptcy*) bilan *m* (de l'actif et du passif) **3.** (*a*) plan *m* (d'exécution d'un travail, etc.); programme *m*; **to be on schedule,** se poursuivre suivant le planning; **to be behind schedule,** avoir du retard/être en retard sur les prévisions; **to be ahead of schedule,** être en avance sur l'horaire prévu/sur les délais prévus/sur le programme établi; **schedule work,** travail de régime; **tight/detailed schedule,** horaire (strictement) minuté; **work schedule/production schedule,** planning *m*/planification *f*/programme *m* de fabrication.

schedule[2], *v.tr.* **1.** (*a*) *Jur:* ajouter (un article) comme annexe (aux statuts d'une société, etc.) (*b*) ajouter (une note) en bordereau **2.** inscrire (un article, etc.) sur une liste/sur un inventaire; **progressive scheduled tax,** barème d'imposition progressive; **scheduled prices,** prix *m* tarif; **scheduled taxes,** impôts *m* cédulaires **3.** dresser un plan/un programme de (qch.); arrêter (un programme).

scheduling, *n. Ind:* établissement *m* d'un programme/planification *f*; programmation *f*; ordonnancement *m*.

scheme, *n.* **1.** (*a*) *Jur:* **scheme of composition (between debtor and creditors),** concordat préventif (à la faillite) (*b*) système *m*; **bonus scheme,** système de primes d'encouragement; **incentive scheme,** système de stimulants salariaux; **profit-sharing scheme,** système de participation aux bénéfices; **social benefit schemes for employees,** système de prestations en faveur des employés **2.** plan *m*/projet *m*; **preliminary scheme,** avant-projet *m*.

science, *n.* science *f*; **management science,** science de la gestion.

scientific, *a.* scientifique; **scientific management,** gestion *f* scientifique; organisation *f* scientifique du travail; **scientific research,** recherche(s) *f* scientifique(s).

scientist, *n.* scientifique *mf*; homme/femme de science.

scrap¹, *n.* **scrap dealer,** marchand *m* de ferraille; casseur *m*; **scrap value,** valeur *f* à la casse; **to sell sth. for scrap,** vendre qch. à la casse.

scrap², *v.tr.* mettre (qch.) au rebut; **to scrap a project,** abandonner/rejeter/renoncer à un projet.

screen, *v.tr.* trier/sélectionner (du personnel).

screening, *n.* sélection *f* (du personnel).

scrip, *n. Fin:* (*a*) **scrip (certificate),** certificat *m* d'actions provisoire (*b*) *coll.* valeurs *fpl*/titres *mpl*/actions *fpl*; **registered scrip,** titres nominatifs (*c*) **scrip issue,** actions *f* gratuites.

scripholder, *n. Fin:* détenteur, -trice de titres.

sea-going, *a.* **sea-going trade,** commerce *m* maritime.

seal¹, *n.* (*a*) (*on deed, etc.*) sceau *m*; (*on letter*) cachet *m*; **contract under seal,** convention scellée (*b*) cachet (de bouteille de vin, etc.); **customs seal,** plomb *m* de la douane; **lead seal,** (*i*) capsule *f* (de bouteille de vin) (*ii*) plomb (pour sceller une caisse, etc.).

seal², *v.tr.* (*a*) sceller (un acte, etc.); cacheter (une lettre, une enveloppe); **sealed tender,** soumission cachetée (*b*) *Cust:* (faire) plomber (des marchandises, etc.).

seaport, *n.* port *m* maritime.

season, *n.* **1.** (*a*) saison *f*; **in season,** pendant la saison; **out of season,** hors saison; **low season price,** prix hors saison; **the busy season,** la haute saison; **the slack season/the off season,** la morte-saison/la saison creuse; **the tourist season/the holiday season,** la saison touristique/des vacances; la haute saison (*b*) **end of season sale,** vente *f* de fin de saison **2.** **season (ticket),** carte *f* d'abonnement (pour un an).

seasonal, *a.* (commerce) saisonnier; **seasonal demand,** demande saisonnière; **seasonal fluctuations,** fluctuations saisonnières; **seasonal unemployment,** chômage saisonnier.

seasonally, *adv.* **seasonally corrected (rate),** (taux) désaisonnalisé/corrigé des variations saisonnières.

second, *a.* second/deuxième; **second mortgage,** deuxième hypothèque *f*; **second debentures,** obligations *f* de deuxième rang; **second endorser,** tiers porteur; **second half-year,** deuxième semestre *m*.

secondary, *a.* secondaire; **secondary industry,** le secteur secondaire/le secondaire; **secondary market,** marché *m* secondaire.

second-class, *a.* **second-class hotel,** hôtel *m* de deuxième classe; **second-class mail** = tarif *m* réduit; **to travel second-class,** voyager en seconde.

second-grade, *a.* **second-grade article,** article *m* de second choix/de qualité inférieure.

second-hand, *a.* (marchandises) d'occasion/de revente; **second-hand bookshop,** librairie *f* d'occasion; **second-hand car,** voiture *f* d'occasion; **second-hand dealer,** brocanteur *m*; revendeur, -euse; **the second-hand market,** le marché *m* de revente; **second-hand shop/market,** brocante *f*.

second-rate, *a.* (*a*) médiocre/inférieur; de qualité inférieure/de qualité médiocre (*b*) **second-rate stock,** titre *m* de second ordre.

seconds, *n.pl.* articles *m* de qualité inférieure.

secretarial, *a.* **to do a secretarial course,** suivre un cours/faire des études de secrétariat; **secretarial work,** travail *m* de secrétaire.

secretary, *n.* (*a*) secrétaire *mf*; **private secretary,** secrétaire particulier, -ère (*b*) **company secretary,** secrétaire général (d'une société).

section, *n.* (*a*) section *f* (d'un département etc.); division *f* (d'un document, etc.) (*b*) *StExch:* rubrique *f*.

sector, *n.* secteur *m*; **economic/industrial sector,** secteur économique/industriel; **the private sector,** le secteur privé; **the public sector,** le secteur public.

secure[1], *a.* **secure investment,** placement sûr/de tout repos.

secure[2], *v.tr.* nantir (un prêteur); garantir; **to secure a debt by mortgage,** hypothéquer une créance; garantir une créance par une hypothèque.

secured, *a.* garanti; nanti; **secured creditor,** créancier privilégié; **secured loan,** emprunt garanti.

security, *n.* **1.** (*a*) sécurité *f*/sûreté *f*; **security of employment/job security,** sécurité de l'emploi (*b*) **security police (in firm, etc.),** services *mpl* de sécurité (*c*) **security margin,** marge *f* de sécurité (*d*) *Adm:* **social security,** sécurité sociale **2.** (*a*) caution *f*; cautionnement *m*; gage *m*; garantie *f*/nantissement *m*; **account opened without security,** compte ouvert sans garantie/sans provision; **security for a debt,** garantie d'une créance; **to give a security,** verser une caution/cautionner; **to pay in a sum as a security,** verser une provision/un cautionnement; **to lodge stock as additional security,** déposer des titres en nantissement; **as security for the sum,** en couverture de la somme; **to lend money on security,** prêter de l'argent sur nantissement/sur garantie; **to lend money without security,** prêter de l'argent à découvert (*b*) (*pers.*) caution *f*/

garant(e); accréditeur *m*; *Jur:* répondant(e); **to stand/become security for s.o.,** se porter caution/se porter garant pour qn; répondre de/cautionner qn; **to stand security for a signature/for a debt,** avaliser une signature; assurer une créance **3.** *Fin:* **securities,** (*i*) titres *m*/valeurs *f*/fonds *mpl* (*ii*) portefeuille *m* titres/*F:* portefeuille; **gilt-edged/government securities,** fonds d'État; **outstanding securities,** titres en circulation/non amortis; **registered securities,** titres nominatifs; **transferable securities,** valeurs négociables/cessibles; **securities department,** service *m* des titres (d'une banque).

seize, *v.tr. Jur:* confisquer/saisir (qch.)/opérer la saisie de (qch.); **the goods were seized,** les marchandises ont été confisquées.

select, *v.tr.* sélectionner/choisir (un candidat).

selection, *n.* sélection *f*/choix *m*; **promotion by selection,** promotion *f* au choix; **selection board/committee,** comité *m* de sélection.

selective, *a.* sélectif.

self-employed, *a. & n.* (travailleur) indépendant.

self-financing[1], *n.* autofinancement *m*; **self-financing ratio,** coefficient *m* d'autofinancement.

self-financing[2], *a.* **the firm is self-financing,** l'entreprise pratique un système d'autofinancement.

self-liquidating, *a.* auto-amortissable.

self-management, *n.* autogestion *f.*

self-service, *n.* (magasin) libre-service *m*; (restaurant) self-service *m*/*F:* un self.

self-sufficiency, *n.* **economic self-sufficiency,** indépendance *f* économique; **national self-sufficiency,** autarcie *f.*

self-sufficient, *a.* indépendant/autosuffisant; **Britain is self-sufficient in oil,**

la Grande Bretagne est économiquement indépendante du point de vue
pétrole.

sell[1], *n. F:* vente *f*; **hard sell**, vente agressive; **soft sell**, vente facile/vente a publicité discrète.

sell[2], *v.tr.* (*a*) vendre (qch.); **to sell sth. back
to s.o.**, revendre qch. à qn; **to sell goods
easily**, écouler facilement des marchandises; **difficult to sell**, de vente/d'écoulement difficile; **to sell sth. by auction**,
vendre qch. à la criée/aux enchères; **to
sell sth. for cash**, vendre qch. (au) comptant; **to sell sth. on credit**, vendre qch.
à terme/à crédit; **to sell sth. at a loss**,
vendre qch. à perte; **to sell sth. dear**,
vendre qch. cher; **to sell sth. cheap**, vendre qch. (à) bon marché; **he sold it to
me for a pound**, il me l'a vendu (pour) une
livre; *StExch:* **to sell short/to sell a bear**,
vendre à découvert (*b*) **goods that sell
well**, marchandises *f* qui se vendent bien;
**these pencils are selling at/sell for 8p
each**, on vend ces crayons 8p chacun/8p
pièce; **certain to sell**, d'un débit assuré;
what are plums selling at? combien valent
les prunes?/quel est le prix des prunes?

sell-by-date, *n.* date *f* limite de vente
(d'un produit).

seller, *n.* 1. (*pers.*) (*a*) vendeur, -euse;
StExch: **seller's option**, prime *f* vendeur/
pour livrer; **seller's market**, marché *m* à
la hausse (*b*) marchand(e)/débitant(e)
(de tabac, etc.) 2. (*article*) (**good**) **seller**,
article *m* de vente/qui se vend bien; **bad
seller**, article hors de vente/qui ne se
vend pas.

selling, *n.* vente *f*/écoulement *m* (de
marchandises, etc.); **direct selling**, vente
directe; **hard selling**, vente agressive;
selling cost, frais *mpl* commerciaux; **selling point**, avantage spécial (d'un produit)
susceptible d'intéresser un client; **selling
price**, prix *m* de vente; prix marchand/
fort; (**conventional**) **selling weight**, poids
vénal; **unique selling proposition (USP)**,
proposition exclusive de vente (*b*) **sell-**

ing off, liquidation *f* (des stocks); *Fin:*
(re)vente *f*/réalisation *f* (de titres, etc.).

sell off, *v.tr.* solder/écouler/vendre à bas
prix (des marchandises); se défaire de
(marchandises); liquider (son stock,
etc.).

sell out, *v.tr.* (*a*) *Fin:* réaliser (un portefeuille) (*b*) vendre tout son stock de
(qch.); **the shop sold out all their furniture**, tous les meubles (du magasin) ont
été vendus; **we're sold out of eggs**, nous
n'avons plus d'œufs, tout est vendu; **the
book is sold out**, l'édition est épuisée (*c*)
to sell out one's business, vendre/se
défaire de son commerce.

sellout, *n. F:* **this line has been a sellout**, cet
article s'est vendu à merveille (et il ne
nous en reste plus); **it was a sellout**, nous
avons absolument tout vendu.

sell up, *v.tr.* (faire) vendre les biens (d'un
failli); **he went bankrupt and was sold up**,
il a fait faillite et tout ce qu'il possédait a
été vendu.

semi-automated, *a.* semi-automatisé.

semidetached, *a. & n.* **a semidetached
(house)/a semi**, maison jumelée.

semi-finished, *a.* **semi-finished products**,
produits semi-finis/semi-produits *m*.

semi-manufactured, *a.* semi-ouvré/
semi-fini.

semi-manufactures, *n.pl.* semi-pro-
duits *m*.

semi-skilled, *a.* **semi-skilled worker**, ouvrier, -ière spécialisé(e).

semi-variable, *a.* (*of costs*) semi-variable.

send, 1. *v.tr.* (*a*) envoyer (qn) (*b*) envoyer/
faire parvenir (qch.); expédier (une let-
tre, un paquet, etc.); remettre (de l'argent, un chèque, etc.); **to send a parcel by
post**, expédier un colis par la poste 2.
v.i. **to send for s.o./sth.**, envoyer chercher qn/qch.

sender, *n.* expéditeur, -trice (d'une lettre, de marchandises); **return to sender**, retour à l'envoyeur.

send in, *v.tr.* **he has sent in his bill**, il nous a envoyé/fait parvenir son compte; **applications should be sent in before the end of the year**, les demandes devront être reçues avant la fin de l'année; **to send in one's resignation**, envoyer/donner sa démission.

send off, *v.tr.* expédier (une lettre, etc.).

send on, *v.tr.* faire suivre (une lettre).

send out, *v.tr.* (*i*) expédier (*ii*) mettre à la poste.

senior, 1. *a.* (*i*) plus âgé (*ii*) qui a plus d'ancienneté (*iii*) plus élevé (en grade); supérieur; **senior clerk**, premier commis/commis principal; chef *m* de bureau; **senior partner**, associé principal; associé majoritaire; **senior in rank**, de grade supérieur; *Fin:* **senior securities**, titres prioritaires 2. *n.* (*i*) le (la) plus âgé(e) (*ii*) qui a le plus d'ancienneté (*iii*) le (la) plus élevé(e) (en grade).

seniority, *n.* 1. priorité *f* d'âge; **he is chairman by seniority**, il est président d'âge 2. ancienneté *f* de service; **to be promoted by seniority**, avancer (en grade)/être promu à l'ancienneté.

sensitive, *a.* **sensitive market**, marché sensible/instable/prompt à réagir.

sequester, sequestrate, *v.tr.* *Jur:* séquestrer (les biens d'un débiteur, etc.); mettre (un bien) en/sous séquestre.

sequestration, *n.* *Jur:* séquestration *f*; mise *f* en/sous séquestre; **writ of sequestration**, séquestre *m* (judiciaire).

serial, *a.* **serial number**, numéro *m* de série; numéro d'ordre; *Ind: etc:* numéro matricule (d'un moteur, etc.).

series, *n.inv.* série *f*; collection *f*.

servant, *n.* **public servants**, employé(e)s d'un service public; **civil servant**, fonctionnaire *m* (de l'État).

serve, *v.tr. & i.* 1. **to serve one's apprenticeship**, faire son apprentissage 2. (*a*) (*in shop*) **to serve a customer**, servir un(e) client(e); **are you being served?** est-ce qu'on s'occupe de vous? (*b*) *v.i.* **to serve in a shop**, être vendeur, -euse.

service[1], *n.* 1. (*a*) service *m*; **ten years' service**, dix années de service; **promotion according to length of service**, avancement *m* à l'ancienneté *f* (*b*) (*in restaurant, etc.*) service *m*; **service included**, service compris (*c*) *Mkt:* **after sales service/back up service**, service aprèsvente; **customer service**, service à la clientèle; **service agreement**, contrat *m* de service; **service charge**, frais *mpl* administratifs/frais d'administration; **rent plus service charge**, loyer *m* plus charges; **24-hour service**, service permanent/de 24 heures; permanence *f* (*d*) **to bring/put (a machine, a vehicle) into service**, mettre (un appareil, un véhicule) en service; **service life**, durée *f* de vie/longévité *f* (d'un matériel); durée/potentiel *m* d'utilisation (*e*) *Veh:* **service speed**, vitesse commerciale 2. *PolEc:* **goods and services**, biens *m* et services; **service bureau**, société *f* de services; **service fee**, prestation *f* de service; **service industry**, (*i*) secteur *m* tertiaire (*ii*) société de services 3. **the civil service**, l'administration *f*/la fonction publique 4. (*a*) **public services**, services publics; **postal service**, service postal (*b*) **goods/freight service**, service de marchandises (*c*) **motorway services**, relais *m* d'autoroute (*d*) *NAm:* **service center**, ville commerciale (qui dessert toute une région) 5. (*of car*) révision *f*; **service department**, service de réparation/d'entretien; **service engineer**, technicien *m* d'entretien; **service manual/handbook**, manuel *m* d'entretien; **service station**, station *f* service.

service[2], *v.tr.* 1. réviser/vérifier; **to service a car**, réviser une voiture 2. **to service a loan**, assurer le service d'un emprunt.

session, *n.* (*a*) session *f*; séance *f*; **to have/to hold a session**, se réunir (pour

discuter, etc.) (*b*) *StExch:* séance/
session; **closing session,** session de
clôture.

set[1], *n.* ensemble *m*; jeu *m* (d'outils, de
boîtes, etc.); série *f* (de poids, de
conférences); batterie *f* (d'ustensiles de
cuisine); service *m* (à thé, etc.).

set[2], *a.* **set price,** prix *m* fixe.

set[3], *v.tr.* **to set a value on sth.,** évaluer qch.

set against, *v.tr.* **set against your invoice,**
à valoir sur votre facture; **to set (off)
losses against tax,** déduire les pertes des
impôts.

setback, *n.* revers *m*; **to suffer a setback,**
essuyer un revers (de fortune).

set off, *v.tr.* **to set off a debt,** compenser une
dette.

set-off, *n.* compensation *f* (d'une dette);
Book-k: écriture *f* inverse; **as a set-off
against . . .,** en compensation de . . .; en
dédommagement de . . . .

set out, *v.tr.* étaler/disposer (ses marchandises, etc.).

set-out, *n.* étalage *m* (de marchandises,
etc.).

setting up, *n.* (*a*) implantation *f* (d'une
nouvelle industrie, etc.) (*b*) établissement *m*/création *f*/fondation *f* (d'un
comité, d'une maison de commerce).

settle, 1. *v.tr.* (*a*) fixer/déterminer (un
jour, un endroit, etc.); **the terms were
settled,** on a convenu des conditions; **your
appointment is as good as settled,** votre
nomination est presque une affaire faite
(*b*) résoudre (une question); arranger/
liquider (une affaire) (*c*) conclure/
terminer (une affaire); régler/solder (un
compte); acquitter/régler (une facture);
payer (une dette, une amende, un
compte, etc.); **to settle (one's bills)/to
settle up,** payer/régler ses comptes (*d*) **to
settle an annuity on s.o.,** constituer/
assigner une annuité à qn; asseoir une
annuité sur qn **2.** *v.i.* **to settle for sth.,**

accepter qch.; **I settled for £100,** j'ai
accepté £100.

settled, *a.* (*a*) (*of question, etc.*) arrangé/
décidé (*b*) (*of bill, etc.*) réglé/soldé/
acquitté.

settlement, *n.* (*a*) règlement *m* (d'une
affaire, d'un litige); solution *f* (à un
problème); détermination *f* (d'une date,
etc.) (*b*) règlement/paiement (d'un
compte); **settlement of account,** arrêté *m*
de compte; **in (full) settlement,** pour
règlement de tout compte; **cheque in
settlement of an account,** chèque *m* en
paiement d'un compte (*c*) *StExch:* liquidation *f*; **the settlement,** le terme; **dealings for settlement,** négociations *f* à
terme; **settlement day,** jour *m* de (la)
liquidation/du règlement; **yearly settlement,** liquidation de fin d'année (*d*)
**legal settlement (between merchant and
creditors),** concordat *m*/règlement *m* judiciaire (après faillite) (*e*) **settlement of
an annuity,** constitution *f* de rente (**on,** en
faveur de).

settling, *n.* (*a*) conclusion *f*/terminaison *f*
(d'une affaire); **settling (up),** règlement
m (d'un compte) (*b*) *StExch:* liquidation
f; **settling day,** jour *m* de (la) liqui-
dation/du règlement.

set up, 1. *v.tr.* (*a*) créer/organiser/insti-
tuer/constituer (un comité/etc.); fonder
(une maison de commerce); monter (un
magasin) (*b*) **to set s.o. up in business,**
établir qn/lancer qn dans un commerce **2.**
v.i. **to set up as a chemist,** s'établir
pharmacien.

set-up, *n.* organisation *f*/établissement *m*;
structure *f*.

severally, *adv. Jur:* **severally liable,** responsable isolément/individuellement;
jointly and severally, conjointement et
solidairement; par divis et indivis.

severance, *n.* **severance pay,** compensation *f*/indemnité *f* pour perte d'emploi.

shade, *v.tr. NAm:* **to shade prices,** établir
des prix dégressifs; **prices shaded for
quantities,** tarif dégressif pour le gros.

shake-out, *n.* réorganisation *f*/remaniement *m* du personnel (avec licenciements).

shake-up, *n. F:* remaniement *m* (du personnel).

shaky, *a.* **shaky business/shaky undertaking,** entreprise qui périclite.

sham, *a. Fin:* **sham dividend,** dividende fictif.

share[1], *n.* **1.** part *f*/portion *f*; **to have a share in/of the profits,** participer aux bénéfices; **to have a share in a business,** avoir des intérêts dans une affaire **2.** (*a*) contribution *f*/cotisation *f*/quote-part *f*; **to pay one's share,** payer sa (quote-)part (*b*) **to go shares with s.o.,** partager avec qn **3.** *Fin:* (*in a company, etc.*) action *f*/titre *m*/valeur *f*; **bonus share,** action gratuite; **deferred share,** action différée; **dividend share,** action de jouissance; action de bénéficiaire; **founder's share,** part *f* de fondateur; **fully paid (-up) share,** action entièrement libérée; **ordinary/common share,** action ordinaire; **participating share,** action de participation; **partnership share,** part d'association; **personal/registered share,** action nominative; **preferred/preference/senior share,** action privilégiée/de priorité; **to hold shares,** posséder/détenir des actions; être actionnaire; **share capital,** capital *m* actions; **share certificate,** titre d'action(s); certificat *m* d'action(s)/de titre(s); certificat provisoire; **the share index reached an all-time low,** l'indice des actions est descendu à son plus bas niveau; **share pusher,** courtier marron; placeur *m*/placier *m* de valeurs douteuses.

share[2], **1.** *v.tr.* partager; **to share an office with s.o.,** partager un bureau avec qn **2.** *v.tr. & ind.tr.* **to share (in) sth.,** prendre part à/avoir part à/participer à/s'associer à qch.; **to share in the profits,** participer/avoir part aux bénéfices; **to share out the work,** répartir/distribuer le travail.

shareholder, *n. Fin:* actionnaire *mf*/sociétaire *mf* (d'une société anonyme);

shareholders' equity, fonds *m* propres/avoir *m* des actionnaires; **shareholders' meeting,** réunion *f* d'actionnaires.

shareholding, *n.* **1.** possession *f* d'actions/de titres; **employee shareholding,** actionnariat ouvrier; **he has a major shareholding in the company,** il est un des principaux actionnaires de la société **2.** *pl.* **shareholdings,** actions *f*.

share-out, *n.* partage *m*/distribution *f*/répartition *f*.

sharing, *n.* **1.** partage *m* (de ses biens, etc.) **2.** participation *f*/partage; **profit sharing,** participation aux bénéfices; association *f* capital-travail; *Cmptr:* **time sharing,** partage de temps/temps partagé.

sharp, *a.* **sharp rally,** reprise vigoureuse; **sharp rise/drop in prices,** forte hausse/baisse des prix.

sheet, *n.* feuille *f* (de papier); **order sheet,** bulletin *m*/bon *m* de commande; bordereau *m* d'achat; **sale sheet,** bordereau de vente; *Ind:* **time/work/job sheet,** feuille de présence; **(workman's) time sheet,** semainier *m*.

shelf, *n.* (*a*) rayon *m*/étagère *f*; **shelf space,** rayonnage *m* (*b*) (*in supermarket, etc.*) **shelf filler,** réassortisseur, -euse; **shelf life (of a product),** espérance *f*/durée *f* de vie (d'un produit); (*of goods*) **to stay on the shelves,** être difficile à vendre.

shift, *n.* (*a*) équipe *f*/poste *m*/brigade *f*/relais *m* (d'ouvriers); (*esp. of dockers*) shift *m*; **day shift,** équipe de jour; **night shift,** équipe de nuit; **to work in shifts,** travailler par équipes/se relayer (*b*) journée *f* de travail; **an eight-hour shift,** une période de relève de huit heures; **to work eight-hour shifts,** se relayer toutes les huit heures; faire les trois huits; **I'm on first shift,** je suis du premier huit.

shiftwork, *n. Ind:* travail *m* par équipes/par relais.

ship[1], *n.* navire *m*; **container ship,** (navire)

porte-conteneurs *m*; **passenger ship,** paquebot *m*; **refrigerator ship,** navire frigorifique.

ship^2, *v.tr.* **1.** embarquer (une cargaison, etc.); mettre (des marchandises) à bord **2.** envoyer/expédier (des marchandises, etc., par voie de mer; *esp. NAm:* par chemin de fer, par la poste, etc.); **to ship coal to France,** expédier du charbon en France.

shipbroker, *n.* courtier *m* maritime.

shipbrokerage, *n.* courtage *m* maritime.

shipment, *n.* **1.** (*a*) embarquement *m*/mise *f* à bord (de marchandises, etc.) (*b*) expédition *f*/envoi *m* (de marchandises) par mer; **overseas shipment,** envoi outre-mer **2.** (*goods shipped*) chargement *m*.

shipping, *n.* transport *m* maritime; *esp. NAm:* transport routier/par chemin de fer; **shipping agent,** agent *m* maritime; (*for goods*) expéditeur *m*; commissionnaire chargeur; **shipping bill,** connaissement *m*; **shipping charges,** frais *mpl* de transport; *NAm:* **shipping company,** entreprise *f*/entrepreneurs *mpl* de transport routier; **shipping office,** agence *f* maritime.

shoot up, *v.i.* (*of prices, costs*) augmenter rapidement/brusquement; monter en flèche.

shooting up, *n.* **the shooting up of prices,** la flambée des prix.

shop^1, *n.* **1.** magasin *m*; (*small*) boutique *f*; **baker's shop,** boulangerie *f*; **grocer's shop,** épicerie *f*; **mobile shop,** camionnette-boutique *f*; **shoe shop,** magasin de chaussures; **to open a shop/to set up shop,** ouvrir un magasin; **to keep a shop,** tenir un magasin; **to close a shop,** fermer boutique; **shop front,** devanture *f* de magasin; **shop window,** vitrine *f*; devanture (de magasin); étalage *m*; **in the shop window,** dans la vitrine/en étalage; **shop assistant,** vendeur, -euse (de magasin); employé(e) de magasin **2.** *Ind: etc:* atelier *m*; **the shop floor,** les ateliers; les

ouvriers *m*; **assembly shop,** atelier de montage/d'assemblage; **repair shop,** atelier de réparations; **shop foreman,** chef *m* d'atelier; **shop steward,** délégué(e) syndical(e); délegué(e) d'atelier/d'usine/du personnel; **closed shop** = monopole syndical de l'embauche; **open shop,** entreprise qui admet du personnel non syndiqué **3.** *StExch:* introducteurs *mpl*; **shop shares,** actions *f* à introduction.

shop^2, *v.i.* **to shop/to go shopping,** (aller) faire ses courses/des achats; (*for food*) faire son marché/aller aux provisions; **to shop around,** chercher des occasions; chercher les prix les plus avantageux.

shopgirl, *n.f.* vendeuse/employée de magasin.

shopkeeper, *n.* (*a*) commerçant(e); boutiquier, -ière (*b*) le (la) propriétaire (du magasin).

shoplifter, *n.* voleur, -euse à l'étalage.

shoplifting, *n.* vol *m* à l'étalage.

shopper, *n.* acheteur, -euse; client(e).

shopping, *n.* achats *mpl*; courses *fpl*; **to do one's shopping,** faire ses courses; (*for food*) faire son marché/aller aux provisions; *PolEc:* **shopping basket,** panier *m* de la ménagère/panier *m* à provisions; **shopping centre,** (*i*) quartier commercial (*ii*) centre commercial/*FrC:* centre d'achats; **shopping precinct,** (*i*) centre commercial (*ii*) aire piétonnière; **shopping street,** rue commerçante; **window shopping,** lèche-vitrine(s).

shop-soiled, *a.* (article) défraîchi/abîmé (en magasin)/qui a fait l'étalage.

shopwalker, *n.* (*a*) chef *m* de rayon (*b*) inspecteur, -trice/surveillant(e) (de magasin).

short, 1. *a.* (*a*) *Fin:* **short bills/bills at short date,** billets *m*/traites *f* à courte échéance; billet à vue; **deposit/loan at short notice,** dépôt *m*/prêt *m* à court terme (*b*) (*of weight, measure, etc.*) insuffisant; **to give short weight,** ne pas donner le poids/tricher sur le poids; **the**

weight is 50 gram(me)s short, il manque 50 grammes au poids/il y a 50 grammes en moins; **short delivery,** livraison partielle; **to prevent short delivery,** éviter des manquants *m* dans la marchandise *(c)* **to be short of staff,** manquer de/être à court de main-d'œuvre; **I'm short of money,** je suis à court d'argent/je manque d'argent *(d) StExch:* **short selling,** vente *f* à découvert/à terme **2.** *n. StExch:* vendeur à découvert/à terme **3.** *adv. StExch:* **to sell short/selling short,** vendre à découvert/à terme.

shortage, *n.* insuffisance *f*; manque *m*; **shortage of staff/of labour,** manque de personnel/pénurie *f* de main-d'œuvre; **dollar shortage,** pénurie de dollars: **to make up/make good the shortage,** combler le déficit.

short-dated, *a. Fin:* (billet) à courte échéance.

shortening, *n. Fin:* **shortening of credit,** amoindrissement *m* de crédit.

shortfall, *n.* déficit *m*; manque *m*.

shorthand, *n.* sténographie *f*; **take this letter down in shorthand,** prenez cette lettre en sténo; **shorthand typist,** sténodactylo *mf*.

shorthanded, *a.* à court de personnel/de main-d'œuvre/d'ouvriers; **to be short-handed,** manquer de personnel.

shortlist[1], *n.* **he's on the shortlist,** il a été retenu/sélectionné (comme candidat).

shortlist[2], *v.tr.* **to shortlist a candidate/an applicant,** sélectionner un candidat/ retenir une candidature.

shortlisted, *a.* être parmi les candidats sélectionnés/dont on a retenu la candidature.

short-staffed, *a.* **to be short-staffed,** manquer de personnel/de main d'œuvre.

short-term, *a. Fin:* **short-term loan,** prêt *m* à court terme/à courte échéance.

short-time, *a.* **1.** (contrat, etc.) à court terme **2. short-time working,** chômage partiel; **to be on short-time,** être en chômage partiel.

shot, *n.* **mailing shot,** envoi *m*/prospectus *m*/dépliant *m* (de publicité directe).

show[1], *n. (a)* exposition *f* (de marchandises, etc.); concours *m*/comice *m* (agricole, etc.); **fashion show,** présentation *f* de collections; **the Motor Show,** le Salon de l'Automobile *(b)* **show house/flat,** maison *f* témoin/appartement *m* témoin.

show[2], *v.tr.* **to show a profit/a loss,** se solder par un profit/un déficit; **the accounts show a net profit of . . .,** les comptes *m* se soldent par un bénéfice net de . . ..

showcard, *n. (i)* pancarte *f (ii)* étiquette *f* (de vitrine, etc.); affiche *f* à chevalet *(iii)* carte *f* d'échantillons.

showcase, *n.* vitrine *f*/montre *f*.

showroom, *n.* salle *f*/salon *m*/magasin *m* d'exposition (d'une maison de commerce); salle de démonstration (de voitures, etc.).

shrink, *a.* **shrink film,** film *m* rétractable; **shrink packaging,** emballage *m* sous film rétractable; **shrink packed/wrapped,** emballé sous film rétractable.

shut, *v.tr.* **1.** fermer (un magasin, etc.) **2.** *(on transfer books of banks, etc.)* **shut for dividend,** clôture *f* pour dividende.

shut down, 1. *v.tr.* fermer (une usine, etc.) **2.** *v.i. (of factory, etc.) (i)* chômer *(ii)* fermer ses portes.

shutdown, *n. Ind: (i)* fermeture *f*; immobilisation *f (ii)* chômage *m* (d'une usine).

shut-out, *n. Ind:* lock-out *m inv.*

shutting, *n.* **shutting down of a factory,** *(i)* fermeture *f (ii)* chômage *m* d'une usine.

sick, *a.* malade; **sick leave,** congé *m* de maladie; **sick pay,** indemnité *f*/allocation *f* de maladie.

sickness, *n.* maladie *f*; **sickness benefit,** prestation *f* en cas de maladie; assurance maladie; **to draw sickness benefit,**

bénéficier de l'assurance maladie; avoir droit à l'assurance maladie.

side, *n.* **1.** *Book-k:* **credit side,** crédit *m*/ avoir *m*; **debit side,** débit *m*/doit *m* **2.** (*on packing cases, etc.*) **this side up,** haut *m* **3. reverse side (of a letter of credit)**/dos *m* (d'une lettre de crédit).

sideline, *n.* (*a*) occupation *f*/travail *m* secondaire (*b*) (*of product*) seconde spécialité.

sight, *n.* (*a*) **bill payable at sight,** effet *m* payable à vue; **bill/draft at sight**/*NAm:* **sight draft,** effet/papier *m*/traite *f* à vue; **three months after sight,** à trois mois de vue; *StExch:* **sight quotation,** cotation *f* à vue (*b*) **on sale sight unseen,** à vendre tel quel/sur description/sans inspection; *Cust:* **sight entry,** déclaration *f* provisoire.

sign *v.tr.* signer (son nom, un document, un chèque, etc.); **the letter was signed by the president,** la lettre portait la signature du président; **to sign a bill,** accepter une traite; **to sign a contract,** signer/passer un contrat; **to sign for (reception of) goods,** signer à la réception (de marchandises).

signatory, *a. & n.* signataire (*mf*).

signature, *n.* signature *f*; **stamped signature,** griffe *f*; **to put one's signature to a letter,** apposer sa signature à une lettre/ signer une lettre; **for signature,** pour signature; **joint signature,** signature collective; signature des parties intéressées; **the signature of the firm,** la signature sociale.

signing, *n.* signature *f* (d'un document); acceptation *f* (d'une traite); **signing fee,** jeton *m* de signature (d'un directeur de société); **signing officer,** fondé *m* de signature/signataire officiel.

sign off, *v.i.* (*of workers in factories, etc.*) signer le registre (en quittant le travail); pointer au départ.

sign on, 1. *v.tr.* embaucher (un ouvrier) **2.** *v.i.* (*a*) (*of workers*) s'embaucher (*b*) (*of workers in factories, etc.*) signer le regis-

tre (en arrivant au travail); pointer à l'arrivée (*c*) *F:* s'inscrire au chômage.

silent, *a.* **silent partner,** associé *m* commanditaire/commanditaire *m*; bailleur *m* de fonds.

silver, *n.* argent *m*; **silver (money),** argent monnayé; **silver coin,** (*i*) pièce *f* d'argent (*ii*) *coll.* (pièces d')argent; **to give a pound in silver,** faire de la monnaie pour une livre (*b*) **silver export point,** silver-point *m* de sortie; **silver import point,** silver-point d'entrées.

simple, *a.* (*a*) **simple interest,** intérêts *m* simples (*b*) *Jur:* **simple contract,** convention verbale/tacite; obligation *f* chirographaire; acte *m* sous seing privé; **simple contract creditor,** créditeur *m* chirographaire.

sincerely, *adv. Corr:* **yours sincerely =** veuillez agréer, Monsieur, Madame, etc., l'expression de mes sentiments respectueux/de mes sentiments distingués/de mes sentiments les meilleurs; je vous prie/nous vous prions de croire, Monsieur, Madame, etc., à l'expression de mes/nos sentiments distingués.

single[1], *n. Trans:* billet *m* simple/aller *m* (simple); **a single to Waterloo,** un aller pour Waterloo.

single[2], *a.* **1.** *Ins: etc:* **single premium,** prime *f* unique; *Book-k:* **single-entry book-keeping,** comptabilité *f* en partie simple **2. single ticket,** billet *m* simple/ aller *m* (simple).

singly, *adv.* séparément; un(e) à un(e); **articles sold singly,** articles *m* qui se vendent séparément/à la pièce.

sink, 1. *v.i.* baisser/diminuer/s'affaiblir/ décliner; **prices are sinking,** les cours *m* baissent/s'affaissent/sont en baisse **2.** *v.tr.* (*a*) **to sink a loan,** amortir un emprunt (*b*) **to sink money into a new business,** investir de l'argent dans une nouvelle entreprise.

sinking, *n.* amortissement *m*/extinction *f* (d'une dette); **sinking fund,** fonds *m*/caisse *f* d'amortissement.

sir, *n. Corr:* **(Dear) Sir,** Monsieur; **Dear Sirs,** Messieurs.

sister, *n.* **sister company,** compagnie *f* sœur/société *f* sœur.

sit-down, *n.* **sit-down strike,** grève *f* sur le tas.

sit-in, *n.* (grève avec) occupation de locaux.

situation, *n.* **1.** situation *f*; **financial situation,** situation financière; **overall economic situation,** conjoncture *f* économique **2.** emploi *m*/place *f*/position *f*; **to get/obtain a situation,** obtenir un emploi; (*in advertisements*) **situations vacant** = offres *f* d'emplois; **situations wanted** = demandes *f* d'emplois.

size, *n.* **1.** (*a*) grandeur *f*/dimension *f*/mesure *f*; étendue *f*; grosseur *f*/volume *m* (*b*) *Ind:* cote *f*/dimensions **2.** numéro *m* (d'un article); taille *f* (d'un vêtement); pointure *f* (de chaussures, de gants); **collar size,** encolure *f* (de chemise).

skeleton, *n.* **skeleton organization,** organisation *f* squelettique; **skeleton staff,** personnel réduit.

skilled, *a.* habile; **skilled worker,** ouvrier, -ière qualifié(e); (ouvrier) professionnel (*m*); **skilled labour,** main-d'œuvre qualifiée/professionnelle.

slack, *a.* **trade/business is slack,** les affaires sont calmes/stagnantes; le commerce est stagnant; **slack period/slack time,** période *f* creuse; période de stagnation; **the slack season,** la morte-saison/la saison creuse.

slackness, *n.* stagnation *f*/manque *m* d'activité/marasme *m* (des affaires).

slash, *v.tr.* **to slash prices,** casser les prix.

sleeper, *n.* associé *m* commanditaire; commanditaire *m*; bailleur *m* de fonds.

sleeping, *a.* **sleeping partner,** associé *m* commanditaire; commanditaire *m*; bailleur *m* de fonds.

sliding, *a.* **sliding scale,** échelle *f* mobile (des prix, des salaires, etc.); **sliding-scale tariff,** tarif dégressif.

slip¹, *n.* bordereau *m*/bulletin *m*/bon *m*; **pay (advice) slip,** bulletin *m*/feuille *f* de paie.

slip², *v.i.* glisser; **shares slipped (back) to 125,** le prix des actions *f* a baissé jusqu'à 125.

slogan, *n.* slogan *m* (publicitaire).

slow, **1.** *a.* **slow increase,** augmentation lente; **business is slow,** les affaires *f* ne vont pas/les affaires languissent; **go-slow,** grève perlée **2.** *adv.* **to go slow,** faire une grève perlée.

slow down, *v.tr.* **to slow down production,** ralentir la production.

slow(-)down, *n.* (*a*) ralentissement *m* (des affaires, etc.) (*b*) *NAm:* **slow-down (strike)** grève perlée; travail *m* au ralenti.

slowing down, *n.* ralentissement *m* (de la production, etc.).

slump¹, *n.* baisse soudaine/forte baisse/chute *f*/effondrement *m*/dégringolade *f* (des cours, du marché, etc.); **slump in sales,** mévente *f*; **the slump in the book trade,** la crise du livre; **slump in the pound,** dégringolade de la livre; **the slump,** la crise/la dépression économique.

slump², *v.i.* (*of prices, etc.*) baisser tout à coup/s'effondrer/dégringoler.

slush, *n.* **slush fund,** caisse *f* servant à payer les pots-de-vin/caisse noire.

small, *a.* (*a*) (*in contract, etc.*) **the small print,** ce qui est écrit en petits caractères (*b*) **small income,** revenu *m* modique (*c*) *Journ: F:* **small ads,** petites annonces; **small change,** (petite) monnaie; **banknotes of small denominations,** billets *m* de banque de petites coupures; **the smaller industries,** la petite industrie;

small investors, petits épargnants; **small shopkeeper,** petit commerçant.

small-scale, *a.* **small-scale business,** entreprise peu importante/de peu d'envergure.

smash, 1. *n.* débâcle *f*; effondrement *m*; faillite *f* (commerciale); krach *m* (à la Bourse) **2.** *adv.* **to go smash,** (*of firm*) faire faillite; tomber en faillite; (*of bank*) sauter.

smuggle, 1. *v.tr.* (faire) passer (des marchandises, etc.) en contrebande/en fraude **2.** *v.i.* faire de la contrebande.

smuggler, *n.* contrebandier, -ière; fraudeur, -euse (à la douane).

smuggling, *n.* contrebande *f*; fraude *f* (à la douane).

snake, *n.* *PolEc:* **the (monetary) snake,** le serpent (monétaire).

snap up, *v.tr.* **to snap up a bargain,** saisir une occasion; sauter sur une occasion; **goods that are quickly snapped up,** marchandises *f* qui s'enlèvent vite.

soar, *v.i.* (*of prices*) monter en flèche.

soaring, *a.* (*of prices, etc.*) qui montent en flèche; **because of soaring prices,** en raison de la (forte) hausse des prix.

social, *a.* **social cost,** coût social.

society, *n.* (*a*) société *f*; **consumer society,** société de consommation; **industrial society,** société industrielle (*b*) **benefit society/friendly society,** société de secours mutuels/société mutuelle; **building society,** (*i*) société/coopérative immobilière (*ii*) = crédit foncier; **cooperative society,** société coopérative (de consommation); **loan society,** société de crédit.

soft, *a.* (*a*) **soft sell,** publicité discrète; **soft selling,** vente *f* par des moyens discrets (*b*) **soft currency,** devise faible.

softbound, *a.* (*of book*) broché.

software, *n.* *Cmptr:* logiciel *m*/software *m*.

sola, *n.* **sola of exchange,** seule *f* de change.

sole, *a.* seul/unique; **sole agent,** agent (commercial) exclusif; seul dépositaire (d'une marque, d'un produit); **sole owner,** seul propriétaire; **sole right,** droit exclusif.

solicitor, *n.* avocat *m*; (*in firm*) chef *m* du contentieux; **the solicitor's department,** le bureau du contentieux.

solvability, *n.* solvabilité *f* (d'un commerçant).

solvency, *n.* solvabilité *f*.

solvent, *a.* solvable.

sound, *a.* **1.** (*machine*) en bon état; non endommagé; solide **2.** sain/solide; **sound currency,** monnaie saine; **sound financial position,** situation financière solide.

soundness, *n.* **1.** bon état/bonne condition (des marchandises, etc.) **2.** solvabilité *f*.

source, *n.* source *f* (de revenu, etc.); **income taxed at source,** salaire imposé à la source; **taxation at source,** retenue *f* à la source.

space out, *v.tr.* **to space out payments over ten years,** échelonner des versements/des paiements sur dix ans.

spare, 1. *a.* (*a*) disponible; **spare capital,** capital *m* disponible; fonds *m* disponibles (*b*) **spare parts,** pièces *f* de rechange/pièces détachées **2.** *n.* pièce de rechange/pièce détachée.

spec, *n.* **to buy sth. on spec,** faire des spéculations; risquer de l'argent (en achetant qch.).

special, *a.* (*a*) spécial; particulier; **special line of business/special class of goods,** spécialité *f*; **special price,** prix *m* de faveur (*b*) (article) hors série; **special order work,** travail *m* à façon.

special(i)ty, *n.* spécialité *f* (d'un magasin, etc.).

specialization, *n.* spécialisation *f*; **area of specialization,** secteur *m* d'activité.

specialize, *v.i.* se spécialiser (**in,** dans).

specie, *n.* (*no pl*) espèces (monnayées)/ numéraire *m*; **to pay in specie,** payer en espèces.

specification, *n.* **1.** spécification *f*; **job specification,** spécification de la fonction; **standard specification,** norme *f* **2.** (*a*) description précise; devis descriptif; **specifications of a contract,** stipulations *f* d'un contrat (*b*) *Const: Ind: etc:* **specifications,** cahier *m* des charges.

specify, *v.tr.* spécifier/préciser; **specified load,** charge prévue/prescrite; **unless otherwise specified,** sauf indication contraire.

specimen, *n.* spécimen *m*/échantillon *m*/ exemple *m*; **specimen invoice,** modèle *m* de facture; (*of magazine, etc.*) **specimen copy/number,** numéro *m* spécimen; **specimen signature,** spécimen de signature.

speculate, *v.i. Fin:* spéculer; boursicoter; **to speculate on the Stock Exchange,** spéculer en Bourse/jouer à la Bourse; **to speculate in oils,** spéculer sur les valeurs pétrolières; **to speculate for a fall,** spéculer à la baisse; **to speculate for a rise,** spéculer à la hausse.

speculation, *n. Fin:* spéculation *f*; **risky speculation,** spéculation hasardeuse; **to buy sth. as a speculation,** spéculer sur (le prix de) qch.; *StExch:* coup *m* de Bourse.

speculative, *a. Fin:* spéculatif; **speculative purchases,** achats spéculatifs; **speculative stocks/shares,** valeurs spéculatives.

speculator, *n.* (*a*) spéculateur, -trice; **land bought (up) by speculators,** terrains achetés par des spéculateurs (*b*) *StExch:* personne qui joue à la Bourse; agioteur *m*; **small speculator,** boursicotier *m*.

spend, *v.tr.* dépenser (de l'argent).

spending, *n.* dépense(s) *f(pl)*; **spending money,** argent *m* de poche; argent pour dépenses courantes; *PolEc:* **spending power/spending capacity,** pouvoir *m* d'achat.

sphere, *n.* **spheres of activity,** secteurs *mpl* d'activité.

spin-off, *n.* (*a*) produit *m* secondaire/ dérivé *m* (*b*) avantage *m*/bénéfice *m* supplémentaire (*c*) nouveau marché/ nouveau débouché.

spiral[1], *n.* montée *f* (continuelle et rapide) (des prix, etc.)/spirale *f* inflationniste; **wage-price spiral,** spirale des prix et des salaires/montée en flèche des prix et des salaires.

spiral[2], *v.i.* (*of prices, etc.*) monter en spirale/en flèche.

split[1], *n. StExch:* **three for two stock split,** distribution gratuite d'une action nouvelle pour deux anciennes.

split[2], *v.tr. Fin:* **to split shares,** partager/ fractionner des actions; **the stock was split 50%, one new share for each two shares held,** les actions ont été fractionnées à raison d'une action nouvelle pour deux anciennes; **split stocks,** stocks scindés.

spoil, 1. *v.tr.* avarier (des marchandises) **2.** *v.i.* (*of fruit, fish, etc.*) s'avarier/se gâter/se détériorer.

sponsor[1], *n.* sponsor *m*.

sponsor[2], *v.tr.* parrainer/patronner/assurer le patronage (d'un produit, etc.).

sponsorship, *n. Mkt:* patronage *m*.

spot, *n.* (*a*) **spot cash,** argent comptant; **to pay spot cash,** payer comptant; **spot credit,** crédit spot/à court terme; **spot deal,** opération *f* au comptant; **spot market,** marché *m* du disponible/du comptant; **spot price,** prix du comptant/du disponible; **spot rate,** cours *m* du disponible; **spot sugar,** sucre payé comptant (*b*) message *m* publicitaire/spot *m*.

spread[1], *n.* différence *f* (entre le prix de fabrique et le prix de vente, entre deux tarifs, etc.); *StExch:* **jobber's spread,**

marge *f* (entre le prix d'achat et le prix de vente) d'un contrepartiste.

spread², *v.tr.* **to spread payments over ten months,** échelonner/étaler/répartir des paiements sur dix mois.

squeeze¹, *n.* **credit squeeze,** restriction *f*/resserrement *m*/encadrement *m* du crédit.

squeeze², *v.tr. StExch:* **to squeeze credits,** restreindre le crédit.

stability, *n.* stabilité *f* (des prix, etc.); **economic stability,** la stabilité économique.

stabilization, *n.* stabilisation *f* (de la monnaie, des prix, etc.).

stabilize, 1. *v.tr.* stabiliser (les prix, le marché, etc.) 2. *v.i.* **prices have stabilized,** les prix se sont stabilisés.

stabilizing¹, *a.* stabilisateur; **to have a stabilizing influence on prices,** exercer une influence stabilisatrice sur les prix; **stabilizing policy,** politique *f* de stabilité.

stabilizing², *n.* = **stabilization.**

stable, *a.* stable; **stable currency,** monnaie *f* stable; **stable prices,** prix *m* stables.

staff¹, *n.* (*i*) personnel *m*; employés *mpl*; **to be on the staff,** faire partie du personnel; **clerical staff/office staff,** personnel de bureau; **senior/managerial staff,** cadres *mpl* supérieurs; **shop/workroom staff,** (personnel de) l'atelier *m*; **staff manager,** chef *m* du personnel; **staff management,** direction *f* du personnel; (*on notice*) **staff only,** réservé au personnel/entrée interdite (au public).

staff², *v.tr.* recruter du personnel (pour un bureau).

staffing, *n.* **staffing policy,** politique *f* de recrutement du personnel.

stag, *n. StExch:* loup *m*.

stage¹, *n.* phase *f*/période *f*/étape *f*/degré *m*/palier *m*; **processing stages,** phases de fabrication; **taxation by stages,** taxes imposées par paliers.

stage², *v.tr.* organiser (une exposition, etc.).

stagflation, *n.* stagflation *f*.

stagger, *v.tr.* échelonner/répartir (des versements); étaler (les vacances, etc.).

stagnant, *a.* (*of economy, prices, etc.*) stagnant.

stagnate, *v.i.* (*of trade*) stagner; être/devenir stagnant; être dans un état de stagnation.

stagnation, *n.* stagnation *f*/marasme *m* (des affaires).

stake¹, *n.* **stake (money),** mise *f*/enjeu *m*; **to have a stake in sth.,** avoir des intérêts/des parts dans une affaire.

stake², *v.tr.* mettre (une somme) en jeu/parier/jouer/risquer/hasarder (une somme).

stale, *a.* (*a*) *Fin:* **stale market,** marché lourd/plat (*b*) **stale cheque,** chèque périmé (*c*) **stale goods,** produits *mpl* qui ne sont pas frais.

stamp¹, *n.* (*a*) timbre *m*; **date stamp,** timbre dateur; **rubber stamp,** tampon *m*/timbre humide; cachet *m*; timbre de/en caoutchouc; **stamp pad,** tampon encreur (*b*) timbre/tampon/cachet/marque (apposée); **official stamp,** estampille officielle (*c*) **postage stamp,** timbre(-poste) *m*; **stamp book(let),** carnet *m* de timbres; **revenue stamp,** timbre fiscal; **ad valorem stamp,** timbre proportionnel (*d*) **stamp duty,** impôt *m*/droit *m* de timbre.

stamp², *v.tr.* timbrer (un document, un effet, un reçu); apposer un visa sur/viser (un passeport); apposer un tampon sur/*F:* tamponner (un passeport); timbrer/affranchir (une lettre); estampiller (des marchandises); **stamped addressed envelope (s.a.e.),** enveloppe *f* affranchie; **to stamp "paid" on a bill,** apposer le tampon "pour acquit" sur une facture.

stamping, *n.* timbrage *m* (de documents,

etc.); estampillage *m* (de marchandises, etc.).

stand[1], *n.* (exhibition) **stand,** stand *m* (d'exposition).

stand[2], *v.i.* (*a*) **the agreement stands,** le contrat tient toujours (*b*) **to stand as security for a debt,** assurer une créance; se porter garant/caution d'une créance (*c*) **securities standing in the company's books,** titres portés dans les livres de la société (*d*) **the balance stands at £70,** le reliquat de compte se monte/s'élève à £70.

standard[1], *n.* (*a*) *Fin:* **the gold standard,** l'étalon-or *m*; **gold exchange standard,** étalon *m* de change (*b*) standard *m*/ niveau *m*/norme *f*; **standard of living,** niveau/standard de vie; **budget standards,** standards budgétaires; **price standards,** standards de prix (*c*) **up to standard,** (*i*) conforme à l'échantillon (*ii*) conforme à la norme; **the goods are up to standard in every way,** la marchandise répond à toutes les exigences.

standard[2], *a.* standard/normal; **standard charge,** redevance *f* forfaitaire; **standard costs,** coûts *m* standards; **standard costing/standard cost accounting,** méthode *f* des coûts standards; **standard make,** marque courante; (*of car, etc.*) **standard model,** modèle *m* standard; *Ins:* **standard policy,** police *f* (d'assurance) type; **standard price,** prix *m* standard; **standard production,** production *f* en série; **standard rate of pay,** barème normalisé des salaires; **standard specification,** norme *f*; **standard weights,** poids unifiés.

standardization, *n.* standardisation *f*/ production *f* en série (d'après un modèle standard); étalonnage *m*/étalonnement *m* (des poids, etc.); unification *f*/ uniformisation *f* (des objets de commerce, etc.); normalisation *f* (dans la fabrication); péréquation *f* (des tarifs, etc.).

standardize, *v.tr.* standardiser/normaliser/uniformiser (la production, etc.); **standardized production,** fabrication *f* en

(grande) série/fabrication standardisée; **standardized products,** produits normalisés.

standby, *n.* **standby credit,** crédit *m* de réserve/de soutien.

standing[1], *a.* **standing expenses,** frais généraux; dépenses *f* de maison; **standing order,** (*i*) *Bank:* ordre de transfert permanent (*ii*) (*with bookshop, etc.*) commande *f* permanente; **standing price,** prix *m* fixe.

standing[2], *n.* **1.** **debt of long standing,** dette *f* d'ancienne date **2.** réputation *f*/importance *f* (d'une société, d'une maison); **financial standing of a firm,** situation financière d'une maison; **firm of recognized standing,** maison réputée/reconnue.

stand off, *v.tr.* faire chômer (des ouvriers).

stand over, *v.i.* **to let an account stand over,** laisser traîner un compte.

standstill, *n.* arrêt *m*/immobilisation *f*.

staple, *a.* principal; **staple commodities,** denrées principales; **staple industry,** industrie principale; **staple trade,** commerce régulier.

starting, *n.* **starting price,** prix initial; **starting salary,** rémunération *f* de départ.

state, *v.tr.* **to state an account,** spécifier un compte.

stated, *a.* **stated capital,** capital déclaré.

statement, *n.* **1.** exposition *f*/exposé *m*/ énoncé *m* (des faits, de la situation, etc.); rapport *m*/compte rendu; **false statement,** fausse déclaration **2.** **bank statement,** relevé *m* de compte (bancaire); **financial statement,** situation *f* de trésorerie; état financier; bilan; **statement of account,** état *m* de compte; relevé de compte; bordereau *m* de compte; **monthly statement,** relevé mensuel; **statement of affairs,** bilan *m*; **statement of affairs in bankruptcy,** bilan *m* de liquidation; **statement of expenses,** état/relevé *m* de(s) dépenses.

statistical, *a.* statistique; **statistical control,** contrôle *m* statistique; **statistical expert,** expert *mf* en statistique(s); **statistical tables,** statistiques *f.*

statistician, *n.* statisticien, -ienne.

statistics, *n.pl.* statistique *f*; **statistics expert,** expert *mf* en statistique(s).

statutory, *a.* **1.** établi/fixé/imposé par la loi; réglementaire **2.** statutaire/conforme aux statuts; **statutory dividend,** dividende *m* statutaire.

steadily, *adv.* régulièrement; **steadily increasing output,** augmentation régulière et continue de la production.

steadiness, *n.* stabilité *f*/fermeté *f* (des prix, des cours).

steady[1], *a.* **steady demand,** demande suivie; **steady market,** marché soutenu/marché ferme; (*of market, etc.*) **to grow steady,** se stabiliser; **steady prices,** prix *m* stables.

steady[2], *v.i.* **prices are steadying,** les prix *m* se stabilisent/se raffermissent; **the market has steadied (down),** le marché a repris son aplomb.

steadying, *n.* (*of prices, etc.*) (r)affermissement *m.*

sterling, *n.* sterling *m*; **pound sterling,** livre *f* sterling; **five pounds sterling,** cinq livres sterling; **sterling area/sterling zone,** zone *f* sterling; **in sterling,** en livres sterling.

stevedore, *n.* docker *m*/débardeur *m.*

steward, *n. Ind:* **shop steward,** délégué(e) d'atelier/d'usine/du personnel; délégué(e) syndical(e).

sticker, *n.* étiquette *f* autocollante/autocollant *m.*

stiff, *a.* (*a*) (*of market, commodity*) (valeur) ferme (*b*) **stiff price,** prix très élevé/prix exorbitant/prix excessif.

stiffening, *n.* (*of prices*) raffermissement *m.*

stimulate, *v.tr.* encourager/activer (la production); **to stimulate trade,** stimuler le commerce/donner de l'impulsion au commerce.

stimulus, *n.* stimulant *m*; **competitive stimulus,** stimulant compétitif.

stipulate, *v.tr.* **to stipulate that . . .,** stipuler que . . .; **it is stipulated that construction shall start next month,** il est stipulé que la construction doit commencer le mois prochain; **the stipulated quantity,** la quantité prescrite.

stipulation, *n.* stipulation *f*/condition *f*/clause *f.*

stock[1], *n.* **1.** (*a*) stock *m*/marchandises *f* en magasin; **closing stock,** stock de clôture/stock final; **opening stock,** stock d'ouverture/stock initial; **safety stock,** stock de sécurité; **stock book,** livre de stock; **stock clearance,** liquidation *f* de stock; **stock control,** gestion *f*/contrôle *m* des stocks; **stock turnround/stock turn,** rotation *f* des stocks; **stock valuation,** évaluation *f* des stocks; **stock in hand/stock in trade,** stock existant/fonds de commerce; **to buy the whole stock (of a business),** acheter un fonds (de commerce) en bloc (*b*) **in stock,** en magasin/en stock/en dépôt; **spare parts always in stock,** pièces détachées toujours en stock/toujours disponibles; **to put goods into stock,** stocker des marchandises (*c*) (*of goods*) **out of stock,** (stock) épuisé; **we are out of stock,** nous n'avons plus de . . ./notre stock est épuisé; **we are running out of stock,** nos stocks s'épuisent/diminuent; notre stock s'épuise/diminue (*d*) **to take stock,** faire/dresser l'inventaire (des marchandises en stock) **2.** *Fin:* valeurs *fpl*/actions *fpl*/titres *mpl*; **bank stock,** valeurs de banque; **capital stock,** capital *m* actions; **common stock,** actions ordinaires; **fully paid stock,** titres entièrement libérés; **Government stocks,** fonds *m* d'État/rente *f* sur l'État;

oil stock, valeurs pétrolières; **preferred stock,** actions privilégiées/de priorité; **stock dividend,** dividende *m* (en) actions; **the (British) Stock Exchange,** la Bourse (de Londres); **Stock Exchange, committee,** comité *m* de la Bourse (à Londres); chambre syndicale des agents de change (à Paris); **stock market,** marché *m* des titres/des valeurs mobilières/la Bourse; **stock market price,** cours *m* de la Bourse; **stock option plan/stock purchase plan,** plan *m* d'options sur titres.

stock², v.tr. 1. approvisionner/stocker (un magasin) (**with,** de); **shop well stocked,** magasin bien approvisionné **2.** avoir/tenir/garder (des marchandises) en magasin/en dépôt; stocker (des marchandises); **I don't stock children's bicycles,** je ne tiens pas de bicyclettes d'enfants.

stockbroker, n. *Fin:* agent *m* de change; courtier *m* (en valeurs mobilières); **outside stockbroker,** coulissier *m*; **the outside stockbrokers,** la coulisse.

stockbroking, n. profession *f* d'agent de change.

stockholder, n. actionnaire *mf*; sociétaire *mf*.

stockist, n. stockiste *m*.

stock-keeper, n. magasinier *m*.

stock jobber, n. *StExch:* contrepartiste *m*.

stocklist, n. 1. inventaire *m* **2.** *StExch:* bulletin *m* de la cote.

stockpile¹, n. stocks *mpl* de réserve.

stockpile², v.tr. & i. stocker; constituer des stocks de réserve.

stockpiling, n. stockage *m*; constitution *f* de réserves.

stockroom, n. magasin *m* (de réserve)/entrepôt *m*.

stocktaking, n. inventaire *m* (des stocks);

to do the stocktaking, faire l'inventaire; **stocktaking sale,** solde *m* d'inventaire.

stop, v.tr. (*a*) **goods stopped at/by the customs,** marchandises *f* en consigne à la douane; marchandises consignées par la douane (*b*) **to stop an account,** bloquer un compte; **to stop bankruptcy proceedings,** suspendre une procédure de faillite (*c*) **to stop payment,** suspendre/arrêter des paiements; **to stop (payment of) a cheque,** faire opposition à un chèque/au paiement d'un chèque (*d*) **to stop s.o.'s wages,** retenir le salaire de qn; **to stop £20 out of s.o.'s wages,** retenir £20/faire une retenue de £20 sur le salaire de qn.

stoppage, n. arrêt *m*/suspension *f* (des affaires commerciales, etc.); **stoppage of pay,** retenue *f* sur les appointements/sur le salaire; **stoppage of payments,** suspension/cessation *f* de paiements.

storage, n. entreposage *m*/emmagasinage *m*/magasinage *m*; **storage capacity,** capacité *f* d'emmagasinage **2.** entrepôts *mpl*/magasins *mpl* (d'une maison de commerce); **cold storage,** entrepôt frigorifique; **he left his furniture in storage,** il a mis son mobilier au garde-meuble/il a entreposé ses meubles.

store¹, n. 1. entrepôt *m*/magasin *m*; **bond store,** entrepôt (sous douane); **cold store,** entrepôt frigorifique **2.** magasin; **cash store,** magasin qui ne fait pas de crédit (à ses clients); **chain stores,** magasin à succursales multiples; **co-operative store(s),** (société) coopérative *f* de consommation; **department store,** grand magasin; **village store,** alimentation *f*/épicerie *f* du village.

store², v.tr. mettre (des marchandises) en magasin/entreposer (des marchandises, des meubles).

storehouse, n. magasin *m*/entrepôt *m*/dépôt *m*.

storekeeper, n. 1. magasinier *m* **2.** *NAm:* marchand(e); boutiquier, -ière.

storing, n. entreposage *m*.

straight-line, *a. Fin:* **straight-line method (of depreciation),** méthode *f* (de l'amortissement) linéaire/méthode de l'amortissement constant.

strategy, *n.* stratégie *f*; **business strategy,** stratégie des affaires; **company/corporate strategy,** stratégie de l'entreprise; **financial strategy,** stratégie financière; **marketing strategy,** stratégie commerciale/de marché.

streamline, *v.tr.* moderniser/rationaliser (des méthodes, etc.); **to streamline production,** rationaliser la production.

streamlined, *a.* (*a*) (*of car, etc.*) aux lignes aérodynamiques/au profil aérodynamique (*b*) **streamlined production,** production rationalisée.

streamlining, *n.* modernisation *f*/rationalisation *f* (des méthodes, de la production, etc.).

strict, *a.* **strict cost price,** prix de revient calculé au plus juste.

strike[1], *n. Ind:* grève *f*; **go-slow**/*NAm:* **slow-down strike,** grève perlée; **lightning strike,** grève surprise; **official strike,** grève officielle; **sit-down strike,** grève sur le tas; **strike breaker,** briseur de grève; *Ins:* **strike clause,** clause *f* pour cas de grève; **strike pay,** allocation *f* de grève/allocation-gréviste *f*; **sympathy strike,** grève de solidarité; **token strike,** grève d'avertissement/grève symbolique; **unofficial strike/wildcat strike,** grève sauvage; **to be on strike,** faire grève/être en grève; **to go/to come out on strike,** se mettre en grève.

strike[2], *v.i. Ind:* se mettre en grève; déclencher une grève; **to strike in sympathy,** se mettre en grève par solidarité; **to strike for better conditions,** se mettre en grève en vue d'obtenir des conditions de travail plus avantageuses.

striker, *n. Ind:* gréviste *mf*.

structure[1], *n.* structure *f*; **corporate/**

company structure, structure de l'entreprise; **cost structure,** structure des coûts; **market structure,** structure du marché; **price structure,** structure des prix; **salary/wage structure,** structure des salaires.

structure[2], *v.tr.* structurer.

structuring, *n.* structuration *f* (du travail, etc.).

stub, *n.* souche *f*/talon *m* (de chèque).

stunt, *n.* **publicity stunt,** coup *m* publicitaire.

style, *n.* (*a*) **style of a firm,** raison sociale; nom social/commercial (*b*) **made in three styles,** fabriqué en trois genres/en trois modèles.

sub[1], *n.* **1.** avance *f* (de salaire) **2.** = subscription **3.** = subeditor.

sub[2], *v.tr.* **1.** (*a*) obtenir une avance (sur son salaire) (*b*) accorder une avance (d'argent) à un employé **2.** = subedit.

sub-agency, *n.* sous-agence *f*.

sub-agent, *n.* sous-agent *m*.

subcommittee, *n.* sous-comité *m*; sous-commission *f*.

subcontract[1], *n.* contrat *m* de sous-traitance.

subcontract[2], *v.tr.* sous-traiter (une affaire)/donner en sous-traitance.

subcontracting, *n.* sous-traitance *f*.

subcontractor, *n.* sous-entrepreneur *m*/sous-traitant *m*.

subedit, *v.tr.* corriger/mettre au point (un article, un manuscrit).

subeditor, *n.* correcteur, -trice.

subject, *a.* **prices subject to 5% discount,** prix sous réserve d'une remise de 5%; prix bénéficiant d'une remise de 5%; **transaction subject to a commission of 5%,** opération *f* passible d'un courtage de

5%; **subject to stamp duty,** passible du droit de timbre; soumis au timbre.

sub-lease[1], *n.* sous-bail *m*; sous-location *f*.

sub-lease[2], *v.tr.* sous-louer (un appartement); (*i*) donner en sous-location (*ii*) prendre en sous-location.

sub-leasing, *n.* sous-location *f*.

sub-lessee, *n.* (*a*) sous-locataire *mf* (à bail) (*b*) sous-traitant *m* (d'un travail à l'entreprise).

sub-lessor, *n.* = locataire *m* principal.

sub-let, *v.tr.* (*a*) sous-louer (un appartement) (*i*) donner (un appartement) en sous-location (*ii*) prendre (un appartement) en sous-location (*b*) sous-traiter (un travail, un contrat)/donner en sous-traitance.

sub-letting, *n.* (*a*) sous-location *f* (*b*) sous-traitance *f*.

sub-office, *n.* succursale *f* (d'une banque, etc.); filiale *f*; bureau *m* auxiliaire.

subordinate, 1. *a.* (rang) inférieur subalterne/secondaire **2.** *n.* subordonné(e)/subalterne *mf*.

subordinated, *a.* **subordinated debt,** dette de second rang/subordonnée.

sub-rent, *v.tr.* sous-louer/prendre (un appartment) en sous-location.

subscribe, *v.i.* (*a*) *Fin:* **to subscribe for a hundred shares in a company,** souscrire à cent actions d'une société; **to subscribe to a loan/to an issue,** souscrire à un emprunt/ à une émission; **subscribed capital,** capital souscrit (*b*) **to subscribe to a newspaper,** être abonné à un journal.

subscriber, *n.* (*a*) *Fin:* **subscriber (for shares),** souscripteur *m* (à des actions) (*b*) **(magazine) subscriber,** abonné(e) (à une revue) (*c*) **telephone subscriber,** abonné(e) du téléphone; *Tp:* **subscriber trunk dialling (STD),** l'automatique *m*.

subscription, *n.* (*a*) *Fin:* **subscription to a loan,** souscription *f* à un emprunt; **subscription by conversion of securities,** sous-

cription en titres; **subscription list,** liste *f* de souscriptions; liste des souscripteurs; **subscription right,** droit *m* de souscription (d'actions) (*b*) **to take out a subscription to a newspaper,** s'abonner/prendre un abonnement à un journal; **subscription form,** bulletin *m* d'abonnement; **subscription rate,** prix *m* de l'abonnement.

subsidiary, *a. & n.* **subsidiary (company),** (*i*) filiale *f*/compagnie affiliée (*ii*) compagnie captive.

subsidize, *v.tr.* subventionner.

subsidy, *n.* subvention *f*; subside *m*; prime *f*; **food subsidies,** subventions à l'alimentation.

substitute[1], *n.* succédané *m*; **substitute products,** produits *m* de remplacement.

substitute[2], *v.tr.* substituer (**for,** à).

substitution, *n.* substitution *f*.

subtenancy, *n.* sous-location *f*.

subtenant, *n.* sous-locataire *mf*.

subvention, *n.* *NAm:* subvention *f*; subside *m*; prime *f*.

subventionary, *a.* (paiement, etc.) subventionnel.

sum, *n.* (*a*) total *m*/montant *m* (*b*) **sum (of money),** somme (d'argent); **large sum,** grosse somme/forte somme; **sum total,** somme totale/somme globale/montant global.

sundry, 1. *a.* divers; **sundry expenses,** frais *mpl* divers **2.** *n.pl.* **sundries,** (frais) divers *mpl*.

supermarket, *n.* supermarché *m*; grande surface.

supertax, *n.* surtaxe *f*.

supervisor, *n.* surveillant(e); agent *m* de maîtrise.

supervisory, *a.* (comité, etc.) de surveillance; **supervisory management,** maîtrise *f*; **supervisory staff,** agent(s) de maîtrise.

supplementary, *a.* supplémentaire (**to,** de); additionnel (**to,** à); *Adm:* **supplementary benefit,** allocation *f*/prestation *f* supplémentaire; *Book-k:* **supplementary entry,** écriture *f* complémentaire; **supplementary taxation,** surimposition *f*; **supplementary wage,** sursalaire *m.*

supplier, *n.* fournisseur/approvisionneur (**of,** en, de); **suppliers' credit,** crédit fournisseur.

supply[1], *n.* (*a*) *PolEc:* **supply and demand,** l'offre *f* et la demande (*b*) **we are expecting a new supply of paint,** nous espérons recevoir bientôt un nouveau stock de peinture; **this paper is in short supply,** ce papier est rare; nous sommes à court de ce (genre de) papier (*c*) *pl.* **supplies,** fournitures *f*; **supplies of money,** fonds *m*/ressources *f.*

supply[2], *v.tr.* **to supply s.o. with sth.,** fournir/approvisionner qn de qch.

support[1], *n.* appui *m*/soutien *m*; **price support,** soutien des prix; **support price,** prix *m* de soutien.

support[2], *v.tr.* soutenir; **to support prices by buying,** soutenir des cours par des achats.

surcharge, *n.* supplément *m*/excédent *m*/ surtaxe *f.*

surety, *n.* (*pers.*) caution *f*/garant(e); répondant(e); donneur *m* d'aval; **surety bond,** cautionnement *m*; **to stand/to go surety for s.o.,** se rendre caution de qn/se porter caution pour qn/se porter garant de qn; **surety for a debt,** garant d'une dette.

surplus, *n.* surplus *m*/excédent *m*; *Fin:* boni *m*; **budget surplus,** excédent budgétaire; **surplus products,** surplus/excédent de produits; **surplus to our requirements,** quantité *f* excédentaire.

surrender[1], *n. Ins:* rachat *m* (d'une police); **surrender value,** valeur *f* de rachat.

surrender[2], *v.tr. Ins:* racheter (une police d'assurance).

surtax[1], *n.* surtaxe *f.*

surtax[2], *v.tr.* surtaxer.

survey, *n.* expertise *f.*

surveyor, *n.* expert *m*; **quantity surveyor,** métreur-vérificateur *m.*

suspend, *v.tr.* (*a*) suspendre; **to suspend payment,** suspendre ses paiements/les paiements; **to suspend work for two days,** interrompre le travail pendant deux jours (*b*) **to suspend (s.o.),** suspendre (qn).

suspense, *n.* (*a*) **bills in suspense,** effets *m* en suspens *m*/en souffrance *f* (*b*) **suspense account,** compte *m* d'ordre.

suspension, *n.* (*a*) suspension *f*; **suspension of payment,** suspension de paiements (*b*) suspension (d'un employé).

swap, *n. Bank:* crédit croisé; swap *m*/ opération de swap; **swaps agreements,** accords d'échanges.

switch, *n.* **switch trading/transaction,** arbitrage *m.*

sympathy, *n.* **sympathy strike,** grève *f* de solidarité; **to come out in sympathy,** se mettre en grève par solidarité.

syndicate[1], *n.* syndicat *m*; consortium *m*; **banking syndicate,** consortium de banques; **financial syndicate,** syndicat financier; **member of a syndicate,** syndicataire *mf*; **underwriting syndicate,** syndicat de garantie; **to form a syndicate,** se syndiquer.

syndicate[2], **1.** *v.tr.* (*a*) syndiquer (une industrie) (*b*) **syndicated shares,** actions syndiquées **2.** *v.i.* se syndiquer.

synthetic, *a.* synthétique/artificiel.

system, *n.* (*a*) système *m*; **accounting system,** système comptable; **computerized information system,** système d'information par ordinateur; **metric system,** système métrique; **integrated management system,** système intégré de gestion; **systems analysis,** analyse *f* des systèmes; **systems analyst,** analyste-programmeur *mf*; **systems engineering,** planification *f* des systèmes; **systems management,** direction systématisée *(b)* **quota system,** contingentement *m*.

systematic, *a*. systématique.

systematization, *n*. systématisation *f*.

systematize, *v.tr.* systématiser.

T

table, *n.* table *f*/tableau *m*/répertoire *m*; **table of contents,** table des matières; **table of weights and measures,** table des poids et mesures; **interest table,** table d'intérêts; *Ins:* **mortality tables/actuaries' tables,** tables de mortalité; **parity table/ table of par values,** table de parités; *Fin:* **redemption table,** tableau d'amortissement.

tabular, *a.* tabulaire; **in tabular form,** disposé en tableau(x).

tabulate, *v.tr.* (*a*) disposer (des chiffres, etc.) en table(s)/en tableau(x) (*b*) classifier (des résultats); cataloguer (des marchandises).

tabulating, *n.* (*a*) = **tabulation** (*b*) **tabulating machine,** tabulatrice *f*.

tabulation, *n.* (*a*) mise *f*/arrangement *m*/ disposition *f* en tableaux (*b*) classification *f* (de résultats); tabulation *f*.

tabulator, *n.* (*a*) (*in punched-card system, etc.*) tabulatrice *f*; **digital tabulator,** tabulatrice numérique (*b*) (*on typewriter*) tabulateur *m*.

tachographe, *n.* tachygraphe *m*/contrôlographe *m*.

tacit, *a.* tacite; **tacit agreement,** accord *m*/convention *f* tacite.

tactical, *a.* tactique; **tactical plan,** plan *m* tactique.

tag, *n.* **(price) tag,** étiquette *f* (indiquant le prix).

take[1], *n.* (*a*) montant reçu/perçu (*b*) part *f* (de bénéfice).

take[2], *v.tr.* (*a*) **to take an amount out of one's income,** prélever une somme sur son revenu (*b*) **to take so much a week,** se faire tant/faire une recette de tant par semaine; **she takes home only £35 a week,** son salaire net n'est que de £35 par semaine (*c*) **he won't take less,** il refuse d'accepter un prix moins élevé (*d*) **to take stock,** dresser/faire l'inventaire (*e*) (*to secretary*) **will you take (down) a letter?** voulez-vous prendre une lettre? (*f*) **to take a partner,** prendre un associé (*g*) **to take legal advice,** consulter un avocat (*h*) **this bottle will take a litre,** cette bouteille contient un litre (*j*) **we take 'The Financial Times',** nous recevons/nous achetons 'The Financial Times' (tous les jours) (*k*) **it will take £8 to buy it,** cela coûtera £8 (*l*) **does the machine take 10p coins?** est-ce que la machine accepte les pièces de 10p?

tak(e)away, *a. & n.* **tak(e)away (shop)** = restaurant qui vend des plats cuisinés (à emporter); **tak(e)away (meal),** plat(s) cuisiné(s) (à emporter).

take back, *v.tr.* reprendre (un employé, des invendus).

take-home, *a.* **take-home pay,** salaire *m* net (après déductions).

take in, *v.tr.* (*a*) *StExch:* **to take in stock,** reporter des titres; **stock taken in,** titres pris en report (*b*) **to take in extra work,** prendre/accepter du travail supplémentaire.

take off, *v.tr.* (*a*) **to take £2 off (the price of sth.),** déduire/rabattre £2 (sur le prix de qch.); **to take 10% off the price,** réduire le prix de 10% (*b*) **to take a day off,** prendre un jour de congé.

take on, *v.tr.* (*a*) engager/embaucher (un

ouvrier); **these workmen have just been taken on,** on vient d'embaucher ces ouvriers (*b*) entreprendre/se charger de/assumer (une besogne, une responsabilité) (*c*) accepter qn (comme client).

take out, *v.tr.* **to take out a patent,** prendre/obtenir un brevet; **to take out an insurance policy,** contracter une assurance/souscrire à une police d'assurance.

take over, *v.tr.* **to take over from s.o.,** relever qn dans ses fonctions; **to take over a business,** prendre la succession d'une maison de commerce/prendre la suite des affaires; **to take over the liabilities,** prendre les dettes à sa charge/prendre le passif; **to take over the receipts and expenditures,** prendre le contrôle des recettes et des dépenses; *Fin:* **to take over an issue,** absorber une émission.

takeover, *n.* prise *f* de contrôle; **takeover bid,** offre publique d'achat (OPA).

taker, *n.* (*a*) (*buyer, lessee*) preneur, -euse (*b*) *StExch:* (*of contangoes*) reporteur *m* (*c*) acheteur, -euse.

take up, *v.tr.* (*a*) **to take up a bill,** honorer un effet; retirer une traite; *StExch:* **to take up an option,** lever une prime; consolider un marché à prime; **to take up a share,** lever un titre; **to take up stock,** prendre livraison de titres (*b*) **to take up a new line of goods,** se charger d'une nouvelle gamme de produits.

takings, *n.pl.* recette *f*/rentrée *f*; **today's takings,** la recette de la journée; **the takings are good,** la recette est bonne.

talk, *n.* **sales talk,** arguments *mpl* de vente; boniment *m*.

tally[1], *n.* (*a*) **the tally trade,** le commerce à tempérament (*b*) pointage *m*; **to keep (a) tally of goods,** pointer des marchandises (sur une liste); **tally clerk/tally keeper,** pointeur *m*/contrôleur *m*/marqueur *m* (de marchandises, etc.); **tally sheet,** feuille *f* de pointage (à la réception des marchandises, etc.); bordereau *m*.

tally[2], **1.** *v.tr.* pointer/contrôler (des marchandises) **2.** *v.i.* correspondre (**with,** à); s'accorder/concorder (**with,** avec); cadrer (**with,** avec); **these accounts do not tally,** ces comptes ne s'accordent pas.

tallying, *n.* pointage *m*/contrôle *m* (de marchandises, etc.).

tallyman, *n.m.* (*a*) pointeur/contrôleur/marqueur (de marchandises, etc.) (*b*) marchand qui vend à tempérament.

talon, *n.* talon *m* (d'une feuille, de coupons); talon de souche.

tangible, *a.* tangible/matériel; **tangible assets,** immobilisations corporelles.

tap, *n.* **bills on tap,** billets placés de gré à gré.

tape, *n.* (*a*) bande *f*/ruban *m*; *Cmptr:* **magnetic tape,** bande magnétique; **perforated tape/punched tape,** bande perforée (*b*) *F:* **red tape,** paperasserie *f*/ bureaucratie *f*.

tare[1], *n.* tare *f*; **actual tare,** tare réelle; **average tare,** tare moyenne/tare par épreuve; **extra tare,** surtare *f*; **to ascertain/to allow for the tare,** faire la tare; **allowance for tare,** (*i*) tarage *m* (*ii*) la tare.

tare[2], *v.tr.* tarer (un emballage, etc.); faire la tare.

target, *n.* but *m*/objectif *m*; **production target,** objectif de production; **target consumers,** consommateurs-cible(s) *m*; **target setting,** fixation *f* des objectifs.

tariff[1], *n.* (*a*) liste *f*/tableau *m* (des prix); **tariff (catalogue),** tarif *m* (*b*) **customs tariff,** tarif douanier/tarif d'importation; **full tariff,** plein tarif; **preferential tariff,** tarif préférentiel; **reduced tariff,** tarif réduit; **tariff agreement,** accord *m* tarifaire; **tariff barriers/tariff walls,** barrières douanières; **tariff laws,** lois *f* tarifaires; **tariff-level indices,** taux *m* indices des tarifs; **multi-part tariff,** tarification séparée des coûts fixes et des coûts mobiles.

tariff[2], *v.tr.* tarifier (des marchandises, etc.).

tariffing, *n.* tarification *f*.

taring *n.* tarage *m*.

task, *n.* tâche *f*; **task force**, groupe d'intervention; **task group**, groupe *m* de travail; **task management**, supervision *f* des travaux; **task work**, travail *m* à la tâche; travail aux pièces.

tax[1], *n.* impôt *m*/contribution *f*/taxe *f*; **(profit) after tax**, (profit) après impôt/(profit) net; **airport tax**, taxe d'aéroport; **betting tax**, taxe sur les paris; **capital gains tax**, impôt sur les plus-values; **capital transfer tax**, droits *mpl* de succession; **corporation tax**, impôt sur les sociétés; **direct/indirect tax**, impôt direct/indirect; **entertainment tax**, taxe sur les spectacles; **exceptional/special taxes**, (*i*) taxes parafiscales (*ii*) parafiscalité *f*; **graduated income tax**, impôt progressif sur le revenu; **income tax**, impôt sur le revenu; **income tax return**, déclaration de revenu/feuille d'impôt; **land tax**, impôt foncier; **luxury tax**, taxe de luxe; **purchase tax**, taxe à l'achat; **turnover tax**, impôt sur le chiffre d'affaires; **value-added tax (VAT)**, taxe à la valeur ajoutée (TVA); **wealth tax**, impôt sur la fortune; **tax adjustment/back tax**, redressement *m* d'impôt; **tax bracket**, tranche *f* d'imposition; **tax code**, cédule *f* d'impôt; **tax collection**, perception *f*/ recouvrement *m* de l'impôt; **tax collector**, percepteur d'impôt; *StExch:* **tax credit**, avoir fiscal/crédit d'impôt; **tax cuts**, dégrèvement *m* d'impôt; **tax deducted at source**, impôt retenu à la base/à la source; **tax exemption**, exemption *f* d'impôt; **tax-free**/*NAm:* **tax exempt**, net d'impôt; exonéré d'impôt; **tax form**, déclaration *f* d'impôt; **tax haven**, asile/paradis fiscal; **tax office**, (bureau de) perception *f*; **tax reduction/tax relief**, dégrèvement d'impôt; **tax rules**, lois fiscales; **tax schedule**, barème *m* d'imposition; **tax shelter**, avantage fiscal; **tax system**, système fiscal; **tax year**, année fiscale; **to pay taxes**, payer des taxes/des contributions; **I paid £500 in tax**, j'ai payé £500 d'impôt; **it gives me £25 interest less tax**, je reçois un intérêt de £25 avant impôt; **this benefit is liable to tax**, ce bénéfice est assujetti à l'impôt; **to levy a tax on sth.**, frapper qch. d'un droit.

tax[2], *v.tr.* (*a*) taxer/imposer (les objets de luxe, etc.); frapper (qch.) d'un impôt; **to tax income**, imposer (des droits sur) le revenu; **highly taxed/low-taxed goods**, marchandises fortement/faiblement taxées (*b*) imposer (qn); **to be heavily taxed**, être lourdement imposé.

taxable, *a.* (revenu, terrain, etc.) imposable/taxable; **taxable article**, bien *m* taxable; **taxable class of goods**, catégorie *f* de biens taxable; **taxable income**, revenu *m* imposable; **taxable year**, exercice fiscal.

taxation, *n.* (*a*) imposition *f* (de la propriété, etc.); taxation *f*; **the taxation authorities**, l'administration fiscale (*b*) charges fiscales; prélèvement fiscal; **commensurate taxation**, équivalence *f* des charges fiscales; **excessive taxation**, fiscalité excessive; **highest scale of taxation**, maximum *m* de perception; **supplementary taxation**, surimposition *f*/surtaxe *f*; **double taxation relief**, suppression *f* de la double imposition; **profit after taxation**, profit après impôt/profit net (*c*) revenu réalisé par les impôts; impôts *mpl*.

taxing, *a.* **taxing authorities**, autorités fiscales.

taxpayer, *n.* contribuable *mf*.

team[1], *n.* équipe *f* (d'ouvriers, etc.); **sales team**, équipe commerciale/de vente.

team[2], *v.tr. NAm:* camionner (des marchandises).

teamster, *n. NAm:* camionneur *m*/routier *m*.

teamwork, *n.* travail *m* d'équipe.

teaser, *n.* **teaser ad**, publicité *f* mystère.

technique, *n.* technique; **management techniques**, techniques de gestion; **marketing techniques**, techniques commerciales; **merchandising techniques,** techniques marchandes.

technology, *n.* technologie *f;* **advanced technology,** technologie de pointe.

Telecom, *n. R.t.m* **British Telecom,** service des télécommunications (en G.-B.).

telecommunication, *n.* télécommunication *f.*

telecopier, *n.* télécopieur *m.*

telegram, *n.* télégramme *m*/dépêche *f* (télégraphique); **to send s.o. a telegram,** envoyer un télégramme à qn.

telegraph[1], *n.* télégraphe *m;* **telegraph service,** service *m* télégraphique.

telegraph[2], *v.tr. & i.* télégraphier; câbler; envoyer un télégramme; **to telegraph an order,** câbler/télégraphier une commande.

telegraphic, *a.* télégraphique; **telegraphic address,** adresse *f* télégraphique.

telematics, *n.* télématique *f.*

teleorder[1], *n.* commande par ordinateur.

teleorder[2], *v.tr.* commander par ordinateur.

teleordering, *n.* (placement de) commandes par ordinateur.

telephone[1], *n.* téléphone *m;* **automatic telephone,** (téléphone) automatique *m;* **house telephone,** téléphone intérieur; **telephone call,** appel *m* téléphonique; coup *m* de téléphone/de fil; **to speak to s.o. on the telephone,** parler à qn au téléphone; **to be on the telephone,** (*i*) être abonné au téléphone (*ii*) parler au téléphone (*iii*) téléphoner; **telephone directory/book,** annuaire *m* des téléphones/annuaire téléphonique/*F:* bottin *m;* **telephone exchange,** centrale *f* téléphonique; **telephone operator,** téléphoniste *mf*/standardiste *mf;* **telephone subscriber,** abonné(e) du téléphone; **telephone order,** commande téléphonique/

par téléphone; **to order sth. by telephone,** commander qch. par téléphone.

telephone[2], *v.tr. & i.* téléphoner (à qn); **we telephoned him the news,** nous lui avons transmis la nouvelle par téléphone.

telephonist, *n.* téléphoniste *mf.*

teleprinter, *n.* téléimprimeur *m*/téléscripteur *m*/(appareil) télétype *m;* **teleprinter operator,** télétypiste *mf.*

teleprinting, *n.* télétypie *f.*

teleprocessing, *n.* télétraitement *m;* téléinformatique *f;* télégestion *f.*

telesale, *n.* vente *f* par téléphone; **telesales person,** télé-vendeur, -euse.

teletypewriter, *n. NAm:* = **teleprinter.**

teletypist, *n.* télétypiste *mf.*

telewriter, *n.* = **teleprinter.**

Telex, *n. Rtm:* (*a*) (poste) Télex *m;* **Telex subscriber,** abonné(e) au service Télex; **Telex user,** usager *m* du Télex; **Telex rate,** tarif *m* Télex; **Telex operator,** télexiste *mf;* **Telex network,** réseau *m* Télex; **to send by Telex,** envoyer par Télex; **we received this order by Telex,** nous avons reçu cette commande par Télex (*b*) (communication) télex *m;* **I received a Telex,** j'ai reçu un télex.

telex, *v.tr.* envoyer par Télex (*Rtm*); **to telex Canada,** envoyer un télex au Canada; **to telex information,** envoyer un renseignement par Télex.

teller, *n.* **1.** caissier, -ière; préposé(e) à la caisse/au guichet; guichetier, -ière **2.** caisse *f; NAm:* **automated teller,** guichet *m* libre-service/automatique.

temp, *n.* secrétaire *mf* qui fait de l'intérim.

temping, *n.* intérim *m.*

temporary, *a.* temporaire/provisoire; *Cust:* **passed for temporary importation,** admis en franchise temporaire; **temporary measures,** mesures *f* provisoires/

temporaires; **temporary post,** (*i*) fonction *f* intérimaire/provisoire (*ii*) travail *m* temporaire; intérim *m*; **temporary secretary,** secrétaire qui fait de l'intérim; **temporary staff,** personnel *m* temporaire.

tenancy, *n.* location *f*; **terms of tenancy,** conditions *f* de location; **during my tenancy,** pendant la durée de mon bail/ pendant que j'étais locataire.

tenant, *n.* locataire *mf*; **sitting tenant,** locataire en possession des lieux; **tenant's repairs,** réparations locatives; **tenant's risks,** risques locatifs.

tendency, *n.* tendance *f*/inclination *f*/ disposition *f* (**to,** à); **deflationary tendency,** tendance déflationniste; **tendencies of the market,** tendances du marché; **strong upward tendency/bullish tendency,** forte poussée vers la hausse; **strong downward tendency/bearish tendency,** forte poussée vers la baisse.

tender[1], *n.* **1.** offre *f*/soumission *f*; **to put a new hospital out to tender/to invite tenders for a new hospital,** faire un appel d'offres pour la construction d'un nouvel hôpital/mettre en adjudication la construction d'un nouvel hôpital; **allocation to lowest tender,** adjudication *f* au rabais; **by tender,** par voie d'adjudication; **to send in a tender/to put in a tender,** soumissioner/faire une soumission; *NAm:* **to make a tender offer,** faire une offre/ une soumission; **sealed tender,** soumission cachetée; **tenders for loans,** soumissions d'emprunt **2. legal tender,** cours légal; (*of money*) **to be legal tender,** avoir cours légal; avoir pouvoir/force libératoire.

tender[2], **1.** *v.i.* **to tender for a contract,** faire une soumission (pour une adjudication)/soumissionner (une adjudication); **to tender for a supply of goods,** soumissionner une fourniture de marchandises; **party tendering for work on contract,** soumissionnaire *m* **2.** *v.tr.* offrir (ses

services, une somme, etc.); **to tender one's resignation,** donner sa démission.

tenderer, *n.* soumissionnaire *m*; **allocation to lowest tenderer,** adjudication *f* au rabais; **successful tenderer for a contract,** adjudicataire *m*.

tendering, *n.* soumission *f*.

tenure, *n.* (période de) jouissance *f*; (période d')occupation *f* (d'une propriété, d'un poste, etc.); **security of tenure,** (*i*) bail assuré (*ii*) stabilité *f*/sécurité *f* d'un emploi.

term, *n.* **1.** (*a*) (terme d')échéance *f* (d'une lettre de change); **term deposit,** dépôt *m* à terme; **term loan,** prêt *m* à terme (*b*) terme *m*/période *f*/durée *f*; **term day,** (jour du) terme *m* (du loyer); **term of a lease,** terme/durée d'un bail; **the loan shall be for a term of ten years,** l'emprunt sera conclu pour dix ans; **during his term of office,** pendant la durée de ses fonctions; (*to employee or employer*) **term of notice,** délai *m* de congé **2.** *pl.* **terms,** (*a*) conditions *f*/clauses *f*/termes/teneur *f* (d'un contrat); *Fin:* **terms of an issue,** conditions d'une émission; **terms and conditions of an issue,** modalités *f* d'une émission (*b*) **cash terms,** paiement *m* (au) comptant; **terms of payment,** modalités *f* de paiement; **terms inclusive,** tout compris; **to buy sth. on easy terms,** acheter qch. avec facilités de paiement.

terminable, *a.* (*of contract, etc.*) résiliable/résoluble; (*of annuity*) terminable.

terminal[1], *a.* (*a*) **terminal charges,** charges terminales (*b*) *StExch:* **terminal market,** marché *m* à terme/du terme; **terminal price,** cours *m* du livrable.

terminal[2], *n.* (*of buses, containers, etc.*) terminus *m*; tête *f* de ligne; **air terminal,** aérogare *f*; **computer terminal,** terminal *m*.

terminate, *v.tr.* (*a*) terminer (*b*) **to terminate a contract,** résilier/résoudre/ annuler/révoquer (un contrat).

termination, *n.* **termination of a contract,** résiliation *f*/annulation *f* d'un contrat.

territory, *n.* **(representative's) territory,** région (assignée à un représentant); **sales territory,** territoire *m* de vente.

tertiary, *a.* tertiaire; **tertiary industries,** secteur *m* tertiaire.

test[1], *n.* (*a*) essai *m*/épreuve *f*; test *m*; **aptitude test,** test d'aptitude; **feasibility test,** essai *m* probatoire; **market test,** test de vente; **test drive (for cars),** essai *m* (de voitures); **test certificate,** certificat *m* d'essai.

test[2], *v.tr.* (*a*) éprouver (qn, qch.); mettre (qn, qch.) à l'épreuve/à l'essai (*b*) essayer (une machine, etc.); contrôler/ vérifier (des poids et mesures, etc.); **to test out a scheme,** essayer un projet.

test-drive, *v.tr.* **to test-drive a car,** faire l'essai d'une voiture.

testimonial, *n.* certificat *m*; (lettre de) recommandation *f*; attestation *f*.

testing, *n.* (*a*) essai *m*/épreuve *f* (d'une machine, etc.); contrôle *m* (des poids et mesures, etc.) (*b*) **field testing,** test *m* sur place; **product testing,** test de produit.

text, *n.* texte *m* (d'une police d'assurance, d'un télégramme, etc.).

theme, *n.* thème *m*; **advertising theme,** thème publicitaire.

theory, *n.* théorie *f*; **information theory,** théorie de l'information; **management theory,** théorie de la gestion de l'entreprise.

third[1], *n.* (*a*) tiers *m*; **to lose a third/two thirds of one's money,** perdre le tiers/les deux tiers de son argent; **discount of a third/a third off,** remise *f* d'un tiers (du prix) (*b*) **third of exchange,** troisième *f* de change.

third[2], *a.* (*a*) troisième; **third copy,** triplicata *m* (*b*) **a third party,** une tierce personne/un tiers; *Jur:* **in the hands of a third party,** en main tierce; **third-party insurance,** assurance *f* au tiers.

threshold, *n. EEC:* **threshold price,** prix *m* du seuil.

thriving, *a.* (*of pers., industry*) prospère/ florissant.

throughput, *n.* (*i*) débit *m*/rendement *m* (*ii*) capacité *f* de traitement.

throw-outs, *n.pl.* rebuts *m*/articles défectueux/pièces *f* de rebut.

tick[1], *n. F:* crédit *m*; **to buy sth. on tick,** acheter qch. à crédit.

tick[2], *v.tr.* (*on a form*) **tick the appropriate box,** cocher la case correspondante.

ticket, *n.* (*a*) billet *m*/ticket *m*; **book of tickets,** carnet *m* de tickets; **entrance ticket,** ticket *m* d'admission; **season ticket,** abonnement *m* = carte *f* (orange, etc.); **single ticket,** aller *m* (simple); **return ticket,** (billet d')aller (et) retour *m* (*b*) **baggage ticket,** bulletin *m*/ticket de bagages; **price ticket,** étiquette *f* (portant le prix) (*c*) *StExch:* fiche *f*; **ticket day,** deuxième jour de liquidation.

tie up, *v.tr.* **to tie up money,** immobiliser des capitaux; **to tie up a block of shares,** bloquer une tranche d'actions.

tie-up, *n.* (*a*) **tie-up of capital,** blocage *m*/ immobilisation *f* de capitaux (*b*) association *f* (de maisons de commerce, etc.).

tight, *a.* (*a*) **tight money,** argent *m* rare (*b*) **tight bargain,** transaction *f* qui laisse très peu de marge; **tight discount,** escompte serré.

till, *n.* tiroir-caisse *m*; **till money,** encaisse *f* (d'un magasin).

time, *n.* (*a*) temps *m*; **idle time,** temps mort; **time and motion consultant,** organisateur-conseil *m*; **time and methods study,** étude *f* des temps et (des) méthodes; **time and motion study,** étude des temps et (des) mouvements (*b*) heure *f*; **closing time,** heure de fermeture; **opening time,** heure d'ouverture; **time card/time sheet,** feuille *f* de présence; semainier *m*; **time of arrival,**

heure d'arrivée; **time of departure,** heure de départ; **time work,** travail *m* à l'heure; **overtime counts (as) time and a half,** les heures supplémentaires sont payées une fois et demie le tarif normal; **to get double time on Sundays,** les heures du dimanche sont comptées double (*c*) terme *m*; *NAm:* **time deposit,** dépôt *m* à terme; **time draft,** traite *f* à échéance; *Ins:* **time policy,** police *f* à terme; police à forfait (*d*) délai *m*; **to ask for time (to pay),** demander un délai/un terme de grâce; **latest time,** délai de rigueur; **prescribed time,** délai réglementaire; **strict time limit,** délai péremptoire; **within a reasonable time,** dans un délai raisonnable.

timetable, *n.* horaire *m*; indicateur *m* (de chemin de fer).

tinned, *a.* (*of food*) en conserve/en boîte.

title, *n.* **title deed,** titre *m* (constitutif) de propriété.

today, *adv.* aujourd'hui; **today's price,** le prix du jour; **today's menu/today's special,** menu *m*/plat *m* du jour.

token, *n.* (*a*) **token payment,** paiement *m* symbolique (*b*) **token money,** monnaie *f* fiduciaire (*c*) **token strike,** grève *f* d'avertissement (*d*) **book token,** chèque-livre *m*; **gift token,** bon-cadeau *m*/chèque-cadeau *m*.

tolerance, *n. Cust:* tolérance (permise).

toll, *n.* (*a*) péage *m*; **toll bridge/road,** pont *m*/route *f* à péage (*b*) *NAm: Tp:* frais *mpl* d'interurbain.

toll free, *adv. NAm:* **to call (s.o.) toll free** = faire un libre-appel.

ton *n.* **1.** tonne *f*; **long ton/gross ton (of 2240 lb** = 1016.06 kg), tonne forte; **short ton/ net ton (of 2000 lb** = 907.185 kg), tonne courte; **metric ton (of 1000 kg** = 2204.6 lb), tonne métrique **2.** *Nau:* (*a*) tonneau *m* (de jauge) (*b*) **measurement ton,** tonne d'arrimage/d'encombrement (*c*) **freight ton,** tonne d'affrètement.

tonnage, *n. Nau:* tonnage *m*/jauge *f*; capacité *f* de chargement (d'un navire);

gross tonnage, tonnage brut; jauge brute; **net tonnage,** jauge nette; **deadweight tonnage,** tonnage réel; **register(ed) tonnage,** tonnage net; tonnage de jauge.

tonne, *n.* tonne *f* métrique.

tool, *n.* outil *m*; **to down tools,** (*i*) cesser de travailler (*ii*) se mettre en grève.

top, *a.* supérieur; **top management,** haute direction/cadres supérieurs/dirigeants; **top priority,** urgence *f*; **top quality,** (de) première qualité/qualité supérieure.

tot, 1. *v.tr.* additionner/faire le total; **to tot up expenses,** faire le compte des dépenses **2.** *v.i.* (*of expenses, etc.*) **to tot up,** s'élever (**to,** à).

total[1]**, 1.** *a.* total; entier; complet; global; **total amount,** somme totale/globale; montant total/global; **total assets,** total *m* de l'actif; **total cost,** prix de revient total; **total expenses,** montant total des dépenses; **total liabilities,** total du passif; **total loss,** perte totale; **total output,** production totale; **total revenue,** recette totale **2.** *n.* total *m*; montant *m*; **sum total/grand total,** total global; **to calculate the total of the amounts,** faire le total des sommes; **the total comes to £105,** cela fait au total £105.

total[2]**,** *v.tr. & i.* (*a*) additionner/totaliser (les dépenses, etc.) (*b*) **to total (up to)** . . .**,** s'élever à/se monter à . . . .

totalization, *n.* totalisation *f*.

totalizator, *n.* (appareil) totalisateur *m*; machine totalisatrice.

totalize, *v.tr.* totaliser/additionner (les dépenses, etc.).

touch, *n.* **to be in touch with s.o.,** être en contact avec qn; **to get in touch with s.o.,** entrer en contact avec qn/contacter qn/ joindre qn.

tour, *n.* visite *f*/voyage *m*/séjour *m* organisé; **conducted tour,** visite guidée; **package tour,** voyage/séjour organisé; **tour operator,** (*i*) agence de voyages

organisés; tour-operator (*ii*) organisateur, -trice de voyages (en groupes).

tourism, *n.* tourisme *m*.

tourist, *n.* touriste *mf*; **tourist bureau/
office,** bureau *m* de tourisme; Syndicat *m*
d'Initiative; *Nau: Av:* **tourist information,** renseignements *m* touristiques; **the
tourist trade,** le tourisme.

town, *n.* ville *f*; cité *f*; **town hall,** hôtel *m* de
ville; **town planning,** urbanisme *m*.

trade[1], *n.* (*a*) métier *m*; **to carry on a trade,**
exercer un métier (*b*) commerce *m*/
négoce *m*/affaires *fpl*; **export trade,**
commerce d'exportation; **foreign trade/
overseas trade,** commerce extérieur/
avec l'étranger; **home trade/domestic
trade,** commerce intérieur; **import
trade,** commerce d'importation; *Nau:*
coastal/coasting trade, cabotage *m*; **to
be in the tea trade,** faire le commerce
du thé; **to do a good trade,** faire de bonnes
affaires; **to do a roaring trade,** faire des
affaires d'or; **to be in trade,** être dans le
commerce; **by way of trade,** commercialement; **trade is at a standstill,** les
affaires ne vont pas/le commerce est nul
(*c*) **trade agreement,** convention *f*/traité
m de commerce; **trade allowance,** remise *f*/
escompte *m*; **trade bank,** banque *f* de
commerce; banque commerciale; **trade
bills,** effets *m* de commerce; **trade card,**
carte *f* d'affaires; **trade catalogue,** tarif *m*;
catalogue général (complet); **trade
credit,** crédit *m* fournisseur; **trade discount,** remise *f* d'usage; **trade gap,** déficit
commercial; **trade name,** nom déposé;
marque *f* de commerce; **trade price,** prix
m de gros; **trade route,** route commerciale; **trade union,** syndicat *m*; **trade
union member,** syndicaliste *mf*; **trade
unionist,** syndiqué(e); **trade unionism,**
syndicalisme *m*; **trade union tariff,** tarif
syndical.

trade[2], *v.i.* faire le commerce (**in,** de);
faire des affaires/entretenir des relations
commerciales (**with s.o.,** avec qn); **he
trades in wines,** il est négociant en vins.

trade in, *v.tr.* donner (qch.) en reprise; **I
am buying a new car and trading in my old
one,** j'achète une nouvelle voiture et
donne ma vieille en reprise.

trade-in, *n.* **trade-in allowance/price,** contre-valeur *f*; prix à la reprise/valeur *f* de
reprise.

trademark, *n.* marque *f* de fabrique; **maker's trademark,** cachet *m* du fabricant;
registered trademark, marque déposée.

trade-off, *n.* échange *m*; compromis *m*/
concession *f*.

trader, *n.* négociant(e)/commerçant(e)/
marchand(e); **private trader,** mar-
chand(e) établi(e) à son propre compte.

tradesman, *n.m.* marchand/fournisseur;
tradesmen's entrance, entrée *f* des fournisseurs.

tradespeople, *n.pl.* commerçants *m*/
marchands *m*/fournisseurs *m*.

trading, *n.* commerce *m*; négoce *m*; **trading account,** compte *m* d'exploitation;
trading area, territoire *m* de vente; **trading assets,** actif engagé; **trading capital,**
capital engagé/capital de roulement;
trading company, entreprise *f*/société *f*
commerciale; **trading estate,** zone industrielle; **trading port,** port *m* de commerce; **trading profit,** bénéfice *m* d'ex-
ploitation/bénéfice brut; **trading stamp,**
timbre-prime *m*; **trading vessel,** navire
marchand/de commerce; **trading year,**
exercice *m* comptable.

traffic, *n.* **freight traffic/goods traffic,** trafic
de marchandises; **passenger traffic,** trafic
de voyageurs/de passagers.

train[1], *n.* train *m*; **goods train,** train de
marchandises; **passenger and goods train,**
train mixte.

train[2], *v.tr.* former/instruire (qn); **to train/
to be training as a bricklayer,** être apprenti maçon; **trained personnel,** personnel qualifié/ayant reçu la formation requise.

trainee, *n.* stagiaire *mf*; apprenti(e).

training, *n.* éducation *f*/instruction *f*; formation *f*; perfectionnement *m*; **booster training/vocational training,** formation professionnelle; **to have had a business training,** avoir reçu une formation commerciale; **on-the-job training,** formation sur le tas; **in-plant training,** formation dans l'entreprise; **training officer,** directeur *m* de formation; **training time,** temps *m* de formation; **vocational training,** formation professionnelle.

transact, *v.tr.* **to transact business with s.o.,** faire des affaires/traiter des affaires avec qn.

transaction, *n.* transaction *f*/opération (commerciale); affaire (faite); **cash transaction,** opération/transaction au comptant; **commercial transaction,** transaction/opération commerciale; **loan transactions,** transactions à crédit; *StExch:* **Stock Exchange transactions,** opérations de Bourse; **transaction for the account,** négociation *f*/opération à terme; **forward exchange transactions,** opérations/négociations de change à terme.

transactor, *n.* négociateur, -trice (d'une affaire).

transfer[1], *n.* (*a*) transport *m*/renvoi *m* (de qch. à un autre endroit); déplacement *m*/mutation *f* (d'un fonctionnaire); **staff transfer,** transfert *m* de personnel; *Rail: Av:* transbordement *m* (de marchandises, de voyageurs) (*b*) transfert/transmission *f* (d'un droit, etc.); **transfer of a debt,** cession *f*/revirement *m* d'une créance; **transfer book/transfer register,** journal *m*/registre *m* des transferts; *StExch:* **transfer of shares,** transfert d'actions; **transfer form,** formule *f* de transfert (*c*) *Book-k:* contre-passement *m*/contre-passation *f* (d'une écriture); transport/ristourne *f* (d'une somme d'un compte à un autre); **transfer entry,** article *m* de contre-passement; *Bank: etc:* **credit transfer,** virement *m* de crédits; **transfer agent,** agent *m* comptable des transferts; **transfer pricing,** prix *m* de transfert interne; **transfer of account (from one bank to another),** transfert-paiement *m*;

transfer of funds, virement *m* de fonds (*d*) *Jur:* **transfer deed,** (*i*) acte *m* de cession; acte translatif (de proprété) (*ii*) *StExch:* (feuille de) transfert.

transfer[2], *v.tr.* (*a*) transférer (des actions, etc.); **to transfer a bill by endorsement,** transférer un billet par voie d'endossement (*b*) *Book-k:* **to transfer a debt,** transporter une créance (*c*) déplacer/transférer/muter (le personnel); transférer (un bureau, un magasin); *Rail: Av:* transborder (des marchandises) (*d*) virer (une somme) (*e*) *Jur:* céder/transmettre (une propriété).

transferable, *a.* transférable/transmissible; *Jur:* (droit, bien) cessible; (droit) communicable/transférable; *Fin:* **transferable securities,** valeurs mobilières négociables/cessibles; (*of ticket, etc.*) **not transferable,** non cessible/personnel.

transferee, *n. Jur: Fin:* bénéficiaire *mf*; cessionnaire *mf* (d'un bien, d'un effet de commerce, etc.).

transference, *n.* transfert *m*.

transferor, *n. Jur:* cédant(e); endosseur *m* (d'un effet de commerce); cessionnaire *mf*.

transient, *n. NAm:* voyageur *m* de passage/*F:* un passage.

transire, *n. Cust:* passavant *m*/laissezpasser *m inv*/acquit-à-caution *m* (délivré au capitaine d'un cabotier).

transit, *n.* (*a*) transit *m*; **(passengers, goods) in transit,** (passagers, marchandises) en transit; **(warehoused) goods for transit,** marchandises de transit; **to convey goods in transit,** transiter des marchandises; (*of goods*) **transit trade,** commerce *m* transitaire; *Cust:* **transit visa/permit,** document *m*/visa *m* de transit (*b*) transport *m* (de marchandises); **damage in transit,** avarie(s) *f(pl)* en cours de route; **loss in transit,** freinte *f* de route.

transmission, *n.* (*a*) transmission *f* (d'un colis, d'un message, etc.) (*b*) **transmis-**

sion of shares, cession *f*/transfert *m* d'actions.

transport[1], *n*. 1. = transportation 2. transport *m*; air transport, transport aérien/par avion; rail transport, transport par chemin de fer; river transport, transport fluvial; road transport, transport routier; transport by sea, transport maritime; means of transport, moyen *m*/mode *m* de transport; transport by lorry/by truck, transport par camion/camionnage *m*; transport agent, transitaire *m*; transport aircraft, avion *m* de transport; transport company, compagnie *f*/société *f*/entreprise *f* de transport.

transport[2], *v.tr.* transporter (des marchandises, des voyageurs); to transport goods by lorry/by truck, camionner des marchandises/transporter des marchandises par camion; to transport goods by rail/*NAm*: by railroad, transporter des marchandises par chemin de fer.

transportable, *a*. (*of goods, etc.*) transportable.

transportation, *n.* transport *m*; transportation method, méthode *f* des transports.

transporter, *n.* (*pers.*) transporteur *m*/entrepreneur *m* de transports.

travel[1], *n.* voyages *mpl*; travel agency, agence *f* de voyages; agence/bureau *m* de tourisme.

travel[2], *v.i.* to travel for a firm, représenter une maison de commerce; être représentant d'une société.

travel(l)er, *n.* 1. travel(l)er's cheque, chèque *m* de voyage 2. (commercial) travel(l)er, représentant(e) (de commerce)/délégué(e) commercial(e).

travelling, *n.* voyages *mpl*; travelling allowance, indemnité *f* de déplacement; travelling expenses, frais *mpl* de représentation; frais de déplacement.

treasurer, *n.* trésorier, -ière; treasurer's report, rapport financier; treasurer's office, trésorerie *f*.

treasury, *n.* (*a*) trésor (public); trésorerie *f*; treasury bills/bonds, bons *m* du Trésor (*b*) purchase of shares for Treasury, (r)achat *m* par une société de ses propres actions; Treasury stocks/shares, actions appartenant en propre à une société.

treat, *v.i.* to treat with one's creditors, traiter/négocier avec ses créanciers.

treble[1], 1. *a*. triple 2. *n*. triple *m* 3. *adv*. trois fois autant.

treble[2], *v.tr. & i.* tripler; prices have trebled in two years, les prix ont triplé en deux ans; the value of the house has trebled, la maison a triplé de valeur.

trend, *n.* (*a*) tendance *f*/orientation *f*; the trend of prices, la tendance des prix; downward trend, tendance à la baisse; economic trend, tendance/évolution *f* économique; the general trend of the market, les tendances du marché; upward trend, tendance à la hausse (*b*) the latest trend in footwear, souliers dernier cri.

trial, *n.* 1. essai *m*; to give sth. a trial, faire l'essai de qch.; on trial, à l'essai; trial lot, envoi *m* à titre d'essai; trial order, commande *f* à l'essai 2. *Book-k*: trial balance, balance générale 3. procès *m*; to stand trial, passer en jugement.

tribunal, *n.* tribunal *m*.

trip, *n.* business trip, voyage *m* d'affaires.

triple[1], 1. *a*. triple 2. *adv*. trois fois autant.

triple[2], *v.tr. & i.* tripler.

triplicate[1], *n.* troisième copie; triplicata *m*; invoice in triplicate, facture *f* en trois exemplaires.

triplicate[2], *v.tr.* rédiger (un document) en trois exemplaires.

trouble, *n.* conflit *m*/difficulté *f*; labour troubles, conflits ouvriers.

troubleshooter, *n.* médiateur *m*/conciliateur *m*.

truck[1], *n.* camion *m*.

truck², *v.tr. NAm:* camionner.

trucking, *n. NAm:* camionnage *m.*

trust, *n.* **1.** confiance *f* (**in**, en); **breach of trust**, abus *m* de confiance; **position of trust**, poste *m* de confiance **2.** *Jur:* (*i*) fidéicommis *m* (*ii*) fiducie *f*; **beneficiary of a trust**, fidéicommissaire *mf*; **trust deed**, acte *m* de fidéicommis **3.** *Fin:* (*i*) trust *m*/cartel *m* (*ii*) trust/société *f* holding (*iii*) syndicat *m* (de copropriété); **investment trust**, société de placement(s)/d'investissement(s); **securities in trust**, valeurs mises en trust; **vertical trust**, trust vertical; **to group into a trust**, truster; **organizer/administrator of a trust**, trusteur *m.*

trustee, *n. Jur:* (*a*) (*of testamentary estate*) fiduciaire *mf*/héritier *m* fiduciaire/grevé *m* de fiducie/grevé de restitution (*b*) (*with powers of attorney*) mandataire *mf*; **public trustee** (**in bankruptcy**), syndic *m* (de faillite).

turn, *n. Fin:* (*a*) **turn of the market/jobber's turn**, marge *f* (entre le prix d'achat et le prix de vente) d'un contrepartiste (*b*) **stock turn**/*NAm:* **inventory turn**, rotation *f* des stocks.

turn around *v.tr.* = **turn round**.

turn down, *v.tr.* **to turn down an applicant**, refuser un candidat; **to turn down a claim**, écarter une réclamation; **to turn down an offer**, rejeter une offre.

turnkey, *a.* **turnkey operation/project**, (projet de) bâtiment livré clef en main; **turnkey operator**, ensemblier *m.*

turn out, *v.tr.* produire/fabriquer (des marchandises).

turnout, *n.* rendement *m* (d'une machine, d'une usine, etc.).

turn over, *v.tr.* **he turns over £1 000 a week**, son chiffre d'affaires est de £1 000 par semaine; **to turn over capital**, faire rouler les capitaux.

turnover, *n.* (*a*) (**sales**) **turnover**, chiffre *m* d'affaires; **his turnover is £50 000 per annum**, il fait £50 000 d'affaires par an; **turnover tax**, impôt *m* sur le chiffre d'affaires (*b*) *NAm:* **inventory turnover**, rotation *f* (des stocks); **staff turnover**, rotation du personnel; **turnover rate**, vitesse *f* de rotation des stocks.

turn round, *v.tr.* **the stocks are turned round every four months**, le délai de rotation (des stocks) est de quatre mois.

turnround, *n.* **1.** renversement *m*/revirement *m*/retournement (de situation) **2. turnround of stocks**, rotation des stocks.

tycoon, *n.* magnat *m.*

type, *v.tr. & i.* écrire/taper (à la machine)/dactylographier (une lettre, etc.).

typewriter, *n.* machine *f* à écrire; **golfball typewriter**, machine à écrire à boule/à sphère; **portable typewriter**, machine à écrire portative.

typewritten, *a.* (document, etc.) dactylographié/écrit à la machine/tapé (à la machine).

typing, *n.* dactylographie *f*/*F:* dactylo *f*; **typing error**, faute *f* de frappe; **typing paper**, papier *m* (pour) machine (à écrire); **typing pool**, équipe *f* de dactylos; **shorthand typing**, sténodactylographie *f.*

typist, *n.* dactylographe *mf*/dactylo *mf*; **shorthand typist**, sténodactylo *mf.*

U

ultimo, *abbr:* **ult,** *adv. Corr:* **your letter of 22 ult(imo),** votre lettre du 22 écoulé.

umbrella, *n.* **umbrella committee,** comité *m* de coordination.

unabridged, *a.* **unabridged edition,** édition *f* complète/intégrale.

unaccepted, *a.* **unaccepted bill,** effet non accepté.

unaccounted, *a.* **these sixty pounds are unaccounted for in the balance-sheet,** ces soixante livres ne figurent pas au bilan; **three articles are still unaccounted for,** il manque toujours trois articles.

unallotted, *a. Fin:* **unallotted shares,** actions non réparties.

unanimous, *a.* unanime; **unanimous consent,** consentement *m* unanime; **unanimous vote,** vote *m* à l'unanimité.

unanimously, *adv.* **he was elected unanimously,** il a été élu à l'unanimité.

unappropriated, *a.* (argent, etc.) inutilisé/disponible; fonds *mpl* sans application déterminée.

unassigned, *a.* **unassigned revenue,** recettes non affectées (en garantie).

unassured, *a. Ins:* non assuré.

unaudited, *a.* **unaudited figures,** chiffres non certifiés.

unauthorized, *a.* non autorisé; sans autorisation; (commerce, etc.) illicite; *P.N:* **no entry to unauthorized person/no unauthorized access,** accès interdit à toute personne étrangère au service.

unavailability, *n.* indisponibilité *f.*

unavailable, *a.* (*i*) indisponible/non disponible (*ii*) qu'on ne peut se procurer/épuisé.

unavoidable, *a.* **unavoidable costs,** frais essentiels/nécessaires.

unbalanced, *a. Book-k:* (*of account*) non soldé.

unbankable, *a.* (effet) non bancable/hors de banque/déclassé.

unbought, *a.* en magasin/non vendu.

unbuilt, *a.* **unbuilt plot,** terrain *m* vague/non construit.

unbundle, *v.tr.* tarifer séparément; établir des prix séparés.

unbundling, *n.* séparation *f* des tarifs; facturation/tarification séparée; dégroupage *m* des tarifs.

uncallable, *a. NAm:* **uncallable bonds,** obligations *f* non remboursables/obligations sans possibilité d'amortissement anticipé.

uncalled, *a. Fin:* **uncalled capital,** capital non appelé.

uncashed, *a.* **uncashed cheque,** chèque *m* à encaisser/chèque non compensé.

uncertain, *a. StExch:* **to quote uncertain,** donner l'incertain.

unchecked, *a.* (*of account, etc.*) non vérifié/non contrôlé.

unclaimed, *a.* (*of dividend, etc.*) non réclamé.

uncleared, *a.* (*a*) *Cust:* **uncleared goods,** marchandises non passées en douane (*b*) (*of debt*) non acquitté/non liquidé (*c*) (*of cheque*) non compensé.

uncollected, *a.* non réclamé; **uncollected taxes,** impôts non perçus.

unconditional, *a.* (*a*) *Fin:* **unconditional order,** ordre (de payer) pur et simple (*b*) **unconditional acceptance,** acceptation *f* sans conditions/sans réserve.

unconfirmed, *a.* **unconfirmed credit,** crédit non confirmé.

unconsolidated, *a.* *Fin:* (*of debt*) non consolidé.

uncorrected, *a.* (*of balance, etc.*) non redressé.

uncovered, *a.* (achat, vente) à découvert; **uncovered balance,** découvert *m*; **uncovered advance,** avance *f* à découvert.

uncrossed, *a.* **uncrossed cheque,** chèque non barré; chèque ouvert.

undated, *a.* non daté; sans date; **undated bonds,** obligations *f* sans date d'échéance; **undated debenture,** obligation perpétuelle.

undelivered, *a.* **undelivered goods,** marchandises non livrées; **if undelivered please return to sender,** en cas de non-livraison prière de retourner à l'expéditeur.

underbid, *v.tr.* faire des soumissions/offrir des conditions plus avantageuses que (qn); demander moins cher que (qn).

undercapitalization, *n.* sous-capitalisation *f.*

undercapitalized, *a.* sous-capitalisé.

undercut, *v.tr.* (*a*) faire des soumissions plus avantageuses que (qn) (*b*) vendre moins cher/à meilleur prix que (qn).

underdeveloped, *a.* *PolEc:* **underdeveloped countries,** pays en voie de développement.

underemployed, *a.* sous-employé.

underemployment, *n.* *PolEc:* sous-emploi *m*/chômage *m.*

underequipped, *a.* sous-équipé.

under-estimate[1], *n.* sous-estimation *f*/sous-évaluation *f.*

under-estimate[2], *v.tr.* sous-estimer/sous-évaluer.

underfunded, *a.* sous-capitalisé.

underinsure, *v.tr.* **he is underinsured,** ses assurances ne sont pas suffisantes/ne le couvrent pas suffisamment.

undermanned, *a.* à court de personnel/de main-d'œuvre.

undermentioned, *a.* **could you send us the undermentioned items,** pourriez-vous nous faire parvenir les articles suivants/les articles mentionnés ci-dessous.

underpaid, *a.* mal rétribué/insuffisamment rétribué; **underpaid workers,** ouvriers sous-payés.

underpay, *v.tr.* sous-payer.

underproduction, *n.* *Ind:* production *f* au-dessous du rendement normal/production déficitaire/sous-production *f.*

underquote, *v.tr.* faire une soumission plus avantageuse que celle de (qn).

undersell, *v.tr.* (*a*) vendre à meilleur marché/moins cher que (qn); **we are not knowingly undersold,** à notre connaissance personne ne vend moins cher (que nous); **he undersold his competitors,** il a obtenu le contrat en demandant moins cher que ses concurrents (*b*) vendre (qch.) au-dessous de sa valeur.

undersign, *v.tr.* signer (un document).

undersigned, *a. & n.* soussigné(e); **I the undersigned declare that . . .,** je soussigné(e) déclare que . . . .

understaffed, *a.* qui manque de personnel; **to be understaffed,** manquer de/être à court de personnel.

understanding, *n.* (*a*) accord *m*/entente

f *(b)* condition *f*; **on the understanding that . . .,** à condition que.

undertake, *v.tr.* se charger de/entreprendre/s'imposer (une tâche); assumer (une responsabilité); **to undertake a guarantee,** s'engager à donner une garantie.

undertaking, *n.* entreprise (commerciale, industrielle, etc.); **joint undertaking,** entreprise en participation.

undervaluation, *n.* estimation *f* (de qch.) au-dessous de sa valeur/sous-estimation *f*/ sous-évaluation *f*.

undervalue, *v.tr.* sous-estimer/sous-évaluer (qch.)/estimer (qch.) au-dessous de sa valeur.

underwrite, *v.tr.* *(a)* *Fin:* garantir la souscription d'une émission *(b)* *MIns:* couvrir (un risque, etc.)/garantir (contre un risque) par un contrat d'assurance.

underwriter, *n.* *(a)* *Fin:* membre *m* d'un syndicat de garantie/syndicataire *mf*; **leading underwriter,** apériteur *m*; **the underwriters,** le syndicat de garantie *(b)* *MIns:* assureur *m*/compagnie *f* d'assurance (maritime).

underwriting, *n.* *(a)* *Fin:* garantie *f* d'émission; **underwriting agreement/ contract,** contrat *m* de garantie; **underwriting commission,** commission syndicale; **underwriting share,** part syndicale; part syndicataire; **underwriting syndicate,** syndicat financier/syndicat de garantie *(b)* assurance *f* maritime.

undischarged, *a.* *(a)* *Jur:* **undischarged bankrupt,** failli non réhabilité *(b)* **undischarged debt,** dette non acquittée/non liquidée/non soldée.

undiscountable, *a.* **undiscountable bill,** billet *m*/effet *m* inescomptable.

undisposed of, *a.* **stock undisposed of,** marchandises non écoulées/non vendues.

undistributed, *a.* non distribué; non

réparti; **undistributed earnings,** bénéfices non distribués; **undistributed profit,** bénéfice non distribué.

undivided, *a.* non partagé; **undivided profits,** bénéfices non répartis; **undivided property,** biens indivis.

unearned, *a.* **unearned income,** revenu non professionnel (provenant d'un capital)/rente *f*; **unearned increment of land,** plus-value foncière.

uneconomic, *a.* peu économique; **uneconomic proposition,** projet *m* non rentable/peu rentable.

unemployed, *a.* **1.** *(a)* sans travail/sans emploi; en chômage *(b)* *n.pl.* **the unemployed,** les chômeurs *m*; les sans-travail *mf inv*/les sans-emploi *mf inv* **2.** *(of capital)* inemployé; **unemployed funds,** fonds inactifs/dormants/inemployés/improductifs.

unemployment, *n.* chômage *m*; **unemployment benefit/compensation/relief,** secours *m*/allocation *f*/prestation *f*/indemnité *f* de chômage; **unemployment fund,** caisse *f* de chômage.

unendorsed, *a.* *(of cheque)* non endossé.

unenforceable, *a.* (contrat, etc.) non exécutoire.

unexchangeable, *a.* *Fin:* **unexchangeable securities,** valeurs *f* impermutables/ inéchangeables.

unexpended, *a.* *Fin:* **unexpended balance,** solde non dépensé.

unfair, *a.* **unfair competition,** concurrence déloyale.

unfavourable, *a.* défavorable/peu favorable; *(of terms, etc.)* peu avantageux/ défavorable **(to,** à); **unfavourable balance of trade,** balance commerciale défavorable; *Fin:* **unfavourable exchange,** change *m* défavorable.

unfunded, *a.* *Fin:* **unfunded debt,** dette flottante/non consolidée.

ungeared, *a.* (*of firm*) sans endettement.

unilateral, *a.* unilatéral; **unilateral contract,** contrat unilatéral.

uninsurable, *a.* non assurable.

uninsured, *a.* non assuré (**against,** contre); *Post:* (colis) sans valeur déclarée.

uninvested, *a.* (argent) non placé/non investi.

union, *n.* (*a*) union *f*; **customs union,** union douanière (*b*) **trade union,** syndicat *m*; **union agreement,** convention collective; **union card,** carte syndicale; **union meeting,** réunion syndicale; **union member,** syndiqué(e).

unionism, *n.* syndicalisme *m.*

unionist, *n.* syndicaliste *mf.*

unionized, *a.* **non unionized labour/ workers,** ouvriers non syndiqués.

unisex, *a.* **unisex shops/fashion,** boutique/mode unisexe.

unissued, *a.* **unissued shares,** actions non encore émises.

unit, *n.* **1.** (*a*) unité *f*; **each lot contains a hundred units,** chaque lot contient cent unités; **unit cost,** prix *m* de revient unitaire; **unit price,** prix de l'unité/prix unitaire; **unit value index,** indice *m* de la valeur unitaire (*b*) **visual display unit (VDU),** console *f* de visualisation/visuel *m* (*c*) unité (de longueur, de poids, etc.); *Pharm:* unité (*d*) *PolEc:* **monetary unit,** unité monétaire; **unit of consumption/of production,** unité de consommation/de production; **unit of labour/man work unit,** unité de travail; *EEC:* **unit of account,** unité de compte **2. unit trust** = société *f* d'investissement à capital variable (SICAV).

unitary, *a.* unitaire.

unlawful, *a.* illégal.

unlisted, *a. StExch:* non inscrit (à la cote officielle)/hors cote; **unlisted securities,** valeurs non cotées.

unmanufactured, *a.* (à l'état) brut; non manufacturé; **unmanufactured materials,** matières premières/matières brutes.

unmarketable, *a.* (*of goods*) invendable; d'un débit difficile; **unmarketable assets,** fonds *m* non réalisables/actif *m* non réalisable.

unmortgaged, *a.* libre d'hypothèques; franc/franche d'hypothèques.

unnegotiable, *a.* (*of cheque*) non négociable; **unnegotiable bill,** effet *m* non négociable.

unobtainable, *a.* (*of article*) qu'on ne peut obtenir/se procurer.

unofficial, *a.* non officiel/non confirmé; (renseignement) officieux; **unofficial strike,** grève *f* sauvage.

unpaid, *a.* **1.** (*of pers.*) non salarié; (*of post*) non rétribué; **unpaid agent,** mandataire *m* bénévole; **unpaid services,** services à titre gracieux/non rétribués/ bénévoles **2.** (*a*) (*of bill*) impayé; (*of debt*) non acquitté; **to leave an account unpaid,** laisser traîner un compte/laisser un compte impayé (*b*) (*of money*) impayé; non versé.

unpriced, *a.* (article) sans (indication de) prix.

unproductive, *a.* (capital, travail) improductif.

unproductiveness, *n.* improductivité *f.*

unprofitable, *a.* peu profitable/peu lucratif/peu rentable; (travail, etc.) inutile.

unquoted, *a. StExch:* **unquoted securities,** valeurs non cotées.

unrealizable, *a.* **unrealizable capital,** fonds non réalisables.

unrealized, *a.* (*of assets, etc.*) non réalisé.

unreceipted, *a.* non acquitté/sans la mention "pour acquit".

unredeemable, *a.* non remboursable.

unregistered, *a.* non enregistré/non inscrit; (*of trademark*) non déposé.

unremunerative, *a.* peu rémunérateur; peu lucratif; peu profitable.

unrepaid, *a.* (emprunt, argent, etc.) non remboursé/non rendu.

unsafe, *a.* *Fin:* **unsafe paper,** papier *m* de valeur douteuse.

unsaleable, *a.* (*of goods*) invendable.

unsecured, *a.* (*of loan, overdraft, etc.*) non garanti/à découvert; (*of debt, creditor*) sans garantie; chirographaire.

unsettled, *a.* (*a*) **the unsettled state of the market,** l'incertitude *f* du marché; les fluctuations *f* du marché (*b*) **the debt remained unsettled,** la dette est restée impayée.

unskilled, *a.* non qualifié/non spécialisé; **unskilled labour,** main-d'œuvre non spécialisée; **unskilled job,** travail de manœuvre; **unskilled worker,** manœuvre *m*.

unsold, *a.* invendu; **unsold goods,** marchandises invendues; invendus *m*.

unsound, *a.* **it is unsound finance,** c'est de la mauvaise finance; *Ins:* **unsound risk,** mauvais risque.

unspent, *a.* (*of sum, balance, etc.*) non dépensé.

unsteady, *a.* (*of prices*) variable; (*of market*) agité/irrégulier.

unsubscribed, *a.* (capital) non souscrit.

unsubsidized, *a.* non subventionné/sans subvention.

untaxed, *a.* exempt/exonéré d'impôt; (produit) non imposé/non taxé.

up, *adv.* **1.** (*on packing case*) **this side up,** haut *m*/dessus *m* **2.** (*of shares, etc.*) **to be up,** être en hausse (**at,** à); **shares are up at £5,** les actions ont monté jusqu'à £5; **profits are up 25%,** les profits ont enregistré une hausse de 25%/ont augmenté de 25%.

update, *v.tr.* mettre à jour.

updating, *n.* mise *f* à jour.

upkeep, *n.* (frais d')entretien *m* (d'un établissement, etc.).

upset, *a.* (*at auctions, etc.*) **upset price,** mise *f* à prix.

upward, *a.* **an upward trend/tendency,** une tendance à la hausse; **an upward movement,** un mouvement de hausse.

urgent, *a.* urgent; **urgent order,** commande urgente.

usance, *n.* *Jur:* usance *f*; **bill at double usance,** effet *m* à double usance; **at thirty days' usance,** à usance de trente jours; **usance bill,** effet *m* à usance.

use¹, *n.* emploi *m*/usage *m*; **direction for use,** mode *m* d'emploi; **in use,** en usage; **joint use,** utilisation *f* en commun; *Cust:* **articles for personal use,** effets usagers/effets personnels; **to make use of sth.,** se servir de qch./faire usage de qch./employer qch./utiliser qch.; *Cust:* **home use entry,** sortie *f* de l'entrepôt pour consommation; **goods for home use,** marchandises mises en consommation.

use², *v.tr.* employer/utiliser/user de/se servir de/faire usage de (qch.).

user, *n.* usager, -ère/utilisateur, -trice.

usual, *a.* usuel/habituel/ordinaire; **usual terms,** conditions *f* d'usage; **it is usual to pay in advance,** il est d'usage de payer d'avance/on paie habituellement d'avance; **the usual practice,** la pratique courante/l'usage courant; **usual hours (of business),** heures *f* réglementaires (d'ouverture).

utilization, *n.* utilisation *f* (de qch.); **utilization of a patent,** exploitation *f* d'un brevet (d'invention); *Ind:* **utilization percent,** taux *m* du rendement; **capacity utilization,** capacité d'emploi.

utilize, *v.tr.* utiliser/se servir de (qch., qn); tirer profit de qch./mettre (qch.) en valeur.

V

vacancy, *n.* **1.** vacance *f*/poste *m* (à pourvoir)/poste vacant; **to fill a vacancy,** pourvoir à un emploi/suppléer à une vacance; nommer qn à une vacance **2.** *pl.* (*a*) **vacancies** = chambres *f* à louer; **no vacancies** = complet (*b*) offres d'emploi(s).

vacant, *a.* vacant; (*of room, apartment, etc.*) **to be vacant,** être libre; **vacant possession,** libre possession *f* (d'un immeuble); **house to be let with vacant possession,** maison *f* à louer avec jouissance immédiate; (*of job*) à pourvoir; (*in advertisements*) **situations vacant,** offres *f* d'emploi(s).

vacate, *v.tr.* quitter (une maison, etc.); *Jur:* **to vacate the premises,** vider les lieux.

vacation, *n. NAm:* vacances *fpl*; **on vacation,** en vacances; **vacation with pay,** congé(s) payé(s).

valid, *a.* (contrat, etc.) valide/valable; (passeport) valide/en règle; **valid receipt,** quittance *f* valable; **to make valid,** valider/rendre valable (un contrat, etc.); **ticket valid for one month,** billet bon/valable pour un mois.

validate, *v.tr.* valider/rendre valable.

validation, *n.* validation *f* (d'un document, d'une signature, etc.)

validity, *n.* validité *f* (d'un contrat, d'un passeport, etc.); **to extend the validity of a credit,** proroger/prolonger la durée d'un crédit.

valorization, *n.* valorisation *f.*

valorize, *v.tr.* valoriser.

valuable, *a.* précieux; de valeur; **valuable article,** objet *m* de valeur; *Jur:* **for a valuable consideration,** à titre onéreux.

valuables, *n.pl.* objets de (grande) valeur.

valuation, *n.* (*a*) évaluation *f*/estimation *f*/appréciation *f*/expertise *f*; *Jur:* prisée *f* et estimation; **stock valuation,** évaluation des stocks; **to make a valuation (of goods, etc.),** faire l'expertise/expertiser (des marchandises, etc.); **to ask for a valuation,** faire estimer/faire expertiser/soumettre à une expertise (*b*) valeur *f* (estimée); **at a valuation of,** d'une valeur de; **it is worth £500 at (a) valuation,** l'expertise a établi la valeur à £500; **to set too high/too low a valuation on goods,** surestimer/sous-estimer la valeur de marchandises.

valuator, *n.* expert *m*; commissaire-priseur *m.*

value[1]**,** *n.* (*a*) valeur *f*/prix *m*; **to be of value,** avoir de la valeur; **this watch is of little/of great value,** c'est une montre de peu de valeur/de grande valeur; **of no value,** sans valeur; **goods to the value of £50,** marchandise d'une valeur de £50; **to lose value/to fall in value,** perdre de sa valeur/diminuer de valeur; se déprécier/se dévaluer/s'avilir; *Fin:* se dévaloriser; **loss of value/loss in value/fall in value,** perte *f*/diminution *f* de valeur; *Fin:* dévalorisation *f*; **to set a value (up)on sth.,** évaluer qch.; **to set a low value on the stock,** estimer à un bas prix la valeur des stocks/évaluer les stocks à un bas prix; **to set too high a value on sth.,** surévaluer qch./surestimer qch. (*b*) **book value,** valeur comptable/*FrC:* valeur aux livres; **commercial value/market value,** valeur vénale/valeur marchande/valeur

225

négociable; *Fin:* cours *m*/valeur en Bourse; **of no commercial value,** sans valeur commerciale; **customs value,** valeur en douane; **decrease in value,** moins-value *f*; **exchange value,** valeur d'échange/contre-valeur *f*; **face value,** valeur nominale; **increase in value,** plus-value *f*; **insured value,** valeur assurée; (*of bond, etc.*) **redemption value,** valeur de remboursement; **surrender value of a policy,** valeur de rachat d'une police; **value at maturity,** valeur à l'échéance; **for value received,** valeur reçue (*c*) *Bank:* **capital value,** valeur en capital; **value in account,** valeur en compte; **value in gold currency,** valeur-or *f* (*d*) **to get good value for one's money,** en avoir pour son argent; **it is very good value,** c'est à un prix très avantageux/ce n'est pas cher.

value², *v.tr.* **to value (goods, damages),** évaluer/estimer/expertiser (des marchandises, des dégâts); faire l'expertise/l'évaluation (de marchandises, de dégâts); **to value furniture,** faire l'expertise/dresser l'état appréciatif d'un mobilier; **to have sth. valued,** soumettre qch. à une expertise/faire évaluer qch.

value-added, *a.* **value-added tax (VAT),** taxe *f* à la valeur ajoutée (TVA).

valueless, *a.* sans valeur; **valueless stock,** non-valeurs *fpl.*

valuer, *n.* expert *m*; **official valuer (of property, etc.)** commissaire-priseur *m*.

valuing, *n.* évaluation *f*/estimation *f*.

variability, *n.* variabilité *f* (des taux d'intérêt, etc.)

variable, 1. *a.* variable; **variable expenses,** frais *m* variables/proportionnels; **variable yield securities,** valeurs *f* à revenu variable; **income from variable yield investments,** revenu *m* variable; **to quote variable exchange,** coter l'incertain **2.** *n.* variable *f*; *pl.* **variables,** éléments *m* variables.

variance, *n.* variance *f*/écart *m*; **budget variance,** écart budgétaire; **cost va-**

riance, variance/écart des coûts; **variance analysis,** analyse *f* des écarts.

variation, *n.* (*a*) variation *f*; **annual/seasonal variations,** variations annuelles/saisonnières (*b*) *Ins:* **variation of risk,** modification *f* de risque.

variety, *n.* variété *f*; diversité *f*; *NAm:* **variety store,** bazar *m*.

vary, *v.tr.* **to vary the terms of a contract,** modifier les clauses d'un contrat.

VAT, *n.* (= **value added tax**), TVA *f* (= taxe à la valeur ajoutée); **subject to VAT,** soumis à la TVA.

vehicle, *n.* véhicule *m*; **commercial vehicles,** véhicules commerciaux/utilitaires; **freight vehicle/goods vehicle,** véhicule de transport de marchandises; **heavy goods vehicle (HGV),** poids lourd *m*; **motor vehicle,** voiture *f* (automobile).

vend, *v.tr. esp. Jur:* vendre.

vending, *a.* **vending machine,** distributeur *m* automatique.

vendor, *n.* (*a*) vendeur, -euse (**of,** de); **street vendor,** marchand(e) des quatre saisons; vendeur ambulant (*b*) *Fin:* **vendor's shares,** actions *f* d'apport/de fondation (*c*) *Jur:* vendeur, -eresse.

venture, *n.* entreprise *f*/affaire *f*; projet *m*; **it is a new venture,** c'est une entreprise nouvelle/une affaire nouvelle/un projet nouveau; **joint venture,** affaire en participation; **joint venture assistance,** subvention *f* de groupe; **venture capital,** capital *m* risque.

verbal, *a.* verbal; **verbal agreement,** convention/entente verbale; **verbal offer,** offre verbale.

verification, *n.* vérification *f*/contrôle *m*.

verify, *v.tr.* vérifier/contrôler (des renseignements, des comptes).

vertical, *a.* vertical; **vertical concentration/merger,** concentration verticale; **vertical integration,** intégration verticale;

vertical trustification, cartellisation verticale.

vested, *a.* **vested interests,** droits acquis; **to have a vested interest in a concern,** avoir des capitaux investis dans une entreprise/être intéressé dans une entreprise.

viability, *n.* viabilité *f* (d'une entreprise, etc.).

viable, *a.* (*of plan, etc.*) viable; durable; **commercially viable,** rentable.

vice-chairman, *n.* vice-président(e).

vice-chairmanship, *n.* vice-présidence *f.*

vice-presidency, *n.* vice-présidence *f.*

vice-president, *n.* *NAm:* vice-président(e).

vintage, *n.* **vintage wine,** vin *m* d'appellation; **guaranteed vintage,** appellation contrôlée.

visa¹, *n.* visa *m*; **transit visa,** visa de transit.

visa², *v.tr.* viser (un passeport)/apposer un visa à (un passeport).

visible, *a.* visible; **visible exports,** exportations *f* visibles; **visible imports,** importations visibles.

visual, *a.* **visual display unit (VDU),** console *f* de visualisation/visuel *m.*

vitiate, *v.tr.* vicier (un contrat, etc.); **to vitiate a transaction,** rendre une opération nulle.

vocational, *a.* professionnel; **vocational guidance,** orientation professionnelle; **vocational training,** formation professionnelle.

void¹, *a.* (*of deed, contract, etc.*) nul; **to render null and void,** rendre nul et non avenu; **to make void,** annuler/rendre nul.

void², *v.tr.* résoudre/résilier/annuler (un contrat, etc.); annuler (une facture).

voidable, *a.* (contrat, etc.) résiliable/annulable.

voidance, *n.* annulation *f* (d'un contrat, etc.).

volume, *n.* volume *m*; **sales volume,** volume de ventes; chiffre d'affaires; **volume of business,** volume des affaires; **volume of output,** volume de la production; **profit volume ratio,** rapport *m* profit sur ventes.

voluntary, *a.* (*a*) volontaire; bénévole; **voluntary liquidation,** liquidation *f* volontaire (*b*) facultatif; **voluntary insurance,** assurance facultative.

vote¹, *n.* (*a*) vote *m*/scrutin *m*; **postal vote,** vote postal; **to take the vote,** procéder au scrutin; **to cast one's vote,** voter; **secret vote,** scrutin secret; **to pass a vote of thanks to s.o.,** voter des remerciements à qn (*b*) (*individual vote*) voix *f*/suffrage *m*; **to give one's vote to s.o.,** donner son vote/sa voix à qn; voter pour qn; **to put a question to the vote/to take a vote on a question,** mettre une question aux voix; **number of votes (cast),** nombre *m* de voix; **(chairman's) casting vote,** voix prépondérante (du président); *coll.* **to lose the trade-union vote,** perdre les suffrages/le vote des syndicalistes (*c*) **to have the vote,** avoir le droit de vote (*d*) motion *f*/résolution *f*; **to carry a vote,** adopter une résolution.

vote², **1.** *v.i.* voter (**for, against,** pour, contre); donner sa voix/son vote (**for sth.,** pour qch.); prendre part au vote; **to vote by (a) show of hands,** voter à main levée; **to vote by proxy,** voter par procuration **2.** *v.tr.* (*a*) **to vote a sum,** voter une somme (*b*) **to vote s.o. in,** élire qn; **to vote s.o. out,** rejeter qn.

voter, *n.* votant *m.*

voting¹, *a.* (*of assembly, member*) votant.

voting², *n.* (participation au) vote; scrutin *m*; **voting paper,** bulletin *m* de vote.

---

voucher, *n.* (*a*) pièce justificative; *Book-k:* pièce comptable (*b*) **voucher for receipt,** récépissé *m*/quittance *f* (*c*) fiche *f*/reçu *m*/reconnaissance *f*/bon *m*; **cash voucher,** bon de caisse; **gift voucher,** chèque-cadeau *m*; bon-cadeau *m*; **luncheon voucher,** chèque-repas *m*/chèque-restaurant *m*.

W

wage, *n.* salaire *m*/paie *f*/paye *f*; **current rate of wages/current wage rate,** taux actuel des salaires; **fixed wage,** salaire fixe/*F:* fixe *m*; **general level of wages/ general wage level,** niveau général des salaires; **index-linked minimum wage =** salaire minimum interprofessionnel de croissance(SMIC); **hourly wage,** salaire horaire; **real wage,** salaire réel; **supplementary wage,** supplément *m* au salaire normal; sursalaire *m*; **wage(s) agreement,** convention *f* des salaires; **wage(s) bill,** masse salariale/charges salariales; **wage claims,** revendications *f* de salaire; **wage differentials,** écart *m* des salaires; hiérarchie *f* salariale; **wage freeze,** blocage *m* des salaires; **wage fund,** fonds *m* disponible pour la rétribution du travail; **wage negotiations,** négociations salariales; **wage(s) policy,** politique salariale/politique des salaires; **wage rate,** taux *m* des salaires; **wage scale,** échelle *f* des salaires; **wage sheet,** feuille *f* de salaire/de paie; **wage structure,** structure *f* des salaires; **weekly wage(s),** salaire hebdomadaire.

wage-earner, *n.* salarié(e).

wage-earning, *a.* **wage-earning population,** les salariés *m.*

waiver, *n.* **waiver of a claim,** désistement *m* de revendication; **waiver clause,** clause *f* d'abandon/de désistement; *Jur:* **waiver of a right,** abandon *m* d'un droit; renonciation *f* à un droit.

walk out *v.i.* se mettre en grève.

walk-out, *n.* grève *f* (surprise).

wall, *n.* **tariff walls,** barrières douanières.

wanted, *a.* (*in ads*) **secretary wanted,** on demande une secrétaire; **situations wanted,** demandes *f* d'emploi; *Fin:* **stocks wanted,** valeurs demandées.

war, *n.* guerre *f*; **tariff war,** guerre de tarifs.

warehouse[1], *n.* (*a*) entrepôt *m*; magasin *m*; **bonded warehouse,** entrepôt de douane; **ex warehouse,** à prendre en entrepôt; **warehouse keeper,** magasinier *m* (*b*) **furniture warehouse,** garde-meuble *m.*

warehouse[2], *v.tr.* entreposer/mettre en entrepôt.

warehousing, *n.* entreposage *m*; magasinage *m*; **warehousing charges,** droits *mpl* de magasinage/d'entreposage; **warehousing system,** système *m* d'entrepôt.

warrant[1], *n.* (*a*) **warrant for goods/ warehouse warrant,** certificat *m* d'entrepôt/warrant *m*; **to issue a warehouse warrant for goods,** warranter des marchandises; **issuing of a warehouse warrant,** warrantage *m*; **goods covered by a warehouse warrant,** marchandises warrantées (*b*) **dividend warrant,** chèque *m* dividende; **interest warrant,** mandat *m* d'intérêts; **warrant indenture,** contrat *m* de droits d'achat d'actions; **share warrant,** warrant/droit d'achat d'actions; **warrant for payment,** ordonnance *f* de paiement.

warrant[2], *v.tr.* garantir; warranter.

warranted, *a.* garanti; warranté.

warrantee, *n.* porteur d'une garantie.

warrantor, *n.* répondant *m*/garant *m.*

warranty, *n.* (bulletin de) garantie *f*; **under warranty**, sous garantie.

wastage, *n.* **1.** (*a*) perte *f*; coulage *m* (*b*) gaspillage *m* **2.** *coll.* déchets *mpl*/rebuts *mpl*.

waste[1], *a.* (matière, marchandises, etc.) de rebut; (produit) non utilisé/perdu; **waste material**, déchet *m*.

waste[2], *n.* **1.** gaspillage *m* (d'argent, etc.); coulage *m* **2.** déchets *mpl*, rebut(s) *m(pl)*.

waste[3], *v.tr.* gaspiller (son argent, son temps, etc.).

wasteful, *a.* **wasteful expenditure**, dépenses *fpl* en pure perte; gaspillage *m*.

waybill, *n.* lettre *f* de voiture/de mouvement; feuille *f* de route; bulletin *m*/bordereau *m* d'expédition.

weaken, *v.i.* **the market has weakened**, le marché a fléchi.

wealth, *n.* richesse(s) *f(pl)*; opulence *f*; luxe *m*; **wealth tax**, impôt *m* sur a fortune.

wear, *n.* usure *f*/détérioration *f* par l'usure; **wear and tear**, usure; dépréciation *f*/détérioration; dégradation *f* (d'un immeuble); **fair wear and tear**, usure normale.

week, *n.* semaine *f*; **earnings per week**, salaire *m* hebdomadaire.

weekly, **1.** *a.* hebdomadaire **2.** *adv.* par semaine; tous les huit jours; hebdomadairement **3.** *n.* journal *m*/revue *f* hebdomadaire/hebdomadaire *m*.

weigh, **1.** *v.tr.* peser (un colis, etc.) **2.** *v.i.* peser; avoir du poids; **parcel weighing two kilos**, paquet qui pèse deux kilos.

weighing, *n.* pesée *f* (de denrées, etc.); **weighing machine**, appareil *m* de pesage *m*; balance *f*.

weight, *n.* **1.** poids *m*; **to sell by weight**, vendre au poids; **net weight**, poids net; **two kilos in weight**, pesant deux kilos/d'un poids de deux kilos **2.** **weights and measures**, poids et mesures *f*.

weighting, *n.* **London weighting allowance**, indemnité *f* pour Londres.

wharf, *n.* débarcadère *m*/quai *m*/entrepôt *m* maritime; **ex wharf**, à prendre sur quai; **wharf dues**, droits *m* de quai.

wharfage, *n.* droits *mpl* de quai.

wholesale, **1.** *n.* (vente en) gros *m*; **wholesale and retail**, le gros et le détail **2.** *a.* (*a*) en gros/de gros; **wholesale dealer**, marchand *m*/commerçant *m* en gros; grossiste; **wholesale goods**, marchandises *f* de gros; **wholesale price**, prix *m* de gros; **wholesale trade**, commerce de gros/le gros; **wholesale shop**, maison *f* de gros (*b*) **wholesale manufacture**, fabrication *f* en série **3.** *adv.* en gros; **to buy/to sell wholesale**, acheter/vendre en gros.

wholesaler, *n.* (*a*) commerçant(e)/marchand(e) en gros; grossiste *m* (*b*) **wholesaler's**, maison *f* de gros.

widening, *n.* **widening of capital**, élargissement *m* du capital.

wildcat, *a.* **wildcat strike**, grève *f* sauvage.

winding up, *n.* liquidation *f* (d'une société); **voluntary winding up**, liquidation volontaire; **winding up order**, ordre *m* de mise en règlement judiciaire.

window, *n.* (**shop**) **window**, vitrine *f*; **window display**, étalage *m*.

wind up, *v.tr.* liquider (une société); régler/clôturer (un compte); **to wind up a meeting**, clore une séance.

wipe off, *v.tr.* **to wipe off a debt**, annuler une dette.

withdraw, *v.tr.* (*a*) **to withdraw a sum of money**, retirer une somme d'argent (de la caisse d'épargne, etc.)/faire un retrait; **sum withdrawn from the bank**, somme retirée/retrait (d'une somme d'argent) d'un compte bancaire (*b*) **to withdraw an order**, annuler une commande.

withdrawal, *n.* retrait *m*; **withdrawal of a sum of money**, retrait d'une somme d'argent; **withdrawal of capital**, retrait de fonds; *Bank: etc:* **withdrawal notice**, avis *m* de retrait de fonds.

witholding, *n. NAm:* **witholding tax**, impôt retenu à la source/retenue fiscale.

within, *adv.* **within 10 days**, dans un délai de 10 jours/d'ici 10 jours.

work[1], *n.* **1.** travail *m*/ouvrage *m*; **clerical work**, travaux administratifs; **day's work**, (travail d'une) journée; **factory at work**, usine *f* en activité; **work assignment**, distribution *f* des tâches; **work in progress**, (*i*) travail en cours (*ii*) produit *m* semi-fini; **work study**, étude *f* du travail **2.** (*employment*) travail/emploi *m*; **to be out of work**, être sans travail/sans emploi; en chômage **3. work to rule**, grève *f* du zèle **4.** *pl.* **works**, usine *f*/atelier *m*; **chemical works**, usine de produits chimiques; **engineering works**, atelier de construction de machines; **steel works**, aciérie *f*; **works committee**, comité *m* d'entreprise.

work[2], *v.i.* **1.** travailler; **to work to rule**, faire la grève du zèle **2.** (*of machine, etc.*) fonctionner.

workable, *a.* (projet, plan) réalisable/exécutable/pratique.

worker, *n.* ouvrier, -ière; **worker participation**, participation ouvrière; **worker representation**, représentation *f* du personnel.

working[1], *a.* **1.** (*of machine, etc.*) qui fonctionne **2. working agreement (between two firms)**, accord *m*/entente *f*/convention *f* (entre deux sociétés).

working[2], *n.* **1.** travail *m*; **working day**, jour ouvrable; **usual working hours**, heures (habituelles) de travail **2. working account**, compte *m* d'exploitation; **working capital**, capital *m* d'exploitation; fonds *mpl* de roulement; **working capital fund**, compte *m* d'avances; **working expenses**, frais généraux; frais d'exploitation; **working interest**, participation d'exploitation; **working party**, groupe *m* de travail **3.** marche *f*/fonctionnement *m* (d'un appareil); **to be in (good) working order**, (bien) fonctionner.

workload, *n.* travail (assigné).

workman, *n.m.* ouvrier/artisan; **workmen's compensation insurance**, assurance *f* contre les accidents du travail.

workmanship, *n.* exécution *f* (d'un travail); fini *m*; façon *f*; **expert workmanship**, travail de spécialiste; **sound/fine workmanship**, construction soignée.

work off, *v.tr.* **to work off a stock of goods**, écouler un stock de marchandises.

work out, **1.** *v.tr.* (*a*) élaborer (un projet); **the plan is being worked out**, le projet est à l'étude (*b*) examiner (un compte); établir/calculer (un prix) **2.** *v.i.* **the total works out at £9**, le montant s'élève à £9.

workshop, *n.* atelier *m*.

world, *n.* (*a*) **the commercial world**, le commerce; **the financial world**, le monde de la finance; **the world of high finance**, la haute finance (*b*) **world exports**, exportations mondiales; **world markets**, marchés mondiaux; **trends in world trade**, tendances *f* du commerce mondial.

worldwide, *a.* universel/mondial.

worth, **1.** *a.* **to be worth so much**, valoir tant; **to be worth nothing**, ne rien valoir; **what is the franc worth?** combien vaut le franc? **two diamonds worth £50 000 each**, deux diamants *m* valant £50 000 chacun **2.** *n.* valeur *f*; **net worth**, situation *f* nette; **of great worth**, de grande valeur; **of little worth**, de peu de valeur; **of no worth**, d'aucune valeur; **give me five pound's worth of petrol**, donnez-moi pour cinq livres d'essence; **£50 worth of goods**, des marchandises *f* pour une valeur de £50.

worthless, *a.* sans valeur; **worthless bill**, titre *m* sans valeur; non-valeur *f*.

write, *v.tr.* écrire (une lettre, etc.).

write down, *v.tr.* **1.** noter (qch.) par écrit; marquer/noter (ses dépenses, etc.) **2.** *Fin:* réduire (la valeur du capital, des stocks); **written down value**, valeur comptable/*FrC:* valeur aux livres.

write off, *v.tr.* (*a*) *Fin:* **to write off capital**, réduire le capital; amortir le capital (*b*) **to write off a bad debt,** défalquer une mauvaise créance; passer une créance par profits et pertes; **to write so much off for wear and tear,** déduire tant pour l'usure; **my car had to be written off,** ma voiture est une perte totale.

write-off, *n.* perte sèche; **my car is a complete write-off,** ma voiture est une perte totale.

write out, *v.tr.* **to write out a cheque (to s.o.),** établir/faire/libeller un chèque (à l'ordre de qn).

write up, *v.tr.* mettre (son agenda, sa comptabilité etc.) à jour.

writing down, *n.* **1.** inscription *f* **2.** *Fin:* réduction *f* (de capital, de stocks).

writing off, *n.* **1.** amortissement *m* (du capital) **2.** défalcation *f* (d'une créance).

X

xerography, *n.* xérographie *f.*

Xerox, *n. R.t.m.* Xerox copy, copie *f*

xérographique; Xerox machine, machine *f* Xerox.

Y

year, *n.* an *m*/année *f*; **the year of a wine,** le millésime d'un vin; **calendar year,** année civile; **company's financial year,** exercice *m* comptable; **financial year/fiscal year/ tax year,** année budgétaire; année d'exercice; exercice (financier); **year end,** fin *f* d'exercice; **year end audit,** vérification *f* comptable de fin d'exercice; *Book-k:* **year ended 31 Dec. 1980,** exercice clos le 31 déc. 1980; **year of assessment,** année d'imposition; **the year under review,** l'exercice écoulé; **valid for one year,** valable pour un an.

yearbook, *n. StExch: etc:* annuaire *m.*

yearly, 1. *a.* annuel; **yearly accounts,** comptes annuels; **yearly payment,** annuité *f*; **debt redeemable by yearly payments,** dette *f* annuitaire; **yearly premium,** prime annuelle **2.** *adv.* annuellement.

yellow, *a. Tp:* **yellow pages,** les pages *f* jaunes de l'annuaire téléphonique.

yield[1], *n.* rendement *m* (d'un capital, etc.); revenu *m* (d'une mise de fonds, etc.); **earnings yield,** rendement; **annual interest yield gross,** taux *m* de rendement actuariel brut; **fixed yield investment,** placement *m* à revenu fixe; (*of industry, etc.*) **in full yield,** en plein rapport/en plein rendement; **tax yields,** montant *m* des recettes fiscales; **variable yield investment,** placement à revenu variable; **yield capacity,** productivité *f*; **yield method,** méthode *f* du rendement effectif; **yield to maturity,** rendement à (l')échéance.

yield[2], *v.tr.* rapporter/produire/donner; **money that yields interest,** argent *m* qui produit des intérêts/argent qui rapporte; **shares that yield high interest,** actions *f* à rendement élevé; **to yield (a) 5% (dividend),** produire/rapporter un dividende de 5%.

Z

Z, n. Z chart, diagramme en Z/graphique *m* en dents de scie.

zero, n. zéro *m*; (*of shares, etc.*) to fall to zero, tomber à zéro.

zero-rated, *a.* books are zero-rated (for VAT), il y a un taux zéro (de TVA) sur les livres.

zero-rating, n. taux *m* zéro.

zip code, n. *NAm:* zip code, code postal.

zone, n. zone *f*; free zone, zone franche; sterling/franc zone, la zone sterling/la zone franc; wage zone, zone de salaires.

COMMON ABBREVIATIONS—ABRÉVIATIONS USUELLES

a.a.r.	**against all risks,** contre tous risques
a/c, A/C	**account,** compte, c(pte)
acc.	**accepted,** accepté
acce.	**acceptance,** acceptation
acct	**account,** compte, c(pte)
accy	**accountancy,** comptabilité
a.c.v.	**actual cash value,** valeur effective au comptant
ad.	**advertisement,** annonce
ad val.	**ad valorem,** ad valorem, ad val.
agcy	**agency,** agence, agce
agt	**agent,** commissionnaire, caire
a/o.	**account of,** pour le compte de
Apr.	**April,** avril
appro.	**approval; on appro.,** à l'essai
approx.	**approximately,** approximativement
a/r.	**all risks,** tous risques
ass.	**assurance,** assurance, asse.
a/s.	**at sight,** (payable) à vue
Aug.	**August,** août
av.	**average,** (*i*) moyenne (*ii*) avaries
avdp.	**avoirdupois,** avoirdupois
back.	**backwardation,** déport, D.
bal.	**balance,** balance, bce; solde
b&b	**bed and breakfast**
b/d.	**(balance) brought down,** solde à nouveau
b/e., B/E	**bill of exchange,** lettre de change, l/c; traite, T/.
b/f, B/F	**(balance) brought forward,** (solde) reporté/report
bkge	**brokerage,** courtage, cage
B/L	**bill of lading,** connaissement, connt
BO	**1. branch office,** agence/succursale **2. buyer's option**
b/o., B/O	**(balance) brought over,** (solde) reporté
b.p., B/P	**bill payable,** billet à payer, b. à p.; effet à payer, e. à p.
b.r., B/R	**bill receivable,** billet à recevoir, b. à r.; effet à recevoir, e. à r.
b.s., B/S	**1. balance-sheet,** bilan **2. bill of sale,** acte/contrat de vente
c.	**1. coupon,** coupon, c. **2. centime,** centime, c., cent.
c.a., CA	**1. current account,** compte courant, c/c **2. current assets,** actif
C/A, c/a.	**1. capital account,** compte de capital **2. current account,** compte courant, c/c
c.&f., C&F	**cost and freight,** coût et fret, CF
CB	**cash book,** livre de caisse
c.d.	**cum dividend,** coupon attaché, c. at(t).
c/d., C/D	**carried down,** à reporter
cent.	**centime,** centime, c., cent.
cert.	**certificate,** certificat, certif.
CF	**carriage forward,** port dû, p.d.
c/f., C/F	**(to be) carried forward,** à reporter
c.i.f., CIF	**cost, insurance and freight,** coût, assurance, fret, CAF, c.a.f.
cl	**centilitre,** *NAm:* **centiliter,** centilitre, cl
cm	**centimetre,** *NAm:* **centimeter,** centimètre, cm
C/N	**1. credit note,** note de crédit **2. cover note,** lettre de couverture
Co.	**Company,** compagnie, Cie; société, Sté
c/o.	**care of . . .,** aux (bons) soins de . . .

c.o.d.	**cash on delivery,** *NAm:* **collect on delivery,** livraison contre remboursement
com(m)	**commission,** commission, com.
cons.	**consols,** consolidés
convd	**converted,** converti, conv.
corr.	**correspondence,** correspondance, corresp.
cp.	**coupon,** coupon, coup.
CP	**carriage paid,** franco, fco; port payé, p.p.
cr.	**credit,** avoir, Av.; crédit, cr.
cum.	**cumulative,** cumulatif, cum.
c.w.o.	**cash with order,** payable à la commande
cwt	**hundredweight** = 50kg
DA	**documents against acceptance,** documents contre acceptation, DA
D/A	**deposit account**
DAP	**documents against payment,** documents contre paiement, DP
db.	**debenture,** obligation, obl.
d.b.	**day book,** journal, jl
d.d.	**days after date,** jours de date, j/d
DD	**direct debit,** prélèvement automatique
Dec.	**December,** décembre, déc.
def.	**deferred,** différé, dif.
del.	**delegation,** délégation, dél.
dely	**delivery,** livraison, livr.
denom.	**denomination,** coupure, coup.
dept.	**1. department,** service, serv. **2. depot,** dépôt
dft	**draft,** traite, T/.
disc.	**discount,** ecompte, esc.
div.	**dividend,** dividende, div.
dol.	**dollar,** dollar, dol.
doz.	**dozen,** douzaine, douz., dz.
dr., Dr	**debtor,** débiteur, débit, dr.
E&OE, e.&o.e.	**errors and omissions excepted,** sauf erreur ou omission, s.e.&o.
ed.	**edition,** édition, éd(it).
e.g.	**exempli gratia/for example,** par exemple, p.ex.
enc., encl.	**enclosure(s)/enclosed,** pièce(s) jointe(s), PJ; inclus, incl.
est.	**established,** fondé
ex.	**1. example,** exemple, ex. **2. exchange,** échange **3. extra,** extra; supplément
Exch.	**1. exchange,** échange; Bourse **2. Exchequer,** Échiquier
excl.	**1. excluding 2. exclusive**
ex cp.	**ex coupon,** ex-coupon, ex-c(oup).
ex div.	**ex dividend,** ex-dividende, ex-d.
exec.	**1. executive 2. executor**
exp.	**1. expense(s),** dépense(s) **2. export,** exportation, exp.
f.a.a.	**free of all average,** franc de toutes avaries
f.a.s.	**free alongside ship,** franco quai
f/c.	**for cash,** comptant
Feb.	**February,** février, fév.
fed.	**federation,** fédération
f.g.a.	**free of general average,** franc d'avaries communes, FAC
f.o.b.	**free on board,** franco de bord, FOB, f.o.b./franco à bord, f. à b.
f.o.c.	**free of charge,** franco, fco/ gratis
f.o.r., FOR	**free on rail,** franco sur rail/franco gare/franco wagon, FOR
f.p.	**fully paid,** libéré, lib.
f.p.a.	**free of particular average,** franc d'avaries particulières, FAP
Fri.	**Friday,** vendredi

F/S	**financial statement,** situation de trésorerie/état financier
ft	**foot, feet,** pied(s)
g	**gram,** gramme, g
g/a.	**general average,** avaries communes, a.c.
gal	**gallon,** gallon
gds	**goods,** marchandise, mise
GRT	**gross register ton,** tonneau de jauge brute
gr.wt	**gross weight,** poids brut
GT	**gross tonnage,** tonnage brut
HO	**head office,** siège social
HP	1. **hire purchase,** vente à crédit/à tempérament 2. **horse power,** cheval-vapeur, c.v.
hr(s)	**hour(s),** heure(s), h
i.e.	**id est/that is to say,** c'est-à-dire, c.-à-d.
imp.	**import,** importation, imp.
in(s)	**inch(es),** pouce(s)
Inc.	**Incorporated**
incl.	1. **included,** inclus, incl. 2. **including,** y compris 3. **inclusive,** inclusivement
info.	**information,** information/renseignements
ins.	**insurance,** assurance, asse
inst.,	**instant,** courant, ct
int.	**interest,** intérêt, int.
inv.	**invoice,** facture, fre
IOU	**I owe you,** reconnaissance de dette
J/A	**joint account,** compte (con)joint
Jan.	**January,** janvier, janv.
jnr, jr	**junior,** jeune/fils
Jul.	**July,** juillet
Jun.	**June,** juin
kg	**kilo(gram),** kilo(gramme), kg
kl	**kilolitre,** *NAm:* **kiloliter,** kilolitre, kl
km	**kilometre,** *NAm:* **kilometer,** kilomètre, km
km/h	**kilometres per hour,** kilomètre heure, km/h
kt	**kiloton,** kilotonne, kt
l	**litre,** *NAm:* **liter,** litre, l
lb	**pound (weight),** livre, lb
l/c	**letter of credit,** lettre de crédit, l/cr.
led.	**ledger,** grand(-)livre, g.l.
Ltd	**Limited (company),** (*i*) (société) anonyme, SA (*ii*) (société) à responsabilité limitée, SARL; (compagnie) limitée
m	1. **metre,** *NAm:* **meter,** mètre, m 2. **month,** mois, m
m/a	**my account,** mon compte, m/c.
Mar.	**March,** mars
max.	**maximum,** maximum, max.
memo.	**memorandum,** memorandum
min.	**minimum,** minimum, min.
MO	1. **mail order (business),** vente par correspondance, VPC 2. **money order,** mandat-poste, MP
m/o	**my order,** mon ordre, m/o.
Mon.	**Monday,** lundi
mortg.	**mortgage,** hypothèque, hyp.

mpg	**miles per gallon**=litres au cent (kilomètres)
MS	**manuscript,** manuscrit, MS
M/U	**making-up price,** cours de compensation, cc.
n.	**1. name,** nom, N **2. nominal,** nominal, N
NB	**nota bene**
n.c.v.	**no commercial value,** sans valeur commerciale
NF, N/F	**no funds,** défaut de provision
no.	**number,** numéro, nº
nos	**numbers,** numéros, nos
Nov.	**November,** novembre, nov.
NRT	**net register ton,** tonneau de jauge nette
n.s.f.	**not sufficient funds,** insuffisance de provision
Oct.	**October,** octobre, oct.
o/d., O/D	**1. on demand,** sur demande, à vue **2. overdrawn,** à découvert; **overdraft,** découvert
offs	**offices,** bureaux, burx
o/h	**overheads,** frais généraux, FG
ono.	**or near(est) offer**
o.p.	**out of print,** épuisé
o.s.	**out of stock,** manque en magasin; épuisé
OT	**overtime,** heures supplémentaires
Our ref.	**our reference,** notre référence, N/Réf.
oz	**ounce,** once
p	**1. penny, pence 2. page,** page, p. **3. premium,** prime
p.a.	**1. per annum,** par an, p.a. **2. particular average,** avaries particulières, a.p.
p&p	**postage and packing,** port et emballage
pat.	**patent,** brevet
pat.pend.	**patent pending,** demande de brevet déposée
pc.	**1. per cent.** pour cent **2. petty cash,** petite caisse **3. price current,** prix courant
pd	**paid,** acquitté
PG	**paying guest,** pensionnaire
pkg.	**1. package,** paquet **2. packing,** emballage
pkt	**packet,** paquet
PN, P/N	**promissory note,** billet à ordre, B/.
PO	**postal order,** mandat-poste, MP
p.p.	**1. per procurationem,** par procuration, p.pon **2. prepaid,** prépayé **3. postpaid,** affranchi
pp.	**pages,** pages, pp.
pr.	**price,** prix, px
pref.	**preference,** (actions de) préférence, préf.
prox.	**proximo,** (mois) prochain, pr.
PS	**postscript,** post-scriptum, PS
pt	**1. payment,** paiement **2. pint,** pinte, *FrC*: chopine
p.v.	**par value,** valeur au pair/parité
qnty, qty	**quantity,** quantité, q.
qt	**quart**
qtr	**1. quarter,** quart **2. quarterly,** trimestriel
RD	**refer(red) to drawer,** retour au tireur
rd	**road,** rue, r.
rcvd	**received,** reçu; pour acquit
re.	**regarding,** en ce qui concerne
red.	**redeemable,** amortissable; remboursable, remb.
ref.	**reference,** référence, Réf.

regd	**registered,** recommandé, r.
rly	**railway,** chemin de fer, ch. de f.
RSVP	**please reply,** répondez s'il vous plaît, RSVP
s.a.e.	**stamped addressed envelope,** enveloppe timbrée/affranchie
Sat.	**Saturday,** samedi
sec.	**secretary,** secrétaire
Sept.	**September,** septembre, sept.
sgd	**signed,** signé, s.
sh., shr.	**share,** action, act.; titre, t.
sit.	**situation,** emploi; **sits.vac.,** offres d'emploi
Snr	**senior,** aîné; père
s.o.	**1. seller's option,** prime vendeur **2. standing order,** ordre de transfert permanent
s.o.p.	**standard operating procedure**
St	**street,** rue, r.
ster.	**sterling,** livre sterling
stk	**stock, 1.** titre, t.; valeur, val., V/. **2.** stock (en magasin)
Sun.	**Sunday,** dimanche
t.	**1. tare,** tare, t. **2. ton,** tonne, t.
TA	**telegraphic address,** adresse télégraphique, ad(r). tél.
tel.	**telephone,** téléphone, tél.; **tel.no., telephone number,** numéro de téléphone, n° tél.
temp.	**temporary secretary,** dactylo intérimaire
Thurs.	**Thursday,** jeudi
tr.	**transfer,** transfert, virement, virt.
TT	**telegraphic transfer,** transfert télégraphique, tt.
Tues.	**Tuesday,** mardi
Tx	**Telex,** Télex
ult.	**ultimo,** (mois) écoulé
u.s.c.	**under separate cover,** sous pli séparé
U/W	**underwriter,** membre d'un syndicat de garantie
vo.	**verso,** verso, vo., v°
WB	**waybill,** feuille de route/lettre de voiture
w.c.	**without charge,** sans frais/gratis
Wed.	**Wednesday,** mercredi
wt	**weight,** poids, p.
xc.	**ex coupon,** ex-coupon, ex-c(oup).
xd.	**ex dividend,** ex-dividende, xd., ex-d.
yr	**1. year,** an/année **2. your,** votre
Your ref.	**your reference,** votre référence, V/Réf.
&	**ampersand,** et commercial
@	**at,** à
©	**copyright,** droit d'auteur
®	**registered trademark,** marque déposée
%	**per cent,** pour cent

AAAA	American Association of Advertising Agencies
AACCA	Associate of the Association of Certified and Corporate Accountants
AAIA	Associate of the Association of International Accountants
ABAA	Associate of the British Association of Accountants and Auditors
ABTA	Association of British Travel Agents
ACAS	Advisory, Conciliation and Arbitration Service
ACGI	Associate of the City and Guilds of London Institute
ACIS	Associate of the Chartered Institute of Secretaries
ACMA	Associate of the Institute of Cost and Management Accountants
ACPA	Associate of the Institute of Certified Public Accountants
ACRA	Associate of the Corporation of Registered Accountants
ACTU	Australian Council of Trade Unions
ADG	Assistant Director General
ADP	Automatic Data Processing, traitement automatique de l'information
AEA	American Economic Association
AFE	Authorization for expenditure
AFL-CIO	American Federation of Labor and Congress of Industrial Organizations
AG	1. Accountant General, Chef de la Comptabilité 2. Attorney General 3. Agent General
AGM	Annual General Meeting, assemblée générale annuelle
AIA	1. American Institute of Accountants 2. Associate of the Institute of Actuaries
AIAA	Associate of the Institute of Accountants and Actuaries
AIB	American Institute of Bankers
AID	US: Agency for International Development
AIWM	American Institute of Weights and Measures
ALGOL	Cmptr: algorithmic language
AMEX	American Express Company
ANPA	American Newspaper Publishers' Association
ANSI	American National Standards Institute = Association française de normalisation, AFNOR
AO	1. Accounting officer 2. Administration officer
AOB	Any other business
AP	Associated Press
APT	Advanced Passenger Train = train grande vitesse, TGV
AR	Annual return, revenu annuel
ARAMCO	Arabian-American Oil Company
ARICS	Associate of the Royal Institute of Chartered Surveyors
ASA	1. Advertising Standards Authority, Bureau de la vérification de la publicité, BVP 2. American Standards Association
ASE	American Stock Exchange
ASTMS	Association of Scientific, Technical and Managerial Staff
ATA	US: 1. Air Transport Association 2. American Trucking Association
BA	British Airways
BB	US: Bureau of the Budget
BCom	Bachelor of Commerce
BEcon	Bachelor of Economics
BHRA	British Hotels and Restaurants Association
BID	Bachelor of Industrial Design
BIF	British Industries Fair
BIM	British Institute of Management
BIS	Bank for International Settlements
BL	British Leyland

BLL	**Bachelor of Laws**
B of E	**Bank of England**
BNOC	**British National Oil Corporation**
BP	**British Petroleum**
BR	**British Rail**
BRS	**British Road Services**
BSBA	**Bachelor of Science in Business Administration**
BSc	**Bachelor of Science**
BSC	**British Steel Corporation**
BSCP	**British Standard Code of Practice**
BSI	**British Standards Institution** = Association française de normalisation, AFNOR
BSIR	**Bachelor of Science in Industrial Relations**
BSS	**British Standard Specification**
BST	**1. British Summer Time,** heure d'été britannique **2. British Standard Time,** heure légale britannique
BTA	**British Travel Association**
BUPA	**British United Provident Association**
CA	**1. Chartered Accountant**/*US:* **Certified Accountant,** expert comptable **2. Consumers Association**
CAC	*US:* **Consumers' Advisory Council**
CAP	**1. Common Agricultural Policy,** Politique agricole commune, PAC **2. Code of advertising practice**
CARIFTA	**Caribbean Free Trade Area**
CBI	**Confederation of British Industry** = Conseil national du patronat français, CNPF
CC	**Chamber of Commerce**
CCA	**Current cost accounting**
CCC	**Canadian Chamber of Commerce**
CED	**Committee for Economic Development**
CEEC	**Council for European Economic Co-operation**
CEGB	**Central Electricity Generating Board**
CEO	**Chief Executive Officer**
CGI	**City and Guilds Institute**
CIA	*US:* **Certified Industrial Accountant**
CICA	**Canadian Institute of Chartered Accountants**
CIO	*US:* **Congress of Industrial Organizations**
CIS	**Chartered Institute of Secretaries**
CITB	**Construction Industry Training Board**
CM	**Common Market,** marché commun
COBOL	*Cmptr:* **common business oriented language**
COD	**Cash on delivery**/*NAm:* **collect on delivery,** livraison contre remboursement
COI	**Central Office of Information**
COMECON	**Council for Mutual Economic Aid,** Conseil de l'aide économique mutuelle, COMECON
COSIRA	**Council for Small Industries in Rural Areas**
CPA	*NAm:* **Certified Public Accountant** = expert comptable
CPI	**Consumer Price Index**
CPM	**Critical Path Method,** méthode du chemin critique
CPR	**Canadian Pacific Railway**
CS	**Civil Service,** Administration civile
CSC	**Civil Service Commission**
CSE	**Certificate of Secondary Education**
CWS	**Co-operative Wholesale Society,** société coopérative de consommation
DA	*US:* **District Attorney**
DAP	**Documents against payment,** documents contre paiement, DP

DAP	**Documents against payment,** documents contre paiement, DP
DCF	**Discounted cash flow,** cash flow actualisé
DCom	**Doctor of Commerce**
DComL	**Doctor of Commercial Law**
DDD	*NAm:* **Direct distance dialing** = le téléphone automatique/l'automatique
DEcon	**Doctor of Economics**
DERV	**Diesel engined road vehicle**
DHSS	**Department of Health and Social Security**
DIM	**Diploma in Industrial Management**
DipCOM	**Diploma of Commerce**
DipEcon	**Diploma of Economics**
DipPA	**Diploma in Public Administration**
DipTech	**Diploma in Technology**
DPP	**Director of Public Prosecutions**
DPR	**Director of Public Relations** = chef du service des relations publiques
EAAA	**European Association of Advertising Agencies**
E&OE	**Errors and omissions excepted,** sauf erreur ou omission, s.e.&o.
ECE	**Economic Commission for Europe,** Commission économique pour l'Europe, CEE
ECU	**European currency unit,** unité de compte européenne, UCE
EDP	**Electronic data processing,** informatique
EEA	**Exchange Equalization Account**
EEC	**European Economic Community,** Communauté économique européenne, CEE
EEOC	**Equal Employment Opportunities Commission**
EFTA	**European Free Trade Association,** Association européenne de libre-échange, AELE
EGM	**Extraordinary general meeting,** assemblée générale extraordinaire
EIB	**European Investments Bank,** Banque européenne d'investissement, BEI
EMA	**European Monetary Agreement,** Accord monétaire européen, AME
EMS	**European Monetary System,** Système monétaire européen, SME
EPU	**European Payments Union,** Union européenne des paiements, UEP
ERNIE	**Electronic Random Number Indicator Equipment**
ETA	**Estimated time of arrival**
ETO	**European Transport Organization**
FACCA	**Fellow of the Association of Certified and Corporate Accountants**
FAO	**Food and Agriculture Organization,** Organisation pour l'alimentation et l'agriculture
FBAA	**Fellow of the British Association of Accountants and Auditors**
FBIM	**Fellow of the British Institute of Management**
FCA	**Fellow of the Institute of Chartered Accountants (of England & Wales)**
FCGI	**Fellow of the City and Guilds of London Institute**
FCI	**Fellow of the Institute of Commerce**
FCIA	**Fellow of the Institute of Insurance Agents**
FCMA	**Fellow of the Institute of Cost and Management Accountants**
FDA	*US:* **Food and Drug Administration**
FIA	**Fellow of the Institute of Actuaries**
FIAC	**Fellow of the Institute of Company Accountants**
FIB	**Fellow of the Institute of Bankers**
FIFO	**First in first out,** premier entré premier sorti, PEPS
FIPM	**Fellow of the Institute of Personnel Management**
FORTRAN	*Cmptr:* **formular translation**
FRICS	**Fellow of the Royal Institute of Chartered Surveyors**
FSVA	**Fellow of the Incorporated Society of Valuers and Auctioneers**
FT	**Financial Times**
FTC	*US:* **Federal Trade Commission**
GAO	**General Accounting Officer**

GATT	**General Agreement on Tariffs and Trade,** Accord général sur les tarifs douaniers et le commerce, AGTDC
GCE	**General Certificate of Education**
GMT	**Greenwich Mean Time,** temps civil de Greenwich
GMWU	**General and Municipal Workers Union**
GNI	**Gross National Income**
GNP	**Gross National Product,** produit national brut, PNB
HEW	*US:* **Department of Health, Education and Welfare**
HGV	**Heavy goods vehicle,** poids lourd
HMSO	**His/Her Majesty's Stationery Office**
HNC	**Higher National Certificate**
HND	**Higher National Diploma**
HST	**High speed train,** train grande vitesse, TGV
IAF	**International Automobile Federation,** Fédération internationale de l'automobile, FIA
IAM	**Institute of Administrative Management**
IATA	**International Air Transport Association,** Association internationale des transports aériens, AITA
IBM	**International Business Machines**
IBRD	**International Bank for Reconstruction and Development,** Banque internationale pour la reconstruction et le développement, BIRD
ICA	**Institute of Chartered Accountants**
ICAO	**International Civil Aviation Authority Organization,** Organisation internationale de l'aviation civile, OIAC
ICMA	**Institute of Cost and Management Accountants**
ICI	**Imperial Chemical Industries**
IDD	**International Direct Dialling** = l'automatique international
IFC	**International Finance Corporation**
IFTU	**International Federation of Trade Unions,** Fédération syndicale internationale, FSI
ILO	**International Labour Organization,** Organisation internationale du travail, OIT
IMF	**International Monetary Fund,** Fonds monétaire international, FMI
IOB	**1. Institute of bankers 2. Institute of Book-keepers**
IOM	**Institute of Office Management**
IOU	**I owe you,** reconnaissance de dette
IPM	**Institute of Personnel Management**
IPR	**Institute of Public Relations**
IR	**Inland Revenue** = le Fisc
IRS	*NAm:* **Internal Revenue Service** = le Fisc
ISBN	**International Standard Book Number**
ISFA	**Institute of Shipping and Forwarding Agents**
ISO	**International Standards Organization**
ITO	**International Trade Organisation**
JAL	**Japan Airlines**
JP	**Justice of the Peace**
KAL	**Korean Airlines**
KLM	**Royal Dutch Airlines,** Société royale d'aviation des pays bas, KLM
LC	**Library of Congress**
LIFO	**Last in first out,** dernier entré premier sorti
LLB	**Bachelor of Laws**
LLD	**Doctor of Laws**
LR	**Lloyds Register**
LSE	**1. London Stock Exchange 2. London School of Economics**
LV	**Luncheon Voucher** = ticket-repas/ticket-restaurant

MBIM	**Member of the British Institute of Management**
MBO	**Management by objectives,** direction par objectifs, DPO
MCom	**Master of Commerce**
MD	**Managing Director** = Président-Directeur Général, P-DG
MEcon	**Master of Economics**
MIS	**Management Information System**
MLR	**Minimum Lending Rate**
MMB	**Milk Marketing Board**
MRP	**Manufacturer's recommended price**
MSc	**Master of Science**
NALGO	**National and Local Government Officers Association**
NATO	**North Atlantic Treaty Organization,** Organisation du traité de l'Atlantique du nord, OTAN
NC	**National Carriers**
NEB	**National Enterprise Board**
NEC	**National executive committee**
NEDC	(*also* **Neddy**) **National Economic Development Council**
NHS	**National Health Service**
NI	**National Insurance**
NPA	**Newspaper Publishers' Association**
NSB	**National Savings Bank** = Caisse Nationale d'Épargne, CNE
NUPE	**National Union of Public Employees**
NYSE	**New York Stock Exchange**
O&M	**Organization and Methods,** organisation et méthodes, OM
OAP	**Old age pensioner**
OECD	**Organization for Economic Co-operation and Development,** Organisation de coopération et de développement économique, OCDE
OHMS	**On His/Her Majesty's Service**
OIT	**Office of International Trade**
OPEC	**Organization of Petrol Exporting Countries,** Organisation des pays exportateurs de pétrole, OPEP
OR	**Operational Research,** recherche opérationnelle, RO
PA	**1. Press Association 2. Publishers Association 3. Personal Assistant,** assistant(e) particulier(-ière), AP **4. Public Address System,** sonorisation extérieure
PABX	**Private automatic branch (telephone) exchange**
PAYE	**Pay as you earn** = impôt retenu à la source/à la base
PBDS	**Publishers and Booksellers Delivery Service**
PER	**Price earnings ratio,** taux de capitalisation des bénéfices
PERT	**Programme, evaluation and review technique** = méthode de programmation optimale, PERT
PLA	**Port of London Authority**
PLC	**Public Limited Company**
PLR	**Public lending right**
PMG	**1. Postmaster General,** directeur général des Postes **2. Paymaster General**
PO	**Post Office** = Postes et Télécommunications, P et T
POB	**Post Office Box,** Boîte postale, BP
POP	**Post Office Preferred (envelopes)** = formats postaux normalisés
PPBS	**Planning, programming and budgeting system** = rationalisation des choix budgétaires, RCB
PPP	**Private Patients Plan**
PR	**Public Relations,** relations publiques, RP
PRO	**Public Relations Officer**
PSBR	**Public sector borrowing requirement**

PSV	**Public Service Vehicle**
QANTAS	**Queensland and Northern Territory Aerial Services (Australian International Airline)**
QC	**Queens Counsel** = *FrC:* Conseiller de la Reine, CR
QUANGO	**Quasi autonomous non-governmental organization**
RE	**Royal Exchange,** Bourse du Commerce
RFD	*US:* **Rural free delivery service**
RO	**Receiving Office** = bureau des messageries
ROI	**Return on Investment**
RPM	**Resale/retail price maintenance**
RRP	**Recommended retail price**
RSVP	**please reply/answer,** répondez s'il vous plaît, RSVP
SAS	**Scandinavian Airlines System**
SAYE	**Save as you earn**
SDR	**Special drawing rights,** droits de tirage spéciaux, DTS
SEC	*US:* **Securities and Exchange Commission**
SICA	**Society of Industrial and Cost Accountants of Canada**
STD	**Subscriber Trunk Dialling,** l'automatique
TASS	**Telegraphic News Agency of the Soviet Union,** agence TASS
TGWU	**Transport and General Workers Union**
TO	**Telegraphic Office**
TT	**Telegraphic transfer,** transfert télégraphique, TT
TU	**Trade Union,** syndicat
TUC	**Trades Union Congress**
TWA	**Transworld Airlines**
UAW	*US:* **United Automobile Workers**
UN	**United Nations,** Nations Unies, NU
UNCTAD	**United Nations Conference on Trade and Development,** Conférence des Nations Unies pour le commerce et le développement, UNCTAD
UNIDO	**United Nations Industrial Development Organization**
UNO	**United Nations Organization,** Organisation des Nations Unies, ONU
UPI	**United Press International**
UPU	**Universal Postal Union,** Union postale universelle, UPU
USDAW	**Union of Shop, Distributive & Allied Workers**
USIA	**United States Information Agency**
USM	**1. United States Mint 2. Unlisted Securities Market**
USP	**Unique selling proposition**
USPO	**United States Post Office**
VAT	**Value-added tax,** taxe à la valeur ajoutée, TVA
VDT	**Visual Display Terminal,** écran de visualisation/visuel
VDU	**Visual Display Unit,** écran de visualisation/visuel
VIP	**Very important person**
WEU	**Western European Union,** Union de l'Europe occidentale, UEO
WFTU	**World Federation of Trade Unions,** Fédération syndicale mondiale, FSM
ZIP	*US:* **Zone improvement plan**

COUNTRY	PAYS	CURRENCY	MONNAIE
Afghanistan	Afghanistan *m*	Afghani	Afghani *m*
Albania	Albanie *f*	Lek	Lek *m*
Algeria	Algérie *f*	(Algerian) **Dinar**	Dinar *m* (algérien)
Angola	Angola *f*	(Angolan) **Escudo**	Escudo *m* (d'Angola)
Argentina	Argentine *f*	(Argentinian) **Peso**	Peso *m* (argentinien)
Australia	Australie *f*	(Australian) **Dollar**	Dollar *m* (australien)
Austria	Autriche *f*	Schilling	Schilling *m*
Bahamas	Bahamas *mpl*	Dollar	Dollar *m*
Bahrain	Bahrein *m*	Dinar	Dinar *m*
Bangladesh	Bangla-desh *m*	Taka	Taka *m*
Belgium	Belgique *f*	(Belgian) **Franc**	Franc *m* (belge)
Bermuda	Bermudes *fpl*	Dollar	Dollar *m*
Bolivia	Bolivie *f*	(Bolivian) **Peso**	Peso *m* (bolivien)
Brazil	Brésil *m*	Cruzeiro	Cruzeiro *m*
Bulgaria	Bulgarie *f*	Lev	Lev *m*
Burma	Birmanie *f*	Kyat	Kyat *m*
Burundi	Burundi *m*	(Burundi) **Franc**	Franc *m* (du Burundi)
Cameroon	Cameroun *m*	CFA Franc	Franc CFA
Canada	Canada *m*	(Canadian) **Dollar**	Dollar *m* (canadien)
Central African Republic	République centrafricaine	CFA Franc	Franc CFA
Chad	Tchad *m*	CFA Franc	Franc CFA
Chile	Chili *m*	Escudo	Escudo *m*
China	Chine *f*	Yuan	Yuan *m*
Colombia	Colombie *f*	(Colombian) **Peso**	Peso *m* (colombien)
(Brazzaville) Congo	Congo-Brazzaville *m*	CFA Franc	Franc CFA
Costa Rica	Costa Rica *m*	Colon	Colon *m*
Cuba	Cuba	(Cuban) **Peso**	Peso *m* (cubain)
Cyprus	Chypre	(Cyprus) **Pound**	Livre *f* (chypriote)
Czechoslovakia	Tchécoslovaquie *f*	Koruna	Couronne *f*
Dahomey	Dahomey *m*	CFA Franc	Franc CFA
Denmark	Danemark *m*	Krone	Couronne *f*
Dominican Republic	République Dominicaine	Peso	Peso *m*
Ecuador	Équateur *m*	Sucre	Sucre *m*
Egypt	Égypte *f*	(Egyptian) **Pound**	Livre *f* (égyptienne)
El Salvador	Salvador *m*	Colon	Colon *m*
Ethiopia	Éthiopie *f*	(Ethiopian) **Dollar**	Dollar *m* (éthiopien)
Finland	Finlande *f*	Markka	Mark *m* (finlandais)
France	France *f*	(French) **Franc**	Franc *m* (français)
Gabon	Gabon *m*	CFA Franc	Franc CFA
Gambia	Gambie *f*	CFA Franc	Franc CFA
Germany (Federal Republic-GFR)	République Fédérale Allemande-RFA	Mark/Deutschmark	Mark *m* Deutschmark *m*
Germany (Democratic Republic-GDR)	République Démocratique Allemande-RDA	Mark/Ostmark	Mark *m* Ostmark *m*
Ghana	Ghana *m*	Cedi	Cedi *m*

COUNTRY	PAYS	CURRENCY	MONNAIE
Greece	Grèce *f*	Drachma	Drachme *m*
Guatamala	Guatemala *m*	Quetzal	Quetzal *m*
Guinea	Guinée *f*	Suli	Suli *m*
Guyana	Guyane *f*	(Guyana) **Dollar**	Dollar *m* (guyanais)
Haiti	Haïti *m*	Gourde	Gourde *f*
Honduras	Honduras *m*	Lempira	Lempira *m*
Hong Kong	Hong Kong *m*	(Hong Kong) **Dollar**	Dollar *m* (de Hong Kong)
Hungary	Hongrie *f*	Forint	Forint *m*
Iceland	Islande *f*	Krone	Couronne *f*
India	Inde *f*	Rupee	Roupie *f*
Indonesia	Indonésie *f*	Rupiah	Rupiah *m*
Iran	Iran *m*	Rial	Rial *m*
Iraq	Irak *m*	(Iraqui) **Dinar**	Dinar *m* (irakien)
Irish Republic	Irlande *f*	(Irish) **Pound/Punt**	Livre *f* (irlandaise)
Israel	Israël	(Israeli) **Pound**	Livre *f* (israëlienne)
Italy	Italie *f*	Lira	Lire *f*
Ivory Coast	Côte d'Ivoire *f*	CFA Franc	Franc CFA
Jamaica	Jamaïque *f*	(Jamaican) **Dollar**	Dollar *m* (jamaïcain)
Japan	Japon *m*	Yen	Yen *m*
Jordan	Jordanie *f*	(Jordanian) **Dinar**	Dinar *m* (jordanien)
Kampuchea	Kampuchea	Riel	Riel *m*
Kenya	Kenya	Shilling	Shilling *m*
Korea (North)	Corée *f* (du nord)	Won	Won *m*
Korea (South)	Corée *f* (du sud)	Won	Won *m*
Kuwait	Kuweit *m*	(Kuwaiti) **Dinar**	Dinar *m* (du Kuweit)
Laos	Laos *m*	Kip	Kip *m*
Lebanon	Liban *m*	(Lebanese) **Pound**	Livre *f* (libanaise)
Liberia	Libéria *m*	(Liberian) **Dollar**	Dollar *m* (libérien)
Libya	Libye *f*	(Libyan) **Dinar**	Dinar *m* (libyen)
Luxemburg	Luxembourg *m*	(Luxemburg) **Franc**	Franc *m* (du Luxembourg)
Malagasy Republic	République Malgache *f*	(Malagasy) **Franc**	Franc *m* (malgache)
Malawi	Malawi *m*	Kwacha	Kwacha *m*
Malaysia	Malaisie *f*	(Malaysian) **Dollar**	Dollar *m* (malais)
Mali	Mali *m*	(Mali) **Franc**	Franc *m* (du Mali)
Malta	Malte	(Maltese) **Pound**	Livre *f* (maltaise)
Mauritania	Mauritanie *f*	CFA Franc	Franc CFA
Mauritius	Île Maurice	Rupee	Roupie *f*
Mexico	Mexique *m*	Peso	Peso *m*
Morocco	Maroc *m*	Dirham	Dirham *m*
Mozambique	Mozambique *m*	Escudo	Escudo *m*
Nepal	Népal *m*	Rupee	Roupie *f*
The Netherlands	Les Pays Bas	Guilder	Florin *m*
New Zealand	Nouvelle-Zélande	(New Zealand) **Dollar**	Dollar *m* (néo-zélandais)
Nicaragua	Nicaragua *m*	Cordoba	Cordoba *m*
Niger	Niger *m*	CFA Franc	Franc CFA
Nigeria	Nigeria *m* or *f*	Naira	Naira *m*

COUNTRY	PAYS	CURRENCY	MONNAIE
Norway	Norvège *f*	Krone	Couronne *f*
Oman	Oman *m*	Rial (Omani)	Riel *m* (omani)
Pakistan	Pakistan *m*	Rupee	Roupie *f*
Panama	Panama *m*	Balboa	Balboa *m*
Paraguay	Paraguay *m*	Guarani	Guarani *m*
Peru	Pérou *m*	Sol	Sol *m*
Philippines	Philippines *fpl*	Peso	Peso *m*
Poland	Pologne *f*	Zloty	Zloty *m*
Portugal	Portugal *m*	Escudo	Escudo *m*
Qatar	Qatar *m*	Riyal	Riel *m*
Romania	Roumanie *f*	Leu	Leu *m*
Rwanda	Ruanda *m*	(Rwanda) **Franc**	Franc *m* (du Ruanda)
Saudi Arabia	Arabie Saoudite	Riyal	Riyal *m*
Senegal	Sénégal *m*	CFA Franc	Franc CFA
Sierra Leone	Sierra Leone	Leone	Leone *m*
Singapore	Singapour *m*	(Singapore) **Dollar**	Dollar *m* (de Singapour)
Somalia	Somalie *f*	Shilling	Shilling *m*
South Africa	Afrique du Sud	Rand	Rand *m*
Soviet Union/USSR	Union Soviétique/URSS	Rouble	Rouble *m*
Spain	Espagne *f*	Peseta	Peseta *f*
Sri Lanka	Sri Lanka *m*	(Sinhalese) **Rupee**	Roupie *f* (cingalaise)
Sudan	Soudan *m*	(Sudanese) **Pound**	Livre *f* (soudanaise)
Surinam	Surinam *m*	Guilder	Florin *m* (du Surinam)
Sweden	Suède *f*	Krona	Couronne *f*
Switzerland	Suisse *f*	(Swiss) **Franc**	Franc *m* (suisse)
Syria	Syrie *f*	(Syrian) **Pound**	Livre *f* (syrienne)
Taiwan	Taiwan	(Taiwan) **Dollar**	Dollar *m* (de Taiwan)
Tanzania	Tanzanie *f*	Shilling	Shilling *m*
Thailand	Thaïlande *f*	Baht	Baht *m*
Togo	Togo *m*	CFA Franc	Franc CFA
Tunisia	Tunisie *f*	Dinar	Dinar *m*
Turkey	Turquie *f*	(Turkish) **Lira**	Livre *f* (turque)
Uganda	Ouganda *m*	Shilling	Shilling *m*
United Arab Emirates	Émirats Arabes Unis	Dirham	Dirham *m*
United Kingdom/UK	Royaume Uni *m*	Pound (sterling)	Livre *f* (sterling)
United States of America/USA	États-Unis *mpl* d'Amérique	(US) **Dollar**	Dollar *m* (US)
Upper Volta	Haute-Volta *f*	CFA Franc	Franc CFA
Uruguay	Uruguay *m*	Peso	Peso *m*
Venezuela	Venezuela *m*	Bolivar	Bolivar *m*
Vietnam	Vietnam *m*	Dong	Dong *m*
Yemen (Sana)	Yémen *m* (Sanaa)	(Yemei) **Riyal**	Rial *m*
Yemen (Aden)	Yémen *m* (Aden)	Dinar	Dinar *m*
Yugoslavia	Yougoslavie *f*	Dinar	Dinar *m*
Zaire	Zaïre *m*	Zaire	Zaïre *m*
Zambia	Zambie *f*	Kwacha	Kwacha *m*

CFA Franc/Franc CFA = Franc de la communauté financière d'Afrique

UNITED STATES: POST OFFICE ABBREVIATIONS—
ABRÉVIATIONS POSTALES: US

AL	ALABAMA		NC	NORTH CAROLINA
AK	ALASKA		ND	NORTH DAKOTA
AR	ARKANSAS		NE	NEBRASKA
AZ	ARIZONA		NH	NEW HAMPSHIRE
CA	CALIFORNIA		NJ	NEW JERSEY
CO	COLORADO		NM	NEW MEXICO
CT	CONNECTICUT		NV	NEVADA
DE	DELAWARE		NY	NEW YORK
FL	FLORIDA		OH	OHIO
GA	GEORGIA		OK	OKLAHOMA
HI	HAWAII		OR	OREGON
IA	IOWA		PA	PENNSYLVANIA
ID	IDAHO		RI	RHODE ISLAND
IL	ILLINOIS		SC	SOUTH CAROLINA
IN	INDIANA		SD	SOUTH DAKOTA
KS	KANSAS		TN	TENNESSEE
KY	KENTUCKY		TX	TEXAS
LA	LOUISIANA		UT	UTAH
MA	MASSACHUSETTS		VA	VIRGINIA
MD	MARYLAND		VT	VERMONT
ME	MAINE		WA	WASHINGTON
MI	MICHIGAN		WDC	WASHINGTON DISTRICT
MN	MINNESOTA			OF COLUMBIA
MO	MISSOURI		WI	WISCONSIN
MS	MISSISSIPPI		WV	WEST VIRGINIA
MT	MONTANA		WY	WYOMING

US ZIP CODES: TOWNS WITH A POPULATION GREATER THAN 300 000— NUMÉROS DE CODE DES VILLES LES PLUS IMPORTANTES (AU-DELÀ DE 300 000 h.)

ATLANTA	GA	30301	MINNEAPOLIS	MN	55401
BALTIMORE	MD	21233	NASHVILLE	TN	37202
BIRMINGHAM	AL	35203	NEWARK	NJ	07101
BOSTON	MA	02109	NEW ORLEANS	LA	70140
BUFFALO	NY	14240	NEW YORK CITY	NY	10001
CHICAGO	IL	60607	NORFOLK	VA	23501
CINCINNATI	OH	45202	OAKLAND	CA	94617
COLUMBUS	OH	43216	OKLAHOMA CITY	OK	73125
DALLAS	TX	75221	OMAHA	NE	68108
DETROIT	MI	48226	PHILADELPHIA	PA	19104
EL PASO	TX	79940	PHOENIX	AZ	85026
FORTH WORTH	TX	76101	PITTSBURG	PA	15230
HONOLULU	HI	96819	PORTLAND	OR	97208
HOUSTON	TX	77052	SAN ANTONIO	TX	78205
INDIANAPOLIS	IN	46204	SAN DIEGO	CA	92101
JACKSONVILLE	FL	32201	SAN FRANCISCO	CA	94101
KANSAS CITY	MO	64108	SAN JOSE	CA	95113
LONG BEACH	CA	90801	SEATTLE	WA	98101
LOS ANGELES	CA	90053	ST LOUIS	MO	63166
LOUISVILLE	KY	40202	ST PAUL	MN	55101
MEMPHIS	TN	38101	TOLEDO	OH	43601
MIAMI	FL	33101	TULSA	OK	74101
MILWAUKEE	WI	53201	WASHINGTON	WDC	20013

NUMÉROS DE CODE DES DÉPARTEMENTS FRANÇAIS
CODE NUMBERS OF FRENCH DEPARTMENTS

01 Ain	25 Doubs	48 Lozère	72 Sarthe
02 Aisne	26 Drôme	49 Maine-et-Loire	73 Savoie
03 Allier	27 Eure	50 Manche	74 Savoie (Haute-)
04 Alpes (Basses-)	28 Eure-et-Loir	51 Marne	75 Paris (Ville de)
05 Alpes (Hautes-)	29N Nord-Finistère	52 Marne (Haute-)	76 Seine-Maritime
06 Alpes-Maritimes	29S Sud-Finistère	53 Mayenne	77 Seine-et-Marne
07 Ardèche	30 Gard	54 Meurthe-et-Moselle	78 Yvelines
08 Ardennes	31 Garonne (Haute-)	55 Meuse	79 Sèvres (Deux-)
09 Ariège	32 Gers	56 Morbihan	80 Somme
10 Aube	33 Gironde	57 Moselle	81 Tarn
11 Aude	34 Hérault	58 Nièvre	82 Tarn-et-Garonne
12 Aveyron	35 Ille-et-Vilaine	59 Nord	83 Var
13 Bouches-du-Rhône	36 Indre	60 Oise	84 Vaucluse
14 Calvados	37 Indre-et-Loire	61 Orne	85 Vendée
15 Cantal	38 Isère	62 Pas-de-Calais	86 Vienne
16 Charente	39 Jura	63 Puy-de-Dôme	87 Vienne (Haute-)
17 Charente-Maritime	40 Landes	64 Pyrénées (Basses-)	88 Vosges
18 Cher	41 Loir-et-Cher	65 Pyrénées (Hautes-)	89 Yonne
19 Corrèze	42 Loire	66 Pyrénées-Orientales	90 Belfort (Territ.)
20 Corse	43 Loire (Haute-)	67 Rhin (Bas-)	91 Essonne
21 Côte-d'Or	44 Loire-Atlantique	68 Rhin (Haut-)	92 Hauts-de-Seine
22 Côtes-du-Nord	45 Loiret	69 Rhône	93 Seine-St-Denis
23 Creuse	46 Lot	70 Saône (Haute-)	94 Val-de-Marne
24 Dordogne	47 Lot-et-Garonne	71 Saône-et-Loire	95 Val-d'Oise

NUMÉROS POSTAUX DES VILLES DE FRANCE
FRENCH POSTAL CODES

80100 Abbeville	62100 Calais	53000 Laval	64000 Pau
47000 Agen	59400 Cambrai	93350 Le Bourget	24000 Périgueux
13100 Aix-en-Provence	06400 Cannes	76600 Le Havre	66000 Perpignan
20000 Ajaccio	11000 Carcassonne	72000 Le Mans	86000 Poitiers
61000 Alençon	51000 Châlons/Marne	43000 Le Puy	07000 Privas
80000 Amiens	73000 Chambéry	59000 Lille	29000 Quimper
49000 Angers	74400 Chamonix	87000 Limoges	51100 Reims
16000 Angoulême	08000 Charleville-	14100 Lisieux	35000 Rennes
74000 Annecy	Mézières	65100 Lourdes	17300 Rochefort
06600 Antibes	28000 Chartres	69001 Lyon	59100 Roubaix
33120 Arcachon	36000 Châteauroux	71000 Mâcon	76000 Rouen
13200 Arles	50100 Cherbourg	13001 Marseille	17200 Royan
62000 Arras	63100 Clermont-Ferrand	77000 Melun	22000 Saint-Brieuc
15000 Aurillac	68000 Colmar	57000 Metz	42000 Saint-Étienne
89000 Auxerre	60200 Compiègne	40000 Mont-de-Marsan	50000 Saint-Lô
84000 Avignon	14800 Deauville	34000 Montpellier	35400 Saint-Malo
60000 Beauvais	76200 Dieppe	03000 Moulins	44600 Saint-Nazaire
90000 Belfort	21000 Dijon	68100 Mulhouse	08200 Sedan
25000 Besançon	59500 Douai	54000 Nancy	67000 Strasbourg
64200 Biarritz	59140 Dunkerque	44000 Nantes	83100 Toulon
41000 Blois	88000 Épinal	11100 Narbonne	31000 Toulouse
33000 Bordeaux	74500 Évian	58000 Nevers	59200 Tourcoing
62200 Boulogne/mer	27000 Évreux	06000 Nice	37000 Tours
01000 Bourg-en-Bresse	38000 Grenoble	30000 Nîmes	10000 Troyes
18000 Bourges	06160 Juan-les-Pins	79000 Niort	59300 Valenciennes
29200 Brest	44500 La Baule	45000 Orléans	56000 Vannes
14000 Caen	02000 Laon	94310 Orly	78000 Versailles
46000 Cahors	17000 La Rochelle	75001 Paris	03200 Vichy

NUMÉROS POSTAUX DES VILLES DE BELGIQUE ET DE SUISSE
BELGIAN AND SWISS POSTAL CODES

BELGIQUE

9300 Aalst (Alost)
5220 Andenne
2000 Antwerpen (Anvers)
6700 Arlon
7800 Ath
6650 Bastogne
7130 Binche
2650 Boom
1420 Braine-l'Alleud
7490 Braine-le-Comte
8000 Brugge (Bruges)
1000 Bruxelles
6000 Charleroi
6071 Châtelet
6460 Chimay
1010 Cité administrative de l'État Bruxelles
9330 Dendermonde (Termonde)

3290 Diest
5500 Dinant
4700 Eupen
5800 Gembloux
9000 Gent (Gand)
1500 Halle (Hal)
3500 Hasselt
5200 Huy
8900 Ieper (Ypres)
5100 Jambes
8500 Kortrijk (Courtrai)
3000 Leuven (Louvain)
4000 Liège
2500 Lier (Lierre)
4890 Malmédy
5400 Marche-en-Famenne
2800 Mechelen (Malines)
8600 Menen (Menin)
7000 Mons
7700 Mouscron
5000 Namur

6620 Neufchâteau
1400 Nivelles
1100 Office des Chèques Postaux Bruxelles
8400 Oostende (Ostende)
9600 Renaix
8800 Roeselare (Roulers)
6900 Saint-Hubert
2700 St-Niklaas (St-Nicolas)
7400 Soignies
4880 Spa
4970 Stavelot
3300 Tienen (Tirlemont)
3700 Tongeren (Tongres)
7500 Tournai
2300 Turnhout
4800 Verviers
1800 Vilvoorde (Vilvorde)
1300 Wavre (Waver)

SUISSE

5400 Baden
4000 Bâle
6500 Bellinzona
3000 Berne
2500 Biel/Bienne
2300 Chaux-de-Fonds
8500 Frauenfeld
1700 Fribourg
1200 Genève
2540 Grenchen
3800 Interlaken
8700 Küsnacht ZH

1000 Lausanne
6600 Locarno
6000 Lucerne
6900 Lugano
1820 Montreux
2000 Neuchâtel
4125 Riehen
9000 Saint-Gall
7500 Saint-Moritz
8200 Schaffhouse
1950 Sion

8800 Thalwil
3600 Thun
8610 Uster
1800 Vevey
8820 Wädenswil
5430 Wettingen
8400 Winterthur
1400 Yverdon
4800 Zofingen
6300 Zug
8000 Zürich

WORLD TIME ZONES—FUSEAUX HORAIRES

GMT = 1200 hours/heures

	Hours/Heures		Hours/Heures
ADELAIDE	2130	LUXEMBOURG	1300
ALGIERS/ALGER	1300	MADEIRA/MADÈRE	1100
AMSTERDAM	1300	MADRID	1300
ANKARA	1400	MALTA	1300
ATHENS/ATHÈNES	1400	MEXICO CITY	0600
BEIRUT	1400	MONTEVIDEO	0830
BELGRADE	1400	MONTREAL	0700
BERLIN	1300	MOSCOW/MOSCOU	1500
BERNE	1300	NAIROBI	1500
BONN	1300	NEW ORLEANS	0600
BOMBAY	1730	NEW YORK	0700
BRASILIA	0900	OSLO	1300
BRISBANE	2200	OTTAWA	0700
BRUSSELS/		PANAMA	0700
BRUXELLES	1300	PARIS	1300
BUCHAREST	1400	PEKING/PÉKIN	2000
BUDAPEST	1300	PERTH (Austr.)	2000
BUENOS AIRES	0800	PRAGUE	1300
CAIRO/LE CAIRE	1400	PRETORIA	1400
CALCUTTA	1730	QUÉBEC	0700
CAPE TOWN/LE CAP	1400	RANGOON	0530
CARACAS	0800	RIO DE JANEIRO	0900
CHICAGO	0600	RIYADH/RIYAD	1500
COLOMBO	1730	ST LOUIS (USA)	0600
COPENHAGEN	1100	SAN FRANCISCO	0400
DELHI	1730	SANTIAGO	0800
DUBAI	1600	SINGAPORE	1930
DUBLIN	1200	STOCKHOLM	1300
GIBRALTAR	1300	SUEZ	1400
HELSINKI	1400	SYDNEY	2200
HOBART	2200	TEHRAN/TÉHÉRAN	1500
HONG KONG	2000	TOKYO	2100
ISTANBUL	1400	TORONTO	0700
JERUSALEM	1400	TUNIS	1300
KUWAIT CITY	1500	VALETTA	1300
LAGOS	1300	VANCOUVER	0400
LENINGRAD	1500	VIENNA/VIENNE	1300
LIMA	0700	WARSAW/VARSOVIE	1300
LISBON	1300	WELLINGTON (NZ)	2400
LONDON/LONDRES	1200		

WEIGHTS AND MEASURES—POIDS ET MESURES

Metric Measures—Mesures métriques

Length—Longueur

1 millimètre (mm)		= 0.0394 in
1 centimètre (cm)	= 10 mm	= 0.3937 in
1 mètre (m)	= 100 cm	= 1.0936 yds
1 kilomètre (km)	= 1000 m	= 0.6214 mile

Weight—Poids

1 milligramme (mg)		= 0.0154 grain
1 gramme (g)	= 1000 mg	= 0.0353 oz
1 kilogramme (kg)	= 1000 g	= 2.2046 lb
1 tonne (t)	= 1000 kg	= 0.9842 ton

Area—Surface

1 cm²	= 100 mm²	= 0.1550 sq. in
1 m²	= 10 000 cm²	= 1.1960 sq. yds
1 are (a)	= 100 m²	= 119.60 sq. yds
1 hectare (ha)	= 100 ares	= 2.4711 acres
1 km²	= 100 hectares	= 0.3861 sq. mile

Capacity—Capacité

1 cm³		= 0.0610 cu. in
1 dm³	= 1000 cm³	= 0.0351 cu. ft
1 m³	= 1000 dm³	= 1.3080 cu. yds
1 litre	= 1 dm³	= 0.2200 gallon
1 hectolitre	= 100 litres	= 2.7497 bushels

Imperial Measures—Mesures britanniques

Length—Longueur

1 inch		= 2.54 cm
1 foot	= 12 inches	= 0.3048 m
1 yard	= 3 feet	= 0.9144 m
1 rod	= 5.5 yards	= 5.0292 m
1 chain	= 22 yards	= 20.117 m
1 furlong	= 220 yards	= 201.17 m
1 mile	= 1760 yards	= 1.6093 km
1 nautical mile	= 6080 feet	= 1.8532 km

Weight—Poids

1 ounce	= 437.5 grains	= 28.350 g
1 pound	= 16 ounces	= 0.4536 kg
1 stone	= 14 pounds	= 6.3503 kg
1 hundredweight	= 112 pounds	= 50.802 kg
1 ton	= 20 cwt	= 1.0161 tonnes

Area—Surface

1 sq. inch		= 6.4516 cm²
1 sq. foot	= 144 sq. ins	= 0.0929 m²
1 sq. yd	= 9 sq. ft	= 0.8361 m²
1 acre	= 4840 sq. yds	= 4046.9 m²
1 sq. mile	= 640 acres	= 259.0 hectares

Capacity—Capacité

1 cu. inch		= 16.387 cm³
1 cu. foot	= 1728 cu. ins	= 0.0283 m³
1 cu. yard	= 27 cu. ft	= 0.7646 m³
1 pint	= 4 gills	= 0.5683 litre
1 quart	= 2 pints	= 1.1365 litres
1 gallon	= 8 pints	= 4.5461 litres
1 bushel	= 8 gallons	= 36.369 litres
1 fluid ounce	= 8 fl. drachms	= 28.413 cm³
1 pint	= 20 fl. oz	= 568.26 cm³

US: Dry Measures—Mesures US: matières sèches

1 pint	= 0.9689 UK pt	= 0.5506 litre
1 bushel	= 0.9689 UK bu	= 35.238 litres

US: Liquid Measures—Mesures US: liquides

1 fluid ounce	= 1.0408 UK fl oz	= 0.0296 litre
1 pint (16 oz)	= 0.8327 UK pt	= 0.4732 litre
1 gallon	= 0.8327 UK gal	= 3.7853 litres

CONVERSION TABLES
TABLEAUX DE CONVERSION

LENGTH/LONGUEUR

centimètres	cm or inches	inches
2.54	1	0.39
5.08	2	0.79
7.62	3	1.18
10.16	4	1.58
12.70	5	1.97
15.24	6	2.36
17.78	7	2.76
20.32	8	3.15
22.86	9	3.54
25.40	10	3.94
50.80	20	7.87
76.20	30	11.81
101.60	40	15.75
127.00	50	19.69
152.40	60	23.62
177.80	70	27.56
203.20	80	31.50
228.60	90	35.43
254.00	100	39.37

WEIGHT/POIDS

kilogrammes	kg or pounds	pounds
0.45	1	2.20
0.91	2	4.41
1.36	3	6.61
1.81	4	8.82
2.27	5	11.02
2.72	6	13.23
3.18	7	15.43
3.63	8	17.64
4.08	9	19.84
4.54	10	22.05
9.07	20	44.09
13.61	30	66.14
18.14	40	88.19
22.68	50	110.23
27.22	60	132.28
31.75	70	154.32
36.29	80	176.37
40.82	90	198.41
45.36	100	220.46

kilomètres	km or miles	miles
1.61	1	0.62
3.22	2	1.24
4.83	3	1.86
6.44	4	2.49
8.05	5	3.11
9.66	6	3.73
11.27	7	4.35
12.88	8	4.97
14.48	9	5.59
16.09	10	6.21
32.19	20	12.43
48.28	30	18.64
64.37	40	24.86
80.47	50	31.07
96.56	60	37.28
112.65	70	43.50
128.75	80	49.71
144.84	90	55.92
160.93	100	62.14

tonnes	tonnes or tons	tons
1.02	1	0.98
2.03	2	1.97
3.05	3	2.95
4.06	4	3.94
5.08	5	4.92
6.10	6	5.91
7.11	7	6.89
8.13	8	7.87
9.14	9	8.86
10.16	10	9.84
20.32	20	19.68
30.48	30	29.53
40.64	40	39.37
50.80	50	49.21
60.96	60	59.05
71.12	70	68.89
81.28	80	78.74
91.44	90	88.58
101.60	100	98.42

Conversion tables

Tableaux de conversion

AREA/SURFACE			CAPACITY/VOLUME		
hectares	hectares or acres	acres	litres	litres or gallons	gallons
0.41	1	2.47	4.55	1	0.22
0.81	2	4.94	9.09	2	0.44
1.21	3	7.41	13.64	3	0.66
1.62	4	9.88	18.18	4	0.88
2.02	5	12.36	22.73	5	1.10
2.43	6	14.83	27.28	6	1.32
2.83	7	17.30	31.82	7	1.54
3.24	8	19.77	36.37	8	1.76
3.64	9	22.24	40.91	9	1.98
4.05	10	24.71	45.46	10	2.20
8.09	20	49.42	90.92	20	4.40
12.14	30	74.13	136.38	30	6.60
16.19	40	98.84	181.84	40	8.80
20.23	50	123.56	227.31	50	11.00
24.28	60	148.27	272.77	60	13.20
28.33	70	172.98	318.23	70	15.40
32.38	80	197.69	363.69	80	17.60
36.42	90	222.40	409.15	90	19.80
40.47	100	247.11	454.61	100	22.00

SPEED–VITESSE

MPH	20	30	40	50	60	70	80	90	100	$(\times\ ^8/_5)$
KMPH	32	48	64	80	96	112	128	144	160	$(\times\ ^5/_8)$

TEMPERATURE–TEMPERATURE

Centigrade

$-18°\ -10\quad 0\quad\quad 10\quad\quad 20\quad\quad 30\quad\quad 40°$

$0°\ 10\ 20\ 32\ 40\ 50\ 60\ 70\ 80\ 90\ 100\ 110°$

Fahrenheit

$$C = \frac{5}{9}(F-32) \quad F = \frac{9}{5}C + 32$$

Balance sheet and statement of a large multinational company

Bilan et résultats d'une grande mulinationale

Consolidated Balance Sheet Assets

SCHLUMBERGER
LIMITED
(SCHLUMBERGER N.^v
INCORPORATED IN
THE NETHERLANDS
ANTILLES) AND
SUBSIDIARY
COMPANIES

	DECEMBER 31,	
	1980	1979
	(Stated in thousands)	
CURRENT ASSETS:		
Cash	$ 18,445	$ 16,694
Short-term investments	1,217,448	1,006,959
Receivables less allowance for doubtful accounts		
(1980—$24,004; 1979—$23,373)	1,050,792	875,891
Inventories	589,882	488,357
Other current assets	55,147	44,920
	2,931,714	2,432,821
INVESTMENTS IN AFFILIATED COMPANIES	167,582	191,886
LONG-TERM INVESTMENTS AND RECEIVABLES	47,222	52,248
FIXED ASSETS less accumulated depreciation	1,758,592	1,334,920
EXCESS OF INVESTMENT OVER NET ASSETS OF		
SUBSIDIARIES PURCHASED less amortization	296,270	305,915
OTHER ASSETS	40,622	32,651
	$5,242,002	$4,350,441

SEE NOTES TO CONSOLIDATED FINANCIAL STATEMENTS

Bilan consolidé
actif

SCHLUMBERGER
LIMITED
(SCHLUMBERGER
N.V., ANTILLES
NEERLANDAISES)
ET SOCIETES
FILIALES

	AU 31 DECEMBRE	
	1980	1979
	(en milliers de dollars)	
VALEURS REALISABLES OU DISPONIBLES:		
Caisses et banques	$ 18.445	$ 16.694
Dépôts à terme et titres de placement	1.217.448	1.006.959
Clients et autres débiteurs, moins provisions		
pour créances douteuses (1980-$24.004; 1979-$23.373)	1.050.792	875.891
Stocks	589.882	488.357
Autres valeurs réalisables ou disponibles	55.147	44.920
	2.931.714	2.432.821
PARTICIPATIONS DANS LES SOCIETES AFFILIEES	167.582	191.886
TITRES DE PARTICIPATION ET CREANCES A LONG TERME	47.222	52.248
IMMOBILISATIONS, moins amortissements cumulés	1.758.592	1.334.920
PRIMES D'ACQUISITION DES TITRES DE PARTICIPATION,		
moins amortissements cumulés	296.270	305.915
AUTRES ACTIFS A LONG TERME	40.622	32.651
	$5.242.002	$4.3.0.441

VOIR NOTES SUR LES ETATS FINANCIERS CONSOLIDES

Consolidated Balance Sheet Liabilities & Stockholders' Equity

	DECEMBER 31,	
	1980	1979
	(Stated in thousands)	
CURRENT LIABILITIES:		
Accounts payable and accrued liabilities	$ 730,666	$ 650,464
Estimated liability for taxes on income	642,940	491,528
Bank loans	193,488	123,183
Dividend payable	47,772	34,978
Long-term debt due within one year	68,092	66,681
	1,682,958	1,366,834
LONG-TERM DEBT	237,701	489,629
OTHER LIABILITIES	86,851	81,158
MINORITY INTEREST IN SUBSIDIARIES	16,091	12,493
	2,023,601	1,950,114
STOCKHOLDERS' EQUITY:		
Common stock	281,470	268,172
Income retained for use in the business	3,110,664	2,295,680
Deduct Treasury stock at cost	(173,733)	(163,525)
	3,218,401	2,400,327
	$5,242,002	$4,350,441

SEE NOTES TO CONSOLIDATED FINANCIAL STATEMENTS

Bilan consolidé
passif et fonds propres

	AU 31 DECEMBRE	
	1980	1979
	(en milliers de dollars)	
DETTES A COURT TERME:		
Fournisseurs, autres créanciers et frais à payer	$ 730.666	$ 650.464
Provisions pour impôts sur les bénéfices	642.940	491.528
Emprunts bancaires	193.488	123.183
Dividendes à payer	47.772	34.978
Fraction des dettes à long terme payable à moins d'un an	68.092	66.681
	1.682.958	1.366.834
DETTES A LONG TERME	237.701	489.629
AUTRES ELEMENTS DE PASSIF	86.851	81.158
INTERETS MINORITAIRES DANS LES FILIALES	16.091	12.493
	2.023.601	1.950.114
FONDS PROPRES:		
Capital—actions ordinaires	281.470	268.172
Bénéfices réinvestis	3.110.664	2.295.680
Actions rachetées par la Société (évaluées au prix d'achat)	(173.733)	(163.525)
	3.218.401	2.400.327
	$5.242.002	$4.350.441

VOIR NOTES SUR LES ETATS FINANCIERS CONSOLIDES

Consolidated
Statement of Income

		YEAR ENDED DECEMBER 31,	
	1980	1979	1978
		(Stated in thousands)	
REVENUE:			
Operating	$4,883,944	$3,549,647	$2,619,245
Interest and other income	153,333	91,791	64,697
Gain on sale of Rowan shares (before income taxes, $30,131)	99,838	—	—
	5,137,115	3,641,438	2,683,942
EXPENSES:			
Cost of goods sold and services	2,813,089	2,061,392	1,498,939
Research & engineering	188,152	131,334	90,519
Marketing	217,685	173,192	119,565
General	299,731	209,981	160,089
Interest	101,752	52,175	17,962
Taxes on income	522,359	354,968	294,895
	4,142,768	2,983,042	2,181,969
NET INCOME	$ 994,347	$ 658,396	$ 501,973
Net income per share*	$ 5.21	$ 3.45	$ 2.63
Average shares outstanding (thousands)*	190,764	190,676	191,223

*Adjusted for three-for-two stock split in September 1980
SEE NOTES TO CONSOLIDATED FINANCIAL STATEMENTS

Résultats consolidés

| | EXERCICE CLOS LE 31 DECEMBRE | | |
	1980	1979	1978
	(en milliers de dollars)		
CHIFFRE D'AFFAIRES:			
Exploitation	$4.883.944	$3.549.647	$2.619.245
Intérêts et autres revenus	153.333	91.791	64.697
Plus-value sur vente des actions Rowan (avant impôts de $30.131)	99.838	—	—
	5.137.115	3.641.438	2.683.942
DEPENSES:			
Coût des ventes et des services	2.813.089	2.061.392	1.498.939
Frais d'études et de recherche	188.152	131.334	90.519
Frais de vente	217.685	173.192	119.565
Frais généraux	299.731	209.981	160.089
Frais financiers	101.752	52.175	17.962
Impôts sur les bénéfices	522.359	354.968	294.895
	4.142.768	2.983.042	2.181.969
BENEFICE NET	$ 994.347	$ 658.396	$ 501.973
Bénéfice net par action*	$ 5,21	$ 3,45	$ 2,63
Nombre moyen d'actions en circulation (en milliers)*	190.764	190.676	191.223

*Ajustés pour tenir compte de la distribution gratuite d'une action nouvelle pour deux anciennes en septembre 1980.
VOIR NOTES SUR LES ETATS FINANCIERS CONSOLIDES

Consolidated Statement of Stockholders' Equity*

	COMMON STOCK				INCOME RETAINED FOR USE IN THE BUSINESS
	IN TREASURY		ISSUED		
	SHARES	AMOUNT	SHARES	AMOUNT	
		(Dollar amounts in thousands)			
Balance, January 1, 1978	7,538,260	$ 77,765	199,407,336	$246,334	$1,381,316
Purchases for Treasury	1,597,050	54,900			
Sales to optionees			416,442	9,209	
Net income					501,973
Dividends declared ($0.56 per share)					(106,172)
Balance, December 31, 1978	9,135,310	132,665	199,823,778	255,543	1,777,117
Purchases for Treasury	609,450	30,860			
Sales to optionees			573,774	12,629	
Net income					658,396
Dividends declared ($0.73 per share)					(139,833)
Balance, December 31, 1979	9,744,760	163,525	200,397,552	268,172	2,295,680
Purchases for Treasury	136,800	10,208			
Sales to optionees			487,870	13,298	
Net income					994,347
Dividends declared ($0.94 per share)					(179,363)
Balance, December 31, 1980	9,881,560	$173,733	200,885,422	$281,470	$3,110,664

*Shares and per share amounts adjusted for three-for-two stock split in September 1980
SEE NOTES TO CONSOLIDATED FINANCIAL STATEMENTS

Etat consolidé des fonds propres*

| | ACTIONS ORDINAIRES | | | | |
| | RACHETEES PAR LA SOCIETE | | EMISES | | |
	NOMBRE D'ACTIONS	VALEUR	NOMBRE D'ACTIONS	VALEUR	BENEFICES REINVESTIS
	(valeurs exprimées en milliers de dollars)				
Solde au 1er janvier 1978	7.538.260	$ 77.765	199.407.336	$246.334	$1.381.316
Rachat par la Société de ses propres actions	1.597.050	54.900			
Exercice des options d'achat d'actions			416.442	9.209	
Bénéfice net					501.973
Dividendes déclarés($0,56 par action)					(106.172)
Solde au 31 décembre 1978	9.135.310	132.665	199.823.778	255.543	1.777.117
Rachat par la Société de ses propres actions	609.450	30.860			
Exercice des options d'achat d'actions			573.774	12.629	
Bénéfice net					658.396
Dividendes déclarés ($0,73 par action)					(139.833)
Solde au 31 décembre 1979	9.744.760	163.525	200.397.552	268.172	2.295.680
Rachat par la Société de ses propres actions	136.800	10.208			
Exercice des options d'achat d'actions			487.870	13.298	
Bénéfice net					994.347
Dividendes déclarés ($0,94 par action)					(179.363)
Solde au 31 décembre 1980	9.881.560	$173.733	200.885.422	$281.470	$3.110.664

*Le nombre d'actions et les montants par action ont été ajustés pour tenir compte de la distribution gratuite d'une action nouvelle pour deux anciennes en septembre 1980.

VOIR NOTES SUR LES ETATS FINANCIERS CONSOLIDES

Consolidated Statement of Changes in Financial Position

	YEAR ENDED DECEMBER 31,		
	1980	1979	1978
		(Stated in thousands)	
SOURCE OF WORKING CAPITAL:			
Net income	$ 994,347	$ 658,396	$ 501,973
Add (deduct) amounts not affecting working capital:			
Depreciation and amortization	335,313	250,197	186,972
Gain on sale of Rowan shares	(69,707)	—	—
Earnings of companies carried at equity less dividends received (1980—$11,249; 1979—$8,335; 1978—$7,167)	(46,897)	(30,147)	(20,693)
Other—net	(28,355)	(12,474)	(18,766)
Working capital provided from operations	1,184,701	865,972	649,486
Increase in long-term debt	49,605	425,029	44,149
Retirement and sale of fixed assets	24,157	37,148	13,080
Decrease in other long-term investments and receivables	9,265	—	—
Proceeds from sale of shares to optionees	13,298	12,629	9,209
Proceeds from sale of Rowan shares less related income taxes	136,669	—	—
Other—net	4,413	1,396	4,730
Total working capital provided	1,422,108	1,342,174	720,654
APPLICATION OF WORKING CAPITAL:			
Net noncurrent assets of Fairchild Camera and Instrument Corp. acquired and consolidated	—	407,747	—
Investment in Rowan	—	22,379	44,626
Increase in other long-term investments and receivables	—	15,066	7,334
Additions to fixed assets	748,235	503,415	393,312
Dividends declared	179,363	139,833	106,172
Reduction of long-term debt	301,533	66,985	15,061
Purchase of shares for Treasury	10,208	30,860	54,900
Total working capital applied	1,239,339	1,186,285	621,405
NET INCREASE IN WORKING CAPITAL	$ 182,769	$ 155,889	$ 99,249
INCREASE IN WORKING CAPITAL CONSISTS OF:			
Increase in current assets:			
Cash and short-term investments	$ 212,240	$ 239,414	$ 104,995
Receivables	174,901	249,460	129,899
Inventories	101,525	146,364	45,057
Other current assets	10,227	8,753	5,772
Increase in current liabilities:			
Accounts and dividend payable	(92,996)	(259,847)	(93,574)
Estimated liability for taxes on income	(151,412)	(154,560)	(53,065)
Bank loans and debt due within one year	(71,716)	(73,695)	(39,835)
NET INCREASE IN WORKING CAPITAL	$ 182,769	$ 155,889	$ 99,249

SEE NOTES TO CONSOLIDATED FINANCIAL STATEMENTS

Etat consolidé de l'origine et de l'emploi des fonds

	EXERCICE CLOS LE 31 DECEMBRE		
	1980	1979	1978
	(en milliers de dollars)		
ORIGINE DU FONDS DE ROULEMENT:			
Bénéfice net	$ 994.347	$ 658.396	$ 501.973
Ajouter (déduire)—montants n'affectant pas le fonds de roulement:			
Amortissements des immobilisations corporelles et incorporelles	335.313	250.197	186.972
Plus-value sur la vente des actions Rowan	(69.707)	—	—
Participation dans le bénéfice net des sociétés mises en équivalence, moins dividendes reçus (1980—$11.249; 1979—$8.335; 1978—$7.167)	(46.897)	(30.147)	(20.693)
Autres—nets	(28.355)	(12.474)	(18.766)
Fonds de roulement provenant de l'exploitation	1.184.701	865.972	649.486
Accroissement des dettes à long terme	49.605	425.029	44.149
Retraits et cessions d'immobilisations corporelles	24.157	37.148	13.080
Diminution des titres de participation dans les sociétés non consolidées et des créances à long terme	9.265	—	—
Produits de la vente d'actions aux bénéficiaires d'options	13.298	12.629	9.209
Produits de la vente des actions Rowan, nets d'impôts	136.669	—	—
Autres—nets	4.413	1.396	4.730
Total de l'origine du fonds de roulement	1.422.108	1.342.174	720.654
EMPLOI DU FONDS DE ROULEMENT:			
Actif net à long terme de Fairchild Camera and Instrument Corp.	—	407.747	—
Investissement dans Rowan Companies, Inc.	—	22.379	44.626
Accroissement des titres de participation dans les sociétés non consolidées et des créances à long terme	—	15.066	7.334
Achats d'immobilisations corporelles	748.235	503.415	393.312
Dividendes déclarés	179.363	139.833	106.172
Remboursement de dettes à long terme	301.533	66.985	15.061
Rachat par la Société de ses propres actions	10.208	30.860	54.900
Total des emplois du fonds de roulement	1.239.339	1.186.285	621.405
AUGMENTATION NETTE DU FONDS DE ROULEMENT	$ 182.769	$ 155.889	$ 99.249
L'AUGMENTATION DU FONDS DE ROULEMENT SE DECOMPOSE COMME SUIT:			
Augmentation des valeurs réalisables ou disponibles:			
Caisses, banques, dépôts à terme et titres de placement	$ 212.240	$ 239.414	$ 104.995
Clients et autres débiteurs	174.901	249.460	129.899
Stocks	101.525	146.364	45.057
Autres valeurs réalisables ou disponibles	10.227	8.753	5.772
Augmentation des dettes à court terme:			
Fournisseurs, charges et dividendes à payer	(92.996)	(259.847)	(93.574)
Provisions pour impôts sur les bénéfices	(151.412)	(154.560)	(53.065)
Emprunts bancaires et dettes à moins d'un an	(71.716)	(73.695)	(39.835)
AUGMENTATION NETTE DU FONDS DE ROULEMENT	$ 182.769	$ 155.889	$ 99.249

VOIR NOTES SUR LES ETATS FINANCIERS CONSOLIDES

Notes to Consolidated Financial Statements

SUMMARY OF ACCOUNTING POLICIES

The Consolidated Financial Statements of Schlumberger Limited have been prepared in accordance with accounting principles generally accepted in the United States. Within those principles, the Company's more important accounting policies are set forth below.

PRINCIPLES OF CONSOLIDATION

The Consolidated Financial Statements include the accounts of all significant majority-owned subsidiaries. Significant 20%-50% owned companies are carried in investments in affiliated companies on the equity method. The pro rata share of revenue and expense of Dowell Schlumberger, a 50% owned oilfield services company, is included in the individual captions in the Consolidated Statement of Income. Schlumberger's pro rata share of after tax earnings of other equity companies is included in interest and other income.

TRANSLATION OF NON-U.S. CURRENCIES

Balance sheet items recorded in currencies other than U.S. dollars are translated at current exchange rates except for inventories, fixed and intangible assets and long-term investments which are translated at historical rates. Revenue and expenses are translated at average exchange rates during the year except for those amounts related to balance sheet items translated at historical rates. Translation adjustments and gains or losses on forward exchange contracts are recognized in income currently.

SHORT-TERM INVESTMENTS

Short-term investments are stated at cost plus accrued interest, and comprised mainly U.S. dollar time deposits.

INVENTORIES

Inventories are stated principally at average or standard cost, which approximates average cost, or at market, if lower.

Notes sur les états financiers consolidés

METHODES COMPTABLES ADOPTEES

Les états financiers consolidés de Schlumberger Limited ont été préparés conformément aux principes comptables généralement admis aux Etats-Unis. Dans ce cadre, les principales méthodes comptables en vigueur dans le groupe sont exposées ci-dessous.

PRINCIPES DE CONSOLIDATION

Les états financiers consolidés intègrent les comptes de toutes les filiales importantes dans lesquelles Schlumberger détient une participation majoritaire. Les principales sociétés dans lesquelles Schlumberger détient une participation comprise entre 20% et 50% sont incluses dans le bilan sous la rubrique "Participations dans les sociétés affiliées", pour une valeur égale à la quote-part de Schlumberger dans leurs actifs nets (mise en équivalence). Les recettes et dépenses de Dowell Schlumberger, société du secteur des Services pétroliers détenue à 50%, ont été incluses dans les rubriques appropriées des "Résultats consolidés", au prorata de la participation de Schlumberger. La quote-part des bénéfices après impôts des autres sociétés mises en équivalence est incluse à la rubrique "Intérêts et autres revenus".

CONVERSION DES DEVISES AUTRES QUE LE DOLLAR

Les éléments du bilan comptabilisés en devises autres que le dollar des Etats-Unis ont été convertis aux taux de change en vigueur à la clôture de l'exercice (taux de change courants), à l'exception des stocks, des immobilisations corporelles et incorporelles et des titres de participation qui ont été convertis à des taux en vigueur au moment de leur acquisition ou création (taux historiques). Les éléments du compte de résultats ont été convertis à des taux de change moyens, hormis les amortissements des immobilisations corporelles et incorporelles et les stocks qui ont été convertis aux taux de change en vigueur au moment de leur acquisition ou création. Les ajustements résultant de ces conversions, ainsi que les profits ou les pertes réalisés sur les opérations de change à terme, sont comptabilisés dans les résultats de l'exercice.

PLACEMENTS A COURT TERME

Les placements à court terme sont comptabilisés au prix d'achat majoré des produits financiers à recevoir, et concernent essentiellement des dépôts à terme en dollars.

STOCKS

Les stocks sont généralement évalués au prix de revient moyen ou standard (ce dernier étant alors équivalent au prix de revient moyen), ou au prix du marché si celui-ci est inférieur au prix de revient.

FIXED ASSETS AND DEPRECIATION

Fixed assets are stated at cost less accumulated depreciation, which is provided for by charges to income over the estimated useful lives of the assets by the straight-line method. Fixed assets include the cost of Company manufactured oilfield technical equipment for use in wireline operations. Expenditures for renewals, replacements and betterments are capitalized. Maintenance and repairs are charged to operating expenses as incurred. Upon sale or other disposition, the applicable amounts of asset cost and accumulated depreciation are removed from the accounts and the net amount, less proceeds from disposal, is charged or credited to income.

EXCESS OF INVESTMENT OVER NET ASSETS OF SUBSIDIARIES PURCHASED

Costs in excess of net assets of purchased subsidiaries having an indeterminate life are amortized on a straight-line basis over 40 years. Accumulated amortization was $25 million and $16 million at December 31, 1980 and 1979, respectively.

DEFERRED BENEFIT PLANS

The Company and its subsidiaries have several voluntary pension and other deferred benefit plans covering substantially all officers and employees, including those in countries other than the United States. These plans are substantially fully funded with trustees in respect to past and current services. Charges to expense are based upon costs computed by independent actuaries.

In France, the principal pensions are provided for by union agreements negotiated by all employers within an industry on a nationwide basis. Benefits when paid are not identified with particular employers, but are made from funds obtained through concurrent compulsory contributions from all employers within each industry based on employee salaries. These plans are accounted for on the defined contribution basis and each year's contributions are charged currently to expense.

TAXES ON INCOME

Schlumberger and its affiliated companies compute income taxes payable in accordance with the tax rules and regulations of the many taxing authorities where the income is earned. The income tax rates imposed by these taxing authorities vary substantially. Taxable income may differ from pretax income for financial accounting purposes. To the extent that differences are due to revenue and expense items reported in one period for tax purposes and in another period for financial accounting purposes, appropriate provision for deferred income taxes is made. The provisions were not significant in 1980, 1979 or 1978.

Approximately $3.0 billion of consolidated income retained for use in the business at December 31, 1980 represents undistributed earnings of consolidated subsidiaries and Schlumberger's pro rata share of 20%-50% owned companies. It is the policy of the Company to reinvest substantially all such undistributed earnings and, accordingly, no provision is made for deferred income taxes on those earnings considered to be indefinitely reinvested.

Investment credits and other allowances provided by income tax laws of the United States and other countries are credited to current income tax expense on the flow-through method of accounting.

IMMOBILISATIONS ET AMORTISSEMENTS

Les immobilisations sont évaluées à leur prix d'acquisition diminué des amortissements; les amortissements sont calculés et imputés aux résultats selon le mode linéaire basé sur la durée probable d'utilisation des immobilisations. L'équipement technique pétrolier fabriqué par la Société et utilisé pour les opérations de mesures dans les sondages est inclus, au prix de revient, dans les immobilisations. Les dépenses encourues pour les remises en état, remplacements et modernisations des immobilisations sont capitalisées. Les dépenses d'entretien et de réparation sont imputées immédiatement aux frais d'exploitation. Lors de la vente ou de la cession d'une immobilisation, son prix d'acquisition et les amortissements cumulés correspondants sont déduits des comptes du bilan et le montant net, diminué du prix de vente, est passé en perte ou en profit dans les comptes de résultats.

PRIMES D'ACQUISITION DES TITRES DE PARTICIPATION

L'excédent du prix d'acquisition sur la valeur raisonnablement estimée de l'actif net des sociétés acquises représente une prime d'acquisition; ces primes sont en général amorties linéairement sur 40 ans. Les amortissements cumulés constatés à ce titre étaient respectivement de 25 millions et de 16 millions de dollars aux 31 décembre 1980 et 1979.

PLANS DE RETRAITE ET D'INTERESSEMENT DIFFERE

La Société et ses filiales ont adopté plusieurs plans bénévoles de retraite et d'intéressement différé en faveur de la presque totalité de leurs cadres et de leur personnel, aux Etats-Unis comme dans les autres pays. Ces plans sont presque intégralement couverts par les versements effectués auprès de trustees, tant pour les services passés que présents. Les charges comptabilisées dans l'exercice sont déterminées par des actuaires indépendants.

En France, les principaux régimes de retraite sont établis par des conventions collectives négociées pour l'ensemble du pays par tous les employeurs et les syndicats d'un même secteur d'activité. Les pensions, lorsqu'elles sont payées, ne le sont pas par l'employeur lui-même; elles sont prélevées sur des fonds alimentés par les cotisations payées obligatoirement par les employeurs dans chaque secteur d'activité et déterminées en fonction du salaire des employés. Les cotisations de l'année sont comptabilisées dans les charges de l'exercice.

IMPOTS SUR LES BENEFICES

Schlumberger et ses filiales calculent l'impôt à payer sur les bénéfices en fonction des divers codes et règlements fiscaux en vigueur dans les nombreux pays dans lesquels les bénéfices sont réalisés. Les taux d'imposition fixés par les autorités fiscales de ces pays varient considérablement. Le bénéfice imposable peut être différent du bénéfice avant impôts tel qu'il ressort des états financiers. Dans la mesure où la différence est due au fait que certains revenus et certains frais peuvent être imputables à un exercice donné pour le calcul de l'impôt, et à un autre exercice pour la détermination du résultat comptable, des provisions appropriées pour impôts différés sur les bénéfices sont constituées. Ces provisions n'ont pas été significatives en 1980, 1979 et 1978.

Au 31 décembre 1980, environ 3 milliards de dollars de bénéfices consolidés réinvestis représentaient les bénéfices non distribués des filiales consolidées ainsi que la quote-part des bénéfices non distribués revenant à Schlumberger dans les sociétés détenues de 20% à 50%. La politique de la Société étant de réinvestir la quasi-totalité de ces bénéfices, il n'a donc pas été constitué de provision pour les impôts qui seraient dus sur la répartition de ceux-ci, ces bénéfices étant considérés comme réinvestis indéfiniment.

Les crédits d'impôts pour investissements et autres déductions fiscales prévus par les législations fiscales des Etats-Unis et des autres pays sont déduits de l'impôt sur les bénéfices de l'année au cours de laquelle ils ont pris naissance.

NET INCOME PER SHARE

Net income per share is computed by dividing net income by the average number of common shares outstanding during the year.

RESEARCH & ENGINEERING

All research & engineering expenditures are expensed as incurred, including costs relating to patents or rights which may result from such expenditures.

ACQUISITION OF FAIRCHILD CAMERA AND INSTRUMENT CORPORATION

In 1979 the Company acquired Fairchild Camera and Instrument Corporation at a cost of $425 million (including expenses). The acquisition was accounted for as a purchase and the accounts of Fairchild have been consolidated with those of Schlumberger since July 1, 1979. Cost in excess of the fair value of net assets acquired of $253 million is being amortized on a straight-line basis over 40 years.

The following pro forma consolidated amounts combine the historical accounts of Schlumberger and Fairchild for 1979 and 1978 and reflect all purchase accounting adjustments as though Fairchild had been acquired January 1, 1978.

	YEAR ENDED DECEMBER 31,	
	1979	1978
	(Stated in millions)	
Revenue	$3,956	$3,208
Net income	$ 666	$ 506
Net income per share (dollars)	$ 3.49	$ 2.65

GAIN ON SALE OF ROWAN SHARES

During the fourth quarter of 1980, the Company sold 4.8 million shares out of total holdings of approximately 5.5 million of Rowan common stock. The gain before income taxes amounted to $100 million. Income taxes amounting to $30 million are included in the taxes on income caption in the Consolidated Statement of Income. The Company's net income for the year and for the fourth quarter of 1980 was increased by $70 million as a result of the sale which had the effect of increasing earnings per share by $.36.

FIXED ASSETS

A summary of fixed assets follows:

	DECEMBER 31,	
	1980	1979
	(Stated in millions)	
Land	$ 46	$ 37
Buildings & improvements	384	321
Machinery and equipment	2,439	1,843
Total cost	2,869	2,201
Less accumulated depreciation	1,110	866
	$1,759	$1,335

Estimated useful lives of buildings & improvements range from 8 to 50 years and of machinery and equipment from 2 to 15 years.

BENEFICE NET PAR ACTION
Le bénéfice net par action est calculé en divisant le bénéfice net par le nombre moyen d'actions ordinaires en circulation au cours de l'exercice.

FRAIS D'ETUDES ET DE RECHERCHE
Tous les frais d'études et de recherche, ainsi que les dépenses relatives aux brevets et aux droits qui pourraient en résulter, sont pris en charge immédiatement.

ACQUISITION DE FAIRCHILD
CAMERA AND INSTRUMENT
CORPORATION
La Société a racheté en 1979, pour un total de 425 millions de dollars y compris les frais afférents à cette acquisition, la société Fairchild Camera and Instrument Corporation. Cette acquisition a été comptabilisée comme un achat ("purchase accounting") et les comptes de Fairchild ont été consolidés avec ceux de la Société à partir du 1er juillet 1979. L'excédent du prix d'achat sur la valeur raisonnablement estimée des actifs nets (prime d'acquisition des titres de participation), soit 253 millions de dollars, est amorti selon le mode linéaire sur une période de 40 ans.

Le tableau présenté ci-dessous pour information comprend les comptes consolidés de Schlumberger et de Fairchild pour 1979 et 1978, compte tenu de toutes les corrections qui auraient été apportées si Fairchild avait été acquis le 1er janvier 1978.

| | 31 DECEMBRE | |
| | 1979 | 1978 |
	(en millions de dollars)	
Chiffre d'affaires	$3.956	$3.208
Bénéfice net	$ 666	$ 506
Bénéfice net par action (en dollars)	$ 3,49	$ 2,65

PLUS-VALUE SUR
LA CESSION DES
ACTIONS DE ROWAN
Au cours du quatrième trimestre 1980, la Société a vendu 4,8 millions d'actions de Rowan sur une participation totale d'environ 5,5 millions d'actions. La plus-value avant impôts s'est élevée à 100 millions de dollars. Le montant de l'impôt sur cette plus-value s'est élevé à 30 millions de dollars et est inclus dans les Impôts sur les bénéfices des Résultats consolidés. Cette cession a eu pour effet d'accroître le bénéfice net de l'exercice (et celui du quatrième trimestre) d'un montant de 70 millions de dollars, soit une augmentation du bénéfice net par action de 0,36 dollar.

IMMOBILISATIONS
Les immobilisations corporelles se répartissent comme suit:

| | 31 DECEMBRE | |
| | 1980 | 1979 |
	(en millions de dollars)	
Terrains	$ 46	$ 37
Immeubles et agencements	384	321
Matériel et équipement	2.439	1.843
Prix de revient total	2.869	2.201
A déduire: amortissements cumulés	1.110	866
	$1.759	$1.335

Les durées de vie estimées des immeubles et agencements vont de 8 à 50 ans, et celles du matériel et de l'équipement de 2 à 15 ans.

LONG-TERM DEBT

Long-term debt, excluding amounts due within one year, consisted of the following:

	DECEMBER 31, 1980	1979
	(Stated in millions)	
Bank loan due 1982-1985, interest 105% of U.S. prime rate	$200	$425
Other bank loans, interest 5.75%-13%	38	65
	$238	$490

Long-term debt at December 31, 1980 is payable principally in U.S. dollars and is due $62 million in 1982, $54 million in 1983, $59 million in 1984, $53 million in 1985 and $10 million thereafter.

LINES OF CREDIT

Effective January 1, 1981, the Company's principal U.S. subsidiary entered into a Revolving Credit Agreement with a group of banks, which provides that the subsidiary may borrow up to an additional $300 million until December 31, 1985 at prime or other money market based rates.

At December 31, 1980 the Company had unused short-term lines of credit of $225 million. There are no material compensating balances or significant conditions, such as commitment fees or other restrictions, in connection with short-term bank borrowings.

COMMON STOCK

Common Stock, par value $1.00 per share, comprised the following number of shares adjusted for the three-for-two stock split in September 1980:

	DECEMBER 31, 1980	1979
Authorized	300,000,000	300,000,000
Issued	200,885,422	200,397,552
In Treasury	(9,881,560)	(9,744,760)
Outstanding	191,003,862	190,652,792

Options to officers and key employees to purchase shares of the Company's Common Stock were granted at prices equal to 100% of fair market value at date of grant.

Options previously granted by Fairchild to its employees which were assumed by the Company were converted to options to purchase shares of the Company's Common Stock at prices not less than 50% of fair market value at date of assumption in accordance with the terms of the 1979 Stock Option Plan.

Transactions under stock option plans were as follows:

DETTES A LONG TERME

Les dettes à long terme, nettes des montants venant à échéance à moins d'un an, s'analysent comme suit:

| | 31 DECEMBRE | |
| | 1980 | 1979 |
	(en millions de dollars)	
Emprunt bancaire remboursable en 1982-1985 (intérêts: 105% du taux de base bancaire américain)	$200	$425
Autres emprunts bancaires (intérêts: 5,75%-13%)	38	65
	$238	$490

Ces dettes sont remboursables principalement en dollars selon l'échéancier suivant exprimé en millions de dollars: 62 (1982), 54 (1983), 59 (1984), 53 (1985), 10 (les années suivantes).

LIGNES DE CREDIT

La principale filiale de Schlumberger aux Etats-Unis a passé avec plusieurs banques un accord de crédit renouvelable lui donnant la faculté d'emprunter, jusqu'au 31 décembre 1985, 300 millions de dollars supplémentaires, au taux de base bancaire ou à un autre taux du marché monétaire. Cet accord est effectif au 1er janvier 1981.

Sur les lignes de crédit à court terme dont pouvait disposer la Société, 225 millions de dollars n'avaient pas été utilisés au 31 décembre 1980. Les emprunts à court terme sont accordés sans que soit requise en contrepartie la création de montants compensatoires importants, et ne sont pas soumis à des conditions particulières d'octroi comme le paiement de commissions d'engagement, ou à des limitations d'autre sorte.

CAPITAL

Le tableau ci-dessous donne la répartition des actions ordinaires de la Société, d'une valeur nominale de 1 dollar, après correction pour tenir compte de la distribution d'une action nouvelle gratuite pour deux anciennes intervenue en septembre 1980:

| | 31 DECEMBRE | |
	1980	1979
Nombre d'actions autorisées	300.000.000	300.000.000
Nombre d'actions émises	200.885.422	200.397.552
Nombre d'actions possédées par la Société	(9.881.560)	(9.744.760)
Nombre d'actions en circulation	191.003.862	190.652.792

Les options d'achat d'actions ordinaires de la Société accordées aux directeurs et cadres supérieurs le sont à un prix égal à 100% du cours de l'action à la date où le droit à option a été octroyé.

Les options octroyées par Fairchild à ses employés préalablement à son acquisition, ont été reconnues par Schlumberger et converties en options d'achat d'actions ordinaires de la Société à des prix ne pouvant pas être inférieurs à la moitié du cours de l'action à la date à laquelle le droit d'option a été octroyé, conformément aux termes du programme d'options d'achat d'actions de 1979.

Les transactions intervenues au titre des plans d'options d'achat d'actions ont été les suivantes:

	NUMBER OF SHARES*	OPTION PRICE PER SHARE*
Outstanding Jan. 1, 1979	1,711,335	$18.77- 39.86
Granted	1,187,922	$28.63- 63.75
Exercised	(573,774)	$18.77- 36.89
Lapsed or terminated	(65,982)	$20.83- 44.86
Outstanding Dec. 31, 1979	2,259,501	$21.13- 63.75
Granted	339,292	$60.83-108.06
Exercised	(487,870)	$21.13- 63.75
Lapsed or terminated	(54,300)	$25.08- 85.58
Outstanding Dec. 31, 1980	2,056,623	$21.13-108.06
Exercisable at Dec. 31, 1980	700,322	$21.13- 63.75
Available for grant:		
Dec. 31, 1979	6,550,114	
Dec. 31, 1980	6,265,121	

*Adjusted for three-for-two stock split in September 1980

INCOME TAX EXPENSE

The Company is incorporated in the Netherlands Antilles where it is subject to an income tax rate of 3%. The Company and its subsidiaries operate in over 100 taxing jurisdictions with statutory rates ranging up to about 50%. Consolidated operating revenue of $4.9 billion in 1980 shown elsewhere in this report includes $2.0 billion derived from operations within the United States and Canada. On a worldwide basis, the Company provided income taxes at an effective rate of 34% in 1980, 35% in 1979 and 37% in 1978.

CONTINGENCY

During 1980, a floating hotel, the Alexander Kielland, functioning as a dormitory for offshore work crews in the North Sea, capsized in a storm. The substructure of the floating hotel had been originally built as a drilling rig by an independent shipyard from a design licensed by a subsidiary of the Company. The Company's subsidiary was not involved in the ownership or operation of the drilling rig or in its conversion or use as a floating hotel. The accident is being investigated by a Commission appointed by the Norwegian Government, which has not yet rendered its report.

While the Company does not believe it has liability in this matter, litigation may ensue which would involve complex international issues which could take several years to resolve and would involve substantial legal and other costs. In the opinion of the Company, any liability that might ensue would not be material in relation to its financial position or results of operations.

INVESTMENTS IN AFFILIATED COMPANIES

Investments in affiliated companies are principally 20%-50% owned companies.

At December 31, 1980 and 1979, equity in undistributed earnings of 20%-50% owned companies amounted to $150 million and $112 million, respectively.

LEASES AND LEASE COMMITMENTS

Total rental expense was $93 million in 1980, $68 million in 1979 and $52 million in 1978. Future minimum rental commitments under noncancelable leases for years ending December 31 are: 1981—$30 million; 1982—$24 million; 1983—$18 million; 1984—$12 million; and 1985—$9 million. For the ensuing three five-year periods, these commitments decrease from $31 million to $12 million. The minimum rentals over the remaining terms of the leases aggregate $20 million. Noncancelable rental commitments are principally for real estate and office space.

	NOMBRE D'ACTIONS*	PRIX D'OPTION PAR ACTION*
Solde au 1er janvier 1979	1.711.335	$18,77- 39,86
Options accordées	1.187.922	$28,63- 63,75
Options exercées	(573.774)	$18,77- 36,89
Options caduques ou annulées	(65.982)	$20,83- 44,86
Solde au 31 décembre 1979	2.259.501	$21,13- 63,75
Options accordées	339.292	$60,83-108,06
Options exercées	(487.870)	$21,13- 63,75
Options caduques ou annulées	(54.300)	$25,08- 85,58
Solde au 31 décembre 1980	2.056.623	$21,13-108,06
Options pouvant être exercées au 31 décembre 1980	700.322	$21,13- 63,75
Disponibles pour les plans d'options d'achat d'actions: Au 31 décembre 1979	6.550.114	
Au 31 décembre 1980	6.265.121	

*Après correction pour tenir compte de la distribution d'une action nouvelle gratuite pour deux anciennes en septembre 1980.

DETERMINATION DE L'IMPOT SUR LES BENEFICES

La Société est constituée selon les lois des Antilles Néerlandaises, où elle est passible d'un impôt sur les bénéfices au taux de 3%. La Société et ses filiales exercent leurs activités dans plus de 100 juridictions fiscales différentes, avec des taux d'imposition allant jusqu'à 50%. Sur le chiffre d'affaires d'exploitation consolidé de 4,9 milliards de dollars réalisé en 1980, 2 milliards ont été réalisés aux Etats-Unis et au Canada. Le taux effectif d'impôts sur les bénéfices mondialement réalisés ressort à 34% en 1980, 35% en 1979 et 37% en 1978.

PASSIF EVENTUEL

En 1980, l'Alexander Kielland, un hôtel flottant utilisé pour l'hébergement des équipes travaillant en mer du Nord, a chaviré lors d'une tempête. L'infrastructure de cet hôtel flottant était à l'origine celle d'une plate-forme de forage, construite par un chantier naval indépendant, d'après des plans fournis sous licence par une filiale de la Société. Cette filiale n'a jamais été propriétaire et n'a jamais participé à l'exploitation de la plate-forme lorsque celle-ci était utilisée pour les forages; elle n'a pas non plus participé à sa transformation en hôtel flottant, ni à l'exploitation de celui-ci. Une commission nommée par le gouvernement norvégien enquête actuellement sur cet accident; elle n'a pas encore déposé son rapport.

Bien que la Société pense n'avoir aucune responsabilité dans cette affaire, des actions en justice peuvent s'ensuivre; ces actions porteraient sur des points complexes de droit international et pourraient s'étendre sur plusieurs années, entraînant ainsi des frais importants de procédure ou autre. La Société pense que le passif qui pourrait éventuellement être mis à sa charge à l'issue de cette affaire ne devrait pas avoir d'effet significatif sur sa situation financière ou ses résultats.

PARTICIPATIONS DANS LES SOCIETES AFFILIEES

Les participations dans les sociétés affiliées comprennent principalement les sociétés dans lesquelles Schlumberger détient une participation de 20% à 50%.

Aux 31 décembre 1980 et 1979, la part de la Société dans les bénéfices non distribués de ces sociétés affiliées s'élevait respectivement à 150 millions de dollars et 112 millions.

BAUX ET ENGAGEMENTS DE LOCATION

Le montant total des dépenses de location s'est élevé à 93 millions de dollars en 1980, 68 millions en 1979 et 52 millions en 1978. Les engagements minima de location non résiliables pour les prochains exercices sont les suivants: 30 millions de dollars en 1981, 24 millions en 1982, 18 millions en 1983, 12 millions en 1984 et 9 millions en 1985. Ces engagements passeront de 31 millions de dollars à 12 millions pour les trois périodes quinquennales suivantes. Pour la durée des baux restant à courir ensuite, le montant total des engagements s'élève à 20 millions de dollars. Les engagements de location non résiliables concernent principalement des immeubles et des bureaux.

TAX ASSESSMENTS

As previously reported, the Company contested assessment of additional tax by the U.S. Internal Revenue Service with respect to its U.S. income tax returns for 1967-1969. The principal parts of the assessment arose from nonrecurring transfers of assets from a subsidiary to the parent company and from continuing wireline operations on the U.S. outer continental shelf. In 1980 these issues wer settled with the U.S. Government. The settlement had a negligible effect on ne income.

For years subsequent to 1969, including 1970 through 1975 where the Internal Revenue Service has completed its examinations, the Government has or is expected to propose additional assessments based upon income from continuing wireline operations on the U.S. outer continental shelf. The determination for the earlier years does not resolve the taxability of this income subsequent to 1969. Management is of the opinion that the reserve for estimated liability for taxes on income is adequate and that any adjustments which may ultimately be determined will not materially affect the financial position or results of operations.

PENSION AND DEFERRED BENEFIT PLANS

Expense for pension and deferred benefit plans was $79 million, $55 million and $39 million, and for compulsory contributions for French retirement benefits $26 million, $22 million and $17 million in 1980, 1979 and 1978, respectively.

Actuarial present value of accumulated benefits at January 1, 1980 and 1979 for U.S. and Canadian defined benefit plans was $124 million and $116 million, respectively, substantially all of which were vested. Net assets available for benefits at January 1, 1980 and 1979 for such plans were $175 million and $145 million, respectively.

The assumed rate of return used in determining the actuarial present value of accumulated plan benefits in both years was between 6% and 6.5%.

SUPPLEMENTARY INFORMATION

Operating revenue and related cost of goods sold and services comprised the following:

| | YEAR ENDED DECEMBER 31, | | |
	1980	1979	1978
	(Stated in millions)		
Operating revenue:			
Sales	$2,128	$1,557	$1,004
Services	2,756	1,993	1,615
	$4,884	$3,550	$2,619
Direct operating costs:			
Goods sold	$1,393	$ 998	$ 636
Services	1,420	1,063	863
	$2,813	$2,061	$1,499

The caption "Interest and Other Income" includes interest income, principally from short-term investments, of $135 million, $82 million and $60 million for 1980, 1979 and 1978, respectively.

Accounts payable and accrued liabilities are summarized as follows:

| | DECEMBER 31, | |
	1980	1979
	(Stated in millions)	
Payroll, vacation and employee benefits	$205	$180
Trade	285	231
Other	241	239
	$731	$650

RAPPELS D'IMPOTS

Ainsi qu'il a déjà été indiqué, la Société a contesté le redressement fiscal opéré par l'U.S. Internal Revenue Service (direction des impôts aux Etats-Unis) à l'issue de son examen des déclarations fiscales de Schlumberger aux Etats-Unis concernant les exercices 1967 à 1969. L'essentiel de ce redressement concernait des transferts exceptionnels d'actifs d'une filiale à la société mère et l'activité des services de mesures dans les sondages (logging) sur le plateau continental des Etats-Unis. Ce contentieux avec l'administration fiscale américaine a été réglé en 1980, et l'incidence de cette affaire sur le bénéfice net a été négligeable.

L'U.S. Internal Revenue Service a terminé son examen des déclarations fiscales de Schlumberger aux Etats-Unis pour les exercices postérieurs à 1969 (1970 à 1975 inclus), et a proposé (ou le fera probablement ultérieurement) des redressements supplémentaires au titre des bénéfices résultant des activités des services de mesures dans les sondages (logging) sur le plateau continental des Etats-Unis. La position finalement adoptée par l'administration fiscale pour les exercices antérieurs à 1970 ne sera pas nécessairement celle qui sera suivie pour les exercices postérieurs. La direction de la Société estime cependant que les provisions pour impôts sur les bénéfices sont appropriées et que tout ajustement éventuel qui pourra finalement se révéler nécessaire n'affectera pas de manière significative la situation financière ou les résultats de la Société.

PLANS DE RETRAITE ET D'INTERESSEMENT DIFFERE

Les charges comptabilisées au titre des plans de retraite et d'intéressement différé se sont élevées en 1980, 1979 et 1978 à 79 millions, 55 millions et 39 millions de dollars; en France, les cotisations versées au titre des régimes obligatoires de retraite se sont élevées, pour les mêmes exercices, à 26 millions, 22 millions et 17 millions de dollars.

La valeur actuelle des avantages acquis par les bénéficiaires des plans constitués aux Etats-Unis et au Canada (calculée à partir de bases actuarielles) s'élevait à 124 millions de dollars au 1er janvier 1980 et à 116 millions de dollars au 1er janvier 1979; ces montants représentent dans leur quasi-totalité des avantages acquis sans condition ultérieure d'attribution. La valeur totale des actifs nets représentant les investissements faits au titre de ces plans s'élevait à 175 millions et 145 millions de dollars aux 1er janvier 1980 et 1979.

Pour les deux années, la valeur actuelle des avantages acquis a été calculée sur la base d'un taux d'actualisation se situant entre 6% et 6,5%.

INFORMATIONS SUPPLEMENTAIRES

Le chiffre d'affaires d'exploitation et le coût correspondant des produits vendus et des services fournis s'analysent comme suit:

	EXERCICE CLOS LE 31 DECEMBRE		
	1980	1979	1978
	(en millions de dollars)		
Chiffre d'affaires d'exploitation:			
Ventes	$2.128	$1.557	$1.004
Services	2.756	1.993	1.615
	$4.884	$3.550	$2.619
Coûts directs d'exploitation:			
Produits vendus	$1.393	$ 998	$ 636
Services	1.420	1.063	863
	$2.813	$2.061	$1.499

Dans les Intérêts et autres revenus sont inclus les produits financiers, perçus principalement sur les placements à court terme, qui se sont élevés à 135 millions, 82 millions et 60 millions de dollars en 1980, 1979 et 1978.

Le poste Fournisseurs, autres créanciers et frais à payer se ventile comme suit:

	31 DECEMBRE	
	1980	1979
	(en millions de dollars)	
Rémunérations, congés payés et autres frais de personnel	$205	$180
Fournisseurs	285	231
Autres	241	239
	$731	$650

FRENCH-ENGLISH

A

abaissement, *n.m.* lowering; abaissement (des prix, des barrières douanières), lowering (of prices, of tariff barriers); abaissement de la valeur du franc, fall/drop in the value of the franc.

abaisser, *v.tr.* to lower/to reduce (prices, cost, etc.); abaisser le taux de l'escompte, to lower the minimum lending rate.

abandon, *n.m.* renunciation (of goods, rights, etc.).

abandonner, *v.tr.* to abandon/to surrender/to renounce/to give up; abandonner la prime, to relinquish the forfeit/the option money; abandonner ses biens à ses créanciers, to surrender one's goods to one's creditors.

abattement, *n.m.* abatement (on declared income); allowance (against tax); abattement à la base, basic personal allowance.

abîmé, *a.* marchandises abîmées, damaged/shop-soiled goods.

abonné, -ée, *n.* (*a*) subscriber (to newspaper, etc.); abonné du téléphone, telephone subscriber; je suis abonné à cette revue, I have a subscription to this magazine (*b*) *Rail: etc:* season-ticket holder (*c*) consumer; les abonnés du gaz, gas users/consumers.

abonnement, *n.m.* (*a*) subscription (to newspaper, etc.); bulletin d'abonnement, subscription form; prendre un abonnement d'un an à une revue, to take out a year's subscription to a magazine; prix de l'abonnement/tarif d'abonnement, subscription rate; *Ins:* police

d'abonnement, floating policy (*b*) *Rail: etc:* (carte d')abonnement, season ticket/*NAm:* commutation ticket.

abonner, *v.tr.* abonner qn à un journal, to take out a subscription to a newspaper for s.o.; être abonné à (une revue, un journal), to subscribe to (a magazine, a newspaper).

s'abonner, (*a*) s'abonner à un journal, to subscribe/to take out a subscription to a newspaper; je me suis abonné à cette revue, I have taken out a subscription to this magazine (*b*) *Rail: etc:* to buy a season ticket.

abrogation, *n.f.* abrogation/repeal.

abrogatoire, *a.* annulling/rescinding (clause, etc.).

abroger, *v.tr.* to abrogate/to annul/to repeal/to rescind.

absentéisme, *n.m.* absenteeism.

absorber, *v.tr.* to take over (a company).

absorption, *n.f.* take-over (of one company by another).

accalmie, *n.f.* slack time/lull (in business).

accaparement, *n.m.* accaparement du marché, cornering of the market.

accaparer, *v.tr.* to corner (the market).

acceptabilité, *n.f.* acceptabilité de la marque, brand acceptance.

acceptant, -ante, *n.* acceptor.

acceptation, *n.f.* acceptance; banque d'acceptation, accepting/acceptance house; (*sur une traite*) bon pour accepta-

tion, accepted; **présenter un effet/une traite à l'acceptation,** to present a bill for acceptance; **refus d'acceptation,** non-acceptance (of goods, bill).

accepter, *v.tr.* to accept; **accepter un effet,** (*i*) to accept/to sign a bill (*ii*) to honour a bill; **ne pas accepter un effet,** to dishonour a bill.

accepteur, *n.m.* acceptor/drawee (of bill).

accessoire, 1. *a.* accessory; **avantages accessoires,** fringe benefits; **frais accessoires,** incidental expenses; **garantie accessoire,** collateral security **2.** *n.m.pl.* accessories; (*dans un magasin*) **accessoires de/pour la toilette,** toilet requisites.

accident, *n.m.* accident; **accidents du travail,** industrial injuries; **la loi sur les accidents du travail** = the Health and Safety at Work Act/the Factory Acts.

accompagnateur, -trice, *n.* (tourist) guide/courrier.

accord, *n.m.* agreement/contract; treaty; **accord commercial,** trade agreement; **Accord général sur les tarifs douaniers et le commerce,** General Agreement on Tariffs and Trade (GATT); **accords internationaux sur les produits de base,** international commodity agreements; **accord tarifaire,** tariff agreement.

accrédité, *n.m.* (*a*) holder of a letter of credit; person having credit facilities with/at a bank (*b*) agent.

accréditer, *v.tr.* (*a*) **notre représentant dûment accrédité,** our duly authorized representative (*b*) *Fin:* **accréditer un client,** to open credit facilities for a customer; **il est accrédité auprès de la BNP,** he has credit facilities with/at the BNP.

accréditeur, *n.m. Fin:* surety/guarantor.

accréditif, 1. *a.* **carte accréditive,** credit card; **lettre accréditive,** letter of credit **2.** *n.m.* (*a*) letter of credit (*b*) **accréditif**

permanent, permanent credit; **loger un accréditif sur une banque,** to open credit facilities with a bank.

accroissement, *n.m.* growth/increase/increment; **accroissement de la demande,** increase in demand; **accroissement global net,** aggregate net(t) increment; **accroissement de la productivité,** growth of productivity; **accroissement des ventes,** sales growth; **accroissement spontané du capital,** self-induced increase of capital; **coût d'accroissement,** incremental cost; **taux d'accroissement,** rate of increase.

accroître, *v.tr.* to increase/to add/to augment; **accroître le capital,** to increase capital; **accroître la productivité,** to increase/to raise productivity.

accumulé, *a.* accumulated/accrued; **intérêts accumulés,** accrued interest.

s'accumuler, *v.pr.* (*des intérêts, etc.*) to accrue.

accusé, 1. *n.m.* **accusé de réception,** (*i*) (*d'une lettre*) acknowledg(e)ment (of receipt) (of a letter) (*ii*) (*d'un colis, etc.*) receipt (of a parcel, etc.); **envoyer un accusé de réception,** to send an acknowledg(e)ment; to acknowledge (sth) **2.** *a.* **baisse (très) accusée,** sharp fall.

accuser, *v.tr.* **1.** to show/to reveal/ to indicate; **compte qui accuse une perte,** account which shows a loss **2.** **accuser réception de qch.,** to acknowledge (receipt of) sth.; **j'accuse réception de votre lettre,** I acknowledge receipt of your letter.

achalandage, *n.m.* (*a*) customers; clientele (*b*) stock; goodwill; **l'achalandage se vend avec l'établissement,** the goodwill is to be sold with the business.

achalandé, *a.* **magasin bien achalandé,** (*i*) shop with a large clientele (*ii*) well-stocked shop.

achat, *n.m.* purchase; **achat au comptant,** cash purchase; **achat d'impulsion/achat**

spontané, impulse buying; **achat à crédit/à terme,** (*i*) purchase on credit (*ii*) buying on hire purchase/*NAm:* on the instalment plan; **chef des achats,** purchasing manager; chief buyer; **facture d'achat,** invoice; *Book-k:* **journal/livre des achats,** bought ledger; **ordre d'achat,** indent; **pouvoir d'achat,** purchasing/spending power; **prix d'achat,** cost price/purchase price/actual cost/prime cost; **aller faire ses achats,** to go shopping; **faire un achat/faire l'achat de qch.,** to make a purchase/to purchase sth./to buy sth.

acheminement, *n.m.* (*a*) **acheminement d'un colis,** route to be followed by a consignment of goods (*b*) flow/routing (of goods, etc.) (*c*) forwarding/sending/dispatch(ing) (of goods, etc.); **durée d'acheminement,** forwarding time.

acheminer, *v.tr.* **acheminer qch. sur/vers un endroit,** to send/to forward/to dispatch/to route sth. to a place; **marchandises acheminées sur Nantes,** goods dispatched to Nantes.

achetable, *a.* purchasable.

acheter, *v.tr.* **acheter qch.,** to buy/to purchase sth.; **j'ai acheté ce livre cinq francs,** I bought this book for five francs; **acheter qch. à qn,** (*i*) to buy sth. from s.o. (*ii*) to buy sth. for s.o.; **acheter qch. (à) bon marché,** to buy sth. cheap; **acheter (au) comptant,** to pay cash (for sth.)/to buy for cash; **acheter à crédit/à tempérament,** to buy on credit; to buy on hire purchase/*NAm:* on the instalment plan; **acheter au détail,** to buy retail; **acheter en gros,** to buy wholesale; **acheter qch. chez l'épicier/chez Martin,** to buy sth. at the grocer's/at Martin's.

acheteur, -euse, *n.* **1.** buyer/purchaser; customer; *Jur:* vendee; **acheteur potentiel,** potential buyer; **on n'a pas pu trouver d'acheteurs pour . . .,** there are no buyers for/there is no market for . . .; **je suis acheteur,** I'll take it **2.** buyer (for

department store, etc.); **acheteur principal,** head buyer.

achèvement, *n.m.* completion/finishing/conclusion (of work); **date d'achèvement,** completion date; **date prévue d'achèvement,** target date.

acompte, *n.m.* instalment/down payment/payment on account; advance; **acompte provisionnel,** advance payment; **payer tant en acompte,** to pay so much on account; **recevoir un acompte sur son salaire,** to receive an advance on one's salary; **verser un acompte de cent francs,** to pay a hundred francs on account (**sur,** on)/to make a down payment/to give an advance of a hundred francs.

acquéreur, -euse, *n.* purchaser/buyer; *Jur:* vendee.

acquis, *a.* **droits acquis,** vested interests.

acquisition, *n.f.* **1.** acquisition; acquiring; **acquisition de données,** data acquisition; **faire l'acquisition de qch.,** to acquire/to purchase sth. **2.** thing bought/acquired; purchase.

acquit, *n.m.* (*a*) receipt; (*sur une facture, etc.*) **pour acquit,** received (with thanks)/paid (*b*) *Cust:* clearance (of ship).

acquit-à-caution, *n.m. Cust:* permit/transire/excise-bond/bond-note.

acquittement, *n.m.* payment/discharge (of bill, debt, etc.).

acquitter, *v.tr.* (*a*) **acquitter une dette,** to pay/to settle/to discharge a debt; **acquitter les droits sur qch.,** to pay the duty on sth. (*b*) **acquitter une facture,** to receipt a bill; **acquitter un chèque,** to endorse a cheque.

s'acquitter, *v.pr.* **s'acquitter d'une dette,** to pay off/to settle/to discharge a debt.

acte, *n.m. Jur:* (*a*) instrument/deed/

agreement; **acte de vente,** bill of sale; sale contract; **acte notarié/acte sur papier timbré,** deed executed and authenticated by a notary; **rédiger/dresser un acte,** to draw up a document (*b*) **acte judiciaire,** writ (*c*) *pl.* **actes,** records (of transactions, proceedings, etc.).

actif[1], *a.* (*a*) **population active,** working population (*b*) **dettes actives,** accounts receivable/debtors.

actif[2], *n.m.* assets; credit (account); **actif circulant,** current assets; **actif immobilisé/stable,** fixed assets; **actif net,** net(t) assets; **actif incorporel,** intangible assets; goodwill; **actif liquide/disponible/négociable/réalisable,** liquid assets/*NAm:* quick assets; **actif réel,** real assets; **excédent de l'actif sur le passif,** excess of assets over liabilities; **mettre qch. à l'actif de qn,** to credit s.o. with sth.; **valeur des actifs,** asset value.

action, *n.f.* **1.** *Fin:* share/stock; **actions de capital/de priorité,** senior shares; **actions de dividende,** junior shares; **actions de jouissance,** dividend shares; **action différée,** deferred share; **action gratuite,** scrip issue/bonus share; **action libérée,** fully paid-up share; **action non entièrement libérée,** partly paid-up share; **action nominative/au porteur,** registered share; **action ordinaire,** ordinary share/*NAm:* common stock; **action privilégiée,** preference share/preferred share/preferred stock; **compagnie par actions,** joint-stock company **2.** *Jur:* **action judiciaire,** action/proceedings; lawsuit; **intenter une action à qn,** to bring an action against s.o./to institute proceedings against s.o./ to sue s.o.; **action en paiement,** action for payment; **action en dommages et intérêts,** action/claim for damages; **mandat d'action,** receiving order (in bankruptcy) **3.** *SwFr:* **vente action,** bargain offer.

actionnaire, *n.m. & f. Fin:* shareholder/ *NAm:* stockholder.

actionnariat, *n.m.* shareholding; **actionnariat ouvrier,** worker participation/ employee shareholding; industrial co-partnership.

activité, *n.f.* **1.** (*a*) briskness; **marché sans activité,** dull market; **le peu d'activité du marché,** the dullness/the slackness of the market (*b*) **graphique des activités,** activity chart; **rapport d'activité,** progress report **2.** (*a*) **en activité,** in action/in operation/in progress; **l'usine est en activité,** the factory is in production; **en pleine activité,** in full operation (*b*) **les activités d'une entreprise,** a firm's operations.

actuaire, *n.m. Ins: Fin:* actuary.

actualisé, *a.* discounted; **cash flow actualisé,** discounted cash flow; **valeur actualisée,** discounted present value.

actuariat, *n.m. Ins: Fin:* (*a*) functions of an actuary (*b*) profession of actuary.

actuariel, *a.* (*a*) *Ins:* actuarial (calculation, etc.) (*b*) **taux de rendement actuariel brut,** annual interest yield gross/gross annual interest return.

actuel, *a.* present-day/prevailing/current; **prix actuels,** ruling prices; **valeur actuelle (nette),** (net(t)) present value.

addition, *n.f.* (*a*) adding up; **faire l'addition des chiffres,** to add up the figures (*b*) **en addition au paragraphe 2 . . .,** further to paragraph 2 . . . (*c*) (*au restaurant, etc.*) bill/*NAm:* check.

additionner, *v.tr. & i.* to add up.

additionneuse, *n.f.* adding machine.

adjoint, -ointe, *a. & n.* assistant/deputy; **directeur adjoint,** deputy manager/assistant manager; **directeur général adjoint,** deputy managing director.

adjudicataire, *n.m.* (*a*) successful tenderer for a public contract; company which has been awarded a public contract; contractor; **être déclaré adjudicataire de qch.,** to secure the contract for sth. (*b*) highest bidder/purchaser (at auction).

adjudication, *n.f.* (*a*) adjudicating/adjudging/awarding (public contracts) (*b*) adjudication/allocation/award (of public contract); **obtenir l'adjudication de qch.,** to be awarded a public contract (*c*) knocking down (of sth. to s.o.); **mettre qch. en adjudication,** (*i*) to invite tenders for sth./to put sth. out to tender (*ii*) to put sth. up for sale by auction; **adjudication au rabais,** allocation to lowest tender(er); **adjudication à la surenchère,** allocation to the highest bidder; **par voie d'adjudication,** (*i*) by tender (*ii*) by auction.

adjuger, *v.tr.* adjuger qch. à qn, (*i*) to adjudge/to award/to allocate sth. to s.o.; **adjuger les fournitures de bureau,** to give the contract for office furniture (after tender) (*ii*) (*aux enchères*) to knock sth. down to s.o.

admettre, *v.tr.* to allow; **admettre un recours,** to allow a claim.

administrateur, -trice, *n.* (*a*) (non-executive) director (of company, bank, etc.); business manager (of newspaper, etc.) (*b*) **administrateur judiciaire,** trustee/(official) receiver (of estate, business, etc.).

administratif, *a.* administrative; **bâtiment administratif,** office building/office block; **détails d'ordre administratif,** administrative details; **frais administratifs,** administration expenses; **méthodes administratives,** systems and procedures.

administration, *n.f.* **1.** (*a*) administration/direction/management (of business, etc.); **l'Administration,** the board of directors; the management; **administration du personnel,** personnel management; **administration des ventes,** sales management; **l'administration du théâtre,** the management of the theatre; **conseil d'administration,** board of directors/executive board; **frais d'administration,** administration expenses; **mauvaise**

administration, mismanagement; **président du conseil d'administration,** chairman of the board; **réunion du conseil d'administration,** board meeting (*b*) *Jur:* trusteeship **2. l'Administration,** the Civil Service.

administrer, *v.tr.* to manage/to direct (business, undertaking, estate).

admission, *n.f.* **1.** *Cust:* entry (of goods); **admission en franchise,** duty-free entry; **admission temporaire,** duty-free entry (of products destined for re-export after processing) **2.** *StExch:* **admission à la cote,** admission to quotation.

adopter, *v.tr.* **adopter une résolution,** to adopt a resolution; **adopter un rapport,** to accept a report; **adopté à l'unanimité,** carried unanimously.

adoption, *n.f.* adoption (of a resolution); acceptance (of a report).

adresse, *n.f.* address; (*d'une société*) **adresse du siège social**/(*d'une personne*) **adresse de bureau,** business address; **adresse du domicile,** home address; **mettre/écrire l'adresse sur une enveloppe,** to address an envelope.

adresser, *v.tr.* to address (letter, parcel, etc.).

ad valorem, *Lt.a.phr.* **payer un droit ad valorem,** to pay an ad valorem duty.

aérien, *a. Av:* **compagnie aérienne,** airline; **par voie aérienne,** by air; **poste aérienne,** airmail; **transports aériens,** air transport.

aérogramme, *n.m.* air letter (form).

affacturage, *n.m.* factoring; **commission d'affacturage,** factoring charges.

affaire, *n.f.* **1.** (*a*) business/deal/transaction/bargain; **affaire d'or,** first-class speculation; splendid bargain; **bonne affaire,** sound transaction; good speculation/good bargain/good buy; **grosse affaire,** big deal; **mauvaise affaire,** bad deal/bad bargain; **petite affaire,** small deal; **faire affaire avec qn,** to do business with s.o./to deal with s.o.; **faire/conclure une affaire,** to make/to conclude a deal; **faire une bonne affaire,** to get a bargain; to do a good piece of business; **traiter une affaire avec qn,** to transact business with s.o. (b) business; **une grosse affaire,** a large firm; **son usine est une grande affaire,** his factory is a large concern; **administrer/conduire/gérer/diriger une affaire,** to run a business; **lancer une affaire,** to start a business **2.** pl. **affaires,** business/trade; **affaires courantes,** routine business; **agent d'affaires,** (business) agent; **bureau/agence/cabinet d'affaires,** (general) agency; **carte d'affaires,** business card; **centre d'affaires,** business centre; **chiffre d'affaires,** turnover; volume of business/sales volume; **déjeuner d'affaires,** business lunch; **homme/femme d'affaires,** businessman/businesswoman; **le monde des affaires,** the business world; **lettre d'affaires,** business letter; **visite d'affaires,** business call; **voyage d'affaires,** business trip; **entrer dans les affaires,** to go into business; **être dans les affaires,** to be in business; **faire des affaires avec qn,** to do business with s.o./to deal with s.o./**faire de bonnes affaires,** to be successful (in business)/to do good business; **faire de mauvaises affaires,** to be doing badly; to be in difficulties; to work at a loss; **faire des affaires importantes,** to do business on a large scale; to have a big turnover; **parler affaires,** to talk business/F: to talk shop; **comment vont les affaires?** how's business? **les affaires vont mal,** business is bad; **je vais à Londres pour affaires,** I am going to London on business; **quel est son genre d'affaires?** what's his line of business?/what line of business is he in? **s'absenter pour affaires,** to go away on business **3.** Jur: case/lawsuit.

affectation, n.f. (a) **affectation d'une somme à un projet,** assignment/attribution/allotment of money to a purpose; appropriation/earmarking for a purpose; **affectation aux dividendes,** sum available for dividend; **affectations**

budgétaires, budget appropriations; **affectation de fonds,** appropriation of funds; **affectation hypothécaire,** mortgage charge (b) **affectation des tâches,** job assignment.

affecter, v.tr. **affecter des crédits à un certain usage,** to assign funds to; to appropriate/to set aside/to earmark/to allocate funds for a certain use.

affermage, n.m. **1.** (a) renting (of farm, land, etc.) (b) leasing (c) contracting (for advertisements, etc.) **2.** rent (of land, farm).

affermer, v.tr. **1.** (a) to lease (farm, etc.) (b) to let out (sth. on contract) **2.** (a) to rent; to take (farm, land, etc.) on lease (b) to contract for (sth.).

affichage, n.m. (a) sticking up (posters)/bill-sticking/bill-posting; **panneau d'affichage,** hoarding/NAm: billboard (b) **publicité par affichage,** poster advertising (c) display; **unité d'affichage,** display unit.

affiche, n.f. **affiche publicitaire,** poster/bill.

afficher, v.tr. to stick (up)/to display (bill, etc.); **afficher une vente,** to put up a poster advertising a sale/to advertise a sale/NAm: to post a sale; PN: **défense d'afficher,** no billsticking/stick no bills/NAm: post no bills.

affidavit, n.m. Jur: affidavit.

affiliation, n.f. affiliation.

affilié, 1. a. affiliated; **société affiliée,** associate/affiliate(d) company **2.** n. (affiliated) member/associate.

s'affilier, v.pr. **s'affilier à,** to become a member of (a syndicate, etc.).

afflux, n.m. inflow/influx (of goods, gold, etc.).

affranchir, v.tr. to pay the postage on/of (sth.); to frank/to stamp (letter); **colis affranchi,** parcel with postage paid; **lettre insuffisamment affranchie,** letter with insufficient postage; **machine à affran-**

chir (les lettres), franking machine/*NAm:* postal meter.

affranchissement, *n.m.* (*a*) stamping/franking (*b*) postage (of letter, parcel, etc.).

affrètement, *n.m.* chartering (of ship, aircraft, etc.); **acte/contrat d'affrètement,** charter-party; **affrètement coque nue,** bareboat charter; **affrètement à temps,** time-charter; **affrètement au voyage,** trip-charter.

affréter, *v.tr.* to charter a ship/an aircraft, etc.

affréteur, *n.m.* charterer.

agence, *n.f.* (*a*) agency (office); bureau; **agence d'affaires,** (general) business agency/office; **agence de location,** letting agency; **agence de placement,** employment agency/employment bureau; **agence de renseignement(s),** information bureau; **agence de voyages,** travel agency; **agence (de voyages) à prix réduits,** bucket shop; **agence en douane,** customs agency; **agence immobilière,** estate agency/*NAm:* real estate agency; **agence maritime,** shipping/forwarding agency; **Agence nationale pour l'Emploi (ANPE)** = Job Centre; **compte d'agence,** agency account; **contrat/mandat d'agence,** agency agreement/contract (*b*) branch office; **la maison a plusieurs agences à l'étranger,** the company has several agencies overseas.

agent, *n.m.* (*a*) agent; **agent à demeure,** agent on the spot; **agent comptable,** accountant; **agent d'affaires,** general agent/(business) agent; **agent d'assurance(s),** insurance broker/agent; **agent de location,** letting agent/estate agent; **agent de publicité,** advertising agent/publicity agent; **agent en douanes,** customs agent; **agent immobilier,** (*i*) land agent (*ii*) estate agent/*NAm:* realtor/real estate agent; **agent maritime,** shipping agent; **seul agent/agent commercial exclusif d'une maison,** sole agent/sole representative of a firm; **il est l'agent exclusif**

de Toyota, he has the Toyota agency (*b*) *Fin:* **agent de change,** (*i*) stockbroker/bill broker/exchange broker (*ii*) mercantile broker (*c*) **agent de liaison,** contact man; **agent de maîtrise,** supervisor; **agent de recouvrement,** debt collector.

agio, *n.m. Fin:* **1.** agio (of exchange); *Bank:* premium (on gold)/premium offer **2.** (*a*) money-changing (*b*) jobbery/speculation.

agiotage, *n.m. Fin: Pej:* stock-jobbing/agiotage/speculation/gambling (on the Stock Exchange).

agioter, *v.i.* to speculate/to gamble (on the Stock Exchange).

agioteur, -euse, *n.* speculator/gambler (on the Stock Exchange).

agréé, 1. *a.* **agent agréé,** authorized agent/dealer; *FrC:* **comptable agréé (CA),** chartered accountant (CA) **2.** *n.m. Jur:* solicitor/counsel/attorney (before a *tribunal de commerce*).

agréer, *v.tr.* to accept/to recognize/to approve (of)/to agree to (sth.); **agréer un contrat,** to approve an agreement; *Corr:* **veuillez agréer/je vous prie d'agréer l'expression de mes sentiments distingués,** yours truly/yours faithfully; yours sincerely.

agricole, *a.* agricultural (country, produce, etc.); **comice(s) agricole(s)/exposition agricole,** agricultural show; **grande exploitation agricole,** (*i*) large scale farming (*ii*) large farm; **petite exploitation agricole,** (*i*) small-scale farming (*ii*) small farm/smallholding; **office commercial des produits agricoles,** agricultural marketing board; **produits agricoles,** agricultural produce.

agriculteur, *n.m.* agricultur(al)ist; farmer.

agriculture, *n.f.* agriculture; farming.

agro-alimentaire, *a. & n.* food industry based on agriculture.

agronome, *n.m.* agronomist/agricultural economist; **ingénieur agronome,** agricultural engineer.

agronomie, *n.f.* agronomy; agronomics.

aide-comptable, *n.m.* accounts assistant.

ajourner, *v.tr.* **ajourner une réunion,** to adjourn/to postpone a meeting.

ajustement, *n.m.* adjusting/adjustment (of wages, prices, etc.); **ajustement saisonnier,** seasonal adjustment.

ajuster, *v.tr.* to adjust (an account, etc.).

aléatoire, *a.* aleatory (contract, etc.); risky/uncertain; **sondage/échantillonnage aléatoire,** random sampling.

aliénation, *n.f.* *Jur:* transfer (of rights, property, etc.).

aliéner, *v.tr.* to transfer (rights, property, etc.).

alignement, *n.m.* making up/balancing (of accounts, etc.); **alignement (des traitements),** bringing (salaries) into line; pay comparability; *Fin:* **alignement monétaire,** (re)alignment of currencies.

aligner, *v.tr. Fin:* to align (**sur,** with)/to bring into line; **aligner les salaires des mineurs sur ceux de l'industrie,** to bring the salaries of miners into line with those of industry; to give miners pay comparability with industry.

aliment, *n.m.* **1.** *Ins:* interest/risk value **2.** food; **aliments et boissons,** food and drink.

alimentaire, *a.* **l'industrie alimentaire,** food industry; **produits/denrées alimentaires,** foodstuff/food products.

alimentation, *n.f.* **produits d'alimentation,** foodstuff/food products; **(magasin d')alimentation,** grocer's (shop); **(rayon d')alimentation,** food counter/department.

aller, *n.m.* outward journey; **cargaison d'aller,** outward cargo; **un aller (simple),** a single (ticket)/*NAm:* a one-way ticket; **un aller (et) retour,** a return (ticket)/*NAm:* a round-trip ticket; **voyage (d')aller et retour,** return journey/*NAm:* round trip; *MIns:* **police à l'aller et au retour,** round policy; *StExch:* **aller et retour,** bed and breakfast deal.

allocataire, *n.m. & f.* recipient of an allowance.

allocation, *n.f.* **1.** (*a*) allocation/assignment/granting (of sum of money, etc.); **allocation de fonds,** appropriation of funds (*b*) *Fin:* allotment (of shares, etc.) **2.** allowance/grant; **allocations familiales** = child benefit; **allocation (de) chômage,** unemployment benefit; **allocation de vieillesse,** old-age/retirement pension; **allocation par tête,** capitation grant.

allonge, *n.f.* **allonge d'une lettre de change,** allonge to a bill of exchange; **allonge d'un document,** rider to a document.

allouer, *v.tr.* to allocate a sum (for a purpose); to grant (a pension); to allocate (shares, etc.); **allouer à qn une somme à titre de dommages-intérêts,** to award s.o. a sum as damages.

amende, *n.f.* fine; **amende pour retard de livraison, etc.,** penalty.

amendement, *n.m.* amendment.

amender, *v.tr.* **amender une proposition,** to amend a resolution.

amiable, *a. Jur:* (*a*) conciliatory; **amiable compositeur,** arbitrator (*b*) *a. phr.* à **l'amiable,** by mutual agreement; *Jur:* **règlement à l'amiable,** out-of-court settlement; **vente à l'amiable,** sale by private treaty.

amont, *n.m. Mkt:* upside (potential).

amortir, *v.tr.* (*a*) *Fin:* to redeem/to pay off/to extinguish/to amortize (debt); **amortir un emprunt,** to repay a loan (*b*) to allow for depreciation; **amortir (pro-**

gressivement), to write down; **amortir (totalement)**, to write off.

amortissable, *a. Fin:* redeemable (stock, etc.).

amortissement, *n.m. Fin:* (*a*) redemption/amortization/repayment (of a debt); **fonds/caisse d'amortissement**, sinking fund (*b*) (amount written off for) depreciation; amortization; **amortissement accéléré**, accelerated depreciation; **méthode de l'amortissement constant méthode linéaire/méthode en ligne droite**, straight line method of depreciation; **provision pour amortissement**, depreciation allowance.

amovible, *a.* **personnel amovible**, transferable/mobile staff.

analyse, *n.f.* analysis; **analyse des coûts/analyse du prix de revient**, cost analysis; **analyse coût-profit/analyse des avantages-coûts**, cost-benefit analysis; **analyse coût-volume-profit**, cost-volume-profit analysis; **analyse des écarts**, variance analysis; **analyse des marchés**, market research; **analyse des tâches**, job analysis; **analyse des ventes**, sales analysis; **analyse de(s) système(s)**, systems analysis; **analyse de la valeur**, value analysis.

analyste, *n.m. & f.* analyst; **analyste-programmeur, -euse**, computer analyst.

analytique, *a.* analytic(al); **comptabilité analytique**, analytic(al) accounting/cost accounting.

animateur, *n.m.* **animateur des ventes**, marketing executive.

animation, *n.f.* **animation des ventes**, sales drive.

animé, *a.* **marché animé**, brisk/buoyant market.

année, *n.f.* year; **année civile**, calendar year; **année budgétaire**, financial/fiscal year.

annexe, 1. *a.* **document annexe**, attached document; **industries annexes**, subsidiary industries; **lettre annexe**, covering letter; **revenus annexes**, supplementary income **2.** *n.f.* annexe (to a contract); attached document.

annexer, *v.tr.* to append/to attach (document, etc.).

annonce, *n.f.* **annonce (publicitaire)**, advertisement/ad/advert; **annonces classées/petites annonces**, small ads/classified ads/classified advertisements; **demander qch. par voie d'annonces**, to advertise for sth; **faire paraître une annonce pour recruter les services d'un traducteur**, to advertise for a translator; **insérer une annonce dans les journaux**, to put an advertisement in the papers.

annonceur, *n.m.* advertiser.

annuaire, *n.m.* yearbook; **annuaire du commerce**, commercial directory; **annuaire des téléphones**, telephone directory.

annualité, *n.f.* yearly recurrence (of tax, etc.).

annuel, *a.* annual/yearly; **rente annuelle**, annuity.

annuellement, *adv.* annually/yearly.

annuitaire, *a.* (debt) redeemable by yearly payments.

annuité, *n.f.* (*a*) *Fin:* annual instalment (in repayment of debt) (*b*) year of service.

annulable, *a. Jur:* voidable/rescindable (contract, etc.); (contract, etc.) that can be annulled/cancelled.

annulation, *n.f. Jur:* annulment; cancelling/cancellation (of contract).

annuler, *v.tr.* to annul/to cancel (contract, etc.); to call off (a deal); to void (a bill, etc.).

anonyme, *a.* anonymous; **société anonyme (par actions)**, joint-stock company/limited (-liability) company.

anticipation, *n.f.* anticipation; **payer par anticipation,** to pay in advance; **paiement par anticipation,** advance (payment)/prepayment.

anticiper, *v.tr.* (*a*) *Fin:* **anticiper un paiement de dix jours,** to anticipate a payment by ten days; **dividende anticipé,** advanced dividend; **remboursement anticipé,** redemption before due date (*b*) **ventes anticipées,** expected sales.

antidater, *v.tr.* to antedate (contract, cheque, etc.).

anti-dumping, *a.* **législation anti-dumping,** anti-dumping legislation.

anti-inflationniste, *a.* anti-inflationary; **measures anti-inflationnistes,** anti-inflation(ary) measures.

antiprotectionniste, 1. *a.* free-trade (policy, etc.) **2.** *n.m.* & *f.* anti-protectionist; free-trader.

anti-trust, *a.inv.* anti(-)trust.

apériteur, *n.m. Ins:* leading underwriter.

appel, *n.m.* **1.** *Fin:* **appel d'offres,** invitation to tender; **faire un appel d'offres,** to invite bids/tenders; **avis d'appel de fonds,** call letter; **faire un appel de fonds,** to call up capital **2.** telephone/*F:* phone call; **appel avec préavis,** person to person call; **appel en PCV,** transfer charge call/*NAm:* collect call; **prendre un appel,** to take a (phone) call; **recevoir un appel,** to receive a phone call.

appelé, *a. Fin:* **capital appelé,** called-up capital.

appellation, *n.f.* **appellation contrôlée,** (*i*) (*d'un vin*) guaranteed vintage (*ii*) guaranteed trade mark; **appellation d'origine** = place of origin guaranteed; **vin d'appellation,** vintage wine.

appoint, *n.m.* (*a*) **faire l'appoint,** (*i*) to make up (a sum) (*ii*) to pay the right amount/the exact fare; **monnaie d'ap-**point, divisional/fractional money (*b*) **salaire d'appoint,** extra salary.

appointements, *n.m.pl.* salary; **toucher ses appointements,** to draw one's salary.

appointer, *v.tr.* to pay/to give a salary to; **commis appointés,** salaried clerks.

apport, *n.m.* **actions d'apport,** founder's/promoter's shares; **apport d'argent frais,** injection of new money; **apport de capitaux,** contribution of capital; **capital d'apport,** initial capital.

appréciateur, *n.m.* valuer.

appréciatif, *a.* **devis appréciatif,** estimate; **dresser l'état appréciatif d'un mobilier,** to draw up the valuation of/to value furniture.

appréciation, *n.f.* **1.** valuation/assessment/estimation/estimate/appraisal; **appréciation du personnel,** staff assessment/appraisal; **appréciation des risques,** risk assessment; **faire l'appréciation des marchandises,** to value/to appraise/to make an appraisal of goods **2.** appreciation/rise in value.

apprécier, *v.tr.* to appraise/to estimate the value of (sth.); to value (sth.)/to set a value on (sth.).

apprenti, -ie, *n.* apprentice.

apprentissage, *n.m.* apprenticeship; **mettre qn en apprentissage chez qn,** to apprentice s.o. to s.o.; **faire son apprentissage chez qn,** to serve one's apprenticeship with s.o.; **contrat d'apprentissage,** contract of apprenticeship; indentures; **taxe d'apprentissage,** training levy/(employers') tax levied as a contribution to training schemes.

approbation, *n.f.* (*a*) approval/approbation; **pour approbation,** for approval/subject to approval; **soumettre à l'approbation (de qn),** to submit for approval (by s.o.) (*b*) certifying (of accounts, of document); passing (of accounts).

appropriation, *n.f.* appropriation; **appropriation de fonds,** embezzlement.

approuver, *v.tr.* to approve; to sanction (expenditure, etc.); **approuver les comptes,** to approve the accounts; **approuver un contrat,** to ratify a contract; **approuver une facture,** to pass an invoice; **approuver une nomination,** to confirm an appointment; **lu et approuvé,** read and approved.

approvisionnement, *n.m.* **1.** provisioning/supplying; procurement; stocking (of shop) **2.** (*a*) supply/stock/store; **approvisionnements de réserve,** reserve stocks; **faire un approvisionnement de qch.,** to stock up with sth./to lay in a supply of sth. (*b*) *Ind:* raw materials and component parts (used in processing industry).

approvisionner, *v.tr.* to supply (**de,** with); to furnish with supplies; to provide with stores; to provision; to procure; to victual (a ship).

s'approvisionner, *v.pr.* to take in/to lay in (stock, a supply of); to stock up with sth.; to lay in stores; **s'approvisionner (chez qn),** to get one's supplies from (s.o.)/to stock up/to shop (somewhere, at s.o.'s).

approvisionneur, -euse, *n.* supplier.

approximatif, *a.* approximate/rough (calculation, estimate); **ces chiffres sont très approximatifs,** these figures are only a rough estimate.

après-vente, *a.inv.* **service après-vente,** after-sales service/back up service.

apurement, *n.m.* auditing/agreeing (of accounts).

apurer, *v.tr.* to audit/to pass/to agree (accounts).

arbitrage, *n.m.* **1.** arbitration; **conseil d'arbitrage,** conciliation/arbitration board (in industrial dispute); **règlement par arbitrage,** settlement by arbitration; **soumettre une question à un arbitrage,** to refer a question to arbitration **2.** *Bank: etc:* arbitrage; **arbitrage de/du change,** arbitrage/arbitration of exchange; *StExch:* **arbitrage en reports,** jobbing in contango(e)s; **faire l'arbitrage de place en place,** to shunt.

arbitral, *a. Jur:* arbitral; **commission arbitrale,** board of referees; **procédure arbitrale,** procedure by arbitration; **solution arbitrale/règlement arbitral,** settlement by arbitration; **tribunal arbitral,** arbitration court/tribunal of arbitration/court of arbitration.

arbitre, *n.m. Jur:* arbitrator/referee/adjudicator; **arbitre rapporteur,** referee (in commercial suit).

arbitrer, *v.tr. Jur:* to arbitrate.

archives, *n.f.pl.* archives.

argent, *n.m.* **1.** silver; **encaisse or et argent d'un pays,** gold and silver holding of a country **2.** money; cash; **argent liquide,** cash (in hand)/ready money; **payer en argent,** to pay (in) cash; **placer son argent,** to invest one's money; **somme d'argent,** sum/amount of money; **trouver de l'argent,** to raise money.

arrangement, *n.m.* agreement; settlement; arrangement; **arrangement avec ses créanciers,** composition with one's creditors; **sauf arrangement contraire,** unless otherwise agreed.

s'arranger, *v.pr.* **s'arranger avec qn,** to come to an agreement/to terms with s.o.; **s'arranger avec ses créanciers,** to compound with one's creditors.

arrérager, **1.** *v.i.* (*du loyer, etc.*) to remain unpaid; to be in arrears **2.** *v.pr.* **laisser s'arrérager (les termes de) son loyer,** to let one's rent fall into arrears.

arrérages, *n.m.pl.* **arrérages de loyer,** rent arrears/back rent.

arrêté, *n.m.* **arrêté de compte,** settlement of (an) account.

arrêter, *v.tr.* to close/to settle (an account); **arrêter les comptes de l'exercice,** to close the yearly accounts.

arrhes, *n.f.pl.* (*a*) deposit/down payment; advance payment; **verser des arrhes,** to pay a deposit; to give an advance.

arriéré, 1. *a.* late/in arrears; **paiement arriéré,** overdue/outstanding payment; **intérêt arriéré,** outstanding interest **2.** *n.m.* arrears (of account, correspondence, etc.); backlog (of orders); **arriéré de loyer,** rent arrears/back rent.

arrière-boutique, *n.f.* back of the shop/*NAm:* back-store.

arriérer, *v.tr.* to postpone/to delay/to defer (payment, etc.).

s'arriérer, *v.pr.* to fall into arrears.

arrivage, *n.m.* arrival; consignment (of goods).

arrivée, *n.f.* arrival (of goods).

arrondir, *v.tr.* to round up (a sum of money).

article, *n.m.* **1.** item (of bill, etc.); **articles de dépense,** items of expenditure; **articles divers,** sundries **2.** article/commodity/item; *pl.* goods/wares; **article (en) réclame,** special offer; **articles d'exportation,** export goods/exports; **articles de ménage,** household requisites; **articles de toilette,** toilet requisites/toiletries; **articles de voyage,** travel goods; **je ne fais pas cet article,** I don't deal in that line; **faire l'article,** *F:* to plug one's products.

assainir, *v.tr.* to stabilize (a budget, etc.); **assainir les finances,** to reorganize the finances; **assainir la monnaie,** to stabilize the currency.

assemblée, *n.f.* assembly/meeting; **assemblée générale annuelle,** Annual General Meeting (AGM); **assemblée (générale) extraordinaire,** extraordinary general meeting (EGM); **assemblée générale**

d'actionnaires, general meeting of shareholders.

asseoir, *v.tr.* **asseoir un impôt,** to calculate the basis for a tax.

assiette, *n.f.* **assiette d'un impôt,** basis of a tax; taxable income; **assiette d'une hypothèque,** property/funds on which a mortgage is secured.

assigner, *v.tr.* **assigner une somme à un paiement,** to earmark a sum for a payment/to allocate a sum to a payment.

association, *n.f.* (*a*) association; **Association Française des Banques (AFB),** French Bankers' Association (*b*) partnership; **entrer en association avec qn,** to enter into partnership with s.o.

associé, -ée, *n.* partner; **associé principal,** senior partner; **associé (en second),** junior partner; **associé commandité,** active partner; **associé commanditaire,** sleeping partner; **prendre qn comme associé,** to take s.o. into partnership.

s'associer, *v.pr.* **s'associer à/avec qn,** to enter/to go into partnership with s.o.

assortiment, *n.m.* stock; assortment (of goods).

assortir, *v.tr.* to stock/to supply (shops, etc., with goods); **magasin bien assorti,** well-stocked shop.

assujetti, 1. *n.m.* **les assujettis à l'impôt,** the tax-payers **2.** *a.* **être assujetti à l'impôt,** to be liable to tax.

assurance, *n.f.* (*a*) insurance/assurance; **agent d'assurances,** insurance agent; **compagnie/société d'assurances,** insurance company; **courtier d'assurances,** insurance broker; **frais d'assurance,** insurance charges; **police d'assurance,** insurance policy; **prime d'assurance,** insurance premium; **payer les primes d'assurance/payer l'assurance d'une voiture,** to pay the insurance on a car; **il est dans les assurances,** he's in insurance (*b*) **assurance (contre les) accidents,** accident insurance; **assurance (des patrons) contre les accidents du travail,** employers' liability insurance; = workmen's compensation insurance; **assurance auto(mobile),** car/motor insurance; **assurance collective,** group insurance; **assurance à cotisations,** contributory insurance; **assurance crédit,** credit insurance; **assurance en cas de décès/assurance décès,** whole life insurance; **assurance incendie/assurance contre l'incendie,** fire insurance; **assurance contre l'invalidité,** insurance against injury; personal accident insurance; **assurance maladie,** medical insurance; **assurance maritime,** marine insurance; **assurance multirisques,** comprehensive insurance; all-risks insurance; **assurance mutuelle,** mutual insurance; **assurance responsabilité civile,** personal (liability) insurance; **assurance aux tiers/assurances vis-à-vis des tiers,** third-party insurance; **assurance tous risques/***SwFr:* **assurance casco,** comprehensive insurance; all-risks insurance; **assurance sur la vie/assurance vie,** life assurance/life insurance; **assurance en cas de vie,** endowment insurance; **assurance contre le vol/assurance vol,** insurance against theft; **contracter une assurance,** to take out an insurance (policy); **il y a assurance,** the property is insured (*c*) *Adm:* **assurance invalidité,** disability pension; **assurance maladie** = sickness benefit; **assurances sociales** = National Insurance/Social Security; **assurance vieillesse** = old age pension.

assuré, -ée, *n.* **1.** (*a*) *Ins:* policy-holder; insured person (*b*) *Adm:* **assuré social,** member of the National Insurance scheme **2.** *a. Ins:* **la maison est assurée,** the house is insured/covered by an insurance.

assurer, 1. *v.tr.* (*a*) to ensure; **assurer un service,** to provide a service; **assurer une rente à qn,** to settle an annuity on s.o. (*b*) *Ins:* **assurer qn,** to insure s.o.; **la Compagnie n'assure pas contre les dégâts causés par la pluie,** the Company will not insure against damage caused by rain; **assurer un immeuble contre l'incendie,** to insure a building against fire **2.** *v.pr.* **s'assurer,** to take out an insurance (policy) (**contre,** against); **s'assurer sur la vie,** to take out a life insurance (policy).

assureur, *n.m. Ins:* (*a*) insurer (*b*) underwriter.

atelier, *n.m.* **1.** (work)shop/workroom; **atelier de constructions navales,** shipyard; **il est monté contre-maître après cinq ans d'atelier,** he became a foreman after five years on the shop floor; **chef d'atelier,** (shop) foreman **2.** (*a*) (shop, workroom) staff (*b*) industrial unit; work group.

attaché, *n.m.* **attaché commercial,** commercial attaché; **attaché de presse,** press attaché.

attribuer, *v.tr.* to assign; to allot; **attribuer des actions,** to allot shares.

attributaire, *n.m. & f. Jur:* assignee; *Fin:* allottee.

attribution, *n.f.* assigning/allotment/allocation; **attribution d'actions,** allotment of shares.

audio-copiste, *n.m. & f.* audio typist.

audio-magnéto, *n.m. & f.* **dactylo audio-magnéto,** audio typist.

audit, *n.m.* (*a*) audit; **audit interne,** internal audit (*b*) auditor; **audit interne,** internal auditor.

augmentation, *n.f.* increase; *Adm:* increment; **un salaire de 80 000 F avec augmentation annuelle de . . .,** salary of 80 000 F with annual increments of . . .; **augmentation de salaire,** increase in salary/rise/*NAm:* raise; **augmentation des prix,** increase in prices; **être en augmentation,** to be on the increase; **chiffre d'affaires en augmentation sur l'année dernière,** turnover showing an increase on last year('s).

augmenter, 1. *v.tr.* to increase; to enlarge; **augmenter le prix de qch.,** to raise/to put up the price of sth.; **cela**

augmente nos dépenses, this adds to our expenses; **augmenter qn,** to raise/to increase s.o.'s salary; to give s.o. a rise/ *NAm:* a raise; **j'ai été augmenté,** I've had a rise; **édition revue et augmentée,** edition revised and enlarged **2.** *v.i.* to increase; **empêcher les frais d'augmenter,** to keep expenses down; **tout a augmenté de prix,** everything has gone up in price; **le chiffre d'affaires a augmenté de 10% par rapport à l'année dernière,** the turnover is 10% up on last year('s).

auteur, *n.m.* (*a*) author; **droit d'auteur,** copyright (*b*) **droits d'auteur,** royalties; **recevoir des droits d'auteur de 10%,** to receive royalties/a royalty of 10%.

authentifier, *v.tr.* (*a*) to authenticate/to certify (a signature) (*b*) to legalize (a document, etc.).

authentique, *a.* (*a*) authentic/genuine (*b*) **copie authentique,** certified copy; *Fin:* **cours authentique,** official quotation.

authentiquer, *v.tr.* = **authentifier.**

auto-amortissable, *a.* self-liquidating.

autofinancement, *n.m. Fin:* self-financing; ploughing back of profits; **marge brute d'autofinancement (MBA),** cash flow.

auto-gestion, *n.f.* self-management.

autolimiter, *v.tr.* **les Japonais autolimitent leurs exportations de voitures,** the Japanese set voluntary limits to their car exports.

automation, *n.f.* automation.

automatique, 1. *a.* automatic; **distributeur automatique,** (*i*) vending machine (*ii*) cash dispenser; *Bank:* **guichet automatique,** cash dispenser **2.** *n.m.* **l'automatique,** subscriber trunk dialling (STD)/direct dialling; **l'automatique international,** international direct dialling.

automobile, *n.f.* car/*NAm:* automobile; **Salon de l'Automobile,** Motor Show; **l'in-**dustrie automobile, the motor/the car industry.

autorisation, *n.f.* authorization/ permission; permit/licence; **autorisation spéciale,** special permit; **autorisation d'exporter,** export permit; **avoir l'autorisation de vendre qch.,** to be licensed to sell sth.

autoriser, *v.tr.* to authorize.

autorité, *n.f.* (*a*) authority; **agir de pleine autorité,** to act with full powers (*b*) **l'autorité fiscale,** the (income) tax authorities; **autorités financières,** financial authorities.

aval, *n.m.* (*a*) *Fin:* endorsement (on bill); **donner son aval à un billet,** to endorse/to back a bill; **donneur d'aval,** guarantor/ backer (of bill) (*b*) *Mkt:* downward (risk).

avaliser, *v.tr.* to endorse/to guarantee/to back (a bill).

avaliste, *n.m.* surety/guarantor/backer.

à-valoir, *n.m.inv.* advance (payment).

avance, *n.f.* **accorder à qn une avance sur son salaire,** to give s.o. an advance on his salary; **avance (de fonds),** advance/loan; **avance bancaire,** bank advance; **avances en devises,** foreign currency loan; **à titre d'avance,** by way of an advance/as an advance; **faire une avance de mille francs à qn,** to advance s.o. a thousand francs; **payé d'avance,** paid in advance/prepaid; **payable à l'avance,** payable in advance.

avancer, *v.tr.* (*a*) to advance/to bring forward; **la réunion a été avancée du 14 au 7,** the meeting has been brought forward from the 14th to the 7th (*b*) **avancer de l'argent à qn,** to advance money to s.o./to lend s.o. money; **avancer un mois d'appointements à qn,** to advance s.o. a month's salary/to pay s.o. a month's salary in advance.

avantage, *n.m.* **avantages sociaux,** fringe benefits; perks.

avantageux, *a.* advantageous/favourable; **prix avantageux,** low price; good price.

avant-contrat, *n.m.* preliminary contract.

avarie, *n.f. MIns:* (*a*) **déclaration d'avaries,** (ship's) protest (*b*) **avarie(s)/avaries-frais,** average; **avaries communes/grosses avaries,** general average; **avaries simples/particulières,** particular average; **compromis d'avarie,** average bond; **franc d'avaries,** free from average; **règlement d'avaries,** adjustment of average; **répartiteur d'avaries,** average adjustor.

avarié, *a.* damaged/spoiled (goods).

avarier, *v.tr.* to damage/to spoil (goods, etc.).

avenant, *n.m.* endorsement/additional clause (to insurance policy).

avenu, *a.* **nul et non avenu,** null and void.

avertissement, *n.m.* demand note; tax bill demand.

avilir, *v.tr.* to depreciate/to lower/to bring down (currency, prices, etc.).

s'avilir, *v.pr.* to lose value; to fall/to come down (in value, in price); to depreciate.

avilissement, *n.m.* depreciation; fall (in price).

avion, *n.m.* aircraft/aeroplane/*F:* plane/*NAm:* airplane; **en avion,** by air/by plane; **par avion,** (by) airmail; **avion commercial,** commercial aircraft; **avion de transport de marchandises,** freighter.

avion-cargo, *n.m.* freighter/*NAm:* freight plane.

avis, *n.m.* notice/notification; warning; announcement; **avis par écrit,** notice in writing; **donner avis de qch.,** to give notice of sth./to notify s.o. of sth.; **donner avis que . . .,** to give notice that . . .; **note/lettre d'avis,** advice note/notification of dispatch; **avis de livraison,** delivery note; **suivant avis,** as per advice; *StExch:* **avis d'exécution,** contract note.

aviser, *v.tr.* **aviser qn de qch.,** to notify s.o. of sth.

avocat, *n.m. Jur:* barrister(-at-law)/counsel; *NAm:* lawyer; *Scot:* advocate; **consulter un avocat,** to take legal advice.

avoir, *n.m.* (*a*) property (*b*) **avoir fiscal,** tax credit (on dividends); **doit et avoir,** debit and credit (*c*) *pl.* **avoirs,** assets.

B

bagages, *n.m.pl.* luggage/*NAm:* baggage; **bagages à main,** hand/cabin luggage; **excédent de bagages,** excess luggage; **franchise de bagages,** luggage/baggage allowance.

bail, *n.m.* lease; **bail à loyer,** rental agreement; **bail à long terme,** long lease; **bail emphytéotique,** long lease (18–99 years)/ = leasehold; **prendre une maison à bail,** to take out a lease on a house; to rent a house (for a stated period); **céder/donner une maison à bail,** to lease (out) a house/to let a house; **signer/ passer un bail,** to sign a lease/an agreement; **renouveler un bail,** to renew a lease; **expiration de bail,** expiration of (a) lease; **mon bail expire en mai,** my lease expires/runs out in May.

bailleur, -eresse, *n.* (*a*) *Jur:* lessor (*b*) **bailleur de fonds,** (*i*) sleeping partner (*ii*) (financial) backer/sponsor.

baisse, *n.f.* **baisse (de prix),** fall/drop/ decline (in prices); **baisse accusée,** sharp fall; **baisse des blés,** drop in wheat; **baisse du franc,** fall in the value of the franc; **baisse du taux officiel de l'escompte de 14% à 13%,** lowering of the minimum lending rate from 14% to 13%; *StExch:* **jouer/spéculer à la baisse,** to operate/to speculate for a fall; to go a bear; **joueur à la baisse,** bear; **marché à la baisse,** falling/bearish market; buyer's market; **spéculations à la baisse,** bear speculations; **mouvement de baisse des valeurs,** downward movement of stocks; **acheter en baisse,** to buy on a falling market; **les actions sont en baisse,** shares are falling.

baisser, 1. *v.tr.* **baisser le prix de qch.,** to lower/to reduce/to cut/to bring down the price of sth.; **baisser les loyers,** to lower/to bring down the rents; **baisser le taux officiel de l'escompte,** to lower the minimum lending rate; **faire baisser le coût de la vie,** to reduce/to cut the cost of living; **la concurrence fait baisser les prix,** competition brings prices down **2.** *v.i.* (*a*) **nos stocks baissent,** our stocks are running low/down (*b*) (*des prix*) to fall/to come down/to go down/to drop; **la valeur de ces maisons a baissé,** the value of these houses has gone down/these houses have gone down in value; **le dollar a baissé,** the dollar has weakened; **ses actions baissent,** his shares are going down.

baissier, *n.m. StExch:* bear.

balance, *n.f.* **1.** scale/scales; weighing machine; **balance à bascule,** pair of scales; **balance automatique,** shop scales/ weighing machine **2.** (*a*) **balance d'un compte,** balance of an account; **balance de caisse,** cash balance; **balance (reportée) de l'exercice précédent,** balance (brought forward) from the previous account; **balance générale/de vérification,** trial balance; **balance d'inventaire,** balance-sheet; **faire la balance,** to make up the balance(-sheet); **balance de l'actif et du passif,** credit and debit balance; balance of assets and liabilities (*b*) *PolEc:* **balance du commerce/balance commerciale,** trade balance/balance of trade; **balance générale des comptes/ balance des paiements,** balance of payments; **balances sterling,** sterling balances.

balancer, *v.tr.* **balancer un compte,** to balance an account; **balancer les comptes,** to close/to make up/to balance the books.

balle, *n.f.* bale (of cotton, etc.); **mise en**

balle, baling; **marchandises en balles,** goods in bales.

bancable, *a. Fin:* bankable/negotiable.

bancaire, *a.* **chèque bancaire,** bank cheque; **commission bancaire,** bank commission; **compte bancaire,** bank/*NAm:* banking account; **crédit bancaire,** bank credit; **dépôt bancaire,** bank deposit; **frais bancaires,** bank charges; **opérations bancaires,** banking operations/transactions; **traite bancaire,** banker's draft; **virement bancaire,** bank giro transfer.

banquable, *a. Fin:* bankable/negotiable.

banque, *n.f.* (*a*) bank; **banque d'escompte,** discount house; **la Banque de France,** the Bank of France; **la Banque Mondiale,** the World Bank; **banque d'affaires,** merchant bank; **banque centrale,** central bank/issuing bank; **banque de placement/banque d'émission,** bank of issue/issuing house; **les grandes banques centrales,** the High Street banks; **billet de banque,** banknote/*NAm:* bill; **carnet/livret de banque,** bank book/pass-book; **avoir un compte en banque,** to have a bank account/*NAm:* banking account; to bank with . . .; **avoir un compte en banque au Crédit Lyonnais,** to have an account with/to bank with the Crédit Lyonnais; **crédit en banque,** bank credit; **directeur de banque,** bank manager; **employé(e) de banque,** bank clerk (*b*) banking; **opérations de banque,** banking business/transactions; **la haute banque,** high finance.

banqueroute, *n.f. Jur:* **banqueroute simple,** bankruptcy (with irregularities amounting to a breach of the law); **banqueroute frauduleuse,** fraudulent bankruptcy (amounting to crime); **faire banqueroute,** to go bankrupt.

banqueroutier, -ière, *a. & n.* bankrupt (*usu.* fraudulent).

banquier, *n.m.* banker.

barème, *n.m.* (*a*) ready reckoner (*b*) scale (of salaries, etc.) (*c*) (printed) table/schedule (of prices, charges, etc.); (price) list.

baril, *m.* barrel (of petrol, etc.).

barré, *a.* **chèque barré,** crossed cheque; **chèque non barré,** uncrossed cheque/open cheque.

barrer, *v.tr.* **barrer un chèque,** to cross a cheque.

barrière, *n.f.* barrier; **barrière commerciale,** trade barrier; **barrières douanières,** customs barriers.

bas¹, *a.* **les prix les plus bas,** rock-bottom prices; **les prix sont au plus bas,** prices have touched rock bottom; **maintenir les prix bas,** to keep prices down/low; **le (taux du) change est bas,** the rate of exchange is low; **marché à bas taux d'intérêt,** cheap money market; **prix basse saison,** low season fare/price; **vendre qch. à bas prix,** to sell sth. cheap.

bas², *adv. StExch:* **les cours sont tombés très bas,** prices have fallen very low.

base, *n.f.* (*a*) basis; **sur une base nette,** on a net(t) basis (*b*) **contrat de base,** principal contract; **prix de base,** base price/basic price; **produit de base,** basic commodity; **tarifs de base,** basic rates; *Bank:* **taux de base,** base rate; **traitement/salaire de base,** basic salary.

bâtiment, *n.m.* (*a*) building; premises *pl.*; **nous avons une cantine dans le bâtiment,** we have a canteen on the premises (*b*) building trade; **entrepreneur de/en bâtiment,** building contractor/builder.

bénéfice, *n.m.* profit/gain; **bénéfices imposables,** taxable profits; **bénéfice brut,** gross profit/pre-tax profit/profit before tax; **bénéfice net,** clear profit/net profit/profit after tax; **bénéfices non distribués,** undistributed profits/unappropriated profits; **bénéfice par action,** earnings/income per share; **participation aux bénéfices,** profit-sharing scheme; **part de bénéfice,** bonus; **petits bénéfices,** perks; **rapporter des bénéfices,** to yield (a) profit; **réaliser**

un bénéfice, to make a profit; **vendre qch. à bénéfice,** to sell sth. at a profit/at a premium.

bénéficiaire, 1. *a.* **bilan bénéficiaire,** balance-sheet showing a profit; **capacité bénéficiaire,** earning power; **compte bénéficiaire,** account showing a credit balance/account (which is) in credit; **marge bénéficiaire,** profit margin; **solde bénéficiaire,** profit balance **2.** *n.* (*a*) *Ins: etc:* beneficiary (*b*) recipient/payee (of cheque, money order); **bénéficiaire d'options,** optionee.

Bénélux, *Pr.n.m.* Benelux; **les pays du Bénélux,** the Benelux countries.

bénévole, *a.* unpaid/honorary; **il est employé à titre bénévole,** he is unpaid.

besoin, *n.m.* need; requirement; **analyse des besoins,** needs analysis.

bien, *n.m.* (*a*) possessions/property/ assets/wealth/goods (*b*) *Jur:* **biens meubles/mobiliers,** personal property/chattels/movables; **biens immeubles/immobiliers,** real estate; *PolEc:* **biens de consommation,** consumer goods; **biens manufacturés,** manufactured goods; **biens permanents,** durable goods; **biens de production/d'équipement,** capital goods.

bien-fonds, *n.m.* real estate/landed property.

bilan, *n.m.* (*a*) *Fin:* balance-sheet; **bilan consolidé/de groupe,** consolidated balance-sheet; **contrôle du bilan,** balance-sheet auditing; **dresser/établir/faire un bilan,** to draw up a balance-sheet (*b*) **le bilan hebdomadaire,** the weekly trading report; **dresser le bilan de ses pertes,** to reckon up one's losses (*c*) *Fin:* schedule (of assets and liabilities); **déposer son bilan,** to file one's petition (in bankruptcy) (*d*) *Fin:* balance (of an account); balance; total amount.

bilatéral, *a.* bilateral; **accord/contrat bilatéral,** bilateral agreement/contract.

billet, *n.m.* (*a*) *Trans:* ticket; **billet d'aller (et) retour,** return ticket/*NAm:* round-trip ticket; **billet simple,** single/one-way ticket; **billet de 1ère classe,** 1st class ticket; **billet d'abonnement,** season ticket (*b*) note/bill; **billet à ordre,** note of hand/ promissory note; IOU; **billet au porteur,** bill payable to bearer/bearer bill; **billet à présentation,** bill payable on demand; **billet à vue,** bill payable at sight/sight draft; **billet du Trésor,** Treasury bill (*c*) **billet de banque,** banknote/*NAm:* bill; **billet de 50F,** 50F note; *NAm:* **billet de $10,** 10 dollar bill.

billion, *n.m.* billion (10^{12})/*NAm:* trillion.

bimensuel, *a.* fortnightly/bi-monthly; **revue bimensuelle,** magazine which comes out every fortnight/every two weeks.

bimestriel, *a.* bi-monthly/two-monthly; **une revue bimestrielle,** a magazine which comes out every other month/every two months.

biodégradable, *a.* biodegradable.

blanc, 1. *a.* **affaire blanche,** profitless/ break-even deal **2.** *n.m.* blank (space); **chèque en blanc,** blank cheque; **endossement en blanc,** endorsement in blank/blank endorsement.

blanc-seing, *n.m.* paper/document signed in blank.

bloc, *n.m.* (*a*) **bloc monétaire,** currency bloc; **bloc sterling,** sterling bloc (*b*) *Ind:* **bloc technique,** design department (in a factory) (*c*) **bloc de marchandises,** job lot of goods; **acheter qch. en bloc,** to buy the whole stock of sth./to buy sth. in one lot/to buy sth. in bulk.

blocage, *n.m. PolEc:* pegging; *Fin:* freezing; **blocage des prix et des salaires,** price and wage freeze.

bloc-notes, *n.m.* note-pad/memo-pad.

bloquer, *v.tr.* to stop (a cheque, an account); to block/to stop (an account); **bloquer les salaires,** to freeze wages; **crédits bloqués,** frozen crédits.

blue chip, *n.m.* blue chip.

boîte, *n.f.* (*a*) **boîte (de carton),** cardboard box (*b*) **boîte de conserve,** tin/*NAm:* can; **fruits en boîte,** tinned/*NAm:* canned fruit (*c*) **boîte aux lettres,** letter box/post box/*NAm:* mail box (*d*) **boîte postale,** post office box; **BP 57 Lyon,** PO Box 57 Lyons.

bon, 1. *a.* (*a*) good/right/sound; **en bon état de marche,** in good working order (*b*) good/profitable/advantageous (investment, etc.); **bonne affaire,** good deal/good speculation/bargain; **acheter qch. à bon marché,** to buy sth. cheap/at bargain price (*c*) good/sound/safe (security, credit, etc.); **billet bon pour trois mois,** ticket valid for three months **2.** *n.m.* (*a*) order/voucher/ticket; **bon d'achat,** gift voucher/gift token; **bon de caisse,** cash voucher; **bon de commande,** purchase order; **bon de commission,** commission note; **bon de livraison,** delivery order (*b*) *Fin:* bond/bill/draft; **bon au porteur,** bearer bond; **bon nominatif,** registered bond; **bon du Trésor,** Treasury bond/Exchequer bill; **bon à vue,** sight draft.

boni, *n.m.* (*a*) (unexpected) profit (*b*) bonus; **recevoir 100F de boni,** to get a 100F bonus.

bonification, *n.f.* (*a*) allowance/rebate/reduction (*b*) bonus.

bonifier, *v.tr.* to give a bonus (to s.o.).

bon-prime, *n.m.* free-gift coupon.

bonus, *n.m. Ins:* **un bonus de 35% sur mon assurance,** a 35% no claims bonus.

boom, *n.m. Fin:* boom.

bordereau, *n.m.* memorandum/(detailed) statement; invoice/account/docket (of goods, cash, etc.); consignment note; tally sheet; schedule; **bordereau de paie,** pay slip; **suivant bordereau ci-inclus,** as per enclosed statement; *Trans:* **bordereau de chargement,** cargo list; **bordereau**

d'expédition, dispatch note/consignment note; **bordereau de livraison,** delivery note; *Bank:* **bordereau d'encaissement,** list of bills for collection; **bordereau d'escompte,** list of bills for discount; **bordereau de versement,** paying-in slip; *StExch:* **bordereau d'achat,** bought note/list of purchases; **bordereau de vente,** sold note/list of sales; **bordereau de crédit,** credit note; **bordereau de débit,** debit note.

bourse, *n.f.* (*a*) **des prix à portée de votre bourse,** prices to suit your pocket (*b*) **La Bourse (des valeurs),** the Stock Exchange; **Bourse de commerce,** commodities exchange; **la Bourse de Londres,** the London Stock Exchange; **à la Bourse/en Bourse,** on the Stock Exchange; **jouer à la Bourse,** to speculate on the Stock Exchange; **coup de Bourse,** deal on the Stock Exchange/speculation; **le cours de la Bourse,** the market rate; **valeurs cotées en Bourse,** quoted shares (*c*) **bourse de l'emploi,** job centre.

boursicotage, *n.m.* speculation; speculating; dabbling on the Stock Exchange.

boursicoter, *v.i.* to speculate in a small way/to dabble on the Stock Exchange.

boursicoteur, -euse, *n.,* **boursicotier, -ière,** *n.* speculator.

boursier, -ière, 1. *a.* **operations boursières,** Stock Exchange transactions **2.** *n.* (*i*) *F:* stockbroker (*ii*) speculator (on the Stock Exchange).

boutique, *n.f.* (*a*) shop/*NAm:* store; **tenir boutique,** to keep/to run a shop; **fermer boutique,** to close down/to fold up (*b*) boutique (small shop selling fashionable clothes) (*c*) **boutique (en plein vent),** stall in a market.

boutiquier, -ière, *n.* shopkeeper/tradesman/tradeswoman.

brader, *v.tr.* (*a*) to sell off/to sell cheaply (*b*) to get rid of sth. at any price.

braderie, *n.f.* (*a*) clearance sale (*b*) open-air market/street market.

branche, *n.f.* branch/sector (of industry, etc.).

brevet, *n.m.* (*a*) patent; **agent en brevets,** patent agent; **brevet d'inventeur/brevet d'invention** (letters) patent; **bureau des brevets,** patent office; **demande de brevet deposée,** patent pending/patent applied for; **prendre un brevet,** to take out a patent; **titulaire d'un brevet,** patentee (*b*) *Jur:* **acte en brevet,** contract delivered by notary in original.

breveté, *a.* (*a*) patented (invention); **breveté sans garantie du Gouvernement (SGDG),** patented without Government warranty (of quality) (*b*) **inventeur breveté,** inventor holding letters patent.

breveter, *v.tr.* to patent (an invention); **faire breveter une invention),** to take out a patent for an invention.

briseur, *n.m.* **briseur de grève,** scab/black-leg.

brocante, *n.f.* antique shop; junk shop.

brocanter, 1. *v.i.* to deal in second-hand goods **2.** *v.tr.* *F:* **brocanter ses meubles,** to sell one's furniture (to a second-hand or antique dealer).

brocanteur, -euse, *n.* antique dealer; second-hand dealer; **magasin de brocanteur,** antique shop; junk shop.

brochure, *n.f.* brochure; **brochure publicitaire,** publicity brochure/leaflet/booklet.

brut, 1. *a.* (*a*) raw (material); crude (oil, etc.); **produit brut,** primary product (*b*) gross (profit, value, weight, etc.); **marge brute,** gross margin; **produit national brut (PNB),** gross national product (GNP); **recette brute,** gross receipts/gross returns (*c*) *PolEc:* **chiffres bruts,** un-weighted figures; **données brutes,** raw data **2.** *n.m.* **le (pétrole) brut,** crude (oil).

budget, *n.m.* budget; **budget commercial,** sales budget; **budget équilibré,** (well) balanced budget; **budget familial,** household budget; **budget global,** master budget; **budget de publicité,** advertising/publicity budget; **budget de trésorerie,** cash budget; **boucler son budget,** to make both ends meet; **établissement/préparation d'un budget,** budgeting; **inscrire qch. au budget,** to budget for sth.

budgétaire, *a.* **année budgétaire,** fiscal/financial year; **comptabilité budgétaire,** budgeting; **contrainte budgétaire,** budget(ary) constraint; **déficit budgétaire,** budget deficit; **excédent budgétaire,** budget surplus; **gestion/contrôle budgétaire,** budgetary control; **prévision budgétaire,** budget forecast(ing); **situation budgétaire de l'année,** budget statement for the year.

budgétisation, *n.f.* *Fin:* inclusion (of an item) in the budget; budgeting.

budgétiser, *v.tr.* to include (sth.) in the budget/to budget for (sth.).

bulletin, *n.m.* (*a*) periodical publication (of a firm, etc.); *Fin:* **bulletin des cours,** official (Stock Exchange) price-list (*b*) ticket/receipt/form/certificate; **bulletin de bagages,** luggage ticket/*NAm:* baggage check; **bulletin de commande,** order form; **bulletin d'expédition,** dispatch note; **bulletin de paie,** pay (advice) slip; **bulletin de souscription,** application form; **bulletin de vente,** advice note/slip; sales note; *Rail:* waybill; *Bank:* **bulletin de versement,** paying-in slip.

bureau, *n.m.* (*a*) desk (*b*) office; **bureau central/principal,** head office; **garçon de bureau,** office boy; **fournitures de bureau,** stationery; **personnel de bureau,** office staff; **travail de bureau,** office work; clerical work; **après les heures de bureau,** after office hours; **organisation des bureaux,** office management (*c*) **bureau de douane,** custom(s) house; **bureau d'expédition,** forwarding office;

Th: **bureau de location,** box office; **bureau de placement,** employment agency; **bureau de poste,** post office; **bureau de publicité,** advertising agency; **bureau de renseignements,** information/ inquiry office; inquiries/information; **bureau de tourisme,** tourist office (*d*) (office) staff (*e*) board/committee/governing body/executive; **constituer le bureau (d'une société, etc,),** to set up a committee (*f*) department; **bureau d'études,** design/planning department; design office; research department; **bureau administratif,** government depart-

ment/bureau; **bureau international,** international bureau.

bureaucratie, *n.f.* bureaucracy/officialdom/*F:* red tape.

bureaucratique, *a.* bureaucratic; **style bureaucratique,** formal/official style; officialese.

but, *n.m.* goal/target/object(ive); **organisation à but lucratif,** profit-making/ profitable organization; **organisation à but non lucratif,** non-profit-making organization.

C

cabinet, *n.m.* office; chambers (of judge, barrister); (doctor's) surgery.

câble, *n.m.* cable; **envoyer un câble (à qn);** to send a cable (to s.o.)/to cable (s.o.).

câbler, *v.tr.* to cable (a message); **câbler à qn,** to send a cable to s.o./to cable s.o.

câblogramme, *n.m.* cable.

cabotage, *n.m. Nau:* coastal trade.

caboteur, *n.m. Nau:* coaster.

cachet, *n.m.* (*a*) seal/stamp (on letter, document); **cachet de douane,** customs seal (*b*) mark/stamp; **cachet d'un fabricant,** maker's trade mark; **cachet de poste,** postmark.

cacheter, *v.tr.* to seal (up) (letter, etc.); **soumission cachetée,** sealed tender.

cadastrage, *n.m.* land registration.

cadastral, *a.* cadastral (register, survey); **extrait cadastral,** land registry certificate.

cadastre, *n.m. Adm:* land register; cadastral survey; cadastre; **bureau du cadastre,** Land Registry Office.

cadastrer, *v.tr.* to enter (property) in the land register.

cadre, *n.m.* 1. (*a*) (*sur un formulaire etc.*) space/box; **cadre réservé à l'administration** = for office use only (*b*) framework; **dans le cadre de ce programme d'expansion,** as part of this expansion programme 2. executive; manager; **cadre commercial,** sales executive; **cadres dirigeants/supérieurs,** managerial staff/senior executives/top management; **cadres de maîtrise,** supervisory staff; **cadres moyens,** middle management; **jeune cadre,** junior

executive; **figurer sur les cadres,** to be on the (company's) books.

caduc, *a. Jur:* **contrat déclaré caduc,** agreement declared to have lapsed; **dette caduque,** debt barred by the Statute of Limitations.

caducité, *n.f. Jur:* lapsing/nullity.

caisse, *n.f.* **1.** (*a*) (packing-)case; tea chest; box; **caisse à claire-voie,** crate; **caisse en carton,** cardboard box; **mettre des marchandises en caisse,** to case/to crate goods **2.** (*a*) float; cash-box (*b*) **caisse enregistreuse/caisse comptable,** cash register; till; **caisse rapide,** quick service till; **ticket de caisse**/*FrC:* **reçu de caisse,** (till) receipt (*c*) cash desk/checkout (in supermarket); cash(ier's) office; **payez à la caisse,** please pay at the desk; **c'est elle qui tient la caisse/qui est préposée à la caisse,** she's the cashier (*d*) (*i*) cash (in hand) (*ii*) takings; **livre de caisse,** cash book; **mouvements de caisse,** cash transactions; **petite caisse,** petty cash; **recettes de caisse,** cash receipts; **solde de caisse,** cash balance; **faire la/sa caisse,** to do the till/to cash up; **avoir tant d'argent en caisse,** to have so much money in hand (*e*) *Bank:* **facilités de caisse,** overdraft facilities (*f*) fund; **caisse d'amortissement,** sinking fund; **caisse de retraite,** pension fund/superannuation fund; **caisse noire,** slush fund (*g*) **Caisse (nationale) d'Épargne** = (National) Savings Bank (*h*) *Adm:* **caisse de la Sécurité sociale,** social security office.

caissier, -ière, *n.* (*a*) cashier (in shop, cinema, etc.) (*b*) *Bank:* cashier/*NAm:* teller; **caissier principal,** chief cashier/head cashier.

calcul, *n.m.* calculation/reckoning; **faire/ effectuer un calcul,** to calculate/to work out (a calculation)/ to reckon; **faux calcul/ erreur de calcul,** miscalculation.

calculateur, -trice, 1. *n.m.* **calculateur (électronique),** (electronic) computer; **calculateur numérique/arithmétique,** digital computer; **calculateur universel,** general purpose computer **2. calculatrice,** *n.f.* calculator; **calculatrice de bureau,** desk calculator; **calculatrice de poche,** pocket calculator; **calculatrice imprimante,** print-out calculator/calculator with a listing.

calculer, *v.tr.* (*a*) to calculate/to work out/to reckon; **calculer un prix,** to arrive at a price/to work out a price; **machine à calculer,** calculator; adding machine; **l'impôt se calcule sur . . .,** tax is calculated on . . ..

calendrier, *n.m.* (*a*) calendar; **bloc calendrier,** tear-off calendar (*b*) timetable; **mon calendrier ne le permet pas,** my timetable does not allow it.

calibrage, *n.m.* grading (of eggs, fruit, etc.).

calibrer, *v.tr.* (*a*) to gauge/to measure (*b*) to grade (eggs, fruit, etc.).

cambial, *a.* Fin: relating to exchange; **droit cambial,** exchange law.

cambiste, Fin: **1.** *n.m.* foreign exchange dealer/broker **2.** *a.* **marché cambiste,** exchange market.

camelote, *n.f.* F: cheap goods/shoddy goods.

cameloter, *v.i.* F: (*i*) to deal in cheap goods (*ii*) to manufacture cheap goods.

camion, *n.m.* lorry/truck; **camion de déménagement,** removal van; **camion semi-remorque,** articulated lorry.

camionnage, *n.m.* (*a*) (*prix*) haulage/ carriage/NAm: truckage (*b*) (*service*) carrying/NAm: trucking (trade); **une entreprise de camionnage,** (a firm of) hau-

liers/haulage contractors/NAm: a trucking business.

camionner, *v.tr.* to carry/to haul/NAm: to truck (goods).

camionnette, *n.f.* (delivery) van/NAm: pick-up (truck).

camionnette-boutique, *n.f.* travelling/mobile shop.

camionneur, *n.m.* (*a*) carrier/(road) haulier; haulage contractor (*b*) van driver/lorry driver/truck driver/NAm: trucker/teamster.

campagne, *n.f.* campaign; **campagne de productivité,** productivity campaign/ drive; **campagne publicitaire/de publicité,** advertising campaign/publicity drive; **campagne de vente,** sales campaign.

canal, *n.m.* channel; **canaux de communication,** communication channels; **canaux de distribution,** distribution channels.

candidat, -ate, *n.* candidate/applicant (**à un emploi,** for a job).

candidature, *n.f.* **formulaire de candidature,** application form; **poser sa candidature à (un poste)/faire acte de candidature,** to apply for (a post); **retirer sa candidature,** to withdraw one's application.

capacité, *n.f.* (*a*) **capacité d'achat,** purchasing power; **capacité bénéficiaire,** earning power; **capacité d'emprunter,** borrowing power; **capacité de production,** manufacturing capacity (*b*) (*d'un tonneau, etc.*) content/capacity; **capacité de storage,** storage capacity.

capital, *n.m.* Fin: capital/assets; **accumulation de capital,** capital accumulation; **capital(-)actions/capital social,** share capital; **capital appelé,** called-up capital; **capital d'apport,** initial capital; **capital circulant/roulant,** circulating capital; **capital émis,** issued capital; **capital engagé,** tied-up capital; **capitaux exigibles,** current liabilities; **capital d'exploitation/de**

roulement, working/*NAm:* operating capital; **capitaux fébriles/flottants,** hot money; **capital et intérêt,** capital and interest; **capital nominal,** authorized capital; **capital non-appelé/non-libéré,** uncalled capital; **capital obligations,** debenture capital; **capitaux permanents/fixes,** fixed capital; **capitaux propres,** shareholders'/stockholders' equity; **capital de réserve,** reserve capital; **capital risques,** venture capital/risk capital; **capital souscrit,** subscribed capital; **capital technique,** (technical) equipment; **capital versé,** paid-up capital; **compte de capital,** capital account; **dépenses en capital,** capital expenditure; **marché des capitaux,** capital market/money market; **mouvements des capitaux,** capital movements; **société au capital de . . .,** company with a capital of. . ./company capitalized at . . .; **avoir des capitaux dans une affaire,** to have vested interests in a business; **faire un appel de capital,** to call for funds; **investir/mettre des capitaux dans une affaire,** to invest/to put capital into a business; **association capital-travail,** profit-sharing scheme.

capitalisable, *a.* capitalizable (interest, etc.).

capitalisation, *n.f.* capitalization (of interest, etc.); **capitalisation boursière,** market capitalization.

capitaliser, *v.tr.* to capitalize (interest, etc.); **valeur capitalisée,** capitalized value.

capitaliste, *n.m.* capitalist; investor.

captif, *a.* **compagnie captive,** daughter company/subsidiary company/dependant company.

cargaison, *n.f. Nau:* cargo; freight; **cargaison mixte,** mixed cargo; **cargaison d'aller,** outward cargo; **cargaison de retour,** homeward cargo.

cargo, *n.m.* (*a*) *Nau:* freighter; cargo-

ship; **cargo mixte,** passenger and cargo ship (*b*) **avion cargo,** (air) freighter.

carnet, *n.m.* (*a*) notebook; **carnet de commandes,** order book; **carnet de dépenses,** account book/housekeeping book; **carnet de dépôt,** deposit book; *Bank:* **carnet de banque,** pass book/bank book (*b*) **carnet de chèques (à souche(s)),** cheque book (with counterfoil/with stub(s)); **carnet de tickets (d'autobus, de métro),** book of (bus, underground) tickets; **carnet de timbres,** book of stamps (*c*) *Aut: etc:* **carnet de route/de bord,** log book.

carrière, *n.f.* career; **perspectives de carrière,** job expectations.

carte, *n.f.* (*a*) **carte d'abonnement,** season ticket; **carte d'affaires,** business card; **carte accréditive/de crédit,** credit card; **carte de commerce,** trading licence (*b*) **carte perforée,** punch(ed) card (*c*) **carte d'échantillons,** sample card (*d*) **carte postale,** post card (*e*) *Ins:* **carte verte,** green card (*f*) (*pour le métro*) **carte orange** = monthly season ticket.

cartel, *n.m.* cartel/trust; combine; ring; **cartel horizontal,** horizontal combine.

cartellisation, *n.f.* cartel(l)ization.

carton, *n.m.* (*a*) cardboard; **carton ondulé,** corrugated cardboard (*b*) cardboard box; carton.

case, *n.f.* (*a*) **case postale,** post office box/PO box (*b*) (*sur un formulaire*) **cocher la case correspondante,** tick the appropriate box.

cash flow, *n.m.* cash flow; **cash flow net,** net cash flow; **cash flow actualisé,** discounted cash flow (DCF); **cash flow marginal,** incremental cash flow.

casse, *n.f.* (*a*) breakage; damage; **payer la casse,** to pay for breakages; **assurance contre la casse,** insurance against breakage (*b*) **vendre à la casse,** to sell for scrap.

casuel, *n.m.* perks.

catalogue, *n.m.* catalogue/*NAm:* cata-log; list; **catalogue illustré,** illustrated catalogue; **catalogue de vente par cor-respondance,** mail order catalogue; **achat/vente sur catalogue,** mail order.

catégorie, *n.f.* category; quality; **viande de première catégorie,** best quality meat/choice cut; **viande de deuxième catégorie,** poor quality meat/cheap(er) cut.

caution, *n.f.* (*a*) (*pers.*) surety/guarantor; **être caution de qn/se porter caution pour qn,** to stand surety for s.o. (*b*) surety/guarantee/security; **caution de banque,** bank guarantee; **demander une caution,** to ask for security; **fournir caution,** to give security (*c*) deposit; **verser une caution,** to pay a deposit.

cautionnement, *n.m.* (*a*) surety/bond/guarantee (*b*) security/caution money/guarantee/guaranty.

cautionner, *v.tr.* to stand surety for (s.o.).

cavalerie, *n.f.* **traite de cavalerie,** accom-modation bill/note.

cédant, **1.** *a.* **partie cédante,** granting/assigning/transferring (party) **2. cédant, -ante,** *n.* (*a*) grantor/assignor/trans-feror/transfer(r)er (of shares, etc.) (*b*) preceding party (to bill).

céder, *v.tr.* (*a*) to give up/to surrender (right); **les droits à eux cédés,** the rights granted to them (*b*) to transfer/to make over/to assign (à, to); to dispose of/to sell (lease); **céder à bail,** to lease; **commerce à céder,** business for sale.

Cedex, *n.m.* **courrier d'entreprise à distri-bution exceptionnelle,** commercial PO box service.

cédulaire, *a.* **impôts cédulaires,** sched-uled taxes.

cédule, *n.f.* *Adm:* schedule; **cédule d'im-pôts,** tax code.

cellulaire, *a.* **gestion cellulaire,** divisional management.

cent[1], *num.a.* (*a*) hundred; **elle a perdu cent francs,** she lost a/one hundred francs (*b*) **pour cent,** percent; **intérêt de sept pour cent,** seven percent interest; **cent pour cent,** a/one hundred percent (100%).

cent[2], *n.m.* (*pièce de monnaie*) cent.

centaine, *n.f.* (about) a hundred; **une centaine de francs,** about a hundred francs/a hundred francs or so; **quelques centaines de francs,** a few hundred francs.

centième, **1.** *num.a. & n.* hundredth **2.** *n.m.* hundredth (part); **trois centièmes de la somme globale,** three hundredths of the total amount.

centile, *n.m.* *Stat:* centile.

centime, *n.m.* centime; **un million de cen-times** (= *un million d'anciens francs*) = (about) £1 000/US$2 5000.

central, **1.** *a.* **banque centrale,** central bank; **bureau central,** head office/main office **2.** *n.m.* **central téléphonique,** tele-phone exchange; **central automatique,** automatic exchange **3.** *n.f.* **centrale d'achats,** central purchasing office; **cen-trale (syndicale),** group of affiliated trade unions.

centralisation, *n.f.* centralization/cen-tralizing.

centraliser, *v.tr.* to centralize.

centre, *n.m.* centre/*NAm:* center; **cen-tre commercial,** commercial centre/shopping precinct; *FrC:* **centre d'a-chats,** shopping centre; **centre des af-faires,** business centre; **centre de traite-ment de l'information,** data process-ing centre; **centre de tourisme,** tourist centre; **centre de tri,** sorting office; **centre industriel,** industrial centre.

céréale, *n.f.* cereal; grain.

certain, **1.** *a.* definite/fixed (price, date) **2.** *n.m.* *Fin:* **le certain de la livre est de 8,68 F,** the rate of exchange for the pound is 8.68 F.

certificat, *n.m.* (*a*) *Nau:* **certificat de chargement,** certificate of receipt; **certi-**

ficat de jauge, tonnage certificate (*b*) *Fin:* **certificat d'action(s),** share/stock certificate; *Ins:* **certificat d'avarie,** statement of loss; *Cust:* **certificat d'entrepôt,** warrant; **certificat d'homologation,** certificate of approval; *Fin:* **certificat de trésorerie,** treasury bond; **certificat d'origine,** certificate of origin; **certificat nominatif d'action(s),** registered share certificate; **certificat provisoire,** share certificate/(provisional) scrip (*c*) (employer's) testimonial; **certificat d'aptitude professionnelle (CAP),** technical/professional diploma.

certification, *n.f.* certification/authentication; **certification d'une signature,** witnessing of a signature.

certifier, *v.tr.* (*a*) *Jur:* to certify/to attest; **certifier une signature,** to witness/to authenticate a signature; **copie certifiée,** attested/certified copy (*b*) **certifier une caution,** to guarantee a surety (*c*) **chiffres (non) certifiés,** (un)audited figures.

cessation, *n.f.* stoppage; termination; **cessation d'un contrat,** termination of a contract; **cessation de paiements,** insolvency; **être en état de cessation de paiements,** to be insolvent; **cessation de travail,** stoppage (of work).

cessibilité, *n.f.* *Jur:* transferability/assignability (of estate, etc.); negotiability (of pension).

cessible, *a.* *Jur:* transferable/assignable; (*d'une traite etc.*) negotiable; (*d'un billet*) **non cessible,** not transferable.

cession, *n.f.* *Jur:* cession/transfer/assignment; **(acte de) cession,** deed of transfer/of assignment; **cession de bail,** lease-back/transference of lease; **cession de biens,** assignment of property (to creditors); **cession d'une créance,** transfer of a debt; *Fin:* **cession de parts,** stock transfer; **cession de parts en blanc,** blank transfer.

cession-bail, *n.f.* lease-back/transference of lease.

cessionnaire, **1.** *n.m.* transferee/assignee; holder (of bill); *Jur:* cessionary **2.** *a.* *Jur:* cessionary.

chaîne, *n.f.* **1. chaîne de fabrication,** production line; **chaîne de montage,** assembly line; **travail à la chaîne,** assembly line work/production line work; **travailler à la chaîne,** to work on an assembly line/on a production line **2. chaîne de magasins/de restaurants/etc.,** chain of stores/restaurants/etc.

chambre, *n.f.* (*a*) **chambre froide/frigorifique,** cold (storage) room/cold store (*b*) **travailler en chambre,** to work at home (*c*) **Chambre de commerce,** Chamber of Commerce; **Chambre de métiers,** Chamber of Trade; *Fin:* **chambre de compensation/de clearing,** clearing house (*d*) **chambre d'hôtel,** hotel room.

change, *n.m.* *Fin:* **agent de change,** (*i*) stockbroker (*ii*) exchange broker/dealer; **bureau de change,** bureau de change; **contrôle des changes,** exchange control/currency control; **cote des changes,** exchange list; **change du dollar,** dollar exchange; **cours/taux du change,** rate of exchange/(foreign) exchange rate; **lettre de change,** bill of exchange; **marché des changes,** foreign exchange market; **opération de change,** foreign exchange transaction; **prix du change,** exchange premium; agio.

changer, *v.tr.* to change; to exchange; **changer un billet de banque,** to change a (bank)note; **changer des dollars contre des francs/en francs,** to change dollars into francs.

changeur, *n.m.* (*a*) (*pers.*) money-changer (*b*) **changeur de monnaies,** change machine.

chantier, *n.m.* yard/depot/site; **chantier (de construction),** building site; *Nau:*

chantier de construction navale/chantier naval, shipyard.

charge, *n.f.* **1.** (*d'un véhicule, etc.*) load/ cargo; capacity; **charge admise/limite,** load limit/*Av:* commercial load; **charge d'un camion/charge complète,** lorry load/ *NAm:* truck load; **charge maximale,** maximum load; **charge normale,** normal load/ capacity; **charge par essieu,** axle load; **charge utile,** (*i*) (load-) carrying capacity (*ii*) pay-load/commercial load; *Av:* **charge en vol,** flight load; *Nau:* **charge d'un navire,** shipload; **ligne de charge,** load-line/plimsoll line; **navire de charge,** freighter; **navire en charge,** ship being loaded/ship loading; **prendre charge,** to load (up)/to take in cargo; **rompre charge,** (*i*) to unload cargo (*ii*) to transfer cargo/to transship **2.** (*a*) charge/responsibility; **prendre en charge,** to take over/to be in charge (*b*) office; **charge d'avoué,** solicitor's practice **3.** (*i*) charge/expense (*ii*) tax; **cahier de charges,** (*i*) (building) specifications (*ii*) articles and conditions (of sale, etc.); *Ind:* **charges d'exploitation,** working expenses/running costs; **charges fiscales,** tax (burden); **charges sociales,** National Insurance contributions (paid by employer); **livre des charges,** cost book; **le loyer plus les charges,** rent plus service charge; **les frais de transport sont à notre charge,** the cost of transport is borne by us/payable by us/chargeable to us; **les réparations sont à la charge du locataire,** the repairs are to be paid for by the tenant.

chargé, 1. *a.* (*a*) loaded/laden (*b*) *Post:* **lettre chargée/paquet chargé** = registered letter/parcel **2.** *n.* **chargé de budget,** account manager/executive.

chargement, *n.m.* **1.** (*a*) loading(-up) (of lorry, etc.); shipping/loading (of cargo); **navire en chargement,** ship being loaded (*b*) *Post:* registration (of letter, parcel) **2.** (*a*) load/consignment/cargo/freight; **chargement complet,** full load; **chargement réglementaire,** regulation load;

Nau: **prendre chargement,** to take on cargo (*b*) *Post:* registered letter/ parcel.

charger, *v.tr.* (*a*) to load (up)/to fill (a lorry, a truck, a ship); **charger des marchandises sur un train,** to load goods onto a train; **navire qui charge pour Londres,** ship taking in freight for London (*b*) **charger un compte,** to overcharge (on) an account.

chargeur, *n.m.* (film) cartridge.

chariot, *n.m.* (*au supermarché*) trolley.

charte, *n.f.* charter; **compagnie à charte,** chartered company.

charte-partie, *n.f. Nau:* charter-party.

charter, *n.m.* **(avion) charter,** charter plane; **vol charter,** charter flight.

chef, *n.m.* (*a*) **chef d'atelier,** shop foreman; **chef de bureau,** head clerk/chief clerk; office manager; **chef comptable,** chief accountant; **chef d'établissement,** works/plant manager; *Publ:* **chef de fabrication,** production manager; **chef du personnel,** personnel/staff manager; **chef de rayon (d'un magasin),** department manager; *Ind:* **chef de service,** department(al) manager; **chef des ventes,** sales manager; **ingénieur en chef,** chief engineer (*b*) **les chefs d'industrie,** the captains of industry.

chemin, *n.m.* **1. chemin de fer,** railway/ *NAm:* railroad; **envoi par chemin de fer,** dispatch by rail **2.** *Cmptr:* **méthode du chemin critique,** critical path method (CPM).

chemise, *n.f.* **chemise (cartonnée),** folder/ cardboard file.

chèque, *n.m.* cheque/*NAm:* check; **carnet de chèques,** cheque book/*NAm:* check book; **chèque de £60,** cheque for £60; **chèque bancaire,** bank cheque; banker's draft; **chèque barré,** crossed cheque; **chèque en blanc,** blank cheque; **chèque visé**/*FrC:* **certifié,** marked cheque/certified cheque; **chèque ouvert/non**

barré, open/uncrossed cheque; **chèque périmé,** out of date cheque; **chèque au porteur,** cheque made payable to bearer/ bearer cheque; **chèque postal,** post office cheque; **chèque postdaté,** post-dated cheque; **chèque sans provision,** unpaid cheque/dud cheque; **il a payé avec un chèque sans provision,** he paid with a cheque that bounced; **chèque de voyage,** traveller's cheque; **service de chèques postaux** = National Girobank; **émettre/ faire un chèque,** to write a cheque; **encaisser/toucher un chèque,** to cash a cheque; **établir/libeller un chèque à l'ordre de . . .,** to make a cheque out to . . .; **faire opposition au paiement d'un chèque,** to stop a cheque; **payer par chèque,** to pay by cheque; **refuser d'honorer un chèque,** to refer a cheque to drawer; **remettre/déposer un chèque à la banque,** to pay a cheque into the bank.

chèque-cadeau, *n.m.* gift cheque/gift token.

chèque-dividende, *n.m. Fin:* dividend warrant.

chèque-repas, *n.m.,* **chèque-restaurant,** *n.m.* luncheon voucher.

chéquier, *n.m.* cheque book/*NAm:* check book.

cher, 1. *a.* (*a*) dear/expensive/high-priced/ costly; **une voiture chère,** an expensive car; **indemnité de vie chère,** cost-of-living allowance; **ce magasin est trop cher,** this shop is too expensive/this shop charges too much; **c'est trop cher pour moi,** I can't afford it; **un hôtel pas cher,** a reasonably priced/an inexpensive/a cheap hotel (*b*) *Corr:* **Cher Monsieur,** Dear Mr X **2.** *adv.* cela s'est vendu cher, it reached/fetched a very high price; **cela ne vaut pas cher,** it's not worth much; *F:* **je l'ai acheté pas cher,** I got it cheap.

cherté, *n.f.* **la cherté de la vie,** the high cost of living; **indemnité de cherté de vie,** cost-of-living allowance.

chiffre, *n.m.* (*a*) figure/number/numeral/

digit; **en chiffres ronds,** in round figures; **calculatrice avec (un) affichage de huit chiffres,** calculator with an eight-digit display (*b*) amount/total; **les dépenses de la société atteignent un chiffre de 4 millions (de francs),** the company's spending reaches a figure of/amounts to 4 million (francs); **chiffre d'affaires,** turnover/*NAm:* revenue; **la société a un chiffre d'affaires d'un million de francs,** the company has a turnover of a million francs.

chirographaire, *a. Jur:* depending on a simple contract; **créance chirographaire,** unsecured debt; **créancier chirographaire,** unsecured creditor/simple-contract creditor; **obligation chirographaire,** simple debenture.

choix, *n.m.* (*a*) choice/selection; **ce magasin a un très grand choix de chaussures,** this shop has a good selection/a wide range of shoes; **au choix de l'acheteur,** at the buyer's option (*b*) **article de choix,** choice article; **de tout premier choix,** (of the) best quality/first-class/high-grade (*c*) **au choix** = all at the same price.

chômage, *n.m.* unemployment; **en chômage,** out of work; **être/s'inscrire au chômage,** to be/to go on the dole; **allocation/indemnité/secours de chômage,** unemployment benefit/*F:* dole; **caisse de chômage,** unemployment fund; **chômage saisonnier,** seasonal unemployment; **chômage technique,** lay off; **être en chômage technique,** to have been laid off; **être en chômage partiel,** to work short time/to be on short time/to be on short-time working.

chômer, *v.i.* to be unemployed; **les usines chôment,** the works are at a standstill; **laisser chômer son argent,** to let one's money lie idle.

chômeur, *n.m.* unemployed; **les chômeurs,** the unemployed; **chômeur partiel,** short-time worker.

chute, *n.f.* **chute des prix,** (heavy) fall/ drop in prices; **chute des ventes,** fall-off in sales.

cible, *n.f.* target; objective; **détermination de la cible**, target setting.

ci-contre, *adv. Book-k:* **porté ci-contre**, as per contra.

ci-inclus, *a. Corr:* **la copie ci-incluse**, the enclosed copy; **(vous trouverez) ci-inclus copie de sa lettre**, (please find) herewith/enclosed a copy of his letter.

ci-joint, *a.* attached/herewith/hereto (annexed); **les pièces ci-jointes**, the enclosed/attached documents; **vous trouverez ci-joint mon chèque**, please find cheque enclosed.

circuit, *n.m.* circuit; **les circuits commerciaux**, commercial/trading/marketing channels; **circuit de distribution**, distribution/marketing network; chain of distribution.

circulaire, 1. *a.* circular (letter, etc.); **billet circulaire**, (*i*) circular note (*ii*) *Trans:* return/*NAm:* round-trip ticket 2. *n.f.* circular (letter); memorandum.

circulant, *a. Fin:* **billets circulants**, (bank)notes in circulation; **capitaux circulants**, working capital/circulating capital.

circulation, *n.f.* (*a*) circulation; **mettre un livre en circulation**, to put a book into circulation (*b*) *Fin:* **circulation monétaire**, money in circulation (*c*) **actions ordinaires en circulation**, common shares outstanding.

circuler, *v.i.* (*de l'argent*) to be in circulation; **faire circuler des effets**, to keep bills afloat.

civil, *a.* civil; **année civile**, calendar year; **droit civil**, civil law; **état civil**, civil status.

clair, *a.* **profit tout clair**, clear profit.

classe, *n.f.* (*a*) class/division/category/order; *Adm: etc:* rank; grade; **produits de première classe**, top quality goods; **hôtel de première classe**, first class hotel (*b*) **classe de revenu**, income bracket (*c*)

Trans: **compartiment de première classe**, first class compartment; *Av:* **classe affaires**, club class; **classe économique**, economy class; **classe touriste**, tourist class.

classement, *n.m.* (*a*) classification (*b*) filing (of documents).

classer, *v.tr.* (*a*) to class/to classify/to rate; *Fin:* **valeurs classées**, investment stock (*b*) to file (documents).

classeur, *n.m.* loose-leaf file; jacket-file; filing cabinet; **classeur à fiches**, card-index file; **tiroir classeur**, filing drawer; *Adm:* **classeur des entrées et sorties**, tally file.

classification, *n.f.* classification/classifying; **classification de fonctions**, job classification; **classification des impôts locaux**, rating.

clause, *n.f. Jur:* clause; **clause additionnelle**, additional clause; rider; **clause compromissoire**, arbitration clause; **clause échappatoire**, escape clause; **clause pénale**, penalty clause; **clause résolutoire**, avoidance clause; **clause restrictive**, restrictive clause; **clause de sauvegarde**, saving clause.

clé, *n.f.* = **clef.**

clearing, *n.m. Fin:* (*a*) clearing house (*b*) clearing; **accord de clearing**, clearing agreement; **banque de clearing**, clearing bank.

clef, *n.f.* (*a*) key; **industrie clef**, key industry; **poste clef**, key post (*b*) **(projet de bâtiment) livré clef en main(s)**, turnkey operation/project.

client, **-ente**, *n.* customer/client; **client mystère**, mystery shopper; **client régulier**, regular customer/patron; **comptes clients**, receivables.

clientèle, *n.f.* (*i*) custom (*ii*) customers; **attirer la clientèle**, to attract custom; **clientèle de passage**, irregular customers; passing trade; **service à la clientèle**, customer service; **avoir une grosse clientèle**, to have a large clientele/a lot of customers; **accorder sa clientèle à . . .,** to patronize . . ..

clos, *a.* **exercice clos le 31 déc. 1980,** year ended 31 Dec. 1980.

clôture, *n.f.* (*a*) *StExch:* **cours/prix de clôture,** closing price; (*des prix*) **être ferme en clôture,** to close firm (*b*) closing (of account); making up/balancing (of books).

clôturer, 1. *v.tr.* to close (accounts, etc.); *Jur:* **clôturer une faillite,** to close a bankruptcy **2.** *v.i.* **le dollar a clôturé à 4,35F,** the dollar closed at 4.35F.

coacquéreur, *n.m.* joint purchaser.

coacquisition, *n.f.* joint purchase.

coadministrateur, -trice *n.m.* co-director; *Jur:* co-trustee.

coassocié, -ée, *n.* copartner/joint partner.

coassurance, *n.f.* mutual assurance; co-insurance/coassurance.

cocher, *v.tr.* to tick/*NAm:* to check; (*sur un formulaire*) **cocher la case correspondante,** tick/check the appropriate box.

cocontractant, -ante, *a. & n. Jur:* contracting (partner).

code, *n.m.* code; **code de commerce,** commercial law; **code postal,** postcode/*NAm:* zip code.

code-barre, *n.m. Mkt:* bar code.

codébiteur, -trice, *n. Jur:* joint debtor.

codétenteur, -trice, *n. Jur:* joint holder.

codirecteur, -trice, *n.* co-director; joint manager.

codirection, *n.f.* joint directorship; joint management.

coefficient, *n.m.* coefficient/factor; **coefficient d'activité,** activity ratio; **coefficient d'exploitation,** working coefficient/operating ratio; **coefficient de liquidité,** liquidity ratio/ratio of liquid assets to current liabilities; **coefficient saisonnier,** seasonal index; **coefficient de solvabilité,** solvency coefficient; **coefficient de trésorerie,** cash ratio.

coffre, *n.m. Bank:* safe-deposit box.

coffre-fort, *n.m.* safe; **dépôt en coffre-fort,** safe deposit.

cogérance, *n.f.* joint management; co-administration.

cogérant, -ante, *n.* joint manager/manageress; co-administrator.

cogérer, *v.tr.* to manage jointly.

cogestion, *n.f.* joint management.

colicitant, *n.m. Jur:* co-vendor.

colis, *n.m.* parcel/package; **(envoyer qch.) par colis postal,** (to send sth.) by parcel post.

collectif, *a.* (*a*) collective/joint (action, report, etc.); **billet collectif,** group ticket (*b*) **contract collectif,** collective contract; **convention collective,** collective bargaining agreement.

colocataire, *n.m. & f.* joint tenant/co-tenant.

colonne, *n.f.* column (of figures, etc.); **colonne créditrice,** credit column; **colonne débitrice,** debit column.

combler, *v.tr.* to make up/to make good (a loss).

comestible, 1. aliments/denrées comestibles, consumable goods **2.** *n.m.* **les comestibles,** consumables.

comité, *n.m.* committee/board; **comité consultatif,** advisory board/commission; **comité de direction,** board of directors/

executive board; **comité d'entreprise,** works council.

commande, *n.f.* (*a*) order; **bon/bulletin de commande,** order form; **commande par téléphone,** (tele)phone order; **commande(s) par ordinateur** (*i*) teleorder(s) (*ii*) teleordering; **commande pour l'exportation,** export order; **carnet de commandes,** order book; **faire/passer une commande (de qch.) au fabricant,** to place an order (for sth.) with the manufacturer/ to order (sth.) from the manufacturer; **passer une commande de qch. à qn,** to indent on s.o. for sth.; **fait sur commande,** made to order; **payable à la commande,** cash with order (*b*) **livrer une commande,** to deliver an order.

commander, *v.tr.* to order (goods, etc.); **commander qch. chez un fournisseur,** to order sth. from a supplier/a stockist; **commander qch. par téléphone,** to order sth. by telephone/to (tele)phone an order; **commander par ordinateur,** to teleorder; (*au café, etc.*) **il a commandé une bière,** he ordered a beer.

commanditaire, *a. & n.m.* (**associé**) **commanditaire** = sleeping partner.

commandite, *n.f.* (*a*) (**société en**) **commandite simple,** limited partnership; **commandite par actions,** partnership limited by shares (*b*) interest of capital invested by sleeping partner(s).

commandité, *a. & n.m.* (**associé**) **commandité,** active partner.

commanditer, *v.tr.* to subscribe capital to/to finance (a firm, etc.) (as a sleeping partner).

commerçant, 1. *a.* commercial/business (district, etc.); **rue commerçante,** shopping street **2.** *n.* tradesman; shopkeeper; merchant; dealer; **commerçant en détail,** retailer; **commerçant en gros,** wholesaler; **petit commerçant,** small trader/shopkeeper; **être commerçant,** to be a shopkeeper/to be in business;

les commerçants, tradespeople/business people.

commerce, *n.m.* (*a*) commerce/trade; **le commerce,** (*i*) trade (*ii*) the commercial world; **le petit commerce,** (*i*) small traders (*ii*) shopkeeping; **être dans le commerce,** to be in trade; **Chambre de commerce,** Chamber of Commerce; **commerce extérieur,** foreign trade; **commerce intérieur,** home market; **effet de commerce,** bill of exchange; **hors commerce,** not for retail sale/not for general sale/not on sale to the general public; **livres de commerce,** account books; **registre de commerce,** trade/commercial register; **représentant/voyageur de commerce,** (sales) representative/*F:* rep (*b*) business; **commerce à céder,** shop/business for sale; **fonds de commerce,** goodwill; **maison de commerce,** firm; **tenir un commerce,** to run a business; **vendre un fonds de commerce,** to sell a business (as a going concern).

commercer, *v.i.* to trade/to deal (**avec,** with).

commercial, *a.* commercial; **attaché commercial,** commercial attaché; **cadre commercial,** sales/marketing executive; **directeur commercial,** sales manager/ marketing manager; **direction commerciale,** sales management; **droit commercial,** commercial law; **effet commercial,** commercial paper; **nom commercial,** trade name; name of a shop; **recherche commerciale,** market research; **service commercial,** sales department; **tendances commerciales,** trade trends.

commercialement, *adv.* commercially.

commercialisation, *n.f.* (*a*) commercialization (*b*) marketing; **accord de commercialisation,** marketing agreement.

commercialiser, *v.tr.* (*a*) *Fin:* to negotiate (a bill) (*b*) to commercialize; **produit non encore commercialisé,** product not yet on sale to the public/not yet marketed/not yet on the market.

commettant, *n.m. Jur:* principal (to a deal)/actual purchaser/actual vendor (when represented by agent); **commettant et mandataire,** principal and agent.

commis, *n.m.* **1.** clerk; **commis aux écritures,** accounting clerk/accounts clerk; **commis d'agent de change,** stockbroker's clerk; **commis principal/premier commis,** head/chief clerk **2.** (*dans un magasin*) sales assistant/shop assistant; salesman/*NAm:* sales clerk.

commissaire, *n.m.* **commissaire aux comptes,** auditor.

commissaire-priseur, *n.m.* (*a*) appraiser/valuer (*b*) auctioner.

commissariat, *n.m.* **commissariat des comptes,** auditorship.

commission, *n.m.* **1.** (*a*) commission; factorage; brokerage; **commission de change,** agio (*b*) **il reçoit une commission de 5% sur chaque vente,** he gets (a) commission of 5% on each sale **2.** commission/order; **maison de commission,** (firm of) commission agents/commission agency; **courtier à la commission,** commission agent; **vente à la commission,** sale on commission.

commissionnaire, *n.m.* commission agent; **commissionnaire d'achat,** buyer; **commissionnaire en gros,** factor; *Fin:* **commissionnaire en banque,** outside broker; **commissionnaire en douane,** customs broker; **commissionnaire expéditeur/de transport/de roulage,** forwarding agent/carrier; **commissionnaire exportateur,** export agent; **commissionnaire d'importation,** import agent.

commissionner, *v.tr.* (*a*) to commission; to appoint (s.o.) as buyer (on commission) (*b*) to order (goods).

commun, *a.* (*a*) common (to two or more); **créer une société en commun avec qn,** to start a company in partnership with s.o./jointly with s.o.; **faire bourse commune,** to share expenses; to pool resources; **mise en commun de fonds,** pooling

funds (*b*) **tare commune,** average tare/mean tare.

communauté, *n.f.* **la Communauté Économique Européenne (CEE),** the European Economic Community (EEC).

communication, *n.f.* (*a*) communication; **demander communication des livres d'une société,** to demand access to the books of a company; **se mettre en communication avec qn,** to get in touch with s.o. (*b*) **réseau de communications,** communications network (*c*) **communication téléphonique,** (telephone) call; **communication interurbaine,** trunk call/*NAm:* long distance (call); **communication urbaine,** local call; **obtenir une communication par voie automatique,** to dial direct.

commutatif, *a. Jur:* commutative (contract, etc.).

compagnie, *n.f.* (*a*) company; **compagnie de navigation,** shipping company; **compagnie aérienne,** airline (*b*) **(la maison) Thomas et Compagnie** (*usu.* **et Cie**), (the firm of) Thomas and Company (*usu.* & Co.).

compensation *n.f.* (*a*) compensation (for damages) (*b*) *Fin:* clearance (of cheques); **accord de compensation,** clearing agreement; **chambre de compensation,** clearing house; *StExch:* **cours de compensation,** making-up price.

compensatoire, *a.* compensatory; **demande compensatoire,** counterclaim; *EEC:* **montant compensatoire monétaire,** monetary compensation amount.

compenser, *v.tr.* to compensate/to make up for (sth.)/to offset; **compenser une perte,** to make good a loss; *Fin:* **compenser un chèque,** to clear (a cheque through a clearing house).

compétence, *n.f.* competence/proficiency/skill/ability; **degré de compétence,** standard of efficiency; **compétence technique,** technical skill.

compétent, *a. Jur: etc:* competent (tribunal, authority, etc.); **commis compétent,**

(*i*) competent clerk (*ii*) qualified clerk; **transmettre au service compétent,** to pass on to the department concerned.

compétitif, *a.* competitive; **prix compétitifs,** competitive prices.

compétition, *n.f.* competition.

compétitivité, *n.f.* competitiveness.

complaisance, *n.f.* **billet/effet de complaisance,** accommodation bill.

complémentaire, *a.* (*a*) **pour renseignements complémentaires s'adresser à** . . ., for further information apply to . . . (*b*) *Book-k:* **écriture complémentaire,** supplementary entry.

complet, *a.* complete/whole/full; (*à l'hôtel*) **complet,** no vacancies; **rapport complet et détaillé,** comprehensive report.

complexe, *n.m.* **complexe industriel,** industrial complex/industriel estate.

comportement, *n.m.* behaviour; **comportement du consommateur,** consumer behaviour.

composé, *a. Fin:* **intérêt composé,** compound interest.

composer, **1.** *v.i.* to compound (**avec,** with); to make a composition (with creditors, etc.) **2.** *v.tr.* **composer un numéro (de téléphone),** to dial a (phone) number.

comprendre, *v.tr.* to comprise/to cover/to include; **service compris,** service (charge) included; **service non compris,** service not included/service extra; **six mille francs par mois tout compris,** six thousand francs a month (all) inclusive/all in.

compression, *n.f. Fin:* **compression des dépenses budgétaires/compressions budgétaires,** retrenchment; cuts in budgetary expenditure; **compression de personnel,** reduction of staff.

compromis, *n.m.* compromise/arrangement; **mettre une affaire en compromis,**

to submit a matter to arbitration; **obtenir un compromis,** to compound (with creditors); *MIns:* **compromis d'avarie,** average bond.

compromissaire, *n.m. Jur:* arbitrator.

compromissoire, *a. Jur:* **clause compromissoire,** arbitration clause (in agreement).

comptabiliser, *v.tr.* to account for (sth.)/to enter (sth.) in the accounts.

comptabilité, *n.f.* (*a*) book-keeping; accountancy; **comptabilité en partie double,** double-entry book-keeping; **comptabilité en partie simple,** single-entry book-keeping; **comptabilité analytique des coûts variables,** direct cost accounting; **comptabilité de coût de revient,** cost accounting; **comptabilité de gestion,** management accounting; **comptabilité publique,** public accountancy; **commission de comptabilité,** audit committee; **livre de comptabilité,** account book; **tenir la comptabilité d'une maison,** to keep the books/the accounts of a firm; *Ind:* **comptabilité matières,** stock record/stores accounts; (**service de) la comptabilité,** accounts department; **chef de la comptabilité,** chief accountant.

comptable, **1.** *a.* accounting (work, etc.); **caisse comptable,** cash register; **machine comptable,** accounting machine; **méthode comptable,** accounting policies/method; **pièce comptable,** accountable receipt; voucher; **plan comptable,** accounting system; **quittance comptable,** formal receipt; **service(s) comptable(s),** accounts department; **valeur comptable,** book value **2.** *n.m.* accountant; **chef comptable,** chief accountant; **expert comptable/**FrC:* **comptable agrégé (CA),** (*i*) = chartered accountant (CA)/*NAm:* certified public accountant (*ii*) auditor; **comptable agréé** = certified accountant; **vérificateur comptable,** auditor.

comptant, **1.** *a.* **argent comptant,** ready money/cash; **payer cent francs comptant(s),** to pay a hundred francs cash (down)/in cash **2.** *adv.* **payer comptant,** to pay (in) cash/in ready money **3.** *n.m.* **acheter qch. (au) comptant,** to buy sth. for cash/to pay cash for sth.; **marché/opération au comptant,** cash transaction; **payable (au) comptant,** (*i*) cash terms (*ii*) payable on presentation; **paiement (au) comptant,** cash payment; **valeurs au comptant,** securities dealt in for cash; **le marché du comptant,** spot market.

compte, *n.m.* (*a*) reckoning/calculation; **faire le compte des dépenses,** to add up/to reckon (up)/to work out expenses; **le compte y est,** the total/the amount is correct; **compte rond,** round sum/even money; **acheter qch. à bon compte,** to buy sth. cheap (*b*) account; **compte d'achats,** purchase account; **compte (de) caisse,** cash account; **compte de capital,** capital account; **compte de contrepartie,** contra account; **compte créditeur,** credit account; **compte débiteur,** debit account; **compte d'actif/comptes clients,** accounts receivable/*NAm:* receivables; **compte de passif/comptes fournisseurs,** accounts payable/*NAm:* payables; **compte des dépenses et des recettes,** income and expenditure account; **compte détaillé,** detailed/itemized account; **compte d'exploitation,** working/trading account; *NAm:* operating account; **compte de pertes et profits,** profit and loss account; **livres de comptes,** account books; **arrêter un compte,** to close an account; **faire ses comptes,** (*i*) to do one's accounts (*ii*) (*dans un magasin*) to do the till/to cash up (*c*) **compte crédit/compte d'abonnement,** budget account; **compte permanent** = credit account/*NAm:* charge account; **compte client,** customer account; **être en compte avec qn,** to have an account with s.o.; **se faire ouvrir un compte chez qn,** to open an account with s.o.; **payer/régler un compte,** to pay a bill/ to settle an account; **j'ai payé mon compte de gaz,** I paid my gas bill; **passer une somme en compte/mettre qch. sur le compte de qn,** to enter sth./to put sth. down to s.o.'s account; **mettez-le/ inscrivez-le à mon compte,** charge it to my

account; **publié à compte d'auteur,** published at the author's (own) expense; **la Cour des comptes** = Audit Office (*d*) **être à son compte,** to work for oneself/to have one's own business; **s'installer/ prendre/se mettre à son compte,** to set up in business on one's own account (*e*) *Bank:* **compte à découvert,** overdrawn account; **compte à vue,** demand deposit; **compte bancaire/compte en banque,** bank account/*NAm:* banking account; **compte courant,** current account; **compte courant postal/compte chèque postal (CCP)** = (National) Giro-bank account; **compte (de caisse) d'épargne/compte sur livret,** (*i*) = savings account (*ii*) = deposit account; **compte de dépôt,** cheque account; **compte (de) chèques (CC),** (personal) cheque account/*NAm:* checking account; **compte de prêt/d'avances,** loan account; **compte (con)joint,** joint account; **compte professionnel/commercial,** office/business account; **numéro de compte,** account number; **relevé de compte,** bank statement; statement (of account); **se faire ouvrir un compte en banque,** to open a bank account; **verser de l'argent à son compte,** to pay money into one's account.

compter, 1. *v.tr.* (*a*) to count (up)/to reckon (up) (numbers, etc.); to add up; **mal compter,** to miscount **2.** *prep.phr.* **à compter de . . .,** (reckoning) from . . .; **à compter du 1ᵉʳ janvier,** as from January 1st/starting from January 1st (*b*) to charge; **je vous compterai cent francs pour cet article,** I'll charge you a hundred francs for this article.

compteur, *n.m.* **compteur à gaz,** gas meter.

comptoir, *n.m.* **1.** counter **2.** (*en Extrême-Orient*) go-down **3.** *Fin:* (*a*) bank; **comptoir d'escompte,** discount house (*b*) branch (of bank).

comptoir-caisse, *n.m.* pay desk/cash desk.

concentration, *n.f.* concentration; integration (of enterprises).

concepteur, *n.m.* project designer; **concepteur rédacteur,** copywriter.

conception, *n.f.* design; **conception de(s) produit(s),** product design; **conception par ordinateur,** computer design; **étude de conception,** design engineering.

concerner, *v.tr.* **en/pour ce qui concerne . . ,** as regards . . ./with regard to . . ./in respect of . . ./in relation to . . . .

concessible, *a.* concessible.

concession, *n.f.* concession.

concessionnaire, **1.** *a.* concessionary (company, etc.) **2.** *n.m.* (*a*) concessionnaire/licence-holder (*b*) dealer/agent; **consultez votre concessionnaire le plus proche,** see your nearest dealer.

conclure, *v.tr.* to conclude (an agreement); **conclure un marché/une affaire,** to make a deal; to settle a deal.

concordat, *n.m.* (bankrupt's) certificate; **concordat préventif (à la faillite),** (*i*) scheme of composition (*ii*) composition/legal settlement (between businessmen and creditors).

concordataire, *a.* **failli concordataire,** certificated (bankrupt); **procédure concordataire,** composition proceedings.

concurrence, *n.f.* competition; **capacité de concurrence,** competitive power/rivalry; **concurrence acharnée,** cut-throat competition; **concurrence déloyale,** unfair competition; **être/entrer en concurrence avec qn,** to compete with s.o.; **nos prix défient toute concurrence,** our prices are unbeatable/our prices are the lowest; **articles sans concurrence,** unrivalled goods.

concurrencer, *v.tr.* to compete with (s.o., sth.) (in trade, in the open market); **leur nouvelle gamme ne peut concurrencer la nôtre,** their new line can't compete with ours.

concurrent, *n.m.* competitor; rival (company); **analyse des concurrents,** competitor analysis.

concurrentiel, *a.* **prix concurrentiels,** competitive prices.

condition, *n.f.* (*a*) condition; stipulation; *pl.* terms; **condition à remplir/nécessaire/requise,** requirement; **conditions d'emploi,** conditions of employment; **conditions de faveur,** preferential terms; **conditions de paiement,** terms (of payment); **condition(s) provisionnelle(s),** proviso(s); **conditions d'un contrat,** terms/articles of a contract; **conditions d'une vente,** conditions of a sale; **faire de meilleures conditions,** to give s.o. better terms; **marchandises envoyées à condition,** goods sent on approval/*F:* on appro; **marchandises sous condition,** goods on sale or return; **offre sans condition,** unconditional offer; **signer qch. sans condition,** to sign sth. unconditionally/*F:* with no strings attached; **signer un engagement sous condition,** to sign an agreement conditionally/provisionally (*b*) **conditions de travail (dans une usine, etc.),** working conditions (in a factory, etc.); **les conditions économiques (du marché),** the economic situation.

conditionné, *a.* **viande conditionnée,** prepack(ag)ed meat.

conditionnement, *n.m.* (*a*) package (*b*) packaging; **industries de conditionnement,** packaging industries.

conditionner, *v.tr.* to package; to prepack.

conditionneur, -euse, *n.* (*pers.*) packer.

confection, *n.f.* (ready-to-wear) clothing industry; **magasin de confection,** shop/store selling ready-to-wear clothes; **vêtements de confection,** off-the-peg clothes.

confectionner, *v.tr.* to manufacture (clothing, etc.); **confectionnés sur demande,** made up to order.

conférence, *n.f.* conference; meeting; **conférence de presse,** press conference; **il est en conférence,** he's in a meeting/he's busy.

confidentiel, *a.* confidential; (*sur document, lettre, etc.*) private and confidential.

confirmation, *n.f.* confirmation (of a credit, a booking, a telephone message, etc.).

conflit, *n.m.* dispute; **conflits du travail,** labour disputes.

conforme, *a.* **copie conforme (à l'original),** true copy; **pour copie conforme,** certified true copy; **conforme à l'échantillon,** up to sample; *Book-k:* **écriture conforme,** corresponding entry.

conformément, *adv.* in accordance/in compliance (à, with); **conformément à votre demande du 13 courant,** in accordance with your request of 13th inst. .

conformité, *n.* **certificat de conformité,** clear report of findings.

confrère, *n.m.* colleague; fellow member (of association, profession, society, etc.).

congé, *n.m.* **1.** (*a*) leave (of absence); **congé de maladie,** sick leave; **congé de maternité,** maternity leave; **congé de paternité/de naissance,** paternity leave (*b*) holiday/*esp. NAm:* vacation; **congé annuel,** annual leave/annual holiday(s); **congé payé,** holiday with pay/paid leave; **congé sans solde,** unpaid leave/holiday; **être en congé,** to be on holiday; **prendre un congé d'une semaine,** to take a week off/a week's holiday; **un après-midi de congé,** an afternoon off **2.** (*a*) (notice of) dismissal; **donner (son) congé à qn,** to give s.o. notice/to dismiss s.o.; **demander son congé,** to hand in one's resignation; to give in one's notice (*b*) **donner congé à un locataire,** to give a tenant notice to quit; **donner congé à son propriétaire,** to give one's landlord notice of leaving **3.** (*pour un apprenti*) **recevoir son congé d'acquit,** to take up one's indentures **4.** authoriza-

tion/permit; **congé pour le transport des vins,** release of wine from bond.

congédiement, *n.m.* dismissal/sacking (of employee).

congédier, *v.tr.* to dismiss (employee); **congédier tout le personnel,** to dismiss/to sack the whole staff.

congelé, *a.* frozen; **produits congelés,** frozen foods.

conjoint, *a.* joint; **compte conjoint,** joint account; **dette conjointe,** joint debt.

conjoncture, *n.f.* *PolEc:* **conjoncture économique,** economic situation; **fluctuations de la conjoncture,** fluctuations in the market; **(période de) basse conjoncture,** slump; **haute conjoncture,** boom; **ralentissement de la conjoncture,** slowing down of economic activity.

conjoncturel, *a.* *PolEc:* cyclical (unemployment, fluctuations, etc.); **prévisions conjoncturelles,** economic prospects.

connaissement, *n.m.* *Nau:* bill of lading/shipping bill; **connaissement direct (avec rupture de charge),** through bill of lading (with transhipment).

conseil, *n.m.* **1.** (*a*) *Jur:* **avocat-conseil,** counsel (*b*) **ingénieur conseil,** consulting/consultant engineer; **cabinet d'ingénieur(s) conseil(s),** consultancy/firm of consultants; **conseil fiscal** = financial adviser; tax consultant; **conseil en recrutement,** recruitment consultant **2.** council/committee/board; **conseil d'administration,** board of directors; **réunion du conseil d'administration,** board meeting; **salle de réunion du conseil d'administration,** boardroom; **la banque fait partie du conseil,** the bank is represented on the board; **conseil de surveillance,** board of trustees; **Conseil de l'aide économique mutuelle (COMECON),** Council for mutual economic aid (COMECON); **Conseil national du crédit,** National credit council.

conseiller, *n.m.* counsellor/adviser; **conseiller de direction/de gestion**, management consultant; **conseiller fiscal** = financial adviser; tax consultant; **conseiller juridique**, legal adviser; **conseiller technique**, technical adviser.

consentement, *n.m.* consent; **consentement exprès**, formal consent; **par consentement mutuel**, by mutual consent.

consentir, 1. *v.i.* to consent/to agree (à, to); **assurances sur la vie consenties par l'industrie automobile**, life assurances agreed (to) by the motor industry 2. *v.tr.* **consentir un prêt**, to grant a loan; **consentir une remise à qn**, to allow a discount to s.o./to give s.o. a discount.

conserve, *n.f.* tinned/canned food.

conserverie, *n.f.* canning industry.

considération, *n.f. Corr:* **veuillez agréer l'assurance de ma haute considération**, yours faithfully.

consignataire, *n.m. & f.* (*a*) *Jur:* depository; trustee (*b*) consignee.

consignateur, **-trice**, *n.* consignor/ shipper.

consignation, *n.f.* 1. lodging/deposit (of money) 2. consignment (of goods); **envoyer qch. à qn en consignation**, to consign sth. to s.o./to send sth. to s.o. on consignment; **marchandises en consignation**, goods on consignment; **facture de consignation**, consignment invoice.

consigne, *n.f.* (*a*) **marchandises en consigne à la douane**, goods stopped/ held up at the customs (*b*) left luggage (office); *NAm:* checkroom (*c*) deposit (on a bottle).

consigner, *v.tr.* (*a*) to deposit (money, etc.); **bouteille non consignée**, non-returnable bottle (*b*) **consigner sa valise**, to leave one's suitcase at the left luggage (office) (*c*) to consign (goods, etc.) (*d*) **marchandises consignées par la douane**, goods stopped/held up at the customs.

consolidation, *n.f.* (*a*) consolidation (of accounts, position, power, etc.) (*b*) *Fin:* funding (of floating debt).

consolidé, *a. Fin:* **bilan consolidé**, consolidated account; consolidated balance-sheet; **chiffre d'affaires consolidé**, group turnover; **dette consolidée**, funded debt; **dette non consolidée**, floating debt; **les fonds consolidés/n. les consolidés**, the funded debt/consolidated debt/consols.

consolider, *v.tr.* 1. to consolidate (position, etc.) 2. *Fin:* to fund (debt); to consolidate (accounts, rates).

consommable, *a.* consumable (goods).

consommateur, **-trice**, *n.* (*a*) consumer; **consommateur cible**, target consumer; **producteurs et consommateurs**, producers and consumers (*b*) customer (in restaurant, etc.).

consommation, *n.f.* 1. consumption (of wheat, petrol); **biens de consommation**, consumer goods; *Aut:* **consommation d'essence aux 100 kilomètres** = petrol consumption (in miles per gallon); **concours de consommation**, economy run; **crédit à la consommation**, consumer credit; **dépenses de consommation**, consumer expenditure; **société de consommation**, consumer society 2. drink/snack (in café, bar).

consomptible, *a.* consumable (goods).

consortial, *a.* relating to a consortium.

consortium, *n.m.* consortium.

constat, *n.m. Jur:* **constat à l'amiable**, agreed statement of facts (on motor vehicle accident)/accident statement.

constaté, *a. Fin:* **valeur constatée**, registered value.

constituer, *v.tr.* to set up (committee, etc.); to form/to incorporate (a company).

constitutif, *a.* constitutive/conferring a right; **titres constitutifs (d'une propriété)**, title deeds.

constitution, *n.f.* constitution/establishing; **frais de constitution (d'une société),** preliminary expenses (in promoting a company); **constitution d'un comité,** setting up of a committee.

constructeur-promoteur, *n.m.* property developer.

consultatif, *a.* consultative/advisory/consulting (committee, board, document, etc.); **avoir une voix consultative,** to be present in an advisory (but nonvoting) capacity; **à titre consultatif,** in an advisory capacity.

container, *n.m.* = **conteneur.**

conteneur, *n.m. Trans:* container; **transports maritimes par conteneurs,** container shipping.

conteneurisation, *n.f. Trans:* containerization.

conteneuriser, *v.tr. Trans:* to containerize; to put into containers.

contenir, *v.tr.* (*a*) to contain; to hold (*b*) to control; **contenir l'inflation,** to check inflation.

contentieux, *n.m.* **bureau/service du contentieux,** legal department (of bank, company, etc.); disputed claims office; **chef du contentieux,** (company's) solicitor.

contenu, *n.m.* content(s) (of parcel, bottle, etc.); **le contenu de sa lettre,** the subject matter/the content of his letter.

contingent, *n.m.* quota; **contingents (d'exportation, d'importation),** (export, import) quotas.

contingentement, *n.m. Adm:* (*i*) quota system of distribution (*ii*) apportioning/fixing of quotas.

contingenter, *v.tr. Adm:* to establish/to fix quotas for (imports, etc.).

contractant, *Jur:* 1. *a.* contracting (party) 2. *n.m.* contracting party.

contracter, *v.tr.* (*a*) to incur/to contract (debt) (*b*) **contracter une assurance,** to take out an insurance policy; **contracter un emprunt,** to contract a loan.

contractuel, *a. Jur:* contractual (obligation, etc.); **action contractuelle,** action for breach of contract; **date contractuelle,** contract date/date of agreement; **main-d'œuvre contractuelle,** contractual labour; **droits contractuels,** rights granted by contract.

contrat, *n.m.* contract/agreement; deed; **contrat d'assurance,** (*i*) contract of insurance (*ii*) insurance policy; **contrat collectif,** collective agreement/group contract; **contrat de location,** hiring/leasing agreement; **contrat de société,** deed/articles of partnership; **contrat de travail,** contract of employment/*NAm:* labor contract; **contrat de vente,** bill of sale/(sales) agreement; **contrat translatif de propriété,** conveyance; **rupture de contrat,** breach of contract; **lié par contrat,** bound by contract/under contract; **passer un contrat (avec qn)/s'engager par contrat,** to enter into/to conclude an agreement (with s.o.); **rédiger/dresser un contrat,** to draw up a contract; **résilier un contrat,** to annul/to terminate/to cancel a contract; **signer un contrat,** to sign a contract.

contre-analyse, *n.f.* check analysis.

contre-assurance, *n.f.* reinsurance.

contrebalancer, *v.tr.* to counter-balance/to offset.

contre-écriture, *n.f. Book-k:* contra-entry.

contre-épreuve, *n.f.* cross-check.

contre-expertise, *n.f.* re-survey/counter-valuation.

contrefaçon, *n.f.* 1. counterfeiting; fraudulently copying or imitating (trade mark, etc.); infringement (of patent, copyright)/*F:* piracy; **procès en contrefaçon,** action for infringement (of copyright, etc.) 2. forgery/fraudulent imitation; pirated edition of book.

contremaître, -tresse, *n.* foreman/fore-woman.

contrepartie, *n.f.* **1.** *StExch:* **contrepartie dissimulée/occulte,** market-making; **faire de la contrepartie,** to operate against one's client **2.** (*a*) *Book-k:* contra; **en contrepartie,** per contra (*b*) counterpart/duplicate (of document).

contre-passation, *n.f.,* **contre-passement,** *n.m.* **1.** *Fin:* return (of bill to drawer) **2.** *Book-k:* (*a*) reversing/transferring (of item, entry) (*b*) contra entry.

contre-passer, *v.tr.* **1.** *Fin:* to return/to endorse/to back (bill to drawer) **2.** *Book-k:* to reverse/to contra/to transfer (item, entry).

contre-poser, *v.tr. Book-k:* to enter (item) on the wrong side of the ledger.

contre-position, *n.f. Book-k:* mis-entry (in ledger).

contreseing, *n.m.* counter-signature.

contresigner, *v.tr.* to countersign.

contre-valeur, *n.f. Fin:* exchange value.

contribuable, *n.m. & f.* taxpayer; **contribuable à l'impôt foncier** = ratepayer.

contribution, *n.f.* tax; rate; **contributions (directes, indirectes),** (direct, indirect) taxation; **contribution foncière,** land tax; **(bureau des) contributions,** tax office/ = Inland Revenue/*NAm:* Internal Revenue; **lever/percevoir une contribution,** to collect/to levy a tax; **payer ses contributions,** to pay one's taxes.

contrôle, *n.m.* **1.** (*a*) control; **contrôle de (la) qualité,** quality control; *Fin:* **contrôle des changes,** exchange control; **contrôle des prix,** price control; **contrôle des stocks,** stock control/*NAm:* inventory control; **contrôle budgétaire,** budget control; **contrôle financier,** financial control (*b*) **prise de contrôle,** takeover **2.** (*a*) auditing/checking (of accounts, etc.) (*b*)

contrôle (de gestion), management control (*c*) **contrôle de présence,** timekeeping **3. cachet de contrôle,** hallmark (on gold and silver).

contrôler, *v.tr.* **1.** to check/to audit (accounts) **2.** to hallmark (gold, silver).

contrôleur, -euse, *n.* (*a*) **contrôleur des contributions,** inspector of taxes; **contrôleur des comptes d'une société,** auditor of a company's accounts (*b*) inspector/examiner/supervisor (of work, etc.)

contrôlographe, *n.m. Trans:* tachograph.

convenir, *v.i.* to agree; to come to an agreement; **convenir du prix avec qn,** to agree on a price/to settle on a price with s.o.; **prix convenu,** agreed price.

convention, *n.f.* (*a*) agreement; covenant; **convention par écrit,** agreement in writing; **projet de convention,** draft agreement; **convention collective** = collective bargaining agreement/union agreement (*b*) *Jur:* article/clause (of deed, etc.).

conversion, *n.f.* (*a*) *StExch:* conversion; **conversion de titre(s),** conversion of stock (*b*) **conversion de la rente de 5% en 3½%,** conversion of Government 5% stock into 3½%.

convertibilité, *n.f.* convertibility (of currencies, etc.).

convertible, *a.* convertible (**en,** into); **obligation convertible (en actions),** convertible bond; **monnaies convertibles,** convertible currencies.

convertir, *v.tr.* to convert (**en,** into); **convertir des rentes,** to convert stock.

convertissement, *n.m. StExch: Fin:* conversion (of securities into money).

convoquer, *v.tr.* to convene (meeting); to call (creditors); to summon (shareholders).

coopé, *n.f. F:* (the) co-op.

coopératif, *a.* **société coopérative,** co-operative society.

cooperative, *n.f.* co-operative stores/*F:* co-op; **coopérative agricole,** agricultural co-operative; **coopérative de consommation,** (*i*) consumers' cooperative (*ii*) co-operative stores; **coopérative immobilière** = building society; **coopérative ouvrière,** workers' co-operative; **coopérative de production,** producers' co-operative.

coparticipant, -ante, *n.m. Jur:* copartner.

coparticipation, *n.f. Jur:* copartnership; *Ind:* **coparticipation des employés dans les bénéfices,** profit-sharing by the employees.

copie, *n.f.* (*a*) copy/transcript; *Jur:* **pour copie conforme,** certified true copy (*b*) carbon copy (of letter).

copieur, *n.m.* (photo)copier.

coporteur, *n.m. Fin:* joint holder (of stock).

coposséder, *v.tr.* to own jointly/to have joint ownership of (sth.).

copossesseur, *n.m. Jur:* (*a*) joint owner (*b*) co-tenant.

copossession, *n.f. Jur:* (*a*) joint ownership (*b*) co-tenancy.

copreneur, -euse, *n. Jur:* co-lessee/co-tenant.

coproduction, *n.f.* coproduction.

copropriétaire, *n.m. & f. Jur:* coproprietor; joint owner/part owner/co-owner.

copropriété, *n.f. Jur:* co-property; joint ownership/co-ownership.

copyright, *n.m.* copyright.

corporation, *n.f.* corporation/corporate body/public body.

correspondance, *n.f.* correspondence; **entrer en correspondance avec qn,** to enter into correspondence with s.o.; **mai**son de vente par correspondance, mail-order firm; **vente par correspondance (VPC),** (*i*) mail order (selling) (*ii*) mail order (sales).

correspondancier, -ière, *n.* correspondence clerk; **secrétaire correspondancière,** (correspondence) secretary.

cosignataire, *n.m.* co-signatory.

cotation, *n.f. Fin:* quotation; quoting.

cote, *n.f.* (*a*) quota/share/proportion (of expense, taxes, etc.); **cote mal taillée,** compounding in gross (of account)/ rough and ready settlement (*b*) *Adm:* assessment; **cote foncière,** assessment on land; **cote mobilière,** assessment on property (*c*) *StExch:* quotation; **cote des prix,** (*i*) official (share-) list (*ii*) (*dans le commerce*) list of prices; **actions inscrites à la cote/valeurs admises à la cote (de la Bourse),** listed shares/shares quoted on the Stock Exchange; **(actions) hors cote,** unlisted (shares)/(shares that are) not (officially) quoted on the Stock Exchange; **admission à la cote,** admission to quotation/to the official list; **faire une demande d'admission à la cote,** to seek a share quotation/quote.

coter, *v.tr.* to quote (price, etc.); **valeurs cotées en Bourse,** shares quoted on the Stock Exchange/listed shares.

cotisant, -ante, *n.* paying member; subscriber (**de,** to).

cotisation, *n.f.* (*a*) quota/share; contribution (to common fund); **assurance à cotisations,** contributory insurance; **cotisations maladie** = health insurance contributions; **cotisation patronale,** employer's contribution; **cotisation ouvrière,** employee's contribution; **cotisations sociales,** (National Insurance and National Health) contributions; **cotisations à la Sécurité sociale** = National Insurance contributions; **régime de retraite financé par les cotisations patronales et**

ouvrières, contributory pension plan (*b*) subscription (to club, etc.).

cotiser, *v.tr.* to pay one's share; **cotiser à la Sécurité sociale** = to pay one's National Insurance (contributions).

coulage, *n.m.* **tenir compte du coulage,** to allow for (*i*) wastage (*ii*) petty theft.

coulisse, *n.f. StExch:* **la coulisse,** the outside market.

coulissier, *n.m. StExch:* outside broker.

coupe, *n.f.* (drastic) cut (in personnel, in estimates).

coupon, *n.m.* **1.** remnant (of material) **2.** coupon; *Fin:* **coupon d'actions,** coupon; **coupon d'intérêt,** interest coupon; **coupon de dividende,** dividend coupon; **coupon attaché,** cum dividend; with/cum coupon; **coupon détaché,** ex dividend/ex coupon; **coupon arriéré,** coupon in arrears.

couponnage, *n.m.*, **couponing,** *n.m.* couponing.

coupon-prime, *n.m.* gift voucher.

coupon-réponse, *n.m. Post:* **coupon-réponse international,** international reply coupon.

coupure, *n.f. Fin:* (bank)note/*NAm:* bill; **coupure de dix francs,** ten-franc note; **petite coupure,** note of small denomination.

cour, *n.f.* court/tribunal; **la Cour des comptes,** the Audit Office.

courant, 1. *a.* (*a*) *Bank:* **compte courant;** current account (*b*) **l'année courante,** the present/current year; **le cinq du mois courant/le cinq courant/le 5 ct.,** the 5th inst.; **fin courant,** at the end of this month (*c*) **affaires courantes,** (*i*) routine/everyday business (*ii*) business in/on hand; **dépenses courantes,** running expenses; **dette courante,** floating debt; **marchandises de vente courante,** goods that have a ready sale; **monnaie courante,** legal currency; **prix courant,** current price; **prix courants,** (current) price list

(*d*) **marque courante,** standard make; **taille courante,** standard size **2.** *n.m.* **le courant économique actuel,** the present economic situation.

courbe, *n.f.* curve; graph; **courbe des ventes,** sales chart/graph.

courir, *v.i.* **les intérêts courent à partir de . . .,** interest accrues (as) from . . .; **les intérêts qui courent,** the accruing interest; **intérêts courus,** accrued interest; **le bail n'a plus qu'un an à courir,** the lease has only one year to run.

courrier, *n.m.* mail/post; letters; **par retour du courrier,** by return (of post); **dépouiller son courrier,** to open/to go through one's mail.

cours, *n.m.* **1. année en cours,** current year; **affaires en cours,** outstanding business; **négociations en cours,** negotiations in progress; **travail en cours,** work in progress; work in/on hand; **en cours de production,** in production **2.** circulation (of money); (*d'une devise*) **avoir cours (légal),** to be legal tender; to be in circulation; **cours forcé,** forced currency **3.** *StExch:* quotation/price; **bulletin des cours,** official list of quotation; **cours au comptant,** price for cash; **cours commerciaux,** commodity prices; **cours de clôture/dernier cours,** closing price; **cours d'ouverture/premier cours,** opening price; **le cours de l'or,** the price of gold; **cours du change,** rate of exchange; **cours du comptant,** spot price/rate; **cours du marché/cours de la Bourse,** market price/rate; **cours étranger,** foreign exchange; **cours des devises,** foreign exchange rate; **cours à terme,** price for the account; **cours d'achat/cours acheteur,** offer price/buying price; **cours vendeur,** selling price; **cours de rachat,** buying-in price; **cours de compensation,** making-up price; **cours en bourse/cours officiel,** (*i*) official price (*ii*) (*à Londres*) house price; **cours hors Bourse/cours hors cote,** unofficial price; **acheter au cours (du jour),** to buy at the price/rate of the day; **cours (des changes) à terme,** forward (exchange) rates; **quel est le cours du sucre?** what is sugar quoted at?

court, *a.* short; **crédit à court terme,** short-term credit; **effet à courte échéance,** short-dated bill; *Fin:* **papiers courts,** short-dated bills.

courtage, *n.m.* (*a*) broking/brokerage; **faire le courtage,** to be a broker; **courtage en immeubles,** real estate agency (*b*) **droit/frais de courtage,** brokerage/commission.

courtier, *n.m.* broker; agent; **courtier d'assurances,** insurance broker; **courtier de change,** bill broker; **courtier de commerce/de marchandises,** general broker/commercial broker; **courtier en valeurs mobilières,** (stock)broker; **courtier libre,** outside broker; **courtier maritime,** ship broker; **courtier marron/non autorisé,** outside broker; **bureau de courtier marron,** bucket-shop; *Publ:* **courtier en librairie,** trade sales rep(resentative)/*NAm:* book agent.

couru, *a. Fin:* **intérêts courus,** accrued interest.

coût, *n.m.* (*a*) cost; **coût, assurance, fret (c.a.f.),** cost, insurance, freight (c.i.f.); **coût d'accroissement,** incremental cost; **coûts constants/fixes,** fixed costs; **coût du capital,** capital cost; **facteur coût,** cost factor; **méthode de coûts variables,** direct costing; **méthode de capitalisation du coût entier,** full costing; **structure des coûts,** cost structure (*b*) **le coût de la vie,** the cost of living; **indice du coût de la vie,** cost of living index.

coûtant, *a.m.* **au/à prix coûtant,** at cost price.

coût-efficacité, *n.f.* cost-effectiveness.

coûter, *v.i.* to cost; **cela coûte cinq francs,** it costs five francs; **coûter cher,** to be expensive; **ne pas coûter cher,** to be inexpensive.

coûteux, *a.* costly/expensive; **peu coûteux,** inexpensive.

couvert, *n.m.* **1. être à couvert,** to be covered (for a credit); *St Exch:* **vendre à couvert,** to hedge **2.** (*au restaurant*) **(frais de) couvert,** cover charge.

couverture, *n.f.* (*a*) cover; margin; **commande sans couverture,** order without security/without cover; **exiger une couverture de 20% en espèces,** to claim a margin of 20% in cash; **opération de couverture,** hedging; **opérer avec couverture,** to operate with cover; to hedge (*b*) *Ins:* covering (of risks) (*c*) coverage; **couverture du marché,** sales coverage.

couvrir, 1. *v.tr.* to cover; **le prix de vente couvre à peine les frais,** the selling price barely covers the cost; **cette assurance ne couvre pas les risques de vol,** this insurance doesn't cover us against theft; **couvrir un emprunt,** to cover a loan; **couvrir les frais de port,** to refund the postage/the carriage; **couvrir une enchère,** to make a higher bid **2.** *v.pr. StExch:* to cover (oneself)/to hedge; **se couvrir en achetant à long terme,** to hedge by buying at long date; **se couvrir en rachetant,** to cover oneself by buying back.

covendeur, -euse, *n.* co-vendor/joint seller.

créance, *n.f.* **1. lettre de créance,** letter of credit **2.** debt; *Jur:* claim; **créances exigibles,** debts due; **créance garantie,** secured debt; **créances gelées,** frozen credits; **créance privilégiée,** preferential/preferred debt; **nos créances,** monies owing to us; receivables; **mauvaises créances/créances douteuses,** bad debts; doubtful accounts.

créancier, -ière, *n.* creditor; holder of debt claim; **créancier hypothécaire,** mortgagee.

création, *n.f.* **création d'emploi,** job creation (scheme); **création d'une entreprise,** founding/establishment (of a company, a firm); **création d'un nouveau produit,** creation of a new product; **création de produits,** product generation; **nos dernières créations,** our latest models; our latest creations.

crédirentier, -ière, *n. Jur:* recipient of an allowance/of an income/of an annuity.

crédit, *n.m.* **1.** (*a*) credit; **crédit bancaire,** bank credit; **crédit en blanc/à découvert,** blank/open credit; **crédit de campagne,** seasonal loan; **carte de crédit,** credit card; **crédit à la consommation,** consumer credit; **crédit à court terme/à long terme,** short/long term credit; **crédit croisé,** swap; **crédit différé,** deferred credit; **crédit documentaire,** documentary credit; **crédits d'équipement,** equipment financing; **crédits à l'exportation,** export credit; **crédits de trésorerie,** (short term) credit facilities/cash advances; **crédit d'impôt,** (*i*) tax rebate (*ii*) tax credit (*iii*) allowance; **lettre de crédit,** letter of credit; **note de crédit,** credit note; **acheter/vendre à crédit,** to buy/to sell sth. (*i*) on credit/*F:* on tick (*ii*) on hire purchase/*NAm:* on the installment plan; **faire crédit à qn,** to give s.o. credit; **ouvrir un crédit à qn,** to open a credit account in s.o.'s favour/in s.o.'s name; **ouvrir un crédit chez qn,** to open a credit account/*F:* an account with s.o. (*b*) **banque de crédit,** credit bank; **établissement/société de crédit,** loan society/credit establishment/credit bank; **crédit foncier** = (government-controlled) building society **2.** credit side (of ledger, balance-sheet); **porter une somme au crédit de qn,** to credit s.o. with a sum/to enter a sum to s.o.'s credit.

crédit-bail, *n.m* leasing; **crédit-bail mobilier,** equipment leasing.

créditer, *v.tr.* **créditer qn du montant d'une somme,** to credit s.o./s.o.'s account with a sum; **créditer un compte,** to credit an account.

créditeur, -trice, 1. *n.* creditor **2.** *a.* **compte créditeur,** account in credit; **solde créditeur,** credit balance.

créneau, *n.m.* gap/opening/opportunity in the market.

creux, *a.* **année creuse,** poor year; **heures creuses,** off-peak hours; **marché creux,** sagging market; **saison creuse,** slack season.

criée, *n.f.* auction; **chambre des criées,** (public) auction room/saleroom/*NAm:* salesroom; **vente à la criée,** sale by auction.

crier, *v.tr.* to put (furniture, etc.) up for auction/to auction (furniture).

crise, *n.f.* crisis; **crise économique,** economic crisis; slump; **crise de l'emploi,** unemployment crisis/job shortage; **la crise du logement,** the housing shortage/crisis.

croissance, *n.f.* growth; **croissance économique,** economic growth; **courbe de croissance,** growth curve; **industrie en croissance rapide,** growth industry; **ralentissement du taux de croissance,** slowing down of the growth rate; *Fin:* **valeur de croissance,** growth stock.

croissant, *a.* increasing (wealth, etc.); **coût croissant,** increasing cost; **rendements croissants,** increasing returns.

croître, *v.i.* to grow/to increase.

culbute, *n.f. F:* **faire la culbute,** (*i*) to go bankrupt (*ii*) to make 100% profit.

cumulatif, *a.* cumulative (shares, etc.); **assurance cumulative,** double insurance.

cycle, *n.m.* cycle; **cycle économique,** business/trade cycle; **cycle de vie (d'un produit),** life cycle (of a product).

D

dactylo, 1. *n.m. & f.* typist; **équipe/pool de dactylos,** typing pool **2.** *n.f.* typing **3.** *n.m. FrC:* typewriter.

dactylographie, *n.f.* typing.

dactylographier, *v.tr.* to type; **lettre dactylographiée,** typed/typewritten letter.

datation, *n.f.* dating; **datation d'un contrat,** dating of a contract.

date, *n.f.* date; **la lettre porte la date du 12 juin,** the letter is dated June 12th/12th (of) June; **en date du 15 courant,** dated the 15th inst.; **en date de Paris,** dated from Paris; **à trente jours de date,** thirty days after date; **date d'échéance,** date of maturity/due date; **date d'émission,** date of issue; **date de naissance,** date of birth; **date d'entrée en vigueur,** effective date (of regulation, etc.); **date limite,** deadline; **date limite de vente,** sell-by date; **date de valeur,** value date; **sans date,** undated (letter, etc.).

dater, 1. *v.tr.* to date (letter, etc.); **votre lettre datée d'hier,** your letter dated yesterday; **lettre datée du 13 mars,** letter dated the 13th (of) March/dated March 13th **2.** *v.i.* to date (de, from); **à dater de ce jour,** (*i*) from today (*ii*) from that day; **à dater du 15,** on and after the 15th; (starting) from the 15th/as from the 15th/as of the 15th.

dateur, *a.* **timbre dateur,** date stamp.

débâcle, *n.f. Fin:* **débâcle (financière),** crash.

déballage, *n.m.* unpacking.

déballer, *v.tr.* to unpack (goods, etc.); to display (goods for sale).

débattre, *v.tr.* to discuss; **débattre un prix,** to discuss a price; **prix à débattre,** price to be agreed/price by arrangement; **salaire à débattre,** salary negotiable.

débauchage, *n.m. Ind:* laying off (of workers).

débaucher, *v.tr. Ind:* to lay off (workers)/ to make (workers) redundant.

débet, *n.m. Fin:* debit balance.

débit[1]**,** *n.m.* (*a*) (retail) sale; **marchandises de bon débit/d'un débit facile,** goods with a ready market/which sell well; **ces marchandises ont peu de débit,** there is little demand for these goods (*b*) (retail) shop; *esp.* **débit de tabac,** tobacconist's (shop); **débit de boissons** = pub/bar.

débit[2]**,** *n.m.* debit; *Book-k:* debit side; **note/bordereau de débit,** debit note; **inscrire/porter au débit,** to debit; **porter une somme au débit de qn/au débit d'un compte,** to debit s.o. with an amount/to debit s.o.'s account with an amount.

débiter[1]**,** *v.tr.* **1.** to retail/to sell (goods) retail; **on débite beaucoup dans cette boutique,** this shop has a large turnover **2.** to yield; **machine qui débite beaucoup d'ouvrage,** machine with a large output.

débiter[2]**,** *v.tr.* to debit; **débiter le compte de qn,** to debit s.o.'s account (with); **débiter qn (d'une somme),** to debit s.o. with an amount; **débiter les frais de poste au client,** to charge (the) postage to the customer.

débiteur, -trice, 1. *n.* debtor **2.** *a.*

colonne débitrice, debit column/debit side; **compte débiteur,** debit account; **solde débiteur,** (*i*) debit balance (*ii*) *Bank:* overdraft.

déblocage, *n.m. Fin:* unblocking/release/unfreezing (of credits, capital); decontrolling (of wages, prices).

débloquer, *v.tr. Fin:* to unblock/to release/to unfreeze (credits, capital, etc.); **débloquer (les prix, les salaires),** to decontrol (prices, wages).

débouché, *n.m.* (*a*) outlet/opening/market; **créer de nouveaux débouchés pour un produit,** to open up new markets/to create new outlets for a product; **examen des débouchés,** market analysis (*b*) job opportunity; **l'industrie offre des débouchés aux économistes,** industry has (job) prospects/job opportunities for economists.

débours, *n.m. usu. pl.* out-of-pocket expenses/outgoings; **faire des débours,** to lay out/to pay out money; **rentrer dans ses débours,** to recover one's outlay.

déboursement, *n.m.* outlay/disbursement; expenditure.

débourser, *v.tr.* to spend/to lay out/to pay out (money).

débudgétisation, *n.f.* debudgeting.

débudgétiser, *v.tr.* to debudget.

décaissement, *n.m.* withdrawal of a sum of money/of funds (for payment).

décaisser, *v.tr.* to withdraw a sum of money/funds (for payment); to pay out.

décentralisation, *n.f.* (*a*) decentralization; **décentralisation administrative,** devolution (*b*) relocation of offices.

décentraliser, *v.tr.* (*a*) to decentralize (administration) (*b*) to relocate (offices, etc.) (away from large towns).

décharge, *n.f.* **1. décharge d'un impôt,** tax rebate **2. porter une somme en décharge,** to mark a sum as paid **3.** discharge/release (from debt, etc.).

déchargement, *n.m.* unloading (of ship).

décharger, *v.tr.* **1.** to unload (a ship, cargo, goods) **2. décharger qn d'un impôt,** to exempt s.o. from (paying) a tax; **décharger qn d'une dette,** to remit a debt; **failli (non) déchargé,** (un)discharged bankrupt; **décharger un compte,** to discharge an account.

déchéance, *n.f.* forfeiture (of rights, etc.); **déchéance de titres,** forfeiture of shares; **action en déchéance de brevet,** action for forfeiture of patent.

déchet, *n.m.* **1.** loss/decrease/diminution (of weight, value, quantity); **déchet de route,** loss in transit **2.** waste product; *usu. pl. Ind: etc:* **déchets,** waste/refuse.

décideur, *a.* **organisme décideur,** decision-making body.

décile, *n.m. Stat:* decile.

déclaration, *n.f.* (*a*) declaration; statement/report; **déclaration sous serment,** affidavit; **déclaration de revenu/déclaration fiscale,** income-tax return; **envoyer sa déclaration à l'inspecteur des contributions directes** = to make a tax return/*NAm:* to file one's tax return; **fausse déclaration,** (*i*) misrepresentation (*ii*) false return/false declaration; *Adm:* **déclaration de versement/de quittance,** receipt; *Rail:* **déclaration d'expédition,** invoice (*b*) *Cust:* **déclaration de/en douane,** customs declaration/bill of entry; **déclaration d'entrée en entrepôt,** warehousing entry; **déclaration de transit,** transit entry (*c*) *Nau:* **déclaration d'avarie,** (ship's) protest (*d*) *StExch:* **jour de la déclaration des noms,** ticket day.

déclarer, *v.tr.* to declare; **déclarer un dividende,** to declare a dividend; **déclarer ses revenus au fisc** = to make one's tax return/*NAm:* to file one's tax return; *Cust:* **avez-vous quelque chose à déclarer?** (have you) anything to declare? **rien à déclarer,** nothing to declare; **valeur déclarée,** declared value; *Fin:* **transferts déclarés,** certified transfers; *StExch:* **se déclarer vendeur,** to put the shares.

déclassé, *a. Fin:* **valeurs déclassées,** displaced stock.

déclassement, *n.m. StExch:* displacement (of shares).

décommander, *v.tr.* **décommander (une commande, une livraison),** to cancel (an order, a delivery); **décommander une réunion,** to cancel/to call off a meeting.

décomposer, *v.tr.* **décomposer un compte,** to analyse/to break down an account.

décomposition, *n.f.* **décomposition des dépenses,** breakdown of expenses; **décomposition des tâches,** job breakdown.

décompte, *n.m.* **1.** (*a*) **faire le décompte,** to deduct sth. (from the price); to make a deduction (from sum to be paid) (*b*) **payer le décompte,** to pay the balance due (on an account) **2.** detailed account; breakdown (of account).

décompter, *v.tr.* to deduct (sum from price).

déconcentration, *n.f.* **déconcentration industrielle,** relocation of offices/businesses (away from large towns).

déconcentrer, *v.tr.* to relocate (offices, businesses) (away from large towns).

déconfiture, *n.f.* financial collapse; *Jur:* insolvency; bankruptcy (of non-trader).

déconsigner, *v.tr.* (*a*) to return/to pay back the deposit on (bottles, etc.) (*b*) **déconsigner ses baggages,** to take one's luggage out of (the) left luggage (office).

décote, *n.f.* (*a*) tax relief; tax exemption; tax credit (*b*) *Fin:* value (of currency) below rate.

découvert, 1. *n.m.* (*a*) *Bank: etc:* overdraft; overdrawn balance; **accorder à qn**

un découvert de £100, to allow s.o. an overdraft of £100/to allow s.o. to overdraw to the amount of £100; **avoir un découvert de 2 000 francs à la banque,** to have an overdraft of 2 000 francs/to be 2 000 francs overdrawn at the bank; **découvert en blanc,** unsecured overdraft (*b*) *Ins:* parts/things not covered by insurance (*c*) *Adm:* (budgetary) deficit; *PolEc:* **découvert de la balance commerciale,** trade gap; *StExch:* **chasser le découvert,** to raid the bears **2.** *adv. phr. Bank:* **compte à découvert,** overdrawn account; **mettre (son compte) à découvert/tirer à découvert,** to overdraw (one's account); **crédit à découvert,** unsecured credit; **vente à découvert,** sale for futures/short sale/short selling; **vendre à découvert,** to sell short; to go a bear.

dédit, *n.m.* forfeit/penalty (for breaking contract, etc.).

dédommagement, *n.m.* indemnity/compensation/damages; **réclamer un dédommagement,** to claim compensation; **recevoir une somme en dédommagement (de qch.)/à titre de dédommagement,** to receive a sum in/by way of compensation (for sth.).

dédommager, 1. *v.tr.* to indemnify/to compensate (s.o.) (**de qch.,** for sth.) **2.** *v.pr.* **se dédommager de ses pertes,** to recoup one's losses.

dédouanage, *n.m.* **dédouanement,** *n.m. Cust:* (*i*) customs clearance (*ii*) taking out of bond.

dédouaner, *v.tr. Cust:* (*i*) to clear through customs (*ii*) to take out of bond (*iii*) to remove the customs duty from an article.

déductible, *a.* deductible.

déduction, *n.f.* (*a*) deduction; allowance; **après déduction des impôts,** after deduction of tax; **déduction faite des frais,** after deducting the expenses; **faire déduction des sommes payées d'avance,** to allow for/to deduct sums paid in advance; **somme qui entre en déduction de . . . ,**

amount deductible from . . .; **sous déduction de 10%,** less/minus 10% (*b*) *Adm:* allowance; tax relief.

déduire, *v.tr.* to deduct; **déduire 5%,** to take off/to allow/to deduct 5%; **les frais de poste sont à déduire du prix total,** postage to be deducted from the total price.

défaillance, *n.f. Fin:* **défaillance du franc,** weakening of the franc; **défaillance du marché,** sagging of the market.

défaillant, -ante, 1. *a.* **partie défaillante,** defaulting party **2.** *n.* defaulter.

défalcation, *n.f.* (*a*) deduction/deducting; writing off (of bad debt); **défalcation faite des frais,** after deducting the expenses (*b*) sum/weight deducted; allowance; abatement (from income tax).

défalquer, *v.tr.* to deduct/to take off (sum from total); **défalquer une mauvaise créance,** to write off a bad debt.

défaut, *n.m.* **1.** (*a*) default/absence/deficiency/insufficiency/(total) lack (of sth.); **à défaut de paiement,** failing payment/in default of payment; **défaut de paiement,** failure to pay/non(-)payment; **intérêts pour défaut de paiement,** default interest; *Bank:* **défaut de provision,** no funds (*b*) *Jur:* default; *StExch:* **agent en défaut,** defaulter **2. défaut de fabrication,** fault/defect (in manufacture); flaw (in fabric, etc.).

défavorable, *a. Fin:* **balance de paiements défavorable,** adverse trade balance; **change défavorable,** unfavourable exchange.

défectueux, *a.* **articles défectueux,** imperfect goods/rejects; seconds.

défendeur, -eresse, *n. Jur:* defendant.

déficit, *n.m.* deficit/shortfall (in cash, balance-sheet); deficiency (in revenue); shortage (in cash, weight); **être en déficit/accuser un déficit/présenter un déficit,** to show a deficit; **combler un déficit,** to make up/to make good a deficit; **compte qui présente un déficit,**

debit balance; **déficit budgétaire,** budget deficit; **déficit commercial,** trade gap; trade deficit; **déficit de la balance commerciale,** trade deficit.

déficitaire, *a.* showing a deficit; **balance/ solde déficitaire,** adverse balance/debit balance; **être déficitaire,** to show a deficit/*F:* to be in the red; **rétablir un budget déficitaire,** to balance an adverse budget.

déflation, *n.f.* deflation; **politique de déflation,** deflationary policy.

déflationniste, *a. PolEc:* **mesures déflationnistes,** deflationary measures.

défraîchi, *a.* **articles défraîchis,** shop-soiled goods.

défrayer, *v.tr.* **défrayer qn,** to pay/to meet/to settle s.o.'s expenses.

dégeler, *v.tr.* to unfreeze/to unblock (assets, credits, etc.).

degré, *n.m.* degree; **degré de liquidité,** degree of liquidity/liquidity ratio.

dégressif, *a.* decreasing/graded; **impôt dégressif,** sliding scale taxation/graduated tax; **tarif dégressif,** decreasing tariff/sliding scale tariff.

dégrèvement, *n.m.* (*a*) reduction (of tax); **dégrèvement pour entretien d'immeubles,** allowance for repairs (*b*) relief from taxation/derating (of industry); **quotité du dégrèvement fiscal,** extent of taxation relief.

dégrever, *v.tr.* to reduce tax/duty (on products); to relieve (s.o.) of a tax; to reduce (s.o.'s) taxes; to derate (industry); to reduce the assessment on (a property).

dégringolade, *n.f.* **dégringolade du franc,** collapse of the franc; **dégringolade des prix,** slump in prices.

dégringoler, *v.i.* (*des prix*) to slump.

délai, *n.m.* (*a*) delay; *Corr:* **veuillez nous répondre sans délai,** please reply immediately/without delay (*b*) time allowed (for completion of a job, etc.); **dans un délai de trois ans,** within three years/within a three year limit; **dans le plus bref délai/le plus court délai/dans les meilleurs délais,** in the shortest possible time/as soon as possible/at your earliest convenience; **dans les délais prescrits,** within the prescribed/required time; **délai de livraison un mois,** delivery within a month/allow one month for delivery; **délai de paiement,** term of payment; **délai de récupération (du capital investi),** payback period (of capital invested); **livrable dans un délai de trois jours,** can be delivered at three days' notice/within three days (*c*) *Jur:* **un délai franc de 5 jours,** 5 clear days' grace; **délai de grâce,** days of grace; **délai de préavis/de congé,** period of notice (to employee, to employer).

délai-congé, *n.m. Jur:* term/period of notice (to employee or employer).

délaissé, *a. StExch:* **valeurs délaissées,** neglected stocks.

délaissement, *n.m.* abandonment (of ship to insurer).

délégation, *n.f.* **1.** (*a*) delegation (of authority) (*b*) *Jur:* assignment/transfer (of debit) **2.** delegation; **une délégation commerciale japonaise,** a Japanese trade delegation/mission.

délégué, -ée, *a. & n.* (*a*) **administrateur délégué,** acting managing director (*b*) **délégué commercial,** sales representative/sales rep; *Ind:* **délégué syndical,** (trade) union representative; **délégué d'usine/du personnel/d'atelier,** shop steward.

déléguer, *v.tr.* (*a*) **déléguer ses pouvoirs/son autorité,** to delegate one's powers/one's authority (*b*) **déléguer une créance,** to assign a debt.

délivrance, *n.f.* delivery/issue (of patent, certificate, etc.).

délivrer, *v.tr.* to deliver (goods, etc.); to deliver/to issue (certificate, ticket, re-

ceipt); **délivrer un brevet à qn,** to grant a patent to s.o.

déloyal, *a.* unfair (practice, proceedings); **concurrence déloyale,** unfair competition.

demande, *n.f.* (*a*) request/application (de, for); **(faire une) demande d'argent/de crédits,** (to put in a) request for money/for funds; **faire une demande (d'emploi, etc.),** to apply for (a job, etc.); **faire une demande par écrit,** to write (off) for/to send for; **suite à votre demande,** as requested; **sur demande,** on application/on request; **(envoi d')échantillons sur demande,** samples (are sent) on request/on application; **argent remboursable sur demande,** loan payable at call; **chèque payable sur demande,** cheque payable on demand/at sight; *Journ:* **demandes d'emploi,** situations wanted (*b*) demand; *Ind: etc:* **construit/fabriqué sur demande,** made to customer's specifications/custom-built/custommade; **demande croissante,** increasing demand; **demande régulière,** steady demand; **évaluation de la demande,** demand assessment; *PolEc:* **l'offre et la demande,** supply and demand; **travailler à la demande,** to work to order (*c*) *Ins:* **demande d'indemnité,** claim.

demander, *v.tr.* **1.** to ask (for); **demander des dommages-intérêts,** to claim damages; **combien demandez-vous de l'heure?** how much do you charge per hour/an hour? **demander un emploi/un poste,** to apply for a job; **demandez notre catalogue,** write for/send for our catalogue **2.** to want/to need/to require; **article très demandé,** article in great demand; *Journ:* **on demande vendeuse,** sales assistant wanted/needed.

démarchage, *n.m.* door-to-door selling.

démarcher, *v.tr.* to canvass.

démarcheur, -euse, *n.* canvasser; door-to-door salesman/saleswoman.

démarque, *n.f.* marking down (of goods in sales).

démarquer, *v.tr.* to mark down (goods in sales).

démettre, 1. *v.tr.* **démettre qn de ses fonctions**, to remove s.o. from his post 2. *v.pr.* **se démettre**, to resign; **se démettre de ses fonctions**, to resign/to hand in one's notice.

demi-douzaine, *n.f.* half-dozen.

demi-gros, *n.m.inv.* **libre-service de demi-gros**, cash and carry.

demi-page, *n.f.* (*d'une annonce*) half-page (advertisement).

demi-pension, *n.f.* (*dans un hôtel*) half(-)board.

demi-produit, *n.m. Ind:* semi-manufactured product.

demi-salaire, *n.m.* half-pay/half-salary.

démission, *n.f.* resignation; **donner sa démission**, to tender/to hand in one's resignation.

démissionner, *v.i.* to resign (**de**, from).

demi-tarif, *n.m. & a.* **billet (à) demi-tarif**, half-price ticket; half fare.

démonétisation, *n.f.* demonetization; calling in/withdrawal from circulation (of coinage, etc.).

démonétiser, *v.tr.* to demonetize; to call in/to withdraw (coinage, etc.) from circulation.

démonstrateur, -trice, *n.* demonstrator.

démonstration, *n.f. Mkt:* demonstration (of an article on show or for sale); **appareil de démonstration**, demonstration model; **démonstration sans engagement**, (ask for) free demonstration; **salle de démonstration**, showroom.

dénationalisation, *n.f.* denationalization (of an industry, etc.).

dénationaliser, *v.tr.* to denationalize (an industry, etc.).

dénommer, *v.tr.* to name/to designate; *Ins:* **personne dénommée**, nominee (for life annuity); (*dans un contrat, etc.*) **ci-après dénommé . . .**, hereinafter referred to as . . . .

denrée, *n.f. usu. pl.* commodity; *esp.* foodstuff/produce; **denrées alimentaires**, food products/foodstuffs; **denrées du pays**, home produce; **denrées périssables**, perishable goods; *StExch:* **matières premières et denrées**, commodities.

dépareillé, *a.* odd/unmatched; **articles dépareillés**, oddments/job lot.

départ, *n.m.* (*a*) **courrier au départ**, outgoing mail (*b*) **départ d'un compte**, opening/starting date of an account; **prix départ usine**, price ex works; (*à une vente aux enchères*) **prix de départ**, upset price; **salaire/rémunération de départ**, starting salary; **valeur de départ**, initial value (*c*) **départ volontaire**, voluntary redundancy.

département, *n.m.* department; **département commercial**, sales department.

dépens, *n.m.pl.* (legal) costs; **être condamné aux dépens**, to be ordered to pay costs.

dépense, *n.f.* expenditure / expense / spending/outlay (of money); **compte des dépenses**, expense account; **dépenses courantes**, current expenditure; **dépenses diverses**, general/sundry expenses; **dépenses d'établissement/dépenses d'investissement/dépenses en immobilisations**, capital expenditure; **dépenses d'exploitation/de fonctionnement**, operating costs/working expenses; **dépenses publiques**, government expenditure; **pièce de dépenses**, cash expenditure note; **recettes et dépenses**, income and expenditure; **contrôler les dépenses**, to check expenditure; **faire des**

dépenses, to incur expenses; **faire trop de dépenses,** to overspend; **les dépenses excèdent les recettes,** expenditure exceeds income; **on ne regardait pas à la dépense,** no expense was spared.

dépenser, *v.tr.* to spend (money); **trop dépenser,** to overspend.

déplacement, *n.m.* (*a*) **frais de déplacement,** (*i*) travelling expenses (*ii*) removal expenses (*b*) **déplacement de l'offre et de la demande,** shift/swing in supply and demand.

déplafonnement, *n.m.* removal of the upper limit (of prices, etc.).

déplafonner, *v.tr.* to remove the upper limit of (prices, etc.).

dépliant, *n.m.* folder/brochure; leaflet.

déport, *n.m. StExch:* (*i*) backwardation (*ii*) premium (of exchange).

déporté, *a. StExch:* backwardation/backwardized (stock).

déposant, -ante, *n.* (*a*) depositor (of money in bank, etc.) (*b*) *Jur:* **(témoin) déposant,** witness who testifies.

déposer, *v.tr.* (*a*) to deposit (documents, etc.) (in a safe place); **déposer de l'argent à la banque,** to deposit money (at the bank)/to pay money into the bank (*b*) **déposer une demande de brevet,** to file an application for a patent; **modèle déposé,** registered design/pattern; **déposer une marque de fabrique,** to register a trade-mark; **marque déposée,** registered trade-mark (*c*) *Jur:* **déposer son bilan,** to file one's petition (in bankruptcy).

dépositaire, *n.m. &f.* (*a*) trustee; **dépositaire de valeurs,** holder of securities on trust (*b*) dealer/stockist; **(seul) dépositaire des produits de qn,** sole agent for s.o.'s products.

dépôt, *n.m.* **1.** (*a*) registration (of trade-mark); **effectuer/opérer le dépôt d'une marque (de fabrique),** to register a trade-mark (*b*) *Publ:* **dépôt légal,** legal deposit

2. (*a*) depositing; deposit (of money, etc.); **dépôt à échéance fixe,** fixed deposit; **dépôt à sept jours de préavis,** deposit at seven days' notice; **dépôt a terme,** short-term investment; **dépôt à vue,** demand deposit; **dépôt de garantie,** deposit of guarantee/security; **dépôt en coffre-fort,** safe-deposit; **dépôt en banque/dépôt bancaire,** bank deposit; **effectuer un dépôt de fonds à la banque,** to deposit/to lodge funds at a bank/with a bank (*b*) **banque de dépôt,** (deposit) bank; **bordereau de dépôt,** paying-in slip; **compte de dépôt,** cheque account; **livret de dépôt,** deposit book (*c*) **en dépôt,** on/in trust; **mettre (des documents, des valeurs) en dépôt dans une banque,** to deposit (documents, securities) with a bank; **marchandises en dépôt,** (*i*) *Cust:* goods in bond (*ii*) goods on sale or return **3.** warehouse/depot; **dépôt de marchandises,** warehouse/goods depot; **en dépôt chez . . .,** stocked by . . . **4.** stock.

dépouillement, *n.m.* **dépouillement d'un compte,** breaking down of an account; **dépouillement de la correspondance,** opening of the mail; **dépouillement d'un rapport,** examination/analysis of a report.

dépouiller, *v.tr.* **dépouiller un compte,** to break down an account; **dépouiller le courrier,** to open/to go through the mail; **dépouiller un rapport,** to examine/to analyse a report; **dépouiller des renseignements,** to process information.

dépréciation, *n.f.* (*a*) depreciation; fall/drop in value; **comptabilité de la dépréciation,** depreciation accounting; **dépréciation fonctionnelle,** obsolescence; **provisions pour dépréciation,** allowance(s) made for depreciation (*b*) wear and tear.

déprécier, 1. *v.tr.* (*a*) to depreciate (currency, gold, etc.) (*b*) to undervalue (goods, etc.) **2.** *v.pr.* **se déprécier,** (*de l'argent, etc.*) to depreciate/to fall in value.

déprédation, *n.f.* misappropriation/corrupt administration (of funds, etc.).

dépression, *n.f. StExch:* depression (of stock); **dépression du marché,** market depression; *PolEc:* **dépression économique,** economic depression/slump/recession.

déprimé, *a.* **marché déprimé,** depressed market.

dérivé, *a. & n.m.* **(produit) dérivé,** by-product.

dernier, *a.* (*a*) last; *StExch:* **derniers cours,** closing prices; **dernier paiement,** final payment; **dernier rappel,** final demand; **le plus offrant et le dernier enchérisseur,** the highest bidder (*b*) **voiture dernier modèle,** car of the latest design.

désaisonnalisé, *a.* seasonally adjusted.

désassortir, *v.tr.* **désassortir un marchand de qch.,** to buy all the stock of a shop(keeper).

description, *n.f.* description; **conforme à la description,** as represented; **description de brevet,** patent specification; **description de poste,** job description.

désemballage, *n.m.* unpacking/unwrapping (of goods).

désemballer, *v.tr.* to unpack/to unwrap/to undo (parcel, goods, etc.).

déséquilibre, *n.m.* **déséquilibre de la balance commerciale,** unfavourable/adverse trade balance; **déséquilibre financier,** financial imbalance/instability.

déshypothéquer, *v.tr.* to disencumber/to free (a property) from mortgage.

désignation, *n.f.* **désignation de marchandises,** description of goods.

désintéressement, *n.m.* buying out (of partner, etc.); satisfying/paying off (of creditor, etc.).

désintéresser, *v.tr.* to buy out (partner); to satisfy/to pay off (creditor); to reimburse (s.o.).

désinvestissement, *n.m.* disinvestment; **désinvestissement marginal,** marginal disinvestment.

dessin, *n.m.* (*a*) **dessin publicitaire,** publicity drawing (*b*) design/pattern; **dessin du produit,** product design; **dessin industriel,** design engineering.

destinataire, *n.m. & f.* addressee/recipient (of letter, etc.); consignee (of goods).

destination, *n.f.* destination; **marchandises à destination de la province et de l'étranger,** goods for consignment to the provinces and abroad; **navire à destination de Bordeaux,** ship bound for Bordeaux.

destiner, *v.tr.* **destiner une somme d'argent à un achat,** to allot/to assign a sum of money to a purchase; **marchandises destinées à l'exportation,** goods (intended) for export.

déstockage, *n.m.* destocking/reduction of stock.

désuet, *a.* **équipement désuet,** obsolete equipment.

désuétude, *n.f.* **désuétude calculée,** planned/built-in obsolescence.

détacher, *v.tr.* **détacher un coupon d'une action,** to detach a coupon from a bond; **le coupon de ces actions se détache le 1er août,** this stock goes ex-coupon on (the) 1st (of) August.

détail, *n.m.* **1.** (*a*) **pour de plus amples détails s'adresser à . . .,** for further particulars apply to . . .; **faire le détail d'un compte,** to itemize an account/to break down an invoice; **paiements dont détails ci-dessous,** payments as per details/as specified below (*b*) **détails techniques,** technical features/specifications **2.** retail; the retail trade; **le commerce en gros et au détail,** the wholesale and retail business/trade; **magasin de détail,** retail shop; **marchand au détail/marchand qui fait le détail,** retail dealer/retailer; **prix**

de détail, retail price; **vente au détail,** retail; **vendre au détail,** to retail.

détaillant, -ante, *n.* **(marchand) détaillant,** retailer/shopkeeper.

détaillé, *a.* **état détaillé de compte,** detailed/itemized statement of account.

détailler, *v.tr.* (*a*) to retail/to sell retail (*b*) to itemize (an account).

détaxe, *n.f.* (*a*) remission of tax/of duty; **détaxe postale,** refund on postage paid in error (*b*) decontrolling (of the price of sth.).

détaxer, *v.tr.* (*a*) to take the duty/the tax off (sth.) (*b*) **détaxer la viande,** to decontrol the price of meat.

détenir, *v.tr.* **détenir des titres,** to hold stock; **société détenue à 50%,** 50% owned company.

détenteur, -trice, *n.* (*a*) holder (of securities, etc.); **détenteur de titres,** shareholder/stockholder/scrip-holder (*b*) owner (of copyright, etc.).

détournement, *n.m.* misappropriation/ fraudulentmisuse/embezzlement; **détournement de fonds,** misappropriation of funds.

détourner, *v.tr.* to misappropriate/to embezzle (funds) (à, from).

dette, *n.f.* debt; **acquitter une dette,** to pay off a debt; **avoir des dettes,** to be in debt; **avoir pour 10 000 francs de dettes,** to be 10 000 francs in debt; **contracter/faire des dettes,** to run into debt; **dettes à court terme,** current liabilities; **dettes actives,** debts owed to us/assets; **dettes bancaires,** bank debts; **dettes compte,** book debts; **dette consolidée,** funded debt/ consolidated debt; **dette exigible,** debt due for (re)payment; **dette flottante/non consolidée,** floating debt/unfunded debt; **dettes passives,** debts owed by us/ liabilities; **dette privilégiée,** privileged debt; **dette véreuse,** doubtful debt; **la dette de l'État/la dette publique,** the National debt; **le Grand(-)livre de la dette publique,** the National Debt Register.

deuxième, *a. & n.* second; **deuxième de change,** second of exchange.

dévalorisation, *n.f.* (*a*) fall in value/loss of value (*b*) *Fin:* devaluation (of currency).

dévaloriser, 1. *v.tr. Fin:* to devalue (currency); **dévaloriser une monnaie de 10%,** to devalue a currency by 10% 2. *v.pr.* se **dévaloriser,** to fall in value/to depreciate.

dévaluation, *n.f. Fin: PolEc:* devaluation.

dévaluer, *v.tr.* to devalue (currency).

devanture, *n.f.* (*a*) shop front/shop window (*b*) goods in the window.

développement, *n.m.* development; expansion; **développement d'un commerce/d'une entreprise,** growth/expansion of a business; **développement du produit,** product development; **développement des ventes,** sales expansion; **programme de développement,** development programme; **zone de développement,** development area.

devis, *n.m.* estimate (of work to be done, etc.); quotation; **devis descriptif,** specification; **établir un devis estimatif,** to draw up an estimate (of quantities and costs); **le devis des réparations s'élève à trois mille francs,** the estimate/the quotation for the repairs comes to three thousand francs.

devise, *n.f. Fin:* currency; **le yen est la devise japonaise,** the yen is the Japanese currency; **cours officiel des devises,** official exchange rate; **devise convertible,** convertible currency; **devises étrangères,** foreign currency; **devise faible,** soft currency; **devise forte,** hard currency; **effet en devise(s),** bill in foreign currency; **marché des devises (étrangères),** foreign exchange market.

devoir, *v.tr.* **devoir qch. à qn,** to owe s.o. sth.; **il me doit mille francs,** he owes me a thousand francs; **la somme qui m'est due,**

the amount owing to me/owed to me/due to me.

diagramme, *n.m.* diagram; chart; graph; **diagramme de circulation,** flow (process) chart; **diagramme en bâtons,** bar chart/bar diagram.

dictaphone, *n.m. Rtm:* Dictaphone.

dictée, *n.f.* dictation; **écrire qch. sous la dictée de qn,** to take down a dictation.

dicter, *v.tr.* to dictate; **dicter une lettre à sa secrétaire,** to dictate a letter to one's secretary; **machine à dicter,** dictating machine.

différé, *a.* deferred (payment, etc.); **crédit différé,** deferred credit.

différentiel, *a.* differential; **droits différentiels,** differential duties; **tarif différentiel,** differential tariff.

différer, *v.tr.* to defer/to postpone/to put off/to hold over (payment, etc.); **différer l'échéance d'un effet,** to let a bill lie over.

diffuser, *v.tr.* to distribute/to circulate (books, newspapers, etc.).

diffusion, *n.f.* distribution/circulation (of books, newspapers, etc.).

dilapider, *v.tr.* to waste/to squander (public money, etc.); to misappropriate (trust funds, etc.).

diminuer, *v.tr.* **montant net diminué du prix de vente,** net amount less purchase price.

diminution, *n.f.* reduction/decrease/lowering (of price, etc.); cutting down (of expenses); **diminution d'impôts,** (*i*) lowering of taxation (*ii*) drop in yield of taxation; **diminution de prix/sur le prix,** reduction in price; **faire une diminution sur un compte,** to allow a rebate on an account.

direct, *a.* direct; **impôts directs,** direct taxes; **publicité directe,** direct advertising/direct mail; **vente directe,** direct selling.

directeur, -trice, 1. *n.* director; *NAm:*

officer; executive manager/manageress; head (of industrial concern, etc.); **directeur adjoint,** deputy manager; **directeur commercial/directeur des ventes,** sales manager/marketing manager; **directeur général,** general manager/managing director; **président-directeur général (P-DG),** chairman and managing director/*NAm:* chief executive officer (CEO); **directeur d'hôtel,** hotel manager; **directeur de la publicité,** advertising/publicity manager; *Bank:* **directeur de banque,** bank manager; **directeur de succursale,** branch manager; **directeur du personnel,** personnel manager; **directeur régional,** district manager **2.** *a.* **prix directeur,** price leader.

direction, *n.f.* (*a*) direction; management (of company, etc.); **conseil en direction,** management consultant; **direction commerciale/des ventes,** sales management; **direction générale,** general management/top management; **direction par objectifs (DPO),** management by objectives (MBO); **équipe de direction,** management team; **haute direction,** top management; **secrétaire de direction,** director's secretary/private secretary (*b*) (*i*) board (of directors) (*ii*) administrative staff; **la direction,** the management (*c*) (*i*) offices (of the board); director's/manager's office (*ii*) head office (of firm, etc.); **direction régionale,** district/regional headquarters.

directorial, *a.* **bureau directorial,** manager's/director's office.

dirigé, *a.* controlled/planned; **économie dirigée,** planned economy; *Fin:* **monnaie dirigée,** managed/controlled currency.

dirigeant, *n.m.* executive; director; manager; **les dirigeants (d'une société),** (the) management.

diriger, *v.tr.* to manage; to run (business, etc.); **diriger la production,** to control production.

dirigisme, *n.m.* (*a*) *PolEc:* planning; **dirigisme économique,** economic planning (*b*) controlled finance.

dirigiste, *n.m. & f. PolEc:* advocate/ exponent of planned economy.

disant, *n.m.* **le moins disant,** the lowest bidder.

discontinu, *a.* discontinuous; **production discontinue,** production in batches.

discount, *n.m.* discount; **(magasin) discount,** discount store.

dispache, *n.f. MIns:* average adjustment/ statement.

dispacheur, *n.m. MIns:* average stater/ average adjuster.

dispendieux, *a.* expensive/costly (product, etc.).

disponibilité, *n.f.* (*a*) *pl.* liquid assets; **disponibilités monétaires,** money supply (*b*) **disponibilités du stock,** items available in stock.

disponible, 1. *a.* available; disposable; **actif disponible/valeurs disponibles,** available assets/liquid assets/current assets; **capital disponible,** spare capital; **encaisse disponible,** cash in hand; **fonds disponibles,** available funds; **revenus disponibles,** disposable income **2.** *n.m.* **le disponible,** (*i*) items available in stock (*ii*) *Fin:* available assets/liquid assets.

disposer, *v.tr.* (*a*) **disposer de capitaux importants,** to have a large capital at one's disposal (*b*) **disposer sur qn,** to draw on s.o.

disposition, *n.f.* **disposition(s) du marché/de la Bourse,** tone of the market.

dissimulation, *n.f. Jur:* **dissimulation d'actif,** (fraudulent) concealment of assets.

dissolution, *n.f. Jur:* termination (of contract); winding up (of company).

distraire, *v.tr.* to misappropriate (funds, supplies, etc.).

distribuable, *a.* **bénéfices distribuables,** distributable profits.

distribuer, *v.tr.* to distribute; **bénéfices non distribués,** undistributed profit(s)/ retained earnings.

distributeur, *n.m.* (*a*) distributor; **distributeur agréé,** authorized stockist/ distributor (*b*) **distributeur automatique,** vending machine; **distributeur automatique (de billets),** (*i*) *Bank:* cash dispenser/*NAm:* automatic teller (*ii*) *Rail:* etc. ticket machine.

distribution, *n.f.* distribution; allotment (of shares); *Post:* delivery; **distribution de dividendes (aux actionnaires),** distribution of dividends (to the shareholders); **circuit de distribution,** distribution channel; **réseau de distribution,** distribution network.

divers, 1. *a.pl.* **articles divers,** sundry articles/sundries; **frais divers,** sundry expenses/sundries **2.** *n.m.pl.* sundries.

diversification, *n.f.* diversification; **diversification industrielle,** diversification/ lateral integration of industry; **diversification des produits,** product diversification.

diversifier, *v.tr.* **diversifier sa production,** to diversify production.

dividende, *n.m.* dividend; **avec dividende,** cum div(idend)/*NAm:* dividend on; **sans dividende/ex-dividende,** ex div(idend)/*NAm:* dividend off; **acompte de dividende/acompte sur dividende/ dividende intérimaire,** interim dividend; **chèque-dividende,** dividend warrant; **dividende cumulatif,** cumulative dividend; **dividende d'actions,** dividend on shares; **dividende fictif,** sham dividend; **dividende privilégié,** preference dividend; **solde de dividende,** final dividend; **politique de dividendes,** dividend policy; **toucher un dividende,** to draw a dividend.

division, *n.f.* division; *Adm:* department/branch; **gestion de division,** divisional management.

divisionnaire, *a.* **monnaie divisionnaire,** fractional/divisionary coins.

dock, *n.m.* **1.** *Nau:* (*a*) dock (*b*) dock(s)/dockyard; **droits de dock,** dock dues **2.** (dock) warehouse; bonded warehouse.

docker, *n.m.* docker; stevedore; *NAm:* longshoreman.

document, *n.m.* document.

documentaire, *a.* documentary; **crédit documentaire,** documentary credit; **traite documentaire,** draft with documents attached; documentary bill of exchange.

documentation, *n.f.* (*a*) documentation (*b*) documents; information; literature.

documenter, *v.tr.* to document (material); **rapport bien documenté,** well-supported report/statement.

doit, *n.m.* debit/liability; **doit d'un compte,** debit (side) of an account; **doit et avoir,** debit and credit/debtor and creditor.

dollar, *n.m.* dollar; **dollar des États-Unis/dollar américain,** US dollar; **billet de 5 dollars,** 5 dollar note/*NAm:* 5 dollar bill; **prime sur le dollar,** dollar premium; **zone dollar,** dollar area.

domaine, *n.m.* **ouvrage tombé dans le domaine public,** work on which the copyright has lapsed/run out; work out of copyright; **invention tombée dans le domaine public,** invention the patent of which has expired.

domicile, *n.m.* (*a*) domicile; permanent residence (*b*) **prise de colis à domicile,** collection of parcels; **notre épicier livre à domicile,** our grocer has a delivery service.

domiciliataire, *n.m.* paying agent (of bill of exchange).

domiciliation, *n.f.* domiciliation (of bill of exchange).

domicilier, *v.tr.* (*a*) to domicile (bill of exchange, etc.) (*b*) **être domicilié à Londres,** to be domiciled in London.

dommage, *n.m. usu. pl.* (*a*) damage (to goods, property, etc.); **réparer les dommages,** to repair/to make good the damage; to make up the losses (*b*) *Jur:* **dommages et intérêts = dommages-intérêts.**

dommages-intérêts, *n.m. pl. Jur:* damages; **poursuivre qn en dommages-intérêts,** to sue s.o. for damages/to bring an action for damages against s.o.; **se faire accorder/obtenir des dommages-intérêts,** to be awarded damages.

données, *n.f.pl. Cmptr: Stat:* **banque de données,** data bank; **collecte de données,** data acquisition; **données brutes,** raw data; **rassemblement de données (statistiques),** data gathering; **recherche/récupération de données,** information retrieval.

donneur, -euse, *n.* (*a*) *Fin:* **donneur d'aval,** guarantor/backer of bill; **donneur de caution,** guarantor; **donneur d'ordre,** principal (*b*) *Fin:* seller; *StExch:* **donneur d'ordres,** client (of a broker).

dormant, *a.* (*d'un capital*) unproductive/lying idle.

dos, *n.m.* **signer au dos d'un chèque,** to endorse a cheque/to sign (on the back of) a cheque.

dossier, *n.m.* dossier; file; **dossier de candidature,** application; application form.

dotation, *n.f.* **dotation au compte de provisions,** appropriation to the reserve.

douane, *n.f.* customs; **bureaux de douane,** customs (house); **déclaration de/en douane,** customs declaration; bill of entry; **(droits de) douane,** customs duties/customs dues; **exempt de douane/(importé) en franchise de douane,** duty-free; **préposé(e) à la douane,** customs officer/employee; **soumis aux droits de douane,** dutiable; **visite de la douane,** customs examination/formalities; **acquitter la douane,** to pay the (customs) duty (on sth.); **passer des marchandises en douane,** to clear goods; **passer par la**

douane, to pass/to get through (the) customs; **procéder aux formalités de la douane,** to effect customs clearance.

douanier, 1. *a.* (pertaining to the) customs; **barrières douanières,** tariff walls; **poste douanier,** (frontier) customs (post); **tarif douanier,** customs tariff; **union douanière,** customs union; **visite douanière,** customs examination/customs formalities **2.** *n.m.* customs officer.

double, 1. *a.* double (quantity, etc.); *Book-k:* **article qui fait double emploi,** duplicated item; **comptabilité en partie double,** double-entry book-keeping; **quittance double,** receipt in duplicate **2.** *n.m.* (*a*) double; **je l'ai vendu pour le double de ce qu'il m'a coûté,** I sold it for twice as much as it cost me/for double the price/for twice the price (*b*) duplicate; carbon copy; **facture en double,** invoice in duplicate.

douzaine, *n.f.* dozen; **une douzaine d'oeufs,** a dozen eggs; **à la douzaine,** by the dozen; **trente francs la douzaine,** thirty francs a dozen/per dozen.

drainage, *n.m.* drain (of money, capital).

drainer, *v.tr.* to tap (capital, etc.); to draw/to attract (trade, workers, etc.).

drawback, *n.m. Cust:* drawback.

dresser, *v.tr.* to prepare/to draw up (plan, report, contract, bill, etc.); to make out (invoice, etc.); to make out/to draw up (list).

droit, *n.m.* **1.** (*a*) *Publ:* right; **exemplaires hors droits,** royalty-free copies; **tous droits réservés,** all rights reserved; copyright reserved (*b*) fair claim; **ce qui revient de droit,** entitlement; **être dans son droit,** to be within one's rights; **faire droit à une réclamation,** to allow a claim; to satisfy a claim; **faire valoir ses droits,** to establish one's rights; **renoncer à ses droits,** to waive one's rights (*c*) *Jur:* **les ayant droit,** rightful claimants; beneficiaries; **à qui de droit,** to whom it may concern **2.** (*a*) charge/fee/due; **droits d'auteur,** royalties (*b*) *Cust:* **droit de douane,** duty; **droit d'entrée,** import duty; **marchandises assujetties aux droits,** dutiable goods; **marchandises exemptes/en franchise de droits,** duty-free goods; **droits de port,** harbour dues (*c*) *Jur:* **droits de succession,** death duties (*d*) **droit d'inscription,** registration fee; *Adm:* **droit de timbre,** stamp duty **3.** law; **droit civil,** civil law; **droit commercial,** commercial law; **droit maritime,** maritime law; **droit des obligations =** contract law; **droit des sociétés,** company law.

dû, 1. *a.* (*a*) owing; **en port dû,** carriage forward (*b*) proper; **contrat rédigé en bonne et due forme,** contract drawn up in due form/formal contract **2.** *n.m.* due(s); **payer son dû,** to pay the amount owed/to pay one's dues.

ducroire, *n.m.* (*a*) del credere (commission)/guarantee commission (*b*) del-credere agent.

dûment, *adv.* duly/in due form; **dûment expédié/reçu,** duly dispatched/received; **représentant dûment accrédité,** duly authorized representative.

dumping, *n.m.* dumping; **faire du dumping,** to dump (goods).

duplicata, *n.m.inv.* duplicate (copy); **duplicata de reçu,** duplicate receipt; **reçu en duplicata,** receipt in duplicate.

duplicateur, *n.m.* duplicator (of circulars, etc.)/duplicating machine; copier.

durée, *n.f.* duration; **durée d'un bail,** duration/term of a lease; **durée (utile) de vie d'un produit,** product life expectancy/shelf-life.

E

écart, *n.m.* (*a*) discrepancy/divergence/ disparity/gap/variance; **analyse des écarts,** variance analysis; **écart de cent francs entre deux comptes,** discrepancy of a hundred francs between two accounts; **écart budgétaire,** budgetary variance; **écart des bénéfices,** profit gap; **écart des coûts,** cost variance; **écart déflationniste,** deflationary gap; **écart inflationniste,** inflationary gap (*b*) **écart de prix,** price differential; **écarts de salaire,** wage differentials.

échange, *n.m.* (*a*) exchange; **échange d'actions,** exchange of shares; **valeur d'échange,** exchange value (*b*) barter trading.

échangeable, *a.* exchangeable (**contre, for**).

échanger, *v.tr.* (*a*) to exchange; **on n'échange pas les articles achetés,** no goods exchanged (*b*) to barter.

échangiste, *n.m. Jur:* exchanger.

échantillon, *n.m.* sample (of cloth, etc.); **conforme à l'échantillon,** up to sample; **échantillon gratuit,** free sample; **échantillon type,** representative sample; **échantillon représentatif,** true/fair sample; **paquet échantillon,** sample packet; *Post:* **échantillons sans valeur,** samples of no (commercial) value.

échantillonnage, *n.m.* **1.** (*a*) making up of samples (*b*) range of samples (in a salesman's suitcase) **2.** verifying/checking against the samples.

échantillonner, *v.tr.* **1.** to prepare patterns/samples of (sth.) **2.** to verify/to check (articles) by the samples.

échappatoire, *a.* **clause échappatoire,** escape clause.

échéance, *n.f.* (*a*) **dépôt à échéance fixe,** fixed deposit; **échéance commune,** equation of payment (of bill of exchange); **échéance moyenne,** average due date; **effet à courte échéance,** short-dated/ short-term bill; **effet à longue échéance,** long-dated/long-term bill; **emprunter à courte échéance,** to borrow short; **prêter à longue échéance,** to lend long; **à trois mois d'échéance,** at three months' date/ three months after date; **faire face à une échéance,** to meet a bill; **il n'a pas pu faire face à l'échéance,** he couldn't meet his end of (the) month payments; **l'intérêt n'a pas été payé à l'échéance,** the interest is overdue; **payable à l'échéance,** payable at maturity; **venir à échéance,** to fall due/to mature (*b*) expiration (of tenancy, etc.).

échéancier, *n.m. Fin:* bills-receivable book/bills-payable book; bill book/bill diary.

échéant, *a. Fin:* falling due.

échelle, *n.f.* (*a*) scale; **économies de grande échelle,** large-scale economies (*b*) **échelle mobile,** (*i*) sliding scale (of prices, of salaries, etc.) (*ii*) escalator clause; **échelle des prix,** price range; **échelle des salaires,** salary scale.

échelonnement, *n.m.* (*a*) spreading out (of payments) (*b*) staggering (of holidays).

échelonner, *v.tr.* (*a*) to spread out (payments); **versements échelonnés sur dix ans,** instalments spread over ten years (*b*) to stagger; **congés échelonnés,** staggered holidays.

échoir, *v.i.* (*a*) *Fin:* to fall due/to become due/to mature; **billets échus,** bills (over)due; **capitaux dont la date de paiement est échue,** matured capital; **intérêts échus,** outstanding interest; **intérêts à échoir,** interest falling due (b) (d'un bail) to expire.

économat, n.m. (a) staff shop (provided by employer) (b) bursar's office.

économe, n.m. bursar.

économie, n.f. **1.** (a) economy; management; **société d'économie mixte,** semi-public company (b) **l'économie de la France,** (i) the French economy (ii) the French economic system; **économie active,** buoyant economy; **économie dirigée,** controlled economy; **économie mixte,** mixed economy; **économie planifiée,** planned economy; **économie politique,** political economy; **économie stagnante,** run-down economy **2.** economy/saving; **économie de main d'œuvre,** labour-saving; **vous faites une économie de 20%,** you make a saving of 20% **3.** pl. savings; **faire des économies,** to save (money); to cut down (on) expenditure; to save (up); **politique d'économies,** policy of retrenchment.

économique, a. **1.** (a) economic; **conjoncture économique,** economic situation/trend; **crise économique,** economic crisis; **croissance économique,** economic growth; **reprise économique,** economic recovery; **sciences économiques,** economics; **série économique,** economic batch; **série economique de production quantité économique de fabrication,** economic manufacturing quantity; **vie économique (d'un produit),** economic life (of a product) (b) **Communauté économique européenne (CEE),** European Economic Community (EEC) **2.** economical/inexpensive; **une voiture économique,** an economical car to run; Av: **voyager en classe économique,** to travel economy class.

économiquement, adv. (a) economically; **les économiquement faibles,** the lower-income groups/(people in) the lower-income bracket (b) inexpensively.

économiser, v.tr. to economize/to save (money, time); **il faut économiser sur qch.,** we must economize/cut down on sth.

économiste, n.m. & f. (political) economist; **économiste d'entreprise,** business economist.

écoulé, a. (a) of last month/ult(imo); **votre lettre du 25 écoulé,** your letter of 25th ult(imo); **payable fin écoulé,** due at the end of last month (b) **l'exercice écoulé,** the last financial year; the year under review.

écoulement, n.m. sale; selling; **marchandises d'écoulement facile,** goods which sell well/that have a ready sale.

écouler, 1. v.tr. to sell (off)/to dispose of/to get rid of (goods, etc.); **écouler (qch.) à bas prix,** to sell (sth.) off at a low price/cheaply **2.** v.pr. **notre stock s'écoule rapidement,** our stock is (i) selling fast (ii) running low.

écrire, v.tr. (a) to write; **écrire à qn,** to write to s.o.; **écrire une lettre à qn,** to write s.o. a letter (b) **écrire une lettre à la machine,** to type a letter; **écrit à la machine,** typewritten/typed; **machine à écrire,** typewriter (c) to write (sth.) down; **écrire l'adresse de qn,** to write down s.o.'s address (d) **écrire la comptabilité,** to write up the books.

écrit, 1. n.m. (a) writing; **consigner/coucher qch. par écrit,** to put sth. down in writing; **convention par écrit,** agreement in writing/written agreement (b) (written) document; **signer un écrit,** to sign a document **2.** a. written; **convention/déclaration écrite,** written agreement/statement.

écriture, n.f. **1.** handwriting **2.** (a) pl. (legal, commercial) papers/documents/records (b) **commis/employé aux écritures,** book-keeper/(invoicing) clerk; **tenir les écritures,** to keep the accounts/

the books (c) entry/item; **arrêter les écritures,** to close the accounts; **écritures en partie double,** double-entry book-keeping; **passer une écriture,** to make an entry (in the books).

éditeur, *n.m.* **1.** (book) publisher **2.** *Cmptr:* **éditeur de textes,** word processor.

édition, *n.f.* (book) publishing.

effectif, 1. *a.* effective; *Fin:* **circulation effective,** active circulation; **monnaie effective,** effective money; **valeur effective,** real value **2.** *n.m.* (*a*) **effectif budgétaire,** budgetary strength/*NAm:* authorized strength; **crise d'effectifs,** shortage of manpower; **gestion des effectifs,** manpower management (*b*) *Ind:* stock (of material, etc.) (*c*) **effectif de série économique,** economic batch quantity.

effectuer, *v.tr.* to effect/to carry out; to effect/to make (payment); **paiements effectués par la caisse,** cash payments.

effet, *n.m.* **1.** effect/result; **les effets de la crise économique,** the effects of the economic crisis **2.** (*a*) **facture avec effet rétroactif,** backdated bill; **nul et sans effet,** null and void; **prendre effet,** to become operative (*b*) *Ins:* commencement (of policy) **3.** **effet de commerce,** bill (of exchange)/negotiable instrument; **effets à payer,** bills payable; **effets à recevoir,** bills receivable; **effet à vue,** sight draft; **effet de complaisance,** accommodation bill; *Fin:* **effets au porteur,** bearer securities; **effets nominatifs,** registered stock; **effets publics,** government stock/securities **4.** *pl.* **effets mobiliers,** personal effects.

efficace, *a.* effective; efficient; **direction efficace,** effective management.

efficacement, *adv.* effectively/efficiently.

efficacité, *n.f.* effectiveness; efficiency; **efficacité économique,** economic efficiency; **efficacité de la direction,** managerial effectiveness; **efficacité publicitaire,** advertising effectiveness.

efficient, *a.* efficient/effective.

effondrement, *n.m.* *StExch:* **effondrement des cours,** slump in prices/collapse of prices; **l'effondrement du dollar,** the collapse of the dollar.

effondrer (s'), *v.pr.* (*des cours, etc.*) to slump/to collapse.

effritement, *n.m.* *StExch:* **effritement des cours,** crumbling of prices.

effriter (s'), *v.pr.* *StExch:* (*des cours, etc.*) to crumble.

égal, *a.* equal (à, to).

égalité, *n.f.* equality; **principe d'égalité des salaires,** principle of equal pay.

élaborer, *v.tr.* **élaborer un plan,** to elaborate/to work out/to think out/to prepare/to formulate/to draw up a plan.

élasticité, *n.f.* *PolEc:* **l'élasticité de l'offre et de la demande,** the elasticity of supply and demand.

élastique, *a.* *PolEc:* **offre/demande élastique,** elastic supply/demand.

électronique, 1. *a.* electronic; **calculateur électronique,** electronic computer; **industrie électronique,** electronics industry **2.** *n.f.* electronics.

élément, *n.m.* component/constituent (of sth.); factor; **élément du prix de revient,** cost factor; **élément d'un compte,** item of an account.

élévation, *n.f.* rise; **élévation des prix,** rise in prices/price rise/escalation (of prices).

élevé, *a.* **devise à change élevé,** hard currency; **les dépenses sont élevées,** expenditure is running high; **(à des) prix élevés,** (at) high prices; **taux d'intérêt élevé,** high interest rate.

élever, 1. *v.tr.* to raise (prices); **élever qn à un rang supérieur,** to promote s.o. **2.** *v.pr.* (*a*) **chaque mois les prix s'élèvent un peu,** prices are going up a little every month (*b*) **le compte s'élève à mille**

francs, the bill comes to/amounts to a thousand francs.

émargement, *n.m.* receipting/initialling/ signing (of account, etc.) in the margin; **feuille/liste d'émargement,** payroll.

émarger, *v.tr.* (*a*) *Adm: etc:* **émarger un compte,** to receipt/to initial an account (in the margin) (*b*) to draw one's salary; **émarger au budget,** to be on the payroll.

emballage, *n.m.* (*a*) packing/packaging/ wrapping (of parcels, goods, etc.) (*b*) packing department (*c*) container/pack/ packing cases/crates; **l'emballage est consigné,** there is a deposit on the container; **emballage géant,** giant pack; **emballage sous film rétractable,** shrink-wrap(ped) pack; **emballage perdu,** no-deposit/non-returnable container; disposable/throw-away container; **emballage transparent,** blister pack (*d*) **frais de port et d'emballage,** postage and packing; **poids net à l'emballage,** net weight when packed.

emballage-bulle, *n.m.* bubble pack/ blister pack.

emballer, *v.tr.* to pack (goods, etc.); to wrap up (article in paper, etc.).

embarcadère, *n.m. Nau:* landing stage; wharf/quay; loading dock.

embargo, *n.m. Nau:* embargo; **lever l'embargo,** to raise the embargo; **mettre l'embargo (sur un navire),** to lay an embargo (on a ship)/to place (a ship) under (an) embargo; **mettre un embargo sur l'importation de qch.,** to put an embargo on the import(ation) of sth.

embarquement, *n.m.* (*a*) *Nau:* embarkation (of passengers); shipment/shipping (of goods); **port d'embarquement,** port of embarkation (*b*) *Rail: Av:* loading/ putting (goods) into (a train, a plane); **quai d'embarquement,** loading platform (for goods) (*c*) boarding; **heure d'embarquement,** boarding time.

embarquer, 1. *v.tr.* (*a*) *Nau:* to embark (passengers); to ship (goods)/to take (goods) aboard (*b*) to load up; to put (goods) into/onto (a lorry, train, plane, etc.); **poids net embarqué,** loaded net weight **2.** *v.pr.* **s'embarquer,** to go aboard/to go on board/to board (a ship, a train, a plane, etc.).

embarras, *n.m.* difficulty/trouble; **des embarras d'argent,** financial difficulties.

embauchage, *n.m.* taking on/engaging/ *NAm:* hiring (of workers).

embauche, *n.f.* **1.** = **embauchage 2.** *F:* job; **chercher de l'embauche,** to look for a job.

embaucher, *v.tr.* to take on/to engage/ *NAm:* to hire (staff, workers).

emboîtage, *n.m. Publ:* box/casing.

émetteur, -trice, 1. *n. Fin: etc:* issuer (of banknotes, shares, etc.) **2.** *a.* issuing; **banque émettrice,** issuing bank.

émettre, *v.tr.* to issue (banknotes, shares, cheques, etc.); **émettre un emprunt,** to issue/to float a loan; **capital émis,** issued capital; **le chèque a été émis le 24 mars,** the cheque is dated 24th March.

émission, *n.f. Fin: etc:* (*i*) issue (*ii*) issuing (of banknotes, shares, etc.); (*i*) issue (*ii*) floating (of loan); **prix d'émission,** issue price; **banque d'émission,** issuing bank; **émission de timbres-poste,** issue of postage stamps.

emmagasinage, *n.m.* **emmagasinement,** *n.m.* (*a*) (*i*) storage (*ii*) storing/ warehousing (of goods) (*b*) storage (charges)/warehouse charges.

emmagasiner, *v.tr.* to store/to warehouse (goods).

émoluments, *n.m.pl.* fee / salary / pay / emoluments.

empaquetage, *n.m.* **1.** packing (of goods, etc.); doing up (of goods) into parcels; **empaquetage automatique,** automatic packaging; **poids net à l'empaquetage, 250 g,** net weight when packed, 250 g **2.** packing (material).

empaqueter, *v.tr.* to package; to pack (sth.) up/to make (sth.) into a parcel.

emphytéose, *n.f. Jur:* long lease (18 to 99 years).

emphytéote, *n.m. & f. Jur:* holder of a long lease.

emphytéotique, *a. Jur:* **bail emphytéotique,** long lease (18 to 99 years)/ = leasehold; building lease; **redevance emphytéotique,** ground rent.

emplette, *n.f.* (*a*) shopping; **faire ses emplettes,** to do one's shopping (*b*) (*objet acheté*) purchase.

emploi, *n.m.* **1.** (*a*) **mode d'emploi,** directions for use (*b*) **emploi du temps,** timetable/schedule (of work) (*c*) *Book-k:* **double emploi,** duplication (of entry); **faire double emploi avec . . .,** to duplicate with . . . **2.** employment/occupation/ post/job; **chercher un emploi,** to look for a job; **créer de nouveaux emplois,** to create new jobs; **la crise de l'emploi,** the unemployment crisis; **emploi à temps complet/à plein temps,** full-time employment/job; **emploi à temps partiel,** part-time employment/job; **être sans emploi,** to be unemployed; *PolEc:* **planification de l'emploi,** manpower planning; **plein emploi,** full employment; **sécurité de l'emploi,** job security; *Journ:* **demandes d'emploi,** situations wanted; **offres d'emploi,** situations vacant.

employé, -ée, *n.* employee/member of (the) staff; **employé de magasin,** sales assistant/shop assistant/*NAm:* clerk; **employé de banque,** bank clerk; **employé de bureau,** office worker; **employé au classement,** filing clerk; **employé aux écritures,** book-keeper; **employé de l'expédition,** dispatch clerk; shipping clerk; **employé d'administration,** government employee/civil servant; **employé de la régie,** customs and excise officer.

employer, *v.tr.* **1.** *Book-k:* **employer une somme en recette,** to put/to enter an amount in the receipts **2.** to employ (workers, etc.); **employer qn comme secrétaire,** to employ s.o. as secretary.

employeur, -euse, *n.* employer.

emporter, *v.tr.* to take away; **plats (cuisinés) à emporter,** food to take away/take away food.

empressé, *a. Corr:* **veuillez agréer mes salutations empressées,** (I remain) yours faithfully.

emprunt, *n.m.* **1.** borrowing; **capital d'emprunt,** borrowed capital; **faire un emprunt à qn,** to borrow money from s.o.; **j'ai fait un emprunt de 2000F à la banque,** I borrowed 2000F from the bank **2.** loan; **emprunt à 8%,** loan (bearing interest) at 8%; **emprunt consolidé,** consolidated loan; **emprunt à découvert,** unsecured loan; **emprunt d'État,** government loan; **emprunt forcé,** forced loan; **emprunt garanti,** secured loan; **emprunt indexé,** indexed loan; **emprunt obligataire,** debenture loan; bond issue; **emprunt or,** gold loan; **emprunt perpétuel,** perpetual loan; **emprunt personnel,** personal loan; **emprunt remboursable sur demande,** call loan/loan repayable on demand; **emprunt à terme,** loan at notice; **emprunt à court terme,** short term loan; **emprunt à long terme,** long term loan; **amortir un emprunt,** to redeem/to repay a loan; **contracter un emprunt,** to raise a loan; **couvrir un emprunt,** to cover a loan/ to subscribe to a loan; **émettre un emprunt/lancer un emprunt,** to issue/to float a loan; **placer un emprunt,** to place a loan; **procéder à un nouvel emprunt,** to make a new issue of capital/a new loan issue; **rembourser un emprunt,** to repay/to redeem a loan.

emprunter, *v.tr.* to borrow; **emprunter (de l'argent) à qn,** to borrow (money) from s.o.; **la société a dû emprunter pour s'acquitter de ses dettes,** the company had to borrow to pay off its debts; **emprunter (de l'argent) sur titres,** to borrow (money) on securities; **emprunter à intérêt,** to borrow at interest.

emprunteur, -euse, 1. *n.* borrower **2.** *a.* borrowing (corporation, etc.).

encadrement, *n.m.* (*a*) *Ind: Adm:* management; **personnel d'encadrement,** managerial staff (*b*) **encadrement du crédit,** credit squeeze/credit ceilings/credit control(s).

encaissable, *a.* *Fin:* (en)cashable/collectable (bill); **ce chèque est encaissable à la banque,** this cheque can be cashed at the bank.

encaissage, *n.m.* boxing/casing/packing (of goods).

encaisse, *n.f.* cash (in hand); cash balance; **encaisse d'un magasin,** money in the till/takings; **encaisse or et argent de la Banque de France,** gold and silver reserves/holdings of the Bank of France; **encaisse métallique,** gold and silver reserves; bullion; *Bank:* **pas d'encaisse,** no funds.

encaissement, *n.m.* *Fin:* cashing (of cheque); receipt/collection (of money or bills).

encaisser, *v.tr.* to cash; to receive/to collect (money, bill); **encaisser un chèque,** to cash a cheque.

encaisseur, 1. *n.m.* collector/receiver (of bill, cheque, money, etc.); payee (of cheque, etc.); (bank) cashier **2.** *a.* collecting (banker, etc.).

encan, *n.m.* (public) auction; **mettre qch. à l'encan,** to put sth. up for auction; **vendre qch. à l'encan,** to auction sth./to sell sth. by auction.

enchère, *n.f.* bid(ding); **couvrir une enchère,** to make a higher bid/*F:* to up the bidding; **l'enchère a monté jusqu'à deux cents francs,** the bidding rose to two hundred francs; **faire une enchère de cent francs,** to bid another hundred francs; **mettre qch. aux enchères,** to put sth. up to/for auction; **mettre une enchère,** to make a bid (on sth); **vente aux enchères,** (sale by) auction/auction sale.

enchérir, *v.i.* to make a higher bid;

enchérir de dix francs, to bid another ten francs; **enchérir sur qn,** to outbid s.o.

enchérisseur, -euse, *n.* bidder; **vendre au plus offrant et dernier enchérisseur,** to sell to the highest bidder.

encombrement, *n.m.* glut (of goods on the market).

encombrer, *v.tr.* **encombrer le marché,** to glut/to overstock the market.

encourir, *v.tr.* **encourir des frais,** to incur expenses.

en-cours, *n.m.* **1.** *Bank:* total of the bills (remitted by the customer to the bank) outstanding at any one time; **en-cours de crédit,** outstanding credits; **l'en-cours de la dette,** the outstanding debt **2.** *Ind:* **en-cours de fabrication,** material undergoing processing; **en-cours de route,** material/stock awaiting transfer (to another department).

endetté, *a.* in debt.

endettement, *n.m.* (*a*) running into debt (*b*) **ratio d'endettement,** gearing; **diminution/réduction du ratio d'endettement,** degearing.

endetter, 1. *v.tr.* **l'achat de sa maison l'a endetté,** the purchase of his house got him into debt **2.** *v.pr.* **s'endetter,** to get/to run into debt; to run up bills.

endos, *n.m.* endorsement (on bill, cheque); **endos en blanc,** blank endorsement.

endossataire, *n.m. & f.* endorsee.

endossement, *n.m.* (*a*) endorsing (*b*) endorsement (on bill, cheque); **endossement en blanc,** blank endorsement.

endosser, *v.tr.* to endorse (cheque, bill, etc.); to back (bill).

endosseur, -euse, *n.* endorser (of bill, etc.).

engagement, *n.m.* **1.** (*a*) pawning/pledging; mortgaging (of property) (*b*) tying up/locking up (of capital); **engagement bancaire,** (bank) commitment; **en-**

gagement hors bilan, contingent liabilities; *Adm:* **engagement de dépenses,** commitment of funds (*c*) receipt (for object pledged) **2.** (*a*) promise/agreement; contract; liability; commitment; **sans engagement,** without obligation; **contracter/prendre un engagement,** to enter into a contract/into an agreement (*b*) engagement/appointment (of employee); indenture.

engager, 1. *v.tr.* (*a*) to pledge/to pawn; to mortgage (property); **tous les frais engagés seront remboursés,** all expenses incurred will be reimbursed; **cette lettre ne vous engage pas,** this letter does not bind you/does not commit you (*b*) **engager du personnel,** to take on/*NAm:* to hire staff; **nous avons dû engager une nouvelle vendeuse,** we had to take on a new sales assistant (*c*) *Fin:* **engager son capital,** to lock up/to tie up one's capital (*d*) to begin/to start; **engager des négociations,** to enter into negotiations; *Jur:* **engager des poursuites,** to bring an action against/to take legal action/to take legal proceedings (**contre,** against) **2.** *v.pr.* **s'engager,** to bind oneself (by contract).

engorgement, *n.m. PolEc:* **l'engorgement (des marchés),** glutting (of markets).

engorger, *v.tr. PolEc:* to glut (the market).

enlever, 1. *v.tr.* (*a*) **enlever des marchandises,** to snap up goods; *Fin:* **enlever une émission d'actions,** to snap up an issue of shares (*b*) **il a enlevé l'affaire,** he got the order/the contract **2.** *v.pr.* **marchandises qui s'enlèvent,** goods that sell quickly/that are snapped up.

enquête, *n.f.* inquiry/investigation; **enquête d'opinion,** attitude/opinion survey; **enquête par sondage,** sample survey; opinion poll; **enquête pilote,** pilot survey.

enregistrement, *n.m.* registration/record(ing); **enregistrement d'une commande,** booking/entering (up) of an order; **enregistrement d'une compagnie,**

incorporation of a company; **enregistrement des bagages,** registration of luggage; *Av:* **se présenter à l'enregistrement,** to check in; *Adm:* **l'Enregistrement,** (the) Registration department.

enregistrer, *v.tr.* to register/to record; **enregistrer une commande,** to book/to enter (up) an order; **société enregistrée,** incorporated company; **(faire) enregistrer ses bagages,** (*i*) to register one's luggage (*ii*) *Av:* to check in one's luggage.

ensemblier, *n.m.* turnkey operator.

entente, *n.f.* (*a*) agreement/understanding (**entre,** between) (*b*) **entente (industrielle),** restrictive practice.

en-tête, *n.m.* heading (of letter, document, bill, etc.); **papier à en-tête,** headed notepaper.

entièrement, *adv.* entirely/completely; **capital entièrement versé,** fully paid(-up) capital.

entrée, *n.f.* **1.** (*a*) entry (in account books, etc.) (*b*) *pl.* (*i*) goods received (*ii*) takings/receipts **2.** (*a*) admission/admittance; entrance fee; **billet d'entrée,** entrance ticket; **entrée gratuite,** free admission; **entrée libre,** (*i*) = no obligation to buy (*ii*) admission free (*b*) import(ation); *Cust:* entry; **droit d'entrée/ taxe à l'entrée,** import duty; **entrée en douane,** clearance inward/entry inward **3.** way in/entrance; **entrée des fournisseurs,** tradesman's entrance.

entre-fin, *a.* medium-quality (goods).

entreposage, *n.m.* warehousing/storing; *Cust:* bonding.

entreposer, *v.tr.* to warehouse/to store; *Cust:* to bond; to put (goods) in bond; **marchandises entreposées,** bonded goods.

entreposeur, *n.m.* warehouse keeper/ warehouseman; *Cust:* officer in charge of a bonded store.

entrepôt, *n.m.* (*a*) warehouse/store/

repository; **entrepôt frigorifique,** cold store; **marchandises en entrepôt,** goods in store; **à prendre en entrepôt,** ex-warehouse (b) Cust: **entrepôt réel/ entrepôt de la douane,** bonded warehouse; **entrepôt fictif,** unbonded warehouse; **marchandises en entrepôt,** bonded goods/goods in bond; **mettre des marchandises en entrepôt,** to bond goods; to put goods in bond (c) entrepôt; **Londres est un grand centre d'entrepôt,** London has a large entrepôt trade; **port d'entrepôt,** entrepôt port.

entrepreneur, n.m. (a) contractor; **entrepreneur (en bâtiments),** building contractor; **entrepreneur de transports/de roulage,** carrier/haulage contractor (b) entrepreneur.

entreprise, n.f. **1.** (a) undertaking/venture; **entreprise en participation,** joint venture (b) firm; **chef d'entreprise,** head/manager (of company, firm, etc.); **entreprise artisanale,** (i) small-scale enterprise (ii) cottage industry; **entreprise commerciale,** business undertaking/ business concern; **entreprise familiale,** family business/firm; **les grosses entreprises,** big/large(-scale) industry; **petites et moyennes entreprises (PME),** small and medium-sized firms; **entreprise privée,** private enterprise; **entreprise publique,** public corporation; **la libre entreprise,** free enterprise (c) **comité d'entreprise,** works council; **croissance de l'entreprise,** corporate growth; **formation dans l'entreprise,** in-plant training; **planification de l'entreprise,** company planning (d) **entreprise de transports/de roulage,** road haulage company/haulage contractors **2.** (contrat d')entreprise, contract (for work, supply of goods, etc.); **entreprise de travaux publics,** contract for public works; **travail à l'entreprise,** contract work; **mettre/ donner qch. à l'entreprise,** to put sth. out to contract; **prendre qch. à l'entreprise,** to contract for sth.; **avoir l'entreprise de construire une route,** to hold a contract for building a road.

entrer, 1. v.i. (a) to enter; **entrer en association avec qn,** to enter into partnership with s.o.; **entrer en correspondance avec qn,** to enter into correspondence with s.o. (b) to import; **les marchandises qui entrent en France sont soumises à des droits de douane,** goods entering France are subject to customs duty (c) **entrer en vigueur,** to come into force/to take effect **2.** v.tr. **entrer des marchandises en fraude,** to smuggle in goods.

entretenir, v.tr. to keep (sth.) in good repair/in good (working) order; to maintain (sth.).

entretien, n.m. **1.** upkeep/maintenance (of property, machines, etc.); **entretien systématique,** planned maintenance; **entretien et réparations,** servicing; **personnel d'entretien,** maintenance staff **2.** (a) interview; **j'ai demandé un entretien avec les directeurs,** I asked to talk to the managers/I asked for a meeting with the managers (b) pl. **entretiens,** talks/negotiations.

enveloppe, n.f. **1.** envelope (of letter); wrapper/wrapping (of parcel); **mettre une lettre sous enveloppe,** to put a letter in/into an envelope; **enveloppe autocollante,** self-seal envelope; **enveloppe à fenêtre,** window envelope; **enveloppe gommée,** adhesive envelope; **enveloppe-réponse,** reply-paid envelope; **joindre une enveloppe timbrée pour la réponse,** enclose a stamped addressed envelope (s.a.e.) for reply **2.** Fin: **enveloppe budgétaire,** provision; budget allocation; appropriation.

envoi, n.m. **1.** (a) sending/dispatch(ing)/ forwarding/consignment; **envoi (par mer, par terre, par fer, par air),** shipment; **envoi à titre d'essai,** sent on approval; **envoi contre remboursement,** cash on delivery (c.o.d.); **j'ai bien reçu votre envoi du 10 octobre,** I acknowledge receipt of your dispatch/consignment of 10th October; **faire un envoi tous les mois,** to send/to dispatch goods every month; **bordereau d'envoi,** dispatch note; **lettre d'envoi,** advice letter/note (b) **envoi de**

fonds, remittance (of funds); **faire un envoi de fonds à qn,** to remit funds to s.o. **2.** consignment; parcel; shipment; **faire un envoi de fleurs,** to send flowers.

envoyer, *v.tr.* to send; to dispatch; **envoyer une lettre à qn,** to send s.o. a letter; **envoyer qch. par (chemin de) fer,** to send sth. by rail; **envoyer qch. par la poste,** to post/to mail sth.; **je lui ai envoyé un chèque par la poste,** I sent him a cheque by post.

envoyeur, -euse, *n. Post:* sender/forwarder (of goods, letter, etc.); **retour à l'envoyeur,** return to sender.

épargnant, *n.m. & f.* saver/investor; **petits épargnants,** small savers/small investors.

épargne, *n.f.* saving; economy; **caisse d'épargne,** savings bank; **Caisse nationale d'épargne,** = National Savings Bank; **livret de caisse d'épargne,** savings bank book; **plan d'épargne,** savings account; savings plan; **l'épargne privée,** private investors; **la petite épargne,** small savers/small investors.

épargne-logement, *n.m.* **plan d'épargne-logement** = building society (savings) account; **prêt d'épargne-logement** = (building society) mortgage/loan.

épargner, *v.tr.* to save (up); to economize.

épicerie, *n.f.* **1.** groceries **2.** grocer's (shop)/*NAm:* grocery **3.** the grocery business/trade.

épongeage, *n.m. Fin:* absorbing/mopping up/draining off.

éponger, *v.tr. Fin:* to absorb/to mop up/to drain off; **éponger le pouvoir d'achat excédentaire,** to mop up excess purchasing power.

épuisé, *a.* (*a*) **lettre de crédit épuisée,** invalid letter of credit (*b*) (*d'un produit, etc.*) out of stock; sold out; (*d'un livre*) out of print.

épuisement, *n.m.* running out (of stocks, goods, etc.); **jusqu'à épuisement des stocks,** while stocks/supplies last.

épuiser, 1. *v.tr.* to run out of (goods, stocks, etc.); **épuiser un stock,** to sell out (of) an article **2.** *v.pr.* **s'épuiser,** (*i*) to run out (*ii*) to run low.

équilibration, *n.f.* balancing (of the budget).

équilibre, *n.m.* **parvenir à rétablir l'équilibre budgétaire,** to manage to balance the budget.

équilibrer, *v.tr.* **équilibrer le budget,** to balance the budget.

équipe, *n.f.* (*a*) **équipe de jour,** day shift; **équipe de nuit,** night shift; **travailler par équipes,** to work in shifts; **travail par équipes,** shift work; **chef d'équipe,** foreman (*b*) team; **équipe de direction,** management team; **équipe de vente/équipe commerciale,** sales team/force; **travail d'équipe,** teamwork.

équipement, *n.m.* equipment; **biens d'équipement,** capital goods; **budget d'équipement,** capital budget; **équipement industriel,** plant.

équivalent, *a. & n.m.* equivalent (à, to).

ergonomie, *n.f.* ergonomics/biotechnology/human engineering.

erreur, *n.f.* error/mistake; **il y a une erreur dans votre compte,** there is a mistake in your account; **sauf erreur ou omission,** errors and omissions excepted (e. & o.).

escalade, *n.f.* escalation (of prices, etc.); **escalade des taux d'intérêt,** escalation of interest rates.

escomptable, *a. Fin:* discountable (securities, etc.).

escompte, *n.m* **1.** discount; **accorder/faire un escompte,** to allow a discount; **escompte (sur paiement) au comptant/ escompte de caisse,** discount for cash; **escompte d'usage,** trade discount **2.** *Fin:* **banque d'escompte,** discount house;

escompte (de banque), discount; taux (officiel) de l'escompte, minimum lending rate (MLR); *NAm:* prime rate; escompte en dedans, true discount; escompte en dehors, commercial/bank discount; faire escompter une traite/présenter une traite à l'escompte, to have a bill discounted; prendre à l'escompte un effet de commerce, to discount a bill of exchange 3. *StExch:* call for delivery (of securities) before settlement.

escompter, *v.tr.* (*a*) *Fin:* escompter un effet, to discount a bill (*b*) *StExch:* to call for delivery of (securities) before settlement.

escompteur, 1. *n.m. Fin:* discounter/discount broker 2. *a.* banquier escompteur, discounting banker.

espèces, *n.f.pl. Fin:* payer en espèces, to pay in cash.

espérance, *n.f.* espérance de vie d'un produit, product life expectancy; shelf life (of a product).

essai, *n.m.* (*a*) trial/test(ing); à titre d'essai, subject to approval; acheter qch. à l'essai, to buy sth. on approval/on appro; commande d'essai, trial order; essai gratuit, free trial; faire l'essai d'un produit, to test/to try out a product; faire l'essai d'une voiture, to test-drive a car (*b*) prendre/engager à l'essai (un employé), to take on (an employee) for a probationary period/for a trial period.

essayer, *v.tr.* to try; essayez notre nouvelle voiture, test-drive our new car.

essor, *n.m.* essor économique, economic expansion; industrie en plein essor, booming/expanding industry; période d'essor, boom.

estampillage, *n.m.* stamping/marking (of goods, etc.).

estampille, *n.f.* (*sur un document, etc.*) (official) stamp; (*sur un colis, un produit, etc.*) identification mark; brand; trade-

mark; postmark; l'estampille a oblitéré le timbre, the postmark has cancelled the stamp.

estampiller, *v.tr.* to stamp (weights, documents, etc.); to mark (goods); to hallmark (gold, silver).

estimateur, -trice, *n.* appraiser/valuer.

estimatif, *a.* estimated (cost, etc.); devis estimatif, estimate.

estimation, *n.f.* (*a*) estimation/estimate (of the value, price, of sth.); valuing/appraising (of goods, etc.); assessment (of damage); estimation approximative/estimation au jugé, rough estimate/*F:* guesstimate (*b*) estimate/valuation; estimation faite par un expert, expert valuation.

estimer, *v.tr.* to estimate/to value/to appraise (goods); to assess (damage).

établir, 1. *v.tr.* (*a*) to establish/to set up (firm, etc.) (*b*) to draw up; établir un budget, to draw up/to work out a budget; établir un compte, to draw up/to make up an account; établir un contrat, to draw up a contract; établir un prix, to price (sth.) 2. *v.pr.* s'établir à son compte, to start up (a business) on one's own/to set up in business on one's own; to become self-employed.

établissement, *n.m.* (*a*) drawing up/making up (of accounts, contract, etc.); établissement des prix, pricing; établissement des prix de revient, costing (*b*) setting up (of a business, a firm, etc.); frais d'établissement/coût de premier établissement, initial outlay/investment/expenditure; set-up costs; *Ind:* capital d'établissement, invested capital (*c*) chef d'établissement, works manager; établissement commercial, commercial premises; établissement industriel, factory; industrial premises; établissement principal, main branch/head office (of a business); les établissements Renault, the Renault works.

étalage, *n.m.* (*a*) display (of goods, etc.); étalage de marchandises sur la voie pu-

blique, street trading (b) tax paid by street trader; stallage (c) window-display; window-dressing; **faire l'étalage,** (i) to put (goods) on display (ii) to dress the window(s); **mettre qch. à l'étalage,** to display sth. in the window; **article qui a fait l'étalage,** shop-soiled article.

étalager, v.tr. to display (goods) for sale; to put (goods) on display (in shop window, on counter, etc.).

étalagiste, n.m. & f. (a) street trader/stall-holder (b) window-dresser.

étalement, n.m. 1. displaying (of goods, etc.) 2. staggering (of holidays).

étaler, v.tr. 1. **étaler sa marchandise,** to display one's goods (for sale) 2. to stagger/to spread out (holidays, payments); **versements étalés sur deux ans,** instalments spread (out) over two years.

étalon, n.m. standard (of weights, measures, etc.): Fin: **l'étalon or,** the gold standard; **l'étalon de change-or,** the gold exchange standard.

étalonnage, n.m. **étalonnement,** n.m. standardization (of weights, etc.).

étalonner, v.tr. to standardize (weights, etc.).

état, n.m. 1. state/condition; **machine en bon/mauvais état (de marche),** machine in good/bad working order 2. (a) statement/report/list/return; **état de compte,** statement of account; **état détaillé d'un compte,** breakdown of an account; **état financier,** financial statement; Jur: **état de frais,** bill of cost; **état de paiements,** schedule of payments (b) **état 'néant',** 'nil' return (c) **état des lieux,** inventory of fixtures (as between landlord and tenant) (d) Ind: etc: **état périodique,** progress report (e) Adm: **état civil,** (i) (civil) status (ii) registry office (f) **état estimatif/appréciatif,** estimate 3. **l'État,** the State; **banque d'État,** State bank.

étatisation, n.f. nationalization.

étatisé, a. State-controlled/State run/

State owned/government run/nationalized; **industrie étatisée,** nationalized industry.

étatiser, v.tr. to establish State control over (industry, etc.); to nationalize.

état-major, n.m. top management (of factory, etc.).

étiquetage, n.m. labelling (of luggage, etc.); ticketing (of goods, etc.).

étiqueter, v.tr. to label (luggage); to ticket (goods).

étiquette, n.f. label/docket/ticket; **étiquette à bagages,** luggage label; **étiquette auto-collante,** stick-on label; **étiquette à œillets,** tie-on label; tag; **étiquette de prix,** price ticket/price tag; **étiquette de qualité,** quality label.

étoile, n.f. **un hôtel deux étoiles,** a two-star hotel.

étranger, a. foreign; **monnaie/devise étrangère,** foreign currency.

étude, n.f. (a) research (work); investigation; survey; **bureau d'études,** (i) research department (ii) design department; **étude de conception,** design engineering; **étude de marché,** market research/survey; **étude de produit,** product analysis; **étude des charges,** cost analysis; **étude des méthodes,** methods analysis; **étude du travail,** work study; **étude économique,** economic research; **étude préliminaire,** preliminary/pilot study; **étude des temps et des mouvements,** time and motion study; **études et recherches,** research and engineering 2. office (of solicitor); chambers (of barrister).

eurochèque, n.m. Eurocheque; **carte eurochèque,** Eurocheque card.

eurodevise, n.f. **marché des eurodevises,** Eurocurrency market.

eurodollar, n.m. Fin: Eurodollar.

euromarché, n.m. Euromarket.

euro-obligation, *n.f.* Eurobond.

évaluable, *a.* appraisable / assessable (goods, property).

évaluation, *n.f.* evaluation; valuation (of stock); appraisement (of property, etc.); appraisal (of the market); assessment (of demand, project, damages); estimate (of weight, losses, etc.); **évaluation des coûts,** cost analysis/costing; **évaluation d'un emploi,** job evaluation; **évaluation approximative,** rough estimate/*F:* guesstimate; **évaluation prudente,** conservative estimate.

évaluer, *v.tr.* to evaluate/to value/to appraise/to estimate; to assess (damages).

évasion, *n.f.* **évasion des capitaux,** flight of capital; **évasion fiscale,** tax avoidance.

éventail, *n.m. PolEc: etc:* range; **éventail des prix,** price range; **éventail de produits,** range of products; **éventail des salaires,** salary range.

éventualité, *n.f.* possibility/contingency/eventuality.

éventuel, *a.* possible/contingent; *Fin:* **passif éventuel,** contingent liabilities; **client éventuel,** potential/prospective customer.

évolutif, *a.* **poste évolutif,** post with possibility of advancement.

évolution, *n.f.* **graphique d'évolution,** flow chart.

examen, *n.m.* examination; **examen des comptes,** inspection/scrutiny of accounts; **examen financier,** financial review; **la question est à l'examen,** the question is under consideration/we are looking into it.

examiner, *v.tr.* to examine; to investigate; to look into/to go into; **examiner les comptes,** to go through/to inspect the accounts; **examiner une question,** to look into /to go into/to consider a matter.

excédent, *n.m.* excess/surplus; **budget en excédent,** budget showing a surplus; **nous avons un excédent de dépenses,** we are overspending; we have a deficit; **excédent de l'encaisse,** over in the cash; **excédents et déficits,** overs and shorts; **excédents de 10%,** 10% overs; **payer 50 francs d'excédent,** to pay (a) 50 francs excess (charge)/to pay a surcharge of 50 francs; **excédent de bagages,** excess luggage; **excédent de production d'un pays,** surplus produce of a country; **excédent des exportations sur les importations,** excess of exports over imports; **excédent (de production) de blé,** wheat surplus.

excédentaire, *a.* (in) excess/(in) surplus; **la balance commerciale est excédentaire,** the trade balance shows a surplus/a credit; **écouler la production excédentaire sur les marchés extérieurs,** to dump surplus/excess production on foreign markets.

excéder, *v.tr.* to exceed/to go beyond (a certain limit); **excéder le montant de son compte (en banque),** to overdraw one's account; **nos pertes excèdent nos profits,** our losses are greater than our profits.

exceptionnel, *a.* **profits exceptionnels/pertes exceptionnelles,** extraordinary items; **taxe exceptionnelle,** special/exceptional tax.

excès, *n.m.* excess; surplus; **excès des dépenses sur les recettes,** excess of expenditure over revenue; **excès de l'offre sur la demande,** excess of supply over demand; *StExch:* **excès de vendeurs,** sellers over.

exclusif, *a.* exclusive/sole (right, etc.); **agent exclusif,** sole agent; **importateur exclusif pour la France,** sole importer (of a product) for France; **produit exclusif,** exclusive article; speciality.

exclusivité, *n.f.* sole/exclusive rights; **nous avons l'exclusivité de la vente de ce produit,** we have the (sole) rights for this product.

ex-coupon, *adv.phr. Fin:* ex coupon.

ex-dividende, *adv.phr. Fin:* ex dividend; **actions citées ex-dividende,** shares quoted ex dividend.

ex-droit, *adv.phr. Fin:* **titre ex-droit,** stock ex rights.

exécuter, *v.tr.* **1.** to carry out (work, etc.); to put (project, etc.) into action **2.** (*a*) *Jur:* **exécuter un débiteur,** to distrain upon a debtor (*b*) *StExch:* **exécuter un spéculateur,** to hammer a defaulter; **exécuter un client,** (*i*) to buy in (*ii*) to sell out against a client.

exécutif, 1. *a.* executive; **comité exécutif,** executive committee; **le pouvoir exécutif,** the executive **2.** *n.m.* (*a*) executive committee; **un exécutif de cinq membres,** an executive of five (*b*) **l'exécutif,** the executive.

exécution, *n.f.* **1.** carrying out (of plan, agreement, etc.); **travaux en voie d'exécution,** work in progress **2.** (*a*) *Jur:* distraint (*b*) *StExch:* hammering (of defaulter).

exécutoire, *Jur:* **1.** *a.* (*d'un contrat, etc.*) enforceable; to be carried into effect; **obligation exécutoire,** operative obligation **2.** *n.m.* writ of execution; **exécutoire des dépens,** order to pay costs.

exemplaire, *n.m.* (*a*) copy (of books, etc.); *Adm:* **exemplaire d'archives,** file copy (*b*) **en double exemplaire,** in duplicate; **en triple exemplaire,** in triplicate.

exempt, *a.* exempt (from tax, etc.); *Cust:* **exempt de droits,** free of duty/duty-free; **lettre exempte de port,** letter free of postage; **exempt de frais,** free of charge.

exempter, *v.tr.* **exempter qn d'un impôt,** to exempt s.o. from a tax.

exemption, *n.f.* exemption (**de,** from); immunity (from tax, etc.); *Cust:* **lettre d'exemption,** bill of sufferance.

exercice, *n.m.* **1.** exercise; **dans l'exercice de ses fonctions,** in the exercise of one's duties **2.** visit of inspection (of excise officer) **3.** (*a*) (*i*) financial year/year's trading/account period (*ii*) budgetary year/fiscal period; **clôture d'un exercice,** year end/end of financial year; **exercice comptable/exercice social,** company's financial year; **l'exercice de ce mois,** this month's trading; **fin d'exercice,** year end; **bilan de fin d'exercice,** end of year balance-sheet (*b*) **exercice 1981 attaché,** cum dividend 1981.

exigence, *n.f.* demand(s)/requirement(s); **exigences de poste,** job requirements; **la marchandise répond à toutes les exigences,** the goods are up to standard in every way; **satisfaire aux exigences de ses clients,** to meet one's customers' requirements.

exiger, *v.tr.* to exact/to demand/to require (**de,** from); **exiger un paiement,** to exact a payment.

exigibilités, *n.f.pl.* current liabilities.

exigible, *a.* claimable (**de,** from); (payment) due; **dette exigible,** debt due for payment; **passif exigible,** current liabilities.

existant, 1. *a.* existing; **majorer les tarifs existants,** to increase existing tariffs **2.** *n.m.* **l'existant en caisse,** (the) cash in hand; **l'existant en magasin/les existants,** stock (in hand).

existence, *n.f.* **existence en magasin,** stock (in hand).

exode, *n.m. PolEc:* **exode des capitaux,** flight of capital.

exonération, *n.f.* exemption (**de,** from) (fees, taxes, etc.).

exonérer, *v.tr.* (*a*) to exonerate (**de,** from); **être exonéré de l'impôt sur le revenu,** to be exempted from income tax (*b*) **exonérer des marchandises,** to exempt goods from import duty.

expansion, *n.f.* expansion (of a firm, etc.); **expansion monétaire,** currency expansion; **industrie en pleine expansion,** booming/expanding industry; **taux d'expansion économique,** economic growth rate.

expansionnisme, *n.m. PolEc:* expansionism.

expansionniste, *a. & n. PolEc:* expansionist.

expatrier, *v.tr. Fin:* **expatrier des capitaux,** to invest money/capital abroad.

expédier, *v.tr.* (*a*) *Jur:* to draw up (contract, deed) (*b*) to forward/to send (letter, parcel, goods); to dispatch; **expédiez ceci par le premier courrier,** get this off by the first post; **expédier des marchandises par navire,** to ship goods; **expédier (un colis) par la poste,** to post/to mail (a parcel); to send (a parcel) through the post by post.

expéditeur, -trice, *n.* 1. sender (of telegram, letter, etc.); (*sur une enveloppe, etc.*) (*abbr.* **exp.**) from . . ./ sender . . . 2. (*a*) shipper/consignor (of goods) (*b*) forwarding agent (*c*) dispatcher.

expédition, *n.f.* (*a*) *Jur:* copy (of deed, contract, etc.); **première expédition,** first authentic copy; **en double expédition,** in duplicate (*b*) dispatch(ing)/forwarding/sending/consignment (of parcels, etc.); **bulletin/bordereau d'expédition,** waybill; **expédition par mer,** shipping/ shipment; **maison d'expédition,** forwarding house; **expédition franco à partir de 1000 francs,** orders of 1000 francs and over delivered free.

expert, 1. *a.* expert/skilled (**en, dans,** in); **la main d'œuvre la plus experte,** the most highly-skilled labour 2. *n.m.* (*a*) expert (*b*) valuer/appraiser.

expert-comptable, *n.m.* = chartered accountant/*NAm:* certified public accountant.

expert-conseil, *n.m. Ind: etc:* consultant.

expertise, *n.f.* 1. (expert) appraisal/ valuation; *Nau:* survey (of ship for damage); **expertise d'avarie,** damage survey; **faire l'expertise des dégâts,** to appraise the damage; **faire une expertise,** to make

a valuation/a survey 2. expert's report/ expert opinion.

expertiser, *v.tr.* 1. to appraise/to value/to estimate; *Nau:* to survey (ship for damage); **faire expertiser qch.,** to have sth. surveyed/to obtain an expert opinion on sth. 2. to give an expert opinion.

expiration, *n.f.* expiry/expiration/termination/end (of lease, contract, term of office, etc.); **venir à expiration,** to expire; **l'expiration des délais,** time limit.

expirer, *v.i.* to expire; **notre bail a expiré hier,** our lease expired/ran out yesterday; **ce passeport expire le 5 mai,** this passport expires on May 5th.

explicatif, *a.* explanatory; **note/notice explicative,** instructions/directions for use.

exploitant, 1. *a.* **société exploitante,** development company 2. *n.m.* (*a*) **exploitant agricole,** farmer; **les petits exploitants,** small farmers/smallholders (*b*) owner/ manager (of a cinema, *etc.*).

exploitation, *n.f.* 1. (*a*) running/operation (of company, etc.); **bénéfices d'exploitation,** trading/*NAm:* operating profits; **exploitation agricole,** farming; **frais d'exploitation,** working costs/running/*NAm:* operating expenses; **société d'exploitation,** development company (*b*) **compte d'exploitation,** trading account/*NAm:* operating report; **budget d'exploitation prévisionnel,** forecast(ed) operating budget; **capital d'exploitation,** working capital 2. (*a*) **exploitation commerciale,** commerce; commercial enterprise; **exploitation industrielle,** industrial concern/undertaking (*b*) farm; **petite exploitation,** smallholding.

exploiter, *v.tr.* (*a*) to run/to operate/to work; **exploiter un commerce,** to run/to carry on a business (*b*) **ouvriers exploités,** sweated labour.

exportable, *a.* exportable.

exportateur, -trice, 1. *n.* exporter 2. *a.*

exporting (country, etc.); **les pays exportateurs de pétrole,** the oil exporting countries.

exportation, *n.f.* export/*NAm:* exportation; **articles d'exportation,** exports; **faire l'exportation,** to export; **les exportations,** (*i*) the export trade (*ii*) exports; **commerce d'exportation,** export trade; **exportation de capitaux,** export of capital; **exportations visibles/invisibles,** visible/invisible exports; **nos exportations de beurre s'élèvent à deux millions de tonnes,** our butter exports total two million tons; **licence d'exportation,** export licence/*NAm:* license; **prime d'exportation,** export subsidy.

exporter, *v.tr.* to export (goods) (**à, en, to**).

exporteur, *n.m.* = **exportateur.**

exposant, -ante, *n.* exhibitor (of goods at show, trade fair, etc.).

exposer, *v.tr.* to exhibit/to show/to display (goods, etc.); **exposer des marchandises en vente,** to display goods for sale.

exposition, *n.f.* exhibition/show (of goods, etc.); **exposition internationale,** international exhibition; **salle d'exposition,** (*i*) (large) exhibition hall/exhibition room (*ii*) showroom.

exprès, *a.inv. & n.m. Post:* (**lettre, colis**) **exprès,** express (letter, parcel); **par exprès,** by special delivery.

expropriation, *n.f. Jur:* expropriation; compulsory purchase of private property; compulsory surrender (of real estate).

exproprier, *v.tr.* to expropriate (*i*) a proprietor (*ii*) property.

ex-répartition, *adv.phr. Fin:* ex allotment.

extérieur, 1. *a.* foreign/external (trade, etc.); **déficit extérieur,** external deficit/balance of payments deficit; **dette extérieure,** foreign/overseas debt **2.** *n.m.* **nos relations commerciales avec l'extérieur,** our (commercial) dealings with foreign countries.

extinction, *n.f.* paying off/wiping out (of debt); termination (of contract).

extourner, *v.tr. Fin:* to reverse (a debit, etc.).

extrabudgétaire, *a. Fin:* extra-budgetary/outside the budget.

extrait, *n.m.* abstract (of deed, account); **extrait de compte,** statement of account.

extraordinaire, *a.* extraordinary; **assemblée (générale) extraordinaire,** extraordinary (general) meeting; **budget extraordinaire,** emergency budget; **frais/dépenses extraordinaires,** (*i*) extras (*ii*) non-recurring expenditure; **impôt extraordinaire,** emergency tax; exceptional tax.

F

fabricant, *n.m.* maker/manufacturer; **fabricant de chaussures,** shoe manufacturer.

fabrication, *n.f.* (*a*) manufacture/making/production (of sth.); workmanship; **article de bonne fabrication,** well-made article/article of good workmanship; **contrôle de fabrication,** manufacturing control; **coût de fabrication,** manufacturing cost; **défaut de fabrication,** defect/fault/flaw (in the manufacture of an article); faulty workmanship; **fabrication à la chaîne,** mass production; **fabrication en série,** mass production; **fabrication par lots,** batch production; **frais de fabrication,** manufacturing/factory overheads; **numéro de fabrication,** serial number; **programme de fabrication,** production plan/schedule sheet; **(produit) de fabrication française,** (product, article) made in France/French-made (product, article); **secret de fabrication,** trade secret; **unité de fabrication,** factory unit (*b*) *Publ:* **chef de fabrication,** production manager (*c*) manufactured goods; **notre fabrication,** our products.

fabrique, *n.f.* **1.** making/manufacture; **prix de fabrique,** cost price/manufacturer's price; **marque de fabrique,** trade mark/brand **2.** factory/works; **fabrique de chaussures,** shoe factory; **valeur en fabrique,** cost price.

fabriquer, *v.tr.* to manufacture (cloth, bicycles, etc.); **fabriqué en France,** made in France; **fabriqué en grande série,** mass-produced; **fabriqué sur commande,** made to order; **fabriqué sur mesure(s),** made to measure.

façade, *n.f. Ins:* fronting.

face, *n.f.* **opération de face à face,** back to back loan.

facial, *a.* **valeur faciale (d'une action),** face value/nominal value (of a share).

facilité, *n.f. Bank:* **facilités de caisse,** overdraft facilities; **facilités de crédit,** credit terms; **facilités de paiement,** easy terms/easy payments.

façon, *n.f.* (*i*) making; fashioning (of jewellery, etc.) (*ii*) workmanship/labour; **tailleur à façon,** bespoke tailor; **travail à façon,** suits/dresses made to measure.

fac(-)similaire, *a.* (copy, etc.) in facsimile; **contrat fac(-)similaire,** contract in facsimile.

fac-similé, *n.m.* facsimile/exact copy (of signature, etc.).

factage, *n.m.* (*a*) carriage (and delivery); transport (of goods); **entreprise/service de factage,** delivery service; **payer le factage,** to pay the carriage (*b*) delivery (of letters).

facteur, *n.m.* factor; **analyse des facteurs de profit,** profit factor analysis; **facteur coût/prix,** cost factor; **facteur de charge,** load factor; **facteur d'utilisation,** duty factor/cycle.

factorerie, *n.f.* foreign trading post/depot.

facturation, *n.f. Book-k:* invoicing; **service de facturation,** invoice department.

facture, *n.f.* invoice/bill (of sale); **acquitter une facture,** (*i*) to pay a bill (*ii*) to receipt an invoice/a bill; **facture détaillée,** itemized invoice; **faire/dresser/établir une facture,** to make out an invoice; **facture pro forma,** pro forma invoice; **payer/régler une facture,** to settle an invoice/to pay a bill; **prix de facture,** wholesale price; **selon/suivant facture,** as per invoice; **valeur de facture,** invoice value.

facturer, *v.tr.* to invoice; to charge for (sth.) (on an invoice)/to put (sth.) on a bill/*NAm:* to bill s.o. for (sth.); **le papier nous a été facturé 60 francs,** we were charged 60 francs for the paper; **marchandises facturées,** invoiced goods; **machine à facturer,** invoicing machine.

facturier, 1. *n.m.* sales book **2.** *n.m. & f.* invoice clerk **3.** *n.f.* **facturière,** invoicing machine **4.** *a.* **dactylo(graphe) facturière,** invoice typist.

faculté, *n.f.* option/right; **louer un immeuble avec faculté d'achat,** to rent a building with the option of purchase; *StExch:* **faculté du double,** call of more.

faible, 1. *a.* **faible demande,** slack demand; **prix faible,** (*i*) low price (*ii*) discount price; **faible quantité,** small quantity; **faible revenu,** low/small income **2.** *n.m. & f. pl.* **les économiquement faibles,** (people in) the lower-income bracket/ lower income groups.

failli, 1. *a.* **commerçant failli,** bankrupt businessman **2.** *n.* (adjudicated) bankrupt; **failli (non) réhabilité,** (un)discharged bankrupt.

faillite, *n.f.* bankruptcy/insolvency; **être en faillite/en état de faillite,** to be bankrupt/insolvent; **être près de la faillite,** to be on the verge of bankruptcy; **maison en faillite,** bankrupt firm; **mettre qn en faillite,** to bankrupt s.o.; **prononcer la faillite de qn,** to adjudicate/to adjudge s.o. bankrupt; **tomber en faillite/faire faillite,** to go bankrupt/to fail; **se mettre en faillite,** to file a petition in bankruptcy.

faire, *v.tr.* **1.** (*a*) to make; **faire un paiement/un versement,** to make a payment (*b*) **faire un chèque,** to write a cheque/ to raise a cheque; **faire un chèque de £10,** to make out a cheque for £10 (*c*) **nous**

ne faisons que le gros, we only trade wholesale/we only deal (in) wholesale (*d*) **faire sa fortune,** to make one's fortune; **faire des pertes,** to meet with/to sustain losses; **il se fait 10 000 francs par mois,** he makes 10 000 francs a month **2.** (*a*) to do; **faire des affaires avec qn,** to do business with s.o.; **faire les cuirs,** to deal in leather (*b*) **faire son apprentissage,** to serve one's apprenticeship; **faire les magasins,** to go round the shops (*c*) to amount to; **combien cela fait-il?** how much does that come to?/does it amount to? **3. faire monter/baisser les prix,** to force prices up/down; **faire coïncider le prix avec le coût marginal,** to equate price with marginal cost; **faire marcher un commerce/une affaire,** to run a business.

faisabilité, *n.f.* **étude de faisabilité,** feasibility study.

faisable, *a.* practicable/feasible.

falsification, *n.f.* falsification; forgery/ faking (of documents, etc.).

falsifier, *v.tr.* to falsify; to forge/to fake (documents, etc.); **falsifier les comptes,** to falsify/to fake the accounts.

familial, *a.* (*a*) *Adm:* **allocation familiale,** family allowance; **revenu familial,** family income (*b*) **entreprise familiale,** family firm/business (*c*) **pot familial,** family-size(d) jar.

fantaisie, *n.f.* **objets de fantaisie,** fancy goods; **magasin de fantaisies,** novelty shop.

faux, 1. *a.* false; forged; **fausse déclaration,** false declaration/misrepresentation; **faux chèque,** forged cheque; **faux bilan,** fraudulent balance-sheet **2.** *n.m. Jur:* forgery; **s'inscrire en faux contre qch.,** to take action to dispute the validity of sth.

faveur, *n.f.* favour; **billet de faveur,** complimentary ticket; **prix de faveur,** preferential/special price; **taux de faveur,** special rates; **le solde est en votre faveur,** the balance is in your favour.

favorable, *a.* favourable; **à des conditions favorables,** on favourable terms; **balance commerciale favorable,** favourable trade balance.

favoriser, *v.tr.* to help/to encourage (sth.); **favoriser l'essor de la production,** to encourage production; **favoriser la croissance,** to promote growth.

fédération, *n.f.* federation; **fédération de syndicats,** amalgamated union; **fédération syndicale,** trade(s) union.

férié, *a.m.* **jour férié** = public holiday/ *Adm:* bank holiday.

ferme[1], **1.** *a.* (*a*) firm/steady; **maintenir ses prix fermes,** to keep one's prices steady; **le marché reste très ferme,** the market continues very steady (*b*) **acheteur ferme,** firm buyer; **offre ferme,** firm/ definite offer **2.** *adv.* **vendre ferme,** to make a firm sale **3.** *n.m. StExch:* **valeur ferme,** firm stock.

ferme[2], *n.f.* farming lease; **prendre une terre à ferme,** to take lease of/to rent a piece of land; **donner à ferme,** to farm out.

fermer, 1. *v.tr.* to close/to shut; **fermer boutique,** to close down; **fermer un compte,** to close an account; **fermer une usine,** to close down a factory **2.** *v.i.* **les magasins ferment à cinq heures,** the shops close/shut at five (o'clock); **hôtel qui ferme pour l'hiver,** hotel that closes down for the winter; *StExch:* **les actions ont fermé à . . .,** shares closed at . . ..

fermeté, *n.f.* firmness/steadiness (of stocks, etc.).

fermeture, *n.f.* (*a*) **fermeture des ateliers,** (*i*) period when a workshop is closed (*ii*) closing down of the workshops (*iii*) lock-out (*b*) **fermeture annuelle,** annual closure/annual holiday; **heure de fermeture,** closing time (of shop) (*c*) **fermeture d'un compte,** closing of an account.

fête, *n.f.* **fête légale** = public holiday/*Adm:* bank holiday.

feuille, *n.f.* **feuille de paie/des salaires/des appointements,** payroll/pay sheet; **feuille d'impôt,** notice of tax assessment; **feuille de présence,** time sheet; attendance list; **feuille de route,** waybill; **feuille de service,** (duty) roster; *Bank:* **feuille de versement,** paying-in slip.

fiche, *n.f.* (*a*) (*i*) docket/slip (of paper) (*ii*) card/form/list/sheet; **fiche de contrôle,** docket; check-list/check sheet/tally sheet; **fiche de pesage,** weight slip; **fiche technique,** data sheet; **remplir une fiche,** to fill in/(*esp. NAm:*) to fill out a form (*b*) (index) card; **boîte à fiches,** card-index box; **fiche de renseignement,** data card/ information card; **fiche perforée,** perforated/punch(ed) card; **jeu de 100 fiches,** packet of 100 cards; **mettre (des informations) sur fiches,** to card-index; **mise sur fiche(s),** card-indexing.

fichier, *n.m.* (*a*) card-index cabinet/file/ box; filing cabinet; **fichier principal,** master file (*b*) card index.

fichiste, *n.m. & f.* card indexer.

fictif, *a.* (*a*) false/fictitious; *Fin:* **actif fictif,** fictitious assets; **compte fictif,** impersonal account; **dividende fictif,** sham dividend; **prix fictif,** nominal price (*b*) **profits fictifs,** paper profits; *Fin:* **valeur fictive (de la monnaie fiduciaire),** face value (of notes, coinage).

fidéicommis, *n.m. Jur:* trust.

fidéicommissaire, *n.m. Jur:* beneficiary (of a trust).

fiduciaire, 1. *a.* (*a*) fiduciary (loan, etc.); **monnaie fiduciaire,** fiduciary currency (= paper money, coinage of low intrinsic value); **circulation fiduciaire,** fiduciary currency (= paper money); **avoirs des banques en monnaie fiduciaire,** cash holdings of banks; **une circulation fiduciaire excessive entraîne l'inflation,** too much paper money (in circulation) leads to inflation; **titres fiduciaires,** paper securities (*b*) **certificat fiduciaire,** trustee's certificate **2.** *n.m.* trustee.

fiducie, *n.f. Jur:* trust; **grevé de fiducie,** trustee.

figer, *v.tr. PolEc:* to freeze; **les salaires ont été figés,** (the) salaries have been frozen.

figurer, *v.i.* to appear/to figure; **ces articles figurent dans le catalogue,** these articles appear/are listed in the catalogue; **faire figurer la réserve au passif,** to show the reserve among the liabilities.

filiale, *n.f.* subsidiary (company); affiliated firm/*NAm:* affiliate.

filière, *n.f.* **1. il faut que cette demande passe par la filière administrative,** this request must go through the usual official channels **2.** (*a*) transfer note (*b*) *StExch:* **établir la filière,** to draw up the succession of previous holders (of shares).

fin, *n.f.* (*a*) **fin courant,** the end of the (current) month; **fin du mois,** end of the month; **fin prochain,** the end of next month; **facture payable fin juin,** bill payable at the end of June; *Bank:* **sauf bonne fin,** under reserve (*b*) **fins de série,** discontinued line; oddments.

final, *a.* (*a*) **règlement final,** final settlement; **solde final,** final balance (*b*) **compte final,** account for the financial year (*c*) **produit final,** end-product.

finance, *n.f.* (*a*) finance; **le monde de la finance,** the financial world; **la haute finance,** (*i*) (the world of) high finance (*ii*) the financiers/the bankers (*b*) *pl.* finances/financial resources; **les finances de la compagnie vont mal,** the company's finances are in a bad state; **les finances publiques,** public resources/funds; **ministère des Finances** = the Treasury; **Inspecteur des Finances** = (high) Treasury official.

financement, *n.m.* financing; **financement (à court, à long terme),** (short-term, long-term) financing; **le financement du projet sera assuré par la compagnie,** the financing of the project will be undertaken by the company/the company will finance the project.

financer, *v.tr.* to finance (undertaking, etc.); to put up the money for (sth.)/to back (s.o.); **projet financé par . . .,** project financed by . . . .

financier, 1. *a.* (*a*) financial (system, etc.); **contrôle financier,** financial control; **crise financière,** financial crisis; **embarras financiers/difficultés financières,** financial difficulties/trouble; **examen financier,** financial review; **directeur financier,** financial director; **direction/gestion financière,** financial management; **frais financiers,** interest (to pay); **société financière,** finance company; **stratégie financière,** financial strategy; **solide au point de vue financier,** financially sound (*b*) **groupe financier,** group (of interrelated companies) (*c*) **le marché financier,** (*i*) the money market (*ii*) the stock market **2.** *n.m.* financier.

financièrement, *adv.* financially.

firme, *n.f.* business/firm/concern.

fisc, *n.m.* the Inland Revenue/*NAm:* the Internal Revenue; **les employés du fisc/le fisc,** Inland Revenue officials/tax officials/*F:* the tax people/the taxman; **frauder le fisc,** to evade tax(es).

fiscal, *a.* fiscal; **administration fiscale,** the taxation authorities/the tax authorities/*NAm:* the taxing authorities; **asile/paradis fiscal,** tax haven; **avantage fiscal,** tax shelter; **avoir fiscal,** tax credit (on dividend); **charges fiscales/prélèvement fiscal** taxation; **dans un but fiscal,** for tax purposes; **dégrèvement fiscal,** tax reduction; **droits fiscaux,** State dues; taxes; customs and excise dues; **évasion fiscale,** tax avoidance; **exercice fiscal,** financial year; **fraude fiscale,** tax evasion/*F:* tax dodging; **politique fiscale,** fiscal policy; **recettes fiscales,** revenue derived from taxes; **montant des recettes fiscales,** tax yields; **ressources fiscales de l'État,** financial resources of the State; **système fiscal,** tax system.

fiscaliser, *v.tr.* to tax.

fiscalité, *n.f.* financial and taxation system (of a country); **fiscalité excessive,**

excessive taxation; **poids de la fiscalité,** tax burden.

fixation, *n.f.* fixing (of date, indemnity, etc.); setting (of date); **fixation des impôts,** assessment of taxes; **fixation des indemnités,** determination of compensation; **fixation des objectifs,** target setting; **fixation des prix,** price fixing/pricing.

fixe, *a.* fixed/regular/settled; **actif fixe,** fixed assets; **agent fixe,** local agent; **capital fixe,** fixed capital; **coûts fixes,** fixed costs; **dépôt à terme fixe,** fixed deposit; **frais fixes,** fixed expenditure; **placement à revenu fixe,** fixed-yield investment; **prix fixe,** fixed price; **repas à prix fixe,** set menu/meal; **traitement/salaire fixe/***n.m.* **le fixe,** fixed salary; **valeurs à intérêt fixe,** fixed-interest securities.

fixer, *v.tr.* to fix/to determine; to set/to arrange (time); **fixer le prix de qch.,** to determine/to fix the price of sth.; **fixer un jour pour la réunion,** to fix a day/a date for the meeting; **fixer des conditions,** to lay down conditions/to stipulate terms; *StExch:* **fixer un cours,** to make a price.

flambée, *n.f.* **flambée des prix,** price escalation.

flèche, *n.f.* **les prix sont montés en flèche,** prices have shot up/rocketed/soared.

fléchir, *v.i.* to weaken; **les prix des actions fléchissent,** share prices are easier/are down today.

fléchissement, *n.m.* (*a*) **fléchissement des dépôts en banque,** falling off of bank deposits (*b*) falling (of prices); *StExch:* **fléchissement des cours,** sagging/easing of prices.

flexibilité, *n.f. Fin:* **flexibilité (d'une entreprise),** flexibility (of a company).

flexible, *a.* flexible (budget, prices, etc.); **horaire flexible,** flexible (working) hours/flexible time-table/flexi-time.

flottant, *a.* floating/fluctuating; **capitaux flottants,** floating capital/assets; **dette flottante,** floating debt; *Ins:* **police flottante,** floating policy; **titres flottants,**

shares on the market; **taux de change flottant,** floating exchange rate.

flotte, *n.f.* **flotte de vehicules,** fleet of cars.

flotter, *v.i. & tr.* **les prix flottent entre . . . et . . .,** prices fluctuate between . . . and . . .; **faire flotter la livre,** to float the pound.

fluctuation, *n.f.* fluctuation; **fluctuations du change,** fluctuations in exchange dealings; **fluctuations du marché,** market fluctuations/ups and downs of the market; **fluctuations saisonnières,** seasonal fluctuations.

fluctuer, *v.i. Fin:* to fluctuate.

fluidité, *n.f. PolEc:* fluidity/free interplay of supply and demand.

flux, *n.m.* flow; *Fin:* **flux monétaire,** flow of money; **flux réel,** flow of goods.

FOB, *a.inv.* **(vente) FOB,** (sale) free on board (FOB).

foi, *n.f.* **acheteur de bonne foi,** bona fide purchaser; **détenteur de mauvaise foi,** mala fide holder.

foire, *n.f.* (trade) fair; **foire du livre,** book fair.

foire-échantillon, *n.f.* trade fair.

foire-exposition, *n.f.* trade fair.

foncier, *a.* **crédit foncier,** mortgage/loan (on property or land); **Crédit foncier = building society; Crédit foncier de France,** government-controlled building society; **impôt foncier/***n.m.* **le foncier,** land tax/property tax; **propriété foncière,** landed property; real estate; **petite propriété foncière,** smallholding; **registre foncier,** land register; **rente foncière,** ground rent.

fonction, *n.f.* **1.** job; **classification de la fonction,** job classification; **définition de la fonction,** job description; **entrer en fonction,** to take up one's appointment/to start one's job; **se démettre de ses fonctions,** to give in one's notice/to resign;

spécification de la fonction, job specification; voiture de fonction, company car 2. (*a*) les fonctions de président, the functions/duties of a chairman; fonctions de direction, managerial functions; fonctions complémentaires, support activities (*b*) en fonction de, according to/with respect to; les appointements offerts seront fonction de l'expérience, the salary offered will be commensurate with/according to/in accordance with experience.

fonctionnaire, *n.* official/*esp.* civil servant; hauts fonctionnaires, top/high ranking civil servants; petits fonctionnaires, minor officials/minor civil servants.

fonctionnariser, *v.tr.* (*a*) to organize on the lines of the civil service (*b*) to transfer to the civil service/to make part of the civil service.

fonctionnarisme, *n.m.* officialdom/*F:* red tape.

fonctionnel, *a.* functional; organisation fonctionnelle, functional staff/organization; responsabilité fonctionnelle, functional responsibility.

fonctionnement, *n.m.* (*a*) bon fonctionnement d'une entreprise, efficiency/smooth running of a firm (*b*) operation/running/working (of a machine, etc.); en (bon) état de fonctionnement, in (good) working order; frais/coûts de fonctionnement, operating costs/expenses.

fondateur, -trice, *n.* founder (of a business, etc.); *Fin:* promoter/founder (of a company); membre fondateur, founder member; parts de fondateur, founder's shares.

fondé, 1. *a.* funded (debt) 2. *n.m. Jur:* fondé de pouvoir(s), agent (holding power of attorney); proxy; il est le fondé de pouvoir (de), he holds a power of attorney (for).

fonder, *v.tr.* (*a*) to found/to establish (business, etc.); fonder un commerce/une maison de commerce, to start/to set up a business; fonder une société, to float/to launch a company; fondé en 1928, established in 1928 (*b*) *Fin:* to fund (debt).

fondre (se), *v.pr.* to amalgamate; to merge; une société qui se fond avec une autre, a company which amalgamates with another.

fonds, *n.m.* 1. fonds (de commerce), business/goodwill; fonds (de commerce) à vendre, business for sale (as a going concern); fonds d'épicier, grocery business/shop; fonds social, company funds 2. *pl.* (*a*) funds; fonds de roulement, working capital; fonds disponibles, liquid assets; fonds propres, shareholders'/stockholders' equity; faire les fonds, to provide for a bill of exchange; faire/fournir les fonds d'une entreprise, to supply the capital for an undertaking; faire un appel de fonds, to call up capital; mettre des fonds dans une entreprise, to invest money in a business; mise de fonds, (*i*) putting up of capital (*ii*) paid-in capital; ma première mise de fonds a été de £1 000, my initial outlay was £1 000; rentrer dans ses fonds, to recover one's outlay/to get one's outlay back/to get one's money back (*b*) fonds communs, pool; fonds communs de placement, investment fund; mutual fund; fonds d'amortissement, sinking fund; Fonds Monétaire International (FMI), International Monetary Fund (IMF); fonds de prévoyance, contingency reserve; fonds de stabilisation des changes, exchange equalization account (*c*) means/resources; cash; placer son argent à fonds perdus, to purchase a life annuity; prêter à fonds perdus, to lend money without security; dépôt de fonds, depositing (of money in a bank); retrait de fonds, withdrawal; taking money out of a bank account; *Adm:* subvention à fonds perdu, capital grant; être en fonds, to be in funds; fonds de caisse, cash in hand (*d*) *Fin:* stocks/securities/funds; fonds consolidés, funded/consolidated debt; consols; fonds publics/fonds d'État, Government stock.

force, *n.f.* (*a*) **forces économiques,** economic forces; **forces du marché,** market forces (*b*) *Ins:* (**cas de**) **force majeure,** force majeure/act of God (*c*) *Mkt:* **force de vente,** sales force.

forcé, *a.* forced/compulsory; **cours forcé,** forced currency; **emprunt forcé,** forced/compulsory loan; **liquidation forcée,** compulsory liquidation; **vente forcée,** forced/compulsory sale.

forfait, *n.m.* (*a*) (contract for a) fixed price; flat rate; lump sum; **travailler à forfait,** to work by contract; **voyage à forfait,** (all-)inclusive/package tour; **verser un forfait,** to pay a fixed sum (*b*) **vente à forfait,** outright sale.

forfaitaire, *a.* (*a*) **prix forfaitaire,** fixed price; flat rate; inclusive price; contract price; **voyage à prix forfaitaire,** package tour (*b*) **vente forfaitaire,** outright sale.

formalité, *n.f.* formality; **formalités de douanes,** customs formalities.

format, *n.m.* format/size; **grand format,** large-size(d); **petit format,** small size(d); **format de poche,** pocket-size(d); **papier format A4,** A4 (size) paper; **formats postaux normalisés,** Post Office preferred.

formation, *n.f.* (*a*) forming; development; **formation des prix sur le marché,** market pricing; **formation de réserves,** building up of reserves; **société en voie de formation,** developing company (*b*) education/training; **formation professionnelle,** professional/vocational training; **formation dans l'entreprise,** in-house/in-plant training; **formation des cadres,** management training/executive training; **formation sur le tas,** on-the-job training.

forme, *n.f.* **la quittance est en (bonne) forme,** the receipt is in order; **un reçu en bonne et due forme,** a regular receipt.

former, *v.tr.* to form; **former une société,** to form a company.

formulaire, *n.m.* (printed) form; questionnaire; **formulaire de candidature,** application form; **remplir un formulaire,** to fill in a form/(*esp. NAm:*) to fill out a form.

formule, *n.f.* **1.** *Jur:* **formule d'un contrat,** wording of a contract **2.** method; **il existe trois formules de paiement,** there are three methods of payment/you can pay in three different ways; **nous offrons deux formules différentes de voyage organisé,** we can offer two different types of package tour **3.** (printed) form (to be filled up); **formule d'effet de commerce,** form for bill of exchange; **formule de chèque,** cheque form; **remplir une formule,** to fill in/(*esp. NAm:*) to fill out a form.

formuler, *v.tr.* to formulate; **formuler un acte,** to draw up a document in due form/to formulate a document.

fort, *a.* (*a*) strong; *Fin:* **devise forte,** strong currency (*b*) **forte baisse des prix,** sharp/big drop in prices; **forte hausse des prix,** sharp/big rise in prices; **prix en forte hausse,** soaring prices; **forte perte,** heavy loss; **forte somme,** large sum of money; **il a un fort salaire,** he has a high salary/he is highly paid (*c*) **prix fort,** full price/catalogue price/list price.

fortement, *adv.* strongly/heavily/highly; **fortement rémunéré,** highly paid; **fortement taxé,** heavily taxed.

Fortran, *n.m. Cmptr:* Fortran.

fortune, *n.f.* **1.** fortune/chance; *MIns:* **fortune de mer,** (*i*) perils of the sea; accidents at sea (*ii*) goods on which a maritime lien applies **2.** fortune/wealth; **faire fortune,** to make a fortune; **impôt sur la fortune,** wealth tax.

fourchette, *n.f. Stat:* bracket; range; **fourchette salariale/de salaire,** wage bracket; **une fourchette de 10 à 20%,** a 10 to 20% band.

fournir, **1.** *v.tr.* to supply/to provide; to find (a security); **fournir qch. à qn/fournir qn de qch.,** to supply s.o. with sth.; **fournir**

un restaurant en pain, to supply a restaurant with bread; **ce magasin nous fournit tout le matériel de bureau,** this shop supplies us with all our office equipment (b) **fournir une lettre de crédit sur qn,** to issue a letter of credit on s.o.; **fournir en nantissement,** to lodge as collateral; **fournir une traite sur qn,** to draw a bill on s.o.; **fournir sur la BNP,** to draw (a cheque) on the BNP (c) **magasin bien fourni,** well-stocked shop **2.** v.i. **fournir aux dépenses,** to contribute to the expenses **3.** v.pr. **il se fournit chez nous,** he is a customer of ours/he's one of our customers; we supply him.

fournissement, n.m. Fin: **1.** contribution in shares (to a company); holding in shares **2. compte de fournissement,** repartition account.

fournisseur, -euse, n. (a) supplier/purveyor; dealer/stockist; caterer; **fournisseur exclusif,** sole supplier (b) **les fournisseurs de cette ville,** the tradesmen of this town; **entrée des fournisseurs,** tradesmen's entrance (c) Fin: **comptes fournisseurs,** accounts payable/NAm: payables; **crédit fournisseur,** supplier's credit/trade credit.

fourniture, n.f. (a) supplying/providing (b) pl. supply of goods/supplies/requisites; **fournitures de bureau,** office equipment/(office) stationery; **contrat de fourniture,** supply contract; **main-d'oeuvre et fournitures/façon et fournitures,** labour and material.

fraction, n.f. fraction; **par 10 francs ou fraction de 10 francs,** for each 10 francs or fraction/or fractional part thereof.

fractionnaire, a. fractional; **couvertures fractionnaires,** fractional reserves; **livre fractionnaire,** day book/book of prime entry.

fractionner, v.tr. to divide into parts; to split (up) (shares, etc.).

frais, n.m.pl. expenses/cost; **frais d'administration/de gestion,** administration costs/management expenses; Nau: **frais**

d'agence, agency fees/attendance fees; **frais d'amortissement,** (i) amortization charges (ii) (amount written off for) depreciation (of building, plant, etc.); **frais de bureau,** office allowance/office expenses; **frais de déplacement,** travel allowance/ travel expenses; **frais directs,** direct costs; **frais divers,** sundry charges/ sundries; **frais d'entreposage/de magasinage,** storage charges/warehouse charges; **frais d'entretien (du matériel, etc.),** upkeep/maintenance expenses; cost of upkeep/of maintenance; **frais d'établissement,** capital expenditure; **frais d'exploitation,** operating costs; current expenditure; **exempt de frais/sans frais,** free of charge; no expenses; **frais de fabrication,** production costs; **faux frais,** incidental/additional expenses; contingencies; extras; **frais fixes/permanents,** fixed charges; standing costs/expenses/ charges; **frais généraux,** general (running) expenses; overheads/oncost; **à grands frais,** at great cost; expensively; **à peu de frais,** at little cost; inexpensively; **frais d'installation,** initial/preliminary expenses; **frais de justice,** legal costs; Ind: **frais de lancement d'une fabrication,** set-up costs; **frais de main-d'œuvre,** labour costs; **aux frais de la maison,** at the firm's expense; **frais de manutention,** handling costs/expenses; **menus frais,** petty expenses; **frais à payer,** outstanding expenses; **frais de port,** carriage; **frais de représentation,** (i) business expenses (ii) entertainment allowance; **frais de transport,** transport charges; **frais de trésorerie,** finance costs; **total des frais effectués/ encourus,** total expenses incurred; **tous frais payés,** (i) all expenses paid (ii) all-inclusive; **le voyage (organisé) coûte 2 400 francs tous frais payés,** the (package) holiday costs 2 400 francs all-inclusive; **faire les frais de qch.,** to bear the cost of/the expense of sth.; **faire/couvrir ses frais,** (i) to cover one's expenses/to get back one's money (ii) to get out of a transaction without loss (iii) to pay its way; **se mettre en frais,** to go to (great) expense; **rentrer dans ses frais,** to get one's money back.

franc[1], *n.m.* franc; **franc (belge, français, suisse),** (Belgian, French, Swiss) franc; **franc or,** gold franc; **franc vert,** green franc; **compte (tenu) en francs,** franc account; **pièce de 5 francs,** 5 franc piece.

franc[2], *a.* **1.** free; **franc de tout droit,** duty-free/free of duty; **franc d'impôts,** exempt from taxation; **franc de port,** carriage paid; *Cust:* **zone franche,** free zone; *Nau:* **franc d'avaries,** free of average; **port franc,** free port **2.** complete/whole; **huit jours francs/délai franc de huit jours,** eight clear days.

franchisage, *n.m.* franchising; **contrat de franchisage,** franchise.

franchise, *n.f.* **1.** exemption; **importer/faire entrer qch. en franchise,** to import sth. free of duty/duty-free; **franchise de bagages,** (free) luggage/baggage allowance; *Post:* **(en) franchise postale (f.p.)** = official paid; **en franchise d'impôt,** exempt from tax/tax free **2.** **franchise d'assurance,** (*i*) excess clause (*ii*) franchise.

franchisé, *n.m.* franchisee.

franchiseur, *n.m.* franchisor.

franco, 1. *adv.* **franco (de port),** free/carriage free; carriage paid/postage paid; **livré franco/franco (à) domicile,** delivery free; carriage paid; **franco de bord (FOB),** free on board (f.o.b.); **franco long du bord (FLB)/franco quai,** free alongside ship (f.a.s.); free on quay/at wharf; *NAm:* ex quay/ex wharf; **franco gare,** free on rail; **livraison franco frontière française,** delivered free as far as the French frontier **2.** *n.m.* *StExch:* single commission (on double operation).

frappe, *n.f.* (*a*) minting (of coins) (*b*) typing; **faute de frappe,** typing error.

frapper, *v.tr.* (*a*) **frapper des marchandises d'un droit,** to impose/to levy a duty on goods (*b*) to mint (coins) (*c*) to type (letter, etc.).

fraude, *n.f.* **1.** fraud/deception; *Jur:* **fraude civile,** fraud/wilful misrepresentation; **fraude fiscale,** tax evasion; tax dodging; **fraude douanière,** illegal entry/illegal importation (of goods)/smuggling; **en fraude,** (*i*) fraudulently/unlawfully (*ii*) secretly; **faire entrer/introduire qch. en fraude,** to smuggle sth. in/to smuggle sth. through (the) customs **2.** fraudulence/deceit; **par fraude,** under false pretences.

frauder, *v.tr.* to defraud/to swindle/to cheat (s.o.); **frauder la douane,** to defraud the customs/to smuggle; **frauder le fisc,** to evade/to dodge tax.

fraudeur, -euse, *n.* (*a*) defrauder/cheat/swindler (*b*) smuggler (*c*) tax dodger.

frauduleusement, *adv.* fraudulently/by fraud.

frauduleux, *a.* fraudulent; *Jur:* **banqueroute frauduleuse,** fraudulent bankruptcy.

freiner, *v.tr.* to curb (inflation); **freiner la production,** to check/to restrain production.

freinte, *n.f.* loss in weight (during transit, manufacture).

fret, *n.m.* **1.** freight (for sea, air, road, transport); **fret aérien,** air freight; **payer le fret,** to pay the freight/freight charges; *Rail: etc:* **fret au poids,** freight by weight; **taux du fret,** freight rates **2.** chartering; **donner un navire à fret,** to freight (out) a ship; **prendre un navire à fret,** to charter a ship **3.** load/cargo (of ship, aircraft, lorry); **prendre du fret,** to take in freight/to embark cargo; **fret d'aller,** outward freight; **fret de retour,** home freight; **faux fret,** dead freight.

fréter, *v.tr.* to freight (out) a ship; to hire a car/a lorry.

fréteur, *n.m.* person who freights (out) a ship/shipowner; **fréteur et affréteur,** owner and charterer.

fuite, *n.f.* **fuite des capitaux à l'étranger,** flight of capital abroad.

fumeur, *n.m.* *Trans:* **compartiment fumeurs,** smoking compartment/smoker; **compartiment non fumeurs,** non-smoking compartment/non-smoker.

fusion, *n.f.* *Fin:* merger; **fusion entre deux compagnies,** merger of two companies; **opérer une fusion,** to amalgamate.

fusionner, *v.i.* to amalgamate/to merge.

futur, *a.* **futur acheteur,** intending purchaser/prospective customer; **ventes futures,** future sales; **valeur future,** prospective value.

G

gâchage, *n.m.* **gâchage des prix,** price cutting.

gage, *n.m.* (*a*) security; *Jur:* **contrat de gage,** bailment (*b*) pawned article; pledge; **laisser qch. en gage,** to leave sth. as security/on deposit; to pledge sth. as security; **mettre qch. en gage,** to pawn/to pledge sth.; **mise en gage,** pawning/pledging; **prêteur sur gages,** pawnbroker; **ma montre est en gage,** my watch is in pawn.

gagé, *a. Jur:* **créance gagée,** secured loan; **recettes non gagées,** unassigned/unpledged revenue.

gager, *v.tr.* to guarantee/to secure (loan, etc.).

gagiste, *n.m.* **(créancier) gagiste,** secured creditor; pledgee.

gagner, *v.tr.* to earn; **gagner de l'argent,** to earn money; **gagner cinq mille francs par mois,** to earn five thousand francs a month; **gagner gros,** (*i*) to earn a lot of money (*ii*) to make large profits; **il gagne bien sa vie,** he earns a good salary/he makes good money.

gain, *n.m.* (*a*) gain/profit; **gains d'une entreprise,** profits of a company (*b*) earnings; **gains d'un ouvrier,** a worker's earnings; **gain de la femme mariée,** wife's earned income/wife's personal income.

gamme, *n.f.* (*a*) range/series/scale; **gamme de produits,** range/line of products; **gamme des prix,** price range/scale of prices (*b*) **haut de gamme,** up market; **bas de gamme,** down market; **quartier de haut de gamme,** up market area/ fashionable area.

garant, -ante, *n.* guarantor/(*esp. NAm:*) warrantor; surety/bail; **garant d'une dette,** surety for a debt; **se porter garant pour qn,** to stand/to go surety for s.o.

garantie[1], *n.f. Jur:* guarantee/(*esp. NAm:*) warantee.

garantie[2], *n.f.* (*a*) guarantee/pledge (of execution of contract); guaranty (of payment); **garantie accessoire,** collateral (security); **garantie bancaire,** bank guarantee; **garantie d'exécution,** contract bond; **fonds déposés en garantie,** funds lodged as security; *Fin:* **garantie de la circulation,** backing of the currency (*b*) guarantee/ warranty (of quality, etc.); **bulletin de garantie,** (certificate of) guarantee; **avec garantie,** guaranteed; **sans garantie,** having no guarantee/no warranty; **sous garantie,** under guarantee (*c*) *Fin:* underwriting; **syndicat de garantie,** underwriters; **contrat de garantie,** underwriting contract (*d*) **caisse/fonds de garantie (d'un emprunt),** guarantee fund.

garantir, *v.tr.* (*a*) to warrant/to guarantee; **créance garantie,** secured debt; **garantir le paiement d'une dette,** to guarantee a debt (*b*) **montre garantie (pour) deux ans,** watch under a two-year guarantee/guaranteed for two years (*c*) *Fin:* to underwrite (issue of shares, etc.); **garantir un contrat,** to underwrite a contract (*d*) **garantir un emprunt,** to back a loan (*e*) **son assurance le garantit contre le vol,** his insurance covers him against theft/he is covered against theft (by his insurance).

garçon, *n.m.* **garçon de bureau,** office boy; (office) messenger.

garde, *n.f.* **garde (en dépôt),** (safe) keeping/(safe) custody; **déposer des titres en garde,** to place securities in safe custody.

gare, *n.f.* (*a*) railway/*NAm:* railroad station; **gare d'arrivée,** (*i*) (*pour passagers*) arrival station (*ii*) (*pour marchandises*) receiving station; **gare de départ,** (*pour passagers*) departure station; **gare d'expédition/gare expéditrice,** forwarding station/dispatch station; **gare de marchandises,** goods depot/goods station/*NAm:* freight depot (*b*) **gare routière,** (*i*) (bus, coach) station/terminal (*ii*) road haulage depot.

gas-oil, *n.m.* diesel oil.

gâter, *v.tr.* to spoil/to damage; **gâter le marché,** to spoil the market.

gelé, *a.* frozen; *Fin:* **capitaux gelés,** frozen capital; **dettes gelées,** frozen debts.

général, *a.* general; **assemblée générale,** general meeting; **directeur général,** (*i*) managing director (*ii*) general manager; **frais généraux,** overheads/general (running) expenses; **hausse générale des prix,** general increase in prices; *PolEc:* **commerce général,** total/global trade (including entrepôt trade).

gérance, *n.f.* (*a*) management (of business); **contrat de gérance,** management agreement (*b*) managership/administratorship; **pendant sa gérance,** during his period as manager/under his administration.

gérant, -ante, *n.* manager/manageress; **gérant d'une succursale,** branch manager.

gérer, *v.tr.* **gérer un commerce,** to manage/to run a business; **mal gérer ses finances,** to mismanage one's finances.

gestion, *n.f.* management; administration; control; **comptabilité de gestion,** management accounting; **conseil en gestion,** management consultant; **contrôle de la gestion,** management audit; **gestion administrative,** administration; **gestion autonome,** independant administration; **gestion cellulaire/par département,** divisional management; **gestion financière (d'une affaire),** financial administration (of a business); **gestion prévisionnelle/budgétaire,** budgetary control; **gestion des affaires,** business management; **gestion des effectifs,** manpower management; **gestion de la production,** production control; **gestion de portefeuille,** portfolio management; **gestion des stocks,** stock control/*NAm:* inventory control; **rapport de gestion,** management report; **science de la gestion,** management science; **techniques de gestion,** management techniques.

gestionnaire, 1. *a.* **compte gestionnaire,** management account 2. *n.* manager/manageress; administrator; **gestionnaire de(s) stock(s),** stock controller/*NAm:* inventory controller.

global, *a.* total/overall; gross; lump (sum); **budget global de publicité,** overall publicity budget; **contrat global,** package deal; **montant global/somme globale,** total amount; **revenu global,** gross income.

gold-point, *n.m. Fin:* gold point; **gold-point d'entrée/d'importation,** import gold point; **gold-point de sortie/d'exportation,** export gold point; **maintenir le change au-dessus du gold-point,** to maintain the exchange above the gold point.

gondole, *n.f. Mkt:* gondola; island shelves.

gracieux, *a.* free (of charge); **à titre gracieux,** gratis/free of charge; **billet donné à titre gracieux,** complimentary ticket.

gramme, *n.m. Meas:* gram (*abbr:* g) (= 0.0353 oz.).

grand(-)livre, *n.m.* (general) ledger; **grand(-)livre d'achats,** bought ledger; **grand(-)livre de ventes,** sales ledger; **porter qch. au grand(-)livre,** to post an entry/to enter an item in the ledger.

graphique, *n.m.* diagram; graph; chart; **graphique d'acheminement,** flow (process) chart; **graphique des activités,** activity chart; **graphique à secteurs/graphique circulaire,** pie-chart.

gratis, 1. *adv.* gratis/free (of charge) **2.** *a.* free (ticket, etc.); **entrée gratis,** admission free.

gratuit, *a.* free (of charge); **échantillon gratuit,** free sample; **essai gratuit,** free trial; **crédit gratuit,** interest-free credit.

gratuitement, *adv.* free of charge.

gré, *n.m.* **au gré de l'acheteur,** at buyer's option; **au gré du vendeur,** at seller's option; **bail renouvable au gré du locataire,** lease renewable at the option of the tenant; **de gré à gré,** by (mutual) agreement; **vendre de gré à gré,** to sell by private contract.

grève, *n.f.* strike/walkout; **allocation de grève,** strike pay; **briseur de grève,** strike breaker/*F:* blackleg/scab; **grève d'avertissement/symbolique,** token strike; **grève générale,** general strike; **grève perlée,** go-slow; **grève sauvage,** unofficial strike; **grève surprise,** lightning strike; **grève sur le tas,** sit-down strike; sit-in; **grève tournante,** staggered strike; **grève du zèle,** work to rule; **piquet de grève,** (strike) picket; **faire la grève du zèle,** to work to rule; **faire grève,** to (be on) strike; **lancer un ordre de grève/ordonner une grève,** to call a strike; **se mettre en grève,** to go/to come out on strike; to take strike action; **ils se sont mis en grève par solidarité avec les mineurs,** they came out (on strike) in sympathy with the miners.

grever, *v.tr.* to burden/to encumber; **contribuable grevé d'impôts,** taxpayer saddled with taxes.

gréviste, *n.m. & f.* striker.

grille, *n.f.* grid; **grille de gestion,** managerial grid; **grille des salaires,** salary scale.

gros, 1. *a.* (*a*) big/large; **gros bénéfices,** large profits; **grosse somme d'argent,** large sum of money; **la plus grosse partie** de nos affaires, the bulk of our business (*b*) **gros propriétaire,** big landowner **2.** *adv.* **gagner gros,** to make a lot (of money) **3.** *n.m.* (*a*) bulk/mass; **le gros de la cargaison,** the bulk of the cargo (*b*) **en gros,** roughly/broadly/approximately; **évaluation en gros,** rough estimate (*c*) wholesale (trade); **faire le gros et le détail,** to deal wholesale and retail; **maison/commerce de gros,** wholesale business; **commerçant en gros,** wholesale dealer/wholesaler; **prix de gros,** wholesale price.

grosse, *n.f.* (*a*) gross/twelve dozen; **six grosses de crayons,** six gross (of) pencils (*b*) *Jur:* engrossed document/engrossment/written instrument; **grosse (exécutoire),** first authentic copy of agreement or title).

grossiste, *n.m. & f.* wholesaler/wholesale dealer.

group, *n.m. Bank:* sealed bag of cash/of specie (for transmission to or from branch office).

groupage, *n.m.* bulking (of parcels); consolidation (of orders, etc.); **service de groupage,** joint cargo service/consolidation service.

groupe, *n.m.* group (of companies); **le Groupe Shell,** the Shell Group; **comptes de groupe,** group accounts; *PolEc: Ind: etc:* **groupe de pression,** pressure group; **groupe de travail,** working party.

groupement, *n.m.* **1.** (*a*) *Stat:* **groupement de données,** classification/grouping of data (*b*) pooling (of interests, etc.) **2.** (*a*) group (of companies); **groupement de consommateurs,** consumer group; **groupement syndical,** trade union bloc (*b*) *Ind:* pool.

grouper, *v.tr.* to group; to consolidate (orders, etc.); **grouper des colis,** to collect parcels (for forwarding in bulk).

groupeur, *n.m.* forwarding agent.

guelte, *n.f.* commission/percentage (on sales).

guerre, *n.f.* war; **guerre des prix,** price war; **guerre des tarifs,** tariff war.

guichet, *n.m.* (*a*) *Bank: Post:* position; **guichet fermé,** position closed; **payer au guichet,** to pay at the counter (*b*) booking office (window); *Th:* box office (window) (*c*) *Bank:* **guichet automatique,** cash dispenser/*NAm:* automatic teller.

guichetier, -ière, *n. Bank:* counter clerk/*NAm:* teller; *Post:* counter assistant/clerk; *Th: Cin:* booking clerk; box office assistant.

H

habillage, *n.m.* (*a*) packaging (of goods) (*b*) **habillage du bilan,** window-dressing of the balance-sheet.

habiller, *v.tr.* (*a*) **habiller un article pour la vente,** to label/to box/to package an article for sale (*b*) **habiller le bilan,** to window-dress the balance-sheet.

***hallage**, *n.m.* **(droits de) hallage,** market dues; stallage.

***halle**, *n.f.* (covered) market; **halle aux blés,** corn exchange; **halle aux poissons,** fish market; **halle aux vins,** wine market.

***hausse**, *n.f.* (*a*) rise; **les affaires sont à la hausse,** business is looking up (*b*) **hausse du coût de la vie,** rise in the cost of living; **hausse des prix,** rise in prices; **les prix sont à la hausse,** prices are hardening; prices are going up; **les prix ont subi une forte hausse,** prices have gone up considerably/prices have shot up; **hausse du prix du pain,** rise/increase in the price of bread; **(la) hausse du prix du pétrole,** (the) increase in oil prices (*c*) **hausse du taux officiel de l'escompte,** the raising of the minimum lending rate; **accuser une hausse,** to show a rise; to go up (*d*) *StExch:* **actions en hausse,** shares that are rising/that are going up; **marché à la hausse,** rising market; **spéculateur à la hausse,** bull; **tendance à la hausse,** bullish tendency; **jouer/spéculer à la hausse,** to speculate on a rising market/to go a bull; **provoquer une hausse factice,** to rig the market.

***hausser**, **1.** *v.tr.* to raise; **hausser les prix,** to raise/to put up prices; **hausser le taux (officiel) de l'escompte,** to raise/to put up the minimum lending rate **2.** *v.i.* to rise; to go up/to increase; **faire hausser les prix,** to send up/to force up prices.

***haussier**, *n.m. StExch: F:* bull.

***haut, 1.** *a.* (*a*) high; **la haute direction,** top management; **la haute finance/la haute banque,** (*i*) high finance (*ii*) the financiers/bankers; **haut fonctionnaire,** top civil servant (*b*) **haut salaire,** high salary; **les prix sont hauts,** prices are high **2.** *n.m.* top/upper part; (*sur une boîte, etc.*) **haut,** this side up.

hebdomadaire, 1. *a.* weekly; **bilan hebdomadaire,** weekly return/weekly (trading) report; **salaire hebdomadaire,** weekly salary/wage **2.** *n.* **un hebdomadaire,** a weekly (paper, magazine).

heure, *n.f.* hour; time; **heure d'arrivée,** arrival time/time of arrival; **heure de départ,** departure time/time of departure; **aux heures de bureau/d'affaires,** during office hours; **en dehors des heures d'affaires/de bureau,** out of office hours; **heures d'ouverture/heures d'affaires,** (*i*) times of opening/opening hours (*ii*) business/office hours; **heures d'affluence/de pointe,** rush hour/peak period(s); **heures creuses,** off-peak hours; **engager qn à l'heure,** to employ s.o. by the hour; **être payé à l'heure,** to be paid by the hour; **il est payé 15 francs (de) l'heure,** he is paid 15 francs an hour; **ouvrier à l'heure,** hourly-paid worker; casual worker; **heure de travail/heure d'ouvier,** man-hour; **la semaine de quarante heures,** the forty-hour week; **il travaille 8 heures par jour,** he works an 8-hour day; **heures supplémentaires,** overtime.

*hiérarchie, *n.f. Adm:* classification of grades/ranking; managerial structure.

*hiérarchique, *a.* cadre hiérarchique, line officer; directeur hiérarchique, line director; line manager; structure hiérarchique, line organization.

*hiérarchiser, *v.tr.* hiérarchiser le personnel, to grade the staff.

histogramme, *n.m.* histogram.

*holding, *n.m. Fin:* holding; société holding, holding company.

homme-sandwich, *n.m.* sandwich man.

homologation, *n.f. Ind:* homologation d'un prototype, type approval/type certification.

homologuer, *v.tr.* (*a*) to ratify; to approve; to obtain legal ratification (of document); to probate (a will) (*b*) *Adm:* prix homologués, authorized charges/prices.

honneur, *n.m.* (*a*) honour; *Fin:* faire honneur à une traite, to honour/to meet a bill; ne pas faire honneur à une traite, to dishonour a bill; acceptation par honneur, acceptance (of a bill) for honour (*b*) prêt d'honneur, loan on trust.

honorabilité, *n.f.* maison d'une honorabilité reconnue, firm of recognized standing.

honorable, *a.* maison honorable, firm of high standing.

honoraire, 1. *a.* honorary (member, etc.) 2. *n.m.pl.* fee(s) (of doctor, lawyer, etc.); honorarium.

honorer, *v.tr. Fin:* to honour/to meet/to retire (bill); ne pas honorer une traite, to dishonour a bill; *Jur:* refuser d'honorer un contrat, to repudiate a contract.

horaire, 1. *a.* hourly; *Ind:* débit horaire, hourly output/output per hour; puissance horaire, output per hour; salarié horaire, hourly-paid worker 2. *n.m.* timetable; schedule; times of opening (of a shop);

horaire souple/variable/flexible, flexitime/flex-time/flexible working time/ flexible working hours.

horizontal, *a.* (*a*) organisation horizontale, functional organization/staff organization (*b*) concentration horizontale, horizontal merger; intégration horizontale, horizontal integration.

*hors, *prep.* 1. hors pointe, off-peak (hours); prix hors saison, off-peak prices/fares; modèle hors série, made-to-order model/custom-built model; hors taxe (HT), exclusive of tax 2. *prep. phr.* mettre un associé hors d'intérêt, to buy out a partner; c'est hors de prix, it is too expensive; the price is prohibitive.

*hors-cote, *a.* actions hors-cote, unlisted shares/shares not quoted on the Stock Exchange; marché hors cote, unofficial market/over-the-counter market.

hôtel, *n.m.* 1. l'Hôtel de la Monnaie, the Mint 2. (*a*) hotel; hôtel de luxe, luxury hotel/first-class hotel; hôtel de tourisme, tourist (class) hotel (*b*) hôtel meublé/garni, lodging house/residential hotel/ *NAm:* rooming house.

hôtelier, -ière, 1. *n.* hotelier/hotel manager/hotel proprietor 2. *a.* l'industrie hôtelière, the hotel trade.

hôtellerie, *n.f.* l'hôtellerie, the hotel trade.

humidité, *n.f.* humidity; (*sur un colis*) craint l'humidité, keep in a dry place/to be kept dry.

hypermarché, *n.m.* hypermarket.

hypothécable, *a.* mortgageable; biens hypothécables, mortgageable property.

hypothécaire, *a.* contrat hypothécaire, mortgage deed; créancier hypothécaire, mortgagee; débiteur hypothécaire, mortgagor; garantie hypothécaire, mortgage security; obligation hypothécaire, mortgage bond/debenture; prêt hypothécaire, loan on mortgage.

hypothécairement, *adv.* by/on mortgage; **créance garantie hypothécairement,** debt secured by mortgage; **emprunter hypothécairement,** to borrow on mortgage.

hypothèque, *n.f.* mortgage; **première hypothèque/hypothèque de premier rang,** first mortgage; **deuxième hypothèque,** second mortgage; **hypothèque générale,** blanket mortgage; **prêt sur hypothèque,** mortgage loan; **avoir une hypothèque sur une maison,** to have a mortgage on a house/to have one's house mortgaged; **emprunter sur hypothèque,** to borrow on mortgage; **prendre une hypothèque,** to raise a mortgage; **purger une hypothèque,** to pay off/to redeem a mortgage.

hypothéquer, *v.tr.* **1.** to mortgage (estate, etc.); **hypothéquer des titres,** to mortgage securities; to lodge stock as security **2.** to secure (debt) by mortgage.

I

identité, *n.f.* identity; **carte d'identité,** identity card; **papiers d'identité,** identification papers.

illégal, *a.* illegal/unlawful.

illégalement, *adv.* illegally/unlawfully.

illégalité, *n.f.* **1.** illegality/unlawfulness **2.** unlawful act.

illicite, *a.* illicit; **profits illicites,** illicit profits.

illimité, *a.* unlimited; **crédit illimité,** unlimited credit; *Fin:* **responsabilité illimitée,** unlimited liability.

ilôt, *n.m. Mkt:* **ilôt de vente,** (display) stand/island.

image, *n.f.* image; **image de marque,** (*i*) brand image (*ii*) corporate image; **image de produit,** product image.

imbattable, *a.* unbeatable; **prix imbattables,** (highly) competitive prices/unbeatable prices/lowest prices.

immatériel, *a.* **valeurs immatérielles,** intangible assets/intangibles.

immatriculation, *n.f.* registering/registration (of deed, company, etc.); **plaque d'immatriculation (d'une voiture),** registration plate (of a car).

immatricule, *n.f.* registration (of deed, etc.).

immatriculer, *v.tr.* to register (document, company, etc.).

immeuble, 1. *a. Jur:* **biens immeubles,** real estate/property; immovable property/immovables **2.** *n.m.* (*a*) real estate/landed property/(*esp. NAm:*) realty;

gérant d'immeubles, property manager; **immeuble(s) de rapport,** rented property; **placer son argent en immeubles,** to invest in property (*b*) building; **immeuble (de bureaux),** office block (*c*) premises *pl;* **immeuble commercial,** business premises.

immobilier, 1. *a. Jur:* **biens immobiliers,** real estate/(*esp. NAm:*) realty; immovable property/immovables; **agence immobilière,** estate agency/*NAm:* real estate agency; **agent immobilier,** estate agent/*NAm:* real estate agent/realtor; **marché immobilier,** property market; **société immobilière,** (*i*) = building society (*ii*) = real estate company; **vente immobilière,** sale of property **2.** *n.m.* (*a*) real estate/realty; immovable property/immovables (*b*) (the) property/real estate business; **il a fait (sa) fortune dans l'immobilier,** he made his money in property.

immobilisation, *n.f.* **1.** (*a*) *Jur:* conversion (of personalty) into real estate (*b*) *Fin:* capitalization (of expenditure) **2.** (*a*) immobilization/locking up/tying up/tie-up (of capital) (*b*) *pl.* **immobilisations (corporelles),** tangible assets/fixed assets/capital assets; **immobilisations incorporelles,** intangible assets; **faire de grosses immobilisations,** to carry heavy stocks.

immobilisé, *a.* **actif immobilisé/valeurs immobilisées,** fixed assets.

immobiliser, *v.tr.* **1.** *Jur:* to convert (personalty) into real estate **2.** to immobilize/to lock up/to tie up (capital).

impasse, *n.f.* (*a*) deadlock (*b*) *Fin:* **impasse (budgétaire),** budget deficit.

impayé, (*a*) *a.* unpaid (debt, bill, etc.); **comptes impayés,** unsettled accounts (*b*) *a. & n.m.* dishonoured (bill); **les impayés,** outstanding payments; dishonoured bills.

impenses, *n.f.pl. Jur:* expenses incurred for the maintenance or improvement of property; **impenses nécessaires,** maintenance expenses; **impenses utiles,** expenditure on improvements (which give increased value to the property); **impenses voluptuaires,** expenditure on luxury items (which do not really increase the value of the property).

implantation, *n.f.* (*a*) **l'implantation d'une industrie dans une région,** the setting up/establishment of an industry in a region (*b*) layout (of factory, equipment, etc.); **implantation fonctionnelle,** functional layout.

implanter, *v.tr.* **implanter une industrie nouvelle,** to set up/to establish a new industry.

importable, *a.* **produits importables,** importable products/products that may be imported.

importance, *n.f.* (*a*) size; extent; **usine de moyenne importance,** medium-sized factory; **importance des dégâts,** extent of the damage (*b*) position/standing; **importance d'une société,** standing of a company.

important, *a.* large/considerable; **une somme importante,** a considerable/large sum of money; **nous ne pouvons pas vous accorder un crédit plus important,** we cannot allow you credit beyond this limit.

importateur, -trice, 1. *n.* importer; **importateur exclusif pour la France,** sole importer for France **2.** *a.* importing (firm, etc.); **les pays importateurs de pétrole,** the oil-importing countries.

importation, *n.f.* **1.** importing (of goods); **contingents d'importation,** import quo-

tas; **droit d'importation,** import duty; **excédent/surplus d'importation,** import surplus; **importation en franchise,** duty-free import; **licence d'importation,** import licence; **maison d'importation,** importer; **prix à l'importation,** import price; **restrictions d'importation,** import restrictions; **tarifs d'importation,** import tariffs **2.** (**article d')importation,** import; *pl.* **importations,** imports/imported goods; **importations visibles,** visible imports; **importations invisibles,** invisible imports; **contingentement des importations,** import quota system.

importer, *v.tr.* to import (goods); **importer des marchandises des États-Unis en France,** to import goods from the United States into France; **la France importe du café,** France is an importer of coffee.

import-export, *n.m. or f.* **une entreprise d'import-export,** an import-export business.

imposable, *a.* (*a*) taxable/liable to tax; **matière imposable/revenu imposable,** taxable income (*b*) rateable/assessable (property); **valeur locative imposable,** rateable value.

imposé, 1. *a.* **prix imposés** = resale price maintenance (RPM) **2. marchandises imposées,** taxed goods **3.** *n.* (*a*) taxpayer (*b*) ratepayer.

imposer, *v.tr.* (*a*) *Adm:* **imposer des droits sur qch.,** to impose/to put a tax on sth.; to tax sth.; **objets lourdement imposés,** goods heavily taxed (*b*) **imposer qn,** (*i*) to tax s.o. (*ii*) to rate s.o.; **imposer qch.,** to make sth. liable to tax; to tax sth./to put a tax on sth.; **imposer les automobiles,** to tax cars; **imposer un immeuble,** to levy a rate on a building.

imposition, *n.f.* taxation; **barème d'imposition,** tax schedule; **double imposition,** double taxation; **taux d'imposition,** rate of taxation.

impôt, *n.m.* tax/duty; **avant impôt,** before tax(ation); **après impôt,** after tax(ation);

(être) assujetti à l'impôt, (to be) liable to tax; **cédule d'impôt,** tax code; **crédit d'impôt,** tax credit; **exempt d'impôt,** tax-free/exempt from tax; **déclaration/feuille d'impôts,** income tax return; tax form; **dégrèvement d'impôt,** tax cuts; tax relief/reduction; **impôt direct,** direct tax; **impôt foncier,** land tax; **impôt indirect,** indirect tax; **impôts locaux,** rates; **impôt progressif,** graduated income tax; **impôt retenu à la base/à la source,** (*i*) pay as you earn (tax)/PAYE/ *NAm:* pay as you go (*ii*) tax deducted at source; **impôt sur le capital,** capital levy; **impôt sur le chiffre d'affaires,** turnover tax; **impôt sur la fortune,** wealth tax; **impôt sur le revenu,** income tax; **impôt sur les dividendes,** tax on dividend; **impôt sur les plus-values,** capital gains ·tax; **impôt sur les sociétés,** corporation tax; **impôt du timbre,** stamp duty; **frapper qch. d'un impôt,** to tax sth./to levy a tax on sth.; **perception/recouvrement de l'impôt,** tax collection; **payer mille francs d'impôts,** to pay a thousand francs in tax(es); **les impôts sont très élevés,** taxation is very high.

imprévu, *a.* unforeseen/unexpected; **dépenses imprévues,** unforeseen expenses; incidental expenses/extras.

imprimante, 1. *n.f. Cmptr:* printer; **calculatrice à imprimante,** calculator with a listing; **sortie d'imprimante,** print-out; listing **2.** *a.* **calculatrice imprimante,** print-out calculator.

imprimé, 1. *a.* printed **2.** *n.m.* (*a*) printed paper; **remplir un imprimé,** to fill in a form; **imprimé publicitaire,** advertising leaflet/publicity handout (*b*) *Post:* **imprimés,** printed matter; **tarif imprimés,** printed paper rate.

improductif, *a.* unproductive/non-productive (assets); **argent improductif,** money earning no interest/yielding no returns.

improductivité, *n.f.* unproductiveness (of capital, etc.).

impulsion, *n.f.* **achat d'impulsion,** impulse buying.

imputable, *a.* chargeable; **frais imputables sur un compte,** expenses chargeable to an account.

imputation, *n.f.* **imputation des charges,** cost allocation; **imputation d'un paiement,** appropriation of money to the payment of a debt.

imputer, *v.tr.* **imputer qch. sur qch.,** (*i*) to deduct sth. from sth. (*ii*) to charge sth. to sth.; **imputer des frais sur un compte,** to charge expenses to an account.

inabordable, *a.* prohibitive (price); **l'essence est inabordable cette année,** the price of petrol is astronomical/prohibitive this year.

inacceptation, *n.f.* non-acceptance (of a bill, etc.).

inacquitté, *a.* unreceipted (bill, etc.).

inactif, *a.* inactive; **fonds inactifs,** unemployed capital; **marché inactif,** dull market; **population inactive,** non-working population.

inamovible, *a.* (*a*) **fonctionnaire inamovible,** civil servant holding an appointment for life (*b*) (post) held for life.

inanimé, *a.* **marché inanimé,** dull market.

incapacité, *n.f.* (*a*) **incapacité (professionnelle),** inefficiency/incompetence (of person in his work) (*b*) **incapacité de travail,** (industrial) disablement.

incertain, *n.m. Fin:* variable exchange; **coter/donner l'incertain,** to quote uncertain.

incertifié, *a.* uncertified.

incessible, *a.* not negotiable; non transferable.

inchangé, *a.* unchanged (price, etc.).

incidence, *n.f.* (*a*) **incidence d'un impôt**

sur le consommateur, the incidence of a tax on the consumer (b) **l'incidence des salaires sur les prix de revient,** the impact/the repercussion of wage levels on production costs.

incitation, n.f. **incitation à la vente,** sales incentives.

inclure, v.tr. (a) to enclose; **inclure un chèque dans une lettre,** to enclose a cheque with/in a letter (b) to include; **le service est inclus (dans le prix),** (the) service is included (in the price) (c) Jur: to insert (clause in contract, etc.).

inclus, a. enclosed; **chèque inclus dans la lettre,** cheque enclosed with the letter.

inclusivement, adv. inclusively; **du vendredi au mardi inclusivement,** from Friday to Tuesday inclusive/NAm: Friday through Tuesday; **jusqu'au 30 avril inclusivement,** up to and including April 30th/NAm: through April 30th.

incompensé, a. uncompensated (loss, etc.).

incompétent, a. (a) Jur: not competent (to deal with sth.) (b) incompetent/inefficient.

inconvertible, a. inconvertible (paper money, etc.).

incorporation, n.f. Fin: **incorporation de réserves au capital,** capitalization of reserves.

incorporel, a. **actif incorporel/valeurs incorporelles,** intangible assets; **biens incorporels,** intangible property.

incoterms, n. incoterms.

indemnisable, a. entitled to compensation.

indemnisation, n.f. indemnification; compensation.

indemniser, v.tr. to indemnify/to compensate; **indemniser totalement qn,** to pay full indemnity/compensation to s.o.;

indemniser qn de ses frais, to reimburse s.o. his expenses/to pay s.o.'s expenses.

indemnitaire, 1. n.m. & f. receiver of an indemnity/of compensation **2.** a. **prestation indemnitaire,** allowance/benefit.

indemnité, n.f. (a) indemnity/indemnification/compensation (for loss); **indemnité en argent,** cash compensation; **indemnité de licenciement,** redundancy pay; **demander une indemnité (en dommages-intérêts),** to put in a claim (for damages) (b) compensation to the other party; penalty (for delay, non-delivery, etc.) (c) allowance; **indemnité pour accidents de travail,** industrial injury benefit; **indemnité de cherté de vie/de vie chère,** cost-of-living allowance; **indemnité de chômage,** unemployment benefit/F: dole; **indemnité de déplacement/de route,** travelling expenses/allowance; **indemnité kilométrique =** mileage allowance; **indemnité de maladie,** sickness benefit; **indemnité de résidence/de logement,** housing allowance.

indépensé, a. unspent.

indexation, n.f. PolEc: index-linking (of prices, salaries, pensions, etc.).

indexer, v.tr. PolEc: to (index-)link (prices, salaries, pensions, etc.); **assurance indexée,** index-linked insurance; **emprunt indexé,** index-linked loan; **salaires indexés sur l'indice du coût de la vie,** salaries linked to the cost of living/index-linked salaries.

indicateur, 1. a. **chiffre indicateur,** index number **2.** n.m. (railway, bus) timetable **3.** n.m. indicator; **indicateur statistique,** statistical indicator; PolEc: **indicateurs d'alerte,** economic indicators.

indicatif, n.m. Tp: (dialling) code; **indicatif interurbain/départemental/FrC:** régional, area code/STD code; **indicatif du pays,** country code.

indication, n.f. **indication de provenance/ d'origine,** place of origin.

indice, *n.m.* (*i*) index (number) (*ii*) factor/coefficient (*iii*) rating; *PolEc:* **indice de croissance**, growth index; **indice du coût de la vie**, cost-of-living index; **indice des prix de gros**, wholesale price index; **indice des prix de détail**, retail price index; **indice pondéré**, weighted index; **indice des prix à la consommation**, consumer price index; *StExch:* **indice des actions**, share index; **indice général des cours**, all-items indicator.

indirect, *a.* indirect; **dépenses indirectes**, indirect expenses; **impôts indirects/contributions indirectes**, indirect taxation; **vente indirecte**, indirect selling.

indisponibilité, *n.f.* unavailability/nonavailability (of funds, etc.).

indisponible, *a.* unavailable (capital, etc.).

individuel, *a.* (*a*) individual; private (fortune, etc.); **consommateur individuel**, individual consumer (*b*) *Jur:* **responsabilité individuelle**, several liability.

individuellement, *adv.* (*a*) individually (*b*) *Jur:* severally; **responsables individuellement**, severally liable.

indivis, *a.* (*a*) *Jur:* undivided/joint (estate) (*b*) **actions indivises**, joint shares/shares held jointly; **propriétaires indivis**, joint owners.

indivisaire, *n.m. & f. Jur:* joint owner.

indivisément, *adv. Jur:* jointly.

indivisible, *a. Jur:* joint (obligation, etc.).

indivision, *n.f. Jur:* joint possession.

indu, *n.m.* **paiement de l'indu**, payment of money not owed.

induit, *a.* induced; **demande induite**, induced demand; **investissement induit**, induced investment.

industrialisation, *n.f.* industrialization.

industrialiser, 1. *v.tr.* (*a*) to industrialize; **pays industrialisé**, industrialized country (*b*) **fromage industrialisé**, processed cheese 2. *v.pr.* **s'industrialiser**, to become industrialized; **le (commerce du) lait s'industrialise**, the milk trade is becoming industrialized.

industrialisme, *n.m.* industrialism.

industrialiste, 1. *a.* industrial 2. *n.m. & f.* industrialist.

industrie, *n.f.* (*a*) industry; **industrie artisanale**, cottage industry; **industrie de base**, basic industry; **industrie de consommation**, consumer goods industry; **industrie de pointe**, advanced technology industry; **industrie de précision**, precision industry; **industrie légère**, light industry; **industrie lourde**, heavy industry; **industrie de luxe**, luxury goods industry; **industrie manufacturière**, manufacturing industry; **industrie nationalisée**, nationalized industry/state-owned industry; **industrie primaire**, primary industry; **industrie de transformation**, processing industry (*b*) **industrie aéronautique**, aircraft industry; **industrie alimentaire**, food industry; **industrie agro-alimentaire**, food industry based on agriculture; **industrie automobile**, car/motor industry; **industrie du bâtiment**, building trade/building industry; **industrie chimique**, chemical industry; **industrie hôtelière**, hotel trade/industry; **industrie des constructions navales**, shipbuilding industry; **industrie du livre**, book trade; **industrie mécanique**, engineering; **industrie minière**, mining/industry; **industrie pétrochimique**, petrochemical/plastics industry; **industrie pétrolière/du pétrole**, oil industry; **industrie textile**, textile industry (*c*) firm/business; **diriger une industrie prospère**, to run a successful business.

industrie-clef, *n.f.* key industry.

industriel, 1. *a.* (*a*) **centre industriel**, industrial centre; **complexe industriel**, industrial complex/industrial estate; **établissement industriel/société industrielle**, manufacturing firm; **faubourg industriel**, industrial suburb; **génie indus-**

triel, industrial engineering; **produit industriel,** industrial product; **secteur industriel,** branch/sector of industry; **véhicule industriel,** industrial vehicle/goods vehicle; **ville industrielle,** industrial town; **zone industrielle,** (i) industrial estate (ii) industrial area (b) *Fin:* **banque industrielle,** industrial bank; **valeurs industrielles,** industrial shares/industrials 2. *n.m.* manufacturer/industrialist.

industriellement, *adv.* industrially; (produced) in industry.

inéchangeable, *a.* unexchangeable; **valeurs inéchangeables,** unexchangeable securities; **les articles vendus en solde sont inéchangeables,** sales goods cannot be exchanged.

inemployé, *a.* unemployed/unused (capital, etc.).

inescomptable, *a. Fin:* undiscountable.

inexact, *a.* inaccurate/incorrect; wrong.

inexécuté, *a.* unfulfilled (contract, etc.); **travaux inexécutés,** work not carried out.

inexécution, *n.f.* non-fulfilment (of contract, etc.).

inexécutoire, *a.* unenforceable/non-enforceable (contract, etc.).

inexigible, *a.* (*d'une dette*) (i) not due (ii) not claimable.

inférieur, 1. *a.* (a) inferior; **d'un rang inférieur,** of a lower rank/inferior in rank (b) poor; **des marchandises inférieures/de qualité inférieure,** poor quality/second rate goods (c) **votre paiement est inférieur de 1 000 francs à la somme prévue,** your payment falls short of the agreed amount by 1 000 francs 2. *n.* subordinate.

inflation, *n.f. PolEc:* **inflation par les coûts,** cost-push inflation; **inflation par la demande,** demand-pull inflation; **inflation fiduciaire,** inflation of the currency; **inflation galopante,** galloping/rampant inflation; **inflation monétaire,** monetary

inflation; **politique d'inflation,** inflationary policy; **inflation des prix,** price inflation; **inflation rampante,** creeping inflation; **inflation des salaires,** wage inflation; **taux d'inflation,** rate of inflation; **tendances à l'inflation,** inflationary tendencies; **contenir l'inflation,** to contain inflation; **le gouvernement a eu recours à l'inflation,** the government resorted to inflation.

inflationnisme, *n.m. PolEc:* inflationism.

inflationniste, 1. *n.m. & f.* inflationist 2. *a.* inflationary; **politique inflationniste,** inflationary policy; **tendance inflationniste,** inflationary tendency.

informaticien, -ienne, *n.* computer scientist; **ingénieur informaticien,** computer engineer.

information, *n.f.* (a) information; **service d'informations,** information service; **centre d'information(s),** information centre; **je vous l'envoie à titre d'information,** I am sending it to you for your information (b) *Cmptr:* **traitement de l'information,** data processing; **théorie de l'information,** information theory.

informatique, 1. *n.f. Cmptr:* data processing/information processing 2. *a.* **gestion informatique,** computer control; **service informatique,** computer service.

informatisation, *n.f.* computerization.

informatiser, *v.tr.* to computerize; **informatiser les salaires,** to computerize salaries/wages.

infrastructure, *n.f. Adm: PolEc:* infrastructure.

infructueux, *a.* unprofitable (investment, etc.).

ingénierie, *n.f. Ind:* (i) engineering (ii) engineering department.

ingénieur, *n.m.* (a) (graduate, qualified) engineer; **ingénieur chimiste,** chemical engineer; **ingénieur constructeur / in-**

génieur des travaux publics, civil engineer; **ingénieur électricien**, electrical engineer; **ingénieur mécanicien**, mechanical engineer (b) specialist engineer; **ingénieur commercial**, sales engineer; **ingénieur conseil**, (i) engineering consultant/consulting engineer (ii) patent engineer; **ingénieur d'études/ingénieur projecteur**, design engineer; **ingénieur informaticien**, computer engineer; **ingénieur en organisation**, work study engineer.

initial, a. (a) initial (cost, capital, etc.) (b) **prix initial**, starting price.

initiative, n.f. **Syndicat d'Initiative** = tourist (information) office.

injecter, v.tr. **injecter du capital dans une entreprise**, to inject capital into a business.

innommé, a. Jur: **contrat innommé**, innominate (contract).

inondation, n.f. **l'inondation du marché par des produits étrangers**, the flooding of the market with foreign goods.

inonder, v.tr. to flood/to glut (the market).

inopérant, a. Jur: inoperative/invalid; **clause inopérante**, inoperative clause.

inscription, n.f. 1. (a) entering/recording (in account book, etc.) (b) registration/enrolment; **inscription d'une entreprise au Registre de Commerce**, registration of a firm in the Register of Companies 2. entry (in account book, etc.) 3. (a) Fin: scrip; **inscription sur le grand(-)livre**, (French) Treasury scrip (b) StExch: **inscription à la cote**, quotation in/on the (official) list; **faire une demande d'inscription à la cote**, to seek a share quotation/quote.

inscrire, v.tr. (a) Fin: **valeur inscrite à la cote officielle**, listed stock; **valeur non inscrite**, unlisted stock/over-the-counter stock; **la dette inscrite**, the Consolidated Debt.

insérer, v.tr. to insert; **insérer une clause dans un contrat**, to insert a clause in an

agreement; **insérer une annonce dans un journal**, to put/to insert an advertisement in a newspaper.

insertion, n.f. insertion; **tarif des insertions**, advertising rates.

insignifiant, a. unimportant; nominal (rent); trifling (sum, loss).

insolvabilité, n.f. insolvency.

insolvable, a. insolvent.

inspecter, v.tr. to inspect/to examine (factory, machine, company books, etc.).

inspecteur, -trice, n. inspector; supervisor (in shop); foreman (in factory, etc.); **inspecteur du travail**, factory inspector; **inspecteur des contributions directes**, tax inspector; **inspecteur des contributions indirectes**, customs and excise official; **Inspecteur des Finances** = (high) Treasury official.

inspection, n.f. 1. (a) inspection; inspecting; examination; examining; **faire l'inspection de . . .**, to inspect, to examine . . .; **inspection du travail**, factory inspection; **effectuer/passer une inspection**, to make an inspection/to inspect (b) tour of inspection 2. (a) inspectorship; **obtenir une inspection**, to be appointed inspector (b) inspectorate; body of inspectors.

inspectorat, n.m. Adm: (a) inspectorship (b) inspectorate; body of inspectors.

instabilité, n.f. **l'instabilité du marché**, the unsettled state of the market; **l'instabilité du change**, fluctuation in the rates of exchange.

instable, a. unsteady (prices, etc.); **marché instable**, jumpy market.

installation, n.f. 1. installing/setting-up (of machine, etc.); fitting out/equipping (of workshop, etc.) 2. (a) fittings (in workshop, etc.); **installations électriques**, electrical fittings/equipment (b) plant; equipment; facilities; **installation frigorifique**, refrigerating plant.

installer, v.tr. to install; to set up (machine, etc.); to fit out/to equip (factory, etc.).

institut, *n.m.* (*a*) institute/institution; **l'Institut d'Assurances Maritimes de Londres** = the Institute of London Underwriters (*b*) establishment; **institut de beauté,** beauty parlour.

institution, *n.f.* (*a*) instituting/establishing (*b*) institution.

institutionnel, *a.* **investisseurs institutionnels,** institutional investors.

instructions, *n.f. pl.* **instructions permanentes,** standing instructions/*NAm:* standard operating procedure; **conformément aux instructions,** as directed; **aux termes des instructions qui lui avaient été données, la commission était chargée de . . .,** under its terms of reference the commission was instructed to . . .; *Corr:* **nous attendons vos instructions,** we await your instructions.

instruire, *v.tr.* **instruire qn de qch.,** to inform s.o. of sth.

instrument, *n.m.* (*a*) instrument; **instrument de commerce/de crédit,** instrument of commerce/of credit (*b*) *Jur:* (legal) instrument (deed, contract, writ, etc.) (*c*) **instruments de précision,** precision instruments.

insuffisance, *n.f.* insufficiency; shortage; **insuffisance de personnel,** shortage of staff.

insuffisant, *a.* insufficient; inadequate; **poids insuffisant,** short weight; **salaire insuffisant,** inadequate salary.

intégral, *a.* entire/complete; **paiement intégral,** payment in full; **libération intégrale d'une action,** payment in full of a share.

intégralement, *adv.* completely/fully/ in full; **rembourser intégralement une somme,** to repay a sum in full; **capital intégralement versé,** fully paid(-up) capital.

intégration, *n.f.* integration; **intégration économique,** economic integration; **intégration horizontale,** horizontal integration; **intégration verticale,** vertical integration.

intégré, *a.* integrated; **système intégré de gestion,** integrated management system.

interbancaire, *a.* interbank; **dépôt interbancaire,** interbank deposit; **taux de référence interbancaire,** interbank reference rate.

interdépartemental, *a.* interdepartmental.

interdiction, *n.f.* **interdiction d'exportation,** export ban; **interdiction d'importation,** import ban.

interdire, *v.tr.* to forbid/to prohibit; **l'exportation de l'or est formellement interdite,** the export of gold is strictly prohibited; *PN:* **entrée interdite (au public)** = no admittance.

inter-entreprises, *a.* inter-firm.

intéressé, 1. *a.* interested; **être intéressé dans une entreprise,** to have a financial interest in a venture; **les parties intéressées,** the interested parties **2.** *n.m.pl.* **les intéressés,** the interested parties.

intéressement, *n.m.* profit-sharing (scheme); benefit (plan); **intéressement du personnel aux fruits de l'expansion,** profit-sharing by the employees.

intéresser, *v.tr.* **intéresser les employés (aux bénéfices),** to initiate a profit-sharing scheme; **je ne suis pas intéressé dans cette entreprise,** I have no financial interests in this firm.

intérêt, *n.m.* **1.** share/stake (in business, etc.); **avoir des intérêts dans une compagnie,** to have a financial interest/vested interests in a company; **mettre qn hors d'intérêt,** to buy s.o. out **2.** advantage; **agir dans l'intérêt de la société,** to act in the interest(s) of the company **3.** *Fin:* **intérêt du capital,** interest on capital; **intérêt composé,** compound interest;

intérêt couru, accrued interest; **intérêts échus,** outstanding interest; interest due/payable; **intérêt élevé,** high interest; **intérêt fixe,** fixed interest; **intérêt simple,** simple interest; **intérêt sur mille francs,** interest on a thousand francs; **intérêt sur prêt,** interest on a loan; **coupon d'intérêt,** interest coupon; **prêt à intérêt,** interest-bearing loan; **revenu d'intérêt,** earned interest/interest income; **sans intérêt,** interest-free; **taux d'intérêt/de l'intérêt,** interest rate/rate of interest; **taux d'intérêt de 4%,** interest rate of 4%; **taux d'intérêt à long terme,** long-term interest rate; **emprunter à intérêt,** to borrow at interest; **laisser courir des intérêts,** to allow interest to accumulate; **payer des intérêts,** to pay interest; **placer son argent à 7% d'intérêt,** to invest one's money at 7% interest; **porter intérêt** to bear interest/to yield; **actions qui portent intérêt au taux de 5%,** shares that yield (a) 5% interest.

intérieur, 1. *a.* **commerce intérieur,** home/internal trade; **consommation intérieure,** home consumption; **marché intérieur,** home market; *Post:* **(tarif d')affranchissement en régime intérieur,** inland postage rate **2.** *n.m.* home (country); *Post:* **colis à destination de l'intérieur,** inland parcels.

intérim, *n.m.* interim; **assurer l'intérim,** to take over s.o.'s duties temporarily; **faire l'intérim (de qn),** to deputize (for s.o.); **secrétaire par intérim,** acting secretary/interim secretary; **secrétaire qui fait de l'intérim,** temp.

intérimaire, 1. *a.* temporary/provisional; **directeur intérimaire,** acting manager; **dividende intérimaire,** interim dividend; **dactylo intérimaire,** temp; **personnel intérimaire,** (*i*) personnel from a temp agency (*ii*) temporary staff; **rapport intérimaire,** interim report **2.** *n.* official holding a temporary appointment; deputy.

intermédiaire, 1. *a.* intermediate; **biens intermédiaires,** intermediate products; **commerce intermédiaire,** middleman's

business **2.** *n.m.* (*a*) middleman; broker (*b*) intermediary/agency; **négocier par l'intermédiaire de . . .,** to negotiate through the intermediary/the agency of . . ..

international, *a.* international; **commerce international,** international trade; **droit international,** international law; **réserves monétaires internationales,** international monetary reserves.

interne, *a.* internal; **contrôle/vérification interne,** internal auditing; **vérificateur interne,** internal auditor.

interprofessionnel, *a.* interprofessional; **salaire minimum interprofessionnel de croissance/SMIC** = index-linked minimum wage.

intersyndical, *a. Ind: etc:* inter-union.

interurbain, *a.* **appel téléphonique interurbain,** STD call/trunk call/long-distance call.

intervenant, -ante, *n.* intervening party; acceptor (of bill) for honour.

intervenir, *v.i.* to happen/to occur; **un accord est intervenu entre la direction et les syndicats,** (an) agreement has been reached between management and unions.

intervention, *n.f.* (*a*) *EEC:* **prix d'intervention,** intervention price (*b*) *Jur:* intervention/becoming a third party (in a contract, etc.); **paiement par intervention,** payment on behalf of a third party (*c*) **acceptation par intervention,** acceptance (of protested bill) for honour.

intitulé, *n.m.* (*a*) **intitulé d'un compte,** name of an account (*b*) *Jur:* **intitulé d'un acte,** premises of a deed.

intransférable, *a.* not transferable; *Jur:* unassignable (right, etc.).

introducteurs, *n.m.pl. StExch: F:* the shop.

introduction, *n.f.* (*a*) bringing in; importing (of goods from abroad, etc.) (*b*) **l'introduction de la semaine de cinq jours,**

the introduction of the five-day week; **lettre d'introduction,** letter of introduction **(de la part de,** from; **auprès de,** to) (*c*) *StExch:* bringing out (of shares); **actions à l'introduction,** *F:* shop shares.

introduire, *v.tr.* to introduce; to bring in/to import (goods from abroad, etc.); *StExch:* to introduce/to bring out (shares).

invalidation, *n.f. Jur:* invalidation (of document, contract, etc.).

invalide, *a. Jur:* invalid/null and void.

invalidité, *n.f. Jur:* invalidity (of contract, etc.).

invendable, *a.* unsaleable / unmarketable.

invendu, 1. *a.* unsold **2.** *n.m.pl.* **invendus,** unsold goods; unsold copies (of newspapers, etc.); remainders/*NAm:* overstocks (of books).

inventaire, *n.m.* (*a*) inventory; **faire/ dresser un inventaire,** to draw up an inventory; **inventaire d'entrée,** ingoing inventory; **inventaire de sortie,** outgoing inventory; **meubles dont l'inventaire se monte à 100 000 francs,** the inventory for the furniture comes to 100 000 francs (*b*) stock list; stocktaking/*NAm:* inventory; **inventaire permanent,** perpetual/ continuous/rolling inventory; **nous faisons/nous dressons l'inventaire,** we're stocktaking/*NAm:* we're taking the inventory; **soldes après inventaire,** stocktaking sale (*c*) *Book-k:* **inventaire (comptable),** book inventory; **inventaire de fin d'année,** accounts for/to the end of the financial year; **livre d'inventaire,** balance book (*d*) *Fin:* valuation (of investments, securities, etc.) (*e*) list/schedule.

inventer, *v.tr.* to invent.

inventeur, -trice, *n.* inventor.

invention, *n.f.* invention; **brevet d'invention,** patent (for an invention).

inventorier, *v.tr.* **1.** (*a*) to inventory/to do the stocktaking/*NAm:* to take the inventory (*b*) to value (goods, bills, etc.) **2.** to enter (article) on an inventory/on a stock list.

investi, *a.* **capitaux investis,** invested/ funded capital.

investir, *v.tr.* to invest (money); **investir des capitaux à l'étranger,** to invest capital abroad.

investissement, *n.m.* investment; investing (of capital); **biens d'investissement,** capital goods; **crédit d'investissement,** investment credit; **dépenses d'investissement,** capital expenditure; **gestion des investissements,** investment management; **investissements à l'étranger,** foreign investment/capital movements; **investissements immobiliers,** investments in real estate; **plan d'investissement,** investment plan; **programme d'investissement,** investment programme; **rendement des investissements,** return on investment; **société d'investissements,** investment company; **société d'investissements à capital fixe,** closed-end investment company; **société d'investissements à capital variable/ SICAV,** open-end investment company; unit trust/*NAm:* mutual fund; **faire des investissements,** to invest (money)/to place money.

investisseur, *n.m. Fin:* investor; **investisseur privé,** private investor.

invisible, *PolEc:* **1.** *a.* invisible; **exportations invisibles,** invisible exports; **importations invisibles,** invisible imports **2.** *n.m.pl.* **invisibles,** invisibles.

irréalisable, *a. Fin:* **valeurs irréalisables,** unrealizable securities.

irrégularité, *n.f.* **irrégularité comptable,** accounting irregularity/irregularity in the accounts.

J

jaquette, *n.f.* (*d'un livre*) jacket.

jargon, *n.m.* jargon; **jargon publicitaire,** advertising jargon.

jauge, *n.f.* (*a*) gauge; capacity (*b*) *Nau:* tonnage/burden; **jauge brute,** gross register(ed) tonnage; **jauge nette,** net register(ed) tonnage; **jauge de douane/ jauge de registre,** register(ed) tonnage.

jaugeage, *n.m. Nau:* measurement (of tonnage).

jauger, *v.tr.* **1.** to gauge/to measure capacity; **jauger un navire,** to measure the tonnage of a ship **2.** *Nau:* **pétrolier qui jauge quarante mille tonneaux,** forty thousand ton tanker.

jaune, *a.* **les pages jaunes (de l'annuaire téléphonique),** the yellow pages (of the telephone directory).

jeter, *v.tr.* to throw; to throw away; **jeter des marchandises sur le marché,** to throw goods on(to) the market.

jeton, *n.m.* **jeton de présence,** director's fees.

jeu, *n.m.* (*a*) *StExch:* speculating; **jeu de bourse,** gambling on the Stock Exchange/ Stock Exchange speculations; **jeu sur les reports,** speculating in contangoes (*b*) **jeu d'outils,** set of tools (*c*) *Book-k:* **jeu d'écritures,** paper transaction.

joindre, *v.tr.* (*a*) to add (**à,** to); **joindre l'intérêt au capital,** to add the interest to the capital; **l'échantillon joint à votre lettre,** the sample attached to your letter (*b*) to get in touch with s.o.; **essayer de joindre un client,** to try to get in touch with a client; **j'ai téléphoné, mais je n'ai pas réussi à le joindre,** I phoned but couldn't get in touch with him/get hold of him.

joint, *a.* joined; *Corr:* **pièces jointes (PJ),** enclosures (*abbr.* encl.).

jouer, *v.i.* **1.** *Fin:* to speculate; to play the market; **jouer à la Bourse,** to speculate/to gamble on the Stock Exchange; **jouer à la hausse,** to speculate on a rising market/to bull the market; **jouer. à la baisse,** to speculate on a fall/to bear the market; **jouer sur les mines,** to speculate in mining securities **2.** to be operative/to become operative/to operate; **l'augmentation des salaires joue depuis le 1ᵉʳ janvier,** the rise in salaries has been operative since January 1st.

joueur, -euse, *n. StExch:* speculator/ operator; **joueur à la hausse,** bull; **joueur à la baisse,** bear.

jouissance, *n.f.* (*a*) *Jur:* **jouissance en commun (d'un bien),** communal tenure; **avoir la jouissance de certains droits,** to enjoy certain rights; **maison à vendre avec jouissance immédiate,** house for sale with vacant possession (*b*) *Fin:* right to interest/dividends; **date de jouissance (de bons du Trésor, etc.),** date from which interest begins to run; **action de jouissance,** redeemed share that continues to participate in dividends.

jour, *n.m.* (*a*) day; **jour franc,** clear day; **préavis de dix jours francs,** ten clear days' notice; **quinze jours,** a fortnight (*b*) **intérêts à ce jour,** interest to date; *Fin:* **prêts au jour le jour,** money at call/call money (*c*) **mettre (une liste, etc.) à jour,** to bring (a list, etc.) up to date/to update (a list, etc.); **tenir les livres à jour,** to keep

99

the books/the accounts up to date (*d*) *Adm:* **jour férié** = bank/public holiday; **fixer un jour pour qch.**, to fix a date/to appoint a day/to make an appointment for sth. (*e*) **le prix du jour,** today's price.

journal, *n.m.* **1.** *Book-k:* **(livre) journal,** account book; journal; **journal des achats,** bought ledger; **journal des ventes,** sales ledger **2.** (news)paper; journal; **journal d'entreprise,** company/house magazine.

journalier, *a.* daily (consumption, etc.).

journaliser, *v.tr. Book-k:* to enter/to write up (entry) in the books.

journalisme, *n.m.* journalism.

journaliste, *n.m. & f.* journalist.

journée, *n.f.* **journée de travail,** (*i*) day's work (*ii*) working day; **faire la journée continue,** (*i*) (*d'un magasin*) to remain open at lunchtime (*ii*) (*d'une personne*) to work through lunch; **travailler à la journée,** to work by the day.

judiciaire, *a.* (*a*) judicial/legal; **assistance judiciaire,** legal aid; **frais judiciaires,** legal charges (in an action); **poursuites judiciaires,** (*i*) proceedings (*ii*) prosecution; **vente judiciaire,** sale by order of the court (*b*) **le pouvoir judiciaire,** (*i*) judicial power (*ii*) the Bench.

judiciairement, *adv.* judicially.

juge, *n.m.* judge; **juge d'instruction,** examining magistrate; **juge d'instance,** (*i*) conciliation magistrate (in commercial cases) (*ii*) police-court magistrate; **juge consulaire/juge au tribunal de commerce,** judge in commercial court.

jugement, *n.m.* (*a*) *Jur:* judgement; decision; award; (*dans une cause criminelle*) sentence; **jugement déclaratif de faillite,** adjudication in bankruptcy (*b*) trial (of case).

juger, *v.tr.* (*a*) to judge; *Jur:* **juger un procès,** to try/to judge a case; **juger une réclamation,** to adjudicate a claim (*b*) to adjudicate (**entre,** between).

juridiction, *n.f.* jurisdiction; **question tombant sous la juridiction du tribunal,** matter within the jurisdiction of the court.

juridique, *a.* juridical/judicial; legal; **frais juridiques,** lawyer's fees/legal charges (in a transaction).

juste, **1.** *a.* right/fair; **juste salaire,** fair wage **2.** right/exact/accurate (*a*) **balance juste,** accurate scales; **chiffres justes,** correct figures; **mesure juste,** full measure (*b*) **au plus juste prix,** at rock-bottom price **3.** *adv.* exactly; precisely; **prix calculé au plus juste,** strict price.

justice, *n.f.* (*a*) justice (*b*) law/legal proceedings; **action en justice,** action at law; **recourir à la justice,** to go to law; **poursuivre qn en justice,** to institute legal proceedings against s.o./to take legal action against s.o.

justificatif, **1.** *a.* supporting/justificatory; *Jur:* **pièces justificatives,** (*i*) written proof (*ii*) relevant documents **2.** *n.m.* (*a*) voucher (copy) (*b*) (*d'un journal, etc.*) tear sheet/advertiser's copy.

justification, *n.f. Typ:* justification.

justifier, *v.tr.* **1.** to justify; to warrant (expenditure, etc.) **2.** *Typ:* to justify.

K

kilo, kilogramme, *n.m. Meas:* kilo, kilogram (*abbr.* kg) (= 2.2 lbs); **5 kilos/5 kg de beurre,** 5 kilos/5 kg of butter.

kilométrage, *n.m.* (*a*) length in kilometres (*b*) = mileage.

kilomètre, *n.m. Meas:* kilometre (*abbr.* km) (= 0.624 mile); *Av:* **kilomètre-passager** = passenger-mile; *Rail:* **kilomètre-** **voyageur** = passenger-mile; **tonnes-kilomètres marchandises,** ton kilometres.

kilométrique, *a.* kilometric; *Aut:* **indemnité kilométrique** = mileage allowance.

kiosque, *n.m.* **kiosque à journaux,** newspaper kiosk/stand.

krach, *n.m.* (financial) crash.

L

label, *n.m.* label; seal of approval; trade-union mark; **label d'exportation,** export label; **label de garantie,** guarantee label; **label d'origine,** certificate of origin; **label de qualité,** quality label.

laissé-pour-compte, *a. & n.m.* returned/rejected/unsold (article).

laissez-passer, *n.m.inv.* pass/permit; *Cust:* transire.

laitier, *a.* **l'industrie laitière,** the milk/the dairy industry; **produits laitiers,** dairy produce.

lancement, *n.m.* floating/launching (of company); launching (of new product, publicity campaign); **prix de lancement,** introductory offer/price.

lancer, *v.tr.* to float/to promote (a new company); to float (a loan); **lancer un nouveau produit (sur le marché),** to put a new product on the market/to launch a new product/to market a new product.

lanceur, -euse, *n.* promoter (of company); **lanceur d'affaires,** business promoter.

légal, *a.* legal; **fête légale,** statutory holiday; bank holiday; **monnaie légale,** legal tender; *Fin:* **taux légal,** official rate of interest.

légalement, *adv.* legally/lawfully.

légalisation, *n.f.* legalization; (*d'une signature, etc.*) authentication.

légaliser, *v.tr.* to legalize; to authenticate.

légalité, *n.f.* legality.

législation, *n.f.* legislation; **législation anti-dumping,** anti-dumping laws; **législation anti-trust,** anti-trust legislation; **législation du travail/législation ouvrière,** industrial/labour legislation.

légitime, *a.* legitimate; **propriétaire légitime,** legal owner.

léonin, *a. Jur:* **contrat léonin,** unconscionable/one-sided bargain.

lettre, *n.f.* **1. lettres majuscules,** capital letters/capitals; **écrire une somme en (toutes) lettres,** to write an amount in words (not figures) **2.** (*a*) lettre; **lettre d'affaires/lettre commerciale,** business letter; **lettre d'envoi/lettre d'introduction,** covering letter; *Post:* **lettre exprès,** express letter; **lettre de rappel,** (letter of) reminder; **lettre de réclamation,** (letter of) complaint; **lettre recommandée,** (*i*) registered letter (*ii*) (letter sent by) recorded delivery; **lettre de recommandation,** reference; **lettre de relance (à un client),** follow-up letter (to a customer); **envoyer une lettre à tarif normal,** to send a letter first class; **envoyer une lettre à tarif réduit,** to send a letter second class (*b*) **lettre d'avis,** advice note; **lettre de change,** bill of exchange; **lettre de change à l'extérieur,** foreign bill; *Ins:* **lettre de couverture,** cover note; **lettre de crédit,** letter of credit; **lettre de crédit circulaire,** circular letter of credit; **lettre de crédit documentaire,** documentary letter of credit; *Av:* **lettre de transport aérien,** air waybill; **lettre de voiture,** waybill/consignment note (*c*) *StExch:* **lettre d'allocation,** letter of allotment.

levée, *n.f.* (*a*) lifting (of embargo); closing/adjourning (of meeting) (*b*) levy(ing) (of taxes); *Post:* collection (of letters); *Fin:* **levée des actions,** taking (up) (of stock); **levée d'une option,** taking up (of) an option; *Bank:* **levées de compte,** personal withdrawals.

lever, *v.tr.* **1.** (*i*) to close (a meeting) (*ii*) to adjourn (a meeting); to lift/to raise (embargo, etc.); **la séance a été levée à trois heures,** the meeting (*i*) was adjourned (*ii*) was closed at three o'clock **2.** to levy (tax); *Post:* **lever les lettres,** to collect the mail; *Fin:* **lever des actions,** to take up stock; **lever une option/une prime,** to take up an option.

levier, *n.m. Fin:* **effet de levier,** gearing; *NAm:* leverage.

liaison, *n.f.* (*a*) **liaison aérienne,** air link; **liaison ferroviaire,** rail link; **liaison postale,** postal link; **liaison rail-aéroport,** rail-air link; **liaison routière,** road link; **la liaison téléphonique Paris-Londres,** (telephone) communications between Paris and London; **travailler en liaison avec qn,** to liaise with s.o./to work in conjunction with s.o. (*b*) **liaisons hiérarchiques,** manager-staff relations/line relations.

libellé, *n.m.* wording/terms used (in a document).

libeller, *v.tr.* to draw up/to word (a document, etc.); **libeller un chèque au nom de qn,** to make out/to write (out) a cheque to s.o.; **chèque libellé à l'ordre de Mme X,** cheque made out to Mrs X; **être libellé au porteur,** to be made out to/to be made payable to bearer.

libéralisation, *n.f.* **la libéralisation du commerce,** the easing of trade restrictions; **libéralisation du cours du dollar,** freeing of the dollar.

libéraliser, *v.tr.* to free/to ease (currency, trade restrictions, etc.).

libération, *n.f.* (*a*) payment (in full); discharge; **libération d'une dette,** discharging/redeeming of a debt; *Fin:* **libération d'une action,** paying up of a share; **libération de capital,** paying up of capital (by shareholders) (*b*) **libération des échanges commerciaux,** relaxing/freeing of exchange controls.

libératoire, *a.* (*a*) **paiement libératoire,** payment in full discharge from debt (*b*) (*de l'argent*) **avoir force/pouvoir libératoire,** to be legal tender.

libéré, *a. Fin:* (fully) paid-up (share); **non (entièrement) libéré/partiellement libéré,** partly paid-up.

libérer, 1. *v.tr.* to free (s.o., an institution, etc.) from/of debt; **libérer qn de la responsabilité légale,** to relieve s.o. of legal liability; **titre de 1000 francs libéré de 750 francs/libéré à 75%,** 1000 franc share of which 750 francs are paid (up) **2.** *v.pr.* **se libérer (d'une dette),** to redeem a debt/to clear oneself of a debt; **se libérer d'un engagement,** to free oneself from a commitment/an obligation.

liberté, *n.f.* (*a*) **liberté du commerce,** freedom of trade (*b*) **liberté syndicale,** right of a worker to belong to a union of his own choosing.

libraire, *n.m. & f.* bookseller.

librairie, *n.f.* bookshop.

libre, *a.* (*a*) free; **cours libre,** free market rate; **libre concurrence,** free competition; **libre entreprise,** free enterprise; **marché libre,** free market; **marché libre des capitaux,** open money market; **produit en vente libre,** product on general sale (*b*) **entrée libre,** (*i*) admission free (*ii*) no obligation to buy (*c*) **libre possession,** vacant possession.

libre-échange, *n.m. PolEc:* free trade; **politique de libre-échange,** free-trade policy; **zone de libre-échange,** free-trade area.

libre-échangiste, 1. *n.m.* free trader **2.** *a.* **politique libre-échangiste,** free-trade policy.

libre-appel, *n.m.* Freephone/*NAm:* Toll Free.

libre-réponse, *n.f. Post:* Freepost.

libre-service, *n.m.* self-service; **(magasin) libre-service,** self-service store; **(res-**

taurant) **libre-service,** self-service restaurant.

licence, *n.f.* licence/*NAm:* license; **détenteur d'une licence,** licensee; **licence de débit de boissons,** licence to sell beer, wines and spirits/*NAm:* liquor license; **licence d'exploitation d'un brevet,** licence to use a patent; **licence d'exportation,** export licence; **licence de fabrication,** manufacturing licence; **licence exclusive,** exclusive licence; **fabriqué sous licence,** made/manufactured under licence; **licence d'importation,** import licence.

licenciement, *n.m.* dismissal; laying-off/lay-off (of workers); **licenciement économique,** redundancy; **indemnité de licenciement,** redundancy pay/compensation; **lettre de licenciement,** notice of dismissal; **licenciement sans préavis,** dismissal without notice.

licencier, *v.tr.* to make s.o. redundant/to dismiss s.o.; to lay s.o. off.

licite, *a.* licit/lawful/permissible.

licitement, *adv.* licitly/lawfully.

lier, *v.tr.* (*a*) to bind; **contrat qui lie qn,** agreement binding (up)on s.o.; **ce contrat vous lie,** you are bound by this agreement (*b*) **marchés liés,** related markets; **opération liée,** combined deal.

lieu, *n.m.* **1.** (*a*) locality; place; **lieu de livraison,** place of delivery; *Adm:* **lieu de naissance,** place of birth; *Mkt:* **lieu de vente,** point of sale (*b*) *pl.* **lieux,** house/premises; **état des lieux,** inventory of fixtures (as between landlord and tenant); **vider les lieux,** to vacate the premises **2. avoir lieu,** to take place; **la réunion aura lieu vendredi,** the meeting will take place/will be held on Friday.

ligne, *n.f.* (*a*) line; *Fin:* **ligne de crédit/de découvert/d'escompte,** line of credit (*b*) **amortissement en ligne droite,** straight-line depreciation (*c*) **ligne aérienne,** airline; **ligne maritime,** shipping line; **ligne d'autobus,** bus route; **ligne de métro,** underground route/line (*d*) *Tp:*

telephone line; **vous avez Paris sur la ligne,** you have Paris on the line.

limitatif, *a.* limiting; restrictive; *Jur:* **clause limitative,** limiting clause.

limitation, *n.f.* limitation/restriction; **limitation des prix,** price control; **limitation de responsabilité,** limitation of liability; **limitation des salaires,** wage restraint.

limite, *n.f.* **1.** limit; **limite d'âge,** age limit; **limites de prix,** price limits; **limite de poids,** weight limit; **prix limite,** upper price limit **2. cas limite,** borderline case; **date limite,** latest date/deadline; (*sur un produit*) **date limite de vente,** sell-by date.

limité, *a.* limited; *StExch:* **cours limités,** limited prices; *Publ:* **édition à tirage limité,** limited edition; **société à responsabilité limitée (SARL),** limited liability company; *FrC:* **Desrochers et Cie Ltée,** Desrochers and Co. Ltd.

linéaire, *a.* (*a*) **programmation linéaire,** linear programming (*b*) **mode/méthode linéaire,** straight line (depreciation) method.

lingot, *n.m.* **lingot d'or,** gold ingot/bar; **or en lingots,** gold bullion.

liquidateur, -trice, *n.* **1.** *Jur:* liquidator; **liquidateur d'une société,** liquidator of a company **2.** *Fin:* **liquidateur officiel (à la Bourse),** official assignee (on the Stock Exchange).

liquidatif, *a.* *Jur:* pertaining to liquidation; **acte liquidatif de société,** winding-up resolution/order; **valeur liquidative,** value at liquidation.

liquidation, *n.f.* **1.** (*a*) liquidation; **frais de liquidation,** closing-down costs; **liquidation forcée,** compulsory liquidation; **liquidation volontaire,** voluntary liquidation; **entrer en liquidation,** to go into liquidation; to wind up a business (*b*) clearing (of accounts); *StExch:* settlement; **chambre de liquidation,** (bankers') clearing house; *StExch:* **jour de la liquidation,** account day/settlement day; **liquidation**

de quinzaine, fortnightly account 2. selling off (of stocks); clearance sale.

liquide, 1. *a.* liquid; **actif liquide,** liquid assets; **argent liquide,** ready money/cash; **capital liquide,** liquid capital; **dette liquide,** liquid debt **2.** *n.m.* (*a*) liquid/fluid; **measures (de capacité) pour les liquides,** fluid measures (*b*) ready money/cash; **je n'ai pas de liquide,** I haven't any cash.

liquider, *v.tr.* **1.** (*a*) to wind up (a business); to wipe out (a debt) (*b*) to clear/to settle (account); to close (transaction); to settle (a deal) **2. liquider le stock,** to sell off stock/to have a clearance sale.

liquidité, *n.f.* **1.** liquidity; **coefficient/taux de liquidité,** liquidity ratio **2.** *pl.* **liquidités,** liquid assets; **liquidités excédentaires,** excess liquidities.

listage, *n.m. Cmptr:* listing.

liste, *n.f.* list; register; **liste d'attente,** waiting list; **liste de candidats,** list of applicants; **liste de contrôle/de vérification,** checklist; **liste d'envoi/liste des abonnés/liste d'adresses/liste de diffusion,** mailing list; **liste des importations,** import list; *Cust:* **liste des marchandises importées en franchise,** free list; **liste officielle de taux,** schedule of charges; *FrC:* **liste de paie,** payroll; *Fin:* **liste des souscripteurs (à un emprunt),** list of applications; **dresser/établir une liste,** to draw up/to make out a list.

lister, *v.tr. Cmptr:* to list.

listing, *n.m.* = **listage.**

litre, *n.m. Meas:* litre/*NAm:* liter (*abbr.* l) (1000 cubic cm = *approx.* 1¾ pints); **ma voiture consomme onze litres aux 100 kilomètres (11 L/100 km)** = my car does 25 miles per gallon (25 mpg)/25 miles to the gallon.

livrable, *a.* (*a*) *Fin:* deliverable (*b*) ready for delivery; **commandes livrables à domicile,** orders delivered (to your door).

livraison, *n.f.* (*a*) delivery; **bordereau de livraison,** delivery note; **conditions de livraison,** delivery terms; **défaut de livrai-**

son, non-delivery; **délai de livraison,** delivery period/lead time; **délai de livraison un mois,** delivery within a month; **frais à percevoir à la livraison,** charges forward; **livraison à domicile,** door-to-door delivery/we deliver to your door; **livraison franco,** delivered free/free delivery; **livraison immédiate,** immediate delivery; **livraison contre remboursement/ paiement à la livraison,** cash on delivery (COD)/*also NAm:* collect on delivery (COD); **payable à la livraison,** payable on delivery; **voiture de livraison,** delivery van; **faire livraison de qch.,** to deliver sth.; **prendre livraison de qch.,** to take delivery of sth. (*b*) *Fin:* delivery; **livraisons à terme,** future deliveries (*c*) *Const:* **livraison (d'un bâtiment) clé en main,** turnkey operation.

livre[1], *n.f.* **1.** (*poids*) pound (*abbr.* lb) (= 500 grams); **une livre de sucre,** a pound/half a kilo of sugar; **vendre qch. à la livre,** to sell sth. by the pound **2.** (*argent*) **livre (sterling),** pound (sterling); **billet de cinq livres,** five pound note; **livre verte,** green pound.

livre[2], *n.m.* (*a*) book; **l'industrie du livre,** the book trade (*b*) *Book-k:* **livre des achats,** bought ledger; **livre de caisse,** cash book; **livres de commerce/de comptabilité,** account books/the books; **livre des inventaires,** stock book; **livre journal,** journal; **livre de paie,** payroll; **livre de petite caisse,** petty cash book; **livre des ventes,** sales ledger; **teneur de livres,** book-keeper; **tenue de livres,** book-keeping; **tenir les livres,** to keep the accounts/the books.

livre-journal, *n.m.* journal/day book.

livrer, *v.tr.* (*a*) to deliver (goods, etc.); **livrer une commande,** to deliver an order; **livrer à domicile,** to deliver to the customer's address (*b*) *StExch:* **vente à livrer,** sale for delivery.

livret, *n.m.* booklet; catalogue (of exhibition); **livret de dépôts,** deposit book; **livret de Caisse d'Épargne,** savings-bank book; passbook; **compte sur livret,** savings account; **se faire ouvrir un livret,** to open a savings account (at the Caisse d'Épargne).

livret-portefeuille, *n.m.* savings-bank book.

livreur, *n.m.* delivery man/boy.

local, 1. *a.* local (authority, industry, etc.); **impôts locaux,** rates; **classification des impôts locaux,** rating **2.** *n.m.* premises; building; **locaux commerciaux,** business premises; **locaux à louer,** premises to let; **local professionnel,** premises (used) for professional purposes.

locataire, *n.m. & f.* (*a*) (*i*) tenant (*ii*) lodger; *Jur:* **locataire (à bail),** lessee/lease-holder (*b*) hirer/renter (of equipment, etc.).

locateur, -trice, *n.* lessor.

locatif, *a.* **impôts locatifs** = rates; **réparations locatives,** repairs incumbent on the tenant; **risques locatifs,** tenant's risk; **valeur locative,** rental (value).

location, *n.f.* (*a*) (*d'une voiture, etc.*) (*i*) hiring/renting (*ii*) hire/rental; **location d'équipement,** plant hire; **location de voitures (sans chauffeur),** (self-drive) car hire/car rental; **donner qch. en location,** to hire sth. out; **contrat de location,** rental agreement; **prendre qch. en location,** to hire sth.; **verser £200 pour la location d'une salle,** to pay £200 for the hire of a hall; **voiture de location,** hire car/rented car (*b*) (*d'une maison, d'un appartement*) (*i*) renting; tenancy (*ii*) letting; **agent de location,** estate agent/letting agent; **prix de location,** rent (*c*) *Th: etc:* booking/reservation (of seats); **(bureau de) location,** box office/booking office.

location-gérance, *n.f.* agreement with liquidator to manage a company in liquidation.

location-vente, *n.f.* hire purchase (of property, equipment); **contrat de location-vente,** hire purchase agreement; **acheter qch. en location-vente,** to buy sth. on hire purchase.

lock-out, *n.m.inv. Ind:* lock(-)out.

lock-outer, *v.tr. Ind:* to lock out (the personnel).

loco, *adv.* loco; **prix loco,** loco price.

logiciel, *n.m. Cmptr:* software.

logotype, *n.m.* logotype/logo.

loi, *n.f.* law; **loi de finances,** Finance Act; **loi de l'offre et de la demande,** law of supply and demand; **loi des rendements décroissants,** law of diminishing returns; **loi sur les sociétés,** Companies' Act.

long, *a.* long; **bail à long terme/à longue échéance,** long lease; **contrat à long terme,** long-term contract; **crédit à long terme,** long-term credit; **emprunt à long terme,** long-term loan; **effets à longue échéance/F:** **papiers longs,** long-dated bills; **placements à long terme,** long-term investments; **politique à long terme,** long-term policy; **emprunter à long terme,** to borrow long.

longévité, *n.f.* life (of product, etc.); **matériel à longévité élevée,** long-life equipment; **longévité des capitaux durables,** (length of) life of durable assets.

lot, *n.m.* **1.** (*a*) (*dans une loterie*) prize; **gros lot,** first prize/jackpot (*b*) *Fin:* **emprunt à lots,** lottery loan; **obligation à lots,** prize bond **2.** (*a*) (*aux enchères*) lot (*b*) parcel (of goods); batch (of goods, etc.); **contrôle par lots,** batch control; **fabrication par lots,** batch production; **lot d'envoi,** consignment.

loterie, *n.f.* **billet de loterie,** lottery ticket; **loterie (publicitaire),** lottery; **loterie nationale,** national lottery.

lotir, *v.tr.* (*a*) to divide (sth.) into lots/into batches (*b*) to divide (land) into building plots; **terrains à lotir,** land to be sold in lots.

lotissement, *n.m.* **1.** (*a*) dividing (of goods, etc.) into lots; parcelling out (*b*) division into plots (of building land) **2.** (*a*) building plot (*b*) housing estate/development.

lotisseur, *n.m.* (*a*) person in charge of dividing goods into lots (*b*) property developer.

louage, *n.m.* **contrat de louage,** rental agreement/contract; **louage de services,** contract of employment; **voiture de louage,** rented car/hired car/hire car.

louer, *v.tr.* (*a*) to hire out/to let (out) (**à,** to); **louer à bail,** to lease; **maison à louer,** house to let; **voitures à louer,** cars for hire (*b*) to rent (house, car, etc.) (**de,** from); to take on (seasonal workers) (*c*) **louer une place d'avance,** to reserve/to book a seat (in advance).

loueur, -euse, *n.* hirer (out); renter.

lourd, *a.* heavy; **industries lourdes,** heavy industries; **poids lourd,** heavy goods vehicle; *Fin:* **marché lourd,** dull/sluggish market.

loyal, *a.* honest/fair; **qualité loyale et marchande,** fair market/fair average quality; **bon et loyal inventaire,** true and accurate inventory.

loyalement, *adv.* honestly/fairly.

loyauté, *n.f.* honesty/fairness; good faith; **loyauté en affaires,** fair (and square) dealing.

loyer, *n.m.* **1.** rent/rental; **arriéré de loyer,** rent arrears/back rent; **loyer de bureau,** office rent; **loyer élevé/gros loyer,** high rent; **loyer modéré,** fair rent; **devoir trois mois de loyer,** to owe three months' rent; **donner à loyer,** to let; **prendre une maison à loyer,** to rent a house **2.** *Bank: Fin:* **le loyer de l'argent,** the rates of interest (for money on loan)/the price of money.

lucratif, *a.* lucrative/profitable/paying; **(association) à but lucratif,** profit-making (association); **(association) sans but lucratif,** non-profit-making (association); **entreprise lucrative,** profitable/lucrative business; **travail lucratif,** well-paid job; **travail peu lucratif,** badly-paid job.

luxe, *n.m.* luxury; **articles/produits de luxe,** luxury goods; **boutique de luxe,** shop selling luxury goods; **industrie de luxe,** luxury goods industry; **impôt/taxe de luxe,** luxury tax; **voiture de luxe,** de luxe car.

M

machine, *n.f.* (*a*) machine; **machine à additionner,** adding machine; **machine à calculer,** calculator; computer; **machine comptable,** accounting machine; **machine à dicter,** dictating machine/*Rtm:* Dictaphone; **machine à écrire,** typewriter; **machine à écrire à boule/à sphère,** golfball typewriter; **machine à (poly)-copier,** copying machine/duplicator; **écrire/taper une lettre à la machine,** to type a letter; **machine de traitement de texte(s),** word processor (*b*) *Ind: etc:* machine; **les machines,** (the) machinery; **atelier des machines,** machine shop; **fait à la machine,** machine-made; **machine-outil,** machine-tool; **machines agricoles,** agricultural machinery; **production à la machine,** machine production; **travail à la machine,** machine work (*c*) **la machine administrative,** administrative/bureaucratic machinery.

machinerie, *n.f. Ind: coll.* machinery; plant.

macroéconomie, *n.f.* macro-economics.

macroéconomique, *a.* macro-economic.

Madame, *n.f.* **Madame/***abbr:* **Mme, Mrs/ Ms;** *Corr:* **Madame,** Dear Madam; **Chère Madame,** Dear Mrs X; **Madame la Présidente,** Madam Chairman; *pl.* **Mesdames X et Y/Mmes X et Y,** Mrs X and Mrs Y.

Mademoiselle, *n.f.* **Mademoiselle/***abbr:* **Mlle,** Miss/Ms; *Corr:* **Mademoiselle,** Dear Madam; **Chère Mademoiselle,** Dear Miss X; *pl.* **Mesdemoiselles/***abbr:* **Mlles X et Y,** Miss X and Miss Y.

magasin, *n.m.* (*a*) shop/(*esp. NAm:*) store; **chaîne de magasins,** chain of shops; **devanture de magasin,** shop front; shop window; **employé de magasin,** shop assistant/employee; **grand magasin,** department store; **magasin d'alimentation,** grocery shop/store; **magasin de (vente au) détail,** retail shop/store; **magasin à grande surface,** hypermarket; **magasin à libre service,** self-service store; **magasin populaire/magasin à prix unique,** one-price store/popular store; **magasin spécialisé,** specialized store; **magasin à succursales multiples,** chain store/multiple store/multiple; **rayon de magasin,** department; counter; **vitrine de magasin,** shop window; **tenir un magasin,** to keep a shop (*b*) store/warehouse; **magasins généraux,** bonded warehouse(s); **marchandises en magasin,** stock in hand; **avoir qch. en magasin,** to have sth. in stock.

magasinage, *n.m.* **1.** warehousing/storing of goods **2.** **(droits de) magasinage,** warehouse dues; storage charges **3.** *FrC:* shopping.

magasiner, *v.i. FrC:* **aller magasiner,** to go shopping.

magasinier, *n.m.* warehouseman/stock keeper.

magazine, *n.m.* (illustrated) magazine.

magnat, *n.m.* magnate (of industry, etc.)/tycoon.

main, *n.f.* **1.** (*a*) hand; **bagages à main,** hand luggage (*b*) **camion d'occasion de première main,** second hand truck (with only one previous owner); **changer de mains,** to change hands; **la propriété a changé de mains en janvier,** the property changed hands in January (*c*) **payer de la main à la main,** to hand over (the) money directly (without receipt or other formal-

108

ity) (*d*) **faire/fabriquer qch. à la main,** to do/to make sth. by hand; **fait (à la) main,** hand-made (*e*) **travailler de ses mains,** to have a manual job **2.** (*a*) hand(writing) (*b*) **main courante,** rough book; *Bank:* **main courante de caisse,** counter cash book.

main-d'œuvre, *n.f.* **1.** labour; manpower; workforce; **main-d'œuvre directe,** direct/productive labour; **main-d'œuvre féminine,** female labour; **main-d'œuvre indirecte,** indirect labour; **main-d'œuvre qualifiée,** skilled labour; **main-d'œuvre spécialisée,** semi-skilled labour; **embaucher de la main-d'œuvre,** to take on workers **2. frais de main-d'œuvre,** cost of labour; **matériel et main-d'œuvre,** material and labour **3.** workmanship.

mainlevée, *n.f. Jur:* **mainlevée de saisie,** restoration of goods (taken in distraint); replevin; **mainlevée d'une hypothèque,** release of mortgage.

mainmise, *n.f.* **mainmise économique,** economic stranglehold.

maintenance, *n.f. Ind: etc:* maintenance (service); **maintenance périodique,** routine maintenance; **programme de maintenance,** maintenance programme.

maintenir, 1. *v.tr.* to maintain; to keep; **dividende maintenu à 5%,** dividend maintained at 5%; **maintenir le change au-dessus du gold-point,** to maintain the exchange above the gold-point; **maintenir les prix fermes,** to keep prices firm/steady **2.** *v.pr.* **la hausse des prix se maintient à 4%,** the rise in prices remains at/is sustained at 4%; *StExch:* **ces actions se maintiennent à . . .,** these shares remain firm at . . . .

maintien, *n.m.* maintenance/keeping; **maintien de la prospérité économique,** maintenance of economic prosperity; **maintien continu de plein emploi,** continuous full employment.

maison, *n.f.* **1.** (*a*) house; **maison de rap-**

port, block of (rented) flats (*b*) home; **dépenses de la maison,** household expenses; **(fait) maison,** home-made **2. maison (de commerce),** firm/company; **maison affiliée,** affiliated company/affiliate; **maison de détail,** retail company/firm; retailer; **maison d'édition,** publishing firm/house; **maison d'escompte,** discount house; **maison d'exportation,** export(ing) firm; **maison de gros,** wholesale firm; **maison d'importation,** import(ing) firm; **maison(-)mère,** parent company/head office.

maître, *n.m.* (*a*) **être maître du marché,** to lead the market (*b*) skilled tradesman (self-employed); **maître charpentier,** master carpenter (*c*) works owner (*d*) employee in charge; **maître d'œuvre,** (*i*) foreman (*ii*) prime contractor.

maîtrise, *n.f. Ind:* supervisory staff; **agent de maîtrise,** foreman/supervisor.

majeur, *a.* (*a*) major/greater; **la majeure partie de nos exportations,** the major part of our exports (*b*) **affaire majeure,** well-established business (*c*) **(cas de) force majeure,** force majeure; act of God.

majoration, *n.f.* **1.** (*a*) overestimation/overvaluation (of assets, etc.) (*b*) (*sur une facture*) additional charge/surcharge; **frapper un immeuble d'une majoration de cinq pour cent,** to put five per cent on to the valuation of a building **2.** increase (in price); mark-up.

majorer, *v.tr.* **1.** to overestimate/to overvalue (assets, etc.) **2.** (*sur une facture*) to make an additional charge; **majoré de notre commission de 10%,** to which we have added our commission of 10%; **majorer une facture de 10%,** (*i*) to put 10% on an invoice (*ii*) to overcharge by 10% on an invoice **3.** to raise/to put up/to increase/to mark up the price of (sth.); **majorer un prix,** to increase a price.

majoritaire, (*a*) *a.* **vote majoritaire,** majority vote (*b*) *Fin:* majority (shareholder); **participation majoritaire,** majority holding/interest/stake; **se rendre (lar-**

gement) **majoritaire,** to acquire majority interest/to acquire a majority shareholding.

majorité, *n.f.* majority; **majorité absolue,** absolute majority; **une majorité de(s) deux tiers,** a two-thirds majority; **décision prise à la majorité (des voix),** majority decision.

mal, *adv.* badly; **mal calculer un compte,** to miscalculate an account; **mal représenter les faits,** to misrepresent the facts; **il est très mal payé,** he is very badly paid.

maladie, *n.f.* **assurance-maladie/indemnité de maladie,** sickness benefit; **certificat de maladie,** medical certificate; **congé de maladie,** sick leave; **maladie professionnelle,** occupational disease.

malfaçon, *n.f.* (*a*) bad work(manship) (*b*) defect.

malversation, *n.f.* embezzlement/corrupt administration (of funds).

management, *n.m.* management; **système d'information de management,** management information system.

manager, *n.m. Ind:* manager.

mandant, *n.m. Jur:* principal (in transaction); **mandant et mandataire,** principal and agent.

mandat, *n.m.* **1.** (*a*) mandate; commission; terms of reference (of committee) (*b*) *Jur:* power of attorney; proxy **2.** warrant; *Jur:* **lancer un mandat,** to issue a warrant; *Fin:* **mandat du Trésor,** Treasury warrant **3.** *Bank: Post:* order to pay; money order; draft; **mandat sur la Banque de France,** order on the Bank of France; **mandat international,** international money order; **mandat de paiement,** (*i*) order to pay (*ii*) (French) treasury money order; **mandat postal/mandat(-)poste,** postal order; **mandat de virement,** transfer order; **toucher un mandat,** to draw on/to cash a money order.

mandataire, *n.m. & f.* **1.** (*à une réunion*) proxy; representative **2.** *Jur:* authorized agent; attorney; assignee; **mandataire général,** general agent.

mandat-carte, *n.m. Post:* postal order/ money order (in postcard form).

mandat-contributions, *n.m. Post:* (special) money order (for paying income tax).

mandatement, *n.m.* (action of) paying by means of a money order.

mandater, *v.tr.* **1.** to elect/to appoint/to commission (representative, etc.) **2.** (*a*) to write out a money order (*b*) to pay by money order.

mandat-lettre, *n.m. Post:* postal order/ money order (which may be sent as a letter in an envelope).

mandat-poste, *n.m. Post:* postal order/money order.

maniement, *n.m.* handling/management (of business, etc.); **maniement de fonds publics,** handling of public money.

manier, *v.tr.* to handle/to manage/to control (business, etc.).

manieur, *n.m.* **manieur d'argent,** financier.

manifeste, *n.m. Av: Nau:* **manifeste (de douane),** customs manifest; **manifeste de chargement,** (ship's, aircraft's) manifest; **manifeste d'entrée,** inward manifest; **manifeste de fret,** freight manifest; **manifeste de sortie,** outward manifest.

manifold, *n.m.* multi-part form.

manœuvre, *n.f.* (*a*) **manœuvre de Bourse,** manipulation on the stock market (*b*) *pl. Jur:* **manœuvres frauduleuses,** swindling **2.** *n.m.* unskilled labourer/worker; **manœuvre qualifié,** skilled worker; **manœuvre spécialisé,** semi-skilled worker; **travail de manœuvre,** unskilled labour/work.

manquant, -ante, 1. *a.* (*a*) missing/ absent (*b*) lacking (*c*) out of stock **2.** *n.* absentee **3.** *n.m.* deficiency; **manquant**

en caisse, short(age) in the cash; **éviter des manquants dans la marchandise,** to prevent short delivery.

manque, *n.m.* deficiency/shortage; **manque d'affaires,** slackness/slack market; **manque de fonds,** lack of funds; **manque à gagner,** (*i*) lost opportunity of doing business (*ii*) slack period/period with no returns; **manque à l'embarquement,** short-shipped goods; **manque à la livraison,** short delivery; **manque de poids,** deficiency in weight; **dix kilos de manque,** ten kilos short.

manquer, 1. *v.i.* (*a*) **manquer de qch.,** to lack/to be short of sth.; **manquer d'argent,** to be short of money; **manquer de personnel,** to be short of staff/to be understaffed; **manquer de sucre,** to be out of sugar/to have run short of sugar; **il nous manque les capitaux nécessaires,** we lack/are short of the necessary capital (*b*) to be lacking/deficient; **manquer en magasin,** to be out of stock; **il me manque dix francs,** I'm ten francs short; **il manque 50 grammes au poids,** the weight is 50 grams short (*c*) (*d'une personne*) to be absent; **manquer à un rendez-vous,** to fail to keep an appointment **2.** *v.tr.* to miss/to lose; **manquer une affaire,** to miss one's chance of doing business; **manquer un contrat,** to lose a contract.

manuel, 1. (*a*) *a.* manual (labour, etc.) (*b*) *n.m.* manual worker/blue collar worker **2.** *n.m.* manual/handbook/instruction book.

manufacturé, *a.* manufactured; factory-made; **biens manufacturés,** manufactured goods.

manufacturer, *v.tr.* to manufacture (industrial products).

manufacturier, *a.* manufacturing (town, industry, etc.).

manutention, *n.f.* handling (of stores, materials, etc.); **appareils de manutention,** handling equipment/machines; **frais de manutention,** handling charges/

costs; **manutention industrielle,** industrial handling.

manutentionnaire, *n.m. Ind: etc:* warehouseman; handler.

manutentionner, *v.tr.* to handle (stores, materials).

maquette, *n.f.* (*a*) *Publ:* (*i*) dummy (of book) (*ii*) lay-out (of page, etc.) (*b*) *Ind:* mock-up (*c*) (scale) model.

maquignon, *n.m. Pej:* shark/swindler/trickster.

maquignonnage, *n.m.* sharp practice.

maquignonner, *v.tr.* to arrange (business, etc.) by sharp practices; **affaire maquignonnée,** put-up job.

maquillage, *n.m.* forging/faking (of documents, etc.); disguising (of stolen property).

maquiller, *v.tr.* **maquiller un chèque,** to forge a cheque.

maraîchage, *n.m.* market gardening/NAm: truck farming.

maraîcher, *a.* **industrie maraîchère,** market-gardening (industry)/NAm: truck farming; **produits maraîchers,** market-garden produce/NAm: truck.

marasme, *n.m.* **le marasme des affaires,** the stagnation/slackness of business; the slump in business; **économie dans le marasme,** stagnating/sagging economy.

marc, *n.m. Jur:* **au marc le franc,** pro rata/proportionally; **au marc le franc de la valeur,** in proportion to the value.

marchand, -ande, 1. *n.* dealer; shopkeeper; tradesman/tradeswoman; **marchand de biens** = estate agent; property dealer; **marchand au détail,** retailer; **marchand en gros,** wholesaler/wholesale dealer; **marchand de journaux,** newsagent; **marchand de poisson(s),** fishmonger; **marchand de tabac,** tobacconist; **marchand de vin,** wine merchant **2.** *a.* (*a*) **denrées marchandes,** saleable/marketable goods; **prix marchand,** trade price; **qualité marchande,** standard/average quality; **techniques marchandes,** merchandising; **valeur marchande,** commercial value/market(able) value (b) **galerie marchande (d'un aéroport),** shopping arcade; **quartier marchand,** shopping centre; commercial centre; **ville marchande,** commercial town (c) **marine marchande,** merchant navy; **navire marchand,** merchant ship.

marchandage, n.m. (a) bargaining/haggling (b) Ind: Jur: (illegal) subcontracting of labour (whereby the worker receives less than a fair wage).

marchander, v.tr. 1. **marchander qch. avec qn,** to haggle/to bargain with s.o. over sth. 2. Ind: to sub-contract (job) (illegally).

marchandeur, -euse, n. 1. haggler/bargainer 2. Ind: (illegal) sub-contractor of labour.

marchandisage, n.m. marketing/merchandising.

marchandise, n.f. merchandise/commodity/pl. goods; **gare de marchandises,** goods depot/goods station/NAm: freight depot; **marchandises au détail,** retail goods; **marchandises en gros,** wholesale goods; **marchandises en magasin,** stock in hand; **marchandises périssables,** perishable goods/perish-ables; **train de marchandises,** goods train/NAm: freight train; **livrer des marchandises,** to deliver goods.

marche, n.f. (a) running/working (of machine, etc.); **en état de marche,** in working order (b) **bonne marche d'une entreprise,** smooth running of a firm (c) course (of events, etc.); **marche à suivre,** course to be followed/to adopt; procedure.

marché, n.m. 1. (a) **faire son marché,** to do one's shopping (b) deal/bargain/contract; **marché au comptant,** cash transaction; **marché de fournitures,** supply contract; **marché de gré à gré,** mutual

agreement/private contract; **être en marché avec qn,** to negotiate a deal with s.o.; **faire/conclure un marché,** to strike a bargain/to clinch a deal; **faire un marché avec qn pour un travail,** to make/to sign a contract with s.o. for a piece of work (c) **(à) bon marché,** cheap(ly); **articles bon marché,** low-priced/cheap goods; bargains; **à meilleur marché,** more cheaply/cheaper; **acheter qch. à bon marché,** to buy sth. cheaply/cheap; **avoir qch. à très bon marché,** to get a very good bargain; **vendre qch. à très bon marché,** to sell sth. cheap(ly) 2. (a) market; **marché en plein air,** open-air market; **marché couvert,** covered market; **marché aux bestiaux,** cattle market; **marché aux poissons,** fish market; **jour du marché,** market day; **la place du marché,** the market place; **aller au marché,** to go to the market (b) **le Marché commun,** the Common Market; **marché extérieur/d'outre-mer,** foreign/overseas market; **marché gris,** grey/semi-black market; **marché intérieur,** home market; **marché libre,** open/free market; **marché marginal,** fringe market; **marché mondial,** world market; **marché noir,** black market; **faire du marché noir,** to buy and sell on the black market; **marché parallèle,** black market; **marché réglementé,** regulated market (c) StExch: Fin: **marché à la baisse,** buyer's market; **marché calme,** quiet/dull market; **marché des changes/des devises,** foreign exchange market; **marché des changes à terme,** forward exchange market; **marché du comptant/marché du disponible,** spot market; **marché en coulisse,** outside market; **marché des denrées et matières premières,** commodity market; **marché d'équipement,** capital goods market; **marché étroit,** limited market; **marché ferme/soutenu,** steady market; **marché financier/marché des capitaux,** capital market; **marché à la hausse,** seller's market; **marché hors cote,** unofficial market/over-the-counter market; **marché instable,** jumpy market; **marché de l'immobilier,** property market; **marché des matières premières,** commodity exchange/market; **marché monétaire,** money market; **marché officiel,** official market; **marché à options/ à primes,** options market; **marché primaire,** primary market; **marché secondaire,** secondary market; **marché à terme,** forward market; **marché des valeurs mobilières,** stock exchange (d) **accaparement du marché,** cornering of the market; **analyse du marché,** market analysis; **cours du marché,** market price/rate; **étude du marché,** market research; **évaluation du marché,** market appraisal; **forces du marché,** market forces; **prix du marché,** market price; **prévision du marché,** market forecast; **tendances du marché,** market trends (e) **accaparer/monopoliser un marché,** to corner a market; **inonder le marché,** to flood/to glut the market; **mettre/lancer un nouveau produit sur le marché,** to put/to launch a new product on the market; **travailler le marché/agir sur le marché,** to manipulate the market.

marchéage, n.m. (division of) marketing.

marcher, v.i. (a) (d'un projet) to proceed/to progress; **les affaires marchent,** business is brisk; **les affaires ne marchent plus,** business is at a standstill/is slack (b) (d'une affaire, d'un appareil) to work/to run/to operate.

marge, n.f. 1. margin (of page); **écrire une note en marge,** to write a note in the margin 2. (a) **marge d'erreur,** margin of error; **marge de sécurité,** safety margin; **Ind:** **marge de tolérance,** tolerance margin; **laisser une bonne marge pour les déchets,** to make a generous allowance for waste (b) **Fin:** **appel de marge,** margin call/call for additional cover; **marge bénéficiaire,** profit margin; **marge brute,** gross margin (of profit); **marge brute d'autofinancement (MBA),** cashflow; **marge commerciale,** trading profit; **marge de fluctuation (d'une monnaie),** margin of fluctuation (of a currency); **marge d'intérêt,** margin of interest; **marge nette,** net margin (of profit).

marginal, a. 1. **note/annotation marginale,** marginal note 2. **analyse marginale,** marginal analysis; **bénéfice marginal,** marginal profit; **coût marginal,** marginal cost; **comptabilité marginale/méthode des coûts marginaux,** marginal costing/ cost pricing; **entreprise marginale,** firm with only a marginal profit; **marché marginal,** fringe market; **prix marginal,** marginal price; **productivité marginale,** marginal productivity; **rendement marginal du capital,** marginal return on capital; **utilité marginale,** marginal utility.

marginalisme, n.m. PolEc: marginalism.

margoulin, n.m. F: (a) St Exch: petty speculator (b) shark/swindler.

marine, n.f. **marine marchande/de commerce,** merchant navy.

maritime, a. maritime; **agent maritime,** shipping agent; **assurance maritime,** marine insurance; **commerce maritime,** maritime trade; **courtier maritime,** shipbroker; **droit/législation maritime,** maritime law; Rail: **gare maritime,** harbour station; Ins: **risque maritime,** maritime risk.

mark, n.m. (German) mark/Deutschmark.

marketing, n.m. marketing; **chef/directeur du marketing,** marketing manager/director; **marketing(-)mix,** marketing(-)mix; **service de marketing,** marketing department.

marquage, n.m. marking (of price, weight, date, etc.).

marque, n.f. (a) brand/make; **acceptabilité de la marque,** brand acceptance; **bonne marque de cigares,** good brand of cigars; **fidélité à la marque,** brand loyalty; **grande marque,** famous make/well-known brand; **image de marque,** brand image; **marque d'appel,** brand on offer; **marque collective,** label; **marque courante,** standard make; **marque déposée,** registered trade mark; **marque de distributeur,** distributor's brand name; **marque de fabricant,** manufacturer's brand name; **marque de fabrique/**

de commerce, trade mark/brand (name); **marque de garantie,** certification mark; **marque de service,** mark of quality/ quality guarantee (on range of services offered by company or manufacturer); **produits de marque,** (*i*) well known brand of goods (*ii*) branded goods; **publicité de marque,** brand advertising; **vin de marque,** (*i*) wine of a well-known brand (*ii*) vintage wine (*b*) **taux de marque,** mark-up rate.

marquer, *v.tr.* **prix marqué,** (*i*) catalogue price/list price (*ii*) marked price; **acheter un article au prix marqué,** to buy an article at the marked price/at the price marked on the label.

marqueur, -euse, *n.* **1.** (*d'une personne*) marker **2.** *n.f. Ind:* stamping machine (for bars of chocolate, soap, etc.).

marron, *a.* unlicensed (trader, etc.); **courtier marron,** unlicensed broker.

masse, *n.f.* (*a*) *Jur:* **masse des créanciers,** (general) body of creditors; *Fin:* **masse des obligataires,** body of debenture-holders/bondholders (*b*) *Fin:* fund; **masse active,** assets; **masse passive,** liabilities; **masse monétaire,** money supply; **masse salariale,** total wages bill.

mass(-)media, *n.m.pl.* mass media.

matériau, *n.m.* **1.** *Const: Ind:* (building) material **2. matériaux,** *n.m.pl. Const:* materials; **matériaux de construction,** building materials.

matériel, 1. *a.* material; **valeurs matérielles,** tangible assets **2.** *n.m.* (*a*) equipment; material; stock in trade; plant (of factory); **matériel de bureau,** office equipment; **matériel lourd,** heavy equipment; plant; **main-d'œuvre et matériel,** labour and material (*b*) *Mkt:* **matériel de PLV (publicité sur le lieu de vente),** point-of-sale material; **matériel de présentation,** display material; **matériel publicitaire,** advertising material **3.** *n.m. Cmptr:* hardware.

matière, *n.f.* **1.** material; **matières premières,** raw materials; **comptabilité matières,** (raw) materials accounting; **matière brute/non travaillée,** unprocessed/unrefined material; **matières plastiques,** plastics; **matière synthétique,** synthetic material **2.** matter; **matière imposable,** taxable income; **matière juridique,** legal matters; (*dans un catalogue, etc.*) **table des matières,** (table of) contents.

matraquage, *n.m. Mkt:* **matraquage publicitaire,** plugging.

maturité, *n.f.* **économie en pleine maturité,** mature economy.

mauvais, *a.* (*a*) bad; poor; inadequate; **mauvaise administration/mauvaise gestion,** mismanagement; **mauvaise période/ saison,** slack/poor season; **de mauvaise qualité,** of poor quality; inferior; **faire de mauvaises affaires,** to be doing badly (in business); **nous faisons de mauvaises affaires en ce moment,** business is bad/poor at the moment (*b*) wrong; **mauvaise mesure,** short measure (*c*) **mauvaise créance,** bad debt.

maximal, *a.* (*a*) maximum (efficiency, etc.) (*b*) maximal.

maximalisation, *n.f.* maximization/ maximizing; **maximalisation du profit/ des profits,** profit maximization; **la maximalisation de l'utilité totale,** the maximization of total utility.

maxim(al)iser, *v.tr.* to maximize.

maximum, 1. *n.m.* maximum; **maximum de rendement,** highest efficiency/ maximum efficiency; **au maximum,** to the maximum; to the highest degree; **chiffre d'affaires de 3 millions au maximum,** turnover of 3 millions at the most/at the outside; **porter la production au maximum,** to raise production to a maximum/to maximize production **2.** *a.* **prix maximums / maxima,** maximum prices/highest prices; **rendement maxi-**

mum, maximum/peak output; **tarif maximum,** maximum tarif.

mécanisation, *n.f.* mechanization.

mécanisé, *a.* mechanized.

mécaniser, *v.tr.* to mechanize (an industry, etc.).

mécanisme, *n.m.* mechanism/machinery; **mécanisme administratif,** administrative machinery; **mécanisme bancaire,** banking machinery/mechanism; **mécanisme budgétaire,** budgetary mechanism; **mécanismes économiques,** economic machinery; **mécanisme des prix,** price mechanism.

mécompte, *n.m.* miscalculation; error in reckoning/in account.

média, media, *n.m.pl.* **les média,** the media.

médiateur, -trice, 1. *n.* mediator; **agir en médiateur/servir de médiateur entre la direction et les employés,** to act as mediator between management and employees **2.** *a.* mediatory/mediating.

médiation, *n.f.* mediation.

médical, *a.* medical; **certificat médical,** medical certificate; **visite médicale,** medical examination.

meilleur, *a.* **1.** better; **meilleur marché,** cheaper/less expensive; **acheter qch. (à) meilleur marché,** to buy sth. cheaper; **payer (qch.) meilleur marché,** to pay less (for sth.); **obtenir du crédit à meilleur compte,** to obtain cheaper credit; **produit de meilleure qualité,** better quality product/product of a better quality **2.** **le meilleur/la meilleure,** (*i*) the best (of several) (*ii*) the better (of two); *Corr:* **veuillez agréer, Monsieur, l'expression de mes sentiments les meilleurs/de mes meilleurs sentiments** = yours faithfully.

membre, *n.m.* member; **carte de membre,** membership card; **club de mille membres,** club with a thousand members/with a membership of a thousand; **membre du conseil d'administration,** member of the board/board member; **les pays membres de la CEE,** the member countries of the EEC.

mémoire, *n.m.* **1.** (contractor's) account/bill; **présenter un mémoire,** to send a detailed account (of costs) **2. pour mémoire,** as a record/as a memorandum **3.** *n.f.* *Cmptr: etc:* memory; **calculatrice à mémoire,** calculator with memory (function).

mémorandum, *n.m.* **1.** memorandum/note **2.** written order (to a supplier).

ménage, *n.m.* household/family.

ménager[1], *a.* **appareils ménagers,** household equipment/appliances; *NAm:* housewares; **Salon des Arts Ménagers** = Ideal Home Exhibition.

ménager[2], *v.tr.* to use (sth.) economically.

mensualisation, *n.f.* (*a*) paying (of employees) by the month; monthly salary system (*b*) transfer (of employees) to a monthly salary system.

mensualiser, *v.tr.* (*a*) to pay (employees) by the month (*b*) to put (employees) on a monthly salary system.

mensualité, *n.f.* (*a*) monthly payment; **payer par mensualités,** to pay by monthly instalments (*b*) monthly salary.

mensuel, -uelle, 1. *a.* monthly; **rapport mensuel,** monthly report; **publication mensuelle,** monthly publication **2.** (*a*) *n.m.* monthly magazine (*b*) *n.m. & f.* monthly paid employee.

mensuellement, *adv.* monthly/each month/every month; once a month.

mention, *n.f.* (*a*) mention; **faire mention (de qn, de qch.),** to mention (s.o., sth.)/to refer to (s.o., sth.) (*b*) note/comment; *Adm: etc:* **rayer les mentions inutiles,** delete where inapplicable.

mentionner, *v.tr.* to mention; **mentionné ci-dessus,** above-mentioned/aforesaid.

menu, 1. *a.* small/minor; **menus dépôts,** small deposits; **menus frais,** petty/ incidental expenses; **menue monnaie,** small/loose change **2.** *n.m.* menu; **menu à prix fixe,** set menu; **menu touristique,** tourist/economy menu.

mercantile, *a.* mercantile; commercial.

mercaticien, -ienne, *n.* marketing specialist.

mercatique, *n.f.* (division of) marketing.

merchandising, *n.m.* merchandising.

mercuriale, *n.f.* market price-list/market prices (of corn, etc.).

mère, *n.f.* **maison mère/société mère,** parent company; head office.

mérite, *n.m.* merit; **appréciation du mérite,** merit rating.

message, *n.m.* message; *TV: WTel:* **message publicitaire,** spot/commercial; **message téléphonique,** telephone message; **laisser un message pour qn,** to leave a message for s.o.; **je lui transmettrai le message,** I'll give him the message.

messageries, *n.f.pl.* **bureau de messageries,** (*i*) shipping office (*ii*) *Rail:* parcels office; **entreprise de messageries,** parcel delivery firm/company; **service de messageries,** parcel post/delivery service; **messageries aériennes,** air-freight company; **messageries maritimes** (*i*) transport of goods by sea (*ii*) shipping line; **messageries de presse,** press distribution service.

mesure, *n.f.* **1.** (*a*) measure; **mesure de longeur,** linear measure; **mesure de capacité pour les liquides,** fluid measure; **mesure (de capacité) pour les matières sèches,** dry measure; **mesure de superficie,** square measure; **mesure de volume,** cubic measure; **poids et mesures,** weights and measures; **prendre la mesure de qch.,** to measure sth. (*b*) *Tail:* **fait sur mesure,** made to measure; **se faire faire un costume sur mesure,** to have a suit made to measure **2.** measure/step; **mesures déflationnistes,** deflationary mea-

sures; **mesures provisoires,** temporary measures; **mesures de sécurité,** safety measures/safety precautions; **mesures d'urgence,** emergency measures.

mesurer, *v.tr.* **1.** (*a*) to measure (dimensions, quantity); to measure out (corn, etc.); to measure up (wood, etc.); to measure off (cloth, etc.); **mesurer deux kilos de sucre,** to weigh two kilos of sugar (*b*) *Tail:* **mesurer un client,** to take a customer's measurements **2. mesurer ses dépenses sur ses profits,** to proportion one's expenditure to one's profits.

métal, *n.m.* metal; **industrie des métaux,** the metal/metallurgical industry.

méthode, *n.f.* (*a*) method/system/way; **méthodes administratives,** systems and procedures; **méthode de classement,** filing system; **méthode expérimentale,** experimental method; **méthode d'exploitation,** method of working/method of operation; **méthodes et organisation,** organization and methods (O&M) (*b*) **méthode du chemin critique,** critical path method; *Fin:* **méthode de capitalisation du coût entier,** full cost accounting (method); **méthode des coûts variables,** direct costing (*c*) *Ind:* **bureau/service des méthodes,** methods office; **étude des méthodes,** methods engineering/ methods study; **étude des temps et des méthodes,** time and methods study; **ingénieur de méthodes,** methods engineer.

métier, *n.m.* (*a*) trade/craft/profession/ occupation; **argot de métier,** trade/ technical jargon; **Chambre des métiers,** Chamber of Trade; **corps de métier,** guild/trade association; **homme du métier,** expert/professional; **métier manuel,** manual trade/craft; **risques de métier,** occupational hazards; **terme de métier,** technical term; **exercer/faire un métier,** to carry on a trade/a profession; **il est du métier,** he's in the trade/the business (*b*) craftsmanship.

métrage, *n.m.* **1.** (*a*) measuring/measure(ment) (*b*) *Const: etc:* quantity surveying **2.** (metric) length (of fabric).

mètre, *n.m.* (*a*) *Meas:* metre (*abbr.* m)/*NAm:* meter (= 3.281 ft.); **mètre carré,** square metre; **mètre courant,** linear metre; **mètre cube,** cubic metre (*b*) (metre) rule; **mètre à ruban,** tape measure.

métrer, *v.tr.* **1.** to measure (by the metre) **2.** *Const: etc:* to survey.

métrique, *a.* metric; **le système métrique,** the metric system; **adopter le système métrique,** to go metric; **adoption/ introduction du système métrique,** metrication; **tonne métrique,** metric ton; tonne; **unité métrique,** metric unit.

mettre, *v.tr.* **1.** to put/to place; **mettre une annonce dans les journaux,** to put an advertisement/an ad in the newspapers; **mettre sa signature à un contrat,** to put one's signature to a contract/to sign a contract **2. mettre son argent en immeubles,** to put/to invest one's money in property; **mettre en vente une maison,** to put a house up for sale; **je ne peux pas y mettre tant que ça,** I can't afford as much as that.

meuble, 1. *a.* movable; *Jur:* **biens meubles,** movables; personal property/personalty **2.** *n.m.* piece of furniture; **meubles de bureau,** office furniture **3.** *n.m.pl. Jur:* movables; personal property/ personalty; **meubles corporels,** tangible movables; **meubles incorporels,** intangible movables.

meublé, 1. *a.* furnished (room, etc.); **appartement meublé,** furnished flat/ apartment **2.** *n.m.* furnished flat/ apartment.

mévente, *n.f.* slump (in sales)/slack period.

microéconomie, *n.f.* micro-economics.

microéconomique, *a.* micro-economic.

microfiche, *n.f.* microfiche.

microfilm, *n.m.* microfilm.

micro-ordinateur, *n.m.* microcomputer.

microprocesseur, *n.m.* microprocessor.

mieux, *adv.* **acheter au mieux,** to buy at best.

milieu, *n.m.* **milieux commerciaux,** business circles; **milieux financiers,** financial circles.

mille, *num.a. inv. & n.m. inv.* thousand; **mille francs,** a/one thousand francs; **deux mille francs,** two thousand francs; **billet de mille,** thousand-franc note.

millésime, *n.m.* (*a*) date (on coin, etc.) (*b*) year of manufacture; (*d'un vin*) year/vintage.

milliard, *n.m.* a thousand million(s); *NAm:* a billion.

milliardaire, *a. & n.m. & f.* multimillionaire; *NAm:* billionaire.

millier, *n.m.* (about a) thousand; a thousand (or so); **des milliers de francs,** thousands of francs.

milligramme, *n.m. Meas:* milligram(me) (*abbr.* mg).

millilitre, *n.m. Meas:* millilitre/*NAm:* milliliter (*abbr.* ml).

millimètre, *n.m. Meas:* millimetre/ *NAm:* millimeter (*abbr.* mm).

millimétrique, *a.* **échelle millimétrique,** millimetre scale.

million, *n.m.* million; **un million de francs,** a million francs; **chiffre d'affaires de deux millions,** turnover of two million; **une machine coûtant deux millions de livres,** a two-million-pound machine.

millionnaire, *a. & n.* millionaire.

minimal, *a.* minimal; **valeur minimale,** minimal value.

minimarge, *n.m.* **(magasin) minimarge/** discount store.

minimisation, *n.f.* minimization; **minimisation du coût de production,** minimization/minimizing of production costs.

minimiser, *v.tr.* to minimize.

minimum, 1. *n.m.* **réduire les frais au minimum,** to reduce expenses to a minimum; *PolEc:* **minimum vital,** minimum living wage **2.** *a.* **pertes minimums/ minima,** minimum/minimal losses; **poids minimum,** minimum weight; **prix minimum,** minimum price; **quantité minimum,** minimum/minimal amount; **salaire minimum interprofessionnel de croissance (SMIC)** = index linked minimum wage **3.** *adv.phr.* **au minimum,** as a minimum; at least; **il y en aura 5 au minimum,** there will be a minimum of 5.

mini-ordinateur, *n.m.* minicomputer.

minoritaire, *a.* **participation minoritaire,** minority holding/interest.

minorité, *n.f.* minority; **être en minorité,** to be in the/in a minority.

minutage, *n.m.* drafting (of document).

minutaire, *a.* **document minutaire,** document in draft (form); **acte minutaire,** original document.

minute, *n.f.* **1.** (*a*) minute (*b*) **clef minute,** key-cutting (while you wait); **talon minute,** heel bar **2.** (*a*) minute/draft (of contract, etc.); **faire la minute d'un contract,** to minute/to draft a contract (*b*) record (of deed, etc.).

minuté, *a.* timed; **horaire minuté,** (*i*) tight schedule (*ii*) detailed schedule.

minuter, *v.tr.* **1.** (*a*) to minute/to draw up/to draft (agreement, etc.) (*b*) to record (deed, etc.) **2.** to time; **sa journée est soigneusement minutée,** his day is carefully planned; his day is run on a tight schedule.

mise, *n.f.* **1.** (*a*) **mise en place de qch.,** placing/positioning (of sth.); **mise en bouteille,** bottling; **mise en dépôt,** ware-housing; *Typ:* **mise en page,** making-up of page (*b*) *Mkt:* **mise en avant,** special display; **mise en circulation (de l'argent),** putting into circulation (of money); **mise au courant (du personnel),** induction (of staff); *Jur:* **mise en demeure,** formal notice (of summons, etc.); **mise en distribution,** distribution; distributing; **mise à jour,** bringing up to date/updating; **mise en œuvre,** putting into action; **mise au point,** (*i*) (*d'un travail*) clarification/explanation (*ii*) (*d'une construction, etc.*) finishing touch; **mise en service,** putting into service; **mise en vente,** putting up for sale; bringing (of product) onto the market; launching (of new product); publication (of book) **2.** (*a*) (*à une vente aux enchères*) bid; **mise à prix,** reserve price/upset price (*b*) *Fin:* **mise de fonds,** (*i*) putting up of money (*ii*) capital outlay; **faire/fournir une mise de fonds,** to put up capital; **mise en commun de fonds,** pooling of capital; **mise hors,** (*i*) disbursement (of money) (*ii*) sum advanced; **mise en paiement (du dividende),** payment (of dividend); **mise sociale,** capital brought into a business by a partner; **mise en valeur,** (*i*) (*d'un investissement*) turning to account (*ii*) (*d'une propriété*) improving.

miser, *v.tr. & i.* (*a*) to speculate (on a rise, etc.) (*b*) (*à une vente aux enchères*) to bid.

mi-temps, *adv. phr.* **emploi à mi-temps,** part-time job.

mixte, *a.* (*a*) mixed; *Nau:* **cargaison mixte,** mixed cargo; **économie mixte,** mixed economy; **organisation mixte,** line and staff organization; *Ins:* **risques mixtes,** mixed risks (*b*) serving a double purpose; **billet mixte,** combined road and rail ticket.

mobile, 1. *n.m.* (*a*) **mobile d'achat,** buying impulse; purchasing motivator (*b*) *Mkt:* **mobile (publicitaire),** (advertising) mobile **2.** *a.* mobile; **échelle mobile,** (*i*) sliding scale (of prices, salaries, etc.) (*ii*) escalator clause.

mobilier, 1. *a. Jur:* movable; **biens mobiliers,** movables/personal estate/personalty; *Adm:* **contribution mobilière,** movable property tax; **cote mobilière,** assessment on property; *Fin:* **valeurs mobilières,** stock and shares; transferable securities **2.** *n.m.* **mobilier de bureau,** office furniture.

mobilisable, *a.* (capital) that can be made available; **fonds mobilisables,** realizable funds.

mobilisation, *n.f.* mobilization (of real estate); realization (of capital).

mobiliser, *v.tr.* to mobilize; to realize; to unfreeze/to free (capital, money).

mobilité, *n.f.* mobility (of capital, labour, etc.).

modalités, *n.f.pl.* ways and means; *Jur:* **modalités d'application de la loi,** means/method of enforcing the law; *Fin:* **modalités d'une émission,** terms and conditions of an issue; **modalités de financement,** financing terms/conditions; **modalités de paiement,** methods of payment.

mode[1], *n.f.* fashion; **journal de mode(s),** fashion magazine.

mode[2], *n.m.* method; **mode d'emploi,** directions for use; **mode de paiement,** method/means of payment.

modèle, *n.m.* (*a*) model/pattern; **maison/appartement modèle,** show house/flat; **modèle de démonstration,** demonstration model; **modèle déposé,** registered design/pattern; **modèle d'une lettre de change,** form of wording for a bill of exchange; specimen of a bill of exchange; **modèle périmé,** obsolete model/type; **modèle réduit,** (scale) model; **nouveau modèle (d'une voiture),** new model (of a car) (*b*) *PolEc:* **modèle décisionnel,** decision model; **modèle d'entreprise,** corporate model; **modèle prévisionnel,** econometric model (*c*) **(article) grand modèle,** large-size(d) (article); **échantillon modèle,** standard sample.

modération, *n.f.* **modération de droit,** tax reduction/rebate.

modéré, *a.* moderate; reasonable (price); **habitation à loyer modéré (HLM)** = council house/flat.

modernisation, *n.f.* modernization/modernizing.

moderniser, *v.tr.* to modernize.

modicité, *n.f.* **la modicité de son revenu ne lui permet pas d'acheter une voiture,** he can't afford a car with his low income.

modifier, *v.tr. Book-k:* to rectify (an entry).

modique, *a.* modest/low (price, income, rent).

moindre, *a.* **1.** less(er); **vendre une quantité moindre,** to sell a smaller quantity **2. les moindres détails,** the smallest details.

moins, *adv.* (*a*) less; **dix francs de moins,** (*i*) ten francs less (*ii*) ten francs short; **moins de dix francs,** less than ten francs; **paquet qui pèse moins de 10 kilos,** parcel weighing less than 10 kilos; **vendre qch. à moins du prix de revient,** to sell sth. at less than cost price; **je ne peux pas vous le laisser à moins,** I can't let you have it for less; **à moins d'avis contraire,** unless I hear to the contrary (*b*) **le moins,** the least; **le moins disant,** the lowest bidder (*c*) **vous compterez cela en moins,** you may deduct that.

moins-perçu, *n.m.* amount due and not received; short payment.

moins-value, *n.f.* (*a*) capital loss (*b*) depreciation/drop in value.

mois, *n.m.* (*a*) month; **mois civil,** calendar month; **au mois d'août,** in (the month of) August; **le 12 de ce mois,** the 12th of this month/the 12th inst.; **le mois dernier,** last month (*b*) **un mois de crédit,** a month's credit; *Fin:* **papiers à trois mois (d'échéance),** bills at three months; *Bank:* **relevé de fin de mois,** monthly statement (of account); **salaire de cinq mille francs par mois,** salary of five thousand francs a month; **devoir trois mois de loyer,** to owe three months'/a quarter's rent; **être payé au mois,** to be paid by the month; **louer qch. au mois,** to rent/to hire sth. by the month (c) monthly salary; **mois double/treizième mois** = (Christmas) bonus; **toucher son mois,** to receive one's (month's) pay/ salary.

moitié, n.f. half; **à moitié prix,** at half price; **la première moitié de l'année,** the first half of the year; **bénéfices réduits de moitié,** profit(s) reduced by half; **être de moitié dans une entreprise,** to have a half share/a partnership in a business; **perdre la moitié de son capital,** to lose half (of) one's capital.

monde, n.m. (a) world (b) **le monde de la haute finance,** the world of high finance/ the financial world/financial circles.

mondial, a. world(-wide); **commerce mondial,** world trade; **prix mondiaux,** world (market) prices; **production mondiale,** world output.

monétaire, a. monetary; **circulation monétaire,** monetary circulation; **marché monétaire,** monetary market; **masse monétaire,** money supply; **politique monétaire,** monetary policy; **système monétaire d'un pays,** monetary system of a country; **unité monétaire,** monetary unit; **zone monétaire,** monetary area; **Fonds monétaire international (FMI),** International Monetary Fund (IMF); **système monétaire européen (SME),** European Monetary system (EMS).

monnaie, n.f. **1.** (a) monetary unit; **cours d'une monnaie,** rate of a currency; **dévaluation d'une monnaie,** devaluation of a currency; **monnaie étrangère,** foreign currency (b) coinage; currency; money; **fausse monnaie,** counterfeit coinage; **monnaie d'argent,** silver money; **monnaie de compte,** money of account; **monnaie divisionnaire/monnaie d'ap-**

point, divisional/fractional money; **monnaie faible,** soft currency; **monnaie fiduciaire,** (i) token money (ii) = fiduciary currency; **monnaie flottante,** floating currency; **monnaie forte,** hard currency; **monnaie de marchandise,** commodity money; **monnaie d'or,** gold money; **monnaie de papier/papier-monnaie,** paper money/banknotes; **monnaie de réserve,** reserve currency; **monnaie scripturale/ monnaie de banque,** bank deposits; **pièce de monnaie,** coin; **Hôtel de la Monnaie/la Monnaie** = the Mint; **frapper de la monnaie,** to coin/to mint money **2.** change; **petite monnaie/menue monnaie,** small change; **donner la monnaie de mille francs,** to give change for a thousand francs/for a thousand franc note; **faire de la monnaie,** to give change (for a note).

monnayage, n.m. minting/coining.

monopole, n.m. monopoly; **monopole d'État,** state monopoly; **monopole des prix,** price ring; **monopole syndical de l'embauche,** closed shop; **avoir le monopole de qch.,** to have the monopoly of sth./NAm: on sth.

monopoleur, -euse, 1. a. monopolist(ic) **2.** n. monopolist.

monopolisant, a. monopolistic.

monopolisateur, -trice, 1. a. monopolistic **2.** n. monopolist/monopolizer.

monopolisation, n.f. monopolization; monopolizing.

monopoliser, v.tr. to monopolize; to have the monopoly of (sth.)/NAm: on (sth.).

monopoliste, 1. a. monopolist(ic); **compagnie pétrolière monopoliste,** oil company with a monopoly **2.** n.m. monopolist.

monopolistique, a. monopolistic; **contrôle monopolistique,** monopoly control.

monopsone, n.m. monopsony.

Monsieur, n.m. **Monsieur**/abbr: **M.,** Mr; Corr: **Monsieur,** Dear Sir; **Cher Mon-**

sieur, Dear Mr X; **Monsieur le Président,** Mr President/Mr Chairman; *pl.* **Messieurs**/*abbr.* **MM,** Messrs.

montage, *n.m.* **1.** installation; fixture; assembling (of apparatus); fitting out (of workshop); **notice de montage,** instructions for assembly **2.** *Ind: etc:* assembling/assembly; **chaîne de montage,** assembly line.

montant, *n.m.* amount/(sum) total/total amount (of account, bill); proceeds (of sale, etc.); **montant brut,** gross amount/total; **montant net,** net amount/total; **j'ignore le montant de mes dettes,** I do not know what my debts amount to/come to.

monté, *a.* **boutique bien montée,** well-stocked shop.

monte-charge, *n.m.inv.* hoist; service lift/goods lift/*NAm:* elevator.

monter, 1. *v.i.* (*a*) to rise; (*d'un prix*) to rise/to go up/to increase; **empêcher les prix de monter,** to keep prices down; **faire monter les prix,** to raise prices; to send prices up; **les enchères ont monté à cent mille francs,** the bidding went up to a hundred thousand francs; **les prix montent en flèche,** prices are soaring (*b*) **la somme monte à cent francs,** the total comes to a hundred francs **2.** *v.tr.* to fit out/to equip (workshop, etc.); to set up/to install (apparatus, etc.); to assemble (a machine); **monter une affaire,** to set up a business **3.** *v.pr.* **se monter,** to amount; **frais qui se montent à des milliers de francs,** expenses that mount up to thousands of francs; **la note se monte à mille francs,** the bill amounts to/adds up to/comes to a thousand francs.

monteur, *n.m.* **monteur d'affaires,** business promoter.

morale, *n.f.* **morale professionnelle,** business ethics.

moratoire, *Jur:* **1.** *a.* (payment) delayed by agreement; **intérêts moratoires,** interest on overdue payments **2.** *n.m.* moratorium; **décréter un moratoire,** to an-

nounce a moratorium; **le moratoire des loyers,** the moratorium on rents.

moratorié, *a.* (bill, etc.) for which a moratorium has been granted.

moratorium, *n.m. Jur:* moratorium.

mort, *a.* (*a*) **marché mort,** dead market (*b*) **argent mort,** money bringing in no interest/lying idle (*c*) *Stat:* **point mort,** break-even point.

morte-saison, *n.f.* slack season/off season.

motel, *n.m.* motel.

motif, *n.m. Mkt:* **motif d'achat,** buying inducement.

motion, *n.f.* motion/proposal; **faire une motion,** to propose/to bring forward a motion; **adopter une motion,** to carry a motion; **la motion fut adoptée,** the motion was carried.

motionner, *v.i.* to propose a motion.

motivation, *n.f.* motivation; **motivation par le profit,** profit motive; *PolEc: Mkt:* **études de motivation,** motivational research; **motivation du consommateur,** consumer motivation.

mouvement, *n.m.* **1.** (*a*) movement; motion; **étude des temps et des mouvements,** time and motion study; **mouvement de caisse/mouvement d'espèces,** cash transaction; **mouvement de capitaux/de fonds,** movement of capital; **mouvement du personnel,** staff turnover; **mouvement des stocks,** stock turnover/turnround (*b*) traffic; **mouvement d'un aéroport,** air(port) traffic; **mouvement d'un port,** harbour/port traffic; **mouvement des marchandises,** goods traffic **2.** *Fin:* **mouvement de baisse,** downward movement; **mouvement de hausse,** upward movement; **mouvement du marché,** market fluctuations; **mouvement des prix,** change/fluctuation/trend in prices.

moyen¹, *a.* (*a*) middle; **les cadres moyens,** middle management (*b*) average/mean (price, etc.); *StExch:* **cours moyen,** middle price (*c*) medium (quality etc.); **de taille/de grandeur moyenne,** medium-sized; **moyenne entreprise,** medium-sized firm; **prix moyen,** moderate/reasonable price.

moyen², *n.m.* (*a*) means; **moyens de communication,** means of communication; **moyens de paiement,** means of payment; **moyens de transport,** means of transport (*b*) *Fin:* **voies et moyens,** ways and means; **répartition des moyens,** distribution of resources/resource allocation; **vivre au-dessus de ses moyens,** to live beyond one's means.

moyennant, *prep.* for; in consideration of; **moyennant paiement de dix francs,** subject to/on payment of ten francs.

moyenne, *n.f.* average; **au-dessus de la moyenne,** above average; **au-dessous de la moyenne,** below average; **en moyenne,** on average; **il gagne en moyenne 40 francs (de) l'heure,** on average he earns 40 francs an hour; **moyenne pondérée,** weighted average; **les recettes donnent une moyenne de mille francs par jour,** takings average a thousand francs a day; **établir la moyenne (des pertes, etc.),** to average (the losses, etc.).

multilatéral, *a.* multilateral; **accord multilatéral,** multilateral agreement; **commerce multilatéral,** multilateral trade.

multimillionnaire, *a. & n.m. & f.* multimillionaire.

multinational *a. & n.f.* **une (société) multinationale,** a multinational (company).

multiple, *a.* multiple; **direction multiple,** multiple management; **maison à succursales multiples,** multiple store/multiple shop/chain store.

multiplication, *n.f.* multiplication.

multiplier, *v.tr. & v.i.* to multiply (**par, by**); **multiplier deux nombres l'un par l'autre,** to multiply two numbers together.

multipropriété, *n.f.* multiple ownership (of building, etc.).

mutation, *n.f.* (*a*) *Jur:* change of ownership; transfer (of property) (*b*) **mutation de personnel,** transfer of staff (*c*) **mutation d'entrepôt,** transfer of bonded goods (to another bonded warehouse).

mutualiste, *n.m. & f.* member of a mutual insurance company/of a friendly society.

mutualité, *n.f.* mutual insurance; **société de mutualité,** friendly society.

mutuel, 1. *a.* mutual (service, insurance, etc.); **compagnie d'assurances mutuelles,** mutual insurance company **2.** *n.f.* **mutuelle,** mutual insurance company; friendly society.

N

nantir, *v.tr. Jur:* to give security to/to secure (creditor); **créancier entièrement nanti,** fully secured creditor.

nantissement, *n.m. Jur:* (*a*) hypothecation/pledging/bailment; **nantissement d'un fonds de commerce,** pledging of a business (as security) (*b*) pledge/collateral (security)/cover; **avances sur nantissement,** advances against collateral; **droit de nantissement,** lien on goods; **prêt sur nantissement,** loan on collateral; **déposer des titres en nantissement,** tó hypothecate securities/to lodge stock as security; **emprunter sur nantissement,** to borrow on security.

national, *a.* national; **banque nationale,** national bank; **dette nationale,** national debt; **fortune nationale,** national wealth; **produit national brut (PNB),** gross national product (GNP); **revenu national brut,** gross national income; **revenu national net,** net national income.

nationalisation, *n.f.* nationalization.

nationaliser, *v.tr.* to nationalize; **entreprises nationalisées,** nationalized/state-owned industries.

nationalité, *n.f. Adm:* nationality; *Nau:* **acte de nationalité,** (ship's) certificate of registry; **prendre la nationalité française,** to take French nationality.

nature, *n.f.* 1. nature/kind; **nature du contenu,** nature of (the) contents 2. **payer en nature,** to pay in kind.

naval, *a.* **chantier naval,** shipyard; **construction navale,** shipbuilding.

navette, *n.f.* **faire la navette (entre sa résidence et son travail),** to commute.

navigabilité, *n.f. Nau: Av:* **certificat de navigabilité,** (*i*) certificate of seaworthiness (*ii*) certificate of airworthiness.

navigation, *n.f.* navigation; shipping; **compagnie de navigation aérienne,** airline; **compagnie de navigation (maritime),** shipping company; **ligne de navigation,** shipping line.

navire, *n.m.* ship; **navire de charge,** freighter; cargo boat; **navire de commerce/navire marchand,** merchant ship; **navire mixte,** mixed passenger and cargo ship; **navire de passagers,** passenger ship; **navire porte-conteneurs,** container ship; lift-on lift-off ship.

navire-citerne, *n.m. Nau:* tanker.

néant, *n.m. Adm:* none; nothing to report; nil; **état néant,** nil return.

nécessité, *n.f.* necessity; **denrées de première nécessité,** essential foodstuffs; staple commodities.

négatif, *a.* negative; **épargne négative,** negative saving.

négligé, *a. StExch:* **fonds négligés,** neglected stocks.

négligence, *n.f.* (*a*) negligence/carelessness; neglect; **par négligence,** through negligence (*b*) *Jur:* **négligence grave,** gross negligence; **négligence coupable/criminelle,** criminal negligence (*c*) *Ins:* **clause (de) négligence/***MIns:* **négligence-clause,** negligence clause.

négoce, *n.m.* trade/trading/business; **faire le négoce du vin,** to trade in wines/to be a wine trader.

négociabilité, *n.f.* negotiability (of a bill).

négociable, *a.* negotiable; transferable (bond, bill, cheque); **actif négociable**, liquid assets; **négociable en banque**, bankable; **non négociable**, not negotiable/non negotiable; **titres négociables en Bourse**, stocks negotiable on the Stock Exchange; **valeur négociable**, market value.

négociant, *n.m.* wholesale merchant/dealer; wholesaler; **négociant en vins**, wine merchant.

négociateur, -trice, *n.* 1. (*a*) negotiator (*b*) middleman/intermediary 2. transactor (of deal).

négociation, *n.f.* 1. negotiation; negotiating (of loan, bill); **en négociation**, under negotiation; *PolEc:* **négociations (de conventions) collectives**, collective bargaining; **pouvoir de négociation**, bargaining power; *StExch:* **négociations à prime/à option**, option dealings/tradings; **négociations à terme**, dealings for the settlement; **engager/entamer des négociations**, to enter into negotiations; **rompre des négociations**, to break off negotiations; **des négociations sont en cours**, negotiations are in progress 2. transaction; **négociations de Bourse**, Stock Exchange transactions; **négociations de change**, exchange transactions.

négocier, 1. *v.tr. & i.* to negotiate (sale, loan, bill etc.) (*b*) to place (loan) 2. *v.pr.* (*d'un effet, etc.*) **se négocier**, to be negotiated.

net, 1. *a.* (*a*) (**actif, poids, prix, montant, revenu**) **net**, net(t) (assets, weight, price, amount, income); (**perte, marge, valeur**) **nette**, net(t) (loss, margin, value); **bénéfice net**, net profit; after-tax profit; **bénéfice clair et net**, clear profit; **ventes nettes**, net sales; **il reçoit un salaire net de £80 par semaine**, he gets £80 clear a week (*b*) **net de**. . ., free from. . .; **net d'impôt**, tax free 2. *adv.* **cela m'a rapporté 100**

francs net, I cleared/I netted 100 francs; I made a net profit of 100 francs.

neuf, *a.* new (garment, product, etc.); **à l'état (de) neuf**, as new/in new condition; (*d'un timbre, etc.*) in mint condition/mint.

niveau, *n.m.* level (of prices, salaries, etc.); **niveau de vie (élevé)**, (high) standard of living; **niveau sans précédent**, record level; **l'indice des actions est descendu à son plus bas niveau/est monté à son plus haut niveau**, the share index reached an all-time low/an all-time high; **maintenir les prix à un niveau élevé**, to maintain prices at a high level.

niveler, *v.tr.* to level/to even up (prices, rates, etc.); **niveler au plus bas**, to level down.

nivellement, *n.m* levelling (of income, etc.).

nocturne, *n.m.* **nocturne le vendredi**, late opening Friday.

noir, *a.* black; **caisse noire**, slush fund; **liste noire**, black list; **marché noir**, black market; **acheter au noir**, to buy on the black market; **travail (au) noir**, moonlighting; **travailler au noir**, to moonlight; **personne qui travaille au noir**, moonlighter.

nom, *n.m.* 1. (*a*) name; **nom (de famille)**, surname; **nom et prénoms**, full name; **nom de jeune fille**, maiden name (*b*) **nom du bénéficiaire**, name of the payee; **nom commercial**, name of a company; firm/corporate name; **nom déposé**, registered (trade) name; **nom d'un produit**, name of a product (*c*) **agir au nom de qn**, to act in s.o.'s name; **les actions sont à mon nom**, the shares are in my name 2. name/reputation; **un nom bien connu dans le monde des affaires**, a big name in the business world.

nombre, *n.m.* (*a*) number; **nombre élevé**, high number; **nombre de trois chiffres**, three-digit number; **nombre d'heures de travail**, number of hours worked; *PolEc:* **nombre index**, index number (*b*) **le nombre suffisant/voulu (de membres)**, the (full) quorum (at meeting); **ne pas être en nombre,** not to have a quorum.

nomenclature, *n.f.* list; catalogue; schedule; **nomenclature douanière,** customs classification; **numéro de nomenclature,** catalogue number/inventory number.

nominal, *a.* nominal (price, etc.); *Fin:* **capital nominal,** nominal capital/authorized capital; **valeur nominale (d'un effet, etc.),** face value (of bill, etc.).

nominatif, 1. *a. Fin:* nominal; **action nominative,** registered share; **certificat nominatif d'actions,** registered share certificate; **liste nominative (des actionnaires),** nominal list (of shareholders); **porteur d'actions nominatives,** registered shareholder; **titres nominatifs;** registered securities/scrip **2.** *n.m. Fin:* **dividende de tant au nominatif,** dividend of so much on registered securities.

nomination, *n.f.* (*a*) nomination (for an appointment) (*b*) appointment; **recevoir sa nomination,** to be appointed (**à un poste,** to a post).

nommer, *v.tr.* (*a*) to name; to give a name to (sth.); **nommé ci-après . . .,** hereinafter called/named . . . (*b*) **nommer un jour,** to appoint a day (*c*) to appoint/to nominate (s.o. to an office or post); **nommer des experts,** to appoint experts; **nommer qn à un poste,** to nominate s.o. to/for a post; **nommer qn président,** to appoint s.o. chairman/president.

non-acceptation, *n.f.* non-acceptance (of bill); refusal (of goods).

non-accomplissement, *n.m.* non-fulfilment.

non-disponibilité, *n.f.* non-availability (of supplies, etc.).

non-exécution, *n.f.* non-fulfilment (of agreement, etc.); non-performance.

non-lieu, *n.m. Jur:* withdrawal/dismissal (of case, suit, etc.); non-suit.

non-livraison, *n.f.* non-delivery (of goods).

nonobstant, *prep. Jur:* notwithstanding; in spite of.

non-paiement, *n.m.* non-payment; **en cas de non-paiement,** in case of non-payment.

non-réception, *n.f.* non-delivery (of goods).

non-reconduction, *n.f. Adm:* failure to renew (a contract, etc.).

non-responsabilité, *n.f. Jur:* non-liability; **clause de non-responsabilité,** non-liability clause.

non-salarié(e), *n.* non-wage-earning person.

non(-)syndiqué(e), 1. *a.* non-union; **employé non(-)syndiqué,** non-union employee **2.** *n.* non-member of a union/non-union worker.

non-valeur, *n.f.* **1.** (*i*) bad debt (*ii*) worthless security; *Adm:* **fonds de non-valeur,** provision for possible deficit (in budget estimates) **2.** unproductiveness; **terres en non-valeur,** unproductive land.

non-vente, *n.f.* no sale.

normal, *a.* (*a*) normal; **prix normaux,** normal prices; **valeur normale,** normal value (*b*) standard; **échantillon normal,** average sample; **poids normal,** standard weight.

normalisation, *n.f.* normalization; standardization (of manufacture, etc.); **commission de normalisation,** standardization committee.

normaliser, *v.tr.* to normalize; to standardize.

norme, *n.f.* norm/standard/(standard) specification; **conforme à la norme,** up to standard/up to specification; **normes financières,** financial standards; **norme de prix de revient,** cost standard; **normes de**

production, production standards; **normes publicitaires,** advertising standards.

notaire, *n.m. Jur:* (*i*) notary (public) (*ii*) = solicitor; **dressé par-devant notaire,** drawn up before a notary.

notarial, *a. Jur:* notarial (function, etc.).

notarié, *a. Jur:* **acte notarié,** deed executed and authenticated by a notary.

notation, *n.f.* (*a*) notation (*b*) markings/scoring/rating; **notation du personnel,** personnel rating.

note, *n.f.* (*a*) note/memo(randum); **note d'avis,** advice note; *Ins:* **note de couverture,** cover note; **note de crédit/note d'avoir,** credit note; **note de débit,** debit note; *Cust:* **note de détail,** details/description (of parcel, etc.); **note de frais,** (note of) expenses; **note de poids,** weight note; **note de service,** memorandum; **prendre note d'une commande,** to book/to make note of an order (*b*) annotation; **note marginale,** marginal note (*c*) notice (*d*) account/bill/invoice; **note d'hôtel,** hotel bill; **suivant la note ci-jointe,** as per account enclosed; **régler/payer une note,** to pay a bill/to settle an account; **faut-il le porter sur la note?** shall I put it on the bill?/shall I charge (for) it on the bill?

noter, *v.tr.* (*a*) to note; **il est à noter que . . .,** it should be noted that . . . (*b*) to jot down (sth.)/to write down (sth.)/to make a note of (sth.).

notice, *n.f.* information; directions; **notice explicative,** (*i*) directions for use (*ii*) instructions book; **notice publicitaire,** (*i*) advertising brochure (*ii*) (*dans un journal*) advertisement; **notice technique,** technical instructions/technical handbook; data sheet; *Fin:* **notice (d'information),** (information) prospectus.

notificatif, *a.* **lettre notificative,** letter of notification.

notification, *n.f.* notification/notice; **recevoir notification de qch.,** to be notified of sth.

notifier, *v.tr.* **notifier qch. à qn,** to notify s.o. of sth.; **veuillez notifier par écrit,** please advise in writing.

notoriété, *n.f.* (*a*) *Fin:* **avances sur notoriété,** unsecured advances; **crédit sur notoriété,** unsecured credit (*b*) *Mkt:* **notoriété de la marque,** brand awareness; **notoriété publicitaire,** advertising awareness.

nourrir, *v.tr.* **cinq cents francs par mois logé et nourri,** five hundred francs a month with board and lodging.

nouveau, *a.* (*a*) new; **deux actions nouvelles pour cinq anciennes,** two new shares for each five shares held; a seven-for-five stock split; **modèle nouveau,** up-to-date model; **nouvelle émission d'actions,** new issue of shares; **créer de nouveaux débouchés au commerce,** to open up new channels for trade (*b*) new/recent/fresh; **vin nouveau,** new wine (*c*) another/further/additional; **jusqu'à nouvel ordre,** until further notice; **un nouvel acompte de cent francs,** a further hundred francs on account; **pour une nouvelle période de trois mois,** for a further period of three months (*d*) *Book-k:* **solde à nouveau,** balance brought forward; **report à nouveau (de l'exercice précédent),** balance brought forward (from previous account).

nouveauté, *n.f.* **1.** new invention; new publication **2.** *pl.* **nouveautés,** (*i*) fancy articles/fancy goods (*ii*) latest fashions.

nouvelle, *n.f.* (piece of) news; **nouvelles économiques,** economic intelligence.

novation, *n.f. Jur:* novation/substitution (of new obligation, contract, for an old one); **novation de créance,** substitution of debt.

nover, *v.tr. Jur:* to substitute (debt).

nue-propriété, *n.f. Jur:* bare ownership/ ownership without usufruct.

nuit, *n.f.* night; **être de nuit,** to be on night shift; to work nights; **travail de nuit,** night work.

nul, *a.* (*a*) **solde nul,** nil balance; *Jur:* **nul et de nul effet/nul et non avenu,** null and void; **considérer une lettre comme nulle et non avenue,** to consider a letter as cancelled (*b*) non-existent; **capitaux presque nuls,** almost non-existent capital.

nullité, *n.f.* **1.** invalidity/nullity (of deed, etc.); *Jur:* **action en nullité,** action for avoidance of contract; **nullité de l'assurance,** invalidity of the insurance; **frapper une clause de nullité,** to render a clause null and void **2.** (*a*) non-existence (of means); **nullité des affaires,** slackness/standstill in trade (*b*) incompetence (of employee, etc.).

numéraire, 1. *a.* (*d'une pièce de monnaie*) **valeur numéraire,** legal-tender value **2.** *n.m.* metallic currency/specie; cash; **actions en numéraire,** cash shares; **avance en numéraire,** cash advance; **numéraire fictif,** paper currency; **versement en numéraire,** payment in cash; **payer en numéraire,** to pay in cash.

numérique, *a.* (*a*) numerical (value, ratio, list, etc.) (*b*) **analyse numérique,** numerical analysis; **calculateur numérique,** digital computer; **données numériques,** numerical data.

numériquement, *adv.* numerically.

numéro, *n.m.* (*a*) number; **numéro de chèque,** cheque number; **numéro de commande,** order number; **numéro de compte,** account number; **numéro d'immatriculation,** registration number; **numéro de lot,** lot number; **numéro de référence,** reference number; **numéro de série/numéro de fabrication,** serial number (*b*) *WTel:* **numéro de téléphone,** telephone/phone number; **faux numéro,** wrong number; **composer/faire un numéro,** to dial a number (*c*) issue/ number (of magazine, etc.); **le dernier numéro,** the latest issue.

numérotage, *n.m.,* **numérotation,** *n.f.* numbering (of pages, etc.); allocation of a (classification) number (to document, etc.).

numéroter, *v.tr.* to number (consecutively).

numéroteur, *n.m.* numbering machine/ numbering stamp.

nu-propriétaire, *n.m. Jur:* bare owner.

O

objectif, *n.m.* aim/target/objective; **direction par objectifs (DPO),** management by objectives (MBO); **établissement des objectifs,** target setting; **objectif à court terme,** short-term objective; **objectifs globaux de l'entreprise,** overall company objectives; **objectif lointain,** long-term objective; **objectif de production,** production target; **objectif de profit,** profit target; **objectif de vente,** sales target.

objet, *n.m.* (*a*) object/aim; **la société a pour objet . . .,** the aim of the company is . . . (*b*) article/thing; **objet de luxe,** luxury article; **objet de valeur,** valuable/article of value.

obligataire, 1. *n.m. Fin:* (*a*) bondholder/debenture holder; **registre des obligataires,** debenture register (*b*) *Jur:* obligee (whose bill has been backed, etc.) **2.** *a.* **créancier obligataire,** bond creditor; **dette obligataire,** debenture debt; **emprunt obligataire,** debenture loan; **intérêts obligataires,** bond interest.

obligation, *n.f.* **1.** *Fin:* bond; debenture; **certificat d'obligation,** debenture bond; **obligations amortissables,** redeemable bonds; **obligation cautionnée,** guaranteed bond; **obligations convertibles en actions,** convertible bonds; **obligation hypothécaire,** mortgage debenture; **obligation indexée,** indexed bond; **obligation au porteur,** bearer bond; **obligation à revenu variable,** variable income bond; **porteur d'obligations,** bondholder **2.** *Jur:* (*a*) obligation; bond; **contracter une obligation (envers qn),** to enter into a binding agreement (with s.o.) (*b*) **obligation contractuelle,** privity of contract.

obligé, *n.* (*a*) person under obligation; *Jur:* obligee (*b*) *Fin:* obliger (guaranteeing a bill).

obsolescence, *n.f.* obsolescence; **obsolescence calculée/obsolescence prévue (systématiquement),** built-in obsolescence.

obsolescent, *a.* obsolescent.

obtenir, *v.tr.* to obtain/to get; to secure; to achieve (result); **obtenir du crédit à meilleur compte,** to get cheaper credit; **obtenir un délai,** to obtain an extension (of time); **où peut-on l'obtenir?** where can you get it?

occasion, *n.f.* (*a*) bargain; **occasions exceptionnelles,** outstanding sales bargains (*b*) **voiture d'occasion,** secondhand/used car; **acheter qch. d'occasion,** to buy sth. secondhand.

occasionnel, *a.* **travailleur/employé occasionnel,** casual worker.

occupant, 1. *a.* occupying/in possession (of property, etc.) **2.** *n.* occupier; occupant; *Jur:* **premier occupant,** occupant.

occupation, *n.f.* (*a*) occupancy/occupation/possession (of a house, etc.); **grève avec occupation d'usine,** sit-in (strike) (*b*) business/work/employment; **occupation pendant les heures de loisir,** spare-time job; **être sans occupation,** to be unemployed/to be out of work.

occupé, *a.* busy; *Tp:* **la ligne est occupée,** the line's engaged/busy.

occuper, 1. *v.tr.* **occuper un poste important,** to occupy/to hold an important post (*b*) to give employment to; **occuper vingt ouvriers,** to employ twenty workmen

2. *v.pr.* **est-ce qu'on s'occupe de vous?** are you being attended to?/are you being served?

octroi, *n.m.* concession/grant(ing) (of a privilege, etc.); **octroi de crédits**, credit grant.

octroyer, *v.tr.* to grant/to allow (à, to).

office, *n.m.* (*a*) office/post; **faire office de secrétaire**, to act as secretary (*b*) bureau/ office; **office de publicité**, advertising agency; **office de régularisation de vente**, marketing board; **office du tourisme**, tourist board (*c*) *adv.phr.* **être nommé d'office**, to be automatically appointed/ to be appointed as a matter of course; **être mis à la retraite d'office**, to be automatically retired.

officiel, 1. *a.* official (statement, journal, source); **congé officiel**, official holiday; *Fin:* **cote officielle**, official quotation; **marché officiel**, official market; **réserves en or officielles**, official gold reserves; **le taux officiel de l'escompte**, the minimum lending rate; **à titre officiel**, officially/formally 2. *n.* official.

officiellement, *adv.* officially.

offrant, *n.m.* (*à une vente aux enchères*) **le plus offrant (et dernier enchérisseur)**, the highest bidder.

offre, *n.f.* (*a*) offer; proposal; **offre par écrit**, offer in writing; *Journ:* **offres d'emploi**, situations vacant; **offre d'essai**, trial offer; **offre ferme**, firm offer; *Fin:* **offre publique d'achat (OPA)**, takeover bid; **offre publique d'échange (OPE)**, exchange offer; *Mkt:* **offre spéciale**, special offer (*b*) (*à une vente aux enchères*) bid (*c*) *PolEc:* **l'offre et la demande**, supply and demand (*d*) (**appel**) **d'offre**, tender.

offrir, *v.tr.* (*a*) **offrir ses services**, to offer one's services; **on lui a offert un emploi**, he has been offered a job (*b*) **offrir cent francs**, (*i*) to offer 100 francs (*ii*) to bid 100 francs; **combien m'en offrez-vous?** how much will you offer me/how much will you give me for it? **offrir des marchandises en vente**, to offer goods for sale; **enchérir sur les prix offerts**, to improve on the prices offered; **être offert à . . .**, to be on offer at . . .; *StExch: etc:* **cours offerts**, prices offered.

oisif, *a.* **capital oisif**, uninvested/idle capital.

oligopole, *n.m. PolEc:* oligopoly.

oligopoliste, *a. PolEc:* oligopolistic (market, etc.).

omission, *n.f.* **sauf erreur ou omission**, errors and omissions excepted (E & OE).

omnium, *n.m. StExch:* (*a*) the aggregate value of the different stocks in which a loan is funded (*b*) **omnium (de valeurs)**, omnium investment company.

once, *n.f. Meas:* ounce (*abbr.* oz) (= 28.35 grammes).

onéreux, *a.* heavy (expenditure, tax, etc.); **charge onéreuse pour le budget**, heavy charge on the budget; *Jur:* **à titre onéreux**, subject to certain liabilities; subject to payment.

open-market, *n.m.* open-market; **politique d'open-market**, open-market policy.

opérateur, -trice, *n.* (*a*) (machine) operator (*b*) *StExch:* **opérateur à la hausse**, operator for a rise; bull; **opérateur à la baisse**, operator for a fall; bear.

opération, *n.f.* 1. (*a*) *Bank: Fin:* transaction; deal; operation; **opération blanche**, break-even transaction; **opération de clearing**, clearing transaction; **opération comptable**, accounting operation; **opération au comptant**, cash transaction; **opération d'escompte**, discount operation; **opération de prêt**, loan transaction (*b*) *StExch:* transaction; deal; speculation; **opérations de Bourse**, Stock Exchange business/transactions; **opération à la baisse**, bear transaction; **opération de change**, exchange transaction; **opération de change à terme**, forward exchange transaction; **opération au comptant**, spot deal/spot transaction; **opération à la hausse**, bull transaction; **opérations à prime**, option dealing(s); **opération à**

terme, credit operation **2. gestion des opérations,** operations management; **planification des opérations,** operational planning **3. le procédé comporte trois opérations,** the process involves three operations.

opérationnel, *a.* (*a*) **coûts opérationnels,** operational costs; **efficacité opérationnelle,** operational efficiency; **recherche opérationnelle,** operational research (*b*) **ce système sera opérationnel en 1984,** this system will be operational/will be in operation in 1984.

opérer, 1. *v.i.* **opérer à découvert,** to operate without cover **2.** *v.tr.* (*a*) *PolEc: etc:* **opérer un sondage,** to take a sample test; to conduct an opinion poll (*b*) to make/to effect (payment, etc.).

opinion, *n.f.* opinion (**de,** of; **sur,** about); view/judgment; **sondage d'opinion (publique),** opinion poll/survey.

opportunité, *n.f.* **coût d'opportunité,** opportunity cost.

opposition, *n.f.* (*a*) **faire opposition à un chèque/au paiement d'un chèque,** to stop (payment of) a cheque; *StExch:* **opposition à la cote,** objection to mark.

optimal, *a.* **conditions optimales,** optimum conditions; **répartition optimale des ressources,** optimal resource allocation.

optim(al)isation, *n.f.* **optim(al)isation du profit,** profit optimization.

optim(al)iser, *v.tr.* to optimize.

optimum, 1. *n.m.* optimum **2.** *a.* **emploi optimum des ressources,** optimum employment of resources.

option, *n.f.* **1. option d'achat,** option of purchase; **prendre une option sur l'achat d'un immeuble,** to have the option of purchase on a building **2.** *StExch:* option; **double option,** double option; **marché à options,** options market; **opérations à option,** option dealing/trading; **option d'achat,** call option; **option de vente,** put option; **lever une option,** to take up an option.

optionnel, *a.* **plan optionnel d'achat d'actions,** stock option plan.

optique, *n.f.* outlook; **optique de la direction,** top management approach; **optique publicitaire,** advertising approach.

or, *n.m.* **1.** *Fin: StExch:* gold; **cours de l'or,** price/rate of gold; **encaisse or et argent,** gold and silver holdings; **étalon(-)or,** gold standard; **étalon change-or,** gold exchange standard; **franc or,** gold franc; **marché de l'or,** gold market; **obligation or,** gold bond; **or en barres/en lingots,** gold bars; ingots; gold bullion; **réserves d'or,** gold reserves; **(acheter, vendre) à prix d'or,** (to buy, to sell) at an exorbitant price; **marché/affaire d'or,** (*i*) excellent deal/business (*ii*) excellent bargain **2. or monnayé/monnaie d'or/pièces d'or,** gold specie/gold coins.

ordinaire, *a.* *Fin:* **actions ordinaires,** ordinary shares/*NAm:* common stock.

ordinateur, *n.m.* *Cmptr:* computer; **comptabilité par ordinateur,** computer accounting; **gestion par ordinateur,** computer control; **ordinateur analogique,** analog computer; **ordinateur électronique,** electronic computer; **ordinateur individuel,** small (business) computer; **unités d'ordinateur,** computer equipment; **mettre (des données) sur ordinateur,** to computerize/to put (data) on computer; **mise (de données) sur ordinateur,** computerization.

ordonnance, *n.f.* *Adm:* **ordonnance de paiement,** order/warrant for payment.

ordonnancement, *n.m.* (*a*) scheduling/sequencing (of production, orders, etc.); **ordonnancement de la production des pièces de rechange,** scheduling/sequencing of spares (*b*) *Adm:* order to pay.

ordonnancer, *v.tr. Adm:* to pass (account) for payment; to sanction (expenditure); to initial (account).

ordonnateur, -trice, *n.* person authorized to pass accounts.

ordre, *n.m.* **1.** (*a*) **ordre alphabétique,** alphabetical order; **certificats délivrés par ordre de date,** certificates issued in order of date; **numéro d'ordre,** serial number (*b*) *Jur:* **ordre utile,** ranking (of creditor) **2. ordre du jour,** agenda (of a meeting); **questions à l'ordre du jour,** items/business on the agenda **3.** class/category; **de premier ordre,** first-class/first-rate (firm, employee, etc.); *Fin:* **obligation de premier ordre,** prime bond; **la hausse de l'inflation sera de l'ordre de 5%,** the rise in inflation will be in the region of 5% **4.** (*a*) *Bank: Fin:* **billet à ordre,** promissory note; bill of exchange payable to order; **chèque à ordre,** cheque to order; **compte d'ordre,** suspense account; **ordre de Bourse,** (Stock Exchange) order/instruction; **ordre de transfert permanent,** banker's order; standing order; **ordre de virement,** order/instructions for transfer (of money, funds, etc.); (*sur un chèque*) **non à ordre,** not negotiable; **libeller un chèque à l'ordre de qn,** to make a cheque payable to s.o./to make out a cheque to s.o.; **payez à l'ordre de . . .,** pay to the order of . . ..

organe, *n.m.* (*a*) **organe de publicité,** advertising medium (*b*) *Adm:* **organe distributeur,** distributing agency.

organigramme, *n.m.* (*a*) administrative chart (of organization etc.); organization chart (*b*) *Cmptr:* flowchart/flow diagram.

organisateur, -trice, 1. *a.* organizing; **efficacité organisatrice,** organizational effectiveness **2.** *n.* organizer.

organisateur-conseil, *n.m.* time and motion consultant.

organisation, *n.f.* **1.** (*a*) organizing; organization; planning; **comité d'organisation,** organizing/planning committee (*b*) organization/management; **organisation fonctionnelle/horizontale,** functional organization/staff organization; **organisation hiérarchique/verticale,** line organization; **organisation mixte,** line and staff organization; **organisation scienti-** fique du travail (OST), scientific management; **organisation du travail,** organization of work **2.** (*a*) organization; **organisation (internationale, politique, etc.),** (international, political, etc.) organization/body (*b*) (business, etc.) organization/*F:* set-up.

organisé, *a.* organized; **voyage organisé,** package trip/tour.

organiser, *v.tr.* to organize; to arrange (a meeting, etc.).

organisme, *n.m.* organization/body; **organisme professionnel,** professional body.

orientation, *n.f.* **orientation du client,** customer orientation; **orientation du marché,** market trend; **orientation professionnelle,** vocational/careers guidance.

orienté, *a.* oriented; **économie orientée vers les exportations,** export-oriented economy; **marché orienté à la baisse,** falling market; **marché orienté à la hausse,** rising market.

originaire, *a.* **membre originaire,** original member; founder member; **vice originaire,** original defect.

original, -aux, 1. *a.* original (text, etc.); **facture originale,** original invoice **2.** *n.* original; *Corr: etc:* top copy; **original d'une facture,** original of an invoice; **copier qch. sur l'original,** to copy sth. from the original.

origine, *n.f.* (*a*) **pays d'origine,** country of origin; **produits d'origine nationale,** home(-grown) produce (*b*) *Fin:* **capital d'origine,** original capital; *Cust:* **certificat d'origine,** certificate of origin; **emballage d'origine,** original packing; **marchandises d'origine** = origin of goods guaranteed; *Ind:* **pièce d'origine,** original/factory-installed component; **valeur à l'origine,** original value.

oscillant, *a. Fin:* fluctuating (market).

oscillation, *n.f. Fin:* **les oscillations du marché,** the fluctuations of the market/ the ups and downs of the market.

osciller, *v.i.* to fluctuate/to swing; *Fin:* (*du marché, des valeurs*) to fluctuate.

outillage, *n.m.* plant/equipment/machinery (of factory).

outre-mer, *adv.* overseas; **commerce d'outre-mer,** overseas trade.

ouvert, *a.* (*a*) open; **les bureaux sont ouverts de dix heures à cinq heures,** the offices are open from ten to five (*b*) *Fin:* **compte ouvert,** open account; **crédit ouvert,** open credit; *Trans:* **billet ouvert,** open ticket (*c*) *PolEc:* **politique de la porte ouverte,** open-door policy.

ouverture, *n.f.* (*a*) opening (up) (of a shop, business, etc.); opening (of an account, of a credit); **ouverture de négociations,** opening of negotiations; **l'ouverture de nouveaux débouchés,** the opening (up) of new markets/of new channels (of trade) (*b*) **heures d'ouverture,** business hours (of shop) (*c*) *StExch:* **cours d'ouverture,** opening price; *Book-k:* **écriture d'ouverture,** opening entry.

ouvrable, *a.* **jour ouvrable,** working day.

ouvrage, *n.m.* (*a*) workmanship (*b*) piece of work/product (*c*) **il n'a pas d'ouvrage,** he is out of work/out of a job.

ouvragé, *a.* worked; finished (product).

ouvré, *a.* worked (jewellery, timber); finished/manufactured (article, product).

ouvrier, -ière, 1. *n.m. & f.* worker/ workman; operative; **ouvrier agricole,** agricultural worker; **ouvrier hautement qualifié (HQ),** highly skilled worker; **ouvrier à la journée,** day labourer; **ouvrier aux pièces,** piece worker; **ouvrier professionnel (OP)/ouvrier qualifié,** skilled worker; **ouvrier spécialisé (OS),** semiskilled worker; **ouvrier syndiqué,** worker belonging to a union **2.** *a.* **agitation ouvrière,** industrial unrest; labour unrest; **association ouvrière,** workers' association; **législation ouvrière,** industrial legislation; **participation ouvrière,** worker participation; **syndicat ouvrier,** trade union.

ouvrir, 1. *v.tr.* (*a*) **ouvrir une région au commerce,** to open up a region to trade (*b*) **ouvrir boutique,** to set up shop; **ouvrir des négociations,** to open/to begin negotiations; **ouvrir un nouveau magasin,** to open a new shop (*c*) *Fin:* (**se faire**) **ouvrir un compte bancaire,** to open a bank account; **ouvrir un crédit,** to open a (line of) credit; **ouvrir un emprunt,** to open a loan **2.** *v.i.* (*a*) **nous ouvrons tous les jours à huit heures,** we open every day at eight (o'clock); **les banques n'ouvrent pas les jours de fête,** the banks do not open on public holidays (*b*) *StExch:* **les valeurs pétrolières ont ouvert ferme,** oils opened firm.

P

pacte, *n.m.* **le pacte pour l'emploi** = job creation scheme (for young people); *Jur:* **pacte de paiement,** pay(ments) agreement; **pacte de préférence,** preference clause.

page, *n.f.* page; **annonce en première page,** front page advertisement; *Tp:* **pages jaunes,** yellow pages.

paie, *n.f.* pay/wages; **feuille/bulletin de paie,** pay (advice) slip; **jour de paie,** pay day; **livre de paie,** payroll; **toucher sa paie,** to draw one's pay/to be paid.

paiement, *n.m.* (*a*) payment; **défaut de paiement,** non(-)payment; **délai de paiement,** deferment of payment; **facilités de paiement,** credit facilities/easy terms; **paiement anticipé,** advance payment; **paiement comptant,** cash payment; **paiement différé,** deferred payment; **paiement d'un compte,** settlement of an account; **autoriser le paiement d'un compte,** to authorize the payment of an account; **paiement d'un impôt,** payment of a tax; **paiement intégral,** payment in full; **paiement libératoire,** payment in full discharge; **paiement par chèque,** payment by cheque; **faire opposition au paiement d'un chèque,** to stop (payment of) a cheque; **paiement partiel,** payment on account; **paiement par versements,** payment by/in instalments; **plan/programme de paiement,** payment plan/schedule; *Jur:* **être en état de cessation de paiements,** to be insolvent (*b*) **paiement en espèces/en numéraire,** payment in cash; **paiement en nature,** payment in kind; **contre paiement de 100 francs,** on payment of 100 francs; **effectuer/faire un paiement,** to pay for sth.; to

make a payment; **recevoir un paiement,** to receive (a) payment; **suspendre/cesser les paiements,** to stop payments.

pair, 1. *a.* even (number) **2.** *n.m. Fin:* par; **au-dessous du pair,** below par; **au-dessus du pair,** above par; **pair du change,** par of exchange; **remboursable au pair,** repayable at par; **valeur au pair,** par value; **émettre des actions au pair,** to issue shares at par.

palette, *n.f.* pallet; **marchandises sur palette(s),** palletized goods.

palettisation, *n.f.* palletization (of goods).

palettiser, *v.tr.* to palletize (goods).

palier, *n.m.* stage/level; **l'inflation a atteint un nouveau palier,** inflation has reached/found a new level; **taxes imposées par paliers,** graduated taxation.

panel, *n.m. Mkt:* panel; **panel de consommateurs,** consumer panel.

panier, *n.m.* **1.** (*a*) *PolEc:* **le panier de la ménagère,** the shopping basket (*b*) *Mkt:* **panier (présentoir)/panier vrac,** dumpbin; **panier à la sortie,** checkout display (stand) (*c*) *PolEc:* **panier de monnaies,** basket of currencies **2.** package deal.

panneau, *n.m.* board/panel; **panneau d'affichage/panneau à affiches/panneau publicitaire,** hoarding/*NAm:* billboard.

panneau-réclame, *n.m.* hoarding.

paperasserie, *n.f.* **paperasserie** (administrative), red tape.

papeterie, *n.f.* **1.** (*a*) paper manufacturing (*b*) paper mill/factory (*c*) paper trade 2. (*a*) stationery trade (*b*) stationer's (shop) (*c*) stationery.

papier, *n.m.* **1.** paper; **feuille/morceau de papier**, sheet/piece of paper; **papier buvard**, blotting paper; **papier carbone**, carbon paper; **papier d'emballage/papier kraft**, wrapping paper/brown paper; **papier à en-tête**, headed notepaper; **papier journal**, newsprint; **papier à lettres**, writing paper/notepaper; **papier pour machine à écrire/***F:* **papier machine**, typing paper; **papier pelure**, air mail paper; flimsy **2.** (*a*) *Adm: etc:* document/paper; **papier de bord**, ship's papers; **papiers d'expédition**, clearance papers; **papiers d'identité**, identity papers; **papier libre**, official paper on which stamp duty has not been paid; **papier timbré**, official paper on which stamp duty has been paid (*b*) *Fin:* bill(s); **papier bancable/papier non bancable**, bankable paper/unbankable paper; **papier commercial/de commerce**, commercial/mercantile/trade paper; **papier de complaisance**, accommodation bill; **papier à court terme/papier court**, short (-dated) bill; **papier sur l'étranger**, foreign bill; **papier fait**, guaranteed paper/backed bill(s); **papier à long terme/papier long**, long (-dated) bill; **papier négociable**, negotiable paper; **papiers valeurs**, paper securities.

papier-monnaie, *n.m.* paper money/paper currency.

paquebot, *n.m.* **paquebot mixte**, mixed passenger and cargo boat; **paquebot transatlantique**, liner.

paquet, *n.m.* (*a*) parcel/package; **expédier un paquet par la poste**, to post a parcel/to send a parcel by post (*b*) **paquet (de lessive, de cigarettes, etc.)**, packet/*NAm:* pack (of washing powder, of cigarettes, etc.); **paquet géant**, giant packet/*NAm:* pack (*c*) *Fin:* **paquet d'actions**, block of shares.

parafe, paraphe, *n.m. Adm: Jur:* signature; initials.

parafer, parapher, *v.tr. Adm: Jur:* to initial (a document).

parafiscal, *a. Adm:* **taxe parafiscale**, exceptional tax; special levy.

parafiscalité, *n.f. Adm:* special levies.

paragraphe, *n.m.* (*a*) paragraph (of letter, etc.) (*b*) sub-clause/paragraph (of contract, etc.).

parallèle, *a.* parallel (**à**, to/with); **économie parallèle**, black economy; **marché parallèle**, parallel/black market.

paralyser, *v.tr.* to paralyse; **grèves qui paralysent l'industrie**, strikes that cripple industry.

parc, *n.m.* **parc automobile**, (*i*) (*d'un pays*) number of cars on the road (*ii*) (*d'une entreprise*) fleet (of cars); **parc d'ordinateurs**, computer population/(the total) number of computers in service.

parère, *n.m. Jur:* expert opinion/advice (on commercial problems).

pari passu, *Lt. phr.* pari passu (**avec**, with).

paritaire, *a.* **commission paritaire**, equal representation committee; **négociations paritaires**, joint negotiations; **réunion paritaire**, round-table conference.

parité, *n.f.* parity; equality (of value, etc.); *Fin:* **change à (la) parité**, exchange at par/at parity; **parité de change**, exchange parity/equivalence of exchange; **parité fixe**, fixed parity; **rapport de parité**, parity ratio.

Parquet, *n.m. StExch:* **le Parquet** = (*i*) the Ring (*ii*) the stockbrokers.

part, *n.f.* **1.** (*a*) *Fin:* share/part; **associé à part entière**, full partner; **part d'association**, partnership share; **parts de fondateur/parts bénéficiaires**, founder's share(s); **part du marché**, share of the market/market share (*b*) **avoir part aux bénéfices**, to have a share in the profits/to share in the profits; **mettre qn de part (dans une affaire)**, to give s.o. a share in the profits **2. faire part de qch. à qn**, to inform s.o. of sth. **3. de la part de,** on behalf of; (*au téléphone*) **c'est de la part de qui?** who's calling, please?

partage, *n.m.* division (into shares); allotment/distribution (of goods, etc.); *Jur:* partition (of real property).

partager, *v.tr.* **1.** (*a*) to divide (into shares); to parcel out; to apportion (property, etc.) **2.** to share; **partager les bénéfices avec son associé,** to share the profits with one's partner; *Fin: etc:* **partager proportionnellement,** to divide pro rata.

participant, -ante, 1. *n.* participant; contributor (to a fund, etc.) **2.** *a.* **action participante,** participating share.

participation, *n.f.* (*a*) participation (à qch., in sth.); **participation aux frais,** cost sharing; **participation ouvrière,** worker participation (*b*) share/interest (à, in); (part of) ownership (in a company); **participation aux bénéfices,** profit sharing; **participation des travailleurs aux bénéfices,** profit-sharing scheme; **participation majoritaire,** majority shareholding; **participation minoritaire,** minority shareholding/minority interest.

participer, *v.i.* (*a*) **participer (aux bénéfices, etc.),** to have an interest/a share, (in the profits, etc.) (*b*) **participer (aux frais, etc.),** to pay one's share (of the costs, etc.)/to contribute to (the costs, etc.) (*c*) **participer (à la gestion d'une entreprise, à une réunion),** to take (a) part in (the running of a firm, a meeting).

particulier, -ière, 1. *n.* (simple) particulier, (private) individual **2.** *a.* private; personal (account); **assistant(e) particulier (-ière),** personal assistant (PA); **secrétaire particulier/particulière,** private secretary/personal assistant.

partie, *n.f.* (*a*) part; **faire partie du personnel,** to be on the staff/to be a member of staff (*b*) **comptabilité en partie double,** double-entry book-keeping; **comptabilité en partie simple,** single-entry book-keeping (*c*) *Jur:* party (to a dispute, a suit, etc.); **les parties contractantes,** the contracting parties.

partiel, *a.* (*a*) partial/incomplete; **acceptation partielle d'une traite,** partial acceptance of a bill; *Nau:* **expédition partielle/chargement partiel,** part shipment; **paiement partiel,** part payment; **perte partielle/sinistre partiel,** partial loss (*b*) **employé(e) qui travaille à temps partiel,** part-time worker/part-timer; **être en chômage partiel,** to be on short time; **travailler à temps partiel,** to work part time/to have a part-time job.

partiellement, *adv.* partially/in part; **créancier partiellement nanti,** partially secured creditor; **payer partiellement,** to pay in part.

partir, *v.i.* (*a*) to start; **à partir d'aujourd'hui,** starting from today/from today (onwards); **à partir du 15,** on and after the 15th; **le directeur sera libre à partir de 10 heures,** the manager will be free from ten (o'clock) onwards/any time after ten; **robes à partir de 100 francs,** dresses from 100 francs.

parution, *n.f. Publ:* publication; **date de parution,** publication date.

parvenir, *v.i.* to arrive; **faire parvenir qch. à qn,** to send/to forward sth. to s.o.; **votre lettre m'est parvenue,** your letter has reached me; I (have) received your letter; **votre demande doit nous parvenir avant la fin du mois,** your application must reach us by the end of the month.

pas, *n.m.* **pas de porte,** (*i*) goodwill (of shop) (*ii*) key money.

passage, *n.m.* (*a*) **passage d'un représentant,** call of a representative (*b*) **nous n'avons que la clientèle de passage/F: que les passages,** we only get the passing trade.

passager, -ère, *n.* passenger; traveller.

passation, *n.f.* (*a*) drawing up/signing (of an agreement); making (of a contract);

entering into (a contract, a lease, etc.)
(*b*) *Book-k:* making (of entries); entering
(of items).

passavant, *n.m. Adm:* permit; *Cust:* transire.

passe, *n.f.* **passe de caisse,** allowance to
cashier for errors.

passeport, *n.m.* passport.

passer, 1. *v.i.* (*a*) **notre chiffre d'affaires est
passé de deux millions à trois millions en
cinq ans,** our turnover has increased from
two million to three million in five years
(*b*) (*d'un représentant*) **passer chez un
client,** to call on a client/a customer
2. *v.tr.* (*a*) **passer des marchandises en
fraude,** to smuggle in goods (*b*) **passer
une commande,** to place an order (**de qch.
à qn,** for sth. with s.o.)/to order sth. (*c*)
Tp: **passez-moi M. Lecuyer,** put me
through to/get me Monsieur Lecuyer (*d*)
Jur: **acte passé par-devant notaire,** document drawn up before a solicitor;
passer un accord, to sign a contract; to
enter into a contract (*e*) *Book-k:* **passer
un article au grand(-)livre,** to post an
entry in the ledger; **passer écriture d'un
article,** to post an entry; **passer une
somme au débit,** to debit (an account)
with a sum; **passer (une somme) en perte,**
to charge (an amount) to an account;
passer (une somme) en profit, to credit
(an amount) to an account.

passif, 1. *a. Fin: Book-k:* **dettes passives,**
liabilities; creditors; **solde passif,** debit
balance **2.** *n.m. Fin: Book-k:* liabilities/
debt(s); **l'actif et le passif,** assets and
liabilities; **passif éventuel,** contingent liabilities; **passif exigible,** current liabilities;
passif à long terme, long-term liabilities;
passif reporté, deferred liabilities.

patentable, *a.* (trade, etc.) subject to a
licence/*NAm:* license; requiring a licence.

patente, *n.f.* (*a*) licence (to exercise a
trade or profession) (*b*) tax (paid by

merchants and professional men); **payer
patente,** to be duly licensed.

patenté, *a.* licensed (trader, etc.).

patenter, *v.tr.* to license.

patron, -onne, *n.* employer; head;
owner; *F:* boss (of firm, of business);
proprietor/proprietress (of hotel).

patronage, *n.m. Mkt:* sponsorship/spon-
soring.

patronal, *a. Ind:* of/pertaining to employers; **cotisation patronale,** employer's contribution; **organisation patronale,** organization of employers; **syndicat patronal,**
employers' federation.

patronat, *n.m Ind:* (the) employers.

patronner, *v.tr. Mkt:* to sponsor/to back.

payable, *a.* payable; **effet payable au 1er
juillet,** bill due on July 1st; **payable sur
demande,** payable on demand; **payable à
30 jours,** payable at 30 days' date; **payable à la commande,** cash with order;
payable à la livraison, payable on delivery; **payable à l'échéance,** payable at
maturity; **payable au porteur,** payable to
bearer; **payable à présentation,** payable
on presentation; **payable à vue,** payable
on sight.

payant, 1. *a.* (*a*) (agency, etc.) charging a
fee; **téléphone payant,** pay phone (*b*)
affaire payante, business that pays/that is
profitable; **travail payant,** paid work **2.** *n.*
payer.

paye, *n.f.* =**paie.**

payement, *n.m.* =**paiement.**

payer, 1. *v.tr.* (*a*) to pay sth.; **payer (une
facture, des impôts, des intérêts, son
loyer),** to pay (a bill, tax(es), interest,
one's rent); **payer (une dette, une
amende, etc.),** to pay (off)/to settle/to
discharge (a debt, a fine, etc.); **payer un
effet,** to honour a bill; **refuser de payer
une traite,** to dishonour a bill (*b*) **payer
qch.,** to pay for sth.; **payer 100 francs à qn,**
to pay s.o. 100 francs; **il le lui a payé 50
francs,** he paid him 50 francs for it;

combien payez-vous le thé? how much do you pay for tea? **vous l'avez payé trop cher,** you've paid too much for it; **payer d'avance,** to pay in advance; **payer (argent) comptant/au comptant,** to pay cash (down); **payer par chèque,** to pay by cheque; **payer à l'échéance,** to pay at maturity/at due date; **payer en espèces,** to pay in cash; **payer intégralement/en totalité,** to pay in full; **payer des marchandises,** to pay for goods; (*sur un chèque*) **payer à l'ordre de . . .,** pay to the order of . . .; **payer à l'ordre de moi-même,** pay cash/pay self; **payer(-)prendre,** cash and carry; **payer à vue/à présentation,** to pay on demand/at sight/on presentation; *Post:* **port payé,** carriage paid/post paid; *Tg:* **réponse payée,** reply paid (*c*) to pay s.o.; **payer un créancier,** to pay a creditor; **payer l'épicier,** to pay the grocer (*d*) **payer un employé,** to pay an employee; **être payé (à l'heure, à la semaine, au mois),** to be paid (by the hour, by the week, by the month); **être payé à la pièce,** to be on piece work; **congé payé,** paid holiday/holiday with pay; **maison qui paie mal,** firm which pays badly/which doesn't give very good wages; **travail bien payé,** well-paid work/job 2.*v.i. F:* **un métier qui paie,** a job that pays well/a well-paid job.

payeur, -euse, 1. *n.* payer; **c'est un bon payeur,** he is a good payer/a prompt payer 2. *n.m. Adm: etc:* paying cashier.

pays, *n.m.* (*a*) country; **pays de provenance,** country of origin (*b*) region/district/locality; **denrées du pays,** home (-grown) produce; **vin de pays/du pays,** local wine.

péage, *n.m.* **pont à péage,** toll bridge; **route à péage,** toll road/*NAm:* turnpike; **télévision à péage,** pay TV.

PCV, *abbr: Tp:* **appel en PCV,** transfer(red) charge call; **faire un appel en PCV,** to reverse the charges (on a call)/to make a transfer(red) charge call.

pécuniaire, *a.* pecuniary; **aide pécuni-**

aire, financial help; **embarras pécuniaires,** financial difficulties; **peine pécuniaire,** fine; **perte pécuniaire,** pecuniary loss; **améliorer sa situation pécuniaire,** to improve one's financial position.

peine, *n.f.* **1.** penalty; **peine contractuelle,** penalty for non-performance (of contract).

pénal, *a.* **clause pénale,** penalty clause (in contract).

pénétrer, *v.tr.* **pénétrer des marchés étrangers,** to penetrate foreign markets.

pension, *n.f.* **1.** pension/allowance; **pension sur l'État,** government pension; **pension de retraite,** retirement/old-age pension; **pension viagère,** life annuity **2.** (payment for) board and lodging; **chambre et pension,** room and board; **chambre avec demi-pension,** room with half board; **chambre avec pension complète,** room with full board.

pensionnaire, *n.m. & f.* boarder; guest/resident (in hotel); **prendre des pensionnaires,** to take paying guests.

pensionné, 1. *a.* pensioned (employee) **2.** *n.* pensioner.

pensionner, *v.tr.* to pension; to grant a pension to (s.o.).

pénurie, *n.f.* scarcity/shortage/(severe) lack (of money, goods, staff, etc.); *PolEc:* **pénurie de dollars,** dollar gap; **il y a pénurie de matières premières,** there is a scarcity of raw materials.

percée, *n.f.* **percée commerciale,** market thrust; **percée technologique,** technological breakthrough.

percepteur, *n.m.* collector of taxes/tax collector.

perception, *n.f.* collection/receipt (of taxes, duties, rents); levying (of tax); **(bureau de) perception,** tax collector's office/revenue office.

percevoir, *v.tr.* to collect (taxes, rents, etc.); to levy (taxes); **cotisations à perce-**

voir, contributions still due; **percevoir des intérêts,** to receive interest.

perdre, *v.tr.* (*a*) to lose (one's money, a court case, etc.); **perdre un client,** to lose a customer (*b*) **perdre de sa valeur,** to lose value.

perdu, *a.* **argent placé à fonds perdu,** money invested in an annuity; **emballage perdu,** no-deposit/non-returnable/throw-away (container, pack(ing), bottle).

père, *n.m. Fin:* **valeurs de père de famille,** gilt-edged securities; blue chips.

péréquation, *n.f.* equalization (of taxes, salaries); *Rail: etc:* **péréquation des prix,** standardizing of freight charges/of tariffs; **faire la péréquation des salaires,** to equalize wages.

perfectionnement, *n.m.* (*a*) perfecting (of machine, method, process); improving; **brevet de perfectionnement,** patent relating to improvements (*b*) further training; **perfectionnement des cadres,** management/executive training; **perfectionnement en cours d'emploi,** in-service training.

perfectionner, *v.tr.* to improve/to perfect (machine, method, process).

performance, *n.f.* performance; achievement; **appréciation des performances,** performance appraisal.

performant, *a.* efficient; with a high degree of (efficiency, productivity, etc.); **entreprise performante,** highly competitive firm.

péril, *n.m. Ins:* **péril de mer,** risk and peril of the seas; sea risk.

périmé, *a.* out-of-date (coupon, etc.); expired (bill, passport); (ticket) no longer valid; lapsed (money order, ticket, etc.); **matériel périmé,** out-of-date/old-fashioned equipment.

périmer, *v.i. Jur:* to lapse/to become

out-of-date; **laisser périmer un droit,** to allow a right to lapse; to forfeit a right.

période, *n.f.* **1.** period; **pendant une période de trois mois,** for a period of three months/for a three month period; **période de récupération/de remboursement,** payback period **2. période comptable,** financial period/accounting period.

périodique, 1. *a.* periodic(al); **publication périodique,** periodical (publication) **2.** *n.m.* periodical (publication)/magazine.

périssable, *a.* perishable; **denrées périssables,** perishable goods/perishables.

perlé, *a.* **grève perlée,** go-slow; **faire la grève perlée,** to go slow.

permanence, *n.f.* (*a*) (duty) office (*b*) **il y a une permanence le dimanche,** there is a 24 hr service on Sundays; the office is manned on Sundays/a skeleton staff is (always) on duty on Sundays; **être de permanence,** to be on duty/on call.

permanent, 1. *a.* permanent (job, etc.); standing (committee); **capitaux permanents,** fixed assets; **instructions permanentes,** standing instructions/*NAm:* standard operating procedure; **inventaire permanent,** perpetual inventory/continuous stocktaking; *Bank:* **ordre de transfert permanent,** standing order/banker's order **2.** *n.m.* paid staff (of organization).

permis, *n.m.* permit; licence/*NAm:* license; *Cust:* **permis de chargement,** loading permit; *Aut:* **permis de conduire,** driving licence; **permis poids lourds,** heavy goods vehicle (HGV) licence; **permis de travail,** work permit.

personnaliser, *v.tr.* to personalize; **chèque personnalisé,** personalized cheque; **publicité personnalisée,** personalized sales technique.

personne, *n.f.* person; **le prix est de 20**

francs par personne, it costs 20 francs per head/per person; *Jur:* **personnes physiques ou morales,** individual and legal entities.

personnel, 1. *a.* personal (business, letter, etc.); *Jur:* **biens personnels,** personal estate/property; **fortune personnelle,** private means/personal wealth; **prêt personnel,** personal loan **2.** *n.m.* (*a*) personnel/staff/employees (of factory, firm, shop, etc.); staff/employees (of hotel, etc.); **personnel administratif,** administrative staff/personnel; **personnel amovible/volant,** mobile/transferable staff; **personnel de bureau,** office staff/clerical staff/secretarial staff; **personnel dirigeant/d'encadrement,** managerial staff/supervisory personnel; *Av:* **personnel rampant,** ground staff; **personnel volant,** flight staff; **personnel réduit,** reduced/skeleton staff; **personnel de service,** staff on duty (*b*) **appréciation du personnel,** staff appraisal/personnel rating; **bureau/service du personnel,** personnel department/office; **chef/directeur du personnel,** personnel manager/officer; **mouvement/mutation du personnel,** (*i*) staff transfers (*ii*) staff turnover; **réduction du personnel,** staff reduction/cutbacks; **faire partie du personnel,** to be on the staff/to be a member of staff/to be on the payroll; **manquer de personnel,** to be understaffed/short-handed.

personnellement, *adv.* personally; in person.

perspective, *n.f.* prospect/outlook; **perspectives de carrière,** job expectations; **perspectives commerciales,** market prospects; **perspectives de profit,** profit outlook.

perte, *n.f.* **1.** loss; **perte de clientèle,** loss of custom; **perte de marché,** loss of market (*b*) *Ins:* loss/damage; **perte présumée,** presumptive loss; **perte totale,** (*i*) total loss (*ii*) (*d'un véhicule*) write-off **2.** deficit; loss (of money); **compte de pertes et de profits,** profit and loss account/*NAm:* profit and loss statement; **dépense en**

pure perte, wasteful expenditure; **pertes et profits exceptionnels,** extraordinary items; **vente à perte,** sale at a loss; **passer une perte par profits et pertes,** to write off a loss; **subir de grandes pertes,** to suffer heavy losses; **vendre qch. à perte,** to sell sth. at a loss.

petit, *a.* small; minor; **petites annonces,** classified advertisements/small ads; **petite caisse,** petty cash; **petit commerçant,** small-trader; **petite entreprise,** small firm; **petits épargnants,** small savers; **la petite industrie,** small-scale industry.

pétrodollar, *n.m.* petrodollar.

pétrole, *n.m.* petroleum/oil; *StExch:* **les pétroles,** oil/oil shares.

pétrolier, 1. *a.* **l'industrie pétrolière,** the petroleum/the oil industry; *StExch:* **marché pétrolier,** oil market; **prix pétroliers,** oil prices; **produits pétroliers,** oil products; **valeurs pétrolières,** oil shares/oils **2.** *n.m.* **pétrolier,** tanker.

phase, *n.f.* phase, stage; *Ind:* **phases de fabrication,** processing stages.

photocopie, *n.f.* photocopy.

photocopier, *v.tr.* to photocopy.

photocopieur, -euse, *n.* photocopier.

photostat, *n.m.* photostat.

photostyle, *n.m. Cmptr:* light pen.

pièce, *n.f.* **1.** (*a*) **pièce de monnaie,** coin; **pièce de deux francs,** two-franc piece (*b*) **ils coûtent dix francs la pièce,** they cost ten francs each; **ils se vendent à la pièce,** they are sold separately/singly (*c*) **travail à la pièce,** piece work; **être payé à la pièce,** to be paid piece work (rates); **travailler à la pièce/aux pièces,** to be on piece work/to do piece work (*d*) *Jur: Adm: etc:* document; **pièce annexe/pièce jointe (PJ),** enclosure (enc.); **pièces justificatives,** (*i*) written proof (*ii*) relevant documents **2. pièces de rechange/pièces détachées,** spare parts/spares.

pignoratif, *a. Jur:* **contrat pignoratif,** contract of sale with option of redemption.

pilote, *n.m.* experimental/pilot (factory, farm, store, study); **échantillon pilote,** pilot sample; **prix pilotes,** experimental/trial prices.

piquet, *n.m. Ind: etc:* picket; **piquets de grève,** strike pickets; **piquets de grève volants,** flying pickets.

piquetage, *n.m.* picketing (by strikers, etc.).

piqueter, *v.tr.* to picket (approaches to factory, place of work, etc.).

placard, *n.m.* poster/bill; *Typ:* **épreuves en placards,** galley proofs; **placard (de réclame),** advertisement (in newspaper).

place, *n.f.* 1. job/position; **perdre sa place,** to lose one's job; **trouver une place de sténodactylo,** to find a job as a shorthand typist 2. (*a*) **sur place,** on-the-spot; **achats sur place,** local purchases; **personnel engagé sur place,** staff engaged locally; **prix sur place,** loco price; *Mkt:* **test sur place,** field test(ing) (*b*) *Bank: Fin:* **affaires sur la place de Paris,** business on the Paris market; **chèque encaissable sur la place,** cheque cashable locally; (*d'un commerçant, etc.*) **avoir du crédit sur la place,** to have credit (facilities) locally/with local banks (*c*) **place du marché,** market place 3. *Th: Trans:* seat; **réserver une place,** to reserve/to book a seat.

placement, *n.m.* 1. *Fin:* investment; **titres de placements,** investments; *F:* **placement de père de famille,** gilt-edged investment; blue chip; **revenus d'un placement,** returns on an investment; **faire des placements,** to invest (money)/to make investments; **faire un bon placement/un placement avantageux,** to make a good investment 2. **agence/bureau de placements,** employment agency/bureau.

placer, 1. *v.tr.* (*a*) to place (s.o.); to find a job/a post for (s.o.) (*b*) to invest (capital, money); to place (shares); **placer (de l'argent) dans les pétroles** to invest in oils (*c*) to sell (goods); **marchandises qui**

se placent facilement, goods that sell readily; **valeurs difficiles à placer,** bills difficult to negotiate 2. *v.pr.* **se placer,** to obtain/to find a post; **chercher à se placer chez qn,** to try to find a job/employment with s.o.

placier, -ère, *n.* (*a*) sales representative/travelling salesman/*NAm:* drummer (*b*) door-to-door salesman; **placier en librairie,** (publisher's) trade representative.

plafond, *n.m.* ceiling; **plafond de crédit,** credit ceiling/limit; **prix plafond,** ceiling (price); **crever le plafond,** to exceed the limit; **fixer un plafond à un budget,** to fix a ceiling to a budget.

plafonné, *a.* **salaire plafonné,** wage ceiling (above which no percentage reduction is made for national insurance contributions).

plafonnement, *n.m.* **protester contre le plafonnement des salaires,** to protest against the ceiling imposed on salaries.

plafonner, *v.i.* **les prix plafonnent à . . .,** prices have reached the ceiling of . . .; **la production plafonne,** output has reached its ceiling.

plan, *n.m.* 1. plan; blueprint 2. (*a*) plan/scheme/project; **plan de campagne,** plan of campaign; **plan d'échantillonnage,** sampling project; *Mkt:* **plan de marketing,** marketing plan; **plan média,** media planning; **plan de travail,** planning (*b*) *Fin: PolEc:* **plan d'austérité,** austerity policy; **plan comptable,** accounting plan; **plan économique,** economic plan; **plan d'épargne,** savings account/plan; *StExch:* **plan d'options sur titres,** stock option plan; **plan quinquennal,** five-year plan; **plan de trésorerie,** cash plan.

plancher, *n.m.* **prix plancher,** bottom price.

planificateur, 1. *a.* planning; **autorité planificatrice,** planning authority 2. *n.m. PolEc: etc:* planner.

planification, *n.f. PolEc: etc:* **planifica-**

tion (**à court terme, à long terme**), (short-term, long-term) planning; **planification économique,** economic planning; **planification de l'entreprise,** company/corporate planning; **planification de l'emploi,** manpower planning; **planification de produit,** product planning; **service de planification,** planning department.

planifié, a. PolEc: **économie planifiée,** planned economy.

planifier, v.tr. PolEc: etc: to plan (production, etc.).

planisme, n.m. PolEc: planning.

planiste, n.m. PolEc: planner.

planning, n.m. (a) Ind: PolEc: planning; scheduling; **bureau/service de planning,** planning department; **planning de distribution,** distribution planning; **planning de la production,** production planning (b) Ind: (**tableau de**) **planning,** work schedule.

plein, 1. a. (a) Nau: **plein chargement,** full cargo; **valeur pleine,** full value (b) **avoir plein(s) pouvoir(s),** to have full power/Jur: to have power of attorney; (d'une usine) **être en plein travail,** to be in full production; **travailler à plein temps,** to work full-time/to have a full time job 2. n.m. **faire le plein (d'essence),** to fill up (with petrol).

plein-emploi, n.m. PolEc: full employment.

pli, n.m. cover/envelope (of letter); **sous pli cacheté,** in a sealed envelope; **sous pli séparé,** under separate cover; **nous vous envoyons sous ce pli . . .,** please find enclosed/herewith . . ..

plus, 1. adv. (a) more; **gagner plus de mille francs,** to earn more than/over a thousand francs (b) (**le**) **plus,** most; **le taux le plus élevé,** the highest rate of interest (c) plus/in addition; **deux cents francs d'amende plus les frais,** two hundred francs fine plus costs; **le prix du repas plus la TVA,** the price of the meal plus VAT

(d) **en plus,** in addition/extra; **le vin est en plus,** the wine is extra.

plus-value, n.f. (a) increase in value/appreciation (of property, shares); **actions qui ont enregistré une plus-value,** shares that show an appreciation; **impôt sur les plus-values,** capital gains tax (b) surplus; excess (of receipts over expenses); profit.

poids, n.m. 1. weight; **poids de 5 kilo(gramme)s,** 5 kilo(gram) weight; Adm: **poids et mesures,** weights and measures; **vendre au poids,** to sell by weight; **vendre à faux poids,** to give short weight 2. load; **poids brut,** gross weight; **poids en charge,** laden weight; Aut: **poids lourd,** heavy goods vehicle (HGV); **poids mort,** dead weight; **poids net,** net weight; **poids utile,** payload/load-carrying capacity.

poinçon, n.m. (sur l'or et l'argent) hallmark.

point, n.m. 1. (a) point/place (of arrival, departure); **point de chargement,** loading point/place; **point de déchargement,** unloading point/place (b) Fin: **point mort,** break-even point (c) **point de vente,** point of sale (POS); sales outlet; stockist; **plus de 400 points de vente en France,** over 400 stockists/outlets in France 2. Fin: (**hausse, baisse, d'**)**un point,** one point (up, down); **amélioration de trois points,** improvement of three points/three-point improvement.

pointage, n.m. (a) checking/ticking off (of items, account, names on list, etc.) (b) Ind: clocking (in, out); **carte de pointage,** time card.

pointe, n.f. (a) **heures de pointe,** (i) (de consommation de gaz, etc.) peak period/peak hours (ii) (de la circulation) peak hours/rush hour(s) (b) **industrie de pointe,** advanced technology industry.

pointer, v.tr. (a) to check/to tick off (items, names on a list, etc.); to tally (goods) (b) Ind: **pointer à l'arrivée,** to clock in/on; **pointer à la sortie,** to clock out/off.

pointeur, *n.m.* checker; tallyman; time-keeper.

police, *n.f.* (*a*) *Ins:* policy; **police d'assurance (sur la) vie,** life (insurance) policy; **police conjointe,** joint policy; **police à forfait,** policy for a specific amount; **police générale,** master/general policy; **police au porteur,** policy to bearer; **police tous risques,** all risks/fully comprehensive policy; **police type,** standard policy; **titulaire/détenteur d'une police,** policy holder; **établir une police,** to draw up/to make out a policy; **souscrire à/prendre une police d'assurance,** to take out an insurance policy (*b*) *MIns:* **police d'assurance maritime,** marine insurance policy; **police d'abonnement/police flottante/police ouverte,** floating policy/open policy; **police sur corps,** hull/ship policy; **police à temps/police à terme,** time policy; **police au voyage,** voyage policy.

politique, 1. *a.* **économie politique,** political economy; economics 2. *n.f.* (*a*) **politique déflationniste/de déflation,** policy of deflation/deflationary policy; **politique inflationniste/d'inflation,** policy of inflation/inflationary policy; **politique de libre échange,** free-trade policy; **politique de la porte ouverte,** open-door policy; **politique des prix et des salaires,** prices and incomes policy (*b*) **politique économique,** economic policy; **politique en matière de change,** exchange policy; **politique de l'entreprise,** company policy; **politique financière,** financial policy; **politique d'investissement,** investment policy; **politique de lancement d'un produit,** product policy; **politique de promotion,** promotional policy; **politique de vente,** sales policy; **nous avons pour politique de satisfaire nos clients,** our policy is to satisfy our customers/we try to keep our customers satisfied (*c*) **la politique,** politics.

polycopie, *n.f.* duplicating (process).

polycopié, *n.m.* (duplicated) copy.

polycopier, *v.tr.* to duplicate; **machine à polycopier,** duplicating machine.

pondérateur, *a.* balancing/stabilizing; **éléments pondérateurs du marché,** stabilizing factors of the market.

pondération, *n.f.* balance; weighting; *PolEc:* weighting (of index).

pondéré, *a. PolEc:* **indice pondéré,** weighted index; **moyenne pondérée,** weighted average; **moyenne non pondérée,** unweighted average.

pondérer, *v.tr. PolEc:* **pondérer un indice,** to weight an index.

pont, *n.m.* **faire un pont d'or à qn,** to give s.o. incentives to make him accept a job.

pool, *n.m.* (*a*) *PolEc:* pool; common stock/fund; combine; syndicate; **pool bancaire,** banking pool; **pool de l'or,** gold pool (*b*) **pool de dactylos/pool dactylographique,** typing pool.

population, *n.f.* population; **la population active,** the working population.

port[1], *n.m.* harbour/port; **droits de port,** harbour dues/port charges; **port autonome,** independent/autonomous port; **port de commerce/port marchand,** commercial port; **port d'escale/port de relâche,** port of call; **port franc,** free port; **port fluvial,** river port; **le port de Paris,** the port of Paris; **port ouvert,** open port; **port de pêche,** fishing port; **port pétrolier,** oil port.

port[2], *n.m.* 1. cost of transport; carriage/shipping (charges); delivery charges; postal charges/postage (of parcel, letter); **port compris,** postage included; **(en) port dû,** carriage forward; **port et emballage,** postage and packing; **(en) port payé/franco de port/franc de port,** carriage paid/free; post paid 2. *Nau:* (*a*) burden, tonnage (of ship) (*b*) **port en lourd,** dead weight.

portable, *a.* **dette portable,** debt payable at the address of payee.

portage, *n.m.* *StExch:* **société de portage,** nominee company.

portatif, *a.* portable; **machine à écrire portative,** portable typewriter.

porte(-)à(-)porte, *n.m.* door-to-door (transport, selling); **faire du porte à porte,** to be a door-to-door salesman/saleswoman.

porte-conteneurs, *n.m.inv.* *Trans:* **(avion) porte-conteneurs,** container aircraft; **(navire) porte-conteneurs,** container ship; **poste à quai pour navire porte-conteneurs,** container berth; **(train) porte-conteneurs,** container train.

porte-documents, *n.m.inv.* document case/brief case/executive case.

portée, *n.f.* **1.** *Nau:* burden/tonnage (of ship); **portée en lourd,** deadweight (capacity); **portée utile,** load-carrying capacity **2.** range/reach; **des prix à la portée de tout le monde,** prices to suit every pocket.

portefeuille, *n.m.* (*a*) portfolio (for papers, etc.) (*b*) wallet/notecase/*NAm:* billfold (*c*) *Fin:* **effets en portefeuille/ portefeuille effets,** bills in hand/holdings; **gestion de portefeuille,** portfolio management; **portefeuille (titres),** investments; securities; **société de portefeuille,** holding company; **société de gestion de portefeuille,** unit trust; **valeurs/titres en portefeuille,** securities (in portfolio) (*d*) **portefeuille d'assurances,** portfolio (of insurance broker)/insurance book.

porter, 1. *v.tr.* (*a*) **la lettre porte la date du 28 novembre,** the letter is dated 28th November (*b*) **placement qui porte intérêt,** interest-bearing investment (*c*) **je porterai votre proposition à la connaissance du conseil d'administration,** I shall bring your suggestion to the notice of the board (*d*) to enter/to inscribe; **porter qch. en compte à qn,** to charge sth. to s.o.'s account; **portez cela sur/à mon compte,** put that down on my account/charge it to my account/*NAm:* bill it to me/bill it to my account; **portez-le sur la note,** put it/ charge it on the bill; **porter une somme au crédit de qn,** to credit s.o.'s account with a sum (*f*) to raise/to carry; **porter la production au maximum,** to raise production to a maximum; **si vous pouviez porter la somme à deux mille francs,** if you could raise/increase the amount to two thousand francs (*g*) to declare/to state; **avec une clause conditionnelle portant que . . .,** with a proviso to the effect that . . . .

porteur, -euse, *n.* **1.** (*a*) bearer/carrier (of message, etc.); **prière de donner la réponse au porteur,** please hand the reply to bearer (*b*) (railway, etc.) porter (*c*) *Fin: etc:* holder/bearer; (*sur un chèque*) **payer au porteur,** pay bearer; **effets au porteur,** bearer stocks; **payable au porteur,** payable to bearer; **porteur d'actions,** shareholder/stockholder; **porteur d'un chèque,** bearer/payee of a cheque; **porteur d'un effet,** bearer/holder/payee of a bill of exchange; **porteur d'obligations,** debenture holder; bondholder; **titre au porteur,** bearer bond; negotiable instrument **2.** *n.m.* *Av:* **(avion) gros porteur,** airliner/large transport aircraft.

portuaire, *a.* **autorité portuaire,** port authority; **capacité portuaire,** port capacity; **équipement/installation portuaire,** harbour/port equipment; **Montréal est une ville portuaire,** Montreal is a port.

position, *n.f.* (*a*) position; **position concurrentielle,** competitive position; **position clef,** key position (*b*) *StExch:* **position acheteur,** bull position/account; **position de place,** market position; **position vendeur,** bear position/account (*c*) *Fin: Bank:* position/situation; **feuille de position,** statement; **position de trésorerie,** cash (flow) situation; **demander la position de son compte (en banque),** to ask how one's account stands/to ask for the balance of one's account.

positionnement, *n.m.* **1.** *Bank:* calculation of the balance of an account **2.** *Mkt:* **positionnement du produit,** product positioning.

positionner, *v.tr.* **1.** *Bank:* to calculate the balance of (an account) **2.** *Mkt:* to position (a product)/to define the market (of a product).

positionneuse, *n.f. Bank:* calculating machine (used for working out the balance of an account).

possesseur, *n.m.* possessor/owner; occupier; holder (of shares).

possession, *n.f.* possession (of property, shares, etc.); *Ind:* **coût de possession d'un article (en stock)**, storage (cost); **libre possession d'un immeuble**, vacant possession (of a property); *Jur:* **possession de fait**, actual possession; **être en possession de qch.**, to be in possession of sth.; **prendre possession d'une maison**, to take possession of a house.

possibilité, *n.f.* possibility; **possibilités d'exportation**, export possibilities.

possible, *a.* possible; **aussitôt que possible/le plus tôt (qu'il vous sera) possible**, at your earliest convenience; as early/as soon as possible.

postal, *a.* **boîte postale 270**, post office box 270/PO Box 270; **carte postale**, postcard; **code postal**, postcode/*NAm:* zip code; **mandat postal**, postal order; **service postal aérien**, airmail service; **tarifs postaux**, postage/postal rates/postal charges.

postdater, *v.tr.* to postdate (cheque, etc.).

poste[1], *n.f.* (*a*) post; **les Postes et Télécommunications (P et T)** = the Post Office; **par poste aérienne**, by airmail; **poste restante**, poste restante; **envoyer (une lettre, un paquet) par la poste**, to send (a letter, a parcel) by post/*NAm:* by mail; **mettre une lettre à la poste**, to post/*NAm:* to mail a letter (*b*) **(bureau de) poste**, post office; **employé(e) des postes**, post office clerk/post office employee.

poste[2], *n.m.* **1.** (*a*) post, station (of worker); **poste de travail**, operation station (in factory) (*b*) **poste de nuit**, night shift;

poste de 12 heures, 12-hour shift **2.** *Tp:* **poste (intérieur, supplémentaire)**, extension; **poste 106**, extension 106 **3.** post/position/job; **description de poste**, job description; **exigences de poste**, job requirements; **poste vacant/poste à pourvoir**, (job) vacancy **4.** *Book-k:* (*a*) entry (in books) (*b*) heading.

poster, *v.tr.* to post/to mail (letter, etc.).

pot-de-vin, *n.m.* *F:* bribe; hush money.

potentiel, **1.** *a.* **acheteur potentiel**, potential buyer; **marché potentiel**, potential market; **ressources potentielles**, potential resources **2.** *n.m.* potential; **potentiel de croissance**, growth potential; **potentiel industriel**, industrial potential; **potentiel du marché**, market potential; **potentiel publicitaire**, advertising potential; **potentiel de vente**, sales potential.

pourboire, *n.m.* tip/gratuity.

pourcentage, *n.m.* percentage (of commission); rate (of interest); **pourcentage de bénéfices**, percentage of profit.

pourchasser, *v.tr.* *StExch:* **pourchasser le découvert**, to raid the shorts/the bears.

pour(-)compte, *n.m.* undertaking to sell goods on behalf of a third party.

poursuite, *n.f. usu.pl. Jur:* lawsuit/action/prosecution; suing (of a debtor); **engager/intenter des poursuites (judiciaires) contre qn**, to take/to institute proceedings against s.o.; to take (legal) action against s.o.

poursuivre, *v.tr.* *Jur:* **poursuivre qn (en justice)**, to prosecute s.o./to take legal action against s.o.; to sue (debtor).

pourvoir, *v.i.* (*a*) **pourvoir aux frais d'un voyage**, to pay the cost of a journey (*b*) **pourvoir à un emploi**, to fill a vacancy/a post; **poste à pourvoir à Paris**, (job) vacancy in Paris.

poussée, *n.f.* **poussée inflationniste**, inflationary surge.

pousser, *v.tr.* **pousser la vente de qch.**, to

push the sale of sth.; **pousser un article aux enchères,** to up the bidding for sth.

pouvoir, *n.m.* **1. pouvoir d'achat,** purchasing power **2.** authority; **les pouvoirs publics,** the authorities; **pouvoir exécutif,** executive power; **le pouvoir judiciaire,** the judiciary; **pouvoir législatif,** legislative power **3.** *Jur:* **être fondé de pouvoir,** to have power of attorney.

pratiquer, *v.tr.* **pratiquer des prix trop élevés,** to be too expensive; **prix pratiqués sur le marché,** current market prices.

préalable, 1. *a.* (*a*) **accord préalable,** prior agreement; **sans avis préalable,** without prior notice (*b*) preliminary (agreement, arrangement, etc. **2.** *n.m.* prerequisite/precondition; preliminary.

préavis, *n.m.* (*a*) prior notice/advance notice; (*au travail*) **préavis (de congé),** notice; **donner un préavis d'un mois,** to give a month's notice; **exiger un préavis de trois mois,** to require three months' notice (*b*) *Bank:* **dépôt à sept jours de préavis,** deposit at seven days' notice.

précaution, *n.f.* **ils font des achats de précaution,** they're panic buying.

précompte, *n.m. Fin:* (*a*) advance deduction (from an account) (*b*) deduction at source (of income tax, national insurance, etc., from wages).

précompter, *v.tr.* (*a*) to deduct in advance (*b*) to deduct (income tax, etc.) at source; **précompter la Sécurité Sociale sur le salaire de qn,** to deduct National Insurance from s.o.'s pay.

préconditionné, *a.* pre-packed/pre-packaged (goods).

préconditionner, *v.tr.* to pre-pack/to pre-package (goods).

préemballé, *a.* pre-packaged.

préemballer, *v.tr.* to pre-package (goods).

préférence, *n.f.* (*a*) *Jur:* **droits de préférence,** priority rights/preferential

claims; **pacte de préférence,** preference clause; **préférence d'un créancier,** priority of a creditor (*b*) *Fin:* **actions de préférence,** preference/preferred shares; *PolEc:* **préférence pour la liquidité,** liquidity preference (*c*) *Cust:* **préférences douanières,** (customs) preference/preferential duty.

préférentiel, *a.* (*a*) preferential (treatment); *Cust:* **tarif préférentiel,** (*i*) preferential tariff (*ii*) *Adm:* concessionary fare/tariff (*b*) *Fin:* **droit préférentiel de souscription,** rights issue.

préfinancement, *n.m.* prefinancing; **(crédits de) préfinancement d'exportations,** prefinancing of export transactions.

préjudice, *n.m.* prejudice/detriment; **au préjudice de . . .,** to the prejudice of . . .; **sans préjudice de mes droits,** without prejudice (to my rights).

prélèvement, *n.m.* (*a*) deduction in advance; setting aside (of a certain portion); *EEC:* **prélèvements agricoles,** agricultural levies; **prélèvement sur le capital,** capital levy; **prélèvement à l'exportation,** export levy (*b*) amount deducted; *Bank:* **prélèvement automatique,** direct debit.

prélever, *v.tr.* to deduct/to set aside (portion or share from whole) (in advance); **prélever dix pour cent sur une somme,** to make an advance deduction of 10% from a sum of money/to deduct 10% in advance; **prélever une commission de deux pour cent sur une opération,** to charge a commission of 2% on a transaction; **dividende prélevé sur le capital,** dividend paid out of capital.

premier, -ière, 1. *a.* (*a*) first; **le premier juin,** the first of June; **coût premier,** prime cost; **frais de premier établissement,** initial outlay/initial expenses; **premier cours,** opening price; *Publ: Journ:* **première édition,** first edition; **première page,** front cover (*b*) *Ind:* **matières premières,** raw materials (*c*) best; **(produit de) premier choix/première qualité,** best/first quality (product); *Fin:*

obligation de premier ordre, prime bond; *Trans:* **billet de première classe,** first class ticket; **voyager en première,** to travel first class **2.** *n.* (*a*) *n.m.* **premier entré, premier sorti (PEPS),** first in first out (FIFO) (*b*) *n.f.* **première de change,** first of exchange.

prenant, *a. Fin:* **partie prenante,** (*i*) payee (*ii*) receiver/recipient.

prendre, *v.tr.* **1.** (*a*) **prendre la direction d'une affaire,** to take over the management of a business (*b*) **prendre mille francs sur son salaire du mois prochain,** to get an advance of a thousand francs on next month's salary (*c*) **prendre 40 francs (de) l'heure,** to charge 40 francs an hour (*d*) **prendre (de l'essence, etc.),** to get/to buy (petrol, etc.); **prendre une chambre,** to take/to reserve/to book a room; **prendre (une place, un billet),** to book/to buy (a place, a ticket) **2.** (*a*) **prendre un jour de congé,** to take a day's holiday/to take a day off; **prendre rendez-vous/prendre date,** to fix a date (for a meeting, etc.); **voulez-vous prendre une lettre?** will you take (down) a letter?/take a letter, please! (*b*) **prendre un associé,** to take a partner; **prendre un ouvrier,** to take on/to engage/*NAm:* to hire a worker; **prendre qn comme secrétaire,** to engage s.o. as one's secretary (*c*) **prendre des marchandises,** to take in cargo **3.** *Trans:* **prendre (l'avion, le bateau, le train),** to take/to catch (the plane, the boat, the train); to go (by air, by boat, by train).

preneur, -euse, *n.* (*a*) buyer/purchaser; **avoir (trouvé) preneur pour qch.,** to have (found) a purchaser for sth.; **je suis preneur,** I'll take it (*b*) **preneur d'une lettre de change,** payee of a bill (*c*) *Jur:* **preneur (à bail),** lessee/leaseholder.

préparation, *n.f.* preparation; **préparation des commandes,** order preparation; *Ind:* **préparation d'un travail,** organization of a job; **temps de préparation,** tooling-up time.

prépayer, *v.tr.* to prepay; **réponse prépayée,** prepaid answer.

préposé, -ée, *n.* (*a*) employee; clerk; **préposé(e) à la caisse,** cashier; *Rail:* **préposé(e) à la distribution des billets,** booking clerk; **préposé(e) des douanes,** customs officer (*b*) postman (*c*) *Jur:* **commettant et préposé,** principal and agent.

préposer, *v.tr.* **préposer qn à une fonction,** to appoint s.o. to a position; to put s.o. in charge of a job; **préposer qn à la direction d'un service,** to appoint s.o. (as) head of department.

pré-retraite, *n.f.* early retirement.

présentateur, -trice, 1. *n.* presenter (of a bill, etc.) **2.** *a.* **banque présentatrice,** presenting bank.

présentation, *n.f.* (*a*) presentation (of bill, etc. for payment); **payable à présentation,** payable on demand/on presentation/at sight (*b*) *Mkt:* display; exhibit (at trade fair, etc.); **présentation du produit,** product display; **présentation en masse,** mass display; **presentation au sol,** floor display; **présentation à la sortie,** checkout display; **présentation en vrac,** dump display.

présenter, *v.tr.* (*a*) **présenter une traite à l'acceptation,** to present a bill for acceptance; **présenter un chèque à l'encaissement,** to cash a cheque (*b*) **présenter une motion à l'assemblée,** to put a motion to the meeting; **compte qui présente un solde créditeur de 50 000 francs,** account that shows a credit balance of 50 000 francs (*c*) *Mkt:* to display (goods).

présentoir, *n.m. Mkt:* display (stand, unit); **(panier) présentoir,** dumpbin; dump display; **présentoir au sol,** floor display/floor stand; **présentoir à la sortie,** checkout display.

présérie, *n.f. Ind:* (*a*) pre-production/pilot run (*b*) test series; pilot series.

présidence, *n.f.* chairmanship/presidency; **être nommé à la présidence de . . .,** to be appointed chairman of . . ..

président, -ente, *n.* (*a*) chairman/chair-person/chairwoman/president (of a meeting, committee, etc.); **être élu président,** to be voted into the chair/to be elected president (*b*) **président (du conseil d'administration),** chairman (of the board)/ *NAm:* president; **président-directeur général (P-DG),** Chairman and Managing Director/*NAm:* Chief Executive Officer (CEO).

présider, *v.tr. & i.* to preside/to be in the chair/to chair; **présider (à) une réunion,** to preside at/over a meeting; to chair a meeting.

presse, *n.f.* **la presse,** the press; the (news)papers; **presse (nationale, régionale),** (national, provincial) press/papers; **(agence, attaché, campagne, conférence) de presse,** press (agency, attaché, campaign, conference) (*b*) *Typ:* **(livre, journal) sous presse,** (book, newspaper) in the press; **prêt à mettre sous presse,** ready for press; **nous mettons sous presse,** we're going to press.

pression, *n.f.* pressure; **groupe de pression,** pressure group; **pression inflationniste,** inflationary pressure.

prestataire, *n.m. Adm:* person receiving benefits/allowances.

prestation, *n.f.* (*a*) *Ins:* benefit; *Adm:* allowance/benefit; **prestations familiales** = family allowances, maternity benefits, rent allowance; **prestations sociales** = national insurance benefits; **verser les prestations,** to pay out benefits (*b*) fee; service; finder's fee; **prestation de service,** service fee/charge.

prestige, *n.m.* **publicité de prestige,** prestige advertising.

préstockage, *n.m.* prestocking.

prêt¹, *a.* ready; prepared; **vêtements prêts à porter,** ready-made/ready-to-wear clothes.

prêt², *n.m.* **1.** loan; **prêt conditionnel,** tied loan; **prêt à découvert,** unsecured loan/ loan on overdraft; **prêt sur gage/sur nantissement,** loan on collateral/against security; **prêt garanti,** secured loan; **prêt à la grosse,** bottomry loan; **prêt d'honneur,** loan on trust; **prêt hypothécaire,** loan on mortgage; **prêts immobiliers conventionnés (PIC),** property loan discounted by the Crédit Foncier; **prêt à intérêt,** loan at interest; **prêt à la petite semaine,** loan by the week; **prêt au jour le jour,** money at call/call money; **prêt à terme,** loan at notice; **prêt à court terme,** short(-term) loan; **prêt à long terme,** long(-term) loan; **prêt sur titres,** advance on securities; **demande de prêt,** application for a loan; **intérêt sur prêt,** interest on a loan; **maison de prêt,** loan office/ company; **titre de prêt,** loan certificate; **accorder/consentir un prêt,** to allow/to grant a loan; **demander/solliciter un prêt,** to apply for a loan **2.** advance (on salary, wages).

prêt-à-porter, *n.m.* ready-to-wear clothes; **magasin de prêt-à-porter,** shop selling ready-to-wear/off-the-peg/ready-made clothes.

prétention, *n.f.* (*a*) claim (à, to); **exposé détaillé des prétentions du demandeur,** detailed statement of claim (*b*) (*dans une annonce d'offre d'emploi*) **envoyer curriculum vitae et prétentions (de salaire),** send curriculum vitae/CV and state salary requirements/expected salary.

prêter, *v.tr.* to lend/*esp. NAm:* to loan; **prêter de l'argent à intérêt,** to lend money at interest; **prêter sur garantie/ sur gage(s),** to lend against security; **prêter à la petite semaine,** to make a short-term loan at a high rate of interest.

prétest, *n.m.* pretest; pretesting.

prêteur, -euse, *n.* lender (*esp.* of money); *Jur:* bailor; **prêteur sur gages,** (*i*) *Jur:* pledgee (*ii*) pawnbroker.

préventif, *a.* preventive; **entretien préventif,** preventive maintenance; **mesures préventives,** preventive measures.

prévision, *n.f.* forecast(ing); **prévisions budgétaires,** budget estimates/budget forecasts; **prévision du marché,** market forecast(ing); **prévision des ventes,** sales forecast(ing)/sales projections.

prévisionnel, *a.* (*a*) estimated/provisional (costs, etc.) (*b*) **budget d'exploitation prévisionnel,** forecast operating budget; **gestion prévisionnelle,** budgetary control; **plan prévisionnel,** forecast plan.

prévoir, *v.tr.* (*a*) to foresee/to forecast; **ventes prévues,** projected sales; **l'installation de cet ordinateur est prévue pour l'année prochaine,** this computer is scheduled/is due for installation next year; **la réunion est prévue pour demain,** the meeting is arranged for/will be held tomorrow (*b*) to provide in advance for (sth.); **dépenses prévues au budget,** expenses provided for/allowed for in the budget.

prévoyance, *n.f.* **caisse de prévoyance,** (*i*) contingency fund (*ii*) *Adm:* (staff) provident fund/scheme; **société de prévoyance,** provident society.

prier, *v.tr. Corr:* **je vous prie de bien vouloir accepter l'assurance de mes sentiments les meilleurs** = yours sincerely; *Ind: etc:* **le personnel est prié d'arriver à neuf heures précises,** staff are requested to arrive punctually at nine o'clock.

prière, *n.f.* request; **prière de nous couvrir par chèque,** kindly remit by cheque; *Post:* **prière de faire suivre,** please forward.

primaire, *a.* primary; *PolEc:* **secteur primaire,** primary industries (agriculture and extractive industries).

prime, *n.f.* **1.** (*a*) *Ins:* premium; **assurance à prime réduite,** low-premium insurance; **prime annuelle,** annual premium; **prime nette,** pure premium (*b*) *Fin: StExch:* premium; option; **acheteur/vendeur de prime,** giver/taker of an option; **marché à primes,** option market; **opérations à prime,** options dealing/trading; **prime de**

conversion, conversion premium; **prime d'émission,** issue premium; **prime de l'or,** premium on gold; **prime de remboursement,** premium on redemption; **(jour de la) réponse des primes,** declaration of options/option day; **abandonner la prime,** to forfeit/to surrender the option (money); **acheter à prime,** to give for the call; **donner la réponse/répondre à une prime,** to declare an option; **lever la prime,** to take up an option **2.** subsidy; grant; *Ind:* **prime spéciale d'équipement,** (government) development subsidy (to firms setting up factories in development areas) **3.** (*a*) bonus; **prime (payée) aux employés,** bonus paid to employees; **prime de déménagement,** removal allowance; **prime de rendement,** productivity/output bonus; **prime de transport,** travel/transport allowance; **prime de vie chère,** cost-of-living bonus (*b*) *PolEc:* **prime à l'exportation,** export bonus **4.** *Mkt:* free gift; **prime échantillon,** free sample; **recette donnée en prime avec ce produit,** free (gift) recipe given with this product/when you buy this product.

principal, 1. *a.* principal/chief; **agent principal,** main agent; **associé principal,** senior partner; **produit principal d'un pays,** main/staple commodity of a country; **un des principaux actionnaires,** a major shareholder **2.** *n.m.* principal.

principe, *n.m.* (*a*) principle; **principes économiques,** economic principles (*b*) **aboutir à un accord de principe,** to reach an agreement in principle.

prioritaire, *a.* priority; **action prioritaire,** preference share/preferred stock; **droits prioritaires,** priority rights; **être prioritaire,** to have priority.

priorité, *n.f.* priority; *Jur:* priority of claim; *StExch:* **actions de priorité,** preference shares/preferred stock; **créancier de priorité,** secured creditor; **droits de priorité,** priority rights; **dividende de priorité,** preferential dividend; **avoir la priorité,** to have priority.

prise, *n.f.* (*a*) **prise de contrôle,** takeover; **prise de décision(s),** decision making; *Fin:* **prise de participation,** acquisition of shareholding; takeover (*b*) *StExch:* **prise de bénéfices,** profit taking.

prisée, *n.f. Jur:* **prisée (et estimation),** valuation (of goods); appraisal (before auction).

privé, *a.* private (bank, enterprise, property, etc.); **le secteur privé,** the private sector (of industry).

privilège, *n.m.* **1.** licence/charter; **le privilège de la Banque de France,** exclusive right of the Bank of France to issue banknotes **2.** preferential right; **privilège du créancier,** creditor's preferential claim; **privilège général,** general lien; **avoir un privilège sur qch.,** to have a lien/a charge on sth.

privilégié, *a.* (*a*) licensed; **banque privilégiée,** chartered bank (*b*) **action privilégiée,** preference share/preferred stock; **créance privilégiée,** preferential debt/preferred debt/privileged debt; **créancier privilégié,** secured/preferential creditor.

privilégier, *v.tr.* to license; to grant a charter to (bank, etc.).

prix, *n.m.* (*a*) price; consideration; quotation; **bas prix,** low price; **prix élevé,** high price; **affichage des prix,** displaying of prices; *PolEc:* **blocage des prix,** price pegging/price freezing; **contrôle des prix,** price control; **détermination des prix,** pricing/price fixing; **différences des prix,** price differentials; **éventail des prix,** price range; **guerre des prix,** price war; *PolEc:* **indice des prix,** price index; **magasin à prix unique,** one-price store/popular store; **monopole des prix,** price monopoly; **prix affiché,** displayed price; **prix d'achat,** purchase price/cost; **prix d'appel,** cut/reduced price; **prix catalogue/prix public/prix fort,** catalogue price/list price; **prix chocs,** drastic reductions/incredible bargain prices; **prix (au) comptant,** cash price; **prix compétitif,** competitive price; **prix conseillé,** manu-

facturer's recommended price (MRP)/recommended retail price (RRP); **prix convenu,** agreed price; **prix courant,** current price; **prix de détail,** retail price; **prix de demi-gros,** trade price; cash-and-carry price; **prix directeur,** price leader; **prix à l'exportation,** export price; **prix de fabrique,** cost price/manufacturer's price; **prix ferme,** firm/steady price; **prix fixe/prix forfaitaire,** fixed price; **prix de gros,** wholesale price; **prix à l'importation,** import price; **prix imposés** = retail price maintenance (RPM); **prix initial,** prime cost; *EEC:* **prix d'intervention,** intervention price; **prix de lancement,** introductory price; **prix du marché,** market value; **prix marqué,** marked price; **prix minimum,** minimum price; **prix modéré,** moderate price; **prix net,** (*i*) net price (*ii*) (*sur un menu*) price inclusive of service; *PolEc:* **prix plafond,** ceiling price; *PolEc:* **prix plancher/prix seuil,** floor price; minimum price; **prix préférentiel,** preferential price; **prix à la production/prix départ usine,** price ex warehouse/factory price; **prix de rabais/prix réduit,** cut/reduced price; **prix réel,** actual price; **prix de revient/prix coûtant,** cost price; **comptabilité de prix de revient,** cost accounting; *EEC:* **prix du seuil,** threshold price; **prix tout compris/prix tous frais compris/prix toutes taxes comprises (TTC),** all-inclusive price; **prix unitaire,** unit price; **prix de vente,** selling price; **régime des prix/mécanisme des prix,** price mechanism/system; **réglementation des prix,** price regulation; **acheter qch. à bas prix,** to buy sth. at a low price/to buy sth. cheap; **augmenter de prix,** to increase in price; **augmenter/baisser les prix,** to mark up/to mark down prices; **coûter un prix fou,** to cost the earth; **déterminer/fixer le prix de qch.,** to price sth.; **établir le prix (de revient) d'un travail,** to cost a job; **faire un prix,** to quote/to name a price; **faire un prix à qn,** to quote s.o. a price; **je vous ferai un prix (d'ami),** I'll let you have it cheap/I'll give you special terms; **faire monter les prix,** to push up prices; **mettre** un prix à qch., to price sth./to put a price to sth.; **quel est le prix de ce livre?** what is the price of this book? how much is this book? (*b*) *StExch: Fin:* **actions cotées au prix de . . .,** shares quoted at the rate of . . .; **effondrement des prix,** price slump; **hausse/baisse des prix,** rise/fall in prices; **prix du change,** (exchange) premium; agio; **prix de l'argent,** price of money; **prix d'émission (d'actions, etc.),** issue price (of shares, etc.); **prix du marché,** market price; **prix du report,** contango rate (*c*) charge; *Trans:* **prix d'un trajet/ du voyage,** fare; **le prix des places est de 25 francs,** the seats are 25 francs each.

prix-courant, *n.m.* price list; catalogue.

prix(-)étalon, *n.m.* standard cost/price.

problème, *n.m.* problem; **évaluation de problème(s),** problem appraisal.

procédé, *n.m. Ind: etc:* process/way; method (of working); **procédé de fabrication,** manufacturing process; **procédé de travail,** operating process.

procédure, *n.f.* **1.** procedure; **(mode de) procédure,** procedure (at a meeting, etc.) **2.** *Jur:* proceedings; **procédure de faillite,** bankruptcy proceedings.

procès, *n.m.* proceedings at law; action (at law); case; **intenter un procès à qn,** (*i*) to file a suit against s.o.; to institute proceedings against s.o.; to sue s.o. (*ii*) to prosecute s.o.

processif, *a. PolEc:* **processif ou récessif,** progressive or recessive.

processus, *n.m.* method/process; **commande/régulation de processus,** process control.

procès-verbal, *n.m.* (official) report; proceedings/minutes (of meeting); **dresser un procès-verbal,** to draw up a report; **tenir le procès-verbal des réunions,** to keep the minutes of the meetings; **le procès-verbal de la dernière séance a été approuvé,** the minutes of the last meet-

ing were approved; *Nau:* **procès-verbal des avaries,** protest.

procuration, *n.f.* procuration/proxy; power of attorney; **procuration générale,** full power of attorney; **signé par procuration (pp°ⁿ),** signed by proxy/on behalf of/per pro/pp; **agir par procuration,** to act by proxy.

procurer, *v.tr.* **où puis-je me procurer ce livre,** where can I get/buy that book? **il est impossible de se procurer ce livre,** this book unobtainable.

producteur, -trice, 1. *a.* productive (de, of); producing; **capital producteur d'intérêt,** interest-bearing capital; **les pays producteurs de pétrole,** petrol producing countries; **régions productrices d'un pays,** productive regions of a country **2.** *n.* producer.

productif, *a.* productive; *PolEc:* **personnel productif/main-d'œuvre productive,** productive labour.

production, *n.f. PolEc: Ind: etc:* production/output; (*a*) **chaîne de production,** production line; **chute/baisse de production,** fall/drop in production; **excédent de production,** surplus production; **production agricole,** agricultural production; **production à la chaîne,** production line system/mass production; **production sur commande,** production to order; **production continue,** continuous flow production; **production dirigée/ planifiée,** planned production; **production par lots,** batch production; **production en masse/en série,** mass production; **taux de production,** rate of production; **augmenter la production,** to increase production/output; **ralentir la production,** to slow down production/to reduce output (*b*) **biens de production,** (*i*) capital goods (*ii*) producer goods; **capacité de production,** production capacity; **chef/directeur de la production,** production manager; **coûts/frais de production,** production costs; **gestion de production,** production control; **moyens de**

production, means/method of production; **organisation de la production,** production engineering; **production intérieure brute (PIB),** gross domestic product; **service de la production,** production department.

productivité, *n.f.* productivity; productive capacity/yield capacity; **campagne de productivité,** productivity drive/productivity campaign; **contrat de productivité,** productivity deal; **prime de productivité,** productivity bonus; **productivité financière d'une entreprise,** productiveness of a firm.

produire, *v.tr.* **1.** to produce (documents, etc.) **2.** to produce/to yield; **argent qui produit de l'intérêt,** money that yields interest; **produire mille voitures par jour,** to produce/to turn out a thousand cars a day.

produit, *n.m.* (*a*) product; produce; **produits agricoles,** agricultural produce; *Mkt:* **produit d'appel,** loss leader; impulse item; **produit de base,** (*i*) basic (*ii*) staple commodity/product; **produits de consommation,** consumer goods; **produits dérivés,** by-products/derivatives; **produits étrangers,** foreign produce/goods; **produit fini/ouvré,** finished product; **produit industriel,** industrial product; **produits manufacturés,** manufactured goods/products; **produits du pays,** home produce; **produits de rejet,** waste products; **produit semi-fini/semi-ouvré,** semi-finished/semi-manufactured product; **analyse de produit,** product analysis; **conception de produit,** product design (*b*) proceeds/yield; **produit net,** net earnings/proceeds; **produit brut,** gross earnings/proceeds; *PolEc:* **produit national brut (PNB),** gross national product (GNP); *Fin:* **produits accessoires,** sundry income; **produits financiers,** interest income.

profession, *n.f.* profession/occupation/trade; **les membres des professions libérales,** professional people.

profil, *n.m.* profile; **profil de la clientèle,** customer profile; **profil d'entreprise,** company profile; **profil du marché,** market profile.

profit, *n.m.* profit; **profit brut,** gross profit; **profit net,** clear profit; **profits et pertes,** profit and loss; **objectif de profits,** profit target; **optimisation des profits,** profit optimization; **vendre à profit,** to sell at a profit.

profitabilité, *n.f.* (*i*) profitability (*ii*) earning power.

profitable, *a.* profitable; advantageous; **affaire profitable,** paying concern; profitable business.

profiteur, -euse, *n. Pej:* profiteer.

pro forma, *a.phr.inv.* **facture pro forma,** pro forma invoice.

progiciel, *n.m. Cmptr:* package; **progiciel de comptabilité,** accounting package.

programmation, *n.f.* (*a*) programming; scheduling; planning; **programmation à long terme,** long-range planning; **programmation linéaire,** linear programming; **programmation de la production,** production scheduling; **personnel chargé de la programmation,** scheduling staff; **service (de la) programmation,** programming department (*b*) *Cmptr:* programming; **langage de programmation,** computer language.

programme, *n.m.* (*a*) programme/*NAm:* program; schedule; **programme de développement,** development programme; **programme de fabrication/de production,** production programme/schedule; *Fin:* **programme d'investissement,** investment programme; **programme à long terme,** long-range plan; **programme de recherche(s),** research programme; *Mkt:* **programme des ventes,** sales programme/schedule; **arrêter un programme,** to draw up/to arrange a programme (*b*) *Cmptr:* program.

programmé, *a. Cmptr:* programmed;

gestion programmée, programmed management.

programmer, *v.tr. Cmptr:* to program.

programmeur, -euse, *n. Cmptr:* programmer.

progrès, *n.m.* progress.

progressif, *a.* (*a*) progressive; **impôt progressif,** progressive/graduated tax (*b*) gradual (growth, development); **l'amélioration progressive du rendement,** the gradual improvement in productivity.

progression, *n.f. Fin:* **progression des bénéfices,** increase in profits.

progressivité, *n.f. Fin:* **progressivité de l'impôt,** progressive increase in taxation.

prohibé, *a.* prohibited; **marchandises prohibées,** prohibited goods.

prohibitif, *a.* prohibitive (price, duty).

prohibition, *n.f.* **prohibition d'entrée,** import prohibition/ban; **prohibition de sortie,** export prohibition/ban.

projection, *n.f.* projection; **projection des ventes,** sales projection.

projet, *n.m.* (*a*) plan/project; scheme; **étude de projet,** project analysis; **étude de projet d'investissement,** capital project evaluation.

projeter, *v.tr.* to plan.

promesse, *n.f.* promise; **promesse d'achat,** agreement/undertaking to purchase; **promesse de payer,** undertaking/promise to pay; **promesse de vente,** undertaking/promise to sell.

promoteur, -trice, *n.* promoter; **promoteur de construction/promoteur immobilier,** property developer; **promoteur des ventes,** sales promoter.

promotion, *n.f.* **1.** promotion; **promotion à l'ancienneté,** promotion by seniority; **promotion des cadres,** executive pro-

motion **2. promotion immobilière,** (promoting of) property development projects; *Mkt:* **promotion des ventes,** sales promotion; **promotion sur le lieu de vente (PLV),** point-of-sale (POS) promotion; **en promotion,** on promotion/on offer.

promotionnel, *a. Mkt:* **équipe promotionnelle,** promotion team; **vente promotionnelle** = special offer/bargain offer.

promouvoir, *v.tr.* (*a*) to promote (s.o.); **être promu,** to be promoted (*b*) to promote (sales, products); **promouvoir la recherche scientifique,** to encourage scientific research.

pronostic, *n.m.* forecast; **pronostic du marché,** market forecast.

propension, *n.f. PolEc:* **propension à consommer,** propensity to consume; **propension moyenne à épargner,** average propensity to save.

proportion, *n.f.* proportion; ratio; percentage.

proportionnalité, *n.f. Fin:* **proportionnalité de l'impôt,** fixed rate system of taxation.

proportionnel, *a.* proportional (à, to); **compensation proportionnelle au dommage subi,** compensation proportional to the damage; **distribution proportionnelle,** proportionment; *Cust:* **droit proportionnel,** ad valorem duty; *Fin:* **impôt proportionnel,** tax at a fixed rate/percentage.

proportionnellement, *adv.* proportionally/in proportion (à, to); pro rata; *Fin: etc:* **partager proportionnellement,** to prorate.

proposer, *v.tr.* to propose/to recommend; **proposer un candidat,** to nominate a candidate; **être proposé pour un emploi,** to be recommended for a job.

proposition, *n.f.* proposal/proposition; **proposition d'assurance,** proposal of insurance; **faire/formuler une proposition,** (*i*) to make a proposal (*ii*) to put/to propose a motion (at a meeting).

propriétaire, *n.m. & f.* **1.** proprietor/proprietress (of business, hotel, etc.); owner (of car, house, etc.); holder; **propriétaire foncier,** (*i*) ground landlord (*ii*) landowner; *Jur:* **propriétaire indivis,** joint owner; **propriétaire unique,** sole owner **2.** landlord/landlady.

propriétaire-occupant, *n.m.* owner-occupier.

propriété, *n.f.* (*a*) proprietorship/ownership; **propriété collective,** collective ownership; **propriété commerciale,** commercial tenant's (right to) security of tenure or compensation; **propriété individuelle,** individual ownership; **propriété indivise,** joint ownership; **propriété industrielle,** patent rights; **propriété littéraire/artistique,** literary property/copyright; **titres de propriété,** title deeds (*b*) property/estate/holding; **propriété foncière,** landed property/landed estate; **propriété immobilière,** real estate/realty; **propriété mobilière,** personal estate; **propriété à vendre,** property for sale.

prorata, *n.m.inv.* proportional part/proportion; **au prorata de qch.,** in proportion to sth./proportionately to sth.; **distribution au prorata,** proportionment; **paiement au prorata,** payment pro rata; **rémunération au prorata du travail accompli,** payment in proportion to work done.

prorogation, *n.f.* extension of time/of time limit (for payment to be made, etc.).

proroger, *v.tr.* to extend (time limit); **proroger l'échéance d'un billet,** to prolong a bill.

prospecté, -ée, *n. Mkt:* (*i*) prospect/prospective customer/potential buyer (*ii*) potential supplier.

prospecter, *v.tr. Mkt:* to investigate/to examine (potential market, etc.); **pros-**

pecter la clientèle, to canvass for customers.

prospecteur, -trice, *n.* canvasser.

prospectif, *a.* prospective; **étude prospective du marché,** market study/survey.

prospection, *n.f. Mkt:* canvassing; **prospection des marchés,** market exploration; **prospection sur le terrain,** field research.

prospectus, *n.m.* (*a*) *Fin:* **prospectus d'émission,** prospectus (*b*) *Mkt:* **prospectus publicitaire,** brochure; (publicity) handout/leaflet.

prospère, *a.* prosperous/thriving (business, etc.).

prospérer, *v.i.* to thrive/to prosper.

prospérité, *n.f.* prosperity; **vague de prospérité,** boom/wave of prosperity.

protecteur, *a. PolEc:* protective (duty, tariff, etc.); **système protecteur,** protection(ism).

protection, *n.f.* (*a*) *Mkt:* **protection du consommateur,** consumer protection (*b*) *PolEc:* protection(ism).

protectionnisme, *n.m. PolEc:* protection(ism).

protéger, *v.tr.* (*a*) to protect; **protéger qch. par un brevet,** to patent sth. (*b*) *PolEc:* to protect (industry, etc.).

protester, *v.tr.* protester (un effet, une lettre de change), to protest (a bill).

protêt, *n.m.* protest; **protêt authentique,** certified protest; **protêt faute d'acceptation,** protest for non-acceptance; **protêt faute de paiement,** protest for non-payment; **dresser/lever/faire protêt (d'un effet, d'une lettre de change),** to protest (a bill); **signifier un protêt,** to give notice of a protest.

protocole, *n.m.* **il a signé le protocole d'accord,** he signed heads of agreement.

prototype, *n.m.* prototype; **voiture prototype,** prototype car.

provenance, *n.f.* (*a*) origin; **de provenance française,** of French origin; **pays de provenance,** country of origin (*b*) *pl. Cust:* **les provenances,** imports.

provenir, *v.i.* to come (**de,** from); to originate (**de,** in); **revenu provenant d'un investissement,** income coming from/accruing from an investment.

provision, *n.f.* **1.** (*a*) *Fin: Bank:* funds/cover/reserve; **insuffisance de provision,** insufficient funds (to meet cheque, etc.); **chèque sans provision,** cheque without cover/*F:* dud cheque; **il m'a payé avec un chèque sans provision,** his cheque bounced; **provision d'une lettre de change,** consideration for a bill of exchange; **faire provision pour une lettre de change,** to provide for/to protect a bill of exchange; **verser une provision,** to pay a deposit/to deposit funds (*b*) *Book-k:* provision/reserve; **provision pour créances douteuses,** reserve for bad debts; **provision pour dépréciation,** provision for depreciation (*c*) retainer (given to lawyer, etc.) **2.** (*a*) store/stock/supply; **provision de papier,** paper supply (*b*) **faire ses provisions,** to do one's shopping.

provisionnel, *a. Fin:* **acompte provisionnel,** payment (of income tax) made on provisional assessment.

provisionner, *v.tr.* to give consideration for (a bill); *Bank:* **provisionner un compte,** to pay money into an account.

provisoire, *a.* provisional; temporary; **dividende provisoire,** interim dividend; **gérant provisoire,** acting manager; **nommé à titre provisoire,** appointed provisionally.

prud'hommes, *n.m.pl.* **conseil de(s) prud'hommes,** conciliation board/industrial tribunal (of employers and workers, in industrial disputes).

psychologie, *n.f.* psychology; **psychologie commerciale,** psychology of marketing;

psychologie industrielle, industrial psychology/psychotechnology; **psychologie de la publicité,** advertising psychology.

psychotechnie, *n.f.,* **psychotechnique,** *n.f.* psychotechnology/industrial psychology.

pub, *abbr.* = **publicité.**

public, 1. *a.* public; **dépense publique,** public expenditure; **la dette publique,** the National Debt; *Jur:* **marché public,** market overt; *Fin:* **offre publique d'achat (OPA),** takeover bid; **relations publiques,** public relations (PR); **secteur public,** public sector; **le Trésor public,** the (French) Treasury **2.** *n.m.* **le public,** the public (sector); (*d'une société*) **placer des actions dans le public,** to go public.

publication, *n.f.* (*a*) publication/publishing (*b*) publication/published work; **publication périodique,** periodical/magazine.

publicitaire, 1. *a. Mkt:* **agence publicitaire,** advertising agency; *Journ:* **annonce publicitaire,** advertisement/*F:* ad; **budget publicitaire,** publicity/advertising budget; **dépenses publicitaires,** publicity/advertising expenses; **espace publicitaire,** advertising space; *TV:* **message publicitaire,** (advertising) spot/commercial; **normes publicitaires,** advertising standards; **supports publicitaires,** advertising media; **vente publicitaire,** promotional sale **2.** *n.m. & f.* advertising executive; publicity man/woman; publicist; *F:* adman.

publicité, *n.f. Mkt:* advertising/publicity; build-up; advertisement; **agence/bureau de publicité,** advertising agency/publicity bureau; **budget de publicité,** (*i*) publicity/advertising budget (*ii*) (advertising) account; **campagne de publicité,** advertising/publicity campaign; publicity drive; **chef de (la) publicité,** advertising manager; **envoi/prospectus/dépliant de publicité (directe),** mailing piece/shot; **frais de publicité,** advertising/publicity costs; **(service de) la publicité,** publicity department; **publicité d'amorçage,** advance publicity; **publicité aggressive,** hard sell; **publicité collective,** group advertising; **publicité directe,** direct mailing; **publicité-médias,** media advertising; **publicité mensongère/trompeuse,** misleading advertising; **publicité subliminale,** subliminal advertising; **publicité télévisée,** television advertising/televized advertising; **faire de la publicité (pour un produit),** to advertise/to publicize (a product).

publipostage, *n.m. Mkt:* mailing.

puce, *n.f. Cmptr:* microchip.

purger, *v.tr.* **purger une hypothèque,** to redeem/to pay off a mortgage.

Q

quadrimestre, *n.m.* *Book-k:* four monthly (accounting) period.

quadruple, *a.* & *n.m.* quadruple; **payer le quadruple du prix,** to pay four times the price.

quadrupler, *v.tr.* & *i.* to quadruple; to increase (one's assets, etc.) fourfold.

quai, *n.m.* (*a*) *Nau:* quay; wharf; pier; **droit(s) de quai,** quayage; wharfage; **marchandises à prendre/livrables à quai,** goods ex quay/ex wharf; **rendu/livré franco à quai,** free on quay (*b*) *Rail:* platform; **billet de quai,** platform ticket; **quai d'arrivée,** arrival platform; **quai de départ,** departure platform; **quai de chargement,** loading platform; **quai de déchargement,** off-loading platform.

qualification, *n.f.* **1.** *Fin:* qualifying (by acquisition of shares) **2.** qualification; **qualifications professionnelles,** professional qualifications; **posséder les qualifications nécessaires pour un poste,** to have the necessary qualifications for a job.

qualifié, *a.* qualified; **ouvrier qualifié,** skilled worker; **ouvrier non qualifié,** unskilled worker; **être qualifié pour faire qch.,** to be qualified to do sth.

qualité, *n.f.* **1.** (*a*) quality; **de bonne qualité/de qualité supérieure,** (of) good/high quality; **marchandises de mauvaise qualité/de qualité inférieure,** poor quality goods; **de première qualité,** high-grade/(of the) best quality; **qualité marchande,** (fair) average quality; **qualité prescrite,** stipulated quality (*b*) **contrôle de la qualité,** quality control; **garantie de qualité,** guarantee/warranty of quality; quality guarantee; **marchandi-**

ses de qualité, quality goods **2.** qualification/capacity; **avoir qualité pour agir,** to be qualified/authorized to act; **posséder les qualités requises pour un poste,** to have the necessary qualifications for a post; to be qualified for a post; **en sa qualité de . . .,** in his capacity as . . ..

quantième, *n.m.* *Adm:* day (of the month).

quantitatif, *a.* quantitative; *PolEc:* **théorie quantitative,** quantity theory.

quantité, *n.f.* quantity; **une petite quantité,** a small quantity (**de,** of); **une (grande) quantité de . . .,** a (large) quantity of . . .; **acheter qch. en quantité considérable/en grande quantité,** to buy sth. in bulk/in large quantities; **remise sur la quantité,** quantity discount; *Cust:* **la quantité permise (de tabac, etc.),** the quantity (of tobacco, etc.) permitted; *Ind:* **quantité économique de production,** economic manufacturing quantity; **quantité économique à commander/ quantité économique de réapprovisionnement,** economic order quantity; **déterminer la quantité de qch.,** to quantify sth.

quantum, *n.m.* amount/proportion/ratio; **fixer le quantum des dommages-intérêts,** to fix the amount of damages/to assess the damages.

quarante, *num.a.inv.* & *n.m.inv.* forty; **semaine de quarante heures,** forty-hour week.

quart, *n.m.* (*a*) quarter/fourth (part); **trois quarts,** three quarters; **remise du quart,** discount of 25%; **je peux l'avoir au quart du prix,** I can buy it for a quarter (of) the price (*b*) **un quart (de beurre, de café),** a quarter of a kilo/250 grammes (of butter, of coffee).

quartier, *n.m.* district; **quartier des affaires,** business district/area/*NAm:* downtown.

quasi-contrat, *n.m. Jur:* quasi contract/ implied contract.

quasi-monnaie, *n.f.* quasi-money/near money.

questionnaire, *n.m.* questionnaire.

quinquennal, *a.* **plan quinquennal,** five-year plan.

quintal, *n.m. Meas:* quintal = 100 kilogrammes; *FrC:* a hundredweight.

quinzaine, *n.f.* **1.** (about) fifteen; **une quinzaine de francs,** fifteen francs or so **2.** (*a*) fortnight (*b*) fortnight's pay/wages.

quinze, *num.a.inv.* (*a*) fifteen; **le 15 décembre,** on 15th December (*b*) **quinze jours,** a fortnight.

quittance, *n.f.* receipt; *Jur:* discharge; **carnet de quittances,** receipt book; **quittance comptable,** accountable receipt; **quittance double,** duplicate receipt; **quittance en double,** receipt in duplicate; **quittance libératoire/finale,** receipt in full (discharge); **quittance de loyer,** rent

receipt; **quittance pour solde,** receipt in full.

quittancer, *v.tr.* to receipt (bill).

quitus, *n.m.* receipt in full; *Jur:* final discharge (from debt, liability, etc.); **donner à qn quitus de sa gestion,** to give s.o. final discharge from his financial administration.

quorum, *n.m.* quorum; **constituer un quorum,** to have/to form a quorum; **le quorum n'est pas atteint,** we don't have/we don't form a quorum.

quota, *n.m.* quota; **quota d'exportation,** export quota; **quota d'importation,** import quota; **quota de ventes,** sales quota; **sondage par quota,** quota sampling; **système des quotas,** quota system.

quote-part, *n.f.* share/quota/portion; contribution pro rata; **quote-part des bénéfices,** share in the profits; **apporter/ payer sa quote-part,** to contribute one's share.

quotidien, *n.m.* daily (newspaper).

quotient, *n.m.* quotient/ratio.

quotité, *n.f.* quota/share/amount/proportion; **impôt de quotité,** coefficient tax; **quotité imposable,** taxable quota; **la quotité du dégrèvement fiscal,** the extent of tax relief.

R

rabais, *n.m.* reduction (in price); allowance/rebate/discount; **rabais de 3 francs,** 3 francs off/reduction of 3 francs; **maison de rabais,** discount store; **acheté à rabais,** bought at a reduced price/bought (on the) cheap; **faire/accorder un rabais sur qch.,** to make a reduction on sth./to reduce sth.; to give a discount on sth.; **vendre qch. au rabais,** to sell sth. at a discount/at a reduced price.

rabaissement, *n.m.* lowering (of prices).

rabaisser, *v.tr.* to reduce/to lower (price).

rabattre, *v.tr.* to reduce; **rabattre 5% du prix,** to take/*F:* to knock 5% off the price; to reduce sth. by 5%.

rachat, *n.m.* (*a*) buying back/repurchase; buying in (of goods); *StExch:* **rachat d'actions,** covering purchases; *Jur:* **pacte de rachat,** covenant of redemption; **(vente) avec faculté de rachat,** (sale) with option of repurchase/of redemption (*b*) *Ins:* surrender (of policy); redemption of annuity, etc.); **valeur de rachat,** surrender value.

rachetable, *a.* repurchasable; redeemable (stock).

racheter, *v.tr.* **1.** (*a*) to repurchase; to buy (sth.) back; to buy (sth.) in (*b*) to redeem (debt, pledge, etc.) (*c*) *Ins:* to surrender (policy); to redeem (annuity) **2.** to buy again; to make a further purchase of (sth.); **racheter du fromage,** (*i*) to buy some more cheese (*ii*) to buy some more of the same cheese.

radiation, *n.f.* erasure/crossing out (of an item in an account, etc.); cancellation (of debt, etc.).

radier, *v.tr.* to erase; to cross (sth., s.o.) off (a list, etc.).

raffermir, 1. *v.tr.* to steady (prices, etc.); **raffermir le crédit d'une maison,** to re-establish a firm's credit **2.** *v.pr.* **les prix se raffermissent,** prices are steadying/are hardening.

raffermissement, *n.m.* hardening/steadying (of prices).

raison, *n.f.* **1. raison sociale,** name/style (of a firm, company); trade name/corporate name **2. travail payé à raison de vingt francs l'heure,** work paid at the rate of twenty francs an hour.

raisonnable, *a.* (*a*) reasonable; **prix raisonnable,** reasonable/fair/moderate price (*b*) **revenu raisonnable,** reasonable/adequate income.

rajustement, *n.m.* readjustment; **les syndicats réclament un rajustement des salaires,** the unions are demanding a readjustment of the wage structure/a wage increase in line with the cost of living.

rajuster, *v.tr.* **rajuster les salaires,** to readjust the wage structure/to bring wages into line with the cost of living.

ralenti, *n.m. Ind:* **travail au ralenti,** go-slow; **travailler au ralenti,** to go slow.

ralentir, *v.tr.* to slow down; **ralentir la production,** to slow down production.

ralentissement, *n.m.* slackening/slowing down; **ralentissement des affaires,** falling off of business; **ralentissement de la demande,** fall-off/slow-down in demand; **ralentissement de la production,** slowing down of production.

ramasse-monnaie, *n.m.* (*au guichet*) tray for change.

ramener, *v.tr.* **ramener le prix d'un article à . . .,** to bring the price of an article down to . . .; **ramener la semaine de 40 à 35 heures,** to reduce the working week from 40 to 35 hours.

rang, *n.m.* (*a*) **se mettre sur les rangs,** to come forward as a candidate; to apply for a job (*b*) **avoir/prendre (le) même rang que . . .,** (*i*) (*une personne, une dette, une hypothèque*) to rank equally with . . . (*ii*) (*une action, etc.*) to rank pari passu with . . .; **actions de premier rang,** preference shares; **obligations de deuxième rang,** junior bonds.

rappel, *n.m.* **1.** payment of arrears **2.** (*a*) reminder (of account, etc.); **dernier rappel,** final reminder (*b*) **rappel de traitement,** back pay **3.** *Mkt:* (*à la radio*) mention (of advertiser's name)/*F:* plug.

rappeler, *v.tr.* **1.** *Corr:* **dans votre réponse rappeler le référence FK/FJ,** when replying quote ref(erence) FK/FJ; **prière de rappeler ce numéro,** (in reply) please quote this number **2.** *Tp:* to call back/to ring back.

rapport, *n.m.* **1.** yield/return/profit; **d'un bon rapport,** profitable/that brings in a good return/that pays well; **actions d'un bon rapport,** shares that yield a good return; **capital en rapport,** interest-bearing/productive capital; **immeuble/maison de rapport,** rented property which brings in income/revenue; **rapport d'un investissement,** return on an investment **2.** *Adm: Jur:* account/report/statement; return (of expenses, etc.); survey; *Nau:* **rapport d'avaries,** damage report; **rapport collectif,** joint report; **rapport du commissaire aux comptes,** auditor's report; **rapport financier,** treasurer's report; **rapport de gestion (d'une société),** annual report (of a company); **rapport périodique/rapport d'avancement des travaux,** progress report; **rapport du président,** chairman's/

president's report; **envoyer un rapport,** to send in a report; **faire/rédiger un rapport sur qch.,** to make/to draw up a report on sth.; **présenter/soumettre un rapport à qn (sur qch.),** to present/to submit a report to s.o. (on sth.) **3. avoir rapport à qch.,** to relate/to refer to sth. **4.** ratio/proportion; **rapport profit sur ventes,** profit-volume ratio **5.** relations (between people); **avoir des rapports avec,** (*i*) to have dealings with s.o. (*ii*) to be in touch with s.o.; **avoir de bons rapports avec la filiale française,** to be on good terms with the French subsidiary; **mettre qn en rapport avec qn,** to bring s.o. into contact with s.o./to put s.o. in touch with s.o.; **rapports patrons-syndicats,** relations between the employers and the unions/union-employer relations.

rapporter, *v.tr.* to bring in/to yield/to bear/to produce; **placement qui rapporte 5%,** investment that yields/brings in/bears 5%; **cela ne rapporte rien,** it doesn't pay; **affaire qui rapporte,** profitable/paying business; **la publicité rapporte,** it pays to advertise.

ratio, *n.m.* *Fin:* ratio; **ratio comptable,** accounting ratio; **ratio de distribution,** distribution ratio; **ratio d'endettement,** gearing; **ratio d'intensité de capital,** capital-output ratio; **ratio de levier,** leverage; **ratio de rentabilité,** profit ratio.

rationalisation, *n.f.* *PolEc:* rationalizing/streamlining (of industry).

rationaliser, *v.tr.* *PolEc:* to rationalize/to streamline (industry).

rationnel, *a.* rational; **l'organisation rationnelle de l'industrie,** the rationalization/streamlining of industry.

rattrapage, *n.m.* *PolEc:* adjustment (of wages in relation to the cost of living, etc.).

rayer, *v.tr.* to strike out/to delete; (*sur un formulaire*) **rayer les mentions inutiles,** delete where inapplicable.

rayon, *n.m.* **1. rayon d'action d'une campagne publicitaire,** range of an advertising campaign; **rayon de livraison,** delivery area; **cette entreprise a étendu son rayon d'action,** this firm has extended its range of activities **2.** (*dans un magasin*) (*i*) department (*ii*) counter; **chef de rayon,** department manager; **magasin à rayons,** department store; **rayon de l'alimentation,** food hall/food department/food counter; **rayon des bagages,** luggage department; **rayon des soldes,** bargain counter/bargain basement; (*au supermarché*) **le cinquième rayon,** the non-food section.

réaction, *n.f.* reaction; *StExch:* **vive réaction du sterling sur le marché des changes,** sharp sterling reaction on the (foreign) exchange market.

réajustement, *n.m.* = **rajustement.**

réajuster, *v.tr.* = **rajuster.**

réalisable, *a.* **1. projet réalisable,** workable plan **2.** *Fin:* realizable; available; **actif réalisable/valeurs réalisables,** current/liquid assets.

réalisation, *n.f.* **1.** realization (of plan, project, etc.) **2.** (*a*) *Fin: Bank:* realization; concluding (of bargain, transaction, etc.); **réalisation d'actions,** selling out of shares (*b*) **réalisation d'un bénéfice,** making a profit (*c*) **réalisation du stock,** clearance sale.

réaliser, *v.tr.* (*a*) to make/to realize (a profit) (*b*) *Fin: etc:* **réaliser des valeurs,** to realize/to sell out shares (*c*) **réaliser des économies,** to economize.

réapprovisionnement, *n.m.* restocking/reordering; **quantité économique de réapprovisionnement,** economic order quantity.

réapprovisionner, 1. *v.tr.* to reorder; to restock (shop) (**en,** with) **2.** *v.pr.* **se réapprovisionner,** to stock up again.

réassortiment, *n.m.* (*a*) restocking (*b*) new stock.

réassortir, *v.tr.* to restock (shop).

réassurance, *n.f.* reinsurance/reassurance; **police de réassurance,** reinsurance policy.

réassurer, *v.tr.* to reinsure/to reassure.

réassureur, *n.m.* reinsurer.

rebaisser, *v.i.* **les prix ont remonté puis rebaissé,** prices have gone up and then fallen again.

rebut, *n.m.* (*a*) waste/scrap; *Ind:* **pièces de rebut/les rebuts,** rejects (*b*) *Post:* **service des rebuts,** dead letter office.

recensement, *n.m. Adm:* (*i*) census (*ii*) inventory.

récépissé, *n.m.* (acknowledgement of) receipt; *Bank: Fin:* **récépissé de dépôt,** deposit receipt; **récépissé de douane,** customs receipt; **récépissé d'entrepôt,** warehouse receipt; **récépissé postal,** postal receipt; *Fin:* **récépissé de souscription à des actions,** application receipt for shares.

réception, *n.f.* **1.** (*a*) receipt (of letter, order, etc.); **accusé de réception,** acknowledgement (of receipt); **accuser réception de qch.,** to acknowledge receipt of sth.; **avis de réception,** advice of delivery (*b*) receipt/reception/taking delivery (of goods); **à la/dès réception de (votre envoi),** on receipt of (the goods forwarded); **payer à la réception,** to pay on receipt (*c*) *Ind:* acceptance/taking over (of equipment, machines, etc., from manufacturer) **2.** (*à l'hôtel, etc.*) reception (desk); **chef de la réception,** chief receptionist.

réceptionnaire, 1. *a.* receiving (agent, clerk) **2.** *n.m. & f.* (*a*) receiver/consignee (of goods, shipment) (*b*) chief receptionist (in hotel).

réceptionner, *v.tr.* to check and sign for (goods on delivery); to take delivery of (parcel, etc.).

réceptionniste, *n.m. & f.* receptionist.

récession, *n.f. PolEc:* recession.

recette, *n.f.* **1.** receipts/returns/takings; **dépenses et recettes,** expenses and receipts; outgoings and incomings; *Fin:*

expenditure and income; **recette nette,** net takings; **la recette d'une semaine,** a week's takings/the weekly takings **2.** (*a*) collection (of bills, by bank messenger, etc.); **faire la recette (des traites, etc.),** to collect money due/owing **3.** tax (collector's) office/(inland) revenue office.

receveur, -euse, *n.* **1.** receiver (of sth.); addressee (of telegram, etc.) **2.** *Adm:* **receveur des contributions,** tax collector/inland revenue officer; **receveur des douanes,** collector of customs; **receveur des Finances,** district collector (of taxes); **receveur des postes,** postmaster.

recevoir, *v.tr.* (*a*) to receive (letter, etc.); **bien reçu,** duly received; *Corr:* **nous avons bien reçu votre lettre,** thank you for your letter/we acknowledge receipt of your letter/we are in receipt of your letter; **recevez, Monsieur, l'assurance de mes sentiments distingués,** yours faithfully (*b*) *Book-k:* **effets à recevoir,** bills receivable; **intérêts à recevoir,** interest receivable/to come; accrued interest.

rechange¹, *n.m.* replacement; **matériel de rechange,** duplicate/standby equipment; **pièce de rechange,** spare part; *pl.* **rechanges,** spares/spare parts.

rechange², *n.m.* *Fin: Bank:* re-exchange (of a bill); redraft.

recherche, *n.f.* research; **recherche appliquée,** applied/industrial research; **recherche des besoins des consommateurs,** consumer research; **recherche commerciale,** market research; **recherche opérationnelle,** operational research; **recherche de produits,** product research; **recherche scientifique,** scientific research; **service/centre de recherche,** research department/centre.

recherché, *a.* **article (très) recherché,** article in great demand; **article peu recherché,** article in limited demand.

réclamation, *n.f.* **1.** complaint; **bureau/service des réclamations,** complaints office/department; **toutes réclamations**

devront être adressées à . . ., all complaints to be addressed to . . .; **faire/déposer une réclamation,** to make a complaint/to lodge a complaint/to complain **2.** claim; **chef du service des réclamations,** claims manager; **formulaire de réclamation,** claim form; *Jur:* **réclamation en dommages-intérêts,** claim for damages; **réclamation d'indemnité,** claim for compensation; **déposer/faire une réclamation,** to make/to put in a claim.

réclame, *n.f.* (*a*) advertising; **en réclame,** on offer; **article (en) réclame,** (*i*) special offer (*ii*) loss leader; **vente réclame,** bargain sale; **faire de la réclame,** to advertise (*b*) advertisement; **réclame lumineuse,** illuminated/neon sign.

réclamer, 1. *v.i.* to complain/to lodge a complaint (**auprès de qn,** with s.o.) **2.** *v.tr.* (*a*) to claim (sth.); **réclamer des dommages-intérêts,** to claim damages; **dividende non réclamé,** unclaimed dividend (*b*) to claim (sth.) back; **réclamer son argent,** to ask for one's money back.

recommandataire, *n.m.* (*pour une lettre de change*) referee in case of need.

recommandation, *n.f.* **1.** recommendation/recommending (of s.o., of hotel, etc.); **(lettre de) recommandation,** (*i*) letter of introduction (*ii*) (letter of) reference/testimonial **2.** *Post:* registration (of letter, parcel).

recommandé, *a.* **1.** approved/recommended (hotel, product, etc.) **2.** *Post:* (*a*) registered (letter, parcel) (*b*) *n.m.* **envoi en recommandé/F:** **un recommandé,** registered letter/parcel.

recommander, *v.tr.* **1.** to recommend; **recommander un hôtel,** to recommend a hotel **2.** *Post:* to register (letter, parcel).

reconduction, *n.f. Jur:* renewal (of hiring agreement, of lease, etc.)

reconduire, *v.tr.* to renew (hiring agreement, lease, etc.).

reconnaissance, *n.f.* (*a*) acknowledgement (of debt, etc.) (*b*) **reconnaissance de dettes,** note of hand/IOU. (*c*) *Mkt:* **test de reconnaissance,** recognition test.

reconversion, *n.f.* (*a*) **reconversion technique,** adaptation to new (economic) techniques (*b*) redeployment (of workers).

reconstitution, *n.f.* reconstitution/reconstruction (of a company, etc.).

record, *n.m.* record (production); maximum/peak (output, etc.); **année record,** peak year; **chiffre record,** record figure.

recouponnement, *n.m. Fin:* renewal of coupons (of share certificate).

recouponner, *v.tr. Fin:* to renew the coupons (of share certificate).

recours, *n.m.* (*a*) recourse/resort; **recours à l'arbitrage,** appeal to arbitration; *Jur:* **se réserver le recours,** to reserve the right of recourse (*b*) **recours contre des tiers,** recourse against third parties; *Ins:* **s'assurer contre le recours des tiers,** to insure against a third-party claim.

recouvrable, *a.* recoverable (money, etc.); collectable (debt).

recouvrement, *n.m.* **1.** recovery/collection (of bill, debts, tax, etc.); **faire un recouvrement,** to recover/to collect a debt **2.** *pl.* outstanding debts; **recouvrements restant à faire en fin d'exercice,** (book) debts outstanding at the end of the financial year.

recouvrer, *v.tr.* to recover/to collect (debts, taxes, etc.); **créances à recouvrer,** outstanding debts (due to us).

recrutement, *n.m.* recruitment/recruiting (of personnel); **conseil en recrutement,** recruitment consultant.

recruter, *v.tr.* to recruit (staff).

rectificatif, 1. *a.* rectifying; *Book-k:* **écriture rectificative,** correcting entry; **facture rectificative,** amended invoice **2.** *n.m. Adm:* corrigendum (to circular, to payroll, etc.).

rectification, *n.f.* rectification; amendment/correction (of document, etc.); adjustment/correction (of account, prices, etc.).

rectifier, *v.tr.* to rectify; to amend/to correct (document, etc.); to adjust/to correct (account, prices).

reçu, *n.m.* (*a*) receipt; voucher; **reçu certifié,** accountable receipt (*b*) **au reçu de votre lettre,** on receipt of your letter.

recul, *n.m.* setback (in business); **les ventes ont subi un recul,** sales have suffered a setback.

récupérabilité, *n.f. Ind:* salvage value.

récupérable, *a. Ind:* **heures récupérables,** time to be made up.

récupération, *n.f.* (*a*) *Jur:* recuperation/recovery (of debt); **récupération du capital investi,** payback; **délai de récupération,** payback period (*b*) *Ind:* recovery (of waste products, etc.); salvage (*c*) recoupment (of losses).

récupérer, *v.tr.* **1.** to recover (debt, etc.) **2.** (*a*) *Ind: etc:* to recover (waste products); to salvage (*b*) to give a new job to/to find alternative employment for s.o. **3.** (*a*) to recoup (a loss) (*b*) to make up (lost time, etc.); **la journée chômée sera récupérée,** the lost day will be made up.

recyclage, *n.m. Ind: etc:* (*a*) retraining (of staff); **suivre un stage de recyclage,** to take a refresher course/to retrain (*b*) recycling/re-processing.

recycler, *v.tr.* **1.** (*a*) to retrain (staff) (*b*) to re-process/to recycle (paper, etc.) **2.** *v.pr.* **se recycler,** to retrain/to take a refresher course.

rédacteur, -trice, *n. Journ: Publ:* (*i*) editor (*ii*) sub-editor; **rédacteur en chef,**

chief editor; **rédacteur publicitaire,** copywriter.

rédaction, *n.f. Journ: Publ:* (*a*) editorial staff (*b*) editorial offices.

reddition, *n.f.* rendering (of account); *Jur:* **action en reddition de compte,** action for an account.

redevable, *a.* **être redevable de qch. à qn,** to be accountable to s.o. for sth.; **redevable de l'impôt,** liable for tax.

redevance, *n.f.* (*a*) dues (*b*) rent; **redevance emphytéotique,** ground rent (*c*) royalty; **redevances d'auteur,** (author's) royalties; **redevance pétrolière,** oil royalty (*d*) fee; (*d'une télévision, etc.*) licence fee; **redevance téléphonique,** rental charge.

redevoir, *v.tr.* to owe a balance of (a sum on an account, etc.); **il me redoit cent francs,** he still owes me a hundred francs; **somme redue,** balance due/amount owed.

rédiger, *v.tr.* to draw up/to draft/to write (out) (agreement, invoice, letter, etc.); **rédiger la correspondance d'une maison,** to conduct the correspondence of a firm.

redressement, *n.m.* (*a*) **redressement économique,** economic recovery (*b*) adjustment (of account); *Book-k:* **écriture de redressement,** correcting entry; **redressement fiscal/redressement d'impôt,** back tax/tax adjustment.

redresser, 1. *v.tr.* to rectify (mistake); to adjust (account) **2.** *v.pr.* (*une action, l'économie*) **se redresser,** to recover/to rally.

redû, *n.m.* balance due/amount owed.

réductible, *a.* reducible (amount, etc.).

réduction, *n.f.* (*a*) reduction (of amount, taxation, etc.); restriction/cutting back (of expenditure); *Fin:* **réduction du capital social,** reduction of share capital; *Ind:* **réduction d'heures de travail,** cut in working hours; **réduction de personnel,** staff cutback; **réduction de salaires,** wage/salary cuts (*b*) **réduction (de prix),** (price) reduction; **réductions sur la quantité,** concessions for quantity; bulk discount/discount on bulk (purchases, orders); **faire une réduction,** to make a reduction/to give a discount/to give a rebate.

réduire, *v.tr.* to reduce; *Fin:* **réduire le capital,** to write down the capital; **réduire ses dépenses,** to reduce/to curtail/to cut back on one's expenses; **réduire le prix d'un article,** to reduce/to lower/to bring down/to cut the price of an article.

réduit, *a.* reduced (price, etc.); *Ins:* **assurance à prime réduite,** low-premium insurance; **billet à prix réduit/à tarif réduit,** cheap ticket/cheap rate/cheap fare; concessionary fare; **débouchés réduits,** restricted market.

réel, *a.* real; **coût réel,** real cost; **revenu réel,** real income; **salaire nominal et salaire réel,** nominal wage rate and net earnings; **valeur réelle,** real value/actual value; *Cmptr:* **temps réel,** real time.

réembaucher, *v.tr.* to re-employ (s.o.).

réemploi, *n.m.* re-employment.

réemployer, *v.tr.* = **remployer.**

rééquilibrer, *v.tr.* **rééquilibrer le budget,** to rebalance the budget.

rééquipement, *n.m.* re-equipment.

rééquiper, *v.tr.* to re-equip.

réescompte, *n.m. Fin:* rediscount/new discount.

réescompter, *v.tr. Fin:* to rediscount; to discount (bill) again.

réévaluation, *n.f.* revaluation (of currency); new assessment/appraisal (of property, etc.); *Fin:* **réévaluation de l'actif (d'une entreprise),** revaluation of the assets (of a company).

réévaluer, *v.tr.* to revalue/to appraise again; to estimate again.

réexpédier, *v.tr.* (*a*) to forward/to send

on/to redirect (a letter, a parcel, etc.) (*b*) to return (to sender).

réexpédition, *n.f.* (*a*) forwarding/sending on/redirecting (of a letter, a parcel, etc.) (*b*) returning (of letter, etc.).

réexportation, *n.f.* (*a*) re-exportation/re-exporting (*b*) re-export.

réexporter, *v.tr.* to re-export.

réfaction, *n.f.* allowance/reduction/rebate/drawback (on goods not up to sample, for loss or damage in transport, etc.).

référence, *n.f.* (*a*) reference; **indemnité fixée par référence au traitement,** compensation fixed according to salary (*b*) *Corr: etc:* reference (on letter, document, etc.); **N/Réf(érence),** our ref(erence); **V/Réf(érence),** your ref(erence); **adresser sous référence RL3U/référence à rappeler RL3U,** when replying please quote ref(erence) RL3U (*c*) sample; pattern (*d*) *pl.* **références,** (employee's) reference/testimonial; **avoir de bonnes références,** to have good references.

référencer, *v.tr.* to classify (sample, pattern) in a sample book.

reflation, *n.f.* reflation (of the economy).

réforme, *n.f.* reform; **réforme monétaire,** monetary reform.

refus, *n.m.* refusal; **refus d'acceptation,** refusal to accept/non-acceptance; **refus de paiement,** refusal to pay/non payment; **il a été condamné à une amende pour refus de paiement,** he was fined for non-payment.

refuser, *v.tr.* to refuse/to decline (sth.); to turn down (offer); **refuser de payer une traite,** to dishonour a bill.

régie, *n.f.* **1.** (*a*) administration (of property, undertaking, etc.); **en régie,** (*i*) in the hands of trustees (*ii*) under State control; **mise sous régie d'une industrie,** bringing of an industry under State control; **régie du dépôt légal,** copyright department (*b*) State-owned company; public corporation; **la régie Renault,** the Renault Company; **la régie des tabacs** = State Tobacco Corporation **2. régie des impôts indirects,** excise (administration); **la Régie,** Customs and Excise.

régime, *n.m.* system/regime/regulations; **régime douanier,** customs regulations; **régime préférentiel,** customs preference/preferential rates of duty/preferential customs duties; **régime de retraite,** pension plan/scheme.

régir, *v.tr.* to govern/to rule; **les prix sont régis par . . .,** prices are governed by . . .; **les conditions régissant votre compte,** the terms for the conduct of your account.

registre, *n.m.* **1.** register/record; **Registre de commerce** = trade register; Register of Companies; **registre de comptabilité,** account book; ledger; **registre d'un hôtel,** hotel register; **registre des salaires,** payroll; **inscrire/rapporter un article sur un registre,** to enter/to post an item in a register **2.** *Cmptr:* register/counter.

règle, *n.f.* (*a*) rule; **règles d'exploitation,** operating rules; **règles de sécurité,** safety regulations (*b*) **passeport en règle,** valid passport/passport in order; **reçu en règle,** formal receipt/receipt in due form; **tenir sa comptabilité en règle,** to keep one's accounts in order.

règlement, *n.m.* **1.** (*a*) settlement (of account, etc.); payment (of bill, debt, etc.); **en règlement de . . .,** in settlement of . . .; **mode/lieu de règlement,** method/place of payment; **pour règlement de tout compte,** in full settlement; **règlement en espèces,** cash payment/cash settlement; **faire un règlement par chèque,** to pay by cheque (*b*) *StExch:* **jour du règlement,** settlement day/ account day (*c*) *Jur:* **règlement à l'amiable,** out-of-court settlement; **règlement judiciaire,** legal settlement; **être en règlement judiciaire,** to be in the hands of the receiver; **se mettre**

en règlement judiciaire, to go into receivership; to call in the receiver **2.** *pl.* regulations; **les règlements de la douane,** (the) customs regulations; **règlements intérieurs,** internal regulations (of a company, etc.).

réglementation, *n.f.* **1.** regulating/regulation; **réglementation des changes,** exchange control; **réglementation des prix,** price control **2.** regulations; rules; **la réglementation du travail,** labour regulations/regulations concerning the employment of labour.

réglementer, *v.tr.* to regulate; to make rules for (sth.); **industries réglementées,** regulated industries; **réglementer les prix,** to control prices.

régler, 1. *v.tr.* to settle (account, deal, debt, etc.); to pay (bill, invoice, supplier, shopkeeper, etc.) **2.** *v.i.* **régler par chèque,** to pay by cheque.

régression, *n.f.* decline (in business, etc.); drop (in sales, etc.); **analyse de régression,** regression analysis.

regrèvement, *n.m.* tax increase.

régularisation, *n.f.* regularizing; *Fin:* equalization (of dividends); **comptes de régularisation d'actif et de passif,** expenses paid in advance/income received in advance; *EEC:* **fonds de régularisation,** equalization fund.

régulariser, *v.tr.* to regularize; to put (document, etc.) into proper order; to equalize (dividends, etc.).

régulateur, *a.* regulating (force, mechanism); *PolEc:* **stocks régulateurs,** buffer stocks.

régulation, *n.f.* regulation/control; *Ind:* **régulation d'un procédé,** process control.

réimportation, *n.f.* (*a*) reimportation/reimporting (*b*) reimport.

réimporter, *v.tr.* to reimport.

réinscription, *n.f.* re-entry/re-entering; re-registering/re-registration.

réinscrire, *v.tr.* to re-enter; to re-register.

réintégration, *n.f.* reinstatement (of civil servant, etc.).

réintégrer, *v.tr.* to reintegrate; to reinstate; **réintégrer qn (dans ses fonctions),** to reinstate s.o.; **réintégrer des employés,** to take employees on again; to re-engage/to reinstate employees.

réinvestir, *v.tr.* to reinvest; **réinvestir les bénéfices,** to plough back the profits; **bénéfices réinvestis,** ploughback.

rejet, *n.m.* rejection (of proposal, etc.); *Jur:* setting aside (of claim, etc.); disallowance (of expenses).

rejeter, *v.tr.* to reject/to refuse (sth.); **rejeter une dépense,** to disallow an expense; **rejeter une offre,** to reject/to turn down an offer.

relais, *n.m.* (*a*) *Ind:* relay/shift; **travail par relais,** shift work (*b*) *Fin:* **crédit de relais,** bridging facility/loan (*c*) **relais d'autoroute,** motorway services.

relance, *n.f.* (*a*) boost; **relance économique,** economic revival (*b*) *Ind: etc:* follow-up (of work in hand); following up (of customer) (*c*) *Mkt:* follow-up; **lettre de relance,** reminder (letter)/follow-up letter.

relancer, *v.tr.* to revive/to boost; **relancer l'économie,** to revive the economy.

relation, *n.f.* (*a*) relation; connection; **relations d'affaires,** business relations; **être en relations d'affaires avec qn,** to have business relations with s.o./to deal with s.o. (*b*) **relations industrielles/syndicales,** industrial relations; **relations ouvrières/du travail,** labour relations (*c*) **relations publiques,** public relations; **chef du service des relations avec le public,** public relations officer.

relevé, *n.m.* abstract/summary/statement; **relevé de caisse,** cash statement; **relevé de compte(s),** statement (of account); **relevé de compte bancaire,** bank statement; **relevé des dépenses,** statement of expenditure; **relevé des dettes actives et passives,** statement of assets and liabilities; **relevé de fin de mois,** end-of-the-month statement; **relevé remis,** account tendered.

relèvement, *n.m.* (*a*) recovery/revival (of business) (*b*) increase (in wages); raising (of tariff, tax, etc.); **relèvement du taux officiel de l'escompte,** raising of/rise in the minimum lending rate.

relever, 1. *v.tr.* (*a*) **relever (les salaires, les prix),** to raise/to increase (wages, prices); **relever le cours du franc,** to raise the value of the franc (*b*) **relever un compte,** to make out a statement of account (*c*) to revive (an industry) (*d*) **relever le compteur (du gaz),** to read the (gas) meter **2.** *v.pr.* **se relever,** to pick up; **les affaires se relèvent,** business is looking up; **les cours se relèvent,** prices are recovering.

reliquat, *n.m.* (*a*) remainder; unexpended balance (*b*) **reliquat d'un compte,** balance of an account.

remballage, *n.m.* (*a*) repacking (of goods) (*b*) new packaging.

remballer, *v.tr.* to repack; to pack (goods) (up) again.

remboursable, *a.* (re)payable/reimbursable/refundable; redeemable (annuity, etc.); **remboursable sur une période de 25 ans,** repayable over (a period of) 25 years.

remboursement, *n.m.* reimbursement/repayment/refund; redeeming/redemption (of annuity, etc.); reduction (of debt); **délai de remboursement,** payback period; **livraison contre remboursement,** cash on delivery/*also NAm:* collect on delivery/COD; *Cust:* **remboursement des droits de douane,** drawback; **remboursement d'un effet,** retirement of a bill; **remboursement d'un emprunt,** repayment of a loan.

rembourser, *v.tr.* (*a*) to repay/to refund (expenses, etc.); to redeem/to pay off (annuity, bond); **rembourser un effet,** to retire a bill; **rembourser un emprunt,** to

pay off/to repay a loan (*b*) **rembourser qn,** to reimburse/to repay s.o.; **on m'a remboursé,** I got my money back.

réméré, *n.m. Jur:* **faculté de réméré,** option of repurchase; **vente à réméré,** sale subject to right (of vendor) to repurchase/sale with option of repurchase.

remettant, -ante, *n. Bank:* person who pays money/cheque into a current account.

remettre, 1. *v.tr.* **remettre un chèque à l'encaissement,** to cash a cheque; **remettre sa démission,** to hand in one's notice **2.** to remit (debt) **3.** to postpone/to adjourn (meeting); to postpone/to put off (decision); to put off/to put back (appointment, delivery date, etc.).

remise, *n.f.* **1.** delivery (of letter, parcel, etc.); remitting (of money); **payable contre remise du coupon,** payable on presentation of the coupon **2.** (*a*) remission (of debt, tax, etc.); **faire remise d'une dette,** to remit/to cancel a debt (*b*) adjournment/postponement (of meeting, etc.) **3.** (*a*) remittance; **faire une remise (de fonds) à qn,** to send s.o. a remittance/to remit a sum to s.o. (*b*) commission (paid to agent) (*c*) discount/rebate; **remise d'usage,** trade discount; **remise sur la quantité,** discount on bulk purchases/orders; **remise de 10%,** discount of 10%/10% off; **faire/consentir/accorder une remise sur un article,** to allow a discount/to make a reduction on an article.

remisier, *n.m. StExch:* intermediate broker/half-commission man.

remonter, 1. *v.i.* **les valeurs pétrolières ont remonté,** oil shares have gone up again **2.** *v.tr.* **remonter un magasin,** to restock a shop.

remplacement, *n.m.* (*a*) replacement; **dactylo qui fait des remplacements,** temporary (typist)/temp (*b*) **coût de remplacement,** replacement cost; **débou-**

chés/**marchés de remplacement,** replacement/alternative markets; **produit de remplacement,** substitute product; *Ins:* **valeur de remplacement,** replacement value (of lost or damaged property).

remplacer, *v.tr.* to replace; to take the place of (s.o., sth.); to deputize for (s.o.).

remplir, *v.tr.* (*a*) to fill in/*NAm:* to fill out/to complete (a form, a questionnaire, etc.) (*b*) to comply with/to fulfil (a condition, an obligation).

remploi, *n.m. Jur:* reinvestment (of the proceeds of a sale of property, etc.).

remployer, *v.tr.* (*a*) to employ (s.o.) again (*b*) to make use of (sth.) again (*c*) *Jur:* to reinvest/to re-use (money, funds).

rémunérateur, *a.* remunerative (work, price, investment, etc.); lucrative/profitable; **peu rémunérateur,** not very profitable/unprofitable; **ce travail n'est pas rémunérateur,** this work doesn't pay.

rémunération, *n.f.* (*a*) remuneration/payment (**de,** of); **en rémunération de vos services,** as payment for your services; in consideration of your services; **rémunération du capital,** return on capital (*b*) salary; **rémunération de départ,** starting salary.

rémunérer, *v.tr.* (*a*) to pay for (services) (*b*) to pay (wages); **employés rémunérés,** paid/salaried employees.

rencaissement, *n.m.* receiving back (of money).

rencaisser, *v.tr.* to receive back (money); to have (money) refunded.

renchérir, 1. *v.tr.* to make (sth.) dearer/to raise the price of (sth.) **2.** *v.i.* (*a*) (*des produits, de la main d'œuvre*) to get dearer; to increase/to rise in price; **tout renchérit,** everything is going up (in price) (*b*) **renchérir sur qn,** to outbid s.o.

renchérissement, *n.m.* rise/advance/increase in price.

rendement, *n.m.* (*a*) *Fin: etc:* yield/return/profit (on transaction); **actions à gros rendement,** shares that bear/yield high interest; **rendement brut,** gross return; **rendement des investissements,** return on investment; **taux de rendement,** rate of return; *PolEc:* **loi du rendement non-proportionnel,** law of diminishing returns (*b*) output (of worker); output/production (of factory, works, etc.); yield; throughput/*NAm:* thruput (of computer); **augmentation de rendement,** rise in production; **diminution de rendement,** fall in output; **rendement d'ensemble/global/total,** aggregate output; **rendement à l'heure/rendement horaire,** output per hour; **rendement individuel,** output per person; **rendement journalier moyen,** average daily output; **rendement maximum,** maximum output; **rendement minimum,** minimum output; **travailler à plein rendement,** to work to full capacity (*c*) (*d'une machine*) efficiency; **rendement économique,** commercial efficiency; **rendement effectif,** performance rating; **rendement global,** overall efficiency.

rendez-vous, *n.m.inv.* appointment; **rendez-vous d'affaires,** business appointment; **fixer un rendez-vous/donner rendez-vous (à qn),** to make/to fix an appointment (with s.o.).

rendre, *v.tr.* **1.** (*a*) to give back/to return; **rendre de l'argent,** to repay/to pay back money; **rendre un dépôt,** to return a deposit; **rendre la monnaie d'un billet de cent francs,** to give change for a hundred franc note; **rendre un article,** to return an article (to a shop) (*b*) (*de la terre*) to yield; (*des impôts, etc.*) to produce/to yield (so much); **placement qui rend 10%,** investment that brings in 10% **2.** to convey/to deliver; **rendre des marchandises à destination,** to deliver goods (to their destination); **rendu à domicile,** delivered to your door; **rendu franco à bord,** (delivered) free on board/f.o.b.; **prix rendu,** delivery price.

rendu, *n.m.* returned article; return; **faire**

un rendu, (*i*) to return an article (*ii*) to exchange an article.

renflouer, *v.tr.* **renflouer une entreprise,** to set a business on its feet again/to refloat a business; *F:* **renflouer qn,** to keep s.o. afloat (financially).

renouvelable, *a.* renewable.

renouveler, *v.tr.* (*a*) **renouveler son personnel,** to renew one's staff (*b*) **renouveler une commande,** to repeat an order; **commandes renouvelées,** repeat orders; **renouveler son passeport,** to renew one's passport (*c*) *Fin: Jur:* to renew/to extend (bill, lease, contract); **renouveler un crédit,** to extend a credit.

renouvellement, *n.m.* (*a*) restocking/reordering (of goods); *Ind:* replacement (of equipment) (*b*) (*d'un bail, d'un contrat*) renewing/renewal; *Ins:* **prime de renouvellement,** renewal premium; **renouvellement d'un crédit,** extension of a credit.

renseignement, *n.m.* (*a*) (piece of) information; *Tp: etc:* **renseignements,** enquiries/inquiries; **bureau de renseignements,** enquiry office/information (bureau); **demande de renseignements,** enquiry/request for information; **tous les renseignements utiles,** all the necessary information; **pour de plus amples renseignements, s'adresser à/écrire à . . .,** for further information/further particulars, apply to . . .; **donner des renseignements (sur qch.),** to give information/particulars (on, about sth.); **prendre des renseignements sur qch.,** to make enquiries about sth.; **je vous envoie à titre de renseignement . . .,** I am sending you for your information/by way of information . . . (*b*) **renseignements (techniques),** data; **renseignements statistiques,** statistical data.

renseigner, 1. *v.tr.* to inform/to give (some) information **2.** *v.pr.* **se renseigner sur qch.,** to get information about sth./to make enquiries about sth.; to enquire/to ask/to find out about sth.

rentabilisation, *n.f.* making sth. pay/making sth. show a profit.

rentabiliser, *v.tr.* to make (sth.) pay/to make (sth.) show a profit; **l'industrie exige de gros investissements longs à rentabiliser,** industry requires heavy investment which takes a long time to show a profit.

rentabilité, *n.f.* profitability/profit-earning capacity; pay-off (of project); **limite de rentabilité,** limit of profitability; **rentabilité des capitaux investis/rentabilité d'un investissement,** return on capital invested/return on an investment; **rentabilité des ventes,** return on sales; **seuil de rentabilité,** break-even point; *PolEc:* **taux de rentabilité,** rate of return/rate of profitability.

rentable, *a.* profitable; profit-earning; paying (proposition); **ce n'est pas rentable,** it isn't profitable/it doesn't pay; **affaire/marché rentable,** profitable deal; **loyer rentable/peu rentable,** economic/uneconomic rent; **société qui devient rentable,** company that moves into profit.

rente, *n.f.* **1. rente foncière,** ground rent **2.** *usu. pl.* (unearned) income; **avoir cent mille francs de rente(s),** to have a private income of a hundred thousand francs; **vivre de ses rentes,** to live on one's private income **3.** annuity/pension/allowance; **rente à paiement différé,** deferred annuity; **rente à terme,** terminable annuity; **rente viagère,** life annuity/life interest **4. rente(s) sur l'État,** Government stock(s)/funds/bonds; **rentes, actions et obligations** = stock and shares; **rentes amortissables,** redeemable stock/loans; **rentes perpétuelles,** perpetual stock/loans.

rentier, -ière, *n.* (*a*) *Fin:* stockholder/shareholder (*esp.* holder of Government stocks) (*b*) **rentier viager,** annuitant (*c*) person of independent means/who lives on unearned income; *PolEc:* rentier.

renting, *n.m.* rental/hire/renting (of machines, material, etc.); plant hire.

rentrée, *n.f.* (*a*) taking in/receipt/encashment (of money); income; revenue (of taxes); **faire des rentrées d'argent,** to get money in; **opérer une rentrée,** to collect a sum of money (*b*) *pl. Bank:* bills and cheques paid in.

rentrer, *v.i.* **rentrer dans ses frais,** (*i*) to get one's money back (*ii*) to get one's expenses (paid).

renvoi, *n.m.* **1.** sending back/return(ing) (of goods, letter, etc.) **2.** dismissal; **menace de renvoi,** threat of dismissal; **renvoi d'un employé,** sacking/dismissal of an employee **3.** putting off/postponement; adjournment **4.** (*a*) referring/reference (of a project, etc. to higher, competent authority) (*b*) **numéro de renvoi,** reference number.

renvoyer, *v.tr.* **1.** to return/to send back (goods, letter, etc.) **2.** to dismiss/to sack (employee) **3.** to put off/to postpone/to adjourn (a matter, decision, meeting) **4.** **renvoyer qch. à qn,** to refer sth. to s.o.

réorganisation, *n.f.* reorganization/reorganizing; redeployment (of staff, resources, etc.).

réorganiser, *v.tr.* to reorganize; to redeploy (staff, resources, etc.).

réouverture, *n.f.* reopening (of a market, a store, etc.); resumption (of negotiations, trading).

réparation, *n.f.* **1.** repair/repairing (of equipment, etc.); **réparation d'entretien,** maintenance; **être en réparation,** to be under repair **2.** *Jur:* **réparation civile,** compensation; **réparation légale,** legal redress.

réparer, *v.tr.* **réparer ses pertes,** to make good one's losses.

répartir, *v.tr.* (*a*) to distribute/to divide/to share out (**entre,** among); **répartir un dividende,** to distribute a dividend; **versements répartis sur plusieurs années,** payments spread over several years (*b*) to apportion/to assess; *Fin:* **répartir des actions,** to allot/to allocate shares; **répartir des impôts,** to assess taxes.

répartiteur, *n.m. Adm:* (**commissaire**) **répartiteur,** tax assessor.

répartition, *n.f.* (*a*) distribution (of wealth, etc.) (*b*) dividing up/sharing out/ allocation (of expenses, responsibilities, work, etc.); distribution/appropriation (of profit); distribution/allotment (of functions); *Jur:* **répartition entre créanciers,** distribution among creditors (*c*) (*distribution pro rata*) apportionment/ allocation (of expenses, losses, rights, liabilities, etc.); assessment (of taxes); *Book-k:* appointment (of costs, expenses, to different accounts); **répartition proportionnelle des pertes entre les commanditaires,** (pro rata) apportionment of losses among the sleeping partners (*d*) *Fin:* allotment (of shares); (**lettre d'**)**avis de répartition,** letter of allotment; **libération/versement intégral à la répartition,** payment in full on allotment (*e*) dividend/distribution; **première répartition,** first dividend/distribution; **nouvelle répartition,** second dividend/distribution; **dernière répartition,** final dividend/ distribution.

répercuter, *v.tr.* **la taxe sera répercutée/ se répercutera sur les consommateurs,** the tax will be passed on to the consumers.

répertoire, *n.m.* index/table/list/catalogue; **répertoire d'adresses,** (*i*) directory (*ii*) address book; **répertoire maritime,** shipping directory.

répertorier, *v.tr.* (*a*) to index (file, etc.) (*b*) to index (item); to enter (item) in an index.

répéter, *v.tr.* to repeat (an order, etc.).

répétition, *n.f. Jur:* claiming back; **répétition d'indu,** recovery of payment made in error.

repli, *n.m. StExch:* fall/drop (in the value of shares).

replier(se), *v.pr. Fin: StExch:* to fall back.

répondant, *n.m.* (*a*) *Jur:* surety/security/guarantor/warrantor (*b*) referee/reference.

répondre, *v.i.* **1.** to reply/to answer; **répondre à une lettre,** to reply to a letter/to answer a letter **2.** *Fin:* **répondre à une prime,** to declare an option.

réponse, *n.f.* **1.** answer/reply; **en réponse à votre lettre du 20 ct,** in reply to your letter/further to your letter of the 20th inst.; *Post:* **réponse payée,** reply paid **2.** *Fin:* **réponse des primes,** declaration of options.

report, *n.m.* **1.** *Book-k:* (*au bas d'une page*) (balance) carried forward; (*au haut d'une page*) (balance) brought forward; **report des exercices antérieurs,** amount brought in; **report à nouveau,** amount carried forward/balance to next account (*c*) posting (of journal entries to the ledger accounts) **2.** *StExch:* (*a*) contango(ing)/continuation; **titres en report,** stock taken in/stock carried over; **prendre des actions en report,** to take in stock (*b*) **(taux de) report,** contango (rate)/continuation rate.

reporté, *n.m. StExch:* giver (of stock); payer (of contango).

reporter, *v.tr.* **1.** *Book-k:* (*a*) to carry forward; to bring forward; to carry over (balance, total) (*b*) to enter up/to transfer (sum to ledger accounts); **solde à reporter,** balance (to be) carried forward **2.** *StExch:* to continue/to contango; to carry over; **(faire) reporter des titres,** to take in/to carry stock; **(faire) reporter un emprunteur,** to take in stock for a borrower; **se faire reporter,** to be carried over/to lend stock.

reporteur, *n.m. StExch:* taker (of stock); receiver (of contango).

repos, *n.m. Fin:* **valeurs de tout repos,** safe investments; gilt-edged securities; blue chips.

reprendre, 1. *v.tr.* (*a*) to take back; **reprendre un employé,** to take back/to re-engage an employee; **reprendre des invendus,** to take back unsold goods; **nous reprendrons les invendus,** the goods are on sale or return (*b*) **reprendre le travail,** to resume work **2.** *v.i.* **les affaires reprennent,** business is improving/is looking up.

représentant, -ante, *n.* **représentant (de commerce),** (*i*) agent (*ii*) (sales) representative/(sales) rep/(commercial) traveller; **représentant exclusif,** sole agent; **représentant à cartes multiples/représentant multicarte,** representative/rep for several firms; general agent.

représentation, *n.f.* **1.** agency; **représentation exclusive d'une maison,** sole agency for a firm; **avoir la représentation exclusive de . . .,** to be sole agents for . . . **2. frais de représentation,** entertainment allowance.

représenter, *v.tr.* (*a*) to represent/to act for (s.o.); **nous représentons la maison X et Cie,** we represent/we are agents for Messrs X & Co. (*b*) to correspond to/to account for; **ceci représente 10% du budget,** this accounts for 10% of the budget.

repris, *a.* **emballage non repris,** non-returnable packing.

reprise, *n.f.* **1.** (*a*) **marchandises en dépôt avec reprise des invendus,** goods on sale or return; **reprise (locative)** = fixtures and fittings (f & f); **reprise d'une voiture,** trade-in (allowance) on a car (*b*) (car, etc., taken in) part exchange **2.** (*a*) resumption (of negotiations, etc.); **reprise de travail,** return to work (after absence); **reprise des travaux,** resumption of work (*b*) **reprise des affaires,** recovery/revival of business; **reprise des cours,** recovery of prices; **mouvement de reprise,** upward movement.

reproduction, *n.f.* reproduction/reproducing; duplicating (of documents, etc.).

reproduire, *v.tr.* (*a*) to reproduce/to duplicate/to copy (document, etc.) (*b*) **modèle reproduit en grande série,** mass-produced model.

rescindable, *a.* that may be annulled/cancelled.

rescinder, *v.tr. Jur:* to rescind/to annul/to cancel/to void (contract).

rescision, *n.f. Jur:* rescission/annulment/voiding (of contract).

réseau, *n.m.* network; **réseau de distribution,** distribution network; **réseau téléphonique,** telephone system/network; **réseau de vente/réseau commercial,** sales network.

réservation, *n.f.* (hotel, plane, etc.) reservation; **bureau de réservation,** booking office.

réserve, *n.f.* **1.** reservation; *Jur:* **sous toutes réserves,** without prejudice; **sous réserve de . . .,** subject to . . . **2.** (*a*) reserve (of provisions, etc.); stock/reserve; **avoir qch. en réserve,** to have sth. in stock/in reserve (*b*) storeroom/warehouse (*c*) *Fin:* reserve (of money, etc.); **réserves bancaires,** bank reserves; **réserve pour créances douteuses,** bad debts reserve; **réserve latente/occulte,** hidden/secret reserve; **réserve légale,** legal reserve; **réserve liquide,** liquid assets; **réserve de prévoyance,** contingency reserve; **réserve statutaire,** statutory reserve/reserve provided for by the articles; **réserve visible,** visible reserve; **fonds de réserve,** reserve fund; **incorporation de réserves,** capitalization of reserves; **mettre de l'argent en réserve,** to put/to set money aside; **puiser dans les réserves,** to draw on the reserves.

réserver, *v.tr.* (*a*) to reserve/to book (hotel room, table in restaurant, etc.); to set aside (goods for a customer, etc.); *Trans:* **réserver une place,** to reserve a seat; *Publ:* **tous droits (de reproduction) réservés,** all rights reserved (*b*) to set aside/to earmark (money for a purpose).

résiliable, *a.* that may be annulled/cancelled.

résiliation, *n.f.* cancelling/cancellation/annulling/annulment/termination (of contract, lease, etc.).

résilier, *v.tr.* to annul/to cancel/to terminate/to void (contract, etc.).

résistance, *n.f. Mkt:* **résistance des consommateurs,** consumer resistance.

résoluble, *a.* annullable/cancellable/terminable/voidable (contract).

résolution, *n.f.* **1.** termination/cancellation/annulment (of contract, owing to breach, etc.); cancelling (of sale); **action en résolution,** action for rescission of contract **2. prendre/adopter une résolution,** to pass/to carry/to adopt a resolution.

résolutoire, *a. Jur:* **clause résolutoire,** avoidance clause; **condition résolutoire,** condition of avoidance (in contract).

résorber, *v.tr.* to absorb (deficit, surplus); to reduce/to bring down (inflation, unemployment).

résoudre, *v.tr.* to annul/to cancel/to void/to terminate/to rescind (contract, etc.).

respecter, *v.tr.* to respect; **respecter une clause dans un contrat,** to respect/to comply with a clause in a contract.

responsabilité, *n.f.* responsibility/liability (**de,** for); *Jur:* **responsabilité civile,** civil liability; **responsabilité de l'employeur,** employer's liability; **responsabilité hiérarchique,** linear responsibility; **société à responsabilité limitée (SARL),** limited (liability) company.

responsable, 1. *a.* responsible/accountable/answerable; **être responsable de qch.,** to be responsible for sth.; **être responsable du dommage,** to be liable for the damage **2.** *n.* (*a*) person responsible (**de,** for) (*b*) person in charge/person authorized to take decisions; **responsable de budget,** account manager/executive;

responsable des relations publiques, public relations officer (PRO); **responsable syndical,** union official.

resserrement, *n.m.* (*a*) *PolEc:* **resserrement du crédit,** credit squeeze (*b*) tightness/scarceness (of money).

ressort, *n.m.* (*i*) jurisdiction (*ii*) competence (of a court, etc.).

ressources, *n.f.pl.* (*a*) resources/means; **affectation/allocation des ressources,** resource allocation; **ressources du budget,** budgetary resources; **ressources de l'État,** government resources; **ressources financières,** financial resources; **ressources personnelles,** private means (*b*) **ressources naturelles (d'un pays),** natural resources (of a country).

restaurant, *n.m.* restaurant; **restaurant libre-service,** self-service restaurant.

restaurateur, -trice, *n.* restaurant owner/restaurateur; caterer.

restauration, *n.f.* catering; **travailler dans la restauration,** to work in catering/ in the restaurant business.

reste, *n.m.* rest/remainder; **payer le reste par versements,** to pay the balance in instalments/*NAm:* installments.

restituable, *a.* returnable/repayable.

restitution, *n.f.* restitution/refund; *Cust:* **restitution des droits d'entrée,** drawback; *EEC:* **restitution à l'exportation,** export restitution/refund; *Jur:* **restitution d'indu,** return of payment made in error.

restreignant, *a.* restricting (clause, etc.).

restreindre, *v.tr.* to restrict/to curb; **restreindre les dépenses,** to restrict/to cut down expenses; **restreindre la production,** to restrict/to cut back production.

restreint, *a.* restricted/limited; **crédit restreint,** restricted credit; **moyens restreints,** limited means.

restrictif, *a.* restrictive (practice); limita-

tive (clause in contract); **endossement restrictif,** restrictive endorsement.

restriction, *n.f.* restriction; limitation (of authority); **restriction de concurrence,** trade restraint; **restriction du crédit,** credit restrictions; **restrictions sur les importations,** import restrictions; **restrictions salariales,** wage restraint; *Fin:* **restrictions de transfert,** transfer restrictions.

restructuration, *n.f.* restructuring; reorganizing the structure (of an industry, etc.).

restructurer, *v.tr.* to restructure; to reorganize the structure (of an industry, etc.).

résultat, *n.m.* result/outcome; **résultat de l'exercice,** statement of income/income statement; **résultat d'exploitation,** trading/*NAm:* operating result; **résultat brut,** gross result; **résultat net,** net result.

rétablir, *v.tr.* to re-establish/to restore; **rétablir un budget déficitaire,** to balance an adverse budget.

retard, *n.m.* delay; **commandes en retard,** back orders; **compte en retard,** account outstanding/overdue; **paiement en retard,** late payment; payment overdue; **être en retard pour payer son loyer,** to let one's rent fall into arrears; **retard de livraison,** delay in delivery.

retarder, *v.tr.* to delay; **retarder un paiement,** to defer payment.

retenir, *v.tr.* (*a*) **retenir une somme sur le salaire de qn,** to keep back/to deduct a sum from s.o.'s salary (*b*) to make a reservation; *Trans:* to reserve/to book (a seat, a place); **retenir (une chambre d'hôtel, une table au restaurant),** to reserve/to book (a hotel room, a table in a restaurant) (*c*) **retenir une offre,** to accept an offer.

rétention, *n.f. Jur:* reservation; retaining (of pledge); **droit de rétention de marchandises,** lien on goods.

retenue, *n.f.* (*sur un salaire*) deduction/ stoppage; **faire une retenue de 5% sur les**

salaires, to stop/to deduct/to withold 5% from the wages; *Adm:* **retenue à la source** = pay as you earn/P.A.Y.E./ *NAm:* pay as you go; (*sur les investissements*); witholding tax; **traitement soumis à retenue,** salary from which a sum is witheld (for pension, etc.).

retirer, 1. *v.tr.* (*a*) **retirer de l'argent de la banque,** to withdraw/to take out (some) money from the bank; **retirer des marchandises de la douane,** to take goods out of bond; to clear goods (*b*) **retirer un profit de qch.,** to derive/to get a profit from sth. (*c*) **retirer un effet,** to retire/to withdraw/to take up a bill **2.** *v.pr.* **se retirer,** to retire; **se retirer des affaires,** to retire from business.

retombées, *n.f.pl.* spin-off effects; **la grève aura des retombées sur les prix,** the strike will have repercussions on prices.

retour, *n.m.* **1.** (*a*) *Trans:* (**billet de) retour/ (billet d')aller et retour,** return (ticket)/ *NAm:* round-trip ticket; **prix/tarif d'aller et retour,** return fare; **voyage (d')aller et retour,** return journey; **prendre un aller et retour,** to buy a return ticket (*b*) *Post:* **par retour (du courrier),** by return (of post); **retour à l'envoyeur,** return to sender (*c*) **cargaison/chargement/fret de retour,** return cargo/freight; homeward cargo/freight; **retour en charge,** loaded return; **retour à vide,** empty return **2.** (*a*) return (of goods, of dishonoured bill, etc.); **marchandises de retour/***F:* **retours,** returned goods/returns; **vendu avec faculté de retour,** on sale or return (*b*) dishonoured bill/bill returned dishonoured **3. en retour d'une somme de 50 francs,** in consideration of a sum of 50 francs.

retourner, *v.tr. Fin:* **retourner un effet impayé,** to return a bill dishonoured; *Post:* **retourner (une lettre, un paquet),** to return/to send back (a letter, a parcel); **marchandises retournées,** returned goods/returns; **prière de nous retourner l'accusé de réception ci-joint, revêtu de votre signature,** please sign and return the enclosed acknowledgment.

retrait, *n.m.* (*a*) withdrawal (of order, bill, licence, etc.); **retrait d'une somme d'argent de la banque,** withdrawal of a sum of money from the bank; **retrait d'espèces,** cash withdrawal; **retrait de fonds,** withdrawal of capital; *Fin:* **lettre de retrait,** letter of withdrawal (*b*) **retrait d'un ordre de grève,** calling off a strike; **retrait de monnaies,** withdrawal of currency from circulation/calling in of currency.

retraite[1]**,** *n.f.* (*a*) retirement (from work); **âge de la retraite,** age of retirement/ retiring age; **retraite anticipée,** early retirement; **retraite sur demande,** optional retirement; **retraite d'office/ forcée,** compulsory/mandatory retirement; **être à la retraite,** to be retired; **mettre qn à la retraite,** to pension s.o. off/to retire s.o.; **prendre sa retraite,** to retire (on a pension) (*b*) **caisse de retraite,** pension fund/superannuation fund; **pension de retraite/retraite de vieillesse,** retirement pension; **régime de retraite,** pension plan/scheme; **régime de retraites complémentaires/retraite des cadres** = graduated pension scheme; **régime de retraite financé par les cotisations patronales et ouvrières,** contributory pension plan; **régime de retraite proportionnelle,** earnings-related pension plan.

retraite[2]**,** *n.f.* re-draft/re-exchange; renewed bill; **faire retraite sur qn,** to redraw on s.o.

retraité, -ée, 1. *a.* retired; pensioned **2.** *n.* (*i*) (old age) pensioner (*ii*) retired person.

retraiter, *v.tr.* to pension off/to retire/to superannuate (s.o.).

rétribuer, *v.tr.* to pay/to remunerate (employee, service); **fonctionnaires bien rétribués,** highly-paid officials; **travail mal rétribué,** badly-paid work.

rétribution, *n.f.* remuneration/reward/ payment (for services rendered); salary.

rétroactif, *a.* retrospective/retroactive; **augmentation avec effet rétroactif au 1ᵉʳ septembre,** increase backdated to September 1st.

rétrocéder, *v.tr.* (*i*) *Jur:* to reassign/to retrocede (*ii*) to sell sth. one has just bought (*usu.* for profit); **rétrocéder une commission,** to return a commission.

rétroprojecteur, *n.m.* overhead projector (OHP).

rétroprojection, *n.f.* overhead projection.

réunion, *n.f.* meeting; **réunion du conseil d'administration,** board meeting.

réunir, 1. *v.tr.* **réunir une somme,** to collect/to get together a sum of money; **réunir un comité,** to convene a committee/to call a committee meeting **2.** *v.pr.* **se réunir,** (*a*) (*pers.*) to meet/to convene (*b*) (*sociétés*) to amalgamate.

revalorisation, *n.f. Fin:* revalorization/ revaluation (of the franc, etc.).

revaloriser, *v.tr.* **1.** *Fin:* to revalorize/to revalue (currency) **2.** to stabilize (prices) at a higher level.

revenant-bon, *n.m.* surplus; bonus; unexpected/casual profit.

revendable, *a.* resaleable.

revendeur, -euse, *n.* (*a*) retailer; middleman; **escompte/rabais pour revendeurs,** trade discount (*b*) secondhand dealer.

revendicatif, *a. Ind:* **action revendicative/mouvement revendicatif,** industrial action; **lutte revendicative,** (wage) claims dispute.

revendication, *n.f.* (*a*) *Ind:* claim/ demand (**sur,** on); **revendications de salaires,** wage claims; **les revendications syndicales,** union demands/claims (*b*) **revendication de brevet,** patent claim; **mener une action en revendication,** to lodge a claim against s.o.

revendiquer, *v.tr.* to claim/to demand (higher wages, etc.).

revendre, *v.tr.* to resell; *Fin:* **revendre des titres,** to sell out stock.

revenir, *v.i.* to cost; **sa maison lui revient à 75 000 francs,** his house cost him 75 000 francs; **cet article vous reviendra à 100 francs,** this article will cost you 100 francs.

revente, *n.f.* **1.** resale; reselling **2.** selling out; *esp. Fin:* **revente de titres,** selling out of stock.

revenu, *n.m.* (*a*) income (of person, of company); revenue (of the State); incomings; **déclaration de revenus,** income-tax return; **impôt sur le revenu,** income tax; **revenu annuel,** annual income; **revenu imposable,** taxable income; *PolEc:* **revenu national brut,** gross national income; **revenu résiduel,** residual income; **revenu du travail,** earned income; **valeur à revenu fixe,** fixed-interest security; **valeurs à revenu variable,** variable-interest securities; equities; **dépenser plus que son revenu,** to live beyond one's income (*b*) yield (of investment, etc.).

reversement, *n.m. Fin:* transfer (of funds from one account to another).

reverser, *v.tr.* to transfer/to carry (an item from one account to another).

réversion, *n.f. Jur:* reversion (à, to); **rente viagère avec réversion,** reversionary annuity.

revient, *n.m.* **(prix de) revient,** cost price/manufacturing cost/prime cost; **établissement des prix de revient,** costing; **établir le prix de revient d'un article,** to cost an article.

révisable, *a.* **prix révisable,** (*i*) price subject to alteration/to modification (*ii*) price open to offer; **prix non révisable,** firm/fixed price.

réviser, *v.tr.* to revise/to check; **réviser un compte,** to (re)check an account.

révision, *n.f.* (*a*) revision/check (of list, account, etc.) (*b*) **clause de révision,** revision clause; **révision des prix,** price review.

révoquer, *v.tr.* **1.** to revoke/to countermand (an order, etc.); **révoquer un ordre de grève,** to call off a strike **2.** to dismiss; to remove (an official) from office.

revue, *n.f.* journal; review; magazine.

riche, 1. *a.* rich/wealthy **2.** *n.* wealthy person.

richesse, *n.f.* wealth; **la richesse publique,** public wealth; **richesse en matières premières,** resources in raw materials; *Mkt:* **la richesse vive,** household/consumer purchasing power.

risque, *n.m.* risk; **capital risque,** risk capital/venture capital; **risques de change,** exchange risks; **risques du métier,** occupational hazards (*b*) *Ins:* **assurance tous risques,** comprehensive/all-risks insurance; **risque assuré,** risk subscribed/taken up; **risque collectif,** collective risk; **risque d'incendie,** fire risk; **risque locatif,** tenant's third-party risk; **risque de mer/maritime,** sea risks; **risque de perte,** loss risk; **risque du recours du tiers,** third-party risk; **risque de vol,** theft risk; **couvrir un risque,** to cover a risk; **souscrire un risque,** to underwrite a risk.

ristourne, *n.f.* (*a*) *Adm: Fin:* refund; return (of amount overpaid) (*b*) rebate/discount (*c*) *MIns:* cancelling/cancellation/annulment (of policy) (*d*) *Ins:* repayment (to party insured) (*e*) commission (*f*) dividend (from co-operative society).

ristourner, *v.tr.* (*a*) to refund/to return (amount overpaid) (*b*) *MIns:* to cancel/to annul (policy) (*c*) to give (s.o.) a discount (on sth.) (*d*) to pay a dividend (to a member of a co-operative society).

ritournelle, *n.f. Mkt:* **ritournelle publicitaire,** jingle.

rompu, *n.m.* fraction (of share, stock).

rond, *a.* round; **en chiffres ronds,** in round figures; **compte rond,** round sum/even figure.

rotation, *n.f.* turnover (of stocks); **rotation des capitaux,** turnover of capital; **rotation du personnel,** turnover of staff; **rotation des stocks,** stock turnround/*NAm:* inventory turn; **le délai de rotation (des stocks) est de quatre mois,** stocks are turned round every four months; **taux de rotation,** rate of turnover.

roulage, *n.m.* carriage/haulage (of goods); **entreprise de roulage,** (firm of) hauliers/haulage contractors/*NAm:* trucking business; **frais de roulage,** (cost of) carriage/haulage.

roulant, *a.* **fonds roulants,** circulating/floating capital.

roulement, *n.m.* **roulement de fonds,** circulation of capital; **fonds de roulement,** working/operating capital.

rouler, *v.i.* **l'argent roule,** money circulates freely.

routage, *n.m.* (*i*) bundling up (*ii*) dispatching/routing (of newspapers, circulars, letters, etc.).

route, *n.f.* (*a*) road; **transport par route,** road transport (*b*) route; **feuille de route,** waybill; **frais de route,** travelling expenses; **marchandises avariées en cours de route,** goods damaged in transit; **route commerciale,** commercial route/trade route.

routier, 1. *a.* **transports routiers,** road transport/road haulage; **gare routière,** road haulage depot **2.** *n.m.* long-distance lorry driver/*NAm:* truck driver/teamster; **(restaurant de) routier(s)** = transport café.

routine, *n.f.* **travail de routine,** routine work.

rouvrir, *v.tr.* to reopen (an account, etc.).

rubrique, *n.f.* heading; column (in newspaper, etc.); **mentionné sous cette rubrique,** mentioned under this heading.

rupture, *n.f.* (*a*) breaking (off); **rupture de contrat,** breach of contract; **rupture des négociations,** breaking off of negotiations; **en rupture de stock,** out of stock (*b*) **rupture de charge,** transhipment of cargo.

rythme, *n.m.* **rythme de livraisons,** delivery rate.

S

sac, *n.m.* bag; **sac publicitaire**, carrier bag/plastic bag (displaying name of shop, etc.).

sacquer, *v.tr. F:* = **saquer**.

saisie, *n.f. Jur:* seizure (of goods, etc.); distraint; embargo; **saisie d'une hypothèque**, foreclosure/foreclosing of a mortgage.

saisir, *v.tr.* 1. *Jur:* to distrain upon (goods); to lay an embargo on sth.; **saisir une hypothèque**, to foreclose a mortgage 2. **saisir un tribunal d'une affaire**, to refer a matter to a court.

saison, *n.f.* (*a*) season; **la saison creuse/la morte-saison**, the off season/the slack season; **la haute saison**, (*i*) the busy season/the high season/the peak season (*ii*) the tourist season/the holiday season; **la saison touristique**, the tourist season (*b*) **hors saison**, off season; low season; **pendant la saison**, in season; **prix hors saison**, low-season price: **vente de fin de saison**, end-of-season sale.

saisonnier, -ière, 1. *a.* seasonal (employment, etc.); **chômage saisonnier**, seasonal unemployment; **demande saisonnière**, seasonal demand; **fluctuations saisonnières**, seasonal fluctuations; (**taux**) **corrigé des variations saisonnières**, seasonally corrected/adjusted rate 2. *n.* seasonal worker.

salaire, *n.m.* salary/wage(s)/pay; **augmentation/hausse de salaire**, salary increase/pay rise; **blocage des salaires**, wage freeze; **écart des salaires**, wage differentials; **feuille/bulletin de salaire**, pay slip; **revendications de salaire**, wage claims; **salaire de base**, basic salary/wage; **salaire brut**, gross pay; **salaire de départ**, starting salary; **salaire élevé**, high salary/wage; **salaire fixe**, fixed salary/wage; **salaire hebdomadaire**, weekly pay/wage; **salaire horaire**, hourly wage/pay; **salaire indexé**, index-linked salary/wage; **salaire indirect**, fringe benefits; **salaire mensuel**, monthly salary; **salaire minimum**, minimum wage; **salaire minimum interprofessionnel de croissance (SMIC)**, index-linked guaranteed minimum wage; **salaire net**, net salary/pay; **salaire nominal**, nominal wages; **salaire réel**, real wage; **structure des salaires**, salary/wage structure; **taux des salaires**, wage rate; **toucher son salaire**, to draw one's wages/one's salary.

salarial, *a.* **dépenses salariales**, wage expenditure; **fourchette salariale**, wage bracket; **hiérarchie salariale**, (*i*) wage differentials (*ii*) salary structure; **masse salariale/charges salariales**, (total) wages bill; **négociations salariales**, wage negotiations/pay talks; **politique salariale**, pay policy; **revenus salariaux**, earned income.

salariat, *n.m.* wage-earning population/the wage earners; salaried staff; **le salariat et le patronat**, employees and employers.

salarié, -ée, 1. *a.* (*a*) salaried/wage-earning; **employé salarié**, wage earner; **personnel salarié**, salaried staff (*b*) paid (work) 2. *n.* wage earner; salaried worker; **les salariés et les patrons**, employees and employers.

salarier, *v.tr.* to pay a wage/a salary to (s.o.)

salle, *n.f.* **salle d'accueil/salle de réception de la clientèle,** reception room; **salle d'attente,** waiting room; **salle de conférence,** conference room; **salle d'exposition,** showroom; **salle des ventes,** auction room/sale(s)room.

salon, *n.m.* trade exhibition/show; **le Salon des Arts ménagers** = the Ideal Home Exhibition; **le Salon de l'automobile** = the Motor Show.

sans-travail, *n.m. & f.inv.* unemployed person; **les sans-travail,** the unemployed.

sapiteur, *n.m. MIns:* valuer (of cargo).

saquer, *v.tr. F:* to sack/to fire (s.o.)/to give (s.o.) the sack; **être saqué,** to get the sack/to be fired.

satisfaction, *n.f.* satisfaction; **satisfaction du consommateur,** consumer satisfaction; **satisfaction dans le travail,** job satisfaction.

saturation, *n.f. Mkt:* **campagne de saturation,** all-out (publicity) campaign; **point de saturation,** saturation point; **saturation du marché,** market saturation.

saturé, *a.* **le marché est saturé,** the market is saturated/has reached saturation point.

saturer, *v.tr.* to saturate (the market).

saupoudrage, *n.m. Adm: Fin:* allocation (of small amounts of credit to a large number of recipients).

sauter, *v.i.* (*d'une banque*) to crash; (*d'une entreprise*) to go bankrupt/to fail.

sauvegarde, *n.f.* **clause de sauvegarde,** saving clause; *PolEc:* **droits de sauvegarde,** safeguarding duties.

sauvegarder, *v.tr.* to safeguard/to protect; **sauvegarder les intérêts des actionnaires,** to protect the interests of shareholders.

savoir-faire, *n.m.* know-how.

schéma, *n.m.* (*a*) summary; outline (*b*) diagram; (sketch) plan; schema.

schématique, *a.* diagrammatic; schematic; **organisation schématique,** skeleton organization; **plan schématique,** outline (plan).

schématiser, *v.tr.* (*a*) to schematize; to simplify (*b*) to make a diagram (of sth.).

science, *n.f.* science; **homme/femme de science,** scientist; **science de la gestion,** management science.

scientifique, **1.** *a.* scientific; **chercheur scientifique,** researcher/research worker; **gestion scientifique,** scientific management; **recherche scientifique,** scientific research **2.** *n.* scientist.

scinder, *v.tr.* to divide/to split (up); *Fin:* **stocks scindés,** split stocks.

scission, *n.f.* **scission d'actif,** splitting/divestment of assets.

script, *n.m. Fin:* scrip/subscription receipt.

scriptural, *a. Bank:* **monnaie scripturale,** bank credit; financial credit; bank deposits.

séance, *n.f.* (*a*) sitting/session/meeting; *StExch:* **séance de clôture,** closing session (*b*) **séance (de travail, d'entraînement),** (working, training) period/session.

second, *a.* second; taking second place/inferior; **article de second choix,** inferior/second-grade article; *Trans:* **billet de seconde,** second-class ticket; **second associé,** junior partner.

secours, *n.m.* help/relief/assistance; **caisse de secours,** relief fund; **société de secours mutuels,** benefit society/friendly society; **secours d'argent,** financial assistance.

secrétaire, *n.m. & f.* secretary; *Adm:* **secrétaire de direction,** director's/executive secretary; private secretary; **secrétaire particulier/particulière,** private secretary; personal assistant (PA).

secteur, *n.m.* (*a*) **graphique à secteurs,** pie diagram/chart (*b*) area/district; **secteur de ventes,** sales area/trading area (*c*)

PolEc: etc: **secteurs d'activité,** field/
sphere of activity; area of specialisation;
secteur de croissance, growth area; **secteur économique,** economic sector; **secteur industriel,** industrial sector; **secteur
primaire,** primary industry; **le secteur
privé,** the private sector; **le secteur public,** the public sector; **secteur secondaire,** secondary industry; **secteur tertiaire,** tertiary/service industries.

section, *n.f. Adm:* section/branch (of department, etc.).

sécurité, *n.f.* (*a*) security; reliability (of
statistics, machinery, etc.); **sécurité de
l'emploi,** security of employment/job
security; *Adm:* **Sécurité sociale** = Social
Security (*b*) safety; **service de sécurité,**
security staff/guards (in firm, etc.); *Ind:
etc:* **co-efficient de sécurité,** security factor; **marge de sécurité,** security margin;
règles de sécurité, safety regulations.

seing, *n.m. Jur:* **acte sous seing privé,**
simple contract; private agreement; contract in writing signed but not sealed or
witnessed.

self, *n.m. F:* = **self-service.**

self-service, *n.m.* (**magasin, restaurant**)
self-service, self-service (store, restaurant).

semaine, *n.f.* (*a*) week; working week;
week's work; **semaine de quarante
heures,** forty-hour week; **faire la semaine
anglaise,** to work a five-day week; to have
Saturday off (*b*) week's pay/weekly
wages.

semainier, *n.m.* (*a*) (workman's) time
sheet (*b*) desk diary (with sections for
each day of the week).

semestre, *n.m.* (*a*) half-year; six-month
period; **bénéfices du premier semestre,**
first-half profits (*b*) six months' pay/
income (*c*) six months' rent.

semestriel, *a.* half-yearly/six-monthly.

semestriellement, *adv.* semi-annually/
half-yearly/every six months; **réviser
les salaires semestriellement,** to review
salaries every six months.

semi-fini, *a.* semi-finished (product).

semi-ouvré, *a.* semi-finished (product).

semi-produit, *n.m.* semi-finished product.

sensible, *a.* marked/noticeable/appre-
ciable/considerable; **amélioration sensible,** marked improvement; **une hausse
sensible des prix,** a big price rise/a
marked rise in prices; **subir des pertes
sensibles,** to incur heavy/extensive/large
losses.

séquestre, *n.m. Jur:* sequestration; **ordonnance de mise sous séquestre,** receiving order (in bankruptcy proceedings).

séquestrer, *v.tr. Jur:* to sequester/to
sequestrate (property).

série, *n.f.* (*a*) set (of documents, tools,
etc.); range (of colours, sizes, samples,
etc.); **numéro de série,** serial number;
PolEc: **série économique,** economic
batch; **valeurs remboursables par séries,**
securities redeemable in series (*b*)
range/line (of goods, products, etc.);
article hors série, custom-made/custom-
built article; **chaîne de fabrication en
série,** production line; **fabrication/
production en (grande) série,** mass
production; **fabrication/production en
(petite) série,** small-scale manufacture/
batch production; **fins de série,** end of
lines; oddments/remnants; *Adm: etc:*
prix de série, contract prices; **série de
produits,** product line; **fabriquer en série,**
to mass-produce.

sérieux, *a.* (*a*) genuine; **acheteur sérieux,**
genuine purchaser; **offre sérieuse,** bona
fide offer (*b*) reliable; **client sérieux,**
good customer; **maison sérieuse,** reliable
firm.

serpent, *n.m. EEC:* **le serpent (moné-taire),** the (monetary) snake.

service, *n.m.* **1.** (*a*) **porte/entrée de service,** tradesmen's entrance (*b*) service/tip (in hotel, restaurant, etc.); **service compris,** service included/inclusive of service; **service non compris,** service not included/exclusive of service (*c*) **libre service,** self-service (in restaurant, shop, etc.) (*d*) **service à la clientèle,** customer service; **service permanent/de 24 heures,** 24-hour service; **service après-vente,** after-sales service; back-up service (*e*) *Adm:* **nécessités de service,** service requirements; **service contractuel,** contract service **2.** duty; **service de jour,** day duty; **service de nuit,** night duty; **tableau de service,** duty roster/chart; **être de service,** to be on duty **3.** *PolEc:* **biens et services,** goods and services; **prestation de service,** service fee/charge; **société de services,** service bureau; company providing a service/providing services; **assurer le service d'un emprunt,** to service a loan **4.** (*a*) *Adm:* branch/department/service; **services publics,** public services; **services administratifs,** administrative department; **service central,** headquarters; **service des douanes,** customs service; **service postal/des postes,** postal service(s); **service des transports,** transport (services); **chef de service,** head of department (*b*) department (of firm); **service des achats,** purchasing department; *Ind:* **service commercial,** commercial department; **service de (la) comptabilité,** accounts department; **service des expéditions,** forwarding/dispatch department; **service de groupage,** joint-cargo service; **service de livraison,** delivery service; **service du personnel,** personnel department; **service de presse,** (*i*) press department (*ii*) *Publ:* (distribution of) press copies/review copies; **service de publicité,** advertising/publicity department; **service technique,** technical branch/engineering department; **service des ventes,** sales department **5.** (*machine, etc.*) **en service,** in use/in operation; **hors de service,** out of order/not in use; **mettre en service,** to put/to bring into service (*b*) *Trans:* service (of train, aircraft, ferry, etc.); **service de marchandises,** goods/freight service; **service régulier,** regular service; **service de voyageurs/de passagers,** passenger service.

servir, *v.tr.* (*a*) **servir un client,** to serve/to attend to a customer; **(est-ce qu') on vous sert?** are you being attended to? are you being served? (*b*) to supply (s.o. with goods) (*c*) **servir une rente à qn,** to pay an annuity to s.o.

seuil, *n.m.* threshold; *EEC:* **prix du seuil,** threshold price; **seuil de réapprovisionnement,** reorder point; **seuil de rentabilité/point de seuil,** break-even point.

shopping, *n.m.* shopping; **faire du shopping,** to go shopping.

siège, *n.m.* **siège social,** head office/registered office (of a company).

signataire, *n.m. & f.* signatory (of a contract, etc.).

signature, *n.f.* **1.** signature; **apposer/mettre sa signature au bas d'un document,** to put one's name to a document; **avoir la signature,** to be authorized to sign (on behalf of firm, etc.); **la lettre portait la signature du président,** the letter was signed by the chairman; **fondé de signature,** signing officer; **pour signature,** for signature; **signature collective,** joint signature; **la signature sociale,** the signature of the firm **2.** *Publ:* signature (of a book).

signer, *v.tr.* to sign (a document, a letter, etc.); **signer un chèque,** to sign a cheque; **signer un contrat,** to become party to an agreement/to sign an agreement; **signer à la réception (de marchandises),** to sign (for goods) on reception; **signez au bas de la page,** sign at the bottom of the page.

situation, *n.f.* **1.** (*a*) *Fin:* state/condition; **quelle est la situation (financière) de la maison?** what is the (financial) position of the firm? **situation de trésorerie,** cash(flow) situation; **situation en banque**

d'un client, customer's financial position/
situation; (*d'une société*) **situation nette,**
net assets/net worth (*b*) report/return; *Fin:*
statement of finances; **situation de caisse,**
cash statement **2.** position/job; **avoir une
belle situation,** to have a good job; **chercher une situation,** to look for a job;
perdre sa situation, to lose one's job.

slogan, *n.m. Mkt:* slogan.

social, *a.* (*a*) **année sociale,** company's
trading year; **capital social,** share capital;
exercice social, accounting period/tax
year; **nom social/raison sociale,** name/
style of a company; **siège social,** head
office (*b*) **assurances sociales** = National
Insurance; **Sécurité Sociale** = Social Security.

sociétaire, *n.m. &f.* (*a*) (full) member (of
corporate body); **carte de sociétaire,**
membership card (*b*) **sociétaire d'une
société anonyme,** shareholder/stock-
holder.

société, *n.f.* company/firm; partnership;
société anonyme (SA), (*i*) public company
(*ii*) limited (liability) company; **société
anonyme par actions,** joint-stock com-
pany/*NAm:* incorporated company;
société en commandite (simple), limited
partnership; **société en commandite par
actions,** limited partnership (with
shares); **société coopérative,** cooperative society; **société de crédit mutuel,**
friendly society; **société d'économie
mixte,** semi-public company; **société
d'exploitation,** development company;
société d'exploitation en commun,
joint-venture company; **société de famille,** family company; **société de finances,** finance company; **société immobilière,** real-estate company; property
developer; **société d'investissement,** investment company; **société d'investissement à capital fixe,** closed-end investment company; **société d'investissement
à capital variable (SICAV),** open-end
investment company; unit trust/*NAm:*
mutual fund; **société mère,** parent company; **société mutuelle,** friendly society;
société de navigation, shipping company;

société en nom collectif, general partnership; **société de personnes,** partnership;
société de placement, investment trust;
**société de portefeuille/société de con-
trôle/société holding,** holding company; **société à responsabilité limitée
(SARL)** = limited liability company;
société de services, company providing a
service/providing services; **société de
transport,** transport company; **acte/
contrat de société,** deed of partnership/
articles of association; **impôt sur les
sociétés,** corporation tax; **loi sur les
sociétés,** company law; **constituer une
société,** to form/to incorporate a company; **liquider une société,** to liquidate/to
wind up a company.

solde, *n.m.* **1.** balance; **solde en caisse,**
balance in hand; **solde de compte,** balance
of account; **solde créditeur,** credit balance; **solde débiteur,** (*i*) debit balance
(*ii*) *Bank:* overdraft; **solde de dividende,**
final dividend; **solde d'une facture,** balance outstanding on an invoice; **solde de
fin de mois,** end-of-month balance; **solde
d'ouverture,** opening balance; **solde
reporté,** balance brought forward; **solde à
reporter,** balance (to be) carried forward; **pour solde,** in settlement; **pour
solde de tout compte,** in full settlement; to
close the account; **régler le solde,** to pay
the balance **2.** (*a*) surplus stock/remnant;
pl. **soldes,** sale goods/bargains (*b*) sale;
reduction; **livres en solde,** remainders;
solde (de marchandises), (clearance)
sale; **solde de fermeture,** closing-down
sale; **soldes de fin de saison,** end-of-
season sales; **solde après inventaire,**
stocktaking sale; **c'est l'époque des soldes,** the sales are on; **prix de solde,** sale
price; **en solde,** to clear; reduced; in the
sale; **mettre du stock en solde,** to put stock
in the sale; **je l'ai eu en solde,** I got it in the
sales; I got it cheap.

solder, *v.tr.* **1.** (*a*) to balance (an account);
**les comptes se soldent par un bénéfice net
de . . . ,** the accounts show a net profit of
. . . (*b*) to settle/to discharge/to pay (off)
(an account) **2.** to sell off (goods at sale
price, at bargain price); to clear (surplus,

unsold stock); *Publ:* to remainder (books).

soldeur, -euse, *n.* person who buys and deals in (*i*) end-of-season fashions (*ii*) seconds/imperfect goods (*iii*) clearance lines; *Publ.* remainders merchant.

solidaire, *a. Jur:* joint and several; jointly liable/responsible; **obligation solidaire,** obligation binding on all parties; **responsabilité (conjointe et) solidaire,** joint and several liability.

solidairement, *adv.* jointly; *Jur:* **conjointement et solidairement,** jointly and severally.

solidarité, *n.f.* **1.** *Jur:* joint and several obligation or liability; joint responsibility **2.** solidarity; **faire grève/débrayer par solidarité,** to come out in sympathy.

solide, *a.* sound; **garantie solide,** reliable/ trustworthy guarantee; **solide au point de vue financier,** financially sound.

solvabilité, *n.f.* solvency; **réputation/ degré de solvabilité,** credit rating.

solvable, *a.* (financially) solvent.

somme, *n.f.* (*a*) sum; total; amount; **la somme s'élève à 100 francs,** the total amounts to 100 francs; **somme totale,** total sum; **somme versée,** amount paid (*b*) **somme (d'argent),** sum of money; **payer une grosse/forte somme,** to pay a large sum/amount of money; **dépenser une somme de 500 francs,** to spend (a sum of) 500 francs.

sommier, *n.m. Adm: etc:* register.

sondage, *n.m.* **contrôle par sondage,** random check; **enquête par sondage,** sample survey; **méthode de sondage,** sampling method; **sondage aléatoire,** random sampling; **sondage d'opinion,** opinion poll.

sonder, *v.tr.* **sonder l'opinion,** to make a survey of public opinion; to carry out/to conduct an opinion poll.

sortant, *a.* **administrateurs sortants (d'une société),** retiring directors (of a company); **membres (de comité) sortants,**

retiring/outgoing members (of a committee).

sortie, *n.f.* (*a*) going out; coming out; departure; exit; *Adm:* issue of stores; **bon/facture de sortie,** issue voucher; *Nau:* **fret de sortie,** outward freight; **inventaire de sortie,** outgoing inventory; *Cust:* **sortie d'entrepôt,** clearing/taking out of bond (*b*) retirement (of official) (*c*) *Mkt:* launching (of new product); publication/ coming out (of book, magazine, etc.) (*d*) export (of goods); **connaissement de sortie,** outward bill of lading; **déclaration de sortie,** entry outwards; **droit de sortie,** export duty; **prohibition des sorties,** export ban/prohibition of exports; **tarif de sortie,** export tariff (*e*) **sorties de fonds,** expenses/outgoings; **ce mois-ci il y a eu plus de sorties que de rentrées,** this month's outgoings have exceeded payments received; we are down on this month's trading/takings (*f*) *Fin:* **goldpoint de sortie,** export goldpoint; **sortie de devises/de capitaux,** currency/capital outflow; flight of currency/ of capital; **les sorties d'or,** gold withdrawals.

souche, *n.f.* counterfoil/stub (of cheque, ticket, etc.); tally (of receipt); **carnet/ livret à souche(s),** counterfoil book.

souffrance, *n.f.* **en souffrance,** pending/in abeyance; *Fin:* **coupons en souffrance,** outstanding/unpaid coupons; **effets en souffrance,** bills held over; bills overdue/ outstanding; **marchandises en souffrance,** goods held up in transit/awaiting delivery; **travail en souffrance,** work waiting to be dealt with/work pending.

soulte, *n.f. Jur:* balance/cash adjustment (to equalize shares, etc.).

soumettre, *v.tr.* to submit/to refer/to put (question, etc.); **soumettre un document à la signature,** to submit/to present a document for signature.

soumis, *a.* subject (à, to); **dividendes soumis à l'impôt sur le revenu,** dividends liable to income tax; **soumis au (droit de) timbre,** subject to stamp duty; **soumis aux**

fluctuations du marché, subject to fluctuations in the market.

soumission, *n.f.* (*a*) tender (for public works, etc.); **par (voie de) soumission,** by tender; **soumission cachetée,** sealed tender; **faire une soumission pour un travail,** to tender for a piece of work (*b*) *Cust:* **soumission (en douane),** bond; **soumission cautionnée,** secured bond.

soumissionnaire, *n.m.* party tendering for work on contract; tenderer.

soumissionner, *v.tr.* to tender for/to put in a tender for (job, public works, etc.); **soumissionner à une adjudication,** to tender for a contract.

source, *n.f.* source; *Fin:* **imposé à la source,** taxed at source; **retenue (de l'impôt sur le revenu) à la source,** pay as you earn (PAYE)/*NAm:* pay as you go.

sous-affrètement, *n.m.* sub-charter (-ing).

sous-affréter, *v.tr.* to sub-charter (ship, etc.).

sous-affréteur, *n.m.* sub-charterer.

sous-agence, *n.f.* sub-agency.

sous-agent, *n.m.* sub-agent.

sous-bail, *n.m.* sublease.

sous-capitalisation, *n.f. PolEc:* undercapitalization.

sous-capitalisé, *a. PolEc:* undercapitalized/underfunded (project).

sous-chef, *n.m.* (*a*) deputy chief clerk (*b*) (*i*) assistant manager (*ii*) under manager.

sous-comité, *n.m.*, **sous-commission,** *n.f.*, sub-committee.

sous-consommation, *n.f. PolEc:* underconsumption.

souscripteur, *n.m. Fin:* (*a*) subscriber; applicant (for shares, etc.) (*b*) drawer (of bill of exchange) (*c*) subscriber (to a magazine, etc.).

souscription, *n.f.* **1.** *Fin:* subscription; application; **souscription à des titres,** application for shares; **bulletin de souscription,** allotment letter; **droits de souscription,** application/subscription rights; **droit préférentiel de souscription,** rights issue; **souscription en titres,** subscription by conversion of securities; **garantir la souscription d'une émission,** to underwrite an issue **2.** subscription; contribution (of a sum of money); **verser une souscription,** to pay a subscription.

souscrire, *v.tr.* **1.** to sign/to execute (deed); to subscribe/to sign (bond, contract, etc.); **souscrire une lettre de change,** to subscribe/to sign a bill of exchange; *Fin:* **souscrire des actions,** to subscribe shares/to apply for shares; **capital souscrit,** subscribed/issued capital; **2.** (*a*) to subscribe; **souscrire à une publication,** to take out a subscription to a publication (*b*) *Fin:* **souscrire à des actions,** to take up shares; **souscrire à une émission,** to apply for/to subscribe to an issue; **souscrire à un emprunt,** to subscribe to a loan; **souscrire à titre irréductible,** to apply as of right for new shares; **souscrire à titre réductible,** to apply for excess shares (*c*) **souscrire pour (la somme de) mille francs,** to subscribe a thousand francs.

sous-développé, *a.* (*a*) *PolEc:* **pays sous-développés,** underdeveloped countries (*b*) underequipped/undermechanized (factory, etc.).

sous-directeur, -trice, *n.* assistant manager/manageress; under-manager/under-manageress.

sous-emploi, *n.m. PolEc:* underemployment.

sous-entrepreneur, *n.m.* subcontractor.

sous-estimation, *n.f.,* **sous-évaluation,** *n.f.,* undervaluation.

sous-estimer, sous-évaluer, *v.tr.* to

underestimate/to undervalue/to under-rate.

sous-fréter, *v.tr.* to underfreight/to underlet (a ship).

sous-locataire, *n.m. & f.* subtenant/sublessee.

sous-location, *n.f.* (*a*) subletting/sub-renting (*b*) subtenancy; sublease.

sous-louer, *v.tr.* (*a*) to sublet/to sublease (house) (*b*) to rent (house) from a tenant.

sous-main, *n.m.inv.* blotting pad; blotter.

sous-palan (en), *adv.phr. Nau:* **livraison en sous-palan**, delivery (of goods) ready for shipping.

sous-payer, *v.tr.* to underpay; **ouvriers sous-payés**, underpaid workers.

sous-production, *n.f.* underproduction.

sous-produit, *n.m.* by-product; second-ary product; spin-off.

sous-seing, *n.m.* private agreement/private contract.

soussigné, -ée, *a. & n.* undersigned; **je soussigné déclare que . . .**, I, the under-signed, declare that . . ..

sous-traitance, *n.f.* subcontracting; **donner en sous-traitance**, to subcontract/to contract out.

sous-traitant, *n.m.* subcontractor; **on a donné le travail à un sous-traitant**, the work was contracted out/farmed out to s.o.

sous-traité, *n.m.* subcontract.

sous-traiter, *v.tr.* to subcontract/to con-tract out.

sous-vendre, *v.tr.* to resell (portion of goods purchased to a third party).

sous-vente, *n.f.* resale (of goods to a third party).

soutenir, *v.tr.* **1.** to support/to back (undertaking, person, etc.); to back (s.o., sth., financially); **soutenir des cours par**

des achats, to support prices by buying **2. soutenir une dépense**, to meet an ex-pense.

soutenu, *a.* sustained; **marché soutenu**, steady market; **marché moins soutenu**, easier market.

soutien, *n.m.* support; **prix de soutien**, support(ed)/pegged price; **soutien des prix**, price pegging.

spécial, *a.* special.

spécialisation, *n.f.* specialization.

spécialisé, *a.* specialized; **ouvrier spéci-alisé (OS)**, skilled worker; **main-d'œuvre non spécialisée**, unskilled labour.

spécialiser(se), *v.pr.* **se spécialiser dans qch.**, to specialize in sth.

spécialiste, *n.m. & f.* specialist; expert; **spécialiste du marketing**, marketing ex-pert.

spécialité, *n.f.* speciality/special feature; special line of business; *Fin:* **spécialité budgétaire**, budgetary speciality; **spéci-alité pharmaceutique**, patent medicine; **c'est la spécialité de la maison**, it's our speciality.

spécification, *n.f.* specification (of pro-duct, etc.); **spécification de la fonction**, job specification.

spécifier, *v.tr.* to specify (conditions, etc.); **compte spécifié**, detailed/itemized account; *StExch:* **spécifier un cours**, to make a price.

spécimen, *n.m.* specimen; sample; *Mkt:* (*d'une revue, etc.*) specimen copy; sam-ple copy; **spécimen de signature**, spe-cimen signature.

spéculateur, -trice, *n. Fin:* speculator; **terrains achetés par des spéculateurs**, land bought up by speculators; *StExch:* **spéculateur à la baisse**, bear; **spécu-lateur à la hausse**, bull.

spéculatif, *a. Fin:* speculative (deal,

etc.); **valeurs spéculatives,** speculative stocks.

spéculation, *n.f. Fin:* speculation; **spéculation à la baisse,** bear operations; **spéculation hasardeuse,** risky speculation; **spéculation à la hausse,** bull operations; **spéculations immobilières,** property speculation.

spéculer, *v.i. Fin:* to speculate; **spéculer en Bourse,** to speculate on the Stock Exchange; **spéculer à la baisse,** to speculate for a fall/on a falling market; to go a bear; **spéculer à la hausse,** to speculate for a rise/on a rising market; to go a bull; **spéculer sur les valeurs pétrolières,** to speculate in oils.

spirale, *n.f.* spiral; **spirale inflationniste,** inflationary spiral; **spirale prix-salaires,** wage-price spiral; *(des prix)* **monter en spirale,** to spiral.

spontané, *a.* **achat spontané,** impulse buying.

spot, *n.m.* (*a*) *Fin:* **crédit spot,** spot credit (*b*) *Mkt:* **spot (publicitaire),** (advertising) spot/commercial; **spot télé,** TV commercial.

stabilisateur, *a.* stabilizing; **exercer une action stabilisatrice sur les prix,** to have/ to exert a stabilizing action on prices.

stabilisation, *n.f.* stabilization (of currency); pegging (of prices, market, etc.); **fonds de stabilisation des changes,** exchange equalization account.

stabiliser, *v.tr.* to stabilize (currency, prices, market, etc.); **les prix se sont stabilisés,** prices have stabilized.

stabilité, *n.f.* stability/steadiness (of prices, etc.); **politique de stabilité,** stabilizing policy; **stabilité économique,** economic stability.

stable, *a.* stable/firm/steady; balanced; **monnaie stable,** stable currency.

stage, *n.m.* period of training; course of instruction; probationary period; **faire un stage,** to attend/to go on a (training) course.

stagflation, *n.f. PolEc:* stagflation.

stagiaire, 1. *a.* training (period); probationary (period) **2.** *n.m. & f.* trainee.

stagnant, *a.* stagnant; **économie stagnante,** stagnant economy.

stagnation, *n.f.* stagnation; *(commerce, marché)* **en stagnation,** at a standstill/ stagnant.

stagner, *v.i.* to stagnate.

stand, *n.m.* **stand d'exposition,** exhibition stand.

standard, 1. *a.* standard; **coûts standards,** standard costs; **modèle standard,** standard model; **prix standard,** standard price **2.** *n.* (*a*) standard; **standards budgétaires,** budgetary standards (*b*) *Tp:* switchboard.

standardisation, *n.f.* standardization.

standardiser, *v.tr.* to standardize; **production standardisée,** standardized production.

standardiste, *n.m. & f. Tp:* switchboard operator.

stand by, *n.m. Fin:* standby agreement.

statisticien, -ienne, *n.* statistician.

statistique, 1. *a.* statistical; **données statistiques,** statistical data **2.** *n.f.* (*a*) statistics (*b*) *pl.* statistical tables; **statistiques pour 1980,** statistics/figures for 1980.

statistiquement, *adv.* statistically.

statut, *n.m.* statute/article (of company, etc.); **statuts d'une société,** (memorandum and) articles (of association) of a company.

statutaire, *a.* statutory; **actions statutaires,** qualifying shares; *Fin:* **dividende statutaire,** statutory dividend; **gérant statutaire,** manager appointed according to the articles.

statutairement, *adv. Fin:* in accordance with the articles; under the articles.

stellage, *n.m. Fin:* double option/put and call.

sténo, *n.f. F:* stenography/shorthand; **prendre en sténo,** to take down in shorthand.

sténodactylo, *n.m. & f.* shorthand typist.

sténodactylo(graphie), *n.f.* shorthand typing.

sténographie, *n.f.* shorthand.

sténographier, *v.tr.* to take down/to write in shorthand.

sterling, *a.m.inv.* sterling; **balances sterling,** sterling balances; **livre sterling,** pound sterling; **cinq livres sterling,** five pounds sterling; **zone sterling,** sterling area.

stimulant, *n.m.* stimulus/incentive; **stimulants de la production,** production incentives; **stimulants de vente,** sales incentives.

stimuler, *v.tr.* to stimulate/to give a stimulus to (trade, etc.); **l'exportation stimule la production,** exports stimulate production.

stipulation, *n.f.* **stipulations d'un contrat,** stipulations of a contract; conditions laid down in an agreement; **stipulation particulière,** special provision.

stipuler, *v.tr.* to stipulate; to lay down (that . . .); **il est stipulé que . . .,** it is stipulated that . . .; **le contrat stipule que toutes les réparations seront à la charge du locataire,** the contract stipulates that the tenant shall be responsible for all repairs.

stock, *n.m.* stock (of goods)/*NAm:* inventory; **évaluation des stocks,** stock valuation; **gestion des stocks,** stock control/*NAm:* inventory control; **liquidation de stock,** stock clearance; **livre de stock,** stock book; **renouvellement des stocks,** restocking; **rotation des stocks,** stock

turnround; **stock de clôture/stock final,** closing stock; **stock de dépannage/de sécurité,** safety stock/buffer stock; **stock existant/stock en magasin,** stock in hand; **stock d'ouverture/stock initial,** opening stock; **avoir en stock,** to have in stock; **pièces détachées toujours en stock,** spare parts always in stock; **constituer des stocks,** to build up stocks; **épuiser les stocks,** to deplete/to exhaust stocks; **notre stock est épuisé,** we are out of stock; **nos stocks s'épuisent,** our stocks are running out/we are running out of stock.

stockage, *n.m.* **1.** stocking/keeping in stock (of goods); storage; **stockage mécanisé,** mechanized stocking **2.** (*a*) stocking/building up of stocks (*b*) stockpiling.

stocker, *v.tr.* (*a*) to stock (goods) (*b*) to stockpile.

stockiste, *n.m.* stockist; agent; dealer.

stratégie, *n.f.* strategy; **stratégie des affaires,** business strategy; **stratégie commerciale/de marché,** marketing strategy; marketing mix; **stratégie de l'entreprise,** company/corporate strategy; **stratégie financière,** financial strategy.

structuration, *n.f.* structuring.

structure, *n.f.* structure; **structure des coûts,** cost structure; **structure de l'entreprise,** corporate/company structure; **structure du marché,** market structure; **structure de(s) prix,** price structure; **structure des salaires,** wage structure.

structurer, *v.tr.* to structure.

subalterne, *a.* subordinate; **employé subalterne,** junior employee; employee in a minor position.

subliminal, *a.* subliminal; **publicité subliminale,** subliminal advertising.

subside, *n.m.* subsidy.

substitution, *n.f.* substitution; **produits de substitution,** substitute products.

subvention, *n.f.* subsidy/grant (of money); **subventions à l'alimentation,** food subsidies; **subventions en capital,** capital grants; **subvention d'équipement,** equipment subsidy; **subvention d'exploitation,** operating subsidy.

subventionnel, *a.* subventionary (payment).

subventionner, *v.tr.* to subsidize; to grant financial aid to (undertaking, etc.); **industries subventionnées,** subsidized industries; **subventionné par l'État,** State-aided.

succès, *n.m.* **succès de librairie,** bestseller.

successeur, *n.m.* successor (de, to).

succursale, *n.f.* branch (of store, etc.); branch (of bank); branch office; **magasin à succursales (multiples),** multiple (store)/chain store.

succursaliste, *n.m.* multiple/chain of stores.

suite, *n.f.* follow-up; *Corr:* **comme suite à votre lettre du 15 août,** with reference to/further to/in response to your letter of 15th August; **(comme) suite à notre conversation téléphonique,** further to your telephone call; **à la suite de votre demande,** in reply to/further to/with reference to your request; (*d'un produit*) **sans suite,** cannot be repeated/discontinued; **donner suite à,** (*i*) to deal with/to carry out (an order) (*ii*) to follow up a letter.

suivant, 1. *prep.* in accordance with/following (instructions); **suivant inventaire,** as per stock-list **2.** *a.* following; **aux conditions suivantes,** on the following terms.

suivi, 1. *a.* close (business relations); steady/persistent (demand); **achats suivis,** consistent buying; **correspondance suivie,** close/regular correspondence **2.** *n.m. Mkt: etc:* follow-up (of product, market, order, etc.).

suivre, *v.tr.* **faire suivre une lettre,** to forward/to redirect a letter; (*sur une lettre*) **(prière de) faire suivre,** please forward; **suivre une affaire,** to follow up

(a piece of) business; **nous n'avons pas suivi cet article,** we have given up/discontinued this line.

sujet, *a.* subject/liable (à, to); **contrat sujet au droit de timbre,** agreement subject to stamp duty; **marchandises sujettes à un droit de . . .,** goods subject to/liable to a duty of . . ..

superbénéfices, *n.m.pl.* excess profits/surplus profits; (very) large profits.

superdividende, *n.m. Fin:* surplus dividend.

supérette, *n.f.* minimarket.

superflu, *a.* superfluous.

supérieur, -eure, 1. *a.* (*a*) superior (à, to); **supérieur à la moyenne,** above average/better than average (*b*) **cadre supérieur,** senior executive; *pl.* **cadres supérieurs,** managerial staff/top management (*c*) **offre supérieure,** higher bid (*d*) (goods, products) of superior quality **2.** *n.* superior; **il est mon supérieur,** he is above me in rank.

supermarché, *n.m.* supermarket.

superprofits, *n.m.pl.* very high/large profits.

supplément, *n.m.* (*a*) supplement/addition; **en supplément,** extra/additional; **vin en supplément,** wine not included/wine extra (*b*) extra/additional payment; **supplément de prix,** extra charge/surcharge; **payer le supplément,** to pay the additional charge/the surcharge/the extra.

supplémentaire, *a.* supplementary/additional/extra/further; **dépenses supplémentaires,** additional expenses; *Ind:* **heures supplémentaires,** overtime; *Post:* **port supplémentaire,** extra postage; **demander un crédit supplémentaire,** to ask for (an) additional credit/for (a) further credit.

support, *n.m.* **support de publicité/ support publicitaire,** publicity medium/ advertising medium.

supporter, *v.tr.* **supporter les frais de** qch., to bear the cost of sth.

suppression, *n.f.* **suppression d'un produit,** abandonment of a product; *Adm:* **suppression de la double imposition,** double taxation relief; **600 suppressions d'emploi,** 600 jobs lost/600 job reductions.

supputation, *n.f.* calculation/reckoning; working out (of interest, etc.).

supputer, *v.tr.* to calculate/to reckon; to work out (interest, expenses).

sûr, *a.* safe/secure; **maison sûre,** firm of good/established standing; **placement sûr,** safe investment.

surabondance, *n.f.* surfeit/glut (of produce, etc.).

surassurance, *n.f.* over-insurance.

surcapacité, *n.f. PolEc:* surplus production capacity.

surcapitalisation, *n.f. Fin:* over-capitalization.

surcapitalisé, *a.* over-capitalized (company).

surcharge, *n.f.* (*a*) *Ind:* overloading; **surcharge permise,** permissible overload (*b*) excess weight (of luggage) (*c*) **surcharge de travail,** excess/extra work (*d*) extra/excess tax (*e*) overcharge/surcharge; additional charge (on account rendered).

surcharger, *v.tr.* (*a*) *Fin:* **surcharger le marché,** to glut the market (*b*) to overtax; to overcharge.

surchauffe, *n.f. PolEc:* **surchauffe (économique),** overheating (of the economy).

surchoix, *n.m.* finest quality; **viande surchoix,** prime quality meat; choice meat.

surconsommation, *n.f. PolEc:* overconsumption.

surcroît, *n.m.* addition/increase; **surcroît de dépenses,** additional expenditure; **avoir un grand surcroît de travail,** to have a great deal of extra work.

surdéveloppé, *a. PolEc:* (*a*) highly developed (economy) (*b*) **un secteur surdéveloppé de l'économie,** an overdeveloped sector of the economy.

surdéveloppement, *n.m. PolEc:* overdevelopment.

surdon, *n.m.* (*a*) compensation (allowable to purchaser) for damage to goods (*b*) right to non-acceptance (of damaged goods).

surélévation, *n.f.* (excessive) increase (of price, etc.).

surélever, *v.tr.* to raise (prices, tariff, etc.) higher; to force up (prices, etc.).

suremballage, *n.m. Mkt:* overwrap; outer wrap(per).

surémission, *n.f.* over-issue (of paper money).

suremploi, *n.m. PolEc:* overemployment.

surenchère, *n.f.* higher bid/outbidding; **faire une surenchère sur qn,** to outbid s.o.

surenchérir, *v.i.* (*a*) to bid higher; **surenchérir sur qn,** to bid higher than s.o.; to outbid s.o. (*b*) to rise higher in price.

surenchérissement, *n.m.* further rise in prices.

surenchérisseur, -euse, *n.* outbidder.

suréquilibre, *n.m.* overbalance; **budget en suréquilibre,** overbalanced budget.

suréquipement, *n.m. PolEc:* overequipment.

suréquiper, *v.tr. PolEc:* to overequip.

surestimation, *n.f.* overestimate/over-valuation.

surestimer, *v.tr.* to overestimate/to over-value (price, cost).

sûreté, *n.f.* (*a*) safety/security/safe-keeping (*b*) *Jur:* surety/security/guarantee; **sûreté (en garantie) d'une créance,** security/surety for a debt; **sûreté personnelle,** surety; **sûreté réelle,** (real) security.

surévaluation, *n.f.* overvaluation/over-estimate.

surévaluer, *v.tr.* to overestimate/to over-value.

surexploitation, *n.f.* over-exploitation/excessive exploitation (of natural resources, etc.).

surface, *n.f.* surface; **les grandes surfaces,** hypermarkets/(large) supermarkets; **surface de présentation (dans un magasin),** display space (in a store); **surface de vente,** sales/selling area.

surfaire, *v.tr.* to overcharge; to ask too much for (sth.).

surfait, *a.* **prix surfaits,** excessive prices; **restaurant surfait,** overrated restaurant.

surfin, *a.* superfine; of the highest quality.

surgelé, *a.* frozen (food).

surimposer, *v.tr.* (*a*) to increase the tax on (sth.) (*b*) to overtax.

surimposition, *n.f.* (*a*) increase of taxation (*b*) overtaxation.

surindustrialisation, *n.f.* overindustrialization.

surinvestissement, *n.m. Fin:* overinvestment.

surmarquage, *n.m.* overpricing; overcharging.

surmarquer, *v.tr.* to overprice (an article); to overcharge.

suroffre, *n.f.* better offer; higher bid.

surpaie, *n.f.* = **surpaye.**

surpasser, *v.tr. Fin:* to oversubscribe (loan, etc.).

surpaye, *n.f.* overpaying/overpayment.

surpayer, *v.tr.* to overpay (s.o.); to pay too much for (sth.).

surplus, *n.m.* surplus/excess; **payer le surplus,** to pay the difference; **surplus agricoles,** agricultural surplus; *Fin:* **surplus monétaire,** monetary surplus; **surplus de productivité,** productivity surplus.

surprime, *n.f. Ins:* extra/additional premium; loaded premium.

surprix, *n.m.* excess price.

surproduction, *n.f. PolEc:* overproduction.

surproduire, *v.tr. & i. PolEc:* to overproduce.

surprofit, *n.m. PolEc:* (*i*) abnormally high profit (*ii*) excessive profit.

surremise, *n.f.* special discount; extra/additional discount.

sursalaire, *n.m.* supplementary wage/extra pay; bonus.

sursaturer, *v.tr.* to supersaturate (the market).

sursis, *n.m. Jur:* respite/delay; **sursis de paiement,** respite of payment.

sursouscrire, *v.tr. Fin:* to oversubscribe (a loan, an issue).

sursouscrit, *a Fin:* oversubscribed.

surtare, *n.f.* extra tare.

surtaux, *n.m.* over-assessment; **présenter une réclamation en surtaux,** to claim a reduction of assessment.

surtaxe, *n.f.* (*a*) surtax/extra tax; **surtaxe à l'importation,** import surcharge; **surtaxe sur les marchandises,** surcharge on goods; **surtaxe progressive,** progressive surtax (*b*) excessive tax; over-assessment.

surtaxer, *v.tr.* to overtax; to over-assess.

survaleur, *n.f.* overvalue (of currencies).

surveillance, *n.f.* (*a*) supervision; *Ind:* personnel chargé de la surveillance, maintenance staff; surveillance de la production, production control (*b*) surveillance des prix, monitoring of prices.

surveillant, -ante, *n.* supervisor; (*dans un magasin*) shopwalker.

survie, *n.f. Ins:* tables de survie, expectation of life/life expectancy tables.

sus, *adv.phr.* en sus, in addition/extra; frais de poste en sus, postage extra.

susdit, -ite, *a. & n. Jur:* aforementioned/above-mentioned/aforesaid.

susmentionné, *a. & n. Jur:* aforementioned/above-mentioned.

susnommé, *a. & n. Jur: Adm:* aforenamed/above-named.

suspendre, *v.tr.* (*a*) to suspend; to stop (payment); suspendre le travail pour deux jours, to stop/to suspend work for two days (*b*) suspendre un fonctionnaire, to suspend an official.

suspens, *adv.phr.* en suspens, pending; in abeyance; effets en suspens, bills held over/bills outstanding.

suspension, *n.f.* (*a*) suspension de paiements, suspension of payment (*b*) suspension d'un employé, suspension of an employee.

symbolique, *a.* loyer symbolique, nominal rent; paiement symbolique, token payment; *Jur:* obtenir le franc symbolique de dommages-intérêts, to be awarded token damages.

syndic, *n.m.* syndic de faillite, official receiver (in bankruptcy).

syndical, *a.* 1. chambre syndicale (des agents de change) = Stock Exchange Committee; commission syndicale, underwriting commission; part syndicale, underwriting share 2. carte syndicale, union card; délégué syndical, shop steward/(trade) union representative; mouvement syndical, trade-union movement; relations syndicales, industrial relations; réunion syndicale, union meeting.

syndicalisme, *n.m.* syndicalisme (ouvrier), trade unionism.

syndicaliste, *n.m. & f.* trade unionist.

syndicat, *n.m.* 1. syndicate; syndicat financier, (financial) syndicate; syndicat de garantie, underwriting syndicate; syndicat industriel, pool; Syndicat d'Initiative = tourist information office; syndicat patronal, employers' federation; syndicat de producteurs, producers' association; syndicat professionnel, trade association 2. syndicat (ouvrier), trade union; les syndicats, the unions; syndicat des mineurs, miners' union.

syndicataire, 1. *a.* of/pertaining to a syndicate 2. *n.* (*a*) member of a syndicate (*b*) *Fin:* underwriter.

syndiqué, *a.* 1. belonging to a syndicate 2. ouvriers syndiqués, trade unionists; travailleurs non syndiqués, non-union workers/workers who are not members of a union.

syndiquer, 1. *v.tr.* to form into a trade union; to unionize (an industry, etc.) 2. *v.pr.* se syndiquer (*a*) to form a syndicate/ to syndicate (*b*) to form a trade union (*c*) to join a union.

synthétique, *a.* synthetic.

systématique, *a.* systematic; entretien systématique, planned maintenance.

systématisation, *n.f.* system(at)ization/ system(at)izing.

systématiser, *v.tr.* to systematize.

système, *n.m.* analyse de systèmes, systems analysis; système bancaire, bank(ing) system; système comptable, accounting system; système de direction, management system; système d'information par ordinateur, computerized information system; **système intégré de gestion,** integrated management system; **système métrique,** metric system; **système monétaire européen (SME),** European monetary system (EMS); **système de traitement de l'information/système informatique,** data processing system/computer system.

T

table, *n.f.* table; *Ins:* **tables de mortalité,** expectation of life tables/life expectancy tables/actuaries' tables; **table d'intérêts,** interest table; **table des parités,** parity table/table of par values; **table de poids et mesures,** table of weights and measures.

tableau, *n.m.* **1.** board; **tableau d'affichage,** notice board; *Rail: etc:* indicator board; **tableau des arrivées,** arrivals board; **tableau des départs,** departures board **2.** (*a*) list/table; **tableau d'avancement,** promotion table; **tableau de bord,** management chart; *Rail: etc:* **tableau des horaires,** timetable; **tableau de marche,** progress schedule; **tableau de prix,** price list; **tableau statistique,** statistical table; **tableau de travail,** work schedule/timetable; **sous forme de tableau,** in tabular form/tabulated; **disposer (des chiffres) en tableau,** to tabulate (figures) (*b*) *Fin:* **tableau d'amortissement,** redemption table; **tableau comptable,** (financial) statement; **tableau emplois-ressources/tableau de financement,** statement of source and application of funds.

tabloïd, tabloïde, *n.m.* tabloid (newspaper).

tabulatrice, *n.f.* tabulator/tabulating machine (in punched-card system, etc.); **tabulatrice numérique,** digital tabulator.

tâche, *n.f.* job; **affectation des tâches,** job assignment; **analyse des tâches,** job analysis/operations analysis; **fixation des tâches,** job specification; **ouvrier à la tâche,** (*i*) piece worker (*ii*) jobbing worker; **travail à la tâche,** (*i*) piece work (*ii*) work (paid) by the job; **travailler à la tâche,** to be on piecework.

tachygraphe, *n.m. Trans:* tachograph.

tachystocope, tachistocope, *n.m. Mkt:* tachistoscope.

tacite, *a.* tacit; **convention tacite,** tacit agreement; *Jur:* **tacite reconduction,** renewal (of lease) by tacit agreement.

tactique, 1. *a.* tactical; **plan tactique,** tactical plan(ning) **2.** *n.f.* tactics; **tactique commerciale,** marketing tactics.

taille, *n.f.* (*d'un vêtement*) size; **les grandes tailles,** the large sizes; outsizes; **petite taille,** small size; **taille courante,** standard size/stock size; **taille de l'entreprise,** size of the firm.

talon, *n.m.* **talon d'un chèque,** counterfoil/stub of cheque; *Fin:* talon (of sheet, of coupons).

tampon, *n.m.* **1.** (*a*) (inking) pad (*b*) rubber stamp; **apposer le tampon "acquitté" sur une facture,** to stamp "paid" on a bill; to receipt a bill (*c*) **tampon de la poste,** postmark **2. stock tampon,** buffer stock/safety stock.

tant, *n.* **le tant pour cent sur cette opération,** the percentage on this transaction; **gagner tant par mois,** to be paid so much a month; **payé à tant par jour,** paid (at a rate of) so much per day/a day.

tantième, *n.m.* percentage/share/quota (of profits, etc.); **tantièmes des administrateurs,** directors' percentage of profit.

taper, *v.tr.* **taper une lettre (à la machine),** to type a letter; **dactylo qui tape au toucher,** touch-typist.

tarage, *n.m.* taring; allowance for tare.

tare, *n.f.* **1.** depreciation/loss in value

(owing to damage or waste) **2.** tare; **tare moyenne/tare par épreuve,** average tare; **tare réelle,** actual tare; **faire la tare,** to allow for/to ascertain the tare.

tarer, *v.tr.* to tare/to ascertain the weight of (packing case, etc.).

tarif, *n.m.* (*a*) tariff/price list; (*dans un café*) **tarif des consommations,** price list/bar prices; *Cust:* **tarif d'entrée,** import list; **tarif de sortie,** export list (*b*) tariff/scale (of charges); rate; **abaissement des tarifs,** lowering of tariffs; **relèvement des tarifs,** raising of tariffs; **tarif dégressif,** sliding-scale tariff/tapering charge; **tarif en vigueur,** rate in force; **tarif forfaitaire,** fixed rate/charge; **tarif d'un impôt,** rate of a tax; *Journ: etc:* **tarif de la publicité,** advertising rates; **tarif réduit,** reduced rate; **tarif uniforme,** flat rate; **taux indices des tarifs,** tariff-level indices (*c*) *Cust:* **tarif ad valorem,** ad valorem tariff; **tarif différentiel,** discriminating duty; **tarif douanier,** customs tariff; **tarif de faveur/tarif préférentiel,** preferential rate/tariff (*d*) *Post:* **tarifs postaux,** postal rates; **tarif (des) lettres,** letter rate; **tarif normal,** ordinary rate/first(-)class (rate); **tarif réduit,** reduced rate/second(-)class (rate) (*e*) *Trans:* **plein tarif,** (*i*) full fare; adult fare (for passengers) (*ii*) full tariff (for goods, etc.); **tarif par kilomètre,** fare/tariff per kilometre; **tarif des marchandises,** goods/freight rate.

tarifaire, *a.* relating to tariffs; **accord tarifaire,** tariff agreement; **lois tarifaires,** tariff laws.

tarifer, *v.tr.* to tariff; to fix the rate of (duties, etc.); to fix the price of (goods, etc.).

tarification, *n.f.* tariffing; fixing the rate (of duties); fixing the price (of goods, etc.).

tas, *n.m.* **formation sur le tas,** on-the-job training; **grève sur le tas,** sit-down strike.

tassement, *n.m. Fin: StExch:* setback.

se tasser, *v.pr.* (*en parlant d'un marché, des valeurs*) to weaken.

taux, *n.m.* **1.** (*a*) rate; **taux de l'impôt,** rate of income tax (*b*) **taux des salaires,** wage rate; **taux horaire,** hourly rate/pay; **être payé au taux de £5 l'heure,** to be paid at the rate of £5 an hour **2.** (*a*) percentage/rate; **taux d'intérêt,** interest rate/rate of interest; **taux d'intérêt facial,** nominal rate; **taux légal,** legal rate; **taux de rendement/de rentabilité (d'un placement),** rate of return (on investment); **prêter au taux de 12%,** to lend at (the rate of) 12% (*b*) *Bank:* **taux de base,** base rate; **taux de l'escompte,** minimum lending rate/ bank rate/*NAm:* prime rate; *FrC:* **taux préférentiel,** *NAm:* prime rate (*c*) **taux de/du change,** rate of exchange/exchange rate; **le taux du jour,** today's rate (*d*) *StExch:* **taux de déport,** backwardation rate; **taux de report,** contango rate **3.** (*a*) *Fin:* ratio; **taux de capitalisation des bénéfices,** price earnings ratio; **taux de couverture,** cover ratio; **taux de marge,** mark-up ratio; **taux de rotation des stocks,** rate of turnover (*b*) **taux de natalité,** birth rate.

taxation, *n.f.* **1.** fixing of prices/wages/etc. **2.** *Adm:* (*a*) taxation (*b*) assessment.

taxe, *n.f.* **1.** (*a*) fixed price; fixed rate (of pay); **marchandises vendues à la taxe,** goods sold at the controlled price (*b*) charge (for service); rate; *Tp:* call charge; **taxe forfaitaire,** flat rate; **taxe postale,** postage; **taxe supplémentaire,** surcharge **2.** tax/duty/rate; **taxe d'aéroport,** airport tax; **taxe sur le chiffre d'affaires,** turnover tax; **taxe à l'importation,** import duty; **taxe locale** = rates; **taxe de luxe,** tax on luxury goods/luxury tax; *Adm:* **taxe parafiscale/taxe exceptionnelle,** exceptional tax/special levy; **taxe professionnelle,** business licence; **taxe sur les spectacles,** entertainment tax; **taxe sur le tabac,** tax on tobacco; **taxe à la valeur ajoutée (TVA),** value-added tax (VAT)/*NAm:* = sales tax; *FrC:* **taxe sur les ventes,** *NAm:* sales tax; **hors taxes (HT),** exclusive of tax; **toutes taxes comprises (TTC),** inclusive of tax.

taxer, *v.tr.* **1.** to regulate/to fix (prices); to regulate the rate of (wages, postage); **taxer une denrée,** to fix a controlled price for a food product **2.** to tax/to impose a tax on (s.o., luxury goods, cars, etc.); **marchandises faiblement taxées,** low-duty goods; **marchandises fortement taxées,** high-duty goods.

technicien, -ienne, *n.* technician.

technico-commercial, *a.* **agent technico-commercial,** sales technician.

technique, 1. *a.* technical; **directeur technique,** technical manager/works manager; **service technique,** engineering department **2.** *n.f.* **techniques commerciales,** marketing techniques; **techniques de gestion,** management techniques; **techniques marchandes,** merchandising techniques; **techniques de la vente,** sales engineering.

techniquement, *adv.* technically.

technocrate, *n.m. & f.* technocrat.

technocratie, *n.f. PolEc:* technocracy.

technocratique, *a.* technocratic.

technologie, *n.f.* technology; **technologie de pointe,** advanced technology.

technologique, *a.* technological; **chômage technologique,** unemployment resulting from automation.

télécommunication, *n.f.* telecommunication(s).

télécopie, *n.f.* telecopy.

télécopier, *v.tr.* to telecopy.

télécopieur, *n.m.* telecopier.

télégestion, *n.f. Cmptr:* teleprocessing.

télégramme, *n.m.* telegram; **envoyer un télégramme à qn,** to send a telegram to s.o.

télégraphe, *n.m.* telegraph.

télégraphier, *v.tr. & i.* to telegraph/to

wire; to cable; **télégraphier à Paris,** to cable/to send a cable to Paris; **j'ai télégraphié la nouvelle,** I cabled the news.

télégraphique, *a.* telegraphic; **addresse télégraphique,** telegraphic address; **dépêche télégraphique,** telegram; **service télégraphique,** telegraph service.

téléimprimeur, *n.m.* teleprinter/*NAm:* teletypewriter.

téléinformatique, *n.f. Cmptr:* teleprocessing.

télématique, *n.f.* telematics.

téléphone, *n.m.* telephone/phone; **abonné du téléphone,** telephone subscriber; **annuaire des téléphones,** telephone directory/phone book; **commande par téléphone,** telephone/phone order; **coup de téléphone,** telephone/phone call; **numéro de téléphone,** telephone/phone number; **téléphone automatique,** STD (system)/automatic telephone system/direct dialling; **téléphone intérieur,** house telephone/house phone/internal phone; **ventes par téléphone,** telesales; **appeler qn au téléphone/donner un coup de téléphone à qn,** to phone s.o./to call s.o. (up)/to ring s.o.; **être abonné au téléphone,** to be on the phone; **commander qch. par téléphone,** to order sth. by telephone/phone; **parler à qn au téléphone,** to speak to s.o. on the phone.

téléphoner, *v.tr. & i.* (*a*) to telephone/to phone (a piece of news, etc.) (*b*) **téléphoner à qn,** to ring s.o. (up)/to phone s.o./to call s.o. (up); **je vous téléphonerai demain,** I'll give you a ring/a call tomorrow; I'll ring you (up)/I'll phone you/I'll call you tomorrow.

téléphonique, *a.* **annuaire téléphonique,** telephone directory/phone book; **appel téléphonique,** telephone/phone call; **cabine téléphonique,** call box/phone box; **centrale téléphonique,** telephone exchange; **commande téléphonique,** telephone/phone order; **redevance télé-phonique,** rental charge; **taxe téléphoni-que,** call charge.

téléphoniste, *n.m. & f.* telephonist; telephone operator.

téléscripteur, *n.m.* teleprinter/*NAm:* teletypewriter.

télétraitement, *n.m. Cmptr:* teleprocessing.

télétypiste, *n.m. & f.* teletypist; teletype(writer) operator/teleprinter operator.

télévendeur, -euse, *n.* telesales person.

Télex, *n.m. Rtm:* (*a*) Telex (machine); **abonné au service Télex,** Telex subscriber; **réseau Télex,** Telex network; **tarif Télex,** Telex rate; **envoyer par Télex,** to send by Telex/to telex; **nous avons reçu cette commande par Télex,** we received this order by Telex (*b*) telex (message); **envoyer un télex au Canada,** to telex Canada/to send a telex to Canada.

télexer, *v.tr.* to send by Telex/to telex.

télexiste, *n.m. & f.* Telex operator.

témoin, *a.* appartement/maison **témoin,** show flat/show house.

tempérament, *n.* **acheter à tempérament,** to buy on credit/to buy by installments/to buy on easy terms/to buy on hire purchase (HP)/*NAm:* to buy on the installment plan; **achat à tempérament,** credit purchase/purchase on credit; **crédit à tempérament,** instalment credit; **vente à tempérament,** sale on hire purchase/on credit.

temps, *n.m.* (*a*) **emploi à plein temps,** full-time employment; **travailler à plein temps,** to work full time (*b*) time/period; *Mkt:* **temps d'antenne,** airtime/airspace/broadcasting time; *Ind:* **temps mort/temps d'arrêt/temps improductif,** down time (*c*) **étude des temps et des méthodes,** time and methods study; **étude**

des temps et des mouvements, time and motion study (*d*) *Cmptr:* **temps partagé,** shared time.

tendance, *n.f.* tendency/trend; **tendance à la baisse,** downward trend/tendency; *StExch:* bearish tendency; **tendance à la hausse,** upward trend/tendency; *StExch:* bullish tendency; **tendance de croissance,** growth trend; **tendance déflationniste,** deflationary tendency; **tendance économique,** economic trend; **tendance générale,** general trend/tendency; **les tendances du marché,** tendencies of the market/the general trend of the market.

teneur[1]**, -euse,** *n.* **teneur de livres,** book-keeper.

teneur[2]**,** *n.f.* **1.** tenor/(exact) wording/terms (of document, etc.) **2.** (*a*) *Ind: etc:* amount/content/percentage (*b*) **teneur payante,** payable grade (of ore); **teneur en or,** gold content.

tenir, 1. *v.tr.* (*a*) to keep; **tenir la caisse,** to be in charge of the cash/the till; **elle tient la caisse,** she is the cashier; **tenir la comptabilité/les livres,** to keep the accounts; **tenir un magasin,** to keep/to run a shop (*b*) to keep/to stock (groceries, etc.) **2.** *v.i.* **mon offre tient toujours,** my offer still stands.

tenu, *a. StExch:* firm/hard (prices).

tenue, *n.f.* **1.** keeping/managing/running (shop, etc.); **tenue de livres,** book-keeping; **tenue de livres en partie double/en partie simple,** double-entry/single-entry book-keeping **2.** *Fin:* steadiness/firmness (of prices); tone (of the market); **la bonne tenue du franc,** the firmness of the franc/the strong position of the franc.

terme[1]**,** *n.m.* **1.** (*a*) **prévisions à court terme/à long terme,** short-range/long-range forecasts (*b*) *Fin: Bank:* **à court terme,** short-term/short-dated; **à long terme,** long-term/long-dated; **argent à court terme,** money at short notice/at call; **crédit à court terme/à long terme,**

short-term/long-term credit; short/long credit; **dépôt à terme,** fixed deposit; **dettes à court terme,** current liabilities; **effet à court terme/à long terme,** short-dated/long-dated bill; **emprunt à court terme,** short(-term) loan; **placement à long terme,** long-term investment; **prêt à terme,** time loan; term loan; **acheter à terme,** to buy on credit (*c*) *StExch:* **le terme,** the settlement; **cours à terme/ taux pour les opérations à terme,** forward rate(s)/price for the account; **livrable à terme,** for future delivery; **livraisons à terme,** futures; **marché à terme,** (*i*) futures market/forward market (*ii*) terminal market; **opérations/transactions à terme,** forward/future(s) transactions; **opération de change à terme,** forward exchange contract; **valeurs à terme,** securities dealt in for the account; **acheter à terme,** to buy forward/to buy for the account; **vendre livrable à terme,** to sell forward (*d*) delay (for payment); *Jur:* **accorder un terme de grâce,** to allow (a debtor) extra time to pay; **terme de rigueur,** latest (possible) date (*e*) instalment; **acheter à terme,** to buy on credit; **remboursable par paiements à terme,** repayable by instalments **2.** (*a*) quarter (of rent); term (*b*) quarter's rent (*c*) quarter day.

terme², *n.m.* (*a*) term; **terme de métier,** technical term (*b*) *pl.* wording (of clause, etc.); terms/conditions; **termes d'un contrat,** terms of a contract; **aux termes de l'article 12,** in accordance with the terms of article 12; by/under article 12.

terminal, *n.m.* (*a*) (air, container, etc.) terminal (*b*) *Cmptr:* terminal.

terminer, 1. *v.tr.* to terminate; to end/to finish/to bring to a close (meeting, etc.) **2.** *v.i.* **les actions ont terminé à . . .,** shares finished/closed at . . . **3.** *v.pr.* **se terminer,** to end/to come to an end; **exercice se terminant au 31 décembre,** year ending 31st December.

terrain, *n.m.* **1.** (*a*) ground; piece of ground; plot (of land); **terrains à lotir,** development site/building land; **un ter-**

rain à bâtir, a building plot; **mettre en valeur un terrain à construire,** to develop a building site (*b*) **la livre a perdu du terrain,** sterling has lost ground **2.** *Mkt:* **sur le terrain,** in the field; **prospection sur le terrain,** field research; **travaux sur le terrain,** fieldwork.

terre, *n.f.* **1.** ground/land; **impôt sur la vente des terres,** tax on the sale of land; **prix courant de la terre,** current price of land **2.** estate/property; **emprunter de l'argent sur une terre,** to borrow money on the security of an estate.

terrestre, *a.* *Ins:* **assurance terrestre,** land insurance.

territoire, *n.m.* *Mkt:* **territoire de vente,** sales territory.

tertiaire, *a.* *PolEc:* **secteur tertiaire,** tertiary industries/service industries.

test, *n.m.* test/trial; **test d'aptitude,** aptitude test; **test auprès des consommateurs,** consumer test(ing); **test sur place,** testing in the field/field testing; **test de produit,** product test(ing); **test de vente,** market test.

testament, *n.m.* *Jur:* will.

texte, *n.m.* (*d'un contrat, etc.*) text/wording; *Cmptr:* **éditeur de textes/machine de traitement de textes,** word processor.

thème, *n.m.* theme; **thème publicitaire,** advertising theme.

théorie, *n.f.* theory; **théorie de l'information,** information theory.

théorique, *a.* **profits théoriques,** paper profits.

ticket, *n.m.* (*a*) ticket; coupon; **ticket d'admission,** entrance ticket; **ticket d'admission dans un parking,** car park ticket; **ticket d'autobus/de métro,** bus/underground ticket; **ticket de caisse,** till receipt (*b*) *Adm:* **ticket modérateur,** patients' contribution towards cost of medical treatment.

ticket-repas, *n.m.,* **ticket-restaurant,** *n.m.* = luncheon voucher.

tierce, *a.f. see* **tiers**.

tiers, **1.** *a.* **tierce caution,** contingent liability; **une tierce personne,** a third person; **tiers porteur,** second endorser (of a bill); *Jur:* **en main tierce,** in the hands of a third party; **déposé en main tierce,** held in escrow **2.** *n.m.* (*a*) third (part); **remise d'un tiers (du prix),** discount of a third/a third off (the price) (*b*) third party; **assurance au tiers/vis-à-vis des tiers,** third-party insurance; **tiers bénéficiaire,** beneficiary (of a cheque, a bill of exchange, etc.); *Adm:* **tiers payant,** direct payment of medical expenses by social security or insurance company; **tiers provisionnel,** interim tax payment (equal to one third of tax paid in the previous tax year); *Fin:* **tiers souscripteur,** third-party subscriber.

timbre, *n.m.* **1.** (*a*) stamp (on document, etc.); **timbre à empreinte,** embossed stamp; **timbre du jour,** date (stamped on document) (*b*) (postage) stamp; **carnet de timbres,** book of stamps (*c*) *Adm:* **droit de timbre,** stamp duty; **timbre fiscal,** revenue stamp; **timbre proportionnel,** ad valorem stamp; **timbre de quittance,** receipt stamp (*d*) **timbre dateur,** date stamp; **timbre humide/timbre de caoutchouc,** rubber stamp **2.** crest/mark (of a firm).

timbre-poste, *n.m.* postage stamp.

timbre-prime, *n.m.* trading stamp.

timbre-quittance, *n.m.* receipt stamp.

timbrer, *v.tr.* (*a*) to stamp (passport, document, etc.); to stamp the postmark on (letter, etc.); **lettre timbrée de Paris,** letter with a Paris postmark/letter postmarked Paris; *Adm:* **papier timbré,** official paper on which stamp duty has been paid (*b*) **timbrer une lettre,** to stamp/to put a stamp on a letter; **joindre une enveloppe timbrée pour la réponse,** to enclose a stamped addressed envelope (s.a.e.) for reply.

tirage, *n.m.* **1.** drawing (of bonds, of

lottery, etc.); *Fin:* **tirage au sort,** drawing of lots; **bons sortis au tirage,** drawn bonds; **les obligations sont rachetées par voie de tirage,** debentures are redeemed by lot **2.** (*a*) *Bank: Fin:* drawing/issue (of cheque, bill of exchange); **tirage en l'air/en blanc,** *F:* kite flying/kiting (*b*) *Fin:* **droits de tirage spéciaux (du FMI),** special drawing rights (of the IMF) **3.** *Publ: Journ:* printing/print-run; circulation (of newspaper); edition (of book); **journal à fort tirage,** newspaper with a large circulation; **un tirage de 30 000 exemplaires,** a circulation/a print-run of 30 000 copies; **tirage limité,** limited edition.

tiré, -ée, *n.* drawee.

tirer, *v.tr.* **1.** to draw/to obtain; **tirer un profit de qch.,** to get/to make a profit from sth. **2.** to draw (bill of exchange, cheque); **tirer un chèque sur une banque,** to draw a cheque on a bank; **tirer à vue sur qn,** to draw on s.o. at sight **3.** *Publ: Journ:* to print; **bon à tirer,** passed for press; **journal qui tire à 30 000 exemplaires,** newspaper with a circulation of 30 000; **tirer un livre à 5 000 exemplaires,** to print 5 000 copies of a book.

tireur, -euse, *n.* drawer (of bill of exchange, of cheque).

tiroir-caisse, *n.m.* till.

tissu, *n.m.* fabric/material.

titre, *n.m.* **1.** title; form of address; *Jur:* **propriétaire en titre,** legal owner/titular owner; **sans titre officiel,** without any official status **2.** (*a*) **titre (de propriété),** title deed (*b*) **titre de créance,** proof/evidence of debt; **titre de crédit,** proof of credit; **titre de paiement,** (document of) payment/remittance; **le titre de paiement doit être envoyé à . . .,** remittance by cheque or money order to be sent to . . . (*c*) *Fin: StExch:* warrant/bond/certificate; *pl.* stocks and shares; **titre à lots,** lottery loan bond; **titres négociables,** negotiable stock; **titre nominatif,** registered security; **titre de participation,** share; participation certificate; **titres de placement,** investment securities; **titres**

en portefeuille, securities (in portfolio); **titre au porteur,** bearer security; **titre de prêt,** loan certificate; **titre provisoire,** scrip certificate; **titre de rente,** government bond; **certificat de titres,** share certificate; **marché des titres,** stock market; **plan d'options sur titres,** stock option plan; **prendre livraison de titres,** to take delivery of stock; **vendre des titres,** to sell stock **3.** claim/right; **titre juridique à qch.,** legal claim to sth. (*b*) **à titre de. . .,** by way of. . .; as a. . .; **à titre gratuit,** free (of charge); *Jur:* **à titre onéreux,** subject to certain liabilities/subject to payment; **à titre provisoire,** provisionally; **marchandises envoyées à titre d'essai,** goods sent on approval.

titulaire, 1. *a.* titular **2.** *n. m. & f.* holder (of passport, etc.); **titulaire d'un brevet,** patentee; *Bank:* **titulaire d'un compte,** account holder; **titulaire d'une carte de crédit,** (credit) cardholder; **titulaire d'un poste,** holder of a post.

titularisation, *n.f. Adm:* establishment (of civil servant, etc.) in a job/post; **en stage de titularisation,** on probation.

titulariser, *v.tr. Adm: etc:* to confirm (s.o.) in his post/appointment.

tolérance, *n.f. Cust:* **tolérance (permise),** tolerance/allowance.

tomber, *v.i.* (*des prix, valeurs, etc.*) to fall (back)/to drop.

tonnage, *n.m.* **1.** tonnage (of ship) **2.** tonnage (of a port) **3. (droit de) tonnage,** (duty based on) tonnage.

tonne, *n.f.* (*a*) ton (= 1 000 kg); **tonne courte,** short ton (= 907.185 kg); **tonne forte,** long ton/gross ton (= 1016.06 kg); **tonne kilométrique,** kilometric ton; **tonne métrique,** tonne/metric ton (*b*) *Nau:* **affrètement à la tonne,** freighting per ton; **tonne de jauge,** gross ton/register ton.

tonneau, *n.m.* **1.** cask/barrel **2.** *Nau:* **tonneau d'affrètement,** freight ton; **tonneau de capacité,** measurement ton; ton measurement; **tonneau de jauge,** gross ton/register ton; **navire de 5 000 ton-**

neaux, 5 000-ton ship/ship of 5 000 tons burden.

tontine, *n.f. Ins:* tontine.

total, 1. *a.* total/complete/entire/whole; **coût total,** total cost; **dépenses totales,** total expenses; **montant total,** total amount; **nombre total d'actions,** total number of shares; **somme totale,** sum total **2.** *n.m.* whole/total; **total global,** sum total/grand total; **le total des recettes et des dépenses,** total revenue and expenditure; **faire le total des bénéfices,** to add up the profits/to calculate the total profit.

totalisation, *n.f.* totalizing/totalization; adding up (of amounts).

totaliser, *v.tr.* to totalize/to total up/to add up; **l'actif se totalise par deux millions,** the assets add up to two million.

totalité, *n.f.* totality/whole; **versements faits en totalité,** payments made in full.

touchable, *a.* (cheque) that can be cashed; collectable (bill).

toucher, *v.tr.* **toucher son traitement,** to be paid; to draw/to receive one's salary; **toucher un chèque,** to cash a cheque; **toucher des intérêts,** to receive interest; **toucher une traite,** to collect a bill.

tourisme, *n.m.* tourism; tourist trade; **agence/bureau de tourisme,** travel agency/tourist agency.

touriste, *n.m. & f.* tourist; *Nau: Av:* **classe touriste,** tourist class.

touristique, *a.* tourist; **menu touristique,** tourist menu; **renseignements touristiques,** tourist information; **ville/centre touristique,** tourist centre.

trafic, *n.m.* **1.** (*a*) illicit trading; trafficking (*b*) *Jur:* **trafic d'influence,** (corrupt) favour trading **2.** *Trans:* traffic; **trafic ferroviaire/des chemins de fer,** rail(way) traffic; **trafic routier/aérien,** road/air traffic; **trafic (de) marchandises,** goods/freight traffic.

trafiquant, -ante, *n.* trafficker; **trafiquant du marché noir,** black marketeer.

trafiquer, *v.tr.* to traffic in sth.

train, *n.m.* train; **train de marchandises**, goods/freight train; **train mixte**, passenger and goods train.

traite, *n.f.* (*a*) *Fin:* (banker's) draft; bill (of exchange); **traite avalisée**, guaranteed bill; **traite à courte échéance**, short-dated bill; **traite à longue échéance**, long-dated bill; **traite en l'air**, fictitious bill/*F:* kite; **traite sur l'étranger/sur l'extérieur**, foreign bill; **traite sur l'intérieur**, inland bill; **traite à vue**, sight bill; **escompter une traite**, to discount a bill; **présenter une traite à l'acceptation**, to present a bill for acceptance; **tirer une traite**, to draw a bill (*b*) (hire purchase) payment/instalment; **je rembourse les traites**, I pay the instalments.

traitement, *n.m.* **1.** (*a*) processing; *Ind:* **capacité de traitement**, handling capacity (*b*) *Cmptr:* **traitement de l'information**, data processing; **traitement de textes**, word processing; **machine de traitement de textes**, word processor **2.** salary; **structure des traitements**, salary structure; **toucher un traitement fixe**, to draw/to be paid a fixed salary.

traiter, **1.** *v.tr.* (*a*) *Ind:* to process (*b*) to handle (business); **traiter une affaire avec qn**, to transact a piece of business with s.o. **2.** *v.i.* to negotiate/to deal; **traiter avec ses créanciers**, to negotiate with one's creditors.

traiteur, *n.m.* (outside) caterer.

tranche, *n.f.* (*a*) **tranche de revenus**, income bracket; **la tranche des salariés moyens**, the middle-income bracket (*b*) block/portion (of an issue of shares, etc.); *Adm:* **par tranche de 1 000 francs ou fraction de 1 000 francs**, for every complete sum of 1 000 francs or part thereof; **émettre un emprunt en tranches**, to issue a loan in instalments.

transaction, *n.f.* (*a*) transaction; **transaction commerciale**, commercial transaction; **transaction au comptant**, cash transaction/cash deal; **transactions à crédit**, loan transactions/credit transactions (*b*) *StExch: etc: pl.* dealings/deals.

transbordement, *n.m.* transhipment (of cargo, passengers from ship, vehicle).

transborder, *v.tr.* to tranship (cargo, passengers from ship, vehicle).

transcription, *n.f.* **1.** transcript/copy **2.** *Book-k:* posting (of journal).

transcrire, *v.tr.* (*a*) to transcribe/to write out (*b*) *Book-k:* **transcrire le journal au grand(-)livre**, to transfer journal entries into the ledger.

transférable, *a.* transferable/negotiable (securities, etc.).

transférer, *v.tr.* to transfer (shares, bills of exchange, etc.); to transfer (funds from one bank account to another); to assign; **transférer un billet par voie d'endossement**, to transfer a bill by endorsement; **transférer le titre de propriété**, to transfer the title deed.

transfert, *n.m.* transfer/making over/assignment (of stock, rights, property, etc.); *Bank:* transfer (of funds); **ordre de transfert permanent**, standing order/banker's order; *Jur:* **acte de transfert**, deed of assignment (in favour of creditors); **formule de transfert**, transfer form; *Fin:* **journal/registre des transferts**, transfer register; **transfert de personnel**, staff transfer.

transfert-paiement, *n.m. Fin:* transfer of account (from one savings bank to another).

transfert-recette, *n.m. Fin:* (*caisse d'épargne*) opening of transferred account.

transformation, *n.f. PolEc:* **industrie de transformation**, processing industry.

transiger, *v.i.* **transiger avec ses créanciers**, to come to terms with one's creditors.

transit, *n.m. Cust:* transit; **visa de transit**, transit permit/visa; **maison de transit**, forwarding agency; **marchandises de transit,** (warehoused) goods for transit; **marchandises en transit,** goods in transit; **passagers en transit,** passengers in transit.

transitaire, 1. *a.* relating to transit of goods; **commerce transitaire,** transit trade; **pays transitaire,** country through which goods are conveyed in transit **2.** *n.m.* forwarding agent/transport agent.

transiter, 1. *v.tr.* to convey (goods) in transit **2.** *v.i.* to be in transit.

transmettre, *v.tr. Jur:* to transfer/to convey (property, etc.); to assign (shares, patents, etc.).

transmission, *n.f.* **1.** passing on/transmission (of message, orders, etc.) **2.** *Jur:* transfer(ence)/conveyance (of estate, etc.); assignment (of shares, patent, etc.).

transport, *n.m.* **1.** (*a*) transport; carriage; haulage; **transport aérien/par air,** air transport; **transport par (chemin de) fer,** rail transport; **transport fluvial,** river transport; **transport de marchandises,** goods transport; **transport maritime,** transport by sea; shipping; **transport routier/**also *NAm:* shipping; **transports en commun,** public transport (*b*) **avion de transport,** transport aircraft; **compagnie/société de transport,** transport company; carrying/forwarding company; **entrepreneur de transports,** haulage contractor/shipping/*NAm:* shipping company; **frais de transport,** freight (charges); carriage **2.** (*a*) *Jur:* = **transport-cession** (*b*) *Book-k:* transfer (from one account to another).

transportation, *n.f.* transport/transportation/conveyance (of goods, etc.).

transport-cession, *n.m. Jur:* transfer/assignment/conveyance (of property, rights, etc.).

transporter, *v.tr.* **1.** to transport/to carry (goods, etc.); **transporter des marchandises (par avion, par chemin de fer, par mer),** to transport goods (by air, by rail, by sea); **transporter des marchandises en camion,** to transport goods by road/by lorry/by truck; *NAm:* to truck goods/to ship goods **2.** (*a*) *Jur:* **transporter (des droits, etc.) à qn,** to transfer/to assign (rights, etc.) to s.o. (*b*) *Book-k:* to transfer.

transporteur, *n.m.* carrier/forwarding agent.

travail, *n.m.* **1.** (*a*) work; **travail en cours,** work in progress; **travail à l'entreprise,** contract work; **travail à façon,** job work; **travail (au) noir,** moonlighting; **travail de nuit,** night work; **travail à la pièce/aux pièces,** piece work (*b*) **étude du travail,** work study; **groupe de travail,** working party; **heure de travail,** man-hour; **organisation scientifique du travail (OST),** scientific management; **planification du travail,** job scheduling (*c*) occupation/employment/job; **être sans travail,** to be out of work/to be unemployed; **Ministère du Travail** = Department of Employment (*d*) place of work; **il est à son travail,** he's at work **2.** (*a*) piece of work; job (of work); **entreprendre un travail,** to undertake a piece of work; to take on a job (*b*) workmanship.

travailler, *v.i.* (*a*) to work; **travailler pour soi-même/pour son compte/à son compte,** to work for oneself; to be self-employed; to work freelance; **travailler huit heures par jour,** to work an eight-hour day (*b*) **faire travailler son argent,** to put one's money out at interest.

travailleur, -euse, *n.* worker; **travailleur indépendant,** self-employed person; **travailleur manuel,** manual worker.

trésor, *n.m.* treasury; **le Trésor (public),** the (French) Treasury; **le trésor public,** public funds/finances; **bons du Trésor,** Treasury bills/bonds.

trésorerie, *n.f.* **1.** treasury; **la Trésorerie générale/la trésorerie,** the Treasury; the Exchequer **2.** (*a*) treasurership (*b*) treasurer's office **3.** funds; cash; **budget de trésorerie,** cash budget; **gestion de trésorerie,** management of funds/cash management; **ils ont des problèmes de trésorerie,** they have cashflow problems.

trésorier, *n.m.* treasurer; **commis trésorier,** treasury clerk; *Adm:* **trésorier-payeur général,** paymaster general (for a department).

tribunal, *n.m.* tribunal; court of law/law court; (the) magistrates; **tribunal de commerce,** commercial court; **tribunal d'instance** = magistrates' court.

trimestre, *n.m.* (*a*) quarter; three months; **par trimestre,** quarterly; **abonnements au trimestre,** quarterly subscriptions (*b*) quarter's salary; quarter's rent.

trimestriel, *a.* quarterly (payment, account, review).

trimestriellement, *adv.* quarterly; every three months.

triple, 1. *a.* treble/triple; **facture en triple exemplaire,** invoice in triplicate **2.** *n.m.* **il gagne le triple de mon salaire,** he earns three times as much as I do/he earns treble my salary.

tripler, *v.tr. & i.* to treble/to triple.

triplicata, *n.m.inv.* triplicate; third copy.

tripotage, *n.m.* *F:* **tripotage financier,** market jobbery.

tripoter, 1. *v.i.* to engage in underhand dealings/in shady business; **tripoter dans l'immobilier,** to engage in shady property deals/speculation **2.** *v.tr.* to deal dishonestly with (money).

tripoteur, -euse, *n.* *F:* shady speculator.

trop-perçu, *n.m.* *Fin:* overpayment (of taxes); **rembourser le trop-perçu,** to refund the excess payment.

trust, *n.m.* *Fin:* trust; **trust de placement,** investment trust; **trust de valeurs,** holding company; **trust vertical,** vertical trust; **valeurs mises en trust,** securities in trust.

truster, *v.tr.* **1.** to group into a trust **2.** *F:* to monopolize.

trusteur, *n.m.* organizer/administrator of a trust.

tuyau, *n.m.* tip; **tuyau de bourse,** stock exchange tip.

type, *n.m.* type; standard model; sample piece; pattern; **échantillon type,** representative sample; **police (d'assurance) type,** standard policy.

U

ultérieur, *a.* later (date, etc.); **commandes ultérieures,** further orders; orders to come.

unanime, *a.* unanimous (vote, etc.); **consentement unanime,** unanimous consent/agreement.

unification, *n.f.* standardization (of weights and measures, tariffs, etc.).

unifié, *a.* unified; standard(ized) (weights, tariffs, etc.).

unifier, *v.tr.* to unify; to standardize (weights and measures, etc.).

uniforme, *a.* uniform; regular; **tarif uniforme,** flat rate.

unilatéral, *a.* unilateral/one-sided (contract, etc.).

union, *n.f.* (*a*) union/association; **union douanière,** customs union; **union économique,** economic union; **union monétaire,** monetary union (*b*) *Jur:* **union des créanciers/contrat d'union,** agreement (on the part of creditors) to take concerted action.

unique, *a.* sole; single; *Adm:* **allocation de salaire unique,** allowance to single-income family; *Ins:* **prime unique,** single premium; **prix unique,** flat price; **articles à prix unique,** articles (all) at one price/at the same price; **magasin à prix unique,** one-price store/popular store.

unitaire, *a.* **prix unitaire,** unit price/price per unit; **indice de la valeur unitaire,** unit value index.

unité, *n.f.* 1. (*a*) unit; **prix de l'unité,** price of one article/unit price/price per unit; *Fin:* **actions émises en unités,** shares issued in ones; **la production a dépassé les 3 000 unités,** production has passed the 3 000 unit mark (*b*) *Adm: Ind: etc:* department; unit; plant; **unité administrative,** administrative unit (*c*) *Cmptr:* unit/module; **unité d'affichage,** display unit; **unité centrale (de traitement),** central processing unit 2. unit (of measure, value, size, etc.); *Fin: EEC:* **unité de compte,** unit of account; *PolEc:* **unité de consommation/de production,** unit of consumption/of production; **unité monétaire,** monetary unit/unit of currency; **unité de poids,** unit of weight; **unité de travail,** unit of labour/man-work unit.

urbain, *a.* urban; *Tp:* **communication urbaine,** local call.

urbanisme, *n.m.* town planning.

urbaniste, *n.* town planner.

urgence, *n.f.* (*a*) urgency; emergency (*b*) *adv.phr.* **d'urgence,** immediately; **veuillez répondre d'urgence,** please reply without delay; **mesures d'urgence,** emergency measures.

urgent, *a.* urgent; **commande urgente,** rush order; **travail urgent,** urgent work.

usage, *n.m.* 1. (*a*) use/using; **à usages multiples,** multi-purpose (equipment, etc.); **locaux à usage commercial,** business/commercial premises; **valeur d'usage,** value as a going concern (*b*) wear/service; **biens/produits d'usage,** durable goods 2. *Jur:* **droit/clause d'usage,** customary right/clause; **avoir l'usage (d'un bien, etc.),** to have the right to (possession of) (property, etc.) 3. usage; custom; practice; **je peux vous fournir les références d'usage,** I can supply (you with) the usual references.

usagé, *a.* used (article); secondhand (car, etc.).

usager, -ère, 1. *n.* user (of sth.) **2.** *a. Cust:* **effets usagers**, articles for personal use; personal effects.

usance, *n.f.* usance; **lettre (de change) à deux usances**, bill payable at double usance; **à usance de trente jours**, at thirty days' usance.

usine, *n.f.* factory; works; plant; **usine d'automobiles**, car factory; **apprentissage/formation en usine**, in-plant training; **directeur d'usine**, works manager; **ouvrier d'usine**, factory worker; **prix (sortie) usine**, price ex works; **travailler dans une usine**, to work in a factory.

usinier, *a.* **groupe usinier**, group of factories; **ville usinière**, factory town.

usufruit, *n.m. Jur:* usufruct.

usure[1], *n.f.* usury; charging of illegal rates of interest.

usure[2], *n.f.* wear and tear (of machinery, etc.); **usure en magasin**, shelf depreciation.

utile, *a.* (*a*) **charge utile,** (*i*) (load-)carrying capacity (*ii*) pay-load/commercial load (*b*) **en temps utile**, in (good) time; within the prescribed time; duly; *Jur:* **jours utiles**, prescribed time; days relevant to an action; **prendre toutes dispositions utiles**, to make all necessary arrangements.

utilisable, *a.* usable; available; **crédit utilisable à vue**, credit available at sight.

utilisateur, -trice, *n.* user/utilizer; **attitude des utilisateurs**, user attitude.

utilisation, *n.f.* utilization/using (of sth.); **frais d'utilisation**, running costs; **mode d'utilisation**, method of use; instructions for use; **période d'utilisation**, economic life.

utiliser, *v.tr.* to use; to utilize; to make use of (sth.).

utilitaire, *a.* utilitarian; **véhicules utilitaires**, commercial vehicles.

utilité, *n.f.* utility/use(fulness); service; **utilité marginale**, marginal utility.

V

vacance, *n.f.* **1.** vacancy; **suppléer à une vacance/nommer qn à une vacance,** to fill a post/a vacancy **2.** *pl.* holiday(s)/ *NAm:* vacation; **un mois de vacances,** a month's holiday/a month off; **les grandes vacances,** the summer holidays; **période/saison des vacances,** holiday period; **étaler les vacances,** to stagger holidays.

vacant, *a.* vacant; **poste vacant,** (job) vacancy.

vague, *n.f.* wave; **vague de baisse,** wave of depression; **vague de hausses de salaire,** wave of wage increases; **vague de spéculation,** wave of speculation.

valable, *a.* valid/good; **billet valable pour un mois,** ticket valid for one month; **quittance valable,** proper receipt; **lettre de crédit valable dans le monde entier,** world-wide letter of credit.

valeur, *n.f.* **1.** (*a*) (relative) value/worth; **mettre une terre en valeur,** to develop a piece of land; *PolEc:* **valeur ajoutée,** added value; **taxe à la valeur ajoutée (TVA),** value-added tax (VAT); **valeur d'échange,** exchange value; **valeur marginale,** marginal value (*b*) (monetary) value/worth; **articles/objets de valeur,** articles of value/valuable articles/valuables; **sans valeur commerciale,** of no commercial value; **date de valeur,** value date; **valeur actuelle,** real value; **valeur comptable,** book value; *Bank:* **valeur en compte,** value in account; **valeur à l'échéance,** value at maturity; **valeur de facture,** invoice value; **valeur marchande/valeur vénale,** market value/ commercial value; **valeur nominale,** face value; **valeur de rendement (d'une entreprise),** profitability value; *Cust:* **valeur en**

douane, customs value; *Post:* **colis/ paquet avec valeur déclarée,** insured parcel (*c*) *Fin:* **valeur d'achat d'une action,** cost of a share; **valeur boursière,** market value; **valeur d'un remboursement,** redemption value (of a bond, etc.) (*d*) *Ins:* **valeur assurable,** insurable value; **valeur assurée,** insured value; **valeur de rachat (d'une police),** surrender value (of policy); **valeur à neuf,** replacement value (as new)/new for old (policy) **2.** *Fin:* (*a*) asset; **valeurs actives,** assets; **valeur en capital,** capital value; **valeur en espèces,** (*i*) cash (*ii*) bullion; **valeurs immobilisées,** fixed assets; **valeurs incorporelles,** intangible assets; intangibles; **valeurs matérielles,** tangible assets; tangibles (*b*) *pl.* shares/securities/stocks; **valeurs au comptant,** securities dealt in for cash; **valeurs cotées,** quoted/listed securities; **valeurs non cotées,** unquoted/unlisted securities; **valeurs de croissance,** growth shares/ stocks; **valeurs immobilières,** real property shares; **valeurs à lot,** lottery bonds/ prize bonds; **valeurs mobilières,** stocks and shares; transferable securities; **valeurs nominatives,** registered securities; **valeurs de placement/de portefeuille,** investment securities/stocks; **valeurs au porteur,** bearer securities; bearer bonds; **valeurs de père de famille/ valeurs de tout repos/valeurs de premier choix/valeurs de premier ordre,** gilt-edged securities; blue chips; **valeurs à revenu fixe,** fixed-yield securities; **valeurs à revenu variable,** variable-yield securities; **valeur à termes,** forward securities.

valeur-or, *n.f. Fin:* value in gold currency.

validation, *n.f.* validation; authentication (of document, signature, etc.).

valide, *a.* (*a*) valid (contract, etc.) (*b*) **billet valide pour un mois,** ticket valid for one month.

valider, *v.tr.* to make valid; to ratify (contract, etc.); to authenticate (document, etc.).

validité, *n.f.* validity (of contract, passport, etc.).

valoir, *v.tr. & i.* (*a*) to be worth (in money, quality); **valoir son prix,** to be worth its price; **valoir cher,** to be expensive; to be worth a lot (of money); **tissu qui vaut douze francs le mètre,** material (which is) worth twelve francs a metre/which sells at twelve francs a metre (*b*) **à valoir sur (qch. une somme),** on account of (sth., a sum); **à valoir sur votre facture,** set against your invoice; **payer 200 francs à valoir,** to pay 200 francs on account (*c*) **faire valoir son argent,** to invest one's money to good account/to invest one's money at a profit; **faire valoir ses droits à. . .,** to assert one's claims to . . . .

valorisation, *n.f.* (*a*) valorization (of product, etc.); stabilization (of price of commodity); **valorisation des stocks,** costing/pricing (of stocks) (*b*) *Bank:* **valorisation (de chèques) sur Paris,** valuing (of cheques) on Paris.

valoriser, *v.tr.* (*a*) to valorize; to stabilize (price of commodity) (*b*) to raise the price of (a commodity) (*c*) *Bank:* to value (cheques, etc.).

variabilité, *n.f.* variability (of interest rates, etc.).

variable, *a.* variable; **frais variables,** variable expenses; **méthode des coûts variables,** direct costing; **revenu variable,** income from variable-yield investments; **valeurs à revenu variable,** variable-yield securities; **société d'investissement à capital variable (SICAV),** open-end investment company; = unit trust.

variance, *n.f. Stat:* variance.

variation, *n.f.* variation; **variations (an-** nuelles, saisonnières),** (annual, seasonal) variations; **variations du cours du franc,** fluctuations of the franc.

varier, *v.i.* to vary; to fluctuate.

variété, *n.f.* variety (**de,** of); **grande variété de produits,** wide range of products.

véhicule, *n.m.* **véhicules commerciaux/ utilitaires,** commercial vehicles; **véhicule de transport de marchandises,** freight vehicle/goods vehicle.

vénal, *a.* **poids vénal,** conventional selling weight; **valeur vénale,** market value.

vendable, *a.* saleable/marketable; **peu vendable,** hard to sell; unsaleable.

venderesse, *n.f. Jur:* vendor.

vendeur, -euse, *n.* **1.** (*a*) seller (*b*) *Jur:* vendor (*c*) salesperson; salesman; saleswoman/saleslady; sales assistant/shop assistant/*NAm:* sales clerk; **vendeur à domicile,** door-to-door salesman; **vendeur, -euse par téléphone,** telesales person (*b*) *StExch:* **vendeur à découvert,** short seller/bear seller.

vendre, *v.tr.* to sell; **vendre qch. à qn,** to sell sth. to s.o.; **vendre à bon marché,** to sell cheap; **vendre comptant,** to sell for cash; **vendre au détail,** to sell retail/to retail; **vendre en gros,** to sell wholesale; **vendre moins cher que qn,** to undersell s.o.; **vendre à perte,** to sell at a loss; **vendre à terme/à crédit,** to sell on credit; *StExch:* **vendre à découvert,** to sell short; **article qui se vend cher,** article that fetches a high price; **articles qui se vendent bien,** articles that sell well/ready sellers; **marchandises qui ne se vendent pas,** slow sellers; **maison à vendre,** house for sale.

vente, *n.f.* (*a*) sale/selling; **vente agressive,** hard sell(ing); **vente au comptant,** cash sale; **vente par correspondance (VPC)/ vente sur catalogue,** mail order selling; **vente à crédit/à tempérament,** credit sale/sale on hire purchase/*NAm:* sale on the installment plan; **vente au détail,** retail sale; **vente directe,** direct selling; **vente aux enchères/à l'enchère,** sale by auction/auction (sale); **vente à l'essai,** sale on approval; **vente de gré à gré/vente à l'amiable,** sale by private agreement/ contract/treaty; private sale; **vente ferme,** firm sale; **vente forcée,** forced sale; **vente de liquidation,** closing-down sale; **vente à perte,** sale at a loss; **vente à prix réduit,** sale at a reduced price; **vente promotionnelle,** promotional sale; **vente publique,** public sale/public auction; **vente pyramidale,** pyramid selling; **vente rapide,** quick/ready sale; **vente réclame,** bargain sale; **vente à réméré,** sale with option of repurchase; **ventes par téléphone,** telesales/telephone selling; *StExch:* **vente à terme,** sale for the account (*b*) **acte de vente,** bill of sale; **bureau de vente,** sales office; **campagne de vente,** sales campaign/sales drive; **contrat de vente,** contract of sale; **directeur/chef des ventes,** sales manager; **équipe des ventes,** sales force; **point/lieu de vente,** point of sale (POS); **publicité lieu de vente (PLV),** point of sale material/POS material; **prévision des ventes,** sales forecast; **prix de vente,** selling price; **promotion des ventes,** sales promotion; **réseau de vente,** sales network; **service des ventes,** sales department (*c*) **en vente,** on sale; for sale; **en vente dans tous les grands magasins,** on sale at all leading stores; **hors de vente,** (*i*) withdrawn from sale/no longer on sale (*ii*) unsal(e)able; **mettre en vente,** to put up for sale; **retirer de la vente,** to withdraw from sale; **articles de bonne vente/de vente facile,** articles which sell well/which have a ready market; **marchandises de vente difficile,** goods that are hard to sell.

ventilation, *n.f. Book-k:* allocation/ apportionment/breakdown (of prices, expenses, etc.); **ventilation des prix de revient,** cost distribution.

ventiler, *v.tr. Book-k:* to apportion/to allocate/to break-down; **ventiler les dépenses,** to break down expenses.

verbal, *a.* **convention verbale,** verbal agreement; *Jur:* simple contract; **offre verbale,** verbal offer.

véreux, *a. F:* **dettes véreuses,** bad debts; **financier véreux,** shady financier.

vérificateur, -trice, *n.* inspector/examiner; **vérificateur de(s) comptes/vérificateur comptable,** auditor; **vérificateur interne,** internal auditor; **vérificateur des poids et mesures,** inspector of weights and measures.

vérification, *n.f.* inspection/examination/checking (of work, measures, etc.); **balance de vérification,** trial balance; **vérification des comptes/vérification comptable,** audit(ing) of accounts; **vérification en douane,** customs examination (of goods); **vérification des stocks,** stock control.

vérifier, *v.tr.* to inspect/to examine/to check (work, measures, etc.); to audit (accounts); **vérifié et revérifié,** checked and double-checked; cross-checked; **vérifier des références,** to take up references.

versement, *n.m. Fin: Bank:* payment/ paying in/deposit; **bulletin de versement,** paying-in slip; deposit slip; **carnet de versement,** paying-in book; **dernier versement,** final instalment; **versement à la commande,** down payment; **versement comptant,** cash payment; **versement en compte courant,** payment into a current account; **versement partiel,** instalment; **payer en plusieurs versements/par versements échelonnés,** to pay by/in instalments.

verser, *v.tr.* (*a*) *Fin:* to pay (in); to deposit (money); **verser des arrhes,** to make a deposit; **verser au comptant,** to pay (in) cash; **verser des fonds dans une affaire,** to invest capital in/to put money into an undertaking; **verser des intérêts,** to pay interest; **verser un salaire,** to pay a salary; **capitaux versés,** paid-up capital (*b*) **verser un document au dossier,** to add a document to the file/to file a document.

verso, *n.m.* verso/back/reverse (of a sheet of paper); back (of a bill, cheque, etc.).

vert, *a. EEC:* **franc vert**, green franc; **livre verte**, green pound; **monnaies vertes**, green currencies; **taux vert**, green rate.

vertical, *a.* vertical; **concentration verticale**, vertical concentration; **intégration verticale**, vertical integration; **organisation verticale**, line organization.

viabilité, *n.f.* viability/workability (of a project, system, etc.).

viable, *a.* viable (plan, project); **l'entreprise est viable**, the firm is paying its way/is viable.

viager, **1.** *a.* for life; **rente viagère**, life annuity/life interest; **rentier viager**, annuitant **2.** *n.m.* life interest; **placer son argent en viager**, to invest one's money in a life annuity; to buy an annuity.

vice, *n.m.* fault/defect/flaw; **vice caché**, hidden/latent defect; **vice de construction**, defect in construction/construction fault.

vice-gérance, *n.f.* deputy managership.

vice-gérant, *n.m.* deputy manager.

vice-présidence, *n.f.* vice-presidency; vice-chairmanship.

vice-président, -ente, *n.* vice-president; vice-chairman.

vie, *n.f.* (*a*) life; **assurance sur la vie**, life assurance; **le coût de la vie**, the cost of living; **indemnité de cherté de vie**, cost-of-living allowance; **niveau de vie**, standard of living; **gagner sa vie**, to earn one's living (*b*) **espérance/durée de vie d'un produit**, shelf life of a product; **vie économique d'un produit**, economic life of a product.

vignette, *n.f.* (*a*) manufacturer's label (of quality, guarantee, etc.) (*b*) *Aut:* = tax disc/road fund licence; *Adm:* price label on medicines for reimbursement by the Social Security.

vigueur, *n.f.* (*en parlant d'un règlement, d'une loi, etc.*) **en vigueur**, in force; **entrer en vigueur**, to come into force/into effect; to become operative; **cesser d'être en vigueur**, to lapse; **taux en vigueur**, current/present rate (of exchange).

virement, *n.m.* (*a*) *Bank:* transfer; **chèque de virement**, giro cheque; **mandat de virement**, order to transfer; **virement bancaire**, bank giro transfer; **virement de crédit**, credit transfer; **virement postal** = Girobank transfer; **payer par virement bancaire**, to pay by bank (giro) transfer (*b*) *Adm:* **virement de fonds**, transfer (often illegal) of funds from one article of the budget to another.

virer, *v.tr. Bank:* to transfer (a sum from one account to another).

visa, *n.m.* (*a*) visa (on passport); **visa de la douane**, customs visa (*b*) signature (on document, etc.); initials (of supervisor, etc., on bankslip, etc.); **visa de chèque**, certification (of cheque).

vis-à-vis, *prep.phr.* **le dollar a gagné 7% vis-à-vis du franc**, the dollar is up 7% against/on the franc.

viser, *v.tr.* (*a*) to visa (passport) (*b*) to countersign/to initial (document); to certify (cheque).

visible, *a.* visible; **exportations visibles**, visible exports; **importations visibles**, visible imports.

visite, *n.f.* **1.** **visites (d'un représentant)**, calls (by a representative) **2.** inspection/examination; *Cust:* **visite de douane**, customs examination.

visiter, *v.tr.* **1.** to call on (a client) **2.** to inspect/to examine (machinery, etc.); *Cust:* to examine (luggage, etc.).

visualisation, *n.f. Cmptr:* **console/écran de visualisation**, visual display unit (VDU)/visual display terminal (VDT).

visuel, *n.m. Cmptr:* visual display unit (VDU)/visual display terminal (VDT).

vitesse, *n.f.* (*a*) (*en parlant de la production, de l'économie*) **perdre de la vitesse**, to slow down/to be losing ground/to flag/to sag (*b*) **expédier un travail à toute vitesse**, to rush a job through (*c*) *PolEc:* **vitesse de transformation des capitaux**, income velocity of capital; *Fin:* **vitesse de rotation (des stocks)**, turnover rate/turnround rate (of stocks).

vitrine, *n.f.* (*a*) shop window/*NAm:* store window/shop front; **articles en vitrine**, goods (on show) in the window; **article qui a fait la vitrine**, article that has been in the window; shop-soiled article; **faire la vitrine**, to dress the window; **lécher les vitrines**, to go window-shopping/to window-shop (*b*) goods displayed in a shop window (*c*) display case.

vivre, *n.m.* (*a*) **le vivre et le couvert**, board and lodging (*b*) *pl.* (food) supplies; provisions.

vœu, *n.m.* wish; **le comité a adopté des vœux demandant que . . .**, the committee has adopted a resolution in favour of . . ..

voie, *n.f.* **1.** way/road; route; **par voie de mer**, by sea; **par voie de terre**, by land; overland; **par la voie hiérarchique**, through the official channels **2.** (*a*) *Adm: Fin:* **voies et moyens**, ways and means; **en voie d'achèvement**, nearing completion; **pays en voie de développement**, developing countries (*b*) *Jur:* **voie de droit**, recourse to legal proceedings; **voie de recours**, grounds for appeal (to a higher court).

voiture, *n.f.* **1.** **lettre de voiture**, waybill/consignment note **2.** (*a*) car/*NAm:* automobile; **voiture de fonction/voiture de société**, company car; **voiture de livraison**, delivery van; **voiture de location/de louage**, hire car (*b*) *Rail:* carriage/car/wagon.

voix, *n.f.* (individual) vote; **donner sa voix à qn**, to vote for s.o.; **mettre une question aux voix**, to put a question to the vote; to take a vote on a question; **voix prépondérante**, casting vote.

vol[1], *n.m. Av:* flight.

vol[2], *n.m.* theft; **assurance vol**, insurance against theft; **vol à l'étalage**, shoplifting.

volant, **1.** *a.* **personnel volant**, (*i*) mobile/transferable staff (*ii*) *Av:* flight/flying staff **2.** *n.m.* **talon et volant**, counterfoil and leaf (of cheque).

voler, *v.tr.* to steal.

volet, *n.m.* (*d'un chèque, etc.*) tear-off/detachable section.

voleur, **-euse**, *n.* thief; **voleur à l'étalage**, shoplifter.

volontaire, *a.* **liquidation volontaire**, voluntary liquidation.

volonté, *n.f.* **billet payable à volonté**, promissory note payable on demand.

volume, *n.m.* volume; bulk; size; **volume des affaires**, volume of business; **volume d'une entreprise**, size of a firm; **volume de la production courante**, volume of current output; **volume de ventes**, sales volume.

votant, **-ante**, *n.* voter.

vote, *n.m.* (*a*) vote; **vote de confiance**, vote of confidence; **vote par correspondance**, postal vote (*b*) **bulletin de vote**, ballot paper; **vote au scrutin secret**, secret ballot; **déclarer le résultat d'un vote**, to déclare the result of the voting; **donner son vote à qn**, to vote for s.o.; **prendre part au vote**, to vote/to take part in the voting.

voter, **1.** *v.i.* to vote; **voter à main levée**, to vote by a show of hands; **voter par procuration**, to vote by proxy **2.** *v.tr.* to vote (money, credits, etc.); **voter une loi**, to pass a law; **voter des remerciements à qn**, to pass a vote of thanks to s.o.

voyage, *n.m.* journey/trip; **agence/bureau de voyages**, travel agency; **chèque de voyage**, traveller's cheque; **frais de voyage**, travelling expenses; **voyage d'affaires**, business trip; **voyage organisé**, organised tour/trip; package tour.

voyager, *v.i.* **1.** (*a*) to travel; to make a journey/a trip; **voyager pour affaires,** to travel on business (*b*) **voyager pour une maison de commerce,** to travel for a firm/to represent a firm **2.** (*en parlant de marchandises, etc.*) to be transported; **vin qui ne voyage pas,** wine that does not travel well.

voyageur, -euse, *n.* (*a*) traveller/*NAm:* traveler; *Trans:* passenger; **train de voyageurs,** passenger train (*b*) **voyageur (de commerce),** (commercial) traveller/representative/rep.

vrac, *n.m.* **en vrac,** loose; in bulk; **cargaison en vrac,** bulk cargo; **marchandises en vrac,** loose goods (not packed); **faire le vrac/transporter le vrac,** to transport goods in bulk.

vue, *n.f.* (*a*) **payable à vue,** payable at sight; **à sept jours de vue,** seven days after sight; **dépôt à vue,** demand deposit; **traite à vue,** draft (payable) at sight; sight draft (*b*) **en vue,** on view; **mettre des marchandises bien en vue,** to display goods prominently.

W

wagon, *n.m. Rail:* (passenger) carriage/ *NAm:* passenger car; **wagon de première classe,** first-class carriage; **wagon de marchandises,** goods van/goods wagon/*NAm:* freight car; **wagon complet,** truckload/ wagon load; **wagon frigorifique,** refrigerated van; **franco wagon,** free on rail; **prix par wagon (complet),** price per truckload; **prix sur wagon,** price on rail.

wagon-poste, *n.m. Rail:* mail van.

wagon-restaurant, *n.m. Rail:* restaurant/dining car.

warrant, *n.m.* (*a*) *Jur:* (warehouse) warrant (*b*) **warrant agricole,** agricultural warrant; **warrant hôtelier,** hotel warrant; **warrant industriel,** industrial warrant.

warrantage, *n.m.* issuing of a warehouse warrant (for goods).

warranter, *v.tr.* to issue a warehouse warrant for (goods); **marchandises warrantées,** goods covered by a warehouse warrant.

X

---

xérographie, *n.f.* xerography.

xérographique, *a.* **copie xérographique,**
 xerocopy/Xerox (*Rtm*) copy.

Xerox, *n.m. Rtm:* **machine Xerox,** Xerox
machine.

Z

zèle, *n.m.* **grève du zèle,** work to rule.

zéro, *n.m.* zero; nought; **valeur qui est tombée à zéro,** share which has fallen to zero.

zone, *n.f.* (*a*) *PolEc:* **zone franche,** free zone; **zone de libre-échange,** free-trade area; **zone monétaire,** monetary area; **zone (dollar, franc, sterling),** (dollar, franc, sterling) area (*b*) **zone industrielle,** industrial estate/trading estate; industrial area; *Adm:* **zone à urbaniser en priorité (ZUP),** priority development area (*c*) *Adm:* **zone de salaire,** wage zone/wage bracket.

ABREVIATIONS USUELLES—COMMON ABBREVIATIONS

ab.	**abandonné,** relinquished (right, etc.)
ac.	**acompte,** (payment) on account
a.c.	**1. argent comptant,** cash **2. année courante,** current year **3. avaries communes,** general average, g/a
acc.	**acceptation,** acceptance (of bill), acc.
act.	**action,** share
ad(r).	**adresse,** address; **ad(r). tél., adresse télégraphique,** telegraphic address, TA
ad val.	**ad valorem,** ad valorem, ad val.
agce	**agence,** agency, agcy
AP	**1. à protester,** to be queried **2. avis de paiement,** advice/notice of payment
a.p.	**avaries particulières,** particular average, p.a.
AR	**accusé de réception,** acknowledgement
asse	**assurance,** insurance, ins.; assurance, ass.
ass.extr.	**assemblée extraordinaire,** extraordinary (general) meeting, EGM
à t.p.	**à tout prix,** at any cost
Av.	**avoir,** credit, cr.
à vdre	**à vendre,** for sale, to be sold
b.	**1. billet,** bill **2. bénéfice,** profit
B/.	**billet à ordre,** promissory note
b. à p.	**billet à payer,** bill payable, b.p.
b. à r.	**billet à recevoir,** bill receivable, b.r.
bce.	**balance,** balance, bal.
beau.	**bordereau,** memorandum, memo
bt.	**1. billet,** bill **2. brut,** gross
bté	**breveté,** patented
c.	**1. centime,** centime, c. **2. coupon,** coupon, c(p). **3. cours,** quotation **4. compte,** account, a/c., A/C, acct
c/.	**contre,** contra
c.à.f.	**coût, assurance, fret,** cost, insurance, freight, c.i.f.
cage	**courtage,** brokerage, bkge
caire	**commissionnaire,** agent, Agt
c.-à-d.	**c'est-à-dire,** that is to say, i.e.
c. at(t).	**coupon attaché,** cum dividend, cum div., c.d.
cc.	**cours de compensation,** making-up price, m/u
c/c.	**compte courant,** current account, c/a, CA
cce	**commerce,** commerce
certif.	**certificat,** certificate, cert.
CF	**coût et fret,** cost and freight, c.&f., C&F
ch. de f.	**chemin de fer,** railway, rly, *NAm:* railroad, RR
ch.f.	**change fixe,** fixed exchange
Cie	**Compagnie,** Company, Co.
c/j.	**courts jours,** short-dated (bills)
cl	**centilitre,** centilitre, cl
cm	**centimètre,** centimetre, cm
c/o.	**compte ouvert,** open account
com.	**commission,** commission, com(m).
connt	**connaissement,** bill of lading, B/L
conv.	**converti,** converted, convd
corresp.	**correspondance,** correspondence, corr.
coup.	**1. coupon,** coupon, cp. **2. coupure,** denomination, denom.
cpt	**comptant,** cash, ready money

cpte	**compte,** account, A/C, a./c.
cr.	**crédit,** credit, cr
ct	*Corr:* **courant,** instant, inst.
cu.	**cours unique,** sole quotation
CU	**charge utile,** payload
cum.	**cumulatif,** cumulative, cum.
c.v.	**cheval-vapeur,** horse power, HP
D.	**1. doit, débit,** debit, debtor, dr **2. déport,** backwardation **3. départ,** starting date
DA	**documents contre acceptation,** documents against acceptance, DA
déb.	**débit,** debit, debtor, dr
déc.	**décembre,** December, Dec.
dél.	**délégation,** delegation, del
dép.	*Adm:* **département**
dest.	**destinataire,** addressee/to . . .
dét.	**détaché,** (coupon) detached
dif.	**différé,** deferred (stock), def.
div.	**dividende,** dividend, div.
DP	**documents contre paiement,** documents against payment, DAP
dr	**débiteur,** debtor, dr
dr.c.	**derniers cours,** last quotation
dz.	**douzaine,** dozen, doz.
e. à p.	**effet à payer,** bill payable, b.p.
e. à r.	**effet à recevoir,** bill receivable, b.r.
en tte. ppté	**en toute propriété,** freehold, F/H
e.o.o.e./e.&o.e.	**erreur ou omission exceptée,** errors and omissions excepted, E.&O.E., e.&o.e.
env.	**environ,** approximately, approx.
esc.	**escompte,** discount, disc.
est.	**estampillé,** stamped
Éts	**établissements,** factory
ex.	**1. example,** example, e.g. **2. exercice**
ex.att.	**exercice attaché,** cum dividend, cum div.
ex-bon.	**ex-bonification,** ex bonus
ex-c(oup).	**ex-coupon,** ex coupon; ex cp; **ex-c.div., ex-coupon de dividende,** ex-dividend coupon; **ex-c.int., ex-coupon d'intérêt,** ex-interest coupon
ex-d.	**ex-dividende,** ex dividend, ex div.
ex-dr.	**ex-droits,** ex rights
exp.	**1. exportation,** export, exp. **2. expéditeur,** sender/from . . .
expn	**expédition,** dispatch(ing)
ex-rép.	**ex-répartition,** ex bonus
F., f.	**franc,** franc, F., f.
f. à b.	**franco à bord,** free on board, f.o.b.
FAC	**franc d'avaries communes,** free of general average, f.g.a.
FAP	**franc d'avaries particulières,** free of particular average, f.p.a.
fco	**franco,** free of charge, f.o.c.; carriage paid, CP
f. ct	*Corr:* **fin courant,** at the end of this month
fév.	**février,** February, Feb.
FG	**frais généraux,** overheads, o/h
FLB	**franco long du bord,** free alongside ship, f.a.s.
FOB	**franco de bord,** free on board, f.o.b.
FOR	**franco sur rail,** free on rail, FOR
f.p.	**1. (en) franchise postale** **2.** *Corr:* **fin prochain,** at the end of next month
fre	**facture,** invoice, inv.
Frs	**Frères,** Brothers, Bros
FS	*Post:* **faire suivre,** please forward

g	**gramme,** gram, g
g.l.	**grand(-)livre,** ledger
h.	**1. heure(s),** hour(s), hr(s) **2.** *StExch:* **hier,** yesterday
h.c.	**1. hors cadre,** not on the staff **2. hors commerce,** not for sale
HS	**hors de service,** not in service/not in use
HT	**hors taxe(s),** exclusive of tax
hyp.	**hypothèque,** mortgage, mortg.
id.	**idem,** idem, id./ditto, do.
imp.	**impayé,** dishonoured (bill, etc.)
incl.	**inclus,** *(i)* enclosed, enc. *(ii)* included, incl.
ind.	**industrie,** industry, ind.
int.	**intérêt,** interest, int.
janv.	**janvier,** January, Jan.
j/d	**jours de date,** days after date, d.d.
Je	**jeune,** junior, jnr, jr
jl	**journal,** day-book, d.b./journal
jr	**jour,** day, d.
j/v	**jours de vue,** days after sight, d.s.
kg	**kilo(gramme),** kilo(gram), kg
kl	**kilolitre,** kilolitre, *NAm:* kiloliter, kl
km	**kilomètre,** kilometre, *NAm:* kilometer, km
kt	**kilotonne,** kiloton, kt
L	**livre sterling,** pound sterling, £
l	**litre,** litre, *NAm:* liter, l
l/c.	**1. leur compte,** their account **2. lettre de change,** bill of exchange, b/e., B/E
LCR	**lettre de change relevé**
l/cr.	**lettre de crédit,** letter of credit, l/c
lib.	**libéré,** fully paid
liq.	**liquidation,** settlement
liv.	**livraison,** delivery
l/o.	**leur ordre,** their order
Ltée	*FrC:* **(compagnie) limitée,** limited (company), Ltd.
M.	**1. Monsieur,** Mr **2. mille,** thousand
m	**1. mètre,** metre, *NAm:* meter, m **2. mois,** month, m
max.	**maximum,** maximum, max
m/c.	**mon compte,** my account
Me	**Maître**
min.	**minimum,** minimum, min
mise.	**marchandises,** goods, gds
Mlle	**Mademoiselle,** Miss, Ms
Mlles	**Mesdemoiselles,** Misses
MM.	**Messieurs,** Messrs
mm	**millimètre,** millimetre, *NAm:* millimeter, mm
m/m	**moi-même,** (my)self
Mme	**Madame,** Mrs, Ms
Mmes	**Mesdames**
mn.	**minute,** minute, min
m/o.	**mon ordre,** my order, m/o
MP	**mandat-poste,** postal order, PO; money order, MO
MS	**manuscrit,** manuscript, MS
mx	**au mieux,** at best

N.	**1. nom,** name **2. nominal,** nominal, n
n.	**notre,** our
NB	**nota bene**
n/c.	**notre compte,** our account
nég.	**négociable,** negotiable
NF	**nouveau(x) franc(s),** new franc(s)
NFC	**nouvelle feuille de coupon,** new sheet of coupons
n°	**numéro,** number, no.; **n° tél.,** **numéro de téléphone,** telephone number, tel. no.
nom.	**nominatif,** registered (security)
nos	**numéros,** numbers., nos
nov.	**novembre,** November, Nov.
N/Réf.	**notre référence,** our reference, Our ref.
o/. . .	**à l'ordre de . . .,** to the order of . . .
OB	**1. opération bancaire,** bank transaction **2. ordre de bourse**
obl.	**obligation,** debenture, bond
oct.	**octobre,** October, Oct.
off.	**offert,** offered
o/m/m.	**à l'ordre de moi-même,** to my/our own order
p.	**1. page,** page, p. **2. pair,** par **3. papier,** paper **4. poids,** weight, wt
PA	**1. pour amplification,** true copy **2. propriété assurée,** insured property
pable	**payable,** payable
p.an.	**par an,** per annum, pa.
p.c.	**1. pas coté,** unlisted **2. pour cent,** per cent
p/c.	**pour compte**
PCC	**pour copie conforme,** certified true copy
p.d.	**port dû,** carriage forward, CF
PJ	**pièce(s) jointe(s),** enclosure(s), encl./enclosed, enc.
p.p.	**port payé,** carriage paid, CP
p.pon	**par procuration,** per procuration, per pro./p.p.
pptaire	**propriétaire,** proprietor, owner
ppté	**propriété,** property
préf.	**préférence,** preference, pref.
priv.	**privilégié,** preferential (share)
pte	**perte,** loss
px	**prix,** price
q.	**1. quai,** quay **2. quantité,** quantity, qnty
QL	**quittance de loyer,** rent receipt
r.	**1. rue,** street, St./road, Rd **2. reçu,** received, rcvd **3.** *Post:* **recommandé,** registered, regd
RA	*Rail:* **régime accéléré,** fast goods service/Rail Express Parcels/Red Star
Réf.	**référence,** reference, ref.
remb.	**1. remboursable,** redeemable **2. remboursement,** redemption
rens.	**renseignements,** information, inf(o).
rep.	**report,** contango
rép.	**répartition,** allotment
RO	*Rail:* **régime ordinaire,** normal, usual goods service
r.p.	**réponse payée,** reply paid, RP
RSVP	**Répondez s'il vous plaît,** please reply, RSVP
s.	**signé,** signed, sgd
s/b.	**son billet,** his bill
s.b.f.	**sauf bonne fin/sous réserve de bonne fin,** under usual reserve
s.c.	**seul cours,** sole quotation

s/c.	1. **son compte,** his account 2. *Corr:* **sous couvert,** under cover
s.e.&o.	**sauf erreur ou omission,** errors and omissions excepted, E&OE
sept.	**septembre,** September, Sept.
serv.	**service,** department, dept.
SF	**sans frais,** no expenses
s.l.	**sauf livraison,** against delivery
s.o.	**sauf omission,** omissions excepted
s/o.	**son ordre,** his order
St^é	**Société,** Company, Co.
s.v.	**sans valeur,** of no value, worthless
SVP	**s'il vous plaît,** please
t.	1. **titre,** security, stock, share 2. **tonne,** (metric) tonne 3. **tare,** tare, t.
T/.	**traite,** draft, dft
t.c.	**toutes coupures,** all denominations (of banknotes)
TC	**taxe complémentaire,** supplementary charge; additional tax
tél.	1. **téléphone,** telephone, tel. 2. **télégraphique,** telegraphic
t.p.	**tout payé,** all expenses paid
tr.	**traite,** draft, dft
TR	**tarif réduit,** reduced rate
TS	1. **tarif spécial,** special rate 2. **taxe supplémentaire,** supplement
tt.	**transfert télégraphique,** telegraphic transfer, TT
t.t.c.	**toutes taxes comprises,** inclusive of tax
u.	**unité,** unit
v.	1. **vendeur,** seller 2. **votre,** your, yr
V/, val.	**valeur,** security, stock, share
v/c.	**votre compte,** your account
virt	**virement,** transfer, tr.
vo., v^o	**verso,** verso, vo.
V/Réf.	**votre référence,** your reference, your ref.
vte	**vente,** sale
XP	*Post:* **exprès payé,** express paid
&	**et commercial,** ampersand
©	**droit d'auteur,** copyright
%	**pour cent,** per cent

AC	1. Appellation controlée 2. Agent de change
ACAC	Administration centrale de l'aviation civile
ACSI	Analyse et Conception de Systèmes Informatiques
ACTIM	Agence pour la coopération technique, industrielle et économique
ADR	Accord pour le transport des marchandises dangereuses par route
AELE	Association européenne de libre-échange, European Free Trade Association, EFTA
AETR	Accord européen de transports internationaux par route
AFB	Association française des banques, French Bankers' Association
AFDEP	Association française pour le développement de la productivité
AFNOR	Association française de normalisation = 1. British Standards, BSI 2. American National Standards Institute, ANSI
AFP	1. Agence France-Presse 2. Association française de prévention des accidents du travail
AG	Assemblée générale annuelle, Annual general meeting, AGM
AGEMCO	Agence européenne d'emballage et conditionnement
AGTDC	Accord général sur les tarifs douaniers et le commerce, General Agreement on Tariffs and Trade, GATT
AID	Association internationale de développement
AITA	Association internationale des transports aériens, International Air Transport Association, IATA
ALE	1. Agence locale pour l'emploi 2. Association de libre-échange, Free Trade association
AME	Accord monétaire européen, European Monetary Agreement, EMA
AMM	Autorisation de mise sur le marché
ANAS	Association nationale des avoués et agréés syndics
AP	Assistant(e) particulier(-ière), personal assistant, PA
ANPE	Agence nationale pour l'emploi = Job Centre
ASSEDIC	Association pour l'emploi dans l'industrie et le commerce
ATC	Assistant technique du commerce
ATI	Assistant technique de l'industrie
ATM	Assistant technique des métiers
ATP	Autorisation de transferts préalable
ATVA	Association de transports et voyages aériens
BAII	Banque arabe et internationale d'investissements
BALO	Bulletin d'annonces légales obligatoires
BB	1. Banque de Bretagne 2. Banque de Belgique
BC	Banque de Commerce
BCI	Banque de crédit international
BEC	Brevet d'enseignement commercial
BEH	Brevet d'enseignement hôtelier
BEI	1. Banque européenne d'investissement 2. Brevet d'enseignement industriel
BF	Banque de France
BFCE	Banque française du commerce extérieur
BFI	Banque de financement industriel
BGL	Banque générale du Luxembourg
BI	1. Brevet d'invention, patent 2. Brevet industriel
BIA	Banque internationale arabe
BIC	Banque internationale du commerce
BIPE	Bureau d'informations et de prévisions économiques
BIRD	Banque internationale pour la reconstruction et le développement, International Bank for Reconstruction and Development, IBRD
BNB	Banque nationale belge

BNP	**Banque nationale de Paris**
BODAC	**Bulletin officiel des annonces commerciales**
BP	**1. Boîte postale,** Post Office box, PO box **2. Brevet professionnel**
BPA	**Bénéfices par action**
BPF	**Bon pour francs,** value in francs
BPGF	**Banque privée de gestion financière**
BSGD	**Breveté sans garantie du Gouvernement,** patent without Government warranty of quality
BT	**Brevet de technicien**
BTS	**Brevet de technicien supérieur**
BVP	**Bureau de la vérification de la publicité,** Advertising Standards Authority, ASA
CA	**Chiffre d'affaires,** turnover
CAP	**Certificat d'aptitude professionnelle**
CAPES	**Certificat d'aptitude pédagogique à l'enseignement secondaire**
CAPET	**Certificat d'aptitude pédagogique à l'enseignement technique**
CCCHCI	**(Caisse centrale de) crédit hôtelier, commercial et industriel**
CC	**Compte courant,** current account, CA, C/A
CCF	**Crédit commercial de France**
CCI	**Chambre de commerce internationale,** International Chamber of Commerce, ICC
CCP	**Compte courant postal/Compte chèque postal** = (National) Girobank account
CE	**1. Comité d'entreprise,** works council **2. caisse d'épargne,** savings bank
CEDEX	**Courrier d'entreprise à distribution exceptionnelle**
CEE	**1. Communauté économique européenne,** European Economic Community, EEC **2. Commission économique pour l'Europe,** Economic Commission for Europe, ECE
CFDT	**Confédération française démocratique du travail**
CGAF	**Confédération générale de l'artisanat français**
CGC	**Confédération générale des cadres**
CGT	**Confédération générale du travail**
CI	**Certificat d'importation,** import certificate
CIC	**Crédit industriel et commercial**
CIDA	**Centre international du droit des affaires**
CISI	**Compagnie internationale de services en informatique**
CITT	**Compagnie internationale du travail temporaire**
CL	**Crédit Lyonnais**
CM	**Crédit mutuel**
CMB	**Crédit mutuel de Bretagne**
CMCC	**Crédit de mobilisation de créances commerciales**
CNC	**Conseil national du crédit**
CNE	**1. Caisse nationale d'épargne** = National Savings Bank, NSB **2. Comptoir national d'escompte**
CNME	**Conseil national des marchés de l'État**
CNPF	**Conseil national du patronat français** = Confederation of British Industry, CBI
CNRS	**Centre national de la recherche scientifique**
CNT	**Confédération nationale du travail**
COFACE	**Compagnie française d'assurance pour le commerce extérieur**
COMECON	**Conseil pour l'aide économique mutuelle,** Council for Mutual Economic Aid, COMECON
CV	**Curriculum vitae,** curriculum vitae, CV
DAB	**Distributeur automatique de billets,** cash dispenser
DEUG	**Diplôme universitaire d'études générales**
DEUS	**Diplôme universitaire d'études scientifiques**
DPO	**Direction par objectifs,** management by objectives, MBO
DTS	**Droits de tirage spéciaux,** Special drawing rights, SDR
EDF, EdF	**Électricité de France**

ENA	1. École nationale d'administration 2. École nationale d'agriculture
ENSET	École normale supérieure de l'enseignement technique
ESC	École supérieure de commerce
EXIM	Exportation–Importation
FAC	Fonds d'aide et de coopération
FCFA	Franc de la communauté financière d'Afrique
FDES	Fonds de développement économique et social
FEOGA	Fonds européen d'orientation et de garantie agricole
FG	Frais généraux, overheads
FMI	Fonds monétaire international, International Monetary Fund, IMF
FSI	Fédération syndicale internationale, International Federation of Trade Unions, IFTU
FSM	Fédération syndicale mondiale, World Federation of Trade Unions, WFTU
GICEX	Groupement interbancaire pour les opérations de crédit à l'exportation
GPL	Gaz de pétrole liquéfiés
HLM	Habitations à loyer modéré
HT	Hors taxes, exclusive of tax
IDI	Institut de développement industriel
IMEX	Importation–exportation
INSEE	Institut national des statistiques et des études économiques
IS	Impôt sur les sociétés
JAL	Japan Airlines
JO	Journal Officiel
KAL	Korean Airlines
KLM	Société royale d'aviation des pays bas, Royal Dutch Airlines, KLM
L.ès L.	Licencié ès lettres = Bachelor of Arts, BA
L.ès Sc.	Licencié ès sciences = Bachelor of Science, BSc
MBA	Marge brute d'autofinancement, cash flow
MM	1. Marine marchande, Merchant Navy 2. Messageries maritimes
MUTI	Mutuelle des travailleurs indépendants
NF	Normes françaises = British Standards
NU	Nations unies, United Nations, UN
OCDE	Organisation de coopération et de développement économique, Organization for Economic Co-operation and Development, OECD
OECE	Organisation européenne de coopération économique, Organization for European Economic Co-operation, OEEC
OHQ	Ouvrier hautement qualifié, highly skilled worker
OIAC	Organisation internationale de l'aviation civile, International Civil Aviation Authority, ICAO
OIC	Organisation internationale du commerce
OIT	Organisation internationale du travail, International Labour Organization, ILO
OM	Organisation et méthodes, Organization and Methods, OM
ONS	Ouvriers non syndiqués, non-union workers
ONU	Organisation des nations unies, United Nations Organization, UNO
OP	Ouvrier professionnel, skilled worker
OPA	Offre publique d'achat, takeover bid
OPE	Offre publique d'échange, exchange offer

OPEP	**Organisation des pays exportateurs de pétrole,** Organization of Petroleum Exporting Countries, OPEC
OS	**Ouvrier spécialisé,** semi-skilled worker
OST	**Organisation scientifique du travail,** scientific management
OTAN	**Organisation du traité de l'Atlantique du nord,** North Atlantic Treaty Organization, NATO
PAC	**Politique agricole commune,** Common Agricultural Policy, CAP
PAP	**1. Port autonome de Paris 2. Prêt à l'accession à la propriété**
PCC	**Pour copie conforme,** true copy
PCV	*Tp:* **appel en PCV,** transfer(red) charge call
P-DG	**President-directeur général,** Chairman and Managing Director/*NAm:* Chief Executive Officer, CEO
PEPS	**Premier entré premier sorti,** first in first out, FIFO
PERT	**Méthode de programmation optimale,** Programme evaluation and review technique, PERT
P et T	**Postes et Télécommunications** = the Post Office, PO
PIB	**Produit intérieur brut/Production intérieure brute,** gross national product, GNP/gross domestic product, GDP
PIC	**Prêts immobiliers conventionnés**
PJ	**Pièce(s) jointe(s),** enclosure(s)/enclosed, enc., encl.
PLV	**Publicité sur le lieu de vente,** point-of-sale advertising, POS
PME	**(Confédération des) petites et moyennes entreprises**
PMI	**Petite et moyenne industrie**
PN	**1. poids net,** net weight **2. prix normal**
PNB	**Produit national brut,** gross national product, GNP
PNN	**Produit national net,** net national product
PP	**1. port payé,** carriage paid, cp **2. payable au porteur,** payable to bearer
PR	**1. Poste restante 2. Procureur de la République 3. Prix de revient,** cost price
PROMODES	**Procédé moderne de distribution et de standardisation**
PV	**Procès-verbal**
RC	**Registre du commerce**
RCB	**Rationalisation des choix budgétaires** = planning, programming and budgeting system, PPBS
RCI	**Rentabilité des capitaux investis,** return on capital employed, ROCE
RP	**Relations publiques,** public relations, PR
RSVP	**Répondez s'il vous plaît,** please reply, RSVP
SA	**Société anonyme,** *(i)* public company *(ii)* limited (liability) company
SARL	**Société à responsabilité limitée** = limited (liability) company
SCM	**Société de caution mutuelle**
SDR	**Société de développement régional**
SERNAM	*Rail:* **Service national des messageries**
SGDG	**Sans garantie du Gouvernement,** (patent) without Government warranty of quality
SI	**1. Syndicat d'Initiative** = tourist (information) office **2. Système international**
SICAV	**Société d'investissement à capital variable**
SICOMI	**Société immobilière pour le développement du commerce et industrie**
SICOVAM	**Société interprofessionnelle pour la compensation des valeurs mobilières**
SIMCA	**Société industrielle de mécanique et de construction automobile**
SL	**Société Lyonnaise**
SM	**Système métrique,** metric system
SME	**System monétaire européen,** European Monetary System, EMS
SMIC	**Salaire minimum interprofessionnel de croissance**
SNC	**Société en nom collectif**
SNCF	**Société nationale des chemins de fer français**
SOCAR	**Société de cartons**

SOFINNOVA	**Société pour le financement de l'innovation**
SOGEBAIL	**Société générale pour le développement des opérations de crédit-bail immobilier**
SS	**Sécurité sociale** = *(i)* National Health Service, NHS *(ii)* Social Security
SVF	**Société des vins de France**
SVP	**S'il vous plaît,** please
TAF	**Taxe sur les activités financières**
TBB	**Taux de base bancaire**
TCA	**Taxe sur le chiffre d'affaires,** turnover tax
TGV	**Train grande vitesse** = advanced passenger train, APT
TIR	**Transports internationaux routiers,** International road transport
TP	**1. Trésor public 2. Tiers provisionnel 3. Taxe à la production 4. Taxe proportionnelle**
TPG	**Trésorier payeur général**
TPS	**Taxe sur les prestations de service**
TR	**Tarif réduit,** reduced rate
TS	**1. Tarif spécial,** special rate **2. taxe de séjour**
TT	**Transfert télégraphique,** telegraphic transfer, TT
TTC	**Toutes taxes comprises,** inclusive of (all) tax
TU	**Temps universel,** Universal time, UT; Greenwich mean time, GMT
TVA	**Taxe à la valeur ajoutée,** value-added tax, VAT
UBAF	**Union des banques arabes et françaises**
UCA	**Unité de compte agricole**
UCE	**Unité de compte européenne,** European currency unit, ECU
UEO	**Union de l'Europe occidentale,** Western European Union, WEO
UEP	**Union européenne des paiements,** European Payments Union, EPU
UFB	**Union française des banques**
UFC	**Union fédérale des consommateurs**
UNEDIC	**Union nationale pour l'emploi dans l'industrie et le commerce**
UPU	**Union postale universelle,** Universal postal union, UPU
UTA	**Union des transporteurs aériens**
VDQS	**Vin délimité de qualité supérieure**
VN	**1.** *Ins:* **valeur à neuf** = new for old (policy) **2. valeur nominale**
VPC	**Vente(s) par correspondance,** mail-order selling/sales
VRP	**Voyageur, représentant, placier,** representative/(travelling) salesman
XP	*Post:* **Exprès payé,** express paid
ZAD	**Zone à aménagement différé**
ZUP	**Zone à urbaniser en priorité,** priority development area